Footprint **New Zealand**

Darroch Donald
2nd edition

Kia Hora Te Marino
Whakapapa-pounamu
Te Moana, Kia tere
Te Karohirohi I mua I
Tou huarahi...

May the calm be widespread
May the sea glisten like greenstone
May the shimmer of light
dance before your path

Maori blessing

New Zealand Highlights

See colour maps at back of book

❶ Experience history and culture combined at Waitangi – the **'birthplace of the nation'**.

❷ Find some relief at Kawakawa's **'Hundertwasser Public Toilets'**, perhaps the artiest in the world.

❸ Admire the vistas, have dinner, climb the mast, or even jump from Auckland's hypodermic **Sky Tower**.

❹ Be the first to see the sunrise from **East Cape**.

❺ Take the real 'underground' in the **'Lost World'** or the **'Haggas Honking Holes'** at **Waitomo**.

❻ Call in at the Devil's Home at the **Wai-o-tapu** Thermal Reserve.

❼ See some tremendous tectonics along the **Tongariro Track**.

❽ Bombard the senses at **Te Papa**, the nation's most celebrated museum.

❾ Find solitude at **Wharariki Beach** and feel guilty leaving footprints.

Tasman Sea

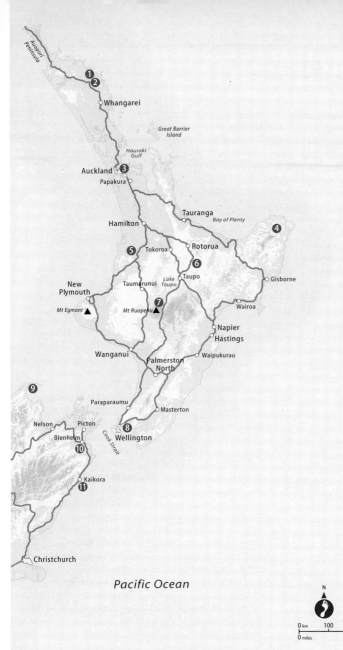

10 See white, red then a bit fuzzy, touring **the vineyards of Marlborough**.

11 It's no 'fluke' spotting whales or dolphins off the **Kaikoura Coast**.

12 Enter the realms of Rohan (Lord of the Rings) in the **Rangitata River Valley**

13 Go glacier walking on **Franz Josef** or **Fox**.

14 Follow the river to the **'Rob Roy'** near Wanaka.

15 Visit the aptly named **Paradise** in the **Dart River Valley**.

16 Admire the grace of the albatross, or the charm of a penguin, on the **Otago Peninsula**.

17 Watch keas dismantle your hire car on the majestic road to **Milford Sound**.

18 Experience the 'sound of silence' while kayaking amidst dolphins on **Doubtful Sound**.

Contents

4

Guide

Northland

Coromandel Peninsula

High pitch
No matter how basic the pitch ('paddock') or the posts, both are a feature of almost every kiwi town and testament to the popularity of rugby union – New Zealand's national game.

A foot in the door

Put Charles Darwin, Claude Monet and JRR Tolkien in a room with six bottles of vodka and a party pack of recreational drugs and combined, they could not come close to the concept of New Zealand. If nature had a design studio, full of her most surreal and stupendous ideas, it would be 'The Land of the Long White Cloud' or more recently aka 'Middle Earth'.

On the map the physical geography of New Zealand looks simple, yet in content it is incredibly diverse and complex. The two main islands North Island and South Island are both quite different. North, which is far less mountainous, is home to more than two-thirds of New Zealanders – or kiwis – who live life to the beat of a faster rhythm than their countrified neighbours to the south. For the tourist North Island generally holds less aesthetic appeal than South Island, but few miss, or indeed forget, the expansive views across Auckland from its hypodermic Sky Tower; the dramatic displays of Maori culture in Northland; or the brooding and colourful thermal features in and around Rotorua.

South Island, however, is said to offer the 'true essence' of New Zealand. To travel through it is like a fun-filled lesson in geography. Vast empty beaches where you feel guilty leaving a single set of footprints; endless mountain ranges blanketed in snow and rainforest; pristine lakes, waterfalls and fiords; giant glaciers; vast limestone caves and arches; natural springs and hot soothing pools…

Whatever your intention, if you choose New Zealand one thing is for sure – never mind 'Middle Earth', New Zealand is heaven on Earth at the end of the Earth. It is like making an appointment with Doctor Nature and her able assistant nurse Adrenaline. And now is the time to 'take the cure'.

Middle Earth or the end of the earth?

New Zealand has a sound, yet muted voice, seldom heard beyond Australasia. Its chronic struggle with relative anonymity within the developed nations has a great deal to do with its geographical position, size and demographics, and is something of a paradox. Ask the average kiwi and they will tell you exactly why they think it is both a blessing and a curse. A blessing because the population density creates an environment lacking the many inherent problems of over-population and a diverse natural environment, which is so obviously well suited to a healthy, outdoor lifestyle. Yet, stuck in the vast shadow of its charismatic neighbour Australia, New Zealand struggles to be taken seriously on the world stage, or to assert much influence both politically and economically. Let's face it, no country wants to be seen as just a 'tourist playground', or that 'place full of sheep, where Lord of the Rings was filmed'.

This paradox also has both positive and negative effects on the personality of its denizens, both collectively and individually. On the positive side kiwis are notoriously friendly and inquisitive, which is one reason they are labelled 'the world's greatest travellers'. They are also well

Game of bridge
A group of trampers (hikers) cross the Hooker River in the Mount Cook National Park.

known for their ingenuity and sound environmental awareness. However, talk to the average kiwi after their much loved and lauded All Blacks rugby team has just 'inexplicably' lost a game and you will almost certainly experience the dark side – the insecure, the moody, and, as they are perceived on the world stage, the historically bereft.

So the commercial gurus and touristical spin doctors have taken to promoting the nation as the 'Home of Middle Earth', and the national airline even emblazons its aircraft with graphics from the *Lord of the Rings* film. And no doubt all this will prove very positive in the long-term, but the ludicrous thing is that the landscape has been like that for millennia and will outlast the life of any book or film. Hordes of 'Rings' fanatics come on an almost religious pilgrimage to see where the filming took place, but in reality all the hype has merely added just another interesting dimension to an already beautiful land. Tolkien buffs now stand, perhaps a little uncomfortably, side by side with the more conventional ecotourists who are, as ever, merely trying to escape into the three dimensions of those traditional picture postcards. Folks, perhaps, who do not know an Orc from a Nazgul and who, frankly, do not care.

Caved in
A huge cavern acts as the portal to the aptly named Cathedral Cove on the Coromandel coast near Hahei.

14 The bungee way of life

Outdoor activities are more than just a tourist attraction in New Zealand, they are a way of life. The national psyche seems to crave adventure and the environment is nothing short of a natural Disneyland. The sheer range of activities on offer is staggering, with a veritable smorgasbord of possibilities from sea kayaking, cruising or flightseeing, to swimming with dolphins, whale watching or tandem skydiving. True, many of these activities can also be found elsewhere in the world, but in such wealth, to such a standard and surrounded by such scenic majesty – almost certainly not. Such is the average New Zealander's love of new and exciting feats of energetic entertainment, that they have become famous for creating their own bizarre and almost unimaginable pursuits. The methods and the modes defy description here except to say that they consistently shift one's adrenaline pumps to overload. Where else in the world can you roll down a hill inside a clear plastic bubble, launch yourself by a bungee cord off the nation's tallest building, or fly at 120 kph strapped to little more than a stretcher with a microlight engine attached? Just how many ways can a country devise to force the unplanned exit of your angst waters?

On a more sedate level (but still with plenty of ups and downs) are the endless opportunities for wilderness tramping (hiking). Many people come to New Zealand to experience some of the best walking on earth. Again, it is no exaggeration to call New Zealand, and the South Island in particular, the walking capital of the world. Not only is the scenery awe-inspiring, but

In the shadow of the Cape Reinga Lighthouse, the most northerly tip of New Zealand.

Golden fall in the orchards of Otago.

also the range of options is vast. With 14 national parks offering everything from hour-long coastal walks, to 10-day wilderness expeditions, you have choices of everything from easy-going strolls to once-in-a-lifetime challenges. Even the names are evocative – Kepler, Dusky, Rees-Dart and Greenstone, to name just a few – each blessed with its own range of extreme features from volcanoes and glaciers to lakes and waterfalls.

Wild world

Experiencing wildlife in New Zealand has been described as being as close to being on another planet as one can get. Millions of years of isolation have resulted in the evolution of a fascinating ark of unique species from the bizarre and whimsical kiwi to the prehistoric tuatara. With so few mammals in a country blanketed by native rain forest, it was the birds that dominated and, with no ground predators, many became flightless. The sights and sounds must have been incredible; to describe it as paradise is totally apt. Yet this is now a biodiversity under siege and a paradise that has essentially been lost forever. From the day that man first arrived, he placed an indelible footprint on the environment; the first step in an almost inevitable journey of destruction. Introduced animals and plants like the rat, the cat and the possum, together with unsustainable hunting and gathering methods, devastated both native flora and fauna, many species becoming extinct or replaced. Today, for example, for every native plant there is one introduced. However, although it will never be the same again and is a mere echo of its former glory, modern-day New Zealand is still home to an incredible range of wildlife, most of which you will see nowhere else on earth. Your encounters will be many and memorable: from enchanting penguins, to graceful albatrosses; cheeky keas to manic fantails, and rotund sea lions to breaching whales. Given the focus and

Though the America's Cup is lost, the City of Sails (Auckland) will always be a 'yachty's Utopia'.

fragility of its species, New Zealand is on the cutting edge of both conservation and ecotourism. As a visitor you will be able to experience both, working separately or in unison, and whether you love wildlife or are indifferent, you will be given a stark insight or reminder into our effect on the world and our place within it.

Kiwi collective

Despite its relatively infant history, New Zealand provides a fascinating cultural mêlée. Before the early European explorers paved the way for widespread colonial immigration, the native Maori had developed their own highly individual way of life. Despite the fact that like any other displaced people, they have struggled to maintain this identity and culture, thankfully 'Maoritanga' (Maoridom) is enjoying something of a renaissance in modern day New Zealand. Maori issues are now taken very seriously within government and in legal circles, especially when it comes to land rights and the harvesting of natural resources. But it is the colourful history and traditions so well presented to tourists, particularly in North Island, that is the modern face of Maoridom in New Zealand. You will be exposed to their different world and traditional lifestyles, and, whether it is through a stay on a 'marae', a cultural performance, a 'hangi' (feast), or simple friendship, it will enhance your visit and a provide a sense of hope that biculturalism has indeed a optimistic future. You will also find that through the solid roots of Maoridom and colonialism a unique 'kiwi' culture and identity is growing both strong and steadfast.

Essentials

Planning your trip

A word of advice about New Zealand: it **is** everything you have heard about it, and an awful lot more besides. If you can only go for two to three weeks, unless you stay put in one area, or visit just a few places, it is going to be an exercise in frustration. Just think about it: you are probably about to travel to the other end of the earth, so make the most of it. Three weeks is pushing it, six is better, and eight weeks about right, short of actual emigration.

If New Zealand presents an irresistible lure, you are probably nature-friendly and also a very active and independent person. The main ingredients of the average 'New Zealand Happy Traveller Cake' is unspoilt nature, stunning scenery, with just a light icing of interesting history. Bake that in a pleasant climate and cover it in lashings of 'great things to do' and voilà – the perfect trip. Start planning well in advance. You will find comprehensive sights and activities listings in each location section throughout this book. The web is also a major source of information. It's a good idea to secure your own transport on arrival, or even before. New Zealand is small and relatively easy to get about, but independence is a major advantage. If you are in a group consider the many campervan options (see page 45). New Zealand is well geared up for this type of travel.

You might also consider buying a car (see page 44). Second-hand cars are cheap in New Zealand and, provided they're still in one piece, you can usually sell them again when you have completed your journey. If you cannot afford your own wheels, then New Zealand is pretty well set up for coach travel throughout both islands. Listings for public transport can be found in the Ins and Outs and Transport sections of the book and also on the official listed websites for each major town or region.

Where to go

Three weeks tends to be the most common 'quick trip' people can afford. However, the 'two to three week' listing below has been divided into 'North Island' and 'South Island', with about 14 days outlined in each. This should give you flexibility and a better idea of the best basic recommendations of each island. As already mentioned, covering the best of both islands in anything under a month is very hard and in reality you would be better focusing on one island (the South preferably) or a particular region. The top regions are Otago, Fiordland and Nelson/Marlborough in the South Island and The Bay of Plenty (Rotorua) and Taupo and Ruapehu in the North.

Two weeks: North Island

You will almost certainly arrive in **Auckland** – the main international airport. Although the Auckland Region has a lot to offer, only spend a day there, then move on quickly. Auckland is a great city – but a city nonetheless. It is modern and in many ways is not at all typical of New Zealand. Take a quick look from the top of the Sky Tower, at the Auckland Museum, followed by Devonport (including a walk to North Head), or one of the West Coast beaches. Then the following day head for Northland and the **Bay of Islands**, where you can cruise the islands in numerous ways or go dolphin watching. Don't miss Russell (the first significant European settlement) and Waitangi (where the **Maori/Pakeha Treaty** was signed). In the evening the live Maori performance at the Treaty grounds is recommended. The following day take a one-day trip to **Cape Reinga,** the northernmost tip of New Zealand. Then return to Auckland and dine in Ponsonby or Parnell. The following day head southwest for a couple of days in the **Coromandel**. If you do not have your own transport consider the day cruise offered by **Kawau Kat Cruises,** T09-4258006, www.kawaukat.co.nz ($99), or road trip with

Coromandel Explorer Tours, T09-8282753, www.coromandeltours.co.nz If you have your own transport in the 'Coro' don't miss Coromandel township (including the Driving Creek Railway), Colville, Cape Colville and Cathedral Cove. From Coromandel head to **Rotorua** for two days of volcanic scenery and a multitude of activities. From Rotorua head southwest to **Taupo** being sure not to miss the Wai-o-tapu Thermal Reserve on the way. Make sure you see the Huka Falls and relax and enjoy a hot pool at De Brett's Thermal Resort. If the weather is fine the following day attempt 'The Tongariro Crossing', a full-day walk (moderate fitness required), or take a cruise on Lake Taupo, followed by a jump out of a plane at 12,000 ft if your nerves can stand it. Alternatively from Taupo, get underground with a day trip to the **Waitomo Caves**. From Taupo take one of two recommended routes south. Either head south on SH1, taking SH47 at Taurangi around the western side of the **Tongariro National Park.** If you can, take a scenic flight above the mountains from Whakapapa Village or drive up the Mountain Road from **Ohakune**. Stay in Ohakune. Next day get to **Wellington** as soon as possible. Alternatively, head southeast to **Napier** and the **Hawkes Bay**. Enjoy Napier itself or visit a winery or Cape Kidnappers and take some time to enjoy the view from Te Mata Peak in **Havelock North**. From Havelock head south through the **Wairarapa** stopping at Mount Bruce Wildlife Centre and, if you can, take in the coast at Castlepoint. The following morning try to visit the remote **Cape Palliser**, the southernmost tip of North Island. Once in **Wellington,** take a trip up the Cable Car, see the view from Mount Victoria and check out the Museum of Wellington City and the Sea and Te Papa – New Zealand's multimillion dollar national museum. For lunch or dinner muse the menus on and around Courtney Place. The following day drive back to Auckland (nine hours) or head across early by ferry for a week in South Island.

Two weeks: South Island

By ferry from Wellington, try to arrive in **Picton** early in the day so you can join one of the trips out into the **Marlborough Sound**s – either dolphin watching, kayaking or a half-day walk to Ship Cove. The following day drive to Blenheim and have a quick look at one or two of the vineyards before heading through Havelock, making your way to **Nelson**. Enjoy the rest of the day in Nelson then make your way to Motueka via Mapua. Next day take a day-walk or kayak trip in the **Abel Tasman National Park**. Then make your way to the West Coast and **Franz Josef** taking a quick look at the Nelson Lakes National Park. In Franz Josef be sure to take a scenic flight around Mount Cook, or at least a glacier walk on the Franz. The following day, drive from Franz Josef, stopping at Ship Creek and Haast to make **Wanaka** by evening. Next day go canyoning, skydiving, or for a walk up the Rob Roy Valley. Alternatively, take a scenic flight to Milford Sound. Head

If you decide to concentrate on one island, or alternatively spend a week in one and then two in the other, South Island has the upper hand.

for **Queenstown** and spend the day deciding what to do. The bungee is an option as is the Shotover Jet and the views from the gondola. Take another day visiting **Milford Sound** – it's best to bus in (to see Te Anau and the **Milford Road**) and fly out.

For the following three days there is an alternative: head for Christchurch first or go via Dunedin. For Christchurch drive from Queenstown to **Mount Cook** village. Spend the rest of the day taking in the scenery by foot, by bike or with a scenic flight. If you are up to it, climb up to the new Muller Hut for the night. Next day drive to Christchurch for a look at Tekapo and the McKenzie Country, arriving in **Christchurch** late evening. Alternatively you could spend the first two days in **Dunedin** and the Otago Peninsula with the following day in the **Catlins**. After a day in Christchurch, head for **Kaikoura** where you can take a whale watching or dolphin swimming excursion, leaving yourself enough time to catch the late ferry from **Picton** that night.

Add to the above these alternatives: In Auckland try to get out on the **Hauraki Gulf**, visit **Tiri Tiri Matangi Island** (a 'must do'), **Rangitoto** or **Great Barrier Island.** Spend some time exploring the Waitakeres and the West Coast beaches. In the city visit Kelly Tarlton's Underwater and Antarctic Encounter and/or the Waterfront and the Maritime Museum. Adrenaline seekers should consider climbing the **Sky Towers** mast (Vertigo) or the controlled bungee from the observation deck (Sky Jump).

In Northland on the way to the Bay of Islands, don't miss the **Whangarei Heads** (Ocean Beach) and/or the **Tutakaka Coast.** While there consider diving the **Poor Knights Islands.** In the Bay of Islands consider a two-day kayak trip on and around the islands or walk to **Cape Brett.** Break your bum on the fast boat to the 'Hole in the Rock'. Heading north, take a peek at historic **Kerikeri** and the delights of the scenic coast road to Whangaroa. After visiting the Cape head southwest to the **Hokianga**. Just south of the Hokianga don't miss 'Tane Mahuta', the 1500 year-old kauri in the magnificent **Waipoua Forest.** Then learn more about the great trees at the **Kauri Museum** in Matakohe. Heading south from Auckland, spend a couple more days exploring the Coromandel. Go fishing from **Whitianga** or spend a day on **New Chums Beach**. Don't miss the Driving Creek Railway in Coromandel Township.

From Coromandel head to the Bay of Plenty. Spend a day enjoying one of the many activities in **Tauranga** or **Mount Maunganui.** There is plenty to detain you in the **Tongariro National Park** and you could also consider a kayaking trip down the Wanganui River in the neighbouring **Wanganui National Park,** before heading south to Wellington. North from Rotorua you can negotiate the **East Cape** via Whakatane. While in **Whakatane** visit the active volcano White Island or swim with the dolphins. If you head west from Rotorua or Taupo, a day underground in the **Waitomo Caves** is well worth your while. If at all possible and you can afford it, try the '**The Lost World**' trip, see page 243. From Waitomo you can follow the coast to **Taranaki** and spend some time around the mountain and the **Mount Egmont National Park** – arguably the most beautiful mountain in the country. From New Plymouth, which is a great town in itself, you could also take in **Wanganui** and a trip on the Wanganui River before heading south to **Wellington**.

If you head west from Rotorua or Taupo, spend more time in **Napier** and consider spending a night at **Lake Waikaremoana** in the Urewera National Park. Then from Napier head south via **Havelock North**, through the Wairarapa taking in Castlepoint, the Waiohine Gorge and **Cape Palliser.** From all these directions you will then end up in Wellington and can spend more time in the city. For a superb day trip go to the wildlife paradise of **Kapiti Island.** From Wellington again it is a nine-hour drive direct via SH1 back to Auckland, though the flight on a clear day between Mount Taranaki on one side and Ruapehu on the other is a delight.

Three weeks: South Island

Added to the above listings under South Island, there are many additional excursions and activities. In Nelson and Marlborough consider an extra day or two in the Marlborough Sounds. Do part of the **Queen Charlotte Track**, or the lesser-known **Nydia Track,** a full-day cruise, a multi-day kayak trip from Havelock or **Picton**, or better still, spend a day or two getting to **French Pass**. From Nelson consider doing the **Abel Tasman Coast Walk** or a multi-day kayak trip. From Motueka, venture over Takaka Hill to **Golden Bay.** Visit the Pupu Springs, Farewell Spit and do not miss **Wharariki Beach**. While in Golden Bay consider doing the **Heaphy Track** or exploring the northern sector of the Abel Tasman or Kahurangi National Parks.

Returning to Motueka, head for the West Coast via the Nelson Lakes National Park. Consider the **Angelus Hut Walk** in the Nelson Lakes then head to **Westport** via the Buller Gorge. From Westport venture north to **Karamea** and see the incredible karst scenery of the **Oparara Basin**. Walk part of the Heaphy Track coastal stretch.

From Karamea head south down the West Coast to **Franz Josef,** taking in the arts and crafts of **Hokitika,** the **white heron colony** near Whataroa and the secluded delights of **Okarito**. Then give yourself an extra two-three days around the Glacier Region. As well as the glaciers be sure to visit **Lake Matheson** (dawn or dusk) and the wild coastline.

Heading south to Haast, stop at **Munroe Beach** and/or Ship Creek. Spend at least two days around **Haast,** take a jetboat trip and/or explore further south to **Jackson's Bay** and the **Cascade Saddle**. Having negotiated the Haast Pass to **Wanaka** spend more time there, enjoying the scenery and wealth of activities, particularly the local walks. From Wanaka head for **Queenstown** via the Cardrona Road and lose yourself in the incredible range of activities.

For a break from the chaos head north and explore the **Glenorchy / Paradise** areas (featured heavily in *Lord of the Rings*), **Arrowtown,** or climb to the top of the **Remarkables**. From Queenstown drive to **Te Anau,** consider the Kepler, Routeburn or Milford Tracks or a multi-day kayak trip on Milford or **Doubtful Sound**. Be sure to make the scenic drive to **Milford Sound** and give yourself an extra day there. Great day or half-day walks include **Key Summit** or **Lake Marian**. Just south of Te Anau, take in the stunning scenery and atmosphere of **Lake Manapouri** and Doubtful Sound. From Manapouri negotiate the Southern Scenic Route to **Dunedin,** and en route consider doing the **Humpridge Track,** visiting **Stewart Island** (to see diurnal kiwi) and certainly give yourself three days exploring the Catlins Coast. Spend two-three days in Dunedin allowing at least one on the **Otago Peninsula**. Take a tour to see the **albatross colony** and the **yellow-eyed penguins**.

From Dunedin head north to Oamaru then inland to **Mount Cook**. Spend some time exploring the area and its activities. If you are fit spend a night up in the new Mueller Hut. Via **Tekapo** and the McKenzie Country, head to Christchurch giving yourself more time in the city. While in Christchurch spend a day exploring the **Banks Peninsula**. West of Christchurch consider the scenic drive to Mt Sunday and Mt Potts Station used for the set for Edoras in *Lord of the Rings*. North of Christchurch, as an adjunct to Kaikoura, head inland to enjoy a hot pool and perhaps a mountain bike ride in **Hanmer Springs.** From Hanmer Springs and Kaikoura enjoy the stunning coastal road that will deliver you back to **Picton** via the **vineyards** of Marlborough.

When to go

For travellers from the Northern Hemisphere spending Christmas Day on the beach, sunbathing while digesting a hearty BBQ, or seeing a Santa Parade under cloudless skies in shorts, is really quite a bizarre experience. The summer or **high season** lasting from **November to March** is, of course, the busiest, and at these times you'll be joining battalions of Kiwis also on holiday throughout the country. At these times, especially over Christmas and for the whole of January, almost the entire country shuts up shop and heads for the beach or the mountains. Accommodation is at a premium and the roads to the major tourist destinations can be busy. But again, 'busy' roads in New Zealand, especially in the more remote parts of South Island, equates to a car passing you every five or ten minutes. In some parts of the country, you get so used to being alone that the sight of other cars can be quite a shock.

The months of late spring (**September/October**) or early autumn (**March/April**) are often recommended. At these times you are almost guaranteed accommodation everywhere and the weather is still pretty favourable. It is also cheaper. The winter or **low season** sits between **April/May to August/September**. At these times prices are often reduced with special deals (especially at weekends) abounding in many, mainly mid-range, accommodation establishments. Bear in mind that some places are closed in winter but generally speaking, in New Zealand, tourism is a year-round affair. Also bear in mind that some places like Queenstown (the principal tourist destination in South Island) are as busy in the winter months with skiing activities as they are with general activities in summer. Taking all the above into account, the best months to visit, unless you enjoy the tourist/holiday buzz, are **October/November** or **March/April**.

Climate

New Zealand has what is called an 'ocean temperate' climate, which basically means that it is generally agreeable. As the country is fairly elongated and lying very much at a north to south angle, the weather varies greatly. The north is consistently a few degrees warmer than the south. As you might expect, the warmest region of the country is generally Northland and the coldest Southland. However, especially in recent years unusual weather patterns have seen the reverse to be true, sometimes for days on end.

In Auckland the winter (June-August) and summer (December-March) average temperatures are 8°C-15°C (48°F-59°F) and 14°C-23°C (57°F-74°F) respectively and in Dunedin 4°C-12°C (39°F-53°F) and 9°C-19°C (48°F-66°F) respectively. But this can be misleading: not too far inland from Dunedin, Alexandra is quite often the hottest spot in the country. When it comes to sunshine, various regions compete closely for the title of 'sunniest place'. For several years now it has been Nelson and Marlborough in the South Island. But next year it could just as easily be Napier on the relatively dry and sunny East Coast of North Island, or even Whakatane in the Bay of Plenty. Wellington and Auckland, too, boast a lot of sunshine with Auckland being far more humid. Wellingtonians also suffer from wind – quite severely too, (thankfully not of the beans variety). The West Coast and Fiordland in Southland, too, have their extremes of wind and rain. But having said that, the beauty of a place like New Zealand is that even in winter, it doesn't rain for long periods. In summary, the weather is very favourable here: you can swim in the sea, wear shorts in summer and will not be forced indoors for days. One other word of advice: thanks to ozone depletion, the sun in New Zealand is **dangerous**, so always wear a hat and the strongest possible sun block: don't forget to slip, slap and slop..

⊘ Tours and tour operators

Although New Zealand is very much the domain of the independent traveller there are a number of specialist tour operators. As you might imagine most of these are either eco- or activity-based. The New Zealand Tourism Board has detailed operator listings on its website, www.purenz.com For operators within New Zealand consult the 'Activities' sections throughout the book. See also ecotourism operators for further information below. For New Zealand operators in your own country see the 'Discount Travel Agents' boxes in the 'Getting there' section. The ones listed below are just a few of the main players:

Backpacker bus tours

Kiwi Experience, *170 Parnell Road, Auckland, T09-3669830, www.kiwiexperience. com*
Contiki, *1st Floor, 15-17 Day Street, Newton, Auckland, T0800-CONTIKI, www.contiki.com*
Stray, *PO Box 14114, Enderly, Hamilton, T07-8243627, www.straytravel.co.nz* and
Magic Travellers, *132-138 Quay Street, Auckland, T09-3585600, www.magicbus.co.nz*

are the four main players all offering flexibility at competitive prices.
Flying Kiwi Wilderness Expeditions, *T0800-693296, www.flying_kiwi.com* offer something a little different, specializing in flexible activity and nature based trips, from 4-27 days.
Bushwise Women, *T04-5626011 www.bushwise.co.nz* For trips especially designed for women.

Coach tours

Great Sights, *180 Quay St, Auckland, T0800-744487, www.greatsights.co.nz* A wide range of tours throughout the country from day city tours to 2-11 day excursions.
Guthreys Tours, *T0800-732528, www.guthreys.co.nz www.vanwaytours.co.nz* Tours from Auckland to Rotorua, Taupo, Waitomo and Bay of Islands.
Scenic Pacific Tours, *T0800-698687, www.scenictours.co.nz* Well-established company offering deluxe (yet good value) coach trips with emphasis on activities as much as sightseeing.
Thrifty Tours, *PO Box 31-257 Milford, Auckland, T0800-803550, www.tourmasters.co.nz* Budget-conscious tours with flexibility. Range of options from 2-16 days in both islands. Thrifty specials to Waitomo, Rotorua and the Bay of Islands.

Ecotourism operators

Auckland
Kiwi Wildlife Tours, *346 Cowan Bay Rd, Warkworth, T09-4222115, www.kiwi-wildlife.co.nz* 11-18 day guided birdwatching trips.
Tiri Tiri Matangi Island, **Tiri Supporters**, *PO Box 24-229, Birkenhead, T09-4794490, peter@naturaledge.co.nz*
Miranda Shorebird Centre, *RD1, Pokeno, T/F09-2322781, shorebird@xtra.co.nz* Specialist wader field centre on internationally significant site, accommodation available.

Northland
Aroha Island Ecological Centre, *PO Box 541, Kerkeri, T09-4075243, F09-4075246, www.aroha.net.nz*

Waikato
Hamilton Zoo and The Free-Flight Sanctuary, *Brymer Rd, Hamilton, T07-8386720, F07-8490293, www.hamiltonzoo.co.nz*

Bay of Plenty
Lakeland Queen Cruises Ltd, *PO Box 1976, Rotorua, T07-3486634, F07-3471766, www.lakelandqueen.co.nz*

Lake cruises and birdwatching trips on a paddle steamer to Mokoia Island Nature Reserve on Lake Rotorua.

Taupo and Ruapehu
Kiwi Encounters, *PO Box 146, Ohakune, T/F09-3859505,whakamanu@hotmail.com* 3-hour guided trips to track kiwi in the Waimarino Forest.

East Coast
Mount Bruce National Wildlife Centre, *RD1, Masterton, T06-3758004, www.mtbruce.doc.govt.nz*
Gannet Beach Adventures, *PO Box 1463, Hastings, T0800-426638, www.gannets.com* 4-hour guided trips to see New Zealand's largest gannet colony.
Gannet Safaris Overland, *RD2, Hastings, T06-8750888, F06-8750893, www.gannetsafaris.com* As above.

Wellington
Nga Manu Nature Reserve, *Ngarara Rd, PO Box 126, Waikanae, T/F04-2934131, www.ngamanu.co.nz*
Kapiti Tours and Kapiti Island Nature Reserve, *T0800-527484, www.kapititours.co.nz* Day trips and overnight stays on a unique island nature reserve. (See Kapiti Coast section, page 421.)

Nelson and Marlborough
Dolphin Watch Marlborough, *PO Box 197, Picton, T03-5738040, www.dolphinwatch marlborough.co.nz* Bird/dolphin watching trips in the Queen Charlotte Sound.
French Pass Sea Safaris, *French Pass, Marlborough Sounds, T/F03-5765204, www.seasafaris.co.nz* Flexible ecotrips to see dolphins and seabirds in the outer Marlborough Sounds.
Original Farewell Spit Safaris, *Tasman St, Collingwood, T03-0800-808257, www.FarewellSpit.co.nz* Trips along the internationally ecologically-significant Farewell Spit to see seabirds including gannets and migrating wading birds.
Albatross Encounter with Ocean Wings, *58 West End, Kaikoura, T03-3196777, www.oceanwings.co.nz* Boat trips to see wide variety of rare seabirds.
Dolphin Encounter, *T03-3196777, info@dolphin.co.nz* Dolphin watching and

Whale Watch Kaikoura, *PO Box 89, Kaikoura, T03-3196767, F03-3196545, www.whalewatch.co.nz* The world-famous whale watching operation in Kaikoura.

Canterbury

Akaroa Harbour Cruises, *Akaroa, T03-3289078, www.canterburycat.co.nz* Dolphin watching cruises including the endangered Hector's dolphin.

Kaki (Black Stilt) Visitor Hide Guided Tours, *Wairepo Rd, Twizel, T03-4353124, kakivisitorhide@doc.govt.nz* Guided trips to see one of the rarest waders in the world.

Heritage Expeditions, *PO Box 6282, Christchurch, T03-3389944, F03-3383311, www.heritage-expeditions.com* Guided birdwatching trips and expeditions throughout New Zealand and the Sub-Antarctic Islands.

West Coast

White Heron Sanctuary Tours, *PO Box 19, Whataroa, T0800-523456, www.whiteherontours.co.nz* Guided boat trips to see New Zealand's only White heron breeding site.

Okarito Nature Tours, *PB 777, Hokitika, T/F03-7534014, www.okarito.co.nz* Specialized boat tours and kayak trips on the wildlife-rich Okarito Lagoon.

Moeraki Wilderness Lodge, *PB Bag 772, Hokitika, T03-7500881, F03-7500882, lakemoeraki@wildernesslodge.co.nz* Accommodation, guided nature walks and kayak trips in World Heritage park.

Otago

Elm Wildlife Tours, *Elm Lodge Backpackers, Dunedin, T03-4741872, F03-4778808, www.elmwildlifetours.co.nz* Superb guided nature tours of the Otago Peninsula. Hooker's sealions, fur seals, albatross and yellow-eyed penguin.

Nature Guides Otago, *PO Box 8050, Dunedin, T03-4545169, F03-4545369, www.nznatureguides.com* Guided trips on the Otago Peninsula, Catlins Coast and Stewart Island, B&B available.

Royal Albatross Centre, *PO Box 492, Dunedin, T03-4780499, F03-4780575, www.albatrosses.com* Observation of the only mainland breeding colony of royal albatross in the world.

Monarch Wildlife Cruises and Tours, *PO Box 102, Dunedin, T03-4774276, F03-4774216, www.wildlife.co.nz* Nature cruises on Otago Harbour, including the renowned albatross colony in the area.

Southland

Catlins Wildlife Trackers, *Papatowai, Owaka, T/F03-4158613, catlinw@es.co.nz*

Catlins Encounters, *Elm Lodge Backpackers, Dunedin, T03-4741872, F03-4778808, www.elmwildlifetours.co.nz* 20-day guided nature tours of the Catlins taking in the best wildlife spots – backpacker orientated. Fiordland Ecology Holidays, *PO Box 40, Manapouri, T/F03-2496600, www.fiordland.gen.nz* Research and holiday cruises around the Fiordland Sounds and Stewart Island.

Ruggedy Range Wilderness Experience, *Oban, Stewart Island, T03-2191066, www.ruggedyrange.com* Guided tours on Stewart Island, where seeing kiwi is one of the highlights.

Kiwi Wilderness Walks, *based in Riverton, T0800-248886, www.riverton.co.nz, (see Riverton section, page 681). Guided nature walks on Stewart Island, again a good trip if you want to see kiwi.*

Nature safaris

Kiwi Wildlife Tours, (see Ecotourism operators above) *346 Cowan Bay Rd, Warkworth, T09-4222115, www.kiwi-wildlife.co.nz* Guided birdwatching tours of New Zealand and the Pacific from 11-18 days.

Manu Tours New Zealand, *106 Ocean Beach Road, Tairua, T07-8647475, www.nzbirding.co.nz* Another one for avid 'twitchers' with a national hunt to see as many endemics as possible in 17 days.

Nature Quest New Zealand, *Dunedin. T03-4898444, www.naturequest.co.nz* Guided or organized independent birding trips with one of the country's best 'twitchers'.

Adventure South, *PO Box 33, 153 Christchurch, T03-9421222, www.advsouth.co.nz* Eco-based 5-23 day cycling and hiking trips and a specialist mid-life adventure tour for 41-55 year olds.

Specialist activity tours

New Zealand Pedaltours Ltd, *PO Box 37-575, Parnell, Auckland, T0800-3020968, www.pedaltours.co.nz* Specialist cycle tours, ecotours, mountain biking, from $595.
Kiwi Kayak Tours, *17H Andromeda Cres, East Tamaki, Auckland, T09-2743142,*

www.kiwikayaktours.com Personalized and professional tours throughout New Zealand.
Ridenz.com, *T0800-413369, www.ridenz.com* Selected riding holidays with operators in both islands.
Active Earth, *T0800-201040, ww.ActiveEarthNewZealand.com* Good guided activity tours of the North Island.

Finding out more

One of the best ways to source information from abroad is on the web. Again the NZTB website is a good place to start, but almost all the regions have excellent, informative websites and these are listed in relevant areas in the text. The national and regional tourist boards and local information centres are generally good at replying to specific enquiries, especially by email, and of course are usually willing to send heaps of useful information by snail mail.

www.purenz.com Official web site of the New Zealand Tourism Board packed with useful information, listings and contacts.
www.searchnz.co.nz One of the countries best national search engines. Great way to access main links through general search.
www.nzcity.co.nz has regional news and a superb weather satellite picture.
www.nzoom.co.nz Useful national web sites with regional news links.
www.yellowpages.co.nz Useful for any national telephone and address listings.
www.maps@mapworld.co.nz Best map supplier in New Zealand including CD-ROMS.
www.travelplanner.co.nz,
www.newzealandvacations.co.nz,
www.destination-nz.com Other useful tourist/visitor based sites with good links.
www.doc.govt.nz The invaluable and fast developing web site of the Conservation Department with detailed information on Regional Conservancies, National Parks, tramping and short walks.
www.travel-library.com Detailed general travel site packed with good tips on buying flight tickets etc.
www.nzherald.co.nz Excellent Web site of the Upper North Island's main daily newspaper, with national, international news, sport, weather and travel.
www.Intercitycoach.co.nz Web site for Intercity Buses with detailed bus information and additional news about fare concessions and package deals.

www.tranzrail.co.nz Provides all your rail and inter-island ferry information needs.
www.auckland-airport.co.nz
www.christchurch-airport.co.nz
Perhaps worth a quick look before you enter the country.
www.hillarysport.org.nz Useful national walks guide.
www.backpack.co.nz www.yha.org.nz
www.kiwiexperience.co.nz The principal backpacker travel organizations.
www.jasons.co.nz
www.aaguides.co.nz Useful general New Zealand travel and sleeping information.
www.nz-travel.co.nz
www.worldtouring.co.nz
www.tourism.net.nz
www.expedia.com
www.travelstore.com
www.lastminute.com
www.firedup.com
www.travelocity.com
www.orbitz.com Good general travel sites with broad information and competitive air fares for NZ.
www.photonewzealand.com
(for author's pictures search: Darroch Donald)
www.andrisapse.co.nz
www.craigpotton.co.nz Some of the best photographers, photographs and pictorial references of New Zealand
www.tolkien.co.uk
www.tolkienonline.com
www.lordoftherings.net Three official *Lord of the Rings* websites.

Language

English is of course the principal language spoken in New Zealand. Maori is the traditional. See also page 726 and Glossary of Maori words on page 742.

Disabled travellers

For travellers with disabilities, visiting New Zealand can, like most places, be a frustrating affair. While most public facilities are well geared up for wheelchairs, older accommodation establishments and some public transport systems (especially rural buses) are not so well organized. However, things are improving and it is now a requirement by law to have disabled facilities in new buildings. The larger airlines like **Air New Zealand** and **Qantas** are well equipped and this applies both to international and domestic flights. Disabled travellers usually receive discounts on travel and some admission charges. Parking concessions are also available for the disabled and temporary cards can be issued on receipt of a mobility card or medical certificate.

You are advised to research options thoroughly before you leave and this can often be done with the assistance of organizations in your own country. For more information within New Zealand contact **Enable,** T0800-171981/T06-9520011, www.enable.co.nz   and in Auckland **The New Zealand Disability Support Group,** T0508-787767

There are few specialist tour companies acting specifically for the disabled. One exception is **Accessible Kiwi Tours Ltd,** owned and operated by Allan and Shona Armstrong, based in Opotiki in the Bay of Plenty, T07-3156988, F07-3155144, info@accessible-tours.co.nz

Gay and lesbian travellers

Homosexuality (except in some rather bigoted rural outposts) is generally well accepted in New Zealand and indeed in some parts it is flourishing. Auckland has a thriving gay and transvestite community heavily focused around the Ponsonby and Karangahape Road (K'Road) areas, where there are many gay and gay-friendly clubs, cafés and pubs. Some specialist publications and independent groups are also in evidence, see page 115 in the Auckland chapter. Each February Auckland hosts the popular 'Hero Parade', which is the national gay event of the year. This popular and growing festival involves a street parade and entertainment in the Ponsonby area. Although not quite on the scale of the world famous Sydney 'Gay Mardis Gras' it can still blow your wig off and is enjoyed by thousands, both gay and straight. From 2004 it is hoped this event will become as much a festival as a mere parade. Not to be outdone, Wellington also has a parade/festival, the 'Devotion Festival' which is usually held in November. See also page 416 in Wellington chapter.

For detailed information on gay and lesbian New Zealand contact the New Zealand Gay and Lesbian Tourism Association, PB MBE P255 Auckland, T09-3742161, info@nzglta.org.nz The **Gay and Lesbian Visitor Information Network Ltd** PB MBE P255, Auckland, T09-3742162/T0800-144296. The following websites www.gaynewzealand.com and **www.gaytravelnet.com/nz** are also excellent sources of information. A few companies offering holiday packages and advice, including: **Budget Travel Parnell,** PO Box 37-259, Parnell, Auckland, T09-3020553, jennyr@budgettravel.co.nz

Student travellers ▸ See also visas section for information on student visas

If you are a student (and can prove it) you will enjoy the usual discounts on public transport and specialist tourist travel, tourist attractions and tourist-based activities throughout New Zealand. There are also some savings to be made on insurance, restaurants, shopping and accommodation. If you are backpacking note however that the main discounts are best secured through the affiliation and membership of one or more of the specific backpacker chains (i.e. YHA, BBH, Nomad or VIP). See also Backpacker Organisations, page 50.

The **International Student Identity Card (ISIC)** is the most widely accepted form of ID and far more effective and hassle-free than an institution-specific identity card. If you do not possess an ISIC consult your educational institution or student travel agency prior to departure for application details. ISIC cards are also available from STA travel, www.statravel.co.uk The **International Student Travel Confederation** (ISTC) is the principal administrator of the scheme and you are advised to consult their website for more information and specific contacts within your own country, www.isic.org NZ T0800-445108, USA T1800-7061333, UK T0800-3762366.

Women travellers ▸ See also section on Safety, page 38

There are few cultural protocols or specific problems that directly or especially affect women or single female travellers in New Zealand. Here equality rules both the landscape and the roost. You are after all in the country that afforded women the vote well before they did in the USA and UK. Traditionally, beyond the male-initated inter-tribal killing and rampant moa killing, Maori women were and are held in high esteem. However, that said, the country is not immune to the usual crime and social problems so all the normal common-sense levels of vigilance and precaution should be adopted. Generally speaking, the average Kiwi male is very similar to his Australian counterpart and can be as sensitive and subtle as a rhino nurturing a particularly nasty and recurrent itch in his nether regions. And although there are of course exceptions to the rule, bear in mind that here it is not often said with flowers, sophistication or indeed panache. Here, like in Australia and the US, it's not so much *Don Juan* as *Roger Ramjet*.

Working in the country ▸ For work visas, see page 29

If you are coming from Europe (especially the UK) or North America and plan to find casual work in New Zealand to pay your way around the country, think again. Given the favourable exchange rates you are far better securing casual work in your own country and saving rather than doing so in New Zealand. Time will be short enough with so much to see and do. However, if you are desperate, backpackers can occasionally work for their keep at some vineyards, orchards and farmstays (see page 49).

One organization that will help you locate these is **Farm Helpers (FhiNZ)**, FhiNZ, 16 Aspen Way, Palmerston North, T0800-327681, www.fhinz.co.nz. Their website is a fine place to start and a booklet listing over 190 associate farms is also available on line for $25. **New Zealand Job Search** is a backpacker recruitment specialist based in Auckland, 229 Queen St, T09-3573996, www.nzjobs.go.nz Another excellent website is www.seasonalwork.co.nz which offers job listings and a host of other information including accommodation, transport and work visas. Obviously do not expect to be paid premium hourly rates. The minimum is around $6.

There is also an option of working voluntarily on organic farms through an organization called **Willing Workers on Organic Farms** (WWOOF). Reports of this network are good and as a member ($30) you can often get free comfortable accommodation in return for a few hours of daily work with associated hosts. For more information and membership details (you receive a comprehensive booklet with operator listings upon receipt of membership) contact WWOOF New Zealand, PO Box 1172, Nelson, T03-5449890, www.wwoof.co.nz

---

Foreign consulates in New Zealand

Auckland
Australia, *7th Floor, 188 Quay St, City,*
T09-0218800. **Canada**, *T09-3098516.*
Croatia, *291 Lincoln Rd, Henderson,*
T09-8365581. **Denmark**, *T09-5373099.*
France, *Level 2, 63 Albert St, T09-3795850.*
Germany, *6th Floor, 52 Symonds St, City,*
T09-9133674. **Ireland** *Level 6, 18 Shortland*
St, T09-9772252. **Japan**, *Level 12, ASB Bank*
Centre, 135 Albert St, City, T09-3034106.
Korea, *Level 10, Toshiba House, 396 Queen*
St, T09-3790818. **Netherlands**, *LJ Hooker*
House, Level 1, 57 Symonds St, City,
T09-3795399. **Peru**, *199-209 Great North Rd,*
Grey Lynn, T09-3769400. **Sweden**, *13th Flr,*

92-96 Albert St, City, T09-3735332. **UK**, *NZI*
House, 151 Queen St, City, T09-3032973. **USA**,
Level 3, Citibank Centre, 23 Customs Street
East, T09-3032724.

Wellington
Australia, *72 Hobson St, T04-4736411,*
Canada, *3rd Floor, 61 Molesworth St,*
T04-4739577, www.voyage.gc.ca **France**, *42*
Manners St, T04-3842555; **Germany**, *90*
Hobson St, T04-4736063; **UK**, *44 Hill St,*
Wellington T04-9242889,
www.britain.org.nz **USA**, *29 Fitzherbert*
Terr, Thorndon, T04-4722068.

New Zealand embassies abroad

Australia **High Commission**:
Commonwealth Ave, Canberra, ACT 2600,
T0262704211 **Consulate General:** *14th*
Floor Goldfields building, 1 Alfred St, Circular
Quay, Sydney, (PO Box 365), NSW 2000,
T0292471999.
Canada **High Commission**: *Suite 727,*
Metropolitan House, 99 Bank St, Ottowa, Ont
K1P 6G3, T6132385991 **Consulate General**:
Suite 1200-888 Dunsmuir St, Vancouver, BC
V6C 3K4, T6046847388.
France **NZ Embassy**: *7ter, Rue Leonard de*
Vinci, 75116, Paris, T0145002411.
Germany **NZ Embassy**:
Bundeskanzlerplatz 2 - 1053113 Bonn,
T228-228-070 **Consulate General**:

Heimhuderstrasse 56, 20148,
Hamburg, T404425550.
Ireland **Consulate General**: *46 Upper*
Mount St, Dublin 2, T016762464.
Netherlands **NZ Embassy**: *Carnegielaan*
10, 2517 KH, The Hague, T703469324
UK **High Commission**: *New Zealand*
House, Haymarket, London SW1Y 4TQ,
T09069100100
USA **NZ Embassy**: *Observatory Circle NW,*
Washington DC, 20008,
T2023284800 **Consulate General**: *Suite*
1150, 12400 Wiltshire Blvd, Los Angeles. CA
90025, T3102071605 **Other Consulate**:
6810 51st Ave NE, Seattle, WA 98115,
T2065259881.

Before you travel

Passports and visas

For detailed visa information consult the Visiting section of the New Zealand Immigration Service (NZIS) website, www.immigration.govt.nz or contact them at NZIS, Private Bag, Wellesley St, Auckland, T09-9144100.

All visitors must be in possession of a passport that is valid for three months beyond the date you intend to leave the country. Australian citizens or holders of an Australian returning resident visa do not need a **visitor's visa** and can stay in New Zealand indefinitely. UK citizens do not need a visa and are automatically issued with a six-month visitor's permit on arrival. To find out the visa status of other countries check out the Visiting New Zealand section of the **New Zealand Immigration Service** website, or ask your travel agent. All visitors making an application for a visitor's permit require: (a) a passport that is valid for at least three months after your departure from New Zealand; (b) an onward or return ticket to a country you have permission to enter; (c) sufficient money to support yourself during your stay (approximately NZ$1000 per month). The sufficient funds factor can be waived if you have a friend or relative in New Zealand (citizen) who officially agrees to sponsor you, ie guarantees to support you financially during your stay. If you have to apply for a visitor's visa you can do so at your nearest New Zealand Embassy or by downloading the relevant forms from the website.

Longer stays and work visas
It is illegal to work on a visitor's permit. Non-residents (with the except of Australian citizens) must obtain a **work visa** which allows you to enter the country, then a **work permit** which allows you to work upon arrival. Applications for both are best made well before arrival. The NZIS website has details and downloadable application forms. One exception to this rule is the **working holiday visa** which is available for those aged 18–30 from a number of countries(including Canada, Japan, Ireland, Germany, France and the UK) and entitles you to work for 12 months. Conditions apply. Student visas come under a separate category. You can also get extensions on your visitor's permit for up to nine months but you must meet certain criteria. For detailed information contact the NZIS direct. For a general **residence visa** an application must be made from your own country. It involves a points system relating to factors such as age, education, occupation. The golden target number required fluctuates depending on the perceived demand for immigrants and, to a degree, politics. For details consult the 'Migration' section on the website or contact the NZIS direct. Be warned – you will need endless supplies of patience. Once a residence Visa is secured you can apply for **citizenship** after three years' residency in New Zealand.

Customs regulations

New Zealand's environment and highly unique biodiversity has literally been decimated by unwelcome and non-native flora and fauna. Not surprisingly, therefore, it has imposed strict bio-security laws. Be extra vigilant about not carrying any fruit, animal or plant matter of any kind without prior permission. Heavy fines are imposed on those who flaunt the rules. You will find details of restricted items on the Customs website. The usual rules and regulations are also in force regarding pets or any live animals, drugs and firearms. Comprehensive advice for travellers is available on the New Zealand Customs Service website, www.customs.govt.nz

Apart from your personal effects and as long as you are over 17 years of age you are allowed the following importation concessions: 200 cigarettes or 250 g of tobacco or 50 cigars, or a mix of all three weighing no more than 250 g; 41/2 litres of wine or beer and one 1125 ml bottle of spirits, liqueur or other libation. Goods of value up to NZ$1000 are duty- and tax-free.

Insurance

Although New Zealand does not exactly suffer from being a crime-ridden society, accidents and delay can still occur. If you can afford it, full travel insurance is advised. For peace of mind, at the very least get medical insurance and coverage for personal effects. The New Zealand Accident Compensation Scheme covers visitors to New Zealand for personal injury by accident. Benefits include some emergency medical expenses, but do not include loss of earnings. **Accident Info Services**, a private company, can give 24-hour advice to visitors on how best to access the New Zealand health system, To800-263345.

Points to note There are a wide variety of policies to choose from, so it's best to shop around. Your local travel agent can also advise on the best and most reliable deals available. Always read the small print carefully. Check that the policy covers the activities you intend or may end up doing. Also check exactly what your medical cover includes, ie ambulance, helicopter rescue or emergency flights back home. Also check the payment protocol. You may have to cough up first (literally) before the insurance company reimburses you. It is always best to dig out all the receipts for expensive personal effects like jewellery or cameras. Take photos of these items and note down all serial numbers. It will also almost certainly be necessary to extend the premium and pay more to cover individual items worth more than NZ$500.

Insurance companies

You are advised to shop around.
STA Travel, *www.statravel.com* and other reputable student travel organisations offer good value policies. Young travellers from North America can try the International Student Insurance Service (ISIS), which is available through **STA Travel**, (USA) *T1-800-7770112, www.statravel.com*

Other recommended travel insurance companies in North America include:
Travel Guard, *T1-800-8261300, www.noelgroup.com*
Access America, *T1-800- 2848300;*
Travel Insurance Services, *T1-800-9371387;*
Travel Assistance International, *T1-800-8212828;* and
Council Travel, *T1-888-COUNCIL, www.counciltravel.com.*

Companies worth trying in the UK other than **STA**, *www.statravel.co.uk* , who specialise in travel for those under 26, include **Direct Line**, *T0845-2468744, www.directline.com*, the **Flexicover Group**, *T0870-990-9292, www.flexicover.net.uk* and **Columbus**, *T020-7375-0011*.

Older travellers should note that some companies will not cover people over 65 years old, or may charge higher premiums. The best policies for older travellers (UK) are offered by **Age Concern**, *T01883-3469; and* **Saga**, *T0800 0565464, www.saga.co.uk* who specifically insure travellers over 50.

Essentials Before you travel

Vaccinations ⤞ *see also Health, page 69*

There are no vaccinations required to enter NZ but as with any country, you are advised to get a tetanus injection or ensure that your boosters are up to date.

Discount travel agents

Discount travel agents in Australia
Flight Centres, *82 Elizabeth St, Sydney, T131600, www.flightcentre.com.au* Branches in other main cities
STA Travel *T1300360960, www.statravelaus.com.au 702 Harris St, Ultimo, Sydney and 256 Flinders St, Melbourne.*
Travel.com.au *80 Clarence St, Sydney, T0292901500, www.travel.com.au*

Discount travel agents in North America
Air Brokers International, *323 Geary St, Suite 4111, San Francisco, CA 94102, T800 8833273, www.airbrokers.com.* Consolidator and specialist on RTW and Circle Pacific tickets.
Council Travel, *205 E 42nd St, New York, NY 10017, T800-COUNCIL,www.counciltravel.com.* Student/budget agency with branches in many US cities.
Discount Airfares Worldwide On-Line, *www.etn.nl/discount.htm.* A hub of consolidator and discount agent links.
International Travel Network/Airlines of the Web, *www.itn.net/airlines.* Offers online information and reservations for a number of airlines.
STA Travel, *5900 Wiltshire Blvd, suite 2110, Los Angeles, CA 90036, T800 7770112, www.sta-travel.com.* Discount/youth travel company with branches in New York, San Francisco, Boston, Miami, Chicago, Seattle and Washington DC.

Travel CUTS, *187 College St, Toronto, ON M5T 1P7, T800 6672887, www.travelcuts.com.* Specialists in student discount fares, IDs and other travel services. Branches in other Canadian cities.
Travelocity, *www.travelocity.com.* Online consolidator .

Discount travel agents in Britain and Ireland
Council Travel, *28a Poland St, London W1V 3DB, T020 7437 7767, www.destinations-group.com*
Ebookers, *www.ebookers.com.* Comprehensive travel booking website.
Expedia, *www.expedia.com.* Another web-only travel site, also withplentiful background information for planning your trip.
STA Travel, *86 Old Brompton Rd, London SW7 3LH, T020 7361 6161, www.statravel.co.uk.* Specialists in student discount fares, IDs and other travel services. Also branches found in most major cities and many university campuses throughout the UK.
Trailfinders, *194 Kensington High St, London W8 6FT, T020 7938 3939, www.trailfinders.co.uk.* Particularly good at organising personalised itineraries and adventure travel.
Usit Campus *19 Aston Quay, Dublin 2, T01 6021777 or 6778117.*Student/youth specialists in Ireland.

What to take

New Zealand is a well-developed nation and all you will need, from pharmaceuticals to camping gear, is readily available throughout the country. There is also a wealth of quality maps and travel books available. Given the favourable dollar rate if you are coming from Europe or North America you may be advised to travel light and buy as you go. Auckland can supply just about all your needs. Backpackers naturally are advised to bring a good sleeping bag and a bed sheet. These are not always provided in hostels and certainly not available in the backcountry tramping huts. A good pair of boots and a large rucksack is a good idea. Bring lots of camera film with you, it will be cheaper than buying it in New Zealand. Remember also to bring a compatible electrical adapter plug. Binoculars are recommended as is a sun hat, sunscreen and sunglasses.

Money

The New Zealand currency is the dollar ($), divided into 100 cents (c). Coins come in denominations of 5c, 10c, 20c, 50c, $1 and $2. New Zealand notes come in $5, $10, $20, $50 and $100 denominations.

Travellers' cheques

The safest way to carry money is in travellers' cheques. These are available for a small commission from all major banks. **American Express** (Amex), **Visa** and **Thomas Cook** cheques are widely accepted. Most banks do not charge for changing travellers' cheques and usually offer the best exchange rates. Be sure to keep a record of your cheque numbers and keep the cheques you have cashed separate from the cheques themselves, so that you can get a full refund of all uncashed cheques should you lose them. It is best to bring NZ$ cheques to avoid extra exchange costs.

Credit cards, ATMs and EFTPOS

All the major credit cards (**Visa**, **MasterCard**, **Amex**, **JCB** and **Diners**) are widely accepted. New Zealand has a wonderful system called EFTPOS (Electronic Funds Transfer at Point of Sale) which is essentially like having thousands of mini-ATMs at points of sale throughout the country. Most hotels, shops, retail outlets and petrol stations have them and it has revolutionized the need to carry around wads of cash. Of course it is best suited to those who have a bank account in New Zealand and carry the various cash/cheque cards, but credit cards can be used with the relevant pin number. The real beauty of the system, other than its sheer convenience, is that you are not charged exorbitant fees for using it. If you intend to stay in New Zealand for a while you may be able to open an account with one of the major banks and secure an EFTPOS/ATM card and PIN. That way your money is in the bank and safe. The standard ATMs are readily available in almost all towns and though they accept non-host bank cards, it's best to stick to your own bank's ATMs so you do not incur hidden fees. Credit cards can of course be used and some banks are linked to foreign savings accounts and cards by such networks as Cirrus and Plus. Check with your own bank and card provider and ask what you can and cannot do before you leave.

*Exchange rates at time of going to press :
$0.587 to the US$
$0.367 to the UK£
$0.521 to the Euro.*

Banks

Almost all towns and villages have at least one of the major bank branches and an ATM. The main banks are the Bank of New Zealand, the National Bank of New Zealand, the ASB Bank, Post Bank and Countrywide Bank, with other trans-Tasman banks, like Westpac Trust and ANZ also in evidence. Major internet banks like Bank Direct also do a healthy business in New Zealand. Bank opening hours are Monday-Friday 0900-1630 with some city branches also remaining open on Saturday mornings until 1230. Exchange offices like Thomas Cook and American Express tend to have longer opening hours, sometimes staying open until 2100 in the cities.

Money transfers

If you need money quickly or in an emergency the best way is to have it wired to you, via any major bank with the Western Union, (NZ)T0800-270000/6492700050 or via Thomas Cook and Moneygram, (NZ)T0800-872893, www.thomascook.com This transfer can be done in less than an hour or up to a week depending how much is being transferred and how much you are willing to pay (about $30-80).Charges are on a sliding scale; it will cost proportionately less to wire out more money.

Cost of living/travelling

If you are coming to New Zealand from the UK or the US you will be amazed at how far a pound or a US dollar will go. In late 2000 the NZ$ dropped to a record low with the US$ and after a slight rally with the UK£ in the mid-1990s the NZ$ is back hovering around £0.35 and about US$0.55. Those travelling from the UK and US will find things generally a lot cheaper, though some things such as beer are about the same price. Eating out is relatively cheap and should be enjoyed to the full. Accommodation can be expensive. Hostel accommodation will range from about $16-22 for a bunk, while a basic single or double room will cost up to double that. A non-powered site in a motor camp will cost from $8-15 per person. A powered site is usually about the same or just a few dollars more. B&B accommodation varies, ranging from $75 for a basic double to over $200 for luxury. Motel prices vary but a double can be secured for as little as $60. A more luxurious motel will cost up to $175. When it comes to transportation petrol is expensive at around $1 per litre ($4 per gallon). Many organized activities are also expensive.

The minimum budget required, if staying in hostels or campsites, cooking for yourself, not drinking much and travelling relatively slowly is about $60 per person per day, but this isn't going to be a lot of fun. Going on the odd tour, travelling faster and eating out occasionally will raise this to a more realistic $80-100. Those staying in modest B&Bs, hotels and motels as couples, eating out most nights and taking a few tours will need to reckon on about $180-275 per person per day. Costs in the major cities will be 20-50% higher. Non-hostelling single travellers should budget on spending around 60-70% of what a couple would spend. However, in New Zealand, despite the highly favourable exchange rates, you will find that money evaporates just as quickly and mysteriously as anywhere else, so it is wise to budget before your arrival.

Youth and student discounts

There are various official youth/student ID cards available. The most useful is the International Student ID Card (ISIC) which will secure discounts in many accommodation establishments, some admissions and activities. In New Zealand you can also secure savings on domestic air travel and reductions on rail and ferry services. For any visitor the numerous and varied backpacker membership and accommodation discount schemes like the YHA (see page 50) are also well worth looking at, with most also managing to securing cheaper rates with many travel and activity operators.

Getting there

Air

There are six airports in the country which handle international flights, but Auckland is the principal international airport. Wellington, Palmerston North and Hamilton in North Island and Christchurch, Dunedin and Queenstown in South Island all offer regular services to eastern Australia.

Buying a ticket

There are now enormous numbers of high street, phone and internet outlets for buying your plane ticket. This can make life confusing but the competition does mean that dogged work can be rewarded with a very good deal. Fares will depend on the season, with prices much higher during Dec-Jan unless booked well in advance. Mid-year tends to see the cheapest fares. **Air New Zealand,** www.airnz.com, is New Zealand's main international airline and flies from a considerable number of capitals and major cities. **Qantas,** www.qantas.com.au, also offers regular flights via New Zealand en route to or from Australia.

The internet is great way of finding a bargain ticket, but can be frustrating unless you just want a straight return or single fare to a single destination. If you are considering a multi-destination journey it is worth checking out 2 or 3 agents in person. **One-way** flight **tickets** are not necessarily a lot more expensive than half a return fare. If you are contemplating a lengthy trip and are undecided about further plans, or like the idea of being unconstrained, then a single fare could be for you. Note that immigration officials can get very suspicious of visitors arriving on one-way tickets, especially on short-term visas. Anyone without long-term residency on a one-way ticket will need to show proof of substantial funds – enough for a stay and onward flight. Discuss this with your local New Zealand Embassy or High Commission before committing to a one-way ticket. **Round-the-World** (RTW) tickets can be a real bargain if you stick to the most popular routes, sometimes working out even cheaper than a return fare. RTWs start at around £800 (1,157 Euros) or US$1,750, depending on the season. Australia is easy to include on a RTW itinerary.

When trying to find the best deal, make sure you check the route, journey duration, stopovers, departure and arrival times, restrictions and cancellation fees. Many cheap flights are sold by small agencies, most honest and reliable, but there are some risks involved when buying tickets at rock-bottom prices. Do not pay too much money in advance and check with the airline directly to confirm your reservation.

Flights from Europe

The main route, and the cheapest, is usually via Heathrow or Frankfurt and the USA (Los Angeles), though fares will also be quoted via other US cities and Asia. Either route usually takes from 20 to 30 hours including stops. There are no non-stop routes, so it's worth checking out what stopovers are on offer: this might be your only chance to see Kuala Lumpur or LA and, besides, a 30-hour journey, only stopping in airports to refuel is, in a word, gruelling. Stopovers of a few nights do not usually increase the cost of the ticket appreciably. The cheapest return flights, off-season, will be around £600 (868 Euros), rising to at least £900 (1,302 Euros) around Christmas.

Flights from Australia

As you might expect there is a huge choice and much competition with trans-Tasman flights. Traditionally most flights used to go from Cairns, Brisbane, Sydney and

Melbourne to Auckland but now many of the cheaper flights can actually be secured to Wellington, Christchurch and Queenstown. Other destinations include Palmerston North, Hamilton and Dunedin. The New Zealand based **Freedom Air** service to Dunedin is cheap (as low as NZ$450) but with only a few flights a week they must be booked well in advance. Flights and especially ski packages to Queenstown can also be cheaper and have been heavily promoted in recent years, but conditions usually apply, giving you limited flexibility. At any given time there are usually special deals on offer from the major players like **Qantas**, **United** and **Air New Zealand** so shop around. Prices range from AUS$450-750. Use the listings in this book, the web, your local travel agent and the national newspapers. From Australia you are likely to be interested in 'open-jaw' tickets that will allow you to fly in to one city and depart from another. This will almost certainly be more expensive and, given the many restrictions and conditions imposed, they are often hard to secure at a good price. Always be careful to check the conditions of the cheaper 'temporary' deals with regard to your minimum or maximum allowed length of stay, cancellations, refunds etc. The flight time between Sydney and Auckland is 3 hours, Melbourne 3 hours 45 minutes.

Flights from the Americas

There are direct **Air New Zealand** and **Qantas** flights from Los Angeles to Auckland. Sadly, one of the cheapest carriers **United** succumbed to the recent financial strains on all airlines and have had to cut services to New Zealand. The cost of a standard return in the high season from LAX starts from around US$1000, from New York from US$1,450 and Chicago from US$1,400. **Air Canada** and **United** connect with **Alliance** partners at LAX from Vancouver, Toronto and Montreal. Prices range from CAN$1500-2700. **Singapore Airlines**, fly direct to Auckland daily from LAX stopping in Singapore. There are also direct flights from Buenos Aires to Auckland with **Aerolinas Argentinas**. The flight time between LAX and Auckland is around 2½ hours.

Major airlines flying to New Zealand

From Australia
Air New Zealand, T0800-0284149, www.airnz.co.uk
Freedom Air, T0800-600500, www.freedomair.co.nz
Qantas, T0845-7747767, www.qantas.com.au
Singapore Airlines, T0870-6088886, www.singaporeair.com

From North America
Star Alliance Partners, T1800-2416522, www.star-alliance.com
Air New Zealand, US T1800-2621234, Canada T1800-6635494, www.airnz.com
Qantas, T1800-2274500, www.qantas.com
Singapore Airlines, T1800-7423333, www.singaporeair.com

From the UK
All Star Alliance Partners, www.star-alliance.com
Air New Zealand, T0800-0284149, www.airnz.co.uk

Qantas, T0845-7747767, www.qantas.co.uk
Thai Airways, T0870-6060911 www.thaiair.com
Garuda–Indonesia, T020-74678600, www.garuda-indonesia.com
Singapore Airlines, T0870-6088886, www.singaporeair.com
Japan Airlines, T0845-7747700, www.jal.com.
Malaysian Airlines, T020-73412000, www.malaysiaairlines.com

From South Africa
Qantas, www.qantas.com.au fly direct from Johannesburg to Sydney with onward connections to New Zealand.
South African Airways, www.saa.co.za do not fly direct to Auckland, but connections can be added on to direct flights to Sydney.

Airline offices in New Zealand

Aerolineas Argentinas, 15th Floor ASB Centre, 135 Albert St, T03-793675.
Air New Zealand, corner of Customs and Queen St, City, T03-362424/ T0800-737000,

Air Pacific, *Level 12/17 Albert St, City,*
T03-792404.
Air Vanuatu, *2nd Floor West Plaza Building,*
corner Customs and Albert St, City,
T03-733435.
American Airlines, *15th Floor Jetset Centre,*
48 Emily Pl, City, T03-099159.
British Airways, *T03-578950.*
Cathay Pacific, *11th Floor, Arthur Andersen*
Tower, 205 Queen St, T03-790861.
Freedom Air, *T0800-600500*
Garuda Indonesia, *Westpac Trust Tower,*
120 Albert St, T03-672324.
Japan Airlines, *Westpac Trust Tower,*
120 Albert St, T03-799906.
Korean Airlines, *92 Albert St, City,*

T09-142000.
Lufthansa Airlines, *T0800-945220.*
Malaysia Airlines, *12th Floor Affco House,*
12-26 Swanson St, T03-793743.
Origin Pacific *T0800-302-302,*
www.originpacific.co.nz
Polynesian Airlines, *Samoa House, 283 K' Rd,*
City, T03-095396.
Qantas Airlines, *191 Queen St, City,*
T03-578900.
Singapore Airlines, *West Plaza Building,*
corner of Albert and Fanshawe St, City,
T03-032129, www.singaporeair.co.nz
Thai Airways, *22 Fanshawe St, City,*
T03-773886.
United Airlines, *17th Floor, 1 Queen St,*
T0800-508648, www.ual.com

Touching down

Airport information

For detailed information on negotiating Auckland International Airport see Auckland ins and outs, page 78. Before you leave your own country check their excellent website www.auckland-airport.co.nz Other airports' websites include: Wellington Airport, www.wellington-airport.co.nz and Christchurch, www.christchurch-airport.co.nz

Taxes

There is a 12.5% GST (Goods and Services Tax) placed on almost every bought item in New Zealand. Prices quoted almost always include GST, but on bigger quotes or services it pays to check. On leaving New Zealand there is a **Departure Tax** of $20-$25 depending on which airport you leave from. This is not included in your ticket price.

Tourist information

The official New Zealand Visitor Information Network is made up of around 100 accredited Visitor Information Centres (VICs) nationally known as I-Sites. **National I-Sites** are based in Auckland and Christchurch as well as the main tourist centres, like Rotorua and Queenstown. Open seven days a week, they provide a comprehensive information service including accommodation bookings and domestic airline, bus and train ticketing. Souvenir shops and occasionally other retail outlets, currency exchange and cafés are often attached. **Regional I-Sites** are found throughout the country and there may be more than one in each region. They provide a general information booking service usually seven days a week and there is also a huge amount of free material. **Local I-Sites** can be found almost anywhere, providing local information as well as assistance in accommodation and transport bookings. They are open at least five days a week, but are subject to varying seasonal and weekend hours. For the purposes of this book the I-Sites are referred to as Visitors Information Centres or VICs.

⦂ Touching down

Business hours
Weekday business hours are usually 0900-1700. Most retail outlets close at 1730 and in the larger towns many are also open at the weekend. Also, in the main centres, the larger supermarket chains are open in the evenings. The modern city malls usually offer one or two late shopping nights, which are usually Thursday or Friday. Almost every town and village has the iconic Kiwi corner 'dairy' whose closing hours are a lottery, but usually late. Most Government offices are open from about 0830-1630.

Electricity
The New Zealand supply is 230/240 volts (50 hertz). Plugs are either two- or three-pronged with flat pins. North American appliances require both an adapter and a transformer; UK an adapter only and Australian appliances are the same. Adapters and transformers are available at local hardware stores or the airport.

Emergencies
For Police, Fire or Ambulance T111

Essential telephone numbers
Emergency: T111
National directory assistance: T018
International directory assistance: T0172
International direct-dial access code: T00

International operator: T0170
Local and national operator: T010
New Zealand country code: T64
Toll help desk: T123

Laundry
Most towns, villages and accommodation establishments have laundries. They tend to operate with $1 or $2 coins. A full wash and dry will cost about $6.

Time
At 1200 in NZ it is 0900 in Sydney, 1100 yesterday in the UK, 0800 in Japan, 1500 yesterday in Los Angeles or 1800 yesterday in New York. Allow for daylight saving i.e. from the first Sunday in October to the third Sunday in March the clock goes one hour forward.

Toilets
Public toilets are readily available and very rarely are you charged for the privilege.

Weights and measures
New Zealand uses the metric system. Distances are in kilometres, petrol is in litres. Ask for a pint in a pub however and you will not be looked at in a funny way.

Well does it?
Yes, the water does go down the plug in an anticlockwise direction in the Southern Hemisphere.

Local customs and laws

Tipping
Tipping in New Zealand is at the customer's discretion and not really expected. However, In a good restaurant you should leave a tip of 10-15% if you are satisfied with the service, but the bill may include a service charge. Tipping is appreciated in pubs and bars and taxi drivers also expect some sort of tip. On a longer journey 10% is fine. As in most other counties, hotel porters, bellboys, waiters and waitresses should all be tipped to supplement their meagre wages.

Smoking
New Zealand is fast catching up with the general 'look there's a leper' attitude to smoking. However, it is still possible to smoke in many restaurants in segregated sections. Many public places, all airlines and most public transport do not allow smoking, but will not have you shot for smoking outside (airport terminals that is).

Thankfully, for the smoker, almost all pubs and clubs still allow smoking. But in 2003 this looks set to change. For the average pub goer the concept of not being able to do so while enjoying a libation is frankly ridiculous.

Responsible tourism

For the vast majority of tourists it is New Zealand's environment and nature that are its greatest attraction. Yet regardless of your interest or your intention, the moment you set foot in New Zealand you are by definition an **Ecotourist**. In essence, though your hosts may not demand it, the environment does. There is no doubt whatsoever that the environment is the biggest and brightest jewel in the tourism crown and a resource that is not only precious but requires considerable protection.

Yet one could argue that environmentalism and tourism is, in essence, a contradiction in terms. Surely what makes New Zealand so special, so attractive, is the very lack of humanity and its areas of almost inaccessible wilderness. There is no doubt this is true, but thankfully the New Zealand psyche is such that it seems to successfully marry tourism and environmentalism and bestow upon the union a blessing that has so far resulted in a congenial, if naturally imperfect relationship. So good in fact, that the country has earned the reputation as one of the best ecotourism destinations in the world. Part of this success is due to the vast area that is protected as forest parks, national parks, nature and marine reserves – almost a quarter of the entire country – all coming under the committed, yet under-resourced advocacy and administration of the **Department of Conservation**.

Before you arrive you can avail yourself of a wealth of information on its excellent website www.doc.govt.nz and throughout your travels you will find dedicated information centres and field stations in all cities, major provincial towns and national parks. If you intend to go walking or to embark on a longer tramp then you will find DoC invaluable and through its system of backcountry huts and campsites an essential aspect of the experience.

Given the country's natural resources New Zealand is, not surprisingly, on the cutting edge of ecotourism. The sheer choice and quality of activities, let alone the location in which they can be experienced are superb, from whale watching at Kaikoura or tramping in Fiordland to exploring the island sanctuaries of Kapiti or Tiri Tiri Matangi. New Zealand is one of very few countries where you can see rare or endangered species (especially birds) at close hand and in solitude. For many this is a new and welcome experience and in deep contrast to the constraints of a being in a busy hide or being surrounded by an orgy of twitchers all falling over each other to compare the size of their telescopes.

Safety

Despite appearances, or what you may have heard, New Zealand has its fair share of crime. There are more guns in New Zealand than there are people and many in the hands of the poor, the drug gangs, the mad and the bad. Tourists are rarely targeted for anything other than petty crime but you still need to be careful. Theft, especially in Auckland, is rife and tourist accommodation establishments are not exempt. Cars and their contents are also regularly targeted. Do not relax your guard, keep money safe and out of sight. Keep your vehicle locked at all times and put valuables in the boot (trunk). It may sound ridiculous but you also need to be wary of other tourists. Having suitable insurance cover is also wise. Urban New Zealand has its fair share of rapes, some brutal, so women should be just as vigilant

For legal advice contact the local Citizens Advice Bureau, in Auckland, T09-5240298

⁝ How big is your footprint?

Ultimately when it comes to being a responsible ecotourist it is of course your own attitude that is crucial. Much of the Environmental Code advocated by the DoC is common sense. Over all, the entire concept can be summed up with two words and an age-old cliché – **respect** and **awareness** and **'take nothing but pictures, leave nothing but footprints'**. Given the unbelievable damage we humans have already inflicted on New Zealand's unique and ancient biodiversity surely that attitude is not only particularly poignant, but also demanded.

For a listing of ecotourist operators throughout the country see page 22.

The independent organization *New Zealand Royal Forest and Bird Society*, 172 Taranaki St, Wellington, T04-3857374, www.forest-bird.org.nz is excellent and produces a quarterly magazine for its members. The monthly *Wilderness Magazine* ($7) or bi-monthly *New Zealand Geographic* ($15), are also good, containing comprehensive outdoors and ecoactivity information and are available in most newsagents and bookshops. For other NZ magazines see www.nzmagazineshop.co.nz

as they need be in the more populous and notorious nations.

Drink driving and speeding laws are very strict in New Zealand: do not even think about driving while under the influence, and keep your speed down. Thanks to the heavy road toll (though some say its principally a major source of government revenue) speed cameras and patrol cars are omnipresent. Drug laws are also strict so don't get caught in possession. One other thing; if you do get lumped with a speeding or parking tickets, as tempting as it may be, it is far less hassle to pay it off and not consider 'doing a runner'. After all, you may well want to return one day!

Getting around

Public transport in all its forms (except rail) is generally both good and efficient. All the main cities and provincial towns can be reached easily by air or by road. Although standard fares, especially by air, can be expensive there are a vast number of discount passes and special seasonal deals available, aimed particularly at the young independent traveller. Although it is entirely possible to negotiate the country by public transport, for sheer convenience you are advised to get your own set of wheels. Many of the country's delights are only to be seen off the beaten track and are certainly a long walk from the nearest bus stop. You will also free yourself of organized schedules. Long term vehicle hire or temporary purchase is generally viable (especially if the costs are shared) and whether you go the way of a standard vehicle or campervan, you will find the country is well geared up for this mode of travel. Having said that, petrol costs are expensive and need to be taken into account.

At the time of going to print domestic air and rail travel in New Zealand is in a state of relative chaos, and has been for months. **Air New Zealand Link** and **Origin Pacific** are currently the two principal domestic air carriers with Qantas (Australia), also providing services between Auckland, Christchurch and Wellington. With the dramatic and unexpected liquidation of **Qantas New Zealand** in April 2001, the skies remain open to a number of interested parties and although none are yet properly established they include **Freedom Air** and **Virgin Blue**. Thankfully, the relative lack of competition has not adversely affected prices. On the contrary, bookings made well in advance over the web with Air New Zealand or Qantas can see you flying from Auckland to Christchurch for as little as $60.

Worse still is the state of rail travel. From 2002 **TransRail** closed all domestic routes except the Auckland/Wellington (**Northerner**), the Christchurch to Greymouth (**TransAlpine**) and the Christchurch to Picton (**TransCoastal**). Again only time will tell whether even these survive. As usual it seems, even here in New Zealand with a modern society becoming so obsessed with speed and the increased pace of life trains, are just too slow.

Air

As well as the principal international airports of Auckland, Wellington and Christchurch, New Zealand has many smaller provincial town airports that are mainly well served. **Air New Zealand Link**, T0800-737000, www.airnewzealand.co.nz, is by far the most dominant carrier. **Origin Pacific**, T0800-302302, www.originpacific.co.nz, also offer a number of domestic services but exist on a lesser footing. All are highly professional and efficient and you will rarely have problems with delays or service.

Apart from the major domestic operators there are many smaller companies with scheduled services. These include: **Great Barrier Airlines** (Great Barrier, Coromandel and Northland), **SoundsAir** (offering a viable alternative to the ferry between North and South Islands) and **Southern Air** (between Invercargill and Stewart Island). All these companies are listed in the relevant sections. Note that flying anywhere in New Zealand is, on a clear day, a scenic delight and often well worth the expense.

Domestic discount fares

If you can, book domestic flights well in advance on the internet or through a travel agent. Most discounted fares can only be purchased in New Zealand and are subject to 12.5% GST (Tax). There are a number of deals available that will make considerable savings depending on season and availability. **Air New Zealand** offers an Airpass system which can offer attractive discounts, which works on a zone and coupon system and can be booked prior to arrival. For more information ask your travel agent or see the website (www.airnewzealand.co.nz) Student and backpacker discounts of up to 50% are available on some domestic flights on presentation of an ISIC, YHA, VIP or BBH card. Conditions and rates vary, so research and book well in advance.

Bus

National bus travel in New Zealand is generally well organized and the networks and daily schedules are good. Numerous shuttle companies service the South Island and these are listed in the Transport sections of the relevant text. There are also many local operators and independent companies that provide shuttles to accommodation establishments, attractions and activities, and these are listed in the Transport sections of the main travelling text.

The two main bus companies are **Intercity**, www.intercitycoach.co.nz, and **Newmans**, www.newmanscoach.co.nz. They often operate in partnership. For information and reservations call the following regional centres: Auckland, T09-9136100; Wellington, T04-4725111; Christchurch, T03-3799020; Dunedin, T03-4749600; and Queenstown, T03-4428238. Intercity is the only truly national company operating in both North and South Islands, while **Newmans** operate throughout North Island, except in Northland where **Northliner Express**, T09-3075873, www.northliner.co.nz, co-operates with **Intercity**. Other companies in North Island:

White Star, T06-3588777, who serve the route between New Plymouth and Wellington, taking in Wanganui and Palmerston North; and the **Little Kiwi Bus Co**, T0800-759999, operating between Auckland and Rotorua via Hamilton. A small company that recently began offering services around Coromandel is **Coromandel Explorer Tours**, T07-8282753, www.coromandeltours.co.nz The principal backpacker bus companies are: **Kiwi Experience**, T09-3669830, www.kiwiexperience.com; **Magic Travellers**, T09-3585600,

www.magicbus.co.nz

Stray, PO Box 14114, Enderly, Hamilton, T07-8243627, www.straytravel.co.nz and the more eco/activity-orientated **Flying Kiwi**, T0800-693296, www.flyingkiwi.com They have a wide range of flexible routes and options available nationally and for reasonable prices. The unfortunately named **Bottom Bus**, T03-4347370, www.bottombus.co.nz, operates a service around the Southern Scenic Route between Dunedin and Milford Sound taking in Queenstown en route.

Concession fares

All the bus companies offer a variety of concession fares. With **Intercity** and **Newmans**, infants less than 2 years travel free and children less than 12 years travel at 33%. Travellers over the age of 60 travel at 20%, backpackers (YHA, VIP, BBH, Nomads cardholders) and students at 15%. There are super fares of 25% and supersaver fares of 50% available but these should be pre-booked. **Intercity** and **Newmans** also operate a **Club Free-Way Card**, similar to Frequent Flyers that accrues points that can later be redeemed for discounts or free tickets. Membership costs $15. **Newmans** also offer attractive discounts but these tend to be more limiting in both timetable and destination. **NB** Economy Fare cancellations must be made up to 2 hrs in advance to avoid a loss of 50% on the ticket price.

Bus passes

Intercity Countrywide bus passes There are a choice of four 'hop on-hop off' routes throughout both the North and South Islands ranging from an Auckland to Christchurch (or reverse) trip from $480 to an Auckland and back deal (or Christchurch and back) from $636. Valid for three months.

Intercity North Island bus passes The 'Twin Coast Discovery' operates in a loop throughout Northland. It takes in the Bay of Islands, Kaitia, the Hokianga, Waipoua Forest and Dargaville; $99, child $67. The 'Coromandel Trail' allows you to travel from Auckland to Rotorua or Tauranga taking in a loop around the Coromandel Peninsula via Thames from $101 (Tauranga $85), child $68/$57. The 'Coromandel Loop' (Thames to Thames) alone costs $54, child $36. The 'Forests Islands and Geysers' takes in a combination of Northland, Coromandel, Bay of Plenty (Rotorua) destinations before offering the choice of southwards travel to Taupo and Wellington or the Waikato (Waitomo Caves) and return to Auckland; $341, child $229. The 'Pacific Coast Highway Traveller' goes from Auckland to Thames (taking in the loop around the Coromandel Peninsula), through Tauranga and Rotorua and then rejoins the coast at Whakatane before travelling through the Waioweka Gorge to Gisborne and Napier to Wellington; $209, child $140. The 'North Island Combo Pass' is a flexi-plan ticket between Auckland and Wellington taking in either the Coromandel or Waitomo; $245, child $164. The 'North Island Value Pass' is a cheaper offer at $147, child $99 but misses out the Coromandel. All passes are valid for three months.

Intercity South Island bus passes The 'West Coast Passport' operates between Picton/Nelson or Greymouth to Queenstown; $169/$149/$104, child $113/ $100/$70. The 'Milford Bound Adventurer' is available on services from Christchurch via Mount Cook to Queenstown and then into Milford Sound; $179, child $120. The 'East Coast

Explorer' allows travel from Picton to Queenstown and Te Anau or Dunedin; $135, child $91. The 'Southern Discovery' departs from either Christchurch or Greymouth taking in Mount Cook, Queenstown and Milford Sound from $320, child $214. This trip is best combined with the famous 'TransAlpine' rail journey between Greymouth and Christchurch (see Rail section below). There are two options taking in the whole of the island; the 'Southern Experience' from Christchurch or Picton return, from $395, child $265 and the 'South Island Extreme' which also departs from Christchurch or Picton from $440, child $295 taking in additional stops including Dunedin. Again, all passes are valid for three months.

Northliner Express passes **Northliner Express** offer discount backpacker passes throughout Northland from the basic 'Bay of Islands Pass' from $53 (valid for one month) to their 'Top Half Pass' taking in Rotorua and the Bay of Islands from $80 (valid for two months) and a 'Northland Freedom Pass' from $115 (valid for a month).

Intercity and Newmans key agents

North Island

Auckland: *Sky City Coach Terminal, 102 Hobson St, T09-9136100*

Gisborne: *Gisborne VIC, Grey St, T06-8686139*

Hamilton: *Hamilton Travel Centre, Cnr Angelsea and Bryce Sts, T07-8343457*

Hastings: *Hastings VIC, Russell Street North, T06-8780213*

Kaitia: *Kaitia Travel, 170 Commerce St, T09-4080540*

Napier: *Napier Travel Centre, Munroe St, T06-8342720*

New Plymouth: *The Travel Centre, Shop 51, Level 2 Centre City Shopping Centre, T07-7599039*

Paihia: *Paihia Travel Centre, Maritime Building, T09-4027857*

Palmerston North: *PN Travel Centre, Cnr Pitt and Main Sts, T06-3546155*

Rotorua: *Tourism Rotorua, 1167 Fenton St, T07-3480366*

Taupo: *Taupo Travel Centre, Gascoigne St, T07-3789032*

Tauranga: *Tauranga VIC, Willow St, T07-5713211*

Thames: *Thames VIC, 206 Pollen St, T07-8687284*

Wanganui: *Wanganui Travel Centre, 156 Ridgeway St, T063454433*

Wellington: *Wellington VIC, 101 Wakefield St, T04-8044860, T044725111*

Whakatane: *Whakatane VIC, Cnr Quay St and Kakahoroa Rd, T07-3086058.*

Whangarei: *Northland Coach and Travel, 11 Rose St, T09-4382653*

South Island

Ashburton: *Ashburton VIC, East St, T03-3081064.*

Blenheim: *Marlborough Travel Centre and Railway Station, SH1, T03-5778080*

Christchurch: *Christchurch Travel Centre, 123 Worcester St, T03-3770951*

Dunedin: *Dunedin Travel Centre, 205 St Andrews St, T03-4778860*

Fox Glacier: *Alpine Guides, Main Rd, T03-7510701*

Franz Josef: *The Glacier Shop, Main Rd, T03-7520242*

Greymouth: *Greymouth Travel Centre, Railway St, Mackay St, T03-7687080*

Hokitika: *Hokitika Travel Centre, 60 Tancred St, T03-7558557*

Invercargill: *Invercargill VIC, Southland Museum, Victoria Ave, T03-2146243.*

Kaikoura: *Kaikoura VIC, West End, T03-3195641*

Nelson: *Nelson Travel Centre, 27 Bridge St, T03-5481538*

Oamaru: *La Gonda Milk Bar, 191 Thames St, T03-4348716*

Picton: *Picton Travel Centre, Ferry Terminal Building, T03-5737025*

Queenstown: *Queenstown VIC and Travel Centre, Cnr Camp and Shotover Sts, T03-4428238*

Te Anau: *Air Fiordland, 70 Town Centre, T03-2497559*

Timaru: *AJ's Station Café, Railway Station, 22 Station St, T03-6847195*

Wanaka: *The Paper Place, 84 Ardmore St, T03-4437885*

Westport: *Craddocks Motors, 189 Palmerston St, T03-7897819*

⦂ Travelling times and distances from Auckland

	Distance(km)	Car	Bus/Coach	Train	Air
Wellington	647	8hrs	9hrs	10½hrs	1hr
Christchurch	1000	2 days	2 days	2 days	1¼ hrs
Dunedin	1358	2-4 days	2-4 days	3 days	2½ hrs
Queenstown	1484	2-4 days	-		2 hrs 35 mins
Bay of Islands	241	3 hrs	4 hrs	-	50 mins
Rotorua	235	2½ hrs	3½ hrs	4 hrs	45 mins

Car

Other than a campervan this is by far the best way to see New Zealand. Petrol is expensive (just over $1 a litre or $4 a gallon), but it will give you the flexibility and freedom neede to reach the more remote and beautiful places. Outside the cities traffic congestion and parking is rarely a problem. In many remote areas, especially in South Island, the roads are single track and unsealed, so a little more driving skill is required. Generally keep the speeds and gears low while on these roads. Also, in most rural areas, you will almost certainly encounter livestock of all shapes and sizes along the road verges, so be careful. At night you should of course take extra care and though there are very few mammals in New Zealand, one thing you will encounter is the cat-sized and brush-tailed possum. But with 70 million of the little critters denuding the countryside of its native vegetation, no one will mind the occasional roadkill.

Rules and regulations

In New Zealand you drive on the left (though some Aucklanders drive where they like). The give way to the right rule applies except when turning left; ie the oncoming car has right of way. This will seem mighty strange for the UK driver, who, if unaware of this rule, will end up on the receiving end of much abuse. If you do come a cropper and everyone is OK then just exchange insurance details. Make sure you avail yourself of the rules before setting out ('NZ Road Code' booklets are available from AA offices).

The accident rate in New Zealand is high, so extra vigilance is definitely required. The speed limit on the open road is 100 kph and in built up areas it is 50 kph. Police patrol cars and speed cameras are omnipresent so flout it and you will almost certainly be caught. A valid driving licence from your own country or an international licence is required to get behind the wheel in New Zealand and certainly must be produced if you rent a vehicle. Finally, never leave or hide valuables in your car and lock it at all times.

Parking in the cities can be very expensive. Do not risk parking in restricted areas or exceeding your time allotment on meters. There are still many old meters in the cities (especially Wellington) which only take 20 or 50 cent coins so take a supply. Also, it is very important to note that you must park with the flow of traffic, never against it.

Motoring organizations The New Zealand Automobile Association (AA) is the principal motoring organization in New Zealand. They have offices in most provincial towns. They also provide a great range of maps and travelling information as well as the usual member benefits. If you have bought a vehicle and intend extensive travel throughout New Zealand the basic annual membership fee of around $60 (which provides the basic breakdown assistance) is recommended. If you intend travelling down the West Coast and to Fiordland and to a lesser extent Southland in South Island, breakdown cover is highly recommended. Members of equivalent motoring organizations in other countries may qualify for reciprocal benefits. For AA enquiries, T09-3774660, membership@nzaa.co.nz For breakdowns, T0800-224357.

Car hire

Almost all the major reliable companies (like **Avis, Budget** and **Hertz**) are represented in New Zealand and you will find offices at airports as well as the major airports, cities and provincial towns (listed in the directory sections throughout the text). There are also many local operators, but if you intend to travel extensively you are advised to stick with one of the major companies as they generally offer better cars, have more extensive networks as well as sound insurance and accident coverage. You must be over 21 and have a valid driver's licence to hire a vehicle and insurance premiums for the under 25s can be high. Small, older and, typically, Japanese cars (1600 cc) start at about $80 per day but rates, naturally, vary depending on season, kilometres covered and the length of time you have the car (getting cheaper the longer you rent it). A medium-sized 2000 cc car will cost around $100 per day with unlimited kilometres. Without unlimited kilometres you are looking at around $0.30 per kilometre.

There are of course cheaper deals out there (up to 50%) but not without risk and you will also find that many companies advertise rates below $50 a day but do so hiding insurance and mileage costs. You can also rent a vehicle in one of the major cities (Auckland being the cheapest) and drop it off at another. This will almost certainly involve a drop-off fee of around $120-$150 but may be worth it for the sheer convenience. In the summer high season, if you are returning to Auckland, it is worth shopping around and trying some bargaining since many operators have a glut of cars needing to be driven back north.

Overall, the choice is vast so you are advised to shop around, but beware of cowboy operators and always read the small print before you sign. Some of the cheaper companies have an insurance excess of $700 even on minor repairs, so be careful. Always go over the car with a company representative and get them to acknowledge and list any dents or scratches that you see on the vehicle. Also if you have a digital camera take a few pics of your own. This may avoid considerable frustration trying to prove you were not to blame. If you do not have a credit card you may also have to leave a substantial cash deposit of between $500 and $1000. Although it comes at extra cost, a 'Collision Waiver' can often be secured, which means you do not automatically lose this deposit in the event of an accident. Note also you may not be covered on certain roads. You will certainly not be covered if you venture onto any of the 'sand highways' on the coast, like Ninety Mile Beach, and many companies do not provide cover in the Catlins (Southland).

There are a few motorcycle rental firms in Auckland (see page 123) and although not cheap, it can be a superb way to see the country, especially in the South Island.

Buying a car

Although not essential, having a set of wheels in order to see New Zealand is highly recommended. Many people take the hired campervan option, but this can be expensive. Given the fact that second-hand cars are cheap, readily available and are not hard to find, it is well worth some serious thought. Many people, even on low budgets, can buy a car, share running costs then resell on leaving. Auckland is a good place to buy, but as with anything second-hand, choose carefully.

Buying procedure and legalities

Licence: A current international or accepted driver's license is essential.

W.O.F (Warrant of Fitness): All cars need a safety certificate to be legally on the road and

to obtain registration. Most garages and specialist 'drive in drive out' Vehicle Testing Stations (VTS) do a WOF test which if passed will last 6 months (see Warrant of Fitness' in the Yellow Pages). It costs about $35. If you buy a car with a WOF make sure it is not more than 28 days old.

Registration: Registration can be gained with legal ownership and a valid WOF certificate for 6 (about $100) or 12 ($200) months.

Change of ownership: The buyer and seller must fill in a MR13A that can be obtained and submitted at any NZ Post Office. Cost $10.

Insurance: Not compulsory but Third Party highly recommended. The AA offer good rates along with breakdown membership.

Highway/Road code: There are a few subtle differences in New Zealand road rules (right of way while turning right a prime example). You are advised to familiarise yourself with the 'Road Code' booklet available from the AA Centres or major bookshops. $15.

Automobile Association: Membership costs around $80 per annum. It covers emergency breakdown service or towing to the nearest garage. You also get free maps, information and insurance discounts. Auckland AA T09-3774660. Breakdown 0800-224357.

Credit check: You are advised to have the car's legalities checked before purchase. AA Auto Report On the web ($25) or T0800-500333. Quote chassis and licence plate numbers.

Vehicle inspections: The AA does a professional and comprehensive inspection as do a number of companies found under 'Vehicle Inspection Services' in the Yellow Pages. Cost $12 (members $95). It is highly recommended, T0800-500333.

Where to buy a car: There are a number of auto magazines available at newsagents but the major daily newspapers (New Zealand Herald, Wed and Sat) and the auctions are also recommended.

Car fairs are held at **Ellerslie Racecourse**, Greenlane (Sun 0900-1200), T09-5292233, www.carfair.co.nz **Manakau Car Market**, Manakau City Centre Car Park (Sun 0900-1300), T09-3585000 and **Sell It Yourself**, 1106 Great South Rd, Otahuhu. 7 days 0800-1830, T09-2703666 and 60 Wairau Rd, Glenfield. 7 days 0700-1900, T09-4433800.

Car Auctions:
Turners Car Auctions, Cnr Penrose and Leonard Rds, Penrose,(Thu/Sat), T09-5251920, www.turnersauctions.co.nz
Hammer Auctions, Cnr Neilson and Alfred Sts, Onehunga, (Mon-Thu, Sat), T09-5792344, www.hammerauctions.co.nz
Guaranteed Buy Back Companies: (read the small print)
Budget Car Sales, 12 Mt Eden Rd, Mt Eden, T09-3794120
Rex Swinburne, 825 Dominion Rd, Mt Roskill, T09-6206587.

Campervans ›› *For major map stockists in Auckland, see page 83*

New Zealand is well geared up for camper van hire and travel and there's an accommpanying glut of reputable international companies. Being a fairly compact country it is certainly a viable way to see the entire country with complete independence. Although hire and petrol costs may seem excessive, once you subtract the inevitable costs of accommodation, and provided you are not alone and can share those costs, it can all work out cheaper in the long run. You will find that motor camps are readily available even in the more remote places and a powered site will set you back around $10-15 dollars per night. Note that lay-by parking is illegal and best avoided, but if you are lost or stuck, you will rarely be confronted. Again, like car rental rates, camper van rates vary and are seasonal. Costs are rated on a sliding scale according to model, season, number of days of hire. The average daily charge for a basic two-berth/six-berth for hire over 28 days, including insurance is around $195/$295 in the high season and $90/$140 in the low season.

The three most popular rental firms are **Britz**, T0800-831900, www.britz.com **Maui**, T09-2753013, www.maui-rentals.com, and **Kea Campers**, T09-4417833, www.keacampers.com There are some lesser known but equally reputable firms that can offer better deals, if not quite such plush vehicles, and these are listed in the Auckland 'Directory' (page 124). Although there are fewer risks involved with camper van hire, the same general rules apply as with car hire. You generally get what you pay for but shop around and check the small print. The average campervan works out at about 14-16 litres per 100 km in petrol costs. Diesel is obviously recommended.

Cycling

Cycling touring in New Zealand is highly recommended and becoming increasingly popular, especially in South Island. Although it is not exactly flat, New Zealand is, let's just say, 'topographically manageable'. Cycle hire companies are listed in each town directory, while specialist cycle tour companies are listed in 'Specialist activity tours' above (page 25).

Combination travel passes

The **New Zealand Travel Pass** T03-9615245, www.travelpass.co.nz offers a range of 5-22 day combined coach, ferry, train and flight options ranging from a 5-day basic unlimited Intercity/Newmans coach travel and one ferry crossing for $348, to a 22-day unlimited Intercity/Newmans coach travel, single ferry crossing, two one-way rail journeys and a one-way long journey domestic flight for $1315.

TransScenic offers the **Best of New Zealand Pass**, T04-4983303/ T0800-692-378, www.bestpass.co.nz which also combines train, coach and ferry services with the bonus of unlimited stops and six months validity. The scheme works on a point purchase system of 600, 800 and 1000 costing $499, $646 and $783 respectively (children around 33% off). Obviously the more points you buy the greater the travel options and top up points are also available from $16 for 20 to $111 for 200. As examples; a trip by coach from Auckland to Rotorua via Waitomo will redeem 115 points, while a single ferry trip from Wellington to Picton 46. Although it may sound complicated once you understand the system it is both convenient and good value for money.

Hitching

Hitching is still quite heavily practised in New Zealand but not entirely safe. As ever, it is not advised for those travelling alone or single women. If you do decide to take the risk, try to keep to the main highways and restrict your hitching to the daylight hours. The usual common sense applies and if in doubt, don't. Another good tip is never take off a rucksack and put that or a bag in the car first. For the opportunist thief this can be like Christmas, and as they speed off you will be left standing there minus gear, feeling a proper Charlie.

Ferry

Other than a few small, harbour-crossing vehicle ferries and the short trip to Stewart Island from Bluff in Southland, the main focus of ferry travel is of course the inter-island services across Cook Strait. The two ports are Wellington at the southern tip of North Island and Picton in the beautiful Marlborough Sounds, in the northern South Island.

There are currently three services: the **Interislander** and the faster **Lynz**, both of which are owned and operated by **Tranzrail**, T04-4983302/T0800-802802, www.interislandline.co.nz; and the new **Bluebridge** T0800-844844/T03-5203086, www.strait.co.nz For details on the inter-island crossing, see page 419; for Stewart Island services, see page 688.

Train

The rail network throughout New Zealand is disappointing and in a seemingly incessant state of flux. New Zealand has struggled for years to maintain anything other than a core network between its main centres of population and provincial towns. Within **North Island** there are two daily services between Auckland and Wellington – the daytime **'Overlander'** and overnight **'Northerner'**. Within **South Island**, there are daily services between Picton and Christchurch (the **'TransCoastal'**) and Christchurch to Greymouth (the **'TransAlpine'**). Also designed specifically as a tourist attraction the Taieri Gorge Railway runs from Christchurch to Middlemarch and back. Having slated the general network the trains are, in themselves, pretty comfortable, the service good and most have a great viewing carriage at the rear. However, unless you are desperate, avoid the overnight Auckland-Wellington service – it is strictly 'lights out' at 2200. But elsewhere any discomfort or boredom will be quickly forgotten when the stunning scenery takes your mind off things. Fares range greatly from Standard to Super Saver so check carefully what you are entitled to and what deals you can secure.

All fares are of a single class. The 'TransAlpine' from Christchurch to Greymouth and the 'TransCoastal ' from Picton to Christchurch are world class journeys offering South Island scenery at its best. Reservations and timetables from the Auckland or Wellington Railway Station Information Centres, accredited Visitor Information Centres (I-Sites) or travel agents throughout New Zealand: TransScenic, T0800-802802 (0700-2200), www.transcenic.co.nz Several specialist travel packages are on offer, including 'Great Train Escapes' and 'Day Escapes', which may sound like a mass breakout from a prison, but is in fact a range of 1-6 day excursions most of which include accommodation. Prices range from $79 for a day excursion to $545 for a 6-day. Children travel for around 40% of the adult fare.

Maps

Detailed urban and rural maps are readily available throughout New Zealand. **Wises** are the major city and provincial town map company producing a range of handbooks and foldout city maps. If you intend to do a lot of travelling, their provincial town maps for both North and South Islands are invaluable. Most large bookshops stock **Wises'** maps and others. Almost all the information centres in the larger towns provide free leaflet maps and the coverage is generally excellent. Department of Conservation (DoC) offices (see also Responsible tourism page 38 above) are also very well stocked with National Park and rural maps. For really detailed maps the **Land Information New Zealand** offices can provide for all your needs. Major libraries have stocks which can be photocopied. **Mapworld** in Christchurch is an excellent outlet and also stocks complete CD-ROMs of all New Zealand national, regional and town maps, T0800MAPWORLD, maps@mapworld.co.nz An excellent source of maps in the UK is **Stanfords:** 12-14 Long Acre, Covent Garden, London, WC2E 9LP, T020-7836 1321, F020-7836 0189, www.stanfords.co.uk Also 29 Corn St, Bristol, BS1 and 39 Spring Gardens, Manchester, M2. Recommended.

Essentials Getting around

Sleeping

Besides actually getting there, accommodation in New Zealand will be your biggest expense. There is generally a wealth of choice and though you will rarely end up without a bed for the night, you are advised to book ahead during the high season. At the present time the New Zealand Tourist Board are heavily plugging the homestay or farmstay options (see below). You are advised to try this at least for a few nights to encounter real Kiwi hospitality and general Kiwi life.

Visitor Information Centres (I-Sites) are a great help with accommodation and generally stock all the highly-illustrated leaflets. They can also offer plenty of good advice regarding the range of options and sort out bookings. The web is also a major source of information with almost all reputable establishments now having at least an email address. There are also many books available including the *AA Accommodation Guides*, www.aaguides.co.nz; *Jason's Motels and Motor Lodges Guide*, www.jasons.co.nz; *The New Zealand Bed and Breakfast Guide*, www.bnb.co.nz; and *Friars B&B Guide*, www.friars.co.nz; as well as numerous motorcamps, motels, camp-sites and backpacker guides (most of which are free). A visit to a national Visitor Information Centre (I-Site) will see you suitably stocked up.

Hotels

The numerous hotels in New Zealand can generally be listed under one of four categories:

Large luxury hotels There are a surprising number of large modern and luxury (four to five star) hotels in the major cities. Auckland in particular seems to benefit the most, with many new establishments like the the **Hilton** being only months old. There are so many luxury rooms and apartment blocks in the city centre it is amazing they can all survive. These major hotels tend to be part of major international or trans- Tasman chains and the prices range from about $250-$500 per night. As you would expect, all rooms are equipped with the latest technology including laptop plug-in ports and Sky TV, etc. They also have restaurants and all the usual leisure facilities, including swimming pools, spa pools and gyms.

Standard chain hotels These range in age and quality and include such familiar names as *Quality Hotels*, *Novotel* and *Copthorne Hotels*. Available in all the major cities and most of the larger provincial towns, their standard prices vary from about $175-$300 but they have regular weekend or off-season deals. Again most have in-house restaurants and additional facilities such as a heated pool.

Boutique hotels These vary in size and price but tend to be modern and of a high and luxurious standard. The smaller, more intimate boutique hotels are beginning to overtake the major chains in popularity. On average double rooms here can cost anything from $175-400.

Traditional pub and budget hotels Many of the rural towns have kept the traditional old wooden hotels. Don't be fooled, however. Some of these may look grand from the outside, but often the interior doesn't match up and neither does the company or the conversation. However, a basic cheap and comfortable room can still be found here generally. Beware the bars in many of these places, unless you're quick on the draw – or know the age of the All Black fly-half that scored in the last minute of the Bledisloe twenty seven years ago at exactly 3.33pm. Also note that prices are often dropped at weekends and during the off-season.

Lodges and B&Bs

There are a growing number of luxury lodges all over New Zealand and most sell themselves on their location or classic 'bush setting' as much as their architecture, sumptuous rooms, facilities and cuisine. Prices tend to be high, ranging anywhere from $200 to the mind-bending $2600 per night of the highly exclusives. Quite how a tariff as steep as that can be justified is an enigma. Put in perspective, it equates to almost eight months in a well-equipped campsite. Most of these luxury lodges are listed.

Although there are not as many B&Bs in New Zealand as there are in Europe, you can still find them in most places. They vary greatly in style, size and quality and can be anything from a basic double room with shared bathroom and a couple of boiled eggs for breakfast to a luxurious ensuite or self-contained with the full breakfast. Again prices vary, with the standard cost being as little as $75-100. Some of the more luxurious, however, are extortionate. When looking at prices bear in mind a full breakfast costs at least $12 in a café or restaurant. Many lodges and B&Bs also offer evening meals. Sadly the Kiwi B&B has still got a long way to go before reaching the standard of its Scottish Highland counterpart, but you will find most hosts to be very congenial and helpful folk.

Homestays and farmstays

The term 'homestay' is often touted about in New Zealand, but its actual meaning is often vague. Generally speaking if an establishment advertises itself as a homestay it will deliberately lack the privacy of the standard B&B and you are encouraged to mix with your hosts. The idea is that you get an insight into Kiwi life, but it may or may not be for you depending on your preferences and personality. Other than that they are very similar to B&Bs, with breakfasts usually standard and an evening meal often being optional. Farmstays of course give you the added agricultural and rural edge and this form of accommodation is generally recommended.

Accommodation can take many forms from being in-house with your hosts or fully self-contained, and breakfasts and evening meals are often optional and included. You will often find yourself helping to round up sheep or milking a cow and if you have kids (and farmstays usually welcome them) they will be wonderfully occupied for hours. Both homestays and farmstays tend to charge the same, or slightly lower, rates as the standard B&Bs. **New Zealand Farm Holidays** based near Auckland also produce a helpful free catalogue listing about 300 establishments, T09-4129649, www.nzfarmholidays.co.nz For farmstay options in Southland (considered the hub of agriculture in New Zealand) contact the very helpful **Western Southland Farm Hosting Group**, T03-2258608, www.nzcountry.co.nz/farmhost The Visitor Information Centres (I-Sites) can help you find homestays or farmstays and the NZTB website also has a detailed listing of nationwide farmstays, www.purenz.com

Motels

Motels are the preferred option of the average Kiwi holidaymaker. They are literally everywhere and reproducing furtively even as you read this. They vary greatly, from the awful, stained 1950s love shacks to the new and luxurious condos with bubbly spa pool. There is usually a range of rooms available and almost all have at least a shower, kitchen facilities (with coffee and tea) and a TV – though whether it actually works and has Sky TV, or doubles as a plant pot, depends on the price. Most are clean and comfortable and nicely appointed, while in others you may find yourself trying to sleep next to the main road. Prices vary from studio units at about $70-$90, one-bedroom units from $80-$100 and suites accommodating families and groups for an additional charge for each adult. Many of the bigger and better establishments have a restaurant and a swimming pool. Many also make the most of the country's thermal features and have spas, sometimes even in your room.

Hostels

Being such a popular destination for the independent traveller/backpacker, New Zealand is well served with hostels and budget accommodation establishments.

Naturally, they vary greatly in age, design, location and quality. Some enjoy a busy atmosphere in the centre of town while others provide a quiet haven of sanctity in the country. They also have a range of types of beds on offer, with many having separate double and single rooms as well as the traditional dormitory. Dorms are usually single sex but sometimes optionally mixed. Camping facilities within the grounds are also common. Generally, hostels are good places to meet other travellers, managers are usually very knowledgeable and helpful, and pick-ups are often complimentary. Bikes, kayaks or other activity gear can often be hired at low cost or are free to use. Wherever you stay you will have access to equipped kitchens, a laundry, games or TV room, plenty of local budget-orientated information, and of course, phones and the internet. Prices vary little for a dorm bed, ranging from $12-$20 depending on season. Single rooms and doubles tend to be under $45 or about $22 per adult. **NB** In the high season and especially over Christmas through to March you are advised to pre-book everywhere at least three days in advance.

YHAs

The Youth Hostel Association NZ is part of a worldwide organization with over 4500 hostels in 60 countries. There are 64 establishments throughout New Zealand. Being part of a large organization, most are on a par if not better than the private or independent backpacker hostels. They all offer very much the same in standard of accommodation and facilities.

YHAs are only open to members but you can join in your home country (if YHA exists) or in New Zealand for an annual fee of $40 ($30 for renewals). Non-members can also stay at hostels for an additional charge of $4 per night for the first 10 nights, by which time you become a member. YHA membership cards are very handy even if you do not intend to stay consistently at YHA hostels. They entitle you to a number of discounts, including up to 30% off air and bus travel. There are also a number of Associate YHA hostels where no membership card is required but where members get a small discount. For information contact the YHA direct T03-3799970, info@yha.org.nz, www.stayyha.com or pick up the YHA Accommodation and Hostel Guide at any major VIC (I-Site).

Backpacker organizations

Other than the YHA, there are three major backpacking membership organizations and networks in New Zealand which provide detailed hostel information listings and certain discounts, including a dollar off each night's stay and other discounts on transport operators and activities. About 100 New Zealand establishments are members of the **VIP** group, *PO Box 60177, Titirangi, Auckland, T09-8168903, www.vip.co.nz* VIP have an annual membership fee of $30.
Budget Backpacker Hostels Ltd (BBH) , *99 Titiraupenga St, Taupo, T/F07-3771568,* www.backpack.co.nz, has nearly 300 member establishments that must meet certain minimum quality criteria. These are listed in their *Blue Book* (free from VICs) along with handy descriptions, contact details and location maps of each hostel. If you choose, you can purchase a BBH Club Card ($40, with $20 free phone card) that guarantees the listed prices. Recommended.
Nomads is the new kid on the block in New Zealand, *www.nomadsworld.com* They offer the same kind of deal but with far fewer hostels for an annual membership of $30. Their principal agent in New Zealand is the **Travellers' Contact Point**, *87 Queen St, T09-3007197*. It is well worth joining one or more of the above.

Motorcamps and cabins

New Zealand's fairly compact size and quality road network lends itself to road touring. Given that so many visitors and Kiwis take the campervan or camping option, New Zealand is very well served with quality motorcamps and campsites. In fact, it is hailed as one of the best in the world. Motorcamps can be found almost everywhere and not necessarily just in towns. The hub of many a remote beach, headland or bay is often the great Kiwi motorcamp. The quality and age does of course vary. Some are modern and well equipped while others are much less so. Almost all motorcamps are equipped with laundry facilities and a few will charge a small fee ($0.20-0.50) for hot showers. Prices are generally very reasonable and range from $8-15 per person (child half price) for non-powered sites. Powered sites are often the same price or less than $5 more.

Most motorcamps have a range of cabins from dog kennels to quite well-appointed alpine-type huts. They vary in price but are rarely more than $60 per night (for two) with an additional charge of $12-15 per person after that.

The **Top Ten** chain of motor camps, which has almost 50 camps nationwide, though up to $3 more expensive per night, are generally highly recommended. If you stick to the Top Ten affiliates you will also find yourself consistently bumping into the same people, which can be great, or conversely, an utter nightmare!

DoC campsites and huts

Naturally most motorcamps cater for campers and the charges are generally the same as a non-powered site ($8-$12). This gives you access to all the facilities. **DoC** (www.doc.govt.nz is also a good source of information) has over 100 basic campsites all over the country with many being in prime locations. They tend to provide clean running water, toilet facilities and BBQ areas, but rarely allow open fires. The National Parks in particular are all excellently facilitated with comfortable well-equipped huts. There is either no camping fee or more commonly a nightly fee of $2-$10 . Fees for huts are anything from $5-$40 per night depending on category and location. If you plan to use DoC campsites and huts you are advised to research their locations, fee structures, rules and regulations and book well in advance, www.doc.govt.nz.

Holiday homes and cottages (baches)

This is one accommodation option very often overlooked by visitors. The country has a wealth of holiday homes and baches (seaside huts, cottages or mansions) which are made available for rent throughout the year. While in summer they will most probably be frequented by the owners, in the off-season in particular you can sometimes find a real bargain. The best place to look is in the national newspapers, travel or house rental sections. The regional VICs can also often be of assistance. Most operate on a minimum weekend or week stay basis and costs vary depending on quality and location. This type of accommodation is of course little use to the single traveller, but if you are a family or a group it is well worth looking into.

Food and drink

Depending on your budget you are in for a treat. The quantity and the quality of food in New Zealand are superb. Although there are many types of traditional cuisine and restaurants in evidence, the principal style is 'Pacific Rim'. It dips into the culinary heritage of many of the cultures of the Oceania region, with inspiration and influences from Thailand, Malaysia, Indonesia, Polynesia, Japan and Vietnam as well as others further afield like Europe. For dishes that have a distinctly Kiwi edge look out for the lamb (arguably the best in the world), pork and venison and freshwater fish like salmon and eel. Despite its reputation as perhaps the best trout-fishing country in the world, you cannot buy trout commercially. Although this is a shame, it does provide the added incentive to go and catch your own, which many restaurants will be happy to cook for you.

Eating categories

In this book eateries are divided into three categories: **expensive** (over $25 for a main/ US entrée); **affordable** ($15-$25 for a main/US entrée) and **cheap** (under $15 for a main/US entrée) All the places listed are recommended as offering relatively good value, quality and standards of service within their respective price category. Some are also noted for having particularly pleasant or unusual surrounds.

As you might expect there is a heavy emphasis on fine seafood. Here, the choice is vast with many warm-water fish like snapper, kingfish, hoki, hapuka and orange roughie. Often you can catch these yourself and done in a BBQ style, fresh off the boat, it will provide a memorable culinary experience. Other seafood delights include crayfish (the South Pacific equivalent to the lobster), fine oysters (the best being from Bluff in South Island), paua (abalone), scallops and the famous green-lipped mussels. These mussels are very substantial, delicious and should not be missed. They are also relatively cheap and readily available. There are also some treats in store from below the ground. The kumara (sweet potato) will shed a whole new light on the humble 'spud', while many of the international vegetables like asparagus and broccoli come cheap (especially while in season) and always fresh. From the tree the fruit of choice is of course the succulent kiwi fruit or 'Chinese gooseberry' which although not exclusively grown in New Zealand is deservedly celebrated. Other fine fruits include feijoa and tamarillo. The celebrated dessert in New Zealand is the pavlova; a sort of mountainous cake made of meringue and whipped cream. For a real traditional feast try a Maori *hangi*. Done properly and without ketchup you will be amazed at just how good and different fish, meat and vegetables can taste when cooked underground.

Where to eat

There are eateries to suit every taste and budget from the ubiquitous fast food joints to world-class seafood restaurants. Auckland and Wellington (which has more cafés and restaurants per capita than New York) are particularly rich in choice with a vast selection of cafés, café-bars, brasseries and traditional and specialist restaurants flying the flag of many countries and styles and giving added puff to the celebrated 'Pacific Rim'. You will find that there is often a very fine line in the distinction between café and restaurant with the vast majority being essentially the same thing. Many cafés, although providing a more informal atmosphere and placing much emphasis on a broader range of cheaper light meals during the day, happily simmer on into the night with more substantial dishes. They also almost always serve coffee, breakfast or brunch, are licensed (or at the very least BYO – which means bring your own) and often provide outdoor seating. The restaurants are similar with few expecting formal attire. You can find up-market, snooty establishments if you wish, but they will not provide the celebrated, laid-back, food-centred focus of the vast majority. Also note that cost does not necessarily relate to quality.

Vegetarians are generally well catered for in the main centres and provincial towns, while the more remote and rural corners of New Zealand still offer the 'half cow on the barbie'. Ask for a vegetarian dish on a South Island backcountry station and you'll most probably be shown the door. Also bear in mind that many of the top hotels, motels and lodges are open to non-residents and often provide fine dining at affordable prices. As well as the vast amount of cafés, café/restaurants and restaurants, you can generally find good 'pub-grub', with the cities and most major towns offering at least one Irish or old English-style pub with everything from the 'Full-Monty' breakfast, and Irish stew to good ol' fish and chips – all for under $18.

Generally speaking, eating out in New Zealand is pretty cheap. For those visitors revelling in the more than favourable dollar exchange rates you are probably going to end up a very happy little hoglet and will certainly need to renew that annual gym sub on your return home. Backpackers on a strict budget will of course fare less well. But no matter what the budget, you should treat yourself at least once. The vast majority of eateries fall into the 'mid-range' bracket ($15-$25 for a main). Price codes for eating out are given in the box above.

As far as opening hours are concerned, again it varies and they are often seasonal. Most cafés open for breakfast between 0700 and 0900 and remain open until at least 1700. Many also remain open until late into the evening or the wee small hours. This usually applies seven days a week with special Sunday brunch hours provided. Most mid-range restaurants open their doors daily for lunch (often 1100-1400) and dinner (from 1800). The more exclusive establishments usually open for dinner from about 1800, with some (especially in winter) only opening some weekday evenings and at weekends.

There are a number of useful (mainly Auckland and Wellington) café and restaurant guides available from the major bookshops, while many VICs provide free promotional leaflets. Note, however, that many of these only list those restaurants that paid for the advertising. Some of the best are therefore not necessarily listed. In summary, nothing beats a stroll around the main café or restaurant areas or streets (often listed) and a stomach-rumbling muse at the menus and interiors before making your decision.

If you intend to do your own cooking and buy in your own food then you will find food shopping is uncomplicated, convenient and offers a wide choice of fare. The main supermarket chains are Big Fresh, Woolworths and New World, with Pac-n-Save and Countdown being marginally cheaper. When buying fresh vegetables and fruit always try to stick to the numerous roadside or wholesale fruit markets where the difference in price and quality can be astonishing.

Drinks

Other than L&P (a fairly unremarkable soft drink hailing from Paeroa) New Zealand lacks a national drink. If there is one, it is the highly sub-standard and over rated beer called Lion Red. This and a number of other equally watery relations are drunk not so much by the pint as the jug, and are all backed by a very 'Kiwi-bloke' image, which is regularly promoted with omnipresent and less-than-PC advertising. Having abused the traditional Kiwi beer you can, however, rest assured that all the main internationally well-known bottled beers are available, as are some good foreign tap ales like Caffrey's and Kilkenny. Depending on which pub and how it is kept and poured, you can also get a good Guinness (see the Pubs and bars sections of cities).

Beer and lager is usually sold by 'the handle', or 'the glass' (pint) or 'the jug' (up to three pints). Half-pints come in a 12-fl oz (350ml) glass. Rarely is a pint a proper imperial pint, it's usually just under. Drinks generally cost from $6-7 for a pint, about $4-5 for a jug of Lion Red and up to $7 for a double shot. Drinks are much cheaper in rural pubs and RSAs (Retired Servicemen's Clubs), where you can usually get yourself signed in. The minimum drinking age has just been reduced from 21 to 18. Liquor shops are everywhere and alcohol can generally (in most places) be bought seven days a week. There is a thriving coffee culture almost everywhere in the main towns and cities, so you will not go without your daily caffeine fix.

Generally speaking, the drinks do not match the food in New Zealand and although the vast majority of Kiwi blokes would argue against it, other than a few exceptions, New Zealand still has a long way to go in offering fine beers, ales and lager. Its wine, however, is an entirely different story.

The Hangi

Pronounced 'hungi', this is the traditional Maori and Pacific Island feast or method of cooking. To the uninitiated, the concept of cooking your dinner in the ground may seem a bit odd, but it is actually incredibly efficient and produces a certain taste and texture in the food that is extraordinarily good. Hangis were designed for the masses and were as much a social occasion as anything else. Traditionally the men would light a large fire and place river stones in the embers. While the stones are heating a pit is dug in the earth. Then the stones are placed in the pit and sacking placed upon them (before sacking it was suitably-fashioned plant material). Then, presumably, the boys went off for a beer while the good ladies of the tribe (bless their wee cotton socks) prepared the meat. Nowadays this includes chicken, wild pig and lamb, but was formerly moa, pigeon and seafood. Vegetables too are added, particularly the traditional sweet potato kumara. Once cleaned and plucked the smaller items are wrapped in leaves (now foil) and the whole lot placed in a basket (traditionally woven leaves from the flax plant, now wire-mesh) and then the whole affair is covered with earth. Then the ladies join said boys for beer and a chat.

Meanwhile, the steam slowly cooks the food and the flavours are sealed in. Then a couple of hours later it is all dug up *et voilà* – it's 'pig-out' time. The succulence and smoked flavours of the food are gorgeous.

Although due to modern-day health and safety requirements it is not really possible to sample a proper hangi, the commercial offerings by the Maori tourist concerns can still be very tasty and well worth the experience. Rotorua is of course the principal venue (see Rotorua section). If you ever have the opportunity of a real one, do not pass it up.

New Zealand wine

New Zealand's rich diversity of climates and soil types has borne an equally rich array of wines and after over a century of development the country now boasts many of internationally recognized standards. Wine is produced the length and breadth of the country but the Hawkes Bay and Nelson/Marlborough areas are the principal wine producing regions. New Zealand Sauvignon Blanc is rated throughout the world as one of the best, but there is growing recognition for its Chardonnay, Pinot Noir, Methode Traditionelle sparkling wine, Riesling, Cabernet Sauvignon and Merlot. Fruit wines, including the unusual 'kiwi fruit wine' are also in evidence. The choice is vast and whether a connoisseur or a novice you are advised to experiment. If you can, visit one of the many vineyards that offer tastings and cellar sales.

Entertainment

Most cities are blessed with numerous venues hosting first-class concerts and shows. **Theatre, orchestral concerts, ballet, dance, comedy, rock and jazz** are all well represented. Many international rock stars now include at least one gig in Auckland in their itinerary. On a smaller scale you will find a vibrant nightlife in New Zealand cities and major provincial towns. Although not necessarily world class, the **nightclubs, cabarets, pubs and local rock concerts** will certainly have you 'shaking your pants'. There's even Country and Western and line dancing (no comment). New Zealand also boasts two large, modern, 24-hour **casinos** in Christchurch and Wellington. **Ticketek** are the national administrators for information and ticketing and a comprehensive listing of up and coming shows and events can be sourced from their website, www.ticketek.co.nz or the website www.nz-events.co.nz

Pubs and bars

The pub scene has come on in leaps and bounds over the last decade with new establishments opening up almost everywhere. Before the 1990s the vast majority of pubs in New Zealand were the archetypal male bastions – establishments where ashtrays were built into the tables, pictures of the local hairy rugby team adorned the walls and the average Saturday night consisted of a good argument about sport, a band playing Deep Purple's 'Smoke on the Water', followed by a fight, copious wall-to-wall vomiting and a failed attempt to get home. Of course such places still exist, but generally speaking pubs and bars are now a much more refined and classy affair yet still retain that congenial and laid-back 'traditional pub' atmosphere. Now you can enjoy a good beer and conversation over an open fire in winter or the sun in summer and women (at least in groups) will not always be hassled by frustrated young farmers or dirty old men. New Zealand has also caught on to the 'Irish pub' fad and although some are the usual gimmicky affairs others are very good, offering fine surroundings and beer to match.

Many drinking establishments are also now attached to restaurants and cafés with outdoor seating. In summer these can be great places to while away an afternoon. If you really must sample the old-fashioned Kiwi pub you will find them often in the hotels or main streets of the rural towns. While not all bad, do not walk in in a pair of pink shorts, or without knowing what an 'All Black' is.

Pubs and bars are generally open from 1100-2230 with many having an extended licence to 2400 and sometimes even 0300 at weekends.

Festivals and events

There are a huge range of organized events and festivals held throughout New Zealand every year, ranging from the bizarre Gumboot Throwing Festival in Taihape (see page 382) to the huge, spectacular Opera in the Park in Auckland (see below). One of the more obscure events is the **Wildfoods Festival** on the South Island's West Coast, an extravaganza of gourmet 'bushtucker' based on natural (or highly unusual) food resources from the land and sea. Some of the most popular national events include the free **'Opera'** and **'Christmas in the Park'**. Held annually in the Auckland Domain over the Christmas period (dates vary), both can attract up to 400,000 people. The many regional and provincial town **Food, Arts and Wine Festivals** are usually held in summer and provide a fitting and lively celebration of the country's wealth of creations. There are also many traditional (if a little commercial) **Maori cultural performances** in the main centres and particularly in Rotorua. In 2002/2003 the world-renowned yachting event, the **America's Cup** was once again defended and hosted by New Zealand in Auckland. This prestigious nautical event had in many ways, since being won for the first time by Team New Zealand in 1995, put both the city and country on the international tourist map and attracted millions of dollars of income, as well as thousands of visitors. Sadly, this time for all sorts of controversial reasons 'Team New Zealand' were white-washed 5-0 by the Swiss 'Team Alinghi' and for a deeply disappointed New Zealand the great era came to an abrupt and embarrassing end.

Local VICs have listings of up and coming events and the NZTB website, www.purenz.com, has a detailed database. Regional and city events are listed in the relevant sections.

Public holidays

If you are a tourist public holidays can be an inconvenience since shops and banks close and cohorts of native kiwis join you. School holidays are particularly bad with the months of January and February being the worst. During these times you should book accommodation and activities well ahead. Bear in mind this also applies to the winter season at the major ski resorts like Tongariro, Wanaka and Queenstown.

Calendar for 2004: **January** 1-2 New Year; **January** 26 Anniversary Day (Auckland/Northland); **February 6** Waitangi Day; **April 9** Good Friday; **April 12** Easter Monday; **April 25** Anzac Day; **June 7** Queen's Birthday; **October 25** Labour Day; **December 25** Christmas Day; **December 26** Boxing Day.

O Shopping

Although on first acquaintance (especially in the cities) you might be forgiven for thinking it is all fluffy sheep or kiwis in rugby jerseys, shopping in New Zealand can be a rewarding and interesting experience. For a country so sparsely populated there is a surprising wealth of quality goods on sale, from international designer label clothing to traditional Kiwi arts and crafts.

Arts and crafts

Beyond the international and the kitsch there are a number of things to look out for. New Zealand arts and crafts consist of a vast array of South Pacific, Maori and contemporary Kiwi styles and influences. Much of the art is very colourful, reflecting the beautiful bright blues and greens of the environment, while two-dimensional works are often beautifully carved panels, figures, bowls and furniture made of native woods like kauri and rimu.

Pottery and ceramics abound. There are Maori pendants (*tiki*) carved from bone (whale bone) and greenstone (*pounamu*). These have been made and worn by the Maori for centuries and often depict sacred animals or spirits. If you buy one, it is customary to offer it as a gift. They are also often associated with *mana* (power or standing) and fertility. Note, however, that there are many cheap and nasty versions on sale, especially in the city souvenir shops and on the street. If you want quality, look in specialist arts and craft or museum shops. Almost everywhere you will also see the stunning hues of the abalone shell (or *paua*). The *paua* is harvested naturally under strict controls and the shells are utilised as a by-product. You can buy the half shells polished and varnished for about $25 or choose from the many jewellery pieces created or inlaid with colourful fragments.

Tapa cloth is a Pacific brown or fawn-coloured material with unique and specific black-dyed designs. This is widely available but the best place to get the cloth is at Auckland's United Tongan Church about one kilometre down Richmond Road, off Ponsonby Road, on Saturday mornings. They are very reasonably priced, original, light and easy to pack. As you might expect, woollen goods are everywhere. There is everything from jumpers and gloves to full sheepskins and cosy slippers. Although not cheap these goods are usually homespun, hand-knitted and of the highest quality.

Clothing

On the clothing front look out for the famous red or blue plaid Kiwi 'swandry'. It's a sort of thick woollen shirt/ jacket and offers the best protection from the cold. You will also see the world-famous All Black rugby jerseys all over the place. Although the real thing is now made by Adidas (in a much less appealing synthetic material) the 'Canterbury' rugby tops have to be the best cotton-made tops in the world and last for years. Make

sure the one you buy is made by the Canterbury Clothing Company (CCC). They have a
factory shop in Christchurch (see page 506). For modern fashion look out for some
award-winning Kiwi labels, like Zambesi, NomD, Karen Walker and World.

Shopping hours
Most shops and businesses are open Monday-Friday, 0900-1700. Many shops are
also open on Saturdays and Sundays. The large mall multi-complexes are also open
daily and offer at least one late shopping night a week. The larger supermarket chains
are open most evenings every day and the humble Kiwi 'dairies' (found in almost
every high street) are often open until 2000-2300. Depending where you are petrol
(gas) stations are open until about 2300 with some remaining open 24 hours. Many
are following the trend of also selling a substantial (if not more expensive) range of
supermarket type items.

▲ Sports and activities

Bungee jumping
The strange practice of attaching a rubber band to your ankles and diving off a very
high bridge has now become synonymous with a visit to New Zealand and the best
known of all this country's weird, wonderful and downright suicidal tourist activities.
The concept was professionally developed, though not invented, by A J Hackett, who
jumped from the Eiffel Tower in 1986 (and more recently from the Sky Tower in
Auckland). It is actually the Papua New Guineans who invented bungee jumping,
apparently as a test of manhood. But, quite how one can impress the gals in such a
manner, with your head planted in the soil looking like a serious road accident is,
frankly, a bit of an enigma. Anyway, there are now bungee sites throughout New
Zealand, varying in type and height from the 'tasters' of about 40 m (from a crane) to
the underwear-soiling 134 m (from a gondola above a canyon). Most are in
Queenstown in South Island. There you can do it from a bridge, suspended high
above a canyon, or even at night, the choice is yours. The latest somewhat over-rated
jumps are in Auckland where you can jump off the Sky Tower or the Harbour Bridge.
(The highest jump in New Zealand was done by A J Hackett himself from the Sky Tower
(192 m) in 1998.) The former is certainly exciting, but is not strictly a proper bungee,
being (understandably) very much more controlled. Other (lower) sites include
Taupo, the Agrodome in Rotorua and Hamner Springs in Canterbury.

Suffice it to say it is indeed mad, but thankfully very safe, though care must be
taken. Your life, after all, is literally in their hands. There are many rumours flying around
that bungee jumping can detach retinas and send various bodily organs into disarray,
but there is little evidence to support these, and although certain bodily parts can go
into uncontrolled fits of clenching, pulsating or shrinking, the rush of adrenaline more
than makes up for it. The bungee is not just the domain of the mad youth either – many
a wonderfully loony pensioner has done it, too. Respect due! There are also many
variations on the theme. Folk have jumped together, in numerous costumes, in canoes,
on bikes and, yes, of course butt naked. The top award, however, has to go to a Scot
who jumped in his kilt, revealing to the world's press just exactly what is worn beneath.
At around $80-$150 a bungee jump is not cheap (so save your dollars) but as a
once-in-a-lifetime experience, it is worth it. The mighty Nevis is recommended.

Caving
The underground world of the **Waitomo Caves** in the Waikato, North Island, is a
magnificent natural wonder as well as a renowned playground. There are over 360
mapped caves – the longest of which is 14 km. Most have underground rivers which

carve a wonderland of caverns, pools, waterfalls and rapids. These are negotiated with a headlamp in a wetsuit, attached to a rubber ring, which is an unforgettable experience. Added to that, there's a 300-m abseil into the **'Lost World'** as well as the spectacle of **glow-worms**. Truly awesome. There are a huge range of activities on offer. Almost all involve getting wet – whether paddling, swimming, floating, abseiling and jumping, or just wetting yourself (in mirth or fear).

Although it may seem dangerous, all the companies take great care of you and are highly professional. **Waitomo Adventures** are particularly recommended. Prices range from a four-hour trip at $85 to a seven-hour trip at $355. If you can possibly afford it, try the seven-hour 'Lost World' experience. Like the bungee, it is a once-in-a-lifetime experience and worth every cent. There are many other caves throughout the Waitomo region and elsewhere in the country, all of which provide an insight into the delicate natural history that lives below.

As in the rest of New Zealand, treat the environment with respect; screaming loonies in wetsuits should really not be down there.

Fishing

New Zealand is fishing heaven. Although noted as one of the best and most unspoilt trout fishing venues in the world, it also provides some superb sea and big game fishing. The lakes of the Taupo and Rotorua regions are the prime trout fishing spots, as is Gore in Southland, and there is ample opportunity to get out on the water. Both the experienced and the novice are well catered for with numerous boat charters and guides from the relatively affordable $60 an hour to the all-mod-cons versions at $150.

The warm Pacific waters that grace North Island's shores also attract a huge range of salt-water species from snapper to massive marlin. Areas particularly well geared up for game and sea fishing include the Bay of Islands, Tutakaka (Northland), Whitianga (Coromandel) and Tauranga/Whakatane (Bay of Plenty). However, there is excellent sea fishing from boat and shore from just about everywhere in New Zealand.

Costs vary from the three-hour novice trip to the highly organized but still affordable three-day 'Hemingway' trips to catch that prize marlin. This is something you might have thought was reserved for the idle rich, but in New Zealand you too can watch the seabirds, the odd dolphin (sometimes even a whale) and the amazing flying fish erupting from the water; then suddenly the line from your rod and barrel-sized reel goes off like the wheel of a formula one car at the start of a race and your jaw drops in sheer awe as you see a huge marlin sail out of the water at incredible speed, and the fight is on. Though big-game fishing is hard work, you do not need to be Arnold Schwarzenegger to do it.

Flightseeing

For those of you who have only ever flown in a commercial jetliner you must try the far more precarious experience of a small fixed-wing aircraft or a helicopter. Even without the stunning views, it is a wonderful experience and one that gives you a far better insight into what flight is all about. There are endless locations countrywide where you can get up in the air with almost every provincial airport, airstrip or local flying club offering flights. It is also surprisingly cheap. A 10-15 minute flight at around $100 by helicopter or a 30-minute flight in a small fixed-wing for the same price may seem expensive, but you will not regret it. In North Island three places are recommended: over the volcanoes of the Tongariro National Park (from Whakapapa); Mount Tarawera (from Rotorua); and White Island (from Rotorua, Tauranga or Whakatane). In South Island, Kahurangi National Park (Nelson) and just about anywhere down 'The Great Divide' and Mount Cook and Fiordland are highly recommended. There are numerous operators in Wanaka, Queenstown, Te Anau and Milford and these are listed in the relevant sections in the main travelling text. If you can only afford one flight, then make it the helicopter flight around the **glaciers** and summit of **Mount**

⁑ Lord of the Rings locations

Listed by region/nearest significant town or village/actual place name and page reference if any/fictional place name and film event/ access method and rating in relation to difficulty or distance (1-10)/ aesthetics (1-10)/ mystical appeal (1-10)/ tour rating (if applicable) (1-10).

1 Waikato/ **Matamata** (page 246) / Piarere / Hobbiton and the Shire, home of Bilbo, Frodo and Sam / Tour only (2) / 4 / 4 / 5

2 Taupo and Ruapehu (National Park) / **Whakapapa Village**/ Pinnacle Ridge, Whakapapa Ski Fields (page 309) / Mordor and the Battle of the Last Alliance / Road and short moderate walk (4) / 8 / 6

3 Wellington / **Wellington city**/ Mount Victoria (page 404) / The Hobbits race to the ferry with the Nazgul in hot pursuit hiding under tree roots as they go / Road and short moderate walk (3) / 8 / 5

4 Wellington / **Upper Hutt**/ Kaitoke Regional Park (page 411) / Rivendell and the Fords of Isen / Road and a short easy walk (3) / 7 / 7

5 Nelson and Marlborough / **Motueka**/ Takaka Hill and Harwood's Hole (page 470) / Chetwood Forest passed as the Hobbits escape from the Black Riders in Bree / Unsealed road and a moderate walk (7) / 8 / 8

6 Canterbury / **Methven**/ Rangitata River Valley, Erewhon and Mount Sunday (page 491) / Edoras / Unsealed road or tour (8) / 9 / 9 / 8

7 Otago / **Wanaka**/ Rocky Mountain and Diamond Lake (page 659) / Fellowship heading south from Rivendell / Road and moderate walk (optional) (4) / 7 / 6

8 Otago / **Alexandra**/ Poolburn Reservoir (page 619) / Unsealed road (7) / 7 / 6

9 Otago / **Arrowtown**/ Kawarau River and Chard Farm (page 626) / River Anduin and site of the Pillars of the Kings / Road (2) / 6 / 6 / 7 (4WD)

10 Otago / **Arrowtown** (page 641) / Arrow River / Ford of Bruinen / Road and short easy walk (3) / 5 / 4 / 7 (4WD)

11 Otago / **Queenstown**/ **Skippers Canyon** (page 635) / Ford of Bruinen; Arwen fleeing the Nazgul / Unsealed road (4WD recommended) (8) / 8 / 8 / 8 (4WD)

12 Otago / **Queenstown**/ **Deer Park Heights** (page 637) (mountain tarn) / Refugees escaping Rohan / Road (entry fee) and short walk (5) / 8 / 8

13 Otago / **Queenstown**/ **Remarkables Ski Fields**, Lake Alta and Queenstown Viewpoint (page 628) / Dimrill Dale / Unsealed road (4WD recommended) (8) / 9 / 8

14 Otago / **Queenstown**/ **Twelve Mile Delta** (page 634) / Ithilien Camp / Road (2) / 7 / 5

15 Otago / **Glenorchy**/ **Paradise and the Dart River Valley** (page 645) / Isengard, Lothlorien and Amon Hen / Unsealed road (6) / 9 / 7 / 9 (flight with landing); 8 (4WD); 9 (jet boat); 8 (horse trek).

16 Southland/Fiordland / **Te Anau**/ **Mavora Lakes** (page 664) / Fanghorn Forest and the Lake of many Mists / Unsealed road (8) / 7 / 6

17 Southland/Fiordland / **Te Anau**/ **Norwest Lakes** / Arwen and Frodo escape the Black Riders / Helicopter only (10) / 9 / 9 / 9

Cook. Most operate out of Franz Joseph or Fox Glaciers. This 30-minute $220 trip on a clear day is truly breathtaking. It really is what New Zealand is all about.

For a more sedate ride you may also like to consider a trip by **hot-air balloon** which, although not so common and more expensive (around $250), is available in a number of locations including Auckland, the Waikato and Canterbury. For the full 'Biggles' experience you can also don the goggles and scarf and get strapped into a **biplane**. Locations include Auckland, Rotorua in North Island and Gore and Wanaka in South Island.

Fly-by-wire

Picture a metal hospital stretcher with a microlight engine on the back, suspended from a wire in a valley and flying like a pendulum, speeding through the air at up to 100 kph. Now imagine yourself strapped to this flimsy device, squealing like a schoolkid. This seemingly suicidal experience is available in Paekakariki, on the Kapiti Coast near Wellington, or in Queenstown. It costs $99 for 10 minutes – pack some spare underwear.

Golf

New Zealand is blessed with hundreds of golf courses, from those that require a cute wedge shot to avoid sheep to others with well-manicured greens fit for an open championship. Have you ever played a steaming golf course? Didn't think so. Well, in Taupo and Rotorua you can. From little fumeroles on the fairways steam vents from the ground. Lose your ball down there and you won't find the solution in the R&A rulebook. There are many world-class courses in New Zealand like the new Gulf Harbour in Auckland, Wairakei in Taupo and the Millbrook in Otago, to name but a few.

Green fees vary, from newer courses costing $200 to some that can be played for as little as $35. No wonder so many Asians come to New Zealand just to play golf. On a New Zealand course, if you go early and in the off-season, it can be rare to even see another player. No doubt you had to leave your clubs at home, but most courses have clubs for hire. A little word of warning – do not come to New Zealand expecting the same strict attitudes to golfing etiquette found in Europe and North America. This is not St Andrews and the courses are not the hallowed turf like the Old Course, or Pebble Beach. In New Zealand when a group of seven (maximum should be four) likely Kiwi lads drop their trousers on the 18th tee to play a 'provisional', just accept it – it's traditional apparently.

Horse trekking

The New Zealand landscape is ideal for horse trekking and it can be experienced around almost every provincial town. Both the experienced and the novice are well catered for, but the latter take note – horses just know when a complete 'buffoon' has climbed on their back. It will only cost around $35 for two hours, after which you'll be walking like John Wayne after a hearty plateful of beans. There are a wealth of operators and horse riding is available throughout the country. For a very informative leaflet and additional information countrywide contact the International League for the Protection of Horses (ILHNZ), PO Box 10-368 Te Rapa, Hamilton, T07-8490678, ilphnz@xtra.co.nz or the national tour organisation www.ridenz.com

One rather unique equestrian option is a tour to the **Glenmorgan Farm** thoroughbred stud at Karaka in South Auckland (See Auckland Activities Section, page 116), T09-2919355, www.glenmorgan.co.nz

Jet boating

You have probably seen it. A red boat packed with tourists, all wearing the same 'well isn't this fun' expression, while thinking 'get me out of here now'. It is quite an unnerving experience whizzing down a river, heading straight at some rocks at insane speeds and closing your eyes in the face of inevitable death, only to open them again to find yourself still, remarkably, alive. Then, as a last hurrah, to be spun about in a 360° turn, just to make sure you are *completely* wet. That said, it is actually great fun and very safe – it just looks scary. There is jet boating available on many North Island rivers, especially the Waikato (Taupo), Wanganui (Wanganui or Taumarunui) and the Motu (Opotiki), but it is the red boats on the Shotover River in Queenstown that are the best-known. Not all are adrenaline-pumping trips with some (especially in North Island) being more scenic affairs. **Jet Boat Safaris** in Glenorchy (see page 644) is a fine example. Costs are reasonable, with a 30-minute trip being around $75.

Kayaking

New Zealand is a renowned playground for this mode of water transport whether on river, lake or sea – even fiord. You can do it from just about every major town. For novices, kayaking just takes just a wee bit of time to get used to, but before you know it, you'll be off and paddling before you can say 'Deliverance'. One word of warning – kayaks and canoes are better designed for little people. Another word of warning – never share a canoe with a loved one. Within five minutes there will be a major argument about technique, threats of violence and floods of tears. If you find it to your taste (the silence, the solitude and the scenery can be heart-warming) then consider a multi-day trip. The best of these are available in the Bay of Islands, Abel Tasman National Park and (most recommended) Fiordland. Inland you also have the Wanganui National Park in North Island. The coastal scenery is often best taken in by kayak and there are some great guides out there. You never know, you might even come across a friendly dolphin or fur seal. Costs again vary slightly but you can hire your own kayak for about $15 per hour while a three-hour trip will cost about $80 and a four-day affair $500.

Marine mammal watching and dolphin swimming

The New Zealand coastline is world famous for its rich variety of marine mammals. Almost everywhere around the coast pods of dolphin can regularly be seen, from the large, common bottlenose to the tiny and endangered Hector's dolphin. Being on the main whale migration routes, the New Zealand coast is also a great place to see these great leviathans. For the tourist, the beauty is not only the whales and dolphins themselves, but also the relative ease in encountering them. The most popular venue is Kaikoura on South Island's northeast coast. Here a deep coastal trench that comes close to shore attracts whales within a short boat-ride from Kaikoura, making it one of the world's best and most convenient whale watching locations. Closer to the shore, huge pods of dolphin frolic in the surf and seem to delight in the prospect of investigating any clumsy human who ventures into the water. Other than Kaikoura, the principal locations for dolphin watching and swimming are the Bay of Islands and Whakatane in North Island and the Marlborough Sounds, Punakaiki, the Catlins Coast and Akaroa (Banks Peninsula) in South Island. Note that encounter success rates (ie finding them) are generally very high in New Zealand. So much so that many operators offer a refund, or another trip, if the whales and dolphins do not turn up. A 2 1/2-hour whale watching trip in Kaikoura will cost $135, $75 for children. A 2-hour dolphin swimming experience (about 30 minutes in the water) anywhere around the coast will cost around $100, $85 for children.

Mountain biking

New Zealand is, as you might expect, a paradise for the avid mountain biker. With its wide range of magnificent landscapes, the country offers numerous tracks, both long and short and mainly through native bush or commercial forest. You can do it almost everywhere. Bike hire is readily available and quite cheap, so at some point you must try it. Whether you go down vertical rock faces and submerge yourself in mud pools, or stick to the straight and not-so-narrow, is up to you. Such is the quality of landscapes, there is perhaps no single place to be recommended for the sport in New Zealand – the exception being, the forests surrounding Rotorua in the North Island and Hanmer Springs, Malborough Sounds or Riverton, in the South Island, all of which are superb. There are several specialist cycle tour operators including **Cycle Touring Company New Zealand** in Whangarei, T021-2255-282, www.cycletours.co.nz They specialise in self-led cycling adventures on routes all over Northland from 2-9 days. Accommodation and food are all inclusive.

Mountaineering

It would take a lifetime to climb all the major peaks in New Zealand. Mount Cook at 3753 m is the country's highest. Although not especially high, the New Zealand peaks are nevertheless spectacular, challenging and potentially dangerous. The majority of peaks are in South Island with the Mount Cook Range, Mount Aspiring (Wanaka) and the peaks of the Nelson Lakes National Park are the most accessible and attractive.

Mount Taranaki in North Island is the country's most-climbed mountain. There is just something about it. To look at it on a clear day is to stand in awe. Its symmetry and isolation just beckons you up its precarious slopes. Other grand peaks in North Island include Mount Ruapehu and the little-climbed (but superb) Mount Hikurangi in Eastland. If you have never done any mountaineering before this is the perfect country in which to catch the mountaineering bug. You are after all in Sir Edmund Hillary's back garden. Like the great man himself and unlimited numbers before you, once you scale that first peak and feel the sense of achievement, you will almost certainly be hooked. But if you are a novice seek advice and above all go well prepared, check the weather forecast and tell someone of your intentions. Many tourist lives have been lost through sheer stupidity and over-confidence. Although it is expensive there are numerous guided trips available especially around Taranaki and Mount Cook (Franz and Fox Glaciers). For specialist enquiries contact the **NZ Alpine Club,** based in Christchurch, T03-3777595. The **NZ Mountain Guides Association,** info@nzmga.co.nz, www.nzmga.co.nz, is also a very good organization to consult for further information and contacts.

Paraflying and tandem parapenting

First question – what is the difference? Well, both involve a bit of hanging around. One is done around hills and coastal slopes, the other is done from the back of a speedboat over water. It's basically a bit like glorified kite flying with you attached to the kite. Paraflying is the easier and more commercial of the two and is practised at many coastal resorts including the Bay of Islands and Mount Maunganui in North Island, but also on inland lakes like Wakatipu (Queenstown) and Lake Wanaka. Basically you are strapped to a cradle below a special parachute and kept in the air by a speedboat. It's great fun and will have you screaming like a banshee and gesticulating wildly to your highly amused compadres. A 10-minute flight will cost about $50.

Parapenting (or paragliding) is great fun but takes a lot to master. Like skydiving the novice is taken in tandem with an expert. There are a limited number of tourist venues, but Te Mata Peak in Hawkes Bay is North Island's top venue while Wanaka and Queenstown are the capitals of the South. A 20-minute flight costs about $140.

Rafting

This is another 'must do' New Zealand activity. The principal locations in the country for whitewater rafting are the rivers of central and east North Island and generally throughout South Island. In North Island the main places are Taurangi and Rotorua and the Tongariro, Rangitaiki, Wairoa, Kaituna, Mohaka and Motu Rivers. In South Island most of the regions have excellent opportunities and the river list is endless. The rivers and the rapids are graded from I to VI.

Although the quick 45-minute trips at about $85 are great fun and packed with adrenaline-pumping moments, the real rafting experience only comes with a multi-day trip (four days will cost around $500). There are many on offer, but if one stands out head and shoulders above the rest it is the four-day trip down the wild and remote Motu in Eastland, North Island. Provided water levels are favourable, this trip has to be one of the best New Zealand outdoor experiences on offer. It is the sheer isolation as well as the scenery and rapids that is so memorable. On a multi-day trip down a river you also experience the growth of the river itself, from the gently flowing headwaters to raging rapids, and then the gentle meander to the coast. The trips are generally well organized and safe. Most will even do the campfire cooking for you.

If the multi-day trip is beyond your budget and your timeline then the best experience is the 45-minute trip down the Kaituna Rapids near Rotorua. The highlight of this trip is the 7-m drop down the Okere Falls, the highest commercially-rafted falls in the world. Here you, your 12-ft raft and all your shipmates are literally submerged headfirst in the chaotic foam before bobbing up again like corks. It is truly unforgettable. There is little time to learn the ropes, but the guides will keep you alive.

River sledding

This is the ludicrously simple but superb concept of rafting down a river on a body-board with little except a wet suit, flippers, a crash helmet and a PhD in lunacy. The prime location for this is again the Kaituna River in Rotorua. However, there is also the option of doing it down the man-made falls of a dam in Hawera, Taranaki. A 40-minute dunking will cost you about $80-$100.

Rock climbing

This exciting activity is on the increase in New Zealand. The principal locations in North Island include the Mount Eden Quarry in Auckland and various locations near Taupo, Cambridge and Te Awamutu. In South Island the main bases are Christchurch and Dunedin for operators, while Fiordland and the Kahurangi National Park offer the most spectacular venues. There are good climbing walls in Rotorua and Palmerston North in the North Island and in Twizel and Frankton (near Queenstown)

Sailing

New Zealand, and Auckland in particular, is famous for sailing. Indeed, between 1995 and 2003 the Kiwis were the proud holders of the world's biggest sailing trophy – the America's Cup – and despite the loss are still considered not only the best sailors in the world but also the best designers and speed racers. Auckland is not called the City of Sails for nothing. An estimated one in four of its inhabitants owns a recreational boat of some kind and this trend is echoed throughout the country. For the experienced sailor New Zealand and especially the Hauraki Gulf off Auckland and the Bay of Islands provides one of the best sailing playgrounds in the world, and for the novice, too, it is highly recommended. It's all great fun, but like any of the favoured sports, a bit of an 'art form'. At least a few hours out on the water are recommended but, if you can, try a multi-day trip. This will give you an insight into what sailing is all about. There are numerous opportunities to get out on the water in a proper yacht, though if you plan a longer trip there must obviously be someone present with the relevant experience and 'tickets' – and the Sir Peter Blakes of this world don't come cheap.

You will find numerous barefoot or skippered yacht charter/hire companies based in Auckland and the Bay of Islands. In Auckland they include: **Charter Link**, *Bayswater Marina, T09-4457114, www.charterlink.co.nz* **Sail Connections**, *PO Box 90961, 8 Madden St, T09-3580556, www.sailconnections.co.nz* and **Charterbase**, *T09-5343991, www.charterbase.co.nz*

Scuba diving

Like sailing, New Zealand has some world-class diving venues including the celebrated Poor Knights Islands off Tutakaka in Northland. Although there are many locations and a number of superb marine reserves all around the country, the Poor Knights is where most budding Jacques Cousteaus gravitate. It is the combination of geology, marine life and perhaps, above all, water clarity that make them so special. With up to 80 m of visibility you can go head to head with a huge grouper or clench your rubbers at the sight of a shark. Of course the trained and the qualified fare better but in many locations local operators will take you for a full or half-day basic first dive experience for around $175 including gear hire. If the thought of all that is too much you can also go snorkelling, which gives you a great insight into the wonders of the deep for minimum effort. There is also some fine wreck-diving available with the old navy frigates *Tui* and *Waikato* deliberately sunk for the benefit of divers off the east Northland coast. Another fine trip is the one to pay homage to the Greenpeace vessel *Rainbow Warrior* that was laid to rest off Matauri Bay. The great *Warrior* was bombed in Auckland by French terrorists in 1985. Other than Northland the main diving locations are the Hauraki Gulf (Auckland), Coromandel (Whitianga), New Plymouth (Taranaki) and the Marlborough Sounds and Fiordland in South Island.

Shark encounters

While the vast majority of the human race still have nightmares at the mere suggestion of a fin surfacing above the water, it appears there is a lunatic fringe who actually wish to have a picnic with them. If you are one of these people and wish to encounter these fascinating creatures in their own habitat from the relative safety of a cage, you can do so in New Zealand. The principal locations are Tutukaka and Napier in North Island and Kaikoura in the South. A four-hour trip will cost about $130, prosthetic limbs extra.

Skiing and snowboarding

New Zealand is the principal southern hemisphere skiing and snowboarding venue and although it is of course seasonal (May-August), the slopes are highly accessible. Most of the major commercial ski-fields are in South Island. They include Coronet Peak and the Remarkables near Queenstown, Treble Cone, Cardrona and Waiorau near Wanaka, Mount Hutt, Mount Potts and Porter Heights west of Christchurch and the Arthur's Pass, Hanmer Springs and Nelson regions. The choice is vast. In North Island the main commercial venues are on the slopes of Ruapehu (Whakapapa and Turoa) in the Tongariro National Park.

Although they vary, the average cost of hire for skis, boots and poles is around $35, snowboard and boots $45. An all-day lift pass will cost anywhere from $35-$75 depending on location, with concessions for both students and children. There are invariably a number of packages available for both adults and children that include lift pass, equipment hire and one or more lessons. There may also be 'Lift and Ski Hire Packages' which cost from $75-$100. A group lesson (2 hr) will cost about $45 while a private lesson (1 hr) will cost about $75. For detailed information consult the websites www.nzski.com, www.snow.co.nz and www.brownbear.co.nz Specific ski-field contact details are listed in the relevant sections of this book.

Surfing

New Zealand is a world-class surfing venue but often overlooked by the surf set and because of this it is quite special. In New Zealand as yet, surfing is pretty uncommercial, but still practised in many locations, with an almost religious following. North Island's West Coast locations of Taranaki, Raglan (Waikato) and Piha (Auckland) are perhaps the most famous venues, but other great surf spots include Whangamata (Coromandel), Eastland, Gisborne and Napier. You can get excellent

⁞ Tramping track classifications

All DoC managed and maintained walks from short 5-minute boardwalks to mountain traverses have a classification, as follows:

Path Easy, generally low-lying and well formed. Suitable for all ages and levels of fitness. No walking boots required.

Walking Track Easy and well formed. Can involve short or steady climbs. Suitable for all ages and the reasonably fit. Shoes are okay, but proper walking boots preferable.

Tramping Track Requires relevant skill and experience. Generally continuous track but may be vague in parts. Expect full range of topographies up to scrambling. Suitable for people of average fitness. Walking boots required.

Route Requires a high degree of skill and route-finding experience. The track may only have markers as guidance. A high level of fitness and equipment (including maps) is required.

Essentials Sports and activities

and relatively cheap tuition in many locations (especially in Taranaki and Raglan). If you want a beginner's taste of what surfing is like, try boogie-boarding or bodysurfing. Boogie-boards are about half the size of a surfboard and made of compressed foam. They are readily available and are cheap to buy or hire. With this and a pair of flippers you can then go pseudo-surfing and take out the difficult bit – standing up.

Swimming

Although swimming in the sea is kept mainly to the summer months, you can do your strokes year round in man-made pools and the numerous hot pools throughout the country. Rotorua and Taupo are the natural hot pool capitals but there are also others in Waiwera north of Auckland, Te Aroha in the Waikato, Tauranga in the Bay of Plenty and numerous other venues throughout the country. There is something quite special about swimming around a large hot pool that is the temperature of a bath tub and for the uninitiated you will be reluctant to ever get out. One word of warning – coastal swimming can be very dangerous and at some popular locations there are notorious rips (currents that carry you off to Australia) so when you are swimming at the beach, take care and if directed swim only 'between the flags'. If in difficulties all you need to do is raise your arm and keep it aloft, and before you know it you'll be hauled into a rubber dinghy by hunky lifeguards (sorry boys, this is not *Baywatch*).

Tandem skydiving

Adrenaline aside, the beauty of taking the jump in New Zealand is the scenic factor. Once you have recovered from that falling feeling the view of the land below hurtling towards you at about 120 kph is truly unforgettable. In New Zealand you can do a tandem in many locations throughout both islands. There is some scant instruction before the actual jump but you are essentially in very safe hands. A location recommended for value and height is Parakai (Auckland) and for scenery it is Taupo, Wanaka and Queenstown. Jumps range in height from 9000 ft to 15,000 ft. The latter will give you about 40 seconds free-fall. At no less than $240 it is undoubtedly expensive but worth it. The price, obviously, increases the higher you go, though commercial operators will generally not take first timers beyond 15,000 ft.

Tramping (hiking)

Even before the *National Geographic* proclaimed the Milford Track as 'the world's best walk', New Zealand could, without doubt, claim to be the tramping (or hiking) capital of the world. Not only is it one of the principal pastimes for many New

Zealanders, it is also the reason many visitors come to the country. There is a vast network of routes and literally thousands of kilometres of track the length and breadth of the country, from the well-formed and trodden highway of the famed Milford Track, to the sporadic trail and markers of the lesser known Dusky Track. The range of habitats is immense, from remote coastlines, through rainforests, beside volcanic lakes, over mountain peaks to island traverses, with most penetrating vast and fully-protected national parks.

Other than the sheer scenic beauty and scope of opportunities in New Zealand, what makes tramping so popular is the ease of access and maintenance of the tracks. Under the administration and advocacy of the Department of Conservation (DoC) all advertised tracks are clearly marked, well maintained and have designated campsites and huts offering clean water, basic accommodation, cooking facilities and toilets. Add to that the wealth of detailed information available, from route descriptions and access to up-to-date weather forecasts, it is little wonder that tramping is perhaps New Zealand's biggest and most uniquely precious tourist asset. Even **safety** is well-managed, with the tracks classified by type and fitness required. Guided trips are available for the more inexperienced and even an 'intentions sheet' system is used for major excursions. All this for as little as $5 per tent or nightly hut fees.

The most famous track is, deservedly, the magnificent **Milford Track**, a 54-km four-day trek that combines lake and mountain scenery. Also in the Te Waipounamu World Heritage Park is the Routeburn, Kepler, Dusky, Greenstone, Hollyford and the newest, the Hump Ridge Track. But these are only a few of the many tasty options.

The most popular tramps come under the heading of New Zealand's (DoC) **'Great Walks'**. In North Island these include the Tongariro Northern Circuit in the Tongariro National Park (including the volcanic delights of the Tongariro Crossing) and the beautiful circumnavigation of Lake Waikaremoana in the Te Urewera National Park. In South Island there are others including the highly popular bays and estuary crossings of the Abel Tasman Coast Track in the Abel Tasman National Park, the beautiful coastal stretches of The Heaphy in the Kahurangi National Park and the muddy delights of the Rakiura Track on Stewart Island (the newest of the country's 14 national parks). Quieter and still spectacular tramps in South Island include the Travers-Sabine in the Nelson Lakes, Rees-Dart-Cascade Saddle between Glenorchy and Wanaka and the stunning, but difficult Dusky Track in Fiordland.

It would be easy just to recommend the likes of the Milford, Kepler and Abel Tasman, but a word of warning: many of the tracks are very busy and are now not so much tracks as public highways. The Milford, Kepler, Heaphy and Abel Tasman are considered the worst in this respect. Of course that does not mean that they should be avoided. They are still worth doing, and no less spectacular, but if you like a bit of solitude with your tramp, consider other options or at the very least go towards the start or the end of the tramping season (October to April). To give you some idea of how busy they are, the Milford now hosts about 10,000 trampers annually and the Abel Tasman up to 300 a day in mid-summer. This not only means a lot of company, it also means you must book accommodation sometimes weeks in advance.

Tramping information, booking and safety For detailed information about all the major tramping tracks and 'Great Walks' contact the local DoC Field Centre (listed under the relevant location) or visit the website www.doc.govt.nz

For accommodation bookings and information call in person or book via the website www.greatwalksbooking@doc.govt.nz

There are two price systems for hut accommodation and four categories. The first are the Great Walks Huts ($15-35 per night) which have bunks with mattresses, basic cooking facilities, usually a log fire plus a clean water supply and long-drop toilets. Categories 2-4 are Backcountry Huts ($5-15) ranging from those offering similar facilities to the above to mere shelters with just water and toilets. An annual Hut Pass can be purchased for $65. All Great Walk Huts must be pre-booked, sometimes

⦂ Tramping – it is no walk in the woods!

If you have never been tramping before and intend to embark on one that involves a number of days, you need to be warned that it will be a challenge. A challenge not only to your physical, but also your mental self. Tramping is not walking the dog or even that long and congenial afternoon jaunt that is followed by 'oh wasn't that lovely, but I'm knackered now dear...can we go home for dinner?' Tramping is all about nature; nature's extremes, and your own. You can, and will, get extremely tired, hot, wet, thirsty, hungry and in New Zealand, bitten alive. But – and here is the big but – the rewards are immense. Not only will you experience nature at its best (or worst), your senses will be bombarded by the all the immensity and richness that offers, from stunning views, to the quiet chuckle of mountain streams – that you could swear are sometimes laughing at you. In many ways it is also a test. You are pitching yourself not against nature, but alongside it, and for many, this is a new and foreign experience, well out of their comfort zone. There will be no lattes, no email or McDonalds, no warm duvets or clean, flush toilets. There will be no hi-fi, no pubs, no dot-coms, stocks and shares, no fingernail polish or powder puff. You're going to get wet and you're going to smell. Again, although your companions may, nature doesn't care – that's natural. You are going to wake up, tired because you were sharing a dorm with what sounded like a small family of warthogs (now that can't be bloody natural!). Everyday you are out there, you are going to eat a meagre breakfast, put those wet boots on again, what feels like a small house on your back, and not for the first time, set off thinking – what the hell am I doing here. And again nature doesn't care. It's not going to take your backpack off, and pat you on the back and say – aw, there, there, there, my poor dear, diddums! No, instead and only if you are receptive to it, somewhere along that track that day nature will remind you exactly why you are there – or shouldn't be. There is also another welcoming and rare factor – appreciating the simple things in life. Once the day's walking is done and you have reached your shelter it is the simple things and simple cravings that really matter – a log fire for warmth, or a cup of tea. And let's face, it almost all of us need to feel a lot more of that! So, in essence you are either going to love it or hate it, but you are going to have to accept the challenge and take the risk to find out which. Above all, like any challenge or any risk, it is the best way to learn a bit more about yourself and others. One word of advice – travel light. I mean really light. Forget the butter, put your toothpaste in a film cartridge, anything to lighten the load, and in the South Island don't forget to take lots of heavy duty insect repellent.

weeks in advance, and all huts (except those run by guided walk companies) operate on a first come first served basis. **Camping** is permitted at some huts or at designated campsites ($5). DoC campsites come in to two catagories; 'serviced' which cost from $6.50-$8 and 'standard' which cost anywhere from $2-$10. Camping is free for children under five. DoC field centres all stock excellent leaflets for each track ($1), maps and can provide up-to-date track and weather reports as required. Most VICs also stock DoC walks leaflets. The website www.doc.govt.nz also hosts comprehensive information about each major walk and its availability, and offers an online booking service.

You are advised to consult the local DoC office before embarking on any of the major tramps regardless of experience and weather conditions and if required fill in an intentions sheet. Always make sure you are well prepared, equipped and of the required level of fitness. Unless you are experienced, tramping on the more remote and quieter tracks alone is not advisable.

Walking

The opportunities are endless. New Zealand is a walker's paradise and most VICs or regional DoC offices compile lists of the most notable long and short walks in each region. There is everything from coastal or bush walks to historical trails. Two of the best one-day walks are the Tongariro Crossing in the Tongariro National Park (best accessed from Taupo) and the Tarawera Falls Walk near Rotorua in North Island. In South Island there are simply too many to list or recommend, but you should at least try the coastal walk at Wharariki Beach, Nelson Region.

Multi-day walks enter the realm of Tramping, the New Zealand term for hiking. The country is world-famous for this, offering some of the best tramping trails in the world (see Tramping above). For more local short or long walks you can also consult the web. The best site is of course the DoC site, www.doc.govt.nz, but another useful one is the independent site www.hillarysport.co.nz

Wildlife watching

Wildlife watching in New Zealand is usually of the bird variety. However, you will also have the opportunity to see dolphins, fur seals and whales. The Bay of Islands and Whakatane are the dolphin-watching and swimming capitals of North Island, while Kaikoura is the world-famous venue for both dolphins and whales in South Island. The endangered Hector's dolphin can also be viewed from Curio Bay in the Catlins, Southland and around Banks Peninsula in Canterbury.

Given the fact that so much of the wildlife of the country and especially the mainland has been pillaged, you are advised to visit at least one of the offshore island reserves. Tiri Tiri Matangi Island north of Auckland and Kapiti Island north of Wellington are easily accessible, world-renowned sanctuaries which are home to many unique and endangered species. On either of these islands you can really get a feel for the paradise that New Zealand once was. With little or no effort, you will also see many of those rare species close up, since many are naturally very tame.

Perhaps the best and most comical is the takahe, an ancient species that looks like a large prehistoric purple chicken. Only about 200 remain. Then of course there is the kiwi – that remarkable nocturnal bird with no wings, an awfully long beak and an ability to lay an egg the size of a small melon. There are many commercial nocturnal houses where you will get a reasonably good view of one, even though it is very dark. The sight of a kiwi in the wild is of course a far more special and intimate experience, but for this you will have either to be exceptionally lucky or to go to Stewart Island or elsewhere on an organized or specialist trip. At night they can sometimes be attracted by taped mating calls.

Sadly, like most of the country's native wildlife, the kiwi is becoming increasingly rare and is fast heading for complete extinction on the mainland. As usual we are to blame. There are very few places in the world where you can see, let alone have such free access to, such rare and beautiful birds, so make the most of it. Overall the scope, opportunities and locations to see and experience New Zealand's incredible wildlife first-hand are endless. DOC's Mount Bruce Wildlife Centre near Masterton in the Wairarapa, North Island, or their Te Anau Wildlife Centre are recommended and of course the city zoos are also great places to see captive native wildlife at close range. While travelling keep your eyes open for organized ecotrips by foot, boat or kayak. For specialist wildlife operators see page 23, and for more information see the Wildlife and Vegetation sections in the Background chapter, pages 727 and 737.

New Zealand is very well suited to the experienced windsurfer and offers endless locations. Windsurfing schools and board hire is available at most of the principal beach resorts.

Zorbing

Last and by no means least is zorbing. This is a most bizarre concept that could only be the creation of incredible Kiwi ingenuity. Described as a 'bi-spherical momentous experience', it involves climbing into a clear plastic bubble and rolling down a hill. Sadly, the organized venture involves a short hill that takes about 10 seconds to roll down and relieves you of about $50 – a bit of a rip-off. But what you could do with your own zorb blows the mind. Although a bit expensive you can have your own momentous experience at the Agrodome in Rotorua. Incidentally, you can also do a wet run and be joined inside the bubble by a bucket of water.

Health

No vaccinations are officially required for entry into New Zealand. You are, however, advised to get a tetanus shot or ensure your booster is up-to-date. The standards of public and private medical care are generally high, but unless you have a genuine accident it is important to note that these services are not free. Health insurance is recommended. A standard trip to the doctor will cost around $40 with prescription charges on top of that. Dentists and hospital services are expensive. For free information on how best to access New Zealand's health system contact the 24-hr Accident Info Services, To800-263345.

Safety precautions

Other than the occasional crazed driver, there are very few dangerous creatures in New Zealand. One exception is the **Katipo Spider**. It's a cute little black number, about 25 mm from leg tip to leg tip, which is found on beaches, under stones and in driftwood throughout North Island and parts of the South. It is not uncommon and can be fatal, with agonizing pain in the vicinity of the bite. Antivenin is readily available in hospitals. Although sharks are a common sight around New Zealand shores, shark attacks are rare. The last fatal attack occurred in Eastland in 1976.

There is one nasty little blighter, which, although not poisonous, will annoy you beyond belief – the dreaded **sandfly**. Particularly common in the wetter and coastal areas of Fiordland (but present almost everywhere), these black, pinhead sized 'flying fangs' have a successful hit rate that makes laser-guided missile systems look archaic. Open your car door and within seconds a vast cloud of the little devils will descend and your entire party will look like a crowd of deranged loonies at a rave. There are numerous environmentally friendly (and reputedly sandfly distinctly unfriendly) creams available such as: *Shoo*, *Botanica* and *Repel*.

Insect repellents generally come in one of two forms: chemical-based and natural. Chemical-based repellents typically contain DEET (N, N-diethyl-m-toluamide) which forms a vapour barrier around the skin that blocks bugs' antennae receptors. Since DEET is essentially a toxic chemical that can be harmful to some composite materials, it should only be used in the lowest concentrations (5-10%) to provide necessary protection. Many people now dispense with DEET factor altogether and opt for natural products which can be just as effective. In New Zealand these are all the rage and come in various brand names. Their effective ingredient is little more than natural oils like eucalyptus or citronella. But whether chemical or natural, maybe one of these days, someone will bring out a brand with two words – to do with sex and travelling – that are far more appropriate.

There are a few other safety factors worth mentioning. **Giardia** is an equally offensive little nemesis of the bacterial variety. He's an ugly wee water-borne parasite on the increase in New Zealand which, if allowed to enter your system, will cause wall-to-wall vomiting, diarrhoea and rapid weight loss. The best bet is not to drink water from lakes, ponds or rivers without boiling it first. The **sun** too is dangerous and you should take care. Ozone depletion is heavy in the more southern latitudes and the incidence of melanomas and skin cancer is above average. Burn times, especially in summer, are greatly reduced so get yourself a silly hat and wear lots of sun block.

Other than that it is very much down to common sense. Bear in mind New Zealand's **weather**, especially at the higher elevations, is changeable and can sometimes be deadly. If you are climbing, tramping, or going anywhere 'bush' make sure you are properly clothed and shod, take maps, a first aid kit and a compass. Above all inform somebody of your intentions.

Volcanic eruptions and **earthquakes** are also an exciting factor. Although major events are rare they can (and have) of course happened and proved fatal. Such is their power and magnificence all you can say here is keep your fingers crossed and hope you are not in the wrong place at the wrong time. In the event of an earthquake, stand in a doorway, get under a table and if you are in the open, get indoors or keep away from loose rock formations and trees.

One other thing. Should you come across any **injured wildlife** call the nearest DoC office and try to ensure the animal is taken to one of the few local wildlife rehabilitators. DoC officers are very busy and the entire department is generally underfunded. Provided the animal is not on the 'Don't touch list' (ask DoC) and you use common sense, capture the animal and put it in a dark, fully enclosed box with some ventilation holes. Then find out the location of the nearest rehabilitator and take it there yourself. If in doubt don't. If you come across a **whale stranding** or an obviously sick seal on the beach call DoC immediately or, in South Island, Marine Watch, T02-5358909 for advice.

Keeping in touch

Internet

New Zealand has contracted that 'love it or hate it' computer disease as badly as any other developed nation. Internet cafés and terminals are now springing up everywhere and if you are amongst the many afflicted, who start walking funny or dribbling if you do not get your daily 'email-inbox-fix' you should be fine. The major cities are very well served with internet outlets and most towns have cafés or terminals somewhere. Libraries and VICs are also a good bet, but unlike the free US system, they charge the same standard rates of $6-12 per hour. Thankfully, due to growing competition, rates are getting cheaper, but you are still advised to shop around. As ever, speeds also vary tremendously and there are plenty of cowboy operators who miraculously seem to have some strange connection problem every day that ensures you stay logged on as long as possible. Internet venues are listed under Information or the Directory sections throughout the guide.

Post

Post offices (most often called 'Post Shops') are generally open from Monday-Friday, 0900-1700, Saturday 0900-1230. Mail can also be sent to 'Post Restante', CPO (Chief Post Office) in the main cities, where it will be held for up to 30 days. If you are being sent any mail make sure the sender marks your surname in capitals and underlines it. There is nothing worse than hanging around town for days waiting for a package that has been sitting there all the time in the wrong pigeonhole, under your first name. Within New Zealand standard (local) post costs $0.45 for medium letters and postcards (2-3 days); $0.80 for airmail (fast post) to domestic centres (1-2 days); $1.50 for airmail letters to Australia and$2 for standard overseas airmail letters to Europe, North America, East Asia, Australia and South Pacific). Domestic mail takes one to two days, perhaps a little longer in rural areas. When sending any cards or letters overseas be sure to use the free blue 'Air economy' stickers. Books of stamps are readily available as are pre-paid envelopes and a range of purpose-built cardboard boxes. Average international delivery times vary depending on the day of the week posted, but a standard letter to the UK can take as few as four days (scheduled 6-12 days). North America is scheduled 4-12 days and Australia and the South Pacific 3-8 days.

Poste Restante pick-up points

Auckland: Wellesley St Post Shop, *Bledisloe St, T09-3796710* (Mon-Fri 0730-1730)
Wellington: *23 Manners St, T04-4735922* (Mon-Fri 0800-1730, Sat 1000-1330).
Nelson: Nelson Post Shop, *Corner of Trafalgar and Halifax Sts, T03-5467818*

(Mon-Fri 0745-1700, Sat 0930-1230).
Christchurch: Cathedral Square Post Shop, *Cathedral Sq, T03-3775411* (Mon-Fri 0800-1800, Sat 1000-1600).
Dunedin: Dunedin Post Shop, *283 Princess St, T03-4773518* (Mon-Fri 0830-1730).
Queenstown: Main Post Office, *15-19 Camp St, T03-4227670* (Mon-Fri 0830-2000, Sat 0900-1600).

Telephone

The international code for New Zealand is 64. There are five area codes: Auckland and Northland **09**; Bay of Plenty, Coromandel, Taupo, Ruapehu and Waikato **07**; Eastland, Hawkes Bay, Wanganui and Taranaki **06**; Wellington **04**; South Island **03**.

The rather attractive Telecom payphones are readily available throughout the country and colour coded. Although there are both coin (blue) and credit card (yellow) booths available, the vast majority are 'phone-card only' so you are advised to stock up. Cards come in $5, $10, $20 and $50 and are available from many retail outlets, post and visitor information offices and hostels. Unless you want to see just how fast digital numbers can disappear on screen, do not use these Telecom cards for anything other than domestic calls within New Zealand. There is now a wealth of cheap international calling cards and call centres available. One of the best is E Phone, www.eph.co.nz, a calling card that accesses the net through an 0800 number. The cards, which again vary in price (usually from $10 to $50), can be bought from many retail outlets (look for the E Phone flag signs outside the shops). They come with simple instructions and can be used from any landline telephone. Voice instructions will tell you what to do and how much credit you have available before each call. Note that local non-business calls are free from standard telephones in New Zealand, so it is not too offensive to ask to use a host's or friend's domestic (non-business) telephone for that purpose. 0800 or occasionally 0508 precede toll-free calls. Try to avoid 0900 numbers as they are usually very expensive. Mobile phones are prefixed by 025 (Telecom) or 021 (Vodaphone).

Media

Although not on the grand scale or blessed with the same choice as countries like the UK, the newspapers in New Zealand are pretty good, featuring fairly comprehensive and factual sections on local, national and international news as well as sport, business and travel.

The principal daily **newspapers** (except Sundays) are the *New Zealand Herald* (Auckland and upper North Island), the *Dominion* (Wellington and lower North Island) and the *Press* (Christchurch and central South Island). If you wish to sample any of these before you leave log on to www.nzherald.co.nz or the general website, www.nzstuff.co.nz is a good site for both national and regional news.

There are a few national **magazines** which may be of interest, including: *North and South* - a magazine covering a wide range of traditional and contemporary issues; *New Zealand Geographic* – the quality New Zealand version of the great US national icon; *New Zealand Wilderness* – a glossy outdoor activity magazine and *New Zealand Outside* – a similar effort. These are readily available at bookshops or post shops while most mainstream international newspapers and magazines can be found at specialist magazine outlets like Maggazino in Auckland and Christchurch (see the Essentials sections of those cities).

Although New Zealand radio is quite good, **television** is a shocker. Whether due to a lack of population, revenue or simple imagination the four principal terrestrial channels have very little to offer. Bar good news and current affairs programmes you are bombarded with the usual insidious UK or US soaps, or the wretched 'Who Wants to be a Millionaire' or 'Survivor'. Most New Zealanders (including tourist accommodation establishments) and the average Kiwi sports fanatic, have now subscribed to Sky TV. Perhaps the most aggravating thing about New Zealand television is the advertising. With such a low population, subsequent lack of variety and ineffective standards authorities, most of the advertising is offensively repetitive. It is not unusual to get the same ad every 10 minutes for days. A number of individuals have also made their fortunes in New Zealand with the use of the off-peak, special offer product advertising. Yes, those heinous 'Only \$29.99'; 'Send no money, we'll bill you' and 'Wait, there's more' products. Sadly, this seems to work.

North Island

Auckland

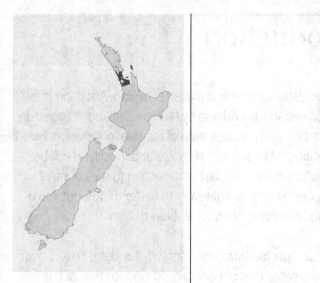

Introduction

With a population of one and a quarter million, Auckland is the largest Polynesian city and also by far New Zealand's biggest. In fact it's the home of almost a third of the total population. For the vast majority of visitors to New Zealand, Auckland will be their arrival point and their first introduction to the country. Many will treat it only as a gateway to better things, but you'd be pleasantly surprised with what it has to offer.

Thanks to its spacious suburban sprawl, Auckland covers over 500 sq km – twice that of London and close to that of Los Angeles – but because the city is built on an isthmus and constantly fragmented by coastline, you are never far from water. The sea pervades almost every aspect of Auckland life, from recreation to cuisine. Aucklanders own more recreational boats per capita than any other city in the world, and it is subsequently and affectionately called the **'City of Sails'** and the 'Nautical Capital of the South Pacific'.

No surprise then that for eight years, between 1995 and 2003 it was the proud home to the world's most prestigious yachting trophy, the **America's Cup**. Most sailing is done in Auckland's backyard, the beautiful aquatic playground and island-studded waters of the **Hauraki Gulf**, one of the most beautiful sailing venues in the world. As well as sailing, you can go fishing, swimming or surfing, all within minutes of the city centre and, in some places, have the beach to yourself. The city also boasts some impressive man-made attractions such as the stunning 360° views from the hypodermic **Sky Tower**, and its bustling city centre streets and trendy suburbs are home to a thousand world-class restaurants.

★ Don't miss...

❶ The 'hypodermic' **Sky Tower** – climb the mast, take in the 360 degree views, dine in the revolving restaurant, or bungee from 192 metres, page 84.

❷ Taking a cruise across Auckland Harbour to historic **Devonport**. Muse in the galleries, enjoy a glass of wine or a flat white in one of the cafés, or walk to take in the views from North Head, page 92.

❸ The **Auckland Museum**, page 90. Introduce yourself to Kiwi history, wildlife and culture.

❹ The café culture and nightlife of **Ponsonby, K'Road** and **Parnell**, page 109.

❺ The solitude of the Waitakere West Coast beaches of **Whatipu, Karekare** or **Bethell's**, page 130.

❻ **Tiri Tiri Matangi Island**, page 134. Mix with rare and endangered species. The stunning **Hauraki Gulf islands**, get there by ferry, yacht or launch, page 134.

❼ The sunrise from the volcanic cones of **Mount Victoria** or **Mount Eden**, pages 92 and 98.

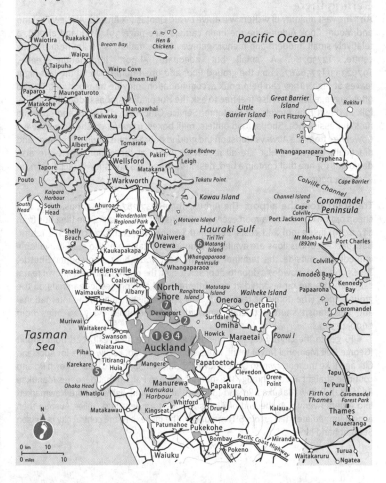

Auckland → *Phone code: 09 Colour map 1, grid C4 Population: 1,250, 000*

Auckland has been labelled a Polynesian city but in reality it enjoys a cosmopolitan make-up of Pacific, European, Asian and indigenous Maori. Modern Auckland is the fusion of four cities: North Shore, an expanding, predominantly European and contemporary area of greater Auckland north of the bridge, with attractive beaches and quiet modern suburbs; Auckland City itself, the heart and hub, with its central business district around Queen Street growing ever skywards, together with the waterfront and its happening inner-city suburbs; Waitakere, to the west, a mix of low and high income suburbs dominated by the bush-clad Waitakere Ranges; and Manakau to the south, with its lively low-income suburbs of predominantly Maori and Pacific Island citizens. All combine to create a huge cosmopolitan sprawl of modern humanity, in which, naturally, it is very easy to get lost.

Ins and outs

Getting there

Air The vast majority of visitors will arrive by air. Qantas (ex Ansett), Air New Zealand and Mount Cook Airlines are the main carriers (see page 39). **Auckland airport**, a relatively small, modern and friendly gateway to the nation, is 20 km from the city centre, T2750789. A small but adequate **Airport Information Centre**, T9792333/T2756467, is on the ground floor and open from 0500 till the last flight leaves at night. They can help book accommodation, provide transport details and offer baggage storage. Also feel free to ask the Hospitality Ambassadors (the smiley folk in bright blue jackets) or Customer Service Officers (red jackets and splendid hats) for assistance. Shops, food outlets, mail boxes, internet, crèche, free showers (towel hire from the Airways Florist on the ground floor $5, plus deposit), phones and practically everything else are all readily available at the airport. There are also dayrooms for hire that contain a bed, desk, TV, coffee, tea and shower facilities, from $30 for 4 hours.

Transport from the airport The Airbus, T0508-247-287, www.airbus.co.nz, is a cheap option leaving the airport every 20-30 mins between 0620-2200 (first bus from city 0440, last 2100) and costs $13, child $6 one way and $22, child $12 return. Backpacker concessions are available. Independent **taxis** are also readily available immediately outside the terminal and will cost you about $40. **Super Shuttle**, T3063960, also provides a door-to-door service. All the regular and well-known rental car operators are represented at both international and domestic terminals on the ground floor. (The domestic terminal is only a short distance from the international and free transit shuttles operate between both terminals every 20 mins from 0600-2230.)

To get to the city **by car** from the airport, take the main exit road from airport (George Bolt Memorial Drive) to the intersection with SH20. Follow signs for Auckland City and take the motorway to Queenstown Rd exit. Turn right in to Queenstown Rd and continue straight ahead, through the roundabout in to Pah Rd that becomes Manukau Rd (SH12). Follow Manukau Rd and turn right at the traffic lights (before Newmarket) into Alpers Avenue. At the end of Alpers Avenue turn right into Gillies Avenue then almost immediately left to join SH1 motorway. The last exit to the central city is Nelson St (right hand lane).

48 hours in Auckland

Many visitors to Auckland make the mistake of giving themselves too little time. Although not entirely representative of the country as a whole, and in many ways, just a modern city like any other, Auckland does have a lot to offer and if you only have 48 hours the following is recommended: forget jet lag – you have no time!

Once you have secured your accommodation, and provided the weather is fine, head straight away for the **Sky Tower** and its all-encompassing view. From the main observation deck you can see the vast sprawl of the city and pinpoint various sights to visit. Note the fact that despite its seemingly endless suburban sprawl, wherever you are in Auckland you are never far from the sea. Also, looking out to the Hauraki Gulf and its Islands, you can instantly see why one in four Aucklanders own a boat and why New Zealand was the proud home of yachting's most prestigious prize-the America's Cup. Adrenaline junkies might like to consider climbing up the mast of the tower or better still taking the plunge from above the observation deck – at 192 m, New Zealand's highest (but highly controlled) bungee jump – welcome to adrenaline country!

Once back down to earth head to the former **America's Cup Village** on the waterfront and have lunch in one of the many, mainly up-market restaurants (Cin Cin in the Ferry Building, Euro on Princess Wharf and Kermadec overlooking the America's Cup Village are recommended). From the Ferry Building then catch a ferry to **Devonport** and take a leisurely walk east to **North Head** from where you will get a memorable view back towards the city centre. Once back in the heart of Devonport, enjoy

a coffee or glass of wine in one of its street-side cafes. If you still have some energy walk to the top of **Mount Victoria** for more good views. Back in Auckland sample the commercial delights of **Queen Street** and/or **Victoria Park Market** and enjoy some retail therapy.

In the evening relax with a stroll along **Ponsonby Road**. Muse at the huge range of cafes and restaurants and decide which best suits you for dinner (see relevant text for recommendations).

The following morning (preferably before the sunrise and if you have your own wheels) grab a picnic lunch and a flask of coffee and head west of Auckland to Scenic Drive and the **Waitakere Ranges**. Stop to watch the sunrise over the city then take a look in the **Arataki Visitors' Centre** (opens at 0900, free). Choose which of the **West Coast beaches** you prefer.

After lunch head back in to Auckland and to the **Auckland Museum** in the Domain where you will get a fine introduction to Maori culture and New Zealand wildlife. Lovers of art could then consider a trip to the **Auckland Art Gallery** (City Centre) while more action can be found with the sharks and penguins at **Kelly Tarlton's Underwater World** and **Antarctic Adventure** near Mission Bay. That evening watch the sunset from the summit of Mount Eden before heading for a local café or restaurant.

Those without independent transport should consider a day-cruise to **Waiheke** or **Rangitoto Island**. Lovers of wildlife should not miss a day-visit to **Tiri Tiri Matangi Island**. If you have a week in Auckland seriously consider 2-3 days on **Great Barrier Island**.

Bicycles, scooters and motorcycles These are a brave option in Auckland, given the way people drive, unless you are a seasoned courier or experienced city cyclist. Within the city stick to walking, buses or a car. Outside the city keep bicycles to the mountain or touring variety. If you want a more unusual mode of transport try a *Tuk-Tuk*, a sort of metal rabbit hutch on wheels with fearless drivers; T9178887, www.tuktuk.co.nz

Outside the central city and major suburbs cycling and motorcycle touring can be a joy. A number of cycle shops offer bikes for hire. There are also a number of motorcycle/scooter rental companies in Auckland, so shop about. ▸▸ *See also Transport page 122.*

Bus Public transport generally is a major bone of contention in Auckland as traffic congestion and higher than average car ownership clogs the city's roads and pollutes the air. Although adequate for the average visitor, it is generally poor and planned improvements are long overdue. Most central and suburban buses stop at the new **Britomart Transport Centre** (BBT), centrally located between Customs and Quay Sts near the waterfront. Information can be obtained from the terminal itself or all major tourist information offices and by phone (**Rideline**, *T3666400, www.rideline.co.nz*).

Greater Auckland

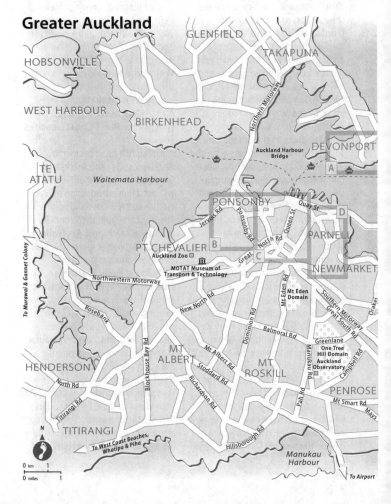

Car Most of the major tourist sights and attractions are centrally located and can be easily accessed by foot, bus or ferry. For longer stays, due to the huge urban sprawl a car is highly recommended. Car ownership per capita in Auckland is one of the highest in the world and you will quickly see that Auckland is not only a 'city of sails' but also a 'city of wheels', many, unfortunately, with certifiable owners (driving in Auckland can be hazardous and rush hour is a nightmare!). Formal metered or multi-storey parking is readily available in the city. Parking costs up to $6 an hr, and traffic wardens are everywhere.

There are more **car rental** companies than you could shake a gearstick at in Auckland, ranging from fully insured, nearly new cars, to rather dodgy-looking rent-a-dents. A new, fully insured vehicle without mileage costs starts from about $75 a day. See page 122 for listings.

Ferries and water taxis Almost all, save the few commuter ferries, depart from around the historic Ferry Buildings on the waterfront, at Quay St. A limited commuter service to some waterside suburbs has been developed and is expanding, but the vast majority of ferry traffic is tourist-based. There are many excellent island or harbour locations, trips and tours to choose from. Fares are generally very reasonable.

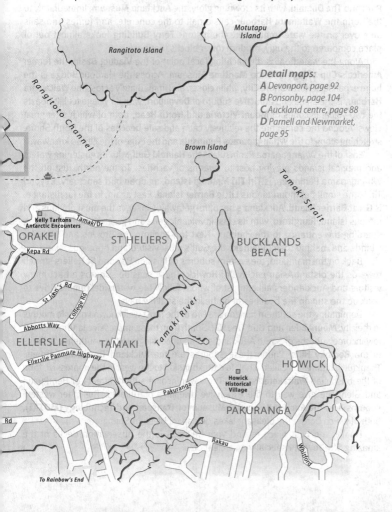

Detail maps:
A Devonport, page 92
B Ponsonby, page 104
C Auckland centre, page 88
D Parnell and Newmarket, page 95

Taxi All Auckland taxi drivers are required to belong to a registered taxi company, which sets standards, but that is no guarantee of good English or not being taken via 'the scenic route'. Meters are usually based on time, not distance, so it often pays to get an estimate first. Typical rates are $2.50 flag call and then about $1.50 per km. Taxis are generally widely available and can be flagged down, ordered by phone or picked up at the numerous city-centre ranks. See page 122 for listings.

Train Local and intercity trains arrive and depart from the new Britomart Terminal centrally located between Customs and Quay Sts near the waterfront. For all information: T0800-802802, www.tranzrail.co.nz Information can also be obtained from all local VICs and the terminal itself. Reservations and information also from all mainstream travel agents. Two main lines west to Waitakere and to South Auckland serve only a few major suburbs. Contact **TranzMetro**, T3666400, www.tranzMetro.co.nz

Orientation and information

The heart of the city centre is the **CBD** (Central Business District) and the main drag of **Queen St**. On either side, the jungle of high-rises gives way occasionally to older buildings like the **Auckland Art Gallery** and the green inner city sanctuaries of **Albert Park** and **The Domain**, with its crowning glory, the **Auckland Museum**. Immediately to the north the **Waitamata Harbour** calls a halt to the concrete, and ferries and sails take over on the **waterfront** where the historic **Ferry Building** looks almost out of place compared to the ugly, modern tower blocks that back it in.

Along the waterfront is the yachting focal point of the **Viaduct Basin**, the former **America's Cup Village** and the **Maritime Museum**. Across the Harbour Bridge is the huge expanse of **North Shore City**, while closer, and immediately across the **Waitamata Harbour**, is the small and attractive suburb of **Devonport**, with its village feel. It boasts the two volcanic cones of **Mount Victoria** and **North Head**, both of which offer great views. Around the corner are the relatively calm and safe **beaches** of the North Shore, stretching along to the **Whangaparaoa Peninsula** and the edge of the city 40 km away.

East of the Whangaparoa Peninsula is the **Hauraki Gulf**, with its glistening waters and magical islands playing host to swarms of yachties. To the north, just off the Whangaparoa Peninsula, is **Tiri Tiri Matangi Island**, an open bird sanctuary. Beyond Tiri is the small but mountainous **Little Barrier Island**. East again, in the far distance, is **Great Barrier Island**, Auckland's beautiful getaway. Closer, is the most obvious and famous island, **Rangitoto**, with its classic volcanic cone and green botanical blanket, guarding the entrance to the Harbour. Next to Rangitoto are Browns and Motuihe Islands and, behind them, **Waiheke** the Gulf's most visited and populous island.

Back on the mainland, the eastern suburbs of Mission Bay and **St Heliers** stretch towards the distant Asian enclave of **Howick**. These seaside suburbs attract many visitors and Aucklanders alike, most of whom follow the waterside **Tamaki Drive** to soak up the sun on the beaches or bathe in the shallow bays.

Dominating the southern horizon are two of the most well known volcanic mounts in the city, **Mount Eden** and **One Tree Hill**. South from these impressive landmarks, the low-income suburbs of South Auckland spread unceasingly to the southern city limits of the **Bombay Hills**. Within these suburbs are the **Auckland Botanical Gardens**. Thankfully, nature has called a halt to city expansion to the west in the impressive form of the bush-clad **Waitakere Ranges**. The lower-income suburb streets of Henderson and Glendene give way to the expensive dwellings of Titirangi. The inner western suburbs host the **Auckland Zoo** and **Museum of Transport and Technology (MOTAT)**, both of which border the pleasant lakeside park of Western Springs.

Finally, the best place to find your bearings is the observation decks of the amazing **Sky Tower**, especially on a clear day.

Maps Perhaps your first purchase in Auckland should be a map. All your needs can be met in that department right in the centre of the city. The **Auckland Map Centre**, 1A Wyndham St, T3097725, has a fine selection of national and local maps of varying scale, as does **Speciality Maps**, 46 Albert St, and **Whitcoulls** on the corner of Queen St and Victoria St. **Whitcoulls** and **Borders**, 291 Queen St, also have comprehensive national travel guide sections.

Various free tourist handouts have some colourful maps of the city, but if you are serious get the *Wises Auckland Compact Handi Map Book* ($24), or at the very least the foldout version ($14). Other than that, you will probably quickly find yourself slipping into the local habit of using the Sky Tower as the seemingly omnipresent beacon, and the main volcanic cones and the harbour as guidance and orientation.

Tourist information There are Visitor Information Centres (VICs) at both airport terminals: **International**, T9792333/T2756467; **Domestic**, T2568480. There are 2 main Auckland Information Centres (*I-Sites*) in the central city: at 287 Queen St, open Mon-Fri, 0900-1800, Sat and Sun 0900-1700, Apr-Oct, Mon-Fri 0900-1700; and the quieter **American Express New Zealand Cup Village** next to the Maritime Museum, T9792333, www.aucklandnz.com, open daily 0900-1700.

If you venture north across the bridge, the North Shore VIC is at 49 Hurstmere Rd, Takapuna, T4868670, www.tourismnorthshore.org.nz, open Mon-Fri 0830-1700, Sat/Sun 1000-1500, or Devonport, 3 Victoria Rd, T4460677, open Mon-Fri 0800-1700, Sat/Sun 0830-1700. All information centres provide piles of free leaflets and handouts, but don't miss the readily available *Auckland A to Z*, *Auckland What's On*, *TNT Magazine* and the *Backpackers' News*, all excellent, up-to-the-minute publications. The *New Zealand Herald* is the main Auckland and North Island daily, www.nzherald.co.nz For all things environmental and ecological, including nature walks, get yourself to the **Department of Conservation** (DoC) Information Centre, Ferry Building, Quay St, T3796467, on the waterfront; open Mon-Fri 1000-1730, Sat 1000-1500, Sun closed.

History

According to Maori legend, when Maui (founder of New Zealand/Aotearoa) fished up the North Island, his efforts to subdue his catch created the islands of the Hauraki (the scales) and the bays and the beaches of the Isthmus (the wounds). Maori Gods of the Ocean and Wind further shaped and modified the geography and created the warm moist climate. It was the Gods of the resident giant, Mataaho, who created the volcanoes (legend has it he was cold) with their most recent piece of central heating being Rangitoto Island which guards the mouth of the Waitamata Harbour.

The first Maoris to settle in the area were thought to be moa hunters (moa being the once numerous, but now extinct, flightless New Zealand bird) before AD 1000. But later, from the 12th to 14th centuries, further migrations and *Waka* (Maori canoes) brought first the Nga-Oho and later the Nga-Tai and Nga-Marama tribes. The latter, led by the ambitious Kiwi Tamaki, ruled the roost for some time, taking up residence in *Pa* (which were Maori settlements, often fortified) on almost every volcano in the district, including a main *Pa* on what is now named One Tree Hill. But his reign did not last and, after an ugly dispute and subsequent brutal conflict with other *hapu* (sub tribes), particularly the Ngati-Whatua from the Kaipara district to the north, he succumbed. This, together with an epidemic of smallpox brought by the early Europeans, meant the area became relatively unpopulated.

This all changed when the first official visit by *Pakeha* (white Europeans) came in 1820 in the form of the Reverends Samuel Marsden and John Gare Butler, two missionaries who were keen to expand their teachings beyond the Bay of Islands. From that point more organized integration and low-key European settlement began. But it was not until 20 years later, in 1840, on the signing of the Treaty of Waitangi, that New Zealand's Lieutenant-Governor, Captain William Hobson, bought a 3000-acre 'pie shaped' part of the Isthmus from the Ngati-Whatua for £55 and a few blankets. He called this area Auckland, after George Eden second Baron Auckland, then Governor General of India, probably in return for giving him command of *HMS Rattlesnake* in which Hobson first visited New Zealand in 1837. Hobson's intention was to create a new capital of New Zealand, the original settlements of the Bay of Islands, particularly Russell, having a distinctly unsavoury and disobedient population.

And so, for a short time, Auckland became the capital and the focus for the invading pioneers. One such pioneer, a Scots medic called Logan Campbell, took full advantage of Hobson's acquisition for the Crown, and in the first years of its existence took almost total control of half the fast-expanding 'pie'. He became mayor of the settlement, and the so-called 'Father of Auckland'.

The rapidly growing demand for more land created great conflict with the Maori, contributing in part to the New Zealand Land Wars of the 1860s. Presumably, the Maori were beginning to realize that, in exchange for a few quid and some basic goods, they were fast losing '*Mana*' (presence, standing, integrity or honour) as well as their indigenous and rightful control.

Thanks to the Land Wars, and the discovery of gold elsewhere in Otago and in the nearby Coromandel, Auckland floundered a little. To add insult to injury in 1865 Auckland lost its status as capital to Wellington and with it the seat of Government.

However, towards the end of the 1800's, thanks to its fertile soils and climate and the brief but explosive 'Kauri' years – when there was widespread deforestation of the Kauri tree – Auckland's fortunes changed and the 'squashed pie' rapidly became the 'full bakery'. The rate at which Auckland continued to develop during the 20th century was astonishing. The irresistible combination of geography, climate, industry, agriculture and business opportunities has seen the population explode, creating the thriving cosmopolitan city we see today.

Sights

City centre

Sky Tower, Sky City and the Casino

① *Enquiries and restaurant bookings; T3636000. For more information, T0800-7592489 or www.skycity.co.nz Theatre information and bookings, Tiketek T3075000. Observation levels open 0830-late. $15, child $7.50, backpackers, $10. Restaurant open for lunch from 1130, dinner 1730, weekend brunch from 1000. Minimum charge $20.*

For many Aucklanders in the early '90s the prospect of a casino and a futuristic 328-m Sky Tower smack bang in the city centre made them quake in their jangles (sandals). Construction began in 1994, on the corner of Victoria and Federal Streets, for the following 32 months and Aucklanders watched with disbelief and awe as Sky City sprouted its great hypodermic into the heavens. It was naturally the talk of the town, finally opening in 1997 in a hail of publicity. No one at the time denied the unbelievable imagination, construction, technology and logistics it took to create, but many still criticized the tower, saying it was too futuristic and a blot on the landscape. But Aucklanders have grown to love it – perhaps because it really is like a beacon. It's an awesome sight and, unless you hate heights, you just have to go up it.

⁞ Sky Tower – some statistics

The Sky Tower was opened in 1997 and took two years and eight months to build. At 328 m tall it is the tallest man-made structure in the Southern Hemisphere and 23 m taller than the AMP Tower in Sydney. The tower's shaft measures 12 m in diameter and its foundations reach 15 m into the earth. It houses the highest weather station, post box and restaurant in the Southern Hemisphere. The restaurant completes a 360° revolution every 60 seconds. It is designed to withstand a 8.0 earthquake and 200 kmh winds. Such winds would only create a 1m sway of the entire structure. During construction the tower was kept absolutely vertical using complex telemetry including three global satellite-positioning systems. There are 1257 steps to the Sky Deck. The fastest recorded time of ascent during the annual 'Sky Tower Vertical Challenge' is 5 minutes – 57 seconds. In 1998 bungee guru AJ Hackett made a 192 m bungee jump from the main observation deck, the highest jump ever attempted from a ground structure.

The Sky Tower has four **viewing decks** and a revolving **restaurant**. A lift takes a mere 40 seconds to reach the main observation deck, where you can walk around the full 360°, taking in the stunning views, while being educated by an audio guide. There is also a **'live weather feed'** and touchscreen computers. If you would like a coffee, go down one level to the lower observation deck. Conversely, if you would like to check that 'weather feed' in person and feel the wind in your hair go up to the outdoor

⁞ *Sky City Hotel is one of the largest in New Zealand (see Sleeping, page 102)*

observation deck above the restaurant. If you are brave and have a few dollars more, why not shoot another few storeys up to the sky deck, the highest available observation point. If you really think you are brave, and have never had the slightest hint of vertigo, you can stand on glass panels in the main observation deck and look down – a most disconcerting experience – or try it at night while enjoying a meal in the Orbit revolving restaurant. The food is great, if you can keep it down long enough to enjoy it!

In the last two years the great tower has become, perhaps inevitably, the focus for some typical Kiwi, lunatic activities. It was really only a matter of time before the hottest tourist entrepreneurs would find some way for tourists to jump off it, or climb out upon its mast and now, alas, with the safety inspectors clearly satisfied, you can do both. The **'controlled' bungee** is known as the Sky Jump (funny that) and the mast climb Vertigo. Details are listed in Activities, page 116.

Sky City claims to be Auckland's largest multi-faceted entertainment and leisure destination. The **main casino** provides all kinds of gambling and gaming options, restaurants, bars and live entertainment 24 hours a day, and has seen the ruin of many. Even if you are not a gambler it is well worth a look. The **Alto Casino and Bar** is a more intimate and sophisticated experience with a more rigourous dress code. One for the real wheelers and dealers. **Sky City Theatre** is a 700-seat, state of the art entertainment venue, staging national and international events and productions. As well as the Tower's Orbit restaurant there are five **other eateries** offering everything from Pacific Rim to Chinese, traditional buffet or café-style options. Ample car parking is provided in a seemingly endless rabbit warren below the complex.

The waterfront and America's Cup Village

The once sandy beaches of the waterfront have now become cliffs of glass and concrete as the city has grown relentlessly outwards and upwards over the last 150 years. Radiating from the historic **Ferry Building**, built in 1912, the waterfront is the place where the city of concrete becomes the City of Sails and where the locals would say she takes on her proper and distinct character. The waterfront has always been a focus of major activity. In the early years it was the point where exhausted immigrants first disembarked to begin a new life in a new land. Later, the immigrant ships gave way to the fleets of log-laden scows bringing kauri to the timber mills. Today, recreation has taken over, as modern ferries come and go and lines of expensive yachts rock gently together in the breeze at the **Westhaven Marina**, the largest in the southern hemisphere.

The waterfront has seen perhaps the most rapid development of all centred around the **Viaduct Basin**, until recently the hallowed home of the America's Cup Village. Even before New Zealand took the cup from the USA's tight grasp in 1995, the Viaduct Basin was a stopover point for the Whitbread Round the World Race (also won by New Zealand in 1994) and the place has become an aquatic stadium of profound celebration. New Zealanders are proud of their yachting heritage and, even outside the fierce competition of the yachting trophy wars, this is reflected on the waters of the Viaduct Basin. Much debate has raged, since the somewhat embarrassing loss of the America's Cup in February 2003, as to what will become of the Viaduct Basin and the site of the former syndicate headquarters. Will it retain something of its former atmosphere? Or merely fade to become just another modern inner city enclave?

New Zealand National Maritime Museum

① *Daily 0900-1800 (winter 0900-1700). Adult $12, child $6 and family concessions. 'Ted Ashby Heritage Cruise' (1 hr 30 min), 1000,1200 and 1400, Tue, Thu, Sat, Sun in summer: adult $15, child $7, museum entry extra. 'Combo' museum entry and Heritage Cruise: adult $19, child $12, concessions available. The New Zealand National Maritime Museum (Te Huiteananui-a-Tangaroa), corner of Quay and Hobson St, on the waterfront and within easy walking distance of the city centre or Britomart Transport Centre. To800-725897/T3730800, www.maritime.org*

Even if you are an committed landlubber and have little interest in boats or sailing, the New Zealand National Maritime Museum is a wonderful museum and well worth a visit. On the waterfront at the entry to the America's Cup Village, it depicts a very important aspect of New Zealand's history and, more importantly perhaps, the particularly maritime flavour of the 'City of Sails'. The museum is well-laid out, chronologically, so that you begin with the replicas and a high video presentation of early Maori, Polynesian arrivals before moving on to European maritime history, including immigration. Here, in the replicated living quarters of an early immigrant ship, complete with moving floor and appropriate creaking noises, you cannot help sympathizing deeply with the brave souls who made the journey.

Moving on again, you then emerge into the galleries of New Zealand's proud yachting history, including the stories of New Zealand's participation and triumphs in the Louis Vuitton Cup, The Whitbread Round the World Yacht Race and, of course, the much-lauded America's Cup. Much of this story is the personal resumé of the late Sir Peter Blake, New Zealand's most famous sailing son who was so tragically murdered in the Amazon in 2002; and more recently Russell Coutts, considered by many after his lucrative move from Team New Zealand to skipper the Swiss challenge Alinghi in 2003, the 'Judas' of Kiwi yacht racing. Naturally, though now almost like a shrine for mourning, is the exhibit and replica of the America's Cup itself. During its proud stay between there 1995 and 2001 the original was housed in the New Zealand Royal Yacht Squadron Headquarters at the Westhaven Marina, but now of course is languishing somewhere in Switzerland. It was of course possible to view the elaborate piece of silverware, but after a delicate and expensive restoration following an axe attack by a self-proclaimed Maori activist in 1997 security became a lot tighter.

The America's Cup

The America's Cup is, to the world of yachting, what the British Open (and the 'Claret Jug') is to golf, or the Ashes (the 'Urn') is to cricket. Although not exactly considered a mainstream spectator sport, it is a sporting prize worthy of considerable international prestige – especially in a small 'yachting-crazy' nation like New Zealand. The Cup has been contested for over a century, usually every four years. For the first 132 years it remained in the possession of the New York Yacht Club, before an Australian challenge lead by magnate Alan Bond took it from American leader Dennis Connor's grasp in 1983. In Australia there was of course considerable celebration, but the party was not to last. Four years later Connor first defeated the New Zealanders for the right to challenge Australia then swept Australia aside, returning the cup to the United States. The win against New Zealand was shrouded with controversy after Conner accused the New Zealanders and their team leader Sir Michael Fay of cheating. This was seen not only as an insult to Fay but to the nation. After three more unsuccessful attempts most of which degenerated into bitter accusations and court cases surrounding the legalities of boat specification and a personal battle between Connor and Fay, New Zealand finally took the cup and settled the score in San Diego, in 1995. It was an achievement that caught the imagination and stirred the passions of New Zealanders to a level normally only associated with the 'All Blacks'. When syndicate leader Sir Peter Blake donned his 'lucky red socks' for the last day of racing many loyal kiwis emulated him, and a sea of red (over 350,000 people) lined Queen Street in Auckland, to welcome their heroes home. Almost immediately the New Zealand syndicate started making plans for the Auckland defence of 2000, an event that would see the transformation of Auckland's Waterfront Basin into the America's Cup Village. The America's Cup was big business.

In February 2000 the New Zealand boat *Black Magic* took the honours in five straight races which only increased the hype and the focus on country, city and the individual team members. Almost immediately after the 2000 campaign foreign syndicates began making offers to key team members that were difficult to refuse. Within weeks the New Zealand team became a shadow of its former self. But despite that, with Auckland set to host a second defence of the cup in 2003, it seemed the hype within New Zealand and the innate confidence arising from such emphatic victories in the past transcended any fears of loss. Once again for the average kiwi it seemed unthinkable that the national team would not out-sail all comers with ease and that new aspects of boat design would prove superior.

When the Louis Vuitton Cup (the preliminary competition that decides who challenges New Zealand for the America's Cup) was won convincingly by Swiss syndicate Alinghi (skippered by former New Zealand team member Russell Coutts) the stage was set for a fascinating duel. Sadly it was to prove a total non-event. With a litany of disasters from tactical mistakes, to the snapping of a mast besetting the New Zealand boat throughout, not to mention the superior sailing skills of Coutts and his team, Alinghi won 5-0 and the cup left New Zealand shores for Switzerland. With red faces rather than socks this was effectively the end of an era for New Zealand yachting and a mighty lucrative honeymoon for Auckland. How the loss of the cup and the honour of hosting the world's most prestigious yachting trophy will affect the city remains to be seen.

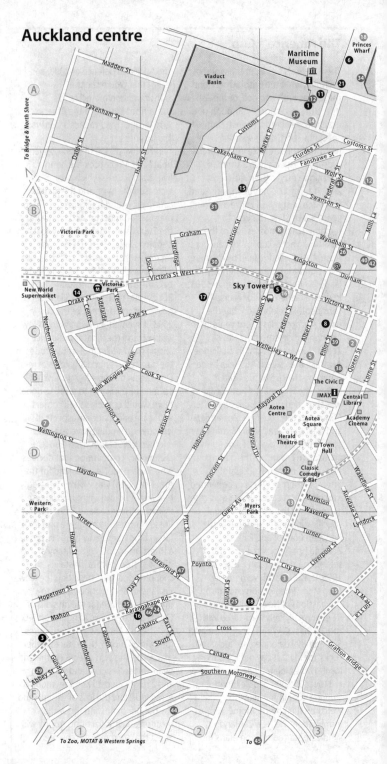

Related maps:
A *Parnell and Newmarket, page 95*
B *Ponsonby, page 104*
Greater Auckland, page 80
Devonport, page 92

N

0 metres   200
0 yards   200

Auckland City centre sights

Sleeping
Albert Park
 Backpackers **1** *C4*
Ascot Metropolis
 10 *C4*
Auckland Central
 Backpackers **2** *C3*
Auckland City
 YHA **3** *E3*
Cintra
 Apartments **4** *E4*
City Central &
 Middle East Café **5** *C3*
Darlinghurst Quest
 Apartments **6** *C5*
De Brett,
 O'Connell Street
 Bistro & Corner
 Bar **9** *B4*
Freemans B & B **7** *D1*
Harbour View **19** *D5*
Heritage **8** *B3*
Hilton & White
 Restaurant **18** *A3*
Oxford
 Apartments **11** *D4*
Quay West & 8
 Over Albert
 Restaurant **12** *B3*
Quest Auckland
 13 *D3*
Sebel **14** *A3*
Sheraton **15** *E3*
Sky City, Orbit
 Restaurant & Sky
 City Theatre **16** *C3*
Whitaker Lodge **17** *E4*

Eating
Cin Cin & Harbourside
 Seafood Bar
 & Grill **4** *A4*
Euro **6** *A3*
Food hall on
 Atrium on Elliot **8** *C3*
French Café **9** *D4*
Gallery Café **10** *D4*

Joy Bong **3** *F1*
Kermadec **11** *A3*
Mecca **2** *C4*
Observatory
 (Sky Tower) **5** *C3*
Rakino's **13** *C4*
Sake Bar Rikka **14** *C1*
Seamart **15** *B2*
Soul **1** *A3*
Sri Pinang **16** *E1*
Toto **17** *C2*
Verona **18** *E2*
Vertigo **7** *A4*
Vivace & Vulcan
 19 *B4*
White Lady **20** *B4*
Wildfire **21** *A3*

Bars & clubs
Bed **24** *E2*
Belgian Beer Café
 22 *B4*
Bomb Shelter **23** *A4*
Calibre **25** *E2*
Cardiac **36** *B4*
Centro **26** *B3*
Club 4:20 **35** *E1*
Danny Doolans **12** *A3*
Deschlers **27** *C4*
Dispensary **28** *C3*
Dogs Bollix Bar **29** *F1*
Empire **30** *B2*
Float **34** *A3*
Galbraith's Ale
 House **45** *F2*
Immigrant **31** *B2*
King's Arms **32** *D3*
Kiwi Tavern **33** *B5*
Loaded Hog **37** *A3*
London Bar **38** *C3*
Margarita's **39** *C3*
Mo's **41** *B3*
Muddy Farmer **42** *B3*
Papa Jack's
 Voodoo Lounge
 43 *C4*
PowerStation **44** *F2*
Staircase **46** *E2*
Supper Club **47** *E2*
Wunderbar **48** *B4*
Wyndham
 Bowling Club **40** *B3*

Link bus route = = =

The museum also houses the scenic and relaxed Big Boat Café as well as a maritime shop with nautical gifts and memorabilia. If you are trying to trace your roots, you can search the computer immigration records and passenger arrivals in 'The Immigrants' section of the museum.

A number of excellent cruises are available from the museum, including the popular 'Ted Ashby Heritage Cruise', aboard the 57-ft traditionally built scow *Ted Ashby*, and six daily excursion options aboard the *Pride of Auckland*. All these wonderful vessels are beautiful replicas or originals and it is an ideal opportunity to get out on to the water in some style.

The Domain

① *T3792020. Domain Winter Gardens and Fernz Fernery, 0900-1730, winter 0900-1630. Free. To get there, see Auckland Museum below.*
The Domain is the venue for a number of major orchestral and operatic outdoor events in summer and over Christmas.

The Domain is one of Auckland's less obvious volcanic cones and New Zealand's oldest park. Originally another enclave and early Maori *Pa*, it was formally put aside as a reserve by Governor Hobson in 1840. Within its spacious grounds are a number of historic features including the **Bledisloe** and **Robert Burns Memorial statues** and its crowning glory, the **Museum** and **War Memorial** (see below). Other points of interest include the **Winter Garden** and **Fernz Fernery** where you can take in the scents of various blooms or study the 300 species of fern on display. The Formal Garden within the Domain was once the site of the Auckland Acclimatisation Society where exotic trees, birds and fish were kept before being released to wreak their havoc on indigenous species. The park also has a number of quiet inner-city bush walks, some with alluring names such as 'lovers walk', which would fool you into the belief you are far from the city, were it not for occasional glimpse of the omnipresent Sky Tower through the branches. If you get hungry during your wanderings or have forgotten a picnic then the Domain kiosk by the duck pond serves basic snacks and refreshments (*open daily 1000-1500*).

Auckland Museum (Te Papa Whakahiku)

① *T3067067, www.akmuseum.org.nz Daily 1000-1700. $5 donation, Maori Concert $15, child $11.25. Most city tour buses stop at the museum, as do buses 63 and 65 from the Britomart Transport Centre and the Link bus from downtown. The Museum is also on the 'Coast to Coast' Walkway.*

The Auckland Museum, an impressive edifice that crowns the spacious surroundings of the Auckland Domain houses some wonderful treasures, displayed with flair and imagination. Its most important collection is that of Maori Taonga (treasures) and Pacific artefacts which, combined, is the largest such collection in the world. Other special attractions include an award-winning Children's Discovery Centre, Social and Settlement History Sections, Natural History Galleries, and 'Scars on the Heart', the story of New Zealanders at war, from the Maori Land Wars in the late 1800s, to the campaigns in Gallipoli and Crete in the two World Wars of the last century. The museum also houses a major national War Memorial and hosts the traditional dawn gathering of veterans on Remembrance (Anzac) Day on the forecourt.

If you are short of time make sure you see the **Maori Court**, a fascinating collection of pieces from woven baskets to lethal hand weapons carved from bone or greenstone, all centred round the huge 25 m Te Toki a Tipiri war canoe (*waka*) and *hotunui*, a beautifully carved meeting house. The authentic Maori concert held three times daily at 1100, 1200 and 1330 (additional performance 1430 January-March) by the Pounamu Maori Performance Group is also worth seeing.

In the **Natural History Galleries** pay particular attention to the 'Human Impacts' section, which will give you a frightening reality check of how New Zealand has been systematically raped of the vast majority of its once huge indigenous biodiversity from the first day man set foot on the shores of this unspoilt paradise. The **Children's Discovery Centre** is a 'sensory learning feast' you, and the kids, might find it hard to drag yourself away from. There are computers, games, things to jump on, look through, poke or prod. The museum café is on the ground floor, and there is a well-stocked museum shop.

Auckland Art Gallery (Toi-O-Tamaki)

ⓘ *Main Building and New Gallery Building, T3077700, www.aucklandartgallery.co.nz Daily 1000-1700. Free guided tours at 1400 daily. Collection displays free; charge for temporary exhibitions. Both galleries are in close proximity and within easy walking distance from Queen St, Central City. The 'Link' bus stops right outside the gallery every 10-20 mins.*

The Auckland Art Gallery is essentially two buildings one in Kitchener Street and the other on the corner of Wellesley and Lorne Streets in the central city. They combine to form the largest and most comprehensive collection of national and international art in the country. The first building and **old gallery** (Kitchener Street) is over 100 years old and, although it has undergone major reconstruction and has added extensions over the years, it retains its French Renaissance revival character and charm.

The gallery spaces within its walls display exhibitions from the permanent collections. These include small collections of some of the better known international masters, particularly 17th-century pieces, but it is the New Zealand works by **Charles Goldie** and **Gottfried Lindauer** that are of particular interest. Goldie and Lindauer were two early European settlers who specialized in oil landscapes and portraits of Maori elders in the late 18th and early 19th century. The works of Goldie are impressive to say the least, with their almost Pre-Raphaelite detail bringing the portraits to life, particularly the delicate detail of the

> ‼ *The independent Gow Langsford Gallery just across the road from the Main Gallery is also worth a look.*

moko, or Maori facial tattoos. However, one has to be a little wary of the romanticism of the depictions of Maori life as seen through early European eyes: the warrior savages being civilized by those who think they know better.

The **New Gallery**, which opened in 1995, is nearby on Wellesley Street. It houses mainly temporary exhibitions and artists' installations that explore new art, new ideas and media. The **Colin McCahon room**, which displays the works of this more contemporary and hugely respected New Zealand artist, demonstrates the often very conceptual nature of these more modern works. The installations can vary from the fascinating to the ridiculous depending on your artistic bent.

For **other Auckland Art Galleries** consult the Auckland Gallery Guide, Art Out West and Parnell Arts Trail leaflets available from main Tourist Information Offices.

Albert Park

Behind the Art gallery is Albert Park, informal lunchtime escape for the city suits and nearby university students. The park was formerly another Maori *Pa* and later, during the Second World War, the site of concrete bunkers. These sites and the park as a whole have now thankfully been replaced by nicely manicured flowerbeds, statues, a floral clock and old spider-like fig trees. It is a great place to bring a sandwich, escape the noise and look up at the Sky Tower. On the park's western fringe, housed in a small cottage, is the **Bruce Wilkinson Collection**, ⓘ *daily 1000-1600,* of ornate clocks and ornaments. Worth a look if only to remind you that it is time to move on.

City North

North Shore City, or the North Shore, as it is better known, is most famous for the miles of coastline and pretty bays that fringe its quiet eastern suburbs. Many British immigrants reside north of the bridge and in summer you will find them on one of the many sheltered beaches enjoying the sun and aquatic delights they never could back home. The commercial centre of the North Shore is **Takapuna**, with its attractive range of modern shops, popular restaurants and bars, but it is **Devonport** with its history, city views and village feel that deservedly attracts most tourists.

Getting there

Car Devonport is 12 km from Mid City across the Harbour Bridge. Take the Takapuna off ramp, turn right on Lake Rd and just keep going. **Bus** Bus #813 from the BBT; T3666400. **Ferry** Fullers Ferry (Ferry buildings, Quay St, Auckland City, T3676892, www.fullers.co.nz), every 30 mins until 1930 weekdays, 2000 weekends and hourly after that until 2300; $8 return, child $4.

The **Devonport Explorer Tour** is a combination of ferry, bus and walking which is personally guided and includes North Head and Mt Victoria 2 hr (hourly 1000-1500, daily; $25). Information and bookings; T3576366. It also offers a tour option with a buffet dinner at the new Watermark Restaurant, from $60 per head, departs 1800. North Shore Information Centre, 49 Hurstmere Rd, Takapuna, T4868670, www.nscc.govt.nz/ www.tourismnorthshore.org.nz

Devonport **Visitor Information Centre** (I-Site) ① *3 Victoria St, T4460677, visitorinfo@nthshore.govt.nz Mon-Fri 0800-1700, Sat, Sun 0830-1700*. Almost next door to the historic Esplanade Hotel. The centre and its friendly staff will provide information on historic sights, the best short walks and places to stay. Internet is available at *Gentronics* 53A Victoria Rd.

Devonport, Mount Victoria and North Head

The heart of North Shore City is in Devonport. This is the shore's oldest and most popular settlement, lying on the shores of its southernmost edge. Devonport's greatest asset is the fact that it is so near yet so far from the city centre, creating a distinct village

Devonport

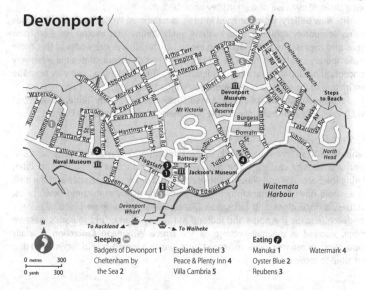

Sleeping 😴
Badgers of Devonport **1**   Esplanade Hotel **3**
Cheltenham by   Peace & Plenty Inn **4**
the Sea **2**   Villa Cambria **5**

Eating 🍴
Manuka **1**   Watermark **4**
Oyster Blue **2**
Reubens **3**

0 metres 300
0 yards 300

feel. It is a popular spot with both locals and visitors, and there is plenty to see and do. Only a 10-minute ferry ride from Mid City, or a 12 km drive across the Harbour Bridge takes you immediately to the heart of this historic and picturesque little suburb. Victorian villas, craft shops, sidewalk cafés and pleasant short walks all lie in wait, dominated by its two volcanoes, Mount Victoria and North Head, both of which offer great views. For a longer stay try one of its many quaint bed and breakfast hideaways.

According to Maori tradition the great ancestral canoe, Tainui, rested here on its coastal explorations in or around the 14th century, before both Mount Victoria and North Head were, not surprisingly, settled by the Maori and used as *Pa*. A village called Flagstaff on the western side of Mount Victoria was one of Auckland's earliest European settlements before land sales expanded in all directions to form eventually the suburb and naval base called Devonport, after its namesake in southwest Devon, England.

If time is short your best bet is to take the short walk to **North Head** which guards the entrance to Waitamata harbour. Follow the shore east along the pohutukawa-lined King Edward Parade from where you can enjoy the view of the harbour, alive with all manner of craft, from jet-skis to huge supply ships. From there you can climb up and all around North Head and enjoy the commanding views back across the city, the North Shore suburbs and out across the Hauraki Gulf. The warren of underground tunnels and bunkers built amidst the hysteria of various potential invasions during both World Wars provide added interest.

From North Head climb down to **Cheltenham Beach**, a popular swimming and sunbathing spot in summer and one that gives the most spectacular and almost surreal view of the volcanic island of **Rangitoto**. It is a particular delight at sunrise. On your return to the village, if you have time and are feeling energetic, try to include a climb to the summit of **Mount Victoria**. Equally stunning views of the city can be had from here, and its slopes retain the remnants of the Maori *Pa*. From there you can go to Victoria Road for a coffee, lunch or some shopping before catching a ferry back to the city.

There are three museums in Devonport. The largest, the **Naval Museum**, ① *Spring St, T4455080, daily 1000-1630, free, 1 hr tours (T4455186) of the naval base are available on weekends at 1300 and 1430*, is best left to those with a specific interest. The more central **Jackson's Museum**, ① *Victoria Rd, T4460466, daily, 1100-1600, adult $10, child $6*, is a better bet with its mish-mash of 'automobilia, sounds, Victoriana and collectibles'. The low-key **Devonport Museum**, ① *31a Vauxhall Rd, T4452661, weekends only 1400-1600, free*, in the Cambria Reserve, is small but still worth a look.

Devonport is famous for its resident artists and there are a number of quality **galleries**. **Art of this World**, T4460926, on the Queen's Parade across the road from the Wharf, is the newest and the best but the **Flagstaff**, T4451142 on Victoria Road, and **Art by the Sea**, T4456665, on King Edward Parade, are all worth a look. The **Devonport Arts Festival** is held every March. Shopping in the village is a delight and there are a number of interesting craft shops, but you may be hard pressed to drag yourself away from the two excellent second-hand bookshops, **Evergreen Books** and **The Hard to Find (but worth the effort) Books** at 15 and 81A Victoria Road respectively. ▸▸ *For Sleeping and Eating in Devonport, see pages 102 and 112.*

‡ *The Devonport Food and Wine Festival is held every February and is a very light-hearted and inevitably alcoholic event with some fine New Zealand wines to be sampled, T4450685*

Auckland City North Sights

City East

Kelly Tarlton's Antarctic Encounter and Underwater World

① *T5280603, www.kellytarltons.co.nz Nov-Feb 0900-2000; Mar-Oct 0900-1800. Adults $25 (expensive but worth it), children free or up to $10 depending on age, family concessions available. There are a number of options to get to Kelly Tarlton's.*

Stagecoach buses #74, #75 or #76 from the Britomart Transport Centre. Fullers 'Harbour Cruise' service includes Underwater World as one of its main stops and departs from the downtown ferry terminal on Quay Street 6 times daily, package available with a return bus, T3679111. Taxis cost about $15 one way. Or for the poor or energetic it is a scenic 6 km walk along the waterfront and Tamaki Drive.

A 10-minute drive east of the city centre beside Tamaki Drive is Kelly Tarlton's Antarctic Encounter and Underwater World. The development is housed within the walls of Auckland City's old disused sewage holding tanks beneath the car park and Tamaki Drive itself. It is a fascinating concept, and typical of the imagination, ingenuity and determination of New Zealand's most famous and best-loved diver, treasure hunter and undersea explorer, Kelly Tarlton, the founder and driving force behind the project. Sadly Kelly died only seven months after it opened.

The attraction is divided into two main parts. The first, **The Antarctic Encounter** (opened in 1994) takes you through a range of informative displays relating the story of early Antarctic exploration, including the triumphs and tragedies of Shackleton, Amundsen and Scott. Before you enter a replica of Captain Scott's 1911 hut in the Antarctic, you are primed by a weather update from the modern-day base. The barely imaginable sub-zero temperatures, wind speeds and familiar words of 'snowing today' make the famous and tragic story of Scott's last expedition in 1910 all the more poignant. The replica hut is an impressive representation, complete with piano.

From there you board a snow cat which takes you through the equally impressive **Penguin Encounter**. A running commentary describes the huge king and smaller, more genteel gentoo penguins in their carefully maintained natural conditions. Such is the standard of the facility and the care of the birds that they breed happily and if you are lucky you will see, at close range, the huge and hilarious down-covered chicks. On the freezing snow they stand upright and dozing in their tatty attire, as if waiting in a queue for a much-needed new fur coat.

After more information about Antarctica and a 'Conservation Corridor', you enter the original **Underwater World**. This is a world-class live exhibit for which Kelly Tarlton pioneered the concept of viewing sea life through fibreglass tunnels. It is a strange mix of distance and intimacy as you walk beneath huge sting rays and sharks gliding gracefully and menacingly right above your head. Other smaller tanks contain a host of other species from beautiful seahorses to ugly moray eels and the highly poisonous scorpion fish. Open rock pools and a separate education facility provide a tremendous learning experience for kids. There is also a well-stocked shop in which to purchase a memento of your visit.

Tamaki Drive, Mission Bay and St Heliers

On a sunny afternoon, especially at the weekend, there is almost no better place to be in central Auckland than somewhere along Tamaki Drive. All along its 9 km length it is both a buzz of activity and a haven of relaxation. Round every corner the view of Rangitoto and yachts plying the harbour predominate. You will see people who rollerblade, walk, jog and cycle in both directions, and leave the road to the vintage cars and city posers. Bike and rollerblade hire is readily available along the route for $6-$10 per hour.

If you have time, take the short walk up the hill to the **M J Savage Memorial Park**, from where the view of the harbour mouth and Rangitoto is wonderful. This is a rather elegant memorial to the nation's first Labour Prime Minister. It was here, at Bastion Point, where one of the most serious recent altercations occurred between Maori and *pakeha* in the late 1970s. The matter, as ever concerning land ownership and sale, was eventually settled after a 17-month stand-off between police and the local Nga-Whatua, whose fine *marae* sits on the southern edge of the park. There are many fine cafés and restaurants along Tamaki and in **Mission Bay** and **St Heliers** from which to sit back and watch the sun set before perhaps taking in a movie at the Art

66 99 On the freezing snow they stand upright and dozing in their tatty attire, as if waiting in a queue for a much-needed new fur coat...

Deco Berkley Cinema in Mission Bay. **Achilles Point**, at the very end of Tamaki Drive, with its secluded beach, is a favourite spot for lovebirds and naturist bathers, and has wonderful views over the Gulf and back towards the city.

Parnell and Newmarket

Trendy Parnell, 2 km east of the city centre, was once a rather insignificant rundown suburb, but in recent years it has undergone a dramatic transformation which has seen it almost overtake Devonport and Ponsonby in the popularity and fashion stakes. It has the same village within a city feel as Devonport, with tiny brick-paved lanes and boutique style outlets, and boasts some of Auckland's finest galleries, speciality shops and restaurants.

At the top of Parnell Rise is the recently finished **Auckland Cathedral of the Holy Trinity**, ⓘ *T3039500, www.holy-trinity.org.nz, both cathedrals open Mon-Fri 1000-1600 Sat, Sun 1300-1700, free,* whose angular structure is aesthetically interesting but nothing compared to the beautiful stained-glass windows and 29 ton organ within. Guided tours and an audio-visual display are both available. The older **Cathedral of St Mary**, which now rests in its big sister's shadow, is one of the largest wooden churches in the world and its wonderfully peaceful interior is a delight. The stained-glass windows are beautiful, as is the entire wooden construction. There is usually a volunteer guide on hand who will proudly explain the 110-year history and show you pictures of how the grand old building was moved to its present site from across the road in 1984. The café (open daily from 0700) on the cathedral forecourt has some great food and is an excellent place to sit and admire its unusual architecture.

Around the corner in Ayr Street you will find **Kinder House**, ⓘ *2 Ayr St, Tue-Sun 1100-1500, $2,* and **Ewelme Cottage**, ⓘ *4 Ayr St, T3790202, Wed-Sun 1030-1200 and 1300-1630, $3.* The former is a recently renovated, two-storey building originally built in 1856 as the home of pioneer churchman and artist John Kinder. It displays some of his art works. A little further down Ayr Street is Ewelme Cottage, built in 1863 as the Auckland home of the family of Archdeacon Vicesimus Lush. It was altered in 1882 but has remained largely unchanged and contains a collection of colonial furniture and household effects.

Back towards the harbour in Judges Bay, is the very cute **St Stephen's Chapel**, one of a number of examples designed by Frederick Thatcher, the favourite architect of the former prominent missionary bishop, George Selwyn. It was one of Auckland's first churches. Although it is not generally open to the public you can have a peek in the window. Access to the park is off Gladstone and Judges Bay Roads. **Parnell Rose Gardens** nearby are a charming escape with rows of scented varieties.

South from the cathedral, Parnell merges into the more modern commercial centre and suburb of **Newmarket** (www.newmarket.net.nz), which is best known for its shopping, quality restaurants, cafés and entertainment (see page 108). Historians may be interested in the grand **Highwic House**, ⓘ *40 Gillies Av, Wed-Sun 1030-1200 and 1300-1630, $5,* the former home (in the 1860s) of 'colonial gentleman of property' Alfred Buckland. For lovers of beer the **Lion Breweries** offer a tour of their facilities. ⓘ *380 Khyber Pass Rd, T3588366, www.lionzone.co.nz Tours of 1 hr 50 mins with*

Auckland City East sights

MECHANICS BAY

Related maps:
A Auckland Centre, p88
Greater Auckland, p80
Devonport, p92
Ponsonby, p104

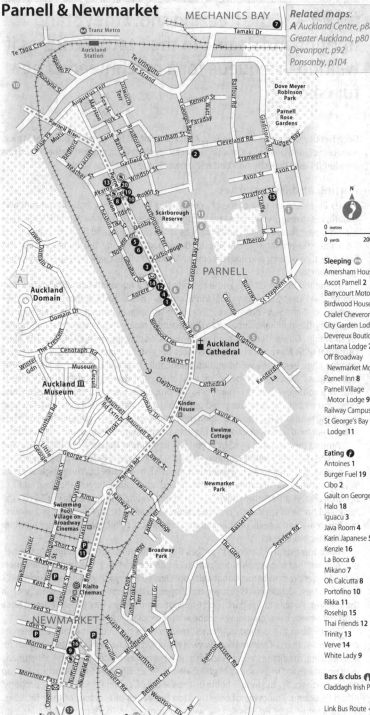

0 metres 20
0 yards 200

Sleeping
Amersham House
Ascot Parnell **2**
Barrycourt Motor In
Birdwood House **4**
Chalet Cheveron **5**
City Garden Lodge
Devereux Boutique
Lantana Lodge **7**
Off Broadway
  Newmarket Mote
Parnell Inn **8**
Parnell Village
  Motor Lodge **9**
Railway Campus **1**
St George's Bay
  Lodge **11**

Eating
Antoines **1**
Burger Fuel **19**
Cibo **2**
Gault on George **2**
Halo **18**
Iguacu **3**
Java Room **4**
Karin Japanese **5**
Kenzie **16**
La Bocca **6**
Mikano **7**
Oh Calcutta **8**
Portofino **10**
Rikka **11**
Rosehip **15**
Thai Friends **12**
Trinity **13**
Verve **14**
White Lady **9**

Bars & clubs
Claddagh Irish Pub

Link Bus Route = =

Bookings essential. It is an interesting tour, but more for an appreciation of the quantity and technology rather than the quality of the product.

Howick

Further east beyond the rather seedy suburb of Panmure is Howick, the largest Asian enclave in Auckland. The suburb is a concrete jungle but it has a pleasant centre with some interesting shops. The biggest attraction in these parts is the award-winning **Howick Historical Village**. ① *Bells Rd, Lloyd Elsmore Park, Pakuranga, T5769506, www.fencible.org.nz Daily 1000-1600. Adult $10, child $5. The Homestead Café, with its suitably historic theme, is also on site. It is served by Howick and Eastern Buses which run a regular service to Mid City, T3666400.* This is a fine example of a restored 'Fencible settlement'. Fencibles were pensioned British soldiers re-enlisted to defend the sites against the Maori and the French in the early years of Auckland settlement and expansion. The village is a 'living museum' where staff in period clothing entertain.

City West

Auckland Zoo

① *T3603819, www.aucklandzoo.co.nz, daily 0930-1730. Adult $13, child $7. Five mins from the Mid City by car. From the Great Western Motorway take the Western Springs off ramp and follow signs. Free car parking. On tour bus route or take Bus 045 from the BBT.*

Situated in pleasant parkland next to Western Springs and 6 km west of the city centre is New Zealand's premier wild animal collection. It has kept pace with the more conservation-minded function of zoos and is worth a visit. The zoo claims to be leading the way in the conservation and captive breeding of native species including kiwi and tuatara – both of which are on display. All the old favourites are also there – elephants (sometimes taken on walkabout around the zoo), giraffes, tigers and orang-utans.

Auckland Zoo has recently developed some imaginative themed exhibits. The huge walk-through aviary, alive with the song of native bird life, is a must-see, as is the McDonald's Rainforest where you feel more captive than the obscenely laid-back spider monkeys. More recent additions include 'Pridelands' the spacious home of the giraffe, lion and zebra with its adjoining 'Hippo River' and a new state-of-the-art seal and penguin exhibit. For the kids 'KidZone' provides the usual touchy-feelies with rabbits and other assorted furry friends.

Museum of Transport, Technology and Social History

① *T8467020, www.akcity.govt.nz/MOTAT Daily 1000-1700. Adult $10, child $5. The Colonial Arms Licensed Restaurant on site serves light lunches and cream teas. You can get to MOTAT by car via the Western Springs Motorway, taking the Western Springs turn off, or take a Yellow bus 045 from Customs St in the city; every 15 mins, 30-min journey.*

The Museum of Transport, Technology and Social History ('MOTAT') is on the Great North Road, 4 km west of the city next to the attractive parklands of Western Springs and near the Auckland Zoo. It was opened in 1967 and is sadly showing its age. A mish-mash of tired-looking buildings over two sites houses many and varied exhibits, from vintage cars, fire engines and motorcycles to telephone boxes and printing presses. It is in great need of a major revamp, but trainspotters, and those looking for somewhere else to take the kids on a rainy day, may find it worth a visit.

The second site, the **Sir Keith Park Memorial Site** (named after New Zealand's most famous war time aviator) concerns all things to do with aviation, rail and the military, including a restored flying boat. The sites are connected by a tramline ($2 return) which passes Western Springs Park and stops at the Zoo on the way.

City South

Mount Eden

At 196 m Mount Eden, the closest volcano to the city centre, provides a spectacular view and the vast, almost surreal crater gets your imagination running wild as you picture it 'going off'. Without doubt the best time to come here is at dawn, especially on misty winter mornings, when it can be a photographer's delight, and you can avoid the coach-loads of visitors.

At the southern base of Mount Eden, **Eden Gardens**, ⓘ *24 Omana Av, T6388395, daily 0900-1630, adult $5, child free, concessions available, café open 1000-1600*, are a great place for lovers of all things green that grow. It is an all-seasons garden with a fine variety of flowering shrubs and New Zealand natives. Mount Eden village itself is worth a look, boasting a fine delicatessen, *Mount Eden Deli* (try a kumara pie), some interesting shops and a number of fine cafés and restaurants. **NB** Mt Eden is a long walk from Mid City, and given the climb you might be better off taking bus No 274 or 275 from the BBT in the CBD.

Cornwall Park and One Tree Hill

ⓘ *Cornwall Park Visitors' Centre, T6308485, www.cornwallpark.co.nz, 1000-1600. Free. Café and free 'points of interest' trail leaflet available.*

Just south of Mount Eden, and 5 km to the south of the Sky Tower, is Cornwall Park, a great escape from the hustle and bustle of city life, as the hordes of joggers and picnic-carrying locals will testify. It is famous not only for its crowning glory, the monument and the tree, but also the well-preserved remains of Maori *Pa* on and around the summit. Kiwi Tamaki the great chief of the Nga Marama lived here during the mid-18th century with his thousands of *whanau* (family) and followers, attracted by the rich pickings of the region's coast and its fertile soils. His claim to the region ended after being routed by sub-tribes from the north and his people being decimated by a smallpox epidemic introduced by the Europeans. Around the summit, if you look carefully, you will see the grass-covered terraces on which sat dwellings and the 'kumara pits' scattered beside them. With the land essentially vacant on the arrival of the first European settlers, it was the Scot, Logan Campbell, the most powerful and well-known of the new capital's residents, who eventually took ownership. Shortly before his arrival, a single Totara tree stood proudly on the summit. This had already given rise to the hill's Maori name, *Te- Totara-a-Ahua*, meaning 'Hill of the single Totara'. This tree was rudely cut down in 1852 by early settlers and it was Campbell who planted several trees in its place, including the lonesome pine you could see until its demise in 2001 (see box). The prosperous Campbell, Mayor and 'Father of Auckland', donated his estate, now the park, to the people of New Zealand to commemorate the visit in 1901 of the heirs to the throne, the Duke and Duchess of Cornwall – hence the name.

At the base of the hill is a visitor centre in **Huia Lodge**, Campbell's original gatekeeper's house. It houses some interesting displays and an introductory video surrounding the natural and human history of the park. Directly across the road is the simple and faithfully restored **Acacia Cottage**, ⓘ *open dawn till dusk, free,* in which Campbell himself lived, though the building itself originally stood in the centre of the city and was relocated here in the 1920s.

If you arrived in Auckland from the airport the chances are **One Tree Hill** (Maungakiekie) was the first New Zealand landmark that you saw – sans tree. Formerly crowning the 186-m cone of this dormant volcano was an old pine, planted by Campbell and shadowing his grave. The monument – a tribute to the relationship of Maori and *pakeha* – had a hard time over the years and was controversially

One Tree Hill becomes None Tree Hill

In October 2000 Auckland lost what was, prior to the futuristic Sky Tower, perhaps its greatest landmark – the beautiful Monterey pine which gave its name to One Tree Hill. Both the tree and the hill have a long and controversial history. Long before the Europeans arrived One Tree Hill, or 'Maungakiekie' as the Maori then knew it, was a strategic *pa* site. Much evidence still remains with clearly visible terraces and kumara (sweet potato) storage pits. Although the Ngati Whatua had all but abandoned the site by 1790, it is said that a totara tree grew upon the hill from a stick used to cut the umbilical cord of a boy named Koroki, born earlier that century. Once this tree grew, the site was known as 'Te-totara-a-ahua', or 'totara which stands alone'. Although early European Documentation suggests the tree may have in fact been a pohutukawa, what is known from newspaper reports is that the remains of this lone tree were felled for firewood by a settler in 1852. The site and the tree were considered *tapu* (sacred) to Maori and its demise at the hands of the European was seen as an affront to their *mana* (integrity). In an attempt to make amends Sir John Logan Campbell, who first purchased the site from the Maori, attempted to replant native totara in 1875. In order to protect the tree from its exposed aspect he also planted Monterey pines around it. The first native tree died and another was planted to replace it in 1910. Sadly, it too died and only a few of the remaining pines took hold. In 1940 there were two pines and in 1960 only one after vandals felled the other. This remaining pine tree grew to form the famous and much loved icon. But, given the site's troubled history, it became the focus of much controversy and a target of Maori activism.

In 1994 the tree was almost completely felled by activist Mike Smith who cut through the main trunk with a chainsaw before being apprehended. Smith was not even a full-blooded Maori nor was he from any Auckland tribe. Despite admirable attempts to save and support the tree with surgery techniques and supporting wires, its days were numbered. After yet another attack in early 1999 the damage proved terminal. In October the following year Auckland City Council made the controversial and rather sudden decision to fell the tree given that high winds posed a significant threat to the public safety. The response was dramatic. Hundreds of people from all walks of life turned out on the day of its demise to say goodbye and to grieve. It seemed everyone had his or her own cherished memory. A Maori *karakia* (farewell service) was held at dawn before the final felling took place. Although there is a plan to plant a native totara, further protected by a ring of pohutukawa, they will all take decades to grow and given the nature of the site there is no guarantee that even a single dominant native will emerge. So for now the historic hill is treeless. For the tourist the name seems to offer nothing but questions, while for Aucklanders it seems the skyline may never look quite the same again. The old pine remains a much-lamented icon kept alive only in story, image and song.

Auckland City South sights

vandalized in 1999 before finally succumbing to an official saw in 2001.

Also within the park boundary at its southern end is the **Auckland Observatory**. ⓘ *T6241246, www.stardome.org.nz, times and events can vary. Standard viewing* session with show $12, child $6. To get there by car: from state Highway 1 take the Greenlane off ramp, the main entrance to the park is off Green Lane West. By Bus: Nos 302, 305 or 312 depart regularly from Mid City. This is the official home of Auckland's star gazers, and also contains the **Stardome Planetarium**, a cosmic multimedia experience played out on the ceiling for the general public. Outdoor telescope viewing sessions and special events are also held, depending on what the weather and the heavens are up to. You can even 'Adopt a Star', an interesting concept that will probably have you trying to find it again, for the rest of your life.

Rainbow's End

① *T2622030, www.rainbowsend.co.nz, daily 1000-1700. All day unlimited rides: adult $35, children from $10. To get there by car, head south and take the Manukau off ramp from State Highway 1 and drive the 1/2 km to the park. By bus take either the 327, 347, 447, 457, 467, 487 or 497 from the Britomart Transport Centre.*

Rainbow's End, near the main Manukau Shopping complex, on the corner of Great South and Wiri Station Road, Manukau, is advertised as '23 acres of fun'. It's New Zealand's largest theme park, and has rides and attractions with such alluring and stomach-churning names as the 'Corkscrew Rollercoaster', 'Goldrush', and the mighty 'Fear Fall'. Along with these are old favourites like dodgems, go-karts, bumper boats, mini golf and an interactive games arcade. Even small kids and cowardly parents are catered for in the more sedate 'Dream Castle'.

Botanical Gardens

① *T2671457, daily 0800-dusk. Free. Visitors' Centre: Mon-Fri 0900-1600, Sat and Sun 1000-1600. Café: 0830-1630. To get there by car: head south, take the Manurewa off ramp from State Highway 1, turn left into Hill Rd. By bus: Stagecoach buses (Papakura, Pukekohe or Drury) leave from the Britomart Transport Centre in the city centre, every 15 min. Alight in Great South Rd, Manurewa, just before Hill Rd.*

In Manurewa, 20 minutes south of the city centre, are the Auckland Botanical Gardens. Since planting first began in 1974 an extensive 64-ha, 10,000-plant collection has sprouted, consisting mostly of New Zealand natives. There is also an ornamental lake, a nature trail and a handsome and wonderfully fragrant display of New Zealand-bred roses. The gardens also have an interpretative visitor centre, an outdoor café and a library. The annual Ellerslie Flower Show, which is the Southern Hemisphere's most illustrious gardening and horticultural event, was recently relocated here from the Ellerslie Showgrounds, and usually takes place during the last week of November.

❦ *Keep your eyes open for some interesting native birds that reside in the gardens, including native pigeon and tui.*

Otara Market

① *T2740830, every Sat 0600-1100. By car, head south and take the Otara off-ramp from State Highway 1. Buses 487/497 from the Britomart Transport Centre (1 hr).*

The southern suburbs are the poorest part of the city. They can be dangerous, and are not a place to stray – especially at night. But they are definitely the place to experience the atmosphere of urban Maori or Pacific Island living. The Otara Market, held every Saturday morning in the Otara town centre car park, 18 km south of the city centre, is ideal for this and is thought to be the largest Maori and Polynesian market in the world. Like most street markets there is always a lot of nonsense for sale but some of the clothes, fabrics and certainly the fruit and vegetables are weird, wonderful and reasonably priced. Try some yams or taro, a type of vegetable and traditional staple diet for many native Polynesians.

🛏 Sleeping

As you might expect of the country's largest city and principal arrival point, Auckland is not short of accommodation. Most of the major **hotels** are to be found in the city centre, particularly on the waterfront or on either side of Queen St. There are also hundreds of **B&Bs** and **homestays** available, but these tend to be concentrated in the better-known suburbs like Parnell and Ponsonby. Homestays are, in effect B&Bs, but tend to involve a closer interaction with the hosts, often under the same roof, as opposed to the traditional B&Bs which tend to be self-contained premises and offer more privacy. Further afield, in the surrounding countryside, the **farmstay** is a growing sector of the accommodation market and one that is being heavily plugged by the Tourist Board. It is said to be the best way to experience real New Zealand life. If you like the sound of this option contact **New Zealand Farm Holidays** based near Auckland. They produce a helpful free catalogue listing about 300 establishments, T09-4129649. There are lots of **motels** throughout the city, mostly in the suburbs of Greenlane and in Manukau and Mangere, the latter two being near the airport.

Self-catering can be readily found in all types of accommodation, but the city centre plays host to a number of plush apartment buildings, most at the higher range of the market. Auckland is huge when it comes to **flatting**, and if you are alone and intend to stay longer this is undoubtedly the best and cheapest way to go. Flats and flat shares are to be found every Saturday in the *New Zealand Herald*, but start hunting early. With New Zealand being such a huge backpacker destination, there are many **hostels**, from the awful to the plush, rowdy to the sedate. They, too, are mostly in the city centre or the more happening suburbs like Parnell. The popular and professional **YHA** has 2 hostels in Auckland and many more throughout the country. There aren't many **motor camps** in Auckland and most **campsites** are where they should be, amidst the beauty of the surrounding countryside parks and on the many islands of the Hauraki Gulf. All the main Tourist Information Offices will help you find what you are looking for and provide a booking service (see page 83).

City Centre *p84, see map p88*

L **Ascott Metropolis**, *1 Courthouse La, T3008800, www.the-ascott.com* The Ascott Metropolis is marketed as 'the definitive' luxury hotel in Auckland. It is an all-suite hotel, well-positioned, and offers a range of rooms from the deluxe to the premiere. Rooms with a view are about $30 a night extra. All the trimmings are there and the recreation area is worth a look in itself.

L **Heritage Hotel**, *35 Hobson St, T3798553, www.heritagehotels.co.nz* The Heritage has more rooms than any other hotel in the country and is indeed more like a village complex than a hotel. It offers a wide range of luxury and standard en suite options, most of which have great views. The indoor and outdoor recreation areas are super. Alas, Henry the Cockatoo who once lived in the foyer has been retired to quiter surroundings. Unlike the concierge, Henry welcomed visitors by biting them when they said 'who's a pretty boy then' and attempted to stroke his chin.

L **Hilton Hotel**, *Princes Wharf, 147 Quay St, T9782000, info_Auckland@hilton.com* Completed in 2002 the Hilton is described with typical corporate spin as a 'contemporary boutique hotel' and sits in an enviable position on Princes Wharf overlooking the harbour on both sides. It opened just in time for the America's Cup and throughout the regatta lived up to practically all the heady expectations to such an extent that it is now the most recognized and talked about hotel in the city. The accommodation and service is of course first class, but for many it is its in-house restaurant, 'White', where one's expectations really surpass themselves.

L **Quay West**, *8 Albert St, T3096000, www.mirachotels.com.au* This unassuming hotel has been a big award winner since its recent opening and it is not hard to see why. The rooms are exquisite, the views even better and the Roman pool and spa is so cute you will probably spend most of your stay there. The 8 over Albert bar and restaurant attached are also first class (see Eating below).

L The Sebel, *corner of Hobson St and Customs St West, T9784000, www.mirachotels.com.au* After the Hilton, the newest hotel in Auckland's centre. It is ideally situated overlooking the Viaduct Basin and former America's Cup Village. It offers the same high standards of suite-style accommodation and service as its sister hotels overseas.

L Sheraton Auckland, *83 Symonds St, T3795132, www.sheraton.com/auckland* This old favourite has had to keep pace with the new hotels with a recent full refurbishment. Although the views are nothing spectacular, it is well-appointed and often the venue for visiting stars. Tom Jones was here recently filling the foyer with cigar smoke and presumably his adoring fans' underwear.

L Sky City Hotel, *corner of Victoria St and Federal St, T3636000, www.skycity.co.nz* The trump card here is the convenience, excitement and 24-hr action, with the casino next door and Sky Tower as an attic. It rates itself as a 4-5 star hotel. Special rates often apply.

AL Freemans B&B, *65 Wellington St, T3765046*. Best known for its location than anything else. Within walking distance of the city centre.

B City Central Hotel, *corner of Wellesley St West and Albert St, T3236000, www.citycentralhotel.co.nz* Another no-nonsense cheaper option, well-placed, clean and comfortable.

B Hotel De Brett, *2 High St, T3772389, www.acb.co.nz/debrett* A cheaper hotel, well sited right in the happening zone of the city centre. Art Deco interior. A good range of clean and spacious rooms from single to family. Breakfast included.

C Auckland City YHA, *corner of City Rd and Liverpool St, T3092802, yhaauck@yha.org.nz* One of 2 YHAs in Auckland, the other is just around the corner, 5 Turner St, T3028200. Both are reliable and a good choice with modern and clean facilities, good kitchen, pleasant friendly atmosphere, in-house bistro. 5- and 4-star Qualmark ratings respectively.

C-D Albert Park Backpackers, *27-31 Victoria St East, T3090336, bakpak@albertpark.co.nz* A smaller slightly quieter version of the below.

C-D Auckland Central Backpackers, *corner of Queen and Darby Sts, T3584877, www.acb.co.nz* Recently relocated to renovated premises this is the busiest backpackers in the central city, with simple clean accommodation, 24-hr reception, security, café, bar, internet and a travel shop attached. The travel shop staff are very knowledgeable and helpful. There's always a buzz of activity and it's the perfect starting point for socialites.

Motels

AL-A Whitaker Lodge, *21 Whitaker Pl, T3773623, www.whitakerlodge.co.nz* Despite the fact this old established motel is out of the sun and does not have very good views, it is otherwise ideally situated and offers large clean rooms, a friendly service and free car parking right in the heart of the city. Winter deals available.

City North *p92, see map p92*

LL Peace and Plenty Inn, *6 Flagstaff Terr, Devonport, T4452925, www.peaceandplentyco.nz* A top B&B on the waterfront offering luxury accommodation and fine food.

L-AL Emerald Inn, *16 The Promenade, Takapuna, T4883500, www.emerald-inn.co.nz* Wide range of options with suites, units, a cottage and villas, close to the beach and all amenities.

L-AL The Spencer on Byron, *9-17 Byron Av, Takapuna, T9166111, www.spencerbyron.co.nz* Auckland's newest hotel and as the highest building on the North Shore never short of good views. Overall a reliable option close to the 'Shore's' major centre and a pleasant alternative to the city centre (8km).

L-AL Villa Cambria, *71 Vauxhall Rd, Devonport, T4457899, villacambria@extra.co.nz* One of the better known and most popular B&Bs in Devonport. Victorian villa with all mod cons. Has a great self-contained 'loft'.

AL Badgers of Devonport, *30 Summer St, Devonport, T4452099, www.badgers.co.nz* Fine villa accommodation with a liberal dash of antiques. Also a nice new self-contained option. Homely and friendly.

AL City of Sails Motel, *219 Shakespeare Rd, Milford, T4869170, city.of.sails@extra.co.nz*

New, with modern, clean rooms. Near Milford cafés and shops.

AL Parklane Motor Inn, *corner of Lake Rd and Rewiti Av, Takapuna, T4861069, www.parklane.co.nz* More a hotel than a motel with modern decor, spa baths available and close to the beach and Takapuna.

A-AL Esplanade Hotel, *1 Victoria Rd, Devonport, T4451291*. One of Auckland's oldest hotels nicely renovated and right on the promenade with fine views of the bustling harbour.

A Amoritz B&B House, *730 East Coast Rd, Browns Bay, T4796338*. Budget rates, close to the beach, shops and transport.

A Cheltenham by the Sea, *2 Grove Rd, Devonport, T4459437*. Contemporary and spacious, ideally situated next to Cheltenham beach. The best on the shore.

A Poenamo Hotel, *31 Northcote Rd, Takapuna, T4806109*. This is a traditional sports hotel and was until recently the temporary home for the All Blacks for pre-match training in Auckland. Adequate facilities. Irish-style bar and restaurant attached. Golf course and range only a wedge away.

City East *p93, see map p95*

LL Amersham House, *corner of Gladstone Rd and Canterbury Pl, Parnell, T3030321, www.amershamhouse.co.nz* Luxurious and elegant with all you would expect for the price, each room wonderfully appointed with a PC to boot. Outdoor pool and spa.

LL Devereux Boutique Hotel, *267 Remuera Rd, Remuera, T5245044, www.devereux.co.nz* A relatively new establishment set in a sprawling historic villa near Remuera and Newmarket, earning a solid reputation. 12 stylish themed rooms with such alluring names as Taj, Cairo or Zambezi. Breakfast included.

L Aachen House, *39 Market Rd, Remuera, T5202329, www.aachenhouse.co.nz* Boutique hotel in an Edwardian mansion full of antiques. Not everyone's cup of tea, but the rooms are spacious with en suite bathroom, and the beds themselves are magnificent.

L St George's Bay Lodge, *43 St George's Bay Rd, Parnell (close to Parnell Rd), T3031050, enquiry@stgeorge.co.nz* Elegant Victorian

villa in a quiet street and tastefully renovated and decorated.

AL Ascot Parnell, *4/32 St Stephens Av, Parnell, T3099012, AscotParnell@compuserve.com* An historic and characterful house with huge rooms. Terrific breakfast included.

AL Barrycourt Motor Inn, *10-20 Gladstone Rd, Parnell, T3033789, www.barrycourt.co.nz* An ugly box of a building, but well-situated in Parnell. Wide range of well appointed rooms with fine views of the harbour. Restaurant within yards, and ample car parking.

AL Birdwood House, *41 Birdwood Cres, Parnell, T3065900, info@birdwood.co.nz* Typical Parnell villa with typical Parnell interior and themed rooms. Tasteful, with Kauri staircase and open fire. Close to Parnell Rd.

AL Chalet Chevron, *14 Brighton Rd, Parnell, T3090290, chaletchevron@extra.co.nz* Charming, well appointed rooms with pleasant views. Very friendly.

AL Seaview Heights, *23a Glover Rd, St Heliers, T5758159, seaview@bitz.co.nz* Two well appointed suites with views towards the harbour and Rangitoto.

A Off Broadway Newmarket Motel, *11 Alpers Av, Newmarket, T5293550, www.off-broadway.co.nz* New and reliable motel with stylish studios or suites with spa, within walking distance of Newmarket shops and restaurants.

A Parnell Inn, *320 Parnell Rd, Parnell, T3580642, parnelin@ihug.co.nz* 16 clean and comfortable studio units, 3 with kitchenettes. Right on Parnell Rd but still quiet. Café attached.

A Parnell Village Motor Lodge, *2 St Stephens Av, Parnell, T3771463*. Perfectly situated with large comfortable rooms and very friendly hosts.

A The Railway Campus, *26-48 Te Taou Cres, Parnell, T3677100, railcamp@auckland.ac.nz* Primarily student accommodation, this place has been cleverly incorporated into the old Railway Building. The entrance is very grand with its huge ceilings, marble floor, ticket office (now reception) and old clock. What used to be the platform corridors now house a café, extraordinary large and well equipped cooking facilities and a laundry, while the old offices house the rooms, the waiting room, a study and library.

C-D City Garden Lodge, *25 St George's Bay Rd, Parnell, T3020880*. A huge mansion of a place with wooden floors and Kauri staircase. Clean, comfortable and friendly with all the necessary facilities. Emphasis is on offering a quiet location in which to escape the city pace or recover from your arduous travels. **C-D Lantana Lodge**, *60 St George's Bay Rd, Parnell, T3734546*. Another quiet option.

Ponsonby

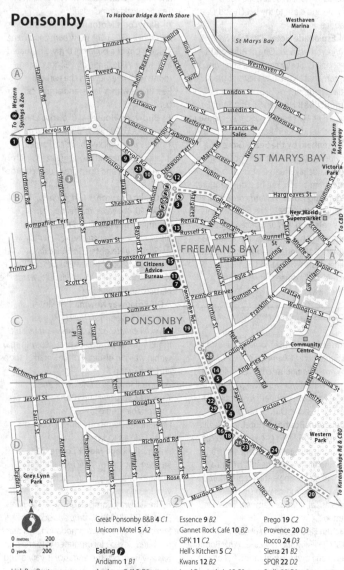

0 metres 200
0 yards 200

Link Bus Route - - -

Sleeping
Abaco Spa Motel **1** *B2*
Brown Kiwi
  Backpackers **2** *B2*
Colonial Cottage **3** *B1*
Great Ponsonby B&B **4** *C1*
Unicorn Motel **5** *A2*

Eating
Andiamo **1** *B1*
Anglesea Grill **2** *D2*
Atlas Power Café **3** *B2*
Atomic Café **4** *D2*
Café Cezanne **6** *B2*
Chandelier **29** *D3*
Dizengoff **7** *C2*
Empress Garden **8** *A1*
Essence **9** *B2*
Gannet Rock Café **10** *B2*
GPK **11** *C2*
Hell's Kitchen **5** *C2*
Kwans **12** *B2*
Lord Ponsonby's **13** *B2*
Masala **14** *C2*
Musical Knives **15** *C2*
Open Late Café **16** *D2*
Ponsonby Fresh Fish
  & Chip Co **17** *D2*
Ponsonby Pies **18** *D2*
Prego **19** *C2*
Provence **20** *D3*
Rocco **24** *D3*
Sierra **21** *B2*
SPQR **22** *D2*
Stella **23** *D3*
Vinnies **25** *B1*

Bars & clubs
Grand Central **26** *D3*
Java Jive **27** *B2*
Surrender Dorothy **28** *C2*

Recently redecorated with various room types. Long-term storage available. Owner looks after his clients well.

City West *p97* *For accommodation further west see page 129*

LL-AL Hastings Hall, *99 Western Springs Rd, T8458550, www.hastingshall.co.nz* Classic, spacious historic villa with a fine range of rooms and suites (most en suite) sumptuously decorated with much love and attention to detail. Sky TV, pool, spa and all the trimmings. Close to Western Springs park and the zoo.

L Waitakere Park Lodge, *573 Scenic Dr, Waitaura, T8149622, www.waitakereparklodge.co.nz* Off the beaten track and situated in 80 acres of bush at the base of the Waitakere Ranges. Close to the vineyards and West Coast beaches. 17 accommodation suites with bush and city views. À la carte restaurant.

AL Great Ponsonby B&B, *30 Ponsonby Terr, Ponsonby, T3765989, www.ponsonbybnb.co.nz* One of the best B&Bs in the city, oozing quality and comfort. Close, but not too close, to Ponsonby Rd. Very friendly, helpful hosts.

A Abaco Spa Motel, *59 Jervois Rd, Ponsonby, T3766850, www.abacospamotel.co.nz* An old motor inn, but comfortable and conveniently situated for Ponsonby and the city centre. Within walking distance of 30 restaurants. Spa rooms available.

A Colonial Cottage, *35 Clarence St, Ponsonby, T3602820.* Olde worlde charm in an old Kauri villa. Alternative health specialists.

A Unicorn Motel, *31 Shelly Beach Rd, Herne Bay, T3762066, unicorn.motel@pin.co.nz* Fine location and recently refurbished.

C-D Brown Kiwi Backpackers, *7 Prosford St, Ponsonby, T3780191, www.brownkiwi.co.nz* The best and most recent Backpackers west of the city. Earning a good reputation and full of character. Close to the happening Ponsonby Rd and link bus service.

City South *p98*

L Central Auckland Airport, *corner of Kirkbride Rd and Ascot Rd, Mangere, T2751059, www.centra.com.au* Only 4 km to the airport,

14 km from the city. Country club style and atmosphere. Winter rates apply.

A Bavaria Guest House, *83 Valley Rd, Mt Eden, T6389641, bavaria@extra.co.nz* Spacious and comfortable with 11 suites, nice deck and garden. German spoken.

A Hotel Grand Chancellor, *corner of Kirkbride Rd and Ascot Rd, Airport Oaks, T2757029, www.grandchancellor.com* A safe bet if you need to be near the airport. All the trimmings, like pool and restaurant.

C-D Budget Travellers Inn, *558 Great South Rd, Manukau, T2788947, www.budgettravellers.co.nz* A highly affordable option close to the airport. Clean and friendly.

C-D Oaklands Lodge, *5a Oaklands Rd, Mt Eden, T6386545, info@oaklands.co.nz* A budget option for those wishing to enjoy the more relaxed atmosphere of this congenial suburb.

There are a huge number of motels on **Great South Rd**. They are all very similar in style and price and include:
A Ascot Motor Lodge, *(92), T5204833, www.ascot.nzco.net*;
A Greenlane Manor, *(353), T5712167*; and
A Oak Tree Lodge, *(104), T5242211, www.oaklodge.co.nz*
There are also lots of motels on Kirkbride and McKenzie Rds in **Mangere**, near the international airport.

Self-catering
Bear in mind that many other types of accommodation (particularly B&Bs) offer self-catering. The following are at the high end of the market, come recommended, and are all located in the city centre.
L Quest Auckland, *363 Queen St, T9809200, www.questauck@extra.co.nz*
AL Darlinghurst Quest Apartments, *52 Eden Cres, T3666500, www.questapartments.com.au*
AL Cintra Apartments, *3 Whitaker Pl, T3796280.*
AL Oxford Apartments, *15 Mount St, TT3674100, www.allfields.co.nz*

Motorcamps
All the following are in the B-D price range.
Avondale Motor Park, *46 Bollard, Av, Avondale, T8287228,*

avondale@kiwicamps.co.nz 15 mins from the city centre, with all the usual facilities.

Manukau Top Ten Holiday Park, *902 Great South Rd, Manukau City, T2668016, www.manukautop10.co.nz* Handy for the airport and a convenient stopover for heading south.

North Shore Motels and Top Ten Holiday Park, *52 Northcote Rd, Takapuna, T4182578, www.nsmotels.co.nz* The most popular holiday park in the city offering lodges, motel and cabin accommodation as well as the usual reliable Top Ten motor camp facilities. 5 mins to the beach.

Remuera Motor Lodge and Inner City Camping Ground, *16 Minto Rd, Remuera, T5245126, remlodge@ihug.co.nz* The only traditional-style motor camp near the city centre. Quiet bush setting with all the usual facilities.

Campsites

Auckland Regional Parks Campsites, *T3031530.* There are 22 Regional Parks in and around Auckland and 39 basic facility vehicle and backpack campsites. From $5 per night. *DoC* also have many regional campsites and administer almost all the Hauraki Island campsites. *For Information contact DoC Information Centre, T3796479.*

🍴 Eating

When it comes to eating, Auckland is said to be on a par with New York and London. With almost 1,000 restaurants in the city it is not surprising to learn that 'dining out' is New Zealand's third biggest retail spend. When looking for a place to eat it is important, in most instances, not to try to differentiate between restaurant and café. Very often, in this part of the world, they are essentially the same thing with the latter perhaps just being a bit more casual. The cafés listed separately below are some of the traditional favourites; those particularly noted for their character, ambience and/or coffee. The central city offers waterside dining indoors and out, with spacious brasseries, intimate silver service, or romantic balconies overlooking the viaduct and harbour. Elsewhere, in High St and Vulcan La, you can find a more casual setting in the many cafés that line these streets. To the west of the city centre, Ponsonby (Ponsonby Rd) has for years managed to hold on to its reputation as the culinary heart of the city, with Parnell coming a close second. Service is generally good and refreshingly friendly. Tipping is not essential but appreciated. BYO means bring your own (bottle).

City Centre *p84, see map p88*

$$$ **Cin Cin**, *Ferry Building, 99 Quay St, T3076966. Mon-Fri from 1100, Sat and Sun from 0930, Fri and Sat until 0300.* It has been established as one of Auckland's top restaurants for years, but has changed hands recently. With its location right next to the ferry DoCks it is very much a happening place, serving Pacific cuisine to the highest standard. The service here is outstanding, as is the wine list. Licensed, outdoor dining available.

$$$ **Euro**, *Shed 22, Princes Wharf, Quay St, T3099866. Daily for lunch and dinner, and brunch Sat and Sun from 1030.* Like many other waterfront restaurants, Euro is one of the new kids on the block that was designed to capture the America's Cup crowds, with a boast of being the best of the best. It has a very luxurious clean-feel interior with a large mesmerizing clock projected onto the wall, and offers new and imaginative cuisine in the revered Pacific Rim style. Excellent it is, but the best? Probably not. Licensed, outdoor dining available.

$$$ **Harbourside Seafood Bar and Grill**, *1st Floor, Ferry Building, T3070556. Daily from 1130, licensed.* Located right above Cin Cin, it is advertised in all the tourist publications and seems to live up to all the praise. This is a good opportunity to try New Zealand snapper or green-lipped mussels.

$$$ **Kermadec**, *1st Floor, Viaduct Quay Building, corner of Lower Hobson and Quay St, T3090412. Mon-Fri for lunch and dinner.* Perhaps the best restaurant in town, and arguably the best seafood venue. Here you can tickle your tastebuds with the many delights of the Pacific Ocean as well as more traditional fare. There are 2 private rooms in

a Japanese-style decor that contain small ponds. Don't miss the seafood platter. Licensed and BYO, private rooms available.

$$$ **Orbit Restaurant,** *Sky Tower, corner Victoria St and Federal St, T3636000. Daily 1730-2200, Sat/Sun 1000-1200, licensed.* Over two thirds of the way up the Sky Tower, so they have the best view of any restaurants in the city, if not the entire hemisphere. The Orbit restaurant revolves, though sadly at a sedate speed. Although the food is not as good as the view, it is comprehensive in selection and has a good reputation. **The Observatory** is the latest edition and offers buffet-style fare. *Open for dinner daily and lunch Thu-Sun.*

$$$ **White (Hilton Hotel) Princes Wharf**, *147 Quay St, T9782000. Restaurant open from 0630.* Throughout the America's Cup White earned a reputation that now places it amongst the very best of Auckland's offerings. There is no doubt the views across the water and classy atmosphere has a lot to do with that just as much as the food and the service. Bellini, the hotel's self-styled cocktail bar, is an added attraction.

$$$ **Wildfire**, *Princes Wharf, Quay St, T3776869. Daily from 1130.* This new addition offers amazing wood-fired pizzas and skewered meats amongst other dishes, all with a Mediterranean flavour. Licensed, outdoor dining available.

$$ **8 Over Albert**, *Quay West Hotel, 8 Albert St, T3096000. Breakfast, lunch and dinner, Mon-Sat, breakfast Sun, licensed.* Shares the same popularity as the hotel and deservedly so, offering a fine menu of Pacific and Mediterranean dishes. The bar downstairs is also commendable.

$$ **The French Café**, *210 Symonds St, T3771911. Lunch, Tue-Fri, dinner Mon-Sat, licensed.* Recently revamped favourite, earning an even better reputation. Fine starters also available as main courses, and excellent fish dishes always available.

$$ **Joy Bong**, *531 Karangahape Rd. Daily from 1700, licensed.* Recently relocated from the edge of Ponsonby this Thai restaurant known affectionately as the 'bong' continues to enjoy a solid reputation. Good value.

$$ **O'Connell Street Bistro**, *corner of O'Connell St and Shortland St, T3771884. Lunch, Mon-Fri, dinner 7 nights, licensed.* Another intimate, tiny venue serving fine

examples of Pacific Rim with a legendary wine list. Express menu for theatregoers.

$$ **Sake Bar Rikka**, *208 Victoria St West, Victoria Park Market, T3778239. Lunch, Mon-Fri, dinner Mon-Sat, licensed.* Some say Sake is now past its best but despite the rumours it remains for now one of the best Japanese restaurants in town. Fine seasonal dishes in a wood-beamed warehouse, in character with the Victoria Park Market.

$$ **Seamart Restaurant**, *corner Fanshawe St and Market Pl, T3028989. Lunch and dinner daily from 1100, licensed.* Being attached to one of the main fresh seafood outlets in town you cannot really go wrong. Great chowder and smoked fish, but something simple and never tried before would be best for newcomers.

$$ **Soul**, *Viaduct Harbour, T3567249. Daily for lunch and dinner.* Much to the chagrin of the considerable local competition (or opposition), owner and chef Judith Tabron was successful in making Soul the place to be during the America's Cup campaign. Doubtless the open-air decks overlooking the harbour had much to do with that but the food is also excellent and affordable. Fish is recommended.

$$ **Toto**, *53 Nelson St, T3022665. Lunch, Mon-Fri, dinner 7 nights, licensed, outdoor dining and private rooms available.* Lavishly decorated Italian-style restaurant offering some of the finest Italian food in the city.

$$ **Vertigo**, *Top Floor, Mercure Hotel, 8 Customs St, T3778920. Daily breakfast, lunch and dinner, licensed.* A bit more down-to-earth than the Orbit restaurant in the Sky Tower, but still an impressive view and good modern dishes to go with it.

$$ **Vivace**, *1st Floor, Norfolk House, corner High St and Vulcan La, T3022303. Lunch, Mon-Fri 1200-1500, dinner Mon-Sat, licensed.* A popular Italian hidden away upstairs in Norfolk House, best known for its candlelight, congenial service and reasonable prices.

$ **Food Hall on Atrium on Elliot**, *Elliot St.* A convenient cheap multi-option venue during the day.

$ **Mexican Café**, *67 Victoria St West, T3732311. Mon-Fri 1200-1430, 1700-late, Sat/Sun 1700-late.* A favourite cheap and cheery café that has been around for years (no mean feat in Auckland), so it must be good.

$ **Middle East Café**, *23a Wellesley St,* *T3794843. Daily 1200-2100.* This Dutch-owned and operated 'camel lovers' café offers the finest cheap meal in the city. The famous Middle East Café shwarma – a $7 lamb shwarma you drown in 2 delectable sauces – is so good it is practically impossible to eat just one.

$ **White Lady**, *corner Queen St and Shortland St. Open all night.* Believe it or not this is a caravan that looks more like a train, which seems to appear from nowhere each night, towed by an old tractor. Within its battered walls are 2 battered-looking gentlemen, serving various battered items of food, most of which look like a serious road accident before you have even sunk your teeth into them. But they taste amazing (as do most things at 0300). The White Lady is the best 'post-drink munchies' venue in the city that is open until the sun rises.

Cafés

Gallery Café, *1st Floor, Auckland Art Gallery, corner of Wellesley St East and Kitchener St, T3779603.* A great café, even without all the in-house artworks.

Mecca, *Chancery Mall, Chancery Lane, CBD, T3567028. Daily 0700-late.* A new restaurant/café/bar worth a mention due to its location in the heart of the new Chancery Centre – a haven for fashion shops and designer labels. Good coffee, attractive menu and a decent vantage point from which to people-watch.

Rakino's, *1st Floor, 35 High St, T3583535.* Hard to find but worth it. Great coffee and traditional café fare.

Verona, *169 Karangahape Rd, T3070508.* Perhaps The K'Rd's favourite café, colourful in character and clientele.

Vulcan, *Vulcan La, T3779899.* Unpretentious old favourite.

City North *p92, see map p92*

$$ **Catalonia**, *129 Hurstmere Rd, Takapuna, T4893104. Lunch and dinner Tue-Sun, no lunch Sat, licensed.* A top French restaurant that is one of the North Shore's favourites. Huge servings and delectable sweets.

$$ **Killarney Street Brasserie**, *2 Killarney St, Takapuna, T4899409. Mon-Fri 1130-late, Sat-Sun 1030-late, licensed.* Extensive menu selection with servings to match.

$$ **Manuka**, *49 Victoria Rd, Devonport, T4457732. Mon-Fri 1100-late, Sat-Sun 0900-late, licensed.* The pick of the bunch in Devonport with its much-loved wood-fired pizzas and laid-back atmosphere.

$$ **On Bourbon**, *59 Victoria Rd, T450085. Daily for lunch and dinner.* A new establishment offering a mixture of good value Creole, French and seafood dishes. Occasional live jazz adds to the atmosphere.

$$ **Oyster Blue**, *58 Calliope Rd, Devonport, T4466646. Dinner Tue-Sat and lunch Fri-Sun.* It remains to be seen if this new Pacific Rim seafood restaurant can maintain the reputation enjoyed by the Porterhouse (its Euro-style predecessor) but doubtless the quiet position and old-fashioned surroundings will help just as before. $20 lunch specials. Licensed.

$$ **Watermark**, *33 King Edward Pde, T4460622. Daily for dinner from 1800, Sun for brunch.* A risky concept outside the city centre, Watermark offers buffet dinners at a set price of $26 and children an even better value $10. Their Sunday brunch is also popular at $16, child $8 Seems to be working and quite classy too.

$ **Shahi Café**, *1/1 Milford Rd, Milford, T4894798. Daily lunch 1200-1430, dinner, 1800-late, licensed.* The North Shore base for good Indian food at affordable prices.

City East *p93, see map p92*

$$$ **Antoine's**, *333 Parnell Rd, Parnell, T3798756. Dinner Mon-Sat. Lunch Mon-Fri, licensed.* Parnell's best and on a par with anything in the city. French cuisine with some firm favourites with the regulars – the duck is apparently exquisite. Professiona.

$$$ **Gault at George**, *144 Parnell Rd, T3582600.* A little pretentious perhaps and strictly for the corporate fat cat or trendsetter, yet despite that, there is no doubting the class, the smooth service, or culinary talents of lauded chef Simon Gault. Good wine list.

$$$ **Hammerheads**, *19 Tamaki Dr, Orakei, T5214400. Daily 1130-2200, licensed.* A tourist seafood favourite sited right next to Kelly Tarlton's Underwater World. A reputation for poor service, but the food makes up for it.

$$$ **Mikano**, *1 Solent St, Mechanics Bay, T3099514. Mon-Fri 1100-late, Sat, 1700-late, Sun 0930-late, licensed.* A little out of the way,

sited next to the helicopter base and container wharves but with a great view across the harbour and serving a very high standard of mainly Asian-inspired fare. Well worth the trip. Has maintained a good reputation for years.

$$ **Bluefins**, *corner of Tamaki Dr and Aitkin Av, Mission Bay, T5284551. Lunch Mon-Fri. Dinner 7 nights, licensed*. The best choice in Mission Bay, with generous, mainly seafood dishes.

$$ **Halo**, *425 Tamaki Dr, St Heliers, T5759969. Daily for lunch and dinner and for the inevitable beach view brekkie and brunches on Sunday*. Licensed. Formerly 'Saints', a total refit and reinvention (if not a complete removal from the ecclesiastical label), orchestrated by ex-Sydney chef Mandy Jackson, has resulted in brasserie-style or fine dining that meets all expectations. Recommended.

$$ **Iguacu**, *269 Parnell Rd, Parnell, T3584804. Mon-Fri 1100-0100, Sat-Sun 1000-0100. Licensed*. Parnell's most popular 'place to be seen', especially with the younger set. Not a place at night for the casually dressed or happily single female, but still immensely popular. Mainly traditional menu from snack size to feast. Top breakfast spot.

$$ **Java Room**, *317 Parnell Rd, Parnell, T3661606. Dinner Mon-Sat 1800-late, licensed and BYO*. Fine selection of Asian and Pacific Rim cuisine at affordable prices.

$$ **Karin Japanese**, *237 Parnell Rd, Parnell, T3567101. Daily lunch 1200-1400, dinner 1800-2200*. Parnell's Japanese offering with a wide range of traditional favourites and prices. If you are a newcomer, take some advice about the options available.

$$ **Oh Calcutta**, *151 Parnell Rd, Parnell, T3779090*. A traditional favourite in Parnell. A fine and reliable one at that.

$$ **Rikka**, *73 Davis Cres, Newmarket, T5225277. Daily 1200-1500, 1800-2400, licensed*. An offshoot of the city-centre Japanese establishment that is no less popular. Fantastic interior. The Tenshin section of the menu is more expensive but highly recommended if you are new to Japanese food.

$ **Burger Fuel**, *164 Parnell Rd, T3773345*. One of several in a chain fast reproducing around the city which is a sure sign that their generous range of burgers from half cow to vege are going down exceptionally well.

$ **La Bocca**, *251 Parnell Rd, Parnell, T3750083. Dinner Mon-Sat 1800-late (summer only), licensed*. A café with a recent and imaginative seafood adjunct. Both café and restaurant (which hopefully will soon open all year round) can boast great quality at very affordable prices.

$ **Portofino**, *156 Parnell Rd, Parnell, T3733740. Lunch and dinner 7 days, licensed and BYO*. Long-standing favourite, reliable and affordable, Italian style.

$ **Thai Friends**, *311 Parnell Rd, Parnell, T3735247. Lunch Tue-Sat. Dinner 7 nights from 1800-2300, licensed and BYO*. A friendly Thai restaurant whose menu will draw you back more than once.

$ **Venus**, *93 Upland Rd, Remuera, T5221672. Tue-Sat 0900-2130, Sun 0900-1500, licensed and BYO*. A popular spot for locals and an intimate venue in the evening. Newmarket's best breakfast.

$ **Verve**, *311 Parnell Rd, Parnell, T3792860. Daily from 0730. Dinner Tue-Sat licensed*. A great 'all rounder' in every way both day and night. Always busy and a top breakfast spot.

$ **White Lady**, *corner of Broadway and Remuera Rd, Newmarket. Open all night*. The sister of the infamous White Lady in the city centre (see above). It has seen its fair share of loonies turning up in the wee hours trying to read the extensive menu, but the stalwart owners remain in control.

Cafés

Café Jazz, *563 Remuera Rd, Remuera, T5240356*. A good place to go if you're in Remuera and need a coffee or lunch.

Kenzie, *17a Remuera Rd, T5222647*. Good 'chill over a coffee and watch the world go by' establishment on the edge of busy Broadway.

Rosehip, *82 Gladstone, Parnell, T3691182*. A bit pricey, but remains a popular haunt, well-situated next to the Rose Gardens and away from busy Parnell Rd. Good coffee.

Trinity, *107 Parnell Rd, Parnell, T3003042*. Prompt no-nonsense service and a good hearty breakfast. Fine coffee.

City West *p97, see map p104*

$$ **Andiamo**, *194 Jervois Rd, Herne Bay, T3787811. Mon-Fri from 0700-late, Sat/Sun from 0800-late, licensed*. Always busy, with a great all-day breakfast selection.

$$ **Anglesea Grill**, *corner of Ponsonby Rd and Anglesea St, Ponsonby, T3604551. Lunch Wed-Fri, dinner Mon-Sat, licensed*. Essentially a seafood establishment with an enthusiastic Scots chef who has applied his fine cooking skills to the fine local produce. Some argue that this is the best seafood restaurant in the city. Don't miss the yellow-finned tuna starter. Also serves good chicken and steak.

$$ **Chandelier**, *152 Ponsonby Rd (next to SPQR), T3609315*. Opened recently next to the infamous and long-established city favourite SPQR, the Chandelier restaurant and lounge bar is predictably and marvellously over the top with Italian-inspired decor and food to draw in a mainly avant-garde clientele. An experience.

$$ **Essence**, *70 Jervois Rd, Herne Bay, T3762049. Daily, 1100-late, Sun brunch 0900-late, licensed*. Relatively small portions – one for those who love an imaginative menu with a highly artistic presentation. Good breakfast or brunch venue.

$$ **GPK**, *262 Ponsonby Rd, Ponsonby, T3601113. Mon-Fri 1100-late, Sat/Sun 0900-late. Licensed*. One of Auckland's most successful restaurants, with another branch in Mt Eden. Always busy with a lively happening atmosphere. The bar is as popular as the menu.

$$ **Hell's Kitchen**, *165 Ponsonby Rd, Ponsonby, T3602656. Thu-Sun lunch and dinner, Tue, Wed dinner only, closed Mon*. With a name like that – originating from a NZ foodies' television series – it seems quite irresistible to try the real thing opened in early 2003. Reports suggest it won't disappoint.

$$ **The Hunting Lodge**, *Waikoukou Valley Rd, Waimauku, T4118259. Lunch and dinner Wed-Sun (daily in summer). Licensed*. Plugged as Auckland's top countryside restaurant, serving traditional fare like beef and lamb and set in the heart of vineyard country. Popular after a day's wine tasting.

$$ **Kwans**, *corner of St Mary's Rd and Jervois Rd, T3781776*. A friendly, reliable Thai option.

$$ **Masala**, *169 Ponsonby Rd, Ponsonby, T3784500. Mon-Fri 1200-late, Sat/Sun 1700-late, licensed and BYO*. Perhaps the best and certainly the busiest Indian restaurant on Ponsonby Rd. Good for a quick late-night supper. Good vegetarian selection.

$$ **Musical Knives**, *272 Ponsonby Rd,*

Ponsonby, T3767354. Tue-Sun from 0830-2230, licensed. So named because the chef and owner has been tour chef for a number of well-known international music stars such as Madonna. Very popular for its health and figure-conscious fare, particularly organic vegetables, herbs and fruits.

$$ **Prego**, *226 Ponsonby Rd, Ponsonby, T3763095. Lunch and dinner 7 days, licensed*. A big favourite with the locals who know they will get good food and good service. Italian-style menu. Great wood-fired pizza and fish.

$$ **Provence**, *44 Ponsonby Rd, Ponsonby, T3768147. Dinner Mon-Sat from 1800, licensed*. Formerly an Irish bar, this property has now taken on a French feel. The Provençal food, fine wines and pleasant decor would certainly seem to suggest it will do better than its predecessor.

$$ **Rocco**, *23 Ponsonby Rd, Ponsonby, T3606262. Mon-Fri from 1200-late and Sun from 1800*. Enjoys a reputation for consistently good Spanish and Italian inspired dishes with a specialization in game and seafood. Cosy private dining upstairs.

$$ **Vinnies**, *166 Jervois Rd, Herne Bay, T3765597. Daily from 1830, licensed*. This is considered to be one of Auckland's finest, with such classics as Russian caviar. Professional in style, quality and presentation. Special menu is available allowing you to sample a wide variety of tastes. Very popular so book ahead.

$ **Dizengoff**, *256 Ponsonby Rd, Ponsonby, T3600108. Daily 0700-1700, unlicensed*. A fine counter service operation offering takeaway or sit-in items that attract a wide-ranging clientele, making it another great people-watching establishment. Light food with a Jewish influence. The breakfasts (especially the salmon and eggs on toast), are hearty and delicious.

$ **Empress Garden**, *227 Jervois Rd, Herne Bay, T3765550. Lunch and dinner daily. Licensed*. One of the city's oldest and most popular Chinese restaurants set out of the way in suburban Herne Bay. The Peking Duck comes highly recommended. Good value.

$ **Lord Ponsonby's**, *267 Ponsonby Rd, Ponsonby, T3765260*. A fine deli, ideal for picnic takeaways.

$ **Ponsonby Fresh Fish and Chip Co**, *127 Ponsonby Rd, Ponsonby, T3787885. Daily*

1100-2130. Always popular and always busy. Try the local Pacific fish, you will probably be back again. Portions were large but are diminishing with time and popularity.

$ Ponsonby Pies, *288 Ponsonby Rd, Ponsonby, T3613685. Daily 0900-1700*. You must not leave Auckland without trying a 'Ponsonby Pie'. This is the base for an operation that distributes the famous pies to food outlets city-wide. The fillings are imaginative, incredibly fresh and for about $3 you can't go wrong. Everything from steak and onion to silverbeet and cheese.

$ Shahi Café, *26 Jervois Rd, Ponsonby, T3788896. Daily, lunch 1200-1400, dinner from 1800-late. Licensed and BYO*. The third Shahi venue and just as good as the others. Small, romantic and intimate.

Cafés

Atlas Power Café, *285 Ponsonby Rd, Ponsonby, T3601295*. A predominantly gay venue serving great coffee.

Atomic Café, *121 Ponsonby Rd, Ponsonby, T3764954*. Another Ponsonby favourite serving good coffee in lively, pleasant surroundings.

Café Cezanne, *296 Ponsonby Rd, Ponsonby, T3763338*. Very popular with students and backpackers. Good hearty fare with the classic Ponsonby atmosphere.

Gannet Rock Café, *38 Jervois Rd, Herne Bay, T3768072. Daily 0700-1530*. New kid on the block offering great seafood lunches.

Open Late Café, *134A Ponsonby Rd, Ponsonby, T3764466. Sun-Wed 1830-0200, Thu till 0300, Fri/Sat till 0400*. A reliable old favourite, not so much for its food as its hours. The place to go if you have got carried away after a long night out and want some café-style fare.

Sierra, *50 Jervois Rd, Herne Bay, T3781273*. Highly popular with locals, excellent coffee and sandwiches.

SPQR, *150 Ponsonby Rd, Ponsonby, T3601710. Mon-Fri 1100-late, Sat/Sun 1000-late, licensed*. One of the oldest and trendiest places in Ponsonby, a favourite with many for food and beverages. Very high posing quotient – daahling.

Stella, *118 Ponsonby Rd, Ponsonby, T3787979. Lunch Tue-Fri, dinner Mon-Sat, licensed*. Small, busy and unassuming café with a cosy fireplace.

City South *p98*

$$ Antiks, *248a Dominion Rd, Mt Eden, T6386254. Lunch and dinner 7 days from 1100, Sun from 1030, licensed and BYO*. Offers a huge selection of mainly European dishes in a bustling, eclectic environment.

$$ Berlin Restaurant, *423 Mount Eden Rd, Mt Eden, T6306602. Dinner Mon-Sat, licensed*. Another favourite with the local residents, German food and decor. Great venison and, of course, sausages and strudel.

$ Crucial Traders, *473 New North Rd, Kingsland, T8463288*. Laid-back café favourite that lures those tired of the Ponsonby scene.

$ Frazers, *434 Mount Eden Rd, Mt Eden, T6306825*. A popular spot for locals, students and backpackers after a good selection of cheap light meals and fine coffee.

$$ Roasted Addiqtion, 487 New North Rd, Kingsland, T8150913. Becoming increasingly popular both for its fine coffee and highly imaginative evening menu.

$$ Sitar Indian Restaurant, *397 Mount Eden Rd, Mt Eden, T6300321. Dinner Tue-Sun 0600, licensed*. The most popular Indian restaurant south of the city centre.

☼ Pubs and bars

Sadly, when it comes to good pubs Auckland is really not in the same league as most other cities of its size. Only in the last decade has the city, and New Zealand as a whole, woken up to the fact that the 'ashtray built into the table, rugby boys and jugs of insipid beer until you're sick' establishments were not everybody's 'pint of ale'. However, whether you are an ardent trend setter, an avid Guinness drinker or cocktail specialist it can still perhaps provide a pub that will suit your needs. With the arrival of the new millennium you can at least find most things, from gay venues, quiet intellectual establishments, and, on occasions, even good beer. New Zealand beer, alas, is like Australian beer: very fizzy, very watery and very cold. Which may, of course, suit your taste. Pubs are well distributed around the city but are concentrated mainly in the city centre and the trendy suburbs of Parnell, Newmarket and Ponsonby, with the odd desirable establishment lying further afield. Centred in High St and Vulcan Lane are a number of Auckland's top spots.

City Centre *p84, see map p88*

Dispensary, *on the corner of Victoria St West and Hobson, T3092118*. Although this 24-hr pub and its decor are nothing spectacular, this can be a very interesting establishment in the wee hours when all the others are shut. From about 0300 the place fills with real party animals and clocked-off bar persons, all with a story to tell.

The Empire, *corner of Nelson St and Victoria St, T3734389*. A fine-looking establishment that is also a real party spot at weekends, offering live music at night and a fine espresso by day in its either frantic or peaceful courtyard.

Float, *Shed 9, Princess Wharf, T3071354, www.float.co.nz* This is a new and highly trendy bar that is cold and clinically decked out. It is designed to host a weekly TV sports programme, and with the cleverly designed fold-away stands of seating can also house a big crowd while presenting live sporting events on a big screen. Definitely for the trendy or sports orientated.

The Loaded Hog, *on the Viaduct Basin, T3664691*. Has been popular since it was opened in 1993 shortly before the Whitbread Round the World Yacht Race. The Viaduct Basin, which acted as the yacht base for both the Whitbread and two America's Cup Regattas, is right outside its doors. Due to its location it has always been popular and is frequented mainly by the well-to-do and trendy both day and night. Its huge interior and interesting agricultural and sailing theme decor is worth a look. They also brew their own beer and serve good food.

Mo's, *on the corner of Wolfe St and Federal St, T3666066*. It is a tiny, very popular bar that is a fine place for conversation, as opposed to posing.

The Muddy Farmer, *14 Wyndham St, T3361265*. A more recent venue, similar in size, popularity and decor as the Loaded Hog and Danny Doolans. The bar is great but the beer is expensive.

Soul, *T3567249* and **Danny Doolans**, *T3582554, both on the Viaduct Basin*. Soul, with its outdoor seating was the perfect place to see and be seen during the most recent America's Cup and Danny's is now considered by many to be the best Irish pub in the city. On weekend nights, along with 'the Hog' (see above), all three go off like a rocket. Danny's in particular has good live music.

With Queen St clubs and a number of major Backpackers nearby, the following bars all rage on well into the night; they are also popular by day and most serve a fine lunch.

Belgian Beer Café, *(Occidental), 6-8 Vulcan La, T3006226*. Tries hard to push the Euro feel with favourable results.

Deschlers, *17 High St*. This is a cocktail lounge with lounge lizard music. A big favourite at the weekend with trendy young things with wandering eyes. At the other end of the waterfront, and far more traditional, is the long-established

Kiwi Tavern, *3 Britomart Pl, T3071717*. It is nicely relaxed and tries hard to push the Kiwi pub feel, but all this may be challenged with the development of the new Britomart Travel Terminal nearby. Time will tell.

City North *p92, see map p92*

The North Shore has its fair share of pubs, and there are a number of favourites that certainly deserve to lure locals and visitors across the Bridge.

The Northcote Tavern, *37 Queen St, Northcote (almost immediately across the bridge), T4807707*. Very popular with both Kiwis and immigrants, who flood in after work before disappearing into the vast suburbs of the shore city. It has two very relaxed contrasting public and lounge bars, the latter with a fine Scots theme. Great Guinness.

Puhoi Hotel and Tavern, *just north of Orewa and 40 km north of the city, in the tiny settlement of Puhoi, T4220812*. May be well out of your range, but worth the trip. It is more an experience than a watering hole, very popular in summer and a favourite haunt of bikers on Sun afternoons. Basic, but richly decorated with an historic interior and interesting clientele.

R'Toto, *134 Hurstmere Rd, Takapuna, T4866330*. Has a huge sports theme bar that fills like the pint glass at the weekends, so it must be popular. The main North Shore base for boy meets girl.

Speakers Corner English Ale House, *7 Anzac Rd in Browns Bay, T4796060*. Next to the beach and hugely popular for its range of fine, mainly British beers and good pub grub which is available daily from 1100.

City East *p93, see map p95*

There are a number of bars nestled in amongst the cafés and shops of the Parnell Rd, which are, along with those in Ponsonby, considered to be the trendiest drinking spots in the city.

The Carlton, *on the corner of Khyber Pass Rd and Broadway, T5290050*. In Newmarket, near Parnell, there are a number of pubs, including this old favourite.

Claddagh Irish Pub, *372 Broadway, T5224410*. The Claddagh, despite the ever-growing competition remains one of the most popular Irish pubs in the city. Owned by the much-loved Noel and Margaret, originally from Limerick (and essentially the founders of Irish bars in Auckland) it is a wonderful homely Irish pub and a favourite haunt of Irish and Scottish visitors and immigrants. Throughout the day it is quiet and welcoming, but as the day progresses and the locals start to come in, it becomes busier and busier, till eventually (especially at weekends) it is jumping to the sound of Irish music late into the night. Along with the Northcote Tavern across the Harbour Bridge (see below), the Claddagh pours the finest pint of Guinness in New Zealand.

Iguacu, *269 Parnell Rd, T3584985*. The old favourite and the kick-off venue for others. From there just follow the designer clothing and the clickity-clack of high heels.

City West *p97, see map p104*

The main drinking venue west of the city centre is Ponsonby, which is similar to Parnell. Here trendy young things parade up and down the sidewalks in and out of the many cafés and bars which fringe them.

Dogs Bollix, *corner of K'Rd and Newton Rd, T3764600*. A wonderful Irish pub, famed not so much for its interior and its beer, but the band of the same name. A weekend night when the boys get going is entertaining.

Garage Bar, *152 Ponsonby Rd, T3788237*. Ideal if you want to escape to a more intimate surrounding.

Grand Central, *126 Ponsonby Rd, T3601260*. Has a highly entertaining Irish manager and less raucous environment.

The Safari, *116 Ponsonby Rd*. A local favourite and gets fairly riotous at weekends.

City South *p98*

Galbraith's Ale House, *2 Mount Eden Rd, Mt Eden, T3793557*. Used to be the old Grafton library and is perhaps the only notable pub south of the city centre. Within its grand exterior a fine range of foreign and home-brewed ales are available (at slightly elevated prices) as is a fine menu. Further south of here beyond Mt Eden and into the depths of South Auckland the pubs are not generally recommended.

⊘ Entertainment

The after-sunset scene in Auckland is getting increasingly better and now boasts some fine venues for dancing, comedy or huge outdoor summer events in the Auckland Domain; infoline, T3671077, the *New Zealand Herald*, www.nzherald.co.nz, or the website www.eventsauckland.com

The Edge is a conglomerate of Auckland's main venues offering the top international performance events. It combines the **Aotea Centre**, **The Civic**, The **Auckland Town Hall**, and **Aotea Square**. For all enquires contact The Edge, T3092677, www.the-edge.co.nz, and ask for the regularly updated event schedule leaflets at all the main information centres. The free publication *What's Happening* is also a very useful guide, again available from information centres. For gigs and clubbing look out for *The Fix* magazine. For up-to-the-minute information and comment tune in to *BFM's* gig guide on the radio or net, www.95bfm.co.nz

Clubbing

Most nightclubs in Auckland are based in the city centre on **Queen St**, **Vulcan La**, **High St** and **Karangahape Rd** (or K' Rd – noted especially for its gay and transvestite scene). Some venues in **Ponsonby** and **Parnell**, although not considered clubs, also remain open well into the wee hours with less emphasis on actual dancing.

Most of the clubs are open nightly, warming up towards the end of the week before going off at the weekend. Venues usually have a cover charge of about $5-$15, and drinks will be at least $6. Dress codes often apply. Pubs vary greatly with their attempts at last orders, but generally speaking the solid drinking stops from midnight to 0300, and from then on it's clubbing till dawn. On K' Rd although most of the clubs are essentially gay orientated, they are very welcoming and popular with all comers. If you are a true party animal head up to the **Dispensary** *on the corner of Victoria and Hobson sts (*see above).

Bed *322 K' Rd*;

Calibre, *basement 179 K' Rd* and

Club 4:20 *at 373 K' Rd* are the top spots and the dance music can be excellent.

If you really want to hit the floor then

The Staircase, aka The Kase, *340 K' Rd, T3744278 (closed Mon)* is good, especially if you go around midnight. Later on, as it gets busy, don't be surprised (or indeed offended) if a very large Pacific Island gentleman called Dina, in the most amazing scarlet number, high heels and a huge fruit filled hat, gives you a cheeky squirt with his large water pistol – it's all done in the best possible taste.

Supper Club, *2 Beresford Sq, T3005040*. Near K' Rd, and is open nightly, DJs Thu, Fri and Sat 2230-late.

For more traditional options, head down to the bottom of **Queen St** and join the queues outside venues in **High St** and **Vulcan La**.

Cardiac, *1 High St* and

Khuja Lounge, *536 Queen St* are popular options. Khuja Lounge has Latino, hip-hop and funk from DJs and live percussionists.

Papa Jack's Voodoo Lounge, *Vulcan La*, is another busy venue with a large bar playing mixed dance music and rock.

Centro, *26 Wyndham St*. It can be excellent, but the dance floor is very small and at times it's like trying to dance in a phone box.

Fever, *2/129 Hurstmere Rd, Takapuna*, across the bridge, is the North Shore City's top night spot.

Margarita's, *18 Elliot St*, which has a larger dance floor and is especially popular as a venue in which to find that temporary 'mate'.

The Wyndham Bowling Club, *18 Wyndham St, T3733433*, is a sophisticated new venue for the over-25s, offering funky house on the main dance floor and more soothing lounge out back. Don't be surprised to see the odd 'All Black' wander in and out with an arrogant swagger.

Comedy

There is a healthy comedy scene in Auckland, and stand-up New Zealand humour (on stage) can be very similar to that found in the US and Europe. Mike King and Brendon Lovegrove are two of the best regular performers. See the *New Zealand Herald* weekend edition for details. There is also an Annual Comedy Festival held generally in late April at various venues throughout the city.

The main venues for comedy are:

Classic Comedy and Bar, *321 Queen St, T3734321*.

The Covert Theatre, *84 K'Rd, T3666637*.

Silo Theatre, *Lower Grays Av, T3660339, www.silo.co.nz*.

Cinemas

There are many cinema complexes throughout the city. New Zealand often receives films before Europe due to film distribution arrangements. For a daily guide to all venues and films consult the *New Zealand Herald* entertainment section, especially in the weekend edition. Admission is around $10, cheap nights are usually Tue.

Academy, *64 Lorne St, T3732761, www.academy-cinema.co.nz* This is the best bet for specialist films.

Devonport 3 Cinema, *48 Victoria Rd, T3679111*. Is quiet and low-key and good if you fancy a ferry journey for added entertainment.

Force Entertainment Centre, *291-297 Queen St T9792400*. Has 12 cinemas and an **IMAX** , *T9792405*. Films change on the hour every hour *Fri and Sat 0900-0300, Sun-Thu 0900-2400*.

Rialto, *167 Broadway, Newmarket, T5292218*.

Theatres

All listings again can be found in the entertainment section of the *New Zealand Herald*, particularly in the weekend edition. Tickets for high profile events can be booked through *Tiketek*, *T3075000*. The prominent theatre venues in the city are:

Bruce Mason Theatre, *corner of Hurstmere Rd and the Promenade, Takapuna, on the North Shore, T4883133*.

The Herald Theatre, *Aotea Square, Queen St, T3092677*.

Maidment Theatre, *corner of Princess St and Alfred St, at the University, T3082383*.

Silo Theatre, *Lower Grays Av, T3660339, www.silo.co.nz* More 'off-the-wall' performances.

Sky City Theatre, *Sky City, corner of Victoria and Federal St, T9126000, www.skycity.co.nz*

Auckland Theatre Company can be contacted for further information: *T3090390, www.auckland-theatre.co.nz*

Gay and lesbian

The Auckland gay scene is kept up to date with the *Express Magazine* ($2.50) which can be bought from the magazine outlets Magazzino (see Shopping below). This publication and the local gossip can also be sought at the

Pride Centre, *281 K'Rd, T3020590*, or in the predominantly gay cafés and clubs including:

Atlas Power Cafe, *285 Ponsonby Rd*.

GAY, *5 High St*.

Surrender Dorothy, *175 Ponsonby Rd, Ponsonby, T3764460*

The Kase, *K'Rd* (see above).

The Wunderbar, *5 O'Connell St*.

The main club venues are listed above in the clubbing section.

Useful websites include:

www.gaysainz.net.nz, www.gaytravel.net.nz/nz/auckland and www.pride.org.nz

Music venues

Auckland is well served with local, national and international gigs and venues. Most major concerts take place (usually as a one night in New Zealand affair) at the **Aotea Centre**; **Western Springs**, **North Shore Events Centre** or **Ericsson Stadium**. Although New Zealand is isolated, it's not unusual to hear Robbie Williams, Moby, or to find oneself throwing one's knickers at an ageing Tom Jones. The traditional local music venues are described below. The best bet for schedules is the *New Zealand Herald*, *www.nzherald.co.nz*

Rock

King's Arms, *59 France St, Newton, T3733240*.

Masonic Tavern, *29 King Edward Par, Devonport, T4450485, every Fri night*.

PowerStation, *33 Mount Eden Rd, Mt Eden, T3773488*.

Rose and Crown, *69 Customs St West*.

Temple Bar, *486 Queen St, T3774866*, live music nightly.

Jazz and Rhythm'n'Blues

Grand Central, *126 Ponsonby Rd, Ponsonby, T3601260*.

Iguacu, *269 Parnell Rd, Parnell, T3584804*. Sun brunch and most evenings.

Java Jive, *12 Pompallier Pl, Ponsonby, T3765870*.

Jazz Bar, *350 Queen St, T3092512. Mon/Fri/Sat*.

London Bar, *corner of Wellesley and Queen St, T3733684, Fri and Sat*.

Manifesto, *315 Queen St, T3034405. Sun*.

General and Irish folk and rock

The Claddagh, *362 Broadway, Newmarket, T5224410*. 'Diddly dee' jam session Mon nights, regular bands most others.

Danny Doolans, *204 Quay St, T3582554*.

Devonport Folk Music Club, *The Bunker, Mt Victoria, Devonport, T4452227. Mon night*.

Dog's Bollix Bar, *corner of K'Rd and Newton, T3764600*. For a great night and a great band – the Dog's Bollix in fact – do not miss Connor and the boys on a Sat and Sun.

● Festivals and events

For up to date details consult the websites www.eventsauckland.com or www.aucklandnz.com

Jan

Sky City Starlight Symphony (last week) – a free open-air event held annually (sometimes with a different name) in the Auckland Domain, attracts over 300,000.
Auckland Anniversary Weekend Sailing Regatta held on th Waitemata Harbour.

Feb

Devonport Food and Wine Festival (*3rd week*), see page 93. Also the
Hero Parade and Festival, a highly entertaining gay festival the highlight being the pageant held along Ponsonby Rd.

Mar

Pacifica Festival (*1st week*). New Zealand's largest Pacific culture festival with food, arts and crafts and music performances.
National Dragon Boat Festival, (*3rd week*), Viaduct Harbour.
Round the Bays Fun Run, a charitable event that attracts over 7000 competitors.

April

Waiheke Jazz Festival (see Waiheke page 136). **Sky Tower Vertical Challenge**. Competitors from 10 years old and up, race up and down the Sky Tower with mixed results.
Rally of New Zealand. Part of the world series. 25 stages that start and finish from Auckland's Mid City.

Jun

New Zealand Boat Show.

Jul

Auckland International Film Festival (*1st week*).

Oct

Auckland Fashion week and the increasingly popular
V8 Super Cars.

Nov

Ellerslie Flower Show (*last week*). The biggest horticultural event in the Southern Hemisphere, held at the Auckland Botanical Gardens.

Dec

Christmas in the Park (*4th week*). A popular and free precursor to the *Starlight Symphony*, again held in the Auckland Domain and hugely popular.
NZ Golf Open (*last week*)and the
Great New Zealand Craft Show (*last week*).

▲ Sports and activities

Bridge climb

For anyone who has been to Sydney and seen the Sydney Harbour Bridge let alone made the ascent of that world famous 'Bridge Climb', the mere sight of Auckland's equivalent will bring about a wry smile if not the full 'Paah'. However, this is Auckland, not Sydney, and besides, the views are still amazing. For details contact **Bridge Climb**, *70 Nelson St, City, T0800-000-808, www.aucklandbridge climb.co.nz* It lasts 2 hrs 30 min and costs from $110, child $55 (night climb $175).

Bungee and rap jumping

There are two opportunities for bungee jumping in New Zealand's largest city, both new, both highly unique and perhaps – given the nation's obsession with the sport – inevitable. The first is the much talked about **Sky Jump**, *from $195 (maximum weight 125 kg), T0800-759-586, www.skyjump.co.nz* from just above the restaurant of the Sky Tower. But there is a 'catch' (thankfully, or sadly, depending how you look at it). Given the incredible jump height of 192 m, not to mention all that nasty hard concrete and people watching you below, it is not possible to jump conventionally with a elastic cord attached to the ankles and to do the 'yoyo' bit. Obviously if you did, in this scenario, you would probably end up like Garfield the ginger cat plastered against somebody's office window. So be advised, watch what is involved first and note that it is a cable-controlled descent in the horizontal, not vertical, position. However, that said, at 20 seconds and about 75kph it is still pants-wetting material.

The second and newest jump opportunity is from the **Harbour Bridge**. **A J Hackett**, *T0800-462-8649, www.ajhackett.com From $125, child (10-15) $89 (spectators can do the 'express climb' to the jump platform for $35, Bungee and Bridge Climb combo, from $199.* Owned and operated by the undisputed leaders in the field, it may not be the highest or the best, but it is still a lot of fun.

Groundrush, *T0800-727-586, www.groundrush.co.nz, from $79,* is a new and revitalized operation that offers the opportunity to rappel 50m down the side of the Mecure Hotel on Customs Street East. Head first is only way to go!

Sky Screamer *based next to Atrium on Elliot on Victoria St, from $35 (second launch $15)* is certainly aptly named and is your chance to be strapped into a seat and launched at high speed heavenwards, having left your stomach and your Sunday best expletives behind. Spectating is actually as good as taking part.

Canyoning

Although Wanaka is generally considered the country's canyoning capital, the streams and waterfalls of the Waitakere Ranges west of the city and the Coromandel Peninsula provide some exciting opportunities and are a worthwhile trip. **Canyonz**, *T0800-422696, www.canyonz.co.nz,* offer a 3-hr excursion with beach visit from $125 and an extended 5-hr trip to Coromandel from $225.

Awol Adventures, *T0800-462965, wwwawoladventures.co.nz,* offer similar half to full day trips with the added option of night and overnight excursions, from $135.

Cruises

A cruise around the inner harbour, or better still, out upon the Hauraki Gulf, gives you the opportunity to experience Auckland's 'other-and-far-more-attractive-half' and is highly recommended. Once 'out there' you will see why Auckland was such an ideal venue for the America's Cup and understand why it is considered such a yachties' heaven. The waterfront and Viaduct Basin is the place to 'cruise shop'.

Fullers, *The Fullers Cruise Centre in the Ferry Building on the Waterfront can supply all the details, T3679111, www.fullers.co.nz* The main operator offering everything from a 2-hr Harbour cruise (taking in the Viaduct Basin, Devonport, the Harbour Bridge etc) from $30, child $15, to island transportation and stop-overs (see Hauraki Islands, page 134. The day trip to Tiri Tiri Matangi Bird Sanctuary is particularly recommended.

Kawau Kat Cruises, *T0800-888006, www.kawaukat.co.nz or ask at the VIC.* Offer a range of cruise options primarily to Kawau Island (day-trip with BBQ lunch from $59, child $24), but also a harbour cruise (from $30, child $15) and a great trip to the Coromandel (recommended as you may miss it by road) from $99, child $45.

Dolphin Explorer, *T3576032, www.dolphinexplorer.com* Trips cost $99, child $50 and depart from Pier 3 on the waterfront. A new outfit offering dolphin watching trips in conjunction with university research projects, so there is no shortage of knowledge. Although it would be denied, and sightings are frequent (reputedly 90%), the Hauraki is not generally as productive as many other sites around the New Zealand coast like the Bay of Islands, Whakatane or the great sea mammal capital Kaikoura. What is guaranteed, however, is stunning scenery and an entertaining day-long cruise.

Ocean Rafting, *Viaduct Basin, T0800-801193, www.oceanrafting.co.nz,* offering the 'fast' cruise option on board a rigid inflatable with trips ranging from a 45-min whirl around the inner harbour from $40, child $20, to a 2-hr trip round the outer islands, from $125, child $62.50.

Golf

Auckland, like much of New Zealand, is golfers' heaven. Green fees are very reasonable (about $35-$50). Club hire is available at most courses. Mid-range, reasonable quiet, scenic and relatively cheap courses that are well worth playing include: **Hauapi**, *Riverhead, West Auckland, T4128809* Murawai, *West Coast beaches, T4118454.* **South Head course**, *west, Kaipara Heads,*

T4202838. Although a good 45-min drive, this course is a delight.

High profile courses like the following tend to be more expensive: **Titirangi**, *West Auckland, T8275749*.

Formosa, *Beachlands, South Auckland, T5365895*.

Gulf Harbour, *Whangaparaoa Peninsula, T4281380, www.gulf-harbour.co.nz*

Hang-gliding

Aqua Air, *T0508-4384444, www.gethigh.co.nz, from $120*, offer conventional tandem hang-gliding but also the rather novel concept of water take-off and landings with contraptions similar to those on floatplanes.

Horse trekking and stud visits

Horse trekking operations are generally focused on the West Coast beaches particularly around Murawai or Parakai. The two main operators are:

South Kaipara Horse Treks, *T4202835, www.horserides.co.nz*

Tasman Rides, *T4208603, www.tasmanrides.co.nz, 1-4hr from $40*.

Glenmorgan Farm, *Karaka in South Auckland (30km). For information contact Jenny Vazey, Glenmorgan Farm-Karaka, 355 Blackbridge Rd, Papakura, T2919355, www.glenmorgan.co.nz From $35*. Unique equestrian tour of the thoroughbred stud, Glenmorgan, one of the country's premier thoroughbred horse farms preparing yearlings and youngsters for the international racing market.

Kayaking

Fergs Kayaks, *12 Tamaki Dr, T5292230, www.fergskayaks.co.nz From $60, departs at 0900 or 1600, 6-7 hr*. Based in the city itself, long established and owned by Olympic champion Ian Ferguson. A range of trips on offer including the deservedly popular day or night guided trips to Rangitoto Island.

Okura Kayak Company, *T4791002, 2 hrs 30 min, from $59 (not including beverage)*. Based on the North Shore beaches offering something slightly different and eminently appealing in the form of a *'Paddle to the Pub'* option to Riverhead, Browns Bay or Devonport.

Given Waiheke Island's (page 136) beautiful and varied coastline it is no surprise to find several operators based there, including the following who offer a range of half to full day guided trips from $60-$125. Independent hire also available:

Ross Adventures, *T3725550, www.kayakwaiheke.co.nz*

Kayak Company, *T3722112, www.thekayakcompany.co.nz*

Leisure centres

Village on Broadway Cinemas, *77 Broadway, Newmarket, T5200806*. Olympic pools and fitness centre right beside the cinema complex.

Quad biking

It would be rude not to have a quad bike operator somewhere around the city and the West Coast beaches and forest trails lend themselves to the pursuit.

4 Track Adventures, *T0800-487-225, www.4trackadventures.co.nz, half to full day trips covering 15km to 55km, from $115*.

Sailing

Naturally, there are numerous opportunities to experience the Hauraki in the best possible way – by sail. Options range from catamarans to racing yachts. The VIC has full listings. Two of the most popular vessels are the racing yachts of *SailNZ* and the tall ship *Soren Larsen*.

SailNZ, *T3595987, www.sailnewzealand.co.nz*, offer cruises and match races between two authentic America's Cup racing yachts the NZL 40 and NZL 41. A basic, yet exhilarating 2-hr sailing costs from $125, child $110, while the full on race between the two during which you have the opportunity to participate, costs $195, child $175.

Soren Larsen, *T4118755, www.sorenlarsen.co.nz*, has been gracing the gulf for a number of years and was (if you are old enough to remember) the vessel that starred in the TV hit series *The Onedin Line*. There are a number of sailing options from a basic day sail on the Hauraki Gulf during which you can take the helm or help raise sails (or simply kick back and watch) (*3hr from $57, 5hr from $97*), or take part in extended 5-night voyages to the Bay of Islands.

Surfing

The best surfing is to be found on the West Coast beaches with the Piha breaks being internationally renowned.

Surf and Beach Tours, *www.newzealandsurftours.co.nz* A new outfit offering surfing trips to the West Coast beaches.

Bodyboard Tours, *T0800-854041*, offer easy-going excursions to Te Henga Beach for a spot of body boarding, walking and lunch, *from $30*.

Swimming

Olympic Pool, *Newmarket, 77 Broadway, T5224414*. Birkenhead on the Shore, *T4183560* and, of course the thermal complexes at **Parakai** and **Waiwera** (see page 126).

'Vertigo'

Established in 2002 this is the exciting opportunity to climb inside the mast of the **Sky Tower** to the 'crows nest' – at 300m, the highest publicly accessible, man-made platform in the southern hemisphere. The view on a clear day is simply unforgettable. *T0800-483-784, www.4vertigo.com, 2 hr from $125, child $70 (14 or over)*, Recommended. **NB** Sadly, no cameras allowed.

Walking

The best walking opportunities in the region are to be found at the **Wiatakeres** and **West Coast beaches**. Refer to the relevant texts in Around Auckland.

The **Arataki Information Centre**, *Scenic Drive, Titirangi, T3031530* (see page 129), is a fine place to visit and gather information before planning a walk. Regional parks and islands like **Rangitoto** and **Tiri Tiri Matangi** also offer excellent walking opportunities. See Hauraki Islands section page 134 or consult the VIC.

○ Shopping

If you fancy some serious retail therapy then Auckland should not disappoint. And given the currency exchange rates, if you are coming from Europe or the US, you are in for a treat. Whatever you're after, Auckland has them all. The most popular shopping spots are to be found in the central city and also **Parnell** and **Newmarket** to the east and **Ponsonby** to the west. But almost every major suburb has the ubiquitous mall that provides both quality and quantity. In recent years Auckland has led the way in the general expansion of opening hours throughout New Zealand. Generally you will find most major stores and malls throughout the city are open from 0900-1730 weekdays and 1000-1600 on weekends – if not longer, with some offering once-weekly night shopping until 2100. The major shopping malls are the:

Downtown Shopping Centre, *11-19 Customs St, City, T9785265*.

Manukau Shopping Centre, *corner of Great South and Wiri Station Rd, Manukau City,* T9785300. This is the largest shopping centre in New Zealand.

The Plaza Pakuranga, *Main Highway, Pakuranga,T5720264*.

St Luke's Shopping Centre, *80 St Luke's Rd, Mt Albert, T9786000*.

Shore City Galleria, *corner of Lake Rd and Como St, Takapuna, T9786300*.

West City Shopping Centre, *Catherine St, Henderson, T9786700*.

If you are looking for products specific to New Zealand, whet your appetite by visiting the **New Zealand Trade Centre**, *105 Queen St, City, T3666879*. Although you cannot buy here, it will give you an insight into what is available. The *'Official Auckland Shopping Guide'* and individual leaflets are available from tourist information centres, and there are even a few specialist shopping tours available. **Maureen O'Sullivan** offers a personalized half-day tour for women from $125 (day tour, $225) with a range of options from designer clothing to fine food and delicacies. Invaluable specialist advice is also available, *T02-1966043, www.psst.co.nz*

There are plenty of quality art galleries in the city, and if you are serious about buying or viewing get the detailed 'Auckland Gallery Guide' or the 'Auckland Art Precinct Map' from the main tourist information centres and allow a full day. Many Auckland artists reside in the western suburbs in and around Titirangi and the Waitakeres. The VIC can supply the useful and attractive 'Art Out West' brochure should you wish to investigate in detail. Pacific and especially New Zealand art is unique, appealing and colourful – reflecting the very nature of New Zealand itself. Prices vary. The best gallery venues are Parnell (ask about the 'Parnell Arts Trail'), Devonport, Titirangi and the Central City. Some quality original artwork is also available on the 2nd floor of the Auckland International Airport at cheaper prices.

Books

Borders, *291-297 Queen St, T3093377*, arrived in 1999, (open until 2200) and it dwarfs the largest of the more traditional stores like **Whitcoulls**, *210 Queen St, T3565400*, or **Dymocks**, on the *Atrium on Elliot, 3799919*.

These majors should meet all your traditional needs, with *Whitcoulls, Dymocks, Bennetts* and *London Bookshops* all having smaller outlets in most major suburbs and shopping malls. For the smaller, more personalized and sedate outlet try:
Unity Bookshop, *19 High St, Auckland City, T3070731*.
The Children's Bookshop, *Corner Jervois and St Mary Rds, Ponsonby, T3767283* and **Auckland Map Centre**, *1A Wyndham St, Mid City* for travel books and maps.
Evergreen, *15 Victoria Rd, Devonport T4452960*. For second-hand books.
Hard to Find, *81A Victoria Rd, Devonport, T4460300*, is good for secondhand books, but the delightful rabbit warren-like interior of the Hard to Find (harder to find your way out!), at *171-173 The Mall, Onehunga, T6344340*, is an experience in itself.
The Woman's Bookshop, *105 Ponsonby Rd, Ponsonby, T3764399*.
For magazines the major bookstores should serve your needs or try:

Magazzino outlets at *123 Ponsonby Rd, T3766933* and at *Extreme on Broadway, Newmarket, T5240604*.

Camping and tramping gear

Although there is a good selection of camping and tramping clothes, boots and equipment to be found in Auckland and New Zealand, surprisingly there does not seem to be the range or the quality that is available in Europe or the United States. However, you may find all you need at **Katmandu**, *151 Queen St, City, T3094615*, and *200 Victoria St West, City, T3777560*.
Bivouac Outdoor, *109 Queen St, City, T3661966*, and *300 Broadway, Newmarket, T5292298*.
Canvas City, *corner of K'Rd and Ponsonby Rd, T3096444*.
Doyles, *66 Hobson St, CBD, T3776998, T5247957*. Good value.

Clothing

Most of the leading international brands and labels can be found in numerous outlets in the central city especially in the new **Chancery Mall** on Chancery Lane (off High St, CBD). Newmarket and Ponsonby are also other favourite spots. For listings get hold of a copy of the 'Auckland Fashion Guide' from the VIC. To source a comprehensive list of clothing stores and other shops in Newmarket visit www.newmarket.net.nz
Atrium on Elliot, *Queen St, T3583052*.
Barkers, *Queen St, T0800-808700*. Menswear.
Country Clothing, *Queen St, T3663940*.
The best factory shops are to be found in the **Dressmart** *outlets in suburban Onehunga*. For specialist advice and tours see Maureen O'Sullivan's tours above.
Ermenegildo Zenga, *Queen St, T3735545*. Menswear.
George Harrison, *Queen St, T3667788*. Menswear.
Kate Sylvester, *Newmarket, T3073282*. Womenswear.
Outdoor Heritage, and **Zambesi**, *T3772220*, are worth a look and have outlets throughout the city. O'Connell and High Streets in the CBD are also famous for its designer fashions – look out for Feline, Tanya Carlson, World, Karen Walker, and Morrison Hotel.

Rodd and Gun *throughout the city,*
T5220607. Menswear.
Saks, *Queen St, T5207630*. Menswear.
Studio Works, *Newmarket, T5290855*.
Womenswear.
Zebrano, *Newmarket, T5232500*.
Womenswear.
There are also numerous specialist boutiques
on Ponsonby Rd including:
Wallace Rose, **Glory** and **State of Grace**.

Gifts, jewellery and souvenirs

Auckland city centre has souvenir shops
everywhere packed with everything from cute
furry kiwis in All Black shirts to the
omnipresent bone or greenstone Maori
pendants – which, traditionally you are
supposed to buy for someone else, not
yourself. So take your pick. **Parnell** and **K' Rd**
are also recommended. But, the more
discerning buyer should wait to see the
smaller more provincial souvenir shops which
tend to offer more specialist, unique stock. If
you like the look of Kauri or other wood crafts
and are heading for Northland wait and buy
there, it may well be better quality and also
cheaper.
Aotea New Zealand Souvenirs, *Lower Albert
St, City, T3795022*.
Breen's, *Tower Centre, 6 Customs St West, City,
T3732788*. For reasonable priced knitwear.
Craftworld, *15 mins from Mid City in West
Auckland in the new Westgate Shopping Centre,
Fernhill Dr, Massey*. One of the newest and
largest craft shops.
The Elephant House, *237 Parnell Rd, Parnell,
T3098740*. One of the best craft shops in town.
Great Kiwi Yarns, *107 Queen St, T3089013*. For
original knitwear.
Marshals, *93 Queen St, City, T3660807*. For
quality New Zealand jewellery.
NtoZ, *Victoria Park Market, Victoria Park, City,
T3772447*.
The Great New Zealand Shop, *Downtown
Shopping Centre, Queen St, T3773009*. For those
looking for the classic Kiwi souvenirs.
Touch the Earth, *Downtown Shopping Centre,
Queen St, T3664474*.
United Tongan Church *about 1 km down
Richmond Rd, off Ponsonby Rd*. On Sat
mornings the original Tapa Cloths for sale are
displayed outside. They are reasonably priced,
light, easy to pack and interestingly original.

Markets

The most famous market in Auckland is the
Victoria Park Market *opposite Victoria Park,
just a few minutes walk west of the city centre.
T3096911, www.victoria-park-market.co.nz* It
provides 7 days a week shopping with a
variety of outlets from shops to stalls that
expand into the car park on Sat. There are a
wide variety of products with a market
theme, a number of good cafés, a food hall
and a pub, all in pleasant surroundings.

K'Rd (or Karangahape Rd), at the
southernmost end of Queen St, is an
excellent area for unusual shops, particularly
Polynesian clothing and craft items. The Sat
morning market on the bridge over the
motorway can also produce the odd unusual
bargain. If you would prefer a less
commercial, raw Polynesian feel then an
excursion to the
Otara Market in the rather dodgy suburb of
Otara in South Auckland is the best place to
go (see page 100).

Photography

Film is readily available throughout the city,
but for specialist film and equipment try
Camera and Camera, *162 Queen St, City,
T3031879*.
PCL, *86 Parnell Rd, Parnell, T3098090*. Although
this is the best professional lab, print film costs
about $10 for 24 and slide $10-$15 for 36. At
up to $30 a roll (36) transparency film is
extortionate and with the $12 processing
once exposed it costs over a dollar every time
you press the shutter.
The Photo Warehouse, *154 Queen St, City,
T3090715*.

Sports

Quality sports stores can be found
throughout the city and suburbs, but in this
land of rugby and for that world-famous
sporting souvenir – the All Blacks Jersey –
head no further than
Canterbury Clothing Company (CCC), *The
Rialto Centre, 165 Broadway, Newmarket,
T5200755*.
Maritime Museum Shop *on the waterfront*,
page 86. For all things nautical, and for the
America's Cup souvenir and clothing range.

⌒ Tours

There are many coach tours to key locations including the Bay of Islands, Waitomo and Rotorua, ranging from simple day tours to activity and accommodation packages. Shop around and compare prices. The VIC has full details. Good local tour companies include:
Action Kiwi, *T5247109, www.actionkiwi.co.nz*, who offer a range of tours from a city tour that includes everything from Mount Eden to an emu farm (*$89*) to kayaking, walking and cycling.
Auckland Wine Tasting Tours, *T6301540, www.winetrailtours.co.nz*, with whom to explore the ever increasing range of

vineyards and vintages springing up around the region, from $120 (includes lunch).
Bush and Beach, *T5751458, www.bushandbeach.co.nz*, specializing in insightful eco-trips to the Waitakeres and West Coast beaches.
Coromandel Explorer Tours, *T8282753, www.coromandeltours.co.nz* For those short of time, or without their own wheels to explore the Coromandel Peninsula. Run by the nature savvy tour guide Nicky. Day tours (0800-1930) are from $145, 2-day from $350, 4-day from $300 (excluding accommodation). Recommended.

● Transport

Bicycle hire

Adventure Cycles, *36 Customs St East, Central Auckland, T3095566,www.adventure-auckland.co.nz* offer a great service and provide a free helmet, lock, tool kit and water bottle, plus maps and tips. Prices range from about $25 a day to $190 a month. They also offer a 50% buyback for up to 6 months, which equates to the rental rate for 1 month when an inexpensive bike is purchased, and is a good deal.

Bus (local)

An *Auckland Busabout Guide*, is available from the bus terminal and all major tourist information offices, showing routes and departure points for the main city attractions. Fares are on a staged system 1-8 and range between $1.20-$7.90. Daily unlimited passes are available on board buses and local ferries for $8; 3-day passes $19.
Rideline, *T3666400*, has a detailed telephone information service on all major local city transport carriers routes, prices and connections with ferry services.
Stagecoach, *T3666400*, www.stagecoach.co.nz are the principal suburban carrier.
'City Circuit' is a red bus providing a free service around the immediate city centre

every 10 min daily from 0800-1800.
An ideal way to get about the city centre is by the excellent **Auckland City Loop 'Link'**. It offers a flat fare of $1.20 to all stops and claims to provide a bus every 10 min, 0600–1900 weekdays and every 15 min evenings and weekends 0700-1800, but you will still feel like a sardine at rush hour. The bus route (goes both ways) runs from: Downtown-Railway-Parnell-Museum-Domain-Newmarket-Hospital-University-AUT-Library-K'Rd-Ponsonby-Victoria Park-Casino/Sky City-Mid Queen St-QEII Square-Downtown.
The **Double Decker 'Explorer'** bus has all day sightseeing with commentary; $20 day pass.

Bus (national)

The 2 main players providing standard coach travel from Auckland to destinations throughout New Zealand day and night are:
Newman's, *T9136200, www.newmanscoach.co.nz*; and
Intercity Coach Lines, *T9136100, www.intercitycoach.co.nz*
All coaches arrive and depart from the **Sky City Coach Terminal**, *102 Hobson St, City (round the corner from the Sky Tower), T9136100, 0700-2200 Mon-Fri, 0700-2000 Sat-Sun.*
Northliner Express, *T3075873,*

www.northliner.co.nz, offer a valued service to a number of North Island destinations, especially Northland. Concession fares apply. They arrive and depart from the **Northliner Travel Centre**, *HSBC Building (opposite the Ferry Building) 172 Quay St.*

Car

Take time to find a good deal, depending on your requirements, through the main visitor information centres. For a cheap, no nonsense deal, try **Scotties**, *Valley Rd, Mount Eden, T09-6302625* – ask about their 'Buy back deals' and drop off arrangements with their sister operation in Christchurch.

If you own a car and have been drinking, there is a wonderful service available in Auckland called **Dial-a-Driver**, *T0800-925-374.* (Similar services are available elsewhere in New Zealand). A sober employee drives you and your car to your chosen destination while another driver follows behind in a company car.The drivers are generally friendly and immensely stoic.

Action Rent-a-Car, *free pick up, 24-hr service, T2622279.*
Affordable Rental Cars and Vans, *48 Carr Rd, Mt Roskill, T0800-454443, afford.rent@extra.co.nz*
Alternative Rental Cars, *115 Beach Rd, City, T3733822.*
Apex Rental Cars, *39 Beach Rd, City/ 30 Rennie Dr, Airport, T2570292/T0800-500660, www.apexrentals.co.nz*
A2B Rentals, *11 Stanley St, City, T0800-616888.*
Avis, *17/19 Nelson St, City, T3792650.*
Big Save Car Rentals, *39-43 The Strand, Parnell, T3033928/ T0800-422771.*
Budget, *83 Beach Rd, City, T0800-652227, www.budget.co.nz*
Hertz, *Airport, T2568695.*
Rent-a-Dent, *45 Union St, Central Auckland , T3090066.*
Thrifty Car Rental, *Airport, T3660562/ T0800-737070, www.thrifty.co.nz*
Scotties, *Valley Rd, Mount Eden, T6302625. Recommended.*

Campervan hire See also p44
Adventure Campervans, *142 Robertson Rd, Mangere, T0800-123555,*

www.nzmotorhomes.co.nz
Backpacker Campervan Rentals, *T0800-422-2672, www.backpackercampervans.com*
Cruise New Zealand Ltd, *T2758921/T0800-111909, www.cruisenewzealand.com*
Britz Motorhomes, *36 Richard Pearse Dr, Mangere, T2759090/T0800-831900, www.britz.com*
Kea Campers, *36 Hillside Rd, T0800-520052/T4417833, www.keacampers.com*
KiwiKombis, *96 Uxbridge Rd, Howick, T5339335, www.kiwikombis.com*
Maui Motorhomes, *36 Richard Pearse Dr, Mangere, T2753013/T0800-651080, www.maui-rentals.com*
Tui Campers, *3 Kingsford Smith Pl, Airport Oaks, Auckland Airport, T0800-324939, T0800-808226, www.tuicampers.co.nz*

Ferry

TIC's can provide all the details for ferry services. The main ferry company is **Fullers**, *information office on the ground floor of the Ferry Building, T3679111 or T3676892, www.fullers.co.nz.*

Though hardly as popular as they are on Sydney Harbour the Viaduct Basin is the place to secure a **water taxi** that can zip you to the North Shore or the Eastern Suburbs, *T0800-829-426, www.yellowboat.co.nz*

Scooter and motorcycle hire

The most convenient is perhaps the award-winning and national **NZ Motorcycle Rentals**, *31 Beach Rd, Downtown Auckland, T3772005, www.nzbike.com* They hire out a range of bikes from the 50cc sensible sewing machines to the 1100cc scary monsters, all at reasonable rates.

Taxi

Alert Taxis, *T3092000.*
Auckland Taxi Co-op, *T3003000.*
Corporate Cabs, *T3770773.*
Discount Taxis, *T5291000.*

● Directory

Airline offices

International Aeorlineas Argentinas, *15th Floor ASB Centre, 135 Albert St, T3793675.* **Air New Zealand,** *corner of Customs and Queen St, City, T3362424/T0800-737000, www.airnz.co.nz* **Air Pacific,** *Level 12/17 Albert St, City, T3792404.* **Air Vanuatu,** *2nd Floor West Plaza Building, corner of Customs and Albert St, City, T3733435.* **American Airlines,** *15th Floor Jetset Centre, 48 Emily Pl, City, T3099159.* **British Airways,** *T3578950.* **Cathay Pacific,** *11th Floor, Arthur Andersen Tower, 205 Queen St, T3790861.* **Freedom Air,** *T0800-600-500.* **Garuda Indonesia,** *Westpac Trust Tower, 120 Albert St, T3672324.* **Japan Airlines,** *Westpac Trust Tower, 120 Albert St, T3799906.* **Korean Airlines,** *92 Albert St, City, T9142000.* **Lufthansa Airlines,** *T0800-945220.* **Malaysia Airlines,** *12th Floor Affco House, 12-26 Swanson St, T3793743.* **Origin Pcific** *T0800-302302, www.originpacific.co.nz* **Polynesian Airlines,** *Samoa House, 283 K' Rd, City, T3095396.* **Qantas Airlines,** *191 Queen St, City, T3578900.* **Singapore Airlines,** *West Plaza Building, corner of Albert and Fanshawe St, City, T3032129, www.singaporeair.co.nz* **Thai Airways,** *22 Fanshawe St, City, T3773886.* **United Airlines,** *17th Floor, 1 Queen St, T0800-508648, www.ual.com*

Domestic **Air New Zealand,** *corner of Customs and Queen St, City, T3362424, T0800-737000, www.airnz.co.nz* **Qantas New Zealand,** *T3578900/T0800-808767.* **Great Barrier Airlines,** *Auckland International Airport (Domestic Terminal), T2759120/T0800-900600.* **Great Barrier Express,** *Auckland International Airport (Domestic Terminal), T0800-900600.* **Mountain Air,** *T0800-222123.* **Helicopter Flights,** *T0800-206406.* **Mount Cook,** *T3095395.*

Banks and currency exchange

American Express Currency Exchange: *105 Queen St, City; NZ Cup Village, Quay St, City; 67-69 Symonds St, City.* **Thomas Cook,** *34 Queen St, T0800-200-232.* **Travelex** *32 and 157 Queen St, T0800-200232.* **ANZ Banking Group,** *corner of Queen and Victoria St, T3589200/T0800-269466,* *www.anz.co.nz* **ASB Bank Ltd,** *corner of Queen and Wellesley Sts, T3063000.* **Bank of New Zealand,** *80 Queen St, T3799900/T0800-275269, www.bnz.co.nz* **Bank of Tokyo Ltd,** *151 Queen St, T3033554.* **Hong Kong Bank,** *290 Queen St, T3670868.* **National Bank of New Zealand,** *205 Queen St, T3599826/T0800-181818, www.nationalbank.co.nz* **Westpac Trust,** *79 Queen St, T3024200/T0800-400600, www.westpac.co.nz*

Communications

Internet Auckland City Library, *44-46 Lorne St, City, T3770209.* Citinet Cyber Café, *115 Queen St, City, T3773674.* Cyber City, *29 Victoria St, City, T3033009.* CyberDatez, *320 Queen St, City, T3770320.* Login 1, *1/12 Rialto Centre, 163 Broadway, Newmarket, T5229303.* Net Central Internet Café, *5 Lorne St, City, T3735186.* Net Zone, *4 Fort St, City, T3773905.* Smile, *Shop 2, 229 Dominion Rd, Mount Eden, T6232237.* One of the best places to email is the **Travellers Contact Point,** *87 Queen St, City, T3007197.* Free coffee. **Post offices** Main post office and post restante, *Wellesly St West, City. Open Mon-Fri 0730-1730, T3796714.*

Disabled facilities

Enable, *T0800-1711981, www.enable.co.nz* New Zealand Disabilities Support, *60 Cook St, T0508-787767.* Auckland Disabilities Resource Centre, *14 Erson Av, Royal Oak, T6258069, drc@disabilityresource.org.nz* Flyability Paragliding Flights, *T4438405.*

Embassies and consulates

Australia, *7th Floor, 188 Quay St, City, T9218800.* Denmark, *T5373099.* France, *Level 2, 63 Albert St, T3795850.* Germany, *6th Floor, 52 Symonds St, City, T9133674.* Ireland *Level 6, 18 Shortland St, T9772252.* Japan, *Level 12, ASB Bank Centre, 135 Albert St, City, T3034106.* Netherlands, *LJ Hooker House, Level 1, 57 Symonds St, City, T3795399.* Sweden, *13th Flr, 92-96 Albert St, City, T3735332.* UK, *NZI House,*

151 Queen St, City, T3032973. USA, *Level 3, Citibank Centre, 23 Customs St East, T3032724.*

Gay and lesbian

Gay Link travel, *177 Parnell Rd, Parnell, T3020553, www.akltravel@gaylink.co.nz* Pride Centre, *33 Wyndham St, City, T3020590, www.pride.org.nz* Express Magazine available from outlets of **Maggazzino** (see page 120).

Laundry

Clean Green Laundromat, *18 Fort St. Open Mon-Sat 0900-2000, T3584370.*

Left luggage

Sky City Bus Terminal, *Hobson St. Open daily 0700-2200.* Downtown Bus Terminal, *corner of Quay and Albert St. Open Mon-Fri 0700-1900, Sat-Sun 0700-1800.* Auckland International Airport. *Open daily 0600-2300, T2756467.*

Libraries

Central City Library, *44-46 Lorne St, City, T3770209. Open Mon-Thu 0930-2000, Fri 0930-2100, Sat 1000-1600, Sun 1300-1700.*

Medical services

Hospitals Auckland Hospital, *Park Rd, Grafton, T3794949.* Greenlane Hospital, *Greenlane Rd West, Greenlane, T6309943.*

Middlemore Hospital, *Hospital Rd, Otahuhu,* *T2760000.* North Shore Hospital, *Shakespeare Rd, Takapuna, T4868930.* Waitakere Hospital, *Lincoln Rd, Henderson, T8390000.* **Accident and medical centres** Shorecare, *209 Shakespeare Rd, Takapuna, T4867777.* Westcare, *57-75 Lincoln Rd, Henderson, T8366000.* Ponsonby Accident and Emergency, *202 Ponsonby Rd, T3765555.* White Cross St Lukes, *52 St Lukes Rd, St Lukes, T8153111.*

Police

Emergency *dial 111.* Main Police Station is at *corner Cook and Vincent St, City, T3974240/ T3024000.*

Supermarkets

New World, *2 College Hill, City (near Victoria Park on the Link bus route), Open daily until 2400.* There are Night Owl or Star 24hr grocery stores on Queen St and the waterfront.

Travel agents

Auckland Central Travel, *Corner Queen and Darby Sts, City, T3584877, F3584872, www.acb.co.nz* Open Mon-Fri 0800-1800, Sat-Sun 0800-1700. Backpacker friendly domestic adventure travel shop, free information and discounted rates on rentals, rail, coaches, ferries, tours. STA Travel, *10 High St, City, T3090458.* Thomas Cook, *159 Queen St, City, T3793924.*

Auckland Directory

North of Auckland → *Phone code: 09 Colour map 1, grid 4A*

The Kaipara Harbour with a combined coastal length that exceeds 3200 km is one of the biggest natural harbours in the world. It was of huge economic significance in the Kauri logging and export days of the mid to late 1800s with the ports of Helensville to the south and Dargaville to the north being of particular importance. Some 40 km north of the city centre (but a mere stone's throw from the northern edge of it) is the Hibiscus Coast – a coastline dominated by the 3-km beach adjacent to the main town, Orewa. Around Orewa there are the more sheltered bays of the Whangaparaoa Peninsula to the south and the Wenderholm Regional Park and Puhoi River to the north.

Ins and outs

Getting there Ritchies go from Auckland BBT, Nos 066, 067, Mon-Sat only, T09-3666400. **Stage-coach** offers a regular daily service to and from Orewa and the

Whangaparaoa Pen- insula from Auckland. By car take State Highway 16 off the Great Western Motorway in the city.

Information **Hibiscus Coast VIC**, ⓘ *on the main drag, the Hibiscus Coast Highway (HCH), adjacent to the Orewa Beach Holiday Park and next door to KFC, T09-4260076, www.orewa-beach.co.nz Mon-Sat 0900-1700, Sun 1000-1600.* Will fill you in on what local activities are available and where to stay. In summer you will struggle to find accommodation, so book ahead.

Southern Kaipara, Helensville and Parakai → *The VIC, 40 Commercial Rd, T09-4207468, www.helensville.co.nz, will help with activity and accommodation bookings.*

Looking at Helensville today, it is hard to imagine it as a buzzing port – these days it is a rather dull place, with little to attract you except perhaps a reminder of yesteryear in the **Pioneer Museum**, on Commercial Street. ⓘ *Daily, 1000-1530 or by arrangement. $3. T09-4207881.* Other than that, most sights and activities are water-based.

Nearby, **Parakai** is most famous for its hot pools at **Aquatic Park Parakai Springs**, ⓘ *150 Parkhurst Rd, T09-4208998, from $12, child $8, open daily 1000-2200.* A long soak is particularly welcome after a horse trek on the beach. ▸▸ *See Sleeping, Eating and other listings, pages127-128.*

Hibiscus Coast and the Whangaparaoa Peninsula

Whangaparaoa Peninsula At the ever-expanding northern fringe of Auckland City is the Whangaparaoa Peninsula. Bar the scenery, it is essentially a rather dull enclave for the northern Auckland suburbanites. There is little on the visitor menu here except the **Whangaparaoa Steam Railway**, ⓘ *400 Whangaparaoa Rd, Stanmore Bay, T09-4245018, www.rail.co.nz Sat-Sun, 1000-1700. $5.* There's also the **Gulf Harbour**, ⓘ *T09-4244735, www.gulf-harbour.co.nz*, with its posh waterfront marina village and golf course. During the America's Cup it was pumping, but if you have ventured this far out and left your BMW and golf clubs at home, then you would be far better off heading for the **Shakespear Regional Park**. There, beyond Gulf Harbour, you will encounter fine views, a few walks and the occasional quiet beach. Alternatively, if your timing is right, take the Fuller's ferry from the Gulf Harbour Marina to the beautiful open bird sanctuary of **Tiri tiri Matangi Island** (see page 134).

Orewa Although the coastal resort of Orewa is not essentially part of Auckland City it has, with the recent motorway connection and ever-encroaching housing developments, become a satellite town. But Orewa is still a staunchly independent community. It boasts a fine beach which lures the city slickers and visitors in increasingly healthy numbers in summer, but otherwise there is not a great deal on offer, except perhaps a coffee and snack before heading north.

Hillary Square is the focus of the town and it boasts a statue of the great man himself. Sir Edmund Hillary is New Zealand's best-known explorer and climber, the first to conquer Mount Everest.

Orewa to Warkworth At the northern end of Orewa you will pass the scenic **Red Beach** before winding your way to **Waiwera**, a small resort built around natural hot springs, where you can laze about in a purpose-built resort that has large pools, spas, and water slides for the kids, and even a separate covered pool where you can take in a movie – presumably to emerge afterwards looking like a walnut. **Waiwera Thermal Resort**. ⓘ *T09-4265369, www.waiwera.co.nz Sun-Thu, 0900-2200, Fri-Sat, 0900-2230. Adult $17, child $10, family $45.*

Just 1 km north of Waiwera is **Wenderholm Regional Park**. This is one of the region's most handsome regional parks, sited on a sand spit deposited by the Puhoi River and now grassed over and dominated by beautiful large pohutukawa trees. The beach is often wild and windswept and offers a wonderful view of the small offshore islands and the mountainous Little Barrier Island to the north. The park has some excellent walking tracks ranging from 20 minutes to 2½ hours. There is a choice of coastal walks, or the more challenging headland walks, where you may see, or hear, the fluid song of the tui and clattering wings of the keruru or native pigeon. If history is your preference, the park's administration block is dominated by the old 1860s colonial homestead **Couldrey House**. ① *T09-5283713. Sat-Sun 1300-1600. The No 895 bus terminates here on summer Suns.*

Puhoi The small and picturesque village of Puhoi is just off State Highway 1, 5 km north of Wenderholm. It has an intriguing history as a Catholic Bohemian settlement established in 1863. Although most of the memories are focused in the **Puhoi Historical Society Museum** ① *in the former convent school, Dec-Apr 1300-1600; Apr-Dec Sat, Sun and public holidays 1300-1530; donation*, much of the story is evident in the historic **Puhoi Tavern**. It is a fascinating little pub full of historic clutter and characters. Provided no one is playing pool you can read all about the early settlers and sympathize with their desperate cause. It is a depressing and unhappy story of a seemingly never-ending struggle with the land, hunger and desperation. Despite the awful stories the pub is very appealing and on the second Friday of each month a local Bohemian band play their toe-tapping tunes. On a fine summer Sunday afternoon the river can be a fine place to be, as you gently wind your way downstream to Wenderholm Regional Park in a canoe or Canadian kayak. ▸▸ *See Activities, page 128.*

● Sleeping

Helensville and Parakai *p126*

A **Kaipara House B&B**, *corner of SH16 and Parkhurst Rd, Helensville, T09-4207462, kaiparah@ihug.co.nz* Offers 3 spacious rooms with thermal baths, and a self-contained summerhouse.

A **Malolo House**, *110 Commercial Rd, Helensville, T09-4207262, malolo@xtra.co.nz* Comfortable old villa-style B&B and backpacker accommodation.

C-D **Point of View**, *T09-4207331, Te Makiri, Helensville, http://homepages.ihug.co.nz/ ~howe/* A pleasant and alternative backpacker farmstay.

Campsites
Parakai Hot Pools, *Parkhurst Rd, Parakai, T09-4208998*. Caravan and campsites and standard facilities.

Hibiscus Coast and Whangaparaoa Peninsula *p126*

LL **The Gulf Harbour Lodge**, *164 Harbour Village Dr, Gulf Harbour, Whangaparaoa Peninsula, T07-4281118, ghlodge@gulf-harbour.co.nz* The main luxury option in the area. Cheaper weekend rates.

L-AL **Moontide Lodge**, *19 Ocean View Rd, Hatfields Beach, T4262374,*

moontde@nznet.gen.nz An excellent B&B choice set on the cliffs above Hatfields Beach north of Orewa. It offers beautifully-appointed rooms with great views and decks. Fine breakfasts, dinner on request. German and French spoken.

Motels dominate the northern end of Orewa and almost all of them can be found on either side of the main drag – the Hibiscus Coast Highway (HCH):

A **Anchor Lodge Motel**, *436, T09-4263410;*
A **Beachcomber Motel**, *246, T09-4265973;*
A **Edgewater Motel**, *387, T09-4265260;*
A **Hibiscus Palms Motel**, *416, T09-4264904.*
A **Coach Trail Lodge**, *Waiwera, T09-4264792*, Offers comfortable accommodation within walking distance of the hot pools, should you need to hang yourself out to dry overnight in Waiwera.

C-D **Marco Polo Tourist Lodge**, *2D Hammond Av, Hatfields Beach, Orewa, T09-4268455, marcopolo_bp@clear.net.nz*, Comfortable backpackers with its palm tree-painted bedroom walls.

C-D **Pillows Travellers' Lodge**, *412 HCH, Orewa, T09-4266338, pillows.lodge@xtra.co.nz*

Motorcamps
The 2 main motor parks in Orewa are the **Orewa Beach Holiday Park**, *265 Hibiscus*

Puriri Park Holiday Camp, *Puriri Av,*
T09-4264648.

❶ Eating

Helensville and Parakai *p126*
$$ **McNutts Farm and Café**, *11km north of*
Parakai, 914 South Head Rd, South Head,
T09-4202853, www.macnut.co.nz A good
alternative in unison with a macadamia
nut orchard tour ($3). Both congenial
and friendly.
$$ **Upper Crust Café**, *46 Commercial Rd,*
Helenville, T09-4208615. Open daily.

Hibiscus Coast and Whangaparaoa
Peninsula *p126*
There are numerous small cafés and
takeaways in Orewa, including:
$$ **The Plantation Café**, *226 HCH, right on*
the waterfront at the southern end of
Orewa, T09-4265083, open Sun-Thu
0700-2100, Fri/Sat 0700-2200. Offers
quality, convenience and a hearty all-day
breakfast.
$$ **Walnut Cottage Café** *Orewa House, 498*
Hibiscus Coast Highway. BYO and licensed.
T09-4275570. Mon-Thu 0930-1630, Fri- Sun
*0930-1800.*Set in some very congenial
grounds.

▲ Activities

Helensville and Parakai *p126*
Several tours leave from Helensville to link
up with others in Dargaville, see p201.
Kaipara Fishing Charters, *T0800-000070,*
bookings@kaiparafishing.co.nz
Kaipara Tours, *T09-4208466.* Have a great
range of options, from 3 hours to 2 days.
South Kaipara Horse Treks, *T09-4202835,*
www.horserides.co.nz
Tasman Rides, *T09-4208603,*
www.tasmanrides.co.nz

Whangaparaoa Peninsula *p126*
Coast Dive Centre, *673 Whangaparaoa Rd,*
T09-4248513. Offers a range of dive trips.
Hibiscus Coast Leisure Centre, *159*
Brightside Rd, Stanmore Bay, T09-4241914.
Serious Fishing Company, *985*
Whangaparaoa Rd, T09-4240588.

Puhoi *p127*
Puhoi River Canoe Hire, *84 Puhoi Valley Rd,*
T09-4220891. $30 for the full river adventure
or $15 per hour.

❷ Transport

Rideline, *T09-3666400.*
Orewa Cycle Works, *12 Bakehouse Lane,*
Orewa, T09-4266958.

West of Auckland → *Phone code: 09 Colour map 2, grid A1*

From the centre of the city the Great Western Motorway straddles the inner inlets of the
Waitemata Harbour before taking you to the western suburbs of Auckland. From these
western fringes of the city the Waitakere Ranges rise to form a huge area of bush with
an extensive network of walking tracks. These seemingly endless hills then eventually
reach the sea and the wild west coast beaches that offer a huge contrast to the quiet
Pacific beaches of the Hauraki Gulf.

Ins and outs
Getting there The Waitakeres, beyond Titirangi to the south and Swanson to the
north and especially the West Coast beaches, are not at all well served by public
transport. The **TranzMetro** train does have a service from the city station to Henderson
and Waitakere, and with a hire bike this could be a workable option. Other than that,
organized tours and car hire are your only option. There is no public transport out to
Whatipu. Those without a car will have to hire their own, or a bike from the city. By bike
you can take your time stopping in Titirangi village before heading out the 27 km to the
point and Whatipu. There is no public transport to Karekare. By car, from the
information centre at Arataki, head north along Scenic Drive before turning left down

Piha Road. 1 km before the road falls down the hill to Piha turn left down Karekare Road. There is no public transport to Piha. **Piha Surf Shuttles** can be of assistance, mainly for groups, T09-6272644. By car it is easily accessible from the Arataki Information Centre on Scenic Drive. For Muriwai take Helensville (**Ritchies**) buses Nos 069 and 067 to Waimauku and flag down a car from there. By car go via State Highway 16, heading north from the Great Western Motorway in the city. Tour operator **Bush and Beach** include Muriwai, T09-5751458, see Auckland Tours page 122.

Waitakere City

West Auckland has a diverse type of suburb that makes up Waitakere City. Te Atatu, Swanson, Henderson, New Lynn and Glendene are relatively low-income areas of little note, except for being home to the 'Westie', a peculiar type of Aucklander who dresses predominantly in black, loves rock 'n' roll, does not believe in hair salons, and simply loves anything on wheels that goes fast, burns rubber and makes lots of noise. The Great Western Motorway pays homage to this almost nightly, with nearly every dawn presenting a trail of abandoned vehicles that never made it home. Further west and south is Titirangi where, on the slopes of the ranges around **Scenic Drive**, the more well-to-do citizens enjoy their secluded, often beautiful bush dwellings, with wonderful views across the city. **Titirangi**, 'the gateway to the Waitakeres', is a very pleasant little village that is worth a visit in itself, with a number of nice cafés, interesting shops and a good art gallery, **Lopdell House**, ① *on the corner of Titirangi and South Titirangi Roads, T09-8178087, www.lopdell.org.nz Daily 1000-1630. Free.* Over all, Waitakere City is most famous for its liberal attitudes, art, vineyards and orchards and its spectacularly wild unspoilt bush and beaches. It has, as a result, proclaimed itself Auckland's Eco–City with the **Kumeu** area being known as the 'Gannet and Grape district'.

The Waitakeres

The 'Waitaks', as they are affectionately known, are one of the region's biggest and most attractive regional parks, offering a 200-km network of walking tracks, many of which hide such scenic delights as large *kauri* trees, waterfalls and large dams. Before embarking on any activities in the area, visit the **Arataki Information Centre**, ①*perched on the hill at the southern end of Scenic Dr, 6 km from Titirangi, T09-3031530, www.waitakerenz.co.nz Daily 0900-1700 (1600 in winter).* It is a newly-renovated centre that provides a vast amount of information, interesting interpretative displays, an audio visual display, nature trail, education centre and, dominating the scene, an impressive Maori *pou* (carving), which lost its rather impressive 'manhood' a few years ago, though another was duly carved, and the glint in his little paua shell eye restored. From here make sure you take detailed advice on all the **walks** in the Waitakeres that you wish to try, and buy the relevant maps. The Waitakeres have seen their fair share of lost trampers over the years. Don't forget to pick up the *Welcome Out West, Art Out West, Artists' and Artisans' Trail* and *Accommodation Out West* leaflets, as well as numerous walking maps and options from the centre, all free.

Sights The 28-km **Scenic Drive** is the best way to get an immediate impression of the area as it winds along the eastern fringe of the Waitakeres, offering stunning views across the city both by day and by night. One of the best views can be seen from the garden of **Hellaby House**, ① *515 Scenic Dr, T09-8149205, gardens daily 0900-1800, house Sat, 1300-1600, Sun, 1100-1700, free,* just below the TV masts. Its elderly owner, Rose, who loved the Waitakeres with a passion, donated Hellaby House to the city, and given the view from her backyard this is not surprising.

West Auckland is one of the best-known wine-producing areas of the country, containing nearly 20 **wineries** with such famous names as Corbans, Coopers Creek, Matua Valley, Nobilo and Babich. The northern areas of Waitakere City host most of these, especially in the Kumeu area. Most wineries offer tours and tastings. **Corbans,**

426 Great North Rd, T09-8384455, being the largest and most accommodating for visitors with the added attraction of art studios and galleries. The newest vineyard **Soljans**, State Highway 16, Kumeu, T09-4125858, www.soljans.co.nz, is also recommended. Shop and café, tours daily at 1130 and 1430, $10. **NZWinePro**, T09-8141112, www.nzwinepro.co.nz, offers one of the best wine tour packages available, as do **Auckland Wine Tasting Tours**, T09-6301540, costing from $85. Copies of the official 'Wine Trail' and *Wineries of Auckland* leaflets can be found at the **Kumeu and District VIC**, ① *Main Rd, T09-4129886*, and main city VICs.

One of the newest and most unusual attractions in the area is the **Watercare Rain Forest Express**, ① *To800-697-246, rainforest@water.co.nz, $20 (Twilight $24), child $10/$12, Bookings essential*, a fascinating and fun trip on the small gauge railway train that still plies the numerous lines and tunnels to service and maintain the local dams. Regular scheduled trips on Sunday 1400 and 'glow-worm special' 1800 (summer only).
▸▸ *See Activities, page 132.*

The Wild West Coast Beaches → *Phone code: 09*

Whatipu
If you are looking for solitude and a real sense of wilderness, without doubt one of the best places to go in the region is Whatipu. Situated 45 km from the city centre, at the southernmost tip of the Waitakere ranges, its huge expanse of sand in part forms the narrow mouth of the **Manukau Harbour**. At the terminus of the winding, unsealed road, past the picturesque little settlements of **Huia** and **Little Huia**, is a small cluster of buildings that make up Whatipu Lodge. The lodge is the last sign of habitation and chance of accommodation before you head north along the 6 km-long beach that stretches all the way to Karekare. If you can pull yourself away from the sound of the surf, head inland across the 700 acres of sand dune and wetland. Hidden in the undulations of dune grasses and cabbage trees are extensive wetlands that are home to noisy paradise shelduck, delicate pied stilts and elegant black swans. At the foot of the bush-clad hills are the remains of the **Parahara Railway** that once hauled huge kauri from Karekare in the 1870s. A boiler and a small tunnel still remain, even though the tracks have long been swallowed by the sand.

If you are on foot you can head north to Piha. Just before the road falls down the hill to Whatipu, take the Donald McLean Road up to the summit of **Mount Donald McLean**. The summit itself is a short 10-minute walk from the road end, and the view across the Waitakeres, the harbour and back across to the tiny Sky Tower is magnificent.
▸▸ *See Sleeping, page 131.*

Karekare → *If you want to swim at Karekare take great care and stay between the flags.*
Like most of the West Coast beaches, the bush-clad hills of the Waitakeres fall dramatically into the sea and form a natural amphitheatre of vegetation and cliff, with the beach as its stage, the wind its song and the surf its applause.

There are a number of short walks and tracks around Karekare, some of which head inland or south to join the extensive Waitakere network. For long inland excursions, make sure you carry a map and supplies. The short walk up the Taraire Track to **Karekare Falls** is worthwhile, especially if you intend to swim in the pool beneath it. Another is the **Colman's Track** from the end of Watchmans Road, where the path creeps up the hill at the northern point of Karekare beach and terminates with a magnificent view. Looking south you can see well past Karekare beach to the huge expanse of Whatipu beach beyond, as well as the tiny, inaccessible Mercer Bay,

● *Karekare beach is now most famous for the fact that the opening scenes of the 1993 film*
● The Piano *were filmed there*

immediately below and north. If you are feeling energetic, keep going along the track which follows the coast to meet Te Ahahu Road eventually, at Piha.

Piha

It is very hard to spend the day at Piha beach without contemplating packing it all in to live here. Piha has been luring dreamers and surfers for years and is, along with Muriwai, one of the West Coast's most popular beaches. And as you climb down the windy road you will quickly realize that, for a few lucky souls, the dream has become reality. Although it can be very busy in summer, it still retains a distinctly isolated charm perhaps due to the lack of public transport. After you are fed up with sunbathing, swimming or trying to hold on to your surfboard in the fierce surf, there are two things you must do. The first and most obvious is to climb **Lion Rock** (a strenuous 30 minutes), the guardian of the beach that looks with menace out to the ocean. From the summit you can look down on the **surfers** bobbing about in search of the perfect wave. The other thing to do, especially in a wild winter storm or at sunset, is to take the **Tasman Lookout Track** at the south end of the beach to **The Gap**. Here you can sit and watch in awe at the power of the breakers as they pound and crash into the narrow gap.

There is also an interesting, if less dramatic, walk at the northern end of Piha Beach, which leads to the isolated and beautiful **White's Beach**. If you have time, also try to see the **Kitekite Falls** from the Kitekite Track down Glen Esk Road behind the main camping ground. If you swim at Piha you can do so in relative safety, but always stay between the flags and in sight of the lifesavers. Piha has been the watery grave for many shore fishermen and uninitiated swimmers. If you get into trouble, raise an arm and keep it aloft – you will be in an inflatable rescue boat before you know it.

▶▶ *See Sleeping and Eating, page 132.*

Muriwai

Muriwai, 15 km north of Piha and 45 km west of the city centre, is the West Coast's most visited beach. On summer weekends it plays host to locals and visitors alike, who nestle down in the black sands to soak up the sun, surf, fish, play, or look over the **gannet colony**. These angry-looking birds have taken up residence on the flat rock outcrops at its southern end to breed, forming a small seabird city. It is a delight in spring, when you can witness at close range the stomachs of the fluffy white chicks being kept full by the comings and goings of their bad-tempered parents. Muriwai boasts the only major north island colony, after Cape Kidnappers on the East Coast, near Napier.

Muriwai itself is well-serviced for locals and tourists and boasts a fine golf course (T09-4118454). If Muriwai beach is too busy for you then try **Maori Bay**, another favourite surf spot just south of Muriwai, reached via Waitea Road. If you find the huge stretch of beach heading north a bit daunting, a good way to venture up it and explore the surrounding bush is on horseback (try **Muriwai Beach Homestay and Horse Riding**, see below). ▶▶ *See Sleeping and Eating, below.*

● Sleeping and eating

For local B&B and Farmstay options contact the Arataki Information Centre, T09-3031530, or consult the free *Staying Out West* leaflet available from all VICs.

Whatipu *p130*

B-D **Whatipu Lodge**, *T09-8118860*. Book a cabin or a tent site which will give you plenty of time to explore the area before heading back to the city the next day.

● *For an explanation of the sleeping and eating price codes used in this guide, see the inside*
● *front cover. Other relevant information is provided in the Essentials chapter, see page 51.*

AL **Piha Lodge**, *117 Piha Rd, T09-8128595, www.pihalodge.co.nz* Award winner with two self-contained units. Large pool and spa.
A **Piha Cottage**, *T/F09-8128514, www.pihacottage.co.nz* A secluded self-contained cottage in quiet bush surroundings.

Motorcamps

Piha Domain Motor Camp, *T09-8128815*. In the heart of the village, tent sites and on-site vans. Bookings advisable.

Muriwai *p131*

There are a number of B&Bs and farmstays in Muriwai.
L-AL Skovholm Country Lodge, *Hinau Rd, Waimauku, T09-4118326, www.skovholm.co.nz* Very comfortable, runby a friendly Danish couple. Close to the city.
AL **Coastal Hideaway**, *459 Oaia Rd, T09-4118392, www.coastalhideaway.com* A delightful self-contained cottage sleeping 2-10. The kind of place you want to return to again and again. Quite secluded in a prime cliff-top position.
B **Muriwai Beach Homestay and Horse Riding**, *781 Muriwai Rd, T09-4117111, www.farmstayauckland.co.nz* Offers the choice of queen, twin or single in a country setting only 2km from the beach. Base for horse trekking – 2 hrs will cost about $55.

Motorcamps

Muriwai Beach Motor Camp, *T09-4119262*.

● Eating

Piha *p131*
RSA, *T09-8128138*, across the river from the motorcamp, and the **Surf Club**, *23 Marine Pde, T09-8128896*, at the southern end of the beach, offers great value meals, but you will have to ask a member to sign you in. *Opening times vary.*
Other than that there are the usual sad-looking pies to be had at the general store near the motorcamp, or burgers and the ubiquitous fish and chips at the burger bar, next to the Surf Club (summer only).

Muriwai *p131*
The Waterfront general store serves light meals and refreshments.
For a more upmarket option try the **Hunting Lodge**, *Waikoukou Valley Rd, T09-4118259, www.thehuntinglodge.co.nz, open for lunch and dinner Wed-Sun.*

▲ Activities

The Waitakeres *p129*
Bush and Beach, *T09-5751458/ T0800-423224, www.bushandbeach.co.nz* An excellent company that opens up the Waitakeres and West Coast beaches to those visitors without their own transport.It offers a wide range of exciting activities and options, both half-day 1230-1700,75, and full-day 0930-1700, $120 and a 2-day trip including accommodation and tour from $185pp double or $295 single.
Action Kiwi, *T09-5247109, www.actionkiwi.co.nz* Offers similar trips.

South of Auckland → *Phone code: 09 Colour map 2, grid B1*

Once you leave the city southbound through the **Manukau City** and **Franklin Districts** there is little to lure you off State Highway 1, which climbs over the Bombay Hills then falls to meet the Waikato River towards Hamilton. However, if you have ample time and are interested in exploring the **Franklin District**, let the folks at the **Franklin VIC**, ① *Mill Rd, Bombay, T09-2360670, tourism.franklin@extra.co.nz*, persuade you to do so.

If you are heading to the Coromandel Peninsula then the best way is to follow the **Pacific Coast Highway** via **Howick** and **Whitford**. The route is generally well marked (with the Pacific Coast Highway logo) and has a number of interesting stops on the way. Just before you hit the coast proper you pass the **Omana Regional Park**. This small park offers outstanding views of the Gulf across to Waiheke and a pleasant beach with a rock platform that provides safe and shallow swimming at high **133** tide and is ideal for kids.

Further south and inland again, is the farming town of **Clevedon**, home to Auckland's Polo Club, T09-2928556, who have games on Sundays in the summer. There are also a number of cafés in which to grab a cup of tea and contemplate a trip to **Montgomerie Farm**, Pioneer Rd, T09-2928724. Here they offer a traditional farm show with a demonstration of sheep-shearing (1100 and 1430), and in spring, lamb-feeding for the kids. Horse trekking is also available. South of Clevedon (but a diversion off the Pacific Coast Highway) is **Hunua**, on the edge of the **Hunua Ranges Regional Park**. These bush-clad ranges contain the watersheds for a number of dams that supply Auckland with most of its water. Although the park and the ranges are not in the same league as the Waitakeres west of Auckland, there are a number of interesting walks – the best of which is an all-day hike that takes in the Wairoa River, Cossey's Dam and the 30-m **Hunua Falls**. For information visit the **Hunua Ranges Park Visitor Centre**, ⓘ *in Hunua, T09-3031530, daily 0800-1630*, or the **Clevedon Information Centre**, ⓘ *9 North Rd, Clevedon, T09-2928660*.

Back on the Pacific Coast Highway east of Clevedon you will hit the coast again. It is a very pleasant drive framed by pohutukawa trees and an area famous for its bird life. Christened the **Seabird Coast**, it is well worth stopping at the **Miranda Shorebird Centre**, ⓘ *Pokeno, T/F2322781, open daily, 0900-1700*, home of the Miranda Naturalists' Trust. The Firth of Thames offers an internationally important habitat and stopover point for thousands of migrating wading birds. The 'target' birds at Miranda (for study not shooting) are the native wrybill – a strange little wader with a crooked beak designed for specialist feeding – and the rare New Zealand dotterel. Both join the near 60 other transitory species that stop over for a short time in spring and autumn to refuel for migration. The godwit, a medium-sized wader that breeds in Alaska, makes the journey to spend the Southern Hemisphere winter in New Zealand. Recent studies suggest that they do this journey non-stop, in a week! They fly at 4,000-6,000 m and reach speeds of 60-70 km per hour. Just a few kilometres south of the Shorebird Centre are the **Miranda Hot Pools and Holiday Park**. ⓘ *T0800-468777, www.mirandahotsprings.co.nz Mon-Thu 0800-2100, Fri-Sun 0800-2230 all year. Adult $7, child $4*. Private spas also available, temperatures up to 40C.

● Sleeping

L **The Inverness Estate**, *Ness Valley Rd, Clevedon, T09-2928710, www.inverness.co.nz* Luxury accommodation in a country setting with fine food and its own estate wine.
A **Miranda B&B**, *Findlay Rd, Miranda, T09-2327735*. Country home in a garden setting. Dinner on request.
A **The Miranda Holiday Park**, *595 Front Miranda Rd, T09-8673205, mirandaholidaypark@extra.co.nz* A fine holiday park with wonderful facilities including its own hot pools. Recommended.

C-D The **Miranda Shorebird Centre**
T09-2322781. Bunk, single/double room and self-contained accommodation is available from $10 to $35. Great value, offers a fine roost if you are looking for accommodatio.

Campsites
Omana Regional Park, *T09-3031530*.

● Eating

$ **Kaiaua Fishery**, *T09-2322779*. Fish and chip shop in Kaiaua, north of Miranda, has a great reputation, and the
$ **Bay View Hotel**, *Kaiaua, T09-2322717. Daily, Sun from 1700*. offers takeaways and snacks as well as a restaurant serving mainly seafood.

Auckland South of Auckland

Hauraki islands → *Phone code: 09 Colour map 2, grid A2*

Ins and outs

Getting there Fullers,To9-3679111, www.fullers.co.nz, ferries from the Ferry Building on Quay St depart daily for Rangitoto at 0900, 1100, 1300 and 1500 adult $20, child $10. Fullers also offer a ferry/tour package with the 'Rangitoto Explorer' – a carriage pulled by a tractor that winds its way around the island, with an interesting commentary and regular photo stops: adult $45, child $25. Bookings essential for all trips. In the winter phone before departure. Be sure to take plenty of water, sun block and a hat – the black scoria can emanate terrific heat. To Tiri tiri Matangi, Fullers run a service to and from Auckland from Pier 3 (adjacent to the Ferry Building) on Thu, Fri, Sat and Sun at 0900; or the same ferry from Z Pier, Gulf Harbour on the Whangaparoa Peninsula, 45 mins later. Trips return by 1645. From Auckland; adult $45, child $23. From Gulf Harbour; adult $25, child $15. Fullers also run a ferry to Motuihe on Sat and Sun in conjunction with the Rangitoto ferry. Additional summer sailings are also available: adult $20, child $10.

Rangitoto Island → *There is a small shop on the island that is open in summer, but you are advised to take your own picnic.*

Rangitoto seems to dominate your views of the Hauraki Gulf from almost every vantage point in the city, so it is only a matter of time before its classically shaped cone lures you across the water to take a closer look. Rangitoto first emerged from the sea in a series of eruptions about 600 years ago, when Maori were known to be inhabiting the area.One Maori myth suggests that the eruption occurred after a casual dispute between the gods of fire and volcanoes, but many years later science put it all down to being the latest of the many eruptions to take place in the area over the millennia. It is only a 30-minute journey by ferry to take a closer look, and to enjoy one of the island's many walks.

Most of these walks culminate at the **summit** from where there is a 360° view of the gulf and the city and you can peer down into its bush-clad crater. The vegetation of the island is of international importance with the recent botanical blanket boasting 200 species of native tree (the most prolific and famous being its pohutukawa) and flowering plants, 40 kinds of fern, some orchids and, of course, many lichens. All this is interspersed with the ankle-breaking mounds of loose laval scoria.

There are a number of **walking** options on the island, all neatly presented in an essential piece of kit – DoC's guide to the island – available from the DoC office in the Ferry Building. If you have plenty of time and want to get away from the crowds that immediately make for the summit (two hours), follow the tracks from the wharf to the summit via McKenzie Bay. It can take six hours but gives you a great feel for the island and its plant life, and provides great sea-level views.

Motutapu Island – the contrasting island connected to Rangitoto by a short causeway – has a few interesting Maori archaeological sites but is best visited as part of the extensive winter replanting programmes that are taking place in conjunction with DoC. As you can see from Rangitoto, Motutapu needs it!

Tiri tiri Matangi → *If you want to join the 'Supporters of Tiri tiri Matangi' and be a part of the island's future and further development, ask on the island or T09-4794490.*

Even if you are not particularly interested in wildlife 'Tiri' (as it is affectionately known) is well worth a visit. This jewel in the Hauraki is one of the few 'open bird sanctuaries' in New Zealand and has become an internationally famous conservation success story. Situated 4 km off the Whangaparaoa Peninsula, north of the city centre, the 220-ha island was originally leased for farming from 1855 to 1971, during which time

the native forest was reduced to 6% of its former glory. Thankfully, the island was
recognized by The New Zealand Wildlife Service (now DoC) as having great potential
as a **wildlife sanctuary**. A nursery was set up in 1983 and from 1984 volunteers from
all walks of life became involved in planting over 250,000 trees and shrubs, and the
island is now 70% revegetated. A vital poison drop rid the island of rats making it
predator free and ready for the arrival of most of its current avian residents. Now Tiri
has become the safe haven for numerous rare and endangered species including the
famous takahe, little spotted kiwi, kokako, whitehead, saddleback, North Island
robin, kakariki, stitchbird and brown teal. Being an open sanctuary, members of the
public can visit and experience what New Zealand used to be like, with the bush alive
with the sound of birdsong. The takahe – those big friendly purple chickens with red
beaks – are perhaps the most famous of its current tenants. These amazing, almost
prehistoric birds, were thought to be extinct until a small group was rediscovered in
the wild Fiordlands of South Island. Since then a successful breeding programme has
increased numbers and, given there are only about 200 of these birds left in the
world, seeing them is an unforgettable experience.

The island has a numerous and varied network of **walks** on which you are almost
certain to 'encounter' takahe and spot many of the other species. The coastal scenery
and sea views are also magnificent. Do not miss the little blue penguin boxes near the
wharf (ask) or the 'Wattle Track'. Kiwi are nocturnal birds, so don't expect to see one
unless you stay at the **bunkhouse** overnight. Ray and Barbara are excellent hosts, as
are the volunteer guides who formed the highly committed and professional outfit
called the **Supporters of Tiri Tiri Matangi**. For details of volunteer work, T09-4794490.
Book well in advance. A guided tour of the island costs $6 extra. There is a souvenir
shop on the island but it does not sell food so take a packed lunch. Coffee and snacks
are available on the ferry, and free coffee and tea is available at the shop on the island.

Other islands in the Hauraki

Motuihe

This small unusually-shaped island of 179 ha lies between Motutapu and Waiheke.
There is archaeological evidence that suggests the island was inhabited and used
extensively by Maori before it was purchased and farmed by European pioneer W H
Fairburn in 1839. Ownership changed hands again a few times before it was finally
bought by the Crown in 1872 and used as a quarantine station. This station would be
used as a prisoner of war camp in the First World War (prisoners included the
infamous German Captain Felix von Lucker), an emergency hospital during the
influenza epidemic in 1918, and a naval training base in the Second World War. In
1967, when the Hauraki Gulf Marine Park was established, the island came under the
control of the Auckland City Council. Today, although the island is still farmed and is a
DoC reserve, it is essentially a recreation venue, popular for swimming, fishing and
escaping the city. A number of walks from 30 minutes to three hours are available,
taking in a number of geological formations, archaeological sites, and the graves of
those who died during the influenza epidemic. ▸▸ *See Sleeping p136.*

Little Barrier Island → *The island can only be visited with permission from DoC, T09-*
3662166. They run a volunteer programme and accommodation is provided, but the waiting list is huge.

On a clear day it is just possible to see the mountainous bush-clad peaks that
make up Little Barrier Island from the city. Little Barrier lies 90 km north of Auckland
and 18 km west of her big sister, Great Barrier. This island is a plant and wildlife

● *The original Maori name, Hauturu, means 'resting place of the winds'.*

reserve of international value and significance. Being predator-free, it is sanctuary to a host of native birdlife, such as black petrel, cooks petrel and brown teal (all endangered). Other unusual inhabitants include the tuatara (a prehistoric native reptile), rare skinks and New Zealand's only bat (and native mammal) – the short-tailed bat. There are also 350 species of native plant on the island. But perhaps the most famous inhabitants are the kakapo. These flightless heavyweights (up to 3½ kg) are the rarest parrot, and one of the most endangered birds, in the world. At present only 62 known individuals remain in captivity or on protected off-shore islands around New Zealand.

● Sleeping

Motuihe
There is a holiday home ($12 per person, $60

minimum), bunkhouse ($7) and camping ($4) available on the island. *T09-5348095*. In summer a small kiosk on the island sells basic snacks and refreshments.

Waiheke Island → *Phone code: 09 Colour map 2, grid A2*

At 93 sq km, Waiheke is the largest island in the gulf and, only 20 km (a 35-minute ferry ride) from the city, it is also the most visited and heavily populated. It has plenty of beaches, activities, easy access, fine restaurants and accommodation, but if you are looking for a real 'island experience' then you are far better going to Great Barrier.

Ins and outs
Getting there Air Waiheke Air Services, T09-3725000, www.waihekeair.co.nz, fly twice daily for $65 return. Scenic flights are also available from $25 (minimum 2). The airport is 3 km east of Ostend and can be reached by local taxi (T09-3728038), or bus (T09-3728823).

Ferry (Passenger only) **Fullers**, T09-3679119, offer a regular (passenger only) service from the Auckland Ferry Building every 2 hrs Mon-Fri from 0530-2330, Sat 0630-2330, Sun 0700-2130; adult $24, child $12. There is also a service from Half Moon Bay in the eastern suburbs. Fullers offer a number of tour packages (see below). **Pine Harbour Ferries**, T09-5365157, www.pineharbour.co.nz, run a fast (20-min) regular passenger service daily from the Beachlands Marina, from $20, child $12 with onward services to Downtown (20 min), from $13, child $7. Passenger and vehicular ferries are also run by **Subritzky Shipping**, T09-5345663. www.subritzky.co.nz, a less salubrious service 6-8 times daily from Half Moon Bay to Kennedy's Point, from 0600, $106 family car and driver, extra passengers $24. Bookings essential. **Pacific Ferries** also offer a new vehicular ferry from Half Moon Bay to Kennedy Point, T3721234.

Getting around Waiheke Bus Service, T09-3728823, offers a 4-route service to and from the main Matiatia wharf and connect with all ferries. Route 1 runs a regular service to and from Onetangi taking in Oneroa, Blackpool, Surfdale and Ostend. Route 2 goes from the wharf to Oneroa, Little Oneroa, Hauraki Store, Palm Beach and Ostend to Rocky Bay and back. Route 3 from the wharf to Oneroa, Blackpool, Surfdale, Hauraki store, Palm Beach, Ostend, Onetangi to Rocky Bay and back. Route 4 to Oneroa, Surfdale, Ostend to Onetangi and back. Tickets and $10 day passes available on the bus. 'Bus and Boat' specials are often available (see Ferries above).

Orientation and information The main village and focus of attention on Waiheke is **Oneroa** at the western end of the island, just a short walk from the **Matiatia Wharf**. From Oneroa east, the settlements generally fade after **Palm Beach** and **Onetangi**,

until the occasional holiday home and residential property gives way to farmland.
Waiheke VIC,① *Korora Rd, in front of the Artworks Complex, in Oneroa, T09-3721234, www.waihekenz.com and www.tourismwaiheke.co.nz Daily 0900-1700, winter 1600.* Other than the necessary island map ($1), publications to look out for are the *Gulf News* $1.50 (Thu), the free *Gulf Islander*, the *Waiheke Marketplace*, the annual *Island Time – A Visitors Guide to Waiheke*. For walks ask for the comprehensive *Waiheke Island Walkways* and for vineyard details, the *Waiheke Island of Wine*. There is also a **left luggage** service available ($2).

History

Waiheke was first settled by the Maori in 1200 AD and over the centuries tribes settled or were ousted by others, with the last bloody invasion coming from the notorious Bay of Islands-based Hongi Hika in the 1820s. European settlement began shortly after missionary Samuel Marsden established a mission near Matiatia in 1818. Sadly, like the rest of the region, Waiheke was cleared of its kauri by the first European settlers before livestock were introduced to create the bare rolling hills we see today. As the population of Auckland steadily grew so did the island's popularity as a holiday destination and by the 1960s clusters of bachs (Kiwi beach holiday homes) were joined by an increasing number of permanents who were looking for that quiet 'alternative' lifestyle. So much so that the island was cruelly called 'Cadbury Island' (after the chocolate bars) – because you had to be either a 'fruit' or a 'nut' to live there!

Oneroa

Near the wharf and sandwiched between the popular Oneroa Bay and Blackpool beaches is the main settlement of Oneroa – a well-known creative haunt. Waiheke has been home to arty types for years and boasts some well-known **artists, poets and writers**, including the internationally renowned Zinni Douglas, Barbara Bailey and ceramist Hilary Kerrod. The VIC can provide more information about open studios and art outlets.

Situated just behind the VIC, the Artworks Complex is a small conglomerate with a cinema, a library, restaurant and the **Whittakers Musical Museum,** ① *T09-3725573, www.musical-museum.org, closed Tue and Fri, casual entry $3; entry and performance $10, child $5,* which displays over 100 musical instruments dating back 500 years, and which has live performances at 1300.

Within a few kilometres of Oneroa are two fine examples of Waiheke's other claim to fame – vineyards. The **Peninsula Estate,** ① *52a Korora Rd, T09-3727866, www.peninsulaestate.co.nz,* offers free tastings and tour by arrangement. The **Mudbrick Vineyard,** ① *2 km west of Oneroa on Church Bay Road, is open daily in summer.* See also Eating, page 141.▸▸ *See Sleeping, Eating and other listings, pages 140-142.*

Beyond Oneroa

Within walking distance east of Oneroa along **Oneroa Bay** and up through the pleasant reserves and back roads is the next 'scommunity', **Palm Beach** (two hours), with its small collection of houses and lovely sandy beach, with a secluded spot for naturists. There is also a General Store that offers bike, boogie board and snorkelling gear hire (from $15 a day). From Palm Beach it is about 3 km to **Onetangi**, site of Waiheke's longest and perhaps most popular beach. The Onetangi Beach Store hires out equipment for watersports from $10 a day. The **Waiheke Island Historic Village and Museum,** ①*165 Onetangi Rd, T09-3729787, Mon, Wed, Sat, Sun (daily on school holidays) 1200-1600, free,* is overlooked by a 700-year-old Maori *Pa* and has cottages and a small museum exhibiting collections of farm machines, engines and assorted bric-a-brac. Also close by on Waiheke Road is the Forest and Bird Society's **Nature Reserve** which may, if you are lucky, produce the odd tui or native pigeon amidst its native tree plantations. South of Onetangi is The **Te Whau Vineyard,** ① *218 Te Whau*

Dr, Rocky Bay, T09-3727191, www.tewhau.com One of the newest on the island and noted not only for its fine labels but also superb views and a classy café. East of Onetangi, the habitation diminishes and farmland, the odd vineyard and secluded bay takes over. If you have time the **Stony Batter Reserve**, on the islands north east headland, is worth a visit (1½-hour walk from the delightful **Cactus Bay**). It consists of an underground complex linked by a series of tunnels which, like others in Auckland, were built in the Second World War in fear of foreign invasion.

Although their reign is now threatened, traditionally the two most famous vineyards on Waiheke are the **Goldwater Estate**, ⓘ *18 Causeway Rd (visits by appointment; T09-3727493, www.goldwaterwine.com)* and **Stonyridge Vineyard**, ⓘ *80 Onetangi Rd, T09-3728822, www.stonyridge.co.nz, tastings daily 0900-1700, tours weekends at 1130.* There is also a fine café (times vary), which produces one of the

Waiheke Island

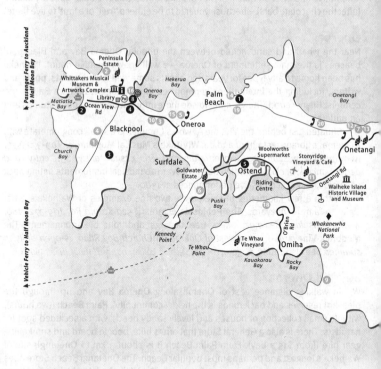

0 km 1
0 miles 1
N

world's most sought-after Cabernets-Larose. You can see these and the other **139**
vineyards on the island on an organized tour (see page 142).

South of Oneroa are the scattered settlements of **Blackpool, Surfdale, Ostend**
and **Omiha,** which provide little in the way of real in interest, though Ostend does
have a market every Saturday from 0800-1300 while Omiha boasts the **Whakanewa
Regional Park** – a pleasant scenic spot with camping facilities and one of the regions
newest parks.⏵ *See Sleeping, Eating and other listings, pages 140-141.*

Sleeping

Given its popularity and proximity to the city,
Waiheke is very well-served with

accommodation, but in recent years the
focus seems to be mainly on vineyard
accommodation luring couples or
honeymooners. **Fullers** provide an

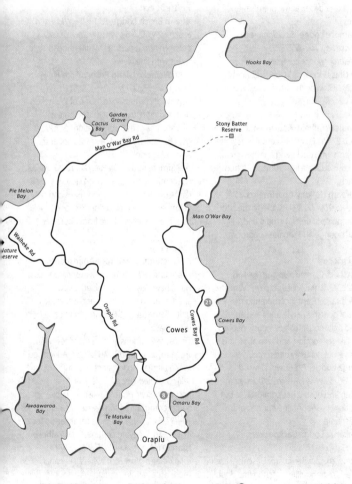

accommodation service and packages from the mainland Information Centre at the *Ferry Building on Quay St, T09-33679111, www.fullers.co.nz*

Waiheke Unlimited, *09-T3727776, www.waihekeunlimited.co.nz* also act as agents for self contained holiday accommodation.

There are also a number of lodges, motels, hostels and over 100 B&Bs to choose from, many with the ever-inviting 4-poster bed. To sample just how exquisite the options are, or see just how well luxury and architecture can combine take a look at the premises and websites of:

LL **Delamore Lodge**, *83 Delamore Dr, Owhanake Bay, T09-3727372, www.delamorelodge.com*; or

LL **The Glass House**, *33 Okoka Rd, Rocky Bay, T09-3723173, www.theglasshouse.co.nz*

Oneroa *p137*

A **Le Chalet Waiheke Apartments**, *14 Tawa St, T09-3727510*. Fully self- contained apartments with decks and fine views in a quiet bush setting, a little further out from the beach.

A **Seadream Holiday Apartments**, *35 Waikare Rd, T09-3728991*. Close to the beach, 2 well-appointed units, 1 studio and 1 larger unit with lounge and separate bedroom.

Little Oneroa

LL **Boatshed**, *Corner Tawa and Huia Sts, T09-3723242, www.boatshed.co.nz* A neat architectural concept incorporating modern individual boatshed-style units and an elevated 'lighthouse' all luxuriously decked out for clients' comfort and relaxation. It is expensive but certainly different.

AL **Punga Lodge**, *223 Ocean View Rd, T09-3726675, www.ki-wi.co.nz/punga.htm* Set in garden and bush it has comfortable but conventional self-contained or bed and breakfast units.

B-D **Hekerua Lodge Backpackers**, *11 Hekerua Rd, T09-3728990, www.ki-wi.co.nz/hekerua.htm* Describes itself as an oasis of tranquillity, offering fine doubles (1 en suite) twins, singles and dorms, an unusual pool and spa, all surrounded by native bush. Bike hire, internet.

Church Bay

Just outside of Oneroa there are a number of luxurious options including:

L **Glenora Estate**, *160 Nick Johnstone Dr, T09-3725082, www.glenoraestate.co.nz* Nestled in its own 8 acres and offering wonderful accommodation in 17th-century style farmhouse and barn – ideal for couples.

AL **The Arderns**, *241 Church Bay Rd, T09-3725487, www.waiheke.co.nz/ ardern.htm* Also offers luxury in more expansive surrounds.

Palm Beach

L **Palm Beach Lodge**, *23 Tiri View Rd, Palm Beach T09-3727763, www.waiheke.co.nz/ palmbch.htm* Spacious Mediterranean-style suites with fine views.

L-AL **Waiheke Island Resort**, *4 Bay Rd, Palm Beach T09-3720011, www.waihekeresort.co.nz* One of Waiheke's better-known luxury establishments with villa and chalet accommodation for 130 people. Attached is a fine restaurant and swimming pool.

A-B **Simkin Lodge**, *54 Palm Rd, T09-3728662*. A recently upgraded ex-backpackers, with a range of balcony rooms and suites and only 50 m from the water's edge. Bike and kayak hire. The bus stops at the front door.

Onetangi

AL **Onetangi Beachfront Apartments**, *27 The Strand T09-3727051, www.onetangi.co.nz* Has 8 new fully self-contained luxury apartments, 9 refurbished and 6 standard units. Barbecues, spas, sauna and free use of kayaks.

There are 2 options among the vineyards:

AL **Miro**, *Browns Rd T09-3727854*. Advertised as the ultimate in romance with a self-contained Tuscan-style villa. A homestay-style double is also available;

AL **Onetangi Road Vineyard**, *82 Onetangi Rd, T09-3726130*. Also offers a similar set-up for 2 in a private vineyard cottage. C-D **Waiheke Island YHA**, *Seaview Rd, T09-3728971, robb.meg@bigfoot.com* Offers a cheaper, more wide-ranging option with doubles (with bathroom), doubles (without), family and twin bunk rooms with 'a $2 million view', TV lounge, BBQ and mountain bikes available.

Ostend

A **The Midway Motel**, T09-3728023, www.waiheke.co.nz/midway.htm Has small and large units, an indoor heated pool, spa and spa room suites.

A **Ridgeview**, 86 Onetangi Rd, T09-3728647, www.ridgeview.co.nz A friendly, animals galore, farmstay option with one bedroom self contained units, just a short stroll from the Stonyridge Vineyard and café.

Elsewhere on the island

L **Te Whau Lodge**, 36 Vintage La, Te Whau Point, T09-3722288. Attached to the Te Whau vineyard overlooking Putiki Bay and provides 4 guest suites in a fine setting, fully licensed, breakfast and dinner included.

L **Waikopou**, Cowes Bay Rd, T09-3727883, www.waikopou.co.nz A luxurious earth-brick lodge retreat in 22 acres of bush with fine views.

AL **Kennedy Point Vineyard Guesthouse**, 44 Donald Bruce Rd, T09-3725600, www.kennedypointvineyard.com Offers another vineyard retreat in affordable well-appointed guest suites.

Campsites

If you have a tent, you can have your own 270-acre retreat with fine views at the **Whakanewa Regional Park**, for $6, T09-3031530, 'Parksline'.

🅱 Eating

There are numerous expensive to mid-range eateries on the island, especially vineyard cafés and restaurants that capture the essence of the island.

Oneroa p137

This is the centre of cuisine on Waiheke.

$$$ **Mudbrick Restaurant** attached to the vineyard, T09-3729050, open daily, bookings essential. Offers great seafood and, of course, a fine wine to wash it down.

$$ **Vino Vino Restaurant**, behind Greenhills Wines and Spirits, T09-3729888, www.vinovino.co.nz Mediterranean fare in relaxed surroundings overlooking the bay.

$$ **Waiheke Resort Restaurant**, near Palm Beach, T09-3727897. Outdoor decks with fine views across the Gulf. Bookings essential.

$$ **Harbour Masters Restaurant and Bar**, Matiatia. If you are worried about catching the ferry and just want a short stroll to the wharf after your evening meal or extended lunch then try this new place to eat.

$$ **NourishCafé**, 3 Belgium St, Ostend. Recommended by locals for fresh light meals, snacks and good coffee at reasonable prices.

Amongst the outlying vineyards the following cafes are recommended:

$$ **Stonyridge**, T09-3728822 (open from 1130-1700 weekends and Thu-Sun in summer).

$$ **Te Whau**, T09-3727191 (open from 1100-1630 weekends and Wed-Mon 1100-1700 in summer).

🎭 Entertainment

Harbour Master's Restaurant and Bar, Matiatia, just a short stroll from the wharf, T09-3722950, www.harbourmasters.co.nz Reputedly where it all happens these days, especially when bands visit from the mainland.

Live performances can also be heard, especially on summer weekends, at a number of low-key eating venues including: **Vino Vino**, T09-3729888, www.vinovino.co.nz and the

Lazy Lounge Cafe 139 Oceanview Rd, Oneroa, T09-3725132.

Artworld Complex, Oneroa (behind the VIC), T09-3722496. Cimema decked out with comfy sofas donated by residents, which after a day wine tasting results in inevitable soporifics.

🎪 Festivals

Waiheke Wine Festival
(www.waihekewine.co.nz) held in February.
Waiheke Jazz Festival
www.waihekejazz.co.nz, held at Easter. Both are hugely popular and the latter attracts top national and sometimes international artists.

🔺 Activities and tours

Club Waiheke Sunset Coral Scenic Rides, Dolphin Point, Church Bay, T09-3726565. Offer trips of the 4-legged variety for $75 for 2 hrs.

Flying Carpet Sailing, *104 Wharf Rd, Ostend, T09-3725621, www.flyingcarpet.co.nz* A pleasant 6 hr 30 min day cruise including buffet lunch on a spacious catamaran from $95 (departs Matiatia 1000).

Ross Adventures Sea Kayaking, *Matiatia, T09-3570550, www.kayakwaiheke.co.nz* Half (4 hr), full, multi-day and night trips, from $65.

The Kayak Company, *T09-3722112, www.thekayakcompany.co.nz* Also offers similar trips from $55.

Windsurfing Waiheke, *T09-3726275, www.windsurfing-waiheke.co.nz* For something a little more demanding, 2 hrs from $45 (independent hire also available).

Out-There Surf, *21 Belgium St, Ostend, T09-3726528.* Hires out dive gear, surfboards and bodyboards.

Fullers, *T09-3679111, www.fullers.co.nz* Offers a number of tour packages inclusive of ferry fare: The *Island Explorer Tour* ticket (departing at 1000) includes an all-day bus pass, from $46, child $22.50; The *Vineyard Tour* (departs 1200) takes in three of the island's best, plus an all-day bus pass for $66. An additional *Beyond and Back* tour (departs 1000, 3hr 30min) in summer only visits the Stony Batter Reserve with a vineyard lunch an additional option, from $55, child $28.

Waiheke Island Adventures Ltd, *T09-3726127, www.waihekeislandadventures.com* and **Waiheke Wine Country Tours**, *T0800-462868, www.gototour.co.nz,* are two local operators that offer a more personal service and flexible itineraries.

Ananda Tours, *20 Seaview Rd, Ostend, T09-3727530, www.waiheke.co.nz/ anadatours.htm,* are the most expensive offering excellent art, eco and scenic tours.

⊜ Transport

Vehicle hire Waiheke Auto Rentals, *T09-3728998, www.ki-wi.co.nz/ auto.htm,* Operates a fleet of cars, station wagons, 4WDs, sports cars and a minibus.
Waiheke Rental Cars, *T09-3728635, www.waihekerentalcars.co.nz* Rent cars, minibuses, jeeps, motorbikes and scooters. Cars start at about $50 a day, scooters $30. Both are a short walk from the wharf at Matiatia.

Taxis Quality Cabs, *T09-372700,* **Waiheke Tuk Tuk**, *T09-3726127, www.waihekeislandadventures.com* The breezy al fresco alternative.
Bike hire Available at the Matiatia Wharf, *T09-3727937, from $20 per day.*

⊙ Directory

Oneroa has banks with 24 hr ATMs, a post office, chemist, grocery shops, petrol station and a number of cafés and bars. Internet access is available at the Lazy Lounge Cafebar, *139 Oceanview Rd (centre of the village), T09-3725132.*

Great Barrier Island → Colour map 2, grid A2

Unlike Waiheke, Great Barrier (or the 'Barrier') has not yet been spoilt by the influences of the city and still offers the visitor a true island adventure. The ferry to the Barrier is a joint island service that at first is packed with commuters and visitors before it empties dramatically at Waiheke and you are left amongst the Barrier locals, and the fishing rods and rucksacks of the odd intrepid backpacker. The bar on the boat suddenly takes a hammering and the conversation turns to local Barrier gossip, kingfish and snapper. The orange glow of the city gradually fades behind Rangitoto and you begin to feel a welcome isolation close in. Great Barrier is the second largest island in the gulf and lies almost 90 km northeast of Auckland. It used to be part of what is now the Coromandel Peninsula and in a way shares the same isolated, under-developed feel, with rugged hills, numerous bays and beautiful quiet beaches. The Barrier is 'possum free' so a precious habitat for some rare and endangered species – the brown teal and New Zealand's largest skink, the cheveron, being the most notable. For those out to do some diving, fishing, tramping, surfing, sailing and relaxing it is unsurpassed in the region.

Getting there   Great Barrier is accessible by sea and air. The main airfield is at **Claris** in the centre east of the island about 17 km from Tryphena's **Shoal Bay Wharf**. Another airfield is at **Okiwi** north of Claris. Ferry services access the island mainly at Tryphena but also **Whangaparapara** and **Port Fitzroy**.

Getting around   A network of mainly metalled roads connects the main settlements, but most of the island remains inaccessible by vehicle. However, transportation around the island is fairly well organized and readily available. A swarm of vehicles will meet you at the Tryphena Wharf (Shoal Bay). Many accommodation centres will also provide their own pick ups but, if you have not yet booked, the taxis and shuttles will take you to the Information Centre in Tryphena or beyond. Both **Great Barrier Airlines** (GBA) and **Mountain Air** also provide shuttles to and from the airport: Tryphena to Claris $10 each way; Claris to Medlands $5 each way. Hitching is generally a safe method of transport – but don't be surprised if you find yourself on a steam roller or a quad bike, or, in fact, anything that goes.

Orientation and information   The main arrival point (by sea) and centre of population on Great Barrier is **Tryphena** which is essentially split into 3 areas or bays – Shoal Bay where the wharf is, Pa Beach and Mulberry Grove. In Pa Beach and Mulberry Grove you will find most of what you need from bread to petrol, accommodation to car hire. Most shops are to be found in the **Stonewall Complex**, including the **Fullers office** ① *next to the Stonewall Store, T09-4290004, open daily 0800-1700*, where long-term resident Tamara is a terrific source of information and advice. The traditional **VIC** ① *is in the post shop in Claris and serves visitors arriving by air; T09-4290033, www.greatbarrier.co.nz, open daily 0800-1800*. (www.greatbarrierisland.co.nz is another useful website.)

It is advisable to take detailed **maps** to Great Barrier if you intend to explore its wild interior. Free handouts are available from the Fullers Information Centre, the main **DoC office**, ①*Port Fitzroy, T09-4290044, Mon-Fri 0800-1630*, and the Information Centre in Claris (the DoC leaflets are the most detailed and informative) but nothing beats the real thing.

Two **publications** are of particular value; *The Essential Guide to Great Barrier* is essential (available from Fullers office and the Information Centre at Claris), $6, and the *Barrier Bulletin* will fill you in on all the latest gossip and events.

History

The Maori name for Great Barrier is *Aotea* meaning 'White Cloud' or 'Clear Day'. Before the Europeans arrived over 12,000 Maori were settled on the island but that population has all but disappeared with only a few descendants of the first tribes still remaining. It was that man Captain Cook again, who on his 1769 voyage renamed the island (along with its more mountainous sister, Little Barrier) –'Great Barrier' being an obvious name for the island's placement between open ocean and the inner gulf. The European history, like that of so much of the upper North Island, was initially centred on the kauri industry and for a while it prospered through sweat and saw. Once cleared, attentions turned underground, to the mineral deposits of gold, silver and copper, which did not prove very productive. The plunder above and below ground complete, the sea became the focus, with a thriving whaling station being set up in Whangaparapara (the remnants of which still remain). Now, 100 years on with the kauri, minerals, whales and human population depleted, the island has been left to the alternative, almost self-sufficient lifestylers – people who thankfully are much more conservation-minded. The DoC now owns and administers over half of the island, The

There is no mains electricity or streetlights on the island , so bring a torch: lights out at 2200. Water is sourced from streams or tank storage but considered safe

Auckland Great Barrier Island

Great Barrier Island

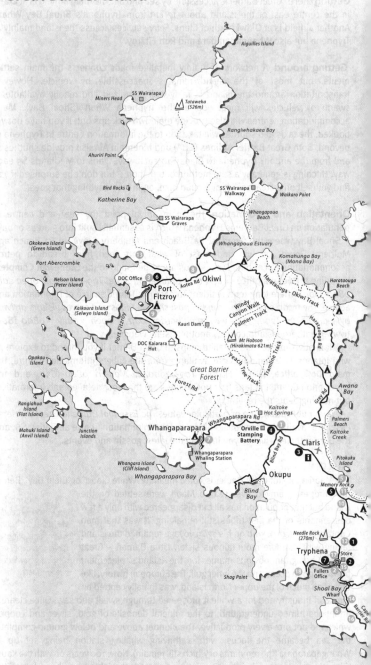

current permanent population of the island juggles around 1000, but increases dramatically with visitors in the summer months.

Sights

Great Barrier is an activities destination, from sunbathing on its beaches, to multi-day tramps within the huge **Great Barrier Forest**, which is where you will find the most notable 'sights' both natural and historical. There are numerous walks or tramps from one hour to two days and the best source of information on these is the DoC office in Port Fitzroy (see above). The *Essential Guide to Great Barrier* (see previous page) also highlights the best walks and routes. Most tramps start or finish from various access points on the road between Port Fitzroy and Whangaparapara. The most popular starting point is Port Fitzroy, where both supplies and information can be gathered at the wonderfully-stocked general store and main DoC office.

> ‼ *Windy Canyon (20 mins) and the Kaitoke Springs (1hr) are two of the best short walks.*

About 4 km north of Tryphena, **Needle Rock** (270 m) is a fine place to start. It is a rough 20-minute scramble to the summit which offers a great view back to Tryphena and the Coromandel to the south and all that awaits you to the north.

Medlands Beach is perhaps the most popular beach on the island, especially with surfies, but it is also a fine place to swim, fish, sunbathe or take a walk around the headlands.

North of Claris, in the heart of the island, is a crossroads. Heading directly north about 3 km is the access point for the **Kaitoke Hot Springs** – a flat, easy one-hour walk past the Kaitoke Swamp to a series of pools in which you can relieve tired limbs.

Located 2 km along and south of the Whangaparapara Road on the Te Ahumata track, the concrete foundations are all that remain of the **Orville Stamping Battery** that once crushed quartz from the Te Ahumata gold field.

Heading east from the Claris

Auckland Great Barrier Island

Rakitu Island
(Arid Island)

Whakatautuna Point

0 km   2
0 miles   2

Medlands
Beach

Windy Hill
(361m)

Rosalie
Bay Rd

Vol Ruahine
(402m)

Cape Barrier

Sleeping 😴
Crossroads Backpackers **1**
Earthsong Lodge **2**
Fitzroy House **3**
Flowerhouse **4**
Foromor Lodge **5**
Gibb's Landing **6**
Great Barrier Lodge **7**
High Tide & Green Grass **8**
Jetty Tourist Lodge **9**
Medlands Beach
 Backpackers & Motel **10**
Medlands Beach House
 & Cottage **11**
Oasis Lodge **12**
Orama Christian
 Community **13**
Pigeon's Lodge **14**
Pohutukawa Lodge **15**
Stray Possum Lodge **16**
Tipi & Bob's
 Waterfront Lodge **17**
Trilliam Lodge **18**

Eating 🍴
Barrier Oasis **1**
Claris Texas Café **3**
Cruisy Café & Bakery **7**
Currach Irish Pub **2**
Great Barrier Island Sports
 & Social Club **4**
Medlands Lodge **5**
Port Fitzroy Boating Club **6**

crossroads you cross the river and up around the headland to **Palmers Beach** with its shroud of pohutukawa trees falling chaotically to the beach. This is a fine beach to explore but access is not easy. The far more accessible **Awana Bay** is another fine spot, popular again for surfing and all other aquatic and beach-orientated activities.

Windy Canyon is about 8 km north of Awana Bay at the top of Okiwi Hill is Palmer's Track. A 20-minute walk through nikau palm groves and up a well-built boardwalk will find you amongst the jagged stacks and spires of the canyon. The summit offers spectacular views. Palmers Track offers perhaps the best access point to Mount Hobson.

At 621 m, **Mount Hobson (Hirakimata)** is the island's highest point. On a clear day its 360° view of the island and beyond is unsurpassed. The summit is the principal nesting site for the rare black petrel. Only about 4,500 remain and they are only found on Great and Little Barrier Islands. They spend most of their life out at sea and are nocturnal on land, so don't expect to see any. They also nest in burrows so make sure you keep to the paths. From the summit the track splits – The Kaiarara track offering a route west to Port Fitzroy (with some fine remains of kauri dams on the way) or south via the Peach Tree Track that terminates at the Kaitoke hot springs.

The well-preserved remains of a **kauri dam** can be seen along the Kaiarara Track. Kauri dams were used by loggers to drive large numbers of kauri downstream, allowing access to remote areas of bush. The lower one at Kaiarara was one of the largest driving dams to be built in New Zealand and is one of the best examples in the region.

The **'SS Wairarapa'** was one of many ships wrecked on the island and certainly the most tragic, with the loss of 130 lives. It ran ashore near Miner's Head in 1894. The 30-minute **walk** along the Whangapoua Beach to Tapuwai Point from the road end takes you to one of two graveyard sites on the island – the other being at Onepoto Beach at Katherine Bay on the west coast.

The **Whangapoua Estuary** is a top spot for wildlife and is home to many interesting coastal and wetland species including spotless crake, banded rail and brown teal. If you spot a brown teal – a rather nondescript little brown duck – consider yourself very lucky as you will have seen one of only about 1200 left in the world. Great Barrier is home to 80% of these.

The remains of the Barrier's old **whaling station** can be seen from the Whangaparapara Harbour. The oceans around the Barrier were the killing fields for thousands of whales from the 1950s before operations thankfully ceased in the 1960s.

▸▸ *For Sleeping, Eating and other listings, see pages 146-150.*

● Sleeping

Great Barrier is both remote and basic, with no mains power, street lights, reticulated water supply or extensive road network, but when it comes to accommodation you can either enjoy that simplicity or be utterly spoilt. Just remember to book well in advance in summer.
Fullers, *Ferry Building, Auckland, T09-3679111*, offer accommodation packages and advice from their office on the mainland. But perhaps your best bet is to contact the Fullers office or the general VIC on the island or the website *www.greatbarrier.co.nz* or *www.greatbarrierisland.co.nz*
Island Accommodation, *T09-4290995,*

www.islandaccommodation.co.nz, are the local holiday accommodation agents.

Tryphena *p143*
LL **Earthsong Lodge**, *T09-4290030, www.earthsonglodge.co.nz* A central, luxury option that overlooks Tryphena Harbour and offers fine cuisine.
LL **Oasis Lodge**, *T09-4290021, www.barrieroasis.co.nz* Set amid a vineyard and is an old favourite. Both luxury and cheaper cottage-style options available, meals included.
LL **Trilliam Lodge**, *24 Schooner Bay Rd, Puriri Bay, T09-4290454.* A beautiful luxury Canadian log-style dwelling offering the full 5-star treatment, 6 double suites.
L **Flowerhouse**, *T09-4290464.* An organic

farm with 1 bedroom. Fine lunch venue.
A **Pigeon's Lodge** *T09-4290437,
www.pigeonslodge.co.nz* A fine B&B with
rooms with bathrooms and set in quiet bush.
A **Tipi and Bob's Waterfront Lodge**,
T09-4290550, www.waterfrontlodge.co.nz An
old favourite with 6 self-contained units,
close to all amenities.
A **Pohutukawa Lodge**, *Pa Beach,
T09-4290211, www.currachirishpub.co.nz*
Close to shops, restaurants and that essential
pint of Guinness. Also offers backpacker
accommodation (**C-D**).
A-D Stray Possum Lodge, *T0800-767786,
www.straypossum.co.nz* The pick of the
budget bunch on the island. An excellent
backpackers near the wharf and offering
bunk-style, double room and chalet options
in a lovely bush setting. Bar, Sky TV, Internet
and pizza café available. Very friendly
management and staff. Tours also available
and bikes, boogie boards and wet suits
for hire.
B Gibb's Landing, *Little Shoal Bay (near the
wharf), T09-4290654,
www.gibbslandinglodge.aotea.org* Beachfront, self-contained accommodation with a
great view. Bike, dive gear and car rent
all available.

Whangaparapara
A **Great Barrier Lodge**, *T09-4290488,
www.greatbarrierlodge.com* Really the only
one place to stay in Whangaparapara.
Accommodation is in cottages in the
grounds and, being out of the way, just
about all you need is available. Car, bike and
equipment hire, licensed bar and restaurant.

Medlands Beach and north
LL **Foromor Lodge**, *T09-4290335*. Another
'helicopter arrival' type venue on a fine
beachfront location at Medlands. Meals and
activities included.
A **Medlands Beach House and Cottage**,
T09-5755725, www.barrierbeachfront.co.nz A
mid-range self-contained accommodation
option, right on the surf beach.
**B-D Medlands Beach Backpackers and
Motels**, *T09-4290320,
www.medlandsbeach.com* A budget option
with bunks and 4 detached double family
rooms with bunks. Boogie boards, fishing and
snorkelling gear available. Get well stocked up
with food – it is remote. Surfies' favourite.
C-D Crossroads Backpackers, *just north of
Claris, T09-4290889*. Well positioned in the
heart of the island. It looks a bit clinical but
offers fine accommodation and has good
facilities and internet access.

Port Fitzroy and around
AL **Jetty Tourist Lodge**, *T09-4290050*. Well
placed and offers self-contained chalets and
backpacker-style dorms. Bar and restaurant,
and within walking distance of the
well-stocked general store.
A **Fitzroy House**, *T09-4290091,
www.fitzroyhouse.co.nz* Two self-contained
cottages in a wonderful setting and has
heaps of activities available.
A **Orama Christian Community**, *Near Port
Fitzroy, T09-4290063, www.orama.org.nz*
Self-contained flats and cottage, guestroom,
cabin and bunkroom accommodation in a
very scenic spot. Has its own library, shop
and laundry facilities.
A-C High Tide and Green Grass, *Okiwi,
T09-4290190*. Set in its own 12 acres of
pasture and bush offering isolation and
peace, backpackers' lodge available.

Camping
There are 6 DoC campsites and 1 DoC hut
available (The Whangaparapara hut having
burnt to the ground recently). Bookings are
advised and current charges (average $6) are
available on enquiry at the **main DoC office**
in Port Fitzroy, *T09-4290044*. Campsites are
available at **Akapoua Bay** (Port Fitzroy),
**Whangaparapara, Whangapoua, Medlands,
Harataonga** and **Awana**. For convenience
Akapoua Bay is advised, and perhaps the
best of the more secluded campgrounds is
Harataonga. The **Akapoua Campsite** also
has a guest lodge which sleeps 8. The
Kaiarara Hut, *$10 per night*. Has 24 bunks.
Private campgrounds are also available at
Great Barrier Island Campground, *Puriri
Bay, Tryphena, T09-4290184, $10*;
Orama Christian Community $10, (see
above);
Sanderson Farm, *Claris, T09-4290264, $7*;
Mickey's, *T09-4290170, $5*. Run by a mad
Irishman and is probably the most
entertaining camping venue on the island.

There are essentially very few restaurants on the Barrier with most eateries being attached to accommodation centres, many of which offer excellent cuisine. Food supplies can be bought at the **Stonewall Village Store**, T4290451, **The Outpost**, T4290610 and the **Mulberry Grove Store and Café**, T4290909 in Tryphena; **The Claris Store**, T4290852; **Great Barrier Lodge**, Whangaparapara, T4290488; **The Port Fitzroy General Store**, T4290056.

Tryphena p143

$$$ **Barrier Oasis**, Stonewall, T09-4290021. Top quality cuisine for guests and visitors, lunch and dinner. Bookings essential.
$ **Cruisy Café and Bakery**, Stonewall Village, T09-4290997. Homemade sandwiches and snacks.
$$ **Currach Irish Pub**, Stonewall Complex, T09-4290421. Good pub food with a wicked seafood chowder.
$$ **Earthsong Lodge**, T09-4290030. Excellent, specializing in French cuisine. Bookings essential.
$$ **Flowerhouse**, Rosalie Bay, T09-4290464. Favourite local lunch spot, pick-ups available.
$$ **Pigeon's Lodge**, T09-4290437. Set menu of mainly French and Italian specialities, bookings essential.
$ **Stray Possum Lodge**, T09-4290109. Pizza kitchen.
$ **Tipi and Bob's**, T09-4290550. Full menu including snacks and fish and chips, licensed (takeaways).

Whangaparapara

$$ **Great Barrier Lodge**, T09-4290488. Restaurant and bar.

Medlands

$$ **Medlands Lodge**, T09-4290352. À la carte French, Provincial and Italian.

Claris

$$ **Claris Texas Café**, T09-4290811. Daily 0900-1600. Fine food all day and from 1800 Thu-Sun evenings. Best coffee on the island.
$ **Great Barrier Island Sports and Social Club**, T09-4290260. Wed, Fri, Sat. Takeaways.

Port Fitzroy

$$ **Jetty Tourist Lodge**, T09-4290050.

Summer only. Kiwi food and seafood.
Port Fitzroy Boating Club, T09-4290072. Daily summer, Sat only in winter. (Takeaways available.)

❼ Entertainment

In summer the bays are alive with the sound of clinking gin bottles and laughter from the parties taking place on yachts and expensive launches, but on the mainland there are 2 fine places to go to drink and have fun.
Currach Irish Pub at the Pohutukawa Lodge, T09-4290211. Live entertainment with an unusual Kiwi/Irish flavour.
The Stray Possum Lodge, T09-4290109. Has a delightful little bar, where the manager and staff will entertain the beer-deprived visitors and occasional locals with a great collection of 80's hits. The odd wild party sometimes ensues.

❼ Festivals and events

The main and increasingly popular annual festival on the Barrier is the **Port Fitzroy Mussel Festival** held in Jan (for details contact the Port Fitzroy Boating Club, T09-4290072).
The long-board **Surf Classic** is held in early Jan (depending on weather), T09-4290966. The Barrier Island Sports and Social Club in Claris hosts a monthly **market** (last Sat), which can be a great way to mingle with the locals, T09-4290260.

▲ Activities

Boating
A wonderland awaits you. Boats can be hired from
GBI Adventure Rentals, Mulberry Grove, Tryphena, T09-4290062; and
Fitzroy House Outdoor Centre, T09-4290091.

Diving
The waters around the Barrier are wonderfully clear. Great diving can be found all around the island, but preferred spots are Tryphena Harbour, around Port Fitzroy and off Harataonga Bay.
Bonadventure Safaris, T09-4799647, www.bonadventure.co.nz Dive safaris from the **MV Friendship**, day from $195,

overnight from $240, gear hire $65 a day.
Dive Gear hire: Mobile Dive Centre,
T09-4290654 ($75 a day). Refills available;
Great Barrier Lodge, *T09-4290488*;
Mobile Dive Centre and
Fitzroy Dive Station (above, *T4290591*).

Eco-tours
Adventure Eco Tours, *T09-4290699,
www.barrieradventures.co.nz* Offer 8-wheel
ATV tours (1hr-1hr 30min) to some of the
best beaches and wetlands to see
endangered species like the brown teal.

Fishing
Generally it is a good idea to bring your own
gear for excellent land and sea fishing.
Charters available include:
Fish'N' Missions, *T09-4290925, from $75
half-day*
Vitamin C, *T09-4290949,
www.currachirishpub.co.nz*
Some of the best land-based spots are
Lighthouse Point (Shoal Bay, Tryphena),
Cape Barrier, **Shag Point**, **'Shark Alley'**
(south headlands of Medlands Beach) and
Haratoanga.

Golf
Yes, the Barrier has a golf course, but mind
the pukekos.
Claris Golf Club, *T09-4290420*. Lessons
(Saturday) and meals available.

Kayaking
The Barrier is a sea kayaking paradise. The
following offer hire and trip options.
Complete circumnavigation of the island
takes about five days and is an awesome trip
needing careful planning, local help and
knowledge.
Bonadventure Safaris, *T09-4799647,
www.bonadventure.co.nz* Kayak safaris from
the **MV Friendship** (The 'mothership'), day
from $195, overnight from $240.
Other operators include:
Aotea Kayaks, *T09-4290664*;
Fitzroy House Outdoor Centre, *T09-4290091*
(hire only);
GB Kayak Hire, *T09-4290520* (guided evening
and night tours);
Great Barrier Lodge, *T09-4290488* (hire only).
Independent hire costs about $45 a day.

This is a great way to explore the island and
both airlines and ferry operators are
bicycle-friendly. For environmental reasons
most tracks are off limits, but a fine track
that is accessible is the DoC Forest 4WD
track off Whangaparapara Rd.
Cycle hire is available with **GBI Hire**;
Claris, *T4290471*;
Great Barrier Lodge, *Whangaparapara,
T4290488*;
Paradise Cycles, *Tryphena, T4290474*.

Tramps
2 Days From the start of Palmers Track at
the top of Okiwi Hill take a look at Windy
Canyon before continuing to the summit of
Mount Hobson. From there check out the
kauri dam remains before continuing along
the track and staying the night at the **DoC.
Kaiarara Hut** (24 bunks, a wood stove, toilet
and cold water, $10, book with, *T09-4290044*).
Then the following day take the Forest Road
and Tramline Tracks to finish your tramp in
style at the Kaitoke Hot Springs. You will need
to arrange pick-up from the Whangaparapara
Road access point.
1 Day Follow the route above but from
Mount Hobson take the Peach Tree Track
directly to the hot springs with pick-up
again from Whangaparapara Rd.
   Both the Harataonga – Okiwi Track (5
hours) and Rosalie Bay Road end to Claris
(5 hours) are also fine walks.

Swimming
Swimming (especially for kids) is best kept to
sheltered **West Coast bays**, but the big
eastern beaches are fine for adults if you are
vigilant. Take flippers and a boogie board.

Surfing
The best spots are **Medlands**, **Kaitoke**,
Palmers and **Awana Bays**.

Tours
Bob's Island Tours, *T4290988*, is a
long-established operator offering an
entertaining trip from $60; **Stray
Possum Bus**, *T0800-767786* is backpacker
oriented and others include **Aotea Tours**,
T4290156 and Adventure Eco Tours
(see above).

⊖ Transport

Air

Great Barrier Airlines (offices at the Auckland Domestic Terminal, T09-2759120, T0800-900600, www.greatbarrierairlines.co.nz, and at the airfield on the Barrier at Claris) are the main carriers; their aircraft are hard to miss with their tails beautifully painted with examples of New Zealand's native bird-life. They offer an efficient service to the island from **Auckland** and **North Shore** airports, as well as connecting flights to the **Coromandel** (Whitianga) and **Whangarei** in Northland. There are 2-4 flights daily 0745,1015, 1500 and 1600 from Auckland, returning 0900,1300,1600 and 1700 from Claris, with extra flights in summer on demand. A standard return will cost you $172, child $110 and a single $99, child $65. Surfboards $35 return, bikes $55. These prices are cheap considering the scenic extravaganza on offer on a clear day. **Mountain Air's Great Barrier Express**, T09-2567025, T0800-222123, www.mountainair.co.nz, offers a similar service and also advertises that dogs, surfboards and bikes are welcome! Both airlines offer pick-up and drop shuttle services throughout the island (see getting around p143) and a 'fly and boat' package for about $115 which is highly recommended. **Waiheke Air Services**, T0800-3725000, also fly to the Barrier but less frequently and on demand; as do **Sunair Aviation**, T0800-685050, to and from **Tauranga** in the Bay of Plenty.

Ferry

Fullers, T09-3679111, www.fullers.co.nz Offer a passenger-only service from the city (2 hrs), on Fri at 1830 and Sun at 1100, additional sailings in summer, from $105, child $52 return, concessions available, bookings essential. **Sealink (Subritzky Shipping)**, T09-3734036, www.subritzky.co.nz A vehicular and passenger service on board the MV Sealink. Sailings daily except Tue and Sat (3 hrs). Additional sailings in summer. Departs from Wynyard Wharf, City, vehicle $440 return, passenger only $75, child $45 return.

The Central Backpackers in Auckland, T09-3584877, www.acb.co.nz, has a sister establishment on Great Barrier – The Stray Possum Lodge, T0800-767786, www.straypossum.co.nz, – which offers the excellent value **Barrier Island Pass** which includes daily transport, tours, use of mountain bikes, body boards, wet suits and snorkel gear. The package costs $125, including travel to and from the island. Recommended.

Car hire Aotea Tours, Okiwi, T09-4290055; Better Bargain Rentals, Tryphena, T09-4290092; GBI Rental Cars, Tryphena, T09-4290061; Medlands Rentals, Kaitoke, T09-4290046; Bob's Island Tours, T09-4290988; and Great Barrier Lodge, Whangaparapara, T09-4290488. All these companies offer rental options with a range of well-used vehicles from hatchbacks to 4WDs, but it is a captive market and prices are not cheap at about $90 per day, dropping slightly for long-term rental.

Cycle hire See activities above.

Taxis Aotea Transport Services, T09-4290055, offer a daily bus service from Tryphena to Port Fitzroy or transfers on demand. Stray Possum Bus, T0800-767786; Sanderson Transport, T09-4290640, and Bob's Island Tours, T09-4290988 offer similar services. The typical fare from Tryphena to Claris is $10.

⊙ Directory

Banks There are no banks on the island but Eftpos is readily available in most shops, cafés, accommodation and restaurants.

Communications Post office: Outpost, Tryphena (Stonewall Complex), T09-4290610. Port Fitzroy Store, T09-4290056. You can even send a message by pigeon at the **Pigeon Post**, Claris, T09-4290242. Telephones: Generally available at main centres and around the island. **Fuel** Petrol and diesel available at Tryphena (Mulberry Grove), Claris, Whangaparapara and Port Fitzroy. Gas: refills at 143 Hector Sanderson Rd, Claris, and 428 Shoal Bay Rd, Tryphena. **Laundry** Claris Fuel and Laundromat, T094290075.

Medical services DoCtor: Health Centre, Claris, T09-4290356. **Pharmacy**: based in Claris, T09-4290006. **Police** Claris, T09-4290343. **Public toilets** Shoal Bay, Whangaparapara, Port Fitzroy Wharves, Mulberry Grove and Pa Beach Tryphena, Medlands, Claris and the Airfield.

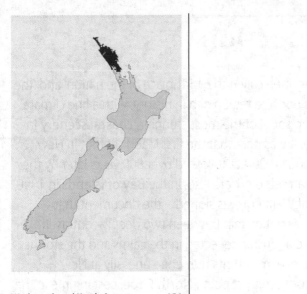

Introduction

Northland is often called the 'birthplace of the nation' and 'the 'winter-less north', a region rich in history, with a fine climate and boasting some of the most stunning **coastal scenery** in the country. It was here that the first Maori set foot in New Zealand, about 1000 AD, followed over 800 years later by the first European settlers. Here also, in the **Bay of Islands** in 1840, the Treaty of Waitangi was signed – the document that launched the relationship between two deeply contrasting peoples. A relationship reflected in the calms and the storms of unsettled ocean currents that unite uneasily at New Zealand's northernmost point, **North Cape**. Lost in time in the Waipoua Forest, making all that human history seem like yesterday, stands one of the few remaining 'ancient' kauri trees, the centuries-old **'Tane Mahuta'**.

All in all, for the modern day visitor, Northland must feature as one of the most aesthetically and historically interesting regions to visit in New Zealand. Most of what it has to offer is signposted and detailed as the aptly named and celebrated **'Twin Coast Discovery'**.

★ Don't miss...

1. Watching the sunrise from **Ocean Beach**, page 166 near Whangarei. Then synchronize watches at the **Clock Museum** in the Town Basin, page 162.
2. Diving the **Poor Knights Islands**, page 167, or sea fishing from **Tutukaka**, page 166.
3. Exploring the Northland Coast from the **Old Russell Road**, page 167.
4. Dolphin swimming, kayaking, sailing, big game fishing or taking a fast jet boat ride in the beautiful **Bay of Islands**, page 172.
5. Discovering the '**Birth of the Nation**' at the Waitangi National Reserve, page 173.
6. **Dune surfing** at Cape Reinga, the northernmost tip of New Zealand, page 191.
7. Standing in awe below the massive 1500-year-old kauri tree '**Tane Mahuta**' in the Waipoua Kauri Forest Park, page 197.
8. Seeing the bizarre garden decorations of **51 Norton Street**, Te Kopuru, near Dargaville, page 199.

Northland Introduction

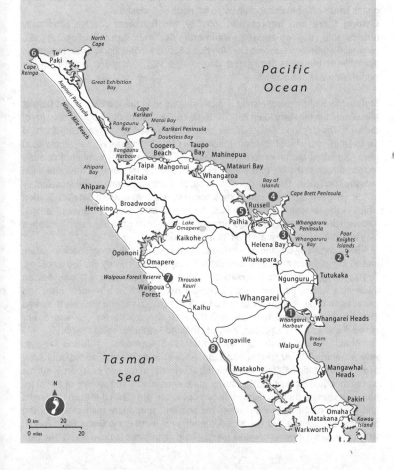

Warkworth and Kowhai Coast

Although not geographically within Northland, it is for most a starting point and a gateway to the region. Most travellers, in their haste to reach Whangarei or the Bay of Islands (on State Highway 1), miss out Warkworth altogether, while others stop for lunch or a coffee by the river before taking the slower and more scenic route north, along the Kowahi coast, via the vineyards of Matakana, then on to the scenic coastal settlements of Leigh, Mangawhai and Waipu. But whatever your intention, Warkworth and the pleasant coastal bays, peninsulas and islands to its east, are certainly worthy of a stop and despite the lure of the north, when it comes to tourism and its associate services, the district is developing at a phenomenal rate.

The Kowhai Coast extends from Wenderholm Regional Park just north of Waiwera to Pakiri Beach and contains three Regional Parks, Kawau Bay, including Kawau Island, the Marine Reserve at Goat Island and over 26 accessible beaches popular for boating, fishing, diving and walking.

Warkworth → *Phone code: 09 Colour map 1, grid C4. Population: 3000*

Although of some historic significance as a former kauri-milling town, Warkworth is now essentially a farming and tourism service centre set in the heart of Rodney District and on the banks of the Mahurangi River, 70 km north of Auckland.

Getting there and information Intercity and **Northliner** coaches stop daily outside the VIC, T09-9136100. **Warkworth VIC**, ⓘ *1 Baxter St, T09-4259081, www.warkworth-information.co.nz Mon-Sat, 0830-1730, Sun, 0900-1500*. **Internet** is available at the town library next door to the VIC. ⓘ *Mon-Thu 0900-1700, Fri 0900-2000, Sat 0900-1200*.

Sights Much of the local history is nicely presented in the **Warkworth and District Museum** within the **Parry Kauri Park**. ⓘ *Tudor Collins Drive on the southern outskirts of the town, T09-4257093. Daily summer 0900-1600, winter 0900-1530. Adult $5, child $1*. The museum, which falls under the shadow of two impressive 6-800 year old kauri trees (the tallest on the east coast of Northland), explores, in a number of carefully recreated rooms, the life of the early pioneers and the influence of the great kauri industry upon them. There is also a small but pleasant nature trail by the museum.

Staying south (4 km), and in stark contrast, is the **Warkworth Satellite Station** which is the Telecom NZ national base for international satellite communications. Although the unmanned visitors' centre has now closed, the two huge satellite dishes may lure still you off the main road for a closer look.

Back on SH1 again, and less than 1 km further south, you can get back to nature and all things sweet and communal at the **Honey Centre**, ⓘ *Perry Rd, T09-4258003, T09-4258003, www.honeycentre.co.nz Daily 0900-1700. Free.* It provides an interesting insight into the industry and a close-up look at a resident hive, and provides an ideal opportunity to buy a tub of the golden stuff for the kids to spread gratuitously all around the hire car. There is also a café on site and a 1-hr **sheep-n-show**, ⓘ *T09-4258942, daily at 1100 and Sat/Sun 1100 and 1400*.

About 4 km north of Warkworth is **Sheepworld**. ⓘ *T0800-227-433, www.sheepworld.co.nz Daily 0900-1700. Show 1100 daily and 1300 Sat/Sun. Adult $10, child $5*. If the foot falls heavy on the accelerator at the very prospect of such a place, then just hold on. It is actually quite entertaining and worthy of the stop. Although chasing them is rightly frowned upon, you are allowed to feed the lambs and get involved in some shearing. The souvenir shop more than caters for the reminder of your visit. Café on site. A further 3 km north is the **Dome State Forest**, which provides a number of walks ranging from 40 minutes to three hours. The best

Auckland Sky Tower on a clear day. All the walks start at the Top of the Dome Café, which is open daily.

To the east of Warkworth, on the scenic Mahurangi Peninsula, are the popular coastal holiday venues of **Snells Beach** (with the Salty Dog Tavern, see page 160), **Algies Bay** and **Martins Bay**, the latter having the best beach, and **Sandspit**, from where the ferry departs to **Kawau Island** (see below).

Short river trips ($20) and self-guided or guided tours of the Matakana vineyards are also on offer from Warkworth. The VIC has further information. ▸▸ *For Sleeping and Eating, see pages 159 and 160.*

Kawau Island → *Phone code: 09 Colour map 1, grid C5*

Kawau island is a popular holiday resort 8 km off the coast on the Mahurangi Peninsula. In summer its sheltered bays are almost more popular than terra firma, as yachties from far and wide drop anchor to enjoy the surroundings, fish, swim, dive or party long into the wee small hours. In pre-European times the island was the headquarters of Maori raiders who made numerous pirate attacks on surrounding tribes from their villages and *pa*.

Getting there From **Auckland** Kawau Kat runs a seasonal **'Paradise Cruise'** departing from the Auckland Waterfront daily at 0930 and leaving Kawau at 1500, arriving back at Auckland at 1630, from $49, child $10 (lunch $10 extra). Alternatively you can try their **'Day Escape'** package by coach via Warkworth to Sandspit (6 km east of Warkworth) where you catch the Mailrun Cruise at 1030 ($39, child $15), returning Sandspit 1400, Auckland 1735. For detailed information call the VIC, T09-4258006, www.kawaukat.co.nz

All other organized trips depart from **Sandspit**. Kawau Kat Cruises have 3 trips: **'The Royal Mail Run'** departs at 1030, adult $39, child $15 ($10 extra for BBQ lunch). The 1-hr trip takes in the scenic bays before landing for a while at the main Wharf. The **'Coffee Cruise'** also departs at 1030 and spends less time cruising the bays allowing you to stay on the island all day if you so wish, from $29, child $12. For thrill seekers there is the seasonal **'Kawau Jet'**, a fast boat which offers a short blast around the island and a spot of dolphin watching before the regulatory stop on the island at the Mansion House, 4 hrs from $99, T09-4258006, www.kawaukat.co.nz Matata Cruises offer a daily **'Coffee Cruise'** departing at 1000 (and 1400 Christmas and Easter); adult $25. There is also a **lunchtime champagne cruise** that departs at 1000 for $35, bookings essential. Both trips allow some time on the island, T0800-225292, matata.cruisesextra.co.nz

There are other irregular ferry sailings from Sandspit. For information, T09-4258006. There is no public transport to Sandspit from Warkworth. For a taxi call T09-425000.

Around the island European ownership dates back to 1837 when the island became the focus for mining activities – first manganese, then copper – with operations ceasing in 1869. There are still remnants of copper mines a short walk from the wharf. In 1862 Sir George Grey in his second term as Governor of New Zealand purchased the island for a mere £3500 and began a 26-year stay in Bon Accord Harbour, where he created perhaps the biggest modern day tourist draw, **The Mansion House**. ① *T09-4228882. Daily 1000-1530. $4, child $2.* Grey was very interested in botany and zoology, developing a small collection of exotic animals and plants and also using the island as an acclimatization centre. He even had a pair of zebra brought from Africa to pull his carriage, which resulted in their death a short time after arriving. Sadly, our George was also blissfully unaware of the monumental environmental damage he was unleashing on the increasingly threatened New

Zealand native flora and fauna. To this day the odd wallaby hops through the bush, accompanied by the laughing of the Australian kookaburra. In 1967, 79 years after Sir George Grey went home to England, the island became part of the **Hauraki Maritime Park**. Some 176 ha were put aside as public domain, the Mansion House turned from guesthouse to museum and the rest of the island went to farmers and the wallabies. ▸▸ *For Sleeping, see page 159.*

Matakana → *Phone code: 09 Colour map 1, grid C4*

Blink and you may miss Matakana, 8 km north of Warkworth on the main Warkworth to Leigh Road, but the surrounding countryside is increasingly famous for its **vineyards**. The **Heron's Flight Vineyard** ① *49 Sharp's Rd, T09-4227915, www.heronsflight.co.nz, daily 1000-1800,* is one of a number in the vicinity producing a fine nationally recognized product. Tours and tastings are available and again a fine café is on site.

Other more recent vineyards worth visiting include: **Ascension**, T09-4229601, www.ascensionvineyard.co.nz; **Hyperion**, T09-4229375 www.hyperion-wines.co.nz; **Matakana Estate**, T09-4258446; **Ransom**, T09-4258862; and the scattering of labels around Mahurangi. The VIC in Warkworth can provide self-guided or guided tour details, T09-4259081.

Also of interest is the **Morris and James Country Pottery and Café**. ① *Tongue Farm Road, T09-4227116. 1000-1700. Pottery tours weekdays at 1130. Café open daily 0830-1630, summer until late, winter Thu-Fri until late.* It uses clay sourced from the Matakana River to produce a wonderful array of terracotta pots and tiles that have become famous throughout the country. There are free weekday pottery tours and the café serves up delicious food and fine local wines in a relaxed garden setting. ▸▸ *For Sleeping, see page 159 .*

Tawharanui → *Phone code: 09 Colour map 1, grid C4 Parksline T09-3031530.*

If you have time, do not miss the biggest countryside and northernmost coastal park in the region, Tawharanui. It takes some getting to via Takatu Road just north of Matakana, but is well worth the effort. Even before you reach the park you are afforded spectacular views of Kawau Island and beyond. Being so isolated, it is quieter than most other parks and offers beaches, walks and scenery unrivalled in many other eastern coastal parks. A heaven for native birds, you are almost sure to see noisy paradise shelduck, together with pied stilts and variable oystercatchers. Plans are afoot to turn Tawharanui into a 'mainland island' protected with predator-free fences: an exciting prospect. The two main beaches are ideal for relaxing or swimming and look out across Omaha Bay to Leigh. Extended walks out to the headland offer even better views. ▸▸ *Permit camping available. For Sleeping, see page 159.*

Leigh and the Goat Island Marine Reserve → *Phone code: 09*
Colour map 1, grid A5

The original name for Leigh was Little Omaha; common sense given its position on the west of Omaha Cove, 13 km from Matakana. However, to avoid confusion with its sister settlement of Big Omaha, slightly inland, the name was changed to Leigh. Why 'Leigh' remains a mystery. Whatever, Leigh is a small fishing community the nature of which is best summed up by its rather mundane street names like 'Wonderview', 'Barrierview', 'Grandview' and, yes, even 'Seaview'!

Matheson's Beach is 1 km to the west of the village and is a popular spot in summer for all beach and aquatic pursuits, but by far the main focus of attention lies 4 km north of Leigh, around **Goat Island** and its associate **marine reserve**. Although the island itself, 300 m offshore, is fairly nondescript, the waters that surround it are very special. These waters were established in 1975 as New Zealand's first marine reserve. Treated essentially like any reserve on land, the entire aquatic flora and fauna is fully protected, and no angling or shell fishing is allowed. Basically, nothing

66 99 In the early days it was possible to feed the fish, but it quickly became obvious a diet of cheese slices and crisps was not conducive to their good health...

can be taken except photographs and scientific samples. The result is an astonishing abundance of marine life that brings hordes of divers to the area all year round. The added allure is that you do not need to be Jacques Cousteau to enjoy it. From the shore swimmers and snorkellers can (particularly in summer) find themselves surrounded by shoals of inquisitive fish looking for an easy meal. In the early days it was possible to feed the fish, but it quickly became obvious a diet of cheese slices and crisps was not conducive to their good health. Indeed a sign just before the beach now states: 'Do not feed the fish, it can make them sick'.

Dive gear can be hired from **Seafriends**, 7 Goat Island Rd, 1 km before the beach, T09-4226212, www.seafriends.org.nz Full dives cost from $75 and can be done daily 0900-dusk. There is also a restaurant on site and a small series of aquariums containing local sea creatures for children to see and for educational purposes. **Goat Island Dive**, 142A Pakiri Rd beside the Sawmill Café, T0800-348369, www.goatislanddive.co.nz, (see page 160 below), also offer charters, training, gear hire and tank refills.

On the surface the glass-bottom boat *Habitat Explorer*, ① *T09-4226334, www.glassbottomboat.co.nz, adult $18*, offers a number of **trips around the island** lasting up to 45 minutes, with a commentary and good views of the fish and abundant marine life below. Trips are weather dependent and can be subject to seasonal schedules. ▸▸ *For Sleeping and Eating, see pages 160 and 161.*

Pakiri → *Colour map 1, grid C5*
The main road north of Leigh splits in to a series of metalled roads that begins to give the first raw impressions of rural Northland life. Just 10 km north of Leigh is the very pleasant and fairly isolated beach at Pakiri. Pakiri is also one of the best bases for **horse trekking** in the North Island. **Pakiri Beach Horse Treks**, ① *Taurere Park, Rahuikiri Rd, Pakiri Beach, T09-4226275, www.horseride-nz.co.nz*, are a popular outfit offering a huge range of trekking options from 1 hr to 7 days safaris and twilight rides. They also provide their own basic or more comfortable homestay accommodation and café. ▸▸ *For Sleeping, see page 160.*

Mangawhai Heads → *Phone code: 09 Colour map 1, grid A4*
From Pakiri the metalled roads wind their way up to Mangawhai, a short distance from the sweeping coast and beaches of the Jellicoe Channel. Slightly inland the rather exposed **Spectacle** and **Tomorata Lakes** play host to local water-skiers and jet-skiers.

The best spot at which to access the beach and coastal views is at **Te Arai Point**, just north of Spectacle Lake. There is little in the way of habitation here, which adds to the peace and isolation. North along the beach from Te Arai there is a wildlife refuge that takes in the impressive sand spit of the **Mangawahi Harbour**, but this is best accessed just south of Mangawhai village on Bull Road (off Black Swamp Road).

Some 10 km north of Te Arai is **Mangawhai**, a small farming village which offers a limited range of motel and motor camp accommodation. Mangawhai Heads, a short distance to the north of the village, is basically a scattering of holiday houses frequented by the wealthy in summer. The beaches around both villages are popular with surfers and beach-goers, and 'The Heads', as it is better known, is also a popular base for deep-sea and game fishing.

There is no information centre in Mangawhai but there is an information booth next to the main drag, Molesworth Drive, near the Golf Club. Consulting the website, www.mangawhaiheads.co.nz can also be very useful. Here you can see the various accommodation options and local activities available. The leaflet *Magical Mangawhai* is also comprehensive and available from Regional Tourist Offices and most local shops and motor parks. ▶▶ *For Sleeping and Eating, see pages 160 and 161.*

Waipu and around → *Phone code: 09 Colour map 1, grid B4*

North of Mangawhai the road negotiates the headland and falls to the beautiful shoreline settlements of Lang's Beach and Waipu Cove at the southern end of Bream Bay, before turning inland to the proudly Scottish enclave of Waipu.

History Waipu was founded in 1853 by a party of 120 Scottish settlers who were part of a group of 400 that originally left their homelands under the resolute leadership of the Reverend Norman McLeod. They did so in desperation during the terrible Highland Clearances, which resulted in mass migrations in the early 1800s. Their first stop was Nova Scotia but after a series of bad winters and crop failures they left for the new colonies in Australia and then New Zealand on board sailing ships they skilfully built themselves. With their resettlement a relative success, word was sent to Nova Scotia and a further 850 followed to settle the area. Hints of the ethnic origins are all around the village with street names like Braemar Lane, Argyll Street and Caledonian Park.

Also, in the village square is the grand war memorial monument which is made of Aberdeen Granite and was shipped especially from Scotland in 1914 to commemorate the 60th anniversary of the town's founding.

Sights The small community is very proud of its Scottish heritage and no visit to Waipu would be complete without a look inside the **Waipu Museum and Heritage Centre**, ① *T09-4320746, www.waipumuseum.com, 0930-1600, $5, child $2*, with its large Nova Scotian flag outside – a flag that combines the ancient Scottish Saltire and Lion Rampant designs. Inside the museum, walls are decked with photographs, and faces of early immigrants, proud and brave, look down on cases full of personal effects, from spectacles to spinning wheels. Logbooks listing the immigrant arrivals and the ships on which they arrived have been carefully created and are being continuously updated. It is little wonder that many Nova Scotians come especially to Waipu to trace their ancestors and at times find family heirlooms amongst the treasured pieces. There has been so much interest over the years that the new Heritage Centre was added in 2002 to house more modern resources with which the public can now trace their lineage. The staff in the museum are very knowledgeable and will, if you linger, tell you many a fine story of both past and present.

Every New Year's Day since 1871 the **Waipu Highland Games** (the largest and longest-running in the Southern Hemisphere) gets into full swing with highland dancers, pipe bands and the statutory kilted, caber-tossing men, all of whom descend on the village from far and wide. ① *For details contact the Waipu Caledonian Society, T09-4320746.*

The **Old Waipu Firehouse Art Gallery** ① *in the old Waipu fire station on West End Street, T09-4320797, 7 days*, is worth a look with some fine examples of local art at affordable prices. And on the eastern edge of Waipu adjacent to Johnston Port Road is the **Waipu Wildlife Refuge**, where you can see a variety of native shorebirds in an easily accessible area situated around the mouth of the Ruakaka River.

The Waipu Caves 13 km to the west of Waipu (via Shoemaker Road), offer a great opportunity to see glow-worms through a 200-m passage, part of an extensive limestone cave system. The cave has free access, so caution is advised. Going alone is not recommended and obviously do not enter without a torch and appropriate footwear. A map giving directions is available in the museum and the cave is signposted from Waipu Caves Road. If you would prefer to see the sights above ground using the four-legged option, or take a guided tour of the cave, **North River Horse Treks** can oblige, T09-4320565/0800-743-344. Again, take appropriate clothing, your swimsuit and a torch.

North of Waipu and back on SH 1 you follow the edge of Bream Bay (beach best accessed at Uretiti 6 km north of Waipu) before turning inland towards Whangarei. At the northern end of Bream Bay and the entrance to Whangarei Harbour is the unsightly **Marsden Oil Refinery** ① T09-4328194, daily 1000-1700. This is where all of New Zealand's crude oil is imported. Sadly, even with all the best technology in the world, the refinery and its tanker traffic poses a significant threat to Northland's pristine coastline and remains a potential environmental disaster. However, see if the **visitors' centre** at the refinery can persuade you otherwise. ▸▸ For Sleeping and Eating, see page 160.

● Sleeping

Warkworth p154
Being in such close proximity to Auckland and city folks looking for a quiet weekend away, the Warkworth offers a vast array of country B&B accommodations. If that is your intention you should call in to the VIC or visit the website www.warkworth-information.co.nz to muse the listings.
LL Kauri Grove Lodge Homestay, Thompson Rd, Kaipara Flats, T09-4225775, www.kaurigrove.co.nz Fine country living, food and wine with 4 luxury guest rooms one with a 4-poster, meals available.
LL Sandpiper Lodge, Takatu Rd Peninsula, Matakana, T09-4227256, www.sandpiperlodge.co.nz Near the beautiful Tawharanui Regional Park. Very classy. Pool and restaurant attached.
L Uhuru Farmstay, 390 Pukapuka Rd, Mahurangi West, T09-4220585, T09-4220545. A spectacular, new and spacious house in farm and bush setting overlooking a private bay. Superb pool.
A Willow Lodge B&B, 541 Woodcocks Rd, T/F09-4257676. Tidy self-contained units 3 mins from the town in a quiet setting, friendly, knowledgeable hosts.
A Central Motel, Neville St, Warkworth, T/F09-4258645. With the Warkworth Inn (below), it's one of the few basic and affordable options.
B-D Warkworth Inn, 9 Queen St, Warkworth, T09-4258569, www.inn@maxnet.co.nz The town's original hotel built in 1860 with comfortable, good value B&B and backpacker-style accommodation. Campervans are also welcome to use the

facilities for a small fee.
Other accommodation worth considering outside Warkworth includes:
L-A Saltings B&B 1210 Sandspit Rd, T09-4259670, www.saltings.co.nz
B His House, Berkah Retreat, 160 Hepburn Creek Rd, T09-4250042, www.hishouse.co.nz
B Cowan Bay Trust Cottage, Cowan Bay, T09-4250133, www.cowanbayfarm.co.nz A self-contained waterside hideaway.

Kawau Island p155
There is a wide range of accommodation options in the satellite coastal villages from B&Bs to motels and motor parks. The VIC in Warkworth has extensive listings and will arrange bookings, T09-4259081, www.warkworth-information.co.nz
A Cedar Lodge, Smelting House Bay, T09-4228700. Self-contained units.
A-D Pah Farm Lodge and Camp, Moores Bay, T09-4228765, pah.farm@ihug.co.nz Fishing lodge, bar and restaurant. There is a restaurant attached to the Pah Farm Lodge and a kiosk on the island, but it is not very well stocked and you would be advised to take your own picnic.

Matakana and Tawharanui p156
The following three **L** category places are all fine top-range options:
L Sandpiper Lodge, Takatu Rd. See Warkworth Sleeping above.
L Hurstmere House, Tongue Farm Rd, Matakana, T09-4229220.
L The Castle, 378 Whitmore Rd, Matakana, T09-4229288, mail@the-castle.co.nz
B Matakana House Motel, 975 Matakana Rd, T09-4227497, www.matakanahouse.co.nz

Mid-range and very tidy.

C-D Matakana Backpackers, *19 Matakana Valley Rd, Matakana, T09-4229264*. Pick-ups available from Warkworth; dormitory and twin share.

Leigh and the Goat Island *p156*

LL-L Tera del Mar, *140 Rodney Rd, Leigh, T09-4226090, www.teradelmar.co.nz* A rambling Victorian villa offering all mod cons including one luxury room with 4-poster bed and open fire.

A-C Leigh Sawmill Café, *142 Pakiri Rd, Leigh, T09-4226019, www.leighsawmillcafe.co.nz* A more affordable and good option in the village offering tidy rooms with en suite bath and also bunks.

C-D Goat Island Backpackers, *Goat Island Rd, T09-4226183*. Another budget option and also has powered sites for campervans, but may be closed in winter.

C-D Whangateau Holiday Park, *559 Leigh Rd, Whangateau, T09-4226305*. On the beachfront and friendly.

Pakiri *p157*

Pakiri Holiday Park, *on the beach, T09-4226199*. Some nice cabins, new luxury cottages, camp kitchen and kayak hire.
Miller's Ark, *just north of Pakiri, T09-4315266*. A rather intriguing homestay or self-contained option.

Mangawhai Heads *p157*

AL Mangawhai Lodge, *4 Heather St, Mangawhai Heads, T09-4315311, www.seaviewlodge.co.nz* Best B&B in the area and good value.

A Milestone Cottages, *Moir Point Rd, Mangawhai, T09-4314018, milestone.cottages@clear.net.nz* An award-winning self-contained option, close to the beach with pool and kayaks.

A Hidden Valley Chalets, *corner of Te Arai Pt Rd, Mangawhai, T09-4315332, www.hiddenvalley.co.nz* Good self-contained chalets in quiet surrounds with outdoor spa.

Motorcamps

Mangawhai Heads Motor Camp, *Mangawhai Heads Rd, T09-4314675*
Riverside Holiday Park, *Black Swamp Rd, Mangawhai, T09-4314825*. Close to the beach and the sand spit wildlife refuge.

Waipu *p158*

There are a number of good B&Bs and lodges in the area mainly in Waipu Cove or Lang Beach to the south of Waipu village.

L Royal Palm Lodge, *19 Highland Lass Pl, Lang's Beach, T09-4320120, www.royalpalmlodge.co.nz* A modern villa with a range of well-appointed rooms and en suite baths, a spa and excellent cuisine. More affordable options include:

A Lochalsh B&B, *Cove Rd, Lang's Beach, T09-4320053*.

A Stone House B&B, *Cove Rd, Waipu, T09-4320432, stonehousewaipu@xtra.co.nz*

A Flower Haven B&B, *53 St Ann Rd, Waipu Cove, T09-4320421*. Self-contained.

A Hinterland Fold Farmstay, *McLeods Rd, Waipu, T09-4320304*. Of particular note: has a good value self-contained studio on a stud for some very horny highland cows.

There are only a few motels, including:

A Waipu Clansman Motel, *30 Cove Rd, Waipu, T09-4320424*, and the beachside

A Waipu Cove Resort, *891 Cove Rd, T09-4320348*.

A-D Waipu Cove Cottages and Camping Ground, *Cove Rd, T09-4320851, covecottages@xtra.co.nz* Tidy and popular.

C-D Ebb and Flow Backpackers Hostel, *Johnston Point Rd, T09-4321288*.

⑦ Eating

Warkworth *p154*

$$$ Kauri Grove Lodge, *T09-4225775*, and **$$$ Sandpiper Lodge**, *T09-4227256* (see accommodation above), are the best options for fine dining. Bookings essential for both.

$$ Warkworth Pizza Company, *Neville St. Daily 1100-1500 and 1700-late*. A popular local favourite.

$$ Pizza Construction, *Mahurangi East Rd, Snells Beach, T09-4255555. Daily 1700-2200*. Also has a good local reputation.

$$ Millstream Bar and Grill Theatre, *15-17 Elizabeth, T09-4222292. Daily*. Something a little different with its appealing à la carte menu and boutique **theatre** showing recent release movies.

$ Salty Dog Tavern, *Snells Beach, T09-4255588*. An old English style pub with good pints of beer and pub grub, just like back home.

Cafés
Arts Café, *Baxter St, T09-4258971. Mon-Fri 0700-1700, Sat-Sun 0900-1500.* With an interesting local art gallery attached.
Queens St Corner Café, *T09-4258749. Daily (opposite the VIC).*
Duck's Crossing Café, *Riverview Plaza, T09-4259940. Daily 0730-1630.*

Leigh and Goat Island *p156*
$$ Sawmill Café, *142 Pakiri Rd, T09-4226019. Summer daily 7 days 0930-late, (winter Thu-Sun late).* The place to go for fresh light meals, good coffee and occasional live music.
$$ Seafriends, *7 Goat Island Rd, T09-4226212.* Has a restaurant open daily for lunches and on Fri/Sat for dinner in summer.
$ Leigh Fish and Chips, *Cumberland St. Daily 1100-2230 (later on weekends).* Given the fishy nature of the village and the area as a whole it would perhaps be rude not to sample these delights.

Mangawhai Heads *p157*
$$ Naja Garden Café, *Molesworth Dr,*

T09-4314111. Daily 0830-1700, and for dinner daily (Thu-Sat in winter). Fully licensed and offers contemporary food and an all-day breakfast.
$$ Sail Rock Café, *12 Wood St, T09-4314051.* Offers an à la carte menu, plus a range of pizzas and café lunches, bar and BYO. Open daily in summer.
$ Salt-e-Air Cyber Café, *7 Wood St, T09-4315430.* Good for a quick coffee and to check your email.

Waipu *p158*
There is not a great deal to tickle the taste buds in Waipu and sadly not a haggis or a 'clooty dumpling' to be had anywhere. However, the following will no doubt all do their best for you with Kiwi fare.
$ Waipu Cove Takeaways, *Cove Rd, T09-4320636.*
$ Granz Café, *45 The Centre, open daily in summer, T09-4320254.*
$$ Pizza Barn and Bar, *3 Cove Rd, Waipu, T09-4321011.*
$$ Clansman Motel and Restaurant, *30 Cove Rd, Waipu, T09-4320424.*

Whangarei and around

→ *Phone code: 09 Colour map 1, grid B4 Population: 40,000*
Given the obvious allure of the Bay of Islands to the north, with its promise of stunning scenery and a whole host of activities, few visitors pay much attention to Northland's largest town. But, despite its rather dull appearance, if you do choose to linger here a while, you will find that it actually has quite a lot to offer – not only in aesthetics (just take a look at the Town Basin) but also in some lesser-known gems only a short drive away. One such pearl is Ocean Beach, Whangarei Heads, the perfect to sit just after a storm, watching the sun rise.

Getting there
Air The district is serviced by **Air New Zealand Link**, To800-737000, www.airnewzealand.co.nz **Great Barrier Airlines**, To9-2759120, www.greatbarrier airlines.co.nz, also run a Fri and Sun service from Whangarei to Claris(on Great Barrier Island) from $189 return **Onerahi Airport**, To9-4370666, is 9 km west of the city and is linked to the city centre by shuttle bus, $10.
Car If you are arriving by car, take extra care on the stretch of road from Waipu to Whangarei. This stretch of road is a notorious black spot and is known locally as 'the killing fields'.
Bus Intercity, To9-4382653, and **Northliner** coaches, To9-4383206, have a daily service to and from Auckland and destinations further north. The depot for both is in Rose St, downtown Whangarei but they can also stop at the VIC at the southern approach to town.

Getting around

Whangarei has a fairly comprehensive bus service operated and administered by the Regional and District Councils. Timetables are available from the VIC or infoline, To9-4384639. Standard fare within the city is adult $2, child $1. The main taxi company is Kiwi Carlton, 24-hr service, To9-4382299. There is no public transport available for getting to **Whangarei Heads** (page 166), but cycling is an option. Cycle hire is available from Town Basin Hire, Jetty One, Town Basin, To9-4372509, costing from $25 a day.

Information

The main **VIC** is just as you come into the town (northbound) in Tarewa Park, ⓘ *Otaika Rd, To9-4381079, www.whangarei.org.nz Weekdays 0830-1700, weekends 0930-1630, extended hours in summer*. The staff are very friendly and helpful and the DoC information centre and a café are attached. The DoC useful pamphlet *Whangarei District Walks* is available from the VIC or DoC office. Believe it or not, the new toilets are also worth a mention if not a sneaky muse.

History

True to the area's tradition it was a Scot, William Carruth, who was the first to buy a block of land from the Maori in 1839 and settle at the mouth of the Hatea River. He was quickly joined by other settlers and before long a small community developed. Like so many other Northland communities they quickly focused their activities on kauri timber milling and for a short while prospered. But after Kororareka (Russell) in the Bay of Islands was sacked in 1845 by the notorious Maori chief Hone Heke, most of the local European settlers fled south to Auckland for safety, only to venture north again a few years later. With these disruptive beginnings initial progress was slow, until the quest for Kauri Gum in the 1850s and the building of a shipyard in the 1860s finally brought prosperity and a rapid expansion to the area. It was not until the 1930s that both road and rail links with Auckland were completed, but by then the busy port had already put Whangarei on the map as the main commercial centre and capital of the north.

Sights

A good place to start your tour of Whangarei's sights is with a fine view of the city and the Harbour itself. **Mount Parahaki** on Memorial Drive (off Riverside Drive) is 241 m high and was once the site of New Zealand's largest Maori *pa*. Today it is crowned with a war memorial and a rather tacky red cross that glows at night. You can also walk up Parahaki (1 hr) via the **Mair Park**, a peaceful park of native bush and well-marked trails. There is an old gold mine and remnants of Maori fortifications within it.

The jewel in Whangarei's scenic crown is the congenial **Town Basin**, where expensive nautical hardware bobs and squeaks on the glistening waters of the Marina. The Basin is an award-winning waterfront development which houses a number of interesting attractions, including museums, art galleries and craft shops, not to mention the odd café and restaurant. There is also a small **information booth** to help you find your way around, ⓘ *To9-4381315*.

Without doubt the best attraction, other than the atmosphere of the Basin itself, is **Clapham's Clock Museum**, ⓘ *To9-4383993. Daily 0900-1700. Adult $8, child $4*. A highly entertaining and ever-growing collection of timepieces from all around the world. The best thing to do is to take a guided tour, otherwise the collection, which is the biggest in the Southern Hemisphere, is a bit daunting.

There are two good art galleries at the Basin. One is **The Marina Gallery**, ⓘ *To9-4388899, Mon-Fri 1100-1700, Sat-Sun 1000-1600*, which has some fine exhibits of local, national and international artists. The other is the gallery in the historic colonial **Reyburn House**, ⓘ *Tue-Fri 1000-1600, Sat-Sun 1300-1600*, (oldest in Whangarei), which features displays of local art. For lovers of beer, the **Brauhaus** offers free beer tasting – but there is a limit!

West of the town Basin, in the peaceful and pleasant **Cafler Park and Rose Gardens**, is the small modern **Whangarei Art Museum**, ⓘ *To9-4307240, www.whangareiartmuseum.co.nz, Tue-Fri 1000-1630, Sat-Sun 1200-1630, donations*, that shows the best of local art past and present and also hosts touring national exhibitions. A short walk will take you to the **Fernery, Conservatory and Cacti House** ⓘ *To9-4384879. Daily 1000-1600. Free*. The Fernery houses New Zealand's largest collection of ferns, while the Conservatory is filled with ever-changing displays of flowers. Near the park on Rust Avenue is the **Forum North Cultural Complex** (see Entertainment, page 170).

On the outskirts of town at the end of Selwyn Avenue is the celebrated creative haven of the **Northland Craft Trust (Craft Quarry)** ⓘ *Daily 1000-1600. Free*. It's an impressive collective of working artists and crafts people producing an array of works from pottery and lithographs to traditional Maori carvings – worth a visit.

Further west and 6 km out of town, in the suburb of Maunu, is the **Whangarei Museum, Clarke Homestead** and **Kiwi House**. ⓘ *To9-4389630, www.whangareimuseum.org.nz, daily 1000-1600, adult $3, $7 all sites*. It is an indoor/outdoor complex with a colonial farming block and homestead and a modern building housing a number of significant Taonga or Maori treasures, including kiwi feather capes and a musket that belonged to the great northern warrior Hone Heke. The display is deliberately indigenous in content and perspective. 'Live Days' are held regularly during the summer with special events like bullock riding, vintage car displays and horse-drawn carriages. The Kiwi House is one of the better examples in the country with exhibits of native flora and live kiwi on show. Note that there is usually only one. This is deliberate as kiwi are solitary birds and fiercely territorial.

Next to the museum is the **Whangarei Native Bird Recovery Centre**, ⓘ *To9-4381457*. Although not freely open to visitors you may be allowed to visit by prior arrangement and for a donation. This charity has the main centre in the north for wild bird rehabilitation and an excellent and successful kiwi egg incubation facility. To the south of the city on State Highway 1 is **The Paper Mill**. ⓘ *To9-4382652. Mon-Sat 1000-1500. Donation; small charge to make paper*. This tourist attraction is growing in popularity and deservedly so. It gives the visitor an insight into traditional craft papermaking using recycled materials in an historical setting, and you can even try to make some yourself.

Just 1 km further south is the **Longview Winery**, ⓘ *To9-4387227, www.longviewwines.co.nz, Mon-Sat 0830-1800 in summer, 0830-1730 in winter*, a 30 year-old estate producing popular and award-winning wines.

To the north of the city on Ngunguru Road, Tikipunga, is the slightly over-rated 23 m **Whangarei Falls** which are worth a peek if you are passing. (Perhaps a better way to experience them is to abseil down them with Northland Outdoors, To9-4303474.) The **AH Reed Memorial Kauri Park** on Whareora Road is the pick of the local parks with some fine examples of native Kauri trees up to 3 m in diameter and 500 years old. They are impressive, but nothing compared to the 1500 year-old Tane Mahuta on the west coast, which in turn is nothing, compared to some monsters that once were. The park has a number of short walks and tracks and a very pleasant waterfall thrown in for good measure.

Although they are hard to find and a bit out of town, the **Abbey Caves** are worth a visit. If you take a right off Memorial Drive (up Mount Parahaki) on to Old Parua Bay Road and on to Abbey Caves Road you will, with a little difficulty, find a DoC sign next to the road. Provided you have adequate footwear, a torch and are not alone (or have kids in tow), then follow the footpath and signs past the weird and wonderful limestone foundations that lead to the caves. Do not venture too far into the caves without a

‣ *If you only do one thing in the Whangarei district, then make sure it's a trip to watch the sunrise at Ocean Beach, 35 km west of the city.*

Whangarei

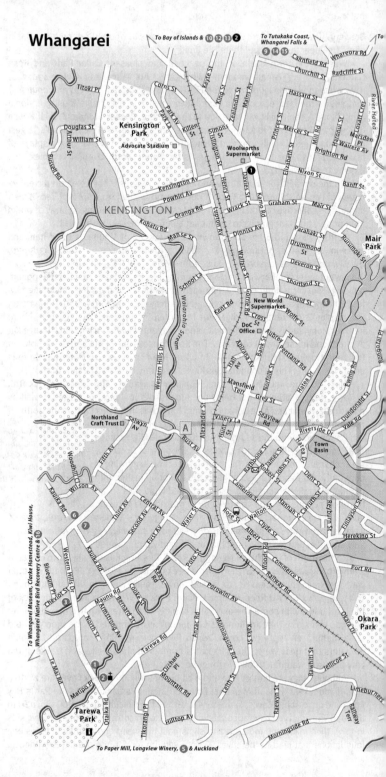

To Bay of Islands & ⑩⑫⑬❷

To Tutukaka Coast, Whangarei Falls & ⑨⑭⑮

To

Cairnfield Rd

Whareora Rd

Churchill St

Radcliffe St

Titoki Pl

Corns St

Keyte St

King St

Zealandia St

Mains Av

Hassard St

River Hatea

Douglas St

Arthur St

William St

Russell Rd

Kensington Park

Park Av

Park La

Killen St

Simons St

Istington St

Princes St

Mercer St

Hill St

TS Imona St

Wairere Av

Marsden Pl

Brighton Rd

Advocate Stadium

Woolworths Supermarket

Elizabeth St

Nixon St

Banff St

❶

KENSINGTON

Kensington Av

Powhiri Av

Oranga Rd

Kohatu Rd

Henry St

Davies St

Kamo Rd

Graham St

Mair St

Lupton Av

Wrack St

Dinniss Av

Parahaki St

Rurumoki St

Mair Park

Manse St

Wallace St

Drummond St

Deveron St

Shortland St

Donald St

Ewing Rd

Horaha Dr

Western Hills Dr

School La

Waiarohia Stream

Kent Rd

Gorrie St

New World Supermarket

Cross St

Wolfe St

❽

DoC Office

Aubrey St

Bank St

Pentland Rd

Hatea Dr

Dundonald St

Yale St

Northland Craft Trust

Selwyn Av

Aparima Av

Hatt Av

Norfolk St

Mansfield Terr

Grey St

Seaview Rd

Vinery La

Riverside Dr

Woodhill

Fifth Av

Wilson Av

Third Av

Central Av

Second Av

First Av

Water St

Rust Av

Alexander St

Hunt St

A

Rathbone St

Bownes St

Robert John St

Dent St

Hatea Dr

Town Basin

❻

❼

Kauika Rd

Western Hills Dr

Bluegum Pl

Chieftoi St

❾

Maunu Rd

Bernard St

Cooke St

Rose St

Cameron St

Walton St

Clyde St

Albert St

Hannah St

Carlisle St

Reyburn St

Ewaxton St

Herekino St

Commerce St

Woods Rd

Spoon Rd

Port Rd

To Whangarei Museum, Clarke Homestead, Kiwi House, Whangarei Native Bird Recovery Centre & ⑯

Armstrong Av

North St

Te Mai Rd

Tarewa Rd

Bays Rd

Pato St

Railway Rd

Parowini Av

Anzac Rd

Orchard Pl

Mountain Rd

Morningside Rd

Kaka St

Tenth St

Rawhiti St

Jellicoe St

Okara Dr

Okara Park

Matipo Pl

❶

❷

Otaika Rd

Tarewa Park

Raewyn St

Tikorangi Pl

Hilltop Av

Morningside Rd

Limeburners

Railway Terr

To Paper Mill, Longview Winery, ❺ & Auckland

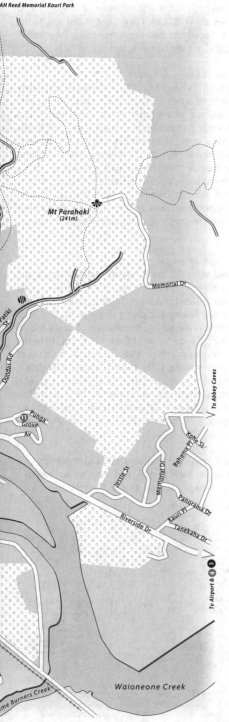

Mt Parahaki
(241m)

Memorial Dr

Patiki St

Dundas Rd

To Abbey Caves

Detail map:
A *Whangarei centre,*
page 166

N

0 metres	300
0 yards	300

Punga Grove Av

Jessie St

Kohe St

Bahama Pl

Memorial Dr

Kauri Pl

Panorama Dr

Riverside Dr

Tanekaha Dr

To Airport & 4 3

Waioneone Creek

Lime Burners Creek

Sleeping

Avenue Heights Motel **7**
Bunkdown Lodge **1**
Channel Vista **4**
Cherry Court Motor Lodge **2**
Cheviot Park Motor Lodge **3**
Graelyn Villa **14**
Kamo Springs Caravan Park **13**
Kingswood Motor Inn **10**
Lupton House **9**
Mulryan's **12**
Otaika Motel &
  Caravan Park **5**
Pohutukawa Lodge **6**
Settlers **8**
Stranded Mariner **16**
Whangarei Falls
  Backpackers & Holiday Park **15**
Whangarei YHA **11**

Eating 🍴

Adriatic Fisheries **1**
Tonic **2**
Topsail Café **3**

Northland Whangarei and around

guide. If you are brave, switch off your torch and amidst the sound of trickling water, enjoy the small galaxy of glow-worms above. It is easy to get lost in and around the caves so the best option is to join a guided tour from Bunkdown Lodge (see below) T09-4388886, $25. ▸▸ *For Sleeping, Eating, and all other listings, see pages 167-172.*

Whangarei Heads → *Phone code: 09 Colour map 1, grid B4*

Ocean beach is one of Northland's best: it's quiet, beautiful and, in a raging easterly wind, a place where the senses are bombarded with nature at its best. On the way you will begin to notice the prevalence of evocative Scots place names like McLeod's and Urquart's Bay and street names like McDonald Road – all family names of the 'overspill' Scots settlers from the Bream Bay and Waipu enclaves. Above these quiet communities and scenic bays are the towering peaks of **Mount Manaia**, the base of which can be accessed from the car park next to the Manaia Club. It is an excellent, but steep walk through native bush that takes about 3 hrs return. You cannot climb to the peak summits themselves – they are tapu (sacred and off limits) – steeped in Maori legend. Other fine coastal walks are to **Peach Cove** (3 hrs) and **Smugglers Cove** (1 hr) both reachable from **Urquart's Bay**. ▸▸ *For Sleeping and Eating sections see pages 168-170.*

The Tutukaka Coast → *Phone code: 09 Colour map 1, grid B4*

Even if fishing and scuba diving did not exist, the Tutukaka coastline would still deserve to be one of the finest coastal venues in Northland. But its rugged scenic bays are best known throughout New Zealand and beyond as the gateway and safe harbour to some of the best deep-sea fishing and diving in the world. The Poor Knights Islands which lie 25 km offshore are an internationally significant A both above and below the waterline, with a wide range of flora and fauna. Here the nutrient-rich currents meet in water of unusually high clarity to create a showcase of marine life much of which is seen nowhere else in the country. Although landing is forbidden without a permit the islands themselves are home to rare terrestrial species, like the prehistoric tuatara, a reptile that has changed little in 60 million years. Most activity in the area takes place from Tutukaka with its large sheltered marina while the village of **Ngunguru**, 5 km before it, has most of the visitor and resident amenities. ▸▸ *For Sleeping, Eating and Activities, see pages 168, 170 and 171.*

Getting there Tutukaka is on the loop road that also takes in Ngunguru and Matapouri before turning inland again back to SH1 and Whangarei. Tutukaka Transport, T0800-488885, offers a weekday coastal shuttle from the Pak-n-Save

Whangarei centre

Sleeping	Eating	Gybe 8	Reva's 4
Quality 1	Barfly 1	Killer Prawn 3	Strand Café 5
	Dickens Inn 2	Mondos 7	Water Street Brasserie 6

0 metres 100
0 yards 100

The Poor Knights Islands

The Poor Knights Islands, lying 24km off Tutukaka, are the remnants of a large volcano, which erupted over 10 million years ago. The islands themselves provide a predator-free refuge for land animals like tuatara, native lizards, giant weta, flax snails, giant centipedes and a wide variety of rare seabirds. They are also home to several species of distinctive plants, including the Poor Knights lily, found only on 'The Knights' and the Hen and Chicken islands off Whangarei Heads. But it is the marine reserve, and the wonderful spectacle below the water, for which the islands are most famous. A rich habitat of caves, arches, tunnels and sheer cliffs attract a wide variety of marine life from sharks to black coral. Sponge gardens, kelp forests and gorgonian fields are inhabited by a myriad of fish, shellfish, urchins and anemones and there even tame grouper, which welcome divers with their distinctively vacuous look. All this combined with the exceptional water clarity make 'The Knights' one of the top dive venues in the world.

supermarket on Walton St at 1200, from $12, child $6. By car from the city suburb of Tikipunga, take the Ngunguru Rd past Whangarei Falls. On the outskirts of the city in Glenbervie the roads become lined by drystone walls giving the area a distinctly British countryside feel (no doubt a legacy of the early settlers) before New Zealand bush takes over once again and you hit the coast at Ngunguru.

Whangarei to the Bay of Islands → *Phone code: 09 Colour map 1, grid B4*
Most people take State Highway 1 to the Bay of Islands, though a far more interesting route is via the **Old Russell Road** which leaves SH1 for the coast at Whakapara, about 26 km north of Whangarei. Here you are entering a mobile phone free zone, on roads with more animals than cars, and on which the children (predominantly Maori) do not mind walking in the rain. Welcome to rural Northland and the simple spirit of the north. After simply enjoying the countryside and its atmosphere you reach the coast at **Helena Bay** which, along with **Whananaki** and **Mimiwhangata** to the south and the **Whangaruru Peninsula** to the north, offer remote and beautiful coastal scenery.

From Whangaruru the road passes the neck of the beautiful **Cape Brett Peninsula** which offers great walking in equally stunning coastal scenery before turning inland and slowly negotiating its way to Russell. If you intend to reach Paihia you can get the vehicular ferry at Opua (last ferry Sat-Thu 2230, Fri 2230).

● Sleeping

Whangarei *p161*
Whangarei has a wide variety of accommodation options but is a little wanting with regard to hotel and luxury accommodation. With most people pressing on northwards to the Bay of Islands pre-booking is generally not essential, but in summer, as ever, still recommended.
AL Quality Hotel, *9 Riverside Dr*, *T09-4380284, quality.whangarei@extra.co.nz* Guest rooms and suites, laundry, licensed restaurant and bar. Overlooks the marina and Town Basin.

A Channel Vista, *254 Beach Rd, Onerahi*, *T/F09-4365529, tancred@igrin.co.nz* Fully self-contained and traditional bedrooms, great harbour views.
A Avenue Heights Motel, *355 Western Hills Dr (SH1), T09-4382737, hayleyk@actrix.gen.nz* New motel conveniently located with 10 tidy luxury units.
A Cherry Court Motor Lodge, *35 Otaika Rd*, *T09-4383128, www.cherrycourt.co.nz* Swimming pool, laundry and licensed restaurant nearby.
A Cheviot Park Motor Lodge, *corner of Cheviot St and Western Hills Dr, T09-4382341, www.cheviot-park.co.nz* Modern, friendly.

A **Kingswood Motor Inn**, *260 Kamo Rd, T09-4375779, F09-4375780*. 5 min north of the city centre, paraplegic units, laundry, spa.

A **Mulryan's**, *Crane Rd, Kamo, T09-4350945, info@mulryans.co.nz* Comfortable B&B style accommodation in a restored kauri villa. Quiet country setting and a great breakfast.

A **Pohutukawa Lodge**, *362 Western Hills Dr, T09-4308634, www.pohutukawalodge.co.nz* New studio units, some with spas, laundry.

A **Settlers Hotel**, *Hatea Dr, T09-4382699, settlers@ihug.co.nz* In a nice setting overlooking the river and within walking distance of the Town Basin. Bedrooms with en suite bath, laundry, pool and private spas, licensed à la carte restaurant.

A **The Stranded Mariner**, *State Highway 14, T09-4389967*. Separate self-contained unit and traditional B&B accommodation. Unusual house with a veritable den of unusual teddy bears and a craft shop.

B **Graelyn Villa**, *166 Kiripaka Rd, T09-4377532, graelyn@extra.co.nz* Nicely restored villa, comfortable and homely.

B **Lupton House**, *555 Ngunguru Rd, Glenbervie, T09-4372989, www.truenz.co.nz/luptonhouse* Traditional kiwi villa in a country setting between the city and Tutukaka with friendly owners. Bathrooms en suite, shared bathrooms, pool.

C-D **Bunkdown Lodge**, *23 Otaika Rd, T09-4388886, bunkdown@ihug.co.nz* Without doubt, one of the best backpackers in the country. Large, modern, more like a B&B and even has a bath. Very helpful friendly hosts who have nothing short of another tourist information centre attached. In-house tours to Abbey Caves $25. Popular, so book ahead.

C-D **Whangarei Falls Backpackers and Holiday Park**, *Ngunguru Rd, Tikipunga, T09-4370609*. A great backpackers that doubles as a small motor camp. It contains all the usual mod cons plus a small pool, spa and TV room.

C-D **Whangarei YHA**, *52 Punga Grove Av, T09-4388954*. Set in peaceful surroundings and spacious grounds overlooking the harbour and Tower Basin, 5 min walk from the town centre. Dorms and doubles with all th eusual facilities including internet. Dive trips to the Poor Knights Islands can also be arranged here.

Motor camps and campsites

A-D **Tropicana Top Ten Holiday Park**, *Whangarei Heads (5 km past Onerahi BP Station and 10 km from the city), T09-4360687*.

Otaika Motel and Caravan Park, *136 Otaika Rd, T/F09-4381459*.

Kamo Springs Caravan Park, *55 Great North Rd, T09-4351208*.

Whangarei Holiday Park, *24 Mair St, T09-4376856, whangareiholiday@actrix.co.nz* This last one is the best bet.

Whangarei Heads *p166*

There is little in the way of accommodation at the heads beyond McLeod's Bay but the small communities of **Parua Bay** just before it, and **Pataua** and **Taiharuru** a few kilometres north, have a number of options.

A **Parua House**, *Parua Bay, T09-4365855, paruahomestay@clear.net.nz* A farmstay with en suite and private facilities, fine views.

A **The Old Lady**, *13 Norfolk Av, Reotahi, T09-4340575*. An historic homestead that offers 2 rooms with their own sitting room and balcony.

A **Tide Song**, *Taiharuru Estuary, Beasley Rd, T09-4361959, www.tidesong.co.nz* Self-contained in a bush and seaside setting.

Motorcamps and campsites

A-D **Tropicana Top Ten Holiday Park**, *Whangarei Heads (5 km past Onerahi BP Station), T09-4360687, www.tropicana. co.nz* Tries hard to live up to all the usual Top Ten standards.

A-D **Treasure Island Trailer Park**, *Pataua South, T09-4362390*. Motorcamp with a beachfront campsite.

Tutukaka Coast *p166*

AL **Waipouri Lodge**, *Tutukaka, T09-4343696, mckillop@extra.co.nz* Self-contained 3-bedroom home.

AL **Poor Knights Lodge**, *Tutukaka, T09-4344405, www.poorknightslodge.co.nz* Two nicely appointed suites with decks overlooking the bay, internet, dinner on request. Dive and fishing trips arranged.

A **Dreamstay**, *Sandy Bay, T09-4343059, dreamstay@homenet.net.nz* B&B, homestay or self-contained options.

A **Pukepoto Orchards**, *521 Ngunguru Rd, Glenbervie, T09-4375433*. Self-contained unit in garden setting.

A **Malibu Mals Divestay**, *Tutukaka Block Rd, Kowharewa Bay, T09-4343450, malibumal@extra. co.nz* Self-contained units or B&B available.

A **Pacific Rendezvous Motel**, *Tutukaka, T09-4343847, www.oceanresort.co.nz* The most celebrated motel in the area with great views across the Tutukaka Harbour.

A **Seabreeze Motel**, *Ngunguru, T/F09-4343844*. Older style motel, overlooking the bay, fully self-contained units and spa pool.

A **The Sands Motel**, *Whangaumu Bay, Tutukaka, T09-4343747*. Spacious self-contained units.

B-D **Tutukaka Holiday Park**, *T09-4343938*. Relatively new park opposite the marina, six cabins, powered and non-powered sites and all the standard facilities.

B-D **Ngunguru Holiday Park and Backpackers**, *Papaka Rd, Ngunguru, (5 km before Tutukaka) T09-4343851*. Standard cabins and facilities with shared facilities for backpackers, water's edge with kayak and bike hire.

Whangarei to Bay of Islands *p167*
Accommodation here is somewhat basic and sparse with the exception of a few luxurious retreats.

LL-AL **Moureeses Bay** *Whananaki North, T09-8465881, moureesesbay@hotmail.com* A peaceful, classy barn-style self-contained house with modern fittings and facilities, just a stone's throw from the beach.

L-A **Robin's Nest**, *Oakura, T09-4336035, www.robinsnest.co.nz* Another tidy self-contained option close to all the activity operators in the village.

C-D **Farm Backpackers and Homestay**, *near Whangaruru, T09-4336894, www.thefarm.co.nz* Although most motor camps in the vicinity welcome backpackers you will also find a warm welcome here. Its very comfortable and friendly but perhaps the biggest attraction here are the activities on offer including **horse trekking**, use of quad and **mountain bikes** and even **yacht racing**. Recommended.

Motorcamps
There are basic motorcamps mainly at Oakura (just north of Helena bay).
C-D **Oakura Motels and Caravan Park**,

Oakura Bay, T09-4336803. Beachside camps with units, cabins, powered and non-powered sites.

C-D **Whangaruru Beachfront Camp**, *Whangaruru, T4336806*. Another alternative.

D **Mimiwhangata Bay** and **Coastal Park**, *bookings can be made through the Tarewa Park Visitor Centre, T09-4302007*. DoC's relatively cheap facilities with a self-contained lodge, cottage, beach house (book well in advance) and a campsite. Basic DoC camping facilities are also available at **Whananaki** and **Whangaruru**; contact DoC, T09-4302007.

❷ Eating

Whangarei *p161*
$$$ **Killer Prawn**, *28 Bank St, T09-4303333*. A swish and busy restaurant/bar considered the best eatery in town, offering a wide selection of traditional and specialist seafood options. Try the namesake 'Killer Prawn' – a small pond of seafood in which to bathe your taste buds.

$$$ **Water Street Brasserie**, *24 Water St, T09-4387464*. Open Tue-Sat, BYO. Fine traditional cuisine in modern surroundings.

$$$ **Tonic**, *239A Kamo Rd, T09-4375558*. Licensed, contemporary French cuisine and a fine Sun brunch from 0900.

$$$ **Topsail Café**, *1st Floor, Onerahi Yacht Club, Beach Rd, Onerahi, T09-4360529*. Open Mon-Sat from 1800, Sun brunch 1000-1500. Serves Continental-style cuisine and is a local seafood favourite.

$$$ **Reva's on the Waterfront**, *Quayside Town Basin, licensed, T09-4388969*. International cuisine in pleasant surroundings, great pizza. Live music.

$$$ **Gybe Restaurant and Bar**, *Quayside Town Basin, opposite Reva's, T09-4597438*. The seafood menu of this nautically orientated restaurant is also worth a look.

$$ **Barfly**, *13 Rathbone St, T09-4388761*. Café-style fare including wood-fired pizza and good coffee.

$$ **Dickens Inn**, *corner of Cameron and Quality St, T09-4300406*. One of Whangarei's most popular pubs. Pub-style cuisine, breakfast, lunch, dinner and snacks, children's menu.

$$ **Mondos Cafe**, *14 Quayside, Town Basin, T09-4300467*. One of the best cafes in the city

set overlooking the quay, ideal for lunch or a light snack.

$ Adriatic Fisheries, *Kensington, 91 Kamo Rd*, *T09-4373874*. Best fish and chippy in town. Supermarket: **Pak-n-Save**, *Walton St Plaza*, *T09-4381488*. Mon-Fri 0830-2000, Sat/Sun 0830-1900.

Whangarei Heads *p166*
There isn't much choice out on the 'Heads' but you can get a good evening meal at the **$$ Flames International Hotel** *in Onerhai (Waverly St)*, *T09-4362107*.
Taurikura General Store, just west of Ocean Beach. A traditional and interesting place to stock up, also has a café in summer. Alternatively get supplies at the supermarket in the **Onerahi Shopping Centre**.

Tutukaka Coast *p166*
$$ Snappa Rock Café *by the marina in Tutukaka*, *T09-4343774*. Open 7 days and nights. People come here from miles around to enjoy the seafood, the atmosphere and talk about the one that got away. One place not to miss.

🍷 Bars and clubs

There are a number of trendy bars and nightclubs in Whangarei.
The Killer Prawn *Bank St*, is the local place to be seen.
Heaven or **Danger Danger** *Vine St*, and **Rynoz** or **Spinners** *Cameron St*, are all pretty lively but, as you would expect, have that small town atmosphere.
Dickens Inn *Cameron St*, **Barfly** *Rathbone* are better for something a little quieter.

🎭 Entertainment

Cinema
Cinema City Five, *James St, T09-4388550*. The main cinema in Whangarai.

Theatre
Forum North Theatre, *Rust Ave*, *T09-4383815*. A well-equipped space and one of the best in the country for cultural and performing arts.

🏔 Activities and tours

Whangarei *p161*
Bone Carving Pacific Carvers, *61 Beazley Cres, T09-4372740*, offer traditional bone carving tuition with the production of your own 'tiki' from $80.

Bush Safaris The Bushwacka Experience, *Highway 14, Maungatapere, T09-4347839*. Thrilling trips in a 4-wheel drive vehicle with frequent stops, barbecue and abseiling. Daily 4-hr trip $85, 2-hr $55. Recommended. **Farm Safaris**, *Maunga- karamea, 20 minutes south of the city on SH1, T09-4323794, fmsafari@ihug.co.nz* Morning, afternoon and twilight tours on 4-wheel bikes. 1 hr (min 4 people) $50, 2 hrs (min 3 people) $90.

Cruises and Kayaking Whangarei Harbour: **Bream Bay Charters**, *Ruakaka, T09-4327484*. Oakura Bay: **Oakura Bay Cruises**, *T09-4336669*. **Town Basin Hire**, *Jetty One, Riverside Dr, Town Basin, T09-4372509*. Hire bikes, rollerblades and leisure craft including kayaks.

Cycling Cycle Touring Company New Zealand, *100 Church St, Whangarei, T021-2255-282, www.cycletours.co.nz* Specializes in self-led cycling adventures on routes all over Northland from 2-9 days. Accommodation and food included.

Diving Pacific Highway Charters, *T09-4373632, www.divenz.co.nz* **Knight Diver Tours**, *30 Heads Rd, T09-4362584, www.poorknights.co.nz* **Dive HQ**, *41 Clyde St, T09-4381075,www.divenow.co.nz* **Dive Connection**, *140 Lower Cameron St, T09-4300818*. Offer full dive courses.

Dolphin, seabird and whale watching
Although viewing success rates are far lower than Kaikoura in the South Island, sightings of a number of whale species are possible. Dolphin trips are also much better catered for in the Bay of Islands but if time is short and you do not intend to head further north **Bream Bay Charters**, *Ruakaka, T09-4327484*, offer trips locally.

⬤ *For an explanation of the sleeping and eating price codes used in this guide, see the inside*
⬤ *front cover. Other relevant information is provided in the Essentials chapter, see page 51.*

Fishing The harbour and more especially the Tutukaka coast offers excellent sea fishing. Big game fishing charters are available at Tutukaka with record catches in summertime. **Bream Bay Charters**, *Ruakaka, T09-4327484*, offer good trips locally.

Scenic flights and Skydiving **Tower Aviation**, *Onerahi Airport, T09-4360886.* Expensive but spectacular.
Northland Districts Aero Club, *Onerahi Airport, T09-4360890.* The latter also offer tandem sky diving, 10,000 feet, from $225.

Tutukaka Coast *p166*
Diving Tutukaka is the main dive base with companies offering personalized tours and equipment hire. Most boats leave for the Poor Knights about 0830 and return at 1600. As well as the Poor Knights, wreck dives are also available to the sunken navy frigate *Tui* just offshore from Tutukaka, and the *Waikato*, another warship sunk in 2000. A 2-dive trip costs about $160-$175 including full gear hire. Tuition, snorkelling and kayaks are also available for the novice.
Dive Tutukaka, *T09-4343867, www.diving.co.nz* The main dive company, run a very professional outfit from their base right on the marina. They offer a variety of over 10 site dives with such evocative names as 'The Labyrinth' and 'Maomao Arch' as well as dive courses, snorkelling, kayak and whale and dolphin watching activities. Full day from $175. See also Whangarei listings for further activities information.
Ecotours **Greensea Eco-Charters**, *T09-4343350, www.greensea.co.nz* Offer a more sedate cruising option on board the 65 year old MV *Wairangi* with marine biologist Lew Ritchie and his charming wife Vicki. Half, full day trips to the Poor Knights or stayaways. Call for prices. Recommended.

Fishing There is no fishing allowed within the marine reserve of the Poor Knights but the surrounding ocean has some of the best deep-sea fishing in the world, with numerous species like shark and marlin. The 'big game' season runs from December to April. A day trip as a group will cost at least $200 a head. Most of the main charter companies are based in Tutukaka including:

Delray Sportsfishing Charters, *T/F09-4343028, delray@igrin.co.nz*;
Lady Jess Charters, *T09-4343758*;
Whangarei Deep Sea Anglers Club, *T09-4343818.*

Horse treks **Whananaki Trail Rides**, *Whananaki T09-4338299.* Trekking in local kauri forests and on the beach, from $25 (free camping and budget accommodation).

Jet-skiing, mountain biking, kayaking, surfing, boogie boarding Equipment hire is available at:
Water Sport Hire, *14 Kopipi Cres, Ngunguru, T09-4343475*,
Ngunguru Holiday Park, *T/F09-4343851.*
Tutukayax, *Marina Beach, T09-4377442.*

Walking One of the best walks in the area is at Tutukaka Head. To reach the car park take the 'right of way' sign right off Matapouri Rd, 400 m past the marina turn-off. From there the track goes over the headland before falling to a small beach and a series of small rock stacks. After negotiating the stacks (beware at high tide), climb the hill to the light beacon (2 km; one hour return), from where there are magnificent views along the coast. A few kilometres north of Tutukaka, just before the road turns inland again, are a number of small settlements and attractive bays and beaches. Matapouri and Whale Bay 1 km to the north are both well worth a stop.

✪ Sport

Golf
Whangarei has some fine golf courses, as listed below:
Whangarei Golf Club, *Denby Cres, T09-4370740*, the best.
Northland Golf Club, *Pipiwai Rd, Kamo, T09-4350042.*
The Pines, *Parua Bay, T09-4362246.*
Sherwood Park, *Millington Rd, Maunu, T09-4346900.*

Rugby
Okara Park in the city is the venue for local and provincial games as well as international test matches.

The Skateboard Park, *William Fraser Memorial Park, Riverside Dr*, has a modern 1500 sq m facility.

Swimming
Whangarei Aquatics, *Ewing Rd (near the Town Basin)*, *T09-4387957*. Olympic-size outdoor pool and a large indoor heated pool, spas and sauna. open daily, $3.50.

🕔 Directory

Banks Most are in Bank St (funnily enough). **Car rentals** Avis, *Okara Dr, T09-4382929*. Budget, *22 Maunu Rd, T09-4387292*. Rent-a-Cheapy, *69 Otaika Rd, T09-4387373*. **Communications** Internet is available at the Library (see below); the VIC (see above); **Cable Action** *at the Town Basin (Post Shop)*, *T09-4307477*. Mon-Fri 1000-1630, Sat/Sun 1000-1600. $6 per hour. **Klosenet**, *34 John St, T09-4388111*. Mon-Sat 1000-2100, Sun 1100-1800. **Main Post Office**, *16-20 Rathbone St*. **Library** *Rust Av, T09-4307260*. **Medical** services **Primecare**, *12 Kensington Av, T09-4371988*. 0830-2200.

The Bay of Islands → *Phone code: 09 Colour map 1, grid B4*

If you arrive in Paihia by road, the Bay of Islands will be a huge disappointment, because all you can see is one – a very little one – just off-shore. What you will certainly see, however, is plenty of 'no vacancy' signs, people and boats – including a ferry that crosses the bay to the small village of Russell – and plenty of sales people in ticket offices, but no islands. Well, don't worry, they are out there. All 150 of them.

The Bay of Islands is one of the major tourist draws in the country offering the visitor a combination of numerous water-based activities and superb coastal scenery. The area is also of huge historic significance in that it is the site of the first European settlement and the signing of the Treaty of Waitangi – the document that began the uneasy 'voyage' of New Zealand's bi-cultural society. You can explore the islands by kayak, yacht, or sailing ship; go big game fishing for marlin or shark; dive amidst shoals of blue maomao; swim with the dolphins; bask in the sun or jump out of a plane.

Getting there
The Bay of Islands airport, accessible via **Air New Zealand Link**, To800-737-000, is between Paihia and Kerikeri. A shuttle bus meets planes ($20). Most people, though, arrive at Paihia on the SH1 from Whangarei. However, a more scenic route on the Old Russell Rd will bring you in 'the back door' via Russell. A **vehicle ferry** connects Russell and Paihia via Opua (see Getting around below). **Northliner**, To9-4027857, and **Intercity**, To9-4027857, run regular daily coach services to the Bay of Islands from Auckland and all major points north and south on SH1. The journey from Auckland takes about 4 hrs. They also link with the **West Coaster** service to Omapere and Dargaville, To9-9136100 / To9-4028989. In Paihia all buses arrive outside the Maritime Building on the Wharf. Book at the **VIC** on the waterfront.

Getting around
Paihia is not big and everything is in walking distance including Waitangi. **Russell** can be reached by **passenger ferry** from the wharf every 30 mins or so from 0720 to 2230 (reduced in winter). Adult $5, child $2.50. A **vehicle ferry** leaves about every 10 mins from Opua, 9 km south of Paihia (daily 0650-2200). Car and driver $8, camper van $13, passenger $1 one way).

Several tour shuttles can get you to **Kerikeri** for the day including Kerikeri Tours, To9-4079904, from $16 one way or cheaper still, Barefoot, (Awesome Adventures) To9-4026985, from $7 (extended tour $55).

Haruru Cabs, To9-4026292, or **Paihia Taxis**, To9-4025064. Bike hire from **Bay**

Bikes from $25 per day.

Orientation and information

Paihia is the main resort town in the Bay, its focus being on the waterfront, where the vast majority of your activities on or around the islands and Bay of Islands Maritime and Historic Park can be booked and boarded. The town was the site of New Zealand's first church and missionary centre. Waitangi, which is a short walk north, is a pleasant contrast as a site of celebrated national heritage. The Treaty of Waitangi was signed here in 1840 at the Treaty House, which is now a national museum and visitors' centre for the Waitangi National Reserve. Paihia is also the base for a number of tours and excursions further north.

The **tourist office** is on the waterfront by the wharf, ① *Marsden Rd, To9-4027345, www.northland.org.nz/www.paihia.co.nz Daily 0800-2000* (reduced in winter). Look out for the free and comprehensive 'Northland Visitors Guide'.

Paihia and Waitangi → *Phone code: 09 Colour map 1, grid B4*

Unless you have a inexplicable fetish for motels there is little in the way of sights in Paihia itself, with the town acting primarily as a base, accommodation and amenity centre for tourists. For the best of land-based attractions you are far better off heading across the water to Russell or the short distance north to the Waitangi National Reserve, possible diversions along the way include the collection of fierce looking Maori *pou* (carvings) and the 1917 sailing ship the *Tui* along the way.

Waitangi Visitor Centre and Treaty House

① *To9-4027437, www.waitangi.net.nz Daily 0900-1700. $10.* A little further along, across the bridge, is Waitangi and the very impressive Waitangi Visitor Centre and Treaty House set in the **Waitangi National Reserve**. This is the heart of New Zealand's historical beginnings. The haunting sound of piped Maori song leads you into the visitor centre where your first stop should be the audio-visual display before taking the pleasant walk around the reserve. This is quite nicely done but does give you a rather politically correct outline of events that led to the signing of the Treaty of Waitangi in 1840 and the significance of the document right up to the present day (see page 714). The main focus of the reserve is the beautifully restored **Treaty House**. It was built in 1833-34 and was once the home of British Resident James Busby who played a crucial role in the lead-up to the treaty signing. The house is full of detailed and informative displays that help clarify the quite confusing series of events surrounding the creation of the treaty. Near the Treaty House the reserve boasts perhaps the most visited **Whare Runanga** (Maori meeting house) in the country. To call this, or any *Whare* merely 'a house' would be rather minimalist. They are essentially artworks, with all the meaning, soul and effort therein and the Whare Runanga at Waitangi is a fine example.

In front of the Treaty House and Whare Runanga is a spacious lawn overlooking the bay to Russell. From the lawn it is a short walk down to the shore where the **war canoe** (*waka*) *The Ngatokimatawhaorua* is housed. This impressive 35-m long craft is named after the canoe in which Kupe, the great Maori ancestor and navigator, discovered Aotearoa (New Zealand), and was commissioned along with the Whare Runanga as a centennial project commemorating the signing of the treaty. The *Ngatokimatawhaorua* continued to be launched every year as part of the high profile Waitangi Day commemoration ceremonies hosted on and around the National Reserve. However, in recent years, after attracting protesters, Waitangi Day was scrapped and there was a call for a more progressive and low key 'New Zealand Day'.

Paihia & Waitangi

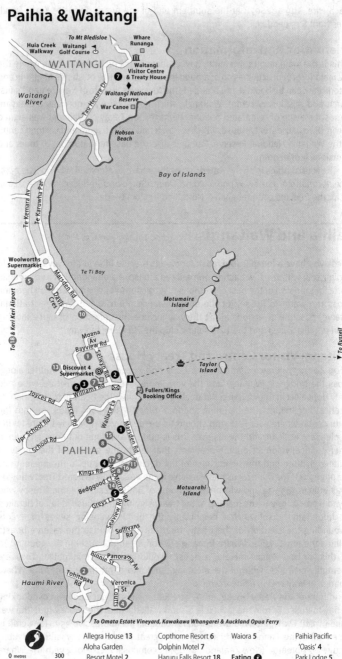

| 0 metres | 300 |
| 0 yards | 300 |

Sleeping
Abri Apartments 1
Admirals View
  Motel 14

Allegra House 13
Aloha Garden
  Resort Motel 2
Bay Adventurer & Bay
  View Apartments 16
Bay Cabinz 3
Beachcomber Resort 4
Captain Bob's
  Backpackers 12

Copthorne Resort 6
Dolphin Motel 7
Haruru Falls Resort 18
Lodge Eleven YHA 8
Mousetrap 9
Paihia Beach Resort 10
Peppertree Lodge 17
Pipi Patch & Bar 11
Saltwater Lodge 15

Waiora 5

Eating
Bistro 40 & Only
  Seafood 1
Caffé Over the
  Bay & Lighthouse
  Tavern 2
Esmae's 3

Paihia Pacific
  'Oasis' 4
Park Lodge 5
Ruffino's 6
Waikokopu
  Café 7

Bars & clubs
Beachhouse 8

To Omata Estate Vineyard, Kawakawa Whangarei & Auckland Opua Ferry

A recent addition to the Waitangi experience is the **Maori Sound and Light Show**,
① *T09-4025990, www.culturenorth.co.nz*, which is staged most evenings and is highly recommended. It is genuine and so far lacking in the commercialism so rife in other tourist locations. If you are looking for the one must-do beyond the islands themselves this is it! Complimentary pick-ups at 1930, from $45, all-inclusive. Returns 2130.

The Huia Creek Walkway, which begins near the Treaty House, is an easy walk (2 hrs) through the reserve to the unremarkable **Haruru Falls**, taking in a fine example of mangrove habitat on the way. Running adjacent to the reserve is the **Waitangi Golf Course**, which along with **Mount Bledisloe** 3 km away, commands fine views across the bay. ▶▶ *For Sleeping, Eating and other listings, see pages 179-186.*

Around Paihia

You might think it ridiculous to recommend a public convenience as a major attraction but if you have time, visit the **Kawakawa 'Hundertwasser' Public Toilets** in the centre of Kawakawa, 17 km south of Paihia. The marvellous and colourful creation of local artist Friedrich Hundertwasser who died in 2000, they are now something of an icon and a monument. South of Kawakawa the **Kawiti Caves**, ① *T09-4040583, daily 0830-1630, $10, child $5, tours hourly on the hour*, are also well worth a visit. Local Maori guides give a very interesting and genuine tour that provides insight into their natural and human history. Recommended.

Russell → *Phone code: 09 Colour map 1, grid B4*

About 2 km across the water from Paihia is the contrasting settlement of Russell which enjoys a village feel and a rich history that eludes its frenetic, tourism-based neighbour. With the advent of the first European settlement Kororareka quickly grew to be the base for whalers, sealers and escaped convicts and soon earned the sordid and notorious reputation as 'the hellhole of the Pacific'. The earliest missionaries tried their best to quell the unholy mob with mixed results. When the Treaty of Waitangi was signed in 1840, although it was the largest European settlement in New Zealand, William Hobson, the then Governor, decided it was not a good marketing ploy to give it capital status and instead bought land in what is now Auckland. To make matters worse, the Treaty was beginning to be seen by local Maori as a fraud and not as beneficial as promised, with financial benefits in particular failing to materialize. Their scorn (led by the infamous chief Hone Heke) was focused on the Flagstaff near Russell, which proudly flew the Union Jack. Heke and his band of not so merry men, duly cut it down, not once but four times, the last felling causing a major battle in which Kororareka was sacked and the first Maori Wars began. Once relative peace returned the authorities decided to make a new beginning and lose the notorious label, calling it Russell.

Today Russell, along with Kerikeri (also in the Bay of Islands), is flaunted as the most historic village in New Zealand and, although it bustles with transitory tourists in the summer and is inundated at New Year, it manages admirably to maintain a sedate and close community feel, which if you stay, can warm the heart.

Getting there

By car via the Opua passenger and vehicular ferry (see page 172) or by the passenger only ferries every 20-30 min from Paihia Wharf, $5 (0730-2230 Oct-March, 2030 Apr-Sep).

● *The original name for Russell was Kororareka, which derived (so legend has it) from the*
● *utterings of a wounded Maori chief who, after being given some penguin soup, said 'Ka-reka-te-korora' (how sweet is the penguin).*

There is no official tourist centre in Russell but the **Bradley's Office** ⓘ *at the end of the wharf, T09-4038020, 0730-1700*, and the **Fuller's Office** ⓘ *Cass St, T09-4037866, daily 0730-1700*, can help with excursion information. For walks information, consult the **DoC Bay of Island's Area Visitor Centre** ⓘ *The Strand, T09-4037685, russellvc@doc.govt.nz daily, summer 0700-1700, winter 0900-1630*, will meet most of your needs. Most of the Paihia-based tours stop off to pick up in Russell on their way out to the islands. For information and times contact tour operators or the VICs. ➤➤ *Also see Activities, page 183.*

Sights

For a detailed historic indulgence head for the **Russell Museum**, ⓘ *on the corner of Pitt and York Sts, T09-4037701, daily, Jan 1000-1700, Feb-Dec 1000-1600, $3, child 50c*. It has an interesting collection of early settler relics and, having being built to commemorate the bicentenary of Captain Cook's visit in 1769, features a host of information on the explorer, including a very impressive 1:5 scale model of Cook's ship *The Endeavour*.

Russell

To ⑤ ⑩ & Tapeka Point Reserve (1500m)

Flagstaff Hill

Tapeka Rd
Flagstaff Rd
Wellington St
Queen St
Prospect St
York St
Kent St
Church St
James St
Long Beach Rd
Beresford Rd
To Long Beach
To ⑨
Kororareka Bay
The Strand
To Paihia
Fullers/ Bradley's Office
Russell Mini Tours
Cass St
Chapel St
Tatau St
Ashby St
Gould St
To ⑩ ⑦, Omata Estate Vineyard & Opua Car Ferry (11 km)
Supermarket
Russell Museum
Anglican
Hazard St
DoC Visitor Centre
Robertson St
Bay of Islands
Pompallier
Matauwhi Rd
Brind Rd
Hope Av
To ⑩ ⑧
Florence Av
Matauwhi Bay

N

0 metres 400
0 yards 400

Sleeping
Arcadia Lodge 1
Duke of Marlborough
  & Restaurant 2
Eagles Nest 5
Inn-The-Pink 3
Kororareka Backpackers 9
Orongo Bay B&B 11
Ounuwhao Harding
  House 7
Pukeko Cottage B&B 8
Pukematu Lodge 10
Russell Top Ten
  Holiday Park 6

Eating
Birdie Num Nums 1
Gables & Bordello
Garden Bar 4
Kamakura 3
York St Café 2

A short distance south along the shore from the museum is **Pompallier**. ⓘ *T09-4039015. Daily 1000-1700. $5.* This historic 1842 dwelling was originally set up by the early missionaries as a printing works. It later served as a tannery and a private home before becoming a small museum in 1990. On the corner of Church and Robertson Streets is the 1836 **Anglican Church** which was one of the few buildings to survive the 1840s sacking and Maori war (bar a few visible musket ball holes) and remains the oldest church in New Zealand. For a grand view it is worth the steep climb to **Flagstaff Hill** (Maiki). Parts of the current pole were erected in the late 1850s over a decade after Hone Heke's attempts at clear felling. A further 1 km north, the earth terraces of the ancient *pa* on the **Tapeka Point Reserve** make a pleasant walk.

Long Beach, 1 km behind the village, is also a nice spot and a fine venue on a hot summer's day. If the history of Russell is of particular interest the Heritage Trails leaflet from the DoC Visitor Centre is useful or you might like to join the excellent Maori guided tour on offer with **Koro Tours**, T09-4038020, from $10. **Russell Mini Tours**, T09-4038044, also offers local tours and depart 3 times daily (1000/1300/1500) from outside the Fuller's Office on Cass St. $17, 1 hr.

➤➤ *See Sleeping and Eating, pages 180 and 182.*

Cape Brett Walk

This is one of the finest walks in Northland following the ridge of Cape Brett to the lighthouse and DoC Cape Brett Hut. With a clear view across the Bay of Islands it provides some spectacular coastal scenery. The well-formed track starts near Rawhiti 29 km from Russell in Oke Bay (secure parking is available at Hartwells, Kaimaramara Bay, end of Rawhiti Road, small fee, T09-4037248). It will take an entire day (about 8 hrs) to walk the 20 km to the Hut but if you cannot face the return journey you can book a water taxi back to Rawhiti from just below the Hut with **Kiwi Eco Tours**, T09-4038823, from $30. **Cape Brett Walkways**, T09-4038823, www.capebrettwalks.co.nz, also offer transportation as part of their walks package (see below). To attempt the walk and stay in the Hut you must first pay a hut fee of $10 and a track fee of $30 at the DoC visitor Centre in Russell. You can also post the fee to the centre (PO Box 134, The Strand, Russell). You will then be given a code for the door lock. Essential maps and all the relevant information are available from there. Basic camping is available near the start of the track in Rawhiti, T09-4037044. Perhaps the best way to tackle the walk is with the new and reputable Cape Brett Walkways (above). They offer a number of attractive alternatives for doing the walk either way, in a day. Transport from Russell and Piahia (guided $175, independent $110) or from Rawhiti (guided $125, independent $60) inclusive of track fee. **NB** The track is on Maori Trust land so stick to the rules.

Kerikeri → *Phone code: 09 Population: 2000 Colour map 1, grid B3*

You have never tasted a mandarin until you have been to Kerikeri. Travelling north from Paihia the rolling hills give way to corridors of windbreaks that hide the laden trees of citrus, grape and kiwifruit for which the area is famous. The word *Keri* means 'dig', and it was here, in pleasant little 'Dig Dig', that the first plough cut into New Zealand soil in 1820. Along with Russell, Kerikeri is rich in Maori and early European history with the Kerikeri Basin, 2 km northeast of the present town, being the nucleus of New Zealand's first European colonization.

Getting there

Kerikeri Airport is about halfway between Paihia and Kerikeri. Arrivals and Departures, T09-4078419 (see Paihia section). Kerikeri is 22 km north of Paihia just off SH1. Both **Intercity** and **Northliner** coaches stop in the centre of town on Cobham Rd.

Getting around For transport to Paihia and guided tours contact **Kerikeri Tours**, T09-4079904, leaves Kerikeri 0815, $16 return or **Barefoot**, (Awesome Adventures) in Paihia, T09-4026985, from $7 (extended tour including Kerikeri from $55).

Information There is a small independent **VIC** in the square off Hobson Ave but you will find that the VIC in Paihia can provide all your needs. (See Paihia page 173). The **DOC** information office, ① *34 Landing Rd, T09-4078474,* can provide advice on local short, or longer, walks in the Puketi Forest. **Rewa's Village Visitors' Centre**, ① *1 Landing Rd, T09-4076454,* can also provide general local information.

Sights

For a sense of history and atmosphere head straight for the **Kerikeri Basin** past the main commercial centre. There the road falls to meet the babbling Kerikeri River and the dominant and attractive **Stone Store**. ① *1000-1700. $3.50.* This was New Zealand's first stone building and was completed in 1835. It was used by the first Anglican bishop George Selwyn as a library in the early 1840s and later as an ammunition store during conflicts between Ngapuhi chief Hone Heke, before assuming its intended purpose as a general mission store. Today it is neatly laid out as testimony to that function with a museum on its top floor.

Almost immediately next door is the two-storeyed **Mission House** or Kemp

House. ① *Daily 1000-1700. $5, combined entry with Stone Store $7, children free.* This is the oldest surviving building in New Zealand (at the very young age of 179). It was established by pioneer missionary Samuel Marsden on land offered to him by the great local Maori warlord Hongi Hika, who accepted 48 felling axes for the land and also offered Marsden and his staff protection from invading tribes. In 1832 it became the home of catechist-blacksmith, James Kemp and his family, generations of whom lived in the house until 1974, when it was passed over to the nation as an historic site. The house is now packed with Kemp family relics.

Overlooking both buildings is the more ancient **Kororipo Pa** which was chief Hongi Hika's more basic domain (until, not surprisingly, he had a European-style house built nearby in the 1820s).

A short stroll across the river is **Rewa's Village**. ① *T09-4076454. Daily, $3, child 50c.* This is an authentic recreation of a pre-European Maori fishing settlement, or *kainga*, named after Hongi Hika's successor. With its very basic ponga tree fern trunk huts and shelters you can only wonder what the early Maori must have thought of the Euro-architecture of the time.

The **Kerikeri Basin** offers a number of pleasant short walks along the river, the most notable of which takes in the 27-m **Rainbow Falls** (also accessible 3 km north from Waipapa Road; leaflet available from DoC). Another fine short walk is to **Ake Ake Point and Pa**, accessible from the pretty Opito Bay, 20 km east of the city.

As well as its fruit, Kerikeri is also famous for its **arts and crafts**. The free leaflet 'Kerikeri Art and Craft Trail' lists a number of venues, the best of which is **Origin Art and Craft Co-op** ① *SH10, T09-4071133, daily 1000-1700.* It has a wide range of works on display and for sale from pottery to stained glass. Well worth a visit is '**Kaleidoscopes**' ① *256 Waipara Rd, T09-4074415. Open most days.* The **Kauri Workshop**, *just as you come in to town on Kerikeri Road, T09-4079196*, has a quality range of kauri and other native wood products. From there you can take a stroll next door to the **Makana Chocolate Factory**, ① *T09-4076800, daily 0900-1730*, where you can watch the stuff being made while wondering why all the employees are not the size of small houses. If natural beauty and skin products are your thing then you can't get more natural than the terrific range on offer from **Living Nature**, ① *just south of the Kerikeri turn off on SH1, T09-4070113, www.livingnature.com Daily 0900-1800.* Beauticians and therapists also available on site.

On an ecological theme is the excellent **Aroha Island Ecological Centre**, ① *on Kurapari Rd, 12 km east of the town , T09-4075243, kiwi@aroha.net.nz (see also Sleeping below). Daily (may be closed 1 month in winter).* Aroha Island and the neighbouring **Rangitane Scenic Reserve** are important remnant habitats of the brown kiwi. The island is kept predator-free and therefore offers a small but valuable sanctuary for a few birds. Alas, with the kiwi being nocturnal, daytime visitors will only be able to see interpretative material in the visitors' centre. However, if you stay overnight you may get the opportunity to see, and certainly hear, the birds after dark on a guided tour. ➤➤ *See Sleeping, Eating and Activities, pages 181-186.*

Kerikeri to Kaitaia

Provided you have your own transport, the roads that branch off SH1 to the coast north of Kerikeri offer stunning coastal scenery and some secluded beaches that are well worth the visit. About 15 km north of Kerikeri the road loops to the coast taking in the small settlements and peaceful hideaways of **Matauri Bay**, **Te Ngaire**, **Wainui**, **Mahinepua** and **Tauranga Bay** before rejoining SH1 again near **Whangaroa**. From there you meet the sweeping shores of **Doubtless Bay** with its mainly retirement communities of **Mangonui**, **Coopers Beach** and **Cable Bay**, before cutting across the picturesque **Karikari Peninsula** on your way to the last significant northern outpost and predominantly Maori enclave of **Kaitaia**.

Matauri Bay → *Phone code: 09 Colour map 1, grid B3*

The views above Matauri Bay are stunning, with the numerous **Cavalli Islands** offering a sight that almost surpasses that of the Bay of Islands. Captain Cook named the islands after travalli (a species of fish) bought by Cook from local Maori. The **Samuel Marsden memorial church** in Matauri Bay commemorates New Zealand's pioneer missionary who first preached the gospel in the Bay of Islands on Christmas Day 1814.

The area remains a top venue for **deep sea fishing** and **diving**. Matauri Bay has always been a popular holiday spot, but assumed additional national fame when the wreck of the Greenpeace Vessel *Rainbow Warrior* was laid to rest off the Cavallis in 1987. The famous flagship was bombed by French secret service through a ludicrous act of terrorism in Auckland in 1985. The intellectually bankrupt idea was to prevent her leading a protest flotilla to the French nuclear test grounds on the Pacific atoll of Mururoa. Her sunken hull, 3 km offshore, provides the poignant home to a myriad of sea creatures while an impressive memorial on the hill overlooking the islands near the beach pays tribute to the ship, her crew (one of which was killed) and the continuing cause for a nuclear-free region. The incident, rightly, caused an international outcry and New Zealanders are in no hurry to forget, or forgive. There is an echo of Maori history, spirit and support in the Bay with the *waka* (war canoe) *Mataatua II* located near the campground. The history of this legendary canoe led to the local tribe, the Ngati Kura, offering the remains and the *mana* of the modern day *Rainbow Warrior* a final resting-place. ▸ *See Sleeping and Activities, page 181 and 186.*

North to Whangaroa

From Matauri Bay the road follows the coast to the picturesque bays and settlements of **Te Ngaire** and **Wainui**. A branch road, just past Wainui, will take you to **Mahinepua Bay**, which provides a classic touch of seclusion, scenery and the only campsite (DoC). From there the road climbs the hill again, offering fine views inland at Radar Heights (an old radar station), before temporarily leaving the coast towards **Tauranga Bay** and **Whangaroa**. ▸ *See Sleeping, page 182.*

● Sleeping

Paihia *p173*

Paihia is well-served with most types of accommodation to suit all budgets, with luxury hotels, a plague of motels and a number of excellent, modern backpackers. Despite a wealth of beds, in summer – especially over Christmas and through Jan and Feb – it is essential to book ahead. Bear in mind the Bay of Islands is also the favoured holiday spot for hundreds of New Zealanders. If you are looking for peace and quiet you would be better staying across the water in Russell where you will find the best lodges and B&Bs.

L-AL Beachcomber Resort, *T09-4027434, www.beachcomber-resort.co.nz* A slightly ageing yet popular hotel resort with New Zealanders, at the southern end of town. Studios and family suites. Right next to the

beach. Fine buffet breakfast.

AL Scenic Circle Copthorne Resort Hotel, *Tau Henare Dr, T09-4027411, wwwcopthornebayofislands,co.nz* 145 guest rooms all recently renovated. Nice location near the Waitangi Reserve. Large and unusual outdoor pools and spas.

AL-L Paihia Beach Resort, *116 Marsden Rd, T09-4026140, www.paihiabeach.co.nz*, and

AL-L Quality Hotel, *also on Marsden Rd, T09-4027416*, are central, reliable and offer views directly across the bay.

There are many **self-contained** accommodation options in town including:

L-AL Abri Apartments, *10 Bayview Rd, T09-4028003, www.abri-accom.co.nz* New and delightful.

L-AL Waiora, *52 Puketona Rd (northern end of town), T09-4026601, www.waiora-valley.co.nz* A peaceful option.

L-AL Allegra House, *39 Bayview Rd,*

T09-4027932, www.allegra.co.nz also a B&B and has stunning views.

AL Bay Cabinz, 32-34 School Rd, T09-4028534. Cosy cedar cabins sleeping 1-4. There are **motels** all over town, mostly centrally located, ranging in both standard and price.

A **Aloha Garden Resort Motel**, 32-36 Seaview Rd, T09-4027540. At the top of the range, has a good reputation.

A **Admirals View Motel**, 2 McMurray Rd, T0800-247234, www.admiralsviewlodge.co.nz Immaculate accommodation.

A **Dolphin Motel**, 69 Williams Rd, T09-4028170, dolphin@extra.co.nz Mid-range option, quiet location, plus private spa pool. There are 8 **backpackers** in Paihia most of which vary only slightly. King St is the main focus and is home to the most modern, happening hostels.

B-D Saltwater Lodge, 14 Kings Rd, T09-4027075 / T0800-002-266, www.saltwaterlodge.co.nz The most popular and busy these days, new and much talked about. It is indeed impressive with all the facilities you might expect to earn its rare 5-star rating. Immaculately clean, very tidy rooms bathrooms, from dorm to double, incredible kitchen, sky TV, internet, gym, kayak and bike hire and even disabled facilities. Off-street parking. Recommended.

B-D The Pipi Patch, 18 Kings Rd, T09-4027111, www.acb.co.nz/pipi.html Also has a great selection of value options from bunks to doubles. There's a popular bar attached, which for travellers is the main focus and meeting venue in town, as well as the haunt of a few good-value locals. Off-street parking.

A-D Bay Adventurer and Bay View Apartments, 28 Kings Rd, T09-4025162, www.bayadventurer.co.nz Another new addition and award winner on the block which marries nicely both self-contained apartments with modern standard backpacker facilities. Pool, spa, internet and off-street parking.

Other reputable backpacker establishments include the quieter and very arty **C-D Mousetrap**, 11 Kings Rd, T09-4028182; **C-D Peppertree Lodge**, 15 Kings Rd, T09-4026122, www.peppertree.co.nz **C-D Lodge Eleven YHA**, corner of MacMurray and King's Rd, T09-4027487,

www.lodgeeleven.co.nz **C-D Captain Bob's**, 44 Davis Cres, T09-4028668, capnbobs@xtra.co.nz Away from the Kings Road hype and perfectly adequate.

With so much competition in these parts all of them have to maintain good standards so you can't go far wrong.

Motorcamps and campsites

Haruru Falls Resort, T0800-757525, 6 km north west of Paihia on the Old Wharf Rd. Has powered sites and camping facilities as well as motel units and a pool. The Haruru Falls are directly in view.

Twin Pines, a short walk up the hill, T09-4027195. Fairly unremarkable but with a pub and restaurant.

Russell p175

Russell has the widest selection of B&Bs north of Whangarei.

LL Eagles Nest, 60 Tapeka Rd, T09-4038333, www.eaglesnest.co.nz One of the best lodges in the country. Impressive architecture, sumptuous beautifully appointed suites and self-contained options, pool, spa, superb cuisine and just about everything a body needs.

L-AL The Duke of Marlborough, T09-4037829, www.theduke.co.nz Well-located right on the waterfront, newly renovated interior and oozing all the gracious charm its 150 years deserve. 28 guest rooms, bar and à la carte restaurant.

L Pukematu Lodge, Flagstaff Hill, T/F09-4038500, www.pukematulodge.co.nz Perched high on the hill with spectacular views this superb B&B is run by a very friendly couple, one of whom is the local Maori policeman. En suite bathrooms. Breakfast almost surpasses the company and the view. Recommended.

L-AL Ounuwhao Harding House, Matauwhi Bay, T09-4037310, www.bay-of-islands.co.nz/ounuwhao Another good B&B in more historic surroundings.

L-AL Triton Suites, 7 Wellington St, T/F09-4038067, www.tritonsuites.co.nz New and very flash boutique motel units in the centre of the village.

L-AL Orongo Bay Homestead, Aucks Rd, T09-4037527, orongo.bay@clear.net.nz Beautiful rooms in what used to be New

Zealand's first American Consulate (1860). Organic gourmet dinners by arrangement. Recommended.

A **Inn-The-Pink**, *1 Oneroa Rd, T/F09-4037347, www.bay-of-islands.co.nz/inthepnk* Self-contained, double and single options with fine views.

A **Arcadia Lodge**, *10 Florence Av, Matauwhi Bay, T09-4037756, arcadialodge@xtra.co.nz* Historic Tudor house with 8 comfy rooms, great breakfast.

For **backpackers** there are two alternatives:

B-D **Pukeko Cottage B&B and Backpackers** *14 Brind Rd, T09-4038498* (book well ahead). Small and cosy.

C-D **Kororareka Backpackers**, *22 Oneroa Rd, T09-4038494, russellbackpackers@hotmail.com* Conveniently located between the village centre and Long Beach. Doubles and dorms, deck with views and relaxing atmosphere.

Motorcamps and campsites

A-D **Russell Top Ten Holiday Park**, *Long Beach Rd, T09-4037826, russelltop10@xtra.co.nz* Offers a range of motels, flats, cabins and backpackers. Reliable and fairly modern.

Kerikeri p177

Accommodation in Kerikeri is plentiful and generally less expensive than Paihia. Although not as busy, you are still advised to book ahead, especially at Christmas and in Jan. Hostels also tend to fill up Apr-Aug due to the fruit harvesting season.

LL **Sommerfields**, *Inlet Rd, T/F09-4079889, www.sommerfields.co.nz* Luxury, modern B&B accommodation set in 5 acres just outside Kerikeri.

LL-L **The Summerhouse B&B**, *T09-4074294, www.thesummerhouse.co.nz* An excellent B&B, peaceful, friendly and full of class set in a citrus orchard with either en suite bathroom or self-contained option. Legendary breakfast.

L-AL **Kerikeri Village Inn**, *165 Kerikeri Rd, T09-4074666, www.kerikerivillageinn.co.nz* New B&B in a contemporary Santa Fe-style house. Fine views and sumptuous breakfast.

AL **Puketotara Luxury Accommodation**, *T09-4077780, moods.holdings@xtra.co.nz* Another countryside retreat with some fine organic cooking.

A **Colonial Cottage**, *Inlet Rd, T/F09-4079240.* B&B in an attractive 1890s cottage.

A **Quilt Cottage**, *128 Waipapa Rd, T/F09-4074212, jenks@igrin.co.nz* Colourful and cosy self-contained cottage with attention to detail, outdoor spa and meals.

A **Kauri Park Motel**, *Kerkeri Rd, T/F09-4077629, kauriprk@igrin.co.nz* Relatively new and set in sub-tropical garden setting. Large nicely appointed units, some with private spa.

B-D **Pagoda Lodge**, *81 Pa Rd, T09-4078617, www.pagoda.co.nz* Unusual property once the domain of an eccentric Scotsman with an obsession with all things Asian. Self-contained units under main pagoda building, boathouse and luxury tents. Not exactly typically kiwi, but all very unique, comfortable and a nice change. Kayak and bike hire.

B **Glenfalloch Homestay**, *Landing Rd, T/F09-4075471.* Variety of nice rooms, swimming pool.

B **Aroha Island Ecological Centre**, *Kurapari Rd, T09-4075243.* Cottage-style accommodation (sleeps 5), B&B, camper vans and campsites. Kayaks and kiwi watching at night.

C-D **Hone Heke Lodge Backpackers**, *65 Hone Heke Rd, T/F09-4078170, honeheke@xtra.co.nz* Dorms, twins and doubles, some with en suite bath, tent sites.

C-D **Kerikeri YHA**, *44 Kerikeri Rd, T09-4079391, www.yha.org.nz* Set in large forested grounds. Double, twin and family rooms, self-contained cottage, campsites.

Motorcamps and campsites

B-D **Aranga Top Ten Holiday Park**, *Kerikeri Rd, T09-4079326.* Modern motor camp, centrally located next to the river. Also campsites at Hone Heke Lodge Backpackers and Kerikeri YHA (above).

Matauri Bay p179

The area, like the Bay of Islands, is very popular so book in advance.

LL **Huntaway Lodge**, *Te Ngaire Bay (4 km north of Matauri Bay), T09-4051611, www.huntawaylodge.com* New exclusive lodge in superb setting overlooking the ocean. 2 rooms with decks. Activities arranged and gourmet breakfast included.

L **Cavalli Beach House**, *T09-4051049, www.cavallibeachhouse.com* Luxurious accommodation in a fine setting and a most

unusual beachfront house. Fine cuisine.
A **Oceans Holiday Village**, *T09-4050417, www.matauribay.co.nz/oceans/* Perfect waterfront location a stone's throw from the beach. A range of self-contained units and family lodges. Boat hire and charter, dive gear and tank refills, kayaks, internet.

Motorcamps and campsites
C-D **Matauri Bay Holiday Park**, *T09-4050525*. Set right on the beach in the shadow of the Rainbow Warrior memorial hill (which sadly affects the view). All the usual facilities for camping and camper vans but no units.
AL-A **Oceans Holiday Village**, *T09-4050417*. Has a fully licensed restaurant/café attached. Fri-Sun in summer, winter hours vary.

North to Whangaroa *p179*
Tauranga Bay hosts a scattering of accommodations.
L **Shearwater Lodge**, *T09-4050089, www.shearwater.com* A luxurious retreat in an enviable position overlooking the ocean, is well-appointed and the pool is as good as they get. Recommended.
A-B **Tauranga Bay Motel**, *T09-4050222*. Back at sea level and basic.
B-D **Tauranga Bay Holiday Park**, *T09-4050436, www.taurangabay.co.nz* New self-contained beachside log cabins. Many come here to join **Northland Sea Kayaking**, *T09-4050381*, a popular sea kayaking outfit offering $70 day trips with an extra $10 for accommodation. They can provide shuttle pick-ups from the main bus route at Kaeo.

● Eating

Pahia and Waitangi *p173*
As you would expect, there are plenty of choices in Paihia, most serving fresh local fish and seafood.
$$$ **Omata Estate Vineyard**, *Aucks Rd, Russell, T09-4038007, info@omata.co.nz* For fine dining it is worth the trip here on a fine summer's day or for an evening treat. It is expensive but superb.
$$$ **Darryl Honey Cruises**, *T09-4027848, darrylsdinnercruises@xtra.co.nz*
Evening cruise including meal, $45.
$$ **'Oasis' Restaurant** *in the Paihia Pacific, 27 King's Rd, T09-4028221*, and

$$ **Park Lodge**, *corner of Seaview and McMurray Rd, T09-4027826*. Open 0700-late. Both offer reliably good à la carte cuisine.
$$ **Esmae's**, *41 Williams Rd, T09-4028400*. Licensed. Good for traditional Kiwi fare.
$$ **Bistro 40**, *T09-4027444* (lunch from 1200, dinner from 1800, licensed), and
$$ **Only Seafood**, *T09-4026066* (open daily from 1700, licensed) *both together at 40 Marsden Rd* The best seafood in town.

Cafés
Waikokopu Café *in the pleasant surrounds of the Waitangi National Reserve, T09-4026275*. Daily 0900-1700, BYO and licensed. Undoubtedly one of the best places for daytime eating. A highly imaginative menu including the sumptuous 'Whalers Breakfast'.
Ruffino's, *39 William's Rd, T09-4027964* (open daily from 1730, licensed). Good if you're just looking for a pizza snack in a central location.
Café over the Bay *right on the waterfront, T09-4028147*. Breakfast from 0800. Has a nice healthy variety of snacks, good coffee and a small deck overlooking all the action.
Supermarkets In town the *Discount 4* is on Williams Rd while *Woolworths*, with all mod cons, is more of a trek at the northern end of town (500m west of the roundabout) on the Kerikeri Rd. Open daily 0700-2200.

Russell *p175*
$$$ **Omata Estate Vineyard**, *Aucks Rd (halfway between Opua and Russell), T09-4038007, www.omata.co.nz* Some of the best eating in the region can be had at this congenial place overlooking the vines and the bay. A great place to be on a summer's day. Expensive lunch and dinner but worth it. Booking essential (closed Mon).
In Russell itself there are some good options along the waterfront (Strand).
$$$ **Kamakura**, *waterfront (Strand), T09-4037771*. One of the region's best restaurants, it's worth a muse of the menu.
$$$ **Duke of Marlborough Hotel** (see above). Open for lunches and dinner. For a bit of tradition the restaurant here is an old favourite, with a great atmosphere and outdoor seating overlooking the bay.
$$$ **Gables**, *T09-4037618, www.gablesrestaurant.co.nz* On the waterfront and has a romantic atmosphere,

fine Mediterranean cuisine and a good wine list, but it is a tad expensive.

$$ York St Café, *York St, T09-4037360*. Open daily 1000-2100. Great pizzas, seafood and breakfasts. Licensed.

$$ Bordello Garden Bar and Bistro, *at the back of the Gables restaurant, T09-4037618*. Also good.

$ Birdie Num Nums, *Cass St, T09-4037754*. And if none of the above appeal then there is always this fish and chippie.

The **supermarket** is centrally located on Cass St. Open daily 0800-1900.

Kerikeri *p177*

$$$ Marx Garden Restaurant, *Kerikeri Rd, T09-4076606*. Try the 'Orgasmic Seafood Platter' for around $30 – speaks for itself.

$$ The Black Olive, *Main Rd, T09-4079693*. Open Tue-Sun 1700 till late. Equally orgasmic pizza etc. Sit in or take away. BYO.

$$ Butler's, *Kerikeri Basin, T09-4078479*. Daily 0900-2100. Across the road from the stone store in a great setting. English pub-style lunches and fine dining in the evening. Beautiful on a sunny day. Occasionally has live music.

$ Café Jerusalem, *Cobblestone Mall, T09-4071001*. Mon-Fri 1100-2300, Sat 1500-2300. Cheap Middle Eastern food, sit-in or take away. Vegetarian snacks.

$ Rocket Café, *Junction SH1 and Kerikeri Rd, T09-4073100*. Award winner offering imaginative fare, good breakfasts, weekend brunches and great coffee.

$ Café Cinema, *Hobson Ave, T09-4079121*. Offers a $22 **movie and meal deal** most nights which is good given the quality of the food (Dutch influenced). The cinema also has lots of character. Recommended.

$ Kerikeri Club, *Cobham Rd, T09-4078585*. Mon-Sat 1300-2200, Sun 1500-2200. Cheap food and lots of it, in the local RSA, bridge and tennis club.

The New World **supermarket** is on Fairway Dr in the town centre. Keri Pies are widely available – try one of Northland's finest here.

☉ Bars and clubs

Pahia *p173*

The best pubs in town are along King Rd amidst all the backpacker establishments.

Beachhouse *next door to Saltwater Lodge*. The place to be.

Pipi Patch Backpackers, *18 Kings Rd*. Most popular with the younger crowd.

Lighthouse Tavern, *upstairs in the Paihia Mall*. Once the bars close, all clubbing (almost literally) takes place here.

☉ Festivals and events

Jan: Tall Ships Race. **Apr**: Bay of Islands Arts Festival. **Aug**: Jazz and Blues Festival. **Sep**: Russell Oyster Festival (recommended), **Food and Wine Festival**.

▲ Activities and tours

Paihia and Waitangi *p173*

The minute you arrive in Paihia you are under pressure to book, book, book and buy, buy, buy. Sadly it has become the nature of the place, as the huge range of tour and activity operators vie for your attention and dollar. The best thing to do is to take your time and to take advice from the unbiased VIC before venturing into the 'booking mall' on the waterfront to be mauled by the sales sharks. It is better not to book ahead, unless you have researched thoroughly, or you will lose much freedom of choice. The two main players are **Fullers**, *T09-4027421, www.fullers-bay-of-islands.co.nz* (not the same company as the ferry operators in Auckland), and **Kings**, *T09-4028288, www.kings-tours.co.nz* Both offer very similar tours around the islands with Cape Brett's famous **'Hole in the Rock'** being the main highlight. Trips generally involve combinations of activities from simple sightseeing to island stops, lunch cruises and swimming with dolphins. Almost all begin with a traditional Maori *powhiri* (welcome) on the wharf before boarding the boat. As you will see, to the unaccustomed, or those who know nothing about Maori protocol, this can initially seem quite threatening.

The booking offices are open daily from 0700-2130, 1830 in winter. Bear in mind there is fierce competition in Paihia. For detailed unbiased information talk to the friendly and congenial staff in waterfront VIC then sit and have a coffee under no pressure and decide on the best option before committing.

Boomnetting Cling on for dear life to a large net slung alongside a cruise boat. The boat stops if dolphins are spotted in the hope that they venture near. Part of a 6-hr cruise trip including the 'Hole in the Rock'.
Kings, (see above). Complete trip: adult $79, child $45.

Cruising A huge choice, again in combination with sightseeing, dolphin encounters and the 'Hole in the Rock' – a massive natural arch in a rock outcrop at the very tip of Cape Brett through which the cruise boats navigate the ocean swell. Trips range from about 3 hrs (adult $62, child $31), or 6 hrs (adult $85, child $50). Some cruise options take in a stop on **Urupukapuka Island**, a favourite haunt of Zane Grey (www.zanegrey.co.nz), the famous American author and big game fisherman. The bay at Otehei is beautiful, spoilt only perhaps by the rather gimmicky yellow submarine *Nautilus* in which you can venture under the water. Adult $12, child $6. If you wish to stay on the island to take in the atmosphere, sights, archaeological walks (see DoC leaflet) and would prefer to pick up a later ferry, there is the basic **Zane Grey Lodge**, *T09-4037009*, or **DOC campsites**. The Zane Grey restaurant in front of the lodge will see you right for a decent meal.
Fullers (above) offers a day-long *Island Escape* package for $45, child $22.50 (departs 0830). Very popular (especially in high swell) is the bone-crunching, high speed 'Hole in the Rock' trips in **Mac Attack**, *T09-4028180*, or Fullers rather lewd sounding **Excitor** *T09-4027020*. Multiple trips daily, 1 hr, $65. There is an informative commentary and stops on the way and both are just as fast. The 'Mac', however, does pride itself on actually threading its way through the Hole, but given the heavy swell this is never guaranteed. You can take a camera but you will probably return with blurred pictures of the posterior of the person in front, and forget wearing specs unless fitted with automatic wipers. If you're prone to seasickness, don't even think about it. For the more traditional, holistic approach **The Rock**, *T0800-762-527*, www.rocktheboat.co.nz, offers an excellent 24 hr cruise on board its own purpose-built craft. It is proving deservedly popular offering a whole host of activities from snorkelling to dolphin watching. The vessel itself is comfortable and well-kitted out with shared (twin or quad) or private cabins, bar and dining area. Meals are inclusive and all in all the experience is a lot of fun. The layout also lets you be as social or as private as you like. From $128. Recommended.

Diving The bay is a fine dive venue and trips are also available for the Greenpeace '**Rainbow Warrior Wreck Dive**'.
Paihia Dive, *T09-4027551*, www.divenz.com, have a very tidy purpose-built launch and offer a 2-dive trip with all gear from $185.
Dive North, *T09-4027079*, divenorth@xtra.co.nz, offer a similar set-up and specialize in trips to the *Rainbow Warrior*. See also Captain Buckos (below).

Dolphin watching The Bay of Islands is a top spot for dolphins, orca and the occasional migratory whale and there is much debate about the impact of tourist activities on the creatures, though the jury is still very much out. Only three companies are allowed actively to approach the dolphins, and all offer a similar experience of observation and encounter, including a scenic trip around the islands and the 'Hole in the Rock'. Limited numbers are allowed in the water at a time, so it can be slow and frustrating, but the animals come first. All 3 companies have high success rates and will take you out again the following day for free if your trip proves to be a 'water encounter'.
Dolphin Discoveries, *T09-4028234*, www.dolphinz.co.nz, offer two trips daily at 0900 and 1300, a 'Discover the Bay' sightseeing / watching trip for $65, child $35, and dolphin swimming trips$95, child $55.
Dolphin Encounters (Fullers), *T09-4027421*, www.fullers-bay-of-islands.co.nz Oct-Apr, depart daily at 0800, returning at 1200 and 1230-1630; May-Sep, 0800-1200. Adult $95, child $48. Trip with stop at Urupukapuka Island, Oct-Apr, daily at 0800-1730.
Awesome Adventures, *T09-4026985*, www.awesomeadventures.co.nz Sep-May, daily at 0800-1200 and 1230-1630; Jun-Aug at 0800-1200. Island stop available (Urupukapuka). Adult $95, child $48.

Fishing The Bay and the upper Northland Coast is the best sea angling and big-game

fishing venue in the country and one of the best in the world. A trip can be just about affordable for the average Joe at about $250-$350 a day. It is a very exciting experience, especially if you are 'in the chair' when you hook a big one. There are numerous reputable charter boats operating from Paihia and Russell. Contact the Paihia VIC for details. For beginners and standard sea-fishing options (including diving) try:
Captain Bucko's, *T09-4027788, cptnbucko@acb.co.nz* Snorkel trip $75, dive $140, fishing $75 (4 hrs);
Wahoo, *T09-4037397,www.sportfishing.co.nz*;
Snapper, *T09-4097123*, offer 4-hr trips suitable for beginners from $50, per person, child $30.
Rent-a-Boat, *T09-4027136, www.rent-a-boat.co.nz* For runabouts suitable for inshore fishing. Around $65/ hr.

Kayaking **Coastal Kayakers**, *T09-4028105, www.coastalkayakers.co.nz*, do half or full day guided trips (some up river to Haruru Falls) and also the excellent 3-day experience. 3 days on a remote bay with a kayak to explore the islands can be a great adventure, and is a fine chance to encounter dolphins alone . All equipment and food provided. Half day trip $45, full day $65, multi day $120-$420; independent hire available $10 per hour, $40 per day.
Sea Kayak Adventures, *T025-2081319, T09-4028596, www.seakayakingadventuresnz.com*, offer an equally excellent service, trips at around $125 per day, occasional specials for backpackers. All equipment and food provided.
Bay Beach Hire, *T09-4026078, kayakfun.win.co.nz*, on the waterfront opposite Kings Rd also offer freedom hire of single and double kayaks and guided trips. Their popular sunset trip costs from $50.

Parasailing, kite surfing and jet skiing
Airtorn, *T09-4026236, www.airtorn.co.nz* Provided the wind is up, why not try the rather tricky sport of kite surfing - a sort of combination of slow water skiing and kite flying with you trying to control both. It's great as long as you love swimming and fancy some colonic irrigation. From $150, 3 hr.
Flying Kiwi Parasail, *T09-4026078, www.parasail-nz.co.nz* A far more sedate option to the tandem skydive which operates

along the foreshore in Paihia; 600 ft from $60, 1000 from $70.
Jet ski hire, *T09-4028118 (Oct-Apr).*

Quad biking and horse trekking
Bush-n-Bike Adventures, *T09-4041142, bush-n-bike-adventures@xtra.co.nz*, offer both 1 hr and 30 min horse treks (suitable for beginner or advanced, from $45) or quad biking (from $65) over farmland, through bush and along the Tirohanga River Valley 15 km south of Paihia. Courtesy pick-ups.

Sailing Again, there are numerous independent sailing charters and options in the Bay, contact the Paihia VIC for advice and details. A day on the water will cost about $70-100. Names to look out for are:
Ecocruz, *T0800-432-6278, www.ecocruz.co.nz* (excellent 3-day trip);
Carino, *T09-4028040, T0800-478-900, bayofislandssailing@xtra.co.nz*, dolphin trips under sail);
Gungha, *T0800-478-900, bayofislandssailing@xtra.co.nz*;
Phantom, *T0800-224-421* both Phantom and Gungha are fast and modern;
Windborne, *T09-4037538, www.windborne.co.nz* Older 1928 schooner. To hire your own yacht try:
Great Escape Yacht Charters, *Opua, T09-4027143, www.greatescape.co.nz*, from $75 per day.

Scenic flights **Salt Air**, *T09-4028338, info@saltair.co.nz* A range of spectacular fixed wing and helicopter scenic flights from a 30-min local jaunt to a top-of-the-range flight to Cape Reinga and back, with a stop and some 4WD. Expensive at $330, but worth it.
Quantum Aviation, *Kerikeri, T09-4077333*, also offer flights both scenic and aerobatic.

Tandem Skydiving and hang gliding
The customary 'But, but, but… what if' here in the Bay of Islands is based at the airport and all perfectly safe.
BOP Skydive Centre, *T0800-427-593, www.skydive4fun.com*;
Sky-Hi Tandem Skydive Ltd, *T0800-427593*. Standard jumps of 9-12,000 ft from $265.
Skywalk, *T088-759-925, skywalk@igrin.co.nz* Tandem hang gliding (motorized) from $150 per 30 min.

Tours Paihia acts as base for a number of full-day coach trips to the far north and **Cape Reinga**. The trips vary a little but usually entail a number of stops to view kauri in the **Puketi Forest**, the lighthouse at the cape and a **dune surfing** experience, whereby you throw yourself down huge sand dunes on a boogie board. **Fullers**, **Kings** (see above) **Northern Exposure**, *T0800-573-875*, and **Awesome Adventures**, *T09-4026985* (recommended), all offer the trip for around about $85. A hefty 'go anywhere' **Dune Rider** that makes the journey for the same price, *T09-4028681*. For a short tour of the local area in an amphibious vehicle contact **Paihia Duck** *(usually parked on the waterfront like some cartoon monster)*, *T09-4028681*, *www.paihiaduck.co.nz* Or for a more conventional road trip to Kerikeri see Getting around (above).

Walking One of the best coastal walks in the North Island is nearby in the very scenic form of the Cape Brett Walk (see Russell, below). Recommended. **Cape Brett Walkways**, *T09-4038823*, *www.capebrettwalks.co.nz*, offer packages for the Cape Brett and other walks in the region.

Kerikeri *p177*
Fishing Black Rocks Charters, *T09-4078505, www.blackrocks.co.nz;* **Earl Grey Charters**, *T09-4077165, www.earlgreyfishing.co.nz* ($80 per hr).

Horse trekking Lakeside Horse Treks, *T09-4079422.* $25 per hr.

Fruit picking If you intend to find work in the orchards of Kerikeri, the hostels will provide advice and occasionally transport.

Walking As well as the attractive short walks along the river from the Basin reserve, further afield (northwest of Kerikeri) the Puketi and Omahuta forests can be accessed between Waipapa and Kapiro on SH1. These forests contain a number of impressive Kauri trees linked a boardwalk. A brief stop here is usually included on the agenda for most of the Cape Reinga coach tours from Paihia. For details on camping and walks contact DoC in Kerikeri, *T09-4078474.*

Matauri Bay *p179*
Diving The *Rainbow Warrior* is a well-known and popular wreck. A number of companies offer trips from Whangarei, Tutukaka and Paihia (see page 184).
Matauri Bay Charters, *Matauri Bay Holiday Park, T/F09-4050525*, is the local company.

Golf Kauri Cliffs Golf Course, *Kauri Cliffs, Matauri Bay Road, T09-4051900, www.kauricliffs.com*, is one of the most scenic golf courses in the country, but expensive at over $200 a round.

---

❶ Directory

Communications Internet and cheap overseas calls available at **Boots Off**, *Selwyn Rd, Pahia, T09-4026632* or the **Waterfront Booking Centre** (Awesome Adventures). **Kerikeri Computers**, *88 Kerikeri Rd (0900-1700)*, or **Eden Internet**, *two doors down from the Cinema at 41 Hobson Rd, Kerikeri (daily 0900-2100).* **Medical services** Doctor in Pahia, *T09-4028407.*

Whangaroa Harbour and Doubtless Bay

Whangaroa → *Phone code: 09 Colour map 1, grid B3*

Whangaroa, on the eastern shoreline of the Whangaroa Harbour, has more the feel of an inland lake than a coastal settlement due to the hills and the subsequent hidden narrow harbour entrance. It is a modern day base for a number of deep-sea fishing charter companies and boasts the historic claim as the site where the sailing ship *Boyd* was sunk after a *Pakeha* / Maori disagreement in 1809. A small **gallery** based in the well-stocked general store will enlighten you. Whangaroa was also home to the first **Wesleyan Mission**, which was established in 1823, and is where the infamous Maori chief Hone Heke died in 1828.

The settlement is dominated by the almost globular volcanic plug, **St Paul**, that provides a great view. It is a short but stiff climb best accessed from the top of Old Hospital Road. ▶▶ *For Sleeping, Eating and Activities, see pages 188 and 189.*

Mangonui and around → *Phone code: 09 Colour map 1, grid B3*

Although historically noted as a port for whaling ships and kauri export, today the congenial waterfront community of Mangonui is most famous for its fish and chips. Once you've tasted them you'll no doubt agree that this is a change for the better.

Getting there All the main Doubtless Bay settlements are serviced by Northliner or Intercity coaches, which stop in Mangonui.

Information There is an independent **VIC** ⓘ *on the waterfront at Mangonui, T09-4062046, www.doubtlessbay.co.nz Daily 0930-1700 (winter hours vary).* The free *Doubtless Bay Visitors Directory* contains a host of local information. Internet is available next door at Mangonui Stationers. ⓘ *Mon-Sat 0830-1700. T09-4060911.*

Around the Bay Just beyond Mangonui are the small beachfront settlements of **Coopers Beach** and **Cable Bay** (a former terminus for ocean cable). This is the habitat of the rich retiree, but the beaches themselves and the view across **Doubtless Bay** make up for their lack of depth and character. Thankfully, history comes to the rescue a little further along the coast at **Taipa**, the spot where Maori legend proclaims Kupe, the discoverer of Aotearoa, first landed. His honourable footprints are now followed by the bucket and spade brigade, who descend in their hundreds in summer. The 1840s **Butler House, Gardens and Whaling Museum**, ⓘ based at Butler Point, towards HiHi, T/F09-4060006, wwwbutlerpoint.co.nz $10, child $2, is worth a visit if you are interested in the local history. ▶▶ *For Sleeping, Eating and Activities, see pages 188 and 189.*

Karikari Peninsula → *Colour map 1, grid A2*

The temptation is to miss the Karikari peninsula and head straight for Kaitaia or the Cape but, if you have time, its isolated and remote beaches have considerable appeal. This T-shaped peninsula separates Doubtless Bay and the mangrove swamps of **Rangaunu Harbour**, with the broad empty sweep of **Karikari Bay** to the north. This bay is a natural danger zone for whale strandings. The last, in 1995, involved over 100 beached pilot whales. Sadly, despite an initial successful refloatation of many, the resilient efforts of locals and DoC were in vain, when almost all rebeached the following day and died. **Whatuwhiwhi** is the main settlement on the peninsula and is serviced by a shop, service station, takeaway and the Whatuwhiwhi Top Ten Holiday Park. The **Cape** itself is worthy of investigation and there is a popular campsite at Maitai Bay (DoC). Rock fishing here is said to be excellent. Karikari Beach can be accessed from a number of marked points along the way. ▸▸ For Sleeping, see below.

● Sleeping

Whangaroa p187
LL Butterfly Bay, T09-4050681, bbay@voyager.co.nz Luxurious self-contained hideaway with its own beach. Fine seafood.
L Kingfish Lodge, T09-4050164, www.kingfishlodge.co.nz This is a famous, 50 year-old establishment that is a favourite isolated haven for sea anglers and only accessible by boat. Has 14 fully serviced rooms, silver service cuisine, gym, sauna and a well-stocked bar (also open to day visitors). Under recent new ownership.
A Whangaroa Motel, Church St, T/F09-4050222. Self-contained units with views across the water.
C-D Sunseeker Lodge, Old Hospital Rd, T/F09-4050496, www.sunseekerlodge.co.nz Peaceful, friendly backpacker accommodation with 2 motel units and doubles. Internet.

Motorcamps and campsites
Whangaroa Harbour Motor Camp, Whangaroa Rd, T09-4050306, DYLEEWhangaroa@xtra.co.nz Usual facilities. Arranges dive and fishing trips and charters.

Mangonui and around p187
L Coopers Beachfront Suites, 18 Bayside Dr, Coopers Beach, T09-4061018, www.coopersbeach.net.nz Two luxury self-contained suites in a quiet location, with great sea views.
AL-A Acacia Lodge, Mill Bay Rd, Mangonui, T/F09-4060417, www.acacia.co.nz Popular lodge on the waterside in the heart of Mangonui. Luxury-standard units, some with spa. Tours and excursions arranged.
AL Carneval, 360 SH10, Cable Bay, T09-4061012, www.carneval.co.nz Fine, all mod cons B&B looking over the Bay and run by a friendly Swiss couple. 2 tasteful rooms with ensuites bathroom. Recommended.
AL Time Out, 6 Heretaunga Cres, Cable Bay, T09-4060101, www.taketimeout.co.nz Lovely beachfront hideaway ideal for couples. Owner volunteers in the VIC so great local info.
A Mangonui Motel, 1 Colonel Mould Dr, T/F4060346, www.mangonuimotel.co.nz Set

in a peaceful location 1 min from the village with good views across the bay, 6 self-contained units.

Motorcamps and campsites
B-C HiHi Beach Holiday Camp, HiHi Beach Rd, HiHi, T/F09-4060307. A peaceful beachfront location (off SH10 7 km south of Mangonui).
A-C Old Oak Inn, Waterfront Rd, Mangonui, T09-4060665. Characterful historic kauri hotel with good value, clean doubles and backpacker accommodation. A café bar and licensed restaurant are also attached.

Karikari Peninsula p187
LL-A Carrington Club, Maitai Bay Rd, T09-4087222, www.carringtonclub.co.nz Luxurious modern lodge or villa option and a host of activities including horse riding, its own 18-hole golf course, vineyard and private beach. The restaurant is also excellent.
A Reef Lodge, Rangiputa Beach, T09-4087100. Self-contained 1 or 2 bedroom studios and conventional units next to the beach, well off the beaten track, spa pool.

Motorcamps and campsites
A-C Whatuwhiwhi Top Ten Holiday Park, Whatuwhiwhi Rd, T09-4087202. Offers a peaceful holiday location next to the beach. There's also a popular campsite located at **Maitai Bay (DoC)**.
A White Sands Motor Lodge, Rangiputa Beach, T09-4087080. Modern units and 1 studio in a beachside location, on site store.

● Eating

Whangaroa p187
$$ Whangaroa Big Game Fish Club, T09-4050399. Has a restaurant and pleasant veranda bar, but winter hours are limited.
$$ Marlin Hotel, across the road, T09-4050347. Provides some rather unremarkable fare.

Mangonui and around p187
There are a number of cafés scattered along the waterfront offering fine local seafood.
$$ Waterfront Café, Beachfront Rd, T09-4060850. Daily 0830-late. A good bet.

$$ Old Oak Inn (see accommodation above) is also good for breakfast, lunch or dinner.
$ Mangonui Fish and Chip Shop, *just north of the village on Beach Rd,* T09-4060478. 0800-2100. In Mangonui, everything revolves around the delights of this popular licensed chippy.

▲ Activities and tours

Whangaroa *p187*
Fishing There are a number of fishing charters available from the marina beside the **Whangaroa Big Game Fish Club**, T09-4050347, and quality, good-value trips can be had aboard the yacht **Snow Cloud** from $70 a day, T09-4050230.

Mangonui *p187*
Many of the Paihia-based Cape tour operators also pass through Mangonui and bookings can be made direct, or through the VICs in Paihia or Mangonui.
A-Z Diving, T09-4087077, *www.atozdiving.co.nz*
Dolphin Rendezvous, T09-4060914, offering local dolphin watching trips.
MV Calypso, T09-4060914, which is popular for general cruising and fishing, from $60.
Paradise Connection, T/F09-4060460, offer the local Cape Reinga day excursion, and its sister operation **4x4 Exclusive Tours**, T09-4060406, takes the personalized approach with day or multi-day tours to the Cape and other local attractions.

Aupouri Peninsula

Kaitaia → *Phone code: 09 Colour map 1, grid B3 Population: 2700*
Almost every night on the national television weather forecast, Kaitaia takes the honours of being the hottest place in the country and, although the place itself is nothing to write home about, the weather and its general friendliness is notable. The town is primarily the main rural service centre for the Far North. It is predominantly Maori with an interesting smattering of Dalmation blood – mainly Croats who came during the kauri gum boom years of the late 1800s. For the tourist it provides a gateway to the Aupouri Peninsula, with its famous, uninterrupted sweep of **Ninety Mile Beach** (actually just over 100 km) to **Cape Reinga** and **North Cape**, the northernmost tip of New Zealand.

Getting there **Kaitaia Airport** is 6 km north of the town and is serviced daily Mon-Fri by **Air New Zealand Link**, T0800-737-000 and **Air Kaitia** (Mountain Air), T0800-222-123, www.mountainair.co.nz **Northliner** and **Intercity** coaches drop off and pick up outside Kaitaia Travel Bureau, 170 Commerce St, who also handle ticketing.
Information Information Far North ① *in the Lighthouse, Jaycee Park, South Rd,* T09-4080879, kaitiainfo@xtra.co.nz *Daily 0830-1700.*

Sights The **Far North Regional Museum** ① *next door to the Information Centre,* T09-4081403, *Mon-Fri 1000-1700, $3.50*, is worth a peek. Although hardly outstanding it is well laid out and proudly boasts a number of important exhibits and Maori *Taonga* including the Kaitaia Carving (one of the earliest Maori carvings in existence) and a very impressive 1500 kg anchor left by de Surville in 1769. Other collections include some interesting Moa remains and the far more modern remnants from the wreck of the *Rainbow Warrior*. There is also the regulation collection of kauri gum and digging items that feature heavily in every museum in Northland. The **Okahu Estate** ① *on the corner of Okahu Road and the Ahipara/Kaitaia highway, 31/2 km from Kaitaia,* T09-4082066, *www.okahuestate.co.nz, 1000-1700 (closed winter weekends)*, is New Zealand's northernmost winery. It is in pleasant surrounds and offers free tastings.

Further field **Gumdiggers Park** ① *on Heath Rd, off SH1 13 km north of Awanui,* T09-4067166, www.gumdiggerspark.co.nz, daily 0900-1730, from $5, child $2, is well worth a look. The result of a local John Johnson's passion to recreate a little piece of

The souls departing

The Northern tip of New Zealand is steeped in Maori legend and tradition. The name Reinga means 'Place of Leaping' and it is here, according to Maori lore, that the souls of the dead depart Aotearoa to the after-life. After travelling up the West Coast to Spirits Bay, the dead are believed to descend the slopes of the headland to the roots of an old, lone pohutukawa tree, before falling in to the sea. From there they are said to re-emerge on Ohaua, the highest point of the Three Kings Islands, where, still within view of Aotearoa, they bid their last farewell, before returning to the lands of their ancestors – Hawaiki.

family history, it is a faithful representation of a gum digger's village around 1900 and depicts what must have been a hard and basic existence. A lot less impressive and far more commercial is the **Ancient Kauri Kingdom**, ① *in Awanui, 8 km north of Kaitaia, T/F09-4067172, www.ancientkauri.co.nz, 7 days. Free,* which lures in the coach loads with its range of kauri furniture and crafts. The shop is perhaps worth a muse but what makes a stop here really worthwhile is the impressive 50-tonne log centrepiece, the old kauri logs drying in the car park, and the date scones in the café. ▸▸ *For Sleeping, Eating, Festivals and events and Activities, see page 191 and 192.*

North to the Cape → *Phone code: 09 Colour map 1, grid A2*

Human nature being what it is, one is naturally drawn up the Aupouri Peninsula to reach the northernmost tip of New Zealand. The peninsula itself, which is bounded by **Ninety Mile Beach** to the west and **Great Exhibition Bay** and the **Rangaunu Bay** and Harbour to the east, used to be covered in kauri forest, but today mainly consists of extensive dune systems and swamps, interspersed with commercial forestry. Although the windswept dunes that back Ninety Mile Beach cannot fail to impress, it is the white silica sands of **Kotoka** – the huge sand spit on the Parengarenga Harbour – that stands out the most. This remote peninsula offers one of the best coastal walks in the country and in spring and autumn is alive with flocks of migratory wading birds. The highest point south of the Cape is the 236 m **Mount Camel** near Houhoura, which stands out like a sore thumb. Sadly, access is some distance from the north and to enjoy its view is a major hike. **Houhoura** is home to the **Wagener Museum** which holds an amazing collection and is a 'must-see'. From Houhoura you pass the village of **Pukenui** before winding your way towards the remote and highly spiritual lands and landscapes of the Cape itself with **Cape Reinga** to the west and **North Cape** – the true northernmost point, to the east.

Getting there With your own wheels it will take about 1½ hrs to reach the Cape from Kaitaia. The road is sealed to Te Paki Station, which is about 21 km from the Cape. Beyond this point the road is metalled so watch your speed – many a budding rally driver in their Maui camper van has come to grief along this stretch. Although Ninety Mile Beach is classified as a highway, you are not advised to take anything other than a 4WD vehicle on to the sand. For those in **rental cars** (that are not insured on the sand) who cannot resist the temptation to do so, it will probably all end in tears. If you are short of time the best way to see the peninsula is to join the many coach tours from Paihia, Mangonui or Kaitaia (see page 192).

Houhoura Houhoura is a small fishing village on the shores of Houhoura Harbour. It is home to the **Wagener Museum** and the **Subritzky/Wagener Homestead** ① *T09-4098850. 0830-1630. $7.50.* The original family residence, the only way to describe this museum is that it is essentially a collection of collections and one of the best in the country. It houses the largest private collection in New Zealand, initiated in 1969 by the Wagener family. Since then the collections have grown to incorporate everything from a stuffed 440-kg (locally caught) marlin, to butterflies, chamber pots, miniature letters, guns and gramophones. It is a delight to wander through or better still take a guided tour (preferably by Owen Wagener himself). Whatever you do, do not leave without asking to see the old washing machine working. Behaves in much the same way as a metal cage would if you locked Mike Tyson in it and then called him names. There is a café attached to the museum.

Pukenui and further north Pukenui is the last major settlement on the way to the Cape, so it may pay to grab some petrol or a coffee at the café and general store, or on your return quench your thirst at New Zealand's northernmost pub the Houhoura Tavern. This is a fine place to mix with the locals. Sharkophobes should not enter – there are very gruesome pictures on the wall. About 25 km north of Pukenui you reach the small Maori enclave of **Te Kao**. This is the best place to park up and access the **Kotoka Sand Spit**. The forestry gate is about 1 km up the road but vehicular access is forbidden. Ensure you have maps and a compass since the myriad forestry roads to reach the sand spit are difficult to negotiate. Eventually you will emerge, preferably on the beach to the west. From there walk north to the sand dunes which are wild, remote and stunning. Allow 8 hrs.

Cape Reinga → *Colour map 1, grid A2*

From Te Kao the road passes through the basic motor camp at Waitiki Landing before entering the huge **Te Paki Station and Recreation Reserve** towards North Cape, Cape Reinga and the lighthouse. This reserve has a total area of 23,000 ha and contains some of the most extraordinary landforms in New Zealand. The Maori call this area *Te Hiku o te Ika* (the tail of the fish) from the legend that tells how the giant fish (North Island) was pulled from the sea by Maui from his canoe (South Island). Geology posits a more prosaic theory. The rocks that form the Cape were formed about 60 million years ago which later separated from the mainland. Then around two million years ago sand moved northwards from Kaitaia forming a huge tombolo and the peninsula we see today. The area supports a wide variety of coastal scenery from cliffs to wide sweeping beaches. There is a great network of short and long walks in the area (information from DoC) but access may be denied, or permission required, T09-4097831. Local Maori own almost a quarter of the land, and areas around North Cape are particularly sacred. The tip of North Cape, the northernmost point of New Zealand, is a scientific reserve with limited access.

For most visitors, sadly, the visit to this amazing area will be all too brief and revolve around Cape Reinga and the **lighthouse**. The views from the hill above the lighthouse are stunning and in stormy weather you can see the Tasman Sea and Pacific in an uneasy union, and as far as the Three Kings Islands, 57 km offshore. The northland coastline has claimed over 140 vessels and many lives since 1808, with the majority falling foul around the Cape. The lighthouse, which is a rather dumpy rotund little unit, was built in 1941 and contains the lens from the original lighthouse built on Motuopao Island to the south. Beside the lighthouse is the obligatory multi-destination signpost for that vital memento for Mum. ▸ *See Sleeping and Eating sections, page 192.*

See Sleeping and Eating sections, page 192.

⬤ Sleeping

Kaitaia *p189*

LL Taharangi Marie Lodge, *700 Sandhills Rd, Ninety Mile Beach, T09-4067462, taharangi@xtra.co.nz* In perfect isolation among the sand dunes of Ninety Mile Beach with a heavenly outdoor spa. Fine base for explorations further north.

A Okahu Vineyard Cottage, *Corner Okahu and Pukepoto Rds, T09-4082066, www.okahuestate.co.nz* Very cosy 3-bedroom

Northland Aupouri Peninsula

cottage amongst the vines.

A Lake Ngatu Countryside B&B, *Sweetwater Rd, Lake Ngatu, Waipapakauri, T/F09-4067300*. Some distance from town, worth the effort.

A Sierra Court Motor Lodge, *65 North Rd, T09-4081461, sierracourt.kaitaia@xtra.co.nz* Basic but comfortable 1 and 2 bedroom units centrally located.

A Wayfarer Motel, *231 Commerce St, T09-4082600*. Centrally located.

C-D Main Street Lodge Backpackers, *235 Commerce St, T09-4081275, mainstreet@xtra.co.nz* Maori-operated and recently revamped with rooms with en suite bath and offering the opportunity of a great cultural experience.

Cape Reinga *p191*
The accommodation north of Kaitaia is fairly basic, with Houhoura, Pukenui and Waitiki Landing offering the best base (the latter being the last available beds before the Cape).

A Houhoura Chalets Motor Lodge, *corner of Far North and Houhoura Heads Rd, T09-4098860, www.chalets@xtra.co.nz* A-frame units near the Wagener Museum.

A-D Pukenui Lodge Motel and Youth Hostel, *SH1, Pukenui, T09-4098837, www.pukenuilodge.co.nz* Offers tidy self-contained motel units and backpackers in an historic lodge, spa and bike hire.

Motorcamps and campsites
B-D Waitiki Landing, *SH1, only 20 km from the Cape, T09-4097508*. Has tent sites, bunks and cabins. Restaurant on site.

Pukenui Holiday Camp, *Lamb Rd, T09-4098803*. This motor camp provides better facilities than the very basic, but more scenic Houhoura equivalent.

D DOC campsites, *T09-4086014*. At Rarawa on the east coast just south of Te Kao, at Kapowairua next to the beautiful Spirits Bay and Tapotupotu Bay, near the Cape.

🍴 Eating

Kaitaia *p189*
$$$ Carrington Club Restaurant, *Maitai Bay Rd, T09-4087222, www.carringtonclub.com* It is a bit of a drive to this luxury resort on the Kari Kari peninsula, but the food, wine and scenery are worth it. Bookings advised.

$$ Beachcomber Restaurant, *The Plaza, 222*

Commerce St, T09-4082010. Mon-Fri 1100-1430, Mon-Sat 1700-late.

$$ Blue House Café, *14 Commerce St, T09-4084935*. Open 7 days from 0700. Seasonal.closing from 1530-2200.

$ Michelangelo's Pizza, *26 Commerce St, T09-4082001*. Open 7 days from 1000, closed from 1700 Tue-Thu.

$ Bushman's Hut Steak House, *corner of Bank St and Puckey Av, T09-4084320*. Open 6 days Tue-Sun 1700-2100. Live music weekends and a good value venue.

Cape Reinga *p191*
The café at the **Wagener Museum** (seasonal hours), the **Houhoura Pub**, the café and takeaway in **Pukenui**, and the restaurant at **Waitiki Landing** are your only hope.

✹ Events

Mar: The annual **Te Houtaewa Challenge** is a gruelling 60-km run up Ninety Mile Beach with added 5 person relay, 42-km marathon, 21 km half marathon and a leisurely 6 km walk for the lazy! The event runs in parallel with a 4-day **Festival of Maori arts and crafts**. For details, **Pop Runner Promotions**, *T09-5702222, poprun@xtra.co.nz*

▲▲ Activities and tours

Kaitaia *p189*
A number of quality day trips leave Kaitaia for the **Cape Reinga/Ninety Mile Beach** circuit. Really good value and generally offer more time at the Cape and various other stops than their distant counterparts operating out of Paihia. Most stop at the Ancient Kauri Kingdom or Gumdiggers Park, the Wagener Museum at Houhoura (see page 190), the Cape and the Te Paki Stream sand dunes (for dune surfing) before running almost the entire length of Ninety Mile Beach. Note that tours run in either direction depending on tides. For other activities near Kaitaia see Ahipara, page 193.

Harrison's Cape Runner, *123 North Rd, Kaitaia, T09-4081033, capetours@xtra.co.nz* Leaves daily at 0900, returning about 1700. Adult $40, child $20, lunch included. *Harrison's* also operate a more personalized *4x4 Reef Runner* tour which takes in a half-day of

4-wheel driving, spectacular views and sand tobogganing. Twin tour discounts apply.

Sand Safaris, *221 Commerce St, T09-4081778, www.sandsafaris.co.nz* Another full-day tour with all the usual stops and activities including the new Gumdiggers Park (see above). Departs daily 0900, returning about 1700. Adult $45, child $25 (includes entry to Gumdiggers Park).

Far North Outback Adventures, *T09-4080927, www.farnorthtours.co.nz* Offer a more personalized luxury 4x4 tour of the Cape. Flexible itinerary, friendly, great food and great value, from $100. Recommended.

Pack or Paddle Fishing and Kayak Adventures, *T09-4098445*. Fine, intrepid, yet a safe and fun day, or multi-day tours with local guide and good bloke Marty, from $90.

Tall Tale Tours, *237A Commerce St,* T09-4080870, www.Tall-Tale.co.nz Offer a unique Maori cultural package including a visit to a *marae* interspersed with learning about protocol, stories, myths and legends. If all that sand does not appeal, you might try your hand with a.22 rifle at the **Far North Indoor Shooting Gallery**, *Hillcrest Rd, T09-4080097 / T027-2869154*. Or better still a scenic flight over the Cape with **Blue Sky Scenics**, *Kaitaia Airport, T09-4067320*. For details about local walking and mountain biking routes consult the *'Kaitaia Area Walks'* leaflet, available from the VIC, $1.

❻ Directory

Internet VIC or Hackers Internet Café, *84 Commerce St, Kaitaia, T09-408499. Mon-Wed 0900-2100, Thu-Sat 0900-late, Sun 1000-2100.* The VIC is cheaper.

South to the Hokianga Harbour

Ahipara and around → *Phone code: 09 Colour map 1, grid B2*

Ahipara forms the southern extremity of Ninety Mile Beach and is 14 km west of Kaitaia. Formerly a 2000-strong gum-digging community it is now a shadow of its former self but still a scenic spot offering a number of beach-based activities. The VIC in Kaitaia will provide all the relevant information or you may wish to visit the local website, www.ahipara.co.nz The hill at the far end of town has fine views up Ninety Mile Beach.

Ahipara to Hokianga Harbour From Ahipara the road turns south to **Herekino**, through Broadwood and **Kohukohu** to **Narrows Landing** on the **Hokianga Harbour**. There you meet the ferry to **Rawene** and the heart of Hokianga. This road is fairly tortuous and once again the familiar Northland Mobile-Phone-No-Service-Zone country sights apply. There is little of interest on the road itself but two venues in the area are of particular note. First is the **Golden Stairs Walkway** on the southern shore of the mouth of the **Whangape Harbour**. If you can muster the courage and tackle the route to the little settlement of Pawarenga, this walk is well worth it. The mouth of the Whangape Harbour is like a small fjord and out of character with the other larger harbours along the west Northland Coast. The walk is fairly short but steep and culminates at the northern tip of the vast and wild beach. From here you could continue down the beach to Mitimiti, where there is a fine and remote backpackers (see below). The following day could be spent exploring the coast before being dropped off at the end of the Golden Stairs Walkway again, from where you negotiate the return to retrieve your car. Be sure to secure all belongings out of sight and lock the car.

The second venue is actually **Mitimiti** and the wild **Warawara Forest**, which is the second largest kauri forest in New Zealand, still containing some whoppers. The 41 km it takes by road to get to Mitimiti from Narrows Landing is quite arduous but worth the drive simply for the views and nature of the remote Northland countryside, not to mention the broad stretch of coast and wild beach at its terminus. Once again, if you stay at the Manaia Hostel at Mitimiti you can just about have 50 km of beach to yourself for fishing, walking or (careful) swimming. The Maori owner of the hostel will happily take you for a 'blat' in the 'sand banger', or eight-wheel quad bike, up and down the beach, and while doing so give you a fascinating insight into the area's Maori history. The Tree House is another fine youth hostel located near the Narrows Landing Ferry. ›› *For Sleeping, Eating and Activities, see page 196 and 196.*

Rawene and Kaikohe → *Colour map 1, grid B3*

Rawene is essentially the gateway to the heart of Hokianga from the north (*To9-4052602, the Rawene Ferry operates daily from 0730-1930, light vehicle $14, foot/car passenger $2*), but has a heart of its own that seems strangely broken. Even in the earliest years of Maori and European settlement, when a large sawmill and shipyard was established in the area, Rawene saw its fair share of conflicts, both internally and externally, that has left it wanting. Today, although it is a pretty place with lots of potential, it struggles with unemployment, drugs and poverty and many think that only tourism and the building of a bridge across the harbour, can come to the rescue. One hopes that it can, but meantime, there is little to hold the visitor back, except the laid-back **Boatshed Café and Gallery**, ① *To9-4057728*, and the historic 1868 **Clendon House**, ① *To9-4057874, 1000-1700 (Nov-Apr). $2*, both on the waterfront. Clendon House is the former residence of James Clendon, a local dignitary who was, amongst other things, the former Hokianga district magistrate.

To the east of Rawene and 14 km north of the small settlement **Taheke** (off SH12) is one of Northland's newest natural tourist attractions, though at almost 3 million years old, new is hardly an apt description. The **Wairere Boulders**, ① *McDonnell Rd, Horeke, To9-4019935, www.wairereboulders.co.nz, daily, $10, child $5*, can loosely be described as a valley of ancient basalt rocks formed by ancient pyroclastic flows that have since eroded and become stacked upon one another, creating a strange geological labyrinth, or 'stream of rocks'. A well-formed path with boardwalks winds through the conglomerate to give the best views from both near and far. Allow 3 hrs.

Just south of Rawene you join the SH12 to Opononi and Omapere and all points south to Dargaville. East of here is the small service town of **Kaikohe** just before SH1. There is a VIC here at Broadway, ① *To9-4011693, daily 0900-1700, closed winter weekends*, but really there is little to stop for. One thing is **Kaikohe Hill**, which offers a good view, perhaps followed by a soak in the wooden hot tubs of the **Ngawha Springs and Waiariki Pools**. ① *Southeast of the town. Daily 0700-1930. $2.50*. The springs, though very basic, are said to cure some rheumatic, lumbago, arthritic and skin conditions. The old Maori warrior Hone Heke recognized the remedial power of the springs, bringing his wounded here for treatment after the British assault on his fortified Ohaeawai *Pa*. Camping and campervan sites available. ›› *For Sleeping and Eating, see page 195.*

Opononi and Omapere → *Phone code: 09 Colour map 1, grid B3*

These two converging waterfront villages are the main resorts in the Hokianga. The villages and the harbour entrance are dominated by the impressive bare sand dunes that grace its northern shore. They rise to a height of 100 m and at sunset glow with an orange radiance. It was here in the Hokianga Harbour, in the 10th century, that the great Polynesian explorer Kupe first set foot in Aotearoa (New Zealand) from his homeland of Hawaiki. After a short stay he went home again leaving a small group behind. Although Kupe himself never returned his ancestors did and it was christened *Hokianganui-a-Kupe* meaning 'the place of Kupe's great return'. The area is also known as *Te Kohanga o Te Tai Tokerau* or 'the nest of the northern tribes'. Indeed it remains the centrepoint from which most Northland Maori trace their ancestry. Both Opononi and Omapere were somewhat insignificant until the appearance of a solitary wild dolphin in 1955. Opo, as she was christened, won the hearts of the nation and subsequently put little Opononi on the map.

Sun) to Paihia and returning south from Paihia (Mon, Wed and Fri). A **Northliner** 'Loop
Pass' is also accepted by Intercity, To800-363-463. **West Coaster** links with the latter
and also offers a service from Paihia to Auckland, To9-9136100/4028989. All buses
stop at the VIC where bookings can be arranged.

Information VIC ① *on the main road roughly between the two communities,
To9-4058869, www.hokiangatourism.org.nz Daily 0900-1700.*

Sights The small **Omapere Museum** ① *0930-1630, free,* housed above the
information centre has some interesting historical stories, pictures and items, of which
the original and highly entertaining 'Tally Ho' video about Opo the dolphin stands out.

You can forget the rather unremarkable **statue of 'Opo'** on the waterfront at
Opononi. It is little improvement on the last that should be outside a supermarket on
springs, with a coin slot. Far better to head for the southern edge of Omapere and the
Arai-Te-Uru headlands. The tip of the headland supported a signal station that for many
years used to help ships negotiate the tricky harbour entrance. The headland offers a
great view across to the sand spit (North Head) or Niua to give it its Maori name. The
Ocean Beach track takes you down to the rocky coast below, where a blow hole and
cave can be explored (turn left and watch the tide). The **Coastal Walkway** also starts
here and winds its way round to the remote and beautiful beaches to the south. **Pakia
Hill** at the southern end of Omapere also offers spectacular views of the Harbour and
the dunes. **The Labyrinth Woodworks and The Amazing Maize Maze** is worth a look,
along Waiotemarama Gorge Road next to the Kauri Forest Walk and with all sorts of
other puzzles to baffle the brain, To9-4054581. There is complimentary tea or coffee
and the **Kauri Forest Walk** is a nice 10-minute amble that takes in a waterfall, but you
can go the full hog with a six-hour hike up to Mount Haturu; To9-4054581. Back in the
centre of Omapere the Mamaku, SH12, is the rather cute-looking local craft co-operative
set up in 1979. Fine wood, fibre, glass works and bone carvings, To9-4058662. ▸▸ *For
Sleeping, Eating and Activities see below and page 196 .*

◑ Sleeping

Ahipara and around *p193*
AL Shipwreck Lodge, *70 Foreshore Rd,
Ahipara, T09-4094929, www.shipwreck
lodge.co.nz* Modern B&B in a superb
beachside location. 3 lovely suites.
AL Beachfront, *14 Kotare St, Ahipara,
T/F09-4094007,
www.beachfront.net.nz* Tidy, beachside
self-contained accommodation. Hosts also
operate a fishing charter boat.
AL Beach Abode, *11 Korora St, Ahipara,
T/F09-4094070, www.beachabode.co.nz*
Wide range of modern self-contained
accommodation options.
B-D Manaia Hostel, *Ahipara, T09-4095347,
mitimiti@xtra.co.nz* Great budget
accommodation, 2 twins and a double, in a
truly remote Northland location. Internet.

B-D Tree House, *West Coast Rd, Kohukohu,
T09-4055855, www.treehouse@xtra.co.nz* A
positive sanctuary of a place set in 17 acres
of bush and orchards. 2 doubles, 2 twins, 2
bunkrooms and a house bus! Camping.

Motorcamps and campsites
A Ahipara Motor Camp and Backpackers,
Takahe St, T09-4094864. For campervans,
tents or backpackers.
A-D Adriaan Lodge Motel, *Reefview Rd,
T/F09-4094888, www.ahipara.co.nz/adriaan*
Also offers backpacker accommodation and
its own quad bike hire.

Rawene *p194*
A Hokianga Homestay, *Clendon Esplanade,
T09-4057554.* Pleasant self-contained
accommodation in an historic villa, just past
Clendon House and not far from the café.

● *For an explanation of the sleeping and eating price codes used in this guide, see the inside
● front cover. Other relevant information is provided in the Essentials chapter, see page 51.*

B **Masonic Hotel**, *Parnell St, T09-4057822*.
Simple, affordable accommodation and
food.
B-D **Rawene Motor Camp**, *1 Marmot St,
T09-4057720*. Small but adequate with
backpacker lodgings. Swimming pool.

Omapere *p194*
AL **Hokianga Haven**, *226 SH12,
T09-4058285, tikanga2000@xtra.co.nz* A
fine beachside B&B, one cosy guestroom.
Friendly art-oriented hosts, dogs and even a
hammock. Recommended.
A **Omapere Tourist Hotel and Motel**,
SH12, T09-4058737. A fine spot right next to
the beach and the wharf. Well-equipped
units are available, as are powered sites and
campsites. Heated pool, nice lawns,
restaurant and bar.
A **B&B in Omapere**, *Signal Station Rd,
T09-4058641, whaley_bnb@paradise.net.nz*
Peaceful spot with great views.
A **Dawn Homestay**, *Omapere
T/F09-4058773*. Nice spot on the hill – quiet,
friendly and secluded. Yacht trips available.
B-D **Globe Trekkers**, *SH12, Omapere,
T/F09-4058183, shirley@xtra.co.nz* Offers
private chalet plus dbl/twin/share/tents,
campervan sites. Bike and scooter hire.
C-D **House of Harmony**, *SH12, Opononi,
T09-4058778*. Small and friendly
backpackers offering scooter hire.

● Eating

Ahipara and around *p193*
$$ **Bayview Restaurant** *at the Adriaan
Lodge Motel (above)*. Open 7 days from
0600, Fri-Sat 1900, Sun 1600.
$ **Waterline Café** *on the waterfront in
Kohukohu, T09-4055552*. Tue-Thu
0930-1630, Fri/Sat 0930-late, Sun
0930-1600.

Rawene *p194*
$ **Boatshed Cafe**, *on Clendon Esplanade,
T09-4057728*. The place to go for lunch or
coffee. Daily 0830-1630.

Opononi and Omapere *p194*
$$$-$$ **Omapere Tourist Hotel** (above)
has a good restaurant offering the
traditional New Zealand fare.
$ **The Opo Beach Takeaway**, *next to the
Opononi Hotel, T09-4058065*. Daily
1000-2100. Does great fish and chips.
There is a 4 Square **supermarket** in
Opononi, T09-4058301.

▲ Activities

Ahipara *p193*
Adventure Centre, *Takahe St, T09-4092055,
www.ahipara.co.nz/adventurecentre* For a
whole host of activities ranging from horse
trekking to sand tobogganing.
Wildcat, *T09-4094129*, Ahipara's own Cape
Reinga coach tour company. From $45,
child $25. By all accounts the trip is as good
as any and the lunch is exceptional!
Tua Tua Tours, *Ahipara Rd, T09-4094875,
tuatuatours@xtra.co.nz* Guided quad bike
tours – lots of fun – 3 hrs $145, 1½ hrs $60.
Fishing Wildcat, *T09-4094729*.

Opononi and Omapere *p194*
Northland Coast to Coast Tours, *T09-4059460*,
offers local tours throughout the Hokianga and
beyond.
Hokianga Express Charters, *T09-4058872*,
trips to the dunes to explore or go
sandboarding ($19). Also fishing and dive trips.
Alma 80 Scow, *T09-4057704,
www.almahokianga@xtra.co.nz* Cruising
the Hokianga aboard a 78-ft kauri ship.
Regular cruise from Rawene on Thu at 1000
and fishing from Opononi on Fri at 1800
Dec-Apr.
Okopako Horse Treks, *Mountain Rd,
T09-4058815*. About $20 per hr.

The Kauri Coast → *Phone code: 09*

Just south of Omapere you bid farewell to the coast and the Hokianga and enter 'kauri country'. Waipoua, Mataraua and Waima Forests make up the largest remaining tract of native forest in Northland, and the Waipoua and Trounson Kauri Forests contain 300 species of tree including the great kauri and the two finest examples and living monuments to these magnificent and awe inspiring trees. The mighty kauri forests used to blanket much of the upper North Island but, thanks to the activities of man, those forests have been plundered and raped and remain a mere suggestion of their former selves. The Waipoua forest is home to the largest remaining individuals, including the much-loved and ancient Tane Mahuta or 'Lord of the Forest'. For lovers of life and for those who have a healthy respect for nature, to visit this great tree is something of a pilgrimage. For those who have never really thought about it, it is a fine place to start.

Waipoua Kauri Forest and around → *Phone code: 09 Colour map 1, grid B3*

The 15,000-ha Waipoua Forest includes the 9105 ha Waipoua sanctuary of which 2639 ha contain mature kauri trees. The original block of forest was bought from the local Maori chiefs for $4,400 in 1876 and, although the original intention was to use the land for 'settlement purposes', most of the forest was reserved for government forestry purposes in 1906. Thankfully, due to much local and national pressure, which came to a head in 1952 with a 70,000-strong petition, the forest is now safely under the administration of DoC. The 20-km drive through the forest is appealing in itself, with roadside kauri and umbrella-like ponga ferns giving you just a hint of what Northland and much of the entire country used to be like.

Walking tracks at the northern end of the forest, immediately next to the highway, give access to the two largest known kauri specimens, **Tane Mahuta**, or 'Lord of the Forest' and **Te Matua Ngahere**, the 'Father of the Forest'. Tane Mahuta can be reached within five minutes and is an awesome sight, with a trunk height of 17.7 m, girth of 13.8 m and total height of 51½ m. It is estimated to be over 1500 years old. 2 km south of Tane Mahuta is a car park where you pay a $2 security fee (such is the level of car theft from the most destructive of New Zealand's introduced mammals – the human). From here, there are a number of short or long walks. Te Matua Ngahere, the second largest tree, can be reached in about 20 minutes, while the 'Four Sisters', a stand of four trees growing together like a huge botanical oil rig, are only 100 m from the car park. The Yakas Track is 6 km in length and takes in another monster, the Yakas Kauri, before emerging at the visitor centre. A lookout point 1½ km from the park's southern boundary is worth a look on the one-hour trek from the visitors centre.

Waipoua Forest Visitor Centre (DoC) ① *off SH12 towards the southern end of the park. T09-4393011, www.doc.govt.nz / www.kauricoast.co.nz Mon-Sun 0830-1700, Sat-Sun 0900-1730.* It contains a small, interesting museum and can provide all walking or sundry information. ►► *For Sleeping, Eating and other listings, see page 200 and 201.*

Trounson Kauri Park and Kaihu → *Colour map 1, grid B3*

There is also a smaller but impressive kauri forest in the 450-ha Trounson Kauri Reserve, which is 17 km south of Waipoua. The road is signposted about 40 km north of Dargaville and goes through Donelly's Crossing, which has everything bar the saloon and stagecoach. A 'tepee' site is available, and facilities include hot showers and a communal cookhouse ($7). Powered sites also available. Guided **night tours** ① *$15. Oct-May T09-4390621,* in summer to hear kiwi (see Kauri Coast Holiday Park below). The forest has a healthy population of North Island browns because of its isolation from other predator-rich forests by a sea of farmland. The camp ① *T09-4390605,* is closed in winter.

Just south of Trounson is the settlement of **Kaihu**. The Nelson's Kaihu Kauri, ① *0900-1700 Mon-Sat*, is a good quality retail outlet for quality kauri crafts. ▸▸ *For Sleeping, Eating and other listings, see page 200.*

Kai Iwi Lakes

About 30 km south of Waipoua and 10 km towards the coast is the aquatic summer playground of the Kai Iwi Lakes. This is a favourite Northland holiday spot for those wanting to enjoy the combination of endless beach and surf, together with the more sedate inland waters of the three main lakes – **Kaiiwi**, **Taharoa** and **Waikere**. Here, mainly in summer, you can enjoy sailing, windsurfing, water-skiing, jet skiing and fishing. Lacking much cover and being so close to the beach, bear in mind the lakes can be a little exposed at times. ▸▸ *For Sleeping, Eating and other listings, see page 200.*

Dargaville and around → *Phone code: 09 Colour map 1, grid B3*

Dargaville is a rather dull township located on the bank of the **Wairoa River**, the Kaipara Harbour's largest and longest tributary. Like many Northland settlements it has, with the exhaustion of the kauri forests, become a shadow of its former self. It was founded in 1872 by Irish timber merchant Joseph Dargaville, when the district was already the enclave of a large group of Dalmation settlers. Kauri timber was again the name of the game and for many years Dargaville was an important export centre. The rivers north of the bustling port were choked with kauri being worked downstream, and it was from here that much of Northland's kauri was shipped to Australia and elsewhere. With the myriad tributaries and branches of the Northern **Kaipara Harbour** inundating the region, access in those days was only possible by boat from the sister port and timber-milling town of Helensville, on the south of Kaipara Harbour, north of Auckland.

Today Dargaville is a main service centre for the farms with their barren fields on which the great kauri once stood, and the river nearby transports little except ducks. The region as a whole is also known as the 'Kumara Capital' of the country producing the best of this sweet potato introduced by the early Polynesian navigators.

Getting there Intercity and **Mainline** have connecting services to Auckland. **West Coaster** run an Auckland to Paihia service and back, *T09-4028989 / T09-9136100*. Buses stop on Kaipa St. Information and ticketing at the VIC.

Information Your best bet is the **Kauri Coast VIC** ① *Normanby St, T/F09- 4398360, www.kauricoast.co.nz Daily in summer 0830-18000; winter, 0830-1700; Sat-Sun 1000-1600.*

Sights Although generally considered principally the gateway to the Kauri Coast, and an important supply or overnight stop on the developing and popular Twin Coast Highway, there is the odd significant thing to see in Dargaville. A number of tour operators and local activities are also based here. The information centre has put together an **Historic River Walk**, with an interesting free leaflet. It is 5 km and takes about an hour. One of the highlights is the **Dargaville Museum**, ① *T09-4397555, daily 0900-1600, $5*, which bears the remnants and relates the sorry tales of the many ships wrecked trying to negotiate the notorious Kaipara Bar. It also has a collection of Maori *taonga* and pioneer exhibits and, at 84 kg, the largest piece of kauri gum in the world (just a few grammes more than a similar piece in the Kauri Museum at Matakohe).

At the reserve there is a 40-minute loop walk that starts near the DoC campsite, taking in some of the finest kauri specimens in the country.

Another useful leaflet from the VIC outlines the **Kauri Coast Craft Trail** which details the various galleries and outlets at which to see kauri and other native woods being crafted, on display or for sale. This is your best chance to buy quality

66 99 It gives a whole new meaning to the words buoy and ballcocks, and makes Barbara Cartland's collection of earrings look tedious. One can only shudder at what goes on in this kind of a disturbed mind...

kauri products at competitive prices. One 'working' studio, the *Woodturners Kauri Gallery* ① *4 Murdoch St, T09-4394975, www.stop.at/rickys, daily*, is run by Rick Taylor, who has been turning and chipping away at kauri for over 23 years.

It is worthwhile taking a look at the coast near Dargaville and the ridiculously long **Ripiro Beach** – if only to have an inkling of what 104 km of almost uninterrupted sand looks like. It is accessible at a number of places, the best serviced being **Baylys Beach**, 14 km west of Dargaville. But if you fancy a look at the local countryside (and the locals) followed by a truly remote walk to the disused 1884 **Kaipara Lighthouse** and the seemingly endless sand dunes of the **Kaipara Heads**, then take the road to the tiny outpost village of **Poutu**. It is a strangely disconcerting 69 km south from Dargaville and gives one an inkling of the staggering length of the Kaipara Harbour's shoreline, at 3,000 km thought to be one of the longest natural harbour coastlines in the world.

Before you leave Dargaville or if you have only an hour or so then head to the rather seedy village of **Te Kopuru** (12 km southwest) and take a look at what must be one of the most interesting and bizarrely decorated gardens on the planet. Located at 51 Norton Street and next door and round the corner in Wilson St, it puts a whole new meaning to the words buoy and ballcocks, and makes Barbara Cartland's collection of earrings look tedious. One can only shudder at what goes on in this kind of a disturbed mind.

If you are not on a tour or cannot be bothered with the 69 km to the Kaipara Heads and the remote walk to the **Kaipara Lighthouse** then there are three interesting peaks to conquer in the vicinity, all of which offer interesting views of the vast Kaipara Harbour. **Mount Tutamoe** is a 4-5 hour walk; the 221 m **Mangaraho Rock** (11 km south of Dargaville) is 45 minutes around base and 30 minutes to summit; and the very knobbly **Toka Toka Peak** (17 km south) is a 20-minute walk. For directions and more information call at the VIC. ▸▸ *For Sleeping, Eating and other listings, see pages 201-202.*

Matakohe and the Kauri Museum → *Phone code: 09 Colour map 1, grid C4*

The village of Matakohe, 45 km south of Dargaville, is the home of the **Kauri Museum**. The museum, at Church Rd, is one of the finest in the country and provides a fitting finale to the Twin Coast Discovery Highway before the SH12 meets the main SH1 at Brynderwyn and heads back south to Auckland.

Getting there The museum is on SH12, 26 km from SH1 at Brynderwyn, which is 114 km north of Auckland. All major coach companies that take the Twin Coast Discovery Highway stop at the museum.

Sights The **Kauri Museum**, ① *T09-4317417, www.kauri-museum.com, daily 0830-1730 Nov-Apr, 0900-1700 May-Oct, $10, child $2.50*, houses a number of highly imaginative displays which offer a detailed insight into the natural history of the kauri and man's exploitation and love affair with the great tree. Starting in the Volunteer Hall one cannot fail to be impressed with the 22½ m cross section of the Balderston Kauri, a local specimen which was killed by lightening. It is a massive example but a relative youngster. On the wall at its base this is dramatically highlighted with life-size circumference outlines of larger recorded trees. The largest outline, depicting a tree that once grew in the Coromandel, has a diameter of 8½ m, which makes the Balderston slice seem like a piece of cress and even dwarfs Tane Mahuta. Around the edges of the hall there are some exquisite examples of kauri furniture and finely crafted models of some of the many kauri scows that used to ply the Kaipara Harbour.

Next to the Volunteer Hall is the **Steam Sawmill**. This is an good working mock-up which takes you through the complex and ingenious methods used to cut the huge logs. Additional displays in the **Smith Wing** outline examples of wood types and ages, the extraction of kauri gum and include some monstrous moving equipment and saws that show what a task it was get the tree from bush to mill. That effort and detail is cleverly and subtly highlighted right down to a bead of sweat from a mannequin's nose!

Other wings of the museum display mock-up pioneer family rooms, machines hall, chainsaw displays, fine kauri furniture, timber panels and carvings. Downstairs is the world's best kauri gum display with some fine (and some not so fine) carvings, busts and ornaments, all carefully fashioned from the tree's resin or sap. This 'amber' (its other name) is of varying ages, some of it hundreds of thousands of years old. Within the museum grounds there are some nicely restored examples of kauri buildings, including the 1867 Pioneer Church and 1909 Post Office. A well-stocked souvenir shop offers a great opportunity to purchase some finely crafted pieces of kauri including some 'Swamp Kauri' pieces, which are tens of thousands of years old.

The museum is well worth a visit and stands as a wonderful tribute to man's imagination and sheer hard work in the extraction and use of the kauri. If there has to be some criticism it is that there is not enough to echo the fact that man's love affair with this great native tree, has been an incredibly damaging and unsustainable affair.

⊕ Sleeping

Waipoua Kauri Forest *p197*
A **Solitaire Homestay**, *SH12, T09-4054891, solitairehomestay@xtra.co.nz* Comfortable B&B with rooms with ensuite bath and standard double in traditional kauri villa, 6 km north of the forest.
A **Waipoua Lodge**, *SH12, T/F09-4390422, www.waipaualodge.co.nz* Fine comfortable self-contained accommodation in former wool shed and stables. Restaurant attached.
B-D Kaihu Farm Backpackers, *Kaihu, T09-4394004*. Backpackers and twin/double. 20 km South of Waipoua. Bus stops outside.
C-D Waipoua DOC, *T09-4390605*. Both 2- and 4-bed cabins available at Waipoua. Hot

and cold showers and some with cooking facilities. Campsites and campervan sites.

Motorcamps and campsites
Kauri Coast Holiday Park, *Trounson Park Rd, Kaihu, T09-4390621*. Powered sites and cabins set in a very pleasant site next to the river. Clean, relatively modern and almost homely. Guided night tours to Trounson Kauri Reserve in summer to perhaps - if you're lucky- hear kiwi but almost certainly to see glow-worms and native eels. $15. Recommended.

Kai Iwi Lakes *p198*
A **Country Cottage**, *Kai Iwi Lakes Rd, T09-4390303*. Two self-contained cottages

● For an explanation of the sleeping and eating price codes used in this guide, see the inside
● front cover. Other relevant information is provided in the Essentials chapter, see page 51.

nearer the lakes than those listed above. They also have jet-skis for hire, $90 per hr.
A Hilltop Studio, *SH12, T09-4396351, rwatt@igrin.co.nz* Single self-contained unit in bush setting, about 10 km from the lakes.
A Waterlea, *T/F09-4390727*. 2 self-contained units right next to the lakes. Host of aquatic activities and relevant equipment. Fishing trips and boat hire, around $70 per hr.

Campsites
Basic facilities available at Pine Beach on the shores of **Taharoa**, and **Promenade Point**, *$6, T09-4398360*. Book at the Dargaville VIC.

Dargaville *p198*
L Lighthouse Lodge, *Pouto Point, T0800-439-515, www.lighthouse-lodge.co.nz* A remote and luxurious hideaway at the very end of the northern Kaipara peninsula at Kaipara Heads, a long drive and most probably not a 1-night stay, but worth the journey. Fishing trips and quad bikes.
AL Kauri House Lodge, *Bowen St, Dargaville, T09-4398082*. Spacious kauri-built house with comfortable rooms with en suite bath.
A Awakino Boutique Hotel, *Awakino Point, Dargaville, T/F09-4397870, apl.j.hyde@xtra.co.nz* Quiet and comfortable, 2 min from town.
A Parkview Motel, *36 Carrington St, Doraville, T09-4398339, www.onward.to/parkview* Pool spa and children's play area.
B Bayly's Beach B&B, *Bayly's Coast Rd, T09-4397157, mlkdh@win.co.nz* Cosy, rural self-contained cottage 1 km from the beach.
C-D Greenhouse Backpackers, *13 Portland St, Dargaville, T09-4396342*. Backpacker accommodation; camping $10.

Motorcamps and campsites
Dargaville Holiday Park, *10 Onslow St, Dargaville, T/F09-4398296, dargavilleholidaypark@xtra.co.nz* Central location with recent upgrades, usual facilities plus backpacker rooms, spa and internet.
Baylys Beach Holiday Park, *22 Seaview Rd, Baylys Beach, T/F09-4396349*. Small and functional near the beach. Also offers quad bike hire.

Matakohe *p199*
A Matakohe House, *Church Rd, T09-4317091, mathouse@xtra.co.nz* Only 50 m from the

museum. Comfortable modern double and twin rooms. Communal lounge, evening meals. Café and art gallery next door.

Motorcamps and campsites
C-D Matakohe Top Ten Motor Camp, *T/F09-4316431*. Fairly modern and 350 m from the museum. Tent sites.
C-D Old Post Office Guest House, *Corner SH12 and Oakleigh, Paparoa. T/F09-4316444*. Old World character and charm homestead with 1 room an ex-prison cell! Located 6 km east of the museum. Backpackers welcome.

● Eating

Waipoua Kauri Forest *p197*
Waipoua Lodge, *T09-4390422, www.waipoualodge.co.nz* For eating out the best and only bet for miles.

Dargaville *p198*
$$ Funky Fish Cafe *34 Seaview Rd, Baylys Beach, T09-4398883*. Daily 1100-late. The best place in the area and well worth the drive.

In Dargaville itself there is not a huge selection beyond the usual takeaways. Other options include the following:
$$ Steakhouse and Bar, *corner of Victoria and Gladstone St, T09-4398460*. Open 7 days. Good family venue.
$$ New Asian Restaurant, *114 Victoria St, T09-4398388*. Open 7 days 1100-2200. Palatable local Chinese.
$$ Blah, Blah, Blah Café and Bar, *101 Victoria St, T09-4396300*. Breakfast, blah blah, blah. Woolworths *on Victoria St, T09-4393935*. Open daily 0700-2200.

Matakohe *p199*
$$ Matakohe House, 50 m from the museum doubles as a café offering quiches, pasta, teas and fine coffee. Also offers smorgasbord on Saurdayst.

▲▲ Activities and tours

Dargaville *p198*
Kaipara Cruises, *T0800-466-793*, link to Helensville on the Southern Kaipara Harbour just north of Auckland and **Kaipara Action Experience**, *T09-4391401, www.kaiparaaction.co.nz*, are the principal

activity operators in the area with a range of options including scenic beach excursions by coach or the 4WD 'Big Foot' along Ripiro Beach daily at 0900, from $55, child $25. Harbour Cruises on board the *Kaipara Kat*, quad bike tours and fishing are additional options. **Baylys Beach Horse Treks**, *T09-4398360*. Ripiro Beach rides, 2 hr from $45. Transport from Dargaville.

Directory

Communications Internet at the VIC or **Kauri Computers**, 85 Victoria St, Dargville. Mon-Fri 0900-1730, Sat 0900-1230. Internet in Matakohe, T09-4317091. Daily from 0900-1730. **Police**, T09-4393400.

Coromandel Peninsula

Introduction

In many ways the Coromandel Peninsula is like a compact and easily accessible mix of Northland and Great Barrier Island. It offers varied and spectacular coastal scenery, rugged mountain bush and a relaxed lifestyle, which together make it the main attraction on the Pacific Coast Highway. The **West Coast**, bounded by the Firth of Thames, is the most undeveloped side of the peninsula. It has a ragged coastline of islands and pebble beaches, lined with some of the best examples of **pohutukawa** in the country. For three weeks in December the olive evergreen leaves that crown the gnarled trunks, flower in a radiant mantle of crimson, earning them the label of New Zealand's Christmas tree. In contrast, the **East Coast** is a plenitude of beautiful bays and sandy beaches, with **Cathedral Cove** and **Hot Water Beach** being two of the most celebrated in New Zealand. Here you will find most of the development, activity and population, from the transitory tourist in the holiday townships of **Whitianga** and **Whangamata** to the rich retiree in the rather sterile resorts of Matarangi and Pauanui. Between the two coasts a dominating backbone of bush-clad mountains make up the **Coromandel Forest Park**, with its wealth of walks and historic logging and mining remains. One word stands out as the key to this almost timeless and beautiful region – relaxation. Enjoy it and respect it – like so much of New Zealand there are few places, so spoilt, yet so unspoilt, on earth.

★ Don't miss...

① **Coromandel Township.** Chill out in the laid-back town and take a ride on the unique **Driving Creek Railway**, page 210.

② **Castle Rock.** Climb up and see the views across the peninsula, page 210.

③ **Coromandel Forest Park.** Explore the **old kauri dams**, then spend a night in the **DoC Pinnacles Hut** in the heart of the park, page 207.

④ **The Pohutukawa Coast** and northern tip of **Cape Colville**. Stop for supplies in the Colville General store, north of Coromandel Township, page 211.

⑤ **New Chums Beach** near Whangapoua, page 211. Go swimming, or take a stroll along the beautiful beach.

⑥ **Sea fishing** or **kayaking** from Whitianga, or try **bone carving** in the town centre, page 214.

⑦ **Cathedral Cove**, page 216. Be the first to see the sunrise, and lay the day's first footprints in the sand

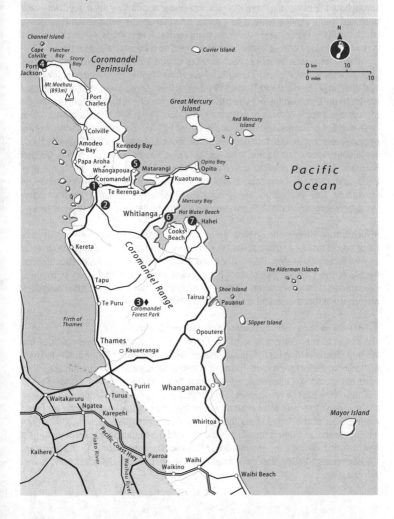

Coromandel Peninsula Introduction

Thames to Coromandel

Ins and outs

Getting there **Air Coromandel** with **Great Barrier Airlines**, T0800-900-600 operate a twice-daily service to and from Auckland (around $100, child $65), for Whitianga and Matarangi. There are also scheduled flights to and from Great Barrier Island and Whangarei in Northland. There are often some combination or sole fly/boat/bus packages with Fullers, Sealink and Intercity. You can visit Coromandel Township on a day-cruise (from $99, child $45) from Auckland with Kawau Kat, T09-4258006, www.kawaukat.co.nz

Getting around The Coromandel Peninsula is the premier destination on the North Island's 'Pacific Coast Highway' tourist route that links Auckland to the north, with Napier and Hawkes Bay to the east. Like the 'Twin Coast Discovery' in Northland, the route is well-signposted, with free leaflets and maps readily available at all VICs. Throughout the peninsula there is a mix of sealed roads (linking the main towns) and unsealed roads (linking west to east and the further up the north of the Peninsula), which results in difficult and time-consuming driving. All the roads are very scenic but very windy and are often affected after heavy rain, so relax and take your time.

There are regular **Intercity** coach services to and from the Coromandel, and two special passes. The 'Peninsula Loop Pass' goes from Thames to Coromandel Township and Whitianga, then back to Thames ($54). With their 'Coromandel Trail' package you can travel the Coromandel SH25 loop then, from Thames, have the option of carrying on to Tauranga and/or Rotorua or returning to Auckland, from $85 (Rotorua, $101). There are a number of peninsula- and Auckland-based bus tour companies offering shuttle, personalized or specialist tour options. These include: **Aotearoa Tours**, T07-8662807, aotearoa@tournz.co.nz (to and from Auckland plus two and three day tours); **Go Kiwi Shuttles**, T8660336, nzwild@xtra.co.nz (Auckland, Thames, Whitianga shuttle plus tours and charter). **Coromandel Explorer Tours**, T07-8282753, www.coromandel tours.co.nz Day tour (0800- 1930) from $145, 2-day from $350, 4-day from $300 (excluding accommodation). Recommended and run by nature-savvy tour guide Nicky.

Information There are visitor information centres (VICs) throughout the Coromandel for free and comprehensive information on all that 'the Coro' has to offer as well as places to stay. They will also book travel and sell local attraction tickets. Details of the VICs are given under the relevant town. You'll find them in Thames, Coromandel Town, Whitianga, Tairua, Whangamata and Waihi. Useful websites include www.thecoromandel.co.nz and www.PacificCoast.co.nz

Thames → *Phone code: 07 Population: 7000 Colour map 2, grid B2*

Thames is at the western base of the Coromandel Peninsula at the mouth of the Waihou River and fringe of the Hauraki Plains. Behind the town rise the bush-clad hills of the **Coromandel Forest Park**. Thames serves as the gateway to the peninsula, either north to Coromandel town and the west coast, or across the heart of the Forest Park to Tairua and the east coast. Thames is the largest town in the Coromandel and was one of the largest towns in New Zealand during the peak of the kauri logging and gold mining eras of the late 1800s, though you would not guess it now. Other than essential services there is little in the town to hold the tourist back, except perhaps a few historic buildings and the old **Gold Mine and Stamper Battery**. On its doorstep, the **Kauaeranga Valley**, the main access point to the Coromandel Forest Park, is well worth a visit.

Information VIC and bus terminal, ① *206 Pollen St, T07-8687284, www.thames-*
info.co.nz Mon-Fri 0830-1700, Sat-Sun 0900-1600. DoC is at the Kauaeranga Valley
Visitor Centre. ① *T07-8679080. Daily 0800-1600.* Most of Thames' amenities are on
Pollen St, which runs the length of the town from south to north. The VIC also provides
free street maps.

Sights Perhaps the best place to start and to get your bearings is the **War Memorial
Monument Lookout** on Waiotahi Creek Road, at the northern end of the town. From
there you can get a fine view of the town and across the Hauraki Plains and Firth of
Thames. Also, at the northern end of town, on Pollen Street, is the **Thames Gold Mine
and Stamper Battery.** ① *Daily 1000-1600. $8, child $4. T/F07-8688514,
rskeet@xtra.co.nz* It offers regular tours which take in the impressive ore-crushing
stamper and various horizontal tunnels, with an informative commentary about the
process and history of gold mining along the way.

   Along the same mining and mineral theme, the **Thames School of Mines and
Mineralogical Museum,** ① *corner of Brown and Cochrane sts, T07-8686227,
Wed-Sun 1100-1600, $3.50, child free,* has a varied and interesting collection of rocks
and minerals from around the world. Given the significance of the area for both kauri
logging and gold mining the small **Thames Historical Museum** ① *corner of Pollen and
Cochrane sts, T07-8688509, daily 1300-1600, $2.50, child $1,* is worth a peek.

   Other places of interest that may (or may not) tickle your fancy include: the
Matatoki Cheese Farm, ① *Wainui Rd (off SH26 7 km south of Thames), T07-8681284,
www.matatokicheese.co.nz, daily 1000-1600 (Sun in winter), from $2;* the very leggy
inhabitants of the **Piako Ostrich Farm,** ① *Piako Rd, Turua (south off SH25),
T07-8675326, tours daily at 1100 and 1400 (closed Tue and Wed Oct-Jun);* or the
wonderfully aromatic products on sale at the **Eco People and Natural Soap Factory,**
① *Corner of Grey and Pollen Sts, T07-8683830, tours from $15.*

   There are also a number of notable **gardens** and **art and craft galleries** in the area
including Lyndell and Stony Creek Gardens, Libby's Pottery, Mahara Garden Pottery
and Sculpture Park and the Maori craft gallery, Te Whare Whakairo. Details of these
plus the historical Thames Heritage Trail leaflet can be obtained from the VIC.

   Market Day in the town is on Saturday and is held in Grahamstown at the north
end of Pollen Street, 0900-1200. ▸▸ *For Sleeping, Eating and other listings, see page 208.*

Coromandel Forest Park (Kauaeranga Valley) → *Phone code: 07*
Colour map 2, grid B2
The Coromandel Forest was, in the late 1800s, one of the most extensive kauri logging
areas in the North Island. At the head of the Kauaeranga Valley, 13 km east of Thames,
there is a fine **DOC Kauaeranga Visitor Centre**, set in a very pleasant recreation area,
accessed via Parawai Rd at the southern end of town. A fascinating audio-visual
display gives you an insight into the life and times of the early pioneer loggers. (If you
do not have your own wheels the **Sunkist Lodge** (see below) in Thames offers a
shuttle service to the park; $20 return, T07-8688808.) From here there are a number
of fine **walks** spread through the Forest Park. These vary from a few hours to a few
days, taking in some of the best scenery the park has to offer and a few remnants of
the old logging days, including the impressive **Dancing Creek Dam**. The **Kauaeranga
Kauri Trail** (leaflet from the Visitor Centre) is the most popular walk taking trampers to
the interesting **Pinnacles** rock formation. ▸▸ *For Sleeping, see page 208.*

Thames Coast and North to Coromandel Town
The coast road to Coromandel township is scenic, but very windy and quite
dangerous, so take your time. On the way, the **Rapaura Watergardens**, ① *6 km up the
Tapu-Coroglen Rd, 0900-1700, $5, T07-8684821, www.rapaurawatergardens.co.nz,*
are worth a look, with numerous paths and lots of 'Monet-like' lily ponds. After your

explorations you can enjoy a cuppa and a snack in the Trellis Tearooms, or even stay the night in the self-catering lodge or cottage.

Just east of the gardens, a little further up the road and along a fairly steep track, is the impressive **'Square Kauri'** estimated to be over 1,000 years old. Ask at the gardens for detailed directions. While on the Tapu-Coroglen Road (on the right about 2 km before the gardens) it is worth a stop to see the quirky work of sculptor Heather Stevens at the Mahara Garden Pottery, T07-8684817. Another pleasant garden with the added attraction of butterflies is the **Butterfly and Orchid Garden**, ① *just 3 km north of Thames, daily summer 1000-1600, winter 1100-1500, from $8, child $4, café and shop, T07-8688080.* If you have not seen a Monarch yet, this is your chance.

Just north of Kereta the SH25 climbs, turns inland and at the crest of the hill, offers a magnificent view of the northern part of the Coromandel Peninsula.

● Sleeping

Thames *p206*
AL **Grafton Cottage**, *304 Grafton Rd, Thames, T07-8689971, www.graftoncottage@xtra.co.nz* Five very smart chalets with fine views.
A **Brian Boru Hotel**, *200 Richmond St, T07-8686523, brianboru@xtra.co.nz* The best hotel option, established in 1868, provides affordable, traditional hotel and standard motel-style accommodation.
A **Coastal Motor Lodge**, *608 Tararu Rd, T07-8686843.* Overlooking the Firth of Thames, just north of the town.
A **Cotswold Cottage**, *Maramarahi Rd, T/F07-8686306.* A restored villa set in spacious grounds and offering a range of rooms.
A **Tuscany on Thames**, *corner of Jellicoe Crescent and Banks St, T07-8685099, www.tuscanyonthames.co.nz* Offers spotless motel units with double spa baths.
B **Brookby Motel**, *102 Redwood La, T/F07-8686663.* A cheaper motel option.
B **Rolleston Motel**, *105 Rolleston St, T07-8688091.* Decent hote, central location. There are also some pleasant B&Bs out of town in the **Kauaeranga Valley**, including the wonderfully spacious
A **Kauaeranga Country B&B**, *Kauaeranga Valley Rd, T07-8686895,* and the 2-bedroom
B **Huia Lodge**, *T07-8686557, huia.lodge@xtra.co.nz*
C-D **Gateway Backpackers**, *209 Mackay St, T07-8686339.* Cheap and comfortable hostel right opposite the VIC. Ideal if you are concentrating on other parts of the peninsula, rather than Thames.
C-D **Sunkist Lodge**, *506 Brown St, T07-8688808, sunkist@xtra.co.nz* Another alternative which offers shuttles to the

Coromandel Forest Park.
B-D **Dickson Holiday Park and YHA**, *3 km north of Thames, T07-8687308, www.dicksonpark.co.nz* Pleasant streamside rooms with shared facilities and ensuite bathrooms with TV. The 3 hr return, 'Rocky's Goldmine Trail' also begins from here.

Coromandel Forest Park *p206*
D **Pinnacles Hut**, *on the park track, T07-8679080.* Run by DoC, a fine place to stay; beds (80) must be booked in advance. DoC campsite near the VIC ($7).

Thames Coast *p207*
If you are beginning to feel dizzy trying to negotiate all the bends in the road, this stretch of coast has some fine accommodation in which to recover.It is also a good place to base yourself to explore the peninsula.
AL **Te Puru Coast View Lodge**, *468 Thames Coast Rd, Te Puru, T07-8682326, tepuru-lodge@xtra.co.nz* A boutique Mediterranean-style getaway with excellent views and fine cuisine.
A **Santa Monica Motel**, *Ruamahanga Bay, T07-8682429.* Has 7 self-contained units and a restaurant.

Campsites and motorcamps
B-D **Te Mata Lodge** *off Te Mata Creek Rd, 20 km north of Thames, T07-8684834, temata@wave.co.nz* Cabins and campsite both on offer.
C-D **Tapu Motor Camp**, *18 km north of Thames, T07-8684837.* Popular but fairly basic beach/riverside location.

🍴 Eating

Thames *p206*
Thames has yet to produce a truly reputable restaurant so don't expect a food fest.
$$ **Brian Boru Hotel** *(see above). Open from 0730, licensed.* Breakfast, lunch and dinner.
$$ **Gold Bar and Restaurant**, *404 Pollen St, T07-8685548.* Good-value all day and evening meal menus. Both are licensed.
$$ **Sola Café**, *720B Pollen St, T07-8688781. Tue-Sun 0900-1600 and 1800-2100 Wed-Sat.* New and already perhaps the most popular café in town with good vegetarian options and the best coffee.
$$ **Food For Thought**, *574 Pollen St, T07-8686065. Mon-Fri 0730-1530.* Good value.
$$ **Kopu Station Hotel**, *just south of Thames.* Standard pub grub and is a good place to mix with travellers coming and going from the Peninsula.
$ **Majestic Fish Shop**, *640 Pollen St.* Try this if it is just a good ol' fish and chippie you are looking for.

🎭 Entertainment

Thames *p206*
Krazy Cow Bar *476 Pollen St,* below the Adventure Coromandel Backpackers is said to be the focus of fun.

🚌 Transport

Thames *p206*
Bike-hire Outdoor Store, *430 Pollen St, T07-8686157.* **Car rental** **Michael Saunders Motors**, *201 Pollen St, T0800-111110,* or **Rent-A-Dent**, *503 Queen St, T07-8688838.* **Taxis** **Thames Gold Cabs**, *T07-8686037.*

ℹ️ Directory

Thames *p206*
Internet VIC (see above).
World-Wide-Wash (laundry), *740 Pollen St, T07-8687912. Mon-Fri 0830-2100, Sat/Sun 1000-2100.* **United Video**, *456 Pollen St. Mon-Thu 1000-2100, Fri/Sat 2200, Sun 2030.*

Coromandel Town and around

Coromandel Town → *Phone code: 07 Population: 2000 Colour map2, grid A2*
Coromandel Town has a wonderful bohemian village feel and a warm atmosphere. The locals, many of whom are artists, are friendly and contented souls who walk about with a knowing smile, as if they are well aware they have come to the 'right' place. It is refreshingly free from the drearily ubiquitous High Street chains or rows of unsightly advertising hoardings, and only a lamppost opposite the road junction as you arrive in the heart of the town bears any signs or place names. The village, and indeed the whole peninsula, derives its name from the visit, in 1820, by HMS Coromandel, which called in to load kauri spars. Again, gold and kauri in the late 1800s were the attraction, and some old buildings remain, though sadly not the beautiful native bush that once cloaked the hills. Just north of the town one of New Zealand's most famous potters, Barry Brickell, has created – along with many fine works from his kiln – a quirky Driving Creek Railway.

Information VIC ① *355 Kapanga Rd, T07-8668598, www.coromandeltown.co.nz Mon-Fri 0900-1700, Sat and Sun 1000-1300 (extended summer hours).* In keeping with the village the staff are very friendly and helpful. The same office also provides DOC information and internet facilities.

Sights
The **Coromandel Mining and Historic Museum**,① *841 Rings Rd, T07-8667251, daily in summer, 1000-1600; winter Sat and Sun, 1330-1600, $2, child $0.50,* is a fairly small affair but provides a worthy insight into the rapacious days of gold mining, when the town had three times the population it does now. The 100 year-old

operational **Coromandel Gold Stamper Battery,** ① *Buffalo Rd, T07-8667933, daily, summer 1000-1700, closed in winter, tours $6, child $3, gold panning $5,* is set in very pleasant surrounds with a waterwheel and stream in which you can (for a fee) try your hand at gold panning.

The **Driving Creek Railway** ① *T07-8668703, www.drivingcreekrailway.co.nz, trains run daily at 1015, 1400, also 1200 and 1600 in summer, $15, child $7, family $35,* created by Kiwi sculptor Barry Bricknell is well worth the visit. Barry has lived in Coromandel for years and his artistic creations, open-air studio and railway line all ooze character and charm. Building began on the narrow-gauge railway in 1975 as a means of transporting clay to the kilns at the base of the hill. Now 25 years on the line winds its way almost 2 km up the hill through regenerating bush to the expansive views from the ridge-top terminus (new Zealand's 'Eiffel Tower'). It is a delight and a construction of budget engineering genius, together with artistic creativity and environmental respect and sensitivity. Tunnels and embankments built of empty wine bottles (the fuel of the railway builders), together with some of Barry's evocative, and at times quite erotic, sculptures, decorate the route. There is an entertaining and informative commentary along the way with the occasional stop (one of which is to see some impressive creepy-crawlies). There are plans to build a spectacular terminus complete with viewing deck at the top and, near the base terminus, a predator-free bush area and museum. The present base terminus, with its brickworks – where all the bricks used along the railway were made – kilns and shop are all fascinating.

The one-hour short walk at **Long Bay Scenic Reserve** west of Coromandel is very pleasant, taking in bush and beach (for the beach turn right to Tucks Bay on reaching the road). It begins at the end of Long Bay Road and is accessed at the Long Bay Motor Camp. The view from the short walk to the **Tokatea Lookout,** at the crest of the hill, up Kennedy Bay Road (via Driving Creek Road) is well worth it.

Don't miss the **craft shops** along Coromandel's main street. The Weta Design Store at 46 Kapanga Road is particularly good. The VIC and the free *Coromandel Craft Trail* leaflet will point the way to others. ▶▶ *For Sleeping, Eating, and other listings, see pages 212- 213.*

South on the 309 Road → *Phone code: 07 Colour map 2, grid A2*
The old 309 road, which starts just south of Coromandel Town, then winds its tricky 22 km to Whitianga, has a number of fine attractions. It is one way to get to Whitianga – the other being the SH25.

First stop on the 309, 4½ km from Coromandel, is the charming **Waiau Waterworks,** ① *T07-8667191, daily 0900-1700, closed in winter, $8, child $4,* which is a garden full of fascinating whimsical water sculptures and gadgets. Like the Driving Creek Railway it is Kiwi ingenuity and imagination at its wonderfully eccentric best. Great for kids.

A short distance further up the road from the waterworks there is a track on the left that takes you a further 2 km to the start of the Castle Rock Walk (standard cars will be fine). The aptly named **Castle Rock** (490 m) is a very knobbly-looking volcanic plug that commands a wonderful view of the northern end of the peninsula. It is a stiff climb and one to two hours return depending how fit you are. Take suitable footwear as the track is more like a stream in winter, but the view is well worth the effort.

Just over 7 km up the 309 are the **Waiau Falls**. It is a 15-minute walk to a very pleasant glade where the falls crash over a rock face. Less than a kilometre further up the road is the **Kauri Grove**, a stand of ancient kauri, some of the very few left alone and protected, and all the more impressive for it. The walk takes about 20 minutes. From here you can return to Coromandel Town or carry on to Whitianga.

North of Coromandel Town, the Colville Road rejoins the coast at **Papa Aroha** (Land of Love) and **Amodeo Bay**. From these charming bays you will be able to feast your eyes once again on Mount Moehau and what is called the **Pohutukawa Cape**. These wonderfully old and gnarled 'pohutas' that grace the shoreline are some of the best examples in the country, and in December flower in a gorgeous crimson mantle. From this point you are entering perhaps the most remote and scenic area of the Coromandel Peninsula with an atmosphere all of its own. The beach at **Waitete Bay**, about 5 km north of Amodeo Bay, is a cracker and a favourite haunt in summer. From here the road climbs over the hill and falls again to the historic settlement of **Colville**, with its amazingly well-stocked **general store**,① *T07-8666805, Mon-Thu 0830-1700, Fri 0830-1800, Sat 0900-1700, Sun 0930-1700*. Next door, the **Colville Café** is a great place to stop for a coffee or a snack.

Just north of Colville you can cross the Peninsula northeast on the Port Charles Road to **Port Charles** or back down southeast to **Kennedy Bay**, then back to Coromandel. Port Charles is the northernmost settlement on the East Side of the Peninsula and has a great bay and beach. Kennedy Bay is less well endowed than Port Charles in both scenery and amenities, but gives the passer-by an insight into real Coromandel Peninsula life. Note St Paul's Anglican Church which must have a very small congregation.

The **Port Jackson Road** which heads north of Colville is an absolute delight with the Moehau Range looming on your right and pebble beaches to the left. The road itself becomes almost completely shrouded by huge gnarled pohutakawa trees. About 13 km north of Colville you will reach the small Te Hope Stream and the beginning of the Mount Moehau Track. **Mount Moehau** is 893 m and the highest peak anywhere near Auckland. Indeed, on a clear day the Moehau range is visible from the city. Mount Moehau is a superb climb, but somewhat frustrating, because the last few hundred metres to the summit (and what must be incredible views) is sacred to the Maori and out of bounds. So if you do make the climb, show suitable respect and settle for nearly reaching the top. The first 2 km of the walk, which follows the river, are still superb with numerous clear pools (sadly swimming is prohibited) and small waterfalls to enjoy. The track, before it starts to make a serious ascent, is a delight and you are almost certain to see native wood pigeon and hear tui.

After negotiating numerous idyllic pebble bays, the road eventually climbs round the northern tip of the cape and falls steeply to **Port Jackson** and **Fletcher Bay**, where the road ends. From here you can enjoy great views of Great Barrier Island, seemingly only a stone's throw away across the Colville Channel. Fletcher Bay marks the beginning of the popular **Coromandel Walkway** which connects Fletcher Bay with Stony Bay and effectively the east coast road and all points south (information about the walkway available at the VIC). There are two tracks about 7 km in length and they take about three hours one way. The steeper of the two tracks offers better views and also doubles as a fine mountain biking route. ➠ *For Sleeping, see page 212.*

SH25 to Whitianga

From Coromandel Town the SH25 winds its way east, over the ranges, offering fine views, before descending steeply to Te Rerenga and Whangapoua Harbour. **Whangapoua village**, 4 km north of the junction at Te Rerenga, is essentially a conglomeration of holiday homes and bachs that come alive in the summer months. A short 30 minute-walk north from the road end in Whangapoua is **New Chums Beach**, which is one of the best beaches in the Coromandel. The fact that you cannot drive there and have to negotiate the headland by foot seems to protect its beauty, enhance its character and make it a truly magical place. Even in bad weather it is worth the walk.

Back on SH25 and east is the sterile real estate settlement of **Matarangi**, which is saved only by its sweeping beach and great golf course. About 6 km further on at the end of the beach is **Kuaotunu** a nice spot in itself, especially for swimming. Kuaotunu also acts as the gateway to **Opito Bay** via the scenic and intriguingly named Black Jack Road. Opito has a lovely beach with magnificent views across to the Mercury Islands and numerous other small Islands. In summer this is a great spot to escape the crowds. (Yeah – who does own that house at the end of the beach!?) ▸▸ *For Sleeping, see page 213.*

● Sleeping

Coromandel Town *p209*
There is a good range of accommodation in and around Coromandel Town, mainly in the form of B&Bs, motels, motor camps and backpackers. The VIC has comprehensive information about B&Bs. In summer you are advised to book ahead everywhere.
LL-L Buffalo Lodge, *860 Buffalo Rd, T/F07-8668960, www.buffalolodge.co.nz* Tasteful, 5-star luxury in a bush setting with sweeping views. Fine cuisine.
AL-A Coromandel Colonial Cottages, *1737 Rings Rd, Coromandel, T/F07-8668857, coromandel_colonial_cottages@xtra.co.nz* Self-contained cottage-style motel units with large grounds and a swimming pool.
AL Karamana Homestead, *84 Whangapoua Rd, Coromandel, T07-8667138, F8667477, karamana@xtra.co.nz* A delightful 1872 kauri villa with three large rooms, antiques, fine food and luxury.
A Te Kouma Harbour Farmstay, *SH25, T07-8668747, www.tekouma.co.nz* If you are looking for a farmstay, although it is some distance back towards Thames, then this offers great value self-contained cottages and a whole host of activities beyond mere animal patting. Recommended.
A The Green House B&B, *505 Tiki Rd, T07-8667303.* Back in Coromandel itself, a tidy B&B with 3 rooms. Friendly hosts who volunteer at the VIC so they can fill you in on all the local information.
A Celadon B&B, *corner of Alfred St and Oxford Terr, T07-8668058, wilsonmc@wave.co.nz* Offers very fine, private and romantic B&B and self-contained options walking distance from the centre.
A Jacaranda Lodge, *SH25, T07-8668002.* Big an d friendly B&B just south of the village.
A Pottery Lane Cottage, *15 Pottery La, T/F8667171, r&bmartin@xtra.co.nz* Well-situated, cute self-contained cottages.
A-D Anchor Lodge Resort, *448 Wharf Rd, T07-8667992, www.anchorlodgecoromandel. co.nz* The newest motel in town and very tidy,

offering 14 luxury units, pool, spa, internet and also backpacker rooms.
A Coromandel Court Motel, *365 Kapanga Rd, T07-8668403, www.coromandelcourtmotel.co.nz* Also relatively new, well-equipped and in a very central location behind the VIC.
B Country Touch B&B, *39 Whangapoua Rd, Coromandel, T07-8668310.* Good value ensuite units in country setting.
There are three **backpackers** in and around Coromandel, all of which are clean and comfortable.
C-D Coromandel Town Backpackers, *732 Rings Rd, T07-8668327.* Small, central and handy for all amenities.
A-D Anchor Lodge Resort *448 Wharf Rd, T07-8667992, www.anchorlodge coromandel.co.nz.* A new option close to the town centre.
C-D Tui Lodge, *60 Whangapoua Rd, T07-8668237.* A wee bit further out but has a good range of accommodation with ensuite bathrooms, a campsite and free bikes.
A-D Tidewater Tourist Park, *270 Tiki Rd, T07-8668888, tidewater@world-net.co.nz* Also offers backpacker accommodation.

Motorcamps
A-D Coromandel Holiday Park, *636 Rings Rd, T07-8668830.* Central and has good facilities and new cabins.
C-D Shelly Beach Top Ten Motels and Holiday Park, *Colville Rd, T07-8668988.* North of town on the beach.
B-D Long Bay Motor Camp, *3200 Long Bay Rd to the west of town, T07-8668720.*

North to Colville and the Cape *p211*
B Pohutukawa Coast Chalets, *near Papa Aroha, just north of Coromandel, T07-8668379.* Comfortable, good value, self-contained 'A Frame' cabins, some of which have fine views. Discounts for 5 days or more.
A Papa Aroha Motel, *Papa Aroha, T07-8668440.* A Spanish-style standard motel with a restaurant.
C-D Papa Aroha Holiday Park, *Papa Aroha.* A

place to camp or park up with the van. Also offers fishing charters, boat and kayak hire.

A-D Anglers Lodge, *Amodeo Bay, T07-8668584 anglers@clear.net.nz*. Offers excellent motel units and a campsite, with swimming pool, spa, shop, kayak hire and charter boat, all on site.

A-D Colville Lodge, *near Colville*. The peninsula's northernmost motel and motor camp. It has a spa and backpacker beds, and campsites are also available.

B-D Colville Farm, *T/F07-8666820*. Popular place with self-contained rooms, lodge, backpackers accommodation and camping facilities.

C-D Fletcher Bay Backpackers, *T07-8666172, js.lourie@xtra.co.nz* The northernmost backpackers which offers a remote but welcome overnight stop if you have done the Coromandel Walkway.

Campsites

DOC operates 5 campsites with basic facilities at Fantail Bay, Port Jackson, Fletcher, Stony and Waikawau Bays. For site information and availability, *T0800-455-466*. $7, child $2. Bookings are essential at Waikawau Bay in summer, *T07-8661106/8679080*.

SH25 to Whitianga *p211*

L-AL Kuaotunu Bay Lodge, *SH25 (Kuaotunu), T07-8664396, www.kuaotunubay.co.nz* A great purpose-built lodge a stone's throw from the beach with twin/double or self-contained unit with a good reputation, owned by long-term and friendly residents.

A Castle Rock Winery, *Te Rerenga, T07-8664542*. This winery has a comfortable flat, and an amazing range of fruit wines (you may never leave!). Open 0900-1800.

A Kaeppeli's, *T07-8662445*. B&B run by a Swiss/ Kiwi family and chef, so they are also renowned for its fine cuisine.

B-D Black Jack Lodge and Backpackers, *at the river mouth, eastern end of Kuaotunu beach, T07-8662988, carl@black-jack.co.nz* Recently upgraded, pleasant and tidy accommodation (new ensuites, free kayaks and bike hire)

B Drift In B&B, *16 Gray's Av, T/F07-8664321*. A good value B&B with great views.

Campsites and motorcamps

There are two holiday parks at Kuaotunu (and a well-stocked store):

B-D Kuaotunu Motor Camp, *T07-8665628*. There is a **campsite** is at Whangapoua (Hamiora), *T07-8667183*, and a general store that can also assist in organising bach rentals, *T07-8668274*

🍴 Eating

Coromandel Town *p209*
The main eateries are all on Kapanga Rd.

$$ Peppertree Restaurant and Bar, *T07-8668211. Open daily from 0900*. Award-winning fine dining with a lunch and mainly seafood dinner menu. It has a pleasant interior, bar and outdoor eating area. On summer evenings book in advance.

$$ Coromandel Café, *T07-8668495* and **$$ Success Café**, *T07-8667100*, are opposite each other and both offer good snacks during the day with the Success being open late for evening dining year round. Again seafood is the speciality (try the mussels).

$$ Umu Café, *22 Wharf Rd (opposite the BNZ), T07-8668618. Daily from 0900-late*. Has good pizza and vegetarian options.

North to Colville and the Cape *p211*
Colville Store and Café, *daily 0930-1600, Fri/Sat/Sun 1800-2000*. This well-stocked place will more than do, considering the location.

SH25 to Whitianga *p211*
See Sleeping above.

🚶 Activities and tours

Activity operators seem to come and go in Coromandel and you are advised to call in at the VIC for the latest listings.

For **fishing or scenic cruises** (around $50 for 3 hr) try **Papa Aroha**, *T/F07-8668818, papa.aroha@xtra.co.nz* Also hires out kayaks.

Snapper Safaris, *T07-8667667*, also offer fishing and scenic cruising, from $35 (departs from the Town Wharf daily 0700, 1230 and 1600). Book at the VIC.

Argo Tours, *T07-8667667*. Tours to mining sites, wetas and tame eels, from $150 for 3 hr.

Horse treks can be arranged with **White Star**, *T07-8666820*.

If you fancy a good **walk** then **Strongman Coaches**, *T07-8668175, www.coromandeldiscoverytours.co.nz* offer a six-pack shuttle service to the Coromandel Coastal Walkway (far north between Fletcher Bay and Stony Bay 3-4 hr), for a manly $65.

⊖ Transport

Intercity runs a service to and from **Thames** and a daily service to **Whitianga** stopping in the town centre. For information and tickets contact the VIC. **Car rental**: Rent-A-Dent, *T07-8668626*, and **bikes** available from **Tide Water Tourist Park**, *270 Tiki Rd, T07-8668888*.

❶ Directory

Internet VIC, see above. **Driving Creek Café**, *Driving Creek Rd, Coromandel. Closed Tue.*

Whitianga and the East Coast

→ *Phone code: 07 Population: 3000 Colour map 2, grid A2*

Whitianga is a very popular holiday town on the shores of beautiful Mercury Bay, which was given its planetary name by Captain Cook during a spot of astronomy on his brief visit in 1769. 'Whiti' (pronounced 'fitty') – as it is affectionately known – has much to offer, including a number of fine beaches within walking distance of the town. But it also acts as a convenient short-cut access point, across the narrow Whitianga Harbour entrance and Ferry Landing, to two fine smaller resorts – Cooks Beach and Hahei. Although there is an abundance of leisure activities to choose from, Whiti is perhaps most famous as a sea and big game fishing base and, like the Bay of Islands, a trip on the water is highly recommended. In summer and especially at Christmas and New Year, Whiti's growing resident population increases dramatically, resulting in excellent tourist services and amenities year round.

Getting there and around

Whitianga airport is 3 kms south of the town and is serviced by **Air Coromandel/ Great Barrier Airlines** (see page 206). **Intercity** buses drop off and pick up outside the VIC in the centre of town and service the local area. Other smaller shuttle companies operate to and from Auckland and around the peninsula (see also page 206). **Go Kiwi**, T0800-446-549, www.whitianga.co.nz/gokiwi offer to Auckland from $54 (return $79) and service the local area. Recommended **Hot Water Beach Connections** are a local company offering a full day hop-on, hop-off service from Ferry Landing to Cooks Beach, Cathedral Cove, Hahei and Hot Water Beach. There are about 5 departures a day and a day pass costs $35. Some buses connect with Auckland services at Dalmeny Corner, T07-8662478. Book all buses at the VIC. The 5-min passenger-only ferry crossing to Ferry Landing operates continuously in summer from 0730-2300. In winter the hours may be reduced; $1, child $0.50. The **ferry to Pauanui**, T027-4970316, leaves from Tairua Wharf on Wharf Rd hourly in summer and every two hours in winter from 0900-1700. $5 return. They also offer good value cruises in summer. **Tairua** is also the main gateway to Alderman, Shoe, Slipper and Mayor Islands. **Opoutere** can be reached by bus from Whangamata, T07-8658613.

Information

'Whiti' VIC, ⓘ *66 Albert St in the centre of town, T07-8665555, www.whitianga.co.nz, daily 0900-1800, Sat 0900-1600*, can give you information about the number of fine craft shops around Whitianga. The new **Tairua VIC** ⓘ *Main St, T/F07-8647575, info.tairua@xtra.co.nz Open summer daily 0930-1600, winter, 1000-1400*, can assist with the plentiful accommodation options or book water-based activity or island trips.

Sights

The **Mercury Bay Museum**, ⓘ *on the Esplanade, daily summer, 1000-1300 Tue-Thu-Sun winter, $5, child 50c*, is fairly small, but nicely showcases the area's rich human history which goes back over 1000 years, when Maori explorer Kupe made landfall here. Cook's visit is also documented. The main waterfront beach is called **Buffalo Beach**, named after *HMS Buffalo* which was wrecked here in 1840. It is a fine beach but gets a little hectic in summer. **Flaxmill Bay** across the water just beyond Ferry Landing, and better still **Lonely Bay**, at the eastern base of the Shakespeare Cliff Scenic Reserve, are often a better bet.

Even if you do not intend to go as far as Cooks Beach and Hahei, the short ferry ride across to **Ferry Landing** is worthwhile. The **wharf** itself was built in 1837 and, though it is one of the oldest in New Zealand, is less than attractive with its concrete coating. However there is a nice café and a number of fine **coastal walks** nearby. Immediately to

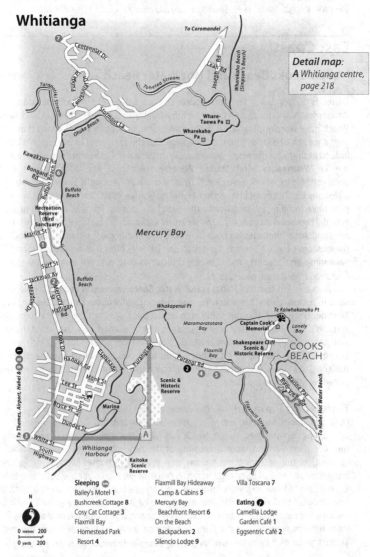

Whitianga

Detail map:
A *Whitianga centre, page 218*

Coromandel Peninsula Whitianga and the East Coast

Mercury Bay

Sleeping 🛏
Bailey's Motel **1**
Bushcreek Cottage **8**
Cosy Cat Cottage **3**
Flaxmill Bay
  Homestead Park
  Resort **4**

Flaxmill Bay Hideaway
  Camp & Cabins **5**
Mercury Bay
  Beachfront Resort **6**
On the Beach
  Backpackers **2**
Silencio Lodge **9**

Villa Toscana **7**

Eating 🍴
Camellia Lodge
  Garden Café **1**
Eggsentric Café **2**

N

0 metres 200
0 yards 200

the right of the wharf is the Whitianga Rock Walk (20 minutes) which takes in a Maori *pa* and offers a great view back over Whiti. The Maramaratotara Bay Walk (40 minutes) joins the Rock Walk and also has good views. A little further down the road opposite the Flaxmill Bay Resort is the access point to the Shakespeare Cliff Scenic Reserve. Climb the path to the right then cross the hill to the viewpoint where you are rewarded with a wonderful view across the Bay.

Whiti has two **Bone Carving Studios** which between them offer the best chance to carve your own bone pendant (traditionally from whale bone but now typically beef bone). **Bay Carving**, ⓘ *next to the museum on the Esplanade, T07-8664021, 0900-1600, evenings by appointment*, is very well-equipped and gives expert tuition (from $35-$60). You choose your own design then test your skills. The other company that offers all-day tuition is the **Bone Carving Studio**, ⓘ *6B Bryce St, T07-8662158, www.carving.co.nz*, which offers full-day courses from $80 and acts as a showpiece for the professional trade. ▸▸ *For Sleeping, Eating and other listings, see pages 218-222.*

East Coast

Hahei, Cooks Beach and Hot Water Beach → *Phone code: 07 Colour map 2, grid A3*

Hahei is a wonderful little unspoiled coastal settlement 35 km by road from Whitianga. A shorter route is via the ferry from Whitianga. Both Hahei and Cooks Beach have wonderful beaches in their own right, especially **Hahei Beach** that looks over a wealth of islands and rock outcrops. But the real jewel in the region's crown, indeed perhaps for the whole peninsula, is the amazing **Cathedral Cove** which guards the **Te Whanganui-A-Hei Marine Reserve**. (Watching the sunrise here is an unforgettable experience.) Access is by boat or a half-hour walk. The track starts from a glorious lookout point just north of Hahei on Grange Road. Tracts of native bush and pine have to be negotiated before the path falls, almost literally, to the beach. It is actually two beaches connected by a natural rock arch (negotiable at low tide). There are sandstone pinnacles on both beaches, with the highest pinnacle, Sail Rock, on the western beach. Although the beach can get very busy it offers great sunbathing, swimming and scenery, and it is very difficult to drag yourself away. ▸▸ *See Sleeping, Eating and other listings , pages 219-222.*

About 15 km south of Hahei is **Hot Water Beach** where you can dig a hole in the sand to access natural hot water. You can only do this for about two hours each side of low tide. Once filled, you can settle in to read a book or watch the surfers doing what you can't. The beach in itself is very pleasant, but be warned: it is also very dangerous with notorious rips. The Hot Water Beach Store hires out spades for $5. Once suitably boiled or if you did not time the tides right, then pop your head into the **Moko Art Gallery**, ⓘ *24 Pye Pl*, just opposite the main car park. The arts and crafts are reasonably priced, very kiwi and top class.

Tairua and Pauanui → *Phone code: 07 Colour map 2, grid B3*

Only the Tairua Harbour and a resulting 20 km-road trip separate these deeply contrasting communities. Tairua, which was settled as a milling and farming town, is the older, smaller and more accessible of the two, situated on SH25. Pauanui, in contrast, is full of expensive holiday and retirement homes with fussy gardens, four-wheel drives and luxury watercraft. A place where men wear polyester shorts and knee-length nylon socks with fawn-coloured dress shoes, and the women sport the latest clinical blue-rinse hairdo. Not exactly the haunt of the happy-go-lucky traveller. Perhaps the best thing about the two towns is the setting and the memorable view from **Paku Hill** which dominates the harbour entrance. It can be accessed from the end of Tirinui Crescent off Paku Drive. ▸▸ *See Sleeping, Eating and other listings, pages 219- 222.*

Opoutere

Opoutere is one of the Coromandel's best-kept secrets. It has a quiet and magical atmosphere with a gorgeous sweeping white-sand **Ocean Beach**, guarded by the Wharekawa Harbour and a narrow tract of forest. At the tip of the sand spit is the **Wharekawa Wildlife Refuge**, where oystercatchers and rare New Zealand dotterel breed in summer. Special care should be taken not to enter this area and disturb the birds (dogs are strictly forbidden). The beach can be accessed from the car park around the corner from the Opoutere Youth Hostel (YHA), see page 219. While you are in the area it is also well worth your while visiting the unusual artworks of Guity and David Evelyn at the **Topadahil Studios**① *Opoutere Rd, T07-8657266.* ▸▸ *See Sleeping, page 219.*

Whangamata

Whangamata is a very popular holiday spot and the main **surfing** venue on the Coromandel. Well-serviced with luxury and budget accommodation, eateries and mainly water-based activities, it acts as a magnet to youngsters, especially at New Year. There are a number of good short coastal **walks**, while south of the town the **Wentworth and Parakiwai Valleys** offer longer walks taking in remnants of the gold mining years and waterfalls. The often busy **beach** at Whangamata is over 4 km long, while the quieter **Whiritoa Beach** and lagoon, 12 km south of Whangamata, also offers a lovely bush walk, heading north. There is a quality **art and crafts** trail in the area (see VIC) and, like Tairua, Whangamata is also a base for trips to the outer islands, including **Mayor Island**. ▸▸ *See Sleeping, Eating, Activities and Directory p220- 222.*

Information Whangamata VIC, ① *616 Port Rd, T/F07-8658340, info-whanga mata@xtra.co.nz Open Mon-Sat 0900-1700, Sun 1000-1600.*

Waihi

Although gold mining once flourished all around the Coromandel, Waihi was in many ways the capital of operations, with 1,200 mines producing half of the country's gold. The scale of operations earned Waihi the reputation as the most famous mining town in New Zealand. The town itself, although well-serviced, is nothing remarkable, but it boasts a heart of gold and seems to retain a sort of Wild West feel.

Information Waihi VIC ① *Seddon St, T07-8636715. Open daily, 0900-1700 in summer, and 0900-1630 in winter, www.waihi.org.nz* Ask for the very useful 'Discover Waihi' brochure.

Sights The most impressive evidence of the town's mining history is the huge **Martha Mine,** ① *The Waihi Gold Mining Company, Barry Road, free guided tours most weekdays, T07-8639880, www.marthamine.co.nz,* which sits like a huge, but strangely discrete bomb crater right in the centre of town. The Martha Mine was one of the originals that reopened after a brief redundancy in the mid-1900s. Today, from a lookout behind the Information Centre, you can watch huge earthmoving trucks relentlessly winding their way in and out of the massive terraced hole. The **Waihi Arts Centre and Museum,** ① *Kenny St, T07-8638386, Mon-Fri 1000-1600, Sat-Sun 1330-1600, $3, child $1.50,* is worth a look. It displays an array of mining memorabilia and interesting working models, including a miniature stamping battery.

Nearby the Ohinemuri River winds its dramatic way west, through the **Karangahake Gorge,** where there are a number of interesting walks and mining relics (DOC leaflet available from the VIC). The **Goldfields Railway,** a vintage steam train, runs 8 km into the gorge from Waihi to **Waikino**. ① *Leaves from Wrigley St, daily at 1100,1230,1400. Adult $12, child $7 return. T07-8638251. There is a café at the Waikino Station. Open daily 1000-1600.*

There are also two wineries in the area, two fine golf courses and a generous collection of gardens, including the pretty **Waihi Waterlily Gardens** ⓘ *Pukekauri Rd, T07-8638267. Daily in summer 1000-1600. $4.50, children free.* If you want to go to the beach, head for the popular surfers' hangout at **Waihi Beach**, 11 km to the east. A pleasant 45-minute coastal walk at the northern end of the beach will take you to the very pretty **Orokawa Bay.** ►► *See Sleeping and Eating page 220-221.*

Sleeping

Whitianga *p214*
There is a huge range of accommodation in Whitianga to suit all tastes and budgets. The TIC has all the information and can pre-book, which is highly recommended in summer.
LL Villa Toscana, *Ohuka Park, T07-8662293, www.villatoscana.co.nz* A superb Italian-style villa set on 2 ha of native bush near Whitianga, with a self-contained designer suite that seems of equal size. Total luxury.
L Silenco Lodge, *T07-8660304, Gavin@enternet.co.nz* Out of town and set in 14 acres of bush. More affordable but still at

the luxury end – spa, log fire, the works.
AL-A Mercury Bay Beachfront Resort, *111-113 Buffalo Beach Rd, T07-8665637, www.BeachfrontResort.co.nz* A prime beachfront location and all mod cons, plus free use of bikes, kayaks and fishing gear. One of the best options in town.
A Whitehouse B&B, *129 Albert St, T07-8665116.* Well-situated and comfortable.
B Cosy Cat Cottage, *41 South Highway, T07-8664488.* Both human- and cat-friendly.
B Bailey's Motel, *66 Buffalo Beach Rd, T07-8665500.* At the lower end of the market but comfortable and on the beachfront and close to town.

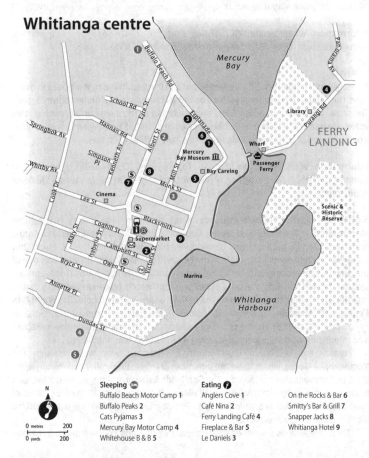

Whitianga centre

Sleeping
Buffalo Beach Motor Camp **1**
Buffalo Peaks **2**
Cats Pyjamas **3**
Mercury Bay Motor Camp **4**
Whitehouse B & B **5**

Eating
Anglers Cove **1**
Café Nina **2**
Ferry Landing Café **4**
Fireplace & Bar **5**
Le Daniels **3**

On the Rocks & Bar **6**
Smitty's Bar & Grill **7**
Snapper Jacks **8**
Whitianga Hotel **9**

C-D Cat's Pyjamas, *4 Monk St, T07-8664663, catspjs@ihug.co.nz* The smallest of 3 back packers in Whiti and a fine one to boot. Buster, the owner, is building a plane in his garage, in which he hopes, one day, to fly to Australia. Well-located and comfortable. Alternative hostels are:

C-D Buffalo Peaks, *12 Albert St, T07-8662933, www.buffalopeakslodge.co.nz*

C-D On the Beach Backpacker's Lodge (YHA), *46 Buffalo Beach Rd, T07-8665380, corobkpk@wave.co.nz* Bike and kayak hire.

C-D Bushcreek Cottage, *1694 The 309 Rd, T07-8665151, www.bushcreek.co.nz* A working organic smallholding with doubles and shared rooms. Campers welcome. Pick-ups from Whitianga. A good and peaceful out of town option.

Motorcamps

B-D Buffalo Beach, *Eyre St, T07-8665854.*

B-D The Mercury Bay, *121 Albert St, T07-8665579.*

Two great alternatives in a quiet and wonderful location near Ferry Landing are:

B-D Flaxmill Bay, Hideaway Camp and Cabins, *T07-8662386;*

B-D Flaxmill Bay Homestead Park Resort, *T07-8665595, www.flaxmillbay-motel.co.nz* Both provide a range of accommodation from log cabins to self-contained units and backpacker bunks, but are only accessible by road via Cook's Beach, or passenger-only ferry ride and walk from Whitianga.

Hahei *p216*

LL-L Island View Villas (Haylyn Park Lodge), *Christine Terr, T07-8663247, view@paradise.net.nz* On the hill on the southern end of the village, the range of self-contained units and rooms are immaculate and the views unforgettable. Swimming pool and spa. Recommended.

A Spellbound B&B, *77 Grange Rd, T07-8663543.* At the opposite end of the village, but is almost as good with equally good views.

A The Church, *87 Beach Rd, T07-8663533, www.thechurchhahei.co.nz* Full of character and offers cottage-style B&B accommodation (ensuite facilities). It also has a fine à la carte restaurant.

A-D Hahei Holiday Resort , *Harsant Ave, T07-8663889, www.haheiholidays.co.nz*

Right on the beach and a fine and spacious facility offering self-contained (beachfront) lodges and backpacker accommodation.

A-D Tatahi Lodge *Grange Rd, T07-8663992, www.dreamland.co.nz/tatahilodge* An excellent motel and backpackers.

Hot Water Beach *p216*

LL-L Moko B&B, *24 Pye Pl, T07-8663367, moko.hotwater@xtra.co.nz* At the top end of the market, very arty and sleeps up to six. Right across the road from Hot Water Beach.

B Auntie Dawn's Place, *Radar Rd, T07-8663707.* A cheaper and friendly option with a couple of units and in-house B&B.

Campsites and motorcamps

C-D Hot Water Beach Holiday Park, *T07-8663735.*

Tairua and Pauanui *p216*

LL Puka Park Lodge, *Pauanui Beach, T07-8648088, www.dreamworld.co.nz* Reputed to provide perhaps the most luxurious accommodation on the peninsula. Fine private bush chalets with a restaurant and bar in the main lodge house.

AL-A Slipper Island Resort, *T07-8648189, www.slipper.co.nz* An opportunity to escape the mainland to a private island with lodge, self-contained chalets and lots of activities.

A Kotuku Lodge, *179 Main Rd, T07-8647040, kotuku@wave.co.nz* A very popular hillside lodge with fine view and great breakfast.

A-AL Pacific Harbour Lodge, *Main Rd, T07-8648581, Pacific.Harbour@xtra.co.nz* One of the best motels with a good restaurant.

A-AL Pauanui Pines Motor Lodge, *174 Vista Paku, Pauanui Beach, T07-8648086, pauanuipines@clear.co.nz* A fine award-winning motel in Pauanui.

C-D Beach Villa Backpackers, *200 Main Rd, T07-8648345.* Very activity-based.

C-D Pinnacles Backpackers, *305 Main Rd, T07-8648446, flying.Dutchman.bp@xtra.co.nz*

Motorcamps

B-D Tairua Estuary Holiday Park, *116 Pepe Rd, T07-8648551.* Central and one of a scattering of motorparks in the area.

Opoutere *p217*

B-D Opoutere Youth Hostel (YHA), *T07-8659072.* A fine, peaceful place to stay and has great facilities, short walks nearby, and a lovely view across the harbour.

Whangamata *p217*

You are advised to consult the VIC and book in advance in summer, well in advance for New Year.

LL Brenton Lodge, *1 Brenton Pl, T/F8658400, brentonlodge@xtra.co.nz* A gorgeous bijou country retreat with romantic, cottage-style suites and lots of pampering.

AL-A Palm Pacific Resort, *413 Port Rd, T07-8659211, www.palmpacificresort.co.nz* A large new motel in the centre of town with tidy deluxe and standard units, restaurant, pool, spas and sauna.

L-AL Bushland Park Lodge, *444 Wentworth Valley Rd, T07-8657468, bushparklodge@xtra.co.nz* Another fine establishment in a lovely location, European in style, emphasis on health and a quality restaurant attached.

A Amber Oaks B&B, *110 Otahu Rd, T07-8656506.* Double or singles, friendly, helpful owners.

AL-A Pipinui Motel, *805 Martyn Rd, T07-8656796, www.pipinuimotel.co.nz* Another new motel set away from the main road and, accordingly, quieter than the larger resorts.

B-D Garden Motor and Tourist Lodge, *Cnr Port and Mayfair, T07-8659580, gardenlodge@xtra.co.nz* Well-maintained, farm-style accommodation with backpacker facilities and 5 min from the beach.

Campsites and motorcamps

B-D Pinefield Top Ten Holiday Park, *207-227 Port Rd, T07-8658791.*

B-D Whangamata Motor Camp, *104 Barbara Av, T07-8659128.*

There is a basic **DOC campsite** at Wentworth Valley, *Wentworth Valley Rd ($7), T07-8657032.*

Waihi *p217*

Waihi and Waihi Beach, 11 km to the east are well-serviced with the full range of accommodation options.

A Ashtree House, *Rifle Range Rd, T07-8636448.* Lovely house and grounds with equally good rooms with ensuite baths. Self-contained unit also available.

A Goose Farm Cottage, *Owahara Falls,*

Karangahake Gorge, T07-8637944. Popular with honeymooners, self-contained, pretty.

A Sea Air Motel and Motor Park, *Emerton Rd, Waihi Beach, T07-8635655, sea-air@paradise.net.nz* Relatively new standard motel.

B Chez Nous B&B, *41 Seddon St, T07-8637538, www.bnb.co.nz/cheznous.html* Central and good value.

Motorcamps

A-D Waihi Beach Top Ten Holiday Park, *15 Main Beach Rd, Waihi Beach, T07-8635504.* Has some fine cabins.

B-D Athenree Holiday Park, *Athenree Rd, T07-8635600, www.athenreehotsprings.co.nz* A little further field and offers all the usual with the added attraction of hot springs.

B-D Waihi Motor Camp, *6 Waitete Rd, T07-8637654.* Chalets, cabins and tent sites.

⊙ Eating

Whitianga *p214*

Whiti is well-served with fine eating establishments; most offer a variety of fresh seafood; the best are along the Esplanade.

$$$ Le Daniels, *21 The Esplanade, T07-8665209. Open daily for lunch and dinner, Sun for brunch.* A little expensive but reputedly the best place in town for quality seafood. Fully licensed.

$$ On the Rocks Bar and Restaurant, *20 The Esplanade, T07-8664833. Open from 1100.* Award-winner specializing in NZ cuisine including seafood and venison.

$$ Fireplace Restaurant and Bar, *T8664828, open from Wed-Sun for dinner. New place also on the Esplanade*, is aesthetically the best with a lovely fire. Pizza and lamb a speciality.

$$ Camellia Lodge Garden Café, *corner of Golf Rd and South Highway, T07-8662253. Daily 1000-1530.* A bit out of town but worth the trip for lunch, it is set in a lovely garden.

$$ Café Nina, *behind the VIC at 20 Victoria St, T07-8665440. Open from 0800 and 1730 for dinner.* The finest café in town. Small and bustling, it covers a great range of healthy and imaginative dishes.

$ Eggsentric Café and Restaurant, *Purangi Rd, Flaxmill Bay (1 km east of Ferry Landing), T07-8660307. Open daily for lunch and dinner Tue-Sun (closed in August).* Without doubt the most colourful place around and at times the liveliest, whose artistic and multi-talented owners put on organized and often impromptu musical performances and poetry readings. Licensed and BYO.

$ Smitty's Bar and Grill, *37 Albert St, T07-8664647*. For good pub grub this is a good bet.

$ Ferry Landing Café, *just a wee walk up the hill from the Ferry Landing wharf, T/F8662820. Open daily 0900-1700 (closed Tue May-Oct)*. Good place to escape the crowds for a quiet coffee or good-value breakfast.

Hahei p216

$$ The Church, *87 Beach Rd, T07-8663797, www.bonappetit.co.nz Open Thu-Tue*. The talents of Swiss chef Andy Schuerch are extremely popular.

$ Café Luna, *nearby at 1 Grange Rd, T07-8663016*. Open 7 days in summer from 0900 until late, with reduced hours in winter. Does a great breakfast for $14.

Tairua and Pauanui p216

The fine dining option has to be at the **$$$ Puka Park Lodge** (see above), bookings are advised.

$ Out of the Blue Café, *Main Rd, Tairua, T07-8648987. 0800-1600*. Serves good coffee, imaginative lunches and snacks and a fine breakfast. About 12 mins north of Tairua the **$$ Colenso Country Café** *on SH25, T07-8663725. 1000-1700*. A top spot for partaking in their fine food.

$$ Shells Restaurant, *Main Rd, Tairua T07-8648811. Closed Sun/Mon*. Convenient for an evening meal.

Whangamata p217

$$$ Nickel Strausse at Bushland Park (see above). Cosy, fine dining.

$$ Café 101, *101 Casement Rd, T07-8656301*. Acceptable breakfasts, lunch and dinner.

$$ Coast, *501 Port Rd, T07-8656999, www.coastrestaurant.co.nz Mon-Sat*. Very 'fresh', a little more upmarket and the place to head for those who like seafood and Pacific Rim cuisine.

$ Vibes Café, *638 Port Rd, T07-8657121*. Good for ight lunches and the best coffee in town.

Waihi p217

$$ Chambers Wine Bar and Restaurant, *22 Haszard St, T07-8637474. Open 1100-late*. In the old 1904 Council Chambers building, offering a mix of Mediterranean and Antipodean dishes.

$$ Grandpa Thorns, *4 Waitete Rd, T07-8638708. Open summer, Tue-Sun from 1730*. Small log cabin-style in a nice setting and good seafood.

$$ Waitete Orchard Café, *Waitete Rd, off SH2, T07-8638980. Daily from 0830-1730*. Great lunch venue with organic flair and fruit wines.

$-$$ Jellyfish and Custard, *31 Wilson Rd, T07-8635840. Daily lunch and dinner*. Serves just about everything but.

$$ Farmhouse Café, *14 Haszard St, T07-8637649. Open daily Sun-Fri*. Also a favourite locally, though this has been mixed with sympathy in recent times since the owner and five family members were so tragically lost in a domestic fire.

▲▲ Activities

Whitianga p214

Cruising, fishing and diving There are numerous charters of all shapes and sizes offering a wide range of trips from fishing and diving to speedboat cruising out into Mercury Bay and beyond. Bear in mind that most coastal fishing charters charge on a 'boat' rather than 'per person' basis, so group bookings are best, or be prepared to join others. The best bet for fishing is to call at the VIC and ask who is going out on any particular day. The Cave Cruzer is a rigid inflatable that can take you on a range of tours around the bay from 1-3 hrs, taking in the main coastal sights including a stop at Cathedral Cove and an evening trip with a spot of cross Maori/Aussie live music from $45, *T0800-427-893 / T025-866744, www.cavecruzer.co.nz* Alternatively the stunning coastal explorations with Hahei Explorer is another excursion well worth considering (see Hahei page 222).

Ecotours Kiwi 4WD Safaris offer 4WD tours that take in the Kuaotunu Peninsula and the kiwi reintroduction program. It is a great opportunity to see these wonderful birds going about their manic noctambulations in a far less commercial setting than the standard kiwi houses. *Day (1100-1500) from $145 or Twilight trips (4-5 hr), from $145, with kiwi feeding $175, T07-8664156, www.trackz.co.nz* **Cathedral Cove Dive**, *T07-8663955,* *www.hahei.co.nz/diving/*, offer trips for certified divers to the Te Whanganui-A-Hei Marine Reserve off Cathedral Cove. The scenery above water is equally stunning.

Golf Whitianga has a fine golf course located about 4 km south of town, *T07-8665479*. Matarangi north of Whitianga is also an excellent course, *T07-8665394*.

Horse Treks **Twin Oaks Riding Ranch** is *9 km north of Whitianga, T07-8665388*. Depart daily at 1000 and 1400 and 1800.
Ace Hi Ranch, *8 km south of Whitianga*, *T07-8664897*, check out their very toe-tapping yee-haaw website -*www.pubcrawlnz.com* offers a very intriguing overnight trip – a pub-crawl by horse, 2 days from $250. More conventional treks available with **Rangihau Ranch**, *Rangihau Rd, Coroglen, T07-8663875*.

Kayaking/windsurfing The coast, with its eroding sandstone scenery and pohutukawa trees is ideal for sea kayaking, and a trip in calm conditions is highly recommended. **Cathedral Cove Sea Kayakings**, *T07-8663877*, *www.seakayaktours.co.nz* based in Hahei, offer kayak hire and half or full day kayak trips at $55/$95 and a sunset trip at $50 with all equipment provided. Courtesy transport to/from Whitianga Ferry. Recommended. **Seafari**, *T07-8660677*, windsurfing tuition. If you want to make a complete and utter Charlie of yourself you should have a go on the **Whiti Banana Boat**. This is a large inflatable yellow 'phallus' that blats around the bay at high speed, with you desperately trying to hold on – and is actually a great laugh. There are a number of trip options including the Hell Bender, the Thrill and Kiddies Ride. Call at the VIC. Otherwise you can always 'hang around' like a chimp at **High Zone** and their 14m ropes course, south of Whitianga near the *309 Road turn-off*.

From $10-$60, T07-8662113, www.highzone.co.nz

Hahei *p216*
If you want to experience Cathedral Cove from the water, an excellent trip is with **Hahei Explorer Tours**, *T07-8663910, haheiexplorer@ paradise.net.nz* and do daily scenic trips on board their nippy inflatable; one hour $55, child $25. The tour also takes in caves and a blowhole not accessible by foot.

Tairua and Pauanui *p216*
There are a number of attractive water- based activities operating mainly out of Tairua, a fine surf beach at Pauanui and the popular Broken Hills Recreation Area walks (leaflet from VIC). For horse trekking contact **Pine Treks**, *T07-8647078*, suitable for beginners.

Whangamata *p217*
Whangamata VIC can assist in finding accommodation and book the numerous water-based trips and activities.
Kiwi Dundee Adventures, *T07-8658809, www.kiwidundee.co.nz* Offers an extensive and imaginative range of eco-tours. Half and full-day trips, taking in natural sights and goldmining remnants, from $190.
Whangamata Surf Shop, *Port Rd*, the focus for the latest surfers' gossip and board hire.

⊖ Transport

Bike hire From VIC from $25 per day. Whitianga Mowers and Cycles, *15 Coghill St*, *T07-8665435*. **Car rental** Rental Car Centre, *32 Campbell St, Whitianga, T07-8665901*.
Taxi Mercury Bay Taxis, *Whitianga*, *T09-8665643*.

⊙ Directory

Internet VIC. Smitty's Inn, Whitianga. Internet and Graphics, *712 Port Road (above Slipper 4 Square), Whangamata, T07-8658832*.

The Waikato

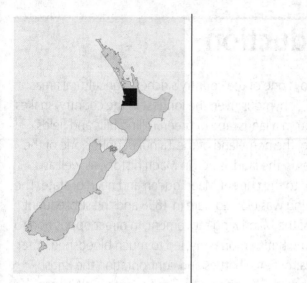

Introduction

The Waikato is one of the country's richest agricultural areas where the eponymous river, the longest in the country, snakes its way through a landscape of green rolling hills and fields. The Waikato, the homeland of the Tainui people – one of the largest tribes in the land, is rich in Maori history, as well as being home to the current Maori queen and head of state. The first Maori king was elected here in 1858 and the subsequent formation of the Maori King Movement, in direct opposition to rule under the British monarchy, led to much bloodshed. After almost a year of fierce battles and confrontation the British finally quashed the Kingites, who fled to southern Waikato, which is now also known as **King Country**. Today, peace reigns, but the memory lives on.

Waikato also boasts New Zealand's fourth largest city, **Hamilton**, which, despite being an unremarkable commercial centre, is increasingly seen as an alternative base to Auckland. Although not a major tourist destination, the Waikato is a region with considerable diversity, from the famous **surf beaches** on its coast, to the jewel in the crown of the King Country, the **Waitomo** District, a wonderland of limestone caves and subterranean activities that deservedly make it one of the North Island's premier tourist attractions. Also of note, since the release of the film *Lord of the Rings*, is the small agricultural town of Matamata, where local farmland was used to create the set of **'Hobbiton'**, home of Frodo and friends. Although very little remains it has become the first stop on the 'tour of homage' for *Lord of the Rings* fanatics.

★ Don't miss...

❶ Otorohanga's famous **Kiwi House**, page 238. Encounter a kiwi, a kea or a kokako.

❷ Going underground with style in the **Haggas Honking Holes** or descending 100m into the awe-inspiring **Lost World**, page 243.

❸ **Woodlyn Park**. Hug an angora rabbit, see the highly entertaining agricultural show, or marvel at glowworms in **Waitomo Caves Village**, page 240.

❹ Taking the back roads from Waitomo to the intriguing coastal village of **Kawhia**, stopping at the misty **Marokopa Falls** on the way, page 233.

❺ Dreaming about VW Beetles and 'left-hand breaks' with the surfies in laid-back **Raglan**, page 234.

❻ Climbing Mount **Te Aroha** then relaxing in a hot pool in the Te Aroha Domain, page 245.

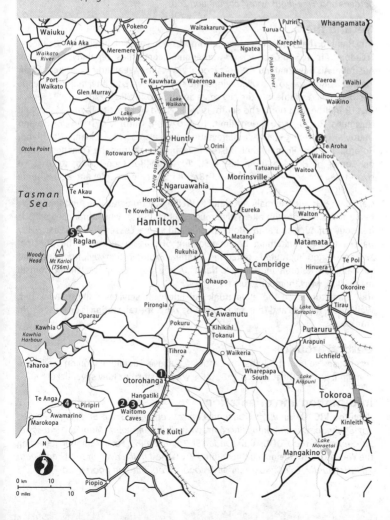

The Waikato Introduction

Hamilton and Waikato North

→ *Phone code: 07 Colour map 2, grid B2 Population: 120,000*

Perched on the serpentine banks of the famous Waikato River, 129 km south of Auckland, Hamilton is New Zealand's fourth largest city and main service centre for the rich fertile agricultural region of the Waikato. Being so close to the major tourist destinations of Auckland and Rotorua, the city struggles to attract visitors for any length of time: it has few major attractions but can be an attractive alternative 'arrival base' to Auckland and is ideally located for explorations around the Waikato Region. Hamilton is also a university town and plays host to some major national events, including the annual National Agricultural Field Days in June and the colourful Hot Air Balloon Fiesta in April. Visitors stopping briefly in the city can enjoy a ride down the Waikato on the MV Waipa Delta paddleboat and visit the celebrated museum, gardens and 'Free-flight Aviary' of Hamilton Zoo.

Getting there

Air Hamilton has a busy international **airport** 15 km south of the city, T07-8433623. **Freedom Air** T0800-600505, www.freedomair.com, flies regularly to Eastern Australia; **Air New Zealand** T0800-737000, www.airnewzealand.co.nz and **Origin Pacific**, T0800-302302, www.originpacific.co.nz, service all the major domestic destinations. A shuttle into the city costs about $10, T07-8437778.

Bus Hamilton (SH1 north and south) is well served by **Intercity** T07-8343457, and **Newmans** T0800-777707. **Northliner**, T09-3075873, **Guthrey's**, T07-8393580 and **Dalroy's**, T0508-465622, www.dalroytours.co.nz, also serve Auckland, Northland, Rotorua and New Plymouth. All buses arrive and depart from the **Transport Centre** on Corner of Bryce and Anglesea St, T07-8393580. Mon-Thu 0700-1815, Fri 0700-1945, Sat 0900-1645, Sun 0900-1845. It has a café, internet and also is home to the VIC.

Car Both SH1 and the main Auckland to Wellington trunk rail line run through the heart of the Waikato. An alternative route south is SH27, which branches off SH1 just south of Auckland at the Bombay Hills and also accesses Waikato East. SH27 passes through Matamata before rejoining SH1 again at Tirau. The principal signposted touring route is called the 'Thermal Explorer Highway', from Auckland via Hamilton, Rotorua and Taupo to Napier. A free touring map is available from all major VICs, www.thermalnz.co.nz

Rail Hamilton is on the main trunk rail line with services daily to Auckland, Wellington, Rotorua and Tauranga, T0800-872467. The **rail station** is on Fraser St, in Frankton.

Getting around

Local buses go from the Transport Centre, see above. For information on services in Hamilton, contact **Busit**, T0800-42875463, www.busit.co.nz (day saver ticket $4).

Information and orientation

Hamilton VIC, ① *Hamilton Transport Centre, corner of Bryce and Anglesea Sts, T07-8393580, www.hamiltoncity.co.nz, www.waikatonz.co.nz Mon-Fri 0830-1700, Sat-Sun 0900-1600.* **DOC**, ① *18 London St, T07-8383363.* For information regarding the Waikato North region, contact **Huntly VIC** ① *next to the river on 160 Great South Rd, SH1, Huntly, T07-8286406, Mon-Fri 0900-1700, Sat-Sun 0900-1500.*

History

The earliest recorded settlers in the Hamilton area were Maori from the Tainui *waka* (canoe) that settled on the banks of the river. At that time, the Waikato River was the major means of communication, transportation and trade with other settled areas. In the 1860s the first Europeans began to settle, during the Land Wars and the notorious 'raupatu' or land confiscations. A military outpost was established in Hamilton East and existed for a number of years before communications and relations improved and agriculture developed. In 1867 the road was opened to Auckland, followed 10 years later by the railway. From that point on settlement began in earnest and the city developed as a major agricultural service centre. The town was named in honour of Captain John Charles Fane Hamilton, the commander of *HMS Esk*, who was killed while leading the naval brigade at the Battle of Gate *pa* near Tauranga in 1864.

Sights in the city

The modern **Waikato Museum of Art and History**, ① *To7-8386533, www.waikato museum.org.nz, daily 1000-1630, donations ($2); Exscite $5, child $3; special exhibitions: adult from $12, child $6*, overlooks the river on the corner of Victoria and Grantham Streets. It presents a wide-ranging programme of both permanent and temporary exhibitions, including a balance of contemporary and historical art of regional significance and national importance. The history of Hamilton and the region is naturally explored with a particularly impressive collection of Tainui Maori *taonga* (treasures). The highlight of the collection has to be the beautiful carved and decorated *waka*, 'Te Wainika', given to the museum in 1973 by Te Arikinui Dame Te Atairangikaahu, the Maori Queen. **'Exscite'** is an adjunct science and technology centre on the ground floor. It offers all the usual whizz-bang earthquake simulation stuff, which is great for little kids and big kids alike. There is also a fine café/restaurant attached to the museum, selling interesting fare such as ostrich antipasto and kangaroo loin, amongst other things.

While near the river it is worth taking a stroll to soak up the almost English atmosphere, with its rowboats and pleasant gardens. On the eastern bank, just across from the museum, the historic paddleboat the **MV Waipa Delta**, ① *To800-472335*, (the original of which first plied the Waikato in 1876) runs various cruises, including a lunch (1200, $39), afternoon tea (1445, $20) and dinner cruise (1830-2200, $55, child $22.50). The food is less than remarkable.

Just south of the city centre and east of Cobham Bridge are the celebrated **Hamilton Gardens**. ① *To7-8563200. Open from 0730-sunset, visitors centre 1000-1600, café from 1030. Free*. These are a conglomerate of Japanese, Chinese and English flower gardens, mixed with numerous smaller and more traditional themed displays. The gardens also host a popular café and restaurant. (The VIC has a free and comprehensive Heritage Trail leaflet, another outlining 'Hamilton's Walkways' and the 'Waikato Vintage Wine Trail'.)

Hamilton Zoo, ① *Daily from 0900-1700, with extended hours in Jan. Adult $8, child $4. To7-8386720, www.hamiltonzoo.co.nz   To get to the zoo, 8 km from the city centre, take the SH23 Raglan Rd, turn right on to Newcastle Rd, then go straight ahead down Brymer, following the signs*. Both modern and progressive in its outlook, the zoo not only acts as a major attraction, but also attempts to mix a considerable collection of native New Zealand species with others important to international conservation breeding programmes. The highlight is the 3,800 sq m, walk-through, 'Free-flight Aviary', which houses 10 species of indigenous, rare and endangered New Zealand birds within a native bush setting. It is often difficult to spot the birds, so take your time and wait. Other attractions include the Sumatran Tigers and the 'Waikato Wetlands' and 'Out of Africa' exhibits, and don't miss the very grumpy Kune pig in the heart of the park. ▸▸ *For Sleeping, Eating and other listings, see pages 229-232.*

⁝ Te Kooti

Te Kooti – or Rikirangi Te Turuki – (1830-93) could arguably be considered the William Wallace (Braveheart) of Maoridom. And although the battles were less bloody, his death far less gruesome, his resolve and integrity (or *mana*) was certainly on a par with the great Scot. Born near Gisborne, of a good family but of no particular chiefly rank, he was given a sound education at the Waerenga-a-hika Mission School before becoming a horse-breaker and later, a seaman on a small schooner trading the East Coast of the North Island. During the Maori uprising and siege of Waerenga-a-hika in 1865, Te Kooti actually supported the *pakeha*, but was accused of supplying the Hauhau Maori rebels with ammunition and intelligence regarding the positions of colonial Government troops.

Without trial and after being essentially set up by a local *pakeha*-allied Maori chief, he was exiled to the Chatham Islands with a group of Hauhau rebels in 1866. Te Kooti had constantly protested his innocence, but his claims were ignored. During his two years on the Chathams Te Kooti studied the New Testament and, after claiming he had experienced a divine revelation, established the tenets of his own 'Ringatu' faith. Convinced that the Government had no intention of releasing him, Te Kooti and a small group of other exiles captured a ship and forced the crew to take them back to the east coast of the North

Island. Now a fugitive and considered dangerous, he was immediately pursued by government forces. Again, after writing to the Government and claiming his innocence, his protestations were ignored. Given little choice, Te Kooti had to fight and, gathering considerable support, he did so with a vengeance.

In a fierce battle at Matawhero against a large force commanded by one Colonel Whitmore, he and his men killed 33 Europeans and 37 allied Maori. Still outnumbered and closely pursued he retreated to the Urewera Forest. Ropata Wahawaha, who was a Maori chief allied to Whitmore, executed 120 of Te Kooti's men. For the following three years Te Kooti was relentlessly pursued and harried not only by government forces, but also European colonials and allied Maori tribes. When battles ensued Te Kooti fought with courage or always managed cleverly to elude his enemies. In 1872 he sought refuge in The Waikato where the Maori 'King Movement' had been established by fellow Maori rebels. There he spent much time peacefully, still proclaiming his original innocence as well as consolidating and spreading the word of his Ringatu religion.

Te Kooti was finally pardoned in 1883 and died back on the East Coast, 10 years later – a free man. To this day his Ringatu religion lives on in the Bay of Plenty and his memory in the hearts of all Maori.

Waikato North

Ngaruawahia   *Phone code: 07 Colour map 2, grid B1 19km north of Hamilton*

Ngaruawahia is the Maori capital of New Zealand, home of the Maori Queen, Te Atairangikaahu (first queen and sixth person to hold office), and one of the best and most significant *maraes* in the country – the **Turangawaewae marae**, beside the river on River Road, and only open once a year in March, during the annual regatta, when a number of *waka* (canoes) are displayed on the river. (The town is located where the

Waipa meets the mighty Waikato.) Another point of interest in Ngaruawahia is the
Mahinarangi House, built in 1929. It is beautifully carved both inside and out, with the royal coat of arms on the giant doors, entitled 'Te Paki o Matariki' announcing the hope of peace and calm between Maori and *pakeha*. Next door is the Queen's official residence. Ngaruawahia also has a number of good walks including the **Hakarimata Walkways** and **Taupiri Mountain**, the site of the Waikato's most sacred burial ground. If you fancy a well-deserved hot soak after your walk or explorations of the town you might like to head 23 km west to the **Waingaro Hot Springs**, ① *T07-8254761, 0900-2200. $6,* featuring large thermal mineral pools and spas.

Huntly → *Phone code: 07 NB: the SH1, both north and south of Huntly, is a notorious accident black spot, so drive with care.*

With its power station and the slow-moving muddy waters of the Waikato, Huntly is not a pretty place. (The underground coal reserves are the largest in New Zealand and the power station produces 20% of the country's needs.) However, the **Waikato Coalfields Museum**, ① *26 Harlock St, T07-8288128, Mon-Fri 1000-1500 and Sat 1300-1500, $4, child $2,* displaying local mining history may tempt you to linger.

In direct contrast to the man-made gloom of Huntly are the numerous **lakes** and wetlands that surround the town. These are popular for both water sports and bird watching. For a detailed description of the lakes and walks ask for the DOC leaflet 'Waikato Wetlands' at the Huntly VIC or DOC offices in Hamilton. If you have kids and can bear it, **Candyland**, ① *75 Henry Rd, about 15 minutes southeast of Huntly, T07-8246818, daily 1000-1700,* is the largest candy shop in New Zealand.

Te Kauwhata → *Phone code: 07 Colour map 2, grid B2*

The main attraction in this mainly grape-growing area is the **Rangiriri Battle Site Heritage Centre**, ① *T07-8263663, 0900-1700, free,* which sits next to the Rangiriri Hotel (with a congenial, old-fashioned country pub that offers a fine pub lunch) just off SH1. Although the place seems to function more as a roadside café than anything else, there are some memorabilia and an information office where you can arrange to see an audio-visual display. The battle that took place in Rangiriri in 1863 was one of the bloodiest of the Maori Land Wars and involved a small group of Maori who made a brave stand against the numerically superior British forces. The remains of the redoubts from which they fought still survive, as does the cemetery. There are also two vineyards here: **Cooks Landing** with a restaurant and wine-tasting tours and direct sales (*T07-8260004*) and **Rongopai Wines** (*tasting and sales T07-8263981*).

● Sleeping

Hamilton *p226*

Hamilton has plenty of mid-range accommodation and you should not have much difficulty finding somewhere to stay without pre-booking. Ulster St, just north of the city centre is the main motel drag and there is certainly plenty of choice. But there are not many B&Bs in Hamilton. The VIC has full listings.

LL-L Novotel Tainui Hotel, *7 Alma Rd, T07-8381366, book_hamilton@novotel. co.nz* This is a modern hotel with all the usual Novotel mod cons, centrally located and overlooking the river. The Café Alma (attached) offers both indoor and outdoor à

la carte dining.

L-A Ambassador Motor Inn, *86 Ulster St, T07-8395111.* With a restaurant attached.

L-A Barclay Motel, *280 Ulster St, T07-8382475, www.barclay.co.nz* Fairly new with all mod cons and spa facilites.

L-A Chloe's, *181 Ulster St, T07-8393410.* Also has a restaurant adjacent.

L-A Sails Motel, *272 Ulster St, T07-8382733, bookings@sails-motorinn.co.nz* Spa facilties.

AL-A Narrows Landing, *431 Airport Rd, Tamahere, T07-8584001, www.thenarrowslanding.co.nz* Also near the airport and offers self-contained accommodation, with country views and a fine restaurant attached.

AL-A Ventura Inn and Suites *23 Clarence St, T07-8380110, www.venturainns.co.nz* Back in town and on the fringe of the Central Business District but quite peaceful nevertheless. It is relatively new and has studio rooms or suites (some with spas) and excellent facilities including a pool.

B Cedar Lodge, *174 Ulster St, T07-8395569.* One of the cheapest on Ulster St.

C-D Flying Hedgehog Backpackers, *1157*

Hamilton

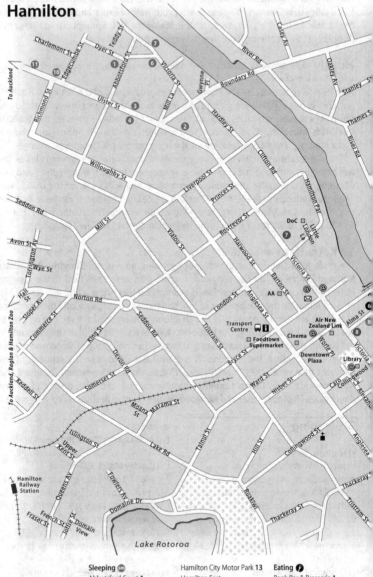

The Waikato Hamilton and Waikato North

Lake Rotoroa

N

0 metres 200
0 yards 200

Sleeping
Abbotsford Court **1**
Ambassador Motor Inn **2**
Barclay Motel **11**
Cedar Lodge **3**
Chloe's **4**
Flying Hedgehog
 Backpackers **6**

Hamilton City Motor Park **13**
Hamilton East
 Motor Camp **9**
Hamilton YHA **7**
J's Backpackers **12**
Novotel Tainui **8**
Sails Motel **10**
Ventura Inn & Suites **5**

Eating
Bank Bar & Brasserie **1**
Iguana **11**
Mr D's **3**
Museum Café &
 Restaurant **2**
Sahara Tent Café & Bar **4**
Scotts Epicurean **5**

Victoria St, T07-8392800,
www.flyinghedgehog. Bravepages.com
Seems to enjoy a good reputation beyond just
the name.
C-D **J's Backpackers**, *8 Grey St, T07-8568934,*

bookme@jsbackpackers.co.nz Another
suburban offering with comfortable dorms,
twins and doubles. They also organize trips
and have internet.
C-D **Hamilton YHA**, *1190 Victoria St, T07-
8380009.* In a quiet location near the river.

Motorcamps and campsites
There are two fairly basic motor camps with
camping facilities in East Hamilton about 3
km from town:
C-D **Hamilton East Motor Camp**, *61
Cameron Rd, T07-8566220.*
C-D **Hamilton City Holiday Park**, *14
Ruakura Rd, T07-8558255.*

Tables on the River **6**

Bars & clubs 🅝
Biddy Mulligan's **7**
Fox & Hounds **8**
Loaded Hog **9**
Outback, Loft & Diggers **10**

🅔 Eating

Hamilton *p226*
Hamilton boasts an amazing number of
café/restaurants (mainly along the southern
end of Victoria St), all trying to outdo each
other in interior design, theme and cuisine.
$$$ **The Bank Bar and Brasserie**, *corner of
Hood and Victoria Sts, further south. Sun-Thu
1100-2300, Fri-Sat 1100-0300.* Another
spacious local favourite, especially with the
suits at lunchtime and trendsetters at night.
Big servings.
$$$ **Iguana**, *Victoria St, T07-8342280,
www.iguana.net.nz Mon-Wed 1000-late,
Thu-Sun 1000-0300.* No bookings. A
well-established, spacious favourite, with a
wide-ranging mainly Pacific Rim menu and
excellent gourmet pizza. The bar is also
popular which just adds to the
establishment's lively atmosphere.
$$$ **Tables on the River**, *12 Alma St,
T07-8396555. Mon-Sat from 1200.* An award
winner – overlooking the river. International
and traditional Kiwi fare.
$$ **Café Alma** (See Novotel Tainui Hotel in
Sleeping above.)
$$ **Museum Café/Restaurant**, *Grantham St,
T07-8397209. Open daily for brunch and lunch
from 1030, for dinner from 1800 Tue-Sat and
has jazz on Thu nights.* You cannot go far
wrong here, with an eclectic menu for lunch
and dinner.
$$ **The Sahara Tent Café and Bar**, *254
Victoria St, T07-8340409.* A Middle
Eastern-style establishment which is worth
seeing, never mind eating in.
$$ **Scott's Epicurean**, *181 Victoria St,*

T07-8396680. A funky little café with a highly imaginative lunch/brunch menu, including, to its eternal credit, a fine bowl of porridge.
$ Mr D's, *opposite Iguana on Victoria St, Daily, 1200-late*. Offers fresh burgers the size of small flying saucers.

♠ Bars

With so many trendy bars and restaurants Hamilton enjoys a lively and friendly social scene and if you mingle with the locals it will probably be a long and interesting night.
Biddy Mulligan's, *724 Victoria St*. Traditional Irish pub, hosting bands at the weekend.
Fox and Hounds *Ward St*. Another favourite.
The Bank *on the corner of Hood St*, or the **Loaded Hog**, *27 Hood St*. The places for trendsetters to be, particularly at weekends, when you can rip your tights and shake your pants to dance music.
For more traditional Kiwi pub atmosphere and for younger crowds, try:
Outback, **Loft** or **Diggers Bar**, *all on Hood St*, which get pretty messy in the small hours!

❷ Entertainment

For information and bookings contact the VIC or Theatre Services, *T07-8386603*.

Casino
Hamilton has succumbed and now has its own casino, the main focus within the flash new **Riverside Entertainment Centre**, *346 Victoria Street, T07-8344900, www.skyriverside.co.nz Daily 1100-0300*. Min age 20, smart casual dress.

Cinema
Village 7 Cinema *in the Centreplace Mall, Ward St*.

Theatres
The Founders, *221 Tristram St*. Offers opera, ballet/dance and musicals
Westpac Community Theatre, *59 Clarence St*. Drama, ballet/dance, concerts, musicals

and comedy.
Meteor, *1 Victoria St*. The smallest, offering drama, dance, bands and comedy.

◎ Shopping

Hamilton has two large shopping centres:
Hamilton Central Shopping Centre, *T07-8342020*; and
Westfield Shopping Centre, *corner of Hukanui and Comries Rd, Chartwell, T07-8548934*.
The two other major shopping malls are:
Downtown Plaza and
Centreplace Shopping Centre.
R&R Sports, *934 Victoria St, T0800-777767 / T07-8393755*. Have a wide range of outdoor equipment for sale and hire, including skis and accessories, tramping gear and boots, wetsuits, surfboards and kayaks.
For New Zealand souvenirs try:
New Zealand World, *24 Garden Pl*.
Crow's Nest Books, *Worley Pl*. A good second-hand bookshop.

⊖ Transport

Bike Rental R&R Sports (see shopping) or **Pack and Pedal**, *corner of Ulster and Liverpool Sts, T07-8380575*.
Car rental Rent-A-Dent and First Choice, *383 Anglesea St, T8391049*.
Waikato Car Rentals, *Brooklyn Rd, T07-8550094*.
Taxis Hamilton Taxi Society, *T07-8477477, T0800-477477*.

❶ Directory

Banks All the main banks have branches on or around Victoria St. For foreign exchange try **Thomas Cook**, *Garden Pl, T07-8380149*. **Communications Internet** At numerous well-advertised city centre locations and also at the VIC and the library on Garden Pl. **Post Office** *36 Bryce St, T07-8382233. Open Mon-Fri 0800-1700, Sat 0900-1400, Sun 0900-1200*. **Medical services** Waikato Health Ltd, *Pembroke St, T07-8398899*.

Waikato coast → *Phone code: 07*

With the well-advertised attractions of Waitomo and its caves, the Waikato coast seldom features very high on the average travelling agenda. Indeed, after some unique subterranean adventures most simply pass through the Waikato on their way south, or east to the capital of all things thermal - Rotorua. But for those with more time, who wish to ride a world-class 'left hand break', or who simply wish to get off the beaten track, then the Waikato coast offers some pleasant surprises. The small laid-back coastal village of Raglan, almost 50 km west of Hamilton, offers a palpable sense of relaxation, not to mention plenty of the aforementioned and near legendary surf breaks, while further south the remote village of Kawhia can offer a highlight on the relaxing, scenic and often solitary diversion off SH1 to the coast and back via the Marakopa Falls to Waitomo.

Getting there and around

The drive to Kawhia from anywhere is quite arduous but scenic. If you are peckish be sure to stop for a homemade pie at the Oparau petrol station (open 0600-2200), T8710683. If you do not have your own wheels try **Kawhia Bus and Freight** who run a service to and from Te Awamutu, T07-8710701. **Perry's Buses** of Te Kuiti also do a weekday coastal run between Kawhia and Te Kuiti, via Wiatomo, T07-8767595, $8 one way. Raglan is 48 km from Hamilton. The commuter-orientated **Hamilton City Buses/Pavlovich** T07-8475343 / T0800-42875463 offer weekday services (3 per day) to Raglan, departing from Hamilton Transport Centre for $11 return (first at 0930) T8564579. In Raglan buses stop at the VIC. For a taxi in Raglan, T8250506.

Information

Kawhia Museum, ⓘ T07-8710161, *www.kawhia.co.nz*, operates as a VIC in the town. **Raglan VIC**, ⓘ *4 Wallis St, T07-8250556, daily from 1000-1600, www.raglan.net.nz* Small but highly efficient.

Kawhia *Population: 600 Colour map 2, grid B1.*

Outside the summer influx of mainly domestic holidaymakers, when the population almost triples, Kawhia (pronounced 'Kafia'), is a sleepy, fairly unremarkable, coastal village on the shores of the Kawhia Harbour southwest of Hamilton. But perhaps due to its remote location and nature's rich pickings, Kawhia seems in no hurry to announce itself as anything more spectacular, and has the contented atmosphere of a place entirely happy with its lot. And it would seem that this has always been the case. Kawhia (which actually translates as 'place of abundance') was home to the Tainui people who first arrived here some 750 years ago. So happy were they with the place and its natural provision, that it took them over 300 years before heading inland to settle other parts of the Waikato. Even then, it was only through inter-tribal disputes, which ironically were over the abundant fishing grounds.

Sights Most of Kawhia's points of interest are on the shoreline in the town and extending around to the harbour entrance and **Ocean Beach**. This is the most popular beach with summer visitors and it is best accessed through the Tainui Kawhia Forest Track southwest of the town centre. Ocean Beach boasts the **Puia Hot Springs** (a far less commercial echo of Hot Water Beach in Coromandel). Here, too, you can dig your own 'spa bath' in the sand, but it's difficult to know where exactly you do this, especially in the off-season. It is perhaps best to join a local tour to access the best spots (see below). Back in town if you want to immerse yourself in Kawhia's interesting history and learn more about the Tainui landing, the small **Kawhia**

① *T07-8710161, www.kawhia.co.nz, seasonal opening times with the regular hours of Wed-Sun 1200-1600 in summer,* which sits next to the Wharf, will proudly oblige. The 'Best of the West' Heritage leaflet will pinpoint and explain specific sites.

When the Tainui people first made landfall they tied their canoe to a pohutukawa tree and named it **Tangi-te-Korowhiti**. Although the specific tree is not marked, it is one of a small grove at the northern end of Kaora Street. What is marked is the site of its burial with two stones **Hani and Puna** which can be seen behind the **Maketu marae** about 500 m south of the landing site (ask for permission at the *marae* to see them).

▶▶ *For Sleeping, Eating and other listings, see pages 234-235.*

Raglan → *Phone code: 07 Population: 3000 Colour map 2, grid B1*

Raglan is the Waikato's main seaside resort, and internationally renowned for its fine surfing. So when you arrive in the heart of the village, with its palm trees and laid-back cafes, don't be surprised if you end up being sandwiched in a queue or sharing your lunch table with a colourful length of fibreglass with 'Ride' em Baby', 'The Big Phallus' or 'No Fear' written on it. In Raglan these strange, almost religious objects seem to make up half the population. The village itself is on the quiet Raglan Harbour with all the surf action on beaches a short drive away heading west. One of those beaches – Manu Bay – has apparently one of the best left-hand breaks in the world.

Sights The main attractions around Raglan are its beaches, the most convenient and safest for swimming being **Te Kopua**, which borders the Raglan campground. Access is via the camp access road west, or across the footbridge at the end of Bow Street in the centre of the village. All the main surf beaches are west of town. **Ocean Beach** is the first and as well as surfing, it is also popular for swimming and the view across the 'Raglan Bar' (harbour entrance). Access is off Wainui Reserve Road via a walking track. Surf lifesavers operate in summer, and as always, you must swim between the flags. The famous left-hand break **Manu Bay** is next and the best spot to surf or spectate. Further still is **Whale Bay**, which is a great spot for both surfers and the uninitiated alike, but it can only be accessed over rocks.

For wild coastal scenery **Ruapuke Beach** is popular but remote. Follow the old coast road (taking in the impressive **Te Toto Gorge** on the way), then follow Ruapuke Beach Road and walk from there. Other beaches near town that are safe and child-friendly are **Cox's Bay** (accessible from Bayview Road and Daisy Street or the walkway along Government Road) and **Puriri Park** (Aro Aro Bay) at the end of Wallis Street.

If you are interested in local history the small **Raglan and District Museum,** ① *Wainui Rd, hours vary and are usually confined to weekends (see the VIC),* has mainly European material. Further afield on SH23 are the aptly named 55 m **Bridal Veil Falls**, which are a bit of a trek but worth it, particularly after heavy rain. If the 756 m summit of **Mt Karioi** beckons it is best accessed from Te Toto Gorge, 12 km southwest (see above). There are fine views from the top; allow six hours. It is known by the Maori as 'the sleeping lady', the reason for which is obvious if you study its outline.

▶▶ *For Sleeping, Eating and other listings, see pages 235-236.*

⬤ Sleeping

Kawhia *p233*
Motorcamps and campsites
B-D **Kawhia Camp Ground**, *73 Moke St, T07-8710863, www.kawhiacamping.co.nz* The newest motor/camping ground, it has cabins as well as powered, non-powered sites and internet access. Also offers 4WD

trips to the hot springs.

B-D **Kawhia Beachside S-Cape**, *225 Pouewe St, as you come into town, T07-8710727, www.kawhiabeachsidescape.co.nz* Offers the usual range of motorcamp accommodation including a self-contained cottage and facilities for backpackers. Bike and kayak hire.

B **Rosamond House B&B**, *T07-8710681*. One

of the few B&Bs. Built in 1901 it was a former residence, boarding house and doctor's surgery, now tastefully renovated.

B Kawhia Motel, *corner of Jervois and Tainui Sts, T07-8710865*. A basic motel.

B Wee Knot Inn, *Jervois St, T07-8710778*. A congenial little pub which also has two affordable self-contained units and a 3-bedroom villa.

Raglan *p234*

The VIC or website www.raglan.net.nz, is a good place to look, also note that both the surf school and horse trekking operators offer accommodation packages. There are plenty of self-contained options all boasting the usual fine views and comforts.

LL-L Solitude Lodge, *349 Wainui Rd, T07-8258045, www.solitude.co.nz* Stands out for both character and sheer peace and quiet. Perfect for romantic couples.

A Luxury Retreat, *6 Upper Wainui Rd, T07-8258684*. One of the better B&Bs.

A-B Raglan Palm Beach Motel, *50 Wainui Rd, T07-8258153*. Popular and nearer the main beaches.

A-C Solscape, *7 km west of the village centre at 611 Wainui Rd, T07-8258268, www.solscape.co.nz* If you are looking for something completely different this really is the only place to stay in Raglan. Here the owners have gone to great pains to relocate and renovate an array of railway wagons as colourful accommodation units from dorm to self-contained. There is also a veritable menagerie of animals on site including a couple of ex-wild kaimanawa horses, saved from the government bullet in central North Island a few years ago. It's good value and highly recommended.

B Harbour View Hotel, *14 Bow St, T07-8258010*. A traditional Kiwi hotel in the centre of town, worth mentioning because it is nicely renovated, cheap, clean and has a good restaurant attached.

B Rangimaarie Seaside Retreat, *78G Moonlight Bay, Greenslade Rd, T07-8257567, Rangimaarieretreat@xtra.co.nz* Self-contained option; specializes in natural therapies and scrumptious organic cooking.

B-D Raglan Kopua Holiday Park, *Marine Pde, T07-8258283*. Almost on an island of its own, with a beach and linked to the village by a short bridge.

Lodge, *6 Nero St, T07-8250515*. The main backpacker accommodation in the village itself, this is quite a small hostel but purpose-built and well situated. Popular of course with the surfing set. Kayak and bike hire.

🍴 Eating

Kawhia *p233*

$$ Annie's Café, *T07-8710198. Wed-Sun 1000-1600 and Fri, Sat 1800-late*. Offers traditional fare.

$ Kawhia Fisheries, *on the wharf*. The best bet, serving fish and chips.

$-$$ Kawhia Hotel, *Powewe St*. Basic meals.

Raglan *p234*

$$ Aqua Velvet, *17 Bow St, T07-8258588. Open for brunch Thu-Tue from 0800-1500, dinner Thurs, Fri and Sat from 1800*. A flash and rather retro new edition to Raglan's culinary scene and no doubt with the talents of ex-Auckland chef Rachel Titchener it will prove a hit.

$$ Tongue and Grove Café, *9 Bow St, T07-8250027. Daily 0830-late*. One of the most popular and affordable eateries in town along with Vinnies.

$$ Vinnies, *7 Wainui Rd, T07-8258289. Daily 1030-late, weekends from 0800-1100*. Serves traditional cuisine with a seafood edge.

$$ Verandabah, *in the Harbour View Hotel, T07-8258010*. Standard pub fare.

$ Raglan Fresh Fish and Takeaways, *35 Bow St*. Has good fish and chips, but it would seem the service is rotten unless you are a local or are attached to a surfboard.

Petchells supermarket, *16-18 Bow St. Mon-Fri 0730-1700, Sat/Sun 0730-1600*.

▲ Activities and tours

Kawhia *p233*

Sand Rover tour, *which operates out of the Kawhia Camping Ground, T07-8710863, dinic@xtra.co.nz $10*. The friendly and enthusiastic four-wheel drive tour will take you fishing and for a picnic at the Te Puia Hot Springs.

Kawhia Harbour Cruises, *T07-8710149. 1000-1300; adult $25, child $10*. Offer a number of trips around the harbour.

KawhiaTrak-N-Paddle, *T07-9570002, www.traknpaddle.co.nz Departs Kawhia Mon/Wed/Sat at 0830. From $100 (day-trip) to $300 (two-day including accommodation).* A new outfit offering a range of tramp, bike and kayak trips amidst the karst scenery west of Waitomo and around Kawhia. If youare without your own transport this is an ideal way to explore this beautiful and lesser-known region of the Waikato.

Raglan *p234*
There are several of fishing and harbour cruise charters including: **Raglan Harbour Cruises**, *T07-8250300, $15.* The latter will take you on a trip to see the unusual Pancake Rock formations (no description necessary there). (The VIC has listings for local fishing charters.)

Magic Mountain, *a 30-minute drive south of* Raglan, *T07-8256892, www.magicmountain.co.nz* The local horse trekking company with treks that take in great scenery, including the Bridal Veil Falls, so make a day of it *(from $70).* Cosy farmstay accommodation *($150 double)* also on offer.
Paragliding, *near Raglan, T07-8257344 on summer weekends.*
Raglan Surfing School, *T07-8257873, www.raglansurfingschool.co.nz A 2-hr lesson will cost around $70.* They also offer independent board rentals and accommodation packages.
Raglan Surf Company, *3 Wainui Rd, T07-8258988.* Surfboard hire and conditions.

Directory

Raglan *p234*
Internet at the Tongue and Groove Café, the library and the video shop, which are all on Bow St. **Police**, *Nero St, T07-8258200.*

Waikato South

Heading south, beyond the gentle meanderings of the Waikato River and the uninspiring urban vistas of Hamilton, the rest of the Waikato takes on the appearance of atypical North Island countryside, with its deliciously green, gently rolling hills replete with plump and contented dairy cows and the odd unsurprisingly smug looking bull. But in these parts, perhaps more than anywhere else in the country looks are deceiving, since beneath the hooves and the haystacks exists a very different world more suited to the stuff of mystical dreams and wild adventures. As Rotorua is to bubbly mud or Kaikoura is to whales, then southern Waikato and Waitomo is to subterranean caves, rivers and glow-worms. Here,you have an ease of access to a labyrinth of incredible limestone caves and underground river systems and more especially all the unique activities that go with them, that rate with the best on earth - or under it. Where else for expmale can you abseil 100 metres into the 'Lost World', or float through the 'Haggas Honking Holes'?

Getting there

Intercity, T09-9136100 and **Guthrey's**, T0800-759999 are just two of several bus companies that run a regular service North and South to Te Awamutu, Otorohanga, Te Kuiti and Waitomoto from Hamilton. **Hodgson Motors**, Ohaupo Rd, offers a regular service to and from Hamilton to Te Awamutu for $5 one-way, T07-8716373. **Perry's Buses** of Te Kuiti is the local bus company serving Waitomo to the coast, T07-8767596. They do a weekday coastal run between Kawhia and Te Kuiti, via Waitomo, $8 one way. They are also on the main North/South trunk rail line, T0800-872467. To get to the Waitomo Caves by bus, locally, the **Waitomo Shuttle**, T07-8738279 / T0800-808-279, $8 one-way, operates a regular service from 0900-1730, between Otorohanga's bus depot, railway station, motels, backpackers, caravan parks and Waitomo. The **Waitomo Wanderer**, T07-3492509 / T07-3485179, www.waitomotours.com, from $30 ($58 return), runs a daily service from Rotorua and

Taupo. It departs Rotorua at 0730 and arrives in Waitomo at 1000, departing Waitomo again at 1545. **Intercity**, T09-9136100, **Newmans**, T09-9136200, **Guthrey's**, T09-3090905 and **Great Sights**, T0800-808226, all offer highly commercial day-trips to the Glow-worm Caves from Auckland and Rotorua and you are advised to shop around. The best idea is to get to Otorohanga on a standard Intercity bus and get to Waitomo independently from there. **Magic Traveller Buses** and **Kiwi Experience** also allow more flexibility than the day-trip option. There is also the train, but the trip from Auckland to Otorohanga alone is pretty dull (from $99 return), T0800-843596. If coming by car, note there is no fuel available in Waitomo Village.

Information

Te Awamutu VIC, ① *1 Gorst Av, T07-8713259. Mon-Fri 0900-1630, Sat-Sun 1000-1500, www.teawamutu.co.nz* **Otorohanga VIC**, ① *on the main SH3 drag at 57 Maniapoto St, T07-8738951, www.otorohanga.co.nz Mon-Fri 0900-1730, Sat/Sun 1000-1600.* Internet here and at the Library. **Te Kuiti VIC**, ① *Rora St in the centre of town, T07-8788077. Open daily 0900-1700 (reduced in winter).* Staff can assist with bus information, tickets and accommodation options in the area. **Waitomo Museum of Caves VIC (I-Site)**, ① *at the heart of operations in the small tourist village of Waitomo, T0800-474-839 / T07-8787640, waitomuseum@xtra.co.nz Daily 0830-1730, 2000 in Jan.* Almost all the above-ground attractions, below-ground activity operators, booking offices and tourist amenities are within walking distance. Although compact it can be confusing, so the best bet (if you have not already researched from other VIC's, leaflets and the web) is to absorb the information at the VIC first and take your time. There are numerous and often very similar activities on offer. Then, let the staff book on your behalf, or go to the relevant tour operator for more information. There is a village store attached to the Waitomo Adventure (Luminoso) booking office, (next to the VIC), that sells limited supplies. The VIC has stamps, internet access and currency exchange. There is also an ATM outside.

Te Awamutu → *Phone code: 07 Colour map 2, grid B2. Population: 9500 You can pick up a detailed Heritage Trail handout at the VIC (see Information above).*
Te Awamutu is in the heart of Waikato dairy farming country and the Waipa District, which also takes in Cambridge to the east. It is most famous for its **Rose Gardens**, which are on Gorst Avenue (across the road from the VIC). The gardens contain hundreds of varieties with such alluring names as 'Disco Dancer', 'Sexy Rexy' and 'Big Daddy' and are nurtured to be at their smelly best for the **Rose and Cultural Festival** held during the end of October or first week in November. Local activities worth looking at here include rock climbing, with the region offering some of the North Island's best, including the challenging 'Froggat Edge'.

Sights

Te Awamutu District Museum, ① *Roche St, T07-8714326, www.tamuseum.org.nz Mon-Fri 1000-1600, Sat-Sun 1000-1300, free*, a bizarre leap of time, culture and theme, with some fine examples of local Maori *taonga* (treasures) mixed with a celebration of the town's two best-loved sons – Neil and Tim Finn, of the rock bands Split Enz and Crowded House. Somehow, it seems a bit like running a video of Freddie Mercury strutting his stuff next to the original Crown Jewels in the Tower of London, but such is the dilemma faced by the New Zealand small town museum.

You can hang around – literally – at the **Wharepapa Rockfields**, about 20 km south east of the town. The crags include the 'Froggatt Edge', which is considered the best sport-climbing crag in the North Island, with over 115 climbs. The VIC will give you information and directions to the fields, as will the Wharepapa Outdoor Centre and the aptly named Boulderfield Café, T07-8722533.

There are numerous walks around Te Awamutu, and the town also acts as the gateway to the **Pirongia Forest Park**. Dominated by the 959 m Mount Pirongia, the park offers some fine long and short walks, including the seven-hour summit track, which rewards you with great views. Again the VIC will provide directions and information (which is best described in the *Go Bush* leaflets or DOC's own *Pirongia Forest Park*). Or pay a visit to the home of the **DB Clydesdale Team**, ① *T07-8719711, open daily*, a team of Clydesdale horses sponsored by New Zealand's largest brewing company. The well- groomed horses and carriages appear regularly on TV along with their fictional owners, who are an annoyingly good-looking couple who call everybody 'mate' and seem to do nothing but mend fences and drink beer. ▸▸ *For Sleeping, Eating and other listings, see pages 241-243.*

Otorohanga → *Phone code: 07 Colour map 2, grid C2 Population 2600*

The small agricultural service town of 'Oto', as it is better known, is so close to Waitomo with its famous caves that it struggles to attract anything other than the passing tourist. However, it does fancy itself as the gateway to the caves and boasts one of the best kiwi houses and displays of native New Zealand birds in the country.

Before heading off to Waitomo or making a beeline for the Kiwi House it is worth looking at the **Kiwiana Displays** at various points along the main street. They are very well presented and chronicle a range of kiwi icons, heritage and heroes, from Sir Edmund Hillary, to rugby and Pavlova. The VIC has a locations leaflet, which comes with a quiz. Recommended.

Established in 1971,The **Otorohanga Kiwi House and Native Bird Park**, ① *Alex Telfer Dr, T07-8737391, www.kiwihouse.org.nz, daily 0900-1700, $10, child $4*, is one of the oldest native bird and reptile parks in the country, housing over 50 species, including three of the four known species of kiwi. It provides the familiar delicate and uneasy balance of visitor attraction with vital conservation activity, attracting thousands of visitors a year and yet, behind the scenes, successfully breeding a number of inmates, including over 65 kiwi since 1975. The park's main attraction is the unique double nocturnal house where you are almost certain to see a kiwi going about its fascinating and comical hunt for food. They do this with their long sensitive beaks, locating grubs with the nostrils which are located at the tip. Once you have reaccustomed your eyes to daylight you can go on to see a number of raptors, waterfowl and reptiles, including the prehistoric tuatara and cheeky native parrot, the kea. The walk culminates with a large walk-in aviary where other rare birds can be spotted. Throughout the park there are also some fine examples of native trees.

❢ Beware – as you sip your coffee or stroll about town, you may be befriended, and highly embarrassed, by the town's summer mascot 'Wiki' – an underpaid and sweaty person in a kiwi suit

If you happen to be in Oto on the second Saturday in February you may catch the **Otorohanga Country Fair**, when the streets are decked with flower baskets and the gumboot-clad locals have fun parading down the street on floats. If you want to see some action at the **livestock saleyards** then Wednesday is the day to go. ▸▸ *For Sleeping and Eating, see page 241.*

Te Kuiti → *Phone Code: 07 Colour map 2, grid C2 Population 4500*

Te Kuiti is fairly unremarkable but is often used as a base for the Waitomo Caves, 19 km to the north. It is a small provincial town known as the sheep-shearing capital of New Zealand (witness the rather grotesque statue at the southern end of town). For a number of years it was home and refuge to the rebellious East Coast Maori chief Te Kooti who built the highly aesthetic **Te Tokanganui-o-noho marae** at the south end of Rora Street. Also worth a stop is the new and magnificent **Te Kuititanga-o-nga-Whakaaro Millennium Pavilion**, which is next to the railway, near the VIC on Rora Street. Its carvings, stained and sandblasted window designs are a great work of art. The big event of the year is the annual **Te Kuiti Muster** in April when the town

⁞ The Formation of Limestone Caves (Karst)

Limestone is a fossil rock made from the layered remains of countless marine animals. The limestone around Waitomo was therefore formerly the seabed, formed about 30 million years ago. Over the millennia these layers have been raised by the action of the earth's plates. In some places the limestone is over 200 m thick. Through its gradual uprising the limestone bends and buckles creating a network of cracks and joints. As rainwater drains into these cracks it mixes with small amounts of carbon dioxide in the air and soil forming a weak acid. This acid slowly dissolves the limestone and the cracks and joints widen. Over time small streams flow through converging cracks and eventually form underground caves.

Once these caves are created the same acidic water seeps from the cave walls or drips from the roof, leaving a minute deposit of limestone crystal. Slowly these deposits form stalactites, stalagmites and various other cave features. The size and rate of their formation depends on the rate of flow. Stalactites form from the drips falling from the ceiling of the cave and stalagmites grow up as the drips fall to the floor. When the two join, pillars are formed and when they spiral around they are called helictites.

Various minerals in the soil like iron oxide can add colouration to the formations. The growth rates of caves and limestone features in general vary considerably depending on topography, vegetation, and of course the weather. It is also important to realize that like everything else the caves have a 'lifespan', eventually collapsing to form gorges, holes or arches. The 'Lost World' near Waitomo is a fine example of part of a cave system that collapsed in on itself. These caves are also home to a unique range of plants and animals of which the New Zealand glow-worm is the most spectacular example.

celebrates its reputation with sheep-shearing championships, the 'bloated sheep race' and street celebrations and entertainment. There are some fine gardens in the area, outlined in the free '*King Country Gardens*' leaflet available from the VIC (see Information above). ▸▸ *For Sleeping and Eating, see page 242.*

Waitomo and the Caves → *Phone code: 07 Colur map 2, grid C2*

The district of Waitomo ('wai' water and 'tomo' hole), with its underground wonderworld of limestone caves, is the region's (and one of North Island's) biggest tourist attractions. Above ground, the typical farmland and the tourist village itself almost completely belie what lies below. Although only the geologically-trained eye would suspect it, there is an astonishing network of over 360 recorded caves in the area, the longest over 14 km. If you come here and have time, and a towel, you should pack a promise to yourself that you will try at least one of the amazing underground activities below and beyond the highly commercialized tour of the Glow-worm Caves. Wherever you go down there, it is pretty unforgettable.

Glow-worm Cave ① *T07-8788227, www.waitomocaves.co.nz Tours begin every half-hour from 0900-1700. Arrive early. Adult $25, child $12. Cave combo ticket (Glow-worm and Aranui) adult $45, child $22.50. Glow-worm Cave and Museum Combo, adult $26, child $12.* This is Waitomo's biggest attraction, but it is also the most commercial. From 0900-1700, lines of buses park outside and group after group are herded underground. The caves were first extensively explored in 1887 by a local Maori, Tane Tinorau, and English surveyor, Fred Mace. Further explorations eventually led to the opening of the caves to tourists in 1889. They now attract almost 250,000 visitors annually. Although the caves remain impressive, you cannot help feeling that you're on some Steven Spielberg film set, about to sit on Santa's knee and ask him for an extension to your MasterCard. Having said that, the highlight of the 45-minute tour – the silent, almost religious homage to see the glow-worm galaxy by boat – is incredible and well worth it, especially if you have never seen these amazing insect larvae before. The cave also has the obligatory shop and café attached.

Aranui Cave ① *A short 3 km drive west of the Glow-worm Cave near the Ruakuri Scenic Reserve. Tours are hourly from 1000-1500 and limited to groups of 20. Book at the Glow-worm Caves or VIC. Adult $25, child $12. Cave Combo Ticket (Aranui and Glow-worm) adult $45, child $22.50.* By contrast this cave is a far more realistic and sedate experience. Its discovery, by Maori hunter Ruruku Aranui, happened by accident in 1910. While out pig hunting, Rukuru's quarry disappeared into the small entrance, followed enthusiastically by his dog. After a year of further explorations and amidst much excitement, the caves were opened to tourists in 1911. Whilst underground, with effective lighting, the colour and variety of the stalactites and stalagmites, and the sound of a thousand drips of water, you can let your imagination run wild and emerge from the cavern satisfied that you have experienced a real limestone cave.

Sights and activities above ground A fine initiation and insight into the area can be found at the **Museum of Caves**. ① *In the VIC, T07-8787640, www.waitomo-museum.co.nz Daily 0830-1700, 1730 in summer. Adult $5, child, free (free entry with some activities).* Now considered the best limestone cave museum in the world, it offers interesting and highly informative displays about cave formation, the history surrounding the local caves and the natural history, including the spectacular and intriguing glow-worms. If you are claustrophobic and shudder at the very thought of going underground then there is also an audio visual display and even a fake cave to crawl through.

The **Waitomo Walkway** (three hours return), begins opposite the Glow-worm caves and follows the Waitomo Stream, taking in a number of limestone features before arriving at the **Ruakuri Scenic Reserve**. This reserve encompasses a short walk that is hailed as one of New Zealand's best. Although it does not deserve quite that billing, it is well worth it, with a circular track taking in interesting caves and natural limestone bridges, hidden amongst lush, native bush. At night, just before the path crosses the stream, you can see a small 'scintilla' of glow-worms. These are the only glow-worms you'll see around here for free! Take a torch.

Another popular walk is the **Opapaka Pa Walk** which takes about 45 minutes return and is 1 km east of Waitomo. The view is memorable and there are also some interesting interpretation points explaining about the *pa* and the medicinal uses Maori made of surrounding flora.

Woodlyn Park ① *Shows are staged on demand, book first. Adult $14, child $8. T07-8786666, woodlyn_park@xtra.co.nz* This is the above-ground entertainment 'must see' in Waitomo, if not the region. Like the Driving Creek railway in the Coromandel it is a typical example of Kiwi imagination, ingenuity and that simple 'can-do' mentality. The 'show', hosted by ex-shearer Barry Woods, is an informative, interactive (and at times comical) interpretation of old and modern-day Kiwi country life, and is very hard to describe. It involves a clever pig, a not so clever pig, an axe, a homemade ingenious computer, dogs, sheep, a 'kiwi bear' and a pair of underpants. Enough said – you'll just have to go and see for yourself! As the visitor book says – 'look out Bill Gates'. Also on the grounds Barry has built a large tyre-lined pond on which you can blat about in a jet boat for $45.

About ½ km north down Waitomo Valley Road from Woodlyn Park, in Waitomo Village, is the **Shearing Shed**, ① *T07-8788371, show held daily at 1245, free, shop open daily 0900-1630*, where cute Angora bunnies are cuddled to within an inch of their little lives and then given a short back and sides so that their highly-prized fur can be used for knitting. Still on the animal theme the **Altura Garden and Wildlife Park**, ① *4 km south of Waitomo village on Fullerton Rd, daily summer 1000-1600, $8, child $4*, provides a diversion if you have kids or wish to stay above ground. A range of animals are on display, with all the regulars, including emus and horses.

▶ *For Sleeping, Eating and other listings, see pages 242-243.*

Waitomo to Kawhia

The **Marokopa Road** that winds its way to Te Anga and the small coastal town of Marokopa, before heading north to Kawhia, is a long but pleasant trip with a number of worthwhile stops on the way. If you have your own wheels the first stop should be the slight diversion to see the impressive view looking back towards Waitomo from 3 km down Waipuna Road. The road is on the left, 11 km from Waitomo. Once back on the main road sit back and enjoy the scenery until you reach the **Mangapohue Natural Bridge Scenic Reserve**. Here a short streamside walk (10 minutes) will take you to an impressive natural limestone arch, complete with unusual stalagmites. This arch was once part of a large cave and it is hard to imagine that the rather inconspicuous little stream essentially created it all. About 5 km further on are the **Piripiri Caves**, accessed by a short but stiff climb up a boardwalk. These caves are in stark contrast to the well-lit, tourist-friendly offerings in Waitomo. They are dark and forbidding, and the path into them is steep and quite dangerous. If you are alone do not venture far and take a torch.

A little further on and about 35 km from Waitomo are the beautiful 32-m **Marokopa Falls** which have to rate as amongst the best in North Island, though due to their remote location they are not celebrated as such. A 15-minute walks descends to a lookout. If you go beyond the lookout to take photographs prepare to get very muddy. From the falls it is a short distance to the small settlement of **Te Anga** where there is a tavern selling lunches.

From Te Anga you have a choice of a very scenic road heading north to Kawhia or carrying on to the coast and **Marokopa**, a small, remote fishing village with black-sand beaches. From Marokopa it is possible to drive all the way to **Awakino**, another small coastal settlement, on the main SH3 New Plymouth road, but it is long, unsealed and fairly arduous. ▶ *For Sleeping, see page 242.*

● Sleeping

Te Awamutu *p237*
Te Awamutu and the southern Waikato is considered the farmstay capital of New Zealand and there are over 500 B&B and farmstay beds in the area. It is therefore a great place to experience New Zealand rural life. The VIC has listings of these and some modern local motels.

B-D Road Runner Motel and Holiday Park, *141 Bond Rd, T07-8717420.*

Otorohanga *p238*
Accommodation in Otorohanga is limited but the VIC can assist.

A Palm Court Motel, *Corner Clarke and Maniapoto Sts (SH3), T0800-686-764, T07-8738289. Modern, clean and comfortable.*

C-D Oto-Kiwi Backpackers, *1 Sangro Cres, T07-8736022, oto-kiwi@xtra.co.nz* Has a good reputation with facilities including campsites and internet. Also offers farm tours and trips, including to the caves and back.

D Otorohanga Kiwi Town Holiday Park, *right next to the Kiwi Park on Domain Dr, T07-8738279.* Basic and tiny and at night you can hear the kiwi screeching away, which is not (strangely) that unpleasant. The park's owner is very helpful and friendly and also runs a shuttle to the caves. There is a great Top Ten motor park at Waitomo (below).

The VIC lists local B&Bs and Farmstays.

C-D **Te Kuiti Camp Ground**, *Hinerangi St*, *T07-8788966*. Basic.

C-D **Casara Mesa Backpackers**, *Mangarino Rd, T07-8786697, casara@xtra.co.nz* Comfortable, has nice en suite doubles as well as the usual share options. Breakfasts, transport and bike hire available.

Waitomo *p239*

There is a wide range of accommodation in Waitomo Village, but in summer pre-booking is essential.

AL-D **Waitomo Caves Hotel** , *T07-8788240, www.waitomocaveshotel.co.nz* On the hill overlooking the village this historic hotel offers a wide range of comfortable standard, ensuite or family rooms and has a restaurant attached.

A **Abseil Inn B&B**, *T07-8787815, www.bnbnzhotels.com* The aptly-named Abseil Inn is up an 'exciting' driveway within walking (or climbing) distance of all amenities. The very friendly hosts are both cave guides, so are full of good tips. Recommended.

A **Te Tiro**, *970 Caves-Te Anga Rd, T07-8786328, www.waitomocavesnz.com* Two modern self-contained timber frame cottages (sleeping 1-5) in the picturesque hills 10 km west of Waitomo. Good value. A **Waitomo Express**, *T07-8786666, www.woodlynpark.co.nz* If it is the unusual you are looking for, look no further than Barry Woods at Woodlyn Park (1 km down Waitomo Valley Rd) and his converted train carriage or ex-WWII aircraft accommodation.

A-B **Glow-worm Motel**, *T07-8738882* and A-B **Caves Motor Inn**, *T07-8738109, are 8 km east of Waitomo Village at the junction with SH3.* Both are fine and the latter has a good restaurant.

B-D **Kiwi Paka YHA**, *behind the VIC and Tavern, T07-8783395, waitomo@kiwipaka-yha.co.nz* New hostel with a wide range of rooms in either lodge or chalets, from shared to double with private bathroom. Excellent café on site, TV lounge, internet. Recommended.

B-D **Juno Hall Backpackers**, *T07-8787649, www.junowaitomo.co.nz* This is a great log-cabin style hostel with a pool and log fire. Courtesy van. Home of Waitomo Caves Horse Treks (see Activities below).

Motorcamps

A-D **Waitomo Caves Top Ten Holiday Park**, *T07-8787639, www.waitomopark.co.nz* A modern, convenient and very friendly motorcamp right in the heart of the village. Spacious, great facilities including internet, pool and spa. Possibly the best showers of any park in the country! Recommended.

Waimoto to Kawhia *p241*

C-D **Lazy Hedgehog Backpackers**, *north of Te Anga, T07-8767508, Closed June-Oct.* Remote and relaxing, two doubles in an old colonial farmstead.

B-C **Camping ground**, *Marokopa, T07-876 7444.* Basic campsite with cottages, backpacker cabins, powered sites, a shop and café.

---

❷ Eating

Te Awamutu *p237*

$-$$ **Ngaroto Nurseries Café**, *208 Ngaroto Rd, 5 km to the north of town, T07-8715695. Daily 0930-1630.* Provides a pleasant rural lunch or coffee option.

$$ **Zest Café**, *201 Alexandra St, T07-8704055.* Locally recommended.

Otorohanga *p238*

$-$$ **Regent Café and Bar**, *Maniapoto St, next to the library, T07-8737370. Sun-Thu 0630-1700, Fri-Sat 0630-2100.* The most popular venue in a limited selection.

Te Kuiti *p238*

There are numerous rather forgettable cafés and eateries on Rora St and the best bet is:

$$ **Riverside Lodge Café Bar and Restaurant**, *east down King St, then turn right before the bridge, T07-8788027. Tue-Sun 0930-late.*

Waitomo *p239*

$$ **Waitomo Caves Hotel** *(see above).* Offers fairly good à la carte traditional cuisine.

$-$$ **Morepork Café** *at the Kiwi Paka Hostel (see above).* The best-value evening meal in town (especially pizza).

$$ **Caves Motor Inn**, *8 km east of Waitomo Village (see above).* Good value for dinner.

$$ **Roselands Restaurant**, *3 km from Waitomo Village up Fullerton Rd, T07-8787611. Daily (summer) 1100-1430.* Best place for lunch. They specialize in hearty BBQ lunches

and salads in a lovely garden setting. There are three other **cafés** in Waitomo run by the operators: the Waitomo Adventures' **Cavelands** *village centre*; Legendary Black Water Rafting Company's **Long Black**, *2 km east*, which does a fine breakfast for around $12; and**Glow-worm Caves Café** *just west of the village. All are open daily from 0800-1730 (later in summer).* **Waitomo Tavern**, *near the VIC, T07-8788448.* The place for cheap and basic pub grub and a pint with the locals. **Village store** next door to Waitomo Luminosa but you are advised to stock up before arriving. Open until 1900.

▲▲ Activities and tours

Te Awamutu *p237* **Castle Rock Adventures**, *1250 Owairaka Valley Rd, T0800-225462, www.castlerockadventure.co.nz* Offers a full day of climbing tuition for an affordable $150 (two people, per person). They also offer self-guided mountain bike hire for $35 (half-day, full-day $50), climbing and lodgings packages from $179. **Pirongia Horse Treks**, *T07-8719960. 1 hour, from $25.*

Waitomo Caves *p239* There is a wide range of choice and competition between operators is fierce; research the options carefully and take your time. Generally speaking with whatever activity or operator you choose, it will be money well spent. A combination of trips that offer value for money, a high level of safety and professionalism, as well as the best mix of activity is the **Lost World Epic** (if you can afford it) followed by the **Haggas Honking Holes**. Both are highly recommended. The activities last from 2-7 hours, are all great fun and usually involve a combination of abseiling, crawling, swimming and floating (note that the water is cold). A brief description of the main tours is listed here followed by a list of the relevant operators. Note that there are also price reductions for trip combinations with some also offering free museum entry. **Tumu Tumu Toobing**, *Waitomo Adventures, daily 1100 and 1530. $85. 4 hrs, about 2 hrs underground.* This trip, along with

the Haggas Honking Holes, is ideal if you are limited for time. The least strenuous of Waitomo Adventures' tours, it involves a highly entertaining walk, swim and float down an underwater stream with glow-worms and interesting rock formations. **St Benedict's Cavern**, *Waitomo Adventures, daily 0800, 1200 and 1600. $100. 3 hrs, about 2 hrs underground (minimum age 10 years).* This cave was discovered in 1962 but was only opened commercially in 2003. It is said to be the prettiest cave in the region and had parts of it christened 'The Hobbit Holes' long before *Lord of the Rings* was filmed in New Zealand. Your exploration of the cave will involve two abseils and a flying fox. Great fun. **Haggas Honking Holes**, *Waitomo Adventures, daily 1115 and 1615. $165. 4 hrs, about 2 hrs underground.* With a name like that who can resist? Slightly more full on, this trip involves an abseil, rock climbing and an intimate encounter with a waterfall, as well as all the usual crawling and scenery. **Lost World**, *Waitomo Adventures, daily 0700 and 1130, $225. 4 hrs.* This is a famous trip in a unique setting. It involves an incredible and mind-bending 100-m (300 ft) abseil into a huge and forbidding hole in the earth. Once negotiated, you follow the river for a short distance into a huge cave system and the aptly named, 'Lost World'. The atmosphere of the place is unforgettable. No abseiling experience necessary, and it is perfectly safe. **Lost World Epic**, *Waitomo Adventures, daily 1130 (min 2 people), dinner included. $355. 7 hrs, 5 hrs underground.* If you can afford it and are fit enough this has to be one of the best and most unusual full-day activity trips in the country, if not the world. It involves the same exciting descent into the gaping hole but is followed by the exhilarating and highly entertaining three-hour negotiation of the cave system and underground river. It involves walking, climbing, swimming, wading, jumping and even racing, with the final stage a quiet reflection on the trip under a galaxy of glow-worms, before emerging, like some intrepid latter-day explorer, at the river entrance. If you can splash out, it's a once-in-a-lifetime trip worth every cent. **Black Labyrinth** *Legendary Black Water Rafting Company, departs every 45 minutes from 0900-1630. 3 hours, 1 hr underground. $75.* Price includes museum entry, showers, soup and bagels. This trip involves floating down a subterranean river by a waterfall on the way and the cave formations and glow-worms.

Black Abyss, *Legendary Black Water Rafting Company, departs 0930, 1100, 1430. 5 hrs, 2 hr 30 min underground, $140.* Price includes museum, showers, soup and bagels.This trip is more adventurous and strenuous than the above, also involving a 30-m abseil.

Waitomo Down Under, *Several trips daily, 2-3 hrs, 1 hr underground. $35-$75 (includes free museum entry). Showers available.* A Maori-run operator offering three cave-tubing adventures similar to those above, with one trip involving a 50-m (150 ft) abseil into the impressive 'Baby Grand' cave.

Long Tomo Rafting, *Waitomo Wilderness Tours, daily, 5 hrs, about 2 hrs underground. $75 (includes free museum entry).* This fairly new adventure involves a 27-m (80 ft) abseil into a cave, then a float through a river system with a great display of glow-worms.

Spellbound, *Legendary Black Water Rafting Company, daily at 0900, 1215 or 1515. 2-3 hrs, about 2 hrs underground. Adult $40, child $20 (includes free museum entry).* Mainly eco-based adventure for those who want to remain dry, with a trip into a cave system.

Tour operators

KawhiaTrak-N-Paddle, *T07-9570002, departs Waitomo Mon/Wed/Sat at 1230.* A new outfit in the area offering a range of tramp, bike and kayak trips amidst the karst scenery west of Waitomo and around Kawhia on the coast. If you do not have your own transport this is an ideal way to explore this beautiful and lesser-known region of the Waikato, from $60 (day-trip) to $300 (2 days including accommodation).

Legendary Black Water Rafting Company, *2 km east of Waitomo Information Centre), T0800-228464, T07-8786219, www.blackwaterrafting.co.nz*

Waitomo Adventures Ltd, *next to the VIC, T0800-924866, T07-8787788, www.waitomo.co.nz*

Waitomo Big Red 4x4, *T07-8787640.* The local quad bike adventure company offering trips to suit all ages and experience; $70 for 2 hrs.

Waitomo Caves Horse Treks, *based at Juno Hall Backpackers, about 1 km east of Waitomo Village, T07-8787649.* Local character 'Juno' will take you on half-day, full-day or overnight trips through the surrounding countryside. These trips are fun and come recommended due to the views and varied limestone scenery. From $40. (Overnight trips possible).

Waitomo Down Under, *office next to the Information Centre), T07-8786577.*

Waitomo Tiki Tours, *book at the VIC.* Will pick you up from your accommodation and transport you to the Ruakuri Scenic Reserve, Marakopa Falls and the Mangapohue Natural Bridge (see below), from $50.

Waitomo Wilderness Tours, *T0800-228372, Simon_Hall@xtra.co.nz*

Waikato East → *Phone code: 07*

The almost English looking countryside of the Eastern Waikato is some of the richest in the nation and over the decades, many a fortune has been secured through its fertile soils. But other than the hot pools in Te Aroha, or horse studs surrounding the pleasant town of Cambridge, there was always a paucity of major tourist attractions. Until, that is, a character called 'Frodo' arrived. In 1999 at the behest of Lord of the Rings film director Peter Jackson, location researchers scoured the area for a plot of land that suited the universal image of Tolkien's 'Hobbiton', home of the Hobbits and central characters in the films, Frodo and Sam. Near the quiet agricultural service town of Matamata a discreet plot was secured and it proved to be the perfect setting for one of the most complex sets created for the film trilogy. Despite the fact almost nothing remains bar a few pieces of hardwood and the mere suggestion of a 'Hobbit Hole' it seems the film's bandwagon has come careering down the hill here more than anywhere in the nation and the much hyped 'Tours to Hobbiton' are proving that the Waikato soil can line pockets in other ways.

Turley-Murphy Connections are the main local bus operator with link services to and from Hamilton and Thames (via Paeroa) most days, T07-8848208, or T07-8848052 (VIC). **Intercity**, T09-9136100, offers services to Matamata from Hamilton or Tauranga stopping outside the Matamata VIC. Most of the main bus operators heading north or south on SH1 stop in Cambridge. For local bus information and Hamilton services contact **Cambridge Travelines**, T07-8277363.

Information

Paeroa VIC, ① *Belmont Rd, T07-8628636. Mon-Fri 0900-1700, Sat-Sun 0930-1430.* **Te Aroha VIC**, ① *in the original Te Aroha Hot Springs Domain ticket office at 102 Whitaker St, T07-8848052, infotearoha@xtra.co.nz   Mon-Fri 0900-1700 (ish), Sat-Sun 1000-1500.* There the under-resourced, friendly and enthusiastic Heath will provide all your local information needs, including maps and advice about accommodation. **Matamata VIC**, ① *45 Broadway, T07-8887260, matvin@nxhost.co.nz Mon-Fri 0830-1700, Sat-Sun 1000-1500.* They can assist with transport and accommodation enquiries or bookings, have internet facilities and also act as agents for the 'Hobbiton' tour. **Cambridge VIC**, ① *corner of Queen and Victoria Sts, T07-8233456, cvc@wave.co.nz Mon-Fri 0900-1700, 1000-1600 weekends.* They also take travel bookings and offer bike hire. Don't leave without the free 'Cambridge Welcomes You' booklet. **Tirau VIC**, ① *next to the Big Sheep in the Big Dog! T07- 8831202, www.tirauinfo .co.nz Daily 0900-1700.* They can assist with all enquiries and bookings. **Putaruru VIC**, ① *75 Tirau St, T07-8837284*, and **Tokoroa VIC**, ① *Leith Pl, T07-886 8872*. Both can assist with enquiries, bookings and details about local walks and attractions.

Paeroa → *Phone code 07 Colour map 2, grid B2*

Poor Paeroa. It's neither here nor there – and that seems to be its problem. People are always rushing through on their way to the Coromandel or the Bay of Plenty and rarely stop. And if they do, it is only very briefly, to get their photograph taken beside a huge plastic bottle of 'Lemon and Paeroa' (L&P), which is New Zealand's only national soft drink. Although not made in Paeroa, the additive spring water was discovered here in 1900 and made the place famous. This old, once thriving port, has little to offer, but don't write the place off entirely. The **Paeroa Museum**, on Belmont Road (Open Monday-Friday 1030-1500), does its best with displays about local history, bone china collections and some Maori artefacts. For view junkies, **Primrose Hill**, near the town centre, offers great views back across the Hauraki Plains – which, alas for poor Paeroa, are flat and boring! If you are in Paeroa on the third Sunday in February you will find the place pumping with the motorcycle extravaganza **'Battle of the Streets'**. This increasingly popular annual event attracts bikers from far and wide, but if the notorious gangs turn up, the event can end up being very aptly named. Lucky this does not coincide with the other major event in the same month – the **Pipe Band Tattoo** – the result would be Mad Max meets Braveheart.

Te Aroha   *Phone code 07 Colour map 2, grid B2 Population 4000*

In 1875 Te Aroha was little more than a single house in the shadow of the mountain, occupied by Irish pioneer Charlie Lipsey, and subsequently known as 'Lipseytown'. With the discovery of gold nearby in 1880 the settlement expanded, but only temporarily, as the mining returns proved relatively poor. Later, with the discovery of the hot soda water geyser, the Hot Springs Domain were born and today this remains the jewel in the crown of this mainly agricultural service town.

Sights There are two major attractions in Te Aroha, **Mount Te Aroha** and the **Hot Springs Domain**. As far as activity goes the two could hardly be more opposite, but the 5-6 hour return climb up the 950 m summit can be rewarded with a dip in the pools, providing the perfect marriage of the two. The mountain path is accessed at the rear of the Domain. The Whakapipi or Bald Spur Lookout about halfway up is easily reached after about 45 minutes and offers a fine view west. But, if you can, carry on to the summit and take in the spectacular 360° view, north across the Coromandel and south to the Bay of Plenty. For track information see *The Te Aroha Mountain Tracks* leaflet from the VIC.

The name of the town and the mountain means 'The Love' and comes from the story of a Bay of Plenty Maori chief who once made those utterings in relief after getting lost and seeing the glorious views south, homewards to his pa

On your return you can fall straight into the **Te Aroha Mineral Pools** ① *near the track entrance, T07-8848717, www.tearohapools.co.nz, daily 1000-2100/2200. From $10-$15, private pools available*. The pools, which were originally created in the late 1800s, are the world's only naturally flowing hot soda spa pools.

The **Wynborn Leisure Pools**, ① *T07-8844498, daily 1100-1900, $6, child $3*, are just a short distance further on. They offer both hot and cold outdoor pools and more modern renovated bathhouses. Next door you can complete your pampering with an hour-long massage and aromatherapy (from around $40). Behind the pools is the **Mokena Geyser**, which is one of very few soda water geysers in the world. Named after the Maori chief and benefactor of the land on which the Domain now stands, the geyser does its 3-m high thing about every half-hour.

Also on the Domain is the **Te Aroha Museum**, ① *T07-8844427. Open weekends 1300-1600, additional hours mid-summer. Donation*. Housed in the original bathhouse (which was once said to be possibly the most attractive building in the country and 'the sanatorium of New Zealand'), it now contains some interesting displays on the mining and agricultural development of the town. Oh, and two rather pretty toilets! Also of considerable historical interest, but not housed in the museum, is the 1712 Queen Anne Pipe Organ in **St Mark's Church,** ① *T07-8848052*. The town has a fairly unremarkable arts and crafts trail, and a gardens and heritage trail; ask for leaflets at the VIC. For a pleasant easy grade short walk there is the wildlife-rich **Howarth Memorial Wetlands Walk**, on the banks of the Waihou River. Ask at the VIC for directions and leaflet. ►► *For Sleeping, Eating and other listings, see page 248.*

Matamata → *Phone code: 07 Colour map 2, grid B2 Population: 8000*

Matamata lies in the heart of Waikato's rich and fertile agricultural landscape and is the epitome of affluent rural Kiwi life. Large ranches and spacious farmsteads would seem to suggest that the domestic and export agricultural worth of New Zealand is alive and well. Although it is pleasant enough, there was never a great deal here to attract the tourist – that is until a film about a little hobbit called Frodo came along!

Sights Long before *Lord of the Rings* hit the world's movie screens, a small plot of private farmland close to Matamata was being transformed into the magical village of **Hobbiton,** ① *tours depart the VIC at 1000, 1230 and 1500, T8886838, www.hobbitontours.com*, home to two of the film's key characters Frodo and Sam. It was felt that the surrounding countryside (which looks something akin to England's rural landscapes) was perfect for portraying 'The Shire' and the plot itself the ideal place to create the unique subterranean homes and busy gardens of Tolkien's Hobbiton. Although there has been a lot of hype about the set and the Hobbiton **tours** are up and running, you must be under no illusions as to what remains. As with all the 'Rings' sets throughout the country there were strict conditions in place to ensure almost all trace of the sets were removed. So now, in essence, a trip to Peter Jackson's Hobbiton is more an exercise in the imagination than reality – and an expensive one at that. There are some remnants, the highlight being an over-grown 'Hobbit Hole' with a plywood frontage but that is essentially it. So for Rings fanatics the $50 for the 2-hr tour may seem worth it, but for the average person it is highly debatable. Also for kids in particular it could really prove a disappoint ment. Until perhaps something credible or more meaningful is recreated at the former set, for most people the sign declaring Matamata as 'Hobbiton', across the road from the VIC is itself more of an attraction. Besides, it costs not a jot, creates a far more meaningful photograph and means the kids won't think Hobbiton was struck down with bubonic plague.

Elsewhere in Matamata (or Hobbiton – whatever you want to call it) a few of the old, low-key attractions remain. The historic and well-armoured landmark **Firth Tower**, on Tower Road, was built in 1882 by Yorkshireman Josiah Firth, and is the town's other main attraction. Why exactly it was so well fortified and therefore cost so much to build, is a matter of debate. The tower is the centrepiece of the historical **museum**, ① *T07-8888369, daily 1000-1600, $5, child $1*, which explains the intriguing history.

About 6 km from Matamata, the **Opal Hot Springs**, ① *T07-8888198*, are a popular spot, and compete with Te Aroha's Domain, with a pool complex of mineral and private spa pools. Back in town if you have an interest in pigeons **Keola Lofts**, ① *428 Hinuera Rd, T07-8881728, daily 1000-1600*, is a lively presentation about them.

Cambridge → *Phone code: 07 Colour map 2, grid B2*
Also on the Waikato River, 20 km south east of Hamilton on SH1, is the pleasant country town of Cambridge, a popular spot to stop at while heading south to Taupo or beyond. Recognized nationally as a centre for thoroughbred horse studs, antiques, arts and crafts, and known locally as 'the town of trees', Cambridge has a distinctly English feel.

Sights The VIC has some excellent leaflets outlining the numerous antique, art and craft outlets in the town. The most famous is the Cambridge **Country Store**, ① *92 Victoria St, T07-8278715, Mon-Sat 0830-1630, Sun 0900-1600*, which is housed in an old church. It has a wide range of crafts including native New Zealand wood pieces, ceramics, knitwear, Maori carvings, wines and foods. The All Saint's Café attached serves fresh snacks and home baking. For horse and pony fanatics the **Cambridge Thoroughbred Lodge**, ① *SH1, Karapiro, 6 km south of the town, T07-8278118, www.racing.net.nz/cambridge, daily 1000-1600, shows at 1030 Tue-Sun, afternoon by arrangement, $12, child $5*, puts on an entertaining hour-long 'New Zealand Horse Magic Show' where a range of horse breeds are shown and perform to order with much horsy humour and audience participation. For more thorough equestrian insight you might like to consider a Thoroughbred Stud Tour with the very vamperian sounding **Barry Lee Bloodstock Ltd**. ① *T07-8275910 (book at the VIC), the tour costs $120 for up to four people and lasts an hour taking in four studs, so it's good value.*

The small **Cambridge Museum** ① *Victoria St, open from 1000-1600 Tue-Sat*, is housed in the old courthouse. There are a number of good **walks** in and around Cambridge. For a short walk the **Te Koutu Lake** on Albert St is very picturesque, while the tramp up **Maungatautari Mountain** (at the terminus of Maungatautari and Hicks Road, off SH1, a few kilometres south of town) is a more strenuous affair, rewarded with fine views of the river and beyond. The mountain is also a very important spot for native wildlife after the creation of 'Warrenheip' – an ecological 'island' of native bush, fenced off and cleared of introduced predators before being left to regenerate and being restocked with native birds, including kiwi. ① *For more information, T07-8237455, www.maungatrust.org* ▸▸ *For Sleeping, Eating and other listings, see page 248.*

Tirau → *Phone code: 07 Colour map 2, grid B2*
Tirau is at the junction of SH1 and SH27 which are the two main routes south – making it a popular coffee stop. The highlight of the town is not hard to miss and comes in the form of a giant corrugated iron sheep and a dog on the Main Road. The sheep houses the **Big Sheep Wool Gallery**, ① *T07-8831954*, which sells an array of New Zealand-made woolly products and kitsch sheep souvenirs. There is a range of other tourist-orientated shops on Main Street selling various New Zealand products.

Tokoroa is a major forestry base and takes its name from a Maori chief who was killed during the Maori Land Wars of the mid 1800s. The main attraction here (other than the toilet or a coffee) are the various walks and mountain biking tracks in the surrounding forest. **Hatupatu Rock** is an interesting place steeped in Maori legend. In Putaruru the **Timber Museum,** ⓘ *3 km south of the village on SH1, T07-8837621, daily 0900-1600,* is the main draw. It has a steam engine and some ancient native logs.

● Sleeping

Te Aroha *p245*
Accommodation is fairly limited in Te Aroha.
AL Aroha Mountain Lodge, *5 Boundary St T07-8848134.* B&B right next to the spas and starting point for the mountain walks.
B Te Aroha Motel, *102 Whitaker St, T07-8849417.* The town's lone motel.
B-D Te Aroha Holiday Park, *217 Stanley Rd, T07-8849567.* Basic facilities.
C-D Te Aroha YHA Hostel, *Miro St, T07-8848739.* Friendly hostel where cooking is a speciality.

Cambridge *p247*
L Houseboat, *T07-8272195, www.houseboatescape.co.nz.* For something different consider a self-drive houseboat, from $600 for two nights excluding fuel.
L Thornton House B&B, *2 Thornton Rd, T07-8277567, www.thorntonhouse.co.nz* A very tastefully renovated historic villa, with 2 well-appointed rooms. Centrally located.
A Birches B&B, *Maungatautari Rd, T07-827 6556.* Farmhouse in a quiet country setting just south of town. In-house or separate cottage options, open fire and spa-bath.
A Erindale Cottages, *42 Queen St, T07- 8273- 369.* Lovely, central, self-contained cottage.
A Riverside Motor Lodge, *27 Williamson St, T07-8276069.* Perhaps the best motel in town.
B-D Cambridge Country Lodge, *20 Peake Rd (north off SH1), T07-8278373.* Self-contained and backpacker bedrooms in rural setting, friendly, good facilities and bike hire available.
B-D Cambridge Motor Camp, *32 Scott St, T07-8275649.* Basic but well-located.

Tokoroa *p248*
B-D Tokoroa Motor Camp and Backpackers, *22 Sloss Rd, T07-8866642.* If you are looking to park up for the night this is your best bet.

ⓕ Eating

Te Aroha *p245*
Two places stand out:
$$ Café Banco, *174 Whitaker St. Wed-Sun 1000-2300.* Stylish place offering good value breakfast, lunch and dinner. It displays interesting antiques and art.
$$ Ironique Café and Bar, *159 Whitaker St, T07-8848489. Open daily.* Serves up a traditional style à la carte menu, light lunches and good coffee.

Cambridge *p247*
$$ Souter House, *19 Victoria St, T07-8273610.* Good for dinner
$$ Alphaz, *72 Alpha St, T07-8276699. Closed Mon.* Worth trying for lunch and dinner.
$-$$ The Gallery, *64c Victoria St, T07-8230999.* Good for a fine breakfast.

Tirau *p247*
The popular eateries and coffee stops are:
$-$$ Alley Cats, *Main Rd, T07-8831107.*
$$ Loose Goose, *7 Main Rd, T07-8831515. Closed Tue.* A new café/restaurant serving gourmet food; and
$$ Oxford Landing, *Main Rd, T07-8831534.*

▲ Activities and tours

Cambridge *p247*
'Camjet', *T0800-226538, www.camjet.co.nz $50, child $35.* For a spin (quite literally) down the river.
The Boatshed Café, *on the shores of Lake Karapiro, south on SH1 then right on Gorton Rd and right again on Amber, T07-8278286, www.theboatshed.net.nz* Kayak hire (3 hr from $20).

ⓖ Directory

Internet Te Aroha Library, *Rewi St, T07-8895689.* All Saints Café, *Cambridge.*

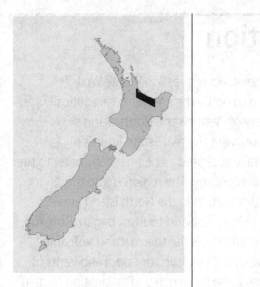

The Bay of Plenty

Introduction

The Bay of Plenty. The obvious question – is it? Well, if statistics are anything to go by the answer is categorically yes. By population, the Bay of Plenty is the North Island's fastest-growing region, with the real estate figures of Tauranga now generally accepted as being a barometer to the health of the national economy. The region is also the most-visited tourist destination in the North Island and is where the very idea of New Zealand tourism began. **Rotorua**, or 'Roto-Vegas' as it is known, is the thermal and **volcanic capital** of New Zealand, with geysers, hot pool and vents of bubbling mud. Rotorua also has a rich and fascinating human history. **Tauranga** is another tourist hot spot. Its sunny climate and beaches, as well as its proximity to Coromandel and Auckland, attract visitors by the busload. Even the cruise ships have started visiting this busy port. The outlying towns, too, get their turn on the tourist merry-go-round. Proud **Whakatane** offers not only a lovely coast and congenial atmosphere but also its own distinct attractions. One minute you can be swimming with **dolphins**, the next reeling in a marlin, or staring down the steaming barrel of **White Island's** volcanic crater.

★ Don't miss...

❶ Touring the incredible **thermal reserves** around Rotorua, not forgetting **Wai-O-Tapu** or **Hell's Gate**. Listen to the gentle fizzing of the 'Champagne Pool' or the therapeutic melody of bubbling mud, page 261.

❷ Cruising or fishing on **Lake Rotorua** or Rotoiti, page 253; rafting the **Okere Falls**, page 270; white-water sledging, page 270; mountain biking in the **Whakarewarewa Forest Park**, page 270; or trying out the infamous 'luge', page 264.

❸ Seeing the trout 'sub-aqua' or the huge, octogenarian native eels at **Rainbow Springs**, page 263.

❹ Seeing the **Tarawera Falls** and walking up the Tarawera River to Lake Tarawera – the best walk in the region (if not the North Island), page 260.

❺ Comparing cameras and doing the tourist thing at the **Agrodome** 'Sheep-Shearing and Sheep Dog Show', page 263.

❻ Experiencing Maori culture, song, dance and food on the **Tamaki Twilight Cultural Tour** and *hangi*, page XXX.

❼ Dolphin watching or visiting the active **White Island** volcano from the congenial seaside town of **Whakatane**, page 282.

The Bay of Plenty Introduction

Rotorua → *Phone code: 07 Population: 70,000, Colour map 2, grid C3*

Rotorua – alias 'Sulphur City' – is the 'thermal and volcanic capital' of New Zealand; a place that can sometimes be smelled before it's seen, though they say you get used to it. Of all the places in 'The Bay of Plenty' nature has indeed given Rotorua 'plenty'. The natural thermal wonders first attracted the Maori in the 14th century and later the Europeans, though nature has not always been so kind. The violent eruption of Tarawera in 1886 led to the loss of 150 lives.

Rotorua is deserving of its 'most visited' tourist status. The city and the region probably offer more unusual sights and activities than anywhere else in New Zealand. And although, like Taupo, it is particularly famous for its thermal and volcanic features, lakes and fishing, the region offers a multitude of other things to do and see. Here you can join in a Maori concert or gorge yourself at a Maori hangi (feast), throw yourself down a 7 m waterfall in a raft, jump out of planes, bike, walk or shop till you drop and then 'take the cure' in one of the city's many hot thermal pools.

Getting there

By air Rotorua is served by **Air New Zealand Link** with daily flights to Auckland, Wellington and other principal domestic centres, To800-737000, www.airnewzealand.co.nz The airport is on the eastern shores of Lake Rotorua, about 10 km from the town centre, To7-3486299. **Super Shuttle**, To7-3493444, and the main taxi companies provide transfers to and from the airport (shuttle $12 one way, taxis about $17).

By rail Rotorua is not directly accessible by rail but **TranzScenic** do offer a daily rail coach link from Hamilton, from $50, To800-843596

By car Rotorua is reached via SH4, which branches off SH1 at Tirua from the North and Taupo from the South. It is a major destination on the sign-posted 'Thermal Explorer Highway' tourist route. **Intercity, Newman's** and **Guthrey's** buses service Rotorua daily and stop outside the VIC on Fenton St. The **Waitomo Wanderer** runs a daily service to the Waitomo Caves (see page 239). It departs Rotorua at 0730 and arrives in Waitomo at 1000, departing Waitomo again at 1545. To7-3492509, To7-34-85179, www.waitomotours.com There is a specialist travel centre within the VIC which handles all enquiries and bookings, To7-3485179, info@tourism.rdc.govt.nz

Getting around

Around town **Ritchies**, To7-3492994, is the local bus company, the main stop being on Pukuatua St. Several local shuttles vie for business in providing daily transportation to the Tamaki Maori Village, Waimangu Volcanic Valley, Waiotapu Thermal Wonderland and Waikite Valley Thermal Pools, with scheduled and flexible non-scheduled pick-ups and drop-offs available, from around $22 return. Contact the VIC for the latest operators, To800-7686782. The **Santa Fe Shuttle**, To7-3457997, leaves for most major attractions several times daily and the fare usually includes entry.Taxis: To7-3481111. ▶▶ *For specific tour buses see Activities and tours, page 268.*

Information and orientation

Tourism Rotorua Travel and Information, ① *1167 Fenton St, To7-3485179, www.rotoruanz.com Daily 0800-1800.* This is one of the oldest and busiest tourist offices in the country. It is the principal base for all local information, as well as the bus arrival and departure point. The in-house travel centre administers local and national bus, coach, air and rail ticketing. There is a currency exchange office (*0800-1730*), toilets, showers, a shop, a café and even a hot thermal footbath outside. **DoC** information is held at the VIC and they also have offices, ① *1144 Pukaki*

① *just a short distance south of the VIC at 1225 Fenton St, T07-3491845, Mon-Sat 0900-1800,* offers a comprehensive range of local and national maps and guides.

History

Ohinemutu on the shores of Lake Rotorua and Whakarewarewa to the south of the present city were first settled by Maori from the Arawa Canoe around the 14th century. These early Maori were quick to utilise the many benefits offered by the local thermal activity and for almost four centuries they thrived happily and peace reigned. Then, in 1823, the Te Arawa were invaded by the Ngapuhi chief Hongi Hika from Northland. Despite the fact that Hika's warriors were armed with European muskets the Te Arawa, determined to defend their little piece of paradise, put up a valiant fight, inflicting heavy losses on the intruders.

By the 1840's the first missions had been established on the shores of Lake Rotorua and Lake Tarawera. However, their sanctity was soon disrupted by more inter-tribal warfare, this time from the Waikato Maori to the west. During the Waikato campaigns and Maori King Movements of the New Zealand Wars, the Te Arawa elected to side with the New Zealand Government and, in 1864, a force of East Coast Ngati Porou attempted to cross Arawa lands to assist the Waikato tribes, only to be repelled by the Te Arawa and sent packing. This led to further reprisals from the Waikato tribes, which were subsequently repelled with Government assistance. It was not until the end of the New Zealand Wars that any substantial European settlement began. With the obvious attraction of both the aesthetic and therapeutic qualities of the thermal sights and waters of the region, the population rapidly expanded and tourism flourished. With the eruption of Mount Tarawera in 1886, settlement was temporarily halted, but as confidence returned so did the tourists and, now over a century on, that attraction and popularity continues.

Sights

Lake Rotorua

Lake Rotorua is the largest of the 17 lakes in the Rotorua thermal region, covering an area of 89 sq km and sitting at a height of 279 m above sea level. It is, as you might expect, a flooded volcanic crater. A feature of many of the launch trips based on the city's lake front is the bush-clad nature reserve of Mokoia Island, scene of the classic love story of the Arawa princess Hinemoa and her suitor Tutanekai. But Mokoia was also the site for far less romantic encounters. During the invasion of Hongi Hika's warriors in 1823, the Arawa *pa* on Mokoia was sacked, but having sustained such heavy losses, the invaders could not hold what they had temporarily conquered. Today the lake is a top venue for recreational activities including boating, water skiing, and above all, trout fishing. For cruising on Lake Rotorua see 'Activities and tours' below.

On the northern shores of the lake are the **Hamurana Gardens**, ① *733 Hamurana Rd*, where the largest spring in the North Island erupts with a beautiful clarity and a volume of over one million gallons an hour. The gardens also feature a tract of giant redwoods and although the gardens are no longer an official tourist attraction the river is worth seeing if you are in the area.

Ohinemutu

Situated on the lakefront within the city, and reached via narrow streets lined with steaming drains, is the former Maori settlement and thermal area of Ohinemutu. The focal point of the village is the **Tamatekapua Marae**, a beautifully carved *whare-runanga* (meeting house), erected in 1939. It is often used as the focus for Maori events and performances, and despite its fairly modern renovation, still contains carvings from the 1800s. It was named after the head of the original Arawa canoe which first made landfall in the Bay of Plenty in the 14th century. Just opposite the *marae* is the Tudor-style **St. Faith's Church**, ① *daily 0800-1700, free*, built in 1910. Its interior pillars, beams, rafters and pews are beautifully carved with Maori designs and on a sandblasted window overlooking the lake a 'Maori Christ' is portrayed,

Rotorua

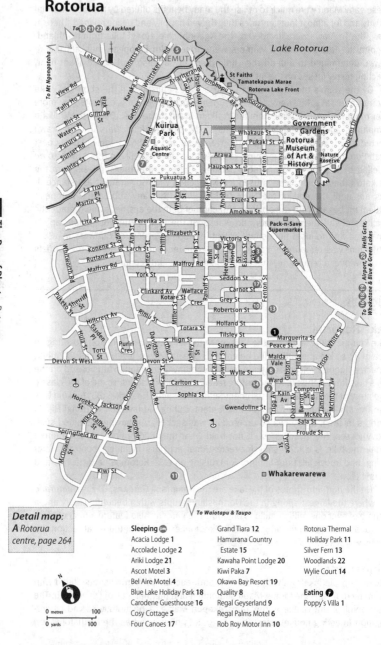

Detail map:
A *Rotorua centre, page 264*

0 metres 100
0 yards 100

dressed in a *korowai* (chief's cloak). Buried in the graveyard are many notable members of the Arawa tribe, among them the only European to be admitted to full chieftainship, the colonial force officer Captain Gilbert Mair (1843-1923). He twice saved the Arawa from inter-tribal attacks. It is interesting to note that the graves are built above ground to protect them from the thermal activity and intense heat. Had they been buried in the conventional style they would have been cooked before the last sod of earth had been replaced. At the entrance of the churchyard is a four-gabled canopy under which a bust of Queen Victoria used to sit. It was presented to the Arawa in 1870 by Prince Albert, the first member of the British royal family to visit New Zealand. The bust recently disappeared in mysterious circumstances. All around the village you can see quite intense thermal activity, that was enjoyed and utilised by the first Maori settlers. There is still a boiling pool near the church that is frequently used for boiling eggs and cooking meat – and perhaps the occasional member of the British monarchy.

Rotorua Museum of Art and History

ⓘ *To7-3494350, www.rotoruamuseum.co.nz Daily 0930-1700 in winter, 0930-1800 in summer. Adult $10, child $4. Guided tours daily at 1100 and 1400. The museum has a shop and a café.* The Rotorua Museum of Art and History is housed in the once-famous **Bath House**. Built in 1908, it was designed along the lines of the European spas and attracted hundreds of clients the world over who hoped to take advantage of the thermal water's therapeutic and curative powers. At the time the soothing waters were thought to be a cure for any ailments, as diverse as anxiety and even obesity. Its popularity in 'taking the cure', together with the added volcanic features and attractions surrounding the city, made the Bath House the focus of the New Zealand Government's first major investment in the new concept of tourism. In one wing of the museum you can see some of the original baths, changing rooms and equipment, together with photographs. Given the rich local Maori history it is not surprising to find a superb collection of Te Arawa *taonga* (treasures) which contrast interestingly with collections of modern artworks by local Maori artists. There are also displays that feature the great Tarawera Eruption of 1886 as well as temporary, national touring exhibitions and more modern dynamic offerings. One display not to miss is the excellent audio-visual display entitled *Rotorua Stories*. It screens every 20 minutes and is a 15-minute introduction to the great historical legends and stories of the area. It comes complete with shuddering pews during the fascinating account and depiction of the Tarawera eruption.

A short distance from the museum are the **Blue Baths** (Blueys). ⓘ *To7-3502119. Daily 1000-1600 in winter, pools open till 2100 in summer. From $5, child $2.* Built in the Spanish Mission style during the Great Depression of 1933, the pools soon flourished as one of the major social and recreational venues in the city, and were one of the first public baths to offer 'mixed' bathing. Sadly, due to competition elsewhere and social change, the Blueys' popularity declined and they were finally closed in 1982. Still much loved, they were restored and re-opened in 1999 as functional hot pools, museum and tearooms. There is an entertaining video presentation relating the story of the pools, and the museum displays are imaginatively set in the former male and female changing room cubicles. You can combine a visit to the museum with a dip in the hot pool or a cuppa in the faithfully-restored tearooms.

Behind the Blue Baths is the highly popular **Polynesian Spa** complex. ⓘ *To7-3481328, www.polynesianspa.co.nz Daily 0630-2300. From $12, child $4.* Rain or shine this is a Rotorua 'must do' and, although often very busy, it is a delight. There is a luxury spa complex and hot springs and pools, private spa pools, a family spa, shop and café. A range of massage treatments are also available. If you cannot afford the luxury spa then the therapeutic adult hot springs will not be a disappointment. Set outside in timber-style tubs, the springs overlook the lake and range in temperature from 33°C to 43°C. It is a great place to ease the aches and pains of your far more active tourist pursuits and a fine place to mix with the locals, though the omnipresent tour groups can make it all very chaotic. The best times to go are at lunch and dinnertime when the tour buses are elsewhere.

Just west of Ohinemutu are the elegant and beautifully-maintained **Government Gardens**. There, as a backdrop to the museum, are the well-manicured bowling greens and croquet lawns, ponds and scented roses, which create a distinctly Edwardian, colonial atmosphere.

Other than the obvious attractions, the Government Gardens are well worth a thorough investigation and a further muse. If you follow the road around the lakeshore you will encounter a thriving **nature reserve** complete with hungry swans and a colony of prehistoric-looking pied shags.

Whakarewarewa

'Whaka' (pronounced 'Fuckka') is the most famous and historic of the region's thermal reserves, with New Zealand's largest geyser, the much celebrated **Pohutu**, being its star attraction. As well as the great spout there are also boiling pools, silica terraces and the obligatory bubbling mud. Also attached to the complex are the **Rotowhio Marae**, the **Mai Ora Village** (a replica of the former Te Arawa Maori settlement) and the modern **Maori Arts and Crafts Institute.**

Although worth the visit to see ol'Pohutu doing its thing and the many interesting Maori aspects, Whaka suffers a little from tourist overkill and is by far the most commercial of the thermal reserves. On entering you have the option of self-guided or a (recommended) Maori-guided tour around the reserve. A series of paths branch out from the main visitors' block and take in a strictly 'showpiece' nocturnal kiwi house before passing the large and at times, fairly inert Ngamokaiakoko ('Leaping Frog') mud pool, before the path delivers you at the geyser formations. There used to be many geysers in Whaka (about 60), but now there are essentially two. The famed Pohutu or 'Big Splash' goes off like a broken water hydrant 10-25 times a day (more recently for days on end), to a height of over 30 m, while the more impotent Prince of Wales (sorry Charles) geyser nearby, is less spectacular. The tracks then negotiate the other small mud pools and volcanic features of the valley before arriving back near the entrance and the Rotowhio *Marae*. There are many features in this functional *marae*, including a banquet and weaving house and a *waka* (canoe).

The *marae* also hosts daily **cultural performances** which feature a traditional *powhiri* (welcome), demonstration of the *taiaha* (warrior's weapon), *haka* (posture dance), *poi* (women's dance) and a range of traditional Maori songs. A longer performance in the evenings includes a *hangi* (feast). The **Maori Arts and Crafts Institute** ⓘ *T07-3489047, www.nzmaori.co.nz, 0800-1800, guided tours (optional) departs hourly from 0900-1700, $18, child $9*, was established in 1963 to ensure that the traditional artist aspects of Maori culture are not lost. A viewing platform allows visitors to see students at work in the woodcarving studio before taking them through other galleries and display areas where pieces of completed work can be seen and are for sale. There is also a shop and a café on site. The Whakarewarewa Valley is about 3 km south of the city centre along Fenton Street (just head for the steam). There are daily cultural performances at 1215 and 1300 and in the evening ('Mai Ora'- 'Essence of Maori' performance, which costs $70, child $40, starts 1815).

Whakarewarewa Forest Park

On the southern outskirts of Rotorua is the recreational playground of the Whakarewarewa Forest Park, well known for its excellent **walking** and **mountain biking** opportunities. The best way to choose from those opportunities is to visit the **Fletcher Challenge Information Centre,** ⓘ *along Long Mile Rd, off Tarawera Road, which in turn is just off SH30 heading east, T07-3462082. Mon-Fri 0830-1800,*

It has a number of interesting interpretative displays as well as all track information and colour-coded track maps. The walks range from 20 minutes to eight hours, with the shortest taking in a tract of giant Californian **Redwoods** (along Long Mile Road) and the longest taking in the shores of the Blue and Green Lakes. For mountain bike hire see 'Activities and tours' section below.

Kuirua Park

If you arrive in the city from the SH4 north, the steam that issues from the thermal features in Kuirua Park will be your first sight and smell (if not taste) of the city's volcanic activity. This park is 25 ha with gardens linked by tracks to a number of low-key thermal pools and features, as well as the cutely named 'Toot and Whistle' miniature steam railway, which is perfect for kids. There is also a miniature golf course and the city's **Aquatic Centre**. ① *0600-2100*. While in the vicinity of Kuirua take a short drive down **Tarawera Road**. On the left heading south, you will see two fenced-off sections that are billowing steam. These were – believe it or not – former properties until 1998, when new boiling springs literally erupted in the driveway. Under a system of Government volcanic damage compensation the families were forced to move and the land given back to nature!

If you want a great view of the city and the region as a whole, then **Mount Ngongotaha** to the west of the city is easily accessible by car. From SH5 heading north, take Clayton Road at the crossroads with the Old Taupo Road. After about 3 km Mountain Road is signposted off Clayton to the right. The Aorangi Peak Restaurant is near the summit. ►► *For Sleeping, Eating and other listings, see pages 265-272.*

Around Rotorua

Blue and Green Lakes → *Phone code: 07 Colour map 2 grid C3*

Southeast of the city, off SH30, Mount Tarawera Road takes you to some of the most celebrated lakes of the Rotorua region. The road runs adjacent to the Whakarewarewa Forest Park, before arriving at the Blue and Green Lakes. Blue Lake (Tikitapu) has a very cheery atmosphere and is used for boating and swimming and walking, with a very pleasant track that circumnavigates its shores, while Green Lake (Rotokakahi) is *tapu* (sacred) and off limits to all recreational activities.

Buried Village → *Santa Fe Shuttles offer a shuttle service from Rotorua several times daily for $30 return including entry, T07-3457997.*

Past these two contrasting lakes the road enters the Te Wairoa Valley, home of the Buried Village. Prior to the 1886 eruption, the Te Wairoa Valley was the focus for Maori-guided tourist trips to see the pink and white terraces at the foot of Mount Tarawera. The sudden and violent eruption of Tarawera on the evening of 10th June 1886 was witnessed by the tourists staying at the village hotel. Sadly for them and many of the settlers, this sight of the mountain was their last. Much of the area, the village and its hotel were laid waste with a blanket of rock and ash falls. Interestingly it was the Maori *whare* (houses) that fared better due to their stronger construction and steeply sloping roofs. There is a small and fascinating **museum**, ① *T07-3628287, www.buriedvillage.co.nz daily 0900-1700, adult $16, children free,* which relates the sorry tale, complete with everyday items excavated from the ash almost a century later. Of particular interest is the treatment of the poor Maori elder who, hours before the eruption, made the prediction that it was about to blow. After the interior displays of the museum a pleasant walk takes you around the remains of some of the original buildings. To complete the walk you have the option of a 10-minute extension to see the 80-m Te Wairoa Falls. You can take a guided or a self-guided tour of the village. There's also the obligatory shop and café on site – not to mention the odd ghost.

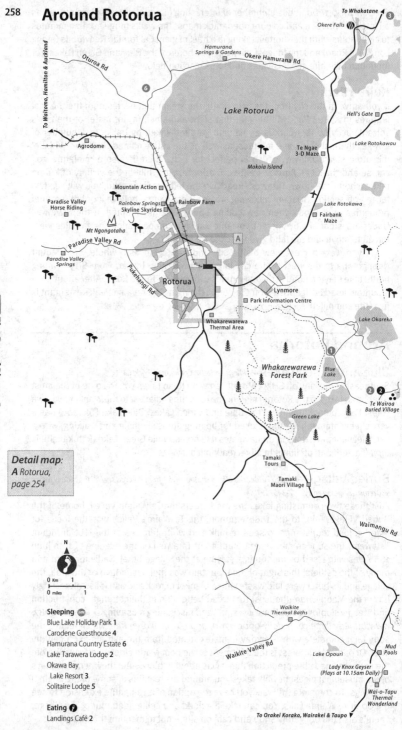

The Bay of Plenty Rotorua

Detail map:
A Rotorua,
page 254

Oturoa Rd

To Waitomo, Hamilton & Auckland

To Whakatane

Okere Falls

Hamurana
Springs & Gardens

Okere Hamurana Rd

Lake Rotorua

Hell's Gate

Lake Rotokawau

Agrodome

Te Ngae
3-D Maze

Mokoia Island

Mountain Action

Rainbow Springs
Skyline Skyrides

Rainbow Farm

Lake Rotokawa

Fairbank
Maze

Paradise Valley
Horse Riding

Mt Ngongotaha

Paradise Valley Rd

Rotorua

Paradise Valley
Springs

Pukehangi Rd

Lynmore

Park Information Centre

Whakarewarewa
Thermal Area

Lake Okareka

*Whakarewarewa
Forest Park*

Blue
Lake

Te Wairoa
Buried Village

Green Lake

Tamaki
Tours

Tamaki
Maori Village

Waimangu Rd

N

0 Km   1
0 miles   1

Waikite
Thermal Baths

Waikite Valley Rd

Lake Opouri

Mud
Pools

Lady Knox Geyser
(Plays at 10.15am Daily)

Wai-o-Tapu
Thermal
Wonderland

To Orakei Korako, Wairakei & Taupo

Sleeping
Blue Lake Holiday Park 1
Carodene Guesthouse 4
Hamurana Country Estate 6
Lake Tarawera Lodge 2
Okawa Bay
  Lake Resort 3
Solitaire Lodge 5

Eating
Landings Café 2

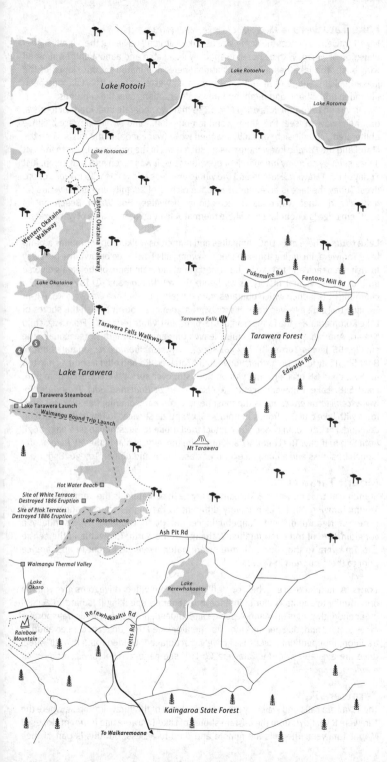

Lake Tarawera is almost the same size as Lake Rotorua and lies at the slightly higher elevation of 315 m. With a shoreline sparsely populated and almost entirely rimmed with bush, the lake has a pleasant atmosphere, dominated by the slopes of the jagged volcanic ridge of Mount Tarawera on its western shore. The lake has been altered in both shape and depth by Tarawera's eruptions over the centuries.

It was on Lake Tarawera on 31 May 1886 that two separate boat loads of tourists, on their way to see the then world-famous Pink and White Terraces (since obliterated), caught sight of a fully-manned *waka* (war canoe) in the mists. Both the Maori and the *Pakeha* knew there was no such *waka* in the region and, due to the fact it was seen by so many independent eyewitnesses, it was taken as a bad omen. Just 11 days later Tarawera erupted and the whole area was laid waste with the loss of 150 lives. Today the lake is an almost deceptive picture of serenity and is the venue for fishing and other water-based recreational activities. **Hot Water Beach** on its southern edge is a popular spot where thermal activity creates an area of warm water.

Lake tours There are 3 DoC campsites and numerous walking opportunities around Lake Tarawera, including the excellent Tarawera Falls Track (see below). The best way to visit the beach and to take in the atmosphere and learn more of the area's diverse and, at times, violent history, is on board the **MV Reremoana**, ① *T07-3628595*, a charming little launch which operates from the jetty just off Lake Tarawera Rd. A 2-hr Eruption Trail cruise leaves daily at 1100 with a 30-min stopover to visit the shores of Lake Rotomahana – the former site of the 'pink' and 'white terraces'). From $27, child $13.50. Another 45-min scenic cruise leaves on demand until dusk (seasonal). The smaller **SS James Torrey**, ① *T07-3628698, www.steamboat.co.nz*, operates out of Boat Shed Bay just a bit further along Mount Tarawera Rd and offer a short 45 min trip for $16, child $8 or a 3-hr trip with an hour stopover at Hot Water Beach from $36, child $18. **Lake Tarawera Scenic**, ① *also based at Boatshed Bay, T07-3628080, www.scenictarawera.co.nz*, is the most flexible company offering free pick-ups from town with lake cruises (from 3 hr from $48) or shuttle services to Hot Water Beach on demand. For Canadian canoe hire contact the **Carodene Guesthouse** (see page 267), from $50 half-day. The **Landing Café**, opposite the jetty, is part of the *MV Reremoana* launch business and a fine place for breakfast, lunch and dinner, T07-3628595.

Mount Tarawera

Standing at 1,111 m, with a 6 km converging gash of craters, is the dormant volcano Mount Tarawera. In looks it is very different to the higher, classic snow-capped cones of Ngauruhoe and Ruapehu in central North Island. It is essentially a conglomerate of three mountains: **Wahanga** to the north, **Ruawahia** in the centre and **Tarawera** to the south. All three were naturally very different in appearance prior to their eruption in 1886.

Tours A number of scenic helicopter flights and four-wheel drive tours give you the opportunity to see its colourful interior, but generally speaking it is hard to access independently and is on Maori Reserve Land. Indeed, there is no public transport for miles around and, due perhaps more to operator greed than upkeep, conservation or tradition, independent access is actively discouraged. Guided tours by four-wheel drive are available with Mt Tarawera Co Ltd, see page 270. ▸▸ *For mountain activity operators see page 268.*

Tarawera Falls

The Tarawera Falls and walkway are set in the heart of the Tarawera Forest, where the Tarawera River flows from the eastern shores of Lake Tarawera and northern slopes of Mount Tarawera. The falls are remote and hard to access, but this is part of their charm, and the effort is definitely worthwhile. The walkway, complete with waterfalls, a disappearing river, beautiful native bush and swimming holes, has to rate as one of North Island's best short to medium walkways. The falls are of particular interest because the river first disappears underground before reappearing from a sheer cliff face. The track can be tackled either from above or below the falls and is accessed from east or west.

Getting there There are three or four ways to get there. By car it is a 70-km drive (one way) from Rotorua via SH30 and the forestry township of Kawerau. Although the roads through the forest are very straight, do not go fast, and keep your headlights on at all times. Once you reach the falls car park it is a 10-minute walk to the base of the falls past the crystal clear waters of the river. From the falls the track then zig-zags up behind them, through native bush, with huge ponga ferns before arriving at the point where the river disappears underground. Then you can continue past a series of other beautiful falls and a swimming hole before emerging at the head of Lake Tarawera. The walk to the Lake is about 4 km (2½ hours one way). You can also access the track via the Eastern Okaitania Walkway, but in total this involves an enjoyable 2-day tramp. The falls are also part of the agenda on the recommended full-day tour with Tekiri Treks, T07-3455016 (see Activities and tours, page 268). You may also be able to negotiate being dropped off and picked up by launch or charter boat from Lake Tarawera (see above).

Information To access the Forest you will need a permit, which is obtained from the **Fletcher Challenge Forests Redwood Grove Visitors' Centre,** ① *Long Mile Rd, Rotorua, T07-3234599, (free)* or from the **Kawerau Information Centre** ① *On Plunket St. Kawarau, T07-3237550. Mon-Fri 0830-1640, Sat/Sun 1000-1500. The permit there costs $2 and is valid for 2 weeks.* They will give you directions on how to access the forest itself and negotiate the unsealed tracks to the falls car park.

Tamaki Maori Village → *Tamaki Tours offer an hourly shuttle from the city.*
About 10 km south of Whakarewarewa, on SH5, Tamaki Maori Village is an award-winning complex created by **Tamaki Tours,** ① *T07-3462823, www.maoriculture.co.nz, daily 0900-1600,* one of the original creators of the Maori concert and *hangi* experience. The village is a faithful recreation of Maori buildings, custom and lifestyle prior to European settlement. It also houses an **art gallery,** specializing in Maori art. There is a daily concert performance at 1230. Perhaps the best way to see the village is to join the 'Twilight Concert and Tour', from $60 (see page 269).

Wai-O-Tapu → *The park is 29 km south of Rotorua off SH5 and is not to be confused with the Waimangu Thermal Valley, which is about 4 km before it.*
① *T07-3485179, www.geyserland.co.nz Daily 0830-1700. Adult $13, child $4. Santa Fe Shuttles offer a shuttle service from Rotorua several times daily for $30 return including entry, T07-3457997.*

Wai-O-Tapu is, without doubt, the best thermal park in the region, with an almost surreal and colourful range of volcanic features, from mud pools and silica terraces to the famous and beautiful 'Champagne Pool'. If you can, time your arrival with the daily 1015 eruption of the **Lady Knox Geyser,** which is signposted on the Wai-O-Tapu Loop Road (off SH5).

Just before the Geyser, again on the Loop Road, are a number or globulous mud pools that are separate from the park itself. These, too, are worth a peek. The thermal park proper is at the southern end of the Loop Road. The full self-guided walk around the park will take about two hours. Along the first section of track there are a number of features including steaming caverns, mud pools and cavernous holes, with evocative names like **Devil's Home** (good one for that photo), the **Devil's Ink Pots** and **Thunder Crater**. The track then arrives at a lookout across the aptly named **Artist's Palette**, a multi-coloured silica field. It really is a wonderful sight to behold with pastel shades of yellow, green and blue, fading in and out of swathes of billowing white steam. A boardwalk takes you across the silica fields, where you can either go on to investigate a silica waterfall, some 'alum cliffs', 'frying pan flat' and some colourful lakes, or (more likely) get entirely engrossed with the **Champagne Pool**. This is hard to describe, but essentially is a bright orange-edged, steaming, fizzing pool of about 60 m in diameter. Without doubt it is the highlight of the park and certainly rates as a 10 out of 10 on the 'awesometer'. What you are looking at is in fact a 62 m-deep flooded volcanic vent, the base of which boils the water to a surface temperature of around 74°C. Hot stuff. From the Champagne Pool it is a short meander past more steaming, gurgling crevasses and a pastel green lake, before returning to the visitors' centre. The visitors' centre also has a shop and café.

Waimangu Volcanic Valley

ⓘ *T07-3666137, www.waimangu.com Daily 0830-1645. There is a walk only or walk and boat option from $20, child $10.*

The volcanic features here in the Waimangu Volcanic Valley, 26 km south of Rotorua, off SH5, are all very recent and were created as a result of the 1886 eruption of Tarawera. Lake Rotomahana is essentially a water-filled crater which, before the eruption, was once the site of the famed pink and white silica terraces. Sadly, both of the terraces were completely obliterated by the eruption, but what were created in their place were the lake and a number of new volcanic features around it. These include the **Waimangu Cauldron** – the world's largest boiling lake – the **Inferno Crater Lake** that rises and falls up to 10 m a month, steaming cliffs, and numerous boiling springs and steaming fumaroles. At the turn of the last century the now inactive **Waimangu Geyser** used to be the largest in the world, spouting water to a staggering 500 m. The park is self-guided and you can see it partly on foot and partly by boat but there are a number of options.

The **Waikite Thermal Pools**, ⓘ *off SH5, between the Waimangu and Wai-O-Tapu thermal reserves, T07-3331861. Daily 1000-2200. From $6, child $2. From SH5 turn west on to Waikite Valley Rd at the Waiotapu Tavern. The pools are about 4 km on the right.* They consist of large family and adult hot pools in a country setting. Ideal for family picnics. Private pools and camping are also available.

Hell's Gate and the Waiora Spa → *Colour map 2, grid C3*

ⓘ *T07-3453151. Daily 0900-1700. No guided tours, but informative leaflet provided. Adult $12, child $6. Spa only $10, child $6, mud bath, $30, child $15. Park entry, mud bath and spa, from $42, child $21. Private mud bath and spa from $50. Massage 1 hr $40. The Santa Fe Shuttle leaves for Hell's Gate from Rotorua several times daily, $30 return, plus entry, T07-3457997. Hell's Gate offers a complimentary shuttle for its Combo and Massage packages.*

The aptly-named Hell's Gate thermal reserve is 15 km from Rotorua on SH30 towards Whakatane. It is not the most colourful of the reserves, but certainly one of the most active, and a thoroughly steamy affair. The 10 ha are set on two levels separated by a tract of bush, yet subtly connected by a warm thermal stream, complete with steaming waterfall. The pools of bubbly mud and water on the lower levels, with such evocative names as 'Sodom and Gomorrah' and 'The Inferno', hiss with menace and are quite scary, reaching temperatures well over 100°C.

The upper level of the reserve is not much better, with steaming lakes and myriad tiny steaming vents, scattered with features including mini mud volcanoes, and

cauldrons of boiling water. Best of all is the **Devil's Cauldron**, a small pit that is home
to a lively globular mud pool which makes the most wonderfully disgusting noises.
Thankfully the entire reserve is connected with a boardwalk, from which, for obvious
reasons, you are encouraged not to stray.

With all that mineral rich bubbly mud about it would seem rude not to create a
mud spa and this is indeed Hells Gate's latest venture. There are a number of
attractive options from massage or sulphur spas, to the wonderfully messy and
therapeutic mud facials, scrubs and (best of all) private mud baths. After all that the
small shop and café which are also on site seem a little mundane.

Agrodome

① *To7-3571050, www.agrodome.co.nz, www.zorb.com Daily 0830-1700. Shows at
0930, 1100 and 1430. Show only $16, child $8. Try to attend the busiest show:
mid-morning or mid-afternoon.*

The Agrodome Complex, 10 km north of Rotorua on SH5, is a principal tourist
attraction on the Rotorua circuit, and deservedly so. It has a wide array of attractions
from the full-on bungee jump to some more sedate farm activities. The focus of the
complex and its principal feature attraction is the **Sheep Show**. If the very thought of
such an event leaves you cold, then think again: it is highly entertaining. This ovine
spectacular features over 19 breeds of sheep – all of which are highly domesticated,
wonderfully tame and very co-operative. Before the show starts the 'stars' are
available for copious stroking, and perhaps an autograph if you're lucky. The actual
animal show is very informative, entertaining and professional. There is much
audience participation and the opportunity to see a sheep fully shorn and bottle-fed
lambs. As for the audience, well, they are almost as entertaining, as they attempt to
video the entire proceedings.

Surrounding the Agrodome there are a scattering of sundry attractions including a
woollen mill and a *paua (abalone)* **pearl farm**. Activities abound including a **farm tour**
(optional extension to the sheep show, combo $20, child $10), **bungee jumping** (43 m,
$99), **helicopter rides** (from $69-$665) and **jet boats** ($35, child $25), as well as the
'Swoop' and **'Zorbing'**. The 'Swoop' is a glorified swing, where you are strapped into a
harness then dropped from a height of 40 m. Apparently somewhere on the way down
you reach over 130 kph, with a G-force of three, which, roughly translated, means your
kidneys seek an unexpected and rapid exit out of your back passage. However, it all
seems to go down very well ($45, child $30). 'Zorbing' is described as a 'biospherical
monumentous disturbance' and is the unique New Zealand invention of rolling down a
hill in a large clear plastic bubble. It can, if you so wish, be filled, with a bucket or six of
water. It is highly entertaining, but a bit of a rip-off as the entire episode lasts about 10
seconds and costs $40. There is a shop and café on site.

Trout Springs

The Rotorua region is rich in freshwater springs, the streams from which are home to
thousands of both brown and rainbow trout. Trout are not native to New Zealand and
were introduced to the region in the 1800s. Some of these springs have been
developed into tourist resorts where you can observe both wild and captive trout
above and below the water or feed the swirling masses. Some streams are also home
to the unbelievably huge native New Zealand eels.

The largest and most popular springs resort is **Rainbow Springs**, ①*5 km from the
city centre on SH5 north, To7-3479301, www.rainbow.co.nz, 0800-1700 (1930 in
summer). $25, child entry free.* Here the attraction of the trout is mixed with other
wildlife treats, including kiwi and other native birds in a free-flight aviary. The underwater viewing area is particularly popular. There are also fluffy farm animals for the kids
to stroke and regular guided tours of the park, farm animal shows and a café on site.

There are also the smaller but quite charming **Paradise Valley Springs**, ① *11 km from the city along Claydon Rd which is straight on at the Koutu Corner intersection, as you head north out of the city on the Old Taupo Rd, T07-3489667, www.paradise.co.nz Daily 0800-dusk. $16, child entry free.* The attraction is very similar; with the same features (and added lions), but it enjoys a quieter, more congenial atmosphere. There is also a small bottling plant which utilizes the pure spring water.

Skyline Skyrides

① *T07-3470027, www.skylineskyrides.co.nz Daily from 0900 until late. Gondola only $15, child $6. Gondola and 2 luge rides $19, child $12. Five luge rides $20.*

If you are physically able, everyone who visits Rotorua should call into the Skyline Skyrides to take a ride up the mountain in the gondolas and have a go on the infamous **luge,** which basically involves throwing yourself down a concrete course on a plastic tray with wheels and primitive brakes. Once down, and if still alive, you can then hitch a ride on a secondary chairlift to repeat the operation. You are given brief instructions, a plastic helmet and a chance to try the 'family' course first, just to get the hang of it. This is very slow – so much so that you can have a conversation with complete strangers, if not tea and cakes on the way down – and once completed you can attempt the main course with its savage turns and precipitous jumps. As well as the luge and scenic gondola there is also a **Sky Swing** that will reputedly fly you (and two others) through the air at 120kph, from $35. Other more conventional activity options include helicopter

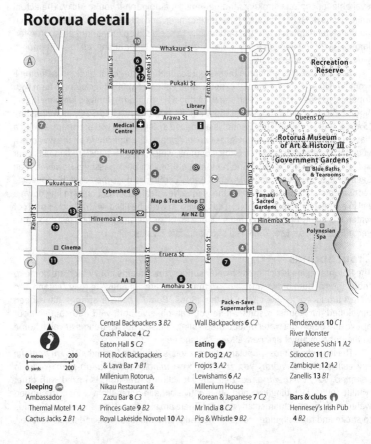

Rotorua detail

N

0 metres 200
0 yards 200

Sleeping ⬤
Ambassador
  Thermal Motel **1** *A2*
Cactus Jacks **2** *B1*
Central Backpackers **3** *B2*
Crash Palace **4** *C2*
Eaton Hall **5** *C2*
Hot Rock Backpackers
  & Lava Bar **7** *B1*
Millenium Rotorua,
  Nikau Restaurant &
  Zazu Bar **8** *C3*
Princes Gate **9** *B2*
Royal Lakeside Novotel **10** *A2*
Wall Backpackers **6** *C2*

Eating ⑦
Fat Dog **2** *A2*
Frojos **3** *A2*
Lewishams **6** *A2*
Millenium House
  Korean & Japanese **7** *C2*
Mr India **8** *C2*
Pig & Whistle **9** *B2*
Rendezvous **10** *C1*
River Monster
  Japanese Sushi **1** *A2*
Scirocco **11** *C1*
Zambique **12** *A2*
Zanellis **13** *B1*

Bars & clubs ⑦
Hennesey's Irish Pub
  4 *B2*

Whirinaki Forest Park → *The nearest town, Murupara, is about 60 km southwest of Rotorua on SH38 (Waikaremoana road off SH5).*

ⓘ *For detailed information of how to access this excellent forest park contact DoC in Rotorua, or better still call in at the DoC Field Centre on the main road in Murupara, which is the nearest township lying at the northern edge of the park, T07-3661080.*
Whirinaki Forest Park is one of New Zealand's finest remaining podocarp forests, aptly described by one famous botanist as a 'dinosaur forest'. The park is off the beaten track but that is part of its charm. There are a number of excellent **walking tracks** taking in the diverse remote forest landscape with giant trees, waterfalls, river valleys and lagoons. There are **DoC campsites** and **huts** within the park to allow longer multi-day tramps. ➤➤ *For organized walking tours within Whirinaki, see the Rotorua activity section page 268.*

⊜ Sleeping

Rotorua Centre
There are over 12,000 tourist beds in Rotorua, so the choice is huge. Many of the main hotel chains are here and there are lots of motels on either side of Fenton St, between the centre of town and Whakarewarewa. Pre-booking is advised throughout the year. Whatever you do and wherever you end up, make sure there is an accessible hot pool in-house or nearby.

LL-AL Royal Lakeside Novotel, *lake-end of Tutanekai St, T07-3463888.* In the heart of town and near Lake Rotorua, and also near Government Gardens. Good reputation with in-house spas, and a popular restaurant and bar. It also offers one of the best hotel Maori concerts and *hangis*.
LL-AL Grand Tiara Rotorua, *Fenton St, T07-3495200, www.grandhotels international.com* One of Rotorua's best and most expensive. Recent renovations have placed it at the forefront of the hotel pack. Close to Whakarewarewa Village and thermal reserve. Pool, spas, gym, café, excellent restaurant and even an Irish pub attached. Maori concert and feasts nightly.
AL Millennium Rotorua, *corner of Eruera and Hinemaru Sts, T07-3471234.* Popular hotel and very tastefully appointed. Only metres from the Polynesian Spa (discounts to guests), reputable in-house bar.
AL-A The Princes Gate, *1057 Arawa St, T07-3481179, www.princesgate.co.nz* An award-winning establishment that describes itself as 'historically boutique' and keeps its

promise. Also in a great location between the city centre and Government Gardens, thermal pool, off-street parking and café. Recommended.
AL-A Quality Hotel, *Fenton St, T07-3480199.* Recently refurbished, comfortable, no-nonsense option with good facilities including brasserie, pool, spa and gym.
AL Regal Geyserland, *424 Fenton St, T3482039.* Famed for its location overlooking the Whakarewarewa Thermal Reserve. You can literally hear the geyser Pohutu going off and look down on a pool of bubbling mud. All the usual facilities and in-house hot pools.

A-B Eaton Hall, *1255 Hinemaru St, T07-3470366, www.eatonhallbnb.cjb.net* Good value, comfortable B&B and close to the Polynesian Spa.
A Accolade Lodge B&B, *30 Victoria St, T07-3482223.* Well-situated, though more a cross between a motel and a B&B, but popular all the same. Has a spa.
B-D Kiwi Paka, *60 Tarewa Rd, T07-3470931, www.kiwipaka-yha.co.nz* The pick of the backpackers bunch, with a fine range of dormitory, unit, motel, camper van and campsite options. The staff are great and the amenities excellent. There's a large kitchen and sitting room, a bar and café and a thermal pool. Activities arranged. It is a bit out of town but most operators provide pick-ups.
B-D Wall Backpackers, *1140 Hinemoa St, T0800-843392, www.thewall.co.nz* Centred around the 20-m climbing wall complex this new, spacious multi-level facility provides tidy modern rooms from 4-8 dorm to doubles with en suite bathroom, a café, large

games room, good kitchen facilities, internet access and a bar overlooking the climbing action. The only drawback is the lack of off-street parking.

C-D Hot Rock Backpackers, *1286 Arawa St, www.hotrock@acb.co.nz* Also popular but ageing, has in-house spa pools and a lively, popular bar on-site.

C-D Central Backpackers, *1076 Pukuatua St, T07-3493285*. A congenial, friendly and more historic establishment that is deservedly growing in popularity. Beds not bunks, single rooms, an in-house spa and off-street parking.

C-D Cactus Jacks, *54 Haupapa St, T07-3483121*. Well-established, its artistic delights seem a little out of place but well-located and friendly with an in-house spa.

C-D Crash Palace, *1271 Hinemaru St, T07-3488842, www.crashpalace.co.nz* Newly renovated, head here for the quieter more homely treatment.

There are almost 100 motels in Rotorua, most on Fenton St, so the choice is vast. Most are modern and very much the same and, given the fierce competition, you will rarely be let down. The best bet is to take a drive down Fenton (if that suits) and literally take your pick. The following are just a few examples, and some that are particularly recommended or well-situated.

AL-A Regal Palms, *350 Fenton St, T07-3503232, www.regalpalmsml.co.nz* One of the newest in town and certainly one of the best. Very classy decor and attention to detail. Suites and apartments, sauna, spa, gym and pool.

AL-A Ambassador Thermal Motel, *corner Whakaue and Hinemaru sts, T07-3479581*. Ideal location close to Polynesian Spa and city centre.

AL Silver Fern, *326 Fenton St, T07-3463849*. Hailed as one of the city's best. Wide range of suites with spa pools.

AL Four Canoes, *273 Fenton St, T0800-422663, www.fourcanoes.com* Hotel/motel that uses the Maori theme and an evening Maori performance and *hangi* to attract custom ($55). Wide range of suites with spa pools and a buffet restaurant.

AL-A Wylie Court, *345 Fenton St, T07-3477879*. A total of 36 suites with pool and also a restaurant.

A Acacia Lodge, *40 Victoria St, T07-3487089*. Well situated close to the city centre, outdoor heated pool and spas.

A Ascot Motel, *247 Fenton St, T07-3487712, www.ascotmotel.co.nz* Spas in all units.

A Bel Aire Motel, *257 Fenton St, T07-3486076*. Good value.

B Rob Roy Motor Inn, *291 Fenton St, T07-3480584*. Offers good rates and has a thermal mineral pool.

Motorcamps and campsites

B-D Cosy Cottage, *67 Whittaker Rd, T07-3483793*. An excellent motorcamp just north of the city centre, almost lakeside. It is one of the only motorcamps in the world that can boast a 'naturally heated' campsite. It has a wide range of cabins, good amenities and spa pools.

B-D Rotorua Thermal Holiday Park, *Old Taupo Rd, T07-3463140*. This campsite is also excellent and well maintained with some fine log cabins and within walking distance of the Whakarewarewa Thermal Reserve and its own free hot pools. Great spacious camping.

Around Rotorua

L-AL Okawa Bay Lake Resort, *SH33, Lake Rotoiti, T07-3624599, www.okawabay.co.nz* A good hotel option out of town, in an idyllic lakeside setting. Full amenities including restaurant and private beach.

There are a number of luxury lodges around town, most lakeside and offering peace and quiet with all mod cons. These include:

LL Solitaire Lodge, *Lake Tarawera, T07-3628208*. Highly celebrated hideaway with 10 luxurious suites overlooking the lake.

LL Hamurana Country Estate, *415 Hamurana Rd, Ngongotaha, T07-3322222, www.hcestate.co.nz* Luxurious mansion, recently fully refurbished, again with luxury suites overlooking Lake Rotorua. Beautifully appointed and noted cuisine.

L Kawaha Point Lodge, *171 Kawaha Point Rd, T07-3463602, www.kawahalodge.co.nz* Lakeside, 5 mins from the airport. Classy kauri lodge with en suite double or twins, two with spa baths, garden with pool.

AL-A Ariki Lodge, *2 Manuariki Av, Ngongotaha, T07-3575532*. Spacious, well-appointed lakeside B&B north of the city.

AL Lake Tarawera Lodge, *Te Mu Rd, Lake Tarawera, T07-3628754, www.laketarawera.co.nz* Beautiful location. Six self-contained country-style cottages, 6-roomed Mission House and campsite. Very popular with the fishing fraternity with trips by arrangement.

A-AL Carodene Guesthouse, *566 Spencer Rd, Lake Tarawera, T07-3628626, www.tarawera.info.co.nz* Quite similar in terms of location and set up with a fully self-contained guesthouse or cabin with lake views. Canadian canoe hire.

Motorcamps and campsites

B-D Blue Lake Holiday Park, *on the banks of Blue Lake on Tarawera Rd, T07-3628120*. If you are looking for a quiet country spot look no further. There is a beach across the road for swimming, kayak hire and a lovely walk around the lake.

● Eating

There are more than 50 restaurants in Rotorua offering a wide range of cuisine to suit all budgets. Most of them are on or around Tutanekai St towards the lake. You should also consider sampling one of the many Maori *hangis* available. Few of them are truly authentic, having neither the time nor the health and safety go-ahead to dig earth pits and cook the food underground, they will still give you just a taste of how good a Maori *hangi* can be (for options see page 269). For dinner afloat don't forget the **Lakeland Queen** paddle steamer that leaves for a cruise/dinner from the lakefront at 1900, *T07-3486634. From $40.*

$$$ Lewisham's Café and Restaurant, *1099 Tutanekai St, T07-3481786. Daily 0930-2200.* Has a good reputation, offering traditional European dishes with a definite Austrian edge. The venison and wiener schnitzel are recommended.

$$$ The Rendezvous, *1282 Hinemoa St, T07-3489273. Daily from 1800.* A popular award-winning restaurant offering fine Pacific Rim dishes in very congenial surroundings. There is venison, quail and even emu on the menu.

$$$ Poppy's Villa, *4 Marguerita St, T07-3471700. Daily from 1800.*

Recommended for Kiwi cuisine.

$$$ Zanelli's, *1243 Amohia St, T07-3484908. Tue-Sun from 1730.* Touted as the best Italian restaurant.

$$$ Nikau Restaurant, *in the Millennium Hotel (see Sleeping above), T07-3471234.* A good reputation for traditional European and Kiwi-style fine dining without being too formal. The bar (Zazu) is also popular.

$$ The Pig and Whistle, *corner of Haupapa and Tutanekai Sts, T07-3473025. Daily from 1130-2130.* Great pub food at affordable prices and you can wash it all down with their own brews.

$$ Freos, *lake end of Tutanekai St, T07-3460976. Daily from 0830.* A busy little café/restaurant that offers traditional Kiwi fare and obviously does it well: it has a loyal following.

$$ Zambique, *also on Tutanekai, T07-3492140. Mon-Sat from 0800-late.* Well known for its creative modern dishes and good coffee.

$$ Mr India, *1161 Amohau St, T07-3494940. Daily from 1130.* Perhaps the best Indian in the city, keeping up the traditions and reputation of other national outlets. All-you-can-eat specials on Sun and Thu.

$$ River Monster Japanese Shusi Bar, *1139 Tutanekai St, T07-3460792. Tue-Sun from 1700.* Four-course specials for $25. Traditional Asian fare.

$$ Millennium House Korean and Japanese, *1074 Eruera St, T07-3493309. Daily 1100-1400, 1800-2300.*

$$ Landings Café, *Spencer Rd, Lake Tarawera, T07-3628502. Daily from 0900. Book for dinner.* A fine, affordable and friendly lunch and dinner spot with a distinctive Scots flavour.

$ Fat Dog, *1161 Arawa St, T07-3477586. Mon-Fri 0900-late, Sat/Sun 0800-late.* The best café in town, always busy and friendly, and offers an imaginative blackboard menu.

$ Scirocco, *1280 Eruera St, T07-3473388.* Another good café.

$ Blue Baths, *Government Gdns, T07-3502119. Daily 1000-1600.* Traditional afternoon teas, and NZ fare in historic tearooms.

$ Robert Harris Coffee House, *227 Tutanekai St. Daily from 0730.* An old faithful, with the usual reliable snacks and breakfast.

⊕ Entertainment

Bars and clubs

Pig and Whistle, *corner Haupapa and Tutanekai Sts, T07-3473025*. Nicely decorated, brews its own ales and has a congenial atmosphere. It also has bands on weekends.
Hennessey's, 1206 Tutanekai St, T07-3437901. Popular Irish pub with good beer, andlive music most nights.
Zazu Bar *in the Millennium Hotel (see Sleeping section), T07-3471234*. The classy place where the locals are apparently secretly hanging out. The happy hours on Fri at 1930 and Sat at 1730 are especially popular.
Lava Bar, *at the Hot Rock Backpackers, 118 Arawa St, T07-3479469* Especially popular with travellers and a younger crowd.
Barbella, *1263 Pukuatua St, T07-3476776*. The place to shake your pants on Wed-Sat from 2200.

Cinema

Cinema complex, *next to the O'Malley's Irish pub on Eruera St, T07-3492994*.

⊕ Festivals and events

Opera in the Pa (*Jan*) World-class opera performed amidst the geothermal splendour of the Rotowhio *Marae*. **Lakeside 2002** (*Feb*) Annual concert and entertainment in the soundshell on the lakeside. **International Two-Day Walk** (*Mar, 3rd week*) 10, 20 and 30-km walks through Rotorua forests and city. **Rotorua Marathon** (*Apr, last week*) 42-km run around Lake Rotorua. **Rotorua Tagged Trout Fishing Contest** (*May, 3rd week*) Catch the tagged trout in Lake Rotorua and become a rich fisher-person. **Catseye Moonride** (*Jul*) A night-time mountain biking event held in the Whakarewarewa Forest Park (unfortunately lights are allowed). **Rally of Rotorua** (*Sep*). **Lockwood Aria** (*Oct*) New Zealand's largest classical singing competition with both classical and contemporary disciplines and Maori cultural music. **New Zealand Trout Festival** (*Oct*) Marks the opening of the Rotorua lakes season. **International Trout Tournament** (*Nov*) 3-day tournament with major prizes attracting anglers worldwide. **New Year's Eve Mardi Gras** (*Dec*) wild shenanigans down at the waterfront.

▲ Activities and tours

In New Zealand, only Queenstown – the reputed activity capital of the world – can claim to have more activities than steamy Rotorua. As the country's second most-visited tourist destination 'Roto Vegas' can certainly satisfy just about everyone, from adrenaline junkies keen to fly upside down in a bi-plane or raft down a waterfall, to those in search of some therapy in the form of a delightfully messy mud bath or a soothing mineral spa.

But before parting with any cash take a long hard look in the VIC to see the vast range on offer and ask about the various combo deals that can save both time and money.

Agrodome

The Agrodome Complex, *just north of Rotorua on SH5, T07-3574350, www.agrodome.co.nz* Offers a wealth of activities including bungee-jumping, jet-boating, 'The Swoop' and the infamous Zorb (see page 263).

Climbing

The Wall, 1140 Hinemoa St, T07-3501400, www.thewall.co.nz *Open daily*. An impressive 20-metre indoor climbing wall. For around $20 you will get some instruction with all the gear. Outdoor trips can also be arranged, full day $100.

Cruising

The two main cruises around Lake Rotorua (including Mokoia Island) and beyond to Lake Rotoiti are provided by the paddle steamer *Lakeland Queen* and the unfortunately named *Scatcat*. The **Lakeland Queen**, *T0800-862784, www.lakelandqueen.co.nz*, offers breakfast, from $28, child $14 (0800-0900); lunch from $30, child $15 (1230-1330); a dinner cruise from $50, child $25 (1900-late); and morning or afternoon cruises from $20, child $10.
Scatcat, *T07-3479852*, offers 1 hr cruises to Mokoia leaving at 1000,1100,1300 and 1400, $25, child free; a two-five hour Mokoia landing trip for $40, child $10 and a two-hour trip to Hamurana Gardens and springs at 1400, $45, child $10.
Kawarau Jet, *T0800-529272*, from Queenstown has now opened operations on

Lake Rotorua and is based on the waterfront. There are also self-drive speedboats available for hire – but alas, a lot slower!

Ecotours

Nature Connection, *based in the city*, *T07-3471705*, offers a range of excellent fully-guided, fully-equipped half to full-day trips to local sights and the Whirinaki Forest Park, from $75.

Whirinaki Escape Walk, *T0800-869255*, *www.rainforest-treks.co.nz* A good local option with Maori guides adding traditional cultural insight into the eco-theme. Full day from $125.

Fishing

As you might expect there are numerous guided and self-guided charters that mainly operate on Lake Rotorua or Lake Tarawera. Ernie Scudder, *T07-3323488*, *www.troutfly.co.nz* A very congenial local fisherman who offers a great trip on the *Silver Hilton*, from $65 an hour. Recommended. Other reputable charters include:
Clearwater (Lake Tarawera), *T07-3628590*;
The Trout Connection, *T07-3472363*;
Parfect, *T0800-8887688*, *www.parfect.co.nz*
Rotorua Trout Safaris, *T07-3620016*, *www.wildtrout.co.nz*
Prices start at about $75 per hour.

4WD and quad bikes

Off Road NZ, *193 Amoore Rd (off SH5 north)*, *T07-3325748*, *www.offroadnz.co.nz* A fine outfit offering a range of thrills and spills in a range of 4-wheel drive vehicles and buggies. From their base near the city you can go uphill and down dale (including a monstrous 15 m 'luge' drop) and through some very large mud pools. There is also clay bird shooting and archery available. Tours daily 0900-1700, from $60.

Land Rover Experience 4WD, *70A Te Manu Rd, Paradise Valley*, *T07-3483007*, *www.landroverexperience.co.nz* The standard muddy tours and expert training in the much-loved Land Rover models (from $145), as well as a challenging 4x4 obstacle course, quad biking, clay bird shooting and mountain biking. Ask about their new 'Jungle Challenge'.

Hill Hoppers, *Longridge Park, near Te Puke*, *well to the north of the city. T07-5331818.*

Offers the complete range of off-road 4WD experiences in a range of vehicles. Trips include the 'Bogs Bunny', the 'Wet Wabbit' and 'Run Rabbit Run' – all from $60. The only drawback is their distance from the city.

Mountain Action, *near Rainbow Springs on SH5 north*, *T07-3488400*, *www.mountainaction.co.nz* The local quad bike operator, and horse trekking also available. From $80. Pick-ups provided.

Golf

There are 6 courses in and around Rotorua.
Arikikapakapa Course, *Rotorua Golf Club, at the southern end of Fenton St*, *T07-3484051*. The best.
Government Gardens, *T07-3489126*, Also has a range and a short 9-hole course.

Horse trekking

Foxwood Park Horse Treks, *Fairbank Rd, at the edge of the Whakarewarewa Forest Park*, *T07-3457003*. Offer trips from 30 minutes to full day, from $20-$120.
Peka Horse Treks, *SH30, T07-3461755*. Ideally situated close to Whakarewarewa Forest Park; 1 hour from $30. Mountain Action (see above) also offers horse trekking (1 hr $30) and are handy to town, but the forest trails are recommended.

Kayaking

Adventure Kayaking, *T07-3489451*, *www.adventurekayaking. co.nz* Half or full-day tours to a number of lakes and rivers in the region, as well as fishing trips and twilight paddles, from $55. Independent hire is also available.
Go Kayaking, *T07-3624222*. Offers similar trips with more emphasis on teaching the beginner; from $65. Independent hire also available from $35 per day.
Kaituna Kayaks, *T0800-465292*, *www.kaitunakayaks.com* Half day from $120 (2-day course $240). Recommended for river kayaking and some very good professional tuition.

Maori concerts and hangis

A trip to Rotorua is not complete without the Maori cultural experience of a concert and/or *hangi* (feast). There are numerous options, some good some not so good. The least commercial and recommended are:

Tamaki Tours Marae Experience, *T07-3462823, www.maoriculture.co.nz*; and the daily Magic of the Maori performance at **World of the Maori (Rotoiti Tours)**, *T07-3488969 (book at the VIC)*. The former involves a daily, twilight *marae* tour, performance and *hangi* with some audience participation; from $65. They provide pick-ups from your accommodation. The latter takes place at the Rakeiao *Marae* on the shores of Lake Rotoiti (20-min drive) but is well worth the trip and caters for smaller groups.

Whakarewarewa Village, *T07-3493463 (see page 256)*. Also has cultural performances during the day and again in the evening at 1115 and 1400.

The major hotels almost all offer *hangis* and concerts, but these tend to be less grand affairs than the above and very commercial. A hotel *hangi* and concert will cost you about $55.

Matariki Hangi and Concert *at the Royal Lakeside Novotel, T07-3463888*. Takes place daily at 1830 and is one of the best on offer, from $58. Others include:
Centra, *T07-3481189*;
Grand Tiara, *T07-3495200*;
Lake Plaza, *T07-3481174*.

Mountain biking
Whakarewarewa Forest Park is just one of many popular and challenging venues for mountain biking around Rotorua, with over 30 km of trails (see page 256).
For organized trips try:
Planet Bike, *T07-3489971, www.planetbike.co.nz* Combo kayak trips and independent bike hire also available. From $50 per-day.
Edzone, *based at the Skyline Skyrides Complex, T07-3461717*. These are another reputable operator.
For more track and operator information, *T07-3484581*.

Rafting and white water sledging
Kaituna Cascades, *T07-3575032, www.kaitunacascades.co.nz* A very professional, safe and experienced company that offers a range of whitewater rafting and tandem kayaking trips, on the Kaituna, Rangitaiki Wairoa Rivers and nearby lakes. The most popular trip is the recommended 45-minute blast down a stretch of the Kaituna (located between Lake Rotorua and Lake Rotoiti) which negotiates 14 falls. The largest of these is the famous and highly entertaining 7-m drop down the Okere Falls – the highest commercial rafted falls in the world. Trips range from $65-$70 (45 minutes) to $385. You also get a photo of the drop down the falls.
River Rats, *T07-3476049 / T0800-333900, www.riverrats.co.nz* A similar company offering a wider scope of multi-activity adventure packages that include jet boating, bungee jumping, 4-wheel drive, the luge, bikes and more.
Wet-n-Wild, *T07-3483191*. Another reputable company offering all the local trips but also specialising in multi-day trips on the Motu and Mohaka Rivers. From $70.

Whitewater sledging is the new and exciting concept of doing all you do in a raft, except alone on a type of 'head-first' water toboggan.
Kaitiaki Adventures, *T0800-338736, www.sledge-it.com* Contact these people to try it and also learn something about Maori culture on a full day tour. Sledge and tour from $120, sledge, raft and tour $140.

Sightseeing tours *For Ecotours see above*. There are a wealth of independent operators and the VIC offers reductions and package deals which are well worth looking at.
Carey's Tours, *1108 Haupapa St, near the VIC, T07-3471197, www.careys.co.nz* A Maori-owned and operated company and one of the largest local tour operators in Rotorua. They offer a wide range of tour options from half to full day and from $38 to $145 (children half price). Carey's also offer the new 'Waimangu Round Trip', which is an adventure worth considering. It combines 5 km of walking and cruising on and around Lakes Tarawera and Rotomahana and includes the Buried Village and the Waimangu Valley Thermal Reserve – all that culminating in a relaxing soak in the Polynesian Spa, from $145, child $80. If you are short of time this is a good all-round trip.
Mt Tarawera NZ Ltd, *T07-3493714, www.mt-tarawera.co.nz* One of the few operators licensed to take tours on to the mountain to see the dramatic Tarewera

craters (or 'gash') left by the violent eruption of 1886. The sight leaves you in no doubt about the ferocity of the explosion. They offer a guided half-day tour (0800-1300) from $110 to a fly/drive option from $390.
Te Kiri Treks, *T07-3455016*. A Maori-operated company that provides an excellent day out in a four-wheel drive, taking in Ohinemutu, Whakarewarewa, Waiotapu, Tarawera and a few secret spots on the way. Lunch is provided in a beautiful self-built bush camp. All for $120. Good value, entertaining and recommended.
Sonny's World, *T07-3490290, www.sonnysworld.co.nz* Another new Maori-operated tour company, also offering the genuine and fun Maori perspective. Half-day $60.
Superia Tours, *T07-3572284, wwwsuperiatours.co.nz* Specialize in flexible personalised trips for small groups with hosts fluent in 7 languages!

Scenic flights
Most scenic flight operators are based at either the airport, Whakarewarewa, the Lake Rotorua waterfront near the town centre (float planes) or at the Agrodome.
Volcanic Air Safaris, *based at the airport and the waterfront, T0800-800848*. Have a fleet of fixed-wing and float plane aircraft as well as helicopters that take in all the local sights and go as far as White Island in the Bay of Plenty, from $50 to $745.
Helipro, *based out at the Agrodome, T3572512, www.helipro.co.nz* Offers a range from a 10-min city flight at $85 to a 1-hr Mt Tarawera trip from $295 and White Island 3-hr flight from $665.
New Zealand Helicopters, *Whakarewarewa Thermal Reserve, T07-3481223, www.newzealandhelicopters.co.nz* Offer local flights from 10 minutes to 4-hour White Island flights, from $270. They are one of the principal operators allowed to land on the summit of Tarawera.
Red Cat, *T07-3459369*, and
Adventure Aviation, *T07-3456780*, offer the old bi-plane option above the city and the lake, and operate from Rotorua airport. Around $100 depending on the level of aerobatics.

Accessed by a scenic gondola there are a number of activities available on the slopes of **Mount Ngongotaha**. These include the infamous luge, a flying fox, flight simulator and helicopter trips, *T07-3470027*. Also see p264.

Tandem skydiving
Rotorua Tandem Skydiving, *operates from the airport, T07-3457520*. Daily, depending on weather conditions. From 9,500 ft for $195 (12,000 ft, $225).

Walking
There are a wealth of walking opportunities in the Rotorua region, ranging from a short walk around **Government Gardens** and the waterfront, to the **Tarawera summit** climb (see page 260), the 20-minute to 8-hour walks through the **Whakarewarewa Forest Park** (see page 256), and the superb **Tarawera Falls** walk (see page 260). Other excellent walking tracks are to be found around Lake Okataina in the **Lake Okataina Scenic Reserve**. These are best accessed from SH30 at Ruato (Lake Rotoiti) or Lake Okareka (Tarawera Falls Rd). The **Okere Falls** walk (30 minutes) is accessed from SH30 east and then SH33 (16 km) and worth the trip, while a great view can be had from the summit of **Rainbow Mountain** (2 hours) which is accessed off SH5, 26 km south of Rotorua. A little further afield is the **Whirinaki Forest**, which is lauded as having an almost prehistoric appearance.
Transport with guided walks is offered by **Whirinaki Escape Walk**, *T0800-869255, www.rainforest-treks.co.nz* and **Whirinaki Trax**, *T07-3664756, from $60*. For a more sedate option you might consider a 2-hour guided walk around town with **Walk About Rotorua**, *T07-3489480*. Sights include Government Gardens and Ohinemutu and there is lots of interesting commentary along the way. Depart the VIC at 0900 and 1300, from $25, child $10. For more local walks information contact the VIC or DoC. Maps can be bought at **The Map and Track Shop**, *a short distance south of the VIC at 1225 Fenton St, T07-3491845*.

✪ Shopping

Outdoor and camping equipment
Outdoorsman Headquarters, *6 Tarawera Rd, T07-3459333*. The best in the city.

Souvenirs
As you might expect, there are plenty of souvenir shops in Rotorua. Most are on Fenton St.
The Souvenir Centre, *1231 Fenton St*. One of the better ones.
Carey's Tours, *1108 Haupapa St*. Has some mainly authentic Maori souvenirs that are also worth a peek.
Maori Arts and Crafts Institute *at the Whakarewarewa Thermal Reserve, SH5*, or the **Maori Art Gallery**, *at Tamaki Maori Village, also on SH5*. Worth looking at for Maori Art.

✪ Directory

Airlines Air NZ, *corner of Fenton and Hinemoa sts, T07-3431100, 3456176*.
Banks All the major branches are in the town centre, on Hinemoa St. **Money exchange**: Travelex, *VIC, T07-3480373. Daily 0830-1800*; Thomas Cook, *corner of Fenton and Hinemoa Sts, T07-3480640. Mon-Fri 0900-1700, Sat 0930-1230*. **Bike hire** Pack and Pedal, *1275 Fenton St, T07-3471157*; Rotorua Cycle Centre, *1120 Hinemoa St, T07-3486588*; Lady Janes, *corner of Tutanekai and Whakaue Sts, T07-3479340*; Planet Bike, *30 Clouston, T07-3489971, 2 hr $30, full-day from $50*.
Car hire Rent-A-Dent, *14 Ti St, T07-3493993*; Budget, *Fenton St, T07-3488127*; NZ Link Rentals, *108 Fenton St, T07-3491629*. **Communications** Internet: Available at numerous city centre outlets including: Cyber World, *1174 Huapapa St*, and Contact Cyber Café, *corner of Pukuatua and Fenton sts, T07-3489440*. Most stay open daily until about 2100. **Post office**: *Hinemoa St. Open Mon-Fri 0730-1730, Sat 0830-1600, Sun 1000-1500*. **Medical services** Lakes Prime Care, *1165 Tutanekai St, T07-3481000. 0800-2200 (24 hr duty doctor T07-3481000)*. **Police** *Fenton St, T07-3480099*.

Tauranga → *Phone code: 07 Colour map 2, grid B3 Population: 66,000*

Tauranga has enjoyed tremendous growth in recent years. So much so that it is used as a barometer of the general state of the economy and national real estate prices. As well as its thriving commercial and business centre, busy port (the name means 'sheltered anchorage') and rich horticultural farmland, it seems Tauranga is also proving the ideal place in which to enjoy the archetypal Kiwi lifestyle. With the combination of location, climate, attractive beaches and the many associated activities, as well as its proximity to the delights of Rotorua, it has much to offer both the native and the visitor. Dominating the scene is the harbour and of course the volcanic dome of Mount Maunganui to the north, which guards its precarious entrance. Nowadays there are almost as many cruise liners negotiating that narrow entrance as there are merchant ships, and the town's tourist allure seems almost set to overtake its popularity with the locals.

Getting there
Tauranga, 210 km southeast of Auckland and 83 km north of Rotorua, is a major destination on the signposted Pacific Coast Highway, which connects Auckland with Napier in the Hawke's Bay region. **Tauranga airport** is 4 km east of the city centre and is served daily by **Air New Zealand Link**, T0800-737000, and **Origin Pacific,** (Wellington) T0800-302302. A taxi to the airport costs about $11, T07-5476177. **Intercity**, T07-5713211, and **Newman's** buses operate daily services to most North Island destinations arriving and departing from the VICs in the city and Mount Maunganui (both handle bookings and ticketing). **Go Kiwi Shuttles**, T0800-446-549, are an excellent company offering regular services to Auckland via Thames, Whitianga and

Rotorua. **Supa-Travel** is a local company that offers a daily service to Auckland (connecting with **Northliner** and **Guthrey's** services to Northland). It also runs from both Tauranga and Mount Maunganui VICs, T07-5710583. **Call-A-Bus**, T0800-100550, www.bus.co.nz, offers a similar daily mini-bus service to Auckland Airport.

Tauranga orientation

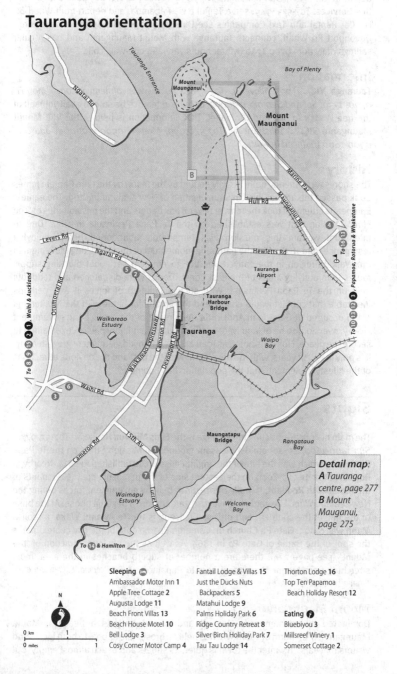

The Bay of Plenty Tauranga

Detail map:
A Tauranga centre, page 277
B Mount Maunganui, page 275

Sleeping 🛏	Fantail Lodge & Villas **15**	Thorton Lodge **16**
Ambassador Motor Inn **1**	Just the Ducks Nuts	Top Ten Papamoa
Apple Tree Cottage **2**	Backpackers **5**	Beach Holiday Resort **12**
Augusta Lodge **11**	Matahui Lodge **9**	
Beach Front Villas **13**	Palms Holiday Park **6**	**Eating** 🍴
Beach House Motel **10**	Ridge Country Retreat **8**	Bluebiyou **3**
Bell Lodge **3**	Silver Birch Holiday Park **7**	Millsreef Winery **1**
Cosy Corner Motor Camp **4**	Tau Tau Lodge **14**	Somerset Cottage **2**

N

0 km 1
0 miles 1

Tauranga city centre is fairly compact and easily negotiable by foot. **Bayline Coaches** (Bay Hopper), T07-5783113 / T0800-44229287 are the local suburban bus company operating regular daily services to Mount Maunganui and east as far as Opotiki. They depart from the corner of Wharf and Willow St beside the VIC. Day pass $6. **Te Puke Bus Services,** T07-5736949, serve Te Puke via Papamoa, and depart from Wharf St. For Car Rental and Taxi Companies see Directory, page 281. **Spirit Harbour Ferry,** Devonport Rd Wharf, connects Tauranga with Mount Maunganui and has regular sailings daily from 0700-1730 (winter hours vary). $6 one-way, child $3.

Information

Tauranga VIC, ① *95 Willow St, T07-5788103, www.bayofplentynz.com Mon-Fri 0700- 1730, Sat and Sun 0800-1600.* For quick reference be sure to avail yourself of the free *What's to See and Do* leaflet. **DOC** information is held at the VIC. **Mount Maunganui VIC,** ① *Salisbury Av, T07-5755099. Mon-Fri 0900-1700, Sat and Sun 0900-1600 (reduced in winter).*

History

The shores were already quite heavily settled by the Maori by the time Captain James Cook passed the area on his circumnavigation of New Zealand in 1769. The earliest European settlement took the form of several flax traders and the missionaries of 'The Elms' mission that was established on the Te Papa Peninsula in 1834. Due to inter-tribal warfare this mission was temporarily abandoned before enjoying resurgence from 1838. With the gathering momentum of the Maori King Movement in the Waikato region in the early 1860s the government set about blocking supply routes from outlying areas of the East Coast. Troops were dispatched and redoubts built on the Te Papa Peninsula. With such a build-up of forces it was perhaps inevitable that conflict would ensue, and the first major battle with the Ngaiterangi Maori occurred at Gate *Pa* in April 1864. As a result of the conflict and government victory, over 20,000 ha of land were confiscated and a military presence remained to secure the peace. From this point, as road access improved, settlement grew steadily. It is only in recent years, with the development of the port and the obvious attractions of the 'lifestyle' element, that the population has boomed.

Sights

The main historical attraction in Tauranga is the **Elms Mission House,** ① *T07-5779772, Sun 1400-1600, $5,* set amidst pleasant grounds on Mission Street on the Te Papa Peninsula, which was the site of the original mission, established in 1834. Nearby in **Robbins Park** on Cliff Road on the eastern side of the peninsula are the remnants of the **Monmouth Redoubt,** ① *daily 0900-1800,* built by government forces during the New Zealand Wars. The gardens have rose gardens and a begonia house. At the base of the hill, at the southern end of Dive Crescent, is the **Te Awanui Waka,** a replica Maori war canoe. **Gate Pa Church** on Cameron Road, south of the city centre, marks the spot of the Battle of Gate *Pa* in 1864. As well as the obvious attraction of **'the Mount'** (see page 274), there are a number of superb **beaches** in the area, most stretching from Mount Maunganui east to Papamoa. ›› *For Sleeping, Eating and other listings, see pages 276-281.*

Mount Maunganui

Dominated by its namesake 'Mount' and graced by golden beaches, Mount Maunganui, 6 km north of Tauranga, has held an irresistible appeal to both locals and visitors for years. In winter the town is quiet, its streets and beach almost empty, but in summer and particularly over the New Year, the place is a tourist battleground with the Mount crowned with an army of view junkies and the beach with battalions of soporific sunbathers. The Mount itself (also known as 'Mauao') is 232 m and guards the entrance to the Tauranga Harbour.

Sights Once an island and an almost impregnable Maori *pa*, the Mount now serves as an obvious tourist attraction and a landmark for ships negotiating the harbour's treacherous entrance. There is a network of pathways which criss-cross the Mount, offering a range of pleasant walks to suit all levels of fitness. The summit climb, which is best accessed from the south of the motor camp, takes about 45 minutes one-way and, as you might expect, is rewarded with a memorable view.

From the narrow neck of the Mount, **Ocean Beach** begins a stretch of sand that sweeps, almost uninterrupted, east to the Cape. Just offshore from Ocean Beach are the two small islands **Moturiki** and **Motuotau**. Moturiki can be reached from the shore and is a popular spot for fishing, while Motuotau is important for its wildlife. Other than the

Mount Maunganui

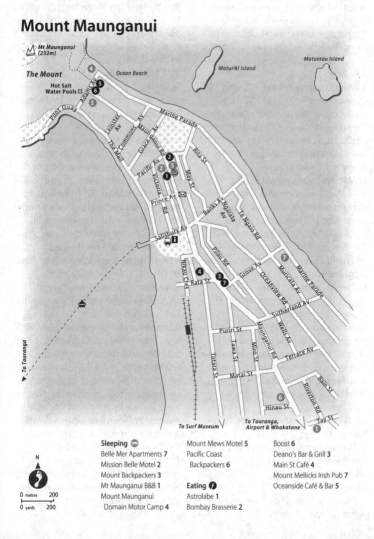

Sleeping 😊
Belle Mer Apartments **7**
Mission Belle Motel **2**
Mount Backpackers **3**
Mt Maunganui B&B **1**
Mount Maunganui
  Domain Motor Camp **4**

Mount Mews Motel **5**
Pacific Coast
  Backpackers **6**

Eating 🍴
Astrolabe **1**
Bombay Brasserie **2**

Boost **6**
Deano's Bar & Grill **3**
Main St Café **4**
Mount Mellicks Irish Pub **7**
Oceanside Café & Bar **5**

N

0 metres 200
0 yards 200

Mount and the beaches the major attraction in the town is the Mount Maunganui **Hot Salt Water Pools**, ① *at the base of the Mount on Adams Av, T07-5750868. Mon-Sat 0600-2200, Sun 0800-2200*. From $2.50, child $1.50. Here, therapeutic salt water is heated to 39°C in a number of large communal and private pools.

Even if you cannot stay up on a board for more than a nanosecond or have never tried surfing the **Mount Surf Museum**, ① *Unit 5, 15 Portside Dr (off Hull Rd or Triton in the Mount Industrial area), T07-5724420, $5, open weekends 1100-1500 or by arrangement*, is worth a look if only to see the huge collection of boards on display and the intriguing 'shrine' to Malibu surfing guru 'Da Cat' (Well, he was never going to be a 'Quentin' was he?). ▸▸ *For Sleeping, Eating and other listings, see pages 277- 281.*

● Sleeping

There is plenty of choice in Tauranga City and Mount Maunganui, but it's best to book ahead in mid-summer when the area is hugely popular with Kiwi holidaymakers. Most of the region's luxury lodges and B&Bs are northwest of the city towards Katikati.

Tauranga *p272*

LL **Ridge Country Retreat**, *300 Rocky Cutting Rd, Welcome Bay, T07-5421301, www.rcr.co.nz* The utmost in relaxation. Beautifully-appointed suites and an overall emphasis on health and beauty with a full range of in-house therapies on offer. You simply won't want to leave.

LL **Matahui Lodge**, *187 Matahui Rd, T07-5718121, www.matahui-lodge.co.nz* A stunning property in a tranquil spot overlooking Tauranga's Inner Harbour and Matakana Island. All the facilities and comforts you might expect and friendly hosts with a passion for fine food and wine. Dinner by arrangement.

LL **Fantail Lodge and Villas**, *117 Rea Rd, T07-5491581, www.fantaillodge.co.nz* Located 25 mins north of the city near Katikati, this country lodge estate, which consistently rates in the country's top 10, offers all-suite luxury accommodation again in beautiful surroundings. Fine cuisine.

L-AL **Taiparoro House B&B**, *11 Fifth Av, T07-5779607, kl.kelly@clear.net.nz* Historic 1882 restored villa close to the city centre. Offers a range of rooms and suites. Organic food a speciality.

L-AL **Puriri Park Boutique Hotel**, *32 Cameron Rd, T07-5771480, www.puriripark.co.nz* Tauranga's principal centrally located hotel. Modern self-contained suites. Good weekend and winter specials.

AL **Durham Motor Inn**, *corner of Cameron Rd and Harrington St, T07-5779691*. One of the best motels in the city centre. 20 clean modern units, pool and spas.

AL-A **Harbour City Motor Inn**, *50 Wharf St, T07-5711435, taurangaharbourcity@xtra.co.nz* One of the city's newest upper-range motels, ideally located with well-appointed rooms and fine facilities.

AL-A **Tau Tau Lodge**, *1133 Pyes Pa Rd, T07-5431600, jevkerry@wave. co.nz* New, good-value boutique lodge located between Rotorua and Tauranga in elevated bush setting. Private suites and spa.

A **Ambassador Motor Inn**, *9 Fifteenth Av, T07-5785665, ambassador.tga@xtra.co.nz* New motel at the estuary end of the Av. Wide range of units, spa and heated pool.

A **Beach Front Villas**, *535 Papamoa Beach Rd, T07-5720816, www.papamoabeach.co.nz* Although a few miles from Tauranga in Papamoa, this complex and villas are on the beachfront and are recommended.

A **Beach House Motel**, *224 Papamoa Beach Rd, T07-5721424, www.beachhouse motel.co.nz* New, award-winning and unusual beachside motel in Papamoa with 18 luxury units, spa, Sky TV.

B **Strand Motel**, *27 The Strand, T07-5785807, strandmotel@xtra.co.nz* Comfortable, basic, budget motel located close to all amenities.

C-D **Bell Lodge**, *39 Bell St, SH2 North (Waihi Rd), T07-5786344, www.bell-lodge.co.nz* Very smart purpose-built complex located north of the city in park surroundings. Large kitchen and comfortable en suite rooms or dorms, open fire, tent sites. Free trips and bikes.

C-D **Tauranga YHA**, *171 Elizabeth St, T07-5785064, yhataur@yha.org.nz* Well-established hostel, comfortable, friendly and centrally located. Twin, doubles, dorm and camping options. Internet.

D Just the Ducks Nuts Backpackers, *6 Vale St, T07-5761366, www.justtheducksnuts.co.nz* Small, but with a name like that an inevitably popular, laid-back hostel with usual facilities including an log fire and free bike hire.

D Apple Tree Cottage Backpackers, *47 Maxwells Rd, T07-5767404, m.j.dek@actrix.co.nz* Small private house located on the edge of the harbour about 1 km from the city centre. Quiet, relaxed and friendly, with hot spa, bike hire and internet.

Motorcamps and campsites
A-D Top Ten Papamoa Beach Holiday Resort, *535 Papamoa Beach Rd, T07-5720816, www.papamoabeach.co.nz* A fine beachfront camp with wide range of options and facilities.

Silver Birch Holiday Park, *101 Turret Rd, SH2, T07-5784603.*

Palms Holiday Park, *162 Waihi Rd, T07-5789337.* Both the above are also adequate options.

Mount Maunganui *p274*
LL Thorton Lodge, *171 Oceanbeach Rd, T07-5755555.* Luxury beachfront lodge with 8 well-appointed apartments, suites and a penthouse with spa.

LL Augusta Lodge, *198 Oceanbeach Rd, T07-5759677, www.augustalodge.co.nz* Modern colonial-style lodge right next to the Mount Maunganui golf course and near the beach, 5 large luxury suites, pool and spa.

AL Mission Belle Motel, *corner of Victoria Rd and Pacific Av, T07-5752578, www.missionbellemotel.co.nz* Modern, luxury Spanish-style motel in the heart of town.

Tauranga centre

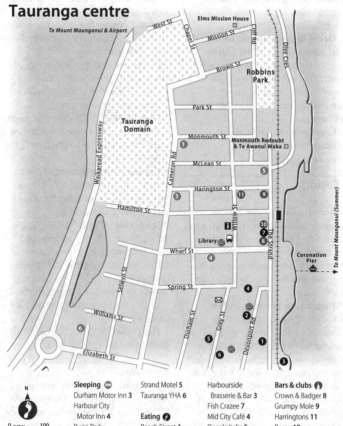

Sleeping	Strand Motel **5**	Harbourside	Bars & clubs
Durham Motor Inn **3**	Tauranga YHA **6**	Brasserie & Bar **3**	Crown & Badger **8**
Harbour City		Fish Crazee **7**	Grumpy Mole **9**
Motor Inn **4**	**Eating**	Mid City Café **4**	Harringtons **11**
Puriri Park	Beach Street **1**	Piccola Italia **5**	Roma **10**
Boutique **1**	Collar & Thai **2**	Stars & Stripes **6**	

0 metres 100
0 yards 100

LL-AL Belle Mer Apartments, *53 Marine Pde, T0800-100235, www.bellemer.co.nz* New tastefully-appointed luxury apartments located opposite the beach and within walking distance of shops and hot pools. Recommended.

A Mount Mews Motel, *8 Maunganui Rd, T07-5757006*. Well established, close to all amenities. Spas.

B Mt Maunganui B&B, *463 Maunganui Rd, T07-5754013, bednbrekkie@ihug.co.nz* Recently refurbished and centrally located, 5 rooms with shared bathrooms, good value.

C-D Pacific Coast Backpackers, *432 Maunganui Rd, T07-5749601, www.pacificcoastlodge.co.nz* Lively with excellent range of comfortable doubles, singles and bunks. Wide range of activities organized, often with price reductions.

C-D Mount Backpackers, *87 Maunganui Rd, T07-5750860*. Smaller more centrally located backpackers. Internet.

C-D Mount Maunganui Domain Motor Camp, *Adams Av, T07-5754471*. Ideally located at the base of the Mount and next to both the beach and the hot pools but charges accordingly and relies too much on that fact to the detriment of its facilities.

C-D Cosy Corner Motor Camp, *40 Oceanbeach Rd, T07-5755899*. Quieter camp further along the beach.

🍴 Eating

Tauranga *p272*

Tauranga has a fine selection of restaurants and cafes to suit all tastes and budgets. Most are on or around The Strand overlooking the harbour. Pick up the free and comprehensive *Dine Out* guide from the VIC.

$$$ Harbourside Brasserie and Bar, *T0800-721714, www.harbourside-tga.co.nz 1130-late*. Enjoys a loyal following and the reputation as Tauranga's best restaurant. Located as much on the water as beside it at the southern end of The Strand, it offers an excellent and imaginative all-day blackboard and à la carte menu, with an emphasis on local seafood.

$$$ Somerset Cottage Restaurant, *away from the city centre, at 30 Bethlehem Rd,*

T07-5766889 (city west). A small, congenial place serving a classic range of international cuisine to suit a wide range of tastes. Bookings essential.

$$$ Mills Reef Winery and Restaurant, *143 Moffat Rd (city west), T07-5768844. Daily from 1000*. Another out-of-town option for lunch and dinner is this renowned restaurant, specialising in seafood and fish delights.

$$$ The Bluebiyou, *559 Papamoa Beach Rd, T07-572209. Daily from 1100*. Right next to the beach in Papamoa, and great if you want to get away from the city (east).

$$ Piccola Italia, *107 Grey St, T07-5788363. Wed-Fri 1130-1430, Mon-Sat from 1800*. A fine Italian restaurant that combines excellent cuisine, congenial authentic atmosphere, fine service and a great Italian wine list. It has a popular local following.

$$ Beach Street, *82 Devonport Rd (on the waterfront), T07-5780745. Daily from 1100-late*. Another fine choice overlooking the harbour. It offers imaginative traditional dishes and great pizzas.

$$ Collar and Thai, *Goddards Centre, 21 Devonport Rd, T07-5776655. Mon-Fri 1130-1400, Mon-Sun 1730-late*. For Thai food you can't go wrong here.

$$ Talk of India, *corner of Cameron Rd and Third Av, T07-5787360. Tue-Sun*. Good Indian food – this is the oldest and reputedly the most popular place.

$ The Stars and Stripes, *Shop 1 and 2 West Plaza, Devonport Rd, T07-5771319*. Has a good selection of traditional steak and burgers at affordable prices.

$ Shiraz Café, *12 Wharf St, T07-5770059. Mon-Sat from 1100*. A great range of lunchtime snacks (try a shwarma or falafel) and a fine cheap breakfast and good coffee.

$ Mid City Café, *Wharf St pedestrian mall*. Popular with the locals for a quick coffee or value breakfast.

$ Fish Crazee, *87 The Strand, T07-5779375. Daily 1800-2100*. Fish and chips.

Mount Maunganui *p274*

$$ Astrolabe (not named after a space ship, but a shipwreck), *82 Maunganui Rd, T07-5748155*. The combination restaurant, bar and café facilities here are to be recommended. It offers breakfast, lunch and dinner with a range of fine and imaginative traditional dishes. Live bands often play at weekends.

$$ Bombay Brasserie, *77 Maunganui Rd (almost directly across the road from Astrolabe), T07-5752539. Daily from 1800*. An excellent, affordable, Indian restaurant.

$$ Boost, *below the Twin Towers on Adams Av, T07-5743360. Open daily*. Modern and trendy, and a safe bet for gourmet and vegetarian pizzas and also serves a fine coffee. Takeaways available.

$$ Deano's Bar and Grill, *305 Maunganui Rd*. Recommended for a good-value steak . There is often entertainment at weekends.

$$ Mount Mellick, *317 Maunganui Rd, T07-5740047. Daily 0900-2200*. A new Irish pub good for traditional European fare with an all-day roast on Sun, live music Fri/Sat.

$ Main St Café, *just south of the roundabout on Maunganui Rd. Open from 0700*. Locals head here for a good, cheap breakfast.

♠ Pubs, bars and clubs

The Crown and Badger, *on the corner of Wharf and The Strand*. A popular spot especially on sunny evenings when the clientele spills out on to the street.

Grumpy Mole, *41 The Strand, T07-5711222*. Another very wooden pub and entertainment venue that has a 'hump-day' every week, whatever that may be.

Roma Nightclub, *Strand, T07-5783100. Thu-Sat til 0500*. Reputed to be the best place to go in the wee hours.

Harrington's, *10 Harrington St, T07-5785427. Thu-Sat until about 0500*. The most comm- ercial club attracting mainly a young crowd.

✹ Festivals and events

Brightstone Blues Brews and Barbecues (*Jan*) Outdoor performances with both national and international celebrities, mixed with boutique brewery product and barbecue food. **Port of Tauranga Half-Iron Man** (*Jan*) Hailed as the country's premier Half-Iron Man event attracting over 1000 national and mainly Australian competitors.

Tauranga Food and Wine Festival (*Feb*) a celebration of fine local and national food and wine. **Zespri Lifestyles Festival of Tauranga** (*Mar*) Held over the entire month, local, national and international events cover beach and surf, harbour and sailing, art exhibitions and shows, food, wine, shopping, sports and leisure activities. **Montana National Jazz Festival** (*Apr*) Considered (after Waiheke Auckland perhaps) to be the country's premier jazz event, performed in the Baycourt Theatre, bars and cafés. **Arts Festival Tauranga** (*Oct/Nov*) Biennial event from 2001 with street performers, dance, theatre, exhibitions and literary events. **Décor Greenworld Garden and Arts Festival** (*Dec*) Another biennial event held early in the month and alternates with the Arts Festival and held over one weekend. Regional gardens are opened to the public and visual art exhibitions are staged throughout the city.

▲ Activities and tours

Abseiling and climbing
Abseil and Bushcraft *a short distance from the city, T07-5410733*. Offers an outdoor 25-m abseiling experience, suitable for beginners. **Rock House**, *9 Triton Av, (opposite the Mount Action Centre), in Mount Maunganui, T07-5724920. Mon 1600-late, Tue-Fri 1200-late, Sat and Sun 1000-1600. Adult $12, child $8*. A rock wall that's proving very popular. Instruction provided.

Bungee Rocket
Bungee Rocket, *on the waterfront, T07-5783057. From $35*. Like most principal centres Tauranga has a 'Bungee Rocket'. The idea is to get strapped into a seat with another lunatic and then shot up into the air on an elastic band. Judging by the expressions on the point of release, it is truly memorable.

Cruising and sailing
South Sea Sailing Company, *T07-5761841, www.southseasailing.com* Offer day and multi-day eco-cruises aboard their luxury catamaran and are licensed to offer dolphin watching and swimming. Eco-cruise day-trip with lunch from $120, overnight

❝❞ Whakatane...has a vibrant atmosphere that is often lacking in many New Zealand towns of the same size. There is just something about it – something that can warm the heart...

from $250. **Blue Ocean Charters**, T07-5789685. Offer a range of half, full or evening, scenic harbour, island and fishing trips from $60.

Diving
Dive HQ , *213 Cameron Rd, T07-5784050, www.divehq.co.nz*; and
Dive Tauranga, *50 Cross Rd, T07-5715286, www.diveunderwater.com*; are the two principal operators based in the city offering snorkelling and dive tours around Mount Maunganui and to local wrecks and Mayor Island.
Eco Divers, *90 Maunganui Rd, Mount Maunganui, T0800-5722784, www.ecodivers.co.nz* Receiving very good reviews and are recommended. Snorkelling from $50, single dive with gear $60, Dolphin- watching and swimming from $100.

Dolphin watching
Tauranga Dolphin Company, *T07-5783197, www.swimwithdolphins.co.nz* $100, child $85. Have been providing dolphin watching and swimming eco-trips for over 10 years. Departs daily for an all-day trip at 0900 from the Port at Tauranga. All gear provided, take your own lunch.
Dolphin Seafaris, *Marina D5 (across the Harbour Bridge) T0800-3268747, www.nzdolphin.com* From $100, child $85. Offering a similar 3-4 hour trip.

Fishing
There are numerous fishing charters (including big game) available and the VIC has full listings and prices.
Blue Ocean Charters *T07-5789685, www.blueoceancharters.co.nz* Offer a wide range of opportunities including dolphin watching, fishing and diving.

Scott Hollis-Johns, *T07-5430555, fishart@xtra.co.nz* Local freshwater fly fishing trips, from $60.

4WD and quad biking
Hill Hoppers, *T07-5331818, www.adventure4wd.co.nz* From $60, child $30. One of the region's best 4-wheel drive activity operators and are based in Te Puke. They have over 3 km of track and a wide range of vehicles. Suitable for the novice and owner.

Golf
Tauranga Golf Club, *Cameron Rd, T07-5788465.*
Mount Maunganui Club, *Fairway Av, T07-5754487.*
If you want to try the relatively new sport of **Golf Cross** where the ball is oval and the hole goalposts then
Ngawaro Golf Cross, *25km southeast of Tauranga on Pyes Pa-Rotorua Direct Rd, T07-5432110, www.golfcross.com,* can oblige.

Horse trekking
Papamoa Adventure Park, *1162 Welcome Bay Rd, T07-5420972.* From $30.
World of Horses, *SH2 between Tauranga and Katikati (14 km), T07-5480404.* Offers not only horse trekking but display, corral, show stables and a café.
Windsong, *161 Peers Rd, Owanawa (off SH29 west), T07-5433132.* A miniature horse stud and training centre for tours and displays.

Jet boating and jet skiing
Jet ski hire:
Bay Marine, *T07-5776005*;
Bay Jet Ski, *T07-5764034.*
Longridge Park, *in Te Puke, T07-5331515.* Offers thrilling jet boat ride amongst its many attractions. $59, child $35.

Kayaking

Oceanix, *in Mt Maunganui, T07-5722196, www.oceanix.co.nz* Offers a range of excursions that take in very different environments from New Zealand's largest port and the Maunganui Heads to the McLaren Falls Park. Sunset and moonlight trips are also an option, from $75.

Waimarino Adventure Park, *Bethlehem, T07-5764233, www.waimarino.com* Also offers a range of guided and self-guided day trips (from $30) to places as far afield as Mayor Island (from $140) and white water courses, from $199.

Mountain biking

Oropi Grove, *3 km up Oropi Rd from SH28 – accessed off Joyce Rd (off Pyes Pa Rd), T07-5773055.* Considered the best track in the area.

Parasailing, waterskiing and kite surfing

Kite Surfing New Zealand, *T07-5701947, www.kitesurfingnz.com*
Parasail BOP, T07-5747333 / T025-791-934. 'The lift of a lifetime', the 'dry' or 'the dunk'.
Water Rox *in Mt Maunganui, Pilot Bay, T07-5747333 / T027-2901125, www.waterrox.co.nz* Offer all sorts of watersport options from parasailing and waterskiing to wakeboarding to the intriguing 'Air Glider'.

Rafting

The Wairoa and Rangitaiki Rivers near Tauranga are major venues for whitewater rafting. For operators see page 270.

Tandem skydiving

Tauranga Tandem Skydiving, *at the airport, T07-5767990, freefall@xtra.co.nz* A drop from 8,000 ft costs $190.

Thermal pools

There are numerous hot pools around Tauranga, with the most popular being the **Mount Maunganui Hot Pools** (see p276). Also hot springs at

Athenree *Athenree Rd, north of Tauranga, on SH2, T07-8635600, daily 0900-1700*; and

Fernland Spa Mineral Hot Pools, 250 Cambridge Rd (SH29), Tauranga, T07-5783081, daily 1000-2200.

Scenic flights and gliding

Island Air Charters, *Hangar 1, Airport, T07-5755795.* Will take you for local flights, or further afield to White Island, Slipper Island, Rotorua and the Coromandel. 1 hour, $120.
Tauranga Aero Club, *Aerodrome Rd, T07-5753210.* Offers similar flights. For weekend **gliding** opportunities call the local gliding club, *T07-5763114 / T07-5752 747, www.gliding.co.nz* 15 min from $80.

Sightseeing and wine tours

The VIC has a full listing of local day trip operators in the area, including:
Tasting Tours, *T07-5441383, tgatastingtours@xtra.co.nz*, An entertaining day of beer and wine tasting with lunch at the very congenial Mills Reef Vineyard Restaurant from $130.

Surfing

Lovely Planet, *T07-5723399, www.lovelyplanet.co.nz* and
New Zealand Surf Schools, *T07-5741666, nzsurfschool@yahoo.com* Both give 1 hr lessons from $45.

Walking

The *Walkways of Tauranga* leaflet is free from the VIC and outlines a number of city and local park walks. The walks around **Mount Maunganui** and to its summit are worthy of being the main walking attraction, but the **McLaren Falls Park** (*about 10 km south of the city on SH29, T07-5431099, Wed-Sun*), and the **Rerekawau Falls (Kaiate Falls)** tracks (signposted from Welcome Bay Road) have other pleasant short walking opportunities. In McLaren Falls Park there are also some interesting animals including very hairy Tibetan yaks. The **Kaimai Ranges**, just to the west of the city, also offer numerous longer and more strenuous walks.

⊙ Directory

Banks All the major branches have offices

For an explanation of the sleeping and eating price codes used in this guide, see the inside front cover. Other relevant information is provided in the Essentials chapter, see page 51.

and ATMs in the city centre. **Car hire** Avis, *325 Cameron Rd, T07-5784204*; **Budget**, *Intercity Building, Dive Cres, T07-5785156*; Johnny's Rentals, *115 Hewletts Rd, T07-5759204*; **Rite Price Rentals**, *25 Totara St, Mt Maunganui, T07-5752726*. **Cycle** hire **Underground Cycles**, *111 Grey St, T07-5780208*, from $20 per day. **Internet** Tauranga Library, *Willow St*, Maunganui Library, *Maunganui Rd*; Cybersurf, *Piccadilly Arcade, Grey St*;

Gateway, *Shop 18, Goddard Centre, Devonport Rd, T07-5711112*; Mount Backpackers, *87 Maunganui Rd, T07-5750860. 0900-2000*. **Medical services** Baycare, *10th St, T07-5788000. 1700-0800*; Hospital, Cameron Rd, T07-5798000. **Post office** *17 Grey St. Mon-Fri 0830-1700, Sat 0900-1200*. **Scooter hire** *T0800-726684*, 2 hr $30. **Taxis** Tauranga Taxis, *T07-5775461, T07-5786086*; Taxi Cabs, *T07-5754054*.

Whakatane and Opotiki

→ *Phone code: 07 Colour map 2, grid B4 Population: 17,000/ 10,000*

Whakatane is the principal town in the Eastern Bay of Plenty, at the mouth of the Whakatane River. It has a vibrant atmosphere that is often lacking in many New Zealand towns of the same size. There is just something about it – something that can warm the heart. Opotiki, 60 km southeast of Whakatane, near the mouths of the Waioeka and Otara Rivers, is a small and fairly unremarkable town (with some fine beaches) but like Whakatane, is rich in Maori history, with settlement taking place before the great migrations of the 14th century. It was the base of the Hauhau – an almost religious sect of Maori rebels who were fierce enemies of the early Pakeha.

Ins and outs

Getting there
Whakatane airport is just northwest of the town off SH2 and is served by **Air New Zealand Link**, T0800-737000. The airport shuttle will get you into town for about $12, T07-3080222. For taxis use the same number or T0800-421829. **Intercity** buses serve Whakatane and the VIC acts as the booking agent. Bay of Plenty company **Bayline** also offers services to Tauranga Mon-Fri, $11.50 and Opotiki Tue/Thu, $7.00, T0800-4229287. You can connect with the East Cape and Opotiki shuttle from Whakatane (see below). For shuttle buses going around the East Cape (SH35) see East Cape section.

Information
Whakatane VIC, ① *corner of Quay and Kakahoroa Dr (to the east of the town centre), T07-3086058, www.whakatane.com Mon-Fri 0900-1700, Sat 0900-1600*. The VIC also holds DoC information. **Opotiki VIC**, ① *corner of St John and Elliot Sts, T07-3158484, www.eastlandnz.com, www.opotiki.org Daily 0830-1700, Sat/Sun 1000-1500*. **DOC** is an adjunct to this office, T07-3156103. The comprehensive and free booklet *Opotiki and East Cape Free Holiday Guide* is a must for anyone touring the area.

History

Whakatane has a rich Maori history going back to 1150 when the Polynesian explorer Toi-te-Hauatahi landed and was reputed to have settled. Later, in the mid 14th century, the ancestral canoe, Mataatua, captained by one Chief Toroa, is believed to

European settlement founded until later in the century, and more especially in the early 1900s, when land drainage opened up the land for farming.

The name Whakatane means 'to act like a man', and it came about after the heroic acts of Wairaka, the high-spirited daughter of Toroa. When the *waka* landed at the river mouth, the men came ashore to investigate. As was the case in those days, the women were instructed to stay in the canoe, but they were so busy nattering away they didn't notice the canoe drifting. This left them in a bit of a predicament as the oars were *tapu* (out of bounds) to the womenfolk. However, young Wairaka, the spirited daughter of the chief, took up the oars and, rowing furiously for the safety of the shore, proclaimed; '*Ka Whakatane au I ahau*' which roughly translated means 'we must now play the part of men'. A very beautiful and evocative statue of Wairaka now stands on a rock at the harbour entrance – a reminder to us all of her heroism.

Sights

Whakatane

The major attraction of Whakatane is as a gateway to visit the active volcano **White Island**, which can, on a clear day, be seen 50 km offshore, steaming away merrily. The other major activities are dolphin swimming, fishing and, to a lesser extent, walking locally and beyond, in the **Urewera National Park**, **Whirinaki Forest Park** and **Tarawera Falls** areas (see Pohutukawa Tours, page 285). The town also enjoys some of the highest annual sunshine hours in the country.

If you have your own transport, perhaps the best thing to do first is to get your bearings. To do this take Hillcrest Road south from the centre of town and the road over the hill west towards Ohope Beach. At the crest of the hill turn left and follow the signs to the **Kohi Point Scenic Reserve**. At the headland (which was the *pa* site of the first Maori settlers) you will get a grand view of the town, the coast and White Island. From here you can also embark on a number of short or long scenic coastal walks.

The island close to shore is **Whale** or **Moutohora Island** (which does indeed look like a whale from the side). Moutohora is another less active volcano which has some hot springs and a number of historic *pa* sites. It is privately owned and a wildlife refuge administered by DoC. Although generally off limits, DoC does offer occasional guided tours in the summer months (contact the VIC).

Back in the town centre another natural feature is the **Pohaturoa**, a large rock outcrop located at the corner of The Strand and Commerce Street. For some six centuries this was used by the Maori as a meeting place and was also where the local Ngati Awa tribe signed the Treaty of Waitangi in the 1840s. While the summit was used as sacred place for the bones of early chiefs, the newborns were given a form of baptism and dedicated to the Gods in a stream at its foot. More local historical information can be gleaned at the **Whakatane District Museum and Gallery**, ① *Boon St, T07-3079805. Tue-Fri 1000-1630, Sat/Sun 1100-1500. Entry by donation*. As well as a wealth of historical displays and a fine dynamic gallery space, it houses a large collection of over 20,000 photographs.

No trip to Whakatane would be complete without a short drive west along to the harbour entrance to see the gorgeous, svelte sculpture of **Wairaka** – a fine tribute to the town's roots and womanhood. There is also an interesting **mural** on the wall at the corner of The Strand and The Quay. It depicts a bi-cultural scene of Maori and *Pakeha* (whites). If you look closely you will see the head of Captain Cook has been defaced a number of times. This is a reflection of some strong feelings which still exist in the area regarding bicultural and land issues. The Tuhoe Iwi, whose lands lie to the south of Whakatane, are well known for their particularly staunch stand.

Just 8 km over the hill from Whakatane, heading east, is the 11 km long sandspit called **Ohope Beach**, guarding the entrance to the Ohiwa Harbour. Principally a beach resort, it is a fine place to while away a few hours in the sun, swimming, sunbathing or just watching White Island billow with steam in the distance. ⮞ *For Sleeping, Eating and other listings, see pages 284-286.*

Opotiki

The **Hukutaia Domain** is about 6 km from the town and signposted to the left after the Waioeka Bridge. It is a hectare of bush with many New Zealand native trees, including a historic 2000 year-old puriri tree called 'Taketakerau', with a girth of about 22 m and a height over 23 m. The hollow in this tree was used by the local Iwi to store the preserved bones of their dead, in an elaborate ritual and as protection from enemy desecration. Also of historical interest is the **Church Of Hinoa** (St Stephen's Anglican Church) at the north end of Church Street. It was originally built for the Church Missionary Society and the Reverend Karl Volkner, who first arrived in 1859. Sadly, given local bad feeling towards the *Pakeha*, he was considered a government spy and killed by Hauhau emissaries in 1865. There naturally followed much unrest in the region.

● Sleeping

Whakatane *p282*

AL-A White Island Rendezvous, *15 Strand East, T0800-242299, T07-3089588, www.whiteisland.co.nz* Part of the Pee Jay White Island Tour operation. New, well-appointed waterfront motel. Café and spa.

AL-A Pacific Coast Motel, *41 Landing Rd, T07-3080100.* Another modern option. Luxury 1-bedroom or studio units. Spa.

AL-A Barringtons Motor Lodge, *34 Landing Rd, T0800-830130, T3084273.* Modern units, some with spa and disabled facilities.

B Nau Mai Motel, *61 Landing Rd, T07-3086422.* Budget motel option close to town centre.

AL Motuhora Rise B&B, *2 Motuhora Rise (off Waiewe) St, T07-3070224, jtspell@xtra.co.nz* Fine B&B on outskirts of town with well-appointed rooms, open fire and spa.

A Clifton Manor Motel and B&B, *5 Clifton Rd, T07-3072145.* B&B in a spacious home and self-contained units within walking distance of town centre. Pool.

A Te Ruru Log Cabin, *659 White Pine Bush Rd, T07-3129069.* Self-contained double with en suite in log cabin style in country location. Horse treks available.

A Briar Rose, *54 Waiewe St, T07-3080314.* Charming cottage in bush setting close to town. Double, single and studio en suite.

B-D Whakatane Hotel, *The Strand, T07-3071670.* Basic but sound backpacker-style accommodation. Singles and shared. Great Irish pub and a noisy nightclub next to that – get a room in the west wing.

B-D Karibu Backpackers, *13 Landing Rd, T07-3078276.* Friendly no-nonsense suburban house hostel in central location. No single rooms. Bus drop-offs right outside, off-street parking, free bike use.

C-D Whakatane Motor Camp, *McGarvey Rd, T07-3088694.* Basic but next to the river.

Ohope *p284*

There are numerous motels along the waterfront, including:

A The Ocean View, *18 West End, T07-3125665*;

A Surfs Reach, *52 West End, T07-3124159*;

A-B Jody's on the Beach, *31 West End, T07-3124616*;

A-B Alfresco Court, *5 Moana St, T07-3125061.*

Good B&Bs include:

AL-A Turney's B&B, *28 Pohutukawa Av, T07-3125040*;

B The Rafters, *261A Pohutukawa Av, T07-3124856.*

Motorcamps

C-D Ohope Beach Top Ten, *367 Harbour Rd.* A good motorcamp in a quiet spot at the west end, right on the beach.

Opotiki *p284*

There are many motels, farmstays, B&Bs and backpackers in Opotiki, the VIC has listings.

AL Capeview Cottage, *167 Tablelands Rd via SH35, T07-3157887, www.capeview.co.nz* Peaceful, modern cottage B&B in country setting cottage 5 km from town.

A Riverview Cottage, *SH2, T07-73155553*,

info@newzealandbestspots.com Well-appointed self-contained cottage, 10 min from Opotiki, next to the Waioeka River. Also offers kayaking trips from $39.

C-D Central Oasis Backpackers, *30 King St, T07-3155165, centraloasis@hotmail.com* A small traditional cottage that is in the heart of town with doubles, twins and dorm. Free use of body boards and bikes and will assist with East Cape transport bookings.

Motorcamps
C-D Opotiki Holiday Park, *Potts Av, T07-3156050*. The only motorcamp within the town – basic but adequate.

⑨ Eating

Whakatane *p282*
There is quite a good choice in Whakatane and all are pretty affordable.

$$ The Wharf Shed, *Strand East, T07-3085698. Daily from 1100*. A fine restaurant with an imaginative, mainly seafood menu.
$$ The Chambers, *also on Strand East (closer to town), T07-3070107. Daily from 1000*. Has a nice ambience and serves a superb lamb dish. Also doubles as a café and has internet.
$$ Where Else Inn, *62 The Strand, T07-3086721*. One of the newest restaurants in town, with reliably good and affordable traditional TexMex dishes.
$-$$ Main St Café, *93 The Strand*. Head here for a cheap snack, street-side coffee and a grand date scone.
Two other reputable eateries are:
$-$$ Go Global, *Commerce St, T07-3089000*;
$-$$ Why Not Café, *below the Whakatane Hotel, T07-3071006*.
New World supermarket, *The Strand West, T07-3088629. Mon-Sun 0800-2000*.

Ohope *p284*
$$ Pohutukawa Café, *on the Main Rd (19), T07-3125292*. Has the best coffee.
$$ Stingray café, *340 Harbour Rd (eastern end of Ohope), T07-3124005*. Has the best harbour views.

Hot Bread Shop Café, *on the main road through town opposite the Eastland Pacific Motel, T07-3156795. Daily 0500-1700*. Has a wide selection of snacks, light meals, good coffee and internet.
New World supermarket is at the western end of Bridge St as you head out of town.

ⓕ Pubs, clubs and entertainment

The Craic, *in the Whakatane Hotel*. A superb small, cosy Irish pub.
Boiler Room, *next door*. Nightclub which hopefully won't ruin the place.
Cinema 5, *The Strand, T07-3087623*.

▲ Activities and tours

Diving and snorkelling
Dive White (Island), *186 The Strand, T0800-348394, www.divewhite.co.nz* The principal operator in the area offering dive trips and snorkel trips off White Island from $120 (snorkel), $225 dive (gear included).
Dolphin Down Under, *(see below)*. Also offers dive trips and snorkel trips off other offshore islands and there are over a dozen other charters available from Whakatane. For details contact the VIC.

Dolphin watching and ecotours
The Bay of Plenty is rich with schools of playful dolphin, and encounters with schools of over 1000 are not uncommon.
Dolphin Down Under, *T07-3084636*. The principal operators, offering a weather-dependent, 5-6 hour trip for around $135, child $75. If a school of dolphins is encountered (highly likely) you can either observe or get in the water. Trips several times daily in summer, by demand in winter. Booking essential.
Ohiwa Harbour Tours, *T07-3087837*. A new local ecotour which encompasses a trip by road to take in natural and human historical facts, followed by a 2½ hour cruise on the wildlife rich Ohiwa Harbour. Light refreshments are provided, but take your own food. Three hours in total. $55. Recommended.

The Bay of Plenty Whakatane and Opotiki

Pohutukawa Tours, *T07-3086495, T025-2218993*. Have an interesting volcanic feature-based tour ($75) as well as trips to the beautiful Whirinaki Forest Park ($95) and Mount Tarawera ($90).

Fishing

There are over 18 fishing charters available ranging from $40-$1350.
Contact the VIC for listings.

Horse trekking

Tui Glen Farm, *2 km from Kawerau, south, T07-3236457*. $35 for 1 hour, $85 for 3 hours.

Hot pools

The nearest hot pools to Whakatane are the **Awakeri Hot Springs**, *which are 16 km away, just off SH30 to Rotorua southwest of the town*, $3 T07-3049117. Basic but relaxing and motor park and camping available.

Jet boating

Kiwi Jet Tours, *T07-3070663*. Offer a 1½-hour trip down the Rangitaiki for $65, child $55.
Motu River Jet Boat Tours, *Opotiki, T07-3158107*. The main jet boat operator for the river. Two hours $85, child $50.

Kayaking

Dolphin Down Under, *see above*, or **KG Kayaks**, *T07-3154005*. Sunset or moonlight trips, 2 hr from $55.

Rafting

Wet n' Wild, *Opotiki, T07-3496567, www.wetnwildrafting.co.nz* Offers one of the North Island's best wilderness expeditions, the multi-day trip down the remote Motu River. Provided the river levels are good, this is an unforgettable experience that will cost around $590. Recommended.

Walking

The VIC has details and leaflets outlining local short and long walks, craft and historic town trails.
Tramplite Walks, *T07-3049893, www.tramplitewalks.co.nz* A local company offering a varied and interesting 3-day hike for a very reasonable $280, which includes accommodation, food and transport.

White Island tours and scenic flights

'**Te Kahurangi**' operating as **Blue Sky Tours**, *T0800-377878 / T07-3237829*. A catamaran leaves at 0830 for a 5-6-hour trip to the island. Lunch provided. $110. Bookings essential.
Pee Jays, *15 Strand East, T07-3089588, T0800-733529, www.whiteisland.co.nz* Highly commercial operator which offers a 5-6-hour trip leaving at 0900. Lunch and refreshments provided. They will often deviate off schedule if dolphins are spotted. $110. Bookings essential.
Vulcan Helicopters, *T0800-804354, www.vulcanheli.co.nz* Operate out of Whakatane airport. Three-hour tour, 1 hour on the island. From $375.
East Bay Flight Centre, *Whakatane airport, T0800-550880, T07-3126204, www.whiteislandair.com* Offers a 50-minute trip in a comfortable fixed wing for $110-$150.
Scott Air, *also based at the airport, T07-3089558, www.scottair.co.nz* Offers similar trips.

❶ Directory

Internet Available at the VIC and also: **Friends Café**, *Ascam Business Services, 88 Strand, Mon-Fri 0830-1700*; **Chambers Café Restaurant**, *Strand East*; and there's a café at *38 King St, Opotiki, T07-3157683*. **Post office** *Commerce St. Mon-Fri 0830-1700, Sat 0900-1200*.

Taupo and Ruapehu

Introduction

From space, **Lake Taupo**, the largest lake in New Zealand, looks like a large bullet-hole shot through the heart of the North Island. This is perhaps fitting given that its placid waters, now world famous for **trout fishing**, mask a frightening heritage of **volcanoes** and **thermal activity** – one that is the trade mark of the Taupo and Ruapehu Region. Here are the remains of the largest volcanic eruption in the last 5,000 years. Now, during its dormancy, Lake Taupo is home to a bustling tourist town, **Taupo**, renowned not only for its **fishing**, but a host of other **activities**, from rafting and mountain biking to tandem skydiving. After exerting yourself, aches and pains can be soothed away in the town's popular **hot pools**.

All around the region is the evidence of ancient and ongoing volcanic activity. Nowhere else is this more apparent than the **Tongariro National Park**, a place that is steeped in Maori legend and spirituality, and New Zealand's oldest national park, boasting the still active volcanoes of **Ngauruhoe** and **Ruapehu** – the North Island's highest peak, which erupted in spectacular fashion as recently as 1996. When both mountains are in less aggressive mood the park provides excellent skiing, tramping and walking opportunites, including the great **Tongariro Crossing**, a walk full of volcanic wonder, considered one of the best day-hikes in the country.

★ Don't miss...

❶ Cruising, sailing or trout fishing on the huge flooded caldera that is now **Lake Taupo**. View it from 9000ft and 200kmph with a man (and parachute) strapped to your back, page 291.

❷ The 'Craters of the Moon', the Volcanic Activity Centre and the thunderous Huka Falls in the **Wairakei Park**, page 295.

❸ A round of **golf** on one of Taupo's first-class 'steaming' golf courses, page 302.

❹ The spectacular view from the summit of **Mount Tauhara** near Taupo, page 295.

❺ The memorable 'Tongariro Crossing' in the **Tongariro National Park** - one of the best day-walks in the country. Follow it up with a relaxing soak in the **Taupo Hot Springs**, page 295.

❻ Peace, and plenty of it at the **Orakei Korako Thermal Reserve**, page 297.

❼ Mount Ruapehu's **Crater Lake** from the **Whakapapa Ski-field** - then ski back down, page 309. Cross your fingers she doesn't blow!

❽ An evening trip to hear wild kiwi from **Ohakune**, page 311.

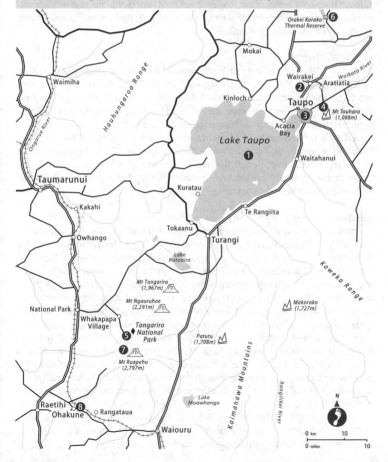

Taupo and around

→ *Colour map 3, grid A4 Population: 20,000*

For the tourist heading south, Taupo is really the first place that begins to satisfy the imagination in terms of what New Zealand is 'supposed' to look like: wide open spaces with snow-capped mountains and clear blue lakes. As you come over the hill into town on a clear day, the scene hits you like the first sip of a fine wine, with the huge expanse of Lake Taupo dwarfing the distant snow-tipped volcanoes of the Tongariro National Park. Take a while to enjoy it from the roadside lookout above the town before merging into the picture in the sure knowledge that it gets even better from here.

Because of its position in the centre of the North Island, Taupo is the commercial headquarters for the central districts of Taupo and Ruapehu, as well as a major tourist resort. The town is very pleasant, busy, friendly and well set out, nestled close to the source of the Waikato River (the longest in the country), and lies on the northernmost bank of the huge lake, once a mighty volcanic crater. The region has a multitude of activities to enjoy. Fishing is, of course, the principal attraction but you can also try the more adrenaline-pumping pursuits of bungee jumping and tandem skydiving, as well as mountain biking, golf, sailing and walking. Beyond the town and its lake, the glorious mountain peaks of the Tongariro National Park (see page 305) will lure you into further investigation, with that omnipresent edge of fear that maybe, just maybe, another volcanic eruption will strike.

Getting there

Taupo is on SH1 280 km South of Auckland and 80 km from Rotorua and is a major stop on the tourist 'Thermal Explorer Highway'. The town is well serviced by both road and by air. The **airport** is just off SH1, 10 km south of the town, T07-3785428. **Air New Zealand Link,** T0800-737000, www.airnewzealand.co.nz, operates direct daily flights to Auckland and Wellington with connections to the South Island. By bus Taupo is served daily by **Newman's** and **Intercity** which arrive and depart from the Travel Centre on Gascoigne St, T07-3789032. **Guthrey's** stop at the VIC, T07-3760027.

Turangi is well served by both **Newman's** and **Intercity** which stop at the Avis Travel Centre on the corner of Ngawaka and Ohuanga Rd, T07-3868918. The VIC in Turangi acts as bus ticketing and AA agents.

Getting around ›› *For taxis, cycle hire and car rentals see Directory, page 304.*

Shuttles and taxis usually meet incoming flights at the airport. Shuttles can also be booked with **Taupo Passenger Services,** T07-3782172. **Tongariro Expeditions,** T07-3770435, www.thetongarirocrossing.co.nz, offers services between Taupo and Tongariro Crossing (summer) and Whakapapa (winter). In summer, departs Taupo 0645, Turangi 0730, returns Taupo 1730, Turangi 1700. In winter, departs 0700. **Alpine Scenic Tours,** T07-3787412, www.alpinescenictours.co.nz, operate between Turangi and Taupo, with additional services to the Tongariro National Park (Tongariro Crossing) daily in summer (on demand in winter). **Kiwi Value Tours,** T07-3789662, T025-750046, offer shuttle services and tours around Taupo and beyond. Hot Pool Shuttle: departs 1800, returns 1930 daily to Orakei Korako Thermal Reserve; departs 0830 to Wairakei Tourist Park; departs 0830, returns 1230 to Waiotapu. The prominent **London Double Decker Bus,** T07-3770774, does 20-min town tours at the weekends and daily in the high season and departs from the lakefront gardens, corner of Tongariro and Redoubt sts (Waterfront near the huge trout statue). Adult $6, child $3. Also look out for the new **Hot Bus,** T07-3771967, www.thehotbus.co.nz, service linking most major attractions. $3 per person, $5 return, $10 day pass. Operates hourly 1000 to 1800 (summer), 1100 to 1700 (winter).

Information

Taupo VIC, ① *Tongariro St (SH1)*, *T07-3760027*, *www.laketauponz.co.nz* *Daily 0830-1700*. It has all the usual information, a good range of maps and also handles DoC enquiries. Specialist information available on the Tongariro Crossing (see Tongariro National Park) with up-to-date weather forecasts. **Turangi VIC**, ① *Ngawaka Pl, just off SH1*, *T07-3868999*, *www.turangivc@laketauponz.com*, *www.laketauponz.com*, *www.ruapehunz.com Daily 0830-1730*. They have the obligatory fishing licences and information about where to catch the 'big ones' ($12.50 day). Internet is available and there is also a wealth of information surrounding the other activities in the Kaimanawa Forest Park and Tongariro National Park. Hut bookings and ski passes can also be arranged. All the local **DoC** information is held at the VIC.

History

Prior to European settlement Taupo was called *Tapuaeharuru*, meaning 'resounding footsteps', and was allegedly named by a Maori chief, who thought the ground felt hollow. The main *pa* site and fortified village was near the lake outlet (the Waikato River). In 1868 an Armed Constabulary force established a garrison on the site of the present township to assist in the national campaign to rout the Maori rebel leader Te Kooti. By the late 1800s the area's thermal activity was already beginning to attract visitors and the land was bought from the Maori and trout introduced into the lake. From that point, it seems, Taupo's destiny was sealed and the tourism trade flourished.

Sights

Taupo's natural sights are mostly outside the town itself (see below and Tongariro National Park). The most immediate and dominant sight in town is of course the huge expanse of **Lake Taupo** itself – 619 sq km. On a calm day it can be almost mirror-like, disturbed only by the wakes of boats and ducks. But it wasn't always like this and the origin of the lake itself will make you quake in your walking boots, for Lake Taupo is in fact the tranquil remains of the biggest volcanic eruptions the planet has created in the last 5,000 years. The latest occurred in AD186 spewing out over 30 cu km of debris at up to 900 kph (about 30 times more than Mount St Helens spewed out). There was so much ash that the effects were seen in China and Rome.

The now placid waters are famous for copious trout and very much the domain of the serious angler. But the lake is of course used for numerous other activities including sailing, cruising, waterskiing and windsurfing. Most of the longer cruises take in the remarkable **Maori rock carvings** (a huge face complete with *moko* or tattoos), which can only be seen from the water and adorn an entire rock face in Mine Bay, 8 km southwest across the lake. Although remarkable, they were only created in recent years, which does somewhat dampen the excitement. For cruising and other lake activities see Activities page 301.

Near the very tacky oriental-style trout statue is the **Taupo Museum and Art Gallery**, ① *Story Pl*, *T07-3789427*. *Daily 1030-1630*. *Donation only*. Here there are some interesting photos and artworks that focus on the early days of the region, and a gallery that features regular exhibitions. Just a little further west the **Waikato River** begins its 425-km journey to the Tasman Sea and winds its merry way north behind the town towards **Wairakei Park**. Before the park proper is **Cherry Island**, ① *off Spa Rd, T07-37894278*. *Daily 0900-1700*. *Adult $8, child $3*. *Licensed café, gallery and shop*. Set in the middle of the river, it has been developed into a small wildlife attraction. There are a few aviaries, fluffy farm animals and some trout pools. Perhaps

Taupo

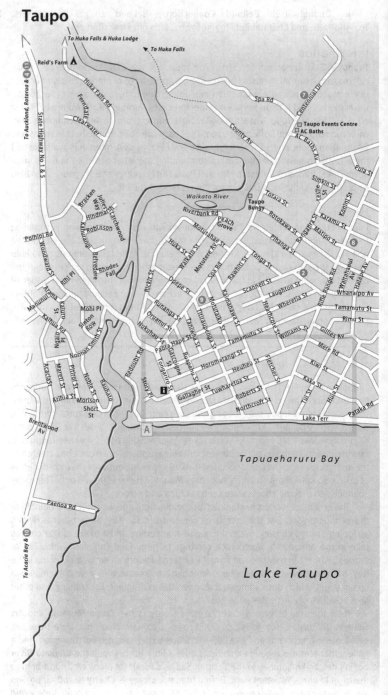

To Huka Falls & Huka Lodge

▼ To Huka Falls

Reid's Farm Λ

To Auckland, Rotorua & 4 5

State Highway No 1 & 5

Huka Falls Rd

Ferndale

Clearwater

Spa Rd

County Av

Centennial Dr

7

Taupo Events Centre
AC Baths
AC Baths Av

Puta St

Simkin St
Kestle St
Komu St

Waikato River

Totara St

Rotokawa St
Rangatira St
Matipo St
Karamu St

Bracken
Hindmarch
Robinson
Julies Way
Larchwood
Kahikatea
Belvedere
Rhodes Fall

Taupo Bungy

Riverbank Rd
Peach Grove

Motutahae St

Pihanga St

8

Pothipi Rd
Woodward St
Rihi Pl

Huka St
Waikato St
Moutere St
Spa Rd
Rawhiti St

Tonga St

Odepe St

Scannell St

Laughton St

Wheretia St

2

Rifle Range Rd
Waitahanui Av
Harper Av
Whanaipo Av

Arama
Mahuhu
Kaihua Rd
Oruanui
Mohi Pl
Simton Row

Rickit St

Runanga St
Oruanui St

Kaimanawa St

9

Moturiki St

Heuheu St

Herthcote St

Tamamutu St
Rimu St

Gillies Av

Norman Smith St

Nukuhau St

Taniwha St

Tamamutu St

Williams St

Mere Rd

Acacia St
Marett St
Pihoi St
Noble St
Tuiwaho
Redoubt Rd
Story Pl

Paora Hape St
Gascoigne
Tongariro St
Ruapehu St
Horomatangi St

Heuheu St
Fletcher St

Kiwi St
Kaka St
Tui St
Hula St

Arihia St
Morison
Short St

1

Gallagher St
Tuwharetoa St

Roberts St

Northcroft St

Lake Terr
Paraka Rd

Brentwood Av

A

Paenoa Rd

Tapuaeharuru Bay

To Acacia Bay & 10

Lake Taupo

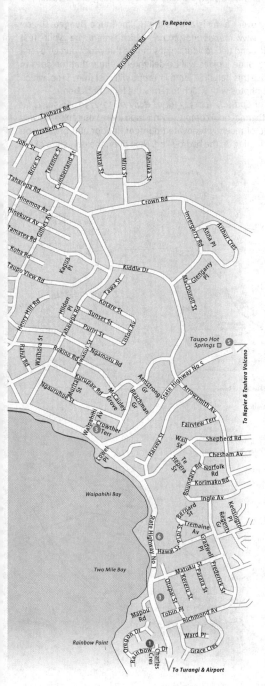

To Reporoa

Broadlands Rd

Detail map:
A Taupo centre,
page 299

Tauhara Rd
Elizabeth St
John St
Terence St
Brice St
Cumberland St
Matai St
Miro St
Manuka St
Taharepa Rd
Hinemoa Av
Hinekura Av
Tamatea Rd
Gillies Av
Koha Rd
Kapia Pl
Taupo View Rd
Crown Rd
Invergarry Rd
Anna Pl
Arthur Cres
Kiddle Dr
Tawa St
Kotare St
MacDonell St
Glengarry Pl
Henry Hill Rd
Hildon Pl
Taharepa Rd
Sunset St
Puriri St
Linton Av
Rahu Rd
Waihora Rd
Rokino Rd
Awanui St
Ngamotu Rd
Taupo Hot Springs 5
Ngauruhoe St
Kuirau St
Kurupae Rd
Beachman Gr
McCauley Gr
Armstrong Gr
State Highway No 5
Arrowsmith Av
To Napier & Tauhara Volcano
Waipahihi St
Crowther Terr
Fairview Terr
Lower Pl
Wall St
Shepherd Rd
Harvey St
Te Heuheu St
Chesham Av
Norfolk Rd
Spa Thermal Rd
Korimako Rd
Waipahihi Bay
Ingle Av
Berkard St
Paul St
Regents Pl
Kensington Pl
Tremaine Av
Gradwell Pl
Hawai St
Two Mile Bay
State Highway No 1
Matuku St
Kereru St
Palaza St
Frederick St
Mapou Rd
Otupai St
Tobin Pl
Richmond Av
Rainbow Point
Oregon Dr
Rainbow Cres
Charles Dr
Ward Pl
Grace Cres
To Turangi & Airport

N
0 metres 200
0 yards 200

Sleeping 🛏
Anchorage Resort Motel **1**
Berkenhoff Lodge **2**
Bramhams **3**
De Brett's Thermal Resort **5**
Drakei Korako Resort **11**
Lakeland **6**
Lake Taupo Lodge **10**
Lake Taupo Top Ten
 Holiday Park **7**
Lochinver **8**
Rainbow Lodge
 Backpackers **9**
Wairakei Resort **4**

Bars & clubs 🍸
Ploughmans Pub **1**

if you are not going to Rotorua where such attractions are on a far grander scale, you might like to pay a visit.

Nearby, almost looking over Cherry Island, is the HQ for **Taupo Bungee**, ⓘ *202 Spa Rd, T0800-888408, www.taupobungy.co.nz*, which might be your first opportunity to get an elastic band tied to your ankles before throwing yourself over a 45 m cliff. Masochistic adrenaline junkies will be delighted to hear that the ones in South Island are at least twice this height. A jump in Taupo will cost from $100, which includes a video and some photos with which to terrify the folks back home.

The **AC Baths**, ⓘ *top of Spa Rd, T07-3773600, daily 0830-2130, $6.50, child $2.50*, are one of two large thermal pool complexes in Taupo. Here you can soak away all your troubles in a range of recently renovated outdoor, indoor and private spa pools while the kids do their thing on the hydro-slide. Next door, the new state of the

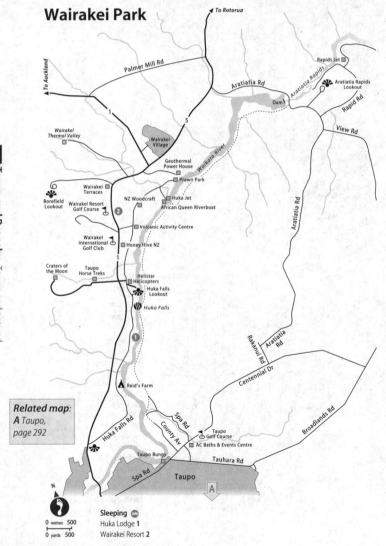

Wairakei Park

To Rotorua

To Auckland

Palmer Mill Rd

Aratiatia Rd

Rapids Jet

Aratiatia Rapids

Aratiatia Rapids Lookout

Dam

Rapid Rd

View Rd

1

5

Wairakei Thermal Valley

Wairakei Village

Geothermal Power House

Waikato River

Prawn Park

Wairakei Terraces

Borefield Lookout

Wairakei Resort Golf Course

NZ Woodcraft

Huka Jet

African Queen Riverboat

Volcanic Activity Centre

Wairakei International Golf Club

Honey Hive NZ

Aratiatia Rd

Craters of the Moon

Taupo Horse Treks

Helistar Helicopters

Huka Falls Lookout

Huka Falls

Rakanui Rd

Aratiatia Rd

Centennial Dr

Reid's Farm

Broadlands Rd

Related map: **A** *Taupo, page 292*

Huka Falls Rd

County Av

Spa Rd

Taupo Golf Course

AC Baths & Events Centre

Tauhara Rd

Taupo Bungy

Spa Rd

Taupo

A

N

0 metres 500
0 yards 500

Sleeping
Huka Lodge **1**
Wairakei Resort **2**

art **Taupo Events Centre**, ① *T07-3760340*, is now set to host major sporting tournaments, exhibitions and trade shows.

The other thermal complex is the excellent and recently refurbished **Taupo Hot Springs**, ① *next to De Brett's just off SH5 (which heads west from SH1, along the lakefront at the southern edge of town)*, *T07-3776502, www.taupohotsprings.com Daily 0700- 2130. $8, child $3.50*. This is the better of the two complexes with all the usual facilities including a massage and beauty treatment centre, hydro-slides and private pools. It's a fine place to relax and mix with the locals, as well as the odd visiting celebrity, including by all accounts Xena Warrior Princess 'aka' Lucy Lawless.

To the east of town looms the dormant volcano **Tauhara** (1088 m). Not only is it a grand site, but also a great walk with superb views which make the three-hour return trip well worth it. The track, which is about one-third grazing paddock to two-thirds native bush, begins from the bottom of Mountain Road, 5 km from Taupo on the Napier SH5 Road. Do not be fooled by the immediate summit in view, which is a false summit. The track enters the bush-filled crater to the true summit beyond it. Adequate footwear and patience are required.

Wairakei Park

Huka Falls
① *The Huka Falls are signposted from SH1 and are accessed via the Huka Falls Rd. There is a new information kiosk in the Falls car park.*

No visit to Taupo would be complete without a muse of utter fear and trepidation at the mighty Huka Falls. In the heart of the Wairakei Park north of the town, these falls are arguably the most spectacular in the country. From a sedate steady flow the waters of the Waikato River are forced through a 15 m-wide cleft of solid rock for 100 m, before falling 7 m into a cauldron of aquatic chaos and foam. From the car park a bridge crosses the rapids before joining a walkway down to the waterfall where, depending on the flow (regulated at Lake Taupo for electricity generation), the falls vary from 9-10 m in height, to a staggering 220 cu m per second of volume. Believe it or not some utter lunatics have attempted the ultimate adrenaline buzz of 'riding' the Huka by canoe. Last time it was attempted in 1994, two canoeists went down. One made it in about 60 seconds. The other disappeared in the torrent and reappeared minus canoe, and life, 40 minutes later.

The **walking tracks** that lead both north and south along the river from here are worthy of a trek on foot or mountain bike. Just up river is the exclusive retreat of Huka Lodge – an exorbitant luxury pad that hosts the filthy rich and visiting dignitaries.

Honey Hive
① *T07-3748553. Daily 0900-1700. Free.*
Carrying along the Huka Falls Loop Road (north) you can take a small diversion to admire the view looking back at the falls, before passing Helistar Helicopters (see page 303) and arriving at the Honey Hive. For honey monsters this is the 'place to bee' with some interesting interpretative displays, a working glass-fronted hive and the Beez Kneez Café. There is also a shop where you can purchase a tub of Manuka Honey, the most delectable toast spread on earth.

Volcanic Activity Centre
① *T07-3748375, www.volcanoes.co.nz Daily 1000-1700. $5, child $2.50. Its website is fascinating and will give you all the latest status reports on national earthquakes and eruptions.*

The next attraction along the road is the geological delights of the Volcanic Activity Centre. It is well worth a peek, if only to get an inkling of the scale and magnitude of the natural powers that lie beneath your feet. The Taupo district is in the heart of one of the most active volcanic zones in the world, the details of which are well presented in the centre. There are models and displays, all with the appropriate shaking and rumbling noises.

Prawn Park

ⓘ *T07-3748474, www.prawnpark.com Daily 0900-1700. $6, child $1.50. Tours leave every 30 min from 1100-1600 daily.*

Carrying along Huka Falls Road you pass **NZ Woodcraft** (a glorified native wood souvenir workshop) before reaching the road end and the riverbank. Here you will find Prawn Park. Hailed as the world's only geothermal Prawn Farm, you can join an informative tour (to meet'em), see the prawns crassly anthropomorphised (and greet'em), before you are encouraged to tuck into a few (and eat'em), in the Riverside Restaurant. After all that you can perhaps understand why their star captive is called 'Grumpy'–apparently the largest prawn in captivity (but who would know?) Perhaps so that poor Grumpy doesn't end it all voluntarily in a hail of salad, prawnless meals are also available in the restaurant.

River trips

Alongside Prawn Park are the headquarters of the highly contrasting *PW Otunui* steamboat and *Huka Jet* river trips. You can take your pick between a sedate and historic trip on the 1907 *Otunui* or the raunchier Huka Jet boats. Both boats go up the river to view the Huka Falls. ⓘ *Otunui, T07-3785828, departs daily at 1030 and 1430 with an additional glow-worm trip at 2100 in summer and 1930 in winter. Adult $30, child $20. The Huka Jet, T0800-485253, www.hukajet.co.nz, is open daily and leaves every half hour, $69, child $39.*

Craters of the Moon Volcanic Reserve

ⓘ *Daily. Free but offer a donation.*

Back on SH1 and almost directly across it, you can access the Craters of the Moon volcanic reserve. This is a very steamy affair somewhat akin to taking a stroll through a smouldering bush fire. From almost every conceivable crack and crater along the 40-minute to one-hour walk, steam quietly billows into the air, with only the faintest hiss giving you an indication of the forces that lie below. The track is easy going, with most of it understandably made up of boardwalk. The reserve and the car park are staffed by friendly thermo-volunteers selling thermo-souvenirs and they will kindly keep a very hot eye on your car.

Heading north again up SH1 you pass the **Wairakei Golf Course** to the left. This is a superb course of international quality and, as far as golf courses go, very cheap and easy to access (if not easy to play). If you just happen to be there in August/September it is also one of the best places in New Zealand to see **tui**, the native bird which features in the course logo. If you go to the trees behind the clubhouse you can often see large flocks of them feeding amongst the flowering branches in an almost hyper feeding frenzy. Their call is one of the most unusual and entertaining in the avian world, with an inconceivable range of whistles, clicks and knocking noises, most of which are beyond the human audible frequency range.

Wairakei Terraces

ⓘ *T07-3780913, www.wairakeiterraces.co.nz 0900-1700. General entry $18, child $9. SH1 7 km north of Taupo. Cultural performances with a traditional* hangi *(feast) are also held Wed-Sat at 1800 subject to bookings, from $75, child $37.50.*

The latest of the region's thermal attractions, the new terraces complex in Wairakei takes a historical and cultural look back in time when the Pink and White Terraces, destroyed during the great Tarawera eruption of 1886, were the region's, and one of the world's, most famous volcanic features. As usual there is lots of steam and boiling water, Maori carvings and a very welcome therapeutic footbath.

Wairakei Thermal Valley

① *Daily. Adult $6, child $2. Borefields Tour, T07-3780254.* Just over 1 km north again is the Wairakei Thermal Valley. Although quite impressive, this area is nothing compared to its former glory, when 22 geysers and almost 250 mud pools used to be scattered around the valley. With the creation of the local geothermal project and the absorption of local subterranean energy, there are now only a few active mud pools and steaming fumaroles.

Aratiatia Rapids

To complete a convenient circuit back into town you can continue up SH1 and on to SH5 for about 2 km, before turning right, following the signs to Aratiatia. This will take you to a dam on the Waikato that tempers the flow of the Aratiatia rapids, a similar gorge the Huka, but more jagged. The dam gates are opened at 1000, 1200 and 1400 daily in winter (plus 1600 in summer and all openings depending on water levels). You can see the rapids from a viewpoint just beside the dam or from a hilltop lookout about 1 km further up the road. From here it is a short drive back into Taupo via the Taupo Golf Club on Spa Road. **Rapids Jet** is at the base of the falls on Rapids Road, T07-3785828. It is similar to the Huka Jet and costs $65, child $35.

Orakei Korako Thermal Reserve

① *0830-1630 (hours vary according to demand). Adult $19, child $7.*
About 40 km north of Taupo (27 km up SH1, then 13 km right on to Tutukau Road, then left on to Orakei Korako Road) is one of the least visited, but best thermal parks in the country. Even without the thermal park, this tranquil lakeside spot, formed by another dam on the Waikato, offers the visitor sanctuary from the hustle and bustle of Taupo and its busy tourist attractions. From the lakeside visitor centre and Geyserland Resort Lodge only plumes of steam and a strange colourful silica terrace across the water give any indication of the numerous interesting volcanic features awaiting you. Once delivered at the terraces by boat you are free to roam the self-guided tracks of the reserve. There is a bit of everything here – colourful algae-covered silica terraces, boiling pools, geysers and lots of bubbling mud. Added to that there is the fascinating Ruatapu Cave which descends into the earth, with the warm Waiwhakaata Pool (Pool of Mirrors) at its base. Apparently, if you put your left hand in the pool and make a secret wish, it will come true. The cave itself is about 40 m deep and from its depths you can look heavenwards towards its gaping entrance and the daylight, shrouded by fronds of silhouetted silver fern. You can stay as long as you like in the reserve before re-boarding the boat back to the visitor centre. If you have any questions about the reserve ask local guide Chris, an entertaining 'geyser' of considerable knowledge.
▸▸ *See Sleeping and Activities, pages 299 and 303.*

Pureora Forest Park → *For maps and more information see the Taupo VIC. There is also a DoC Field Centre in Mangakino, T07-8781080.*

This little-known forest park to the west of Taupo offers a number of easy short walks as well as the more demanding climb to the summit of **Mount Pureora** (1165 m). The park is also the focus for the successful reintroduction of the **kokako** (a native bird with a beautiful haunting song). Most of the main park sights can be taken in on a scenic drive that starts from Kakaho Road, south of the intersection of SH32 and Poihipi Road, to emerge again at Mangakino. ▸▸ *See Activities, page 303.*

Turangi and Tokaanu → *Phone code: 07 Colour map 3, grid A3 Population:*

4000. On SH1, 50 km south of Taupo and 4 km inland from the southeastern edge of Lake Taupo.

Turangi is a small, pleasant village, world famous for trout fishing on the scenic Tongariro River that flows past the eastern edge of the village before quietly spilling into the huge expanses of the lake. The village is well served with accommodation and amenities and is often used as a base for exploring the Tongariro National Park.

The village would not be content without proudly displaying some live trout somewhere and the **Tongariro National Trout Centre**, ① *3 km south of Turangi on SH1, T07-3868607, daily 1000-1600, free,* tries hard. Although there is some way to go before it could be called a major attraction, you can at least see a trout hatchery in operation, some adult fish in a large pool and underwater viewing area and learn about their interesting life cycle.

The neighbouring village of Tokaanu, 5 km to the west along SH41, also provides accommodation, amenities, and basic thermal pools (Mangaroa St, $6, T07-3868575) as well as fishing and boat access to Lake Taupo. ▸▸ *See Sleeping, Eating and other listings, pages 299-303.*

● Sleeping

Taupo *p290*
There is a wealth of motels with the best being the 'lakeview' options on or around Lake Terrace and the waterfront. The cheaper options tend to be a bit 'time warped' and are in the town's western suburbs. There are also many B&Bs, homestays and farmstays available, mainly around town and in Acacia Bay to the east of Taupo. For full details contact the VIC.
LLHuka Lodge, *Huka Falls Rd, T07-3785791, www.hukalodge.com* Luxury at its most lucrative in quiet seclusion beside the river. Mingle with heads of state and visiting stars. Watch your money evaporate.
LLLake Taupo Lodge, *41 Mapara Rd, Acacia Bay, T07-3787386, www.laketaupolodge.co.nz* Another top establishment offering total luxury in 4 suites with dining room, reading gallery, open fire. Includes exquisite cuisine.
L-ALAspen Villas, *9-11 Tui St, T07-3787487, www.aspenvillas-taupo.co.nz* One of the newest motels on the scene, immaculate fully self-contained units with spa.
ALLakeland, *282 Lake Terr, Two Mile Bay, T07-3783893, www.lakeland.co.nz* Mid- to upper-range comfort next to the lake. Restaurant and bar, spas and pool.
AL-ACaboose Taupo, *100-102 Lake Terr, T07-3760116, www.taupo.caboose.co.nz* A new and unusual luxury establishment with a 'colonial African' theme. Log cabin-style architecture and accommodation with an

unusual range of suites and bunkrooms. Spas, pool, restaurant and bar. Recommended.
AL-ATui Oaks, *corner of Lake Terr and Tui St, T07-3788305, www.tuioaks.co.nz* One of the best motels in the upper range, great views across the lake. Pool, restaurant and bar.
AAnchorage Resort Motel, *Lake Front, Two Mile Bay, T07-3785542*. Situated a bit further out along Lake Terr. Good facilities including pool, spas and gym.
ACatelli's Motel, *23-27 Rifle Range Rd, T07-3784477, www.catellis.co.nz* Comfortable mid- to upper-range motel within walking distance of town.
ABramhams, *7 Waipahihi Av, T07-3780064, bramham@reap.org.nz;*
ALochinver *33 Tamatea Rd, T07-3770241, www.homstead/lochinver/lochinverpa.html;* Both are perfectly friendly, comfortable and centrally located.
C-DAction Downunder Hostel, *corner of Kaimanawa and Tamamutu Sts, T07-3783311.* A tidy YHA associate with great modern rooms and facilities. Spa and bike hire.
C-DBerkenhoff Lodge, *75 Scannell St, T07-3784909*. Slightly out of the centre but has a fine 'rambling house' atmosphere and is friendly and well kept. Bar, café, spa and free bikes.
C-DRainbow Lodge Backpackers, *99 Titiraupenga St, T07-3785754, rainbowlodge@clear.net.nz* Well established, popular and congenial backpackers run by one of the longest-serving managers in the

game here. Good dorms and excellent doubles. Recommended.

C-D Taupo Central Backpackers, *corner of Tongariro and Tuwharetoa Sts, T07-3783206*; **C-D Go Global**, *in the former Cob and Co Hotel across the road, T07-3786165, www.go-global.co.nz* The two most central and happening hostels. Do not necessarily have the best, most modern accommodation, but do have top pubs within crawling distance. **Central** has its own terrace with fine view over lake and town.

Motorcamps and campsites
A-D De Brett's Thermal Resort, *Napier/ Taupo Highway (SH5), T07-3788559*. An excellent establishment with great range of cabins as well as powered sites. Modern facilities. Right opposite hot pools complex with a reduction on entry for clients. Recommended.

B-D Lake Taupo Top Ten Holiday Park, *28 Centennial Dr, T07-3786860*. An adequate alternative, closer to town and opposite the newly renovated AC Thermal Baths.

Reid's Farm, *next to the river on the Huka Falls Rd*. Controversial free camping just outside Taupo but it does get busy and can attract less than desirable neighbours.

Orakei Korako Thermal Reserve *p297*
B Orakei Korako Resort, *494 Orakei Korako Rd, T07-3783131, ok@reap.org.nz* Provides

log cabin-style accommodation across the lake from the thermal reserve. Quiet, comfortable with modern facilities. Spa pool on the deck overlooking the lake. Recommended for superb peace and quiet.

Wairakei Park *p295*
LL-L Wairakei Resort, *7 km north of town on SH1 and right in the heart of all the Wairakei Park attractions, T07-3748021, www.wairakei.co.nz* An award winner and one of the few conventional-style hotel resorts in the area. It is both well appointed and laid out with good facilities especially for the sporty, with tennis, golf and squash, plus a spa, pool and sauna in which to relax after all the activity.

Turangi and Tokaanu *p298*
LL Tongariro Lodge, *Grace Rd, T07-3867946, www.tongarirolodge.co.nz* Fine fishy establishment on the banks of the river. Range of very luxurious chalets, some with kitchen facilities. Geared up for anglers with its own resident fishing guides. Restaurant and bar.

AL-A Anglers Paradise Resort, *corner of SH41 and Ohuanga Rd, T07-3868980*. Convenient and well-appointed motel with swimming pool and spas.

A-B Creel Lodge Motel, *183-187 Taupahi Rd, T07-3868081*. Popular due to its position

Taupo centre

Sleeping 🛏	Taupo Central	Finch's Bar &	Thai 9
Action Downunder	Backpackers 6	Bistro 64 2	
Hostel 1	Tui Oaks 7	Lotus Thai 3	Bars & clubs 🍸
Aspen Villas 8		Max Café 8	Finn MacCauls 11
Caboose Taupo 2	Eating 🍴	Misha's 4	Gravity Bar 10
Catelli's Motel 3	Bach 1	Mr India 5	Jolly Good
Dunrovin Motel 4	Burbury's 7	Pimentos 12	Fellow 13
Go Global 5		Replete Café 6	

0 metres 200
0 yards 200

backing on to the Tongariro River, peaceful atmosphere and good value.

A-B Parklands Motorlodge, *corner of SH1 and Arahori St, T07-3867515, info@prklands.co.nz* Modern and comfortable, close to the Rafting Centre. Pool, spa, sauna, restaurant and bar, activities organized.

B-D Bellbird Lodge, *3 Rangipoia Pl, T07-3868281, www.bellbird.co.nz* Smaller of the two budget options with distinctly homely feel. Doubles, share, no singles. Transport arranged to Tongariro Crossing.

B-D Extreme Backpackers, *26 Ngawaka Pl, T07-3868949, ebpcltd@xtra.co.nz* Very tidy lodge-style accommodation with private and shared accommodation. Café, climbing-wall, open fire and internet.

Motorcamps and campsites

C-D Club Habitat, *Ohuanga Rd, T07-3867492.* Large motel, motorcamp, backpackers (YHA) and camping park with good facilities. Restaurant, bar, sauna and spa.

⑦ Eating

Taupo p290

There is a wide selection of restaurants, brasseries and cafés in Taupo, most are in the many motels and in the heart of town, around the waterfront. If you have been looking forward to sampling a big fat juicy trout, you will be disappointed. Under the conservation act it is illegal to buy or sell trout. However, if you have had a successful fishing trip most restaurants will be delighted to cook your catch for you.

$$$ Reflections in the Lake, *Tui Oaks Hotel (see above), T07-3788305.* Can offer a pleasant candlelit affair overlooking said lake.
$$$ Serengeti Restaurant, *in the new Caboose Lodge, T07-3760116.* Has everything short of the full water buffalo.
$$ There is a rash of mid-range eateries all claiming the best menus and views across the lake along the waterfront and Robert Street so a muse at the menus there should secure something to your taste.
$$ Pimento's, *17 Tamamutu St, T07-3774549.* Open from 1800 (closed Tue). New on the scene and creating a bit of a stir by all accounts. Imaginative Pacific Rim menu and tidy aesthetics.

$$ Finch's Bar and Bistro 64, *64 Tuwharetoa St, T07-3772425.* Mon-Fri from 1130, Sat/Sun from 1800. If you are looking for a good traditional beef or lamb dish look no further. An imaginative menu (how about the very tasty Scots smoked fish stew in focaccia) and congenial surroundings including a great open fire.
$$ Villino Restaurant, *45 Horomatangi St, T07-3774478, www.villino.co.nz* Also popular, offering mainly European dishes.
$$ Mr India, *30 Tuwharetoa, T07-3771969. Mon-Sat 1100-1430 for lunch and from 1730 for dinner.* Reliable Indian option.
$$ The Lotus Thai Restaurant, *137 Tongariro St, T07-3769797. Daily from 1200-2100, closed Tue.* Good Thai fare.
$$ Misha's, *28 Tuwharetoa St, T07-3776293. Daily from 1700.* The Indian with perhaps the most loyal following.
$$ Bach Restaurant, *2 Pakata Rd, Lake Terr (away from the centre of town), T07-3787856. Summer daily from 1200-1400 and from 1800; winter Mon-Fri from 1800 and Sat and Sun 1200-1400.* A deserving award winner and has the best pizza in town.
$ The Ploughmans Pub, *43 Charles Cres, T07-3773422.* A pleasant English-style pub just off SH1 heading south out of town. It offers good pub grub in quiet surroundings.
$ Replete Café, *45 Heu Heu St, T07-3780606. Mon-Fri 0845-1700, Sat 0900-1430, Sun 1000-1430.* Considered one of the best cafés and daytime eating establishments.
$ Burbury, *42 Roberts St.* An old favourite, nicely located on the waterfront. Always busy and offers a fine selection of quick snacks, breakfasts and bottomless cups of coffee.

For simple value and choice when all the others have closed try the newly renovated **$ Max Café**, *Roberts St. Open 24 hours.*
Supermarkets: **New World**, *247 Old Taupo Rd, T07-3497720*; **Pak-N-Save**, *Ruapehu St, T07-3771155.*

Turangi and Tokaanu p298

Though you can't buy trout commercially in New Zealand, most establishments in the Taupo region will cook your catch for you. Good food at affordable prices is available at:
$$ Angler's Café *in the Angler's Paradise Resort, T07-3868980, daily from 1800,* or the
$$ Parklands Motorlodge, *see above.* Other than that there is also:

$$ Brew House Bar and Restaurant, *in the Club Habitat Complex, 25 Ohuanga Rd, T07-3867492. Daily, 0700-2100.* Offers good pub grub to wash down with its microbrewery ales. Breakfasts are also good.
$$ Valentino's, *in the town centre, T07-3868821. Open from 1830.* A popular Italian joint.

🎔 Pubs, bars and entertainment

Taupo *p290*
Most of the action emanates from Tongariro and Roberts St (waterfront) and their connecting blocks in the heart of town. The best pubs are both on the corner of Tongariro and Tuwharetoa Sts: the new Irish **Finn MacCauls**, *T07-3786165*, and trendier **Gravity Bar**, *T07-3787624*. Both have bands at the weekends.
Jolly Good Fellows, *80 Lake Terr, T07-3780457.* Fine lake views and a congenial atmosphere.
Ploughmans, *Charles Cres, T07-3773422.* Head here for a quiet (good) pint and traditional pub food.
Cinema, *Horomatangi St, T07-3787515.*

✺ Festivals and events

Taupo *p290*
The biennial **Lake Taupo Arts Festival** (*1st and 2nd weeks of Feb*) swings into action, attracting local and national artists and exhibitions. The street performances are excellent, T07-3771200. Almost immediately afterwards is the **Adidas Great Lake Relay**, a 160 km relay around the lake, www.relay.co.nz **Ironman New Zealand** (*1st week of Mar*) attracts the obscenely fit from all over New Zealand, who compete in a 1-day triathlon event, www.ironman.co.nz April sees the 3-day **Lake Taupo International Trout Fishing Tournament** (*around the 3rd week*). **Taupo half-marathon** (*1st week in Aug*) sees all ages, shapes and sizes running (or crawling) around the lake. The new **Montana Taupo Festival** (*Sep*) is a 5-day blues music festival that went very well in 2003, T07-3760404. The locals on their bikes for the **Great Lake Cycle Challenge** (*late Nov*), T07-3781546. The usual festive spirits of *Dec* always sees at least a few streakers in the lake (travel writers not exempt, apparently.)

🛒 Shopping

Taupo *p290*
Kura, *47A Heu Heu St, T07-3774068.* For interesting New Zealand art and crafts.

⛰ Activities and tours

Taupo *p290*
Bungee jumping Taupo Bungee, *just off Spa Rd, T07-3771135.* From $100 (tandem $160) for 45-m jump.

Charter boats As you might expect there are numerous boat charters plying the lake. The marina office in Taupo at the Boat Harbour, along Storey Place, has all the information. The three main operators are:
Chris Jolly Outdoors, *T07-3780623, www.chrisjolly.co.nz*
Taupo Launchmen's Association, *T07-3783444*; and
Sailing Centre, *2 Mile Bay, T07-3783299, www.sailingcentre.co.nz*

Climbing Rock and Ropes, *based at the fun park Crazy Catz between Rotorua and Taupo on the SH5, T07-3748111, www.rocknropes.co.nz* A low and high ropes course with a giant 15-m swing that is a lot of fun and a good reputation; from $15-$59.
Events Centre, *Spa Rd, T07-3773600. Mon-Fri 1700-2100, Sat/Sun 1200-2100. Excellent new climbing-wall, from $8-$13.* For the real thing see Walking below or try
Wilderness Escapes, *T07-3783413*, Abseiling, climbing and caving from $40, full day $110.

Cruising There are numerous opportunities to cruise the lake in a number of varying craft offering daily trips, most of which leave regularly from the Boat Harbour on Storey Place.
Cruise Cat Scenic Cruises, (Chris Jolly Outdoors), *T07-3780623.* 1½-hour trips (Mon-Sat 1130-1300; Sun 1030-1230), to see the Maori rock carvings in Mine Bay and the picturesque Whakaipo Bay. $28, child $14 (Sunday Brunch Cruise from $42, child $28).
The Barbary, *T07-3783444.* A fine 50-ft

ocean-going yacht which also takes in the Maori carvings and leaves daily at 1000 and 1400; 2 hr 30 min $30, child $10.

Ernest Kemp, *T07-3783444*. A small replica steamboat that leaves from the Boat Harbour daily at 1030 and 1400 (1700 in summer). Again it takes in the Maori rock carvings. $28, child $10.

For steamboat cruising and jet boating on the Waikato River (Wairakei Park) see below.

Ecotours Eco safaris (NZ), *Kinloch near Taupo, T07-3770127*. A national operation with day or multi-day trips from $650.

Chris Jolly, *T07-3780623*. Good nature-based trips of the surrounding area. From $45.

Kayaking Kiwi, *T07-3780909*, *www.kayakingkiwi.com* A range of local ecotours including a half-day guided kayak adventure to the Maori carvings on Lake Taupo from $69, or a half-day kayak and launch cruise combo, from $129 and uided walking adventures to local forest parks from $59.

Fishing As you might expect there is a wealth of operators out there desperately wanting to make a living doing what they love the most and perfectly willing to take you out to try to catch a 'monster trout'. Guides charge about $50 per hour for up to 2 people with a full day costing anything from $200 per head. The obligatory licence is $12.50 per day, $33 per week. A minimum 3-hour trip is recommended to give you at least a chance, especially for beginners. For full listings see the VIC, the following are all recommended.

Mark Aspinall, *T07-3784453*, *www.markaspinall.com*

Ian and Andrew Jenkins, *T07-3860840*, *www.tui-lodge.co.nz*

Paddy Clark, *T07-3781364*, *www.nzflyfishing.co.nz* Fly fishing specialist

Greg Catly, *T07-3770035*, *www.nzflyfish.co.nz*

Poronui Ranch, *T07-3789680*, *www.poronuiranch.co.nz*

Ron Burgin, *T07-3728112*, *www.anglersretreat.co.nz*

Gliding Taupo Gliding Club, *Centennial Drive, Taupo, T07-3785463*,

bartley@reap.org.nz Tandem flights mainly at weekends, with more regular schedules in summer, weather permitting. From $70.

Golf Taupo is one of the best golfing venues in the country.

Wairakei Golf Club, *SH1 North, T07-3748152*, *www.wairakigolfcourse.co.nz*

Wairakei 9 Hole Course, *on SH 1 adjacent to the Wairakei Resort (north), T07-3748021*. If you are a complete novice, this place is 'hacker friendly'. Green fees from $9.

Taupo Golf Club, Spa Rd, then Centennial Dr, T07-3786933, www.taupogolf.co.nz One of the very few 'steaming' courses in the world. Green fees from $35.

Horse trekking Taupo Horse Treks, *Karapiti Rd, Wairakei (near 'Craters of the Moon' reserve), T07-3780356*. 1- and 2-hour treks, from $30.

Moehiwa, *Poihipi Rd (west, just opposite Huka Falls Rd junction), T07-3783727*. A very experienced outfit that really cares about both horses and clients, offering 1-2-hour treks from $35.

Jet boats (See Wairakei Park and Aratiatia Rapids above).

Kayaking Kayaking Kiwi, *T07-3780909*, *www.kayakingkiwi.com* Excellent half-day kayak and kayak/launch eco-based adventures from $69.

Kayak NZ, *T0800-529256, www.kayaknz.com* Guided trips and instruction from $40.

Kiwi River Safaris, *T07-3776597*, *www.krs.co.nz* Try the rather novel idea of glass-bottom kayak trips on the Waikato. Includes a soak in the hot pools, from $40.

Mountain biking There are some excellent tracks nearby, including the recommended riverside track that goes all the way to the Aratiatia Rapids from Spa Road. See also Directory below for bike hire.

Rapid Sensations, *T0800-227238*, *www.rapids.co.nz* Guided trips (1½ hours), from $55.

Parasailing and jet skiing
UFO Watersports *T0800-867272*, *www.fluifo.com* Regular flights along the waterfront from £65. Jet ski hire from $60.

**Quad biking Great Lake 4WD
Adventures**, *T07-3768386;*
Taupo Quad Adventures, *T07-3776404.*
Both offer the usual thrills and spills across
local farmland, also taking in native bush and
forest trails. 1 hour from $60, half day $130.

Rafting Most of the major companies are
based in Turangi, see below.
Kiwi River Safaris, *Taupo, T0800-7238577,
www.krs.co.nz* Raft the Rangitaiki as
opposed to the more famous Tongariro. 2
hours from $85.

Scenic flights Helistar Helicopters, *Huka
Falls Loop Rd, T0800-435478,
www.helistar.co.nz* Flights vary from a quick
5-minute trip hovering near the falls, to
several hours taking in the Tongariro
National Park. From $55-$500.
Skytrek Aviation, *T07-3780172;*
Taupo Air Services, *T07-3785325.* Both offer
a range of flights in fixed-wing from $50.
There are **float plane trips** on offer from the
lake based at Boat Harbour, T07-3787500.
From $60-$390.

Tandem skydiving There are 3
companies that compete and all are very
professional. Jump heights and prices vary
between companies: a jump from 9000 ft
will cost about $195; 12,000 ft $215; and
15,000 ft (Taupo Tandem) $300. You can go
higher, with oxygen assistance, if you have
the money. The recommendation is that if
you have gathered the courage to get up
there at all, for goodness sake splash out and
go as high as you possibly can – you won't
regret it. Pick-ups available from town. **Great
Lake Skydive**, *T0800-373335,
www.freefly.co.nz*
Skydive Taupo, *T0800-586766,
www.skydivetaupo.co.nz*
Taupo Tandem, *T0800-275934,
www.skydive.net.nz*

Town tours Kiwi Value Tours,
T07-3789662, and **Paradise Tours**,
T07-3789955, are both Taupo-based
operators that offer daily tours around town
or further on request. From $40.

Walking The much-celebrated, 1-day
(16-km) Tongariro Crossing, across the
volcanic slopes and landscapes of the
Tongariro National Park, is accessible from
Taupo (see page 305). There are various ways
of tackling the walk, with either the
independent option using local transport
operators and the range of accommodation
around the park, or with specialist guides. The
VIC can also help with information and hut
bookings. Recommended operators offering
'all in' packages from Taupo include:
Tongariro Expeditions, *T07-3770435,
ww.thetongarirocrossing.co.nz* Transport from
$30 return. Leave Taupo at 0545 ($35 return)
and 0620 ($25 return). Pick up from the
mountain 1530.
Whirinaki Rainforest Treks, *T07-3772363.* An
excellent Maori-guided, 2-day, heli-trek. Full
day from $125. Whirinaki lies just east of the
Urewera National Park (west of Taupo) and
has some of the most unspoilt rainforest in
the North Island. There are numerous other
short and long walks in the area including the
excellent climb to the summit of Tauhara
(1088 m), west of the town (see Sights above).
The VIC can provide detailed walking
information and maps.

Orakei Korako Thermal Reserve *p297*
NZ Riverjet, in the Visitors' Centre,
T07-3337111, www.riverjet.co.nz Interesting
jet-boat trips taking in some lovely lake and
river scenery. From $55, child $35. You can
also hire kayaks at the Visitors' Centre,
T07-3783131, www.orakeikorako.co.nz
Paradise Tours, *in Taupo, T07-3789955.* Offer
specialist tours to the reserve.

Pureora Forest Park *p297*
Kayaking Kiwi, *T07-3780909,
www.kayakingkiwi.com* Eco-walking tours to
the summit of Mount Pureora, from $59.

Turangi and Tokaanu *p298*
Climbing Extreme Backpackers, *26
Ngawaka Pl, T07-3868949.* Has an
international standard climbing-wall open to
the public.

Ecotours Tongariro Ecotours, *Atirau Rd
(SH1), T0800-101024.* Although currently only
offered to group bookings this is an excellent
2-hour trip aboard the *Delta Queen*, which
glides serenely through the extensive and
wildlife-rich wetlands of Lake Taupo.

Enter taining commentary, binoculars are provided. Trips go from Atirau Rd daily from 0800, $40.

Fishing Taupo and the Tongariro River is New Zealand's premier trout-fishing region. Provided you have a licence ($12.50 a day available from the VIC or DoC) you can fish all year round, though summer is considered the best time for brown trout, and winter for the rainbow variety. There are numerous boat charters and guided trips (from about $50 per hour, gear included) based in and around Turangi (consult VIC) and tackle can be hired from tackle shops on Taupehi Rd, or **Sporting Life**, *T07-3868996*, **Greig Sports**, *T07-3867713*, both in the town centre. When it comes to guides, names to look out for are **Peter Church** and **Kerry Simpson**.

Horse trekking Kiwi Outback, *T07-3866607*. 2 hours amidst stunning National Park scenery for $75.

Kayaking Rock and River, *203 Puanga St, Tokaanu, T0800-865226, www.RaftingNewZealand.com* Entertaining 3 hr 30 min-trips down the Tongariro, followed by a soak in their own hot pools back at base, from $90. Recommended. **Tongariro River Rafting**, *Atirau Rd, Turangi, T0800-101024, www.whitewaterraft.co.nz* Tours on the Tongariro, with the choice of either a relaxing scenic trip (1 hr 30 min) or a more exhilarating challenge down the Grade II sections of the river. Prices on application.

Mountain biking Tongariro River Rafting, *see above*. Guided trips or guidance on walking some excellent local tracks including the 42 Traverse, considered the best track in the North Island. Independent hire from $60 per day. Prices on application.

Quad biking Kiwi Outback Tours, *T07-3866607, T0800-628642*. 2 hours-full day/overnight. 3 hours, $110. ˘

Rafting The Tongariro River is up to Grade III and has over 50 rapids, while the Rangitaiki further afield, is up to Grade IV, providing a bit more action.

Tongariro River Rafting, *see above*. A range of trips from conventional rafting to raft fishing and also offer trips suitable for families. From $85 for 4 hours.
Rock and River, *see above*. Raft the Tongariro, from 1 hour to overnight. They also have free hot pools. From $85.

Walking One of the best short walks around Turangi is around **Lake Rotopounamu**, which is just off the SH47, 9 km south of the intersection of SH47 and SH41 towards National Park. It is a pleasant 2-hour stroll through native bush around the lake. Sadly there are no views from here south to the volcanoes. For a good view north you can climb **Mount Maunganamu** in about 20-30 minutes. This walk starts at the Scenic Reserve along a track turning right after the Tokaanu Tailrace Bridge on SH41. The VIC in Turangi has details of other walks in the area.

❶ Directory

Taupo *p290*
Banks All the major banks have branches and ATMs in central Taupo. **Car** rental **A1**, *corner of Tamamutu and Gascoigne, T07-3783670*; **Avis**, *61 Spa Rd, T07-3786305*; **Budget**, *corner of Titiraupenga and Tuwharetoa Sts, T07-3789764*; **First Choice**, *7 Nukuhau St, T07-3780985*; **Rent-A-Dent**, *7 Nukuhau St, T07-3782740*. **Cycle hire**: **Rent-A-Bike**, *11 Kereru St T025-322729*. **Internet** Log On, *71 Tongariro St (opposite the VIC, T07-3765901. Open until 2200*. **Cyber Wash**, *117 Tongariro St, T07-3774168* ; **Contact Cyber Café**, *10 Roberts St, T07-3783697*. **Post** office *Horomatangi St, T07-3789090. Mon-Fri 0900-1700, Sat 0900-1200*. **Laundry** Cyber Wash, *see above*. **Library** Story Pl, *T07-3760070*. **Medical services** Hospital, *Kotare St, T07-3788100*; Taupo Medical Centre, *corner of Heu Heu and Kaimanawa Sts, T07-3784080*; Late pharmacy, *Mainstreet, 67 Tongariro St, T07-3782636. 0900-2030*. **Police** Story Pl, *T07-3786060*. **Taxis** Taupo's Top Cabs, *T07-3789250*; Taupo Taxis, *T07-3785100*. **Useful addresses** AA, *93 Tongariro St, T07-3786000*.

Tongariro National Park

→ *Colour map 3, grid A3*

Tongariro National Park is New Zealand's oldest national park, and the fourth oldest in the world. In 1887 Horonuku Te Heuheu Tukino, the then paramount chief of Ngati Tuwharetoa, gave the central portion – essentially the volcanoes of Ruapehu, Ngauruhoe and Tongariro – to the nation. In more recent years the park has been substantially increased in size to cover an area of 75,250 ha, taking in the forest, tussock country and 'volcanic desert'. As well as its stunning scenery, Tongariro National Park offers some excellent walking opportunities, including the Tongariro Northern Circuit, considered one of New Zealand's great day hikes. The Tongariro Crossing (part of the circuit) is hailed as one of the best one-day walks in the country. In winter, skiing is the principal activity here.

Getting there → *See also individual village 'Getting there' sections below*

From Taupo **Tongariro Expeditions,** T07-3770435, www.thetongarirocrossing.co.nz, leave Taupo at 0545 ($35 return) and 0620 ($25 return). From Turangi, depart 0630 ($30 return) and 0715 ($20 return). Return from the mountain (Ketetahi) at 1530. **Alpine Scenic Tours** also offer scheduled daily services to Whakapapa and National Park, Mon-Wed-Fri, depart Taupo 0630, $25 return, (Turangi 0730 from $20), T07-3868918, pick up from Ketetahi track end 1715, www.alpinescenictours.co.nz In Turangi itself **Bellbird Connections,** Bellbird Lodge Backpackers, T07-3868281; and **Club Habitat,** T07-3867492 also offer transport options. From National Park Village, most places to stay offer shuttles including **Howard's Lodge,** T07-8922827, www.howardslodge.co.nz: Whakapapa Village for $12 (return), the start of the Tongariro Crossing for $16. Beware of cowboy operators in the region and try to stick to well-publicised operators. For the latest weather conditions over Ruapehu and Ngauruhoe log on to the 'live' webcam during daylight hours, www.geonet.org.nz

Getting around

The Park is bounded along its north, and western sides by SH47, with the principal settlements of Turangi, National Park and Ohakune, and to the east by SH1 (the famous Desert Road). The small township of Waiouru is to the southeast. Whakapapa Village, at the northern base of Ruapehu, serves as the Park's main headquarters. All the surrounding townships are served by **Intercity,** with Turangi also being served by **Newman's.** The main Auckland/Wellington TranzScenic rail line runs through Ohakune and the National Park. A number of local shuttle bus operators provide access to Whakapapa Village and major tramping drop-off/pick-up points around the park (see the relevant sections below). You can also fly direct to Tongariro National Park from Auckland ($238 return) with **Mountain Air,** T07-8922812, www.mountainair.co.nz The airfield is at the junction of SH47 and SH48.

Information

DoC Whakapapa, ⓘ *Whakapapa Village on SH48, T07-8923729, www.whakapapa .co.nz, www.ruapehunz.com Daily 0800-1700.* It has a wealth of information on the park, interesting displays, maps and weather reports. Park hut bookings/fees are administered here. If you are planning a longer tramp or summit climb you are advised to fill in an intentions sheet at the centre. For sleeping and eating within and surrounding the park see Whakapapa Village, National Park, Turangi and Ohakune listings. DoC hut bookings can be made at all major DoC field centres and the Whakapapa Visitors' Centre. Campsites have been established near each of the huts. Hut fees are $14, youth $7 Nov-May; $10, youth $5 Jun-Oct. Camping fees are around $4-5 cheaper.

History

According to local Maori legend, the volcanoes were formed back around the 14th century, when Ngatoroirangi, a navigator and priest of the Arawa canoe, came to New Zealand. Journeying inland from the Bay of Plenty, Ngatoroirangi saw the majestic peaks and decided to climb them, thus laying claim to all that he saw. As he climbed, Ngatoroirangi was hit by a violent blizzard. Close to death he cried out to the gods in his homeland of Hawaiki to send fire to warm his body and revive him. In response to his plea a great fire was issued forth, forming White Island, Rotorua and Taupo, before erupting from Tongariro and saving his life. Apparently in gratitude, Ngatoroirangi then slew his slave, Auruhoe, who had accompanied him on the climb, throwing the poor soul into the newly formed crater, which later formed Ngauruhoe. The name Tongariro means 'south wind' and 'borne away' and refers to Ngatoroirangi's pleas for help. Science, of course, offers a more boring theory. It suggests that they are in fact andesitic, single and multi-vented volcanoes of recent geological origin, dating back about two million years, reaching their greatest heights during the last ice age, when glaciers extended down the slopes of Ruapehu. Have you ever heard such nonsense?

Tongariro

All of the National Park's sights are of course natural and dominated by the three majestic volcanic peaks of Tongariro, Ngauruhoe and Ruapehu. Although all three mountains are active volcanoes they are quite different in size and appearance.

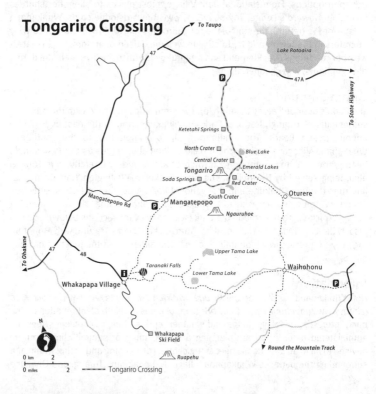

Tongariro Crossing

The Tongariro Crossing

This excellent hike is hailed as one of the best one-day hikes in the country and provided the weather is kind, there is no doubt that the views and the varied volcanic features certainly make it a memorable one. To call it a walk is really an understatement: at about 16 km in length with some steep climbs and the odd bit of scrambling, it is really a mountain hike that can take up to 10 hours. In winter it can be impassable and even in summer dangerous, so despite what you may have heard, don't underestimate it. Having said that, provided you are fit, well-prepared, the weather is looking good and you have the time, you should not pass up the opportunity.

The walk can be tackled from either north or south, with a number of diversions on the way. The usual recommendation is to start from the **Mangatepopo Car Park** (off SH47 on the park's western edge), walk the 10 km north to **Ketetahi Hut**, stay the night (all part of the 'package'), then either descend from the Ketetahi Hut to SH47A (walk terminus), or return the 10 km back to Mangatepopo. There is a hut at the Mangatepopo end but it has neither the character nor the view of the Ketetahi.

From Mangatepopo the track makes a gradual ascent towards the southern slopes of Tongariro, while the steep slopes and lava flows of Ngauruhoe loom to the northwest. Sandwiched between the two mountains the track is then forced to make a steep ascent up the **Mangatepopo Saddle**. Before this ascent there is the choice of a short diversion to the '**Soda Springs**' – a series of cold springs which emerge from beneath an old lava flow, surrounded by an oasis of greenery. Once you have negotiated the Saddle you enter Tongariro's **South Crater**.

The views of Ngauruhoe from here are excellent (and the especially fit can take in the summit diversion from here). A short climb then leads to the aptly named **Red Crater** and the highest point on the crossing (1,886 m). Following the rim of this colourful (and in the odd place steaming) crater you are then treated to a full artist's palette, with the partial descent to the **Emerald Lakes**. (The minerals from Red Crater create the colours in the water.) Just beyond Emerald Lakes the track branches right to **Oturere Hut**, or continues to Ketetahi Hut across the **Central Crater** and alongside **Blue Lake**, another water-filled vent. The track then straddles the **North Crater** taking in the stunning view north across Lake Taupo, before making a gradual zigzag descent to the **Ketetahi Hut**. The hut sits alone on the slopes at an altitude of about 1,000 m, like a first class real estate property: location, location, location and a 'real' view. (It is the busiest and most popular hut in the park. If you have booked your stay in the hut bear in mind it operates on a first come first served basis, so get there early.) The huts all have mattresses, gas cookers (summer only), water supplies and toilet facilities. In the busy seasons wardens can provide information and weather reports. The hot **Ketetahi Springs** are on private Maori land only a few hundred metres away. Until recently a soak in the pools of the stream armed with a gin and tonic was a lighlight of the walk. But sadly disagreements between DOC and the local Iwi mean the springs and stream are now out of bounds.

From Ketetahi it is a two-hour descent through native bush to the SH47A access point. For more information contact the Whakapapa Visitor's Centre, page 305.

Taupo and Ruapehu Tongariro National Park

Tongariro, at the northern fringe, is a fairly complex, flat-topped affair and the lowest at 1968 m. Of the three mountains it is the most benign with only a few mildly active craters, some hot springs, lakes, fumaroles and pools of boiling mud. From a purely aesthetic point of view its most attractive features are the aptly named **red crater** (which is still active) and the small **emerald lakes** at its base. Nearby are the contrasting **blue lakes** of the central crater and the **Ketetahi springs**, which emerge on its northern slopes. All of these interesting features are included on the **Tongariro Crossing**, which can be completed in a day and is considered one of New Zealand's best one-day walks (see box, page 307).

Ngauruhoe → *For a live web cam of Ngauruhoe log on to www.geonet.org.nz/ngauruhoe*
Just 3 km to the south of Tongariro is the symmetrical cone of **Ngauruhoe** (2291 m), the youngest of the three volcanoes. Its classic cone shape is due to its relative youth, but more especially because it has a single vent, as opposed to Ruapehu and Tongariro. Although, Ruapehu and White Island (Bay of Plenty) have been far more active recently, Ngauruhoe has over the years been considered the most continuously active, frequently venting steam and gas and, occasionally, ash and lava in more spectacular displays of pyroclastics. Its last significant eruption occurred in 1954.

There is plenty of evidence of these eruptions to be seen, the most obvious being the old lava flows on its slopes. The Tongariro Crossing Track skirts the eastern flank of Ngauruhoe, while another popular three to four-day tramp is the **Northern Circuit Track**, one of New Zealand's great walks encompassing both Ngauruhoe and Tongariro.

Ruapehu → *For a live web cam of Mt Ruapehu log on to www.geonet.org.nz/ruapehu*
About 16 km south of Ngauruhoe is the majestic shape of Ruapehu, with its truncated cone, perpetually snow-covered **summit peaks** and **crater lake**. It is the North Island's highest mountain, at 2797 m, and over the course of the last century has seen the most violent activity of all the three volcanoes. Between 1945 and 1947, due to a number of eruptions blocking the overflow, the waters of the crater lake rose dramatically. On the stormy Christmas Eve of 1953, without warning, the walls of the crater collapsed and a mighty lahar (volcanic rock and water debris) rushed down the Whangaehu River, wiping out the rail bridge near Karioi. The night train to Auckland arrived moments later and 153 lives were lost. It erupted more recently, in September 1995, thankfully and miraculously without loss of life, and the same thing happened a year later, wiping out the entire ski season for both Whakapapa and Turoa. Ruapehu attracts thousands of visitors each year who come to ski or climb on its slopes, or enjoy its numerous long and short tramping tracks. The longest track is the **Round-the Mountain Track** which takes 5-6 days with overnight stays at a number of DoC huts on the way. Ruapehu is home to three ski fields: **Whakapapa** on its northern flank (serviced by Whakapapa and Iwikau Villages), **Turoa**, on the southern flank (serviced by Ohakune); and **Tukino**, the smallest and least popular of the three on the eastern slopes.

Walking
Tongariro National Park offers numerous walking tracks from a few minutes to six days. There are numerous DoC huts throughout the park. The major tramps are the famed **Tongariro Crossing**, the **Northern Circuit** and the **Round the Mountain Track**. Most of the shorter walks are accessed from Whakapapa Village and the Ohakune Mountain Road, which connects Ohakune with the Turoa Ski Field. Note that a number of local activity operators also offer guided walks and DoC runs an excellent summer programme of organized and guided walks, which usually start from the Whakapapa Village Visitors' Centre; $10-80. T8923729. See Activities, page 315.

Northern Circuit The Tongariro Northern Circuit winds its way over Mount Tongariro and around Mount Ngauruhoe passing through unusual landforms and volcanic features, including lakes, craters and glacial valleys. Taking three to four days to complete (with overnight accommodation provided in DoC huts), it is listed as one of New Zealand's great walks. The track officially starts from Whakapapa Village and finishes at the Mangatepopo Road just off SH47, but can also be accessed from Ketetahi Road (north) or Desert Road (east). Detailed information about the walk can be obtained from the Whakapapa Visitors' Centre (see below), where you can also arrange hut bookings and are also advised to fill in an intentions form. The DoC website, www.doc.govt.nz, also provides excellent details of the walk. If you do not have your own transport, the local shuttle operators will provide transportation (see Getting there above and in relevant town below). If you have your own vehicle do not leave valuables in it.

Round-the-Mountain Track The Northern Circuit can be combined with the full Ruapehu Round-the-Mountain Track to create a mighty six-day tramp around all three mountains. Again comfortable accommodation is available in DoC huts along the way. The track can be accessed from Whakapapa Village or the Ohakune Mountain Road. For information and hut bookings contact the Whakapapa Visitors' Centre (see below) or DoC field centre on Ohakune Mountain Road, Ohakune (see page 311).

Ruapehu Crater Lake Both the summit and Crater Lake of Ruapehu are popular climbs in both summer and winter and are, in part, easily accessible via the Whakapapa Ski Field Chairlift. The climb to the crater and back takes about seven hours (four hours if you use the chairlifts). Once you reach the snowline it is tough going and can be dangerous. Ice axes and crampons are essential kit in winter and recommended even in summer. Whatever your intentions, always obtain all the necessary information before attempting this climb and let DoC know your plans. Ruapehu has claimed many lives (a very close eye is also kept on the mountain's seismic activity, and at the slightest sign of any action, an exclusion zone is placed around the crater). A few local operators offer guided walks to the Crater, T07-8923738 (see VIC).

Whakapapa Village → *Phone code: 07 Colour map 3, grid A3*
Whakapapa Village is essentially the headquarters and information base for The Tongariro National Park and the gateway to the **Whakapapa Ski Field**. It is also home to the magnificent **Grand Chateau Hotel**, built in 1929. As well as the Chateau itself there are a number of accommodation and eating options available in the Whakapapa Village. There is also a store, the DoC field centre and, believe it or not, a golf course. Don't miss the excellent displays in the Whakapapa DoC Visitors' Centre (see below) and especially the seismograph, monitoring the fickle moods of the mighty Ruapehu, which, lest you forget, is an active volcano that last let rip in the mid-1990s.

Getting there and around There is only shuttle bus transportation available to Whakapapa Village. Alpine Scenic Tours are a principal operator with daily schedules, T07-3868918. See also Getting there, page 305. There is a shuttle bus service to the ski fields (Top-o-the-Bruce) from outside the VIC at 0830,1230 (return 1530,1630) $6 return.

Information DOC Whakapapa VIC, ⓘ *SH48, T07-8923729, www.whakapapa.co.nz Daily 0800-1800.* The Centre offers a broad range of information on the park, with many displays and an audio-visual theatre to keep you interested on a rainy day ($3). The staff are expert in advising on walks in the park. Note the seismograph quietly

Taupo and Ruapehu Tongariro National Park

● Look out for the bright yellow kiwi road sign. There are very few of these signs in the
● country. Due to their considerable 'souvenir' appeal the DoC got so fed up replacing them that the signs were almost withdrawn altogether

Ruapehu *n*. lit: *rua* (pit); *pehu* (to explode, as in violent eruption)

It is September 1995 and a beautiful, calm summer's afternoon on the slopes of Mount Ruapehu. Excited skiers descend the slopes while others clamber for chairlifts, or sit in the café and the car park admiring the view. Meanwhile, the needle of the seismograph in the Whakapapa Village Visitors' Centre, twitches. This is not unusual, but will be noted – just like others of late, that along with a rise in the temperature and discolouration of the Crater Lake have a few volcanologists wondering… just wondering mind you! Shadows lengthen across the snow as the late afternoon sun slowly falls towards Mount Taranaki to the west. Again the needle twitches, and again… faster and faster…then she blows.

Caught on amateur video the Crater Lake explodes like a fire hydrant full of black ash and white steam, sliced open by an axe. All eyes look upward, jaws fall downwards, and a whole lot of designer epaulettes get wet from the inside. It's a mighty sight to behold, as the mountain billows ash, steam and rock and everyone suddenly becomes a champion downhill skier. By nightfall, as the mountain continues to rage and everyone is accounted for, an exclusion zone is placed round the slopes; and the nation, and the world, watches and waits. In the US a report gets filed that half of the North Island has gone – wherever that was.

The 1995 eruption was nothing too unusual for Ruapehu and thankfully and perhaps luckily no one died. For a few weeks Ruapehu billowed ash and steam that could be seen for miles around and even from space. Planes were diverted and light ash fell as far away as Whakatane in the Bay of Plenty. During the near-constant emissions of steam and ash more violent spurts of molten rock occurred. The one-time waters of the Crater Lake were displaced and poured down the mountainside forming chocolate-like lahars. And although a catastrophic eruption was possible it didn't occur. After a few weeks the mountain settled down again and the seismic needles returned to their monotonous single line. What was unusual was that the same thing happened a year later, wiping out the entire ski season for both Whakapapa and Turoa and for almost another year, the mountain still vented above average amounts of steam. Now into the new century, it is just another eruption etched in our memory, on film, or documented in the record books, and the 1995/6 eruptions will not go down as the worst of the last century. Between 1945 and 1947, due to a number of eruptions blocking the overflow, the waters of the Crater Lake rose dramatically. On the stormy Christmas Eve of 1953, without warning the walls of the crater collapsed and a mighty lahar rushed down the Whangaehu River, wiping out the rail bridge near Karioi. The night train to Auckland arrived moments later and 153 lives were lost.

To be around such tempestuous and unpredictable forces of nature is awesome indeed. To watch a mountain erupting is more so. You almost look at them, Ruapehu, Ngauruhoe, Tongariro, Taranaki and 'will' them to 'let rip'. But then you look across the huge expanse of Lake Taupo, all 619 sq km of it in the knowledge that it is a crater and was once a volcano that did just that – and you wonder and suddenly accept, that straight monotonous lines on seismographs are in fact a good thing – and not just for your epaulettes.

National Park Village → *Population: 500 Colour map 3, grid A3 Phone code: 07*

The small, unremarkable and almost barren village of National Park is set overlooking Mount Ruapehu and Ngauruhoe, at the junction of SH4 (which links Taumaranui and Wanganui) and SH47. It is also on the main Auckland/Wellington railway line. Graced only by its convenient location to both Tongariro and Wanganui National Parks it has a number of accommodation options, amenities and activity operators and is naturally popular in the winter ski season. Its only notable 'sight' is its own impressive view across to the mountain.

Getting there The Auckland/Wellington **TranzScenic**, T0800-872467, 'Northerner' and 'Overlander' trains stop at the station on Station Rd, while buses stop in Carroll St, the village's main street. Bus tickets can be bought from Ski Haus, Pukenui and Howard's Lodges.

Getting around Alpine Scenic Tours, T07-3868918, www.alpinescenictours.co.nz, operate a daily shuttle to and from National Park to Whakapapa Village (and the ski field), Tongariro Crossing access points and Turangi. They also connect with **Intercity** and **Newman's** buses at Turangi. Summer services may vary but they will run pretty much on demand. Most of the major accommodation establishments offer shuttle services throughout the park. **Tongariro Crossing Transport** is based at Howard's Lodge and will get you to Whakapapa Village for $12 (return), the start of the Tongariro Crossing for $16 and the 42 Traverse (popular mountain bike trail) for $35, T07-8922827, www.howardslodge.co.nz

Information There is no official VIC in the village but the staff at the BP Station on Carroll St (SH4) can be of assistance, T07-8922991, www.nationalpark.co.nz
▶▶ *See Sleeping, Eating and other listings, pages 312-315.*

Ohakune → *Phone code: 06 Colour map 3, grid A3 Population: 1320*

The pleasant little ski resort of Ohakune (meaning 'place to be careful'), near the southern edge of Tongariro National Park, changes its mood according to the season. In winter when (and if) the snows arrive, it attracts skiers in droves. But when winter brings little snow, or when spring arrives and the snow fades, it falls silent. So pretty little Ohakune is unpredictable, but whatever the season or the weather, it is worth lingering.

Getting there Ohakune is served by **Intercity** buses (every day except Sat) which stop in the centre of town at the VIC. About 2 km west of the centre, towards the mountain, is the principal après-ski and mountain access point. The train station is also here, and the daily Wellington/Auckland trains all stop on the way, T0800-872467. For all booking and ticketing contact the VIC.

Getting around Although it has essentially two centres, and shuttling between them is awkward, everything in Ohakune is within walking distance. Shuttles operate up and down the Ohakune Mountain Rd (to the Turoa ski field) or elsewhere within the Tongariro National Park, pretty much on demand. These include **Snowliner**, T07-3858573, and **Dempsey Buses**, T07-3854022; check with the VIC for latest schedules and prices.

Information and orientation Ohakune has essentially 2 centres. The main centre is on Clyde St (SH49, where you arrive into the town) and this is the base for the VIC, the main cafés, restaurants and amenities. The other 'centre' is of the après-ski variety and is about 2 km northwest, towards the mountain, up Goldfinch Street and Mangawhero Terrace. Here the focus is the **Powderhorn Chateau** (principal après-ski base) with the railway station, the mountain access point (Ohakune Mountain Rd) and the DoC Field Centre also here. The **Turoa ski field** is 17 km up the Ohakune Mountain Rd. **Ruapehu VIC** ① *54 Clyde St, T07-3858427, www.ohakune.info, www.ruapehunz.com Mon-Fri 0900-1700, Sat/Sun 0900-1530 (summer).* **DOC Ohakune Field Centre,** ① *at the base of the Ohakune Mountain Rd, T07-3858578. Mon-Fri 0900-1500.* It has some excellent displays, (including video footage of the 1995 Ruapehu eruption), up-to-date weather forecasts and maps, and can advise on any aspect of park activities, including local short walks. For information on the **Turoa Ski field,** T07-3858456, www.snow.co.nz, www.ohakune.info For local **weather** and regular snow updates in winter listen to Peak FM 95.8 FM, T07-3854919, or Ski FM 96.6 FM, T07-3859502.

Sights All of Ohakune's 'sights' are essentially natural and revolve around **Mount Ruapehu** and its associate activities – skiing and walking being the principal pursuits. There are a number of local short walks (mainly around the DoC field centre) as well as longer options, which come under the Tongariro National Park activities. If the weather is good, no trip to Ohakune would be complete without a drive to see the magnificent views from the top of the 17-km **Ohakune Mountain Road** and the **Turoa Ski field**. The road begins at the northwestern edge of town. **Lake Rotokura**, about 12 km south of Ohakune on SH49, is also worthy of a visit. Take the track signposted to the left. There are actually two lakes, one above the other and both reached on foot through native bush (30 minutes). Both have a lovely, tranquil atmosphere, especially the upper lake, which reflects the top of Ruapehu on a clear, still day.

▸▸ *See Sleeping, Eating and other listings, pages 313-317.*

● Sleeping

Whakapapa Village *p309*
All prices rise in winter, and opening and closing times vary. For all winter accommodation, and even in summer, booking is advised.
LL-AL The Grand Chateau, *T07-8923809, www.chateau.co.nz* Traditional luxury in a grand location. 63 rooms, 1 executive suite and 9 villas. Excellent restaurant, bar and café. Pool and golf course. Worth asking about special packages in summer. **AL-A Skotel Alpine Resort**, *T07-8923719, www.skotel.co.nz* Modern facilities with luxury and standard hotel rooms or self-contained chalets. Restaurant and bar. Spa, sauna, gym, internet and tramping gear hire.
C-D Whakapapa Holiday Park, *T07-8923897*. Basic facilities but set in the heart of the village and riverside, close to all amenities. Backpacker accommodation. **D DOC Huts**, *T07-8923729*. There are 9 DoC huts in the park with foot access only. Fees $8-$15.

National Park Village *p311*
All accommodation in National Park is in high demand in the winter ski season, when prices also rise. Booking is advised.
AL-D Howard's Lodge, *Carroll St, T07-8922827, www.howardslodge.co.nz* Fine establishment with a wide range of comfortable rooms. B&B available. Spa.
A-D National Park Lodge and Motel, *Carroll St, T07-8922993, natparklodge@xtra.co.nz* Self-contained units, comfortable backpacker accommodation and campsites available. Activities and transport pick-ups.
A-B Mountain Heights Lodge, *SH4, T07-8922833*. B&B, self-contained, motorcamp and camping just south of National Park Village. Friendly Yorkshire owners with 'reet grand' home cooking. Activities and transport pick-ups arranged.
B-D Pukenui Lodge, *corner of SH4 and Miller St, T07-8922882*. Modern single-storey lodge. Various rooms, quad, double or single, some en suite. Motel units and camping also available. Spa.

● *If the weather is foul you can always warm yourself up briefly with the video of the 1995*
● *Ruapehu eruption in the DoC field centre*

B-D **The Ski Haus**, *Carroll St, T07-8922854, SkiHaus@xtra.co.nz* Family and multi-share rooms, spa pool and bar. Activities and transport arranged.

C-D **National Park Backpackers**, *Findlay St, T07-8922870, www.npbp.co.nz* Modern establishment with dorms and doubles with en suite bathrooms, tent sites and internet. Climbing-wall. Activities and transport to Tongariro Crossing arranged.

Ohakune *p311*
As a main ski resort Ohakune offers a wide range of accommodation, though it operates on a seasonal basis. In winter, especially at weekends, you are advised to book well in advance. If you are stuck or want to avoid the high winter prices the far less salubrious village of **Raetihi**, 11 km to the east, has a number of cheaper options. For information, options and bookings contact the Raetihi VIC, T07-3854805.

AL **Powderhorn Chateau**, *corner of Mangawhero and Thames Sts, T07-3858888, www.powderhorn.co.nz* Alpine-style accommodation in the après-ski base of Ohakune. Spacious, well-appointed rooms. Excellent restaurant and bar attached. Ski/bike hire, indoor pool.

AL **Ruapehu Homestead**, *SH49, Rangataua, T07-3858799.* Well-appointed rooms. In-house restaurant. Base for horse treks.

AL **Whare Ora**, *1 Kaha St, Rangataua, 5 km from Ohakune, T07-3859385, whareora@xtra.co.nz* Beautiful, renovated, 5-level wooden house originally built in 1910. One en suite with spa and sitting room, 1 attic en suite room. Luxuriously appointed with great cuisine.

AL-A **Cairnbrae House** *Mangawhero River Rd, Ohakune, T07-3853002, www.cairnbraehouse.co.nz* Lovely rural homestay 7km southwest of Ohakune. Immaculate rooms with private bathroom. Private guest lounge, SkyTV and internet, not to mention the odd deer in the garden. Dinner on request.

A **Tairoa Lodge**, *144 Magawhero Rd, T/F 3854882, tairoalodge@xtra.co.nz* Modern, spacious single-storey lodge in the centre of town. Range of rooms (with bathroom). Activities arranged.

B **Waireka B&B**, *11 Tainui St, T/F 3858692, richardmilne@xtra.co.nz* Friendly, affordable

B&B with local photographer and qualified naturopath.

There are numerous self-contained chalet-style options in town including:
A **Ossie's Chalets and Apartments**, *corner of Tainui and Shannon St, T07-3858088;*
B **Ruapehu Cabins**, *107 Clyde St, T07-3858608, ruapehu.cabins@xtra.co.nz*
B-D **Rimu Park Lodge and Chalets**, *27 Rimu St, T07-3859023.* Also offers backpackers accommodation).
AL-A **Ruapehu Chalet Rentals**, *23 Clyde St, T07-3858149, accommodation@ruapehu.co.nz*

There are also numerous motels including the newest and recommended:
A **Peaks Motor Inn**, *corner of Mangawhero Terr and Shannon St, T07-3859144, www.thepeaks.co.nz*
A **Hobbit Motor Lodge**, *corner of Goldfinch and Wye Sts, T07-3858248.* Of which has a good in-house restaurant.
B **Sunbeam Motel and Lodge**, *4 Foyle St, T07-3858470.* Bar and restaurant attached, spas and tour services.
A-D **Alpine Lodge Motel**, *7 Miro St, T07-3858758.* A cheap, central motel with backpacker accommodation. Bistro attached. Spa pool.
C-D **Matai YHA**, *15 Clyde St, T07-3858724, maitai.lodge@xtra.co.nz* Central location, recently renovated, good range of rooms and dorms. Bike hire.
D **Station Lodge**, *60 Thames St, T07-3858797.* Basic, laid back and close to all the nightlife. Spa.

Motorcamps and campsites
C-D **Ohakune Top Ten Holiday Park**, *5 Moore St, T07-3858561.* An excellent facility with spotless amenities near the town centre and next to the Mangateitei Stream. Shuttle service available. Spa.
D **DOC Mangawhero Campsite**, *Ohakune Mountain Rd, T07-3858578.* Book with DoC. Basic facilties for purist campers.

Taumarunui *p317*
There is not a huge range of choice when it comes to accommodation but the VIC can advise. The best motorcamp in town is the
B-D **Taumarunui Holiday Park**, *near SH4*

and next to the river, 3 km east of town,
T07-8959345.

🍴 Eating

Whakapapa Village *p309*
$$$ Grand Chateau, *see above.* Restaurant with fine, traditional à la carte dining.

$$ Pihanga Café and Bar, *In the Grand Chateau,* Café attached to the Grand Chateau with good coffee and the best and most varied café menu in the village. Offers lunch and dinner from 1130 daily.

$$ Skotel Resort, *T07-8923719.* Also has a good restaurant and bar that has expansive views across to Ngauruhoe and is open to non-guests for breakfast, lunch and dinner.

$ Fergusson's Café, *opposite the Chateau. 0800-1530.* The best place for a light, cheap snack.

$ Knoll Ridge Café, *up the Top of the Bruce Rd (take the chairlift), T07-8923738. Chairlift $16, child $8. 0900-1600 (last lift 1530 in summer).* Place to head if you fancy a coffee (with a view).

Whakapapa Camp Store, *in the village.* Has light snacks and sells groceries at elevated prices, so stock up before you go.

National Park Village *p311*
$$ Ski Haus and **National Park Backpackers**, *see above,* have in-house restaurants offering breakfast, lunch and dinner to non-guests.

$$ Schnapps Hotel, *Findlay St, T07-8922788. Daily from about 1100.*

$$ Eivin's Café, *on the corner of Carroll St and SH4, T07-8922844. Daily from 0830.* Both are pleasant enough and serve traditional pub-style fare, including pizza.
There is no supermarket in the village. The **BP Station** *on Carroll St, T07-8922879. 0730-1900,* stocks basic supplies.

Ohakune *p311*
$$$ The Matterhorn and **Powderkeg** restaurants, *in the Powderhorn Chateau, corner of Mangawhero and Thames St, T07-3858888. The Matterhorn is open daily year round, while the Powderkeg is closed in summer.* Very popular for a range of fine traditional dishes.

$$ Ohakune Hotel's O Bar, *72 Clyde St, T07-3858268.* Good traditional pub food

both day and evenings throughout the year.

$$ Alpine Wine Bar and Restaurant, *opposite the Okahune Hotel on Clyde St.* More formal dining, again every evening throughout the year from 1800.

$$ Sassi's Bistro, *Miro St, T07-3858758. Open for breakfast from 0700 and dinner from 1800 every night, year round.* Has an intimate, congenial atmosphere.
A number of motels have reputable in-house restaurants including:

$$ The Hobbit, *corner of Goldfinch and Wye St, T07-3858248.*

$$ Turoa Ski Lodge Restaurant, *10 Thames St, T07-3858274. Licensed. Open daily.* Cosy and great value steak.

$ Le Pizzeria and **$ Margarita's**, *on Thames St, at the northwestern end of town. Both open late in the winter evenings.* Can alleviate the post-party munchies.

$ Stutz Café, *Clyde St, T07-3858563.* Slightly dodgy 'caf' that can fill a desperate gap.

$ Utopia Café, *further north up Clyde St. Open 0900-1600 year round (extended hrs in winter).* Good coffee and an altogether better class of snack.

$ The Fat Pigeon Garden Café *on the way back up towards the mountain on Mangawhero Terr. Seasonal opening hours.* A good café with in/outdoor seating.

Taumarunui *p317*
For eating you can't go past
$ Main Trunk Café, *set in an old rail carriage on Hakiaha St. Wed-Sun 1000-2200.*

🏔 Activities and tours

Whakapapa *p309*
Whakapapa can be used as a base for the numerous activities throughout the park. One local operator is **Plateau Adventure Guides**, a quality outfit offering a range of activities from mountaineering to kayaking, T07-8922740. For the luxury treatment you might like to try the **Tongariro Trek Trip** offered by the Grand Chateau, T07-8923809. It includes the Tongariro Crossing and Crater Lake of Ruapehu as well as 4 nights in the hotel itself, all for $1000.

Mountaineering Whakapapa provides the most accessible routes to the Ruapehu summit(s) and the Crater Lake. You can ride

2 chairlifts 2,020 m above sea level to the Knoll Ridge Chalet ($16). You can reach either the Crater Lake and/or the summits from there; 6 km, 4 hours (9 km, 7 hours minus chairlift). The highest summit is **Tahurangi** (2797 m) on the southwest fringe of the crater. The Dome hut, which took a pummelling during the 1990s eruptions, is easily accessible at the crater's northern fringe. As always, make sure you are well-equipped and leave details of your intentions with DoC at the visitors' centre (see also Ruapehu Crater Lake Walk on page 309).

Scenic flights Mountain Air Scenic Flights, *on SH47 at the junction to Whakapapa Village and the Grand Chateau (pick-ups from Turangi)*, *T0800-922812, www.mountainair.co.nz* Operates excellent and affordable flights over the park and beyond. From $70-$145.

Skiing *For ski information, T07-8923738, www.whakapapa.co.nz Snowphone T0900-99333*. From Whakapapa the Bruce Rd continues 6 km up to **Iwikau Village**, *for more information and all bookings T07-8923738, www.whakapapa.co.nz/ www.snow.co.nz 0900-1600*. The North Island's largest ski field, Iwikau is essentially a conglomerate of ski club chalets and lodges, the main focus being the ski field amenity and reception buildings. An all-day lift pass is from $50, youth from $25. Full-day ski, boot and pole hire costs from $32, youth from$22 (snowboard and boots from $45). Various day and beginner packages are available: Ski gear rental and lifts from $94, youth $51; Snowboard equivalent $107, youth $67; 'Sightseeing Package' (from $16, youth $8). There are ski school and crèche facilities available on the mountain as well as a café at Knoll Ridge.

Walking A number of short walks can be accessed from Whakapapa, as well as the longer tramps of the **Tongariro Crossing**, **Tama Lakes**, **Northern Circuit** and the **Round the Mountain** tracks (see above). The **Whakapapa Nature Walk** (1 km, 30 minutes) is an easy and pleasant stroll which starts near the visitors' centre; the **Taranaki Falls Walk** (6 km; 2 hours) crosses low-lying tussock to the 20 m falls of the Wairere

stream; and the **Silica Rapids Walk** (7 km; 2½ hours), is a loop track that follows another stream through beech forest to some coloured silica terraces. Note that a number of local activity operators also offer guided walks and the DoC runs an excellent summer programme of organized and guided walks, which usually start from the Whakapapa VillageVIC; from $55, T07-8923729.

National Park Village *p311*
There are a number of activity operators based in the village, most connected to the various lodges and backpackers. Walking equipment (including boots) can be hired from **Howard's Lodge, Pukenui Lodge** and the **Ski Haus** (see Sleeping above). **Pete Outdoors**, *T07-8922773*, offers a wide range of guided activities.

Climbing wall National Park Backpackers, *Findlay St, T07-8922870. Daily 0900-2100*. An 8-m wall that is open to non-guests. $12.

Kayaking, canoeing and rafting
National Park is often used as a base for Wanganui River Trips; the main lodges and backpackers will assist in arranging trips. For operators see Whanganui National Park section, page 392.

Mountain biking The **42 Traverse** is a 46 km 3-7-hour track and the major biking attraction in the area. The following provide information, guided trips or independent bike hire:
Howard's Lodge, *T07-8922827*, transport from $35, hire from $60 per day;
Pukenui Lodge, *T07-8922882*.

Scenic flights Mountain Air Scenic Flights, *on SH47 at the junction to Whakapapa Village and the Grand Chateau, T0800-922812, www.mountainair.co.nz* Excellent and affordable flights over the park and beyond. From $70-$145.

Skiing For information log on to www.snow.co.nz Equipment hire from:
Pukenui Lodge, *T07-8922882*;
Howard's Lodge, *T07-8922827*;
Ski Biz, *Carroll St, T07-8922717*;
Eivin's, *SH4, T07-8922844*.

T07-3337099, www.tongarironz.com Guided trips of the Tongariro Crossing.

Ohakune *p311*

Ecotours Kiwi Encounters, *T07-3859505*, A local company offering touristy noctambulations into the Waimarino Forest to learn more about kiwi. If you are lucky you may actually see one, but if not, the screeching calls will certainly be forever ingrained in your memory. If you do see one, count your lucky stars: they reckon in 15 years the entire mainland population may be wiped out. 2045-2300, $35, child $20.

Horse trekking Ruapehu Homestead, *SH49, Ohakune, T07-3858799*. The best company for beginners but also caters for advanced riders. 1-hour trek $35, child $25; 3 hours $50.

Kayaking, canoeing and rafting
Ohakune is a popular base for river activities on the Wanganui River. For operators see page 396.

Mountain biking The area is an excellent place for mountain biking of all grades of difficulty. For information on what tracks are available call into the DoC field centre or VIC. Bike hire is available through:
Ski Shed, *Clyde St, T07-3859173*. Full day $35.
Scenic Cycles, *16 Miro St, T07-3858257*. Organized trips including provision of bikes and transport to the ski field for a thrilling ride back down the mountain, from $35.

4WD Lahar Totally Off Road, *Lahar Farm, T07-3854136, www.laharfarm.co.nz* Provides self-guided, guided or training trips for 4-wheel drives, but only if you bring your own. Accommodation available.

Skiing This is the tourist raison d'être for Ohakune, with the Turoa ski field being preferred by many to the larger Whakapapa field on the western slopes of the mountain. As well as offering some great runs and spectacular views, Ohakune sits head and shoulders above the rest in terms of après-ski atmosphere and amenities. Although popular destinations for skiing, both Turoa and Whakapapa have suffered in recent years due to the Ruapehu eruptions in the mid-1990s and a lack of fresh winter snow. As a result, many have gravitated to the South Island ski resorts, with disastrous economic consequences for the town. However, when conditions are right there is no doubt Turoa can offer some of the best skiing in the North Island. There are numerous ski equipment hire shops in Ohakune as well as at the base of the ski field itself. The average cost of hire for skis, boots and poles is around $31, youth $20, and snowboard and boots from $40. An all-day lift pass will cost from $56, youth $28. There are a number of packages available on the mountain, including the 'Discover Skiing' package, which includes lift pass, equipment hire and one-hour lesson for around $49. The 'Lift and Ski Hire Package' is self-explanatory and costs from $94 for the day, youth from $51; snowboard equivalent $107, youth $67. A group lesson on the mountain will cost about $25 while a private lesson will cost $85. For further information on skiing see Whakapapa and National Park Actitivies sections above. Also try to source the Turoa 2002 booklet. For transport services up the mountain see page 311.

Walking The Ohakune Mountain Road provides short and long walks, some of which join the Tongariro National Park's major walking circuits. There are two very pleasant short walks which depart from the DoC field centre at the edge of town. The 15-minute **Rimu Track** with its interpretative information posts is wonderful, even in the rain, while the 1-hour **Mangawhero Forest Walk** follows the river valley up towards the mountain. Further up the road (12 km) the 1-hour **Waitonga Falls Track** is popular, as is the longer (5-hour) **Lake Surprise** tramp, which starts about 16 km up the road. The less active can try the 10-minute **Mangawhero Falls Walk**, also accessed off the Mountain Road. For details, maps and the latest on weather call in at the DoC field centre, T07-3858578. The **Tongariro Crossing** is also accessible from Ohakune. For information see page 305. For shuttle transport see page 311.

⊙ Entertainment

Ohakune *p311*
Without doubt the place to go is the
Powderkeg Bar, *in the Powderhorn Chateau,*
Thames St. It is spacious, nicely decked out in
an Alpine style, very popular, and above all
has a great open fire.
Margarita's *further along Thames St*. Also
popular with the locals.
O Bar, *on Clyde St*. The place to be in the
centre of town.
Ohakune Cinema, *17 Goldfinch St,*
T07-3858488.

❶ Directory

Ohakune *p311*
Internet Snowbird Copy Centre, *92 Clyde*
St. Daily 0930-1700. **The Video Shop**, *Clyde*
St. 1000-2030. **Police** *T07-3850100.* **Post**
office *Goldfinch St.*

Outside the park

Waiouru and the Desert Road → *Phone code: 07 Colour map 3, grid A3*
Population: 2,500
Waiouru is at the junction of SH1 (Desert Road) and SH49 from Ohakune (27 km) on
the southern fringe of the Tongariro National Park. It is essentially an army base and,
for the traveller, a last resort for accommodation when the Desert Road is closed with
snow. During the winter this can happen quite frequently and when it does (if
conditions allow) all traffic is diverted to the west of the mountain via Ohakune and
National Park. If this happens you can expect to add another 1-2 hours to your
journey. The Desert Road is essentially the stretch of SH1 from Waiouru to Turangi (63
km), featuring Ruapehu and Ngauruhoe to the west and the Kaimanawa Mountains to
the east. The broad, flat valley is so called because of its barren landscape, given over
only to grass and ancient volcanic ash fields. It has a strange kind of beauty spoiled
only by the tracks of off-road army vehicles and rows of electricity pylons
disappearing into the horizon. During eruptions, potential ash-falls on these wires
substantially threaten upper North Island electricity supplies.

There are few sights in Waiouru but, if you have time or the snow has fallen, the
QEII Army Memorial Museum, ① *T07-3876911, daily 0900-1630, $10, child $7, café,*
is worth a look. It has a generous collection of army hardware as well as a range of
displays covering New Zealand's military history since the mid-1800s. There is also a
dynamic Roll of Honour to remember those who have died for this great country.

Taumarunui → *Phone code: 07 Colour map 3, grid A3 Population: 5000.*
Taumarunui is a small agricultural service town lying at the confluence of the Ongarue
and Wanganui Rivers, on the western fringes of the Ruapehu District. Although
nothing to write home about, it is often used as an overnight base for skiing in the
Tongariro National Park, and as a base for kayak, canoe and jet-boat tours of the
Wanganui River and the Wanganui National Park. For Wanganui River activity
operators based in Taumarunui see Wanganui National Park section, page 392.

Getting there Taumarunui is served by **Intercity** and **Newman's** and is also on the
main Auckland/Wellington rail line. The VIC administers bookings and tickets.

Information Taumarunui VIC, ① *at the train station on Hakiaha St, the main drag*
through town, T07-8957494, www.middleofeverywhere.co.nz Mon-Fri 0900-1630,
Sat and Sun 1000-1600. It has an interesting working scale model of the 'Raurimu
Spiral' (see below). **DOC**, ① *Cherry Grove, beside the river, T07-8958201.*

Sights The major attraction around Taumarunui is the **Raurimu Spiral**, an impressive
feat of railway engineering on the main north/south trunk line, devised by the late RW

Holmes in 1908. The track falls (or rises) 213 m at an incline of 1 in 50, by means of a complete circle, three horseshoe curves and two tunnels, which double the distance travelled. Check it out from the lookout, 37 km south of the town on SH4, or the working model in the VIC.

There are a number of walks around the town for which the VIC has details. For the very energetic there is the climb to the summit of the flat-topped **Mount Hikurangi** (770 m) behind the town. For detailed directions, and to confirm permission with the local landowner, ask at the VIC. The 155-km **Taumarunui to Stratford Heritage Trail** (scenic drive) begins or ends here, taking you through the Wanganui and Taranaki Regions to Stratford. The highlight of this trip is the tiny settlement of **Whangamomona**, which, after a run-in with regional bureaucracies in 1995, declared itself a republic. It is an unremarkable little place with a population of less than 100. The village opens its borders on the anniversary of the great uprising in October each year, when there is a weekend of celebrations. No passport control or baggage checks necessary, just a pint glass. There is also an alternative scenic route from Taumarunui, across the hills via Ohura and SH40 to SH3 and New Plymouth. This is a rugged trip over remote country so make sure you are stocked up. ▸▸ *For Sleeping and Eating see pages 313 and 314.*

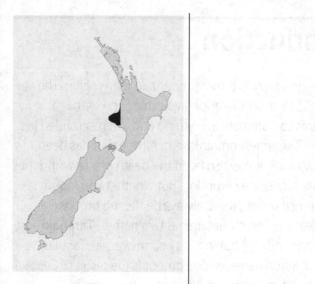

Taranaki

Introduction

In many ways Taranaki is more mountain than region. The awesome 2518 m snow-capped volcanic cone of the same name seems to dominate everything and, even shrouded in mist, it is still strangely omnipresent. Although it has been enjoyed by many, it has also been the death of a few, and they say it is due for another eruption. But whether you look at it with reverence or fear, it will always be the region's one defining feature. The mountain has two names, **Taranaki** and **Egmont**, both official, but in a way controversial. Taranaki is the original Maori name, while Egmont is the result of Captain Cook's habit of renaming anything in sight during his explorations in 1770. The largest town is **New Plymouth**, a proud, prosperous and modern centre that lies in the shadow of the great mountain on the northwest coast. Although a little bit out of the way, those who make the effort to visit the region will not be disappointed. As well as the superb scenery and range of activities on or around the mountain itself, the region boasts a fascinating history, fine parks, gardens, arts and crafts and a coastline internationally recognized for its excellent surfing.

★ Don't miss...

❶ The great **Mount Taranaki**, perhaps the most beautiful mountain in the country: climb it, ski down it, walk or drive around it, or stroll through its 'Goblin Forest', page 330.

❷ Taking a stroll through the **Pukeiti Rhododendron Gardens** or New Plymouth's **Pukekura** and **Brooklands Parks**, page 326 and 323.

❸ 'Dam-Dropping' in **Hawera**, page 329.

❹ The bizarre contemporary artworks at the **Govett-Brewster Gallery** in New Plymouth, page 323.

❺ **Paritutu Rock** above the New Plymouth Power Station, page 324. See if you can see Mount Ruapehu. Then see if you can get down!

❻ **Surfing lessons** in Oakura, page 326.

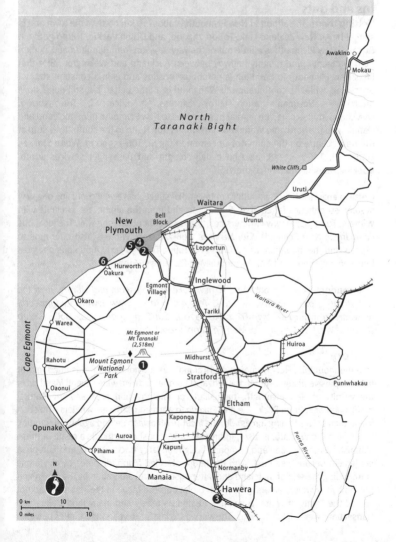

New Plymouth → Colour map 3, grid A1 Population: 67,000

Based on resources of rich agricultural land and natural gas and oil supplies, lively New Plymouth enjoys considerable prosperity and it's the main service town and population base of the New Plymouth district and Taranaki Region. Like the entire region, the town is dominated by the mountain, which seems to dictate the general mood, like some huge meteorological barometer. On a clear day, when the mountain radiates, its sheer size and stature are mirrored proudly in the town and all around the region. But, when shrouded in mist and rain, both are equally dull and sombre. As well as being a fine base from which to explore the recreational delights on and around the mountain and the region as a whole, New Plymouth itself has an excellent art gallery, some interesting historic buildings and a fine marine and public park.

Ins and outs

Getting there The airport at New Plymouth is about 10 km north of the town and is served by **Air New Zealand Link**, T0800-737000, and **Origin Pacific**, T0800-302302. By road, New Plymouth is a little out of the way: 254 km from Hamilton and 172 km from Wanganui, and roughly halfway between Auckland and Wellington. SH3 that links New Plymouth to Hamilton is notorious for slips and is in a constant state of upgrading, while its continuation to Wanganui is a little better, but still quite slow. **Intercity, Newman's** and **Dalroy Express**, 7 Erica Pl, T06-7550009, www.dalroytours.co.nz, run regular bus services to New Plymouth from Auckland and Hamilton to the north and Wanganui and Palmerston North to the south. They stop at the travel centre on the corner of Queen and King St, T06-7599039. **White Star**, 25 Liardet St, T06-7583338, also have daily freight and passenger services south. Bookings and information at the VIC.

Getting around New Plymouth's central grid of streets has a very confusing one-way system, so patience is required. Shuttles to and from the airport are available with **Withers**, T06-7511777, www.withers.co.nz, and cost about $12 one-way. The local bus company is **New Plymouth City Services**, T06-7582799. Wither's also offer runs to hostels and the mountain, as do **Cruise NZ Tours**, T06-7583222. A minibus operates between Inglewood and New Plymouth Mon-Fri, T06-7566193.

Information New Plymouth VIC, ① *new Puke Ariki Museum and Library, near the waterfront on Egmont St, T06-7596080, www.newplymouthnz.com, www.taranakinz.org.nz Mon-Fri 0830- 1700, Sat/Sun 0900-1700.* **DoC,** ① *220 Devon St West, T06-7590350. Mon-Fri 0800-1600.*

History

Like the mountain, New Plymouth and Taranaki as a whole has an unsettled and at times explosive history. Prior to the arrival of Europeans there were several Maori *pa* in the vicinity of New Plymouth, particularly around the port area and the natural fortification of Paritutu Rock. The first *Pakeha* to arrive in 1828 were whalers who soon found themselves joining forces with the local Te Ati-awa to defend against marauding tribes from the Waikato. In 1841, in an area now almost deserted as a result of these skirmishes, the New Zealand Company bought up large tracts of land, and European settlement began in earnest. With the return of exiled Maori, disputes quickly arose surrounding the sale of their land and, after unsuccessful arbitration by the crown and fuelled by the white settlers' greed, war broke out. The Maori in the Taranaki had not signed the Treaty of Waitangi so were treated as rebels and many land claims and transactions were highly dubious. The war was to last for 10 years, and battles between the Europeans and the Maori were amongst the fiercest ever fought in the country. As a result, most settlers deserted the area leaving New Plymouth little more than a military settlement. It was not until 1881 that formal peace was made and New Plymouth and the region as a whole settled down and began to prosper through its rich agricultural lands. New Plymouth was named after Plymouth in Devon, England, from where many of the first settlers came. Today, as well as agriculture, economic booms have been enjoyed through the discovery of natural gas and oil.

Sights

One of the town's most celebrated institutions is the **Govett-Brewster Gallery**, ① *corner of Queen and King sts, T06-7585149, www.govettbrewster.org.nz Daily 1030-1700. Free*. Although it opened 30 years ago you could be forgiven for thinking the paint was still wet. The interior is on three levels and looks very modern, befitting its reputation as the premier contemporary art gallery in the country. Although perhaps not to everyone's taste, the mainly three-dimensional and highly conceptual pieces are well worth a look. The gallery doyen is Len Lye, a poet, writer and multi-media artist who specialized in pioneering animation work in the 1930s. His mainly abstract film works are regularly shown.

The rather flash new **Taranaki Museum and Library (Puke Ariki)**, ① *Egmont St, T06-7589583, www.pukeariki.com, Mon-Fri 0900-1630, Sat and Sun 1300-1700, free*, is worth a visit and houses an interesting collection of Maori artefacts and displays, mixed with the usual pioneer exhibits and wildlife specimens. The quaint little **Richmond Cottage**, ① *on Ariki St, open in summer, Mon, Wed and Fri 1400-1600 and all year round on Sat and Sun, 1300-1600*, now almost absorbed by the museum, is a furnished colonial cottage built in 1853.

There are some other notable historic buildings and sites in the city, including the oldest stone church in the country, **St Mary's**, on Vivian Street. The original church was built in 1846. The interior contains some lovely Maori carvings and stained-glass windows. The cemetery echoes the military theme, with several soldiers' graves being a testament to the town's and area's colourful and, at times, bloody past.

The **Fitzroy Pole** (Pou Tutaki) which stands proudly at the northern end of town on the corner of Devon Street East and Smart Road was erected by the Maori in 1844. It was done to commemorate Governor Fitzroy's decision to question the legalities of white settlers and forbid their acquisition of huge tracts of land. Although not the original, the carving speaks for itself.

In distinct contrast and far more contemporary is the **'Wind Wand'** on the waterfront near the museum. Created for the 2000 millennium celebrations by local multi media artist Len Lye it is a 45-m, 900-kg kinetic sculpture that is designed to sway gently in the breeze. The bulb at the end is lit at night to enhance this effect though watching it at any time can prove quite therapeutic. For more information log on to www.windwand.co.nz: seems even artworks have their own websites these days.

New Plymouth is famous for its parks, the oldest and finest of which are **Pukekura** and **Brooklands**, which merge. They are best accessed at Fillis Street, just east of the town centre. Pukekura, opened in 1876, is a well-maintained 20 ha of lakes and assorted gardens, with a cricket ground, fernery and tea-room serving refreshments and light meals daily except Tuesday. From here, on a clear and calm day, you will see the reflection of Mount Taranaki across the main lake, which is crossed by a Japanese-style bridge. Brooklands has an outdoor amphitheatre, ponds

Taranaki New Plymouth

● *The VIC can give details of a number of Heritage Trails, including an interesting 2-hr*
● *walk in town starting at Puke Ariki Landing, a park with sculptures and the lofty 'wind wand' by the shoreline.*

studded by lily pads, English-style and rhododendron gardens, an historic colonial hospital museum/gallery and a 2000-year-old puriri tree. There is also a small children's zoo, ① *daily from 0900-1800*, with all the usual inmates, including kune-kune pigs, goats and miniature horses, as well as monkeys and a fine collection of parrots and parakeets.

Near the ugly towers of the power station and the busy port is the **Sugar Loaf Island's Marine Park**, with its eroded, volcanic rock islands. Designated in 1986, the park is home to New Zealand fur seals and a variety of nesting seabirds. Boat trips to visit the park and view the wildlife are available (see Activities below). The shoreline of the park is part of an interesting 7-km Coastal Walkway, the highlight of which is the climb up **Paritutu Rock** – if you can. The climb requires considerable effort and involves pulling yourself up by a steel cable, but the view (though spoilt slightly by the power station and oil storage tanks) is worth the effort, with the ever-present Taranaki cone to the east and the town to the north, and Ruapehu and Ngauruhoe just visible on a clear day. Then you're faced with the descent, which is not so much a scramble, as an abseil. If the climb is too daunting, a fine view can also be had from Marshland

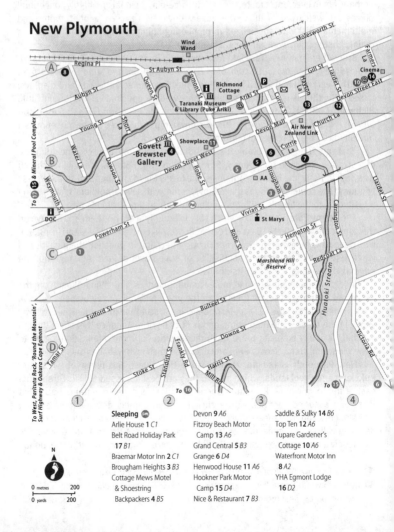

New Plymouth

Sleeping 😴
Arlie House **1** *C1*
Belt Road Holiday Park **17** *B1*
Braemar Motor Inn **2** *C1*
Brougham Heights **3** *B3*
Cottage Mews Motel & Shoestring Backpackers **4** *B5*

Devon **9** *A6*
Fitzroy Beach Motor Camp **13** *A6*
Grand Central **5** *B3*
Grange **6** *D4*
Henwood House **11** *A6*
Hookner Park Motor Camp **15** *D4*
Nice & Restaurant **7** *B3*

Saddle & Sulky **14** *B6*
Top Ten **12** *A6*
Tupare Gardener's Cottage **10** *A6*
Waterfront Motor Inn **8** *A2*
YHA Egmont Lodge **16** *D2*

N
0 metres 200
0 yards 200

Hill, off Robe Street, which was formerly the Pukaka *Pa*. It is also home to the **New Plymouth Observatory**. ① *To6-7587886. Open to the public on Tue 2000-2130 (winter 1930-2100). $2.* ▸▸ *See Sleeping, Eating and other listings, pages 327-330.*

Around New Plymouth

North on SH3

There are a few attractions, walks and viewpoints along this road that are definitely worth a visit. Heading north past Waitara and Urenui, which have some popular beaches in themselves, is the **White Cliffs Brewing Company**, ① *To6-7523676, Mon-Fri 1000-1700, Wed 1500-1700*, a boutique beer brewery offering tastings and sales of some fairly heady brews.

The **Whitecliffs Walkway** is the most celebrated in North Taranaki. The Whitecliffs, (named after the famous Dover cliffs in England), although not on the same scale or grandeur as their namesake, are nonetheless quite impressive and dominate the shore for some 7 km. The track can be accessed from the south at the Pukearuhe Historic Reserve at the end of Pukearuhe Road, north of Urenui. The total length of the track is 9.5 km, terminating at the northern access point, on Clifton Road at the mouth of the Tongaporutu River. Much of the track is along the shoreline, so make sure you check the tides.

The immediate coastline either side of the **Tongaporutu River** is scattered with rock towers, caves and arches, though they are not easily accessed (low tide only). For a superb view of them head just north of the Clifton Road, across the bridge and up the hill on the other side. Turn left onto Cemetery Road. From the end a short walk across an accessible field will take you to the headland. There is also a fine view of the Whitecliffs from there.

Just north of Tongaporutu are **Mokau** and **Awakino**. Both are popular but remote holiday spots especially good for coastal walks and fishing. For canoe trips and cruises on the Mokau River (see Activities page 329).

A lengthy diversion off SH3 along SH40 will take you to the 74-m **Mount Damper Falls**, the highest waterfall in the North Island. From SH40 take the Okau Road to the Mount Damper Falls car park, which is well marked. The 15-minute walk will take you to a lookout platform. The falls are best viewed after heavy rain. ▸▸ *See Sleeping page 328.*

To North, Airport, Fitzroy Pole & ⑨⑩⑪⑫⑬
Gover St
State La
Courtenay St
Woolworths ☐Supermarket
Eliot St
Leach St
P
New World Supermarket
Lemon St
Gover St
Cameron St
Pendarves St
Gilbert St
Fillis St
Gover St
Pukekura Park
To Brookland's Park
To South (SH 3), Mt Egmont National Park, Around the Mountain Circuit & ⑭

Taranaki New Plymouth

⑤
Eating ⊙
Agra **1** *A5*
Blow Fish **15** *B1*
Burtons & Bar **2** *A5*
El Condor **3** *A5*
Espresso **4** *B2*
GCR & Bar **5** *B3*
India Today **13** *A4*
L'Escargot **6** *B3*

⑥
Mill Rock & Bar **7** *B3*
Ozone **14** *A4*
Sandwich Extreme **12** *A4*
Simply Read **8** *A1*
Steps **9** *A5*

Bars & clubs ⊙
Crowded House **10** *A4*
Peggy Gordon's **11** *B2*

Carrington Road (off Victoria Road) heads southwest out of New Plymouth towards the mountain. It has a number of sights worth visiting. **Hurworth Cottage,** ⓘ *827 Carrington Road, T06-7533593, viewing by appointment,* was built originally in 1856 by young lawyer Harry Atkinson, who was also New Zealand's Prime Minister, not once, but four times. Young Harry and his family had to flee the house and the area during the Taranaki Wars in 1860. The house today is a well-renovated tribute to the family. Further along is the **Pouakai Zoo Park,** ⓘ *1296 Carrington Rd, T06-7533788, daily (except Mon) 1000-1600, $5, child $2,* a small, private, enthusiastically run zoo, exhibiting a number of native and non-native species including meerkats and gibbons.

The highlight on the Carrington Road, however, is the **Pukeiti Rhododendron Trust Gardens.** ⓘ *T06-7524141. Daily summer 0900-1700, winter 1000-1500. $8 ($5 in winter), child free.* This is a 4-sq km garden surrounded by bush that is world renowned for its beautiful displays of 'rhodies' and azaleas, which are best viewed in the spring/summer and especially during the Rhododendron Festival in late October. There is a restaurant, and a shop selling plants and souvenirs.

If you continue on Carrington Road you will join the network of roads that surround the mountain. There is a fine walk and views of the mountain on the Stony River and **Blue Rata Reserves**. From Carrington take a left onto the Saunders Road dirt track and follow it to the end. From there, by foot, negotiate your way through the bush following the sound of the river. You will emerge onto the Stony River boulder field. From here you can walk carefully east or west, under the shadow of the mighty mountain. The large Blue Rata, from which the reserve takes its name, is hard to find, about 100 m into the bush, on the river-side of the track, about halfway up its length.

Before rejoining SH45 and heading north or south, take a discreet peek at the memorial to the great man, prophet and Maori chief, Te Whiti, which is at **Parihaka Pa**, on Mid-Parihaka Road (signposted). ▸▸ *See Sleeping page 328.*

Lake Mangamahoe

There is something you simply must do on your visit to New Plymouth (weather permitting) and that is to soak up the beauty and serenity of Lake Mangamahoe. Just 10 km southeast on SH3, this scenic reserve is one of the very best places where you can see a reflection of the mighty mountain on water. After enjoying the lake itself, with its numerous swans, ducks and geese, head to the road end and take the right hand track up the steps to the lookout point. From here at sunset, or anytime when the mountain is clear, the view is magnificent. Take your camera.

'Surf Highway 45'

If you fancy doing the 175-km trip around the mountain, it involves at least a full day via the 'Surf Highway 45' and SH3. But on a clear day the mountain will be good company throughout, and there are a number of interesting places to see and visit on the way.

Heading south from New Plymouth the view of the mountain is shielded by the Kaitake and Pouakai Ranges for a short while, then you arrive in **Oakura**, famous for its surf, windsurfing and swimming beach. There is also an interesting craft shop called the Crafty Fox in the heart of town next to the Main Road. Various local art and craft pieces are for sale and there is a railway wagon café next door. ▸▸ *See Sleeping and Surfing Activities, pages 328 and 329.*

Lucy's Gully, 3 km south of Oakura, is a pleasant picnic spot with exotic trees and ferns including redwoods. There are also walking tracks into the Kaitake Range.

● *The 'Scenic 3 Highway' has a number of attractions described in the free 'Scenic 3 Highway'*
● *leaflet available from the VIC. For detailed information try 'Walks in north Taranaki' from DoC or the VIC, $1.*

Around the small settlement of **Okato** the mountain comes back into view and the road edges its way closer to the coast. You can satisfy your desire to see it again at the **Cape Egmont Lighthouse,** about 3 km down Cape Road. Although the lighthouse is closed to visitors it is still worth seeing. It seems strangely out of place, standing in a field with a huge mountain in the background! Just south of Cape Road back on SH45 is Mid-Parihaka Road. Two kilometres up is **Parihaka Pa** (see above).

Back on SH45, you can enjoy the scenery or explore the many side roads until you reach **Opunake**, which has a fine surf and swimming beach and a 7-km walkway, starting at Opunake Lake, which takes in lake, beach and river scenery. See the **VIC** ① *in the Library on Tasman St for accommodation options, T06-7618663. Mon-Thu 0930-1700, Fri 0930-1830.*

The next settlement south of Opunake is **Manaia** which is the place to leave SH45 if you want to get a bit more intimate with the mountain at **Dawson Falls**. There is not a lot in Manaia itself, a small settlement of about 1,000, named after a Maori Chief. Country and Western fans might like to pop into the **Taranaki Country Music Hall of Fame,** ① *11 Surf Highway, T06-2748442. 1000-1600.* Even if you are not a fan, at least try the website www.countrytouchnewzealand.homstead.com/countrytouchnz.com Recommended.

● Sleeping

New Plymouth *p322*
For full listings contact the VIC or www.accommodationtaranaki.co.nz For mountain accommodation see page 332.
LThe Nice Hotel, *71 Brougham St, T06-7586423, www.nicehotel.co.nz* This is a new luxury boutique hotel that is indeed very 'nice' and well situated close to all amenities. There are a range of themed rooms and a quality restaurant attached. They also offer nice tours!
The newest offering in the town centre is the **L-A**Waterfront Motor Inn, *1 Egmont St, T06-7583023, www.newplymouth waterfronthotel.co.nz* Other than its contemporary feel the location and views are hard to beat.
AL-A Devon Hotel, *390 Devon St, T06-7599009, www.devonhotel.co.nz*; and **AL-A**Grand Central Hotel, *42 Powerham St, T06-7587495, www.grandcentralhotel.co.nz* The 2 best options in this range.
ABraemar Motor Inn, *152 Powerham St, T06-7580859.* Well-established motel, fairly modern and has a distinct Scottish theme. Restaurant attached.
ABrougham Heights, *across the road from the Nice Hotel at 54 Brougham St, T06-7579954, www.broughamheights.co.nz* Well located, modern and comfortable motel that seems to absorb some of the niceties from the *Nice Hotel* across the road.

AThe Grange, *44B Victoria Rd, T06-7581540, cathyt@clear.net.nz* Modern, good value B&B, ideally located near the Pukekura Park.
AHenwood House, *314 Henwood Rd, T06-7551212, henwood.house@xtra.co.nz*, and **A**Tupare Gardener's Cottage, *487 Mangorei Rd, T06-7586480*, are 2 B&Bs both a little out of town but quiet, characterful and very pleasant.
AThe Loft, *729 Frankley Rd, T06-7532950.* A lovely rural self-contained option.
BAirlie House, *161 Powerham St, T06-7578866, www.airliehouse.co.nz* A characterful, aptly named historic villa B&B, centrally located and recently very tastefully renovated, with 2 tidy rooms with bathrooms and a self-contained studio, internet.
BCottage Mews Motel, *suites attached to the Backpackers, 48 Lemon St, T06-7580403.* Immaculate, good value and fine folk.
BSaddle and Sulky, *188 Coronation Av, heading southeast on SH3, T06-7575763.* Motel with the standard spas and Sky TV.
B-D Shoestring Backpackers, *48 Lemon St, T06-7580404.* A large traditional villa with a range of rooms and fine facilities. Friendly folk, sauna and internet.
B-DYHA Egmont Lodge, *12 Clawton St, T06-7355720.* Small, very friendly and set in a quiet location a 15-min walk from town (taxi fare refunded).

Motorcamps and campsites
B-D Belt Road Holiday Park, *2 Belt Rd, T06-7580228.* Nearer the water but

overlooking the port.

B-D Fitzroy Beach Motorcamp, *further north on Beach St, T06-7582870*. Less well endowed but more scenic.

B-D 'Top Ten' Motorcamp, *29 Princess St, Fitzroy, T06-7582566, New.Plymouth.TopTen@xtra.co.nz* Small and central.

North on the SH3 *p325*

B Mokau Motel, *SH3, T06-7529725*. Basic.

C-D Palm House, *T06-7529081, palmhouse@taranaki-bakpak.co.nz* A good backpackers, affiliated with the YHA in New Plymouth.

C-D Seaview Motorcamp, *Awakino, just before SH3 turns inland heading north, T06-7529708*. Excellent, with a café attached.

Carrington Road *p326*

A Patuha Farm Lodge, *575 Upper Pitone Rd, Okato, T06-7524469*. This 10-bedroom lodge is well placed in a quiet bush setting on the edge of the Pukeiti Rhododendron Trust Gardens. Overall a fine relaxing retreat.

B-D Hookner Park Motorcamp, *Carrington Rd about 10 km from town, T06-7536945*. The quiet country option. A working dairy farm where you can join in with farm activities.

Oakura *p326*

B Oakura Beach B&B, *1160 SH45, T06-7527320, www.oakura.com* Lovely villa-style B&B belonging to a well-travelled, friendly couple. Recommended.

B Oakura Motel, *53 Wairau Rd, Oakura, T06-7527680*. Basic, 3 mins from the beach.

C-D Oakura Beach Camp, *2 Jans Terr, T06-7527861*. Again basic but has a store and is across the road from the beach.

🍴 Eating

New Plymouth *p322*

$$$ L'Escargot (Andre's), *37-43 Brougham St, T06-7584812. Mon-Sat from 1700*. This is an old favourite offering award-winning, fine French-style cuisine in a congenial setting.

$$$ The Nice Hotel, *71 Brougham St. Mon-Sat from 1600*. Well, it couldn't possibly be horrible could it? Fine à la carte with superb desserts and a good wine selection.

$$$ Steps Restaurant, *37 Glover St,*

T06-7583393. Tue-Sat from 1800, Tue-Fri 1200-1400. Award-winning place and, with its fine Mediterranean cuisine, often hailed as the best in town.

$$ Agra, *151 Devon St, T06-7580030. Daily 1730-late*. A small, good-value Indian diner deserving of its loyal following.

$$ Burtons, *corner of Devon and Gover Sts, T06-7585373. Daily from 0700*. Good pub grub.

$$ GCR Restaurant and Bar, *Brougham St, T06-7587499, Mon-Fri from 0700, Sat and Sun from 0800*. A new modern restaurant and bar specializing in gourmet pizzas.

$$ India Today, *40 Devon St East, T06-7699117. Daily from 1730, lunch 1130-1430*. A little more conventional than Agra.

$$ The Mill Rock, *2 Courtney St, T06-7581935. Mon-Sat from 1100*. Pub that has joined the growing trend of serving a variety of dishes on hot slabs of stone – the 'stone-grill'.

$ El Condor, *170 Devon St East, T06-7575436. Tue-Sat from 1700*. Good value Argentinean pizza joint.

New World and **$ Ozone**, *117 Devon Street East*, or

$ Sandwich Extreme, *52 Devon Street East*, both sell good coffee and light snacks.

$ Simply Read, *2 Dawson St, T06-7578667*. Café in a sunny spot overlooking the sea, with a small bookshop attached.

$ The Espresso, *attached to the Govett-Brewster Gallery, Queen St, T06-7599399*. A firm favourite.

$ The Blow Fish, *406 St Aubyn St, T06-7591314*. No airs and graces; good value. **Countdown** supermarkets are on *Leach St*. **Pack-n-Save**, *Gill St*.

🎭 Entertainment

Pubs and bars

Burtons, *see above*. A firm favourite, with fine ales and a fair weather Fri evening clientele that spills out on to the street.

The Mill Rock, *see above*. Another favourite, with a cosmopolitan clientele and live bands.

Crowded House, *Devon St*. About the size of a football field and claims to be the official bar of the famed Taranaki Rugby Team supporters.

Peggy Gordon's, *corner of Devon and Egmont sts.* The town's Irish-style offering.

Cinema and theatre
Cinema, *125 Devon St East*, T06-7599077.
Showplace, *Devon St*, T06-7584947. Regular national and occasional international acts.
New Plymouth Operatic Society. Puts on about 3 shows annually, and they are of an excellent standard.

⊕ Festivals and events

For events detail log on to www.newplymouthnz.com/calendar.asp
Taranaki Festival of the Arts (*Feb/Mar every 'odd' year*). High profile and quality arts festival, involving dance, music, theatre, literary events, workshops and exhibitions.
The Taranaki Rhododendron Festival (*Oct*) Involves a number of events and tours that take place at various major gardens, www.rhodo.co.nz
New Plymouth Festival of Lights (*Dec-Feb*) Held in Pukekura Park, it involves the illumination of trees, waterfalls and fountains with additional staged events.

▲ Activities and tours

For mountain activities see page 330. New Plymouth offers many of the usual activities, along with dam-dropping and tandem-surfing.

Dam-dropping This is another of those 'Kiwi unique' adrenaline offerings. This time you throw yourself down a dam outlet with only a boogie-board and some other lunatics for company. The experience lasts 3 hours, costs from $50 (dam drop only 1hr) to $100 (full trip) and also takes in some Maori culture.
Kaitiaki Adventures, *based in Hawera*, T06-2785555, www.kaitiaki.co.nz

Fishing, diving and cruising For cruises from Mokau ($30), call T06-7529775. For fishing or diving try:
Compass Rose, T06-7511573,
Taranaki Fishing Charters, T06-7520731, or
Fishy Business, T06-7588095.
Chaddy's Charters, *Lee Breakwater Marina, Ocean View Parade, near the port*, T06-7589133. Offers regular fishing and

cruise trips to the marine reserve. It costs $25, child $10, fishing $60.
New Plymouth Underwater, *16 Hobson St*, T06-7583348. Main diving outfit.

Horse trekking and 4WD tours
Windyglen Farm, *Bertrand Rd, Waitara*, T06-7520603. Treks depart daily 1030, 1330 (and 1830 in summer).
Off the Beaten Track Adventures, T06-7627885. Canoe and 4-wheel drive trips. For kayak/horse trek combos see **Canoe and Kayak** below.

Kayaking **Chaddy's Charters**, T06-7589133. For hire and local shoreline and marine park explorations.
Canoe and Kayak, *corner of McClean St and West Quay*, T06-7548368. For expeditions down the Mokau River in North Taranaki – offers various good options including a 3-hour exploration of the Sugar Loaf Islands (from $40); a full-day scenic trip down the gentle Mokau River; or a 4-hour kayak/horse trekking combo, from $70 ($40 kayaking only).

Mineral pools **Mineral Pool Complex**, *8 Bonithon Rd*, T06-7591666. Mon-Fri 0800-2000, Tue 0900-1700, Sat/Sun 1200-2030. Bookings essential. The new complex is the result of a very tasteful renovation of the former mineral pool that has an artesian mineral well spouting 29,000-year-old water. It offers both communal and private pools (4 people) with a range of professional massages and health treatments. The pools cost $15 for 30 minutes, but this is on a 'per pool' basis and they are freshly filled for each client. Very therapeutic.

Mountaineering, climbing and abseiling
Top Guides, *T0800-448433*, *www.topguides.co.nz*, and
MacAlpine Guides, *T025-417042*, *alpineguidesmac@xtra.co.nz* Both will see you safely up and down the mountain from around $170. Other activities include climbing and abseiling.

Scenic flights and tandem skydiving
Air Taranaki, T06-7544375.
Taranaki Scenic Flights, T06-7550500.

Beck Helicopters, *T0800-336644*.
Taranaki Skydiving Club, *T06-7552426*.
Sightseeing and cultural tours
Waka Tours, *T06-7552068*,
www.4wdwaka.com New operators offering
an interesting mix of Maori culture and
ecology and an even more attractive choice of
transport types including 4-wheel drive, quad
bikes and best of all a 1-hour voyage of
discovery in a traditional *waka* (canoe), from
$60, child $30.
Cruise NZ Tours, *T06-7583222*. Popular city
tours for about $45 and an all-day tour for
around $100.
Newman's, *T06-7584622*. Also offer regular
trips around the city, the mountain and
farther afield for about the same price.
Seaspray, *T06-7589676*. Good value and
caters for small groups, 3 hours from $50.

**Surfing, tandem-surfing and
windsurfing** The Taranaki or Egmont Coast
is one of the best surfing places in the country.
The so-called 'Surf Highway 45' which hugs
the coastline between New Plymouth and
Wanganui has some fine surf beaches,
particularly at **Oakura** and **Opunake**.
Particular gems also include **Ahu Ahu Road**,
the **Kumara Patch** and **Stent Road**. In town,
Footsore Beach is one of the favourites.
Companies offering trips and lessons come
and go as much as the surf, so for the most
recent listings and prices contact the VIC.
Sirocco, *Oakura, T06-7527363*. Private hire and
wave information.
Vertigo, *Oakura, T06-7527363*. Surf board hire
and also offers windsurfing lessons.

O Shopping

Arts and crafts
There are numerous excellent arts and crafts
galleries and outlets in the region, for details
see the VIC.
Rangimarie Maori Art and Craft Centre,
near Paritutu Rock on Centennial Dr,
T06-7512880.
Kina NZ Design and Art Space, *101 Devon St
West, T06-7591201*.

O Directory

Airlines Air New Zealand, *12-14 Devon St
East, T06-7573300*. **Banks** Most main
branches can be found on Devon St. Currency
exchange at TSB Centre, *120 Devon St East,
T06-7595375*. **Car hire** Avis, *113 Gill St,
T06-7559600*. Budget, *25 Liardet St,
T06-7588039*. NZ Rent-a-Car, *Devon Rd,
T06-7587923*. **Cycle hire** Cycle Inn, *133
Devon St East, T06-7587418*. From $30 per day.
Raceway Cycles, *207 Coronation Av,
T06-7590391*. **Internet** New Plymouth
Library, *Brougham St*. Interplay, *Devon St East*.
PC Doctor (Mike's Comp services), *211c Devon
St East, T06-7572754*. **Post office** *Currie St.
Mon-Fri 0730-1730, Sat 0900-1300*. **Medical
services** Hospital, *Taranaki Base, David St.
Accident and Medical Clinic*, *Richmond
Centre, Egmont St, T06-7598915. Daily
0800-2200*. **Useful addresses** AA, *49-55
Powerham St, T06-7575646,*. **Police**,
Powerham St, T06-7575449. **Taxi** New
Plymouth Taxis, *T06-7575665*. Energy Cabs,
T06-7575580.

Mount Egmont (Taranaki) National Park → *Phone code: 06 Colour map 3, grid A1*

*Weather permitting, no trip to Taranaki would be complete without getting close to the
mountain. At 2518 m, Mount Taranaki is not only in the heart of Egmont National Park,
but essentially is the heart. This classically-shaped, dormant volcano was formed by
the numerous eruptions of the last 12,000 years. The most recent happened 350 years
ago and they say she is presently 'overdue', with the potential to 'go off' at any time.
Fatham's Peak, on the southern slopes, is a parasitic outcrop from the main vent,
while the Pouakai and Kaitake Ranges to the west are much older andesite volcanoes
which have eroded for much longer than Taranaki.*

❝❞ The forest and vegetation is called 'goblin forest' (due to its miniature 'hobbit-style' appearance the higher in altitude you go) and the entire mountain is drained by myriad babbling streams...

Getting there

The main access points to the park and the mountain are at North Egmont (Egmont VIC), Stratford (East Egmont) and Manaia (Dawson Falls). Egmont VIC is 16 km from North Egmont Village, at the end of Egmont Rd, which heads towards the mountain. East Egmont is accessed via Pembroke Rd, which heads 18 km towards the mountain from Stratford. Dawson Falls is at the end of Upper Manaia Rd, via Kaponga on the southern slopes of the mountain. Dawson Falls is 24 km from Stratford. **Wither's**, T0800-751177, and **Cruise NZ Tours**, T06-7583222, both offer shuttle services to the mountain from New Plymouth (particularly Egmont VIC); from $40 return.

Information → *For a live webcam of the mountain visit www.geonet.org.nz/taranaki.html*

Before attempting any walks on the mountain you should read all the relevant information. In New Plymouth the VIC (see page 322) can provide basic information particularly about getting there, while DoC office (both in town and on the mountain) can fill in the detail with walking information, maps and weather forecasts. **Egmont VIC**, ① T06-7560990, nevc@doc.govt.nz Daily from 0800-1630. **Dawson Falls VIC**, ① T06-7655144. Mar-Dec Wed-Sun 0800-1630, Jan-Feb daily. **DOC Stratford Field Centre**, ① Pembroke Rd, T06-7655144.

Walks

The 140-km of short or long walks, which range in difficulty and from 30 minutes to four days, are well maintained by DoC. All are easily accessible from the main access points and information centres above. The forest and vegetation is called 'goblin forest' (due to its miniature 'hobbit-style' appearance the higher in altitude you go) and the entire mountain is drained by myriad babbling streams. Beware that the higher you go, obviously, the more dangerous it gets. In winter the slopes are covered in snow and ice, so climbing boots, crampons and an ice axe are essential. Even in summer crampons are advised on the summit, though the main enemy underfoot is the loose scree.

❗ The mountain has numerous walking tracks, two main summit routes, a round-the- mountain track and a ski-field.

To the uninitiated Mount Taranaki looks deceptively easy and the weather is highly unpredictable. Many people have lost their lives on its slopes, so you must be well prepared. DoC has produced a number of leaflets that detail the walks. *Around the Mountain Circuit* and *Short Walks in Egmont National Park* are both excellent. The VICs around the mountain can also advise on routes, hut accommodation options, prices and bookings.

The **Mountain Circuit** takes 3-5 days and is about 55 km in length. (There are a number of huts to stay in en route, but these must be pre-booked at DoC.) At Dawson Falls two of the best short-walk options include the track to the falls which can be accessed via the **Kapuni Loop Track** (one hour). This walk offers some good photo opportunities along the way, as does the **Wilkie's Pools Track** (one hour), which takes in some very pretty 'goblin forest' and a series of plunge pools, formed by sand and gravel running over the lava. At North Egmont the 45-minute walk from the park entrance to the **Waiwhakaiho River** has some beautiful base native bush, while the **Ngatoro Loop Track** (one hour) takes in some beautiful 'goblin forest', and the **Veronica Loop Track** (two hours) some excellent views. Both of these tracks start from the top of the road. If you want to go the full nine yards and climb the summit, good luck: it's quite a hard climb, but boy, is it worth it.

● Sleeping

For all mountain hut bookings contact and pre-book with DoC.

North Egmont
C-D The Camphouse, *North Egmont VIC, T06-7560990*. Basic bunk-style accommodation, with cooking facilities and hot showers near the centre.
C-D Missing Leg Backpackers, *1082 Junction Rd, Egmont Village, T06-7522570, jo.Thompson@xtra.co.nz* Very friendly and relaxed backpackers with doubles and share, log fire, bike hire and shuttle service up the mountain. Recommended.

East Egmont
AL-A Stratford Mountain House, *Pembroke Rd, Stratford, T0800-668682, www.mountainhouse.co.nz* Very popular hotel close to the slopes with an award-winning restaurant attached, Euro-style cuisine.
A Anderson's Alpine Lodge, *922 Pembroke Rd, T06-7656620*. YHA affiliated 3-storeyed Swiss-style chalet with 3 guestrooms.

Dawson Falls
A Dawson Falls Tourist Lodge, *Manaia Rd, Dawson Falls, T06-7655457*. Another Alpine-style lodge, comfortable rooms, log fire and all mod cons, in-house restaurant.
C-D Konini Lodge, *Dawson Falls, T025-430248*. A poor relation of the above, but comfortable nonetheless. DoC owned.

▲▲ Activities

Mountain guides If you want some experienced company and some great information en route then 3 main operators offer guided summit treks and other walks: **Top Guides**, *T0800-448433, www.topguides.co.nz* **MacAlpine Guides**, *T025-417042, alpineguidesmac@xtra.co.nz*; and **Mountain Guides Mount Egmont**, *T06-7588261, mguide@voyager.co.nz* All will see you safely up and down the mountain from around $170-$300 per day.
Other activities include climbing, abseiling and low -level hikes.
Skiing The only ski field on Taranaki is Manganui on the Stratford Plateau 3 km past the Mountain Lodge, Pembroke Road, East Egmont, which is accessed via Stratford (ski hire available, T06-7656100).
Information: **Stratford Mountain Club**, *T06-7655493*, the ski field direct, *T06-7591119*, or *www.snow.co.nz*

Hawera and around → *Phone code: 06 Population: 8000*

Hawera, an interesting little town with many architecturally-significant buildings, is the largest of the southern Taranaki townships and is on the coast at the confluence of SH45 and SH3. It's a good place to stop for a break and take in a few sights and attractions. From here it is about 70 km to complete the circuit around the mountain, north to New Plymouth.

Getting there
Hawera VIC, ① *55 High St (just head for the water tower), T06-2788599, visitorinfo@stdc.govt.nz Mon-Fri 0830-1700, Sat and Sun summer 1000-1500*. Acts as travel and accommodation booking agent.

Sights

The most obvious 'sight' is the **water tower**, built in 1914. Apparently, it was built at the request of insurance underwriters who were getting somewhat dismayed at the town's amazing propensity to burn down, which it did to varying degrees in 1884,1895 and 1912. The VIC has an 'Historic Hawera' heritage trail leaflet that details the major buildings. Strangely enough there is not an old fire station.

The **Tawhiti Museum**, ① *401 Ohangai Rd, Fri-Mon 1000-1600 summer (only Sun in winter), $6.50, child $2*, is an amazing little museum that uses realistic life-size exhibits and scale models to capture Taranaki's past. It is a private museum with an interesting history of its own. Its founders Nigel and Teresa Ogle make the models and figures on site. There is also a narrow gauge railway.

Equally unusual is the **Elvis Presley Memorial Room**, ① *51 Argyle St, phone for appointment, T06-2787624, donation only*, where avid collector and fan Kevin Wasley has amassed memorabilia and 2000 of The King's records. If you have not seen enough of dairy fields and cows, the 'udderly amazing' **Dairyland**, ① *on the corner of SH3 and Whareroa Rd, T06-2784537, daily 0900-1700, $3, child $2*, is the region's equivalent to Sheepworld in Northland or The Agrodome in Rotorua. Here you can take a simulated milk tanker ride and learn how the mechanical mega-suckers have taken over from the old hand-and-bucket method. There are interactive audio-visual displays and also a revolving café, which is supposed to simulate a revolving rotary milking shed!

SH3 from Hawera to New Plymouth

Eltham Eltham is well known for its dairy products, especially its production of cheese, but for the tourist the attractions are mainly its surrounding lakes. **Lake Rotokare** (Rippling Lake), 11 km southeast on Sangster Road, is in a pretty setting with a one-hour walk and picnic sites. Further afield, **Lake Rotorangi** on Glen Nui Road (via Rawhitiroa Road) is 40 km in length and was formed by the damming of the Patea River. It is popular for water sports and fishing. For information regarding other local attractions and accommodation, contact the **Eltham VIC**, ① *Eltham Library, High St, T06-7648838. Mon-Fri 0930-1730*.

Stratford A glance at the street names in Stratford will soon confirm your suspicion that this rural service centre and eastern gateway to the Egmont National Park was named after Shakespeare's birthplace in England. But there the similarity really ends. Stratford, New Zealand, is a pleasant little town but there is little to detain you beyond a meal, a coffee and perhaps a look at the **Glockenspiel** ('Playing clock') on the clock tower in the centre of town. The five-minute performance of life-sized figures depicts a few lines and music from the story of Romeo and Juliet and takes place at 1000, 1300 and 1500. Other than that the main attraction in town is the **Taranaki Pioneer Village**, ① *on SH3, T06-7655399. Daily from 1000-1600, $7, child $3*. It consists of 50 resited buildings on 10 acres, all faithfully equipped to depict the Taranaki of the early 1900s. The on-site café is deservedly popular and open same hours.

For more information on accommodation and local attractions, contact **Stratford VIC**, ① *Broadway, T06-7656708, www.stratford.co.nz Mon-Fri 0830-1700, Sat/Sun 1000-1400*. It also acts as a travel agent. Café and art gallery next door.

If you have kids, Inglewood, 13 km south of New Plymouth, has the **Fun Ho National Toy Museum**, ① *on the corner of Rata and Maitai sts, T06-7567030. Mon-Fri 0900-1700, Sat and Sun 1000-1600. $5, child $2.*. It is small but may keep them occupied for a few milliseconds. To recover, head for the popular MacFarlane's Café on Kelly Street, T06-7566665.

● *Hawera is the base for the imaginative dam dropping experience (see New Plymouth*
● *activities, page 329).*

Taranaki Hawera and around

⊜ Sleeping

Hawera

AL Kingfisher Cottage, *135 Ahipara Rd (north, between Hawera and Eltham) T06-2726630, www.kingfishercottage.co.nz* New well-appointed, self-contained cottage with great views and good fishing nearby.

A-B Kerry Lane Villas Motel, *2 Kerry La, T06-2781918.* The newest motel in Hawera in quiet rural setting 5 mins from town.
C-D Ohangai Backpackers, *Urupa Rd, T06-2722878.* Well-equipped farmstay backpackers 5 km from town (turn right in front of the museum).
B-D King Edward Park Motorcamp, *Waihi Rd, T06-2788544.*

Stratford

B-D 'Top Ten' Holiday Park, *Page St, T06-7656440, stratfordholpark@hotmail.com* The closest motorcamp to the mountain.

⊘ Eating

Hawera

$ Morrison's Café and Bar, *Victoria St, T06-2785647. Daily from 1100.*
Dairyland and the Tawhiti Museum also have cafés attached (see above).

Stratford

Backstage Café, *Main St, T06-7657003. Tue-Fri 1000-late, Sat 1000-1400 and 1800-late.* Considered one of the best bets,

The East Coast

Introduction

The East Coast of the North Island is all about **sun**, **wine** and remote **coastal scenery**. The East Cape (the 'heel' of the 'upside-down boot') is where you can witness the day's first warming rays and a little further south, the coastal town of **Gisborne** prides itself on being the first place Captain Cook set foot in New Zealand in 1769.

Inland from Wairoa (south of Gisborne) and the enchanting Mahia Peninsula, are the dense forests of the **Te Urewera National Park**, a place of almost spiritual beauty and particularly famous for its 'Great Walk' that circumnavigates its most scenic jewel, **Lake Waikaremoana**. Back on the coast you enter the wine country of Northern **Hawke's Bay** and the pretty coastal town of **Napier**, almost completely flattened by an earthquake in 1931 and now reborn as an international showpiece for its art deco buildings.

South again on the bleached cliffs that caress Hawke's Bay is the largest gannet colony in the country, at **Cape Kidnappers**. Further south is one of the most stunningly beautiful and remote parts of North Island, the **Wairarapa**, where, from **Castle Point** to the lighthouse at **Cape Palliser** – the southernmost tip of the North Island – the peace and isolation is unsurpassed anywhere in North Island.

★ Don't miss...

❶ Rafting the wilderness of the **Motu River** and losing contact with civilization for days, page 339.

❷ Being one of the first in the world to see the day's sunrise at the **East Cape Lighthouse**, page 339.

❸ Spiritual **Mount Hikurangi**: see for miles, page 318.

❹ The best of **Napier's** Art-Deco architecture, and re-visiting the day of New Zealand's worst earthquake in the Hawke's Bay Museum, page 354.

❺ Premier **Hawke's Bay vineyards**, page 357, or the gannet colony at Cape Kidnappers, page 356.

❻ The wild scenery of **Castlepoint** on the Wairarapa's remote coastline, page 368.

❼ Crossing the swing bridge at **Waiohine Gorge** near Carterton, page 369.

❽ Exploring the coast road to the **Cape Palliser Lighthouse** – the southernmost tip of the North Island, page 370. Walking into the 'chancel' of the **Putangirua Pinnacles**, page 370.

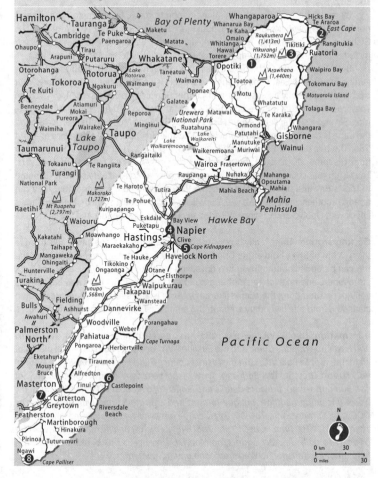

East Cape to Wairoa

→ *Phone codes: Bay of Plenty District 07; Gisborne District 06 Colour map 2, grid B4 Population: 6500*

Those with a healthy imagination and good sense of geography will recognize East Cape as the 'heel' of the 'upside-down boot' that is New Zealand. Along with the Wairarapa, East Cape is the least-visited area in the North Island. This is due not so much to its isolated location but its geography. Almost the entire peninsula is sparsely populated, remote and mountainous. Indeed, much of the Raukumara Range, which makes up most of its interior, remains impenetrable by road, with only wild rivers like the Motu and Mata carving their way through the wilderness.

Ins and outs

Getting there There are five **Air New Zealand Link**, To6-8682700, flights a day to Gisbourne from both Wellington and Auckland. Local operator **Sunair**, To800-786247, www.sunair.co.nz, offers flights from Napier (from $89) and Rotorua (from $190). The airport is about 2 km west of the town centre. **Link Taxis** operate an airport shuttle, To6-8674765, $10.

By car Gisborne is linked with all major points south, to Wellington 550 km and north (via the Waioeka Gorge) to Opotiki 147 km and Auckland (504 km) by SH2. Gisborne is a major stop on the well-signposted 'Pacific Coast Highway' which includes SH35. This 330-km trip terminates at Opotiki, where SH35 re joins SH2.

Both Opotiki and Gisborne are served by **Intercity** buses. Beyond those places getting around the East Cape by public transport is possible, but unpredictable. Your best bet is with **Polly's Passenger and Courier Services**, To6-8644728, To7-3156350. They operate a return service from Hick's Bay (at the top of the Cape) to Whakatane, Mon-Sat and a similar service from Hick's Bay to Gisborne Mon-Sat. The service around the Cape is excellent because it provides a flexible timetable on a single fare of about $60. The bus departs Whakatane VIC at 1230, Opotiki VIC for the Cape at 1430, and from Gisborne VIC at 1300, but check for changes. **Cook's Couriers**, To68-644711, To27-4371364, cook.teararoa@xtra.co.nz, also offer a Mon-Sat service from Gisborne to Hick's Bay and back (departs Gisborne VIC at 1230), from $30 one-way. They can arrange another courier to take you from Hick's Bay to Opotiki and Whakatane. Always check with Opotiki and Gisborne VICs for any changes to schedule and price.

Getting around There really is only one way to explore the Cape and that is to drive the 334 km of SH35 from either Opotiki to Gisborne or do it in reverse. Although the trip can be done comfortably in two days, you may like to absorb the very laid-back atmosphere and take longer, perhaps exploring the numerous bays and beaches as you go, or attempting the climb Hikurangi, North Island's fourth highest peak. On a clear day, from this legendary summit, the entire East Cape is laid out before you.

Information Opotiki VIC (see page 282) has 2 excellent free handbooks, the *Opotiki and East Cape Holiday Guide* and the *Eastland Visitor Guide*, both essential pieces of kit for the trip. **Te Puia VIC**, ① *in the District Council Building, To6-8646853*. **Gisborne VIC**, ① *209 Grey St, To6-8686139, www.gisbornenz.com Mon-Fri 0830-1730, Sat and Sun 0900-1730, provides details and leaflets of a number of interesting gardens, walks (including heritage, antique and art and craft trails) and wineries. Gisborne DOC, 163 Carnarvon St, To6-8678531, echb-conservancy@doc.govt.nz Wairoa VIC, corner of SH2 and Queen St, To6-8387440, wirvin@nzhost.co.nz Nov-Mar 0900-1700 daily, Apr-Oct 0900-1700 Mon-Fri. They act as bus booking agents, can help organise transport to Waikaremoana and have internet.*

▪ Rise and shine

East Cape has earned the label of
North Island's 'last wilderness'. People
come here to get away from it all and
shift down a few gears. But it is not
only the remoteness that attracts
visitors. They also come for the sun.

Not in the sense of soaking up the rays
but to experience the joy and strange
sense of pride at being the first souls
on earth to witness the day's sunrise –
according to human time and
provided it is not cloudy, that is.

Opotiki to East Cape Lighthouse → *Colour map 2, grid B4/5*

The Cape road, SH35, begins at Opotiki (see page 282) and very soon you will be
aware that you are entering another world. Change your watch to 'Cape Time', which
really means taking the batteries out. Maori influences are also almost immediately
apparent in the first small settlement of Torore (24 km) and the beautiful carvings
which adorn the gates to its school.

With the coast now your guide and the steaming volcanic White Island offshore
as companion you continue past **Hawai** and around the mouth of the **Motu River** (49
km). Here, when there has been little rain, the expansive boulder fields of the Motu

East Cape

The East Coast East Cape to Wairoa

riverbed can make it look like an insignificant trickle. But don't be deceived, at times this river can be a raging torrent spewing forth from its mountain wilderness and leaving only huge piles of driftwood as evidence of its fury. All along the coast at this point there seems to be more tangled wood on the beach than there is rock and sand. **Omaio**, the next settlement, has one such beach and is renowned for its good fishing. Just around the corner from the Motu River mouth keep your eyes open for the **Whitianga Marae** at Whitianga Bay (51 km), which again is beautifully carved.

After Omaio is **Te Kaha** (70 km) with its shallow rocky coast and popular beaches. Te Kaha is pleasant and offers the first really credible place to stop for supplies or accommodation. **Whanarua Bay** (88 km), a mere 10 minutes north of Te Kaha, also offers real serenity and is another fine spot to spend your first night on the Cape. As the road climbs into the tiny village take the track on the left (easily missed) which falls abruptly to the beach. This small, secluded bay is stunning. Whanarua has a backpackers hostel, a motorcamp (with organized activities), a store and a petrol stop. There is also a very basic camping ground about 1 km past the village.

Just before **Waihau Bay**, the next settlement, **Cape Runaway** and the northern sweep of the East Cape come into view, where you'll find the idyllic **Raukokore Anglican Church** (99 km) standing by the beach. **Waihau Bay** (107 km) itself offers accommodation, fuel and a well-stocked general store. From **Whangaparoa** (118 km), where the road temporarily leaves the coast and ducks below Lottin Point, it is possible to walk to **Cape Runaway**, but bear in mind that this is Maori land and permission must first be sought. A local farmstead offers guided tours, To7-3253697. **Lottin Point** (140 km), which essentially makes up the northern edge of the East Cape, is named for an officer who sailed with French explorer Jules Sebastian Cesar Dumont d'Urville in 1827 (presumably the latter's name was too long for people to remember). Lottin Point has one of the most remote motels in the country, at the very end of Lottin Point Road, offering sanctuary and also, apparently, fine rock fishing.

From Lottin Point the road meets the coast again at **Hick's Bay** (151 km), this time named for one of Captain Cook's sidekicks. Hick's Bay has a wild surf beach and an old wharf at its northern end. There is also a small store and a petrol stop. Around the corner from Hick's Bay is **Horseshoe Bay**, which is also impressive.

Before reaching East Cape and the lighthouse you pass through the tiny settlement of **Te Araroa** (160 km) before negotiating about 21 km of unsealed road. There are two particular points of interest in and around Te Araroa. The first is the **pohutukawa tree** which dwarfs the school grounds (it is believed to be one of the largest in the country and over 600 years old). The second is the new **Manuka Oil Distillery**, ① *between Te Araroa and Hick's Bay (about 4 km from the Gisborne junction), To6-8644826, www.manuka-products.com Mon-Fri, 0900-1600*. There is a factory shop at the distillery selling the delicious Manuka honey.

If you want to see the sunrise at East Cape, Hick's Bay and Te Araroa are your best (and only) options for accommodation. The coast road to the lighthouse and the most easterly point of New Zealand is beautiful, with numerous rock platforms, small rivers, pohutukawa trees and a long and empty stretch of beach worthy of investigation. The **Coastal Arts Gallery**, ① *To6-8644890, daily*, is also worth a peek.

The **lighthouse**, which only comes into view at the last minute, sits proudly on a hilltop all of its own. It can be easily accessed through a gate and via a set of seemingly never-ending steps, beyond a small group of derelict buildings. ▸▸ *For Sleeping see page 345.*

● *Te Kahu holds a sinister claim to fame as the site of New Zealand's last fatal shark attack in* ● *1976 when a local diver was attacked and killed by a bronze whaler.*

Climbing Mount Hikurangi

Hikurangi is an attractive mountain but does not look the 1,752 m that makes it the fourth highest (and highest non- volcanic mountain in the North Island). The name Hikurangi means 'Sky Peak' and refers to the well-loved peak in Hawaiki, the ancient ancestral home of the Maori. It is relatively accessible and a delightful climb. The summit return will take at least nine hours (13 km) so give yourself plenty of time. If you follow the Tapuwaeroa River Road almost to the end you will see an iron bridge that crosses the boulder fields of the Tapuwaeroa River to several farm buildings on the hill. At the far side of the bridge a sign will remind you that you are on Maori (private) land, but once you park your car down the side road towards the river, you can still use the track that heads up and past the houses, over the hill and beyond, towards the summit. Once you reach the top of this first hill you will clearly see the climb that lies before you. Follow your nose and the stiles up a well-formed sheep station track that goes almost two thirds of the way to the summit. It terminates at Hikurangi's 'well-kept secret' – the Millennium Maori Pou (carvings). These are beautifully crafted pieces that are full of spiritual meaning and

stand in a circle to greet the sunrise. From here head upwards and locate the white bunk- house. From behind the bunkhouse things start to get difficult. Climb up the scree slope to the rock outcrops and the path that leads you through a tract of mountain bush. Keep your eyes open for Tom Tit (no, not a local village idiot who has gone bush, but a native black and white bird that looks like a robin and is particularly fearless). Beyond the bush it is a hard slog to the summit – of which there are many – with the main summit reached after several almost equally high 'false-summits'. On a clear day the view is spectacular. To the north the empty bush-cloaked peaks of the Raukumara Ranges dominate and offshore to the north, White Island's active crater can be seen steaming away.

For more information on the mountain, hut accommodation ($5) and guided tours ($70) contact the local Iwi (tribe), Ngati Porou, T06-8679960, www.ngatiporou.iwi.nz It is both polite and respectful to let the Ngati Porou know that you intend to climb the mountain and seek official permission. If you join a tour it will also save a lot of climbing. Besides if the weather turns nasty it is added security.

East Cape to Gisborne → *Colour map 2, grid B/C6*

The eastern side of the Cape is more populous than the west and for much of the time the road winds its way through countryside between coastal settlements. If you wish to access the coast this is best done at these settlements, or with short diversions using a detailed map. From Te Araroa you head south and gain the first sight of Mount Hikurangi before arriving in **Tiki Tiki**. Here, the Anglican Church with some fine Maori designs is worth a visit. It was built in 1924 as a memorial to local Iwi tribesman (Ngati Porou) who died in the First World War.

Just before the Mata River crossing is the turn-off to **Mount Hikurangi**. Even if you do not intend to climb the mountain it is worth the short diversion to enjoy the river and mountain views. The road which flirts with the Tapuwaeroa River is a bit of an obstacle course as you dodge stray pigs, chickens, horses, sheep and cattle. Back on SH35 it is only a short distance to **Ruatoria** (206 km), the main administrative base of

66 99 One wonders what Captain Cook expected – surely not a group of Maori uttering the words "Oh look it's Captain Cook at last, we've been expecting you"!

the predominant East Cape Iwi, the *Te Runanga O Ngati Porou*. It has a food store and petrol station where you can have a light-hearted chat with the locals.

Turning your back on the mighty Hikurangi, next stop is **Te Puia Springs** (232 km) whose eponymous hot thermal pools are behind the hotel (see below). ① *Access to the pools is available to non-residents but hours are seasonal, T06-8646755*. The village also has a store, VIC (see above) and a petrol station. A short diversion from Te Puia is scenic **Waipiro Bay** with its three *marae*. The beachside holiday resort of **Tokomaru Bay** (243 km) is next, where you can find accommodation and food (see below). Between Tokomaru and Tolaga Bay is **Anaura Bay**, a 7 km diversion from SH35, where there's a very pleasant, relatively easy grade coastal walk (two hours).

Tolaga Bay (279 km) is the largest coastal town and resort on the East Coast. Worth a visit is the 660 m-long wharf (reputed to be the longest in the Southern Hemisphere) which can be accessed down Wharf Road to the south of the town. Also here is Cook's Cove. Our intrepid explorer stopped here to make repairs and gather supplies, though ship's naturalists Banks and Solander were particularly interested in the coastal scenery and unusual rock formations which can be seen on the (three-hour) walkway.

For decades the sleepy little settlement and beach at **Whangara** 29 km north of Gisborne (then 5 km east) was seldom visited by tourists. But due to the recent success of the film *Whale Rider*, in which the location (particularly the beach) was extensively featured, all that has changed. There is no disputing its beauty or spirituality, but what worries the local Iwi now is that its popularity may well prove to be its demise.

From Tolaga Bay the road leaves the coast for a while before reuniting at Tatapouri and Makorori, both well known as fine surfing spots. **Wainui** is essentially a beachside suburb of Gisborne with all the attendant amenities. (On its fine surf beach there is an interesting 'Sperm Whale Grave' which was the inevitable result of a mass stranding of 59 sperm whales in 1970). From Wainui you have just about reached your East Cape journey's end (or beginning) and Gisborne. ▸▸ *For Sleeping, Eating and Activities, see pages 347-349.*

Gisborne → *Phone code: 06 Colour map 2, grid C5 Population: 31,000*

The busy agricultural service town, port and coastal resort of Gisborne attracts many visitors in search of the sun, eager to jump on a surfboard or explore the East Cape. Being the most easterly city in New Zealand, Gisborne prides itself on being the first city in the world to see the sunrise. It is also the first place that Captain Cook set foot in New Zealand. On top of that, it boasts an almost subtropical climate with long hours of sunshine and rich fertile plains. You'd be forgiven for expecting the place to be brimming with pride and vitality, yet somehow Gisborne seems a little tired.

History

The first Maori to settle were thought to be from the Horouta and Te Ikaroa-a-Rauru *waka* (canoes) which landed at the base of the Kaiti Hill in 1350. When Captain Cook made the first European landing at the same site in 1769 he was met by a threatening

‣ Culture clash – Cook's first landing

On the 8th of October 1769 a group of Maori living on a *pa* just to the east of the Turanganui River, looked out to sea and saw an enormous bird on the horizon. It was in fact Cook's ship, *The Endeavour*. The Maori dispatched a party of warriors to investigate, while Cook and his men were rowing merrily ashore in search of supplies and eager to make contact with any 'savages'. Cook disembarked and the first ever footprint of a shoe was made on New Zealand sand. He and his men took some gifts to the local *whare* (meeting house) while others guarded the longboats. As they chatted on the shore the warriors emerged and performed a *haka* (posture dance). Utterly terrified and taking this to be a sign of imminent attack, the *Pakeha* (white Europeans) fired warning shots, one of which felled a Maori warrior. Both warriors and Cook hastily retreated. That night the Maori kept a close watch on the great big bird in both fear and amazement. Next morning Cook tried a second landing. A party of warriors once again met the landing party and performed a *haka* (a traditonal Maori war dance). This time accepting the fearful dance as a bizarre 'welcome' Cook kept his

muskets at bay. For a time warriors and *Pakeha* mixed uneasily and gifts and words were exchanged. But when a gleaming metal sword was snatched from one of Cook's party a shot was fired and another Maori was fatally wounded. Once again Moari retreated to their *pa* and Cook to his ship. Next day it was the Maori who approached Cook in their *waka*, but yet more deaths occurred when the approaching party failed to understand the ships signal volley. The Maori persisted and some were taken on board, fed, given gifts and returned to shore the following morning. After another brief sortie on shore by ship's naturalists Banks and Solander, Cook weighed anchor and the 'great big bird' took flight. Cook named the place 'Poverty Bay' because…. 'It had afforded us not one thing we wanted'. It was October 11th.

In the words of a respected modern day Maori 'One wonders what Captain Cook expected – surely not a group of Maori uttering the words 'Oh look it's Captain Cook, at last, we've been expecting you'! In 1995 the replica of *The Endeavour* retraced its steps around the coast of New Zealand, but its presence in Poverty Bay created uproar.

group of Maori. Cook promptly scarpered, leaving only the name 'Poverty Bay' behind. Although the area was home to a whaling station, European settlement would not occur in earnest until the 1840s with the establishment of several Christian missions. Captain G E Read, who settled in 1852, was a pivotal figure in the town's development. After a period blighted by threats and attacks by Maori, eventually things settled down in the 1860s when steady growth and development continued.

Sights

After the VIC your first stop should be **Cook's Landing Site and National Historic Reserve** next to the main port and the base of Titirangi (Kaiti Hill).To get there, cross to the northern bank of the **Taruheru River** which flows through the centre of the town. The reserve marks the spot where Cook first set foot, on 9 October 1769, to a hostile response from local Maori. Above the reserve the **Titirangi Domain or Kaiti Hill** provides great views across the city and the second of three Cook memorial edifices. At the summit of the hill is the **Cook Observatory**, ⓘ *To6-8677901, Tue only at 1930*, which, frankly, has seen better nights.

Set in trees at the foot of the hill to the west is the **Te Poho-O-Rawiri Marae**, ① *T06-8685364*, which was built in 1930 and is one of the largest carved meeting houses in the country. Nearby is the **Toko Toru Tapu Church**, ① *T06-8672103*.

Before re-crossing the river it is worth taking a look at the Inner Harbour Area. The Works on the Esplanade is home to the well-known **Longbush Wines**, ① *T06-8675764, 1000-1800*, who have been producing a fine range for 35 years. There are tastings, an outlet and also a good restaurant within the renovated warehouse. Opposite the nearby Wharf Café is a wall which has been colourfully adorned with children's self-portraits, created for the millennium.

Head to the beachside reserve on the southern bank of the river to see another Cook memorial. A little further along is a statue of Cook's cabin boy, **Young Nick**, who is credited as being the first to sight land. He was rewarded by having the promontory Young Nick's Head (which forms the southern edge of Poverty Bay) named in his honour. He also apparently won himself a bottle of rum, the customary reward for the first able seaman to see land. These statues are of particular interest simply because of their location with the backdrop of the port and huge steel-hulled cargo ships.

To learn more about young Nick and the region's history head for the small but effective **Gisborne Museum (Tairawhiti)**, ① *Stout St, T06-8673832. Mon-Fri 1000-1600 Sat and Sun 1330-1600*. Entry by donation. It houses all the usual stuff with a particular bent towards the fascinating Maori history and, of course, that man Cook. There are also ever-changing exhibitions of national and international contemporary art. Attached to the museum (quite literally) is the wheelhouse of *HMS Canada*, which foundered at the base of Kaiti Beach in 1912. It forms part of the Maritime section of the museum.

There is one other, less remarkable museum in the city, of particular interest to transport and technology buffs, the **East Coast Museum of Technology**, ① *Main Rd, Makaraka. Daily 0930-1630. $3, child $1*.

There are an increasing number of **vineyards** around the region producing the notable vintages. Names to look out for include **TW Chardonnay**, *T021- 864818*, **Lindaur**, *T06-8682757*, and **Waiohika**, *T06-8674670*. Most offer tastings. Contact the VIC for details. For a self-guided tour of vineyards, restaurants and art studios ask about the *Sunflower Trail – a Tour of Taste and Texture*. ▸▸ *For Sleeping, Eating, and other listings, see page 347-350*.

South to Wairoa → *Colour map 3, grid A6*

From Gisborne, SH2 climbs the **Wharereta Hills** offering great views back across Poverty Bay. On the southern slopes, 60 km south of Gisborne, are the **Morere Hot Springs**, ① *T06-8378856. Dec-Apr 1000-1800. $6*. Here, public and private thermal pools are set among a pleasant bush setting with a number of good short walks. There is accommodation (B-D) and a café across the road.

At the tiny junction settlement of **Nuhaka**, 8 km south of the springs, a scenic coastal road leaves SH2 towards the **Mahia Peninsula**. The Mahia is a barren, windswept peninsula 21 km long and about 12 km wide that marks the coastal boundary between the Pacific and Hawke's Bay. The Mahia used to be an island and is now joined to the mainland by a sandspit or tombolo. Almost totally devoid of trees, infested by sheep and deeply rutted by eroded green valleys, the peninsula has a strange appeal. One of the great Maori migration *waka* (canoes), the *Takitimu*, made landfall here in the 14th century, after circumnavigating the northern and eastern coasts from its first landfall at Awanui near Ninety Mile Beach. Some of its crew never left and the peninsula was also home to one of North Island's biggest whaling stations. Today, at the neck of the peninsula is the small holiday village of **Mahia Beach** which forms a link between two beaches: **Mahanga Beach**, lying to the east, is

exposed to the elements of the open ocean and a popular surf spot; **Opoutama**
Beach, on the Hawke's Bay side (west), is much more sheltered and therefore better
for swimming. On the eastern edge of the peninsula are the settlements of **Oraka** and
Mahia, connected by a rows of holiday baches which hug the shore like a string of
pearls. In summer the peninsula is a very popular spot for surfing, windsurfing,
swimming and fishing, but year round it enjoys the erstwhile island atmosphere,
which makes it an idyllic spot in which to get away from it all. You will need your own
transport. From Mahia it is a 44-km drive to Wairoa past farmland and coastal lagoons
renowned for their birdlife. »» *For Sleeping and Eating, see page 348.*

Wairoa → *Colour map 3, grid A5 Population: 5200*
Wairoa is the eastern gateway to the Te Urewera National Park and sits on the coast at
the junction of SH2 and SH36, roughly halfway between Gisborne (98 km) and Napier
(118 km). Also strategically placed on the banks of the Wairoa River, it was once a
thriving port. These days, however, it has little to hold the visitor except perhaps a
brief peek at the relocated and reconstructed 1877 **lighthouse** which once shone
away on the Mahia Peninsula. Sadly these days, looking somewhat incongruous in
the centre of town next to the river, it only seems to attract local graffiti artists. The
town has a number of shops in which to stock up and small takeaways to grab a
snack before heading north, south or inland to **Waikaremoana** via SH36. There are a
limited number of accommodation options available in town and the VIC has details.

● Sleeping

Opotiki to East Cape Lighthouse *p339*

Torore, Te Kaha and Whanarua Bay
A-B Te Kaha Hotel and Motel,
T07-3252830, www.tekaha.tourguide.net.nz
Rooms and 2 modern beachfront units
overlooking a sheltered beach and bay. Bar
and restaurant serving lunch/dinner
in-house, recommended only for the local
seafood. **A Tui Lodge B&B**, *Copenhagen Rd,*
T07-3252922. Spacious modern home with
tidy twins and doubles, shared facilities.
Dinner on request.
A Waiwaka B&B, *T07-3252070,*
waikawa.bnb@xtra.co.nz In a beautiful spot
2 km north of Te Kaha and 12 km from
Whanarua Bay.
B-D Te Kaha Holiday Park, *T07-3252894.*
Basic amenities with backpacker
accommodation.
B-D Rendezvous Holiday Park,
T07-3252899. Usual amenities but also
offers fish and dive trips and bike hire,
internet. **C-D Robyn's Place**, *T07-3252904.*
Almost next door to the Holiday Camp and
within walking distance to the bay.
Backpacker accommodation.
D Maraehako Camp Ground, *1 km past the*
holiday park, T07-3252047. Beachfront.

Waihau Bay and Lottin Point
A Waihau Bay B&B, *T07-3253674,*
n.topia@clear.net.nz 2 self-contained units
and double overlooking the beach.
A Oceanside Apartments, *at the far end of*
Oruaiti Beach, 3 km northeast of Waihau,
T07-3253699, www.waihaubay.co.nz
Excellent apartments or B&B rooms,
fishing charters.
A Lottin Point Motel, *T06-8644455.*
Amazing location and a great sense of
escape. New and expanding number of
units. Licensed restaurant in summer.
Activities arranged.
B-D Waihau Bay Lodge (Hotel),
T07-3253804. Comfortable rooms with
shared facilities, licensed bar and restaurant.
Backpacker beds and campsite available.
B-D Waihau Bay Holiday Park,
T07-3253844. Located opposite the beach.
Full range of options, camp kitchen, store
and a café with dubious coffee!

Hick's Bay and Te Araroa
B-D Hick's Bay Motel Lodge, *up the hill just*
past the village, T06-8644880.
Licensed restaurant.
B-D Te Araroa Holiday Park, *at the end*
of the bay, west of the village, T06-8644873.
Modern facilities including a store
and off-licence.

Gisborne

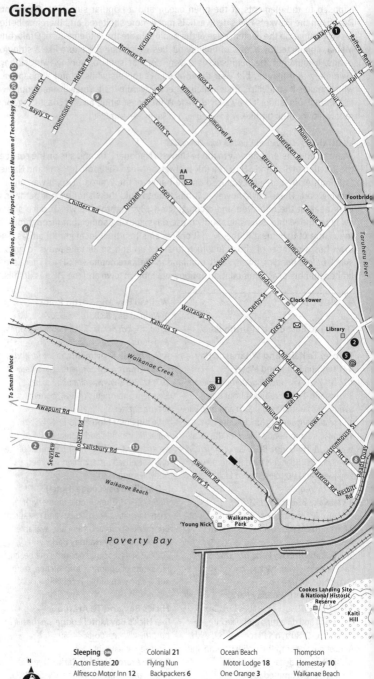

The East Coast East Cape to Wairoa

To Wairoa, Napier, Airport, East Coast Museum of Technology & 12 20 21 15

Balance St
Railway Reserve
Hall St
Norman Rd
Victoria St
Herbert Rd
Stout St
Root St
Hunter St
Roebuck Rd
Williams St
Somervell Av
Thomson St
Dominion Rd
Bayly St
Leith St
Aberdeen Rd
9
Berry St
Childers Rd
Disraeli St
Eden La
AA
Attree Pl
Footbridge
6
Temple St
Taruheru River
Carnarvon St
Cobden St
Palmerston Rd
Waitangi St
Derby St
Gladstone Av
Clock Tower
Kahutia St
Grey St
Library
2
Waikanae Creek
Childers Rd
5
To Smash Palace
Bright St
Peel St
3
Awapuni Rd
Roberts Rd
Kahutia St
Lowe St
1
Salisbury Rd
13
Materoa Rd
Customhouse St
2
Seaview Pl
11
Awapuni Rd
Pitt St
8
Reads Quay
Grey St
Nesbitt Rd
Waikanae Beach
Poverty Bay
'Young Nick'
Waikanae Park

Cookes Landing Site & National Historic Reserve
Kaiti Hill

N

0 metres 200
0 yards 200

Sleeping
Acton Estate **20**
Alfresco Motor Inn **12**
Beach Bach **16**
Beachcomber **1**
Blue Pacific **2**
Cedar House B&B **4**

Colonial **21**
Flying Nun
Backpackers **6**
Gisbourne **17**
Gisbourne
Backpackers **15**
Gisbourne YHA **7**

Ocean Beach
Motor Lodge **18**
One Orange **3**
Pacific Harbour **8**
Studio 4 B&B **5**
Tatapouri Camp
Ground **19**

Thompson
Homestay **10**
Waikanae Beach
Holiday Park **11**
Waikanae Beach
Motel **13**
White Heron **9**

Eating 🍴
Café Villagio **1**
Fettucine Bros **2**
Irish Rover **3**
Marina **4**
Verve Café **5**
Wharf Café **6**
Works **7**

C-D Hick's Bay Backpackers, *Onepoto Beach Rd, T06-8644731, hicksbaybackpackers@xtra.co.nz* Cosy, friendly place set next to bay. Popular with surfers. Internet. Arranges trips/transport.

East Cape to Gisborne *p341*

Te Puia and Waipiro Bay
B-D Te Puia Springs Hotel, *T06-8646755*. Basic but saved by the hot thermal pools.
C-D Waikawa Lodge, *Waikawa Rd, Waipiro Bay, T06-8646719, www.waikawalodge.co.nz* A remote and charming backpackers which although quite small is modern and offers a perfect getaway. Also home to Waikawa Horse Adventures.

Tokomaru Bay
AL Rahiri Homestay, *263 Mata Rd, T06-8645615, www.rahiri.com* Farmstay homestead on sheep and cattle station. Comfortable with great amenities.
B Te Puka Tavern, *T06-8645466*. 2 comfortable motel units close to beer and food.
C-D Brian's Place, *Potae St, T06-8645870*. Intimate and relaxed wee backpackers with friendly host. Loft rooms, fresh crayfish and horse trekking an added bonus.

Tolaga Bay
B-D Tolaga Bay Motor Camp, *167 Wharf Rd, T06-8626716*. A bit tired and basic but the only one for miles.
B Tolaga Bay Motel, *corner of Cook and Monkhouse, T06-8626888*.
Basic but adequate.

Gisbourne *p342*
Gisborne is a popular summer resort so book ahead in the high season.
LL Acton Estate, *577 Back Ormond St, T06-8679999*. The top hotel in town, this is a restored Edwardian-style mansion in spacious grounds, offering period-furnished rooms and fine cuisine.
AL Beach Bach, *52 Wairere Rd, Wainui Beach, T06-8686605*. Your own little bach on Wainui Beach, just north of town.
AL Cedar House B&B, *4 Clifford St, T06-8681902, www.cedarhouse.co.nz* Similar Edwardian-style to Acton Estate but cheaper and central.

AL One Orange, *Wainui Beach, T06-8688062, www.oneorange.co.nz* New and distinctly designer self-contained apartment and studio set right next to the beach in Wainui. Recommended.

A Gisborne Hotel, *corner of Tyndall and Huxley Rd, T06-8684109, info@gisbornehotel.com* One of Gisborne's few hotels. Comfortable with very friendly hosts but not particularly well-located. Tour arrangements a speciality.

There's the usual selection of **motels**, which are mostly on Gladstone Av, which is the main drag (SH35), and Salisbury Rd, which is centrally located near the beach.

A-AL Al Fresco Motor Lodge, *784 Gladstone Av, T06-8632464, www.nzmotels.co.nz/ alfresco* Newest motel in town.

A-AL Teal Motor Lodge, *479 Gladstone Av, T06-8684019, www.teal.co.nz*

A Beachcomber, *73 Salisbury Rd, T06-8689349.*

A Blue Pacific, *90 Salisbury Rd, T06-8686099, www.seafront.co.nz*

A Colonial, *715 Gladstone Av, T06-8679165, www.gisbornecolonial.co.nz*

A White Heron, *474 Gladstone Av, T06-8671108.*

A Waikane Beach Motel, *19 Salisbury Rd, T06-8684139.*

Two exceptions are:

AL-A Pacific Harbour, *on the corner of Reads Quay and Pitt St, by the harbour, T06-8678847.* Very modern and plush.

AL-A Ocean Beach Motor Lodge, *corner of SH35 and Oneroa Rd, Wainui Beach, T06-8686186.* Modern and popular motel a little further afield, in the beachside suburb/ village of Wainui.

B Studio 4 , *4 Heta Rd, T0800-370398, studioart@clear.net.nz* Central B&B with tidy double or single. Artist in residence.

B Thompson Homestay, *16 Rawiri St, T06-8689675.* Well-established cheaper B&B within walking distance of town.

C-D Gisborne YHA, *near the inner harbour at the corner of Wainui Rd and Harris St, T06-8673269, yha.gis@clear.net.nz* Friendly, well-maintained and just a short walk from the town centre. Full range of rooms and all the usual facilities.

C-D Gisborne Backpackers, *690 Gladstone Rd, T06-8681000, gisbornebp@xtra.co.nz* A

vast establishment offering a wide range of accommodation options in an old orphanage. It has beds as opposed to bunks, a bath and Sky TV and all the usual facilities. Long walk into the town centre.

C-D Flying Nun Backpackers, *147 Roebuck Rd, T06-8680461, yager@xtra.co.nz* Looks very colourful and comically ecclesiastical from the outside, and although perhaps not the best backpackers in town, the interior is modern enough and the place certainly has character. Cable TV.

Motorcamps and campsites

B-D Waikanae Beach Holiday Park, *Grey St, T06-8675634.* This is the best equipped and most centrally located motorcamp in town. Short walk to the beach and the VIC.

D Tatapouri Camp Ground, *5 Innes St, T06-8683269, www.tatapouri.co.nz* This is a good camping option 15 mins north and away from the town, right by the beach.

South to Wairoa *p344*

NB Booking ahead in summer is advised.

A Cappamore Lodge, *435 Mahia East Coast Rd, T06-8375523, oconellcappamore@clear.net.nz* This is like Scandinavia by the sea. The log cabin has one double and a twin with full self-catering facilities and a great view across the ocean.

A The Quarters Te Au Farmstay, *Te Au Farm, Nuhaka (Mahanga), T06-8375751, www.quarters.co.nz* Modern isolated farmstay/self-contained cottage.

B-D Mahia Beach Motel and Holiday Park, *43 Moana Dr, Mahia Beach, T06-8375830.* The centre of activity on the peninsula, with café and camp store.

❼ Eating

East Cape to Gisborne *p341*

$ Mountain View Café, *just south of Te Puia Springs on SH3.* Both good food and coffee.

Gisbourne *p342*

$$$ The Acton Estate, *see Sleeping above, bookings essential, T06-8679999.* Open to non-guests and offers a 4-course, à la carte culinary experience prepared by the in-house award-winning chef.

$$$ The Wharf Café, *60 The Esplanade, The*

Wharf, *T06-8684876. Daily 0900-late*. This is not very expensive but still at the high end, very popular, with wide-ranging menu.
The Marina Restaurant, *Vogel St, T06-8685919*. Well-established eatery next to the marina. Fine international cuisine (especially steaks) and good wine list.
$$ The Fettuccine Brothers Restaurant, *12/14 Peel St, T06-8685700. Daily 1800-late*. Mediterranean in decor and food. Popular with the locals.
$$ The Works, *The Esplanade, Inner Harbour, T06-8631285. 1130-late. Wine tasting 1000-1500*. Home of Longbush Wines so no need to recommend the wine list. Good venue for lunch.
$ The Irish Rover, *Peel St, T06-8671112*. The best pub and pub grub in town.
$ Verve Café, *121 Gladstone Rd*, and **$ Café Villagio**, *Balance St Village*, are two of the best cafés in town.
Supermarket Woolworths, *corner of Gladstone Rd and Carnarvon St, Mon-Sun 0700-2200*, and
Pak-n-Save, *Gladstone Rd, Mon-Sun 0800-2000*.

South to Wairoa *p344*
$ Beachfront Café, *Moana St, Mahia Beach, daily 1200-late* or
$ Sunset Point Sports Bar and Bistro, *Newcastle St, Mahia Beach, T06-8375071*.

🍷 Pubs, bars and entertainment

Gisborne *p342*
There are 2 great pubs in Gisborne:
The Irish Rover, *Peel St*, the town's offering to the mighty leprechaun and especially good during happy hours (around 1700-1900) and on Fri evening. Regular live bands.
Smash Palace, *Bank St, T06-8677769*. A local legend and deservedly so, supporting the most amazing decor, best seen from over the rim of a glass. It also has a local wine outlet next door.
Odeon Cinema, *79 Gladstone Rd, T06-8673339*.

🎣 Activities and tours

East Cape to Gisborne *p341*
Fishing Kiwi Boyz Charters, *Waihau Bay, T06-3253850*.

Waikawa Rd, Waipiro Bay, T06-8646719, www.waikawalodge.co.nz
Marae stay Ngati Porou Outdoor Pursuits *T06-8678436, T06-8679960, www.ngatiporou.iwi.nz* (See also Climbing Mount Hikurangi box above.) Summit climbs with a stay in the mountain hut, fascinating cultural information and *marae* stays.

Gisborne *p342*
For the latest surf reports, T06-8681066-1302, or radio 89FM after 0700 news and ZG90.9FM after 0800 news.
Fishing, diving and shark cage experience Surfit Charters, *T06-8672970, www.surfit.co.nz* Another chance to encounter those persecuted denizens of the deep. Fishing half-day from $105, Shark Encounters, from $200.
Shoreline Adventures, *T0800-102298*. A wide range of services from congenial bay cruises raising crayfish pots, to 'biscuit riding' and waterskiing. Great for families.
Horse trekking Waimoana Horse Treks, *a short distance north of Gisborne, T06-8688218, waimoana@ihug.co.nz* Combine bush and beach on 2 trips departing at 1000 and 1400; 2 hours, from $35.
Cultural Te Runganga-o-Turanganui-a-Kiwa, *Nga Wai E Rua, Grey St, T06-8678109, www.trotak.iwi.nz* An introduction to the historical and cultural sites in and around the city by the local mandated tribal authority.
Sightseeing and Flightseeing Trev's Tours, *T06-8639815, trevs.tours@xtra.co.nz* Local knowledgeable tour operator offering a range of trips to a variety of old and modern attractions locally and farther afield. From $45.
Air Gisborne, *T06-8674684*. The local fixed-wing scenic flight operator. From $55.
Ashworth Helicopters, *T06-8677128*. Everything from short scenic flights around the bay to heli-fishing.
Station Experiences and quad biking New Zealand Safari Adventures, *Tangihau Station Enterprise, Rere, T06-8670872, www.tangihau.com* This is an interesting venture offering a range of New Zealand Station life experiences from basic farm tours and shepherd's muster, to ATV quad bike tours and deer hunting. From $75-800.

Gisborne Quad Adventures, *176 Valley Rd, T06-8684394*. Also offer scenic quad biking adventures closer to town. 1-3 hours, from $60.

Surfing Chalet Surf Lodge, *62 Moana Road, T06-8689612, www.chaletsurf.co.nz* Based in Wainui, just north of Gisborne, this company (in association with local surf retailer, **The Boardroom**, *T06-8671684*) can provide a taste of the region's fine surf beaches, from $35. Accommodation and independent board hire are also available.

○ Shopping

Gisborne *p342*
The Ukaipo Art Gallery, *133 Ormond Rd, T06-8671177*. Promotes local Maori artists and often hosts some lovely work. There is a flea market which starts at an ungodly hour every Sat morning in Alfred Cox Park across from the VIC.

● Directory

Gisborne *p342*
Banks All the major banks have branch offices on Gladstone Rd.
Internet Cyberzone, *83 Gladstone Rd*. Verve Café, *121 Gladstone Rd*. **VIC**, Grey St.
Police *corner Childer Rd and Peel St, T06-8690200*. **Post Office** *166 Gladstone Rd, T06-8678220. Mon-Fri 0830-1730, Sat 0900-1600, Sun 1000-1500*. **Taxi** Gisborne Taxis, *T06-8672222*, operate a bus service on weekdays. Car taxi companies include **Sun City Taxis**, *T06-8676767*.

Te Urewera National Park *Phone code: 06*

Te Urewera is daunting and mysterious; a place of almost threatening beauty. The National Park encompasses the largest block of native bush in the North Island and is the fourth largest national park in the country. The main focus of the park is Lake Waikaremoana, the 'Sea of Rippling Waters', while the track which circumnavigates it, the Lake Waikaremoana Circuit, is one of the most popular walks in the country. The vast park is home to a wealth of wildlife: some native and welcome, including kiwi, kaka and kokako (one of New Zealand's rarest and most endangered birds); others introduced and very unwelcome, such as the omnipresent possum, stoats, goats, rats and feral cats. The park is also a favourite haunt for pig hunters, though, thankfully, few known banjo players.

Ins and outs

Getting there and around Frasertown to Waikaremona is about 50 km; Waikaremoana to Murupara is another 75 km. Access to Lake Waikaremoana and the heart of the park is via the hardy SH38. This almost completely unsealed highway links Murupara on the western boundary of the park with Frasertown, near Wairoa to the east. It is pretty heavy going, very windy, often subject to fallen trees and, if you break down, you're on your own. The park and all the amenities of Lake Waikaremoana are best accessed from the east via Wairoa and Frasertown. This will allow you to get intimate with the park on foot from Waikaremoana before building up the strength to explore the western part.

Big Bush Holiday Park, in Wairoa, *T06-8373777, www.lakewaikaremoana.co.nz*, offers a regular shuttle service to and from Rotorua ($60 one way) Mon, Wed and Fri and from Wairoa ($25) depending on demand. They also run a water taxi service on Lake Waikaremoana taking trampers to and from trailheads, from $25 one way. **Waikaremoana Guided Tours** based at the Waikaremoana Holiday Park offer similar services, *T06-8373729, www.lake.co.nz*

Information DOC Aniwaniwa Visitor Centre, *⒈ SH38 at Lake Waikaremoana, T06-8373900, T06-8373722, aniwaniwa-ao@doc.govt.nz Daily 1000-1700*. It has modern displays, an audiovisual show ($2) and a gallery which is entrusted to care for and display the controversial **Urewera Mural** by Colin McCahon. The staff can assist with the limited but surprisingly good accommodation options and also handles all the walk information, fees and hut bookings. **DOC Murupara**, ① *SH38, T07-3661080*.

History
The Te Urewera area is home to the Tuhoe people, known as 'the children of the mist'. They have always been amongst the most determined of Maori tribes. Before the Europeans arrived the Tuhoe effectively ruled over the forest. Even other Maori were fearful of their *mana* (standing, integrity) and legendary bush skills. So when the Europeans arrived to lay claim to the forest it was obvious trouble would ensue.

During the New Zealand Wars of the 1860s and 70s the great Maori leader and rebel, Te Kooti (see page 228) took refuge in Te Urewera with the Tuhoe. From here he fought his enemies until the Tuhoe made peace and Te Kooti was forced to seek exile in the King Country of the Waikato. With the end of the Wars in 1872, and after being pardoned 11 years later, Te Kooti died a free man. But although the official wars ended in the Te Urewera, the troubles and hard feeling did not. Tuhoe religious prophet and leader Rua Kenana, who headed a thriving religious community in Maungapohatu, remained a thorn in the *Pakeha's* side until his arrest in 1916. Thereafter, leadership crumbled and so did the Tuhoe's hold on the region. The kauri fell, the land was 'acquired' and the *Pakeha* took control. Many Tuhoe still live in Te Urewera and although most would say the forest is no longer theirs, in spirit it remains so.

Sights

Lake Waikaremoana → *Colour map 3, grid A5*
This beautiful lake was created only 2000 years ago when the Waikaretaheke River was dammed by a huge landslide between the Ngamoko and Panekiri Ranges. One section of that landslide is claimed to have been 3 km long by 1 km wide. This relatively new addition to the landscape sits beautifully with the equally impressive bush which cloaks its indented shores. The main activities on the lake are trout fishing and boating, but it is most famous for the network of excellent **walks** around its shores.

Most of the short walks radiate from the main settlement of Waikaremoana, which is little more than a scattering of DOC buildings and the motorcamp at the northeastern end of the lake. There are two waterfalls within 15 minutes of the DOC visitors' centre. The first, the **Aniwaniwa Falls**, is less than 1 km from the centre and is accessed from a track right beside it. The slightly higher and more impressive **Papakorito Falls** are up a short track opposite the centre (or by car to within a five-minute walk). There is a short and pleasant 2-km track connecting the visitors' centre with the motorcamp called the **Black Beech Track** (30 minutes). If you fancy something more demanding and scenic, the **Ngamoko Track** (2½ hours) just south of the motorcamp climbs the mountain through a delightful tangle of native bush before emerging at a 1099 m trig and viewpoint.

The lake covers 5500 ha; it stands at a height of 600 m; its deepest point is 256 m

Better still is the four-hour tramp to see the idyllic **Lake Waikareiti**, which is a smaller body of water formed in the same way as Lake Waikaremoana. Set 300 m above Lake Waikaremoana, it is almost like a lost world with a magical atmosphere and shores entirely cloaked by bush. The DOC Sandy Bay Hut is available for an overnight stay (book at the visitor centre, $14) and there is also boat hire. Most serious trampers, however, come to Lake Waikaremona to experience the scenic **Waikaremoana Circuit Track**, a national tramping top 10 (see box next page).

There are numerous other walks and huts in the park including the three to five-day **Whakatane River Round Trip**, the three-day **Manuoha-Waikareiti Track** and

⁝ The Waikaremoana Circuit Track

The Circuit track, a 46-km walk of moderate difficulty, completely circumnavigates the lake. It can usually be completed in 3-4 days taking in a variety of bush types, full of birdlife and rocky or sandy bays ideal for fishing and swimming. Most of the route is fairly easy going except for ascent of the 900 m Panekiri Range, which offers a spectacular view across the lake and national park. There are five modern, comfortable DOC huts and five designated campsites along the route which provide basic amenities. The walk can be tackled in either direction from the southern access point at Onepoto (which climbs Panekiri first), or from the most popular starting point, Hopuruahine, on the lake's northern shores. Although there is parking at both access points most people leave their vehicles at the Waikaremoana Motorcamp ($5) and take the water taxi to either starting point (from $25). The taxi will also pick up or drop off from various designated points along the way, which is ideal for those who only wish to walk part of the circuit. Weather can be very changeable throughout the year and downright ugly in winter, so, as always, go well equipped. The walk is very popular in summer, so either late spring or early autumn is advised. Bookings are essential and conditions apply. The huts cost from $14 per person per night, child $7. Campsites are $10, child $5. For all information, maps, leaflets and bookings contact the DOC Aniwaniwa Visitor Centre (see above). For web bookings and information log on to www.greatwalkbooking@doc.govt.nz

the two-hour **Onepoto Caves Track**. For more information and bookings contact DOC or call at the Aniwaniwa Visitors Centre (see above).

● Sleeping

Accommodation is available at Waikaremoana or the settlements of Kaitawa and Tuai at the southeast entrance to the park. Booking is advised in summer.
B-D Whakamarino Lodge, *Tuai, T06-8373876, www.lakelodge.co.nz* Comfortable self-contained units, rooms 5 km from Waikaremoana.
A-B Homestay, *9 Rotten Row, Tuai, T06-8373701, ykarestay@xtra.co.nz* Thankfully Bev's hospitality and the accommodation does not reflect the street name. Single and double, dinner $25.
B-D Waikaremoana Motorcamp, *T06-8373826, www.lake.co.nz* Well situated right next to the lake near most major short walks and the visitor centre. Modern range of lodges, chalets, cabins and units as well as backpacker beds, powered, non-powered sites, petrol and a well-stocked store. Kayak hire and base for water taxi. Recommended.
D DOC Sandy Bay Hut, *booking from DOC offive, SH38 at Lake Waikaremoana, T06-8373900, T06-8373722, aniwaniwa-ao@doc.govt.nz*. See above.

▲ Activites

Fishing, boat and kayak hire Available at the **Waikaremoana Motorcamp**, *see above* ($45 per day). Fishing (from $55 per hour), fishing licences, hunting trips, and lake cruises (from $20, 1½ hours) can also be arranged from there. **Big Bush**, *T06-8373777, bigbush@xtra.co.nz* Offers similar activities.

Napier and around

→ *Phone code: 06 Colour map 3, grid A5 Population: 54,900*

Napier is a bright, dynamic place with the pleasant vibe of a Mediterranean coastal town. On the surface it seems to enjoy the perfect relationship with nature and the rich fertile land and the warming sun have made it the wine-producing capital of North Island. But even though it paid a heavy price in 1931 when an earthquake almost razed the town, the proud and determined people used this to their advantage and set about its rebuilding with a collection of art deco buildings thought to be amongst the finest in the world. Now, as it enters the new millennium, Napier seems in the best of health.

Ins and outs

Getting there By air Napier is served by **Air New Zealand Link**, T0800-737000 and **Origin Pacific** T0800-302302. There are regular daily flights to both Wellington and Auckland and other principal national destinations. The airport is just north of the town on SH2. There is an **Airport Shuttle**, T06-8447333, service costing around $12 one-way.

By bus, Napier is served by **Intercity** and **Newmans**. Buses arrive and depart from the Napier Travel Centre at the train station on Munroe St, T06-8352720. 0830-1700. All major buses companies serve Hastings too.

By car, Napier is on SH2, 321 km north of Wellington. The junction with SH5 and SH2 is about 6 km north of the town and from there it is 117 km to Taupo and 397 km to Auckland. Napier is the premier east coast destination on both the 'Thermal Explorer' (SH5), www.themalnz.co.nz and 'Pacific Coast Highway' (SH2), www.pacific coast.co.nz, touring routes. These routes are both well signposted and advertised.

Getting around Much of the city is negotiable on foot and, given the architectural appeal, is best appreciated from the street. The local suburban bus company is **Nimbus**, T06-8778133. They operate weekdays only and offer a service to Hastings. For car rental companies, cycle hire and taxis, see page 272.

Information Napier VIC, ① *100 Marine Parade, T06-8341911, www.hawkesbay. nz.com Mon-Fri 0830-1700, Sat and Sun 0900-1700*. It has information and leaflets on local and regional Heritage Walks, Gardens and Art and Craft Trails. **DOC,** ① *59 Marine Parade, T06-8343111, napier-ao@doc.govt.nz Mon-Fri 0900-1615*. It has information about Cape Kidnappers Gannet Colony (plus tide times), as well as Te Urewera and Ruahine National and Forest Parks. **Hastings VIC,** ① *in the Westerman's Building, corner of Russell and Heretaunga Sts T06-8735526, www.hastings.co.nz Mon-Fri 0830-1700, Sat and Sun 0900-1700*. Internet and transport booking.

History

When Captain Cook first mapped the Bay in 1769 Maori were already happily ensconced on local *pa* and harvesting the local marine resources. This harvest was expanded in the 1830s when seasonal whalers arrived from Australia to be joined a decade later by missionaries and another decade after that by the first significant group of European settlers. In 1854 the town was named after British general Charles Napier.

During the New Zealand Land Wars of the 1860s the residents, with the help of local Maori, managed to defend themselves against aggressive tribes from the north and, with the development of agriculture, the settlement flourished. But though the devastating earthquake of 1931 destroyed everything, the subsequent rebuilding led to great improvements. The land surrounding Bluff Hill had been raised several feet and huge tracts of land, previously underwater or covered in swamp, were now

The Big Shake

February 2nd 1931 in Hawke's Bay was a day like any other, but with one notable exception: local farmers noticed that their stock were in a strange and inexplicable state of angst. Dairy cattle, usually so routine in their willingness to stroll to the milking sheds, refused to budge. Instead they wanted only to huddle in the corners of the paddock – usually something they did prior to a thunderstorm. Yet the skies were clear and all was still. It is now thought that some animals can sense the very subtle tremors that often occur before a major earthquake, several days or hours before the main shock. Alas, if only the people of Napier had known that. The following day at around 1030 there was a ferocious quake measuring 7.9 on the Richter Scale. The effect was devastating. Survivors recall that the land became 'almost fluid' and to a deafening roar, buildings were toppled, trees were uprooted and over 3,600 hectares of coastline thrust upwards by several feet. The few buildings the earthquake did not destroy, fires would, and with the loss of any water supply, let alone the organized means with which to fight them, all the shocked survivors could do was watch. By the time it was all over, Napier was essentially flattened and 161 lives had been lost. In Hastings, to the south, the damage was less severe, but older buildings still collapsed and 88 people were killed. In rural areas as far away as the Wairarapa, roads and bridges were destroyed, rivers became lakes and communications were cut off. Aftershocks followed for several weeks afterwards, the biggest, 10 days later, dragging out the terror and suffering of the survivors. But although many lives were lost and the town was destroyed, the spirit and determination of those survivors was not. Despite the enormity of the task, within two years the town was rebuilt and actually benefited from the availability of new land that had previously been seabed. Undoubtedly another benefit was the manifestation of its art deco architecture. Yet the quake remains, for now, the worst in New Zealand's human history.

available for use. The redesign of the city encompassed the widespread creation of earthquake-resistant concrete boxes of art deco design and within a decade the town had a new face and a new future. Although the earthquake remains a painful memory, it has, in many ways, shaped the coastal town that Napier is today.

Sights

Art deco architecture

The main attraction of Napier is its famous art deco architecture. On foot, the two central streets **Emerson** and **Tennyson** have many examples. On Emerson Street is the **ASB Bank** with its incorporated Maori designs and fine doorway, while on Tennyson Street the highlights are (from east to west) the **Daily Telegraph Building**, restored **Municipal Theatre** and the **Desco Centre** (art deco shop).

Before the earthquake of 1931 Napier looked very different. Bluff Hill, which now forms part of the town, was practically an island, surrounded by swamps which formed the estuary of the Tutaekuri River.

Further afield is perhaps the most attractive building of all, the façade and entrance of the 1932 **Rothmans Pall Mall Building** at the corner of Bridge and Osian streets. Although somewhat distant from the town centre (in the port area of Westshore), it is worth the diversion. The building is even more impressive at night, when it is beautifully and imaginatively lit. During the day it is possible to have a look at the interior which hosts just as much attention to detail. For a more modern example of art deco take a wander inside the pharmacy at the southern end of Emerson Street. For tours of the art deco buildings, see Activities and tours, page 364.

Marine Parade

Marine Parade creates an impressive perspective with its long promenade lined with **Norfolk Pines** and old wooden houses (the few that survived the earthquake). There are a number of waterfront attractions to add to its Mediterranean/English ambience. At the northern end are some elegant gardens including the **Centennial Gardens** at the base of Bluff Hill (free). Heading south the newly renovated **Ocean Spa**, ① *To6-8358553, Mon-Sat 0600-2200, Sun 0800-2200, general entry $6, child $4, private spa $8, massage from $35,* has hot pools, private spas, health and beauty therapies and a café.

Almost immediately to the south of the spa complex gardens again predominate with a **floral clock**, the **Tom Parker Fountain** (no Elvis connections here) and **'Pania of the Reef'** statue. The fountain is just your average garden fountain by day but by night comes alive with a multi-coloured aquatic light show. 'Pania' is a small, attractive statue of a Maori maiden, with her legend of love described accordingly in a shower of the fountain's mist.

Heading south is the art deco **Colonnade** and **Sound Shell**. The Colonnade was once used for dancing and skating and is home to the **Veronica 'Bell** and memorial. The *Veronica* was a naval vessel which was in port at the time of the quake and her crew was pivotal in the first attempts to save lives in the rubble. The bell is rung to commemorate their efforts every New Year. Opposite the Sound Shell, which is occasionally used for open-air concerts, is the **Art Deco Tower** (A&B building), which is also nicely lit at night and the art deco **Masonic Hotel**.

Past the modern VIC and Mini Golf Park are the **Sunken Gardens**, complete with ponds of water lily and a lazy waterwheel. Further south is **Marineland**. ① *To6-8344027, www.marineland.co.nz Daily 1000-1630. Shows at 1030 and 1400. $9, child $4. Touch the Dolphins Tour at 0900 ($15, child $8). Swim with the Dolphins, daily sessions ($50). Penguin Recovery Workshop at 1300 ($15).* Here seal and dolphin displays are mixed, perhaps with a twinge of guilt, with an ongoing programme of wild penguin and gannet rehabilitation. You can also touch, feed and swim with the dolphins. Thankfully, all the animals seem to be in caring as opposed to strictly commercial hands.

Although somewhat spoiled by the port, and hard to reach, the view from Bluff Hill at the northern tip of the town is worth the effort. A good view down Marine Parade and across the city can also be had from Lighthouse Road above the Centennial Gardens (accessed up Lucy Road, off Coote)

Continuing south you then encounter the intriguing **Millennium Sculpture** created by local artist, David Trubridge. The work is carefully lined up to where the sun rose at the dawning of the new millennium. One can only wonder if it will still be standing for the morning of January 1st 3000 and if so, what on earth will be reflected in its steel discs.

The newest of Napier's waterfront attractions is the **National Aquarium of New Zealand**, ① *To6-8341404, www.nationalaquarium.co.nz, 0900-1900, from $12, child $6, behind the scenes tours from $20, child $10, tank dives from $45,* which hosts an eclectic mix of native and non-native water and land creatures, from the enchanting seahorse to the iconic kiwi. The design of the building is quite clever, creating the impression that one is descending into the depths. 'Izzy' a remarkably toothy Australian import will also have any unsuspecting herpetophobe breaking into a cold sweat.

The Hawke's Bay Museum, ⓘ *9 Herschell St, T06-8357781, www.hawkes baymuseum.co.nz, daily 1000-1630, $5, children free,* offers a wide range of exhibits relating to the history and art of the region in modern surroundings. *Nga Tukemata* (The Awakening) presents the art and *taonga* of the local Maori and a rare presentation of evidence that dinosaurs once existed in New Zealand. Special attention is of course afforded to the earthquake of 1931. Relics plucked from the rubble go with the audio-visual descriptions and touching memories of survivors. Recommended. ▸▸ *For Sleeping, Eating, and other listings, see pages 358-366.*

Around Napier

Cape Kidnappers Gannet Colony → *Colour map 3, grid B5 All trips are subject to season and tide times. There is a Cape Shuttle between Napier and Clifton or Te Awanga, $20. Contact Kiwi Shuttles, T027-4593669, or the VIC.*

Cape Kidnappers is the jagged white peninsula which marks the southern boundary of Hawke's Bay. It gets its name from another rather unfortunate incident involving Captain Cook and the local Maori. Believing Cook's Tahitian interpreter was being held against his will, the Maori sent a *waka* to bring him back to shore. Doubtless a little confused, the Tahitian captive escaped back to the Cook's ship, which promptly weighed anchor and left, leaving only a name behind – Cape Kidnappers.

The Cape is famous for its colony of gannets. These large, elegant seabirds have lots of attitude, and weighing in at about 2 kg with deadly 6-in beaks designed to spear fish, they have every right to it. They hunt by gliding high over the surface of the water and diving at tremendous speed with wings folded back to catch the unsuspecting fish beneath. In the summer months up to 15,000 gannets gather at Cape Kidnappers to breed, forming the biggest mainland colony in New Zealand, and one of the biggest in the world. Perhaps given their attitude and armoury, gannets are not particularly fearful of anything or anybody, which makes them very approachable, particularly when grouped together and guarding their own little breeding patch. Being so approachable makes them the perfect tourist attraction, as they simply stare at you with an expression of complete contempt. The tourist visiting season runs from October to late April, with the best time to view being early November and late February. The first fluffy white chicks hatch in early November with the last chicks fledging and leaving the colony for their migration to Australia during May.

There are a variety of tours available to see the gannets. Most negotiate the beach and the tides below the peninsula, some others go overland. Provided the tides are right you can **walk** the 8 km to the colony yourself. The walk starts from the Clifton Motorcamp but it is generally hard going. Given the time restrictions due to the tides, you are advised to join a tour operator. If you are determined to go it alone, you can get the latest tide times from the VIC or DOC. ▸▸ *For Sleeping, Eating and other listings, see pages 359-364.*

Other sights

If you missed the National Aquarium or simply fancy something a little different pop into the new **Seahorse Farm,** ⓘ *Main Rd, Awatoto (about 6 km south of the city), T06-8340998, www.theseahorsefarm.co.nz Fascinating and relaxed hour-long tours are available three times daily, but book ahead, from $8, child $4.* It is a working aquaculture farm that supplies marine life for the national and international market with about 75,000 beautiful and delicate seahorses the undisputed main attraction. Recommended.

In stark contrast staunch British 'petrol-heads' should pay homage to the **British Car Museum,** ⓘ *63 East Rd, Haumoana, near Cape Kidnappers, T06-8750561. Daily but call first. $5.* It's quite small but its eccentric owner is very proud of his many old favourites, including the legendary Mini.

Even if you have think you have seen enough sheep, try the **Classic Sheepskins**
Tannery, ① *22 Thames St, Pandora, near Napier airport, T06-8359662, www.classicsheepskins.co.nz Mon-Fri 0730-1700, Sat and Sun 0900-1600. From $8, child $4.50*. It offers tours of the premises at 1100 and 1400 to see just how those hearthrugs and car seat covers are made. Drying lines with row after row of stretched sheepskins is a bizarre sight and conjures up an image of a flock of naked, embarrassed sheep hiding somewhere in the fields beyond.

Hawke's Bay Wineries
Given the climate and the soils in the Hawke's Bay it was inevitable that it would not take long for the first grapevine to be planted by the first Europeans settlers. Back then wine was produced primarily for religious use and it was the Catholic Society who founded a Mission Vineyard, in Taradale in 1851. Since that first harvest, the vines and the industry have boomed, making Hawke's Bay second only to Marlborough as the country's top wine-producing region. The two regions combined produce a range of wines which can compare with the world's best. Hawke's Bay offers a particularly wide range of wines due to the composition of the land and diverse 'sub regions'. Two such established 'sub-regions' are Bay View and the Esk Valley. There are over 25 vineyards in the area so, unless you are a connoisseur, knowing which to visit can be a dilemma. Thankfully the **Hawke's Bay Wine Trail**, as outlined in the free leaflet of the same name, gives details of what each vineyard offers. Some have stunning architecture, some are particularly famous or more established, others have fine restaurants or cafés. Most offer sales and tastings. You can either embark on a tour according to your own choice and itinerary, or join a number of organized tours. If you know little about wines, and New Zealand wine in particular, an organized tour is advised. ▸▸ *See Eating and Activities and tours, pages 362 and 365.*

Hastings → *Phone code: 06 Colour map 3, grid B5 Population: 50,000*
Hastings is a lively, sprawling, mainly agricultural service centre 20 km south of Napier and, like Napier, it was reduced mostly to rubble by the 1931 earthquake, with the loss of 88 lives. In rebuilding the town the architects echoed Napier's art deco and Spanish Mission styles, much of which can clearly be seen in the town centre. The two best examples are the **Westerman's Building** that now houses the VIC on Russell Street and **Municipal Theatre** on Hastings Street. The prominent art deco **clock tower**, right in the centre of town, was erected in 1935 to house the bells from the old 1909 Post Office Tower which collapsed in the quake. Architect Sydney Chaplin won 25 Guineas ($52) for its design. During the summer the town is a blaze of colour for the annual **flower festival**, when row upon row of hanging baskets line the streets providing a tourist attraction in itself and winning the town much praise around the country.

Sights Modern-day attractions in Hastings include the **Hawke's Bay Exhibition Centre**, ① *201 Eastbourne St, T06-8762077. Mon-Fri 1000-1630, Sat and Sun 1100-1600. Usually free depending on exhibitions*. It is the region's premier arts venue offering a varied programme of national and international touring exhibitions. Science and history also feature and there is an in-house café.

Given the dangerous nature of the beaches in the region, **Splash Planet**, ① *Grove Rd, T06-8769856, www.splashplanet.co.nz, daily 1000-1800, from $15, child $10*, a new themed water park, is proving very popular. There is an ice rink, hot pools and the inevitable slides and rides to keep the kids happy for hours. If wine tasting doesn't whet your appetite, the **Pernel Fruitworld**, ① *1412 Pakowhai Rd (north towards Napier), T06-8783383, www.pernel.nzliving.co.nz, daily 0900-1700, $9.50, child $5*, offers an interesting orchard tour and experience, fruit tastings and small animal farm for kids. Especially good in spring when the trees are in blossom. Café on site. ▸▸ *See Sleeping, Eating and other listings, pages 359-366.*

Havelock North is a very pleasant little village nestled amongst vineyards and orchards towards the coast and in the shadow of the 399-m **Te Mata Peak**. The view from the summit of Te Mata on a clear day is a 'must see' and it is easily reached by car via the village and Te Mata Peak Road. Weather permitting, it is also a top spot for **Paragliding** (see page 365).

As well as the wineries surrounding Havelock North it is also home to another one of nature's great delights, honey. **Arataki Honey Ltd**, ① *66 Arataki Rd, T06-8777300, www.aratakihoneyhb.co.nz, Mon-Sat 0830-1700, Sun 0900-1600, $10, children free*, was established in 1944 and is one of the largest beekeeping enterprises in the Southern Hemisphere, with a staggering 17,000 hives. There is a guided tour available daily at 1330, a shop and the spectacular 'wall', with its army of 40,000 live and very busy bees.

The **Village Growers' Market**, ① *at the Black Barn (Lombardi) Vineyard, every Sat 0900-1200*, is worth a visit and where the locals stock up on fresh produce and the latest gossip. ▸▸ *For Sleeping, Eating and other listings, see pages 361-365.*

Southern Hawke's Bay and south to the Wairarapa
▸▸ *Colour map 3, grid B4*

From Hastings SH2 winds its lonely way towards the little-visited, but stunning region of the Wairarapa, before arriving in Wellington. On SH2 there are a number of small towns including **Waipawa, Waipukurau, Dannevirke** and **Norsewood** (the latter two having obvious Scandinavian links). Although these settlements have little to offer the visitor there are plenty of activities available in the area, including ballooning and tramping. The wild **Kaweka** and **Ruahine Ranges** have some fine tramping but you are advised to plan carefully and go well prepared. DOC (Napier) or the field station in the historic village of **Ongaonga**, T06-8566808, 15 km west of Waipukurau, will provide all the necessary information and leaflets. The **VIC**, ① *Waipukurau Railway Station, Railway Esplanade (southern end of town), T06-8586488, chbinfo@xtra.co.nz, Mon-Fri 0900-1700, Sat 0900-1300*, can assist with activity and accommodation bookings.

Before leaving Hawke's Bay region proper, there is one other place worth visiting. But bear in mind it is on the 'alternative' route into the back country of the Wairarapa and involves a bit of a hike. For the sake of it, it is worth the trip to see a sign that points at a distinctly unremarkable hill called '**Taumatawhakatangihangakoauauotamate-aturipukakapikimaungahoronukupokaiwhenuaktanatahu**' and declares it as having the longest place name in the world (88 letters). Roughly translated, it means 'The place where Tamatea, the man with the big knees, who slid, climbed and swallowed mountains (known as land eater) played his flute to his loved one'. As you carefully contemplate both sign, place and meaning, as well as your annoyingly inquisitive nature, you can be sure of one thing – old Tamatea may have been a big eater but he was also a lousy lover if this was his idea of a romantic spot. If you do not have your own transport, tours with exclusive access to the summit (252 m) are available through **Airlie Mount Farm Walks**, T06-8587601.

To getting there from Waipukurau, take the coast road towards Porangahau. After about 40 km take a right. Follow the AA 'Historic Place Sign'. From Porangahau it is possible to take the back road to Wimbledon and undertake the alternative route to the Wairarapa, re-emerging on SH2 at either Eketahuna or Masterton. This will allow you to take in the stunning Castlepoint on the way.

● Sleeping

Napier *p353*
Napier is a popular holiday spot, in summer you are advised to book ahead.

LL **Cobden Villa**, *11 Cobden Rd, T06-8359065, www.cobdenvilla.com* Cosy and tastefully decorated art deco-style accommodation that gives a nice reminder of the local style without being over the top.

LL **Master's Lodge**, *10 Elizabeth Pl, Bluff Hill, T06-8341946, www.masterslodge.co.nz* 2 luxury private suites, solarium, in-house museum and veranda with commanding views. Dinner on request.

LL **McHardy House**, *11 Bracken St, Hospital Hill, T06-8350605, www.mchardyhouse.com* One of Napier's oldest estates, central, with 4 suites and 2 rooms. Luxuriously appointed with fine dining and panoramic views.

LL-L **County Hotel**, *Browning St, T06-8357800, www.countyhotel.co.nz* Restored art deco Edwardian Hotel in the centre of town with 18 tastefully decorated suites. Popular award-winning restaurant Anatole's and Churchill Bar attached.

LL-L **Te Pania Hotel**, *45 Marine Parade, T06-3775767, www.scenic-circle.co.nz* Napier's newest hotel. All very 'Auckland' and clinical in appearance, but ideally close to the town centre and with ocean views.

L **Gladstone Villa**, *21 Gladstone Rd, T06-8356413*. Modern, central, nicely-appointed self-contained unit.

A **Bluewater Hotel**, *10 West Quay, Ahuriri, T06-8358668, bluewaterhotel@xtra.co.nz* A modern hotel in a pleasant location overlooking the Westshore Marina. Spas, restaurant and bar.

A **Villa Fajr Holiday Home**, *Marine Par, T06-8350584, www.villafajr.co.nz* Excellent, modern, self-contained accommodation in traditional wood beachfront house.

There are numerous **motels** in Napier, especially in Auriri (Westshore) and along the promenade.

A **The Beach Front**, *T06-8355220*, and A **Shoreline Motel**, *T06-8355222*, are modern and the best on Marine Pde.

A **Art Deco Masonic Hotel**, *T06-8358689*. A slightly cheaper, older style option.

A **Harbour View Motor Lodge**, *Westshore, T06-8358077*, and

A **The Anchorage**, *26 West Quay, T06-8344318, www.anchorage.net.nz* Both are again modern, well-appointed and look over the harbour and marina.

A **Deco City Motor Lodge** 308 Kennedy Road, *T8434342, www.decocity.co.nz* One of the newest and most well-facilitated motels in town, which is proving popular especially during the Art Deco weekend.

A **Rocks**, *27 Meeanee Quay, Westshore,*

T06-8359626, www.napieraccommodation. com/therocks Perfect if you are hankering after an old-fashioned bath in your motel.

B **Sea Breeze B&B**, *281 Marine Par, T06-8358067, seabreeze.napier@xtra.co.nz* Tidy guesthouse right on the promenade.

C-D **Napier YHA**, *277 Marine Par, T06-8357039*, and

C-D **Waterfront Lodge**, *217 Marine Par, T06-8353429*, are both comfortable and friendly backpackers with internet.

C-D **Criterion Backpackers**, *48 Emerson St, T06-8352059*. A former hotel with spacious rooms and above average amenities.

C-D **Napier Prison Backpackers**, *55 Coote Rd, T06-8359933, nzhomestay@hotmail.com* Here you can 'do time' in a small hostel within the old prison complex. The accommodation is comfortable enough but it is the free jail tour that is the attraction.

Motorcamps and campsites

AL-D **Kennedy Park Top Ten Motor Camp**, *Storkey St, T06-8439126, www.kennedypark.co.nz* For campervans and tents this is a popular and well-established motor park offering a wide range of options. Recommended.

Cape Kidnappers *p356*

C-D **Clifton Motor Camp**, *Clifton Beach (road terminus) T06-8750263*; and

B-D **Te Awanga Holiday Park**, *52 Kuku St, Te Awanga, T06-8750334*, offer adequate beachside accommodation near the Cape and the 2 main operators Gannet Beach Adventures and Gannet Safaris.

Hastings *p357*

LL-L **Olea Cottages**, *101 Ru Collin Rd, T06-8797674, oleacottages@xtra.co.nz* Two modern purpose-built, self-contained cottages in peaceful rural setting between Hastings and Havelock North. Very nicely appointed with great attention to detail. Beds the size of football pitches and baths the size of small swimming pools. Very friendly hosts. L-AL **Hawthorn Country House**, *420 SH2, T06-8780035, www.hawthorne.co.nz* Award- winning luxury B&B again in country setting. Spacious rooms. Sumptuous breakfasts.

A **Angus Inn**, *Railway Rd, T06-8788177*. Large recently renovated complex with

Napier

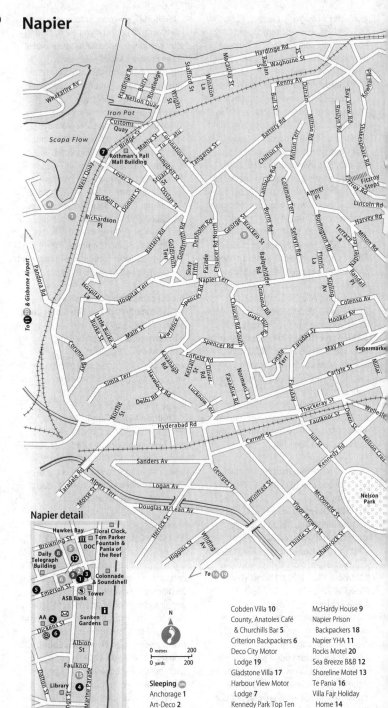

Napier detail

Hawkes Bay
Floral Clock,
Tom Parker
Fountain &
Pania of
the Reef
Browning St
DOC
Daily
Telegraph
Building
Colonnade
& Soundshell
Emerson St
Tower
ASB Bank
AA
Sunken
Gardens
Dickens St
Albion
St
Faulknor
St
Library
Marine Parade
Hastings St

N

0 metres 200
0 yards 200

Sleeping 🛏
Anchorage **1**
Art-Deco **2**
Beach Front **3**
Bluewater **4**

Cobden Villa **10**
County, Anatoles Café
& Churchills Bar **5**
Criterion Backpackers **6**
Deco City Motor
Lodge **19**
Gladstone Villa **17**
Harbour View Motor
Lodge **7**
Kennedy Park Top Ten
Motor Park **16**
Masters Lodge **8**

McHardy House **9**
Napier Prison
Backpackers **18**
Napier YHA **11**
Rocks Motel **20**
Sea Breeze B&B **12**
Shoreline Motel **13**
Te Pania **16**
Villa Fajr Holiday
Home **14**
Waterfront Lodge **15**

on-site restaurant and pool.

A-B Aladdin Motel, *120 Maddison St, T06-8766322.* Slightly cheaper motel option, centrally located.

C-D Travellers' Lodge, *606 St Aubyn St West, T06-8787108, travellers.lodge@ clear.net.nz* One of several budget options in Hastings, locally recommended, with purpose-built facilities, spacious doubles, singles and dorms, sauna, internet, free bike hire and assistance finding seasonal fruit picking work (Feb-Apr).

Motorcamps and campsites
A-D Hastings Top Ten Holiday Park, *610 Winsor Av, T06-8786692.* Wide range of options and good facilities. Within walking distance of Splash Planet so ideal for kids.

Havelock North *p358*
There are a number of magnificent traditional and modern 'country house style' B&Bs and lodges in the area. For full listings contact the VIC.

LL Mangapapa Lodge, *466 Napier Rd, Havelock North, T06-8783234, Mangapapa.lodge@xtra.co.nz* A world-famous small luxury hotel in 100 year-old refurbished country house. Magnificent range of accommodation and fine in-house restaurant. Expensive, but superb.

LL Black Barn (Lombardi Wines), *Havelock North, T06-8777985, lombardi@xtra.co.nz* Lombardi have 2 luxury self-contained options, a barn and a cottage, both situated in the heart of the vineyard.

L-AL Olea Cottages, *101 Ru Collin Rd, T06-8797674, oleacottages@xtra.co.nz* Two excellent, modern self-contained cottages ideal for couples.

L-AL Te Mata Lodge, *21 Porter Dr, Havelock North, T06-8774880, temata.lodge@xtra.co.nz* Comfortable, self-contained and centrally located in the village, spas.

L-B Brompton Apartments, *39 Havelock Rd, T06-8770117, www.brompton.co.nz* Modern self-contained apartment complex in the heart of the village. Classy decor and spas.

AL-A Village Motel, *corner Te Aute Rd and Porter Dr, T06-8775401, www.villagemotel.co.nz* The newest motel offering in the village. Centrally located with very tidy units, spas, Sky TV and internet.

A Havelock North Motor Lodge, *7 Havelock*

Eating 🍴
Acqua Brasserie **1**
Breakers Café **3**
Café Ujazi **12**
Deano's Bar & Grill **4**
Mossy's **6**
Ocean Boulevard
 Foodcourt **2**
Sappho **5**
Shed 2 **7**
Westshore Fish Café **11**

Bars & clubs 🍸
Flaherty's **8**
Rosie O'Gradys **9**

The East Coast Napier and around

Rd, Havelock North, T06-8778627. Another quality, modern motel, well located.

B-D Arataki Motel and Holiday Park, *139 Arataki Rd, Havelock North, T06-8777479.* Peaceful location, good facilities including a heated indoor pool.

C-D Peak Backpackers, *33 Havelock Rd, T06-8771170.* This is a modern establishment, clean, comfortable and well situated right in the heart of the village. Off-street parking, internet.

🍴 Eating

Napier *p353*

$$$-$$ Breakers Café and Bar, *corner of Tennyson St and Marine Par, T06-8358689.* Central location, perhaps a bit over the top on modern 'neon' aesthetics but fine food, again with an emphasis on seafood.

$$$-$$ Acqua Brasserie, *corner of Emerson St and Marine Par, T06-8358689. Open from 1130 daily.* Modern, good seafood and in prime location. Get a seat by the aquariums.

$$$-$$ Shed 2, *West Quay, Ahuriri, T06-8352202.* Waterfront location, imaginative international menu including ostrich, good seafood.

$ Deano's Bar and Grill, *255 Marine Par, T06-8354944.* You can't go far wrong with the $13 meal deal (Mon/Wed) but resisting the 'Rhino'-sized steak will be difficult.

$ Westshore Fish Café, *112a Charles St, T06-8340227. Tue-Sun 1130-late.* The best fish and chips.

There is a small foodcourt in the **Ocean Boulevard Mall**, *off Dickens St.*

$ Mossy's, *88a Dickens St, T06-8356696. Daily 0800-late.* An intimate, cosy café with candles and tasteful decor. Good value and live music on Sat nights.

$ Anatole's Café, *12 Browning St, T06-8357800. Daily 0730-late.* Another award-winner with good coffee, a wicked raspberry tandoori chicken and fine breakfasts.

Places for a reliably good caffeine fix are:

$ Sappho, *222 Emerson St, T06-8343933*; and **$ Café Ujazi**, *28 Tennyson St, T06-8351490.* The latter also does some imaginative vegetarian dishes.

Hawke's Bay Vineyards *p357*

You are advised to try at least one lunch or dinner at one of the vineyards (see also page 365). Perhaps the finest cuisine can be found amidst the amazing architecture and pleasant surroundings of **Sileni Estate**. Although some way from Napier (34 Km) on the Maraekakaho Rd (via SH50), it is well worth the journey. There are 2 restaurants: the **Mesa Alfresco** (from 1130) which caters for daytime cuisine and **RD1** (from 1800) which offers à la carte dinner. *Book ahead, T06-8798768, www.selini.co.nz*

Other vineyards with fine restaurants and cafés include:

Crab Farm, *551 Main Rd North, Bay View, T06-8366678*;

Brookfields, *Brookfields Rd, Meeanee, T06-8344615*;

Te Awa, *Roys Hill Rd, Hastings, T06-8797602*;

Mission Estate, *198 Church Rd, Taradale, T06-8442259*;

Vidal Estate, *T06-8768105*, (recommended);

Craggy Range, *Waimarama Rd, Havelock North, T0508-272449, www.craggyrange.com* (the latest much-hyped addition).

For more detail and a locations map ask at the VIC for the *Hawke's Bay Food Trail* leaflet.

Cape Kidnappers *p356*

Clifton Bay Café and Bar, *T06-8750096, daily in summer, Wed-Sun, winter 1000-1600.* Excellent place near the entrance to the motorcamp and overlooking the beach

Hastings *p357*

For fine dining near Hastings see **Sileni** or **Vidal** vineyards (above).

$$ Corn Exchange, *118 Maraekakaho Rd, T06-8708333. Open daily for lunch and dinner.* A stylish modern café in the old corn exchange building. Gourmet pizza a speciality.

$$ Warren's Bakery, *123 Russell St, T06-8787476.* Historic icon dating back over a century offering a wide range of delicious light snacks, sandwiches, pies and cakes as well as good coffee. Outdoor seating.

$ Rush Munro's, *704 Heretaunga St West.* Old and famous place serving fine ice cream.

Countdown supermarket, *Queen St. Mon-Fri 0800-2100, Sat and Sun 0800-2000.*

Havelock North *p358*

$$ Craggy Range Winery, *east of the village on Waimarama Rd*, *T06-8737126*. Has a classy restaurant offering lunches from 1200 and dinner daily.

$$ Vidals, *913 St Aubyn St East, Hastings, T06-8768105. Open for lunch and dinner daily.*

$$ Peak House Restaurant, *Te Mata Peak Rd, T06-8778663, www.peakhouse.co.nz Wed-Mon 1200-1400 and from 1800 for dinner, licensed.* Magnificent view, but be sure to book ahead and ask for a table by the window.

$ Postina, *in the old village post office on Havelock Rd, T06-8771714. Open for dinner Thu-Mon from 1830.* Affordable Mediterranean dishes with a good blackboard wine list.

$ The Olive Tree, *17 Joll Rd, T06-8770222.* Does snacks and has good coffee.

$$ Rose and Shamrock, *corner of Napier Rd and Porter Dr, T06-8772999. Daily from 1030, lunch 1200-1400 and dinner 1800-2130.* A spacious and delightful Anglo/Irish-style pub in the centre of the village with fine ale and good pub-food. For a good breakfast on a Saturday head for the Farmers' Market (see page 358).

❶ Pubs and entertainment

Napier *p353*
There are 2 Irish pubs in Napier:
Rosie O'Grady's and **O'Flaherty's**, *both on Hastings St*. Although not notable for interior aesthetics, they occasionally 'go off' with bands at the weekends.

Gintrap, *West Quay*. The place to be seen at the moment. It is like a cross between a wool shed and Nasa's mission control centre with music that may well result in 'lift off'.

Churchill's Bar, *below the County Hotel in Browning St*. Great, if you want to have a bit of fun over a fat cigar and G&T. There, the staff are well used to merry clients doing awful Churchill impersonations but quite rightly draw the line when it gets to…
'Never, in the field of human drinking…. '

❀ Festivals and events

Beware, Napier and the Hawke's Bay's famous itinerary of annual events involves an awful lot of food and wine. Here, in hedonistic Napier it seems food, wine and all

things convivial are the one continuum and very core of the region's lifestyle.

Presumeably there are no events scheduled for January because of the over-consumption and sheer excess of the Christmas period. However, you can roll gently into February with the **Harvest Hawke's Bay Harvest Festival**, a weekend of convivial fun and games celebrating the region's wine production. Apparently, grown men race around a park in wine barrels before dispersing for a spot of lunch – tremendous stuff. After an extended feast and drinks party for the winner, it is then time to contemplate the **International Mission Estate Concert** (*Feb*), an outdoor concert at the renowned Mission Estate Winery drawing increasingly large crowds, truckloads of laden picnic hampers and some famous (if ageing) performers. Over the last few years they have included Dame Kiri Te Kanawa, Dionne Warwick, the Beach Boys and most recently, that icon of the ages Clifficus Richardisaurus. Shortly after the Mission weekend is the **Art Deco Weekend** (*Feb*) Napier's biggest and most popular event celebrating the art deco style. It involves vintage cars, period costume, parades, Devonshire teas (and scones) on the promenade and, perhaps best of all, a spot of 'wineglass wanders'. Then to end a hectic month it's time to relax with some more food and wine at the **Weta Wine and Food Fest**, which speaks for itself (burp!).

Edible Arts Fest (*Mar 2004*). Clearly this idea was the result of too many council meetings during the previous event! Apparently, this event will be a world-first (really!) incorporating yet more food and wine with the added attraction, this time, of 'edible art exhibitions', live music and theatre performances. The infamous 'Great Long Lunch' will naturally kick off this great new event in fine style. Then, at last the **Horse of the Year Show** (*Mar*) is cleverly inserted into the itinerary to offer just a hint of the concept of physical exercise. This is actually the largest horse show in the Southern Hemisphere attracting over 1000 riders and a small army of well-fed spectators, we presume all puce, bursting from ill-fitting clothing and watching from collapsed deck chairs. The **Winter Arts Festival/Winter Solstice Fire Festival** (*May/Jun*) is a celebration of the arts, with theatre, restaurant theatre and vocal arts all enhanced by a spectacular fire show at the Sound Shell. All this cleverly intended to mask the inevitable rampant consumption of more food and wine. Then, perhaps in thanksgiving, November receives the title of **Month of Wine and Roses**. A month of private garden tours with a little music and, naturally, lots (and lots) of food and wine.

Finally as local poultry and farm animals are being fattened up for Christmas, amidst gay banter and the popping of wine corks, the city's voluminous population gathers for the **Great Bathroom Scale Busting Fest** a wholesome, distinctly rotund event opened by the winner of the annual Break the Pogo Stick competition…Well, OK only kidding – but surely it's only a matter of time. Cheers….

▲ Activities and tours

Napier *p353*

Art Deco or Earthquake Walks There are several guided or self-guided tour options available. The **morning walk** (1 hour, $8) leaves from the VIC at 1000 daily year round, while the **afternoon walk** (2 hours, $12) leaves at 1400 from the Art Deco Shop, 163 Tennyson St, daily in Oct-Jun, then Sat/Sun/Wed from Jul-Sept. The **Earthquake Tour** (2 hr, from $12) also departs from the VIC daily at 0930 and 1400 Oct-Mar (1400 only Apr-Sep). This entertaining tour concentrates on the history and events surrounding that fateful day in 1931 and concludes with a look at the fascinating pictures and memorabilia of the Earthquake Gallery. Coach tours (1hr) are also available for groups. All the tours are hosted by the Art Deco Trust, an organization set up in 1985 to help preserve and promote art deco in the region. Included in the morning and afternoon walks is an audio-visual and free refreshments at the **Art Deco Shop**, *opposite Clive Square, T06-8350022, www.artdeconapier.com* The shop stocks a wide range of art deco products and is open daily 0900-1700. If you wish to see the best of the buildings on your own, or are pushed for time, pick up a copy of the excellent 'Art Deco Walk' leaflet ($2.50) from the VIC. There are also *Art Deco Scenic Drive* maps available.
Ballooning *T06-8794229*, $230, child,

from $150.
Canoeing Salty Rock Adventure Company, *58 West Quay, T06-8343500, www.saltyrock.co.nz* Trips and hire.
Climbing trips and climbing-wall Salty Rock , *T06-8343500*.
Diving See National Aquarium, page 355.
Fishing Out of the Blue, *T06-8351110*.
Grant Petherick Fly Fishing, *T06-8767467*.
Horse treks Te Awanga, *T06-8750541*.
Riverlands (Mohaka River), *T06-8349756*.
(Accommodation available.) **Coastal Horse Treks**, *Tangoio, T06-8367626*. **Jet boat tours** Riverside Jet, *T06-8743841, www.riversidejet.co.nz*
Paragliding Airplay, *Havelock North, T025-512886*.
Rafting/kayaking Riverlands (Mohaka River), *T06-8349756*. Salty Rock Adventure Company, *West Quay, T06-8343500*.
Sand yachting (Land yachts on wheels) Blokarts, *T0800-946377, info@adventureatwinecountryhb.co.nz*
Scenic flights Napier Airport, *T06-8356192*. From $39.
Sightseeing tours Bay Tours and Charters, *T06-8436953*. **Long Island Tours**, *T06-8770977*. Both offer local and regional tours. **Napier Prison Tours**, *T06-8359933*. Visit the local prison reputed to be the oldest in New Zealand, daily 0930 and 1500, from $10.
Swimming The beach in Napier is pebble, deeply shelved and too dangerous for swimming. However, there is a small lap pool and hot pools at the new **Ocean Spa Complex**, *Marine Parade*. See page 355.
Vineyard tours See page 357.
Walking The **Whana Valley Walk**, *T06-8742860, www.whana-valley-walk.co.nz* A well-organized, good value, 3-day event taking in very pleasant countryside and accommodation lodges (meals optional and extra), $165.
Windsurfing/sailing Sail'n Surf, *T06-8350684*.

Cape Kidnappers Gannet Colony *p356*
There are several tour operators here.
Gannet Beach Adventures, *T06-8750898, T0800-426638, www.gannets.com* The oldest company. This 4-hr tour leaves daily (Oct-May) from Clifton Beach by tractor and allows about 90 mins with the gannets, from $30, child $17.

Gannet and Coastline Tours Ltd, *T06-8444538, www.gannet.co.nz* Offers a similar 4½-hr tour in a 4-wheel drive truck but leaves from Napier giving less time with the gannets, from $30, child $17.

Gannet Safaris Overland, *at the Summerlee Station on the Cape (near Te Awanga), T06-8750888, www.gannetsafaris.co.nz* Go overland by shuttle bus, which involves very little walking. The 3-hr tours depart daily Sep-May at 0930 and 1330, from $45.

Hawke's Bay vineyards *p357*
Sileni, *Maraekakaho Rd, Hastings, T06-8798768, www.selini.co.nz 1000-1700. Restaurant open until late.* Stunning modern architecture, top class restaurant and a fine range of wines.

Mission Estate, *corner Avenue and Church Rds, Taradale, T06-8442259. Mon-Sat 0830-1730, Sun 1100-1600.* The oldest vineyard in New Zealand. Famous labels, restaurant and established tours.

Church Road, *150 Church Rd, Taradale, T06-8442053, www.churchroad.co.nz Daily 0900-1700.* Formerly the McDonald's Vineyard. Owned by the internationally famous Montana Estates. Winemaking museum and restaurant. Hosts excellent jazz concerts.

Te Mata, *Te Mata Rd, T06-8774399, www.temata.co.nz Mon-Fri 0900-1700, 1000 Sat, 1100 Sun.* Another architectural stunner. Reputable label.

Te Awa, *Roy's Hill Rd, SH50, T06-8797602, www.teawafarm.co.nz 0900-1700, Sat and Sun 1000-1800.* Interesting building, fine labels and good café.

Black Barn (Lombardi), *Te Mata Rd, T06-8777985, www.lombardi.co.nz Mon-Fri 0900-1800, Sat and Sun 1000-1800 (reduced winter hours).* Excellent accommodation options, underground cellar and host to the Village Growers' Market every Sat in summer.

Craggy Range, *253 Waimarama Rd, T06-8737126, www.craggyrange.com* The region's newest and much-hyped winery in the shadow of Te Mata Peak. All the grandeur and self-promotion is perhaps a little over the top. Classy restaurant that could make more of the view.

Clearview, *194 Clifton Rd, Te Awanga, Hastings, T06-8750150, www.clearviewestate.co.nz Daily 1000-1700.* One not to miss if you are visiting Cape

Kidnappers. Quality not quantity with a classy Mediterranean-style café.

Vidal Estate, *913 St Aubyn St East, T06-8768105, www.vidal.co.nz Mon-Sat 1000-1800, Sun 1000-1700, winter daily 1000-1700.* Excellent restaurant serving lunch and dinner daily.

Wine tours
Most of the tours available are flexible, and will cater for your needs.

Grant Petherick Wine Tours, *T06-8767467, www.flyfishingwinetours.co.nz* High quality, entertaining and informative, customized tours. From $350 for half day for 2, $600 full day. Recommended.

Hawke's Bay in a Glass, *T06-8432478, www.qualityhb.co.nz* Another quality operator offering flexible tours arranged to your own time schedule and tastes. Price varies.

Bay Tours, *T06-8436953, www.baytours.co.nz* Locally recommended and good value with a flexible itinerary, from $45.

Wine Tours, Napier, *T06-8436953.* Established in 1982. Range of tours from $45.

Vince's Vineyard Tours, *T06-8366705.* Personalized tour with friendly, local, knowledgeable guide. In operation for 10 years. Flexible itineraries from $40.

Vicky's Vineyard Tours, *T06-8439991.* Good range of imaginative tours from added sightseeing to committed connoisseurs. Small groups. From $40.

On Yer Bike Winery Tours, *Hastings, T06-8798735.* The energetic option, by bike (requires supreme coordination and orientation skills towards the end of the day). Other good bike tour companies include:
Bike About, *T06-8439991, www.bikeabouttours.co.nz* and,
Bike D'Vine, *T06-8336697, www.bikedevine.com* Tours are flexible, usually self-guided and sometimes include other less libatious destinations. Lunch is often provided as well as maps, cell phones and even pick ups should you get too tired or weighed down with purchases. Prices start at a very reasonable $40 per day.

Havelock North *p358*
Tandem pargliding Airplay, *T025-512886, airplay@xtra.co.nz* Flights and courses available from $180.

ⓘ Directory

Napier and Hastings
AA *Dickens St, T06-8353725.* **Car hire** *Hertz, T06-8356169.* Xpress, *T06-8358818.* **Cycle hire**: Marineland, *209 Marine Parade, T06-8344027.* Napier Cycle Centre, *Tennyson St, T06-8359528.* Pedal Power, *340 Gloucester St, Taradale, T06-8449771.* **Internet** *Cybers, 98 Dickens St, Napier, T06-8350125. Mon 0830-2100, Tue-Fri 0830-2400, Sat 0900-2400, Sun* 0900-2000. There are additional outlets in the **Ocean Boulevard Mall**, *Dickens St, T06-8340963.* **Internet World**, *102 East Queen St, Hastings, T06-8764876.* **Library** *Station St, T06-8344180.* **Medical services** *30/32 Monroe St, T06-8354696.* **Post office** Napier, *corner Dickens and Hastings Sts, T06-8353725. Mon-Fri 0800-1700, Sat 0930-1230.* Hastings, *The Plaza, Russell St, T06-8789425. Mon-Fri 0830-1800, Sat 0830-1700, Sun 0900-1800.* **Police** *T06-8354688.* **Taxi** Star, *T06-8355511.*

The Wairarapa → Phone code: 06

The Wairarapa is one of the least-visited regions in the North Island. Most visitors miss it out in their rush to reach Wellington via SH1, which lies to the west beyond the natural barrier of the Ruahine and Tararua Ranges. If that simple fact is not appealing enough, the remote and stunning coastal scenery and relaxed atmosphere will, if you make the effort to visit, confirm that this is a place worth getting to know. The highlights, other than the delights of rural towns like Martinborough, which lie like a string of pearls along SH2, are the ever-increasing number of quality vineyards, a terrific range of country B&Bs and the coastal splendour of Castle Point and Cape Palliser, the North Island's most southerly point.

Ins and outs

Getting there By bus, **Tranzit Coachlines**, To800-471227, To6-3771227, wai@tranzit.co.nz, run regular services between Wellington and Palmerston North (including Mount Bruce). The fare from Masterton to Martinborough is around $3.60 one-way. By train, **TranzMetro**, To4-8017000, www.tranzmetro.co.nz, provides regular services from Wellington to Masterton (six a day Mon-Fri, twice daily Sat/Sun) and has the added attraction of the long Rimutaka tunnel across the ranges. There is a special day excursion fare of $15, child $8. Standard fare $13 one way. Masterton train station is on Perry St, about a 15-min walk from the town centre. **Tranzit** coaches link with **TranzMetro** rail services, To800-843596.

Getting around **Wairarapa Coachlines** offer a regular weekday and limited weekend services between Masterton, Martinborough and Featherston, To25-916971, T3782911. There is no public transport to Castlepoint. However, you may be able to hook up with the holiday park or hotel staff on supply trips to Masterton.

Information **Masterton VIC**, ① *5 Dixon St, To6-3787373, www.wairarapanz.com Mon-Fri 0900-1700, Sat/Sun 1000-1600.* The staff are very friendly and it acts as the main accredited VIC in the region. They hold a comprehensive information base on the wealth of B&B beds all over the Wairarapa Region. **DOC Masterton Field Centre**, ① *South Rd (continuation Queen St), To6-3770700.* **Greytown VIC**, ① *in the Council building, 110 Main St, To6-3049008. Fri-Sun 1000-1600.* Small office but the free *Taste of Greytown* leaflet is especially useful. **Martinborough VIC**, ① *18 Kitchener St, To6-3069043, martinborough@wiararapanz.com Daily 1000-1600.* **Featherston VIC**, ① *in the Old Courthouse (SH2) in the village, To6-3088051. Daily 1000-1500.*

Given its relative geographical isolation (thanks to the Tararua Ranges), Masterton was not settled to any great degree until the late 1850s, but with rich fertile soils and a favourable climate, growth was rapid. Today, the town is the chief commercial centre for the Wairarapa Region. Masterton also gives Te Kuiti in the Wiakato (the 'sheep-shearing capital of New Zealand') a run for its money in the big woolly event stakes. The **Golden Shears** is the major date in the local young farmer's calendar and offers moderate fame and fortune to the fastest clipper around. It is held at the beginning of March, lasts about three days and ends with a big dinner and 'cabaret'.

Sights Just opposite the VIC is the new **Aratoi Museum of Art and History**, ① *T06-3700001, www.aratoi.co.nz, daily 1000-1630, admission by donation*, which admirably showcases many aspects of the region's social, cultural and natural history, as well as rapidly blossoming into the main focus for local contemporary artists. The museum also hosts visiting national exhibitions, something the region was missing out on for years. Good in-house café. Also within walking distance of the VIC and town centre is the much-loved and celebrated **Queen Elizabeth Park**. First planted in 1878, today it boasts a lake (with boats for hire), sports grounds, a miniature railway, swing bridge, aviaries, a deer park and the usual tracts of manicured herbaceous borders. A little further out of town, on Colombo Road, is **Henley Park**, with lakes, offering fishing and lakeside walks.

Masterton has a number of interesting gardens and **Heritage Trail Walks** (1-2 hours) which are part of an eight-walk Regional Heritage Trail. Information and leaflets for all can be obtained from the VIC. If you are a budget traveller, or just simply a little tired from your endless travels, be sure to check out the bronze statue and charming story of **Russian Jack**, the erstwhile Wairarapa 'Swag' man, on Queen Street.

For recreational walks the **Mount Holdsworth** area offers access to the Tararua Range with short and long walk options. Details are outlined at the car park. To get there take Norfolk Road just south of the town (17 km). ▸▸ *For Sleeping, Eating and other listings, see pages 371-374.*

Mount Bruce → *Colour map 3, grid C3*

① *T06-3758004, www.mtbruce.doc.govt.nz   The centre is open daily from 0900-1630. $8, children free.*

The main focus of Mount Bruce, 30 km north of Masterton on SH2, is the **Mount Bruce National Wildlife Centre**. This centre is the flagship of DOC's conservation and endangered species breeding programme. Although much of what happens at Mount Bruce takes place behind the scenes, (and involves dedicated staff acting as surrogate mothers) the public can see many species otherwise rarely seen. There is something very special about sitting on the veranda of the cafe, sipping a coffee and overlooking an enclosure with a takahe (a charming prehistoric-looking purple bird, not dissimilar to a large chicken) going happily about its business, in the knowledge that there are only 200 or so left in the world. Likewise, taking a stroll through the native bush, to see other enclosures hiding stitchbirds and kokako, all of which you will probably never see again in your lifetime.

There is a nocturnal kiwi house which rates as amongst the best in the country and leaves you in no doubt as to the numerous threats which this national icon faces in the modern world. Other highlights include the eel feed at 1330 and the kaka feed at 1500. The wild eels live in the stream running through the reserve and gather beneath the bridge at feeding time in a swirling mass. This particular species, native to New Zealand, are far larger than the average eel and live up to at least 80 years. The kaka is a cheeky and at times raucous native bush parrot. There is a small colony at Mount Bruce that have been bred in captivity and now live wild in the area. They all have names and will quite happily nibble your hair or your ear before cracking open a

⁞ Shelling out for paua

The inner shell casing of the sea-mollusc paua has to be one of the most beautiful and colourful things in nature. The paua is very closely related to the abalone, of which there are about 130 species worldwide, and both are related to snails and limpets. The Maori, as a source of both food and decoration, have long valued paua and the same is true for the masses in modern times. To protect paua as a sustainable resource, strict quotas are in place in New Zealand and no paua harvesting is allowed with compressed air. This makes their collection, with only a snorkel, often in cold southern waters over 12 m in depth, quite an art. Dives of up to two minutes are not uncommon. What comes up from those depths is not the radiant casing that you see in the souvenir shops, but a drab coralline coated shell, that once removed of its flesh, must be ground down to reveal the beautiful patterning beneath. The paua industry is well established in New Zealand, not only for seafood, but also more especially for the shell from which the polished jewellery is made. You will encounter the huge range of designs in almost every souvenir shop throughout the land. In some parts of the country the humble paua has even reached icon status. In Bluff, near Invercargill an elderly couple (in that typically eccentric New Zealand style) decided to decorate almost their entire house (in and out) with paua. Why, frankly, remains an enigma. The result is the famous 'paua house', which must feature in many a photo album all over the planet as that 'decidedly weird place' at the bottom of the world.

peanut with their powerful beaks. If you go to the feeding area just before 1500 they will usually be hanging about in the trees, available for interviews and photographs. Within the main building there are some fine displays, a shop and a café.

Castlepoint → *Colour map 3, grid C4*

It is a major diversion to get to this remote coastal settlement (65 km from Masterton) but the trip is well worth it. Castlepoint is considered to be the highlight on the Wairarapa's wild and remote coastline and it certainly deserves the honour. At the eastern end of the main beach a stark rocky headland, from which sprouts the weather-beaten **Castlepoint Lighthouse**, sweeps south to enclose a large lagoon. The picturesque bay, that is itself a popular spot with surfers and swimmers, is dominated at its southern entrance by the aptly named 162-m **Castle Rock**. If you're temped to climb the rock it can be accessed from the southern end of the bay. The lighthouse can be accessed across the sand tombolo which connects it to the mainland via a boardwalk. Parked up on the beach you will see huge tractors and metal rigs which launch the local fishing boats. Just below the lighthouse there is a cave which can be explored at low tide, but beware – Maori legend has it that it is the hiding place of a huge menacing octopus. One word of warning: a small memorial stone testifies to the number of people who have drowned while exploring the offshore reef, so take care. On its eastern side, huge ocean waves can catch you unawares. While contemplating the memorial stone look closely at the rocks that surround it and you will see hundreds of fossil shells embedded therein. ⏵ *For Sleeping, Eating and other listings, see pages 372-374.*

Riversdale Beach and Flat Point

The small coastal resort of Riversdale is 35 km northeast of Te Wharau which is itself east of Masterton, (130 km round trip). The beach is long and sandy and as it's patrolled in summer offers safe swimming as well as surfing, fishing and diving. The Flat Point to Honeycomb Rock section of coast is wilder than Riversdale with interesting rock formations and an old shipwreck. ▸▸ *For Sleeping, see page 372.*

Carterton → *Colour map 3, grid C3*

Carterton acts as a secondary service town to Masterton and is famous in spring for its daffodils (first planted in 1920). Although not aesthetically as pleasing as its neighbouring settlements, it is perhaps worth a stop to see the Paua Shell Factory and use the town as an access point to the Mount Dick Viewpoint and the Tararua Forest park at Waiohine Gorge.

Sights The **Paua Shell Factory**, ⓘ *Kent St, T06-3796777, www.pauashell.co.nz, daily 0800-1700, free,* is one of the few places in the country that converts the stunningly beautiful paua (abalone) shells into jewellery and souvenirs. It is possible to see how the shell is crafted and to watch a video about the paua itself, with complimentary coffee or tea. This is all cleverly designed to get you into the shop, where there is a vast range of paua shell items on sale, some of which are painfully kitsch.

Sporting your new paua shell earrings and key rings, and provided the weather is fair, you can then go and see one of the best views in the Wairarapa, from **Mount Dick**. At the southern end of town turn into Dalefield Road which heads straight towards the hills like a never-ending runway. At the very end of the road keep going and just before its terminus look for a farm track on the left. This track, which is negotiable without four-wheel drive (just), goes about 3 km up to a viewpoint; 14 km total.

The trip to **Waiohine Gorge** (22 km) at the entrance to the **Tararua Forest Park** is well worth it for the scenery itself, let alone the walks on offer and the heart-stopping **swing bridge**, one of the longest in New Zealand. The road is signposted just south of the town on SH2. Eventually an unsealed road connects you with the riverbank which gradually rises high above the river gorge. At the road terminus you can embark on a number of walks from one hour to several days, almost all of which involve the initial negotiation of the swing bridge which traverses the gorge at a height of about 40 m. Even if you do nothing else at Waiohine, a few trips back and forth on the bridge is great fun. Although it is perfectly safe, bear in mind that jelly has less wobble. For **eco-rafting trips** down the Waiohine both day and night contact the Adventure Centre in Greytown, page 374. ▸▸ *For Sleeping and Eating, see pages 372 and 373.*

Greytown → *Colour map 3, grid C3*

Greytown, along with Martinborough, is the prettiest of the Wairarapa settlements and is best known for its antique, art and craft shops and roadside cafés. It's also a great spot to stop and wander around the old buildings and quaint shops. Given its historic village feel it is not surprising to learn that Greytown was one of the first places settled in the area. Settlement began in earnest in the 1850s, on land purchased by Sir George Grey, one of New Zealand's first governors and after whom the town is, of course, named. The **Cobblestones Museum**, ⓘ *169 Main St, T06-3049687, daily from 0900-1630, $3, child $1,* is a collection of buildings and memorabilia from the early settler days. ▸▸ *For Sleeping, Eating and other listings, see pages 372-374.*

Martinborough → *Colour map 3, grid C3*

Martinborough is located towards the coast from SH2, 16 km southeast of Greytown. It is not dissimilar to Greytown but enjoys its country location and a quiet town square

● *While you are in Martinborough don't miss Thrive, 8 Kitchener St, where you will find the*
● *famous 'Thunderpants' – apparently an entirely new concept in modern technology knickers. They are very popular because (by all accounts) they 'do not go up your bum'!*

more (as opposed to the bustling SH2). First settled by a nationalistic Briton, John Martin in the late 1880s, the Village Square and the streets running off it form the shape of the Union Jack. With names like Kansas, Texas and Ohio, it is clear that Martin had as much a love of the US as he did his homeland. Described as a unique 'wine village', with a staggering 20 vineyards within walking distance of the square, and blessed with as many charming B&Bs, it is a favourite romantic haunt for Wellingtonians in search of a quiet weekend followed by a savage headache on the following Monday morning.

Sights Of local historical interest is the Colonial Museum, ① *on the Square, T3069736, Sat and Sun 1400-1600, donation,* which was itself the former village library built in 1894. It is furnished with all the usual early settler artefacts. The *Vintage Village Heritage Walk* leaflet available from the VIC will pinpoint other sites of historical interest like the rather grand and recently restored **Martinborough Hotel**. Again there are a number of 'open gardens' for which the VIC will point the way.

The **Patuna Chasm**, ① *Patuna Farm, Ruakokopatuna Rd, book through the VIC or T06-3069966, www.patunafarm.co.nz,* is an interesting limestone gorge featuring stalactites, fossils and waterfalls and a host of native wildlife. The chasm is on private land but guided walks are available from $15. Along a similar theme the **Ruakokopatuna glow-worm caves** nearby are also on private land but can be accessed with permission from Blue Creek Farm, ① *T06-3069393.* Take a torch and your gumboots. About 20 km southeast of the village are the busy white propellers of the **Hau Nui Wind Farm**, White Rock Road. Although you are not free to wander amongst them there is a viewing platform provided. From there you might consider going all the way to the remote coast at **Tora** or **White Rock** which offers some great walks and coastal scenery.

If you are around in November, your visit may coincide with the immensely popular **Toast Martinborough** celebrations, a festival of fine wine and food toast@toastmartinborough.co.nz

The main attraction is of course the **vineyards** and most offer tastings and some tours, but bear in mind not all of them are open all year round. The most noted labels tend to be Sauvignon Blanc, Riesling and Pino Gris. The new **wine centre** in the heart of the village, ① *T06-3069040, www.martinboroughwinecentre.co.nz,* is a good place to get a feel for what is available and ask about tours. *The Martinborough Wairarapa Wine Trail* leaflet, available from the VIC, will also get your tour started. The website www.nz wine.com is useful. The **Ata Rangi Vineyard** is one of the better known, producing a Pinot Noir, for which the village is now famous. ① *T06-3069570, www.atarangi.co.nz Sep-Mar, Mon-Fri 1300-1500, Sat and Sun 1200-1600.* There are a number of local tour operators who can arrange specialist **wine tours**, including **Burgiss's South Wairarapa Tours**, T06-3089352. ▸ *For Sleeping, Eating, and other listings, see pages 372-374.*

Cape Palliser, Ngawi and Lake Ferry → *Colour map 3, grid C3*

The day-long drive to see the Cape Palliser Lighthouse epitomizes the region and is highly recommended. On the way you can take in the bizarre rock formations of the Putangirua Pinnacles, the charming coastal fishing village of Ngawi and a colony of enchantingly languid fur seals, before the road terminates at the steps of the lighthouse. (From Featherstone or Martinborough make your way down Lake Ferry Rd, towards Lake Ferry. Just before the village turn left for Ngawi. From here the lighthouse is about 40 km. Once the road joins the coast and if it is a clear day, you may be able to see the snow-capped Kaikoura Ranges of the South Island.)

Sights After about 15 km look out for the **Putangirua Pinnacles** car park. The pinnacle formations are a series of gravel spires and turrets. They are about an hour's walk down a streambed, so take proper footwear. Once you reach the entrance to the pinnacles (on the left, after about 30 minutes) you have the choice of climbing a steep path through bush to a viewpoint (30 minutes), or entering the

pinnacles stream bed and going into heart of the formation. You should not miss the
viewpoint but both trips are worth it.

From the car park the road continues, hugging the cliffs before opening out across a
wide coastal plain, with a beautiful shore of rock and sand, well known for its excellent
surfing. The coastal village of **Ngawi** soon comes into view and you
will be struck by the collection of old tractors and bulldozers on the
beachfront with rigs supporting a raft of fishing boats of all shapes
and sizes. It is well worth a stop here to take a closer look and watch
as one of the dearly-loved machines is used to launch a boat.

*The Lake Ferry Hotel is a
fine place to enjoy a meal
or a drink while watching
the sunset and
whitebaiters sifting the
shallows on the banks of
Lake Onoke.*

From Ngawi the red and white tower of the lighthouse can be
seen. On the rocks just before it is a colony of New Zealand **fur
seals**, though you have to look carefully so as not to miss them. Like
fat, brown barrels they doze the day away amongst the boulders. All they're missing is a
TV, a can of beer and a remote. By all means take a closer look, but do not go too near (no
more than 10 m). If you do, be warned: their soporific attitude will evaporate in an
explosion of rippling blubber as they charge towards the surf.

From the seal colony it is only a short distance to the **lighthouse,** with its steep
climb of steps and rewarding views. Here you are at the southernmost tip of the North
Island. Once you return to Lake Ferry Road it is worth the short diversion to see **Lake
Ferry** itself. ►► *For Sleeping, see page 373.*

Featherston → *Colour map 3, grid C3*

Featherston is the southern gateway to the Wairarapa (or the last settlement
depending on which way you came) and sits in the shadow of the Rimutaka range that
was, and continues to be, the 'great divider' between the Wairarapa and Wellington.
Although not particularly remarkable in history or aesthetics, Featherstone is best
known as the 1870s base of operations, in the mammoth task of connecting the
Wairarapa and Wellington by rail.

Sights The main attraction in Featherston is the **Fell Engine Museum,** ① *Fitzherbert
St, T06-3089379. Mon-Fri 0930-1600, Sat and Sun 1000-1600, or on request.
Donation.* It houses the beautifully restored Fell Engine (the only one of its type in the
world) that used to climb the steep 265-m slopes of the Rimutaka Incline.

The railway line now goes through a tunnel and the **Rimutaka Incline** has been
opened up as a walkway, which starts at the end of Cross Creek Road, 10 km south of
Featherston. It takes a whole day to reach the summit or cross the ranges to Kaitoke (17
km). There is a YHA in Kaitoke should you need a bed at the other end, T06-5264626.

As you leave the Wairarapa by road (or indeed arrive) a fine departing (or
introductory) view can be seen from the **Rimutaka Trig** (725 m) at the crest of the
ranges road. The track (one hour return) starts beside the road, just below the summit
café, on the Wellington side. From the top you will get a great view of **Lake Wairarapa**
and the coast. ►► *For Eating, see page 374.*

⬤ Sleeping

Masterton *p367*
The Wairarapa is renowned for its
ever-increasing number of B&Bs which
comfortably cater for the huge numbers of
Wellingtonians, who cross the hills into the
Wairarapa in droves on summer weekends
and during the holiday periods. Given the
sheer number of beds, standards are
generally high and competition is fierce. The
choices, especially around the vineyards of
Martinborough (if not necessarily the prices),
are particularly good.
L The Fresh Egg, *Bute Rd, T06-3723506,
www.freshegg.co.nz* Top of the range B&B
with 2 rooms, a twin sleep-out with private
bath, pool, sauna, and fine cuisine.
L-A Masterton Motor Lodge, *250 High St,
T06-3782585, www.masterton-motor
lodge.co.nz* Wide range of top quality units,
pool, spa, in-house restaurant and bar.

AL **Acorn Cottage**, *Bowlands, Bideford, T06-3724842, www.bowlands.co.nz* Charming, well-appointed,130 year-old cottage in country location. Fully self-contained with log fire.

AL **Victoria House**, *15 Victoria St, T06-3770186*. Good value, centrally located B&B in a restored Victorian villa.

AL-AL **Copthorne Resort**, *High St South, T06-3775129*. Standard, fairly unremarkable hotel accommodation but with an attractive range of amenities including pools, spas, squash courts and solarium. Good for families.

A **Koeke Lodge**, *Upper Plain Rd, T06-3772414, www.bigboulders.com* Huge house close to town and complete with library and snooker room. Good value.

B **Natusch House**, *55 Lincoln Rd, T06-3789252, www.natusch.co.nz* 1893 villa named after a pioneer architect. Tastefully decorated with period furnishings, 4 rooms with shared bathrooms.

B **Empire Lodge**, *94 Queen St, T06-3771902*. Main budget hotel in town, with basic rooms (with bathroom), and restaurant.

Motorcamps and campsites

B-D **Mawley Park Motor Camp**, *15 Oxford St, T06-3786454*. All the usual basic amenities (from cabins to tent sites) situated close to town and beside the river.

Castlepoint *p368*

There is a well-equipped motorcamp, a tidy motel, a beach store at Castlepoint and a number of B&Bs nearby.

A **Okau Station**, *7 km north of Castlepoint, T06-3726892, www.nzhunt.com* Tidy self-contained cottage near the beach with log fire.

B **Whakataki Hotel**, *4 km before Castlepoint, T06-3726852*. Kiwi country pub with budget rooms and cabins available.

A-D **Castlepoint Holiday Park and Motels**, *T06-3726705, holiday@castlepoint.co.nz* Friendly and spacious park with adequate amenities right next to the beach overlooking the headland. Wide range of accommodation options from tent sites to self-contained motel units in the village. Friendly, helpful hosts.

Riversdale Beach and Flat Point *p368*

At Riversdale Beach there is a store, a motorcamp and a number of B&Bs.

A **Blairlogie**, *between Riversdale and Whareama, T06-3723777, www.wairarapa.co.nz/blairlogie* Historic homestead and self-contained cottage in spacious grounds.

A **Caledonia Coastal Farmstay**, *Flat Point Rd, T06-3727553, wendakerr@xtra.co.nz* A well-appointed self-contained cottage in prime position overlooking the beach.

Motorcamps and campsites

C-D **Riversdale Beach Holiday Park**, *T06-3723889, holidaypark@inspire.net.nz* Cabins and sites.

Carterton *p369*

There are numerous friendly B&Bs available. For the full range contact the VIC.

A **Courthouse Cottage**, *16 Hilton Rd, South Carterton, T06-3798030, www.wairarapa.co.nz/courthouse* Very pleasant self-contained option right in the heart of town. As the name suggests the cottage was the former 1860s courthouse.

A **The Bothie**, *Admiral Rd, Gladstone, T06-3727724*. This is a fine cottage, which although in the nearby settlement of Gladstone (as opposed to Carterton) is worth the trip. It has a wonderful ambience, with a nice interior, decks and a log fire.

A **Carrington Cottages**, *T06-3798877, www.carringtoncottages.co.nz* Nearer Carterton, an option also worth considering.

B **Matador Motel**, *187 High St, T06-3798058*. Not as dodgy as the name suggests and the town's only motel.

Motorcamps and campsites

D **Campground**, *Belvedere Rd, T06-3798267*.

Greytown *p369*

Greytown and the immediate area also has its fair share of lovely B&Bs details of which are available at the VICs.

D **Campground**, *Kuratawhiti St, T06-3049837*.

Martinborough *p369*

Martinborough has a huge selection of B&Bs and self-contained cottages very similar in design and focusing on the romantic weekend market. You are advised to visit or call the VIC to choose and book.

LL **Wharekaukau Country Estate**, *Western*

*Lake Rd, Palliser Bay, T06-3077581,
www.wharekaukau.co.nz* This is one of the region's (and one of the country's) top luxury lodges. It is quite simply incredible and in a peaceful part of the North Island.

LL Martinborough Hotel, *The Square,
T06-3069350, www.martinboroughhotel.co.nz*
Recently refurbished, luxury rooms in elegant surroundings, restaurant and bar.

LL-L Aylstone, *Huangarua Rd, T06-3069505,
www.aylstone-martinborough.co.nz* Top-range lodge offering total pampering and fine wine and cuisine.

L Petit Hotel, *3 Kitchener St, T3069350,
www.petithotel.co.nz* Well-appointed suites with 'plump beds and rich furnishings', bound to attract any couple for a lively weekend. Very discreet hosts. There are numerous romantic self-contained cottages.

L-AL Olive Rose, *44 Dublin St, T06-9390169.*
Fully self-contained option in the heart of the village, has a lovely atmosphere, a log fire and clawfoot bath.

AL-A Margaret and Bruce Craig, *Dublin St,
T06-3069930, www.craigievar-
martinborough.co.nz* Have 3 cottage-style B&Bs on offer including the 'Craigievar', set in its own gardens and orchard.

A Claremont Motels, *38 Regent St,
T06-3069162, www.claremont-motels.co.nz*
One of the few places in New Zealand where a motel is hard to find! This one seems to live up to its near singular standing.

Motorcamps and campsites
D Campground, *on the corner of Princess and Dublin sts, T06-3069336.*

Cape Palliser *p370*
AL Hamenga Lodge, *Cape Palliser Rd,
T06-3078010.* Licensed lodge with a range of comfortable rooms, open fire.

B Ann's Abodes-Mangatoetoe,
T06-3077728, N-A.Gray@xtra.co.nz A modern, affordable self-contained house in a perfect spot, near the Ngawi village, the lighthouse and seal colony.

B-C Lake Ferry Hotel, *Lake Ferry Rd,
T06-3077831.* Basic, affordable, hotel accommodation, backpacker beds, good restaurant and bar attached.

Motorcamps and campsites
B-D Lake Ferry Motorcamp, *Lake Ferry Rd,*

T06-3077873. Busy, waterside and within walking distance of the hotel.
DOC also administers a campsite (self-registration) at the Putangirua Pinnacles, *T06-3078230.*

Featherstone *p371*
Featherstone has a number of luxury and mid-range lodges, B&Bs and self-contained cottages. The VIC has full listings.
**C-D Leeway Caravan Park and
Backpackers**, *8 Fitzherbert St, T06-3089811.*

---

❼ Eating

Masterton *p367*
There is not a huge amount of choice in Masterton but for something different try the
$$ Slow Food Café and Bar, *290 High St,
T06-3775100, www.slowfoodcafe.co.nz Open
daily.* Built in a former relocated stables the café has joined an international movement with the philosophy of combating the 'fast food' ethic with a focus on local fare enjoyed on the sit, not the run! Organic beers, dancing to jazz, blues and swing every Sat.
$$ Café Cecille, *in the heart of Queen
Elizabeth Park (eastern end of Park Av or from
Memorial Dr off Dixon St), T06-3701166.* Good choice for either lunch or dinner. Licensed.
$$ Plaza India, *3 Perry St, T06-3705177.* Does an above-average curry.
$ Café Strada, *next to the Regent Theatre on
Queen St (232), T06-3782070. Daily from
1000-late.* Should do for a snack and coffee.

Castlepoint *p368*
There are no restaurants, so the **village store**
T06-3726823, and the **Whakataki Hotel**,
4 km north, are your best bet.

Carterton *p369*
$$ Buckhorn Bar and Grill, *20 Memorial Sq,
T06-3797972. Tue-Sat 1130-late, Tue-Sun 1200-
1430, from 1800.* Pub grub in nice surroundings.
$ Wild Oats Bakery, *127 High St, T06-3795580.
Open from 0630.* Considered the best café.

Greytown *p369*
$$ Main St Deli, *T06-3049022. Daily from
0700-1800, Fri and Sat for dinner.* Has a large outdoor eating area and offers breakfast, lunch and dinner along with some great snacks and coffee, good value.

$$ **Wakelin House**, *123 Main St. Open from 1100 Wed-Mon*. Also very congenial and a favourite throughout the region for both lunch and dinner. Recommended.

Martinborough *p369*
As you might expect Martinborough is not short of choice.
$$ **Marlborough Hotel**, *T06-3069350. Daily 0800-late*. Popular for breakfast, lunch and dinner.

There are a number of good cafés, some within vineyards.
$$ **Old Winery Café**, *on the Margrain Estate, corner Ponatahi Rd and Huangarua Rd, T06-3068333. Open daily for lunch and dinner in summer (winter; Thu-Sun, dinner Fri and Sat)*. One of the most popular.

Featherstone *p371*
$ **Lady Featherstone**, *31 Fitzherbert St, T06-3086565. Mon-Fri 1000-1700, Sat/Sun 0830-1800*. Homemade offerings.

▲ Activities and tours

Masterton *p367*
Argo Tours (eight-wheel quad biking) **Dev Rae**, *T06-3782810, www.argo88.com*
Canoeing and jet skiing Seven Oaks, *T06-3723801*. 2-3 hour guided canoe trips and jet-skiing on the Whareama River, 1030 and 1330, from $25, child $10.
Climbing-wall Oasis, *2 Akura Rd, T06-3788789*.
Jet boat Wet-n-Wild, *T06-3068252, www.wetnwild.co.nz* Thrills and spills on the Ruamahanga and Manawatu Rivers.
Sightseeing and vineyard tours
Tranzit Coachlines, *T06-3771227*. Offer good value daily wine tours throughout the region, from $68.
Swimming Recreation Complex, *Dixon St*. Heated indoor and outdoor pools.
Walking The Kaiwhata Walk, *Ngahape Rd, T06-3722772, www.kawhatawalk.co.nz* Well-organized 3-day walk on private land towards the coast from the Ngahape Valley. Accommodation, food and transport arranged, from $125.

Castlepoint *p368*
Okau Station (see Sleeping above) offers a range of activities in their vast 'Wilderness Park'. The main beach is the venue for a famous horse race in March.
Fishing Legionnaires Charters, *T06-3726613*. There are fishing competitions in summer.

Greytown *p369*
Greytown is the base for
The Adventure Centre, *76 Main St, T06-3048565, www.ecoadventure.co.nz* It offers a wide range of activities including rafting half day and night trip (from $70), kayaking or 'river bugging' (from $70), (abseiling (from $55) and caving (from $85), mainly centred around the Waiohine Gorge. The full-day 'extreme trip', which is a combination of these activities, costs a very reasonable $95.
Ballooning NZ, *T06-3798223*. Will take you up, up and away (if the weather is settled) for an early morning 2-3 hour flight for about $260, breakfast included.

Martinborough *p369*
In an effort to lure the well-heeled Wellingtonians there are a wide range of activity operators around Martinborough. You have the choice of canoeing, quad and mountain biking, skydiving, horse trekking, clay-bird shooting, diving and jet boating. The VIC will fill you in with all the details and book on your behalf.
Tora Walks, *T06-3078862; toracoastalwalk@wise.net.nz* Offer an interesting and varied 3-day coastal tramp with an equal variety of accommodation types. $120 (meals optional extra).

● Directory

Bike hire Christina Estate Vineyard, *T06-3068920*, or **Martinborough Bike Rental**, *T06-3068477*, from $25 half day, $35 full day.
Car hire Graeme Jones Car Rental, *81 Dixon St, T06-3786667*, from $60 per day.
Internet Martinborough VIC and at the library, *Queen St, T06-3789666*.

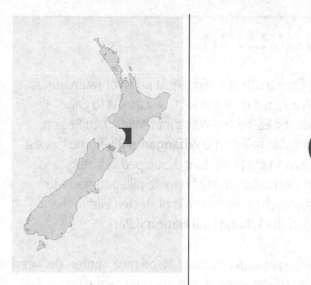

Wanganui and Manawatu

Introduction

Stretching from south of Levin to just north of Taumarunui, and from Wanganui on the West Coast across to Cape Turnagain in the east is the Wanganui/Manawatu Region, scythed almost in half by the **Whanganui River**, the longest navigable river in the North Island. Steeped in history, and supporting a rich watershed of remote hills adorned with native bush, much of the region is protected within the boundaries of the **Whanganui National Park**.

Settlement began with groups of Maori moa hunters between 1400 and 1650, who were in turn followed by the first Europeans; whalers from Kapiti Island. The rich agricultural lands have now made the region the sixth most populous in New Zealand with almost half of that within the urban boundaries of **Palmerston North** and **Wanganui**. Palmerston North, home to New Zealand's largest university, is also an important national seat of learning. Although not blessed with the tourist bounty of other parts, the region still has much to offer and provides a good base to explore the lower North Island and surrounding national parks. The Whanganui National Park is especially popular with kayakers and trampers, who can leave civilization behind for days on end.

★ Don't miss...

❶ Exploring the historic **Whanganui River** (the country's longest navigable waterway) by kayak or jet boat. Take a side trip to the 'Bridge to Nowhere', page 395.

❷ The mail-run up the **Whanganui River Road**, page 394, through the historic mission settlements of Atene, Koriniti, Hiruharama (Jerusalem) and Pipiriki.

❸ The **New Zealand Rugby Museum** in Palmerston North, page 381. Pay homage to the All Blacks.

❹ The township of **Bulls**, page 383.

❺ The **World Annual Gumboot Throwing Festival** in Taihape (November) – the 'Gumboot Capital of the World', page 383.

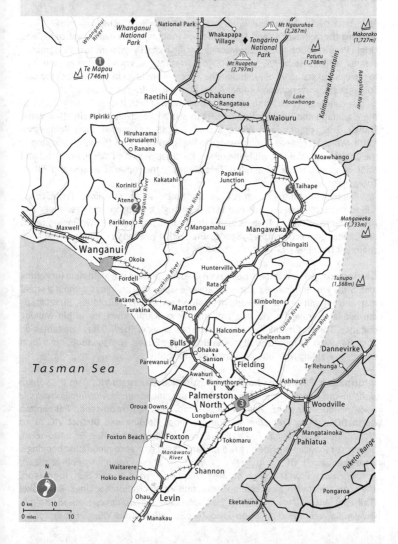

Palmerston North and around

→ *Phone code: 06 Colour map 3, grid B3 Population: 75,000*

On the banks of the Manawatu River and in the heart of flat, rural Manawatu, is the pleasant university and agricultural service town of Palmerston North. Although set away from SH1 and not exactly blessed with a wealth of touristical product, 'Palmy' can provide a good base to explore the southern half of the North Island and is an important gateway west, through the impressive Manawatu Gorge, to the Wairarapa and Hawkes Bay. Other than Massey University, which is the second largest in the country, the town is perhaps most famous for its Rugby Museum, a place of almost spiritual significance, where many New Zealand rugby fanatics come on a pilgrimage to pay homage to their All Black heroes.

Ins and outs → *Palmerston North is 140 km from Wellington and 546 km from Auckland*

Getting there New Zealand Link, T0800-737000, www.airnewzealand.co.nz, and **Origin Pacific**, T0800-302302, www.originpacific.co.nz, fly regularly to most domestic centres, while **Freedom Air**, T0800-600500, T099126801, www.freedomair.com, flies to the eastern seaboard of Australia. The airport is about 4 km northwest of the city, T06-3514415, www.pnairport.co.nz A taxi from the centre costs around $12.

By car, Palmerston North is about 30 km west of SH1. It is the main gateway to the Wairarapa and Hawke's Bay via SH3 to SH2 at Woodville. **Intercity, Newmans, Tranzit**, T06-3554955, and **White Star**, T06-3588777, operate from Palmerston North. White Star runs a regular service to Wanganui and New Plymouth and stop at the Courthouse, Main St, while the others run through to Wellington, Auckland and Napier and stop at the Palmerston Travel Centre at the corner of Main St and Pitt St, T06-3554955.

Palmerston North is on the main north south rail line. **TranzScenic**, T0800-802802, operates only one service through the region, the Overlander and Northerner to Auckland. There is also a daily commuter service to Wellington called the Capital Connection, T06-4983000. The station is about 2½ km from the town centre off Tremaine Av.

Getting around Be warned. Because it is so flat, 'Palmy' is a nightmare for getting lost. Stray too far from the central square and visible tall buildings without a street map and you will be lost in a world of fast food and chain retail outlets. Street maps are available from the VIC. Most of the sights within town are within walking distance. **Tranzit Citylink** is the local area bus service. The VIC has timetables on T050-8446749. Standard adult fare $1.80. **Madge Buses**, T06-3564896, run a local service to Fielding from outside Farmers on King St.

Information **Palmerston North and Destination Manawatu VIC**, ① *in the square right in the heart of the town*, T06-3546593, *manawatu.visitor-info@xtra.co.nz www.manawatunz.co.nz Mon-Fri 0900-1700, Sat/Sun 1000-1500.* **Palmerston North DOC**, ① *717 Tremaine Av*, T06-3509700. **Fielding and District VIC**, ① *10 Manchester Sq, Fielding*, T06-3233318, *www.fielding.co.nz Mon-Fri 0900-1600, Sat 1000-1300*, can provide all the detail and assist with accommodation bookings. **Horowhenua VIC**, ① *93 Oxford St, Levin*, T06-3678440, *horowhenua.visitor@clear.net.nz Mon-Fri 0900-1730, Sat and Sun 1000-1500.* They can assist with all accommodation and transportation bookings. **Rangitikei (Taihape) VIC**, ① *in the Town Hall, Hautapu St, Taihape*, T06-38 80350, *www.rangitikei.com Daily 0900-1700.* 'Access-a-Bull' **Bulls VIC**, ① *113 Bridge St,*

Palmerston North

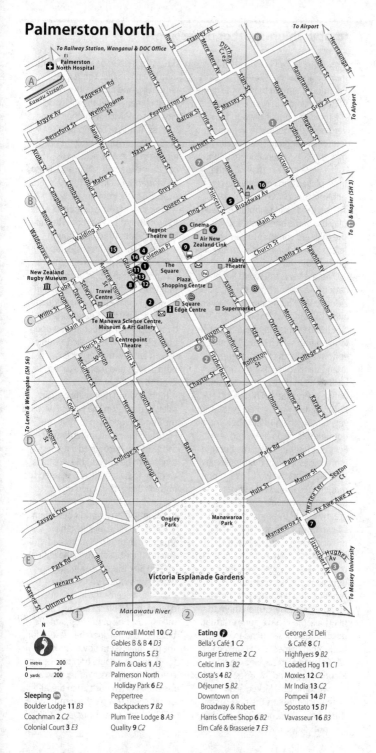

Sleeping 🛏

Boulder Lodge **11** *B3*
Coachman **2** *C2*
Colonial Court **3** *E3*
Cornwall Motel **10** *C2*
Gables B & B **4** *D3*
Harringtons **5** *E3*
Palm & Oaks **1** *A3*
Palmerson North
  Holiday Park **6** *E2*
Peppertree
  Backpackers **7** *B2*
Plum Tree Lodge **8** *A3*
Quality **9** *C2*

Eating 🍴

Bella's Café **1** *C2*
Burger Extreme **2** *C2*
Celtic Inn **3** *B2*
Costa's **4** *B2*
Déjeuner **5** *B2*
Downtown on
  Broadway & Robert
  Harris Coffee Shop **6** *B2*
Elm Café & Brasserie **7** *E3*
George St Deli
  & Café **8** *C1*
Highflyers **9** *B2*
Loaded Hog **11** *C1*
Moxies **12** *C2*
Mr India **13** *C2*
Pompeii **14** *B1*
Spostato **15** *B1*
Vavasseur **16** *B3*

Rugby Union-sport or obsession?

Like Australia, New Zealand finds much of its national identity in sport. Paramount among these is the game of Rugby Union. In New Zealand it is the focus of a public devotion that verges on the obsessive. Although founded in England, New Zealand has over the last century adopted Rugby as if it were its own, making it the most played and certainly the most publicly-supported national sport. The methods and techniques used to play the game effectively and within the rules are complicated and best left to a long discussion with any kiwi bloke in the pub.

Over the years the world famous national team known as the All Blacks – due to their iconic black strip – have added a particular 'Pacific' or 'Southern Hemisphere' flair and style to the game, which to the layman, is epitomized by the fearsome *haka* (Maori dance or challenge) that is performed in front of the opposition before every match. The New Zealand Rugby Union was formed in 1892 and very quickly the All Blacks became a dominant force on the world stage. For decades until the game became more widespread and professional (and like sport the world over more moneyed) the All Blacks were practically invincible and a force greatly feared by any opposition. Drawn from a rich array of national provincial teams the selected 15 players are considered the crème de la crème – like royalty once were in Britain and Hollywood stars are in America, and this places an inordinate amount of pressure upon them to play well. Many have done just that, becoming almost legendary household names, like Colin Meads, who played 55 tests; George Nepia, a Maori who played 32 times; Grant Fox an awesome goal kicker; Sean Fitzpatrick, perhaps the best captain in the history of the game and of course, let's not forget, that man- mountain,

the unstoppable Jonah Lomu (note that Jonah is in fact Tongan by nationality and not a native Maori).

But in many ways the All Blacks have become victims of their own success. With the creation of the Rugby World Cup in 1987 (held every four years) the All Blacks were naturally expected to win and did so, comfortably. But in 1991 they lost to Australia in the semi-finals, which was a cause of some despair, but felt to be merely an aberration. Then in 1995, in South Africa, the bough broke, when a team considered to be unbeatable lost to the South African 'Springboks' in the dying moments of the final. Back home in New Zealand there was subsequently a period of palpable national depression and anger directed upon both players and the coach. Losing was an entirely new experience to both players and more so to the New Zealand public.

It did not end there. Once again salt was rubbed in the wound when in the Rugby World Cup of 1999 the French (considered underdogs) in the semi-finals trounced a team still thought to be unbeatable. Australia went on to beat France. It seemed the unthinkable was happening – Australia was beginning to take over the mantle of the world's best team.

Since 1999 the All Blacks have struggled in the Tri-Nations and against the Australians in the annual one-off Bledisloe Cup. Although many Kiwis would vehemently disagree, it seems the all-conquering days of the All Blacks are over and are merely just one of the best, not the best. For the outsider the reasons for the downfall seem obvious – if the focus on a loss could only be one of gracious acceptance rather than a rapacious witch hunt, then the All Blacks could reverse the trend. The 2003 World Cup will prove crucial.

They can help with finding 'Afford-a Bull' accommodation requirements – and that's no bull.

History

The Maori name for the river, *Manawatu*, is 'still breath' and relates to a lullaby of the coastal tribes from the west coast of the lower North Island. It tells the story of the journey of a cuckolded husband, Hau, to retrieve his wayward wife. Poor Hau named many rivers during his quest to win back his spouse. Sadly, when he eventually found her, she was in the arms of another lover in Wellington – probably a stockbroker. When love-sick Hau came to the Manawatu River, it was so cold it made his breath stand still hence the name, 'still breath'. The local Rangitane Iwi lived in the area for hundreds of years before the Europeans began to settle in the mid 1800s. With the rich surrounding agricultural lands, it did not take Palmerston long to develop and prosper. By 1930 the population was about a third of what it is today.

Sights

The best-known attraction in Palmy is the **New Zealand Rugby Museum**, ① *87 Cuba St, T06-3586947, www.rugbymuseum.co.nz Mon-Sat 1000-1200 and 1330-1600, Sun 1330-1600. Adults $4, child $2.* Established in 1969, it was the first of its kind in the country and contains the largest collection of rugby memorabilia, including shirts, caps, photographs, boots, ties and programmes. There are also videos and detailed accounts of every All Black game since 1870 available for specialist research. If you have a particular question there is (of course) a wealth of fanatics on hand to fill you in on every pass, ruck and maul.

The **Te Manawa Science Centre, Museum and Art Gallery**, ① *396 Main St, T06-3555000, www.temanawa.co.nz, daily 1000-1700, $6, child $4,* is a progressive and modern centre that integrates the usual social, cultural and artistic heritage with hands-on science displays. It is split into three main parts, the museum, gallery and science centre, all of which are worth visiting. There are the some interesting Maori *taonga* and a few nationally significant artworks by contemporary gurus like Colin McCahon and Ralf Hotere. The gallery upstairs often hosts important national touring exhibitions and as always there is a popular hands-on, interactive science section.

If you head west towards the university and the river (Fitzherbert Avenue, then Park Road) you can access the **Victoria Esplanade Gardens**, ① *open dawn to dusk,* a very pleasant mix of bush, lawn and gardens that grace the banks of the river. There are numerous walking tracks and a play park complete with miniature railway for the kids.

As usual there are leaflets available from the VIC outlining other city walks and open gardens in the area. From a historical prospective the **Regent Theatre** is of particular note and a main feature of the city's heritage walk. Elsewhere, horticultural properties feature heavily under the banner of *Health Herbs and Honey.* The **Pohangina Valley Tourist Route,** which takes in a pleasant mix of rural scenery, gardens, craft outlets and the market town of Fielding (see below) is also worth considering (best broken up with an overnight stay). On a rainy day, Mr and Mrs Fit and the wee fitettes can head for the city's climbing-wall at **City Rock**, ① *217 Featherston St, T06-3574552, www.cityrock.co.nz Tue-Thu 1530-2200, Fri 1530-1830, Sat 1000-1900, Sun 1200-1900 1000-2200, $11.* It is a 10-m high top rope and boulder wall.

While you are wandering around Palmerston North you may occasionally glimpse

● *The town is named after a former British Prime Minister Viscount Palmerston, the 'North'*
● *being added in 1871 to distinguish it from another Palmerston in Otago, South Island.*

☷ World Gumboot Festival

It's October and an air of serious anticipation has fallen on the town of Taihape. In a town usually full of chatter and gossip, words are few and the looks distrustful. The town's men-folk gather in the pub and huddle around tables, whispering. When a stranger walks in they don't look up, but down at his feet…it's time.

They disperse and from behind closed doors the 'Skellerup Perth' is coming out of the closet. Muscles are flexed. Into the night and down in the gardens, covert practice sessions take place. Cats scatter and the moonlit sky fills with the silhouettes of hurling Gumboots. The great festival is nigh.

The World Gumboot Throwing Festival is a unique and inevitably highly-entertaining festival that takes place most years in November of in Taihape – the self proclaimed 'Gumboot capital of the world'. Apparently, it involves both 'serious' and 'novelty' throwing for teams and individuals of all ages. How quite one becomes a 'serious', thrower of a gumboot, or throws one 'seriously' is a mystery, but serious, it can be with a prize of $5000 for a new New Zealand record (currently; men 38.66 m, women 24.92 m). Note that the actual world record is held by the Finns, an astonishing men 63.98m, and women 40.78m.

the graceful white blades of the **Tararua Wind Farm** towers, on the hills to the west of town. If you fancy a closer look there is a private access route from Centre and Back Roads (off Fitzherbert East Road from Massey University) and via Jackson's Farm to Hall Block Road on the east side of the Manawatu Gorge (SH3). Bear in mind, however, that access is restricted and you may be best going with a tour operator (see below). ▸▸ *See Sleeping, Eating and other listings, pages 384-387.*

Around Palmerston North

Fielding → *Colour map 3, grid A6*
Fielding sits in the heart of the Manawatu 'flatlands' on the banks of the Oroua River. It is a pretty place, relatively prosperous and particularly well known for its private and public gardens. Indeed, their careful nurturing has played a key role in the town's run of success in the nation's *Most Beautiful Small Town Awards*, which it has won a remarkable 12 times. Although there is not a huge amount to see or do in Fielding there are a scattering of small museums (traction engines being a speciality), craft outlets and of course, **gardens**. But even if that does not appeal and you do not have green fingers, it is a pleasant place to stop and take a wander. Better still take a tour by horse and cart, or watch the local farmers bidding at the **stock sales** on a Friday.

Levin and Foxton → *Colour map 3, grid B3*
Levin and Foxton, both southwest of Palmerston North lie in the heart of the Horowhenua region. This narrow strip of land bordered by the Tararua Ranges to the west and the Tasman Sea to the east is known for its rich alluvial soils and subsequent fruit-and-vegetable growing industries. Earlier industries included flax milling and timber exports.

The **Tokomaru Steam Engine Museum**, ① *on SH57, T06-3298867, Mon-Sat 0900-1500, Sun 1030-1500, $5, child $2*, is the highlight (if not the sum total) of Tokomaru village, 32 km north of Levin. The museum offers the enthusiast or the layperson the chance to see the country's largest collection of working steam engines. There are a number of static displays and the occasional 'Steam Ups' (by all accounts).

The **Lake Papaitonga Scenic Reserve**, 4 km southwest of Levin, offers a delightful short walk (30 minutes) through some superb native bush, before reaching two viewpoints across the lakes. The atmosphere here, particularly at sunset, is magical. The area is rich in both Maori history and birdlife, details of which are outlined at the park's entrance.

Himatangi Beach which is off SH1 between Foxton and Sanson is considered the region's best. The sand dunes here are up to 19 km wide and make up New Zealand's largest expanse of sand country. This sense of wilderness, together with the driftwood strewn along the tide line, make a trip well worth while.

Taihape → *Phone code: 06 Colour map 3, grid B3 Population: 2000*

North of 'Palmy' in SH1, in the odd little region of **Rangitikei**, is Taihape, a fairly nondescript town quietly serving the local dairy farming industry. At first sight, there appears to be little of interest, other than a few unremarkable cafés, motels and shops, but there are some notable activities in the area and some of the major river adventure companies are based in the town. The VIC can provide information about a number of garden visits and heritage tours in the area, and then, of course, there's Taihape's famous and very silly festival, which brings some life and 'sole' to the town. Given the town's love of footwear and completely unique way of abusing it perhaps it would be rude not to take a quick peek at the giant **corrugated gumboot** at the end of Huia St (left off Hautapu heading north). ▸▸ *See Sleeping, Eating and other listings, pages 384-386.*

Mangaweka → *Colour map 3, grid B3*

Mangaweka is best known for its DC-3, which sits next to SH1 and houses a café. It is also the base for the Rangitikei River Adventure Company, which operates a variety of adventure packages on the river. There is a basic **camping** ground in the village and a number of local walks established by DoC. ▸▸ *See Activities, page 386.*

Bulls → *Population: 3898 Colour map 3, grid B3*

The small agricultural service town of Bulls stands of the junction of SH3 and SH1, midway between Wanganui and Palmerston North. Blink and you'll miss it, but take a closer look and you may be surprised to learn that the township was not named after our four-legged friends, but one James Bull, who was one of the first settlers in 1858. By all accounts he was quite the entrepreneur and created so much of the town's infrastructure that in 1872 the government approved the replacement of the original name for the settlement – Rangitikei, with Bulls. But our James has a lot to answer for. In the desperate effort to put Bulls on the map, the community has gone to ridiculous lengths to incorporate its name into every one of its amenities. Take a look around and you'll find the VIC (see page 378) which is 'Inform-a-Bull', the chemist which is 'Dispense-a-Bull', the fire station 'Extinguish-a-Bull', the police station' Const-a-Bull' and the church, which is 'Forgive-a-Bull', and so it goes on. It is interesting to note a few major omissions in town, like the public toilets and pub, and as you head out on SH3 there seems to be the most glaring omission of them all – a sign saying 'Antiques and Collectibles', clearly owned by the black sheep of the town. Annoyingly, this is all very infectious, and for days you will find yourself suffering from this chronic 'Voca-Bull-ary' affliction. Some may find Bulls entertaining, but others may find such behaviour 'Question-a-Bull'.

To the south of Bulls keep an eye open for fields of 'bulltiful' sunflowers which are at their best between January and March

● *For an explanation of the sleeping and eating price codes used in this guide, see the inside* ● *front cover. Other relevant information is provided in the Essentials chapter, see page 51.*

Wanganui and Manawatu Palmerston North and around

At the RNZAF base at Ohakea which is on SH1 between Sanson and Bulls is the **Ohakea Wing RNZF Museum**, ① *T06-3515020. Daily 0930-1630. $8, child $3.* Here there are historical and hands-on displays, as well as a flight simulator, videos and a café. Great for kids.

Just north of Bulls (8 km) signposted off SH1 is the six-hectare **Amazing Maize Maze**, ① *T06-3277615, www.maze.co.nz, Dec-Apr, Sun-Thu 1000-1800, Fri-Sat 1000-2200, $9, child $5,* which has over 10km of paths to baffle your orientation skills. 'Moonlight mazeing' on Fri and Sat (bring a torch!). The maze takes on a different theme each year which if viewed from the air displays exceptional skill.

⦿ Sleeping

Palmerston North *p378*
The town has the inevitable rash of motels most of which are along Fitzherbert Av or the Pioneer Highway.

LL-AL **The Palm and Oaks**, *183 Grey St, T06-3590755, www.thepalm-oaks.co.nz* Modern, luxury self-contained Italian deco- style villa a short walk from the city centre, spa pool, courtyard, decks and off-street parking.

L-A **Quality Hotel/Motel**, *110 Fitzherbert Av, T06-3568059, www.qualitypalmerston.co.nz* The Quality is one of Palmy's few hotels but doesn't let the side down, restaurant, bar, spa and sauna.

AL **Cornwall Motel**, *101 Fitzherbert Av, T06-3549010, www.cornwallmotorlodge.co.nz* One of the newest along the strip and earning a good reputation, spas.

AL-A **Coachman Motel**, *134 Fitzherbert Av, T06-3565065, www.coachman.co.nz* Pleasant and well appointed, with café, gardens and an open fire.

A **Boulder Lodge**, *Pohangina Valley West Rd, Ashurst, T06-3294746, www.boulder-lodge.co.nz* Some distance from Palmerston North this is a popular and isolated self-contained wooden cabin. You arrive by 4-wheel drive and can have a bath outside in an open fire heated tub under the stars. It has no electricity but LPG which provides heating and hot showers. All this is part of the charm.

A **Gables B&B**, *179 Fitzherbert Av, T06-3583209, thegables.pn.nz@xtra.co.nz* Refreshing historic homestead on the main motel drag.

A **Plum Tree Lodge**, *97 Russell St, T06-3587813, plumtreelodge@xtra.co.nz* Well-appointed self-contained lodge close to town centre.

Other slightly cheaper motel options worth considering are:

A **Colonial Court**, *305 Fitzherbert Av, T06-3593888* and

A **Harringtons**, *301 Fitzherbert Av, T06-3547259, www.harringtons.co.nz* Very friendly.

C-D **Peppertree Backpackers**, *121 Grey St, T06-3554054.* This is by far the best backpackers in town. A YHA associate in an old rambling, single storey house, and close to the centre of town. Excellent facilities, open fire and garden where you can view the owner's homemade racing car.

C-D **Palmerston North Holiday Park**, *133 Dittmer Dr, T06-3580349.* Rather tired but next to the river and adjacent to the Esplanade Park.

Taihape *p383*
There are a scattering of good farmstays in the area.

AL-B **Mairenui Farm Holidays** have a number of good value self-contained or B&B options. The VIC can also help with bookings.

A **Aspen Court Motel**, *Mataroa Rd North (SH1), T06-3881999, www.aspencourt.co.nz* The newest motel in town, with above average facilities.

B **Taihape Motels**, *Kuku and Robin St, T06-3880456.* An older, cheaper option with adequate facilities and close to the centre of town.

C-D **River Valley Lodge** , *T06-3881444 (see Activities below).* Recommended backpackers.

Motorcamps and campsites
C-D **Abba Motorcamp**, *Old Abattoir Rd (3 km north of town), T06-3880718.* Campervans and tents basically accommodated.

❶ Eating

Palmerston North *p378*

The town is blessed with good restaurants and cafés. Most are on Broadway Av, George St and Cuba St, just off the main square.

$$$ **Dejeuner**, *159 Broadway*. *T06-9525581, www.dejeuner.co.nz Mon-Sat 1800-late*. A small restaurant that is well established in the town and offers an imaginative blackboard menu.

$$$ **Vavasseur**, *201 Broadway, T06-3593167. Mon-Sat from 1800*. Similar in style and an award-winner, particularly well known for its New Zealand lamb dishes.

$$$ **Spostato**, *213 Cuba St, T06-9523400. Daily from 1800-late*. Italian-style restaurant, at the top end of the Cuba St offerings.

$$$ **Bella's Café**, *2 The Square, T06-3578616. Open for lunch Tue-Sat from 1100 and for dinner Mon-Sat 1800-late*. Another popular choice and offers a mix of Italian, Thai and traditional Pacific Rim dishes. Cosy atmosphere and great service.

Most of the pubs (see below) offer good affordable lunches and dinners.

$$ **Costa's**, *282 Cuba St, T06-9525577. Daily from 1800*. A popular Tex Mex-style restaurant.

$$ **Mr India**, *79E George St, T06-3545075. Daily from 1730*. Has a loyal following.

$$ **Moxies**, *81 George St, T06-3554238. Daily from 0730*. New café already established as a popular spot for breakfast, lunch and dinner offering an interesting blackboard menu.

$$ **Elm Café and Brasserie**, *Fitzherbert St, T06-3554418. Daily 0900-1700 and Wed-Sat 1830-late*. Although a bit away from the centre of town, it is worth the effort with great traditional cuisine in rather grand Tuscan-style surroundings.

$ **George St Deli and Café**, *corner of George and Main St, T06-3576663. Mon-Sat 0630-1730*. Has one of the finest breakfasts and perhaps the best coffee in town.

$ **Pompeii**, *198 The Square, T06-9525575. Daily from 1700 (deliveries available)*. For a pizza you can't go far wrong here.

$ **Burger Extreme**, *at the Old Grand Hotel, 339 Church St, T06-3577224. Daily 1200-1400 and 1700-2100, (deliveries available)*. Extremely huge burgers.

$ **Celtic Inn**, *see below*. About the best cheap pub lunch.

$ **Robert Harris**, coffee shop is good for a quick snack and reliable cuppa and there are various other fast food outlets in the **Downtown on Broadway** shopping mall.

Taihape *p383*

$$ **The Brown Sugar Café**, *Huia St, T06-3881880. Daily 0900-1700, Fri-Sun until 2030*. The best café in town with good coffee, breakfasts and an open fire.

There are a number of restaurants on Hautapu St:

$$ **The Venison Kitchen**, *65B Hautapu St, T06-3881011*. A fairly unique venison café;

Al Centro, *105 Hautapu St, T06-3880593. Tue-Sun from 1700*. Decent Italian fare.

❶ Pubs

Palmerston North *p378*

Celtic Inn, *tucked down the Regent Arcade off Broadway, T06-3575571*. The best bet for traditionalists.

For the trendsetters and modernists:

Highflyers, *on the corner of The Square and Main St, T06-3575155*;

Loaded Hog, *on corner of George and Coleman Sts, T06-3565417*.

❶ Entertainment

Centrepoint Theatre, *corner Pitt and Church St, T06-3545740, www.centrepoint.co.nz* Established in 1974 and one of the few North Island theatres that can boast its own full-time professional theatre company. There are regular shows, many of national importance, covering comedy to classic dramas, with an emphasis on New Zealand plays.

Regent Theatre, *on Broadway, T06-3502100*. Opened in 1998 and with a seating capacity of almost 1500 it hosts larger events such as ballet, musicals, orchestral performances and comedy.

Abbey Theatre, *369 Church St*. Hosts other mainly musical (rock and pop) events For most performances in the town you can get more information and book with **Ticketek**, *T06-3581186*.

❀ Festivals and events

Taihape p383

The **World Gumboot Throwing Festival** (see above) is a serious event. Not just any old 'wellie' can be used. It must be: "A Skellerup Perth size 8 Men's, of ordinary standard stock, and be available from a regular vendor of footwear, and have no structural or design changes. It cannot be weighted or lightened. The height of the gumboot must be a minimum of 36 cm/14 in and weigh not less than 964 grams/34 oz. The boot may not be folded, twisted or distorted. The boot must be approved for throwing by the organizers". As well as the official throwing there are numerous other secondary gumboot events including a 'Gumboot Art Competition', 'Shoot-the- boot', 'Carve-a-boot' and 'Flycast-a-boot'. There are also food, art and craft stalls and some of the other, far more traditional activities of shearing, milking and shoeing to boot. All in all the festival is great fun and highly recommended. If you want to take part and fancy your chances with the size 8, there is a participation fee of $4 for individuals, $20 for groups, *T06-3881126, gumbootcountry@xtra.co.nz*

▲ Activities and tours

Palmerston North and Fielding pp378 and 382

Gliding Weekend flights are available with the local gliding club at the **Fielding Airfield**, *Taonui, T06-3238389*.
Golf There are a number of good courses in the area including **Brookfields**, *Te Matai Rd, T06-3580749*; and **Fielding Golf Course**, *Fielding, T06-3238636*.
Horse trekking Timeless Horse Treks, *Gorge Rd, Ballance, T06-3766157, www.timelesshorsetreks.co.nz* Half- to multi-day trips. **Jet boats** Adventure Jet Tours, *T06-3772114, www.adventurejet.co.nz*
Kayaking Manawatu Gorge Adventures, *T0800-746688, www.teamtactix.co.nz*
Quad bikes Yes, the darn things are here too. **Go 4 Wheels**, *George Rd, Ballance, T06-3767136, go4wheels@amcom.co.nz* From $65 for 1 hr, wind farm 2 hrs from $115.
Scenic flights Helipro, *T06-3571348,*

www.helipro.co.nz Offer a range of flights including the City Panorama, $60, 10 minutes and the Windfarm Wizzer, $95, 20 minutes.
Sightseeing and specialist tours
Bush Pigeon Tours, *T06-3766288*. They also do trips around the town and beyond (including the Tararua Wind Farm).
Tranzit, *T06-3771227*. Offers tours of the Wairarapa vineyards from $68.
Swimming Lido Aquatic Centre, *Park Rd, T06-3572684*. Mon-Fri 0600-2000, Sat and Sun 0800-2000. From $2.50.

Taihape p383

Adrenaline Gravity Action, *based at Mokai Bridge (off SH1) south of Taihape, T0800-802864, www.gravitycanyon.co.nz* Has greatly expanded its adrenaline sapping operations in recent months offering not only the North Island's highest bungee (80m, from $99) but also New Zealand's longest Flying Fox (1 km) and a Giant Swing that swoops into the canyon. Even if you are a big girl's blouse you can still hide in the café and watch from a distance.
Fly fishing Rangitikei Anglers, *Kawhatau Valley, Mangaweka, T06-3825852, www.flyfishers.co.nz* Tarata Fishaway, *T06-3880354, www.tarata.co.nz* Both rafting and fly fishing trips on the Rangitikei. B&B and self-contained accommodation available.
River Adventures River Valley, *T06-3881444, www.rivervalley.co.nz* A range of activities including white water rafting ($109), horse trekking ($49) and kayaking ($109, hire from $25). Accommodation available (A-D). **Rangitikei River Adventures**, *Main Rd, Mangaweka, T0800-655747, www.rra.co.nz* A variety of river trips including rafting, kayaking, overnight campouts and wilderness safaris, 1 hr from $30, half day from $55, full day from $110. Four days from $550. Suitable for families.
Scenic flights Wanganui Aero Works, *Valley Rd, T06-3881696*. Helicopter fishing, hunting and sightseeing trips.

○ Shopping

Palmerston North p378

Books Bruce McKenzie Bookshop, *George St, T06-3569922*. Makes a refreshing change from the large bookshop chains.

New Zealand art and crafts Ivy and Moss, *481 Main St*, and **Something Different**, *117 Victoria Av.* **Fine art** Taylor Jensen Gallery, *39 George St, T06-3554278, www.finearts.co.nz*

❶ Directory

Airline offices Air NZ, *30 Broadway Av, T06-3518800*. **Car hire** Ward Hire, *445 Tremaine Av, T06-3553043*. Rental Car Centre, *320 Rangitikei St, T06-3574316*.

Rent-A-Dent, *T06-3555227*. Internet ECafe, *corner Church St and Fitzherbert (The Square), T06-3537899. Mon-Thu 0900-2400, Fri, Sat 24hr*. Very fast. **Post office** *124 The Square, T06-3569495. Mon-Fri 0830-1730, Sat 0900-1700*. **Medical services** Palmerston North Hospital, *Southern Cross, 21 Carroll St, T06-3569169*. City Health, *22 Victoria Av, T06-3553300*. **Taxi** Taxis Gold and Black, *T06-3555059*. **Useful addresses** AA, *185 Broadway Av, T06-3577039*. Police Church St, *T06-3579999*.

Wanganui → *Phone code: 06 Colour map 3, grid B2 Population: 41,000*

Wanganui lies at the mouth of the Whanganui River roughly half way between Wellington and New Plymouth. Proud of its river and once a bustling port, Wanganui is now principally an agricultural service town and the southern gateway to the Whanganui River National Park. The town boasts a rich heritage and retains some fine buildings as well as a reputable museum and a number of parks and gardens. In summer the main street is ablaze with a thousand hanging baskets of flowers and throughout the year the restored steamboat 'Waimarie' plies the great river, reminding both locals and visitors of days gone by.

Ins and outs

Getting there Wanganui airport is near the coast about 5 km to the southwest of town and is served by **Air New Zealand Link,** T0800-737000. There is an airport shuttle operated by **Ash's Transport,** T06-3477444, (Palmerston North included) or call a taxi (see page 391). By car, Wanganui is on the main SH3 coastal route 162 km southwest of New Plymouth and 196 km north of Wellington (via SH1 which joins SH3 at Bulls). SH4 from Te Kuiti (250 km) terminates in Wanganui. **Newmans** and **Intercity** buses stop at 156 Ridgeway St. **White Star,** T06-3476677, operates a service between New Plymouth and Wellington (via Palmerston North) stopping at 161 Ingestre St. The VIC facilitates all national bus bookings.

Getting around Wanganui has 4 looped bus routes which run Mon-Fri (weekends vary) by **Tranzit Citylink (Horizons),** T0508-446749, www.horizons.mwlp, linking the main suburbs, including Castlecliff on the coast. All start from Maria Place in the centre of town, off Victoria Av. Standard fare is $2. Pick up a timetable from the VIC. Note that there is a **Mail Run** service operating to Pipiriki and the Whanganui National Park via the Whanganui River Rd (see River Road Tours, page 394). **Information** **Wanganui VIC,** ① *101 Guyton St, T06-3490508, www.wanganuinz.com, www.rivernz.com Mon-Fri 0830-1700, Sat and Sun 0900-1500*. They have details about local gardens, the Wanganui Heritage Walk and local Arts Trail. **DOC Wanganui Conservancy Office,** ① *Ingestre Chambers, 74 Ingestre St, T06-3452402*.

History

The Whanganui River was an important focus for the Maori and provided a vital supply route both north and south. Even the great Polynesian explorer Kupe was believed to have travelled up the river in 800 AD and the first Maori settlement dates back to about 1000. Intertribal conflicts were common and came to a head (literally) in the 1830 when Ngati Toa, chief Te Rauparaha from Kapiti Island, sacked the local tribe and celebrated with a cannibal feast. Heads continued to roll with the arrival of the first Europeans in 1831 in the form of trader Joe Rowe, reputed to be a dealer in preserved Maori heads. Sadly for ol' Joe it was a case of what comes around goes around and in a dispute with the Maori his head was also lopped off and preserved, the rest of him providing dinner. Thankfully, in 1840 the missionaries arrived and for a while, everyone began to keep their heads as opposed to losing them. About the same time the New Zealand Company, keen to extend land purchases beyond Wellington, made a rather dubious deal with the local Maori and 'bought' 40,000 acres. Once the Maori realized that this spurious transaction meant the permanent loss of their land, almost a decade of bitter wrangling followed. British troops were brought in, but eventually, after arbitration, an agreed cash payment was made in 1848. The Maori went on to assist the *Pakeha* during the Taranaki Land Wars of the 1860s. With the establishment of a railway linking New Plymouth, via Wanganui to Wellington, together with the importance of the river as a communication link north, the town prospered.

Sights

Queen's Park was a former British stockade site during the New Zealand Wars of the 1860s and is east of Victoria Ave. It is essentially the cultural heart of the city and home to the Wanganui Regional Museum, the War Memorial, the Alexander and District Libraries and the Sargeant Gallery.

The **Wanganui Regional Museum**, ① *T06-3457443, www.wanganui-museum.org.nz, Mon-Sat 1000-1630, Sun 1300-1630, $2, child 60c*, is of particular note due to rich

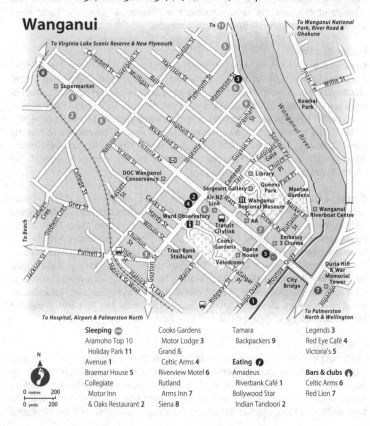

Wanganui

Sleeping		Cooks Gardens	Tamara	Legends 3
Aramoho Top 10		Motor Lodge 3	Backpackers 9	Red Eye Café 4
Holiday Park 11		Grand &		Victoria's 5
Avenue 1		Celtic Arms 4	**Eating**	
Braemar House 5		Riverview Motel 6	Amadeus	**Bars & clubs**
Collegiate		Rutland	Riverbank Café 1	Celtic Arms 6
Motor Inn		Arms Inn 7	Bollywood Star	Red Lion 7
& Oaks Restaurant 2		Siena 8	Indian Tandoori 2	

local history and the influence of the river down the years. There is a fine collection of Maori *taonga* (treasures) in the *Te Atihaunui-a-Paparangi* (the Maori Court) including an inevitable collection of *waka* (canoes), the finest of which is the beautifully carved *Te Mata-o-Houra*. Of particular interest also is the range of displays showing the ingenious methods and traps the early Maori used to catch fish on the river and birds in the bush. Upstairs there is a large and rather tired-looking collection of wildlife exhibits, including numerous native birds and moa bones. Elsewhere temporary galleries feature a programme of changing exhibitions.

A short distance away from the museum, proudly crowning Queen's Park Hill, is the **Sargeant Gallery**, ① *T06-3490506, www.sarjeant.org.nz, Mon-Fri 1030-1630, Sat and Sun 1300-1630, donations,* set in a grand building and reputed to be one of the best in the country. Home to over 4,000 permanent artworks, there is an ever-changing programme of local and national touring exhibitions and occasionally an international show.

The **Wanganui Riverboat Centre**, ① *on the riverbank on Taupo Quay, T06-3471863, www.wanganui.org.nz/riverboats The Waimarie sails Mon-Fri at 1400 (2 hours), Sat and Sun 1400 (3 hours); from $25, child $10, in summer there are often additional lunch and dinner cruises,* has been a hive of activity in recent years as committed enthusiasts have been hard at work fully restoring the old paddlesteamer *The Waimarie*. This steamer worked the river for 50 years, carrying a wide variety of cargoes and tourists, before she came to grief and sank at her moorings in 1952. In 1993 she was removed from the mud and over the next seven years faithfully restored to be relaunched on the first day of the 21st century. Now, she is sailed proudly up the river daily with a loving crew and cargo of admiring tourists. Although the riverboat centre no longer houses *The Waimarie* there are displays of photographs and memorabilia from the river era. If you do go for a trip be sure to ask if you can take a look at the restored steam engine that pumps the pistons below decks. It is quite a sight and testimony to the loving care and attention that is now bestowed upon the old girl since she was pulled from the mud.

Immediately across the road from the Riverboat centre are the **Moutoa Gardens** which, though unremarkable, are famous as the spot where the deed was believed to be signed between the New Zealand Company and the Maori for the dubious land deals of 1840. This notoriety and the continued displeasure felt by Maori regarding land deals led to an occupation of these gardens in 1995. High profile court battles followed and an ugly confrontation with police was only avoided by face-to-face meetings and thankfully a peaceful end to the 83-day occupation.

Cook's Gardens, which grace the western heart of the town on St Hill Street are home to the 1899 colonial-style **Opera House** the modern **Trust Bank Stadium** (with its wooden cycling velodrome) and the **Ward Observatory**, ① *T025-2458066. Open for public viewing on most Fri nights from 2000-2130.* This observatory was originally built in 1901 and houses the largest telescope of its kind still in use in the country.

Just across the bridge from Taupo Quay is the unusual access to the **Durie Hill** and the **War Memorial Tower**. A tunnel, almost immediately across the bridge takes you 200 m into the hillside where you can get the '**Earthbound Durie Hill Elevator**' to the top. ① *This highly considerate service is available Mon-Fri 0730-1800, Sat 0900-1700, Sun 1000-1700 and costs $1.* From the top you can then climb the Durie Hill War Memorial Tower, built of fossilized rock. The view from the top is rather engaging and on a clear day can include Mount Taranaki and Ruapehu, but don't expect to get any photographs of Ruapehu, unless you want a water tower in the way.

There are a number of good **parks and gardens** in the town and surrounding area. At the top end of Victoria Avenue up the hill is the **Virginia Lake Scenic Reserve** with the usual lake, themed gardens and aviary. There is a nice walk that goes around the lake and once completed you might like to celebrate by setting off the coin-operated lake fountain.

If you have kids the star attraction in Wanganui has to be the excellent **Kowhai Park** on the eastern bank of the river just across the bridge to Anzac Parade. Here you can find a wonderful array of interactive attractions including a dinosaur slide, a pirate ship, a flying fox, roller beetles and sea serpent swings, as well as the traditional bike and skateboard tracks, all of which will keep them happy for hours.

Wanganui to Hawera

About 5 km northwest of Wanganui, down Rapanui Road (towards the sea) is **Westmere Lake**. Set aside as a wildlife refuge with native bush, it provides a pleasant spot for a picnic. For the more energetic there is a 40-minute walk that circumnavigates the lake. A little further down Rapanui Road is the **Bason Botanical Gardens**, ① *T06-3429742, daily from 0800-dusk*, bequeathed to the Wanganui Regional Council in 1966 by local farmer Stanley Bason. They consist of 25 ha of gardens, with native and introduced plants, a conservatory, begonia house, camellia garden and lake with a lookout. If you have time you may like to follow the road to the sea (14 km) and the small village of Mowhanau, blessed with the black-sand **Kai Iwi Beach**, which is surrounded by cliffs but still provides a safe spot for swimming.

Back on SH3 and a further 20 km northwest is the **Bushy Park Forest**, ① *daily, $3, child $1, to get to the Bushy Park Reserve turn right at the village of Kai Iwi and follow the signs (8 km)*. It's a picturesque 90-ha reserve with a rich variety of native flora and fauna. Some of the trees are magnificent and they include the great girth and twisted trunk of 'Ratanui', a Northern rata that is thought to be the largest living rata in the Southern Hemisphere.

Ashley Park, 29 km northwest of Wanganui near the village of Waitotara is a similar to Bushy Park, but more commercial, with farm animals, pony rides, a swimming pool and a café. ▸▸ *See also Sleeping, below.*

● Sleeping

Wanganui *p387*
Other than motels there is not a large amount of choice in Wanganui and B&Bs are particularly thin on the ground.
AL-A **Rutland Arms Inn**, *corner Victoria Av and Ridgeway St, T06-3477677, www.rutland-arms.co.nz* Centrally located. Well-appointed suites in the old English style. Bar, restaurant and courtyard café attached.
A-B **Grand Hotel**, *corner St Hill and Guyton Sts, T06-3450955, www.thegrandhotel.co.nz* A 1920s hotel in the heart of town. Nothing spectacular but good value with, spa, bar and good restaurant attached. Internet.
AL-A **Avenue Hotel**, *379 Victoria Av, T06-3450907, www.theavenuewanganui.com* Glorified modern motel with café, bar and outdoor pool, walking distance to the town. There are over 20 motels in Wanganui with the top end of Victoria Av being home to some of the newest and the best including:
AL-A **Siena**, *355 Victoria Av, T06-3459009, www.siena.co.nz;*
A **Collegiate Hotel and Motor Inn**, *122 Liverpool St, T06-3458309, www.collegiatemotorinn.co.nz;*
A **Cook's Gardens Motor Lodge**, *corner of Guyton and Purnell Sts, T06-3456003.*
For a cheaper motel try:
B **Riverview Motel**, *14 Somme Pde, T06-3452888.*
C-D **Tamara Backpackers Lodge**, *24 Somme Pde, T06-3476300, www.tamaralodge.co.nz* An excellent establishment with a locally streetwise manager, set in a large 2-story villa overlooking the river. A range of older rooms or new units with own bathroom. Large garden, free bike hire, internet. River trips organized.
C-D **Braemar House**, *2 Plymouth St, T06-3472529, www.braemarhouse.co.nz* YHA affiliate, recently renovated and round the corner from the Tamara. Also comfortable but quieter and more sedate, off street parking.
C-D **Aramoho Top 10 Holiday Park**, *460 Somme Pde, T06-3438402, T0800-272664, aramoho.holidaypark@xtra.co.nz* A bit out of the centre but worth the drive. Quiet, modern facilities next to the river. Friendly owners.

A-D Bushy Park Homestead, *T06-3429879, www.bushypark-homestead.co.nz* Built in 1906, it provides grand B&B and budget accommodation.

Ashley Park, *T06-3465917*. Motel, B&B, farmstay and campsite accommodation.

● Eating

$$ **Victoria's**, *13 Victoria Av, T06-3477007. Tue-Fri from 1200-1400, Tue-Sun from 1800. Licensed.* Has a good reputation offering traditional New Zealand fare.

$$ **Legends**, *25 Somme Pde, T06-3487450. Wed-Sun 0730-late. Licensed.* Locally popular and offers affordable breakfasts, lunches and à la carte evening dining.

$$ **Oaks Restaurant**, *at the Collegiate Motor Inn, 122 Liverpool St, T06-3458309. Wed-Fri from 1200 for lunch daily for dinner. Licensed.* Also has a good reputation and offers à la carte and café-style cuisine as well as a seafood smorgasbord on Sat.

$$ **Bollywood Star Indian Tandoori Restaurant**, *88 Guyton St, T06-3459996. Open for lunch Tue-Sun 1100-1500 and dinner daily from 1800. Licensed.* The best Indian in town.

$ **Amadeus Riverbank Café**, *69 Taupo Quay, T06-3451538. Mon-Thu 0830-1600, Fri 0830-1900, Sat and Sun 1000-1600. Licensed.* It does a fine value breakfast, good coffee and outdoor seating overlooking the river.

$ **Red Eye Café**, *96 Guyton St, T06-3455646. Tue-Sat 0800-late, Sun 1000-1500.* Has a loyal following and also serves a good coffee.

● Pubs

The Red Lion, *Anzac Pde.* Along with Rutland Arms (below) one of the main pubs in town, also offering à la carte dining.
Rutland Arms Inn, *see above.* Seems to attract a friendly clientele.
Ceilidh Bar, *attached to the Grand Hotel, Guyton St,* and
Celtic Arms, *432 Victoria Av, T06-3477037*, both are fairly dull Irish-style offerings.

● Entertainment

Royal Wanganui Opera House, *on the edge of Cooks Gardens, St Hill St, T06-3490511.* Small but very grand and a regular venue for touring shows from opera to rock.
Embassy 3 Cinema, *34 Victoria Av, T06-3457958.* For details about other up and coming performances contact the VIC.

● Festivals

Wanganui in Bloom (*Dec-Mar*) The streets are adorned with 1,000 hanging baskets of flowers. The highlight is the festival and Heritage Weekend in March, when there are various events including a raft race, vintage car procession and street bands. The nationally recognised **Wanganui Arts Festival** (*end of March 2004*) is a biennial event over a week.

▲ Activities and tours

Mountain biking As well as being the main gateway to the National Park, Wanganui is well known for its excellent mountain biking. Favoured tracks and routes include **Lismore Forest**, **Hylton Park**, **Bushy Park Loop**, the **Whanganui River Road** and **Pauri Village Forest**. The VIC has details about all these venues and the **Wanganui Pro Cycle Centre**, *199 Victoria Avenue, T06-3453715,* hires bikes and will also provide advice. For all river activities based in or around Wanganui see page 394. Note that there is a Mail Run Tour service operating to Pipiriki and the Whanganui National Park via the Whanganui River Road.

● Directory

Airline offices Air NZ, *133 Victoria Av, T06-3483500.* **Bike hire** Wanganui Pro Cycle Centre, *199 Victoria Av, T06-3453715.* From $35 per day. **Car hire** Avis, *161 Ingestre St, T06-3457612.* Rent-a-Dent, *T06-3451505.* **Internet** VIC; the library *Queen's Park, T06-3491000, Mon-Fri 0900-2000, Sat 0900-1630*; and **Computer Care**, *corner of Quay and Vic Av. Mon-Fri 0845-1700, Sat 1000-1230.* **Post office** *226 Victoria Av (between Ingestre and Plymouth Sts), T06-3454103. Mon-Fri 0830-1700.* **Medical services** Wanganui Hospital, *Heads Rd, T06-3481234.* After Hours, *163 Wicksteed St, T06-3480333.* **Taxis** Wanganui Taxis, *T06-3435555.* **Useful** addresses Police: *Bell St, T06-3490600.* AA: *78 Victoria Ave, T06-3489160.*

Whanganui National Park

→ *Colour map 3, grid A3*

Springing from high on the volcanic slopes of Tongariro in National Park, the Whanganui River begins its 290-km journey to the sea, carving its way through some of the most remote and inaccessible country in the North Island. At its most remote mid to lower reaches, it cuts deep in to the soft, sand and mudstone and is joined by tracts of intact lowland forest, which form the heart of the Whanganui National Park. Although the river is not the longest in the North Island (that honour going to the Waikato) it has been the longest navigable river for generations. As a result the river is rich in both Maori and European history, from the first days of early exploration and settlement through to the river's renaissance as a tourist and recreational attraction. Although the entire area is hard to access (which is undoubtedly part of its charm), there is the opportunity to explore the historical sites of the river and enjoy its atmosphere. You can do this, in part on its banks by road and walking tracks, or on the river itself by jet boat or kayak.

Ins and outs

Getting there and around The 3 principal gateway settlements to the river are Taumarunui to the north, Raetihi to the northwest and Wanganui to the south. Physical access to the river and the park is from 6 main access points: from the north, Ohinepane, 21 km down river from Taumarunui; from the East Whakahoro (linked to SH4 by roads from Owhango and Raurimu), Pipiriki (accessible from Raetihi), Ohura Rd (from SH4 north of Raetihi); from the south via the River Rd off SH4 (just North of Wanganui) to Pipiriki, and from the West via way of Stratford/Ohura Rd (SH43) where Brewer Rd and Mangaehu Rd lead on to Kohi Saddle and the Matemateaonga Track. As well as the daily **Mail Run** service from Wanganui to Pipiriki, T06-3442554, most tour operators will provide transportation in and out of the park for about $30-$50 return. Other than that you are on your own.

Note that both the back roads, tracks and the river itself is subject to slips and flooding so always consult the DOC before attempting a major excursion. Summer is undoubtedly the busiest and safest time to visit the park. During this time you are advised to pre-book all accommodation.

Information There are **DoC** offices in Wanganui, T06-3452402, Taumarunui, T07-8958201 and Pipiriki, T06-3855022. For DoC bookings also refer to their website greatwalksbooking@doc.govt.nz They deal with all information enquiries and hut/campsite bookings and fees. You are advised to consult the local office for latest fee structures and conditions. There are a number of good books available about the river and the park (available from main DoC offices) while DoC produces detailed leaflets, including the helpful *In and Around Whanganui National Park* and the *Whanganui Journey*. They also stock the recommended publication *Guide to the Whanganui River* ($8).

History

Legend has it that the Whanganui was created as a result of a mighty love feud between the mountains of Tongariro and Taranaki in the central North Island. When both fell in love with the beautiful Mount Pihanga, a battle ensued. Taranaki lost the fight and, wild with grief and anger, ripped himself from his roots and tore a path towards the coast, where he now stands alone – in a mighty huff. Perhaps through indifference or appeasement, Tongariro created the waters that filled Taranaki's path of destruction and the Whanganui River was born.

Less than 300 years after the great Maori explorer Kupe first explored the healing scars of Taranaki, the descendants of the early canoes began to settle the riverbanks. In time the river became linked by a series of *pa* (Maori settlements) and on almost every bend there was a guardian controlling and protecting the life forces of the river. The 'river people' became expert at utilizing the rivers resources. Sheltered terraces were cultivated and elaborate eel weirs were built and, although not necessarily at harmony with neighbouring tribes, they were certainly in harmony with the environment. The first major European influence came in the form of missionaries in 1840 who created a number of missions on the banks of the river's lower reaches.

Whanganui National Park

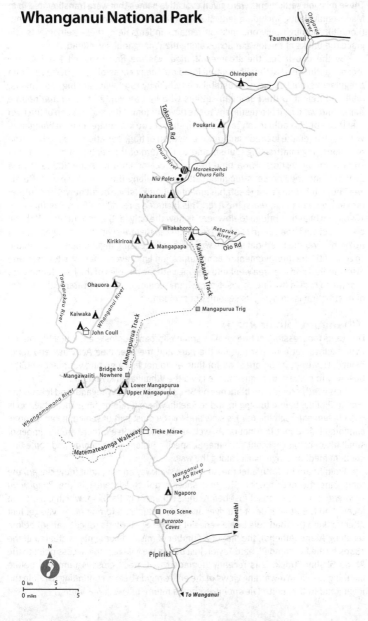

66 99 Legend has it that the Whanganui was created as a result of a mighty love feud between the mountains of Tongariro and Taranaki in the central North Island...

These mission settlements were given evocative names that were transliterated in to Maori equivalents, including Jerusalem (Hiruharama), Athens (Atene) and Corinth (Koriniti). Although only one mission remains in Jerusalem, these settlements still grace the banks of the lower reaches along the Whanganui River Road.

By the mid-1860s the steamer *Moutoa* was the first to reach Pipiriki (now located at the head of the Whanganui Road but then accessible only by boat). Soon a regular riverboat service was established which by 1891, was carrying passengers, mail and freight to the European settlers who had attempted to farm the remote banks and valleys. It is a testimony to the navigational skills and upkeep of the river that these boats could reach Taumarunui, almost 200 km upstream from Wanganui. With such a remote location and unique method of transportation, the area and the river soon began attracting tourists and by the turn of the century there were over 10,000 annual visitors. For a time the river became known as the 'Rhine of New Zealand' and the sparse, struggling settlements along the river prospered. Hotels were built, including a huge establishment at Pipiriki (since burnt down) and further inroads were made to reach the river. This included a road built from Raetihi in the 1930s of which the 'Bridge to Nowhere' is now the only lasting monument. With the creation of such roads and the main trunk railway together with the ceaseless silting up of the river the riverboat service waned, finally ceasing regular operations in the 1920s. With the improvement of communication links everywhere the tourist trade also suffered and the area went into decline with the paddles of the last steamboats ceasing to turn in the late 1950s. Now, when it comes to tourism Taranaki's old tear of destruction is enjoying its second honeymoon.

Whanganui River Road

Due to its inaccessible nature it takes some effort and almost certainly a trip on the river itself to get a proper feel for the park and the river (see Activities and tours below). However, if you are short for time or do not fancy getting your feet wet, the best way to make your acquaintance is via the Whanganui River Road.

This windy scenic road branches off SH4 15 km North of Wanganui and follows the river to Pipiriki, before turning inland to Raetihi where it rejoins SH4. The entire trip is 106 km and although the road is slow and for the most part unsealed, it can be done comfortably in about four hours. As well as the scenery itself, there are a number of small historically significant settlements, specific historic sites, *marae* and some fine short- to medium-length walks along the way.

From South to North after the Aramoana Walkway and Lookout (now closed) the road joins the river proper. The first specific point of interest is the *Pungarehu Wharenui* (meeting house) just before the settlement of Parikino, which used to be located on the other side of the river and now occupies a former Maori village. Just after Parikino the road cuts into a series of **Oyster Shell Bluffs** (once seabed) before reaching **Atene** (Athens), the first of a number of mission settlements created in the 1840s by the Reverend Richard Taylor. Just before the village is the access point to the **Atene Skyline Track**. This recently upgraded DOC track crosses farmland before climbing to take in rewarding views of the entire region before continuing to rejoin the River Road further north (viewpoint 1½ hours return; full walk 6-8 hours).

The next settlement and former mission settlement is **Koriniti** (Corinth). Formerly the Maori settlement of Otukopiri, it still retains a fine *marae* that welcomes visitors. The Anglican Church dates back to 1920. Keep your eyes open here too for flood markers, one of which is half way up a barn, giving you a shocking reminder of the potential dangers of the river. The **Operiki Pa**, just north of Koriniti, was the original home of the Koriniti Maori and the site of the first Anglican Church built in 1840. About 6 km further north is the **Kawana Flour Mill**, a fully-restored example from 1854, complete with miller's cottage. Both the mill and the cottage are a short walk from the main road and well worth a quick look. **Ranana** (London) is the next small settlement. Ranana was one of the largest former mission settlements first established in the 1890s and its church is still in use today.

After Ranana is **Hiruharama** (Jerusalem) the most picturesque of all the former missions. Originally a larger Maori village known as Patiarero, it was once home to famous New Zealand poet James Baxter and French Sister Mary Aubert whose Catholic mission still remains to this day. You can visit the church that was built in the late 1800s. From here the road climbs to a fine viewpoint and the Omorehu Waterfall Lookout before delivering you at **Pipiriki**. Pipiriki used to be the major tourist destination at the turn of the century, complete with a large hotel. These days, although not so blessed with luxurious accommodation, it is still an important settlement, serving as the main southern gateway to the heart of the National Park via the river itself. Although the large hotel, Pipiriki House, that once stood here has long since burnt down, a former **Colonial House**, ⓘ *summer 1000-1600, $1, child 50c,* remains and serves as a small museum and information centre, as well as a reminder of the former glory days.

The small DoC office in Pipiriki can assist with information and also provides overnight parking. On the way you will pass the rather sorry remains of the former 1903 steamer *MV Ongarue*, which plied the river until the late 1950s. Although restored in 1983 and placed high and dry on the hill for all to see, she is clearly much in need of some attention and a new lick of paint. From Pipiriki the road then turns inland and winds its way for 27 km to the small township of Raetihi, where it rejoins SH4.

One of the major man-made 'sights' within the park is the very aptly named **'Bridge to Nowhere'**. Built in 1936 to provide access for a remote rural pioneer settlement, it never really served its intended purpose after the project was abandoned with the advent of the Second World War. Regenerating

Whanganui River Road

bush quickly covered the track and the bridge is all that remains. It is located about 30 km upstream from Pipiriki and can only be reached from the river by jet boat, canoe or by a three-day walk.

◉ Sleeping

Whanganui National Park *p392*
Both the walking tracks and the river itself within the park are well-endowed with DOC huts and campsites. During the period 1 Oct-30 Apr you must buy a hut and campsite pass from DOC (or VIC and some operators) before staring your journey. This pass costs $35 ($25 if bought before your journey), child $12.50 and is valid for 6 days. Concessions are available for some canoe and jet boat trips. Campsites provide a water supply, toilets and shelters with benches for cooking. Huts have bunks with mattresses, stoves, benches, tables and cooking facilities. In winter campsites are free of charge while hut users must have hut tickets or an annual hut pass. The **Teieke Hut** on the eastern riverbank near the Matemateaonga Landing is fairly unique in that it is also a *marae*, (traditional protocol must be observed). Besides the DOC facilities and the *marae* there is the immensely popular

   AL-D **Ramanui Lodge**, *in a very remote spot on the riverbank in the heart of the park and 21 km above Pipiriki, T06-3487122, T025-480308, www.greenstone.co.nz* Access is either by boat, canoe or by foot, which makes the place very special. There is B&B (dinner if required), cabin and campsite accommodation available, along with a bar and positively exquisite home cooking. Guided tours to the 'bridge' also available.

Whanganui River Road *p394*
A-B **Omaka Homestay**, *Parikino, T06-3425597, omakaholiday@xtra.co.nz* 1,000-ha hill farm. Homestay, backpackers (in a comfortable working woolshed) and camping options. Campervans welcome. Very friendly with lots to see and do.
   B **Flying Fox**, *Koriniti, T06-3428160, www.whanganuiriver.co.nz* The Flying Fox is on the western bank of the river and is only accessible by an exciting aerial cableway or by jet boat. The accommodation consists of B&B, 2 self-contained cottages and campsites. There is a very cute outdoor wood-fired bath, some fine 'home brew' to

sample and the home cooking is superb. Recommended.
   B **Operiki Farmstay**, *Operiki, T06-3428159*. Traditional single storey house close to the river. One double and one twin, dinner on request. Good value.
   D **Jerusalem Catholic Church Backpackers**, *Jerusalem, T06-3428190*. Basic but angelic.

Campsites
   D **Kauika Campsite**, *near Ranana, T06-3428061*.
   D **DoC**, *Pipiriki, T06-3855022*.

▲ Activities and tours

There are numerous options available for exploring the river from simple independent and self-guided canoe hire, to single- or multi-day kayak trips, jet boat trips and multi day tramps. The various operators can supply all the necessary equipment (including camping gear). As well as the designated DOC huts and campsites along the way there is a comfortable B&B Lodge (Ramanui) in the heart of the park. Note that if you do go it alone, especially tramping, the tracks essentially end at the river and pick-ups will have to be arranged. If you are alone this may be costly, so careful logistics are sometimes necessary to time your arrivals and departures with scheduled tour trips.

Kayaking The Whanganui is very popular with kayakers and canoeists due to its sheer length, and the 239 listed rapids along the way. But it is fairly unique in this sense, in that for almost its entire length the rapids are of a grade suitable for beginners. There are a wide range of trips available from five days (Taumarunui to Pipiriki) to just a few hours. There are designated DoC huts and campsites with basic amenities, throughout the park for use by kayakers and trampers (see Sleeping below). Note fees apply and bookings are required. Kayaking trips can be done independently or with the various tour operators, most of whom access the river from the north. The best time to embark on a major trip is obviously in the summer, though more experienced canoeists sometimes tackle the river after winter rains. Costs vary but standard independent canoe or kayak (Canadian) hire starts at about $30 a day for a single, to $55 for a double. A trip with a tour operator, which includes all equipment, will cost you about $85-110 per day. DOC charges a flat fee of $25 for hut and campsite use for 2-6 days ($35 if not bought before the journey). NB Operators listed here according to base.

Wanganui Rivercity Tours, *T0800-377311, T06-3442554, www.rivercitytours.co.nz* Daily Mail Coach Tour from $30, 1-4 day guided or independent hire canoe trips (equipment, food and transport with pick-ups included). Independent hire and transport from $55 per day, 2-day (1-night) trip from $240, 4-day trip from $545, jet boat from $40. (camping equipment hire also available).

Omaka Farmstay, *Whanganui River Rd, near Atene, T06-3425597, omakaholiday@xtra.co.nz* 1-3 hr canoe trips available, from $15.

Ohakune Yeti Tours, *T06-3858197, www.canoe.co.nz* Range from luxury to economy 4-6 day trips. From $125. Recommended for the longer excursion.

Canoe Safaris, *T06-3859237, www.canoesafaris.co.nz* Canoe and rafting trips throughout the area. Whanganui 2-5 day guided trips from $290 (all-inclusive).

Raurimu Plateau Adventures, *T06-8922740, T.parker@xtra.co.nz* 2-5 day guided trips (2-day from $275). Independent rentals and transport ($55).

Whakahoro (Wade's landing) Wade's Landing Outdoors, *T06-8955995, wades.landing@xtra.co.nz* Canoe, kayak and jet boat trips, tramping drop-offs. Flexible itineraries.

Taumarunui Blazing Paddles, *T07-8955261, T0800-252946, www.blazingpaddles.co.nz* 1-5 day trips. Canadian or kayak. Self-guided from $50 per day. Guides can be arranged.

Jet boating Since the 1980s jet boats have been the principal fast transport link up and down the river. There are various operators providing sightseeing trips from 15 minutes to two days (including the drop-off for the 40-minute 'Bridge to Nowhere' walk) and pick-ups from the river ends of the Matemateaonga Walkway and Mangapurua Track. Again costs vary but a five-hour trip to the bridge will cost about $85.

Operators are listed below according to base.

Whanganui River Spirit Jetboat Tours, *T06-3421718, www.riverspirit.co.nz* From 2½ hrs, $50. **Scenic Experience Jetboat Tours**, *T06-3425599*. From 2½ hrs, $50, 7 hr 30min from $145. All trips depart from Pungarehu (25 min north of Wanganui).

Whakahoro (Wade's Landing) Wade's Landing Outdoors, *T06-8955995*. Canoe, kayak and jet boat trips. Flexible itineraries.

Pipiriki Bridge to Nowhere Tours, *T06-3854128, www.bridgetonowhere-lodge.co.nz* 20-min to 4-hr bridge trip (4 hr, $80).

Tramping As well as the 'Bridge to Nowhere' track which is accessible only by jet boat canoe or by foot there are 2 main tramps in the park: the Matemateaonga Walkway and the Mangapurua Track.

Matemateaonga Walkway This track which penetrates deep into the heart of the park, traversing an expanse of thick bush-clad hill country between Taranaki and the Whanganui River, is considered one of the North Island's great walks. It uses an old Maori trail and former settlers' dray road and for the most part follows the ridges of the Matemateaonga Range before arriving at the river and the Ramanui Lodge. The highlight is a short 1½ hour diversion up the 730 m Mt Humphries for a fine view. The track is 42 km in length, considered 'moderate' in difficulty and takes about 4 days to complete. There are 3 DOC huts along the way for which a fee must be paid (see Sleeping above). Bear in mind that transport must be arranged with one of the jet boat operators either to pick you up or drop you off at the river end of the track. From the west the track is accessed from SH43 at Strathmore, near Stratford. Look for the signpost that indicates the road to Upper Mangaehu Rd and the track which begins at Kohi Saddle.

Mangapurua Track The Mangapurua

Track is about the same length as the Matemateaonga Walkway and takes 3-4 days to complete. It starts from Whakahoro (easily accessed at the end of the Whakahoro Rd) up the Kaiwhakauka Valley past the Mangapurua Trig (663 m) and then descends through the Mangapurua Valley, via the 'Bridge to Nowhere' to meet the river at the Mangapurua Landing, 30 km upstream from Pipiriki. There is only 1 hut at Whakahoro but a number of good campsites along the way. Again you will need to arrange jet boat transportation back to base.

Introduction

Although Wellington is the nation's capital it enjoys a small-town atmosphere. With its surrounding hills, generally compact layout and well-preserved historical buildings, it has far more character than sprawling Auckland or monotonously flat Christchurch. Wellington is a vibrant, cosmopolitan city, noted for its arts and café culture, with almost as many restaurants and cafés per capita as New York. Its most famous visitor attraction, the multi-million dollar **'Te Papa' Museum**, is on the city's recently revamped and buzzing waterfront. Some of the best shopping in the country can also be found in the compact city centre. If you are heading for the South Island by ferry, you will inevitably encounter Wellington and you are advised to give it more than a cursory glance while waiting for your ferry.

To the east of the city are the rather unremarkable commuter towns of Upper and Lower Hutt, from where you can reach the beautiful, off-the-beaten-track region of the Wairarapa, with its remote coastline. First, though, you must negotiate the **Rimutakas** – 'the hill' – a natural barrier that has always prevented the spread and pace of settlement and development. To the north, both major rail and road links hug the scenic **Kapiti Coastline**, with its pleasant coastal towns and their associated beaches and attractions, the most noteworthy being the nature reserve of **Kapiti Island** looming a short distance offshore.

★ Don't miss...

❶ The impressive **'Te Papa' – The National Museum of New Zealand**, page 407. Try to avoid information overload and make find enough time to explore.

❷ **The Museum of Wellington, City and Sea,** page 406.

❸ Taking the city centre **Cable Car** to the **Botanical Gardens**, page 407. Enjoy the views, stop and smell the roses, then walk back down the city centre via the Parliamentary District, page 404.

❹ Rollerblading on the **Wellington Waterfront** followed by an al fresco lager, page 406.

❺ The city views from **Mount Victoria**, page 404. On a windy day, watch the planes make the tricky landing into Wellington Airport below you.

❻ Wellington's world-class café and restaurants in or around **Cuba Street** or **Courtenay Place**, page 413.

❼ The incredible, wildlife paradise of the old non-human New Zealand, on a day trip to **Kapiti Island** off the scenic Kapiti Coast, page 421.

❽ The fast and funky stretcher-cum-microlight and 'Fly By Wire' at **Paekakariki**, page 421.

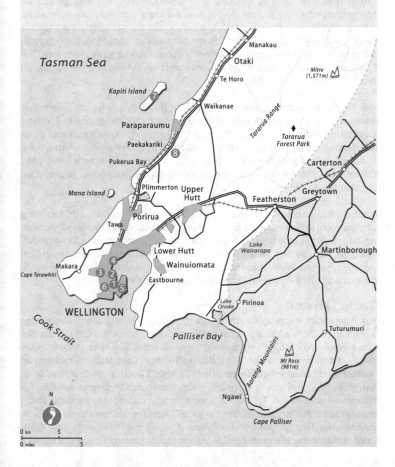

Ins and outs

Getting there

Air Wellington airport, T04-3855100, www.wellington-airport.co.nz, is in the suburb of Miramar, about 6 km to the south of the city centre. It has recently been given a major revamp and is now highly modern and efficient, handling both international and domestic flights. It is perhaps the most infamous airport in the country due to its short runway, nestled precariously between populated hillsides. During southerly storms the nightly news often shows the latest 'interesting' landing from Wellington, whereby the aircraft 'come dancing' into land. That, and the fact you can practically make eye contact with the residents in the houses that nestle on the hillsides, makes a departure or arrival by air rather memorable. Although there are dozens of **Trans-Tasman** and **Pacific Island** flights per week, Wellington primarily operates a busy domestic schedule, with regular daily flights to most principal centres. **Air New Zealand**, T0800-737000, www.airnewzealand.co.nz, and **Origin Pacific**, T0800-302302, www.originpacific.co.nz, are the principal carriers. Additionally, a number of smaller operators fly to upper South Island destinations. These include **Soundsair**, T0800-505005, www.soundsair.co.nz, who offer regular and very reasonable fares from $79 one-way to Picton, Nelson and Blenheim. The new terminal has all the usual facilities including food outlets, shops, left luggage and an information centre, T04-3855123. All the major car rental companies are represented at the airport. There are plenty of taxis to meet you and the standard fare into town is about $22, T04-3844444. Shuttle buses can be shared for about $10, T04-9399590. Both shuttles and taxis depart from directly outside the baggage claim area. The **Stagecoach Flyer** is the regular bus service to and from the airport to the city, $4.50, Mon-Fri 0620-2020, Sat and Sun 0650-2050.

Rail The railway station is next to the Quay on Bunny St and has an information centre, T04-4983000. **TranzScenic** operate a regular daily service north to Auckland (Overlander/Northerner), T0800-872467, T04-4950775, www.tranzscenic.co.nz **TranzMetro**, T04-801-7000, www.tranzmetro.co.nz, also offer regular services to the Wairarapa including Martinborough (bus link) and Masterton direct (six times daily, Mon-Fri, twice daily Sat and Sun).There is a special day excursion fare of $15, child $8. Standard fare $13 one-way.

Road Wellington is 658 km from Auckland. The principal route is via SH1. SH2 is the principal route to the Wairarapa and the East Coast. Wellington is the terminus for all vehicular traffic by ferry to South Island (see page 419). **Intercity**, and T09-9136100, **Newmans**, T04-4993261, are the principal bus companies and arrive and depart from the railway station. **White Star**, T04-4784734, operates services to Palmerston North, Wanganui and New Plymouth. Tickets available from the VIC.

Getting around

Bus Stagecoach Buses operate daily from 0700-2300. City and suburban coverage is good and there is a 'ten-trip' ticket system available. The yellow **City Circular Bus** runs every 10 mins (Mon-Fri 0730-1800, Sat 0900-1800, Sun 0950-1800) from the railway station taking in major sites including **'Te Papa'**, **Cuba Mall**, the **cable car on Lambton**, and **Parliament Buildings**. It costs $2 (child $1) with an $8 'Star Pass' ticket ($10 group of 4) available in conjunction with **Stagecoach Wellington** services. For information call **Ridewell**, T04-8017000, www.wrc.govt.nz, and get your hands on the free *Wellington bus and train guide* from the VIC. Note there is free shuttle service to the Interisland ferry terminal from the railway station. If you intend visiting the **Kapiti Coast** or **Hutt Valley** it is worth considering the **Capital Explorer Pass** which allows a

T04-5692933, is the main public bus operator offering regular daily services to the Hutt Valley, . The **Stagecoach Flyer,** T0800-801700, also offers express services from Hutt City to Wellington CBD and also the airport every 30 min, from $7, child $3.50.
▸ *For taxi, car rental and bike hire see page 420.*

Car Parking can be a nightmare in the city centre. It is heavily metered and mercilessly patrolled. If you struggle to find a spot in the centre, try the 'park and display' areas around the railway station, north and south of the centre, and 'Te Papa' Museum. You can walk from there.

Train **TranzMetro** operate regular daily suburban services between Wellington City and Upper Hutt, Melling and Paraparaumu. There are also additional services further afield to the Wairarapa and Palmerston North. For information call **TranzMetro,** T04-801-7000, www.tranzmetro.co.nz, or **Ridewell,** T04-8017000.

Walking Wellington city centre is quite compact and you should not have much trouble getting around on foot. Indeed, given the road system, with its numerous one-way networks and omnipresent traffic wardens, this seems the best thing to do.

Orientation and information

Wellington is generally easy to negotiate and, unless you are in a car and swept away on its one-way systems, you should not get too lost. All roads lead into the centre since there is nowhere else for them to go. The central city is essentially sandwiched between the hills and the waterfront and those arriving by road will be delivered right into the heart, within a stone's throw of Lambton Quay, the main business and shopping street. Lambton then doubles back north to meet Molesworth St, Thorndon and the Parliament District. The Harbour, with its merging main roads of Quay, Customhouse, Jervois, Cable St and Oriental Parade, sweeps back south and east, encompassing the modern and highly developed waterfront, including the dominant 'Te Papa' Museum. From the heart of the waterfront south, Willis and Jervois connect with Victoria, Cuba and Courtenay Pl, where you'll find many of the restaurants and cafés. Behind the Central Business District (CBD) are the spacious Botanical Gardens and hillside suburbs of Kelburn. Dominating the view southeast is Mount Victoria, a 'must see' lookout and an ideal place to get your bearings.

If all that sounds heinously complicated, *Tourism Wellington* make things pretty simple by promoting a **'four quarters'** map system, which is often referred to on maps or in brochures. The four quarters running in a clockwise direction from Mount Victoria round the bay through the CBD and then north are: **Courtenay, Cuba, Willis** and **Lambton**. There is a specialist **Map Shop**, on the corner of Vivian and Victoria Sts (near Cuba St), as well as the stocks available at major bookshops *Whitcoulls* and *Dymocks* (see page 418).

Wellington VIC, ⓘ *101 Wakefield St (Civic Sq), T04-8024860, www.wellingtonNZ.com Mon-Fri 0830-1730, Sat/Sun 0930-1600.* The VIC also has a shop, a café and internet access. There is also an information centre at the airport, T04-3855123. **DoC,** ⓘ *Government Buildings, Lambton Quay, T04-4727356, www.doc.govt.nz Mon-Fri 0900-1630, Sat and Sun 1000-1500.* **Upper Hutt VIC,** ⓘ *6 Main St, Upper Hutt, T04-5272141, www.upperhuttcity.com Daily 0900-1700.* **Lower Hutt VIC,** ⓘ *10 Andrews Ave, Lower Hutt, T04-5604715, www.huttcity.info Mon-Fri 0900-1700, Sat/Sun 1000-1600.*

Useful free **guides** include: *Wellington Visitors' Guide, What's On Wellington,* the *Wellington Arts Map, Wellington Shopping, Wellington Wine and Food* and the *Wellington Fashion Map.* Also the weekly newspaper *Capital Times* is designed for visitors. The main daily in the lower North Island is the *Dominion*, but the *New Zealand Herald* (Auckland and upper North Island) is also available.

History

According to Maori legend it was Kupe, the great Polynesian explorer, who first made landfall in the region in about AD 950, and his descendants, the Ngai Tara and Rangitane tribes, became the first permanent settlers. The first European ships to enter the harbour were the *Rosanna* and the *Lambton* on a preliminary exploration for the first New Zealand Company in 1826. But it was not until 1839/40 when other ships, the *Tory* and then the *Aurora,* brought the first settlers, that the inevitable dubious land deals with the local Maori were made. Initially the first blocks of land purchased were at the northern end of the harbour towards what are now Petone and the Hutt Valley. But the land was found to be unsuitable for building, so the settlers moved south, to what is now Thorndon, in the heart of modern day Wellington. Along with the rest of the country, Wellington suffered three decades of Maori/*Pakeha* friction surrounding the various land deals. But despite this, and a major earthquake in 1855 (which actually had the positive effect of creating new and ideal flat land for building), Wellington prospered. By the 1860s, with the various inroads being made in to the South Island and the then capital Auckland suffering due to its geographical position, it was decided to move the seat of government and make Wellington the capital in 1865. The name Wellington was bestowed in honour of yet another British general, Arthur Wellesley (1769-1852), the first Duke of Wellington. Although modern day Wellington is a proud buzz of human life and celebrated development, deep down there is an ever-present fear of further earthquakes and the hope that history will not repeat itself.

Sights

Mount Victoria Lookout → *Take a No 20 bus*

Most of Wellington's major attractions are all within walking distance or a short bus ride from each other. Perhaps the best place to start, and an ideal spot to get a sense of place, is the 196 m Mount Victoria Lookout. Although from a distance the wooded sides of the Mount hardly seem in character with the film trilogy *Lord of the Rings,* it proved both a convenient and aesthetically suitable location for several scenes depicting 'The Shire' in the first film, the *Fellowship of the Ring.* It was also here that the four Hobbits hid from the evil Nazgul. Looking southeast from the city centre Mount Victoria is not hard to miss, but to the uninitiated reaching the lookout can be somewhat akin to an expedition up K2. The best ascent is by car. Head straight for the hill up Majoribanks Road at the bottom of Courtenay Place. From Majoribanks turn left on to Hawker, carry on up Moeller , Pallister, and then Thane. The entrance to the lookout is on the right, off Thane. If you get lost in the web of residential hillside streets, just make sure you keep going up and eventually you will reach the summit. You might like to investigate the **Byrd Memorial**, a rather modernist edifice pointing south towards the Antarctic, in honour of the American Admiral Richard Byrd. The view is spectacular at sunrise and after dark. If you are on foot the summit is part of the 'Southern Walkway', details and leaflets from the VIC.

The Parliamentary District

The Parliamentary District is centred on and around Bowen Street, in the Lambton Quarter just west of the rather grand looking **railway station** building. Standing on Lambton Quay or Bowen Street you will be immediately struck by the rather odd and aptly named **Beehive**, which houses the various government offices. Designed by

66 99 The best [cartoon] has to be the less-than-flattering one of Rob Muldoon (perhaps New Zealand's most famous Prime Minister)... looking for all the world like an alien slug – or 'Jabba the Hut' from Star Wars...

British architect, Sir Basil Spence, and built in 1980, it is either loved or hated. Far more pleasing is the 1922 **Old Parliament House**, ⓘ *T04-4719503. Mon-Fri 0900-1700, Sat 0930-1600, Sun 1130-1600. Tours Mon-Fri 1000-1600, Sat 1000-1500, Sun 1200-1500. 1 hr. Free.* And next door to that is the **Parliamentary Library**, which is older still. There is an excellent **visitors' centre** in the ground floor foyer of Parliament House. Regular tours are available and you can also see parliament in session.

While in the vicinity of Parliament House take a peek or stop for lunch in the **Backbencher Pub**, across the road on Molesworth Street facing the High Court. Adorning the walls are some superb cartoons and *Spitting Image*-style dummies of past and present Prime Ministers. The best has to be the less-than-flattering one of Rob Muldoon (perhaps New Zealand's most famous Prime Minister). It is particularly grotesque, looking for all the world like an alien slug – or 'Jabba the Hut' character from *Star Wars*.

Just a short stroll from the Backbencher Pub on Lambton Quay is the historic **Old Government Building**, ⓘ *partially open to visitors, T04-4727356,* built in 1876 to house the Crown Ministers and public servants of the day. It has an interesting interior with a rather grand staircase and cabinet room, but it is worthy of above average scrutiny externally as well. The building was designed to look like stone but actually constructed of wood and is the second largest wooden building in the world (the largest being the Todaiji Temple in Nara City, Japan). An expensive restoration was completed in 1996 and it now houses the Victoria Universities Law Faculty and the DoC information centre. Also in the Parliamentary District is the **National Library**, ⓘ *T04-4743000, Mon-Fri 0900-1700, Sat 0900-1630, Sun 1300-1630,* with its impressive collection of research books, colonial photographs and in-house gallery. It also has a shop and a café.

From the library, heading towards the water are the **Archives New Zealand**, ⓘ *10 Mulgrave St, T04-4995595, www.archives.govt.nz Mon-Fri 0900-1700, Sat 0900-1300. Free.* Within its hallowed walls are a number of important historical documents including the original and controversial *Treaty of Waitangi.*

Also on Mulgrave Street is the **Old St Paul's Cathedral**, ⓘ *T04-4736722, Mon-Sat, Free,* an 1866 Gothic-style church adapted from traditional stone to native timbers. It is worth a look, not only to see the superb timberwork of the interior, but also the impressive stained glass windows.

Nearby the **New Zealand Film Archive**, ⓘ *Level 4, 84 Taranaki St, T04-3847647, www.filmarchive.org.nz Mon-Fri 0900-1700, free, tours by appointment,* houses a collection of New Zealand and overseas film and TV materials of artistic, social and historical value dating back to 1897. It runs frequent specialist exhibitions.

The suburb of Thorndon, to which the Parliamentary District essentially belongs, is the oldest and most historic in Wellington. The *Thorndon Heritage Trail* leaflet (from the VIC, $1) outlines other historical sites in the area. Two notable examples are the

1843 **Premier House** (still the official Prime Minister's residence) on Tinakori Road and, further north at 25 Tinakori Road, the **Katherine Mansfield Birthplace**, ① *T06-4737268. Daily 1000-1600. $5, child $2*. Mansfield is generally hailed as New Zealand's most famous writer, having penned many internationally well-known short stories. Some of those stories (*Prelude* and *A Birthday*) feature this house, where she lived until she was five. The house and gardens have been faithfully restored and there is an interesting video portrait of the writer.

Civic Square and the waterfront

The Civic Square, just behind the VIC, was given a major revamp in the early 1990s and is blessed with some interesting architectural features. These include the instantly striking Nikau Palm columns adorning the modernistic **Public Library** and the imaginative and beautiful silver fern orb, cleverly suspended above the centre of the square. The Civic Square is often used for outdoor events and also houses the **City Gallery**, ① *T04-8013952, www.city-gallery.org.nz   The gallery is open daily 1000-1700 and there is a good café on the ground floor. Free*. With Wellington considered the artistic heart of the nation, the gallery strives (successfully it would seem) to present a regular programme of the very best of contemporary visual arts. There is an impressive array of media on show and the gallery also hosts special events, film screenings and performances.

Also in the square is the kids' paradise of **Capital E**, ① *T04-9133720, www.capitale.org.nz Daily 1000-1700*. Described as 'an inner city childrens' events centre' it offers an ever-changing agenda of experiences, events and exhibitions. You won't be surprised to learn that there is a large and expensive toyshop attached.

From Civic Square it is a short walk across a very arty **City to Sea Bridge** that connects the square with the waterfront. The bridge sprouts a number of interesting sculptures that celebrate the arrival of the Maori in New Zealand.

The **Waterfront** has become a major focus in the city for its museums, aesthetics and recreational activities. On a sunny weekend it is abuzz with tourists and locals alike, simply chilling out, sightseeing, inline skating, kayaking or fishing.

To the north of Civic Square is **Frank Kitts Park** with its impressive childrens' play area complete with model lighthouse and slide. Further north is the classy revamped **wharf**, with its al fresco waterfront cafés and restaurants where you can relax over a beer, see various water based activities taking place and watch the sightseeing helicopter come and go

Museum of Wellington, City and Sea

① *T04-4728904, www.museumofwellington.co.nz Daily Mon-Fri 1000-1700, Sat and Sun 1000-1730. $5, child $2.50*.

Housed in the former Bond Store on Queens Wharf is the recently revitalized Museum of Wellington, City and Sea. Being in such close proximity to Te Papa, you might think its attempts to compete and woo visitors was an exercise in futility, but this museum is actually superb and, in its own way, competes favourably with Te Papa. The interior multi-levelled design is modern yet rustic, maintaining the feel of its former function and the modern dose of sensual bombardment it now houses is very powerful. As the name suggests, the emphasis is on local history, with a particular maritime bent. Of particular note is the **Waihine Disaster Gallery** and the state-of-the-art holographic Maori legends display. The Waihine was a passenger ferry that came to grief at the harbour entrance in 1968 with the loss of 51 lives. Original film footage set to a suitably dramatic score documents the chilling series of events. The 3D and holographic mix of the Maori legend display is simply stunning and leaves you in no doubt how much technology has transformed and injected new life into museums as a whole. Recommended.

① T04-3817000, www.tepapa.govt.nz Daily 1000-1800, Thu 2100. Free. (charge of around $12 for major travelling exhibitions). You will need a half a day at the museum, but much more and you'll suffer from sensory overload.

To the south of Civic Square and gracing the Harbour's eastern bank is the unmistakable Te Papa – Wellington's biggest tourist attraction. As if the exterior was not enough, the interior is also mind-bending. Heavily publicized Te Papa has tried to faithfully represent the nation's heritage since 1998, at a cost of $317 million. Since then over 5 million people have visited – not surprisingly perhaps – the recent *Lord of The Rings* exhibition. They say there is something for everybody and this does seem to hold true. There is a heavy emphasis on Maori heritage and *taonga* (treasures) and biculturalism, mixed with the inevitable early settler material. This reflects the country's relative youth on the scale of world history and events. However, it does provide the usual high-tech sensual bombardment and you will find the hours passing happily by as you become engrossed. Since it's free, it is a good idea to have an initial quick recce and return later for a more in-depth investigation. One word of advice: go early to avoid the processions of noisy children.

There is an excellent shop on the ground floor but the café is less than impressive. Modern ideas may be great, but do we have to sit at our tables and watch a decorative tube of green slime doing what our lunch is about to?

The Botanic Gardens and Cable Car
① Free, open from dawn till dusk, T04-4991903, www.wbg.co.nz The main entrance is on Glenmore St in Thorndon, on the No 12 bus route. The Cable Car, T04-4722199, runs every 10 mins, Mon-Fri 0700-2200, Sat and Sun 0900-2200. $1.80, child $1. Before going anywhere near the gardens you should pick up the free gardens map and leaflet, available from the VIC.

Wellington's Botanic Gardens are really quite magnificent, but excruciatingly hilly, and although well worth the visit and a stroll, almost require oxygen and a base camp support team to do so. Gracing its precarious slopes are 26 ha of specialist gardens, radiant flowerbeds, foreign trees and native bush. Its crowning glories are the **Carter Observatory** and the **Norwood Rose Garden**. By far the most sensible and conventional way to visit the gardens is via the **Cable Car**, at 280 Lambton Quay, first built in 1902 and now a tourist attraction in itself. The almost completely subterranean single line has cables that haul the two lovely red carriages up and down, with four stops on the way. When your carriage glides in quietly to the summit (Kelburn) station you step out into the gardens and are immediately rewarded with a fine view across the city. There is also a small museum (free).

Having arrived in such style you are now in the perfect position to explore the gardens. At the crest of the hill and a short walk from the summit station is the **Carter Observatory**, ① T04-4728167, shows and telescope viewing available at 1945, 2020, 2055 and 2130 on Tue, Thu and Sat, $10-$25, child $5-$17, which has a static displays, planetarium shows and audiovisuals. Be sure to see another fine view over the city on the lawn, just in front of the observatory. The **Norwood Rose Gardens**, with its circular display of over 300 varieties, are at the northern end of the gardens, at the base of the hill and along with the café, ① Mon-Fri 1100-1500, Sat and Sun 1000-1600, should perhaps be your last port of call.

The **Otari Wilton's Bush**, ① 160 Wilton Rd, T04-4991400, www.owb.co.nz, open dawn to dusk, free, in the suburb of Wilton northwest of the Botanical Gardens – take No 14 bus, is another famous garden that concentrates on nurturing a fine collection of native flora.

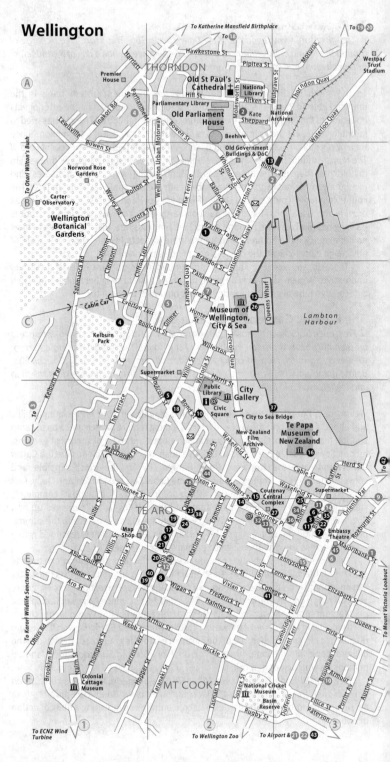

To Katherine Mansfield Birthplace
To 18
To 19 20

THORNDON

Hawkestone St
Pipitea St
Harriet St
Premier House
Westpac Trust Stadium
Moturoa

A

Old St Paul's Cathedral
National Library
Hill St
Parliamentary Library
Kate Sheppard
National Archives
Old Parliament House
Beehive
Old Government Buildings & DoC
13
Bunny St
2

B

Norwood Rose Gardens
Carter Observatory
Wellington Botanical Gardens

To Otari Wilton's Bush
To Karori Wildlife Sanctuary

Cable Car
Everton Terr
5
Kelburn Park
4
Hunter St
7
Grey St
Panama St
Brandon St
John St
1
Waring Taylor St
Museum of Wellington, City & Sea
12
26
Queens Wharf
Lambton Harbour

C

D

Supermarket
Public Library
City Gallery
37
Civic Square
City to Sea Bridge
New Zealand Film Archive
Te Papa Museum of New Zealand
16

MacDonald
17
Ghuznee St
44
Dixon St
28
Cuba Mall
TE ARO
Manners St
15
Coutenay Central Complex
23 38
19
17 9
24
13
Map Shop
21
20 29
40
39
8
12
Wakefield St
Cable St
8
Supermarket
9
Oriental Par
25
34 31
6
36 27
32 33
14
11 22
7
Embassy Theatre
45
6
Levy St

E

F

MT COOK
Colonial Cottage Museum
National Cricket Museum
Basin Reserve

To ECNZ Wind Turbine
To Wellington Zoo
To Airport & 21 22 43

South of the city centre

Wellington Zoo, ⓘ *Manchester St, in the suburb of Newtown, directly south of the city centre, T04-3816755, www.zoo.wcc.govt.nz Daily 0930-1700 (last entry 1630). $9, child $4.* Take a No 10 or 23 bus. Like Auckland and Hamilton, Wellington has embraced the need for the modern-day zoo to be involved in conservation projects as well as be commercially viable. Wellington has some fine exhibits of natives, including **kiwi** (housed in a modern new nocturnal house), **tuatara** and a wide variety of non-natives specie, including **Sumatran tigers, Malayan sun bears** and troupe of **chimps**, the second largest in the Southern Hemisphere.

The **National Cricket Museum**, ⓘ *T04-3856602, daily 1030-1530, weekends only in winter, $3, child $1,* is a small but worthy attraction, particularly for the enthusiast. It is housed in the old grandstand of the Basin Reserve (a ground that has hosted some famous encounters) and displays a range of national and international memorabilia dating back to 1743. Particular emphasis seems inevitably to be placed on the team's encounters with the arch-enemy Australia.

The **Colonial Cottage Museum**, ⓘ *68 Nairn St, Brooklyn, T04-3849122, daily 1200-1600, closed Mon and Tue, May-Dec, $5, children free,* is housed in one of the city's oldest buildings dating back to 1858. Georgian in style, the faithfully restored and furnished interior takes you back to the early settler days. While visiting the Colonial Museum you might like to supplement the trip with a **city view** and the starkly contrasting **ECNZ Wind Turbine**, which slices the air above Brooklyn. From Brooklyn Road turn right in to Todman Street and follow the signs.

Around Wellington

There are a number of attractions around Wellington that are worth a visit. The **Karori Wildlife Sanctuary**, ⓘ *T04-9209200, www.sanctuary.org.nz; Mon-Fri 1200-2000, Sat and Sun*

N

0 metres 200
0 yards 200

1000-2000 Nov-Feb; Mon-Fri 1200-1700, Sat and Sun 1000-1700 Mar-Oct; nocturnal tours by arrangement; from $6, child $3; guided tours available, is located in a valley of regenerating bush in the suburb and hills of Karori. In 1994 an area of 250 ha was set aside and protected with a predator-proof fence. Now, with the eradication of non-native pest species within the boundary of the fence, the benefits are already being seen. Reintroduced species are beginning a comeback and birdsong is returning to bush that once lay silent. The sanctuary has an **information centre** at the end of Waiapu Road in Karori. The area around the perimeter fence is already popular for walking and mountain biking. If you are without your own transport **Wellington Rover Tours** will get you there and back (allowing over 2 hours to explore) for only $10, T021-426211, www.wellingtonrover.co.nz

Set in the middle of Wellington harbour is the **Somes or Matiu Island Reserve**, ① *T04-4991282, www.eastbywest.co.nz Daily from 0830-1700. Ferry $16.50, child $9.* Once a quarantine station, the island is now administered by the DoC and is home to a number of protected native birds. The island can be reached by ferry which leaves from Queen's Wharf and stops off at the island three times a day on its way to Days Bay near the coastal resort of Eastbourne (timetable, T04-4991273).

There are two New Zealand **fur seal colonies** near Wellington. The first and the most accessible is the Red Rocks colony reached from the end of Owhiro Bay to the south of the city (see below). If you do not have your own transport **Seal Coast Safari** or **Wellington Rover Tours** both offer tour options (see Activities, p 417). The second colony, at Turakiae Head to the south east of Pencarrow Lighthouse, requires permission (DoC). To get there take the Coast Road to Baring Head via Petone (Upper Hutt) and Wainuiomata. Then walk east to the headland (it's a half- to full-day trip). There is no public transport to Pencarrow.

There are a number of great **walks** in and around the city and details and free leaflets that cover these are available from the VIC or DoC. The **Heritage Trail** leaflet takes in many of the sights within the city above. There are **Northern, Southern, Eastern** and **Waterfront Walkways**. These range from an hour or two covering just a few kilometres to a full day's jaunt. They take in a range of city, suburb, waterfront, coastal and country scenery with both historic, contemporary or natural sights outlined. **Mount Kaukau** (430 m) to the northwest of the city is a good climb and offers a rewarding view of the region. It can be accessed from Simla Crescent in Khandallah (two hours). One of the most popular walks near the city is the walk to **Red Rocks** and the fur seal colony (see above) which is accessed via the quarry track at the western end of Owhiro Bay (4 km). Owhiro Bay is reached via Brooklyn and Happy Valley Road (take Nos 1, 4 then 9 buses).

Other good **beaches** in the area suitable for sunbathing and swimming can be found to the east of the city. From the airport follow the road round the headland to Palmer Head and **Scorching Bay** on the edge of Seatoun.

The Hutt Valley → *Population: 130,000*

To the east of Wellington, sitting obstinately right on a major fault-line and already split by the Hutt River, are the fairly unremarkable Wellington dormitory towns of Lower and Upper Hutt, or 'Hutt City'. There isn't much on offer for the visitor, but if you can drag yourself away from Wellington or just happen to be passing, there are a few sights and activities that may appeal.

Sights

The main attractions in Lower Hutt are the Maori Treasures Complex, the Petone Settlers Museum and The Dowse Art Museum and café.

The **Maori Treasures Complex**, ① *58 Guthrie St, Lower Hutt, T04-9399630,* *www.maoritreasures.com*, is an exciting new arts-based project comprising studios, an art walk, café and shop. Visitors are encouraged to join one of two tours. The two-hour 'Treasures of Our Ancestors Tour' (*Mon-Fri 1000-1330, from $45*) offers an insight in to the traditional techniques and practices passed down over five generations and used by resident artists in a variety of media. It is very much an interactive, hands-on experience that is both highly informative and a lot of fun. The four-hour 'Journey with Our Ancestors Tour' (*Mon-Fri 1000, from $85*) also includes lunch and allows participants to create something of their own under the expert guidance of the resident artists. The café and shop can be visited independently. A courtesy coach departs from the Wellington VIC 30 mins before each tour. Alternatively, take a train from the Wellington Railway Station (Hutt Valley service) to Waterloo Station or take a taxi, walk (10min) or the #76 bus south.

The **Petone Settlers Museum**, ① *on the waterfront, T04-5688373. Tue-Fri 1200-1600, Sat and Sun 1300-1700, entry by donation,* is quite a small affair but no less effective in adequately highlighting the early historical significance of the area. The **Dowse Art Museum and Cafe**, ① *Civic Centre, Laings Rd, T04-5706500, www.dowse.huttcity.govt.nz, Mon-Fri 1000-1600, Sat/Sun 1100-1700, free,* is a nationally respected showcase of contemporary art and crafts. The coffee in the café is also reputed to be the best in the area.

In Upper Hutt, the **Silverstream Railway Museum**, ① *Reynold Bach Dr, Silverstream, T04-9715747, $5, child $3,* houses a large collection of steam locomotives, some of which operate on a short track on Sundays between 1100-1600. A bit of a trek but still worth it is the **Staglands Wildlife Reserve**, ① *Akatarawa Rd, T04-5267529, www.staglands.co.nz, daily 1000-1700, $10, child $5,* another capable steward and advocate of native New Zealand wildlife conservation. There is also a very pleasant café on site with an open fire in winter. The **Kaitoke Regional Park** (12 km north of Upper Hutt) is a popular recreational spot and since the release of the *Lord of the Rings* trilogy has attracted a steady stream of loyal fans on their national tour of film locations. It was here amidst the native beautiful forest glades and alongside the riverbank that the set of **Rivendell** was created. During filming over 300 crew were on site, which is now hard to imagine since like all the other film locations little remains except the memory, the atmosphere and little Rivendell signs proudly directing you to the right spot. To get there enter the northern entrance to the park off SH2 down Waterworks Rd and follow the signs.

The **Hutt River** also featured in the film as the Great River Anduin that flowed through Middle Earth from the *Misty Mountains* and *Mirkwood*. Locations used for filming were between **Moonshine**, and **Totara Park** was also used in filming. Access is left off SH2 across Moonshine Bridge, just beyond Poets Park.

Upper Hutt also gives access to some short and more challenging walks in the **Akatarawa Forest** and **Rimutaka Forest Park** (camping available).

● Sleeping

Although not as good as Auckland in terms of quantity, Wellington does have the advantage that all types of accommodation are centrally located and within walking distance of most attractions. During festivals and in summer Wellington can get busy so you are advised to book ahead. Upper range hotels seem to dominate but, given the emphasis on weekday business, prices are usually halved at weekends.

LL-AL Hotel Inter-continental Wellington, *corner of Grey and Featherston St, T04-4722722, reservations_wellington @interconti.com* Right in the heart of the city and a stone's throw from the waterfront, the best of the best of the hotel chain links. It has all the usual amenities including 3 restaurants and bars including the western theme Arizona Bar.

LL-AL James Cook Hotel Grand Chancellor, *147 The Terrace, T04-4999500.* Another at the top range, with all mod cons, a fine piano bar and in an ideal spot to climb the steps down to Lambton Quay.

LL-L Ruby House B&B, *14b Kelburn Pde, T04-9347930, www.rubyhouse.co.nz* Elegant villa with 3 classy self-contained rooms, very private and within walking distance from the city centre. Great hosts. Recommended.

LL Shalimares, *9 Shalimares Cres, T04-4791776, www.shalimares.co.nz* Modern house with luxury, tasteful and spacious accommodation overlooking the harbour on the northern outskirts of the city.

L The Lighthouse, *326 The Esplanade, Island Bay, T04-4724177, bruce@sportwork.co.nz* Your chance to stay in a lighthouse (built in 1993). Offers suitably impressive views across the harbour entrance and oozes character. Small kitchen and bathroom on one floor, living and sleeping areas above. Recommended.

L-AL Museum Hotel-Hotel De Wheels, *90 Cable St, T04-3852809, www.museum-hotel.co.nz* A modern establishment ideally located across the road from *Te Papa* and in the heart of the café, bar and restaurant areas.

AL-A Eight Parliament Street, *8 Parliament St, T04-4990808, www.boutique-BB.co.nz* A traditional, well-appointed villa with 3 rooms (ensuite bathrooms). Excellent breakfast.

AL Quality Hotel Oriental Bay, *73 Roxburgh St, T04-3850279.* Situated on the waterfront with wonderful views across the harbour and CBD, it's worth staying here for that reason alone. However it also boasts an indoor pool, licensed restaurant and is close to *Te Papa.*

L-AL Wellesley Hotel, *2-8 Maginnity St, T04-4741308, ThorndonGroup@ compuserve.com* If you are fed up with the flash modern high-rise hotels, the 1920s neo-Georgian style Wellesley offers tastefully appointed period furnished suites right in the heart of the Lambton Quarter. Popular café with regular live entertainment (mainly jazz), gym, sauna.

A Apollo Lodge Motel, *49 Majoribanks St, T04-3851849, www.apollo-lodge.co.nz* Standard modern unit interiors, most with kitchen facilities. Walking distance to Te Papa and Courtenay Pl.

A Edgewater Homestay, *495 Karaka Bay, Karaka Bay, Seatoun, T04-3884446, www.edgewaterwellington.co.nz* Modern and classy, situated near the airport and best city beaches. Popular with *Lord of the Rings* cast and crew.

A Haswell Lodge, *21 Kent Terr, T04-3850196.* Comfortable units sited well off the main street. Walking distance from *Te Papa* and Courtenay Place restaurants and cafés.

A The Victoria Court, *201 Victoria St, T04-4724297, victoriacourt.nz@xtra.co.nz* A new and nicely appointed motel in a perfect location for the mid-city and café, restaurant districts of Cuba and Courtenay.

A Wellington Motel, *14 Hobson St, T04-4720334.* Closest motel to the South Island ferry terminals.

A Trekkers Hotel, *213 Cuba St, T04-3852153, info@trekkers.co.nz* A recently restored establishment right in the heart of the Cuba Quarter with fine facilities and very tidy, good value rooms. Can, however, feel a bit like being in a rabbit warren. In-house restaurant, off-street parking.

A Cambridge Hotel and Backpackers, *corner of Alpha St and Cambridge Terr, T04-3858829, info@cambridgehotel.co.nz* Impressive establishment on the edge of the Courtenay Quarter that feels more like a grand hotel than a backpackers. Full range of rooms from shared to tidy double rooms with ensuite bathroom, standard in-house facilities, Sky TV and a quite remarkable bathroom section. The only drawback is the lack of atmosphere and off-street parking. Otherwise recommended.

C-D Wildlife House Backpackers, *58 Tory St, Courtenay Quarter, www.wildlifehouse.co.nz* It seems everyone in Wellington knows *Wildlife House Backpackers* thanks to the ingenious idea of its owners to paint its exterior in zebra-like stripes. The purpose- built interior is even more notable both aesthetically and functionally. Large living areas, full range of rooms from motel-style double ensuites to dorms, large open plan kitchen, Sky TV room and a 24-hr internet suite, spa, sauna. Off-street parking is also available. Ask about the *Wildlife* $99 starter pack.

C-D Downtown Backpackers, *1 Bunny St, Lambton Quarter, T04-4738482 www.downtownbackpackers.co.nz* Not the most characterful place to be, but it's certainly 'happening', has adequate (ex-hotel) facilities, including an in-house bar and is well located next to the railway station. No off-street parking. Internet. **C-D Rowena's City Lodge**, *115 Brougham St, Mt Victoria, T0800-801414,* www.wellingtonbackpackers.co.nz Pleasant, friendly hostel in large rambling house, far more intimate than many of the larger backpackers. Value single rooms and tent sites are also available.

C-D Rosemere Backpackers, *6 MacDonald Crescent, T04-3843041, www.backpackerswellington.co.nz* Spotless. Colourful and friendly establishment in a quiet location on the edge of the happening Cuba Quarter. Full range of rooms, tent sites, good facilities throughout, internet.

C-D Wellington YHA, *corner of Wakefield St and Cambridge Terr, T04-8017280, yhawgtn@yha.org.nz* Very popular and supporting an impressive new modern expansion. Comfortable rooms with ensuite bathrooms, fine views and all in the heart of the Courtenay Quarter's cafés and restaurants, just a stone throw from *Te Papa*.

Motorcamps and campsites
It is hard to believe that there is, as yet, no motorcamp within Wellington itself.

B-D 'Top-Ten' Hutt Park Holiday Park, *95 Hutt Park Rd, Lower Hutt, T0800-488872, www.huttpark.co.nz* Excellent. Although about 15 km from Wellington city centre it is worth the trek. There really is little choice. See also **backpackers** above for camping alternatives.

❼ Eating

Wellington prides itself on its thriving café and restaurant scene and is often dubbed 'the café crazy capital'. More than 80 new establishments have opened up in the last 5 years and the choice is now vast, which means you are almost guaranteed good quality. The Courtenay Quarter is where most are located (Blair St, off Courtenay Pl is practically wall-to-wall restaurants), though Queen's Wharf on the waterfront and Cuba St are also favourite haunts. For the more expensive restaurants booking is advised.
$$$ Dockside, *Queen's Wharf, T04-4999900;*
$$$ Shed 5, *Queen's Wharf, T04-4999069. Both open daily from 1100.* Two very popular eateries. Although both are fine evening venues they are particularly popular during the day and at weekends, with their al fresco atmosphere and mainly seafood or Mediterranean lunches (or simply a cold beer

while watching the world go by).

413

$$$ *Icon Restaurant, Te Papa, T04-8015300. Daily from 1100.* As you might expect, although not enjoying the same al fresco atmosphere as the above, it is very classy and boasts another fine view – one that can be enjoyed in all weathers. International cuisine with a Pacific Rim influence.

$$$ Logan Brown, *corner of Cuba and Vivian sts, T04-8015114. Open for lunch Mon-Fri and dinner Mon-Sun.* A well established, multi award-winning establishment, offering international cuisine in the old historic and spacious banking Chambers. The interior is spectacular and comes complete with a huge chandelier.

$$$ Bouquet Garni, *corner of Willis and Boulcott sts, T04-4991095. Daily from 1000.* Both a bistro and wine bar set in an old wooden villa. It offers fine or casual dining and is very proud of its beef and lamb dishes for which it has just won a national award.

$$$ Boulcott Street Bistro, *99 Boulcott St, T04-4994199. Open from 1200 Mon-Fri and Mon-Sat from 1800.* Another top restaurant in historic surroundings, this time a period wooden villa. The cuisine is mainly French mixed with some international dishes.

$$ Little India, *Blair St, T04-3852535. Open for lunch Mon-Fri and dinner daily from 1730.* One of the city's best Indian restaurants.

$$ Mondo Cucina, *Blair St, T04-8016615. Daily from 1730.* Popular and modern but with a rich traditional menu and a fine bar. Has some interesting artworks on the walls.

Most of the more classy pubs in the Courtenay Quarter offer fine, reliable and mainly international or Pacific Rim cuisine.

$$ Hummingbird, *corner of Blair St and Courtney Pl, T04-8016336. Mon-Fri from 1100-0300, Sat and Sun 1000-0300.* Attracts a loyal following and is known especially for great tapas.

$$ Brava, *2 Courtenay Pl, T04-3841159. Mon-Fri 0800-late, Sat and Sun 0900-late.* Offers reliable fine dining but is most popular for its breakfasts and brunches at the weekend.

$$ Uncle Changs, *72 Courtenay Pl, at the other end of Courtenay, T04-8019568. Open daily for lunch and dinner.* One of the better Chinese restaurants, it specializes in Taiwanese and Szechuan.

Wellington Eating

$$ **Monsoon Poon**, *12 Blair St, T04-8033555. Open for lunch Mon-Thu 1100-2300, Fri 1100-2400, Sat 1700-2400, Sun 1700-2300.* Considered the pick of Asian restaurants in the city. One of the reasons for this is the neat concept of offering a wide range of Asian dishes from Thai to Vietnamese all in the one place. The chefs do their thing in full view of the dining floor, which is spacious yet designed to accommodate social groups couples, or singles, plus a lively bar. All this creates a great atmosphere. Recommended.

$$ **One Red Dog**, *9-11 Blair St, T04-3849777. Daily 1000-2400.* A bar-cum-restaurant offering some of the best gourmet pizza in town. Fine wine list. The only drawback is its popularity as both restaurant and bar as it can get a little too busy at times.

There are numerous small restaurants and cafés in the **Cuba Quarter**.

Restaurants that stand out include:

$$ **The Café Istanbul**, *156 Cuba St, T04-3854998. Open daily for lunch and dinner.* A Turkish-style restaurant with a very congenial atmosphere and a loyal following.

$$ **Tulsi**, *135 Cuba St, T04-8024144. Open daily for lunch and dinner.* A new Indian restaurant with a very classy modern interior, known for its highly contemporary cuisine and friendly service. Recommended.

$$ **Kopi**, *103 Willis St, T04-4995570. Open daily from 1000.* Perhaps the best Malaysian place in the city offering 'rotis' to die for.

$$ **Sakura**, *corner of Whitmore and Featherstone sts, T04-4996912. Mon-Fri 1200-1400 and Mon-Sat from 1800.* In the heart of the city, this is one of the best traditional Japanese restaurants.

$$ **Tugboat on the Bay**, *in an old tugboat in Oriental Bay, T04-3848884. Daily for lunch and dinner.* If you prefer waterscapes to cityscapes and really wish to get intimate with the harbour, this place offers the usual classy seafood dishes with traditional kiwi backups.

$ **Backbencher**, *34 Molesworth St, T04-4723065.* Characterful place at the northern end of town where you can be assured a good pub lunch.

In the Cuba Quarter there are numerous inexpensive cafés and takeaways:

$ **Midnight Expresso**, *178 Cuba St and*
$ **R&S Noodle House**, *148 Cuba St.* Both are recommended.

$ **K.K. Malaysia**, *54 Ghuznee St and*
$ **Satay Village**, *58 Ghuznee St.* Neither will disappoint in either price or quality.

$ **Molly Malone's Dubliner Restaurant**, *(upstairs), corner of Courtenay and Taranaki, T04-3842896.* You can't go far wrong with a traditional pub lunch here.

$ **Satay Kampong**, *262 Wakefield St. Open for both lunch and dinner.* Basic and immensely popular Malaysian restaurant.

$ **Wellington Seamart**, *220 Cuba St. Mon-Thu 0700-2000, Fri 0700-2100, Sat 0700-2000, Sun 0700-1730.* Fish and chips or fresh seafood.

Finally, if it is late at night, you are desperate and anywhere near the railway station, there is always the 24-hr **Donald's Pie Cart**.

❼ Cafés

Café Lido, *right in the heart of town, just opposite the VIC (which itself has a reputable café). Mon-Wed 0700-1700, Thu-Fri 0700-1900, Sat 0900-1430.* One of the most popular in the city and always busy. It is a fine place to mix with Wellingtonians and watch the world go by over good coffee.

Astoria Café, *corner of Waring Taylor St and Lambton Quay.* A modern, popular café that fills with suits at lunchtime. It is also famous for the weird water sculpture outside that looks for all the world like a stand off between a group of rival sperm!

Cuba St is the focus of the café scene where 'funky' **Fidels** (234), **Café Globe** (213), **Midnight Expresso** (178), **Olive** (170) and **Krazy Lounge** (132) all stand out.

Café L'Affare, *27 College St, T04-3859748. Mon-Fri 0700-1630, Sat 0800-1600.* Well worth the extra walk. It is a thriving coffee business as well as an excellent café, full of atmosphere. As you might expect the coffee (and even the smell of the place) is sublime.

Expressoholic, *128 Courtenay Pl*, is laid back, open late and also serves up great coffee.

Parade Café, *148 Oriental Pde.* Another popular award-winner.

Chocolate Fish, *near the beach at Scortching Bay.* Full of character and hugely popular on sunny summer afternoons. Many from the cast and crew of *Lord of the Rings* chose this as their favourite hangout.

● Pubs, bars and clubs

Pubs and bars

The main hot spots in the city are **Courtenay Pl** and its off-shoots **Blair St** and **Allen St** with the odd reputable drinking hole in **Cuba St**, **Willis St** and the **Central Business District (CBD)**. With the vast range of cafés and restaurants, many of which are licensed, the main pubs tend to remain quiet until late, when, particularly at weekends, they fill with young and old and generally go off well into the wee small hours.

Backbencher, *34 Molesworth St, T04-4723065*. Worth a look for sheer interest's sake, with the *'Spitting Image'* type dummies and cartoons decking the walls keeping the country's politicians in check. It also is a good venue to watch sports, has live bands at the weekend and is a hugely popular venue on Fri nights.

Queen's Wharf is a great daytime drinking venue with a number of fine waterfront cafés providing the ideal spot for that relaxing afternoon libation. These include:

Dockside and **Shed 5** (see Eating above).

The Bodega, *286 Willis, T04-3848212*. A laid back, live music venue.

Barney's Place, *80 Cuba St, T04-3848441*. A similar venue, especially good for cheesy 80s music.

The selection on Courtenay and its off-shoot streets of Blair and Allen are vast but the following are a few of the most popular:

Molly Malone's, *corner Taranaki St and Courtney Pl, T04-3842896*. The city's most popular Irish offering and hosts bands both folk and rock most nights. The beer too is reliably good.

Vespa Lounge, *721 Allen St, T04-3852438*. A popular late night venue and where most bartenders go till well into the wee hours.

One Red Dog and **CO2**, *both on Blair St*. The up-market 'bolly til you're jolly' venues.

Clubs

Wellington enjoys a lively club scene though, like pubs, loyalty and popularity of individual places waxes and wanes. As usual it always pays to talk to the locals.

Opera, *Courtenay Pl*. Rather trendy and uptight but popular dance music venue.

Coyote St Bar, *Courtenay Pl, T04-3856665*. Takes itself less seriously than *Opera*.

Phoenix, *Courtenay Pl*. Especially noted for hosting overseas DJs.

Barney's, *60 Dixon St, T04-3848441*. A laid-back low-key place playing lots of 80s music. Has a loyal and friendly local clientele.

Good Luck Bar, *126 Cuba St*. Often referred to as the 'Chinese Opium den revisited' and the best place to be in this part of town.

● Entertainment

For up-to-date listings contact the VIC or check the daily newspaper *The Dominion*, as well as the tourist papers *City Life* and *Capital Times*. Other useful websites: *www.events.org.nz* or the city's own *www.wellingtonnz.com*

Although Aucklanders would disagree, Wellington probably has the edge when it comes to a good night out. There are numerous venues: large concert halls like the **Michael Fowler Centre** offering both rock and classical; noted theatres like the **St James** and **Circa**, offering contemporary drama, dance and comedy; and a plethora of pubs and clubs, particularly down Courtenay Pl and along Cuba St.

For major events tickets can be booked or bought directly from **Ticketek**, *in the Michael Fowler Centre, 111 Wakefield St, T04-3843840, www.ticketek.co.nz* Also note that the VIC offers discounts on theatre tickets, subject to availability.

Art galleries

Wellington is a major national venue for the visual arts and there are some fine galleries. The VIC produces an excellent free guide – *The Wellington Arts Map* booklet. Dealers in contemporary New Zealand art include:

The Bowen Galleries, *35 Ghuznee St, T04-3810351. Mon-Fri 1000-1730, Sat 1000-1400*.

The Ferner Gallery, *128 Featherstone St, T04-4999446. Mon-Fri 0930-1730, Sat 1000-1600*.

The Tinakori Gallery, *132 Featherstone St, T04-4712636. Mon-Fri 0900-1700, Sat 1000-1500*.

Cinemas

Tuesday night is cheap ticket night and listings can be found in the daily papers.

Paramount, *25 Courtenay Pl, T04-3844080, www.delux.co.nz* Considered the best and most characterful cinema in town. In-house bar.

The Embassy Theatre, *10 Kent Terr, at the bottom of Courtenay Pl, T04-3847657*. Also deserves special mention. Due to its giant screen (which is one of the largest in the Southern Hemisphere) and a recent renovation, it was chosen as the venue for the Australasian premier of Kiwi director Peter Jackson's *Lord of the Rings* trilogy in October 2001. For a number of weeks after the *Two Towers* premier in 2002 a huge model of *Gollum* peered down menacingly at a large replica of the ring from the rooftop – not a pretty sight.

Other mainstream cinemas include:
Reading Theatres, *in the Courtenay Central Complex, Courtenay Pl, T04-8014600*;
Rialto Theatres, *corner of Cable St and Jervois Quay, T04-3851864*; and
Hoyts, *Manners St, T04-3843567*.

Comedy venues

Indigo Bar and Venue, *171 Cuba St, T04-8016797*. Well known for its laid-back comedy nights.

Concert halls

The Michael Fowler Centre, *111 Wakefield St, T04-8014231*. Wellington's largest concert venue hosting a mix of rock and classical performances. Tickets sold on site with *Ticketek*.
Wellington Town Hall, *T04-8014231*, and **Queen's Wharf Events Centre**, *T04-4700190*, are 2 other popular concert venues.

Theatres

There are 4 principal theatres in Wellington, all with good reputations.
Bats Theatre, *1 Kent Terr, T04-8024175, bats@actrix.co.nz* A small characterful venue offering live professional theatre focusing on alternative works and New Zealand drama.
Circa Theatre, *1 Taranaki St, T04-8017992, www.circa.co.nz* Performance times Tue and Wed 1830, Thu-Sat 2000, Sun 1600. Next to *Te Papa* is a well-established theatre that offers lively international drama, comedy and music. In-house café.
Downstage Theatre, *12 Cambridge Terr,*

T04-8016946, www.downstage.co.nz Recently renovated and one of New Zealand's leading professional theatres presenting touring shows of classic contemporary drama, dance and comedy.
Opera House, *111 Manners St, T04-8024060*. Also one of Wellington's favourite venues for touring shows and has recently undergone major renovation.
Westpac St James Theatre, *also on Courtenay Pl, T04-8024060, stjames@stjames.co.nz* Originally built in 1912, after a multi-million dollar refurbishment in 1998 it is now considered a premiere venue and a central focus to the performing arts. The *James* is also home to the Royal New Zealand Ballet.

Gay and lesbian

In the **Cuba Quarter**:
Valve, *154 Vivian St*
Blue Note, *191 Cuba St* and
The Pound, *63 Cuba St* are all popular and go off well in to the night with anything from karaoke to drag performances. For more information on gay and lesbian issues contact the **Gay switchboard**, *T04-3850674*, or **Lesbian Line**, *T04-3851162*.

Live music venues

Jazz

Blondini's Café and Bar, *at the Embassy Theatre on Kent St (see above)*. Offers a dynamic jazz program at weekends from 2200-late.
Beacon Bar, *8 Blair St, T04-8017275*. Another popular venue, Thu and Sat nights.

Classical

Occasional classical concerts are staged at:
University School of Music;
Conservatorium of Music (Polytechnic) and **St Andrews** on the Terrace. See VIC for further details.

Rock

There are numerous pub venues that host mainly weekend rock gigs including:
Opera, *corner of Blair St and Courtenay Pl, T04-3828900*;
Bodega, *286 Willis St, T04-3848212*;
Wellington Sports Café, *corner of Tory St*

and Courtenay Pl, T04-8018015;
Indigo, *171 Cuba St, T04-8016797;*
The Grand, *69-71 Courtenay Pl,*
T04-8017800, (Thu);
Backbencher, *34 Molesworth St,*
T04-4723065;
Matterhorn, *106 Cuba St, T04-3843359.*

Folk
Molly Malone's, *corner of Taranaki and*
Courtenay sts, T04-3842896. Can usually get
the toes tapping most nights.
Kitty O'Sheas, *a few doors down,* less
traditional and coming in a close second.

▲ Activities and tours

Cruising For day trips around the Harbour,
to the Somes Island Reserve and the eastern
harbour seaside resorts of Days Bay and
Eastbourne take the **Eastbourne Ferry**,
T04-4991282 (timetable T04-4943339). It
operates a regular sailing schedule daily from
Queen's Wharf. A day return to Days Bay is
$15, child $8. There are also a number of
charter boats available at Queen's Wharf.
After 5, *T04-4999069, www.shed5.co.nz,* is a
custom-built luxury launch offering fishing
cruises with catering supplied by the *Shed 5*
restaurant, from $45-$75. Tailored cruises
around the harbour or further afield across
Cook Strait to the beautiful Marlborough
Sounds. On-board catering and
accommodation is available, *T025-452641.*
Charter boats for fishing leave just north of
Queen's Wharf.
The former ferry, **M.V. Wellesley**, *based at*
the southern end of the waterfront (just north
of Te Papa), hosts 2 cruise options, an
evening jaunt with a buffet diner ($39)
through the week and 1 hr harbour cruises
departing 1300, 1400 and 1500 Sat and Sun
from $3.

Ecotours Seal Coast Safari, *departs from*
the VIC at 1030 and 1330, T0800-732527,
www.sealcoast.com Offer entertaining tours
of the seal colony and Red Rocks often
taking in the ECNZ Wind Turbine on the way,
$59, child $10, 2 hr 45 min.

Golf Paraparaumu Golf Course, *just north*
of Wellington, T04-9028200. An international
standard golf links ranked 73rd in the world

and graced by Tiger Woods at the NZ Open **417**
in 2001.
Miramar Course, *next to the airport,*
T04-8017651. Average.
Karori Course, *on the outskirts, T04-4767337.*
More challenging.

Horse trekking Country Club Riding
Academy, *Johnsonville (Ohariu Valley),*
T04-4788472. New Zealand's largest
equestrian centre specializing in horse
trekking and tuition.

Inline skating Hugely popular along the
waterfront.
Ferg's Rock 'n' Kayak, *Shed 6 on the Queen's*
Wharf, T04-4998898, www.fergskayaks.co.nz
Mon-Fri 1000-2200, Sat and Sun 0900-2200.
Blade hire from $10 per hour, tuition also
available for $30.
Cheapskates, *60 Cuba St, T04-4990455.* Skate
hire from $10, 1 hr.

Kayaking Ferg's Rock 'n' Kayak, *see*
above. Hugely popular at weekends hiring
out a range of single or double kayaks for
self-guided or organized trips (night
included) on the harbour. Hire from $12 for 1
hr, Basic Skills Course (Sun mornings) from
$60. There is also a **climbing wall** on the
premises reputed to be the highest in the
country, 2 hr instruction, 1 hr coaching with
entry and all equipment, from $30.

Mountain biking There are a number of
good tracks around Wellington including the
Karori Wildlife Sanctuary perimeter fence
(from Brooklyn Hill), **Karori Reservoir**, parts
of the **Southern Walkway**, **Tinakori Hill** and
Mount Kaukau.
Mud Cycles, *T04-4764961,*
www.mudcycles.co.nz Cycle hire and tours
from $25 for a half day.

Scenic flights Helipro, *Queen's Wharf,*
T04-4721550, www.helipro.co.nz Helicopter
flights over the city, harbour or beyond from
$75 for 10 min.

Sightseeing There are a number of
specialist sightseeing operators offering a
range of city (and further afield) tours.
Wally Hammond's Tours, *T04-4720869.*
Scheduled daily trips with a well-established

and entertaining operator, 2½ hours, $40.
Wellington Rover Tours, *T021-426211,
www.wellingtonrover.co.nz* Good value, for a
city tour taking in Mount Victoria, the zoo,
the seal colony at Red Rocks, and a well-
earned coffee stop at the *Chocolate Fish Café*.
Additional venues include the Karori Wildlife
Sanctuary. From $35 (Karori only $10).
Walk Wellington, *T04-3849590,
walkwellington@xtra.co.nz* For informative
and entertaining guided walks around the
city with either an art, heritage or nature
bias. From $20, child $10 (2 hrs). Book at
least 3 days ahead if possible.

Swimming The best beaches are east of
the city around the coast at Seatoun. The
invitingly named **Scortching Bay**, *3 km
north of Seatoun*, is a favourite. If the b
each holds no appeal, head for the **Freyberg
Pool**, *139 Oriental Pde,T04-3843107.
Daily 0600-2100, Fri 1730.*
**Windsurfing/surfing Wild Winds Sail
and Surf**, *at the Overseas Terminal near* Te
Papa, *T04-3841010 (summer only)*. Windsurf
hire and tuition available.

Hutt Valley
**Lower Hutt HangDog Indoor Rock
Climbing Wall**, *based at the Top Adventures
HQ, 453 Hutt Rd, T04-5899181,
www.topadventures.co.nz Casual entry costs
$9. Open daily 0900-2100.* Top Adventures
also offer waterfall abseiling, half day from
$50, a Rap Jump and Abseil (70m) package,
again a half-day trip, from $50 and a full day
Rap, Abseil and Rock Climb combo, from
$75. All great fun, safe and good value.
Upper Hutt Mt Devine Horse Treks,
Russell's Road, T04-5289973.
H20Xtream Aquatic Adventure Centre,
*corner of Blenheim and Brown sts,
T04-5272113. Open daily.* Water slides, a wave
machine and all manner of water activities.

O Shopping

Wellington is reputed to be a fine city for
shopaholics who generally find no difficulty
in getting the right fix in the main shopping
areas of **Lambton Quay, Willis, Cuba**
and **Courtenay Streets**. For quality
souvenirs try the shop on the ground floor at
Te Papa. The VIC has a number of free

shopping leaflets, the *Wellington Shopping
Guide* being the current bible of choice.

Lambton Quay
The highlights on Lambton Quay
(nicknamed 'The Golden Mile') are the
elegant **boutique shops** of the
Old Bank and **Kirkcaldie and Stains**,
Wellington's answer to Harrods. Here you
can indulge, browse or simply try the huge
variety of scents before re-emerging on the
street like a mobile flowerbed.
Sommerfields, *199 Lambton*, is a grand shop
for New Zealand **souvenir** hunters.
Dymocks, *366 Lambton*; and
Whitcoulls, *312 Lambton*, the major
bookshops are also based here.

Willis Street
Well-known for its sheer variety with a
number of popular **clothing stores**
including: **Starfish**, *128 Willis St and
Robin Mathison, 89 Victoria St.
Unity Books, at the far end of Willis St.* An
excellent bookshop specializing in New
Zealand titles.

Cuba Street
As you might expect, Cuba Street's wide
variety of cafés and restaurants are echoed in
the nature of its shops. Whether it is 70s
clothing, second-hand books, utter kitsch, a
pair of skin-tight pink plastic pants or an
erotic device (batteries not included), this is
where to go. It is always good fun to muse at
the other shoppers even if you do not
indulge yourself.

Courtenay Place
A little more upmarket than Cuba but still
retains a wide variety of interesting shops.

☻ Sports venues

WestpacTrust Stadium, *just north of the city
centre on Aotea Quay*. This distinctly spherical
space has become the proud venue for
national and international rugby fixtures,
international rugby sevens tournaments and
cricket.
Basin Reserve, *at the other end of the city on
Buckle Street*. Still used for regional and
national cricket fixtures and home to the
National Cricket Museum (see Sights above).

❀ Festivals and events

It seems that Wellington is happy and proud to host more 'events' than any other town or city in New Zealand and there is always something going on. The Jazz festival and Festival of the Arts are particularly, and deservedly, well celebrated.

Foster's Wellington Cup Week (*Jan*). A major sporting and social event for the city and the region's high point on the annual racing calendar. Usually held in the last week of the month, T04-5284166, www.racingwellington.paradise.net.nz

Wellington Fringe Festival (*Feb/Mar*). An exciting month-long event that begins in the last week of February and celebrates and showcases contemporary and modern theatre, music and dance, T04-4958015, www.fringe.org.nz

Wellington Dragon Boat Festival (*Feb*) Usually held towards the end of the month, this paddle-fest attracts over 2000 competitors, T04-4710205, www.dragonboats.co.nz

New Zealand International Festival of the Arts (*Feb/Mar*). This is a biennial event and Wellington's most celebrated. It lasts for 3 weeks and is currently the country's largest cultural event with a rich and varied pageant of music performers, drama, street theatre, traditional Maori dance, modern dance and visual arts. T04-4730149, www.nzfestival.telecom.co.nz

Tareitanga Sculpture Symposium (*Feb/Mar*). A 2-week event where up to 50 artists create an exciting range of works at Frank Kitts Park on the waterfront, www.tareitanga.org.nz

The Laugh Festival (*Apr*). A national comedy event open to local, national and international talent, www.laugh.nzoom.com

Wellington Film Festival (*Jul*). A showcase of nationally and internationally celebrated films, T04-3850162.

Wellington International Jazz Festival (*Oct, biennial*). An increasingly popular and growing celebration of national and international jazz talent, T04-3859603 www.jazzfestival.co.nz

❍ Transport

Getting to the South Island

The scenic 85 km journey across Cook Strait takes either 3 hrs or 2 hr 15 min depending upon which ferry you take. There are basically 2 services to choose from. The long established **Interisland** and the faster **Lynx** services are both operated by the Interisland Line, *T0800-802802, www.interislandline.co.nz* The latest vessel making the crossing and without doubt the one with the most character is the independently operated **Bluebridge**, *T0800-844844, T03-5203086, www.strait.co.nz* It also tends to be a little cheaper.

In adverse weather conditions the crossing can be a bit of an ordeal. Sailings will be cancelled if conditions are considered too dangerous, but thankfully this does not happen very often. If you can, schedule your trip so it is daylight during the 1 hr scenic and memorable approach through the 'Sounds' to Picton. Also note that access outside on the Lynx is very limited, so if you want to take photographs, go on the older vessels. Pre-booking quite well in advance is advised at all times, but especially in Dec/Jan. Most major VICs and travel agents organise bookings and tickets.

'Arahua' and 'Aratere' ferry schedule

There are 3 vehicle/passenger ferries in the **Interislander** fleet, the *Arahua* (meaning 'Pathway to Dawn') or the *Aratere* (meaning 'Quick Path') and the *Lynx* (see below). On board the Arahua and Aratere facilities include a range of bars, food courts, cafés, a movie theatre and a VIC. There is also a children's play area and nursery and private work desks, although negotiating a laptop on stormy seas can in itself provide much entertainment for fellow passengers. The slightly higher Club Class ticket will give you access to a private lounge, complimentary tea and coffee, magazines, newspapers and a slightly better class of sick bag. A free shuttle bus to the terminal (2 km) is available from the Wellington Railway Station, 35 mins before each scheduled ferry departure. At the Picton end a free shuttle is available to

Wellington Transport

● *For an explanation of the sleeping and eating price codes used in this guide, see the inside*
● *front cover. Other relevant information is provided in the Essentials chapter, see page 51.*

the railway station connecting Picton with Christchurch.

Various day/limited-excursion, family and group fares and standard discounted fares are available but must be booked in advance and are subject to availability. At peak periods (particularly Dec/Jan) discounts are rarely available and whatever the discount, they are offered mainly in winter and for night sailings. **Best of New Zealand Pass** and **Travelpass New Zealand** are accepted, and kids under the age of 4 travel free. Fares for passengers range from the standard $52 (child $31), to the saver $36 (child $23). Vehicles including campervans cost from $129-$179. The vehicle fare does not include the driver. Motorcycles cost from $36-$52, bikes $10.

Lynx Ferry

The **Lynx** is the fast and rather incongruous-looking catamaran that operates daily, taking 2 hr 15 min to do the crossing. On board facilities are the most luxurious of all the services and include a café and bar. Various discounted fares are available subject to availability. **Best of New Zealand Pass** and **Travelpass New Zealand** are applicable with small additional charge. Fares for passengers range from the standard $68 (child $39) to the saver $47 (child $29). Vehicles including campervans cost from $149 to $199. The vehicle fare does not include the driver. Motorcycles cost from $47-$68, bikes $15.

The Bluebridge

The Bluebridge came into service in mid-2002 and has become very popular, not only as a result of its slightly cheaper fares but because it is also considered 'old fashioned'. This is a real ship and unlike the modern, fast and comfy catamarans does not look like something straight out of a Batman movie. Needless to say facilities are basic, but adequate and so far the service is efficient

and the staff amicable. The standard fare is $40 for a passenger (child $25) and $110 for the vehicle.

ⓘ Directory

Bike hire Mud Cycles Karori, *1 Allington Rd, Karori, T04-4764961*. Penny Farthing, *89 Courtenay Pl, T04-3852279*. **Car hire** At the airport, also: Ace, *150 Hutt Rd, T04-4711176*; Darn Cheap Rentals, *14 Seaview Rd, T0800-800327*; Pegasus, *51 Martin Sq, T04-3844883*; Budget, *81 Ghuznee St, T04-8024548*. **Foreign Exchange** Thomas Cook, *358 Lambton Quay, T04-4722848*; American Express, *Cable Car Complex, 280-292 Lambton Quay, T04-4737766*. **Internet** Available at the VIC. Otherwise, Manners, Cuba and Courtney Sts are your best bet. Outlets include: E-Joy, *115 Cuba St, T04-3852153*; Cyber City, *99 Courtenay Pl, T04-3843717*; Cyber Spot, *Lambton Sq, 180 Lambton Quay, T04-4730098*; On Net, *Shop 17, Oaks Complex, Dixon St, T04-3848259*. **Post office** *101 and 284 Lambton Quay, T04-4723301*. Mon-Fri 0830-1700. Post Restante, *43 Manners St, T04-4735922*. Mon-Fri 0800-1730, Sat 1000-1330. **Embassies and consulates** Australia, *72 Hobson St St, T04-4736411, T04-4996393* ; Canada, *61 Molesworth St, T04-4739577* ; France, *42 Manners St, T04-3842555*; Germany, *90 Hobson St, T04-4736063*; UK, *44 Hill St, T04-4726049*; USA, *29 Fitzherbert Terr, Thorndon, T04-4626000*. **Library** *Victoria St (Civic Sq)*. Mon-Fri 0930-2030, Sat/Sun 1300-1700. **Medical services** Wellington Hospital, *Riddiford St, T04-3855999*. A&E Centre (and After Hours Pharmacy), *17 Adelaide Rd, T04-3858810*. Urgent Pharmacies, *Medical Centre Building, 729 High St, T04-9396777*. **Taxi** Wellington Combined, *T0800-384444 / T04-3844444*. Black and Gold, *T04-3888888*. **Useful addresses** AA: *79 Taranaki St, T04-3858859*. **Police** *corner of Victoria and Harris St, T04-3812000*.

Kapiti Coast → *Phone code: 04*

Just north of Wellington, SH1 slices its way through the hills of a major fault-line and passes the rather dull dormitory town of Porirua before joining the picturesque Kapiti Coastline. For the next 30 km the small coast and inland settlements of Paekakariki, Waikanae and Otaki are shadowed by Kapiti Island on one side and the Tararua Forest Park on the other. Kapiti Island itself is well worth a visit while Paekakariki, Paraparaumu and Waikanae offer a number of interesting local sights and activities. Otaki is the principal access point to the Tararua Forest Park.

Ins and outs

Getting there   Paekakariki, Paraparaumu, Waikanae and Otaki are all on SH1 and the main rail line. Both the main bus companies and TranzMetro trains stop at these centres. Note the regional trains to and from Paraparaumu run frequently day and evening services and are relatively cheap. A day rover ticket costs $10. For information and times contact **Ridewell**, T0800-8017000 or the VICs. **Blue Penguin Coaches**, T04-3646899, T025-454164, www.blue-penguin.co.nz, also run Wellington and airport services and may also be able to assist weekdays. It is also worth considering the **Capital Explorer Pass** which allows a day of unlimited travel on regional buses and trains along the Kapiti Coast for $15, T04-8017000.

All access and landing permits for **Kapiti Island** are administered and must be pre-booked with DoC. Only 50 people can land per day and bookings need to be made well in advance. Landing permits cost $9, child $4.50. Although there is a well equipped hut, it is mainly used for research purposes and no overnight stays are allowed. For detailed information call DoC or consult the booklet *Kapiti Island Nature Reserve*, available from the main Wellington DoC Office, see page 403. Private boats are not allowed to land on the island but two principal permitted private operators can get you there for a day trip: **Kapiti Tours Ltd**, T0800-527484, T04-3645042, www.kapititours.co.nz, from $30, child $20 and **Kapiti Marine Charter**, T04-2972585, $30, child $20. Boats depart from Paraparaumu Beach in front of the Kapiti Boating Club at 0900-0930 and return 1500-1600.

Information   **Paraparaumu VIC**, ⓘ *just off SH1 in the Coastlands shopping centre*, T04-2988195, www.kapititourist.co.nz Mon-Sat 0900-1600, Sun 1000-1600. Main **DoC** office for the Kapiti Coast, ⓘ *10 Parata St, Waikanae*, T04-2932191. **Kapiti Coast VIC**, ⓘ *in Centennial Park, SH1, Otaki*, T04-3647620, www.kapititourist.co.nz Mon-Fri 0830-1700, Sat/Sun 0900-1600.

Paekakariki → *Colour map 3, grid C2 Population: 1600*

Paekakariki is a tiny seaside village, popular with visiting train enthusiasts, as well as adrenaline junkies eager to experience the infamous 'Fly by Wire'.

Sights   The first thing to do in Paekakariki is to take a quick diversion up to the **viewpoint** on Paekakariki Hill Road (3 km) and take in the view. On a clear day you can get a great view of Kapiti Island and see the coast right up to Wanganui. At the village railway station is the **Steam Inc Engine Shed**, ⓘ *T04-9057207, Sat and Sun 1100-1500, from $6,* where devoted enthusiasts have painstakingly restored a number of vintage trains, some of which still huff and puff along the tracks. A few kilometres further north is the **Wellington Tramway Museum**, ⓘ *in Queen Elizabeth Park*, T04-2928361. *Open weekends 1100-1700*. Here historical displ- ays and working trams look back at one of Wellington's former modes of transport. Three trams are currently in operation; rides cost $4, child $2, otherwise admission is free.

Paraparaumu is the principal township on the Kapiti coast and has close ties with Wellington both as commuter town and as a seaside resort popular during the summer months. There are two main beaches, Raumati to the south and Paraparaumu Beach to the north. All the usual facilities are here and the town also serves as the gateway to Kapiti Island. A little further north on SH1 is the small satellite town of Waikanae, which also prides itself on its fine beach. Paraparaumu's main claim to fame came in 2001 when the legendary golfer Tiger Woods was lured with a rather attractive $2 million appearance fee to play (or simply to turn up) at the NZ Open golf challenge on Paraparaumu's world class golf course, T04-9028200.

Sights Other than the **beach**, the main attractions are scattered along SH1 just to the north of Paraparaumu and around Waikanae. The **Lindale Centre**, ① *2 km north of town, T04-2970916, $10, child $5,* is essentially a kitsch and coffee stop for coach tours, but there is a farm park for kids with weekend farmy shows and a number of retail outlets, including the shop attached to Kapiti Cheeses. Here a delicious and imaginative array of gourmet products are available to tickle the taste buds. There is also a café nearby that will attempt to do the same.

Just a little further north still on SH1 is the **Southward Car Museum**, ① *T04-2971221, www.southward.org.nz Daily 0900-1630. $6, child $3.* It has a huge collection of 250 vehicles dating from 1895. In addition to cars there are traction engines, motorcycles, bicycles and a model railway, shop and café.

On the outskirts of the pleasant village of **Waikanae**, 5 km north of Paraparaumu is the **Nga Manu Nature Reserve**, ① *T04-2934131, www.ngamanu.co.nz Daily 1000-1700. $7.50, child $3.50. The reserve is quite hard to find but signposted from SH1.* Although principally an educational establishment, this reserve, which is set in delightful bush, with man-made lakes, bush walks and collections of native and non-native wildlife, is definitely worth the detour. Everything is well presented and this is one of the few establishments in the country that is not ashamed to display (as highly effective educational tools) the 'enemy' – the heinous non-native pests. There is a wonderful (well enclosed) display of rats, some possums and the less well advertised, but obligatory, mallard ducks on the lawn, eyeing up your picnic. Added to the refreshing 'pest' displays are the usual collections of native birds, geckos, tuatara and a nocturnal kiwi house. Eel feeds take place at 1400.

At some point along the coast it is well worth taking at least a look at the beach. This can be done at a number of access points, one of which is **Te Horo Beach** just north of Waikanae. The coast is piled high with amazingly sculpted pieces of driftwood.

Kapiti Island → *Colour map 3, grid C2*

Kapiti Island is a very special place, a place that is not only a delight to visit but is like going back in time to when New Zealand was an unspoiled paradise. Lying 5 km offshore from Paraparaumu, it is 10 km long, two km wide and has a total land coverage of 1,965 ha. Its highest point is **Tuteremoana** at 520 m. The island is now one of the most important reserves in the country and has an adjunct marine reserve, all of which is administered, protected and nurtured by DoC. It took a huge budget and six years of hunting and poisoning in the 1980s to rid the island of 22,500 possums, while further exhaustive helicopter poison drops in the 1990s have been successful in keeping rats at bay. After numerous plant and animal reintroductions, the results are the first signs of regeneration and hints of what once was. Here you are in nature's territory – not human. You can walk on a number of well kept tracks through proper New Zealand bush. Inquisitive birds like robin, saddleback and stitchbird flit about your head, while weka and takahe poke about for insects disturbed by your feet. At night you can hear kiwi, or share the coastal path with little blue penguins that do not run in fear, but merely stick their heads in the grass and very lucky, you can hear one of the most beautiful bird songs ever to grace human ears – that of the endangered kokako.

Otaki → *Phone code: 06 Colour map 3, grid C2 Population: 5600*

Otaki is the last (or first) settlement within the Wellington Regional Boundary. Steeped in Maori history, there are a number of *marae* including the 1910 finely carved **Te Pou O Tainui Marae** on Te Rauparaha Street. The **Rangiatea Church** in the town was one of the finest restored Maori churches in the country. Sadly fire destroyed the church in 1995 and another restoration is now complete. Otaki is the main eastern gateway to the **Tararua Forest Park**. Otaki Gorge Road, which is two km to the south of the town, takes you 19 km to **Otaki Forks** where a number of tracks lead into the mountains. Information about the Tararua Forest Park, local sights and accommodation options can be obtained from the VIC (see page 421).

Wellington Kapiti Island

● Sleeping

Paekakariki *p421*
C-D Paekakariki Backpackers, *11 Wellington Rd, Paekakariki, T04-9025967, paekakbackpack@paradise.net.nz* Very pleasant, comfortable wee place set on the hillside above the village. Doubles, twins, singles and dorms.
C-D Paekakariki Holiday Park, *Wellington Rd, Paekakariki, T04-2928292.* This offers above average accommodation and amenities close to the beach.

Paraparaumu and Waikanae *p422*
LL Greenmantle, *214 Main Road North, T04-2985555, www.greenmantle.co.nz* The choice of World No1 golfer Tiger Woods in 2001 during the New Zealand Open. Offering six beautifully appointed private suites, outdoor hot tub, spa, pool and in summary 'the full set of irons', so to speak. B&B or dinner, bed and breakfast.
AL Te Horo Luxury Lodge, *109 Arcus Rd, Te Horo, T04-3643393, tehoro.lodge@xtra.co.nz* Luxuriously appointed homestay with 4 rooms in a peaceful setting near the driftwood beach. Open fire and no shortage of wood.
AL Te Nikau Forest Retreat, *Kakariki Grove, Waikanae, T04-3568460, www.tenikau.co.nz* Contemporary house with wooden interior set in coastal forest, 2 spacious doubles, tree-house spa.
A Killara Homestay, *Ames St, Paekakariki, T04-9055544, www.killarahomestay.co.nz* 2 rooms (queen and twin) in a large comfortable beachfront villa within walking distance of the village. Spa and internet.

A Byron's Resort, *20 Tasman St, Otaki, T04-3648121, www.byronsresort.co.nz* Quality motel units with all resort amenities including restaurant, pool, spa and sports facilities. Camping is also available.
A Copperfield Seaside Motel, *13 Seaview Rd, Paraparaumu Beach, T04-2986414, www.copperfield.com* Modern motel with licensed restaurant 2 mins walk from the beach.
A Sand Castle, *Paetawa Rd (off Peka Rd), Peka Peka, Waikanae, T04-2936072, sandmotel@kapiti.co.nz* A delightful and aptly named motel right next to the beach.

Motorcamps and campsites
C-D Lindale Motor Park, *Main Rd North (SH1), Paraparaumu, T04-2988046.* Ideally located next to all Lindale tourist centre amenities.
D Ngatiawa Campsite, *Terrace Rd, Waikanae, T04-2935036.* A lovely quiet campsite with cabins set in bush next to the Ngatiawa stream.

Otaki *p423*
C-D Toad Hall, *Addington Rd, Otaki, T04-3646906.* Amazing renovated homestead complete with cuddly cats and crafty canines. Dorms and doubles.

● Eating

Paekakariki *p421*
$$ Fisherman's Table Restaurant and Bar, *SH1, Paekakariki, T04-2928125. Daily 1130-2100.* A relaxed and pleasant family seafood restaurant.

$$ Aqua Vitae Wine Bar and Restaurant, *Lindale Tourist Centre just north of Paraparaumu*, *T04-2989889*. Serves New Zealand and international-style cuisine in congenial surroundings.

Waikanae *p422*
$$ Breakers Restaurant, *1 Waimea Rd*, *T04-2935711*. Another pleasant seafood restaurant.

Otaki *p423*
$ Brown Sugar Café, *corner of SH1 and Riverbank Rd*, *T04-3646359*. Lots of delicious home cooking in a garden setting.

▲ Activities

Paekakariki *p421*
Fly by Wire, *behind the BP station on SH1, where bookings can be made. (A courtesy shuttle is available from Wellington.) T0800-359299, www.flybywire.co.nz* This is a very hard 'activity' to describe and is indeed the stuff of dreams – literally. It all came about after founder Neil Harrap had dreamt (one can only presume after way too many lagers) that he was attached to a flying machine with a microlight engine on the back. It went around and around and around, like a dangling weight on a plumb line. On waking, so intrigued was Mr Harrap that he wrote it all down. But it didn't stop there. To cut a long story short, after a phone call to a friend who is a pilot, hours of design,

even more hours of building and more finding a suitable location, the dream began to take shape. Last but not least, after convincing those highly sceptical characters in the government's health and safety department that he wouldn't kill tourists, the dream became reality and 'Fly by Wire' was born. If you want to live Mr Harrap's dream you can do so in perfect safety at speeds of up to 120 km an hour for a budget-denting (but still worth it) $99, 15 minutes, plus video.

Paraparaumu *p422*
Four-wheel quad bikes **Kapiti 4x4 Adventures**, *T04-2990020, www.kapitifourX4.co.nz* More trailblazing bike trips based near Paraparaumu. One-hour ($70), all day ($250) and overnight (POA) trips.
Horse trekking **Ferndale Equestrian Centre**, *Waikanae, T04-2936209, www.ferndalehorses.com* 2-3 hour horse treks over farmland and along the beach.
Scenic flights **Kapiti Aero Club**, *Kapiti Rd, T04-9026536, bj007@paradise.net.nz* Fixed wing 20 min, from $189; helicopter 20-min, from $195 and glider 20-30 min, from $210.

Otaki *p423*
River Rock Centre, *Otaki Gorge Rd, T04-3643110, riverrock@xtra.co.nz* Host an exciting 'menu' of activities including kayaking, abseiling and rafting. They were also the originators of the intriguing concept of 'night rafting'. From $30.

South Island

Nelson and Marlborough

Introduction

The regions of **Nelson** and **Marlborough** have all the classic New Zealand ingredients – **mountains**, **lakes**, golden **beaches** and great **tramping tracks** – all safe within the boundaries of its national parks and warmed by the sunniest climate in the country. If that weren't enough, it also has a relatively low population.

Those who do live here are a diverse bunch: from the farmers, fruit-growers and wine-makers in the valleys, to the artists and writers in the quiet creative havens of the **Marlborough Sounds** and smaller rural towns, like **Motueka** or **Takaka**. Despite the appealing lifestyle and obvious attractions, few foreigners have heard of this 'secret region'. Most simply pass through on their way to the tourist honey pots further south, stopping only briefly in **Picton**, the main ferry port on South Island.

★ Don't miss...

❶ The myriad **Marlborough Sounds**. Explore them by boat, kayak, or on foot, page 430.

❷ The back roads to the remote aquatic maelstrom at **French Pass**, page 440.

❸ The world-class wines of the Marlborough Region **vineyards**. Join the locals in a rain dance, page 436!

❹ The buzz of seaside **Nelson**, the most popular coastal town in New Zealand, page 452.

❺ Lake Angelus in the **Nelson Lakes National Park**, page 481.

❻ A scenic flight from Nelson, taking in all three National Parks and the Marlborough Sounds in one day, page 464.

❼ Arty **Takaka**, **Golden Bay** and the crystal clear waters of its local **Pupu Springs**, page 474.

❽ The spectacular coast from **Cape Farewell to Wharariki Beach**. Explore the caves, the empty bays and feel guilty leaving footprints, page 477.

❾ The strange and lonely sandscapes of **Farewell Spit**, page 476.

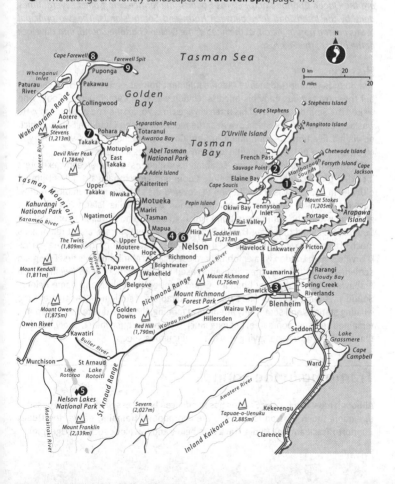

Marlborough Sounds → *Colour map 4, grid B4*

The Marlborough Sounds is like South Island's giant foyer. This vast, convoluted system of drowned river valleys, peninsulas and islets, often dubbed New Zealand's 'little slice of Norway', is the island's scenic introduction where you can enjoy stunning scenery, cruising, tramping, kayaking, wildlife watching or just a few days' peaceful relaxation. The port of Picton is the gateway to the Sounds. From here it is then only a short journey to Blenheim, the region's capital. Although the town itself is fairly unremarkable, the area produces some of the best wines in New Zealand. A day visiting a few of the top vineyards is recommended. South of Blenheim is the pretty coastal settlement of Kaikoura, famous for its whales, dolphins and seabirds, (see page 515 in the Canterbury chapter).

On the map, it may look like the Marlborough Sounds take up a relatively small area of the South Island, but its myriad sounds (drowned river valleys as opposed to fjords, which are drowned glacial valleys) create an astonishing 1500 km of coastline. Although the snow-capped peaks of Norway do not bound the endless inlets and bays, the topography is just as intriguing and very picturesque. Wildlife abounds and the area is particularly well-known for its seabirds and dolphins. The two main inlets are the Queen Charlotte and Pelorus Sounds, the former being plied several times daily by the Interisland ferry between North and South Islands. The two principal towns are the port of Picton, at the head of the Queen Charlotte Sound, and Havelock at the head of the Pelorus.

History

The Sounds exhibit evidence of Maori settlement from as early as the 14th century, but the most famous early historic association was with Captain James Cook, who visited the Sounds on each of his three voyages in 1770, 1773-4 and again in 1777. He was particularly fond of Ship Cove near the mouth of Queen Charlotte Sound, which he visited five times. A monument in Ship Cove commemorates his visits. As you might expect, Cook is responsible for many place names in the area.

Other, more brief and less celebrated, visitations by other early explorers included those of Abel Tasman (before Cook) and French navigator Jules Dumont d'Urville in 1827. It was D'Urville who discovered the chaotic and incredibly narrow passage of water between the mainland and the D'Urville Island (no prize for guessing where the name came from) which guards the northwestern corner of the Sounds. He called this strait French Pass, or Passe des Français, and it remains as much of a threat to shipping today as it did to the early navigators. In the same year as D'Urville's visit, London whaler John Guard established Marlborough's first European settlement, and the countries first land-based whaling station, at Te Awaiti Bay on Arapawa Island in the Tory Channel. Guard went on to explore and name Pelorus Sound in search of other sites that were suitable for settlement. Apart from the whaling stations and some early attempts at farming, the area, due to its topography, remained sparsely populated, keeping much of its native bush intact. Sadly, much of that bush has now gone, giving way to the ubiquitous sheep.

Tramping in the Sounds

Although most of what the Sounds has to offer can be accessed by boat it is possible to explore much of it on foot. There are two popular **tramping** tracks, the **Queen Charlotte Track** and the **Nydia Track** (see below and Havelock section, page 439).

Details of the Queen Charlotte Track are outlined in the relevant DoC leaflets and both the VIC and DoC in Picton can provide more comprehensive information and maps. The website www.qctrack.co.nz is also useful.

The Queen Charlotte Track is a 71 km (3-5 day) well formed track from Ship Cove (Captain Cook's New Zealand base, 1770-1777) to Anakiwa and suitable for most people of average fitness (it's also open in part to mountain bikes, see leaflet from VIC, $2, www.qctrack.co.nz). The track makes its way around sheltered coves, over skyline ridges and through native forest fringing a vast network of sunken river valleys. Sections of the track are suitable for mountain biking. Although the track can be tackled from either Anakiwa or Ship Cove you are advised to walk the track from Ship Cove. The track is also becoming increasingly popular, so plan and book well in advance. There are numerous DoC campsites and independent accommodation establishments to suit the full range of budgets all along the route.

Boat access is also well organized and readily available. Given the ease of water access it is considered best to tackle the route from east to west, from Ship Cove to Anakiwa. Water taxis and cruise operators regularly stop not only at Ship Cove, but also at many of the accommodation establishments or campsites en route so it is possible to do part of the track, or to stay in one place and simply chill out. For the real

The Marlborough Sounds

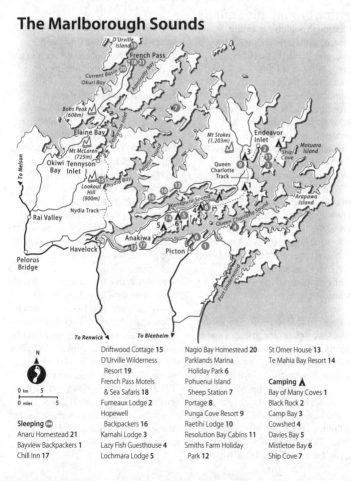

Sleeping
Anaru Homestead **21**
Bayview Backpackers **1**
Chill Inn **17**

Driftwood Cottage **15**
D'Urville Wilderness
  Resort **19**
French Pass Motels
  & Sea Safaris **18**
Furneaux Lodge **2**
Hopewell
  Backpackers **16**
Kamahi Lodge **3**
Lazy Fish Guesthouse **4**
Lochmara Lodge **5**

Nagio Bay Homestead **20**
Parklands Marina
  Holiday Park **6**
Pohuenui Island
  Sheep Station **7**
Portage **8**
Punga Cove Resort **9**
Raetihi Lodge **10**
Resolution Bay Cabins **11**
Smiths Farm Holiday
  Park **12**

St Omer House **13**
Te Mahia Bay Resort **14**

Camping Å
Bay of Many Coves **1**
Black Rock **2**
Camp Bay **3**
Cowshed **4**
Davies Bay **5**
Mistletoe Bay **6**
Ship Cove **7**

cheats you can also arrange to have your pack transported on to your next accommodation or port of call. ▸▸ *For Sleeping and Activities, pages 441-448.*

Nydia Track
Details of the track are outlined in the relevant DoC leaflets and both the VIC and DoC offices in Picton and Havelock can provide more comprehensive information and maps.
The Nydia Track is the lesser known and shorter of the two tramping tracks. It is 27 km in length and takes two days. The track, which is essentially a network of old bridle paths, begins at Kaiuma Bay (near Havelock) and traverses the Kaiuma and Nydia saddles, taking in the sheltered, historic timber-milling site at Nydia Bay, before ending at Duncan Bay. The track is particularly noted for its magnificent forest, much of which is untouched and a fine example of the native bush that once covered the region. Although the Nydia Track is more difficult than the Queen Charlotte and requires detailed planning, it offers a shorter, less busy alternative, though it is not so well served by accommodation and public transport. From Havelock it is 12 km (45 min) drive via SH6 to the turn-off at Dalton's Rd, then another 21 km to Kaiuma car park and the start of the track. Given that, you are far better catch a water-taxi (5 min) to Shag Point from Havelock. Contact the VIC in Havelock for the latest operator listings, T03-5742633. ▸▸ *See also Sleeping, page 444.*

Getting around the Sounds
Marlborough Sounds Adventure Company, *based in Picton (see Activities below)*, offer guided walks (4-day, $965/5-day $1250) and self-guided walks (4-day, including food, transport and accommodation, $535). They also offer kayaking trips and an increasingly popular 3-day walk/paddle/mountain bike adventure from $410, which is recommended. **Southern Wilderness NZ**, *T03-5784531, T0800-266266, www.southernwilderness.com*, organizes trips on the Queen Charlotte Track ranging from a 1-day guided walk (NZ$130) to a 5-day guided gourmet walk with kayaking options (NZ$1690) including luggage transfers and hotel-style accommodation with own facilities and à la carte restaurant dining. Track packages also offered for backpackers and independent walkers.

There are plenty of water-based operators who will drop off or pick up from a number of points along the track, with most offering day-walk options. Sea access is possible at Ship Cove, Resolution Bay, Endeavour Inlet, Camp Bay (Punga Cove), Bay of Many Coves, Torea Bay (the Portage), Lochmara Bay, Mistletoe Bay (Te Mahia) and Anakiwa. **The Cougar Line**, *based on the Waterfront in Picton T0800-504090.* is the most modern and comfortable. They will drop you off at

Ship Cove (departs Picton 0800/1330, $48) and pick up at Anakiwa (Tirimoana, 1430/1645). They can also deliver your pack to your accommodation and offer day-walks.
Endeavour Express, *based in both Endeavour Inlet and at the Waterfront in Picton, T03-5735456, www.boatrides.co.nz*, offer the same service, departing Picton 0900/1030/1315, with single fares starting at $20 and full round trips from $55 and picking up at Anakiwa (Tirimoana) 1715.
Beachcomber Cruises, *based in Picton, T0800-624526, T03-5736175*, have both scheduled trips to Torea and Anakiwa ($45) but will run drop off or pick up at any of the accessible points. They depart Picton 0930 and pick up Anakiwa 1600, $48. Free tea and coffee.
West Bay Water Transport, *based near the Ferry Terminal in Picton, T03-5735597, www.westbay.co.nz*, serve the southern end of the Queen Charlotte Track, from Torea Bay to Anakiwa (single $15). They also offer half-day, track-walk options ($30). Departs Picton 0830/1030/1345/1600/1800.
Arrow Water Taxis, *based in Picton, T03-5738226*, offer flexibility and will go on demand to anywhere in Queen Charlotte Sound or Tory Channel for about the same price. A typical single fare to Anakiwa is $15.

There are also options by road from Picton to Anakiwa. **Sounds Connection**, *T0800-742866* (minimum 4, $50), and **The Rural Mail Run**, from $10, are 2 further options. Both must be booked and pre-paid via the VIC. If you have your own wheels, road access is also possible at Camp Bay (Punga Cove), Torea Bay (The Portage) and Mistletoe Bay (Te Mahia).

Picton → *Phone code: 03 Colour map 4, grid B4 Population: 4000*

Picton is 27 km from Blenheim and 336 km from Christchurch south via SH1

Once you cross the Cook Strait and enter the 'The Sounds', you arrive in the pretty township of Picton, gateway to the the Marlborough Sounds and South Island. In summer Picton is a buzz of activity with visitors coming and going by ferry, car or train, but in winter it reverts to its more familiar role as a sleepy port.

Despite its size, Picton has an interesting history. It was once an important Maori *pa*-site called Waitohi before the first Europeans settled and renamed it Newton. For a while Newton was the proud capital of Marlborough (before Blenheim stole the honours) and later, after being renamed Picton, became a candidate for the country's capital. In more recent times controversy has affected the town. For almost a decade the issue of relocating the ferry port south closer to Blenheim has been hotly debated. Thankfully for 'the Picts' that option was dismissed by the government, who claim it is not financially viable. So, thankfully, as the gateway to both the South Island and the Sounds, pretty Picton looks set to remain.

Ins and outs

Getting there Picton **airport** is about 10 km south of the town and is served by **Soundsair**, *T0800-505-005, www.soundsair.com,* about nine times daily to/from Wellington; $79 one-way, $139 return including a free shuttle to town. Scenic flights and a wide range of 'flight/activity combos' are also available, see page 448.

There are numerous **bus** companies that network their way south or west from Picton. **Intercity**, *T03-5737025, www.intercitycoach.co.nz* (Nelson, Blenheim, Kaikoura and Christchurch); **Atomic Shuttles**, *T03-5737477, www.atomictravel.co.nz* (throughout South Island); **Delux Travel Line**, *T03-5785467, www.deluxetravel.co.nz* (Blenheim and beyond). Other smaller companies offering a range of options include: **South Island Connections**, *T03-3666633, www.southislandconnections.co.nz* (Christchurch and beyond); **Knightline**, *T03-5474733, www.knightlinecoaches.co.nz* (Nelson and the Abel Tasman National Park); **Kiwilink**, *T0800-802300, www.kiwilinks.co.nz* (Nelson, Golden Bay and West Coast); **Kahurangi Bus**, *T0800-881-188 / T03-5259434, www.kahurangi.co.nz* (via Blenheim to Nelson, Abel Tasman). A typical single fare to Blenhiem is $8-$10, Nelson $15-19 and Christchurch $25. Buses all drop-off or pick-up at the railway station, ferry terminal or outside the VIC. For further details and bookings contact the VIC. The main intercity coach agent is the Picton Travel Centre in the ferry terminal building, *T03-9891996.*

The **Interislander**, **Bluebridge** and **Lynx ferries** dock in the rather plush terminal, about 500 m from the town centre. There are at least four sailings daily. For information on these sailings and prices see page 419, or contact *T0800-802802, www.interislandline.co.nz.*

The daily **TranzCoastal** is the only daily **train** service to and from Christchurch and Picton, *T0800-872467, www.tranzscenic.co.nz* It arrives daily at 0050 and departs at 1340, from $55-$70. This trip is famous for its stunning coastal scenery.

Information Picton VIC, ⓘ *on the foreshore*, *T03-5737477, F5735021, www.marlboroughweb.co.nz Open daily 0830-2000 (1700 winter).* Only a short walk from the ferry terminal, very busy but staffed accordingly. There are many useful leaflets on offer including the invaluable *What to Do In Picton* and very useful *The Queen Charlotte Track*. **DoC**, ⓘ *in the same building*. Sells a range of books and maps on the region. The **railway station**, ⓘ *To3-5738857, 0900-1700*, (and ferry terminal) provides comprehensive information about train and ferry departures and prices. Useful websites include: www.picton.co.nz, www.creativemarlborough.co.nz and www.marlborough4fun.co.nz

Sights

If you have arrived on the almost futuristic *Lynx* ferry, with its comfy seats and state-of-the-art radar screens, you will be immediately thanking your lucky stars for progress when you encounter the old teak wooden hulk of the **Edwin Fox**, ⓘ *between the ferry terminal and the town centre, 0845-1700 daily. $6*. The remains of the 1853, once fully-rigged East India trading ship is being lovingly restored to a reminder of her former glory by the Edwin Fox Society. The vessel, which is – apparently – the ninth oldest ship in the world and the only remaining example of her type, was formerly a troop carrier in the Crimean War before being commissioned to bring immigrants to Australia and New Zealand. The interesting displays in the museum include the impressive hulk of the ship. One thing is for sure – they don't make nails like they used to!

Next door is the town's most recent tourist attraction, the **Aquarium of the Marlborough Sounds**, ⓘ *To3-5736030, www.aquariummarlborough.co.nz Daily 0900-1700, $8, child $5*. As one of the few aquariums in the country it is perhaps worth a look, but more fun for kids. A range of displays house the usual characters including an octopus called Larry, some seahorses and rays, and the staff are always

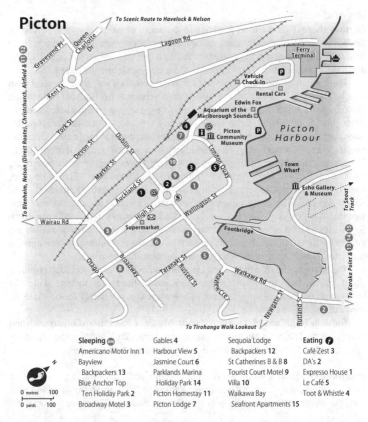

Picton

on hand to enthuse and answer any questions.

Just a little further towards the town on London Quay, commanding prime position overlooking the Waterfront, is the **Picton Community Museum**, ① *Open 1000-1600 daily. $3, child 50c*. Lovingly maintained by the Picton Historical Society, it contains a cluttered but interesting range of items focusing mainly on the 1800s whaling operations in the Sounds (including an evil-looking harpoon gun), as well as the inevitable Maori *taonga* (treasures) and early pioneer settler pieces.

A short walk across the footbridge and the inlet to the eastern side of the Waterfront to Shakespeare Bay will deliver you to the **Echo Gallery and Museum**, ① *Open daily in summer. Adult $3, child $1*. The Echo is a former 'scow' built in 1905 that has now been lovingly and gradually restored after her retirement in 1965. She was formerly a trading vessel, and apparently the last commercial trader under sail in New Zealand before seeing further service in Second World War. There is no doubt that she has led an interesting, if not rather unfortunate existence. Indeed she is perhaps the most unfortunate vessel to sail the high seas. By all accounts she was stranded 15 times, damaged 16 times, had two new engines, propellers and shafts, had fires in 1911 and 1920, seven collisions involving 75 different vessels and was sunk twice. Be careful not to trip going up the gangplank. ▶▶ *For Sleeping, Eating and other listings, see page 444-452*.

Walks around Picton

For a comprehensive guide to the walks around Picton, get hold of the excellent *Picton by Foot* broadsheet, available free from the VIC. There are a number of options, with most traversing the narrow peninsula to the northeast of the town separating Waikawa Bay and Picton Harbour. Most are around two hours return, with the longest being the **Snout Track**, taking in the **Queen Charlotte Lookout**. Other walks taking in fine views are the **Karaka Point Lookout** (20 minutes, on the main road east of Waiwaka) and the **Tirohanga Walk Lookout**, above and south of the town (start point off Newgate St just east of the town centre, two hours return). For the numerous activities based in Picton see page 448.

Blenheim → *Phone code: 03 Population: 22,000*

Although it is depressingly flat and unremarkable looking, Blenheim - Marlborough's largest town - is a popular tourist base, primarily for those intent on sampling the region's fine wines. Most of the wineries lie just to the west of town, on the fertile soils of the Wairau Plains. In Blenheim you can be sure a local winemaker will never be far away. Wine-making in Marlborough is big business and fiercely competitive; it brings new meaning to the phrase 'designer label'.

Ins and outs

Getting there Blenheim **airport** is on Middle Renwick Rd 7 km west of town. It is serviced by **Air New Zealand Link**, T0800-737000, www.airnewzealand.co.nz, and **Origin Pacific**, T0800-302302, www.originpacific.co.nz Flights are met by the **Airport Super Shuttle**, T03-5729910, or **Neal's Shuttles**, T03-5775277; $12.

Blenheim sits on both the main road (SH1) and rail links south, via Kaikoura (129 km) to Christchurch (308 km). An interesting alternative route by car to Blenheim from Picton is via the coast road, Port Underwood and the scenic bluffs of Rarangi. There are a number of fine viewpoints, sheltered bays, a campsite and several good DoC walks. In partnership with Picton there are many **bus** services available to meet the demand for those heading south. There are also services that head northwest via SH6 to Nelson, the Abel Tasman National Park and Golden Bay and west to St Arnaud and the Nelson Lakes National Park. For operators and details see Picton Ins and outs, page 433.

The **TranzCoastal** train service to Picton or south to Christchurch passes through Blenheim once a day (to Picton 0020, Christchurch 1410)., *T0800-872467, www.tranzscenic.co.nz*

Information Marlborough VIC, ① *in the railway station on Grove Rd (SH1), T03-5778080, www.destinationmarlborough.com Daily 0830-1830 (winter Mon-Fri 0900-1730; Sat and Sun 0900-1600).* There is plenty of information on hand surrounding the town, region and, of course, about the wineries. The free *Marlborough Visitor Guide* is useful.

Climate One of the rarest sights you will see in Blenheim is an umbrella. The Marlborough Region and the Blenheim area especially have suffered in recent years from a severe lack of rain. Whether this pattern continues and how much it will affect wine growing in the area remains to be seen, but in the meantime slap on the sunscreen, buy a hat and enjoy the sun.

Sights

Being primarily a service town, Blenheim has little in itself to offer the tourist in the way of sights, with most visitors simply joining the various winery tours based in town, or picking up the information to tour the vineyards themselves. However, of some historical interest is the provincial museum and archives complex at The **Brayshaw Museum Park,** ① *New Renwick Rd, 3 km south of the town. Daily 1000-1600. Entry is free though there is a small charge for some attractions.* The museum is a mainly open-air affair, featuring an interesting reconstruction of an early settlers' village along with the inevitable farm machinery and ancient vehicles. Also of some note back in town is **Pollard Park,** Parker Street – a pretty conglomerate of flowerbeds, ponds and rose gardens. Right in the centre of town is **Seymour Square** with its landmark clock tower. It also hosts the **Millennium Gallery,** ① *T03-5792001, Mon-Fri 1000-1700, Sat-Sun 1200-1630, donation,* which is the main focus for the arts in the region. If you are interested in more regional detail surrounding **arts and crafts** pick up the free *Art and Craft Trail* leaflet from the VIC.▸▸ *See also Sleeping, Eating and other listings, pages 445-452.*

Wineries

The biggest attractions around Blenheim – and arguably the entire region – are the world-class wineries. Sun-baked Marlborough is New Zealand's largest wine-growing region, with over 50 wineries producing highly acclaimed Chardonnay, Riesling, Cabernet Sauvignon, Merlot, Pinot Noir, sparkling Methode Champenoise and some of best Sauvignon Blanc in the world. Montana sowed the first seeds of success in the early 1970s and is now the largest winery in the country. Three decades on, Montana has been joined by many other world-famous names and is a major national export industry.

❣ Most wineries and some tour operators will organize shipping

Like Hawke's Bay in the North Island, the wineries have been quick to take advantage of the tourist dollar, with most offering tours, **tastings** (free or small charge) and good **restaurants**. Although the competition in Marlborough is fierce, the region's vineyards lack the architectural splendour or variety of Hawke's Bay. Perhaps they just leave the wine to do the talking.

If you are a complete novice you are advised to join one of the many excellent **tours** on offer. They generally last a full, or half-day, taking in the pick of the crop and the widest variety of wine types. There is always an informative commentary on offer, very often a lunch stop too and, of course, numerous tastings included in the package. If you know a bit about wines and have particular tastes, many tour operators will create a personal itinerary. If you wish to explore by yourself, there are plenty of maps and leaflets available at the VIC.

Most of the wineries are located off SH6 around the small village of **Renwick,** 10 km west of Blenheim. Should you get sick of all the wine, or pompous 'wine-speak', there are other distilleries, breweries, vineyards and orchards in the area, producing everything from liqueurs and fruit wines to olive oil. There is even a brewery producing its own beer at **The Cork and Keg**, an English-style pub and brewery on Inkerman Street

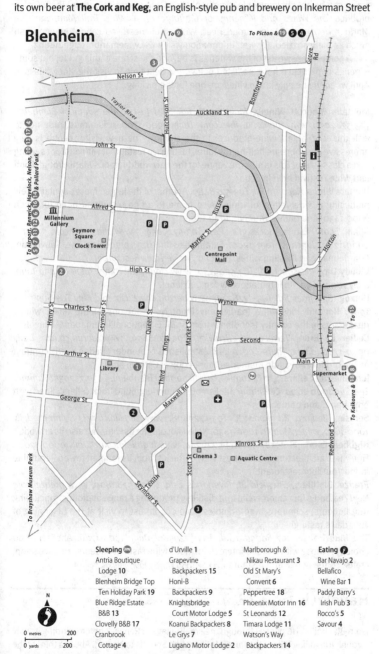

Blenheim

Sleeping	d'Urville **1**	Marlborough &	Eating
Antria Boutique	Grapevine	Nikau Restaurant **3**	Bar Navajo **2**
Lodge **10**	Backpackers **15**	Old St Mary's	Bellafico
Blenheim Bridge Top	Honi-B	Convent **6**	Wine Bar **1**
Ten Holiday Park **19**	Backpackers **9**	Peppertree **18**	Paddy Barry's
Blue Ridge Estate	Knightsbridge	Phoenix Motor Inn **16**	Irish Pub **3**
B&B **13**	Court Motor Lodge **5**	St Leonards **12**	Rocco's **5**
Clovelly B&B **17**	Koanui Backpackers **8**	Timara Lodge **11**	Savour **4**
Cranbrook	Le Grys **7**	Watson's Way	
Cottage **4**	Lugano Motor Lodge **2**	Backpackers **14**	

in Renwick, T03-5729328. Add to this the many fine eating establishments and there is no doubt your visit to the area can get very expensive.

Information Some excellent and detailed information about the region and New Zealand wines generally can be found in the magazine *Campbell's Wine Annual* which can be bought in most leading bookshops and magazine outlets. The VIC also produce *The Wines and Wineries of Marlborough – Wine Trail Map* and *The Marlborough Wine Region* broadsheet. With all of these you cannot go wrong so much as plain sozzled. For web information visit **www.winemarlborough.net.nz**

A comprehensive list of the wineries is beyond the scope of this guide, but some wineries of particular note are listed below. The best time to visit the vineyards is in April when the heavily laden vines are ripe for the picking.

Montana Brancott Winery, *Main South Rd (SH1) just to the south of Blenheim,* T03-5782099, *www.montanawines.com Daily 0900-1700.* It is almost rude not to visit this, the largest wine-producer in the country. The new visitor centre is very impressive and there are half-hourly tours, tastings, a restaurant with outdoor seating and a classy shop. This is also the venue for the now world-famous **Marlborough Food and Wine Festival** held in Feb.

Hunters Wines, *Rapaura Rd,* T03-5728489. Another of the larger, most popular labels producing a wide variety of wines. Also home to a fine restaurant open for lunch (1100-1430) and dinner Thu-Sun, from 1800.

Allan Scott Estate, *Jackson's Rd,* T03-5729054, *www.allanscott.com Daily 0900-1700, lunches from 1200.* Established in 1973, producing fine Sauvignon, Chardonnay and Riesling wines. Popular *Twelve Trees Restaurant.*

Cloudy Bay, *Jackson's Rd,* T03-5209140, *www.cloudybay.co.nz Tastings and tours daily 1000-1630.* An internationally famous label.

Herzog, *81 Jeffries Rd,* T03-5728770, *www.herzog.co.nz Oct-mid May Tue-Sun from 1900.* Not only fine wine (particularly Pinot Noir) but one of the finest winery restaurants in the country (set dinner from $98). Exceptional international wine list.

Cellier Le Brun, *Terrace Rd, Renwick,* T03-5728859, *www.lebrun.co.nz Daily 0900-1700 (dinner Thurs-Sat).* A long-established contender offering a little contrast as the producer of a fine Methode Champenoise. Café on site.

Johanneshof Cellars, *SH1 Koromiko, 20 km north of Blenheim,* T03-5737035. *Summer Tue-Sun 1000-1600. Cellar tour $8.* Famous for underground 'rock cellars', lined with both barrel and bottle.

Seresin, *Bedford Rd, Renwick,* T03-5729408, *www.seresin.co.nz Summer daily 1000-1630, winter Mon-Fri 1000-1630.* Noted not only for its wine, but also its artwork.

Highfield Estate, *Brookby Rd,* T03-5729244, *www.highfield.co.nz Daily 0900-1700.* Fine wine, architecture and the best view of the lot, from its rampart tower. Reputable indoor/outdoor restaurant.

Prenzel Distillery, *Sheffield St, Riverlands Estate,* T03-5782800, *www.prenzel.com* New Zealand's first commercial fruit distillery producing a range of products including fruit liqueurs, schnapps, and brandies. One of contrast to visit at the beginning of your day's tasting!

The Mud House, *197 Rapaura Rd,* T03-5729586. *Daily 1000-1700.* Another good choice for those with a broad interest. Includes wine tasting, liqueurs, an olive shop, crafts, coffee house and restaurant. ▸▸ *See also Winery tours listings, page 450.*

Havelock → *Phone code: 03 Colour map 4, grid B4 Population: 500*

From Blenheim SH6 passes through the small village of Renwick before winding its way through the rolling hills of the Inner Marlborough Sounds to Nelson. About a third of the way (41 km), at the head of the expansive Pelorus Sound, is the enchanting little village of Havelock. Blink and you will miss it, but if you have time a stop here is well worth it.

Ins and outs

Getting there and around Havelock is 41 km from Blenheim and 75 km from Nelson on SH6. By **bus, Intercity; Atomic Shuttles,** T03-5737477; **Kiwilink,** T03-5778332 and **Knightline,** T03-5474733, all service Havelock (Main Rd) on their way back and forth to Nelson. For full service listings see Picton Ins and outs above, page 433. For **track transport** (Nydia included) contact the **Havelock Shuttle Company,** T03-5742114. **Water taxis Sea Lark,** T03-5734272, in conjunction with **West Bay Water Transport,** based near the ferry terminal in Picton, serve the southern end of the Queen Charlotte Track from Torea Bay to Anakiwa (single $15). They also offer half-day track-walk options ($30), T03-5735597, www.westbay.co.nz **Pelorus Water Transport** also offer taxi and charter services, T027-2390000.

Information There are two independent visitor centres in the main street vying for tourists' attention. **Pelorus Enterprises,**① *60 Main Rd, T03-5742633, pmel@xtra.co.nz Daily 0830-1700.* Mandy and Sandy will take good care of you. **Outdoor Centre,**① *65A Main Rd, T03-5742114, www.marlboroughadventures.co.nz Daily 0830-2000 (1700 in winter).* They are also a booking agent for many activities in the area and hold most of the **DoC** information. Bike hire and internet is also available.

Sights

The village itself has little to offer except a friendly welcome, a fine café, restaurant, art and craft galleries, some rugby-playing mussel shells (honest), a small but interesting **museum,** ① *Main Rd, T03-5742176, daily (seasonal) 0900-1700, donation,* and a fine Scottish pub, but it is an ideal base from which to explore the glorious Pelorus and other 'outer sounds'. As the quiet neighbour to the much-hyped Queen Charlotte Sound, the Pelorus does not receive as much attention, but it is no less impressive and, in summer, provides a much quieter alternative. Although you may find it hard to believe, Havelock was once a thriving gold-mining town and also the boyhood home of one of New Zealand's most famous sons, Ernest Rutherford – the man 'who split the atom'. His former home is now the busy Youth Hostel. Havelock was also the latter-day home of another famous New Zealander, the writer Barry Crump. 'Crumpy' was the archetypal 'Kiwi bloke' whose humorous accounts of hunting and life in the bush has had many a proud Kiwi smiling in recognition. These days Havelock's gold is the green-lipped mussel, without doubt the finest-tasting thing in a shell, and a major export industry within the Sounds.

If you intend to explore the Sounds by road you can do this along the **Kenepuru Road**, which starts just past Linkwater (east of Havelock on Queen Charlotte Drive), or the **Tennyson Inlet** and **French Pass** roads, just north of Rai valley, west of Havelock (see below). Maps are available at the Picton or Havelock VICs. If neither water nor road appeal you can of course explore from the saddle with Marlborough Sounds Horse Treks, T03-5742073.▸▸ *See also Sleeping, Eating and other listings, pages 446-451.*

Walks

Havelock is the principal base from which to embark on the increasingly popular **Nydia Track** (see page 432). Both the Outdoors Centre and the YHA can advise. The **Havelock Shuttle Company,** T03-5742114, can help with transportation. About 18 km west of Havelock is the **Pelorus Bridge Scenic Reserve**. This is a pretty little spot where the azure waters of the Rai and Pelorus Rivers carve their way through the surrounding bush-clad hills. There are a number of walks from 30 minutes to 3 hours. A number of DoC information boards or the tearooms near the car park will keep you right. At the very least, stop and have a look at the river from the bridge.

Closer to Havelock itself is the climb to **Takorika Hill**. Located behind the town, its ascent will be rewarded by fine views. The lazy, or pushed-for-time, can reach the transmission tower by car via forest tracks (6 km). The entrance via Wilsons Rd is about 5 km west of Havelock on SH6.

Tennyson Inlet, French Pass and D'Urville Island

→ *Phone code: 03 Colour map 4, grid B4*

The Ronga and Opouri roads which connect the remote corners of the Outer Sounds are well worthy of investigation, offering some stunning coastal scenery of a type that is unsurpassed elsewhere in the country. Both roads can be accessed just beyond the small settlement of Rai Valley 48 km east of Nelson and 27 km west of Havelock. To explore both roads properly you should stock up with food and petrol and give yourself at least two days: one to take in Opouri Road and Tennyson Inlet (40 km), then back to Ronga Road to French Pass (70 km); and the second (or more) to spend some time in French Pass before returning to SH6. From French Pass it is also possible to explore the most remote and largest of the Sounds islands, D'Urville Island, named after the intrepid French explorer who first discovered and named it in 1827.

Getting there If you do not have your own transport you can join **Back Roads Transport** on their mail run to French Pass from Rai (Tue and Thu), T03-5765251.

Tennyson Inlet

About 1 km from SH6, Opouri Road shadows the Opouri River and cuts through paddock upon paddock full of sleepy stock lying in the shade of sheds that have seen better days. Then it suddenly and dramatically straddles **Lookout Hill** (900 m) before falling like a stone to Tennyson Inlet. The view at the crest of the hill is almost as impressive as the hairpin bends which must be negotiated to reach the inlet. But once there, the peace and tranquillity seem reward enough. If you are feeling energetic you might like to walk part of the **Nydia Track** to **Nydia Bay** where there is camping and accommodation available (see page 444).

French Pass

Back on Ronga Road, the route cuts through the paddocks of a river valley before climbing through attractive native bush to reach the first stunning views of Croisilles Harbour and out to the west coast of **D'Urville Island**. The first settlement of any consequence is **Okiwi Bay**, a secret little haunt of many a boatie Nelsonite. Okiwi provides a great base from which to go sailing or fishing in the quiet undisturbed bays of the Sounds westernmost coastline.

Just past Okiwi Bay the road passes through some beautiful tracts of beech forest before becoming unsealed. It is another 40 km to French Pass but after just a few kilometres the views of the Sounds really open up and the damage to your hire car will be the last thing on your mind. From **Elaine Bay** the road clings precariously to bush-clad ridges giving you an occasional glimpse of the scenic splendour, before the trees peter out and D'Urville Island comes into view. You then head along the western side of the now bare ridge to French Pass. On the way take the short detour to the top of the hill with the transmitters. From there you can soak up another stunning vista of Tennyson Inlet.

French Pass is really nothing more than a row of houses and a DoC campsite in a small sheltered bay at the very tip of the mainland. French Pass takes its name from the nautical nightmare that is just around the corner. The best view of this alarmingly slim channel of water can be seen from a path that leads down to a viewing point from the road (about 1 km before the settlement). At anytime, but particularly mid-tide, the

Let's Split

As New Zealand's most eminent scientist, Ernest Rutherford is best known for being the first person to split the atom. He was born at Spring Grove near Nelson in 1876 and after being awarded several scholarships, graduated with a Bachelor of Arts at the age of 17, and a Bachelor of Science two years later. By the age of 22 he was a professor at McGill University in Montreal and was already deeply involved in to research surrounding radioactivity. Within a decade he had discovered the natural transmutation of elements, the development of techniques that allowed the radioactive dating of geological samples and also made the first deduction of the nuclear model of the atom. All this brought him to world prominence and earned him several prestigious awards, including the Nobel Prize for Chemistry in 1908 and a knighthood in 1914. But despite all this, his best work was yet to come, and at the end of the First World War he conducted an experiment which split the atom – something which had far reaching consequences for mankind. Rutherford died in Cambridge, England at the age of 61.

chaotic currents can be seen forcing their way between the mainland and D'Urville Island. First discovered by D'Urville in 1827, this passage is a very important point on the nautical map because it offers an enticing short cut between Wellington and Nelson. If you are lucky you can time your visit to coincide with the passage of a ship. Some are so large you swear they will never make it and you can almost shout hello to the captain on the bridge, wave, and then tell him to watch where he is going.

French Pass is not only famous for its scenery, pass or shipping. Without doubt the most famous sight and resident was Pelorus Jack (see next page). ▸▸ For Sleeping see page 446.

Sleeping

Queen Charlotte Track *p431*
The Queen Charlotte Track is well served with accommodation options with a broad range from DoC campsites ($5), to privately-owned backpackers, self-contained units and luxury lodges. The VIC has full listings and will help you plan your itinerary and book your accommodation, but in summer you are advised to do this well in advance. There are also ample accommodation options elsewhere throughout the Sounds with most offering meals and some having in-house restaurants or at the very least adequate cooking facilities. Some can be reached by water taxi, others by road, or even by air. Again the VIC will advise. Some of the more noteworthy establishments are listed below.
LL-L Raetihi Lodge, *Kenepuru Sound, T03-5734300, www.raetihi.co.nz* An excellent establishment and one of the most modern in the luxury bracket, offering some of the best accommodation in the Sounds. 14 themed rooms, stunning views, licensed restaurant (à la carte from $55). Accessible by road, boat or by air (direct from Wellington with **Soundsair**).
LL-L The Lazy Fish, *Queen Charlotte Sound, T03-5735291, www.lazyfish.co.nz* A superb luxury option set in its own bay, only accessible by boat about 12 km from Picton. Its motto is *'Ubi Dies Omnis Festus'* ('where every day is Sunday') and it is an apt description. It is a renovated, beautifully appointed homestead only a few metres from the water with a range of rooms or cabins set in bush. Excellent cuisine inclusive of the price. There is also an outdoor bathtub, excellent kitchen facilities and windsurfer/canoe/fishing tackle hire.
L-C Punga Cove Resort, *Punga Cove, Endeavour Inlet, T0800-809697,*

• Pelorus Jack

The name and tale of Pelorus Jack has been synonymous with the Marlborough Sounds, and particularly French Pass, for over a century, relating not to some old pirate or explorer, but to a dolphin. And at the time, perhaps the most famous dolphin in the world. It was also this particular dolphin that paved the way for the concept of legal protection for all sea mammals.

As long ago as the late 1800s, the Marlborough Sounds and the route from Wellington to Nelson via the treacherous waters of French Pass were regularly used and negotiated by a vast array of trading and passenger vessels. Although there is no evidence as to the exact date of the strange dolphin's first appearance, by the turn of the century the antics of the 'Great White Fish' or 'Jack' (as he was christened by the local fishermen) were becoming legendary. Almost every vessel that appeared over the horizon, east of French Pass, would be habitually escorted by 'Jack' to its entrance, where he would mysteriously disappear, only to reappear in readiness to escort the next. What was most unusual about 'Jack' (but not initially understood) was that he was a large Risso's dolphin, a rare species which are not the classic 'dolphin' size, shape or colour, having a bumpy forehead and very pale skin. Before long, people from all over New Zealand were making the trip just to see the 'mysterious creature' and many other people, especially the regular seafarers held 'Jack' in high regard. News quickly spread and through word of mouth, letters, postcards and newspaper articles, 'Jack' began to gain notoriety around the world. But of course not all the stories of the day got the details right and almost every aspect of 'Jack' the strange sea creature became exaggerated. Some said he was 40 ft long and others that he was in fact, a mighty whale just like Moby Dick. One article even said he was protected by an Act of Parliament. Remarkably, it was this particular piece that stirred the then tourist office, and one Daniel Bates – a junior clerk in the Government Weather

www.pungacove.co.nz Wide range of options from private chalets and self-contained studios to a backpackers lodge. Facilities and services include a licensed restaurant, shop, laundry, spa and canoe hire. Note the resort is a 500m walk from the road.

L-D Pohuenui Island Sheep Station, *Pohuenui Island, T03-5978161*. A place that comes recommended and represents the Sounds at its best. Remote seclusion on a working farm. Full board or bunkroom. Join in the work and feel a million miles from civilization.

AL-D Portage Hotel, *Kenepuru Sound, T03-5734309, www.portage.co.nz* A wide range of accommodation from luxury spa rooms to bunkrooms. Restaurant, well stocked shop, pool and DoC campsite nearby. Kayak and bike hire available.

A-D Furneaux Lodge, *Endeavour Inlet, T03-5798259, www.furneaux.co.nz* Historic lodge set in idyllic gardens near a waterfall. Self-contained chalets and backpacker accommodation in a lovely stone 'croft'. Campsite available. Restaurant and bar. Ideal for a night stopover from Ship Cove.

A Kamahi Lodge, *Resolution Bay, T03-5799415*. Popular friendly homestay. Dinner on request. Activities arranged.

A-D Lochmara Lodge (Backpackers), *Lochmara Bay, T03-5734554, www.lochmaralodge.co.nz Closed Jun-Oct.* Another popular backpackers with a great, laid-back atmosphere. Dorm and private studio chalets – if you can remove yourself from a hammock. Spa (in the bush where the Punga People live!), open fire, free kayak, windsurfer hire, tea and coffee.

A-D Resolution Bay Cabins, *Resolution Bay,*

Office – to lobby for 'Jack's' official protection. One must remember that at the time, any sea mammal, be it whale, seal or dolphin, was something of a mystery and an animal to be either feared or killed. And given the grandiose details being touted all over the world surrounding the mysterious 'Jack', museum curators were beginning to put a price on his head and desire his brain in a bottle! Already, he was being shot at and surreptitiously hunted for bounty. Thankfully, after much lobbying and personal determination by Bates, an official act of parliament – the first of its kind protecting any sea mammal – was passed in September 1904 and as a result it became illegal to hunt or harm 'Jack' or any of his ilk in New Zealand waters. Of course this only exacerbated 'Jack's' newsworthiness and social standing. Children wrote sack loads of postcards and letters addressed 'To Pelorus Jack – New Zealand' and his visitations were listed in social columns of the national papers. Visiting celebrities like Mark Twain took the Nelson voyage especially to see him and seafarers the world over gave a special toast at gatherings in respect and honour of his protection and guidance. It was the spring of 1912, some 25 years since his first 'official' documented sighting that 'Jack' mysteriously disappeared. Although at the time there was national outrage and a subsequent and unsuccessful witch-hunt to find his 'killer', it is now thought that 'Jack' most probably died of old age. It is also now known that 'Jack' was perhaps the last individual of a once thriving pod of Risso's dolphin that resided in the area and that is why perhaps he turned all his attention to seeking company in the form of shipping and human beings. But it is the Maori who have perhaps the best explanation of the whole phenomenon. To them 'Jack' the dolphin (or *tahu-rangi*) is said to be a *taniwha* – or a spirit sent by the gods to be our guide and helper. Because he is a spirit and therefore magic, he can never die, and has for the last century been merely asleep, resting in his ocean cave between spells of duty. What is most interesting of all are a handful of stories that swear of the

T03-5799411, www.resolutionbaycabins.co.nz Accommodation ranges from cabins to self-contained cottages. Nice atmosphere and fine café. Shop on-site.

A-D St Omer House, *Kenepuru Sound, T03-5734086.* Historic villa with rooms (some shared), units, self-contained cottages, powered sites. Lovely setting with a private beach only yards away. Restaurant on site.

A-D Te Mahia Bay Resort, *Kenepuru Sound, T/F5734089, www.temahia.co.nz* Compact establishment in a peaceful location. Popular new and old self-contained accommodation, backpackers and tent sites available. Store but no bar or restaurant.

B-D Hopewell, *Kenepuru Sound, T03-5734341, www.hopewell.co.nz* Excellent establishment in a remote location on Kenepuru Sound providing the perfect blend of isolation, relaxation, value and comfort.

Although accessible by road from or Picton (85km) it is a tortuous drive. A water taxi is therefore recommended and should be made part of the over all experience, or better still if you can afford it you can fly direct from Wellington (Soundsair) to the local airfield from where you can be picked up. A range of budget options from a self-contained cottage to well-appointed doubles and 4-shares. Attractive grounds right down to the water's edge. Outdoor spa over looking the sound, internet, kayaks and plenty of water-based activities on offer with fishing trips being a speciality. Friendly, caring hosts. Warning: one night is not enough. The secret is out so book well ahead. Recommended.

C-D Chill Inn , *770 Queen Charlotte Dr, T03-5741299, www.thechillinn.co.nz* If you are planning on walking the track and water taxis are not your thing then 'the Chill', which is a short distance from Anakiwa, offers a fine accessible base from which to leave or to return (track transport available). It's a low-key, friendly place with hammocks, cool music and a spa the major factors in its inherently laid-back atmosphere. It is a small place but has all the usual facilities. Free kayak, bikes and breakfast.

C-D Smiths Farm Holiday Park, *Queen Charlotte Dr, Linkwater, T03-5742806*. Self-contained motel units, cabins, powered and tent sites close to the track start at Anakiwa to which there is courtesy transport. Bike hire.

Campsites
D DoC campsites are available at *Ship Cove, Camp Bay, Bay of Many Coves, Black Rock, Cowshed, Mistletoe Bay and Davies Bay*.

Nydia Track *p432*
DoC campsites (from $5) available in the northwestern corner of Nydia Bay: 2 in Tennyson Inlet and 1 in Duncan Bay.
D Nydia Lodge, *on the south coast of Nydia Bay, T03-5203002*. Sleeps 50.
C-D Driftwood Cottage, *Nydia Bay, T03-5798454, driftwood@nydiabay.co.nz* A small, excellent and 'alternative' backpackers with cabins.

Picton *p433*
There are few modern hotels but plenty of motels to choose from.
AL Waikawa Bay Seafront Apartments, *45 Beach Rd, T03-5735220*. A modern establishment located beside the Waikawa Bay marina complex, east of Picton. Since its creation in 2000 it has been receiving good reviews and offers luxury self-contained apartments, pool, spa, and café/restaurant /bar nearby.
AL-A The Broadway Motel, *113 High St, T03-5736563, www.broadwaymotel.co.nz* The town's newest motel, centrally located. Spotless standard and spa units.
A The Jasmine Court, *78 Wellington St, T03-5737110, www.jasminecourt.co.nz* Is another good motel offering a fine range of well-appointed, modern units. Good location.
A Americano Motor Inn, *32 High St, T0800-104104, www.americano.co.nz* Right

in the heart of town this is a large motel with a popular licensed restaurant attached.
A St Catherine's B&B, *123 Wellington St, T03-5738580, www.stcatherines.co.nz* Set in a very relaxing historic former convent it offers 2 rooms, 1 queen with shared bathroom and 1 room (ensuite bathroom) with a 4-poster bed and great views from a private balcony.
A-B The Gables, *20 Waikawa Rd, T03-5736772, www.thegables.co.nz* Enjoys a good reputation and in ideal location with 3 rooms and 2 self-contained cottages on site plus another cottage option in Waikawa Bay.
A-B Picton Homestay, *2 Canterbury St, T0800-274286*. A modern, friendly and good value homestay, in a quiet location. Courtesy car.
Cheaper **motel** options include:
B The Harbour View, *30 Waikawa Rd, T03-5736259*, with 12 fully self-contained studio units and fine views across the harbour.
B Tourist Court Motel, *45 High St, T03-5736331*. One of the better, long-established budget motels, near the centre.
C-D Sequoia Lodge Backpackers, *3A Nelson Sq, T03-5738399, stay@sequoialodge.co.nz* Although about 500 m from the town centre and 1 km from the ferry terminal, this is an excellent hostel run by an enthusiastic manager. Modern, recently renovated facilities with secure parking. Range of dorm and private single, twin and double rooms, some en-suite. Log fire, free tea and coffee and great homemade bread. Free pick-up/drop-off to ferry. Internet.
C-D The Villa, *34 Auckland St, T03-5736598, www.thevilla.co.nz* A deservedly popular, well-established and lively backpackers in a century old villa. Dorms, twins and doubles. Fine facilities and a great outdoor area with spa. The managers are a hive of information on local activities and can assist with plans and bookings. Free 'all you can eat' breakfast, tea, coffee, duvets, bike hire and shuttle service. Internet. Pre-booking advisable.
C-D Picton Lodge, *9 Auckland St, T03-5737788, picton.lodge@xtra.co.nz* The closest hostel to the ferry terminal and close to the VIC and town centre, pub next door. Singles, doubles/twins and small dorms. Large open plan living area. Free breakfast, blankets and bike hire.

C-D **Bayview Backpackers**, *318 Waikawa Rd, T03-5737668, bayview.backpackers@xtra.co.nz* A modern, friendly and rapidly expanding place in Waikawa Bay just east of Picton. Good value dorm beds, single/twin and double rooms some with ensuite bath and TV. It offers the peace and quiet the bustling hostels in the town centre do not. Free pick-up/ drop-off to the ferry. Free bikes, kayaks and sailing trips arranged. Internet. Recommended.

Motorcamps
C-D **Blue Anchor Top Ten Holiday Park**, *78 Waikawa Rd, T0800-277444.* An excellent award-winning holiday park and consequently very popular. It is well located within walking distance from town, has tidy cabins and tourist flats and great facilities. It does, however, get a little crowded at times especially if you are camping so try to arrive early in the day. Another large, but older less salubrious holiday park, the
C-D **Parklands Marina Holiday Park**, *T03-5736343 on Beach Rd, Waikawa.* Is close to the marina.

Blenheim *p435*
There are no shortage of beds in Blenheim with hotels, motels and backpackers. The emphasis, however, is on the many excellent boutique-style lodges, B&Bs and homestays outside the town, often in the vineyards. The VIC has comprehensive listings and can book on your behalf. During the picking season (Apr/May) you are advised to pre-book backpackers in the region.

Blenheim Township
LL **Hotel d'Urville**, *52 Queen St, T03-5779945, www.durville.co.nz* A newly renovated 11-room boutique hotel in a former bank in the heart of the town centre. Individually themed rooms, some with 4-poster beds. Classy restaurant attached.
L **The Marlborough Hotel**, *20 Nelson St, T03-5777333, www.the-marlborough.co.nz* A modern luxury option with range of rooms and suites, heated pool, internet and the quality *Nikau* restaurant.
AL-A **Lugano Motor Lodge**, *corner of High and Henry Sts, T03-5778808.* A modern and popular luxury motel, close to the centre of town. Ever tried a 'thermo-mattress'? Well,

now is your chance!
AL-A **Phoenix Motor Inn**, *174 Middle Renwick Rd, T03-5779002.* A new motel on the block earning a good reputation. 12 studio and 3 luxury units.
A **Knightsbridge Court Motor Lodge**, *112 Middle Renwick Rd, T03-5780818.* Considered one of the better mid-range motels in town.
C-D **Honi-B Backpackers**, *corner Hutcheson and Parker Sts, T03-5778441, honi-b-backpackers@xtra.co.nz* New and centrally located hostel revitalising the town's backpacking scene. Standard modern facilities and wide range of rooms, parking and internet. Recommended.
C-D **The Koanui Backpackers**, *33 Main St, T03-5787487.* A rambling single-storey villa close to town. A bit tired but its friendly manager affords visitors much care and attention. Good value doubles.
C-D **Grapevine Backpackers**, *29 Park Terr, T03-5786062, rob.diana@xtra.co.nz* Another large suburban, single storey villa on the riverbank. Full range of rooms, free canoe and bike hire. Assistance finding seasonal work.
C-D **Blenheim Bridge Top Ten Holiday Park**, *78 Grove Rd, T03-5783667. Located to the north of the town beside SH1, the main railway line and the river.* A bit noisy so close to the main road and railway line but otherwise, well equipped and functional.

Around Blenheim
LL **Old Saint Mary's Convent**, *Rapaura Rd, T/F5705700, www.convent.co.nz* One of the most popular places to stay in the region. A century old, renovated and relocated 2-storey convent set in expansive gardens and surrounded by vineyards. Comes complete with billiard room. Even if you are not in the honeymoon suite ask to see it, it is positively angelic.
LL-L **The Peppertree**, *SH1, Riverlands, T03-5209200, www.peppertree.co.nz* Historic villa with a range of luxury en-suites. Fine breakfast.
LL **Timara Lodge**, *Dog Point Rd, T03-5728276, www.timara.co.nz* Luxury by the lake! 1920s homestead amidst 180 acres of beautiful gardens. Superb rooms, facilities and fine cuisine.
LL **Antria Boutique Lodge**, *276 Old Renwick Rd, T03-5792191,*

www.antria.co.nz Described as a modern European castle, Antria is certainly aesthetically different. But don't expect ramparts or moats. This is a truly modern concept, more Mediterranean in design, with large Gothic timber doors opening up into an open-air courtyard. Stylish, well-appointed rooms and artwork adds to the overall class and atmosphere. The tariff is reasonable in comparison to many other top-range establishments.

L Cranbrook Cottage, *Giffords Rd, T03-5728606*. Without doubt one of the most characterful and gorgeous self-contained cottage B&Bs in the region. Very romantic with breakfast delivered to the door each morning!

L-AL Le Grys, *Conders Bend Rd, Renwick, T03-5729490, www.legrys.co.nz* Self-contained, beautifully appointed mud-block cottage or rooms (with ensuite bath) in the main house, set in the heart of the vineyard.

AL Blue Ridge Estate B&B, *O'Dwyers Rd, T03-5702198, www.blueridge.co.nz* Very classy purpose-designed homestay set in a 20-acre rural property with fine views across some of the best-known vineyards. Well-appointed rooms with earthy colours and an almost minimalist feel. Good value and recommended.

A Clovelly B&B, *2A Nelson Pl, Renwick, T03-5729593, www.clovelly.co.nz* A more affordable B&B option in the sleepy village of Renwick 10 km west of Blenheim. Good value and only 2 minutes from the *Cork and Keg* English-style country pub and brewery.

A St Leonards, *18 St Leonards Rd, T03-5778328, st.leonards@xtra.co.nz* Beautifully appointed self-contained accommodation in a former stables. Great value.

C-D Watson's Way Backpackers, *56 High St, Renwick, T03-5728228*. The most popular backpackers in the Blenheim region. Lots of character, relaxed and well-equipped and within walking distance of numerous vineyards and *The Cork and Keg* English pub and brewery.

Havelock *p438*

There is little in the way of accommodation in Havelock itself, most is out in the Sounds.

B Havelock Garden Motel, *71 Main St, T03-5742387, www.gardenmotels.com* A

fine, newly renovated option set in large gardens close to all amenities.

C-D Rutherford YHA, *46 Main Rd, T03-5742104*. Spacious YHA, the former home of world-famous scientist Ernest Rutherford, run by a caring relative. Double, twin and bunks. Camping available. Internet.

C-D Chill Inn, *Queen Charlotte Dr, T03-5741299, thechillinn@hotmail.com* A laid-back backpackers deserving of growing popularity, especially before or after embarking on the Queen Charlotte or Nydia Tracks. Dorms, twins and doubles. Nice atmosphere and setting.

Motorcamps and campsites

C-D Havelock Motor Camp, *24 Inglis St, T03-5742339*. Powered/tent sites and cabins close to the harbour.

C-D DoC campsite, *T03-5716019*. Cabins and powered sites.

French Pass *p440*

There are a number of places to stay and a surprising amount of activities based in or around French Pass.

A-B French Pass Beachfront Villas and Sea Safaris, *T03-5765204, www.seasafaris.co.nz* Here residents Danny and Lynn Bolton have created the main focus for activity operations in the area and have combined that with some delightful motel-cum-backpacker accommodation. The trips they offer are flexible, half- to multi-day ventures that can include diving, fishing, walking, or wildlife watching, with dolphins a regular sight. Many rare seabirds can also be seen on the trips. Audio-visual presentations and commentary provided. Sea Safaris also offer a water-taxi service to the remote D'Urville Island and the D'Urville Island Wilderness Resort (see below). Overall this operation is very friendly and professional and has the refreshing edge of placing conservation and promotion of the unique environment with utilisation and access. Bookings are essential. Recommended

A-B D'Urville Wilderness Resort, *T03-5765268, www.Durvilleisland.co.nz* It doesn't get much more remote than this! Comfortable accommodation and a waterfront café and bar accessible only by boat. Ideal for that total getaway experience or for exploring D'Urville Island.

A-B Nagio Bay Homestead, *on the western side of the peninsula*, *T03-5765287*. Idyllic B&B with its own private beach. Home-grown, organic produce a speciality.

B-C Anaru Homestead, *T03-5765260*. Large homestead offering budget singles and 4 doubles. Fishing charters available.

Motorcamps and campsites

B-D Okiwi Bay Holiday Park, *T03-5765006*, *www.okiwi.co.nz* A small homestay lodge, powered and tent sites, petrol and a small store.

D DoC Campsite French Pass. Small and basic but, not surprisingly, popular.

⑦ Eating

Picton *p433*

Despite (or perhaps because of) the competition from so many fine vineyard restaurants around Blenheim and resort restaurants out in the Sounds, Picton seems strangely lacking in fine dining options.

$$ Le Café, *on London Quay*, *T03-5735588*. *Open daily for breakfast, lunch and dinner.* Perhaps the best bet, it has a good atmosphere and is well placed on the waterfront but the service can be a little slack.

$$ Expresso House, *58 Auckland St*, *T03-5737112*. *Daily (except Wed) in season from 1100-late (Thu-Tue in winter)*. Offers fine coffee and great value, imaginative lunch and dinner menu.

$$ Café Zest, *31 High St*, *T03-5736616*. *Mon and Thu 0800-1500 and Fri-Sun from 0800-late*. Recommended for breakfast.

$$ DAs, *58 High St*, *T03-5738823*. *Daily 0900-2200*. A reliable mid-range option with a café-style menu, specializing in gourmet pizza but it cannot seem to decide if it is a pokie (slot machine) parlour or a café.

$ Toot and Whistle, *T03-5736086*, *on Auckland St*, *near the ferry terminal*. *0900 till late daily*. The best pub grub and beer to be found in town. A lively place that has seen no doubt seen its fair share of clients miss the ferry.

Supermarket Supervalue, *in the Mariners mall on High St*, *T03-5736463*. *Mon-Wed 0800-1800, Thu 0800-1930, Fri 0800-2030, Sat 0800-1900 and Sun 0900-1700*.

Blenheim

With the influence of the wineries and the many gourmet travellers, the choice and quality are excellent.

$$$ Hotel d'Urville, *52 Queen St*, *T03-5779945*. *Daily 0600-midnight*. The place for fine dining in Blenheim.

$$$ Nikau, *at the Marlborough Hotel, 20 Nelson St*, *T03-5779821*. Recommended poolside fine dining.

$$$ Savour, *corner of SH1 and Mills and Ford Roads (3 km north of the town)*, *T03-5702192*. Also trying to make a mark and developing a solid reputation. The added attraction there is the adjunct Wine and Food Gallery with its range of local wines, gourmet foods, bread and cheese.

$$ Rocco's, *5 Dodson St*, *T03-5786940 Evenings only*. A fine Italian restaurant.

$$ Bellafico Wine Bar, *17 Maxwell Rd*, *T03-5776072*. *Mon-Sat 1000 until late*. European offerings.

$$ Paddy Barry's Irish Pub, *51 Scott St*, or **$$ Bar Navajo** *on Queen St*. *Mon-Wed 1000-late, Thu-Sat 1000-0300, Sun 1000-2200*. Both good for pub grub.

$$ The Store, *at Kekerengu (halfway between Blenheim and Kaikoura)*, *T03-5758600*. *0700-late*. Recommended, fine café-style cuisine with crayfish a speciality.

Supermarket New World, *Main St*. *Daily 0800-2100*.

Wineries *p436 and 450*

Some of the larger wineries have fine restaurants or cafés offering indoor/outdoor seating and lunch and/or dinner. Some of the best can be found at (recommended) :
Hunters, *T03-5728489*,
Allan Scott, *T03-5729054*,
Montana, *T03-5782099*,
Cairnbrae, *T03-5727018*,
Highfield, *T03-5728592*,
Cellier le Brun, *T03-5728859*, and
Wairau River Wines, *T03-5729800*.

Havelock *p438*

$$$ Mussel Boys Restaurant, *73 Main Rd*, *T03-5742824*. *Daily 1100-2130*. A stay in Havelock would not be complete without sampling the green-lipped mussels at this award winning restaurant. A bowl of seafood chowder will cost a value $9 and steamed mussels from $15.

$$ Clansman Scots Pub, *Main Rd*. Recommended for a pint and some fine pub grub.

$$ Slip Inn Café and Wine Bar, *by the main marina, T03-5742345. Mon-Thu 1000-2000, Fri-Sun 1000-2300*. Small but lively place worth checking out if you are planning a trip out on the Sound.

$ Darling Dill Café, *corner of Main Rd and Neil St, T03-5742824*. Good for a coffee or breakfast.

French Pass *p440*
D'Urville Wilderness Resort, *see Sleeping above*. The only place to eat. Other than that, there's a small store and a petrol station.

☻ Festivals and events

For further information on other annual events and specific dates contact the VIC or look up the regional website www.marlborough4fun.co.nz

Blenheim *p435*
The Marlborough Centre, *Arthur St, T03-5782009*. The region's principal entertainment venue with a variety of shows, exhibitions and performances on offer throughout the year.
However, most of the Blenheim and Marlborough events obviously revolve around fine wines and food. The principal event of the year is the now world-famous **BMW-Marlborough Wine Festival** (*2nd Sat in Feb*). A lively (and very alcoholic) celebration of the region's gourmet food and wines. Live music provided. *For more information T0800-228800*.
Blues, Brews and Barbecues annual festival (*1st week Feb*). This is the breweries' answer to their winemaking neighbours, whereby tents are raised and all kinds of ales dismantled to accompanying live entertainment. There is even alcoholic lemonade. *T03-5789457, entry $15*.
Heads are raised from wine glasses at the **Easter Airshow** (*end of Apr*) which stages some mock dog fights between classic fighter planes from both World Wars. Wine and food included – of course, www.classicfighters.co.nz
Bubbles and Balloons (*Jun*). A hot air ballooning festival held over Marlborough,

T03-5778935. Where the bubbles come into it we can only imagine!

▲▲ Activities

Picton *p433*
Most activities are obviously based around cruising, tramping (see page 430) or kayaking, with the odd bit of dolphin and bird spotting thrown in. The VIC in Picton has a comprehensive list of activities, which are cleverly listed by time of day, not operator, and well worth a look. They can also advise on horse trekking, winery tours (see page 450), diving, tandem paragliding, scenic flights (from Picton airfield), fishing and independent boat charters.

Cruises
There are endless bays, coves and islands to explore in the Sounds, with a rich variety of wildlife including dolphins and rare seabirds. As you might expect, there is a mind-boggling range of cruise options available with fiercely competitive operators. Most are based on The Waterfront in Picton. It's a good idea to check at the VIC before parting with your cash.
Beachcomber Cruises, *The Waterfront, Picton, T0800-624526, T03-5736175*, offer 2 popular half-day 'Mail Boat' cruises: the Pelorus Mail Boat departs Tue/Thu/Fri from Havelock at 0930 and Picton at 1015, returning mid-late afternoon, taking in many mail stops and a mussel farm or two on the way, from $90; the Magic Mail Run explores the Queen Charlotte Sound, including a stop at Ship Cove and a salmon farm. It departs Picton daily Mon-Sat at 1330, and returns at 1730; $62. Also on offer is a 2-hr 'Round the Bays' cruise that takes in a number of Queen Charlotte Sound bays, including Double Cove where you stop briefly to feed tame fish. It departs daily at 1015 and 1415; from $38. Another is a 6-hr luncheon cruise to the Portage Resort Hotel and Torea Bay, departing daily at 1015. A one-day 'Freedom Walk' (8 km) taking in part of the Queen Charlotte Track from Torea Bay, departs at 1015 daily (from $42). They also offer a range of half-day or full-day cruise and walk options from $32, Queen Charlotte Track transfers (with pack transfers) from $55 and a Ecotour of

Motuara Island Bird Sanctuary, from $48.

The Cougar Line, *also based on the Waterfront, T0800-504-090, www.cougarlinecruises.co.nz* Offer a similar series of cruises. The most popular is the day trip to Ship Cove where you have the option of a 5-hr bush walk to Furneaux Lodge where you are picked up later in the afternoon. It departs at 0800 and 1000. Various short cruises are also on offer taking in up to 80 km of coastline in 3 hrs with an informative commentary on the way. These depart at 1000 and 1330. Cougar also offer a luncheon cruise to the Punga Cove Resort that leaves at 1000 and a 3-hr twilight tour that departs at 1800. Cruises cost from $48.

Endeavour Express, *based at the Waterfront, T03-5735456, www.boatrides.co.nz,* and **West Bay Water Transport**, *T03-5735597, www.westbay.co.nz* Both offer a similar range of day walking options from $35 as well as tramping track and accommodation transfers.

Sounds Connection, *T0800-742866, www.soundsconnection.co.nz* Also offer a flexible water taxi service.

Day walks

Most of the water-based operators offer a range of half/full-day walking trips. Two of the most popular trips are the Ship Cove to Furneaux Lodge (with **Endeavour Express** and **Cougar**, from $48), which takes in the Captain Cook monument and some lovely native bush and views. The other is the eco-based trip to the Motuara Island Bird Sanctuary (with **Beachcomber Cruises** and **Endeavour Express**, from $48). The VIC or individual operators can advise. Cougar have the best boats and tend to offer the most modern, comfortable service, but competition is fierce.

Ecotours

Dolphin Watch Marlborough, *14 Auckland St, about 200m east of the VIC, T03-5738040, www.dolphinwatchmarlborough.co.nz* They offer a range of trips from 3-4½ hrs including an excellent jaunt to the **Motuara Island bird sanctuary** (departing 0845/1345, from $65) or a **Birdwatchers' Special** (departs daily in winter and twice daily in summer at 0830 and 1330, from $85). The Sounds are not only home to seals and

dolphins but also some rare birdlife such as the king shag (found only in the Sounds), New Zealand robins, little blue penguins and saddlebacks. Many of the land-based birds on the island are typically fearless and will constantly check your route for disturbed insects.

Sea Safaris, *based in French Pass, T03-5765204, www.seasafaris.co.nz* (See page 440). Also offer some superb, flexible wildlife trips.

Flightseeing

Soundsair, *based across the road from the VIC in the old railway station, T0800-505005, www.soundsair.com* Offer an extraordinary number of flight combinations and options that include 1 night's accommodation, lunch, day walks and cruises from around $135-$350. Standard flightseeing trips range from 20 min for $100 to 1 hr 15 min from $220. The standard single fare to Wellington costs from $79, child $67.

Sea kayaking

Most travellers save their NZ kayaking experience for the Abel Tasman National Park (see page 467), the most famous sea-kayaking venue in the country. However, Abel Tasman is now getting very crowded in summer and the idea of having a beautiful golden bay to yourself is a near impossibility. What the Sounds can offer that the Abel Tasman often cannot, is almost guaranteed shelter and relative peace and quiet. Also note that Abel Tasman has about 50 km of coastline, whereas the Sounds have 1500! The principal operator in Picton is the **Marlborough Sounds Adventure Company**, *on the Waterfront, T0800-283283, www.marlboroughsounds.com* They offer a wide range of excellent trips from a few hours (including a twilight trip), a 4-day paddle/walk, to 6 days specialist itineraries and are highly professional and very safe. Mountain bike hire is also available from $50; twilight trip from $50; 1-day guided trip from $90; 4-day guided paddle/walk $965. Another excellent and increasingly popular trip they offer is called the 3-day **Ultimate Sounds Adventure**, a guided 1-day hiking, 1-day sea kayaking, 1-day mountain biking adventure, with an overnight stay at *Portage Resort Hotel*. The trip departs every

Wed from 1 Nov-30 Apr, and costs $410 at a backpacker rate and $595 twin share ensuite. A packed lunch is included in twin share rate. Note there is no other track in NZ where you can walk and mountain bike on the same track. Recommended.

Other companies in the area include: **Sea Kayaking Adventure Tours**, *based in Anakiwa*, *T03-5742765*. 1-day trips from $75 and independent hire from $40; and **The Sea Kayaking Wilderness Company**, *Havelock Youth Hostel, T03-5742610, www.soundswild.com* Trips from $80.

Self-drive

If you are looking for an alternative method of exploring the Sounds you can do so in part by road. Note, however, that the roads throughout the Sounds are tortuous, mostly unsealed and not entirely suitable for campervans, or indeed sightseeing. Perhaps this is the time to have a break from driving and take a boat? The **Queen Charlotte Drive** is (for the passenger) a scenic 35 km drive from Picton to Havelock taking in a number of sheltered bays, campsites and viewpoints on the way. From Linkwater it is possible to then traverse the ridge between Queen Charlotte and Kenepuru Sounds by road (close to the route of the Queen Charlotte Track) before the road joins the main landmass of the Sounds. The intrepid explorer can reach the outermost bays from this road and combine some walking on parts of the Queen Charlotte Track, including the most popular day walk – the **Endeavour Inlet to Ship Cove Track**. On a clear day the half-day to full-day walk to the summit of **Mount Stokes** (at 1203 m the highest point in the Sounds) is recommended for the view. The walk is a moderate expedition involving 500 m of ascent. **Campsites** are available at Mistletoe Bay, Cowshed Bay, Punga Cove (Endeavour Inlet) and at Titirangi Bay. Note that some accommodation establishments are also accessible by road, including Punga Cove, The Portage, Te Mahia, St Omer House and Raetihi Lodge (see page 441).

For another fine and remote exploratory drive in to the Sounds see the French Pass section, page 440.

Blenheim *p435*

The wilderness of the Marlborough backcountry and the remote Molesworth Station (New Zealand's largest cattle station) can be explored with **Back Country Safaris**, *T03-5757525*. One to five-day excursions from $210.

Horse trekking

High Country Horse Treks, *Ardnadam, Taylor's Pass Rd, Redwood Village, T03-5779424*. 1-4 hrs from $30-$100.

River trips

If you fancy a trip along the Opawa River on board a paddleboat, try the very gracious **Marlborough River Queen**, *T03-4383088* 2 hr with dinner with one glass of wine, from $35).

Walking

There are some fine walking venues in the region, particularly around the Richmond Ranges, the **Withers Farm Park** and on the coast road, via Rarangi, to Picton. The ascent of **Mount Richmond** (1760 m) with its memorable views is recommended. For self-guided trips consult DoC or the VIC for their free leaflets.

Winery tours

There are a broad range of tours and many operators available all of whom will look after your every whim. Some offer more formal scheduled trips, while others can design a trip around your personal tastes or take in arts and crafts and garden visits. You can even go by bicycle.

Delux Travel Line, *T0800-500511, www.deluxtravel.co.nz* Marlborough's original Wine Trail Tour taking in Montana, Forrest, Cellier Le Brun, Le Grys, The Mud House and Preznel. Tastings included, meal extra. Available from Picton and Marlborough. Departs daily, Picton 1000, Blenheim 1100. From $49 ($54 Picton).

Highlight Tours, *T03-5779046*. Both full-day or half-day, morning and afternoon tours. Flexibility with venues (including craft and garden venues) and lunch (extra cost) included. From $45.

Barry's Wine Tours, *40 Warwick St, T03-5781494*. Have a solid reputation for offering an entertaining, good value tour of 8 wineries with the option of gardens or craft outlets, half-day from $50 (with lunch $75). Other regional tours are also a feature. Recommended.

Marlborough Wine Tours, T03-5789515, www.marlboroughwinetours.co.nz Personalized tour of up to 8 wineries. Flexible itinerary depending on taste. UK wine delivery service.

Sounds Connection, T03-5738843, www.soundsconnection.co.nz Scheduled and private half to full-day tours. Based in Picton. Half-day from $45, full $55, gourmet (includes food and wine matching, underground cellar tour, olive grove and lunch stop at your own account), from $69.

Marlborough Travel Centre Winery Tours and Wine Line, T03-5779999, T0800-990800, www.marlboroughtravel.co.nz Fleet of hop-on hop-off buses that operate a continuous circuit daily with stops at every venue on an hourly basis. Departs the Marlborough VIC at 1000, last departure 1500, from $40. Daily half-day or full-day tailor-made tour packages can also be arranged.

Wine-Tours-By-Bike, T03-5776954, www.winetoursbybike.co.nz This is the new and delightfully common-sense method of visiting the wineries – by bike. The great attraction here is the slow pace and the greater bombardment of the senses only felt on a bike. The drawback obviously is the steady deterioration of those senses as the day wears on and the inability to pedal in any direction after 10 glasses of wine. You can join a guided tour or hire your own bikes and have them delivered to your door. Half day from $35, full $50, guide from $25 per hr.

Rimu Guesthouse, based in Renwick also hire bikes and can point you in the right direction, T03-5727575, rimuguesthouse@xtra.co.nz

Havelock

Most of what Havelock has to offer and almost all of its services will be found on Main Road or down at the harbour, which is a short walk from centre of the village.

Cruises

Pelorus Sound can be explored by boat or by road. There are numerous opportunities to get on the water from scheduled cruises to charter boats and kayak trips.

Beachcomber Cruises, T0800-624526, T03-5736175. Popular Mail Boat Run leaves Havelock at 0930 on Tue, Thu and Fri, costing from $90, child free. It delivers supplies and mail to a number of the isolated settlements and visits one of the many **mussel farms** before returning at about 1730.

Marlborough Travel, T03-5779997, www.marlboroughtravel.co.nz Also operate daily cruises from Jetty 1A at the marina at 0930 and 1400, from $69, child $29. This is a similar trip with the added appeal of fresh steamed mussels and a glass of wine for lunch. Recommended.

Classic Cruises and **The Mussel Farm Cruise** on board the 40-ft kauri launch MV Mavis, T03-5742114. Two other more sedate and popular trips based in Havelock. Both take in the beautiful scenery of the Sounds and will give you an insight in to how the famous mussels are bred and harvested. It leaves from the marina at 1030 and again at 1330, costing from $49.

Affinity Cruises, T03-5727223, www.affinitycruises.co.nz Day cruise charters or overnight cruises from 2-7 days. The 63-foot vessel has 8 private cabins, all meals are included and activities range from fishing to bush walking.

Note that **water-taxis** are available from Havelock and you can be flexible with your intentions and itinerary (see Ins and outs, page 439). The Outdoors Centre can help you plan and book. There are also **fishing** and **diving** charters available.

Sea kayaking

If this is your thing or you would like to try it, the Sounds provide excellent opportunities. Several companies can oblige including: **Havelock Sea Kayaking Company**, (Outdoors Centre) T03-5742114, www.marlboroughadventures.co.nz; **Soundswild**, T03-5735577, www.soundswild.com (Recommended) **Sea Kayaking Adventure Tours**, Anakiwa, T03-5742765, info@nzseakayaking.com; **Explore Pelorus Sea Kayaks**, Nelson, T03-5765251. Trips are half-day from $70, full- or multi-day from $150 per day. Independent hire is also available from $35.

❶ Directory

Picton *p433*

Car hire There are lots of companies based just outside the ferry terminal, with a few others on High Street in the centre of town. Ace, *T0800-422373*. **Apex**, *T0800-422744*. Budget, *T03-5736081*. **Pegasus**, *T03-5737733*. Rent-A-Dent, *T03-5737787*. **Internet United Video**, *corner of High and Dublin Sts. 0900-2100*. **Scooter hire** The Sounds Connection, *10 London Quay T0800-742-866*. Rent out nifty scooters from $25 per hr. **Taxi** Red Band, *T03-5797072*. **Petrol** (24hr): Shell Picton, *101 High St, T03-5737949*. **Post office** Mariners Mall, *High St, T03-5736900. Mon-Fri 0830-1700, Sat 0930-1230*. **Police** *36 Broadway,*

T03-5203120. **Storage** Sounds Storage, *14 Devon St, T03-5735136, soundsstorage@xtra.co.nz* Offer secure car and boat storage.

Blenheim *p435*

Bike hire Spokesman Cycles, *Queen St*. Bikes for winery tours can be hired from Wine-Tours-By-Bike, *T03-5776954*. **Internet** Chequers Café and Wine Bar, *Scott St, T03-5793242. Daily 0930-late*. **Post office** *corner of Scott and Main Sts, T03-5783904, T03-5783904. Mon-Fri 0830-1715, Sat 0930-1230*. **Taxi** Blenheim Taxis, *T03-5780224*.

Havelock *p438*

Internet is available in the Outdoor Centre and the YHA.

Nelson and around

→ *Phone code: 03 Colour map 4, grid B3 Population: 50,000*

Nelson is known as the sunniest place in the country, though this label could apply to its atmosphere, its people and its surroundings, for as well as its mediterranean climate, Nelson has a great deal going for it. It is lively and modern, yet steeped in history. Surrounding it, all within 100 km, are some of the most beautiful coastal scenery and beaches in New Zealand, not to mention three diverse and stunning national parks, where you can experience some of the most exciting tramping tracks in South Island, plus a host of other activities. Little wonder that Nelson is one of the top holiday destinations in the country as well being considered the best place to live in New Zealand.

Ins and outs

Getting there Nelson is serviced by the small but efficient **airport** about 6 km southwest of the town centre on SH6, in the suburb of Nayland. **Air New Zealand Link,** T0800-737000, www.airnewzealand.co.nz, and **Origin Pacific,** T0800-302302, www.originpacific.co.nz, fly regular scheduled flights to Auckland, Wellington and Christchurch. Also of note are **Abel Tasman Air** who run a quality service with small fixed-wing aircraft throughout the region, T03-5288290, www.abeltasmanair.co.nz **Super Shuttle** operates to and from the airport, T03-5475782 (about $10).

The following **bus** companies provide regular services to/from Nelson and the region as a whole: **Intercity,** 27 Bridge St, T03-5481538, www.nelsoncoaches.co.nz (Christchurch via Blenheim/Picton and the West Coast); **Kiwilink,** T03-5778332 (Christchurch/Blenheim/Picton/Golden Bay/Heaphy Track/Abel Tasman/Kaikoura/ West Coast); **Knightline,** T03-5287798 (Blenheim/Picton/Motueka); **Lazerline,** T0800-220001 (Christchurch via Lewis Pass); **White Star,** T03-5468687 (Christchurch) and **Atomic Shuttles,** T03-3228883 (Blenheim/Picton/West Coast). Operators servicing Motueka and the Abel Tasman National Park include: **Abel**

⦂ Thou Art gorgeous, darling!

In 1987, Nelson sculptor Suzie Moncrieff created and directed a unique stage show called **Wearable Art**. The concept is very simple – to create a piece of themed artwork in any media and in a form that can be worn in motion. The names of previous entries sum up the potential creativity, imagination and fun: The 'Over the Shoulder Boulder Holder' (Bizarre bra Section); 'Queen of the Night' (Man Unleashed section); 'Flaming Avenger' (Illumination Illusion section) and 'Superminx' (Dynasty section).

Almost overnight the first show became a huge success and every year since it has grown in stature attracting more entries, more media coverage, more money and now major sponsorship. The **Montana Wearable Arts Festival** held every September attracts entries representing disciplines as diverse as sculpture, architecture, fabric design, weaving and engineering, from artists and designers based in New Zealand, Australia, Europe, the Pacific and Asia. The prize too has increased with the Supreme Award winner now winning $7000. Award- winning entries can be seen at the new World of Wearable Art and Collectible Cars, *Quarantine Rd, Annesbrook just north of Nelson Airport, T03-5489299, www.worldofwearableart.com*

Tasman Coachlines, 27 Bridge St, T03-5480285, **Knightline,** T03-5287798 and **Kahurangi Bus,** T0800-881-188.

Buses going further northwest to Takaka and Golden Bay are: **Abel Tasman Coachlines** and **Kahurangi,** T03-5259434.

Buses heading south to St Arnaud and the Nelson Lakes National Park and the Rainbow ski area include: **Nelson Leisure Travel,** T03-5475912, **Atomic Shuttles,** T03-3228883 and **Nelson Lakes Shuttles,** T03-5211023, www.nelsonlakes.co.nz

Average fares to Christchurch are from $40, Greymouth from $50, Takaka from $22, Heaphy Track from $44 and Blenheim from $20. Most of the bus services stop right outside the VIC on the corner of Trafalgar and Halifax Streets. *Intercity* drop off at the bus terminal on Bridge Street. The VIC can assist with bookings and information.

By **car** Nelson is 144 km from Picton via SH6, 424 km to Christchurch via SH6, SH65 (Lewis Pass) and then SH1 and 226 km to Westport via SH6.

Getting around The local suburban bus company is **Nelson SBL,** T03-5481539, based at the terminal on Lower Bridge St. SBL run a Summertime bus that does a circuit of the city's major attractions on the hour departing the VIC from 1000-1600, from $5 per circuit or $10 for a day pass. The standard fare starts at $2.

Information
Nelson VIC, ① *corner of Trafalgar and Halifax Sts, T03-5482304, www.nelsonnz.com Daily 0900-1700.* The booklet *Nelson-Live the Day* is very useful and there are also a comprehensive range of activity, dining and shopping brochures. **DoC** has an adjunct office in the same building.

History
The Nelson Region has a rather bloody Maori history, with many of the early tribes who started arriving from the North Island in the 16th century being successively conquered by others migrating south. The Ngati Tumatakokiri (who gave Abel Tasman his hostile reception in 1642) were for a while the largest tribe, but they were effectively wiped out by the Ngati Apa (from Wanganui) and Ngati Tahu (also

from South Island). This transition was short-lived, however, when in the 1820s the Ngati Toa from Kapiti arrived and conquered the lot. So, when the NZ Company's agent, Captain Wakefield arrived about two decades later, it was with Te Rauparaha (chief of the Ngati Toa) that he negotiated land purchase. From the early 1840s Wakefield went on to effectively establish the company's largest New Zealand settlement – Nelson. However, very quickly problems arose when too many migrants arrived to too little work and not enough agriculturally viable land. To counter this, Wakefield and a survey party went in search for more land in the Wairau Valley to the southeast. Wakefield thought this land to be already his, but Te Rauparaha disputed that claim. The misunderstanding and subsequent disagreement lead to what was called the **Wairau Affray** and the death of Wakefield, 21 of his party and four Maori. This incident understandably retarded the development of early Nelson and to make matters worse, the NZ Company went bankrupt in 1844 leaving many destitute and unemployed. Redemption arrived in 1857 when gold was discovered near Collingwood (Golden Bay) and a new impetus was brought to the region. By the end of the century, long after the gold had run out, the rich agricultural potential and sustainability of the region was finally being realised – a natural resource that remains the most important resource in the region to this day.

Sights

Sadly the appearance of central Nelson is spoiled by one thing you cannot miss. The **Civic Tower** across the road from the VIC, which dominates the central city skyline, is

Nelson

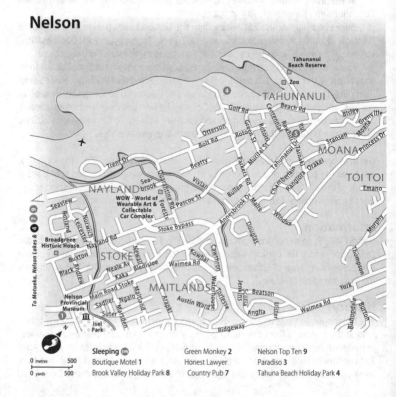

0 metres	500	**Sleeping** 💤	Green Monkey **2**	Nelson Top Ten **9**
0 yards	500	Boutique Motel **1**	Honest Lawyer	Paradiso **3**
		Brook Valley Holiday Park **8**	Country Pub **7**	Tahuna Beach Holiday Park **4**

without doubt the most hideous looking building in the country. An utter mess of concrete and steel, covered with aerials and radar, it looks like something that is about to take off. Whether to the moon or Mars, it would matter not as long as the architect responsible was strapped to it. That aside, there are many more attractive sights to see in and around Nelson.

A fine place to start is a short climb (1 hour return) to the **viewpoint** above the **Botanical Gardens**, which can be accessed off Milton or Maitai Roads. This site is claimed as the geographical centre of New Zealand, but other than offering a fine view of the town and giving you a sense of location, it is also the regular target for some delightful expressions of daring' and protest. Here, it is not at all unusual to see some wonderfully-colourful and frilly lingerie fluttering from the flagpole! More recently it was a flag proclaiming disgust at the use of GM (genetically modified) foodstuffs. Sadly, after that, the attractive botanical gardens are admirable, but far less remarkable. The other heavens of green in Nelson include the very attractive **Queens Gardens** off Bridge Street, complete with the city's fair share of ducks, and the vibrant flowerbeds of **Anzac Park** at the end of Rutherford Street. The **Miyazu Japanese Park** on Atawhai Drive has a traditional 'stroll' garden built to celebrate Nelson's links with sister city Miyazu in Japan.① *Open dawn to dusk, free.* There are numerous other fine gardens to visit in the region and the VIC can provide further information. The leaflet *Gardens of the Nelson Region*, free from the VIC, is a handy guide.

The newest tourist attraction in the Nelson area is the **World of Wearable Art and Collectable Cars**, ① *set in a 1 ha site in Quarantine Road, Annesbrook, just north of Nelson Airport, T03-5489299, www.worldofwearableart.com Daily 1000-1830 (1700 in winter), from $15, child $7.* The complex has two galleries. The first is the Wearable Art Gallery showcasing the historic Wearable Art Garment collection (now an iconic aspect

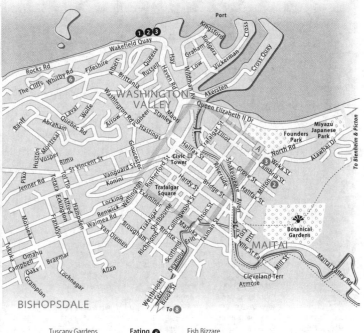

Tuscany Gardens Motor Lodge **5**
Wheelhouse Inn **6**

Eating ❷
Boat Shed **1**
Café 244 **4**

Fish Bizzare
Brasserie & Bar **3**
Passion **2**

of the region). There is a fully-scripted show that uses mannequins rather than live models but with all the usual elements of sound and lighting. The second gallery has an impressive collection of classic cars formerly on view in the town centre.

Although Nelson was one of New Zealand's earliest and largest settlements, there is little architectural evidence. Of obvious notoriety, but hardly historical (having being finally completed in 1965), is the **Nelson Cathedral**, ① *To3-5481008, daily in summer 0800-1900 (winter 0800-1700) tour guides are on duty most days, donation*, which dominates the southern end of town. Although its exterior barely matches the view of Trafalgar Street from the steps that lead up to it, the interior contains some fine stained-glass windows.

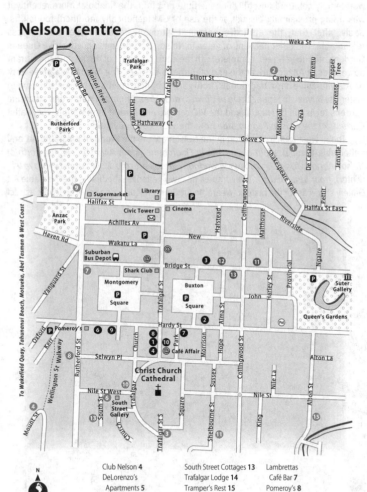

Nelson centre

0 metres 100
0 yards 100

N

Sleeping
Abbey Lodge B&B **1**
Cambria House **2**
Cathedral Inn **3**
Club Nelson **4**
DeLorenzo's
   Apartments **5**
Little Manor **6**
Nelson City YHA **7**
Palace Backpackers **8**
Palms Motel **9**
Rutherford & Miyazu
   Japanese Restaurant **10**
Shelbourne Villa **11**
Shortbread Cottage **12**
South Street Cottages **13**
Trafalgar Lodge **14**
Tramper's Rest **15**

Eating 🍴
Amadeus Café
   & Patisserie **1**
Broccoli Row **2**
Café Verte **3**
Chez Elco **4**
Flinders on Hardy **6**
Lambrettas
   Café Bar **7**
Pomeroy's **8**
Poppy Thai **9**
Victorian Rose **10**

Bars & clubs 🍸
Little Rock Café **11**
Molly McGuire's **12**
O'Reilly's **13**

Also worth a quick look is **Broadgreen Historic House**, ⓘ *276 Nayland Rd, in* *Stoke, which is 6 km southwest of the town centre via the coast road, T03-5470403. Summer Tue-Fri 1030-1630, Sat-Sun 1330-1630 (winter Tue, Wed, Thu, Sat and Sun 1400- 1630). Adult $3, child $0.50.* It is an 11-room 1855 Victorian 'cob' house furnished accordingly and set amongst pleasant gardens.

While in Stoke a far better sense of history can be found at the **Nelson Provincial Museum** set in the lovely **Isel Park**, ⓘ *Exhibitions open Mon-Fri 1000-1600 and Sat-Sun 1200-1600, T03-5479740. Adult $2, child $1. The free leaflet 'Nelson City of History-Trevor Horne Heritage Trail' is available from the VIC.* Accessed via Hilliard Street, it serves as the region's principal museum and contains all the usual suspects covering life from Maori settlement to the present day. It boasts a particularly large photographic collection dating from the 1870s.

With over 300 artists resident in the town **art and crafts** feature heavily in list of attractions. A copy of the *Nelson Regional Guide Book – Art in its Own Place*, is a great guide and available from most bookshops. The **Suter Gallery** (Te Aratoi-o-Whakatu), ⓘ *208 Bridge St, T03-5484699, www.thesuter.org.nz, daily 1030-1630. $2,* heads the list of major art galleries. Located next to Queen's Gardens, it boasts four exhibition spaces that showcase both permanent and temporary historical and contemporary collections. There is also a café, cinema and theatre on site that run a programme of musical and theatrical performances.

There are many other galleries in the area displaying a vast array of creative talent. Of particular note is **The Hoglund Art Glass**, ⓘ *Korurangi Farm, Landsdowne Road, T03-5446500, www.hoglund.co.nz,* home to the Hoglund Glass Blowing Studio. Here the internationally renowned pieces are created for sale and show in the gallery. Tours from $15. There is also a café and the entire set-up is located in a pleasant park-like environment. Also worth a visit is the **South Street Gallery**, ⓘ *10 Nile St West, T03-5488117.* This is the historical home of the Nelson Pottery where 25 selected potters of national and international renown create their various wares. The street itself is also noted for its 16 working-class **historical cottages** built between 1863 and 1867. On a rainy day, you can also try your hand at **bone carving**, ⓘ *87 Green Street, T03-5464275.* At only $55 for the full day course this is good value. ⏭ *For Sleeping, Eating and other listings, see pages 460-467.*

Around Nelson

Beaches

No visit to Nelson would be complete without a trip to the beach and the most popular stretch of golden sand is to be found at the **Tahunanui Beach Reserve**, just a few kilometres southwest of the town centre. Although you will not find the same scenic beauty and certainly not the solitude of the other, more remote beaches in the region, it is a convenient place to lay back and soak up the rays, swim or fly a kite. It is a great spot for kids with a small **zoo**, ⓘ *open 0900-1600; adult $5, child $2*, and a large fun park nearby. Slightly further afield (20 km) towards Motueka (SH60) are the beaches and forest swathe of **Rabbit Island**. This seemingly never-ending beach offers a far quieter and expansive alternative. It is worth checking with DoC, however, to confirm that it is not closed due to fire risk. With recent droughts this is becoming a more regular occurrence.

Wineries

Wineries around Nelson are also a big attraction. Although the region and its fine winemakers perhaps suffer from the reputation and sheer scale of their much-hyped neighbours in Marlborough, the wine they produce can be of a very fine quality. For more information on Nelson Region wineries consult www.nelsonwines.co.nz Some of the better known wineries which all offer (at the very least) tastings, include the following:

Seifried Estate Vineyard, *Redwood Rd, Appleby, T03-5441555, www.seifried.co.nz* The largest and oldest in the region and offers tours and tastings with a fine restaurant.
Grape Escape, *McShane Rd, T03-5444341, www.grapeescape.co.nz* Richmond incorporates a number of facets, producing a wide range of wines including certified organic varieties and housing an art and crafts outlet, a chocolatier (how is that for a job), a café, a nursery and even a candlestick maker. Perhaps it is only a matter of time before they add the proverbial partridge in a pear tree.
Waimea Estate, *22 Appleby Highway, Hope, T03-5444963, www.waimeaestates.co.nz* Which also has a café and is open daily from 1000-1700.
Greenhough Vineyard, *also in Hope T03-5423868.*
In the pretty locale known as Upper Moutere there are a number of fine wineries including:
Moutere Hills, *Sunrise Valley, Upper Moutere, T03-5432288, www.mouterehills.co.nz* Noted not only for its wine but its café, open daily 1100-1800 (weekends only in winter).

Neudorf, *Neudorf Rd, T03-5432643, www.neudorf.co.nz* Offers tastings.
Ruby Bay Wines, *Korepo Rd, T03-5402825.* Very scenic.
Spencer Hill Estate, *Best Rd, T03-5432031.* Popular and well-established.
Glovers Vineyard, *Gardner Valley Rd, T03-5432698, www.glovers-vineyard.co.nz* Owned by the very congenial David Glover, who is considered something of an institution when it comes to producing fine wines and sampling others. The great 'sorcerer' will be delighted to give you a taste, but best pre-book, since there may be a great tasting party raging. If you get lost, just head for the sound of classical music.

Breweries

Lovers of beer will be relieved to learn that some local brewing talent is hot on the heels of the winemakers.
McCashin's Brewery, *660 Main Rd, Stoke, T03-5470526, www.macs.co.nz* Home to the popular Mac's Ales. Open daily and tours are available at 1115 and 1400 daily, from $5 (tastings from $3).
Founders Brewery, *in the Founders Historic Park, 87 Atawhai Drive, T03-5484638, www.biobrew.co.nz* A certified organic brewery offering a range of heady organic brews. It has a good café.

Nelson to Motueka

From Richmond, 14 km southwest of Nelson, SH60 follows the fringe of Nelson Bay west to Motueka. This route – often labelled as 'Nelson's Coastal Way' – is the realm of vineyards, orchards, art and craft outlets and some pleasant seaside spots. One such spot worth a look, particularly around lunch or dinnertime, is **Mapua**. A congenial little settlement at the mouth of the **Waimea Inlet** (and just a short diversion off SH60), it boasts one of the best restaurants in the region, The Smokehouse, see page 463.

Across the road is the fairly unremarkable **Touch the Sea Aquarium and Gift Shop**,ⓘ *T03-5403557, daily, from $5.50, child $3.50,* which is maybe worth a look if you love seahorses or have kids. Far more impressive is the work of local artisans showcased in the **Cool Store art gallery**,ⓘ *Next door, T03-5403778.* When it comes to the quality of work, it is exactly that and well worth a muse.▶▶ *For Sleeping, Eating and other listings, see pages 461-466.*

Motueka → *Phone code: 03 Colour map 4, grid B3 Population: 12,000*

Motueka itself is a rather unremarkable little place of little note, but set amidst all the sun-bathed vineyards and orchards and within a short distance from some of the most beautiful beaches in the country, it seems to radiate a sense of smug satisfaction. Once a thriving Maori settlement, the first residents were quickly displaced by the early Europeans, who were also intent on utilizing the area's rich natural resources. Today Motueka is principally a service centre for the numerous vineyards, orchards and market gardens that surround it, or for the many transitory tourists on route to the Abel Tasman National Park and Golden Bay. With such a seasonal influx of visitors Motueka is also a place of contrast, bustling in summer and sleepy in winter. One thing you will immediately notice on arrival is its almost ludicrously long main street – so long you could land a 747 on it and still have room for error. ▸▸ *See also Abel Tasman National Park, page 467.*

Ins and outs Getting there Motueka has no scheduled services but **Abel Tasman Air,** To3-5288290, www.abeltasmanair.co.nz, can get you there from within the region if you want to arrive in style. The airport is located on College St (SH61) 2 km west of the town centre. By road, Motueka is 51 km from Nelson on SH60 (Coastal Highway). ▸▸ *See also Nelson Ins and outs, page 452.*

Information Motueka VIC, ① *Wallace St in the town centre, To3-5286543, www.abeltasmangreenrush.co.nz Daily 0800-1900.* It is a busy centre that prides itself on providing the best and most up to date information on the Abel Tasman National Park. **DoC field centre,** ① *at the corner of King Edward and High Sts, To3-5281810, www.motuekaao@doc.govt.nz Mon-Fri 0800-1630.* Maps and leaflets available for the entire region plus hut bookings for the Abel Tasman Coastal Walkway, Kahurangi National Park and Heaphy Tracks. You could also call into **Abel Tasman Wilson's Experiences,** ① *265 High St (on the right of the main road into town, next to New World Supermarket), To3-5287801, www.abeltasmannz.co.nz,* for maps, tide information and help with itinerary planning. Operators of beachfront lodges, launch cruises, water-taxi, guided/non-guided sea kayaking and walking.

Sights The best **beaches** near Motueka (and before the national park) are in **Kaiteriteri.** For a local short **walk** try the Motueka Quay accessed via the waterfront west of the town centre. For other walks in the area contact DoC. There's also the small and fairly unremarkable **Motueka Museum,** ① *on High St, To3-5287660. Mon-Fri 1000-1500 (also weekends in summer). Donations.* ▸▸ *See also Sleeping, Eating and other listings, pages 461-464. For activities in the Abel Tasman and Kahurangi National Parks see pages 467 and 480.*

Kaiteriteri and Marahau → *Colour map 4, grid B3.*
Kaiteriteri and Marahau are both on the dead-end road to the southern boundary of the Abel Tasman National Park, which is accessed from SH60 just north of Motueka. **Kaiteriteri** (13 km) is a very pretty village with two exquisite **beaches** of its own and is a popular holiday spot. The main beach is the main departure point for scenic launch trips, water taxis and kayak adventures into the Abel Tasman National Park. If you do nothing else in Kaiteriteri, allow yourself time to take in the view from the **Kaka Pa Point Lookout** at the eastern end of the beach. There is a signpost appended with destinations and distances that will remind you how far you are from home – and how close to paradise. **Breakers Beach** below, looking east towards the park, is truly idyllic.

Marahau, a further 6 km east of Kaiteriteri, is principally an accommodation and activity base at the main access point to the national park. There is a good range of accommodation options, a number of water-taxi and activity operators and a café to satisfy the needs of exhausted, hungry trampers. There is much controversy surrounding a $15 million resort development on environmentally sensitive wetlands, right at the entrance to the national park that has just been given building consent. Should funding be found (which it inevitably will), sadly this sums up the fears of many conservationists that it may be the beginning (or confirmation of the beginning) of the end for the unspoilt beauty of the Abel Tasman. ▸▸ *See Sleeping and Eating, pages 462-464. See also Abel Tasman National Park, page 467.*

Nelson *p452*

Being such a popular holiday destination there is no shortage of beds in Nelson with a few good hotels, numerous B&Bs and homestays, the usual rash of motels and more backpackers than almost anywhere else in New Zealand. Despite this, mid-summer is very busy and you are advised to book ahead.

LL-AL Cambria House, *7 Cambria St, T03-5484681, www.cambria.co.nz* A well established, beautifully appointed and well located B&B in a 130 year-old homestead.

LL-AL Cathedral Inn, *369 Trafalgar St South, T03-5487369, www.cathedralinn.co.nz* Another well-located, historic option with a fine reputation.

LL-AL Shelbourne Villa, *21 Shelbourne St, T03-5459059, www.shelbournevilla.co.nz* Right next to the Cathedral, offering 3 king size master suites and 1 loft with 2 twins. Beautiful garden.

L-AL The Rutherford Hotel, *Trafalgar Square, T03-5482299, www.rutherfordhotel.co.nz* The principal hotel in the city and centrally located. It has all the usual mod cons and a very good Japanese restaurant attached.

AL DeLorenzo's Apartments, *51 Trafalgar St, T03-5489774, www.delorenzos.co.nz* New, well appointed and fully self-contained block of apartments close to town.

AL The Honest Lawyer Country Pub, *1 Point Rd, Monaco, T03-5478850, www.honestlawyer.co.nz* Although out of town (near the airport) this is well worth the effort. Lovely rustic rooms and a quiet characterful pub with restaurant downstairs.

AL Little Manor, *12 Nile St, T03-5451411, a.little.manor@xtra.co.nz* A charming, 2-storey, historic self-contained cottage in the heart of town.

AL-A Palms Motel, *5 Paru Paru Rd, T03-5467770, www.palmsnelson.co.nz* One of the best upper-range motels in the centre of town.

AL South Street Cottages, *1, 3 & 12 South St, T03-5402769.* Compact, self-contained historic cottages in Nelson's most historic street.

AL-A Tuscany Gardens Motor Lodge, *80 Tahunanui Dr, Tahunanui, T03-5485522,* *tuscany@xtra.co.nz* A relatively new luxury motel with a good reputation close to Tahunanui beach.

A Boutique Motel, *7 Bail St, Stoke, T03-5471439, boutique@ts.co.nz* A new and well appointed establishment located in the quiet suburb of Stoke and near the airport.

A Wheelhouse Inn, *41 Whitby Rd, T03-5468391, www.wheelhouse.nelson.co.nz* A new, spacious, timber-style establishment, with self-contained accommodation. Quiet bush setting with a superb view.

B Abbey Lodge B&B, *84 Grove St, T03-5488816, www.abbeylodge.org.nz* Simple, no nonsense budget option 10 min walk from the town centre.

B Trafalgar Lodge, *46 Trafalgar St, T03-5483980, www.trafalgarlodge.co.nz* A fine and well-located budget option with very friendly owners.

The choice of budget accommodation is vast with over 15 to choose from. The following are recommended:

C-D Club Nelson, *18 Mount St, T03-5483466, clubnelson@xtra.co.nz* A huge rambling villa with 45 rooms, a pool and tennis courts.

C-D The Green Monkey, *129 Milton St, T03-5457421 thegreenmonkey@xtra.co.nz* A small, modern and quiet option with great doubles and fine facilities.

C-D Nelson City YHA, *59 Rutherford St, T03-5459988, www.yha.org.nz* A large, modern, purpose built YHA that is deservedly popular. Mainly twin and doubles. A little lacking in atmosphere but well located in the town centre.

C-D Paradiso, *42 Weka St, T03-5466703, www.backpackernelson.webnz.co.nz* Club-Med in Nelson! A bit of a walk from the centre of town but very popular with a pool, spa and sauna. Wide range of rooms, conservatory kitchen and internet. Busy so book ahead. Internet.

C-D Palace Backpackers, *114 Rutherford St, T03-5484691, thepalace@xtra.co.nz* Another popular place set in a spacious historic villa overlooking the town. Wide variety of rooms. Great view, free breakfast/coffee, spa and a nice friendly atmosphere. Internet. Camping available.

C-D Shortbread Cottage, *33 Trafalgar St, T03-5466681.* Another small, homely and friendly backpackers with good facilities.

Shortbread is excellent!

C-D Tramper's Rest, *31 Alton St, T03-5457477*. An excellent home-style backpackers with an owner who is a guru when it comes to tramping information. Small, but very friendly and cosy.

Motorcamps and holiday parks

The pick of the bunch is the
Nelson Top Ten, *29 Gladstone Rd, Richmond, T03-5447323*. Although 14 km away in Richmond it is worth it. Another possibility is the vast.

Tahuna Beach Holiday Park, *70 Beach Rd, Tahunanui, T03-5485159*. Close to the most popular beach in town. Shop on site. The closest motor camp to the town centre is the **Brook Valley Holiday Park**, *about 2km south of the town centre on Brook St, T03-5480399*. It is in a pleasant enough position in the valley beside the river but is pretty basic and the sandflies are a menace.

Nelson to Motueka *p458*

B-D Mapua Leisure Park (clothing optional), *33 Toru St, T03-5402666, www.nelsonholiday.co.nz* An excellent camp, set amidst pine trees and sheltered surroundings, at the river mouth. It has numerous pretty areas to camp in, powered sites, cabins, chalets, sauna, pool and spa. There is also a small café and bar on the beach. If the holiday park is not to your tastes, there are a number of good B&Bs in the area.

LL Jester House, *15 km south of Motueka on the Coastal Highway (SH60), T03-5266742, www.jesterhouse.co.nz* Something completely different and without doubt the most unique accommodation in the region. Quite simply, this could be (and probably will be) your only opportunity to stay in a giant boot!

LL-L Bronte Lodge, *Bronte Rd East, T03-5402422, margaret@brontelodge.co.nz* Another luxury option set in beautiful gardens. 2 luxury suites and self-contained villas with all mod cons.

AL Istana Coastal Cottage, *located just south of Mapua on the Coastal Highway (SH60), T03-5441979, www.istana.co.nz*

Self-contained cottage in a superb position overlooking the coastal inlet, very peaceful and tastefully appointed with Asian antiques and modern furnishings. Swimming pool and free kayaks. Recommended.

A Kina Colada Health Retreat, *Kina Peninsula, T03-5266700*. Enjoy the congenial surroundings, a massage, sauna or an oxygen, hydro and moor-mud therapy (what ever that might be).

Motueka *p458*

The area has many fine lodges, B&Bs and homestays, most of which are located out of town. The VIC has full listings. Given the proximity to the Abel Tasman National Park you are advised to book well ahead in summer.

LL-L Lodge at Paratiho Farm, *545 Waiwhero Rd, T03-5282100, www.paratiho.co.nz* Touted as the most luxurious place to stay in the region. Set on a 900-acre farm in the country, it is rather stunning. It offers just about all a body could need, but at $1600 a night for a single occupancy, it would have to!

LL Motueka River Lodge, *Motueka Valley Highway, Ngatimoti, T03-5268668, www.motuekalodge.co.nz* Another popular establishment of sumptuous luxury near the town.

LL Kahurangi Estate, *Sunrise Rd, T03-5432980, www.kahurangiwine.com*; and **AL Old Schoolhouse**, *Kina Beach Estate, T03-5266252, www.kinabeach..co.nz* Both offer beautiful self-contained cottages amid vinyards.

In Motueka, 3 more affordable options are:

AL-A Blue Moon, *57 School Rd, T03-5286996,www.thebluemoon.co.nz* (self-contained)

A Rowan Cottage Organic B&B, *27 Fearon St, T03-5286492, www.rowancottage.net* and **A The Estuary B&B**, *543 High St, T03-5286391*. All are good value, modern and have good facilities with character.

Motels include:

A-B Avalon Manor, *314 High St, T03-5288320*. A possible exception to a rather unimpressive rule.

B-D Bakers Lodge, *4 Poole St, T03-5280102,*

⬤ *For an explanation of the sleeping and eating price codes used in this guide, see the inside*
● *front cover. Other relevant information is provided in the Essentials chapter, see page 51.*

www.bakerslodge.co.nz An excellent, award-winning establishment with a wide variety of rooms, modern facilities and a nice atmosphere. Very popular so book well in advance.

C-D White Elephant, *55 Whakarewa St*, *T03-5286208*. Popular and spacious old villa backpackers.

Motorcamps

B-D Fernwood Holiday Park, *519 High St (SH60)*, *T03-5287488*. Beside the roundabout at the start of the never-ending main road through the town.

B-D Motueka Top Ten Holiday Park, *10 Fearon St, at the other end of the town*, *T03-5287189, www.motuekatop10.co.nz*

Kaiteriteri *p459*

LL-AL Kimi Ora Holiday and Health Resort, *Martin Farm Rd, T03-5278027*, *www.kimiora.co.nz* 20 modern chalets, pool, spa and a health centre offering a range of treatments. In-house restaurant (open to non-guests) and courtesy pick-ups also available.

AL Bayview, *Kaiteriteri Heights, Little Kaiteriteri, T03-5278090*, *www.kaiteriteribandb.co.nz* Offers exactly that from 2 lovely rooms and while enjoying breakfast on the deck.

A Sea View B&B, *259 Riwaka-Kaiteriteri Rd*, *T03-5289341*. A good value B&B with one queen and one double/single.

A Torlesse Coastal Motels, *Kotare Pl, Little Kaiteriteri Beach, T03-5278063*, *www.torlessemotels.co.nz* The best motel option with a choice of studio or 2-bedroom units.

Motorcamps and campsites

C-D Kaiteriteri Motor Camp, *across the road from the beach, T03-5278010*. Has tent and powered sites and cabins.

Marahau *p459*

A Ocean View Chalets, *T03-5278232*, *www.accommodationabeltasman.co.nz* Neat, self-contained cottages set on the hillside overlooking the bay, about 500 m from the main village.

A Marahau Lodge, *T03-5278250*, *www.abeltasmanmarahaulodge.co.nz* Slightly more up-market with well appointed

units, pool, sauna and spa. Clients are well looked after.

C-D Old McDonald's Farm, *Harvey Rd, further along the road, essentially at the entrance to the park Abel Tasman Park, T03-5278288, ww.oldmacs.co.nz* A large but sheltered holiday camp complete with various animals, including 2 friendly and extremely dosy kune pigs. There are plenty of sheltered tent and powered sites and a range of well appointed self-contained units, cabins and a backpacker's dormitory. Small café on site and internet.

C-D Barn Backpackers, *Harvey Rd, T03-5278043*. A smaller but otherwise similar set up. Both can assist in park accommodation and activity bookings.

C-D Southern Exposure Kayak Company also have budget accommodation on *Moss Rd, T0800-695-295*, *www.southern-exposure.co.nz* A rather unusual option worth considering is

B-D Abel Tasman Aqua Packers, *Anchorage Bay, T0800-430744, wwwaquapackers.co.nz* that offer dormitory style accommodation on board a small ex-WWII naval patrol vessel. Standard or dinner, bed and breakfast options. Plenty of activities and a good base from which to explore the park.

🍴 Eating

Nelson *p452*

There are over 50 cafés and restaurants in Nelson with the centre of town or the waterfront being the prime locations. Ask for the free and comprehensive *Eat, Drink Nelson guide* from the VIC.

$$$ Miyazu Japanese Restaurant, *Rutherford Hotel, Trafalgar Sq, T03-5482299. Mon-Sat from 1800.* An excellent but expensive Japanese restaurant with a loyal regional following.

$$$ The Boat Shed, *350 Wakefield Quay, T03-5469783, www.nelsonwaterfront.co.nz Open daily for breakfast, lunch and dinner.* The flagship of a trio of waterfront restaurants bought up and revitalised by extrovert Israeli Zviki Eschet. Many Nelsonians shun the newcomer's efforts and his progressive style, but there is no denying the quality of the food or the location. Fresh, local seafood is of course a speciality.

Nearby, located at the Nelson Yacht Club is

$$$ Passion - The Restaurant, *322 Wakefield Quay, T03-5391307. Open daily for lunch and dinner*. Another of Zviki's culinary projects, just a tad cheaper than the Boat Shed but with an equally imaginative menu. If you fall in love with the cuisine on offer here you can even join the in-house cookery school.

$$$ Flinders on Hardy, *90 Hardy St, T03-5488589. Daily 1100-late*. A classy minimalist décor establishment clearly under the influence of Auckland waterfront restaurants and of the same ilk. Best wear a tie!

$$ Chez Elco, at *296 Trafalgar St, T03-5487595. Daily from 0700-1900*. One of the oldest cafés in the country with a loyal local following. Fine atmosphere, food, great coffee and breakfasts.

$$ The Fish Bizarre Brasserie Bar, *272 Wakefield Quay, T03-5483361. Daily from 0900-late*. Another Zviki Eschet restaurant popular for the view and with numerous affordable seafood offerings as well as steak, pizza and burgers.

$$ Amadeus Café and Patisserie, *284 Trafalgar St, T03-5457191. Daily 0800-late*. Great for either breakfast, lunch or dinner. Wide-ranging Euro-style menu and a plump range of great pastries and cakes.

$$ Pomeroy's, *276 Trafalgar St, T03-5487524*. Restaurant/wine bar with an imaginative menu and blackboard selection. Good coffee and breakfasts.

$$ Poppy Thai, *142 Hardy St, T03-5488997. Daily 1730-2200*. The pick of the affordable Asian restaurants.

$$ Lambrettas Café Bar, *204 Hardy St, T03-5458555, www.lambrettascafe.co.nz 0900-late*. Another popular, good value café specializing in all things Italian, including scooters. Excellent pizzas.

$$ Café 244, *244 Queen St, Richmond, T03-5449244. Mon-Wed 0900-1800, Thu-Sat 0900-late, Sun 1000-1600*. The pick of the cafés in Richmond should you be staying out in that direction.

$ Café Verte, *123 Bridge St, T03-5457174*. A good café to laze about over a latte and take your pick from an interesting menu.

$ Broccoli Row, *5 Buxton Sq, T03-5489621. Daily 0930-2200*. Known for its seafood and vegetarian offerings. Pleasant outdoor area.

$ The Victorian Rose, *281 Trafalgar St,*

T03-5487631. An Olde English-style pub with very expensive beer but good value food. Cheap all-you-can-eat Sun roasts a speciality.

$ The Honest Lawyer, *1 Point Rd, Monaco, near the airport*. Another fine pub worthy of the ale and steak lover's attention.

Wineries *p457*

There are a number of winery restaurants out of town but worth the trip for a leisurely lunch. These include:

$ Waimea Estates, *22 Appleby Highway, Hope, T03-5444963,www.waimeaestates.co.nz*

$ Seifrieds, *corner of SH60 and Redwood Rd, Appleby, Richmond, T03-5441555, www.seiifried.co.nz* A popular restaurant at the biggest winery.

Supermarket Woolworths, *corner of Paru Paru Rd and Halifax St, T03-5466466;* **New World**, *Montgomery Sq, T03-5489111*.

Nelson to Motueka *p458*

The Smokehouse Restaurant, *Mapua, T03-5402280, www.smokehouse.co.nz Open daily for lunch and dinner, from 1100*. Well known for its fine smoked fish and other seafood delicacies. The restaurant is set overlooking the river with a very pleasant outdoor eating area where you can tickle your taste buds and sample a glass or two of local wine while taking in the view, al fresco. Attached is a very popular fish and chip shop.

Motueka *p458*

$$$ Gothic Gourmet Restaurant, *208 High St, T03-5286699. Daily from 0730-late*. Interesting concept – but lacks atmosphere and is too expensive for what it is.

$$ Grain and Grape, *218 High St, T03-5286103;* and

$$ Hot Mamma's Café, *105 High St, T03-5287039*. Both open daily - 'ate' till late. Both have a loyal local following, good coffee and inviting blackboard menus.

$ Blast Expresso, *145 High St, T03-5280087*. Also a good bet for a quality caffeine hit.

$ Riverside Café, *just out of town on the way to Lower Moutere (Inland Highway 7km), T03-5267447. Tue-Wed 0930-1730, Thu-Sun 0930-late*. A fine option, especially if you have kids, replete with spacious grounds and great staff.

$ **Park Café** *just at the entrance to the park on Harvey Rd, T03-5278270. Daily from 0800 (closed May-Aug)*. Fine blackboard fare, a bar, good coffee and Internet. Great atmosphere.

☺ Pubs, bars and entertainment

Nelson *p452*

When it comes to nightlife, most of the action in Nelson (and it can be considerable) takes place on or around Bridge St. Here you will find the very 'Mad-Max'
Little Rock Café, *165 Bridge St*. It goes off with dancing at the weekend with the young set shaking their pants into the small hours.
Molly McGuire's nearby is Nelson's popular Irish pub featuring regular music sessions.
O'Reilly's is an even better Irish option across the road.
The Shark Club, *132 Bridge St, T03-5466630*. Not, as the name suggests, a haunt for second-hand car salesmen or lawyers but perhaps the town's most popular pool parlour and backpacker hang-out.
Victoria Rose, *Trafalgar St*. The place to head if you are fed up with the noise, like jazz or blues, or just want to watch some sport on the big screen, but the good stuff (Irish and English beer) is expensive.
Honest Lawyer *in Monaco* is again a good venue for conversation and traditional Irish music at the weekends.

Cinema and theatre

State Cinema Centre, *across the road from the VIC, T03-5488123*. Also has a café upstairs.
Suter Gallery, *208 Bridge St, T03-5484699*. The focus for more cultural events, including theatre, dance and non-mainstream films.

Motueka

Dodgy Ref *121 High St, T03-5284101* The best place for a beer in town.

☻ Festivals and events

For up to date events listings consult the website www.nelsonnz.com/events
The most famous event in Nelson is the now world famous **Wearable Arts Festival** (*late Sep – see box, page 453*). Also of note are the **Nelson Jazz Festival** (*between Christmas and New Year*), www.nelsonjazz.co.nz, and the

Festival of Opportunities (*late Feb*) a event that explores and contemplates the mind, the body, the spirit - and probably even your navel, www.nelsonhealthfest.co.nz
The waterfront hosts the **Hooked on Seafood Festival** (*Mar*) offering a showcase for the region's seafood, wine and local produce, www.hookedonseafood.co.nz

▲ Activities

Nelson *p452*

Nelson and the Nelson Region offers a wide range of activities from the crazy to the traditional. The VIC has listings of everything that is on offer.

Cruising and sailing

Cat-O-Nine, *262 Wakefield Quay, T03-5480202, www.cato9.co.nz* A well-established operator offering a range of trips and activities locally or to the Abel Tasman National Park. Half-day to multi-day trips on offer. **Nelson Yacht Charters**, *based at Nelson Port, T0800-738724*. Hire from $220 per day.

Diving

Dive Inn, *175 Haven Rd, T03-5458549, www.diveinn.co.nz* From $25.
Big Blue Dive and Fish, *corner of Akersten and Wildman Av, Port Nelson, T03-5467411, www.bigbluenz.com* From $60.

Fishing

There are a number of private charters and guided trips available for both sea and fly fishing. For details contact the VIC.
Cat-O-Nine Charters, *262 Wakefield Quay, T03-5480202, www.cato9.co.nz* One of the most convenient. From $60 with all gear provided.

Flightseeing

Abel Tasman Air, *Nelson Airport, T03-5288290, www.abeltasmanair.co.nz* An excellent and friendly outfit offering both transportation and flightseeing options in the region. A flight around Abel Tasman and Kahurangi National Parks is recommended. From $35.
Nelson Helicopters, *T03-5418178*. Scenic helicopter flights. Used extensively during the filming of Lord of the Rings for shuttling

cast and crew into the depths of the Kahurangi National Park.

4WD Quad Biking and the Skywire
Four-wheel quad biking is a speciality in the region with one of the oldest and best operators in the country based nearby. **Happy Valley Adventures**, *194 Cable Bay Road, Hira T03-5450304, www.happyvalleyadventures.co.nz* Back-country guided rides, taking in a mighty maitai tree and some superb views. Interesting eco-based commentary. Kids' fun rides in an 8-wheel drive also available and there is a café on site. An excellent wet weather option. From $85 for 2½ hrs.
Skywire is a new addition to the adrenaline cocktail and is essentially a 4person flying-fox that flies 1.6 km across the valley, reputedly at 120 km/ph. A 'Granny Run' is available for the faint-hearted, presumably with tea and scones and classical music playing in the background. From $15-$120. Transportation available.

Golf
Nelson is not short of quality courses.
Greenacres, *Richmond, T03-546441.* From $30.
Nelson Golf Club, *Bolt Rd, T03-5485028.* From $35.
Driving range, *453 Nayland Rd, Stoke, T03-5472227.*

Horse trekking
Western Ranges Horse Treks, *Wakefield, T03-5224178, www.thehorsetrek.co.nz* A good outfit well suited to both beginners and the experienced. They trek the Kahurangi National Park and Northwest Nelson ranges, from $70 half-day.
Stonehurst Farm Horse Treks, *Stonehurst Farm, Clover Rd, T03-5424121, www.stonehurstfarm.co.nz* Treks of 1-4 hrs from $35.
Thorndale Horse Treks, *north of Nelson (near Happy Valley Adventures), on Cable Valley Rd, T03-5451191.* Also recommended. 1 hr to overnight from $35.

Mountain biking
The Nelson area is very popular for mountain biking. A broadsheet outlining the best local and regional rides is available from DoC.

Natural High, *52 Rutherford St, T03-5466936, www.natural-high.co.nz* Offer guided tours and independent hire ($25 to $85 per day).

Rock climbing
Vertical Limits, *34 Vanguard St, T03-5457511, www.verticallimits.com* Offer some excellent rock climbing trips to some notable venues in Golden Bay. From $130. They also have an indoor **climbing wall** for instruction or independent use, from $6.

Sea kayaking
If you intend to go sea kayaking in the Abel Tasman National Park you can organize the trip from the Nelson VIC or direct with operators (see page 471). There are many of operators and plenty of transport. You can also organize trips locally or to the much quieter, sheltered and expansive Marlborough Sounds.
Natural High, *52 Rutherford St, T03-5466936,* Independent hire from $65 per day (guided half- to 3-day trips from $65, local harbour trip from $45).

Sightseeing and wine tours
There are numerous sightseeing and wine tour operators available. Recommended operators include:
JJ's Scenic and Wine Tours, *279 Hill St, T03-5447081.* Half-day from $50.
Nelson Safaris, *T0800-354671.* A new operator offering general sightseeing tours and full-day vineyard tours of the Wairau Valley from $108.
Bay Tours, *48 Brougham St, T03-5457114, www.baytoursnelson.co.nz* Flexible with wine tours a speciality from $40.
Nelson Day Tours, *T03-5484224.* Wine and craft, city and district tours from a very reasonable $35.

Skydiving, paragliding and hang-gliding
If the weather is in your favour you can do your obligatory tandem skydive with:
Skydive Nelson, *16 College St Mouteka, T03-5284091, www.skydive.co.nz* From $260.
Nelson Paragliding, *T03-5441182, www.nelsonparagliding.co.nz* Tandem paragliding from $110, courses from $150.
Adventure Paragliding, *18A Marybank Rd, Atawai, T03-5452006, www.skyout.co.nz*

Tandem from $110, courses from $150.
Tasman Tandems, *Motueka, T03-5289283*.
From $110.
Nelson hang-gliding Adventures,
T03-5489151, gmeadows@clear.net.nz From
$140. Tandem and solo introductory
hang-gliding courses are also available.

Walking

For a short walk the viewpoint above the
Botanical Gardens is recommended, while
for longer excursions and more expansive
views try the **Dun Mountain Walkway**,
which is accessible via the Broom Valley.
From Brook Street take a left on to
Tantragee Road.

Water-skiing and kitesurfing

Natural High, *52 Rutherford St, T03-5466936*.
From $45. The broadsheet *Water Ski Tasman*
is available from the VIC.
Kitesurfing is huge in Nelson with the winds
over Tahunanui Beach often creating the
perfect conditions.
Rig-N-Rip, *T03-5451588*. Owner Tim Wincer
is a local expert. Offer 3-hr lessons from $80
(Oct-April).

Whitewater rafting

Rapid River Rafting Company,
T0800-292466, www.rapid-river.co.nz
Offering half to 5-day trips on the Buller,
Gowan and Clarence Rivers. From $79.

Winery tours

JJ's Wine Tours, *T0800-568-568,
www.jjs.co.nz* Great half or full-day tours
from $50.
Nelson Safaris, *T0800-354671*. A new
operator offering full day vineyard tours of
the Wairau Valley from $108.

Nelson to Motueka *p458*

Mapua Adventures, *opposite the wharf,
T03-5403833, www.mapuaadventures.co.nz*
Very helpful and friendly staff that offer an
exciting range of options centred around
the river estuary, coastline and forests.
These include jet boating (35 min from $39;
1 hr from $49), sea kayaking (2 hr 30 min
from $39; 6 hr from $119) and mountain
biking (2 hr from $20). Independent
mountain bike hire costs from $10 per hr to
$30 per day.

Motueka *p458*

Abel Tasman Wilson's Experiences, *see
page 459*. Offer a wide range of guided/
non-guided sea kayaking, and walking trips
to the Abel Tasman National Park.
The Hire Boat Company, *T03-5286381,
www.totallyboating.co.nz* Local boat hire
from $175 per day.
Bush and Beyond, *35 School Rd,
T03-5289054, www.naturetreks.co.nz* Offer a
variety of conservation-based walks from 1-8
days, mainly in the Kahurangi National Park,
from around $115 a day. For other activities
see Nelson above and Kaiteriteri below.

Kaiteriteri and Marahau *p459*

See also other park-orientated activity
operators based in Marahau (see page 471).
**Marble Hills 4 Wheel Motorcycle
Adventures**, *92 Little Sydney Valley Rd,
T03-5278400, www.marblehills4fun.co.nz*
Provide some excellent scenic trips and 4WD
fun from $45. (Cabin accommodation
available.)
Flying Fox, *on the main road near Kaiteriteri,
T0800-FLYFOX. Daily 0900-1800 in summer.*
This is more of a novel idea than a major
adrenaline rush, but involves being hoisted
700 m up a hillside in a 6-man carriage to
descend at a reputed 100 km per hr into a
small pond – what will they think of next!
$25, child $15.

O Shopping

Nelson *p452*

For detailed information on art and craft
outlets get a copy of the *Nelson Regional
Guide Book - Art in its Own Place*, available
from most bookshops.
Nelson Market, *Sat 0800-1300*.
Monty's Market, *in Montgomery Sq,
T03-5466454. Sun 0900-1300*. Popular and
has a crafts edge. There are many specialist
arts and crafts outlets including:
Höglund Art Glass Gallery, *Korurangi Farm,
Landsdowne Rd, Richmond, T03-5446500*,
The Wood Gallery *69 Point Rd, Monaco,
T03-5477299*, and
Craft Habitat, *SH6, Richmond, T03-5447481*.
A conglomerate of working studios.
Bead Gallery, *18 Parere St, T03-5467807*.
Excellent.
Pomeroys Coffee and Tea Co, *80 Hardy St,*

T03-5466944. Stock up on fine filter coffee or tea.

❶ Directory

Nelson *p452*
Banks You will find all the main branches in or around *Trafalgar St.* **Bikes** can be hired from **Natural High**, *52 Rutherford St, T03-5466936*, from $25 per day. **Hollidays Cycle Centre**, *277 High St, Motueka, T03-5289379*, from $25 per day. **Car hire Budget**, *Nelson Airport, T03-5479586;*

Pegasus, *83 Haven Rd, T03-5480884;* **Hardy Cars**, *8 Bridge St, T03-5481618.* **Internet Email Centre**, *53 Bridge St;* **Aurora Tech**, *161 Trafalgar St,* and **Café Affair**, *295 Trafalgar St.* **Post office** (post restante) *corner of Trafalgar and Halifax, opposite the VIC, T03-5467818. Mon-Fri 0745-1700, Sat 0930-1230.* **Medical services** Nelson Hospital, *Tipahi St, T03-5461800,* **Emergency Pharmacy**, *corner of Hardy and Collingwood Sts, T03-5483897.* **Police** *T03-5488309.* **Taxi** Sun City Taxis, *T03-5482666* and Nelson City Taxis, *T03-5488225.*

Abel Tasman National Park

→ *Colour map 4, grid B3*

The Abel Tasman is the smallest and the busiest national park in New Zealand, and one of the most beautiful, protecting 23,000 ha of some of the finest coastal scenery and beaches in the country. Rolling hills of native bush fall to azure-coloured clear waters and a 91 km coastline, indented with over 50 beaches of golden sand. It is a paradise for trampers and sea kayakers and boasts the famous and increasingly popular 51 km Coastal Walkway. The park is also home to the Tonga Island Marine Reserve.

The park was opened in 1942 after the tireless efforts of conservationist and resident Perrine Moncrieff, and named after the Dutch navigator Abel Tasman who first sighted New Zealand in 1642. Many of the place names are accredited to the explorations and subsequent mappings in 1827 by the French explorer Jules Sebastien Cesar Dumont d'Urville.

With over 170,000 visitors a year and up to 4000 on an average summer's day many feel the great 'Abel Taz' is losing its appeal. More importantly, it is in danger of being placed on an environmental precipice. Part of the problem lies not only in its sheer and understandable popularity, but also that DoC is somewhat powerless to prevent further damaging development. Although they administer the vast majority of the park, the sections between the low and high water mark are essentially council-owned. That does not necessarily mean that the Tasman District Council is intent on ruining the place, but it does mean that development, money and greed can grow to rule the roost, while pure conservation loses its beautiful feathers and gets placed further down the pecking order. What will happen remains to be seen, but as it is the Abel Tasman is everything it is cracked up to be and, if you can stand the company and respect and treat the place as such, it is well worthy of investigation. They say winter is now the best time to visit the park. In summer you must book well in advance for all accommodation and most activities.

Ins and outs

Getting there Marahau, at the park's southern entrance, is the principal gateway to the park. Access from this point is by foot, water-taxi, kayak or launch. The northern (walk) gateway to the park is via Takaka (Golden Bay) at the road terminus on the eastern edge of Wainui Bay. There is road access (unsealed) into the northern sector of the park terminating at Totaranui and Awaroa Bay. Note that you can also fly into Awaroa Bay from Nelson or Motueka, contact **Abel Tasman Air**, Nelson Airport, T03-5288290.

Kaiteriteri and Marahau are served via Motueka by **Abel Tasman Coachlines** (Nelson), To3-5480285; **Kiwilink** (Blenheim), To3-5778332 and **Kahurangi Buses**, To800-881-188. Abel Tasman Coachlines and Kahurangi Bus also serve the northern sector of the park to Totaranui.

There are numerous **water-taxi** operators that offer casual walkers or day trippers the option of being dropped off at one beach to be picked up later at the same, or at another. For trampers this can also provide numerous options to walk some of the **Coastal Walkway** or to retire early in the attempt to walk its whole length. Note also

Abel Tasman National Park

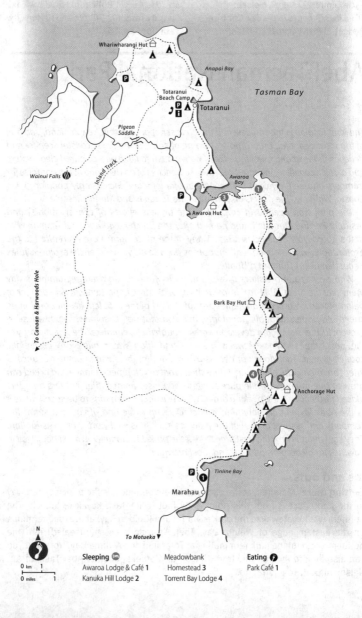

N

0 km 1
0 miles 1

Sleeping
Awaroa Lodge & Café **1**
Kanuka Hill Lodge **2**

Meadowbank
Homestead **3**
Torrent Bay Lodge **4**

Eating
Park Café **1**

that some operators will tow kayaks, giving you the option to kayak and walk or again retire early. Bags and backpacks can also be carried independently, but this tends to be in conjunction with organized trips. Alas, in the Abel Tasman these days it is actually possible to 'hail' a water-taxi, or at least gesticulate wildly to catch one, even though you are not pre-booked! Also note that most water-taxi companies can pick up or help arrange bus transport from Nelson and Motueka to coincide with departures and of course they also offer a huge range of 'suggested' itineraries for a set price. In Motueka itself the principal operator (departing from Port Motueka Marina) is **Abel Tasman Sea Shuttles**, T0800-732748, www.abeltasmanseashuttles.co.nz   A return fare to Tonga Bay will cost from $50 return. In Kaiteriteri the principal beachfront operators are, again Sea Shuttles, above; **Abel Tasman Water Taxis**, T03-5287497, T0800-423397, www.abeltasman4u.co.nz   and   **Abel Tasman Enterprises**, T0800-223582, www.abeltasman.com   In Marahau **Abel Tasman Aqua Taxi**, T03-5278083, T0800-278282, www.aquataxis.co.nz, have an office and café (where you also board your boat-n-first leg by tractor-trailer!). Prices are reasonable and with so much competition kept very much the same. An average fare to Totaranui at the top end of the park will cost from $30-$35 one-way. Most water-taxis depart between 0830 and 1000 from Motueka, Kaiteriteri and Marahau with additional sailings in the early afternoon, depending on the tides.

Information

VIC and **DoC** offices in Motueka (see Motueka Information, page 459) are the best and principal sources of information on the park. They can assist with accommodation bookings and passes, transportation and activities. They can also provide tide times. DoC can also assist with general information, hut bookings, maps, and leaflets. Unmanned DoC information stations and intentions sheets are available at Marahau and Totaranui (seasonal).

Walking and tramping

The most popular walk, and one that is now world-famous, is the 51 km Coastal Walkway, while the Inland Track offers a quieter and more energetic tramp away from both the coast and the hordes of people.▸▸ *See Sleeping, Eating and other listings, page 471.*

The Abel Tasman Coastal Walkway

This two- to five-day, 51 km walk requires medium fitness and the track itself is well maintained (and certainly well trod). The only obstacle encountered and sections that can cause difficulty are the two estuary crossings at Awaroa Inlet and Torrent Bay. Given this fact these two stretches must be negotiated at low tide, otherwise your swimming skills will be tested way beyond your walking.

There are a number of ways to tackle the track in whole or in part. The most popular route is from the south (Marahau) to the north (Wainui), or commonly from Totaranui in the north (by water-taxi from Marahau) back to Marahau in the south. There are plenty of DoC campsites and huts along the way and a few other, more salubrious, independent lodges should you choose the luxury option. Detailed information about the track can be obtained from DoC in Motueka and the website www.doc.govt.nz. Their leaflet *The Abel Tasman Coast Track* ($1) is invaluable and they can provide the essential tide tables. Although the walk does take in many attractive bays, inlets and beaches, it does involve a lot of bush walking, where the view of the sea, never mind beaches, are obscured for long periods of time. So if you are not a seasoned tramper a

● *Given the popularity of the Coastal Walk you must book well in advance. In peak season it is not uncommon to have 200 people in the main campsites alone.*

water-taxi/walk plan over part of the route is perhaps recommended. Although the whole trip is a delight, the most scenic beaches are **Torrent Bay** and the **Awaroa Inlet**. Both of these should not be missed and have the added novelty of the tidal crossing – which will give you a mild taste of what tramping in New Zealand is all about.

A rough outline of the **recommended route**, distances and times (from south to north) is as follows: Marahau to Anchorage: 4 hours, 11½ km; Anchorage to Bark Bay: 3 hours, 9½ km; Bark Bay to Awaroa: 4 hours, 11½ km; Awaroa to Totaranui: 1½ hours, 5½ km; Totaranui to Wharwharangi: 3 hours, 7½ km; Wharwharangi to Wainui: 1½ hours, 5½ km. There are DoC huts at Anchorage, Bark Bay, Awaroa and Wharwharangi and numerous campsites along the way (see below).

Inland Track

The Inland Track is for obvious reasons less popular and links **Marahau** to **Wainui** via the **Pigeon Saddle** on the Takaka-Totaranui Road. It is a 37 km, 3-5 day effort. The main attraction here, other than the fact it is far less trodden than the coastal track, is the beautiful undisturbed and regenerating bush and occasional fine views. You may also hear kiwi at night. The track can be tackled in whole or part and one recommendation is to start at the car park at **Harwood's Hole**. This way you can take in the impressive Harwood's Hole before tackling the remaining 20 km track north over the Pigeon Saddle to Wainui. Note that the track can also be tackled in part with the access point at Pigeon Saddle (Totaranui Road via Takaka). DoC can provide information and an essential broadsheet about the track. There are four huts but no separate campsites but they are not of the same standard (obviously) as those on the Coastal Track.

If you are short of time or cannot stand the sight of a paddle, the following are two day-walks that will provide a pleasant taste to what the Abel Tasman is all about. They are also not too strenuous, having the added fun of getting your feet wet, and take in a lovely cup of tea to boot. The first is accessed from the southern end of the park, the other from the north.

Torrent Bay to Marahau → *14 km, 3-6 hours*

From Marahau take an early morning water-taxi to **Torrent Bay** ($15). Make sure your arrival at Torrent Bay coincides with low tide. Take in the immediate delights here, then take the Coastal Track heading south, for which you need to take off your boots and then follow the markers across the estuary. Return boots to feet and find the track again that climbs the small headland before falling to the exquisite **Anchorage Bay** Beach. Then, from halfway up the beach, climb the hill, not forgetting to look back at the stunning view. Take the sidetrack (15 mins) from the top of the hill down to the incredibly cute (and hopefully quiet) **Watering Cove**. Climb back up to the coastal track and continue south. If you have time check out **Stillwell Bay** and certainly walk along **Appletree Bay** (re-access to main track at far end of the beach). From there complete the walk past **Tinline Bay** to the Marahau entrance point. If the tide is in your favour, you can cross the bay directly just beyond Tinline Bay (where the path descends to beach level). Fall exhausted and happy in to the Park Café, reward yourself with a pint of beer, a glass of wine or the full seafood fettuccine. While there use the email facility to make friends jealous back home.

Awaroa Bay → *6 km, 3-6 hours*

From Takaka take the Totaranui Road via **Pohara**, **Wainui Inlet** and the **Pigeon Saddle**, enjoying the views on the way. From the Totaranui Road take a right on the Awaroa Road to the **Awaroa** car park. Make sure once again that your arrival coincides with an outgoing tide. Digest the view across the inlet and the walk you are about to do. Descend to beach and remove footwear. Cross the inlet in a direct line towards the sea, ignoring the especially muddy bit for the first 100 m. Enjoy the paddle and negotiate the deepest part (should be no more than knee deep) to **Sawpit Point** and the DoC Awaroa Hut. Follow the bay around and if possible extend your walk to the tip of the sandspit. From there walk along Awaroa beach to the far end. Follow the signs to Awaroa Lodge. Enjoy this oasis in paradise and sample the beer, a coffee or a refreshing cup of tea. Then retrace your steps to the Awaroa car park, keeping an eye on the tide.

● Sleeping

See also Marahau Sleeping, page 462.

Abel Tasman National Park *p*467

There are 4 DoC huts and 21 campsites on the Coastal Track plus a number of private B&Bs and lodges. DoC huts have heating, toilets, bunks, mattresses and a water supply (all water should be boiled). Campsites have water and toilets. In summer (Oct-Apr), DoC huts must be booked well in advance and a summer season hut pass ($14 per hut per night) purchased. Campsites cost $7 per night.

LL **Meadowbank Homestead**, *on the beachfront at Awaroa, with Abel Tasman Wilson's Experiences (see pages 459 and 466).* A replica of the original settler's home. It is a relaxed holiday home on the beachfront, providing accommodation primarily for guided walkers and kayakers. Other guests can stay on a space available basis. Price includes twin/double accommodation, ensuite bathroom, chef-prepared meals and launch transfers.

AL-D **Awaroa Lodge**, *Awaroa Inlet, T03-5288758, www.awaroalodge.co.nz* Offers a range of modern suites, ensuite chalets and standard chalets in a remote location in the heart of the park and along the coastal track. A licensed café adds to its appeal, but with the up-grading of the complex it looks as if it will only be a matter of time before trampers in need of a beer or caffeine fix will be actively discouraged. It is a shame since this was the very essence of its atmosphere. Note Awaroa is accessible only by foot, water-taxi, by fixed-wing plane or helicopter.

LL **Torrent Bay Lodge**, *further south, also owned and operated by Abel Tasman Wilson's Experiences (see Meadowbank Homestead above).* Provides the same excellent level of luxury and service.

LL-AL **Kanuka Hill Lodge**, *on a hillside overlooking the beautiful Anchorage Bay, T03-5482863, www.kaukalodge.co.nz* Completes the surprisingly generous list of luxury accommodations in the park. Only accessible by water taxi.

D **Totaranui Beach Camp**, *T03-5288083.* Another popular budget camp right next to the beach. It is accessed from the north by road, or from the south by water-taxi. It is basic (no power) with limited facilities and is administered by DoC ($9). Bookings are essential in the high season.

▲ Activities

The choice is so vast that on initial acquaintance it is all very confusing. You can tramp, walk, kayak, walk/kayak, cruise or even swim with seals, but exactly how you do it and how much you pay is a headache. The advice therefore is to give yourself plenty of time to pre-plan and not to jump at the first option with which you are presented.

Organized trips and cruises

For other water-taxi operators, see page 468. There is a bewildering number of organized trips on offer designed to help make the decisions for you, but they can, if you are indecisive, make it very difficult to choose. All the water-taxi operators offer a range of cruises and half- to full-day trips, with combinations of cruising and walking.

Abel Tasman Wilson's Experiences, *265 High St, Motueka, T03-5287801, www.abeltasman.co.nz,* A professional and reliable outfit. They offer half- to 5-day guided/non-guided options based from the only beachfront lodges in the park, including transport on water-taxi or comfortable launch. A transport-only fare can be as little

● *For an explanation of the sleeping and eating price codes used in this guide, see the inside*
● *front cover. Other relevant information is provided in the Essentials chapter, see page 51.*

Whale Strandings

Although science has yet to confirm the exact reasons for whale stranding, it is an undeniable and sad fact that the coastline of New Zealand is highly prone to this bizarre phenomenon. Almost every year, especially in summer, strandings occur around the country's coastline, with some bays like Keri Keri Bay in Northland, the Mahia Peninsula in the Hawke's Bay and, worst of all, Golden Bay in the Nelson Region being the most notorious. Without doubt it is the geography and enclosed nature of these locations that trap the pods of herding whales, led, it is thought, by just one sick or disorientated adult. Once in shallow tidal waters they quickly become disorientated then ground themselves, often with fatal results. Over the years the most common species affected have been pilot whales, but many other species in fewer numbers have also been stranded. For those species small enough to be physically moved, New Zealand has led the world in the delicate art of re-floating these mammoth, intelligent leviathans. At any given stranding, large numbers of volunteers from all walks of life turn up to help in accordance with strict protocols and a national program lead by DoC and the charitable organization Marine Watch based in Christchurch. Through 'peacetime' training, many Kiwis are now well-versed in how to deal effectively with the emergency. In essence the following takes place: while beached and out of the water, the whales must all be kept upright and wet. If the individual that initiated the stranding can be identified it is usually destroyed to prevent an almost inevitable re-stranding. Then, once the tides turn, they are gently rocked to 're-set' their balance, then re-floated in unison, sometimes on specially built pontoons. As you can imagine this takes considerable skill, logistics and organization. Sadly, despite the huge effort, most whales die, but there have been some major successes, sometimes with almost every whale being returned to the sea successfully. The biggest whale stranding in recent years occurred when a staggering 385 pilot whales stranded in Golden Bay in 1991. Only 15 died, the rest successfully re-floated. To attend a whale stranding is an incredible experience both to witness its effect on people (bringing out both the best and the worst) and to sense the almost haunting presence of these intelligent creatures. For more information contact DoC or Marine Watch in Christchurch, T025-358909. If you encounter a stranded whale or dolphin or even a freshly dead carcass, contact DoC immediately, T0800-362468.

as $20 and a day-cruise from $50, while a 5-day guided walking/sea kayaking trip weighs in at around $1,400, all in.

Abel Tasman Seal Swim, *Sandy Bay Rd, Kaiteriteri, T0800-252925,www.seakayak.co.nz* Swim with the seals at the Tonga Island Marine Reserve (within the park boundary). They are the only operators that have a DoC concession to do so. From $80.

Most water-taxis depart between 0830 and 1000 from Motueka, Kaiteriteri and Marahau, with additional sailings in the early afternoon, depending on the tides. In summer wherever you are in the park it is basically a 0900-1700 operation with water-taxis plying the coast and various stops constantly between those times.

Sea kayaking

The Abel Tasman offers a world-class sea-kayaking experience and it is, without doubt, the top venue in New Zealand. But it is very busy. On a mid-summer's morning the colourful flotilla of kayaks departing from Kaiteriteri and Marahau are a sight to behold and something that would probably even have had the early Maori paddling their *waka* for cover. There is an army of operators offering a wide range of options from simple independent day hire and self-guided day-trips, to multi-day, guided kayak/walking combinations. The choice is yours and the decision difficult.

If walking is not your thing, then a kayak only trip is obviously recommended. But to get the overall essence of the Abel Tasman, a guided combination of both kayaking and walking is recommended. The beauty of the Abel Tasman, other than the scenery, crystal clear waters and the wildlife, is the layout of its myriad bays and beaches, which makes a staged trip and the logistics eminently surmountable. Even if you have never been sea kayaking before, it is relatively safe and easy. The modern day sea kayak is very stable and all the major operators provide training, guidance and have adequate safety standards. Serious sea kayakers tend to leave the Abel Tasman to the novice flotillas and are to be found hiding in the serenity of the Marlborough Sounds or Fiordland. The principal and reputable kayaking companies include:
Abel Tasman Wilson's Experiences, 265

Southern Exposure, *Moss Rd, Marahau, T03-5278424, www.southern-exposure.co.nz* (accommodation available).
Kaiteriteri Sea Kayak, *Kaiteriteri Beachfront, Kaiteriteri, T0800-252925, www.seakayak.co.nz*
Abel Tasman Kayaks, *Marahau Beach, T0800-5278022, www.kayaktours.co.nz*
Abel Tasman Sea Kayak Company, *506 High St, Motueka, T03-8252925, www.seakayaknz.co.nz*
Ocean River Adventure Company, *Motueka, T0800-732529, www.seakayaking.co.nz*
Planet Earth Adventures, *Pohara, Golden Bay, T03-5259095, www.seakayakingnz.com* Popular and slightly different.
Sea Kayak Nelson, *Nelson, T0800-695494.*

Competition is fierce so the best advice is to shop about and research thoroughly before deciding. Prices range from about $35 independent hire per day, $60-$100 for a guided day trip, to $385 for a 3-day trip (camping) with food provided.
Abel Tasman Wilson's Experiences offers civilized adventures staying at the only beachfront lodges, chef-prepared meals and private rooms with ensuite bathrooms. A three-day guided kayak/walk costs $950.

Golden Bay → *Colour map 4, grid B3*

From the pretty township of Takaka the SH60 continues northwest, eventually reaching the coast and the tiny village of Collingwood, the gateway to Kahurangi National Park, the Heaphy Track and Wharariki Beach, one of the most beautiful beaches in the country. From the end of terra firma, 22 km north of Collingwood, the huge 35 km Farewell Spit extends like a golden rainbow out into ocean to envelope the vast mud flats of Golden Bay.

Ins and outs

Getting there Takaka is served from Nelson by **Abel Tasman Air**, T03-5288290, www.abeltasmanair.co.nz This operator also provides excellent scenic flights and air transport from the southern end of the Heaphy Track. The airfield is about 6 km west of the town on SH60. By road, (SH60) Takaka is 109 km from Nelson and 50 km to Farewell Spit. **Bus** companies serving the area include **Abel Tasman Coachlines**, T03-5480285; **Kahurangi Bus**, T0800-881188, and **Kiwilink**, T03-5778332. Buses stop outside the VIC.

Information and orientation Almost all the services the visitor requires can be found along the main street through Takaka, Commercial St. **Golden Bay VIC,**

❗ Te Waikoropupu Springs

Borne of the Takaka Marble Aquifer, the turquoise waters of the 'Pupu Springs' bubbles out at an average rate of 13.2 cubic metres per second, creating a lake that is the clearest of any freshwater body outside Antarctica. To the scientific community they are of interest not only as an unusual landform, but also for the resident aquatic plants and animals. For divers it provides a habitat of unsurpassed clarity and for the Maori they are considered *taonga*, a treasure, and *wahi tapu-a* scared place to be revered. It is a peaceful, beautiful place that has a palpable and rare sense of purity. If you are in the area, a visit is highly recommended.

Nelson and Marlborough Golden Bay

ⓘ *Willow St, at the southern entrance to Takaka, T03-5259136, gb.vin@nelsonnz.com, www.heartoftheparks.net.nz, www.nelsonnz.com Daily 0900-1700*. They stock the full range of information for the entire Golden Bay area, including Collingwood and Farewell Spit. The free *Golden Bay Heart of the Parks Guide* is useful. **DoC**, ⓘ *62 Commercial St, T03-5258026, goldenbay@DoC.govt.nz Mon-Fri 0800-1600*. They have detailed information on both the Abel Tasman and Kahurangi National Parks (including the Heaphy and Abel Tasman Coastal Tracks).

Takaka → *Phone code: 03 Colour map 4, grid B3 Population: 1,1000*

Takaka was founded in 1854 and is the principal business and shopping area for Golden Bay. In summer it is a bustling little place and year round the residence of a colourful and cosmopolitan palette of art and crafts people. It is also home to a large dairy factory. There are a number of interesting attractions around the town including the intriguing 'Pupu' Springs and Rawhiti Cave. The township also serves as the gateway to the northern sector of the Abel Tasman National Park, the vast Kahurangi National Park with its famed Heaphy Track and the remote 35 km Farewell Spit. The small seaside village of **Pohara** about 10 km north east of Takaka on the road to the northern boundary of the Abel Tasman National Park, boasts the best local beach and provides safe swimming.

Sights In the town itself the **Golden Bay Museum and Gallery**, ⓘ *T03-5259990, daily 1000-1600, closed Sun in winter, $1,* displays the usual local treasures and a special feature on early explorer Abel Tasman's unfortunate first encounter with the local Maori. Far more appealing is the gallery next door that showcases the cream of local arts and crafts talent. There are many other independent studios and galleries in the area for which the VIC's free *Arts of Golden Bay* leaflet can point you in the right direction.

The biggest attraction in the immediate area are the beautiful and crystal clear **Te Waikoropupu or Pupu Springs** (see box). ⓘ *The springs are administered by DoC and are open daily. To get there follow SH60 north of Takaka, turning left just after the bridge over the Takaka River. Follow Pupu Valley and Pupu Springs Road to the car park.* There are well-maintained paths and the reserve can be explored thoroughly in about 45 minutes. Nearby the **Pupu Walkway**, which starts at the end of Pupu Valley Road, retraces an old goldmining water race, taking in some interesting features and lovely bush. It is one of the best short walks in the region and takes about half a day.

Of the two limestone cave systems in the area, Te Anaroa (see page 475) and Rawhiti, it is the **Rawhiti Cave** that is the most impressive. It is, however, the least accessible. This ancient cave, with its enormous entrance laden with thousands of coloured stalactites, can be accessed independently, but a guided tour with

Kahurangi Walks is recommended. ① *3 hrs, from $25, child $15. T03-5257177,*
www.kahurangiwalks.co.nz

Also on the limestone theme and closer to Takaka are the odd and shapely 'karst' features of the **Labyrinth Rocks**, ① *just outside the town (3 km) on Labyrinth Lane, Three Oaks, T03-5258434. Daily from 1300-1700. $6.* They will keep the kids occupied for hours.

Also of note in this area, and accessed where Motupipi meets the Clifton Crossroads is the **Grove Scenic Reserve**. Here a short 10 minute walk will bring you to an intriguing spot where massive Rata trees grow out of curiously-shaped karst rock outcrops. Nearby those with green fingers and the love of a fine view will enjoy the **Begonia House** and succulent **gardens**, ① *Rocklands Rd, Clifton, T03-5259058. 1000-1700. Free.*

Again, while in the immediate area, it would be rude not to have a quick look at the **Abel Tasman Memorial** on the headland just beyond Tarakohe (Totaranui Road) and look, then listen, with eyes shut to the pretty **Wainui Falls** (Wainui Bay); an easy 40 minute walk. Note this road can also take you to the northern beaches and tramping access points of the **Abel Tasman National Park**.

Of some novelty are the famous Anatoki **tame eels** at **Bencarri Farm**, ① *6 km south of Takaka (signposted off SH60 on McCallum Rd), T03-5258261, www.bencarri.co.nz Daily 1000-1730, $10, child $5.* The eels are reputed to be the oldest tame eels in the country with some individuals still enjoying a daily snack after 80 years of residence. Bencarri Farm also has a host of touchy-feely animals including llamas and some homesick Scottish 'Heelaan coos'. There is a good café (open 1000-late) and there are also numerous activities on offer including gold panning, 4WD quad biking (from $49) and, yes, the obligatory cow-milking. ▶ *See Sleeping, Eating, Activtities and other listings, pages 477-479.*

Collingwood → *Colour map 4, grid B2*

Collingwood was formerly known as Gibbstown and was (believe it or not) once a booming gold mining town that was promoted as an eminently suitable capital for the nation. But that dream turned to dust when the gold reserves were laid waste and a fire almost destroyed the entire village. Rebuilt and renamed Collingwood in honour of Nelson's second-in-command, fire struck again in 1904 and yet again as recently as 1967 when the town hall, hotel and two shops were reduced to ashes. Despite its fiery history and now void of its once lofty social standing, Collingwood still retains a few historical buildings, including the characterful courthouse, which is now a café where you can sentence yourself to a lengthy tea break. Collingwood itself also has a small and fairly unremarkable **museum**, ① *Tasman St, T03-5248447. Daily 0900-1800. Adult $2, child $1.*

The area has a few other notable attractions worth visiting. South of Collingwood, in the attractive **Aorere River Valley** and back on the limestone theme, are the privately owned **Te Anaroa and Rebecca Caves**, ① *Caves Rd, near Rockville, T03-5248131, www.goldenbaycaves.com One-hour guided tours of the Te Anaroa Caves are available in summer at 1030,1230,1430 and 1630 (winter by arrangement). Dual cave tours of 2-3 hours are also available from $15, child $6.* The Te Anaroa Caves are 350 m in length and include the usual stalactite and stalagmite formations and fossilised shells, while the Rebecca Caves are best known for their glow-worms. At the end of Cave Road are two fairly unremarkable 'karst' (limestone) rock monoliths known as the **Devil's Boots** (presumably because they are upside-down). The walks and mountain bike tracks of the **Aorere Goldfields**, which were New Zealand's first, are accessed from the road end and are of far more interest. (See free DoC leaflet). For something longer and more challenging, the three to four-day hike to **Boulder Lake** is recommended.

● *Access on the spit is restricted so an organized tour is the only way to truly experience the*
● *place, see page 479*

66 99 Wharariki Beach has to be one of the most beautiful beaches in the country... caves, arches and dunes and near perfection. It is so beautiful you almost find yourself feeling a corrupting sense of guilt at leaving your lone footprints in the sand...

If you have time, an exploration of the pretty **Aorere River Valley** (Heaphy Track Road) is recommended. Beyond the pleasures of the drive itself, a stop at the river **gorge** at Salisbury Bridge (Quartz Range Road) and the old **Bainham Store** will both have the camera clicking. Access down to the river is possible, to the right just beyond Salisbury Bridge, while the Bainham Store is an original, store that has changed little in decades and is still open for business. ▸▸ *See Sleeping, Eating and Activities, pages 478-478.*

Farewell Spit → Colour map 4, grid B3

The spit is formed entirely from countless tons of sand ejected in to the northerly ocean currents from numerous river mouths scattered all the way up the West Coast. It is a dynamic, almost desert-like landscape, with sparse vegetation struggling to take root in the dry and constantly shifting sand. The vast majority of the spit is a DoC nature reserve and the vast mud flats that it creates along its landward edge are one of New Zealand's most important wading-bird habitats. Over 100 species have been recorded around the spit, but it is the sheer numbers of each species that are most notable. Migrating flocks of godwit and knot can run well in to the thousands, providing a memorable sight. Black swans also use the food-rich mud flats of Golden Bay, and when the tide is in they gracefully tread the water in vast flocks. There is also a small colony of rapacious gannets at the very end of the spit.

Both Cape Farewell and Farewell Spit were noted by Tasman in 1642 (no doubt a little shorter than it is now) and named by Cook when he left the shores of New Zealand in 1770. The lighthouse at the very tip of the spit was first erected in 1870. It has an interesting history, having been almost washed away once and relocated.

The Spit is a remarkable and memorable landscape if only for its powerful sense of isolation, but to see it from afar and from sea level is a strangely unremarkable experience. With its vast dune system, no more than 20 m in height, its sheer length and the omnipresent coastal haze, its very presence is, to say the least, muted. At best only a small grove of pine trees near its tip can be seen, like some tiny far off island. If you cannot afford to go out on the spit or simply want to get a better impression of its scale from afar, the best place to view it is from the elevated hills around the Pillar Point Light Beacon, accessed from Wharariki Road and Puponga.

At the base of the Spit and just beyond the last small settlement of Puponga is the **Farewell Spit Café and Visitor Centre**, ⓘ *To3-5248454. Daily 0900-1700 (seasonal).* It stocks a range of informative leaflets and has a number of interesting displays surrounding the spit, its wildlife and the rather sad and repetitive whale strandings in Golden Bay. The café sells a range of refreshments and snacks and has a fine deck overlooking the bay and the spit itself. Most of the established **walking tracks** leave directly from the centre. Note you can also book and join the Farewell Spit tours en route to the spit at the visitor centre (from $45).

Wharariki Beach

Wharariki Beach has to be one of the most beautiful beaches in the country. Perhaps it is its very remoteness that makes it so special, but add to that its classic features, including caves, arches and dunes, and you have near perfection. It is so beautiful you almost find yourself feeling a corrupting sense of guilt at leaving your lone footprints on its swathes of golden sand – let alone stripping off entirely and splashing about in the waves. You can access the beach by road from Puponga via Wharariki Road (20 minute walk) or make it the highlight on a longer and stunning coastal walk from **Pillar Point Lighthouse**. ▸ *See Activities, page 479.*

Pillar Point to Wharariki Beach coastal walk → 13 km, 6-8 hrs

From **Puponga** follow Wharariki Beach Road to the turn-off (right) up to **Pillar Point Light Beacon** ('Blinking Billy'). Note this is a rough non-signposted road. Park your vehicle at the base of the hill below the light beacon. Climb the hill to Pillar Point and enjoy your first proper view of Farewell Spit before heading further north towards **The Old Man Rock** (155 m) along the crest of the hill. Take in the views of the Spit and Golden Bay before retracing your steps to Pillar Point. From Pillar Point follow the sporadic orange markers south through a small tract of manuka trees. From there follow the markers and the cliffs taking in all the cliff-top views to **Cape Farewell**. Keep your eyes peeled for fur seals, whose plaintive cries will be probably be first to reach the senses. Continue south along the cliffs before descending to Wharariki Beach. If the tide is in your favour, walk its entire length and investigate the many caves and rock corridors along its length. Once at the base of **Pilch Point** (at the very end of all the beaches) retrace your steps to Pillar Point. Now *that* is a coastal walk!

● Sleeping

Takaka *p474*

The VIC has a full listing of B&Bs and homestays, most of which are near the beaches at Pohara.

L Bay Vista, *Pohara, T03-5259772, www.bayvistahouse.co.nz* A single-storey, spacious and modern B&B with 2 doubles and a deluxe ensuite with private lounge. Just 5 km south of Takaka itself is the
AL-A Rose Cottage Motel and B&B, *Hamama Rd, T03-5259048.* Offers a 3 unit motel and a cute 2-bedroom B&B in a garden/country setting.
A Anatoki Lodge Motel, *87 Commercial St, T03-5258047, anatoki@xtra.co.nz* Pick of the motels providing modern facilities close to all amenities.
A Muscle Farm, *4 Buxton Lane, T03-5259924.* Another good alternative, attached to the local fitness centre into which clients have free access. Elsewhere in Pohara and slightly more affordable, is the great value
B Sans Souci Inn, *Richmond Rd, Pohara, T03-5258663, www.sanssouciinn.co.nz* It is a mud-brick mediterranean-style establishment with lovely bedrooms and a great licensed in-house restaurant.

C-D Annie's, *25 Motupipi St, T03-5258766, T0800-266937.* Well-established and cosy backpackers.
C-D Barefoot Backpackers, *114 Commercial St, T0508-5257078, www.bare-foot.co.nz* The latter offers free trips to the Pupu Springs, has a spa and terrific homemade bread.
C-D Getaway Backpackers, *28 Motupipi St (just opposite Annie's), T03-5256261, T0800-8011120.* Another new alternative in a spacious, well kept suburban house with caring owners, bikes and internet.
C-D Nook, *9 km from Pohara, T03-5258501, thenook@paradise.net.nz* Comfortable dorms, double accommodation in a straw-bale cottage or a 4-berth house truck.
C-D River Inn, *Waitapu Rd, at the other end of town, T03-5259425, www.riverinn.co.nz* Closest to the Pupu Springs, a century-old pub-style place. It has a wide range of rooms with especially cheap singles. Free bike hire and internet.

Motorcamps

B-D Pohara Beach Holiday Park and Motels, *Abel Tasman Dr, Pohara, T03-5259500.* The best motorcamp with tent, powered sites and modern timber motel units, next to the beach.

LL Kahurangi Luxury Retreat, *just before Collingwood township on SH60,* T03-5248312, *retreat@kahuranginz.co.nz* Luxurious and spacious, it is well appointed, and the friendly owners have a genuine desire to make your stay worthwhile; fine cuisine.

A Golden Bay Lodge and Garden, *Tukurua Beach,* T03-5259275, *www.goldenbaylodge.co.nz* A beautiful spot on the cliff-top with self-contained units and B&B rooms.

AL Collingwood Homestead B&B, *Elizabeth St, in Collingwood itself,* T03-5248079, *www.collingwoodhomestead.co.nz* It gets the vote as the best B&B in the entire region. Cheaper options in Collingwood include:

B Skara Brae B&B and Motels, *Elizabeth St,* T03-5248464, *www.accommodationcollingwood.co.nz* and

C-D Somerset House Backpackers, *Gibbs Rd (signposted off the main road in the village),* T03-5248624, *www.backpackerscollingwood.co.nz* Owned by an ex-pat UK dentist, this 16-bed place has totally the opposite effect from a visit to any dentist's chair. It is relaxed and homely and there is not a drill in sight. Good facilities, including internet, kayak and bike hire, a very congenial deck overlooking the village and a hopelessly affectionate cat called 'Somerset'.

C-D Innlet and Cottage, *Main Rd, Pakawau, on the road to Farewell Spit,* T03-5248040, *www.goldenbayindex.co.nz/theinnlet* It oozes character and is in a lovely bush setting offering dorms, twins and doubles and 2 charming self-contained cottages that sleep 3-6. The owners are friendly, dedicated long-term residents. There is bike hire available and excellent harbour/ rainforest kayak trips from $50-$85. Internet.

Motorcamps

C-D Collingwood Motor Camp, *in the centre of the village at the end of William St,* T03-5248149. Very basic.

C-D Pakawau Beach Park, *Pakawau,* T03-5248327. Also an excellent motorcamp with modern facilities and some very colourfu, good value self-contained huts overlooking the beach. There is a fairly unremarkable licensed café across the road.

🍴 Eating

Takaka *p474*

$$ Wholemeal Café, *Commercial St,* T03-5259426. Daily 0730-1930. A bit of an institution in Takaka and the main haunt for the locals. It has good coffee, breakfasts, health-conscious blackboard menu and excellent service.

$$ Dangerous Kitchen, *also on Commercial St (48),* T03-5258686. Daily 0830-late. Does fine pizza.

$$ Milliways, *90 Commercial St,* T03-5259636. Daily from 1000. A good choice with an imaginative menu and pleasant outdoor eating area.

$$ Sans Souci, *Richmond Rd, Pohara,* T03-5258663. Similar and open for lunch and dinner (seasonal).

$ Bencarri Farm, *(south off SH60). Open daily 1000-late.* For a café experience surrounded by a veritable menagerie.

Collingwood *p475*

There are few options but the

$$ Mussel Inn, *Onekaka, (roughly half way between Takaka and Collingwood on SH60),* T03-5259241, *daily from 1100 in summer and 1700 in winter,* offers good pub grub, great value mussels and the best beer around – and a toilet to remember.

$ Courthouse Café, *corner of Gibbs and Elizabeth St, Collingwood,* T03-5248572. Daily 0830-late (seasonal). The best bet in town.

$$ Collingwood Tavern, *Tasman St,* T03-5248160. Serves pub/bistro style food.

$ Visitor centre, *at the very end of the road at Farewell Spit,* T03-5248454. Daily 0900-1730 (seasonal). Hosts a good café with a basic blackboard menu.

⛰ Activities

Takaka *p474*

Barefoot Guided Tours, *114 Commercial St, Takaka,* T0508-5257078, *www.bare-foot.co.nz* For local, regional or national park guided tours from $30-$150.

Bencarri Farm, see page 475.

Collingwood *p475*

Kahurangi Guided Walks, T03-5257177,

www.kahurangiwalks.co.nz Offer guided trips to Boulder Lake for $130 per day.

Wharaiki Beach *p477*
Cape Farewell Horse Treks, *Puponga, T03-5248031, www.horsetreksnz.com* Some of the most scenic routes in the region. One hr to overnight, from $35.

ᕚ Tours to Farewell Spit

All the organized tours to Farewell Spit are based in Collingwood.
The Original Farewell Spit Safari (Farewell Spit Tours), *Tasman St, T03-5248257, T0800-808-257, www.farewellspit.com* Are, as the name suggests, the original tour operator and have been taking people out on to the spit for over 50 years. They are a very professional outfit and now offer a range of 4 tours. The most popular of these is the **Lighthouse Safari** which is a 5 ½-hr excursion to the end of the spit and the lighthouse. Transportation takes the form of robust but comfortable RL Bedford Trucks that can go where conventional wheels cannot. Along the length of the seaward side of the spit you will be introduced to the Spit's wildlife (which can include the odd bleary-eyed basking fur seal) and allowed stops to take in the special atmosphere of the spit, before arriving at the lighthouse. There you can climb to see the rather unremarkable view from the top, before descending again to learning a little of its interesting history over a welcome cup of tea. There is an interesting commentary throughout the tour. This tour costs a very reasonable $60, child $30. **The Gannet Colony Safari** (6 ½ hrs, $85, child

$45) is an extended trip that takes in the above and, as the name suggests, the gannet colony at the very end of the spit (this company are the only operators with the DoC concession to get up close). The **Cape Farewell Eco Tour** (6 hrs) is basically the same trip as the Lighthouse Safari with a diversion to the dramatic cliffs at Cape Farewell, the most northerly point of the South Island, from $70, child $45. The **Wader Watch Safari** (3-4 hrs, $60) is a specialist and fascinating trip to see the wading birds on the spit often numbering into the thousands. Although most suited to birdwatchers and somewhat seasonal (summer only), it would be of considerable interest to any nature lover, especially given the limited access to the spit.
Farewell Spit Nature Tours, *based in Collingwood on Tasman Street, T03-5248188, www.farewell-spit.co.nz* A newer operation offering a similar lighthouse tour (6 hrs) with the exception of a diversion to visit the cliffs and seal colony at Cape Farewell and the elevated view of the spit from Pillar Point with a full meal included, from $80, child $50. Book ahead for all of the tours above.

ᕕ Directory

Takaka *p474*
Bike hire The Quiet Revolution, *7 Commercial St, T03-5259555.* From $25 per day. They also offer local tours from $30.
Internet Golden Bay Net Café, *37 Commercial St, T03-5258355.* Baylink Communications, *6 Commercial St.* The Gazebo Backpackers, *7 Haiwatha Lane (western end of the town), T03-5257233. Daily 1200-2000.*

Kahurangi National Park

→ *Colour map 4, grid B2*

Opened in 1996, Kahurangi is New Zealand's second newest national park (the newest now being Stewart Island, opened in 2001). After Fiordland, it is also the largest. It is a vast and remote landscape of rugged alpine ranges and river valleys, the most notable of which is the Heaphy that meets, in part, the park's most famous tramping route, the Heaphy Track. One of the most interesting features of the park is its ancient geology. It contains some of the country's oldest rock landforms, with spectacular limestone caves, plateaux, arches and outcrops. Kahurangi is home to over half of New Zealand's native plant species (over 80% of all alpine species) and over 18 native bird species, including the stealthy New Zealand falcon, the great spotted kiwi and the huge New Zealand land snail.

Ins and outs

Getting there Transport to the various trailheads is available from Nelson, Motueka, Takaka, Collingwood and Karamea (West Coast). **Kahurangi Bus,**(Nelson) T0800-881188, T03-5259434; **Abel Tasman Coachlines,** (Nelson) T03-5288805; **Wadsworth Motors** (Nelson to the Whangapeka Track),T03-5224248; **Bickley Motors,** (Takaka), T03-5258352, and **Karamea Express,** T03-7826617 (West Coast) are the principal operators. The average fare from Takaka is $15-$20 and from Karamea $6 -$10. **Abel Tasman Air,** Nelson, T03-5288290 offer flights to Karamea and Takaka.

Getting around They say it takes a long time and many walks to acquaint yourself properly with Kahurangi and for many this is its very appeal. One of the best ways to see the park is from above (see Activities below). The **Heaphy Track** is usually the visitor's first and only acquaintance with the park but the **Cobb Valley, Mount Arthur** and the **Tablelands** (accessed from the Cobb River Valley, 50 km south of Takaka and from the Flora car park, 30 km south of Motueka) offer some shorter walk options. The view from Mount Arthur (4 hours, 8 km), which is accessed from Motueka, is particularly recommended.

The eastern **Heaphy Track** trailhead is accessed via Collingwood (28 km) and Bainham (Aorere River Valley) at the end of the Heaphy Track Road. The route is signposted from Collingwood. The eastern trailhead is served daily (see bus operators above) in summer and on demand in winter.

Information The DoC field centres in the **Nelson VIC, Motueka** and **Takaka** (see above) stock detailed information on the park, including access, walking and tramping. On longer walks or tramps you are advised to go well prepared and, in summer, book the huts and passes ahead – especially on the popular Heaphy Track. They also administer hut tickets and bookings.

The Heaphy Track → *Take plenty of insect repellent*

The Heaphy Track is one of New Zealand's most popular 'Great Walks' and the most popular tramp in the Kahurangi National Park. It is a relatively low-level tramp of 82 km taking 4-6 days. The Heaphy is named after Major Charles Heaphy, a noted soldier, who was the first to traverse the coastal portion of the modern track in 1846. Although not famed for its mountainous vistas, the track does provide a wide range of interesting habitats and a superb coastal section. It is also noted for being 'open' for much of its length, providing a fine sense of space and wilderness. **Flannigan's**

Corner (915 m) near Mount Perry (880 m) is the highest point on the track and provides memorable views. The Heaphy is usually negotiated from west to east. The western trailhead starts about 15 km north of Karamea, while the eastern, starts 28 km south of Collingwood.

The approximate walking times are as follows - west to east: Kohaihai River Mouth to Heaphy Hut, 5 hours, 16 ½ km; Heaphy Hut to Lewis Hut, 2 ½ hours, 8 km; Lewis Hut to Mackay Hut, 3 ½ hours, 13 ½ km; Mackay Hut to Saxon Hut, 3 hours, 14 km; Saxon Hut to Gouland Downs Hut, 1 ½ hours, 5 km; Gouland Downs Hut to Perry Saddle Hut, 2 hours, 8 km; Perry Saddle Hut to Brown Hut, 5 hours, 17 km.

● Sleeping

Heaphy Track

The 7 huts along the track are supplied with bunks, heating, water (must be boiled) and toilets. Hut passes are $14. Note a pass does not guarantee a bunk. Camping is $8, child $6. For more information and bookings contact DoC or the major VICs. You can also book direct with DoC website www.greatwalksbooking@doc.govt.nz

▲ Activities and tours

Guided walks Kahurangi Guided Walks,

Takaka, T03-5257177, www.kahurangiwalks.co.nz

Bush and Beyond, Motueka, T03-5289054, www.naturetreks.co.nz and **Barefoot Guided Tours**, also in Motueka, T0508-525-700, www.bare-foot.co.nz, all provide a range of guided walks in the park from $30-$130 per day.

Rock climbing Vertical Limits, Nelson, T03-5457511, www.verticallimits.com Offer some excellent rock climbing trips to Kahurangi, from $130.

Scenic flights Tasman Bay Air Nelson, T03-5288290. Offer flights across the bare mountaintops and remote valleys. A truly memorable experience.

Nelson Lakes National Park

→ Colour map 4, grid C2

The slightly underrated Nelson Lakes National Park protects 102,000 ha of the northernmost Southern Alps range. Its two long, scenic and trout-infested Lakes Rotoroa and Rotoiti, cradled in beech-clad alpine ranges, hiding beautiful tussock valleys and wildflower-strewn meadows, dominate the park. Although a quick look at the lakes are all that most people see of this park, the ranges and river valleys offer some superb walking. The two most noted tramps are the 80 km, 4-7 day Traverse-Sabine Circuit and the excellent 2-3 day Robert Ridge/Lake Angelus Track. There are a number of very pleasant short walks from 20 minutes to two hours that extend into the park from St Arnaud or Lake Rotoroa.

The principal base for the park is pretty village of St Arnaud, which nestles at the northern end of Lake Rotoiti. Almost all accommodation, services, major park access and activities are located here. The park is also accessible from the more remote and sparsely populated Lake Rotoroa.

Ins and outs

Getting there St Arnaud is 90 km from Nelson (via SH6), 100 km from Blenheim (SH63) and 163 km from Westport (SH6/63). To visit Lake Rotoroa, turn off SH6 at Gowan Bridge west of St Arnaud. An 11 km side road takes you up the Gowan Valley to the lake. The West Coast-bound buses (including **Intercity**, T03-5481538; **Atomic Shuttles**, T03-3228883, www.atomictravel.co.nz; and **Lazerline**, T0800-220-001) all stop in Murchison outside Collins Tearooms, Beechwoods Restaurant or the VIC.

St Arnaud is served by **Nelson Lakes Shuttles**, T03-5211023, www.nelsonlakes.co.nz (Nelson); **Wadsworth Motors**, T03-5224248, wadsworthmotors@xtra.co.nz (Nelson): **Atomic Shuttles**, T03-3228883, www.atomictravel.co.nz; and **Nelson Leisure Travel**, T03-5457912 (ski season). **Water-taxis** operate on both Lakes Rotoroa and Rotoiti and offer scenic and/or fishing trips and tramping pick-ups/drop-offs: **Rotoiti Water Taxis**, T03-5211894; **Lake Rotoroa Water Taxi**, T03-5239199. From $30, lake's end one-way.

Information DoC Nelson Lakes National Park, ① *St Arnaud, T03-5211806, starnaudao@doc.govt.nz Daily 0800-1900 (seasonal)*. An excellent centre which provides comprehensive displays and information on the park and local accommodation and transport. **Nelson Lakes Village Centre** ① *on the main road, T03-5211854. 0800-1830 (seasonal hours)*. Serves as the main grocery store, petrol station, postal agency and has EFTPOS. Lake Rotoroa does not have a shop. **Murchison VIC**, ① *on the main road through town, at 47 Wallar St (SH6), T03-5239350, www.murchisonnz.com 1000-1700 (seasonal)*. Nelson Lakes also plays host to the popular Rainbow Valley and Mt Robert ski-fields (only accessible in winter). **Skiing information**, ① *T03-5211861, www.skirainbow.co.nz / www.snow.co.nz* The views from the chairlifts are spectacular.

Mount Robert to Lake Angelus Basin walk → *2-3 days, 30 km*

If you are short for time this walk is touted as one of the best in the park. The destination (and highlight) is the beautiful Lake Angelus Basin and an overnight stay at the Mount Angelus Hut ($10) from which to take it all in. It is a walk that should only be considered by those of average fitness, in good weather conditions. Go prepared and pre-book your hut accommodation (and fill in an intentions sheet) at the DoC Visitors' Centre.

From the Upper Mount Robert car park (accessed from West Bay, 5 km from St Arnaud) climb the steep zig-zag track up the face of Mount Robert to the bushline shelter near the summit (two hours). From there follow the marked route along the ridge and around the **Mount Robert Ski-field** to **Flagtop Summit** (1690 m). Then descend and continue on the saddle beneath **Julius Summit** (1794 m). The route now leaves the ridge briefly, crossing rocky ground before rejoining the ridge. At a small saddle marked by a metal pole, the route drops again to the west side and crosses a steep, rocky slope to another broad saddle at the head of **Speargrass Creek**. From here a short climb to the ridge reveals the beautiful **Angelus Basin** (5 hours).

Stay the night at the Angelus Hut (book at DoC, $10) and get up for sunrise! To return you can either retrace your steps, or descend in to the **Hukere Valley** to join the **Cascade Track** to **Coldwater Hut** at the southern end of the lake. From there the Lakeside Track will deliver you back to the lower Mount Robert car park. If you have no vehicle and have been dropped off, you may consider booking a water-taxi from the southern end of the lake and reward yourself with a scenic cruise back to **St Arnaud**.

Murchison → *Phone code: 03 Population: 750 Nelson 125 km*

Murchison, 65 km further along SH6 from St Arnaud (see Nelson Lakes NP page 481), at the head of the Buller Gorge and junction of the Matakitaki and Buller Rivers, is a service centre for the local farming community and for many, the gateway to the West Coast from the north. Although once an important goldmining town (and famous for being nearly wiped out by a violent earthquake in 1929), it is today a quiet place, primarily of interest to the tourist as the base for a number of interesting activities. It is also the haunt of the odd serious tramper intent on exploring the remote southern wilderness of the Kahurangi National Park. The small **Murchison Museum**, ① *on Fairfax St, daily 1000-1600, donations*, has interesting

● Sleeping

St Arnaud and Lake Rotoiti
At St Arnaud and Lake Rotoiti, the range of accommodation includes hostels, motels, B&Bs and 3 camping areas.

AL-D Alpine Lodge and Chalet, *St Arnaud, T03-5211869, www.alpinelodge.co.nz* The mainstay of quality accommodation and eating in the village and comprises a wide range of options from self-contained studio units in the main lodge to twin, family or dorms in the Chalet. Licensed à la carte restaurant, café, bar and spa. Bike hire from $10 per hr.

A St Arnaud Log Chalets, *T03-5211882, www.nelsonlakes.co.nz* Offer very pleasant modern self-contained log chalet-style units.

C-D Yellow House, *T03-5211887, theyellowhouse@xtra.co.nz* YHA associate which is modern and friendly with good facilities, including a spa. They can also provide good tramping information and gear hire.

A Tophouse, *Tophouse Rd, 9 km north of St Arnaud, T03-5211848, T0800-867468, www.tophouse.co.nz* A very animal- (and people-) friendly, historic farm guesthouse. It has 4 self-contained units and 5 comfortable B&B rooms. At one time it also boasted New Zealand's smallest bar. Café on site, open daily to non-guests 0930-1700.

Other reputable B&Bs in the area include:
B Woodrow Cottage, *Tophouse Junction (5 km), T03-5211212*. Pretty and fully self-contained.

LL Kikiwa Lodge, *Korere, Tophouse Rd, T03-5211020, www.kikiwalodge.co.nz*

Campsites
D DoC campsites with power at the edge of the lake in *West and Kerr Bays, T03-5211806*. Deposit fees at DoC Visitor Centre.

Lake Rotoroa
The very limited options at Lake Rotoroa range from the exclusive and newly refurbished fishing retreat

LL Lake Rotoroa Lodge, T03-5239121, www.lakrotoroalodge.com to the excellent and friendly
Gowan River Holiday Camp, *Gowan River Valley Rd, beside the river (6 km from SH6), T03-5239921.* (Avoid the campsite by the lake, where the sandflies will eat you alive.)

Murchison
LL Maruia River Lodge, *Shenandoah, Maruia River Valley, T03-5239323, www.maruiarivertlodge.co.nz* The most luxurious option in the immediate area offering all mod cons, in a pleasant bush setting next to the river.

A-B Coch-y-Bondhu Lodge B&B, *15 Grey St, T03-5239196, www.homestays.net.nz/ cochybondhu.htm* Pretty B&B with 5 comfortable, well-appointed rooms. Fishing trips are a speciality.

C-D Lazy Cow Homestyle Accommodation *right in the heart of the village at 37 Walker St, T03-5239451.* A warm welcome at this 18-bed backpackers. With all the water activities in the region it is not surprising to find a very welcome in-house spa.

Motorcamps and campsites
A-B Kiwi Park Motel and Holiday Park, *170 Fairfax St, T/F5239248,* which also offers some tidy, modern motel units , or the
C-D Riverview Holiday Park, *T03-5239591, 2 km north of town, by the river.*

● Eating

Murchison
$ Beechwoods Café, *on SH6 where all the buses stop at SH6 southern end of town, T03-5239571.* Daily 0630-2130. Highly commercial, with a wide range of light meals and snacks available.

$$ Commercial Hotel *next to the VIC, T03-5239696.* Ironically, a far less commercial atmosphere here.

$ River Café at *The Adventure Centre, 51 Fairfax St, T03-5239889.* Good for a quick coffee and check of the email. But, beware,

● *For an explanation of the sleeping and eating price codes used in this guide, see the inside*
● *front cover. Other relevant information is provided in the Essentials chapter, see page 51.*

you will be hard pushed to walk out without being lured for a trip down the river. And why not?

▲▲ Activities and tours

Murchison

The principal activities in the area include fishing, white-water rafting, kayaking, caving, mountaineering and walking. The VIC has all the details.

Fishing Russell Frost's Ticklish Trout Tours, *T03-5239868, www.guideflyfishingnz.com* Tours from $360. Independent fishing licences ($33 per week) are available from the VIC.

Horse trekking Tiraumea Horse Treks, *T03-5239341*.

Jet boats Buller Jetboat Tours, *Buller Gorge Swingbridge (see below) T03-5239880, www.murchison.co.nz* Jetboat trips down the Buller from $65 (hourly, Sep-Apr).

Kayaking and rafting Murchison Adventure Centre, *51 Fairfax St, T03-5239899, www.rivers.co.nz* An attractive range of rafting and kayaking trips in the region, with the local Buller River (grade 3-4)

being the main focus. A 4-hr blat down the Buller followed by a soak in the hot tub will cost from $60. The adventure centre also has a shop and a café on-site.

New Zealand Kayak School, *T03-3525786, www.nzkayakschool.com* Offer 4 day introductory, intermediate, advanced and women-only white-water kayaking courses from $595 including accommodation.

Mountain biking Auto Engineering, *27 Grey St, T03-5239425*. Bike hire.

If you feel lucky and want to try **gold-panning**, the VIC hires out pans and shovels for $5 ($20 bond) and will point you in the right direction. The VIC can also provide details and directions of the numerous short and long walking options in the area. The view from the **Skyline Walk** (1 ½ hrs, 6 km) is recommended. If a walk seems too much, worth visiting the Ariki Falls which are located 3 km from O'Sullivan's Bridge heading west down SH6, (turn left down the track 1 km after the statue of three people hugging). The pink rocks are even more attractive than the falls. But beware, take insect repellent.

Canterbury

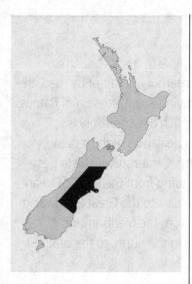

Introduction

Whichever way you arrive in Canterbury, by air or by road, the **Canterbury Plains** dominate, giving an impression of flatness. And yet, despite appearances, much of Canterbury is mountainous and home to New Zealand's highest peak, **Aoraki**, or **Mount Cook** (3754 m). Canterbury is the largest region in the South Island, extending from the Pacific Ocean and the Canterbury Plains in the east to the Great Divide and Southern Alps to the west, and from the Marlborough Mountains and Kaikoura Ranges in the north, to the braided **Waitaki River** in the south.

Central Canterbury is the hub of South Island and its capital, **Christchurch** is the country's second largest city. Dubbed 'The Garden City', it also claims the title of New Zealand's favourite city, although it lacks the architecture and the remarkable friendliness of Dunedin. **North Canterbury** is home to South Island's 'little piece of Rotorua' in the form of the **Hanmer Springs** thermal resort, providing just one good reason to stop en route to the West Coast via the beautiful **Lewis Pass**. Along with **Arthur's Pass** to the south, these form the region's two main portals from the east coast to the west and are also the focus for skiers in winter.

In **South Canterbury** the pleasant coastal port of **Timaru** provides a starting point from where to head west, via Fairlie and **Burke's Pass** to the **MacKenzie Country**. Here you will find the region's most stunning and diverse scenery, culminating in **Pukaki Lake** and **Mount Cook Village**.

★ Don't miss...

1. The oceans 'Who's Who' in **Kaikoura**, page 515.

2. A punt on **Christchurch's Avon River**, page 490.

3. **The Antarctic and Arts Centres** in 'The Garden City', page 495.

4. Taking a **gondola to the crater rim** of the Banks Peninsula, then mountain biking back down, page 498.

5. Exploring the 'Banks' and finding the 'French connection' in **Akaroa**, page 509.

6. A graceful **balloon trip** over the Canterbury Plains at dawn, page 531.

7. Wallaby meat pie with plum sauce in **Waimate**, page 536.

8. Taking **one of the world's most scenic train trips** to the West Coast, page 527.

9. Taking a scenic drive through the hills west of Christchurch en route to the **Mount Hutt ski fields**, page 527.

10. Stargazing at **Lake Tekapo** page 540.

11. Letting the mountains envelop you along SH80 to Mount Cook Village. Then taking an unforgettable scenic flight around **Aoraki (Mount Cook) and the glaciers**, page 548.

12. Seeing one of the **rarest birds in the world (the black stilt)** in **Twizel** page 542.

Christchurch → *Colour map 5, grid C4 Population: 320,000*

What Auckland is to volcanic plugs, stark concrete and Polynesia, or Dunedin is to wildlife, fine architecture and Scotland, Christchurch is to the deciduous tree, gardens and England. Dubbed 'The Garden City', Christchurch is known as the most English of New Zealand's cities. Reminders of these roots are everywhere, from the formal blazers and straw hats of the city's schoolchildren, to the punts on the river and the distant chorus of 'howzatt' from its myriad cricket pitches on lazy summer Sunday afternoons. Without doubt the key to its charm is the immense, tree-lined Hagley Park that borders its centre and has over the decades remained remarkably intact. With the park, its trees and the pretty Avon River that threads it all together, the aesthetics of Christchurch verge on the adorable. But natural aesthetics and its obvious English colonial feel aside, Christchurch has developed its own very Kiwi-orientated atmosphere. It has the buzz and vitality of Auckland, the cosmopolitan 'town' feel of Wellington, and it shares a pride in its heritage and architecture that only Dunedin can beat.

Ins and outs

Getting there Air Christchurch Airport, (domestic terminal VIC, T03-3537774), T03-3537714, www.christchurch-airport.co.nz, is 12 km northwest of the city via Fendalton Rd and Memorial Av. It is a modern airport with both international and domestic terminals in a single easily-negotiated building. The international terminal has direct links with Australia, Singapore and Japan, while the domestic serves all national provincial airports. There are travel and information centres in both terminals, and city transport is to be found directly outside the terminal building. **Air New Zealand**, T03-3630600, T0800-737000, www.airnewzealand.co.nz, and **Qantas**, T0800-808767, www.qantas.co.nz, cover most long haul destinations and Australia, while **Freedom Air**, T0800-600500, www.freedom.co.nz, fly to Brisbane and the Gold Coast. **Air New Zealand** are the principal domestic carrier with **Qantas** and **Origin Pacific**, T0800-302302, www.originpacific.co.nz, also providing some services to major regional destinations. Combined they offer flights to Wellington and Auckland almost every hour.

From the **airport** (12 km) **Metro buses**, T03-3668855 offer regular airport services to the Square (20 min) hourly, Mon-Fri from 0600-2300, Sat and Sun 0800-2300, from $2. **Red Bus City Flyer**, T0800-733287, also offer services hourly Mon-Fri 0600-2300, Sat and Sun 0730-2230. Various shuttles including **Super Shuttle** (door to door), T03-3579950, or **Airport Shuttle**, T0800-7402000 will take you into town for around $12. A taxi costs about $18-$25 (see Directory, page 506).

Road Christchurch is 336 km south of Picton (Kaikoura 183 km) via SH1; 579 km north of Invercargill (Dunedin 362 km/ Timaru 163 km) on SH1. Queenstown is 486 km southwest via SH1/SH8, and Greymouth 258 km via Arthur's Pass and SH73. **Bus Intercity** is the main player, with daily services to most major towns in the South Island including Picton (5 ½ hrs), Dunedin (6 hrs), Mt Cook (5½ hrs), Wanaka (9 hrs), Queenstown (10 hrs). In Christchurch their agent is the **Christchurch Travel Centre**, 123 Worcester St, T03-3770951; reservations T03-3799020, www.intercitycoach. co.nz **Great Sights**, T0800-744487, www.greatsights.co.nz, also offer more tour-based options. There are many smaller shuttle services listed in 'Getting there' sections of the intended destinations. **Atomic Shuttles**, T03-3228883, www.atomictravel.co.nz, are the main Christchurch-based company offering excellent South Island-wide services. **Southern Link**, T03-3588355, also offer services to Picton, Dunedin, Queenstown and Wanaka. **Supa Kut–Price Shuttles**,

T03-3298069, offer an 'unbeatable' price to Dunedin at $20 one-way, $30 return. **Coast to Coast**, T0800-800847, www.coast2coast.co.nz and **Alpine Coaches**, T0800-274888, www.alpinecoaches.co.nz, offer daily services to Greymouth and Westport on the West Coast, while the **Hanmer Connection**, T0800-377378, offer a daily service to Hanmer Springs. **High Country Shuttles**, T0800-435050, are based in Twizel and offer a daily shuttle between Christchurch, Twizel and Mount Cook. They link with the Wanaka/Queenstown Intercity, Atomic and Southern Link services. **Lazerline**, T03-3887652, offer daily services through the Lewis Pass to Nelson. For special deals, including the **Best of New Zealand Pass** which offers a combination of train, ferry and coach travel see 'Getting around', 'Essentials' section, page 39. The VIC has full details on national bus travel and can make bookings on your behalf. Typical prices are: Dunedin $30; Queenstown $50; Invercargill $70; Mount Cook $25; Kaikoura $15; Picton $25; Greymouth $35.

Train The train station is 3 km from the city centre at the southwestern tip of Hagley Park on Addington St. **TranzScenic**, T0800-872467, www.tranzscenic.co.nz operate the northbound TranzCoastal (departs 0730; Kaikoura/Blenheim/Picton, from $35-$80); and the deservingly popular **TranzAlpine** (departs 0900; Greymouth, from $60). For details and fares get the 'times and fares' booklet from the train station or the VIC. **The Best of New Zealand Pass** offers a combination of train, ferry and coach travel (see Getting Around). A shuttle from the station to the city centre costs from $6, a taxi from $10.

Getting around You are far better off on foot or going by public transport within the city than using a **car**. The one-way system is a little confusing, and although there are

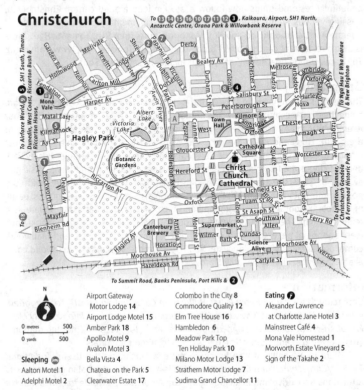

Christchurch

To ⑬ ⑭ ⑮ ⑯ ⑩ ⑰ ⑪ ⑫ ❸, Kaikoura, Airport, SH1 North, Antarctic Centre, Orana Park & Willowbank Reserve

To Summit Road, Banks Peninsula, Port Hills & ❷

N

0 metres 500
0 yards 500

Sleeping 🛏
Aalton Motel **1**
Adelphi Motel **2**

Airport Gateway
  Motor Lodge **14**
Airport Lodge Motel **15**
Amber Park **18**
Apollo Motel **9**
Avalon Motel **3**
Bella Vista **4**
Chateau on the Park **5**
Clearwater Estate **17**

Colombo in the City **8**
Commodore Quality **12**
Elm Tree House **16**
Hambledon **6**
Meadow Park Top
  Ten Holiday Park **10**
Milano Motor Lodge **13**
Strathern Motor Lodge **7**
Sudima Grand Chancellor **11**

Eating 🍴
Alexander Lawrence
  at Charlotte Jane Hotel **3**
Mainstreet Café **4**
Mona Vale Homestead **1**
Morworth Estate Vineyard **5**
Sign of the Takahe **2**

plenty of parking lots and meters they are almost as tightly patrolled as Auckland and Wellington. An hr in the city centre will cost about $2. A good idea is to park your car for free south of Moorhouse Av (the Old Train Station and Hoyts 8 Cinema) and catch the free shuttle from there. Being so flat the city provides easy **cycling**. For bike, motorcycle and car hire, see Directory, page 506.

Christchurch has an excellent public **bus** system with a brand new terminal, the **Bus Exchange**, on the corner of Lichfield and Colombo Sts. For all bus information To3-3668855, www.metroinfo.org.nz, Mon-Fri 0630-2230, Sun 0900-2100, or **Red Buses**, To800-733287, www.redbus.co.nz The buses run on a 2-zone system; zone-1 costs $2, zone-2 $2.70. Monthly passes are available and you can purchase cash fares from the driver as you board the bus (have correct change ready). An excellent way to get around is with a **Red Bus Day Pass**, which covers most of the city centre and major attractions for $7 (family $15) a day. They can also be bought from the driver or from the bus information offices. The electrified **Free Yellow Shuttle** takes in a north-south route from the Casino, through Cathedral Sq and down Colombo St and back, and operates every 10-15 min Mon-Thu 0800-2230; Fri 0800-2400; Sat 0900-2400 and Sun 1000-2000. It's worth jumping on at least once to get your bearings. The **Best Attractions Express Shuttle** continuously links the Christchurch Gondola, Christchurch Tramway, International Antarctic Centre and Willowbank Wildlife Reserve and departs regularly from its stop in Cathedral Square, directly opposite the Tram Stop. An all-day pass (with bonus second day free) allows you to visit each venue as often as you wish. Tickets are available from the driver or from the VIC, adults $10 and children $8. For shuttle services to **Lyttleton** and **Akaroa** see 'Around Christchurch' section, below.

Between 1905 and 1954 Christchurch had a thriving **tram** system. Since 1995 the beautifully restored trams now follow a 2½ km loop around central Christchurch, passing various sights of interest on the way (commentary provided). The trams operate Apr-Oct 0900-1800 and Nov-Mar 0900-2100, from $10, To3-3667830. There is also a restaurant car that offers a daily dining tour, To3-3667511, www.tram.co.nz The trams can be boarded at many stops including Cathedral Square.

Orientation

The heart of Christchurch lies just to the west of **Hagley Park** with **Cathedral Square** being the most recognized focus. The borders of the city centre are known as the ' **Four Avenues'**: Deans Av that borders the western fringe of Hagley Park, **Moorhouse Av** to the south, **Fitzgerald Av** to the east and **Bealey Av** to the north. One of the most attractive features of the city is the **River Avon** that winds its way through Hagley Park and the city centre from west to east. The city is essentially flat and has a basic grid system of streets extending in all directions from Cathedral Square, with the north/south **Colombo St** being the main shopping street. The city centre is easily negotiable by foot using the Cathedral and high-rises around Cathedral Square as a reference point. The VIC has a plentiful supply of free city maps. The major bookshops (see 'Shopping' page 506) also stock Christchurch city map books, and **Mapworld**, corner of Manchester and Gloucester Sts, To3-3745399, www.maps@mapworld.co.nz is an excellent source of city, town, provincial and national maps.

Information

Christchurch VIC, ① *Old Post Office Building in Cathedral Sq (West), To3-3799629, www.christchurchnz.net, www.christchurch.org.nz, www.localeye.info.nz Daily Mon-Fri 0830-1700; Sat-Sun 0830-1600.* There are also VICs in the international (To3-3537783/4) and domestic (To3-3537774/5) airport terminals.

There is a wealth of **free brochure** material, including the useful *Today and Tonight/Christchurch and Canterbury*, which is a must. There are also numerous city attractions and 'drive' maps including the *Top Attractions*; *A Guide to Christchurch's*

❖ The Road to Edoras

For **Lord of the Rings** fans or indeed anyone who wants to see some classic Southern Alpine scenery, then the trip to **Mount Sunday** (Potts Station) in the Rangitata Valley is a great day out. Mt Sunday, which sits predominantly in the **Rangitata River Valley** and in stark contrast against the mountainous skyline of Southern Alps, became the perfect filming location and set for Edoras and King Theoden's grand hall in *The Two Towers*, the second film in the *Lord of the Rings* trilogy. From Mt Somers take the road west through the Ashburton Gorge towards **Lakes Camp and Clearwater**. Just before the lakes the road becomes unsealed and opens up in to the wide tussock valley giving an almost surreal sense of space. From the lakes, which are the favourite haunt for windsurfers and water-skiers, keep heading west towards the end of the valley. There, at the western edge of the Mt Harper Range (Harpers Knob) there is a sudden and dramatic view down

in to the Rangitata Valley and in the far distance, the prominent outcrop known as Mt Sunday (611m). As you get ever nearer you can see why it was the perfect film location and although nothing remains of the set itself and direct access to the hill is forbidden, it still has plenty of impact and offers a great photo opportunity. The best place to take pictures is just past the Mt Potts Station or looking back down the valley as the road climbs the hill towards its terminus at The Erewhon Station.

If you do not have your own transport or do not trust your own vehicle you can join a multi-day tour with **Tussock and Beach Tours** based in Christchurch, *T03-3030880, www.nature.net.nz* (See Christchurch Activities, page 504), or if you are feeling flush even charter a light aircraft and fly in to the valley and the airstrip at Mt Potts. **A** Mt Potts Alpine Lodge, *T03-3039738, www.mtpotts.co.nz* has mid-range accommodation in the form of rooms with shared amenities or a self-contained cottage option. There is a licensed bar and restaurant on site.

City Centre; *The Avon River Drive*; *The Garden Drive*; *The Antarctic Heritage Trail*; *Wine Trail* and *Arts Trail* maps. The **daily paper** in the Central South Island is the Christchurch Press. If you need more contact addresses and numbers, don't forget the www.yellowpages.co.nz website.

DoC, ① *133 Victoria St, T03-3799758. Mon-Fri 0830-1630.* They can provide local, regional and South Island walks and tramping information.

History

Given Christchurch's strong and outwardly obvious English links, it is perhaps ironic that the first European settlers on the Canterbury Plains were in fact Scottish. Although having originally emigrated separately to Nelson and Wellington in 1840 and 1842 in search of better living conditions, brothers William and John Deans arrived on the plains and established themselves on land the local Maori called *Putaringamotu* in 1843, calling it Riccarton after their home town in Central Scotland. Five years later the New Zealand government made a contentious land deal with the local Maori purchasing about 8 million ha of land for – we presume – little more than 'two sticks and a balloon', which paved the way for more concerted settlement.

In 1849 a prestigious 53-member organization called the **Canterbury Association** was founded by Irishman Robert Godley. Comprising two Archbishops (of Canterbury and Armagh), seven bishops, 14 peers, and other notables, mainly from Godley's old university college of Christchurch, in Oxford, its aim was to establish a new utopian Anglican settlement in the new colony of New Zealand. The site of this new settlement was chosen by the association's surveyor, Captain Joseph Banks, who, presumably after seeing the Deans brothers' prize 'neeps' and 'tatties' (turnips and potatoes), saw the obvious potential of the rich alluvial plains for agriculture.

In 1850 the 'first four ships' – The *Charlotte Jane*, *Randolph*, *Sir George Seymour*, and *Cressy* brought 782 colonial souls to the then whaling base of Lyttleton, which had already been established on the Banks Peninsula. Even before their arrival the Canterbury Association had already christened the great settlement-to-be, Christchurch. But perhaps, human nature being what it is, it seems little of either

Around Cathedral Square

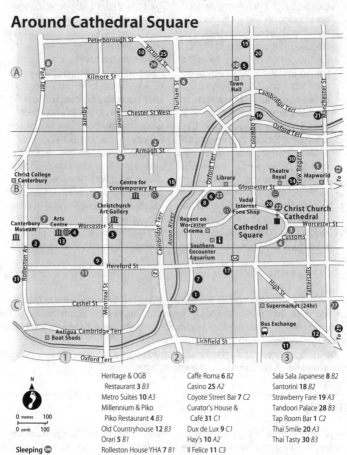

N

0 metres 100
0 yards 100

Sleeping
Christchurch City YHA **1** *B3*
Crown Plaza, Yamagen
 Japanese & Canterbury
 Tales Restaurants &
 Victoria Street Café **6** *A2*
Croydon House **2** *B2*
George & Pescatore
 Restaurant **8** *A1*

Heritage & OGB
 Restaurant **3** *B3*
Metro Suites **10** *A3*
Millennium & Piko
 Piko Restaurant **4** *B3*
Old Countryhouse **12** *B3*
Orari **5** *B1*
Rolleston House YHA **7** *B1*
Thomas's **11** *C1*
Windsor B&B **9** *B1*

Eating
Annie's Wine Bar **2** *B1*
Bon Bolli **3** *B1*
Boulevard Bakehouse **4** *B1*
Café Metro **5** *A3*

Caffe Roma **6** *B2*
Casino **25** *A2*
Coyote Street Bar **7** *C2*
Curator's House &
 Café **31** *C1*
Dux de Lux **9** *C1*
Hay's **10** *A2*
Il Felice **11** *C3*
Java **12** *C3*
Le Café **13** *B1*
Little India Bistro
 & Tandoori **14** *B3*
Oxford on Avon **16** *A3*
Palazzo del Marinaio **17** *C2*
Passport to Asia **29** *C3*
Retour **21** *A3*

Sala Sala Japanese **8** *B2*
Santorini **18** *B2*
Strawberry Fare **19** *A3*
Tandoori Palace **28** *B3*
Tap Room Bar **1** *C2*
Thai Smile **20** *A3*
Thai Tasty **30** *B3*

Bars & clubs
Bailies **22** *B3*
Bard **23** *B2*
Bog **24** *C2*
Jolly Poacher **26** *A2*
Loaded Hog **27** *C3*

the Association's disintegration in 1855 and the effective end to the great Anglican settlement plan.

Despite these hiccups the new colony flourished and today its roots are obvious. One only need look at the trees and cricket pitches in Hagley Park, the gardens, the street names and the punting on the river, the public school boys skipping out of Christ's College in blazers and straw hats, to realize how much of its founding English influence prevails. Indeed, in Christchurch, to be in the slightest way related to anyone on 'the first four ships' is, 'darling', to belong to the city's elite. As for the Deans boys, William drowned in 1851 on a journey to Australia to buy sheep, and John died in the cottage three years later after contracting tuberculosis.

Sights

City centre

Within the **'Four Avenues'**, and easily negotiated on foot, are a number of sights and attractions that easily take up one day. Ask at the VIC about the **Super Pass**, which can combine entry to a number of major venues from $69, child $29.

Cathedral Square Dominated by the Gothic-revival Anglican **Christ Church Cathedral**, Cathedral Square has recently undergone a major revamp that has become the talk of Christchurch. The issue is highly contentious (even nationally), with most feeling the development is an aesthetic disaster and a crass waste of money. Certainly, it does seem hopelessly out of character with the rest of the city, with its sharp angles and dull façades of steel and concrete. And once again it seems to suffer from the scourge of the average New Zealand architect – a severe disregard for trees. Surely it does not take a PhD to realize that it is Christchurch's wealth of flora that is its very appeal, so why create a complete antithesis at its very heart? With so much negative debate, one of New Zealand's most noted architects, Ian Athfield, was brought in to assist in revamping the revamp, and at the time of going to print it would seem that the debates are still raging and the long-term plans still not finalized. However, current aesthetics aside, the main feature worth looking at in the Square is of course the Cathedral itself. ① *To3-3660046. Tours are available Mon-Fri 1100/1400, Sat 1100, Sun 1130. $4, child $1.50 (tour $3).* It houses a number of interesting memorials and boasts an interior design that is an interesting and eclectic mix of Maori and European. The spire can be climbed in part, offering a panoramic and memorable **view** of the city. There is also an audio-visual presentation and a good café attached. The Square is also home to two notable characters: one permanent, made of bronze, a memorial and pleasantly quiet; the other semi-retired, wearing a cloak, a pointy hat and that never stops talking. The former is the statue of **John Robert Godley**, the founder of the Canterbury Association and essentially Christchurch itself; the latter the iconic **Wizard**, a local eccentric who has been 'entertaining' the masses with his views on life, the universe and just about everything contentious for decades. As a wizard he apparently travels without a passport and has been known to get through customs without one, presumably for the sake of some peace and quiet. ① *Although the Wizard officially retired in 2001, he still puts in the odd appearance in the Square between Nov-Mar – he is a wizard after all. For an argument or more information visit his website, www.wizard.gen.nz*

Also in the square is the **'Four Ships Court'**, a memorial to the 'first four ships' which stands outside the 1879 **Old Post Office** (which now houses the Christchurch VIC). Accessed through the VIC is the **Southern Encounter Aquarium**, ① *To3-3590851, www.southernencounter.co.nz, daily 0900-1630, from $10, child $5,* which seems remarkably out of place but is still worth a look, housing an interesting collection of local sea creatures. Trout and salmon feeding 1300, marine tank dive and feeding 1500. **Guided City Walks**, offer informative 2-hr guided walks of the inner city from $8. ① *They depart Oct-Apr 1000 and 1300; May-Sep 1300, from the southeast corner of the Square, T03-3799629 (or book at the VIC).*

The Avon River Heading west from Cathedral Square you immediately encounter (and not for the first time) the pretty Avon River. This is one of the city's greatest assets. The river meanders like a snake from the northwest tip of the 'four avenues' through Hagley Park and the Botanical Gardens, through the city centre, before finally continuing its journey through the city's eastern suburbs to the sea. The river is particularly attractive in autumn when poplar and weeping willows are radiant in golden hues. It offers some lovely inner city walks that are outlined in the free *River Walks of Christchurch* available from the VIC. The *Avon River Drive* is another alternative. On the eastern bank of the river, just beyond Cathedral Square and beside the Worcester Street Bridge, is one base from where you can go **punting** on the river, ① *T03-3799629. The punts operate daily usually from 0900-2100 (winter 1000-1600) and a 30 minute trip will cost from $18, child $9.* Note also the 1917 statue of **Scott of the Antarctic** beside the river – not the first or last reminder that Christchurch is a principal gateway to the Antarctic.

Across the bridge and on the right, further up Worcester Street, is the new **Christchurch Art Gallery (Te Puna O Waiwhetu)**, ① *T03-9417300, www.christchurchgallery.org.nz Daily 1000-1700 (Wed 2100), free (with a charge for major exhibitions).* Immediately christened by some cynics as 'a warehouse in a tutu' it is actually supposed to be 'evoking the sinuous form of the koru and the River Avon that flows through Christchurch'. With over 3,000 square metres of exhibition space, it is over four times the size of the Robert McDougall Gallery that for years struggled to showcase its formidable 5,500 permanent works. So whether you see it as a tutu or as an impressive edifice from the outside is up to you, but what cannot be denied is the quality of its content. Many of the famous New Zealand artists are represented including Charles Goldie, Colin McCahon and Ralph Hotere, but there is also an emphasis on contemporary works and a dynamic schedule of national and international exhibitions. There is a quality retail outlet that specializes in contemporary art and crafts and the obligatory café/bistro.

The **Centre for Contemporary Art**, ① *60 Gloucester St, T03-3667261, www.coca.org.nz Mon-Fri 1000-1700, Sat-Sun 1200-1600. Free.* Also worth visiting, five galleries and over 50 exhibitions per annum. Much of the art is for sale.

The Arts Centre On the opposite side of the road is the Arts Centre of Christchurch, ① *2 Worcester Boulevard, T03-3660989, www.artscentre.org.nz Tours daily from 1030-1530. The free 'What's on at The Arts Centre' and 'Christchurch City Arts Trail' booklets are very useful.* Once the site of the original University of Canterbury, the old Gothic revival buildings now house an excellent and dynamic array of **arts and crafts**, workshops, galleries and sales outlets, as well as **theatres, cinemas, cafés, restaurants** and **bars**. It is well worth a visit, particularly at the weekend when it hosts a lively arts and crafts **market**. It becomes very much the focus of attention for tourists with an international food fair and top local **entertainment**, from a local town crier to city buskers. There are also some notable historical features including the 'Den' of scientist **Ernest Rutherford** (see box in previous chapter), the **Great Hall** with its stained glass windows and the **Townsend Observatory** with its working telescope. Free guided **tours** are available and depart from the Information Centre in the Clocktower foyer.

Hagley Park At the western edge of the Arts Centre, Worcester Street meets Rolleston Avenue and the eastern fringe of Hagley Park. Amazingly intact after all the years of development, Hagley Park (over 200 ha) is divided in two portions by Riccarton Avenue, and comprises pleasant tree-lined walkways, sports fields and in its central reaches the **Botanical Gardens**, ⓘ *0700-dusk, Conservatory Complex 1015-1600*, enclosed by a loop of the Avon River. Well maintained and with a huge variety of gardens from 'herb' to 'rose', these provide a great escape from the buzz of the city year round. Autumn sees the gardens at their most colourful. **Information Centre and Curators House Café**, ⓘ *Rolleston Ave, near the Peacock Fountain, T03-9417590. Daily Sep-Apr 1015-1600; May-Aug 1100-1500. Guided tours are available daily Sep-May, from 1000-1630 departing from the Information Centre ($6, child $4)*.

At the entrance to the Botanical Gardens on Rolleston Avenue is the **Canterbury Museum**, ⓘ *T03-3665000. Daily 0900-1730 (winter 1700). General entry is free but there are charges for the Exhibition Court and Discovery Centre ($2). Guided tours are also available*. Housed in a grand 1870 neo-Gothic building and founded in 1867, it is well worth a visit, the undoubted highlights being its impressive Maori collection and the Hall of Antarctic Discovery. In keeping with other museums in the country, it also hosts a dynamic Discovery Centre for kids and big kids alike. The Exhibition Court displays a changing program of travelling national and international exhibitions. There is also a fine in-house shop and a café overlooking the Botanical Gardens.

Just north of the museum is **Christ College Canterbury**, ⓘ *for information about guided tours in summer, T03-3795570*, which is without doubt New Zealand's most famous historic school. Built in 1850 it is an aesthetic and architectural delight, and in the late afternoon spills forth suitably clad and 'proper' scholars.

At the southern end of Rolleston Avenue are the **Antigua Boat Sheds**, which were built in 1882, making them one of the oldest buildings in Christchurch. The former boat builders' premises now host a café and are the base for **Punting in the Park**, ⓘ *T03-3660337, 30-minute punting trips daily from 1000-dusk, from $20*. You can also hire **canoes**, ⓘ *T03-3665885. 0930-1730 (winter 1600). One hour, $7; also paddleboats, one hour $14; and rowing boats, one hour, $20*.

Canterbury Brewery ⓘ *Near the junction of Riccarton and Hagley Avenues (Hagley Park), at 36 St Asphalt St, T03-3794940. Tours Mon-Thu, from $10, bookings essential*. Founded in 1854, its long established 'CD' is something of a libatious institution in the Canterbury Region. The brewery has a good museum and guided tours with tastings are available.

City North and West

Mona Vale ⓘ *just beyond the northwest corner of the 'Four Avenues' at 63 Fendalton Rd, T03-3489660*. Heading out towards the airport is Mona Vale, a beautiful Elizabethan-style homestead and gardens, built in 1905 on the land first settled by the Scots Dean brothers in 1843. While the Homestead itself now is a fine restaurant and café, the 5½ ha grounds are a spectacular array of features including a lily pond, rhododendrons, azaleas and exotic trees, all set in reverence to the lovely River Avon. The gardens can be reached by punt, and guided tours are available. Phone for details.

International Antarctic Centre and Hagglund Ride ⓘ *at the airport (signposted), Orchard Rd, T03-3589896, www.iceberg.co.nz Daily Oct-Mar 0900-2030; Apr-Sep 0900-1730, from $20, child $10. Guided tours are available from officers who have lived and worked on the ice or you can self-guide with the help of 'snow-phones' ($6). Hagglund Ride from $12, child $9. A combo Visitor Centre/ride costs $30, child $20*. By public transport the City-Airport bus (from Cathedral Square) runs to the Centre every half-hour. Since the turn of the last century and the days of Scott and Shackleton, Christchurch has been a principal 'gateway to the Antarctic'. Today the Antarctic Centre, which opened in 1990, is a working campus and formidable array of buildings. In its

Christchurch's Most Unusual Visitor

He is a rebellious, moody, teenage star that weighs almost two tonnes. He does what he likes, when he likes and has very bad breath. He would not win any beauty contests but he doesn't care. Anything blue he will attack, anything yellow he wants to play with and anything red makes him horny. He loves to throw his weight around and in doing so has destroyed boats, trees, cars, sheds and kayaks – to name but a few. But, he has injured nobody and has no desire to. He has had to be forcibly evicted from a garage several times, a woodshed twice and on one occasion even somebody's bedroom. He has tried to mount and make love with several boats and even a Toyota Corolla car (red, of course).

Yet, despite his behaviour (and perhaps because of it), he is an international star and while in Christchurch has over 6,000 visitors a day. Some fear him; some hate him and some have even attacked him – but most love him dearly. He even has an entourage of carers who look after him, play with him when bored and keep those that want to hurt him away. His name is Dumbo. He is a Southern Elephant Seal. Dumbo first turned up on the beaches of Christchurch in 1993 and for six consecutive years spent each summer there 'in moult' (a natural process of shedding and re-growing pelage that occurs annually in seals). Dumbo was a sub-adult and therefore in a state of 'solitary limbo', before becoming sexually mature and securing his own territory amongst others. Why exactly Dumbo chose the public beaches of Christchurch to moult, where he went in winter, or indeed, where he is now, is not known. But he was certainly a handful and provided an interesting insight into these magnificent creatures and at times, sadly, the darker side of human nature. The summer of 2000 was the first since 1993 that Dumbo failed to return. However, it is now felt that this is entirely natural and that he is now of an age to be elsewhere making love with seals as opposed to cars. But wherever he is now, one thing is for sure – he remains in the hearts of many and will always be the city's most unusual visitor.

For more information about Dumbo, contact his personal NZ agents, minders, secretaries and public relations executives at his 'Christchurch Office' c/o Marine Watch, *T03-3898270*.

entirety, it is home to Antarctica New Zealand (managers of New Zealand's activities in the Antarctic), the Antarctic Heritages Trust, the US and Italian Antarctic programmes, the International Centre for Antarctic Information and Research, and the Antarctic Passenger terminal and aircraft hangers, where you can often see the Hercules that head off into the wild blue and very cold yonder. The Visitors' Centre, which was opened in 1992, is an excellent introduction to the great white continent and a place from which would-be world travellers will emerge dreaming. Overall it is both informative and fun, with an excellent array of displays from the historical to the modern-day. One of the first displays you will encounter are the current Antarctic weather statistics (3832 km away and the temperature on the day – try minus 70° F) that send a shiver down your spine and your hands plunging into your pockets. Then, to get an even better idea of the real thing, you can don jackets and overshoes and enter the **Snow and Ice Experience**, a room kept at minus 5° F, replete with manufactured snow and ice. In contrast is a superb **audio-visual**, which beautifully marries images from the ice with inspiring music. From the displays you then emerge

into the well and unusually stocked **Antarctic shop** and the 60° F **South Café and Bar**.
A recent addition to the centre activities is the **Antarctic Hagglund Ride**. The Hagglund
is a tracked vehicle that was originally used by the US and NZ Antarctic programmes
in Scott and McMurdo bases. During the 45-minute ride you are taken to see some of
the major facilities of the centre before experiencing the all-terrain abilities of the
vehicle on a man-made adventure course. The Centre also forms part of the
interesting **'Antarctic Heritage Trail'** (free leaflet from the VIC). Note that the free
Canterbury museum also hosts an excellent Antarctic display.

Orana Wildlife Park and the Willowbank Reserve While out in the vicinity of the
airport it is worth visiting one (or preferably both) of Christchurch's main wildlife
attractions, **Orana Park**, ① *743 McLeans Island Rd (10 minutes from the airport),
T03-3597109, www.oranawildlifepark.co.nz Daily 1000-1700, from $12, child $6.* This is
New Zealand's largest captive wildlife reserve, set in 80 ha of parkland. It has a good
mix of native and international wildlife with an emphasis on **African** animals. All the
usual suspects are there from the lofty giraffes and horny rhinos to the ever-popular,
inquisitive meerkats. And of course amongst the many New Zealand natives you will
find a nocturnal kiwi house. Also near the airport (five minutes), is the **Willowbank
Wildlife Reserve**, ① *60 Hussey Rd (off Gardiners Rd), T03-3596226,
www.willowbank.co.nz Daily 1000-2200. Entry to the reserve costs $16, child $8. For
transport book at the city VIC or T0800-484485.* It focuses more on native wildlife and
farm animals and provides daily guided tours ($2) and both night and day **kiwi** viewing.
The reserve has a very successful kiwi-breeding programme and you can also see the
cheeky kea (mountain parrots) being fed. There is a good **restaurant** on-site offering
buffet dinner from 1830-2030, from $37.50.

Riccarton Bush and Riccarton House (Putaringamotu) ① *3½ km west of the city
centre on the banks of the Avon River, the main entrance to the reserve is at 16 Kahu
Rd, T03-3486184. Deans cottage is open daily, while the homestead is open Mon-Fri
1300-1600. Tours daily at 1000 and 1400.* Set in 30 acres of parkland is the historic
Riccarton Estate. Once the home of the Scots pioneers and brothers William and John
Deans (the first European settlers on the Canterbury Plains), it features the faithfully
restored and furnished original 1843 **Deans cottage** in which they first lived, and the
grand Victorian/Edwardian **homestead** that was built by the next generation from
1856-74. Within the house, which has recently been restored and redecorated in
period style, you will find the detailed brochure *The Story of Riccarton House* which
gives more details about the family and the lives they led. Café on site.

The Nga Hau E Wha Marae ① *Daily, free. For evening performance and hangi, book
ahead on T03-3887685, nhewmarae@xtra.co.nz Concert and hangi starts 1845 and
ends at 2115, from $65, child $33 (concert and tour only 1845-2000, from $30, child $19,
includes transport from the city. To get there independently from the city, take Hereford
St (northeast), turn right into Linwood Ave then left into Buckleys Rd, continue through
to Pages Rd (250).* The Nga Hau E Wha National Marae or 'Marae of the Four Winds' is
the country's largest *marae*. The meetinghouse (Whare Nui) is beautifully constructed
and comes complete with greenstone (*pounamu*) inlaid steps (which should be rubbed
for good luck). Guided **tours** are available, on which you will be given an introduction to
Maori culture, protocol, history and tradition. You can also extend your visit and stay to
experience the evening **performance** and **hangi** (feast).

City East
East of the city centre the River Avon negotiates suburbia before emptying its
contents into the Pacific. There is a **wildlife reserve** on the estuary that offers good
bird watching and short walk opportunities and a number of fine **beaches**. **New

Brighton is the main focus of activity, with beachside **cafés** and a **pier** decked with hopeful anglers. New Brighton can be reached from the centre of the city, via Cashel St, then Buckleys Pages Road (8 km). South of the estuary via Ferry Rd (SH74) is the coastal resort of **Sumner** (12 km) which also has some fine beaches with safe swimming and plenty of cafés. The **scenic drive** to Lyttleton and the Lyttleton Harbour from Sumner (Evans Pass Road) is recommended.

City South

Airforce World ① *On the old RNZAF Base at Wingram, Main South Road (15 minutes southwest), To3-3439532, www.afw.co.nz daily from 1000-1700, from $10, child $5.* If vintage aircraft are your thing then Airforce World will appeal. It has an impressive collection of 28 classic aircraft including a Spitfire and a Skyhawk. All of the aircraft have been faithfully restored and are theatrically displayed alongside special sections on World War II and the role of the modern-day RNZAF. It is worthy of a visit even if you are not a plane buff, and there is the added attraction of free flight simulators. Guided tours are available (1100, 1300 and 1500) and there is a café on site.

Science Alive ① *Moorhouse Av (Old Train Station), To3-3655199. Mon-Fri 0900-1700, Sat-Sun 1000-1800, from $6 (all day pass).* Although the Discovery Centre in the museum, the Antarctic Centre and wildlife parks are all obvious draws for kids, the Science Alive Centre is a great wet weather attraction. It is very much a hands-on place that could even see your kids waiting outside for you!

The Christchurch (Port Hills) Gondola ① *To3-3840700, www.gondola.co.nz Daily from 1000-2130. From $17, child $8. The Best Attractions Shuttle Bus leaves from the Visitor Centre at 1000, 1400 and 1600 ($8 all day pass) or the #28 bus from the Bus Exchange, from $2.* If only for the stunning **views**, the Christchurch Gondola is well worth the trip. The base terminal is in the Heathcote Valley 10 km southeast of the city via Ferry Road. From there gondolas whisk you 945 m to the top of the Port Hills (1500 m) and the Summit Complex. The complex has all the expected shops and a café but also supports viewpoints from which you can gaze down to Lyttleton and across the Banks Peninsula. North, the view across the city is equally stunning, and on a clear day beyond the Canterbury Plains is the distant line of the Southern Alps. You can embark on a number of **walks** from the complex that explore the crater rim, including the Bridle Path which was once used by the early pioneers as the main route to Lyttleton. An attractive way of descending is by **mountain bike** (see page 505).

On the way or coming back from the gondola you might like to stop off at the **Ferrymead Historic Park**, ① *in the suburb of Ferrymead (Ferrymead Park Dr), To3-3841970, www.ferrymead.co.nz Daily 1000-1630, from $6, child $3 ($8/$4 at weekends when trams are operating).* It's an entertaining mock-up of a 1920 Edwardian township and a working museum with a wide array of period memorabilia including transport displays, Clydesdale horse-drawn carts, and a bakery selling freshly baked food. Trams and trains operate at weekends.

● Sleeping

As you would expect, Christchurch has plenty of accommodation covering all types and all budgets. Almost all the national chain hotels are in evidence in the city centre, with the majority being located in or around Victoria and Cathedral Square. A few independent boutique-style options surround Hagley Park and overlook the River Avon. Likewise there are many B&Bs both in the city centre and a little further out, with some set in historic and spacious villas. Most of the motels are northwest of the city centre along Papanui Road and Bealey Avenue west (to SH1), or on Riccarton Road heading south. Hostels abound in the city centre, from the small purpose-built, or old hotel/pub-style to the large and modern. All the motor parks are on the city fringes in all directions, but mainly close to SH1 north and south. Over all you will find prices above average for South Island, but winter can see a drop in rates and some very reasonable deals, especially with the many competing hotels. Since Christchurch is the starting point for so many South Island travellers you are advised to pre-book in mid summer.

Hotels

LL Clearwater Estate Hotel *Clearwater Av, Harewood, T03-3601000, www.clearwater.net.nz* The Bob Charles designed (and highly aquatic) 72-hole championship golf course layout was opened in 2002 and is proving very popular. The hotel provides luxury lakeside villas with rooms, suites or 2 bedroom villas, spas and a quality restaurant. Discount B&B or golfing packages are often available.

LL-AL Commodore Quality Hotel, *T03-3588129, www.commodore.net.nz* and **LL-AL Sudima Hotel Grand Chancellor**, *T03-3583139, www.sudimahotel.co.nz*. Both are at the end of Memorial Avenue 5 min from the airport and the Antarctic Centre.

L Crown Plaza, *corner Kilmore and Durham sts, T03-3657799, www.crownplaza.com* Aesthetically, from the outside you will either love it or hate it, but there is no denying its prime position at the corner of Victoria Square. The Square acts like a garden and comes complete with river, fountains and a path leading right into the heart of the city. It has all the usual luxuries, a Japanese restaurant, a café and a very spacious, comfy atrium area on the ground floor.

L-AL Metro Suites, *above the Metro Café, corner of Kilmore and Colombo Sts, T03-3664067, www.metrosuites.co.nz* For sheer convenience these 2 new and stylish suites are recommended. One with a historic design complete with claw foot bath, the other in a minimalist style. Breakfast in the café downstairs is included.

L-AL Millennium Hotel, *Cathedral Sq, T03-3651111, central.res@cdlhms.co.nz and* **AL-A Heritage Hotel**, *Cathdral Sq, T03-3779722, www.heritagehotels.co.nz* Both are modern, well-appointed and have all the usual facilities. The restaurants and bars are also popular with non-clients due to their ideal location.

AL Chateau on the Park, *189 Deans Av, T03-3488999, www.chateau-park.co.nz* Still near the river and retaining that 'Garden City' feel at the northwestern edge of Hagley Park. A little further from the action but that is part of its appeal. Its gardens are excellent and the restaurant and bar have a nice cosy atmosphere.

A The George Hotel, *50 Park Terr, T03-3794560, www.thegeorge.com* Also overlooking the river and more expensive. It has a solid reputation with excellent, well-appointed suites, facilities and award-winning cuisine.

A Holiday Inn, *356 Oxford Terr, T03-3791180, reservations@holidayinnchristchurch.co.nz* Right next to the Avon River, smaller, more discreet and better value.

Motels

There are literally dozens, offering affordable prices and located within walking distance of the city. On **Papanui Rd** in order of price:

AL-A Milano Motor Lodge (87), *T03-3552800, milano@xtra.co.nz*

A Adelphi Motel (49), *T03-3556037, adelphi@xtra.co.nz* and

A Strathern Motor Lodge (54), *T03-3554411, spa@xtra.co.nz*

On **Bealey Av**, again in order of price:

AL-A Tuscana Motor Lodge, (74), *T03-3774485, www.tuscana.co.nz*

AL-A Bella Vista (193), *T03-3773445, www.bellavistamotel.co.nz*

AL-A Avenue Motel, (136), *T03-3660582, Email: avenuemotorlodge@ xtra.co.nz;*

A Avalon Motel, (301), *T03-3799681, infoavalonmotel@xtra.co.nz*

On **Riccarton Rd**:

AL-A Apollo Motel (288), *T03-3488786, www.apollomotel.co. nz*

A Aalton Motel (19), *T03-3486700, welcome@aalton.co.nz*

Canterbury Christchurch

● For an explanation of the sleeping and eating price codes used in this guide, see the inside
● front cover. Other relevant information is provided in the Essentials chapter, see page 51.

At the **airport**:

AL-A Airport Gateway Motor Lodge, *45 Roydvale Ave, T03-3587093, www.airportgateway.co.nz*

A Airport Lodge Motel, *105 Roydvale Av, T03-3585119, airport_lodge@clear.net.nz* are recommended.

Convenient for the **town centre**:

AL-A Colombo in the City, *863 Colombo St, T03-3668775, www.motelcolombo.co.nz*

B City Worcester Motels, *336 Worcester St T03-3664491, city.worcester@inet.net.nz*

B Stonehurst Apartments, *241 Gloucester St, T03-3794620, accom@stonehurst.co.nz*

B&Bs and homestays

In or near the **centre**

LL Weston House, *62 Park Terr, T03-3660234, www.westonhouse. co.nz* Neo-Georgian mansion offering luxurious suites and elegant surroundings opposite Hagley Park and the Avon River.

AL Hambledon, *103 Bealey Av, T03-3790723, www.hambeldon.co.nz* A large and well appointed historic 1856 mansion with lovely luxury rooms (with bath), a large collection of antiques and peaceful garden.

L-A Manor House, *82 Bealey Av, T03-3668584, www.themanor.co.nz* Another vast, historic, well appointed mansion with 12 rooms, 10 of which have ensuite bathrooms. The wooden façades and staircase of the ground floor are superb and the open fire gives a lovely cosy atmosphere.

AL Orari, *42 Gloucester St, T03-3656569, www.orari.net.nz* Smaller, slightly cheaper with more modern decor and close to town, and the Arts Centre in particular. Rooms with a private bathroom.

AL Croydon House, *63 Armagh St, T03-366511, www.croydon.co.nz* Another fine choice, friendly and well-located. Again, rooms with private bathroom. Nice to sit and watch the trams rattle past on the street outside. Good breakfast.

A Windsor B&B Hotel, *52 Armagh St, T03-3661503, www.windsorhotel.co.nz* A good value B&B option.

Further out in quieter locations,

L-AL Glenmore House, *6 Pear Tree La, Hillsborough, T03-3328518, www.glenmorehouse.co.nz* (built in 1857);

L-AL Elm Tree House, *236 Papanui Rd,* *Merivale, T03-3559731, www.elmtreehouse.co.nz* Both excellent, equally characterful and recommended.

Hostels

B-D Stonehurst Backpackers, *241 Gloucester St, Latimer Sq, T03-3794620, www.stonehurst.com* The best mainstream large establishment. It has just about everything – a wide range of good double, twin, single and dorm rooms (some with ensuite bathroom and self-contained), clean facilities, a pool, pizza bar, internet and a travel shop. It is deservedly popular so book in advance.

C Foley Towers, *208 Kilmore St, T03-3669720, foley.towers@backpack.co.nz* Also has a great range of rooms and facilities, internet. It is a very friendly place and is more peaceful than the Stonehurst.

C Christchurch YHA, *273 Manchester St, T03-3799535, yhachch@yha.org.nz* The more modern of the two YHA options. It is purpose-built so a little sterile but still has all the right facilities and comfortable rooms.

C-D Rolleston House YHA, *5 Worcester Blvd, T03-3666564, yhachrl@yha.org.nz* Although a little tired it is still popular, with a good atmosphere and well positioned across the road from the Arts Centre.

C-D Thomas's Hotel, *36 Hereford St, T03-3799536, www.thomashotel.co.nz* Ideally located (on the other side of the Arts Centre), well equipped and spotless. Ideal for couples looking for a good value double and some peace and quiet, but perhaps lacking atmosphere if you are alone.

C-D Occidental Backpackers, *208 Manchester St, T03-3799284, freebreakfast@occidental.co.nz* Pub/hotel-style establishment. A little tired but has clean comfortable double, twin, single and dorm rooms and a lively and popular bar downstairs, with great value meals. It's definitely a social place.

C-D Vagabond Backpackers, *232 Worcester St, T03-3799677, vagabondbackpackers@hotmail.com* Very tidy, peaceful and friendly.

C-D Dorset House, *1 Dorset St, T/F3668268, dorsethouse@cyberxpress.co.nz* An historic, upmarket place pitched somewhere between a backpackers and a B&B, with good doubles, twins and singles. It also has

Sky TV and provides pick-ups.

C-D Old Countryhouse, *437 Gloucester St,
T03-3815504*. Another newly renovated villa,
similar in style with doubles and shared
rooms, a very homely atmosphere and a
lovable dog called Murphy. Internet,
off-street parking. Recommended.

D Frauenreisehaus, *272 Barbadoes St,
T03-3662585, jesse-sandra@quicksilver.net.nz*
Bohemian, health-promoting and for
women only. It prides itself in offering beds
not bunks and has internet.

Motorcamps and campsites

A-D Meadow Park Top Ten Holiday Park,
*39 Meadow St (off Papanui Rd at the
northwestern end of the city), T03-3529176,
meadowpark@xtra.co.nz* It has a great range
of options from self-contained motels,
lodges and flats to chalets, cottages and
standard cabins, powered/tent sites. All are
modern and the facilities are equally so
including a spa pool, sauna and weight
training room. Keep your eyes peeled for
the sign off Papanui Road – it is quite
hard to find.

B-D Amber Park, *308 Blenheim Rd, south of
the city centre , T03-3483327,
www.amberpark.co.nz* Older but tidy, it
offers flats, cabins, powered/tent sites in a
quiet garden setting.

---

❷ Eating

While Christchurch can't quite match
Auckland, Wellington or Queenstown in its
range of fine eateries, it is by no means
wanting and overall you will not be
dissatisfied. Generally you will find a wide
range of options to suit all budgets. Most of
the modern eateries are to be found along
the trendy 'Strip' overlooking the river from
Oxford Terrace. This is a fine place for
lunch and is very convenient for the city
centre. **Colombo St** and **Manchester St**
also offer a wide choice. Note Christchurch
has 3 pretty unique dining options. For the
romantic couple you can arrive at your
restaurant by punt (see page 495). Another
unusual option is the **Tramway
Restaurant**, *T03-3667511*, (see Sights
above), while the **Willowbank Wildlife
Reserve**, *T03-3596226*, (see Sights above),
offers dining in view of the deer, before

joining a complementary guided night tour
to see kiwi.

City centre

Hotel restaurants include:

$$$ Yamagen Japanese and
$$$ Canterbury Tales Restaurants in the
Crowne Plaza; and
$$$ The Piko Piko in *The Millennium* or the
$$$ O.G.B in the *Heritage, all growing in
popularity (see Sleeping above)*.
$$$ Pescatore in the *George, T03-3710257*,
is another award-winning hotel option
offering fine Pacific Rim cuisine in a very
pleasant setting.

$$ Victoria Street Café, in the *Crowne Plaza*,
is a good choice for lunch and fits nicely in
the affordable bracket (open from 0630).

$$ Dorothy's Boutique Hotel, *corner of
Latimer Sq and Hereford St, T03-3656034,
www.dorothys.co.nz Mon-Sat from 1800,
lunches Mon-Fri from 1200*. The cuisine in this
characterful and historic hotel also has a fine
reputation.

$$$ The Alexander Lawrence Restaurant
*Charlotte Jane Hotel, 110 Papanui Rd,
T03-3551028, www.charlotte-jane.co.nz*
Offers the same intimate and congenial
atmosphere with the added attraction of
outdoor seating with open fire.

$$$ Retour Restaurant, *in the rotunda,
corner of Cambridge Terr and Manchester St,
T03-3652888. Open for lunch Wed-Fri
1130-1400 and daily for dinner from 1730
Tue-Sun from Apr-Sep*. Another great
romantic option, it is very different
aesthetically, offering a fine imaginative,
mainly NZ menu and, most importantly
perhaps, can be reached by punt from the
city centre. To book a punt see Avon River or
Hagley Park Sights above. A great lunch
option that can also be reached by punt is
the beautiful.

$$$ Mona Vale Homestead, *63 Fendalton
Rd, T03-3489660*. They have an all-day menu
(which is best to appreciate the
surroundings), from 0930-1530 but are also
open for dinner.

$$$ Bon Bolli, *corner of Worcester and
Montreal St, T03-3749444*. A good French
option, too modern in aesthetics but more
than makes up for it with the cuisine.

Two of the best and most popular options
on the Strip (Oxford Terr) are:

$$ Tap Room Bar and Restaurant *(124), T03-3650547, Open breakfast, lunch and dinner* and

$$ Coyote Street Bar and Restaurant *(126), T03-3666055.* Both offer imaginative dishes from seafood to pasta.

$$ Tiffany's Restaurant, *95 Oxford Terr, T03-3791350.* A great choice for NZ cuisine. Elsewhere, good affordable **Asian** choices include:

$$ Thai Smile, *818 Colombo St, T03-3662246;*

$$ The Sala Sala Japanese Restaurant, *184 Oxford Terr, T03-3666755, Mon-Sun for dinner from 1730 and Mon-Fri for lunch from 1200-1400;*

$$ The Little India Bistro and Tandoori, *corner of Gloucester and New Regent Sts, T03-3777997, Mon-Fri for lunch from 1200 and daily for dinner from 1700* and

$$ Tandoori Palace *56 Cathedral Sq, T03-3657816, www.tandooripalace.co.nz Mon-Fri 1130-1700 for lunch and daily for dinner from 1700.*

$$ Il Felice, *56 Lichfield St, T03-3667535, www.felice.co.nz Mon-Sat from 1800.* Recommended Italian.

$$ Santorini, *corner of Gloucester St and Cambridge Terr, T03-3796975.* A good and very colourful Greek option with live entertainment most nights.

$$ Palazzo del Marinaio, *108 Hereford St, T03-3654640.* Daily for lunch and dinner. For seafood it would be rude not to mention this Italian-style restaurant.

$$ Hay's, *63 Victoria St, T03-3797501. Tue-Sat from 1700 and Mon evenings in summer).* Great NZ Lamb.

$$ Dux de Lux, *41 Hereford St, T03-3666919.* A great vegetarian and seafood selection and a good atmosphere.

$$ Annie's Wine Bar and Restaurant, *T03-3650566. Daily from 1100.* Good for light lunches and has a good wine list.

$$ Strawberry Fare Restaurant, *114 Peterborough St, T03-3654897. Mon-Fri 0700-late, Sat and Sun 0900-late.* Lovers of weight-gain and creative desserts should throw caution to the wind here.

$ The Oxford on Avon, *794 Colombo St, T03-3797148.* Huge, great-value lunches and dinners. It's a bit of a Christchurch institution offering set-price, no-nonsense buffet breakfasts, lunches and dinners, from 0700.

For no-nonsense cheap Asian fare try the various eateries:

$ Passport to Asia, *266 High St* or

$ Thai Tasty, *in the Gloucester Arcade, 129 Gloucester St, T03-3797540. Daily until 2200.* Check out their national anthem playing website on www.geocities.com/thaitasty Another value option are the eateries in the

$ Casino, *Victoria St* (see Entertainment below).

Out of the city

$$$ The Sign of the Takahe, *200 Hackthorne Rd, in the Port Hills (south via Colombo St then straight up Dyers Pass Rd) , T03-3324052, www.signofthetakahe.co.nz* Historic country house and restaurant with award-winning cuisine. The views are better than anything in the city. Bookings essential.

$$ Morworth Estate Vineyard, *Broadfield (7 km southwest via Main South Rd, left on Hampton's Rd, then right on Block Rd), T03-3495014, www.morworth.com Open for lunches from Wed-Sun 1000-1600.* A great restaurant/café providing a pleasant escape from the city.

Cafés

Le Café, *The Arts Centre, T03-3667722. Sun-Thu 0700-2400, Fri and Sat 24hrs.* In the heart of the complex this fine café has extended hours, making it one of the most popular social hang outs in town. It also has great coffee, good value breakfasts and internet.

Boulevard Bakehouse, *below Arts Centre, T03-3772162. Daily 0800-2400.* Also popular, especially at lunchtime.

Curator's House Restaurant and Café, *at the edge of the Botanical Gardens at 7 Rolleston Av, T03-3792252, www.curators.com Daily from 1000-late.* Very pleasant and offers local cuisine with a Spanish touch. The tapas are excellent.

Caffe Roma, *176 Oxford Terr, T03-3793879.* Also very popular, being a big breakfast brunch hangout at the weekend.

Café Metro, *corner of Colombo and Kilmore Sts, T03-3744242.* Another place with a loyal following and a good atmosphere.

Java, *corner of High and Lichfield sts, T03-3660195.* Funky and a popular hang-out with the younger and more alternative crowd.

Mainstreet Café, *corner Colombo and Salisbury St, T03-3650421. Daily from 1000-late.* Generous and imaginative vegetarian dishes.

❶ Pubs, bars and clubs

Pubs and bars
Christchurch's main drinking venue is a conglomerate of modern, well-appointed and lively restaurant/bars on **Oxford Terrace** or **'The Strip'**. It is a good spot to be both in the evening and more especially during the day, when you can sup a bottle or glass of your favourite libation while watching the world (and the river) go by. Currently the most popular place is Montieth's own **Tap Room Bar and Restaurant** *(124), T03-3650547,* that serves the full range of South Island brews and also serves great food. Irish pub fans will be satisfied with the **Bog**, *across the road from the Tap Room at the top of Cashel Mall, T03-3797141,* and the older and more spacious **Bailies**, *Cathedral Sq, T03-3665159.* Other popular pubs include:
Loaded Hog, *corner of Manchester St and Cashel St, T03-3666674*
Dux de Lux, *in the Arts Centre, corner of Hereford and Montreal Sts (especially daytime at weekends), T03-3666919, daily from 1100)*
Jolly Poacher, *Victoria St (opposite the Casino), T03-3795635; and*
The Bard, *corner of Oxford and Gloucester Sts, T03-3771493.* An old English favourite. You will find most stay open to at least 2300 with some on 'The Strip' remaining open at weekends until 0230.

Clubs
For listings of local gigs and visiting acts consult *The Press* newspaper. The website www.bethere.org.nz can also be useful. There are plenty of pubs hosting live music, especially at weekends, and overall there is a lively and modern dance/club scene in the city centre. The best bet, if you can stand all the mobile phones, is to gather with the city slickers in the pre-club pubs along 'The Strip' on Oxford Terr, then just tag along.
In **Lichfield St** you will find a few of the main late-night clubs:
Ministry (88-90), popular and large establishment and

Platinum (76), smaller cellar and gay-friendly. Both are good dance venues.
Illusions, *corner of Chancery Lane and Gloucester St.* The 'Trendyphobic's best bet, still putting on the 60s and 80s disco classics.
The Bog, *82 Cashel Mall.* For a good jig, joke and pint, head for this unfortunately christened Irish pub which has live music in the evenings from Wed-Sat.

❼ Entertainment

For performance and cinema listings consult *The Press* newspaper.

Cinema and theatre
If you missed out on the Maori performances and *hangis* (feasts) in the North Island Christchurch provides one of the few opportunities in the South island (see Nga Hau E Wha Marae, page 497).
The Arts Centre, *Worcester Boulevard*, is home to the **Court Theatre**, *T03-9630870, www.courttheatre.org.nz* the **University Free Theatre**, *T03-3745483* the **Southern Ballet and Dance Theatre**, *T03-3797219* and the **Academy Cinema**, *T03-3660167.* There is a dynamic programme of events year-round listed at the Information Centre, *T03-3632836, www.artscentre.org.nz* The Friday Lunchtime Concert Series featuring local, national and international musicians is held in the Great Hall of the Arts Centre, 1310, $8. www.artists.co.nz/concerts.html is a good source of performance dates and venues.
The Theatre Royal, *145 Gloucester St, T0800-474697, T03-3666326, www.artists.co.nz/trve.html* The other major events venue featuring everything from rock to jazz.
Town Hall, *86 Kilmore St, T03-3778899, www.nccnz.co.nz* Has the in-house James Hay Theatre.
Mainstream cinemas include:
Hoyts 6, *Northlands Mall, T03-3666367;*
Cinema 3 Hornby, *Hornby Mall, T03-3492365*
Regent on Worcester Cinemas, *94 Worcester St T03-3660140*
Hoyts, *392 Moorhouse Ave (Old Train Station), T03-3666367*
Rialto *250 Moorhouse Av, T03-3749404.*

Christchurch Casino, *30 Victoria St,
T03-365999*. A well-established institution
and naturally a popular entertainment
venue. Even if you do not get lured to the
'pokies', roulette and card tables, it can be a
fascinating place to watch the desperate,
cool or ecstatic go by. There are also various
bars and good-value food outlets. Dress
code is smart casual, the age limit is 20 years
and it is open 24 hrs. The free yellow shuttle
stops right outside, *T0800-227466*.

⊛ Festivals and events

For details on events have a look at the
useful websites www.bethere.org.nz and
www.showtimecanterbury.org.nz Noted
annual events include:
Summertimes' programme,
www.summertimes.org.nz that includes
summer theatre and retro events, twilight
concerts and even a teddy bears picnic. The
culminating outdoor Rick Armstrong Motors
Classical Sparks in March is the highlight, with
a classical concert and fireworks in Hagley
Park. **World Busker's Festival** (*15-24 Jan*)
www.worldbuskersfestival.com is a lively
event attracting artists of all shapes, sizes and
acts. The Speight's **Coast to Coast**
www.coasttocoast.co.nz (*6-7 Feb*), is a South
Island icon event that is a gruelling
combination of running, kayaking and cycling
to the West Coast. **Festival of Romance** (*14
Feb*). Dancing and jazz in Victoria Square.
**International Garden City Festival of
Flowers** (*13-22 Feb*)
www.festivalofflowers.co.nz Offers over 30
events from garden tours to floral carpet
displays. This event coincides with the **Jade
Wine and Food Festival** (*over a weekend in
Feb*). This is a celebration of local produce
held in Hagley Park. **Festival of Asia** (*Mar -
date pending*). A day of Asian celebration at
the Arts Centre.
Le Race (*27 Mar*) www.lerace.co.nz The
South Island's largest cycling event.
Kidsfest (*3-16 Jul*) www.kidsfest.org.nz This
is an annual fun festival of events, workshops
and performances for children. **Christchurch
Arts Festival** (*Jul-Aug*)
www.artsfestival.co.nz Includes theatre,
dance, classical and jazz concerts, cabaret
and exhibitions of the visual arts throughout

the city. **Montana Christchurch Winter
Carnival** (*Aug*) www.wintercarnival.org.nz A
10-day celebration of winter-themed events.
Showtime Canterbury
www.showtimecanterbury.co.nz (*31 Oct-16
Nov*). An annual carnival full of activities
including the **A&P Agricultural Show**.
National and international **Rugby** 'Super
Twelve' and 'Tri-Nations' (*Mar-Oct*) and Test
matches at Christchurch's recently upgraded
Jade Stadium in the south of the city.

▲ Activities

There is a huge range of tours operating
out of Christchurch, encompassing
everything from sightseeing, activity
combos, wineries, gardens, walking and
motorcycling. The VIC has brochures and
full listings.
Adventure Canterbury, *T03-3852508,*
www.adventurecanterbury.com One of the
main activity operators in Christchurch. They
offer a wide array of trips and activities
including, **rafting** (Sep-May full-day $165);
helicopter flightseeing (from 15 minutes
$140/ Heli-ski $945); **jet boating** on the
Waimakariri (2 hrs $55-$95); **horse trekking**
(2½ hrs $70); **fishing** (5-6 hrs $650); **farm
visits** (3 hrs $55, with lunch $80); **scenic
city and wine tours** from $35-$95.

Ballooning

Ballooning over the Canterbury Plains is
perhaps Christchurch's iconic activity.
Up Up and Away, *T03-3814600,*
*www.ballooning.co.nz and
Aoraki Balloon Safaris, Methven, T03-3028172,
www.nzballooning.com Both offer early
morning flights of about 1 hr, with champagne
breakfast from $190-$285. Recommended.*

Climbing

YMCA, *12 Hereford St, T03-3660689*. Has a
climbing wall that is open to the public for
casual use, from $8. Equipment hire and
instruction are available at extra cost.

Bone carving

229B Fitzgerald Av, *T03-3797530,*
thebonedude@hotmail.com A self-carving
studio where you can carve your own
Maori-style pendants (*tiki*) from $35.
Excellent value.

Cruising

For wildlife and historic/scenic cruises on the **Lyttleton Harbour** see page 511.

Fishing

There are a number of operators offering half-day to full-day trips or tailor-made options from $250. The VIC has listings.

Jet boating

Jet Thrills River Tours, *T0800-277729, www.jetstreamtours.co.nz*
Jet Stream Tours, *T03-3851478, www.jetstreamtours.co.nz*
Waimak Alpine Jet, *T0800-263626, www.waimakalpinejet.co.nz* All offer a range of jetboating trips to the eastern Southern Alps rivers from $55-$95 with transport inclusive. Jetstream also offer a heli-jetboat option from $195.

Horse trekking

Waimak River Horse Treks, *T0800-873577, mcstay@ihug.co.nz* Offer interesting 30 minutes or 1½ hrs horse trek/jetboat combos or trekking only trips from $35.
Longspur Treks, *based near Lake Ellesmere, T03-3290005*. Offer one to 2-hr treks from $35-$60 including pick-up.

Mountain biking and cycling tours

There are some attractive options around Christchurch, with the Port Hills and Banks Peninsula being the main venues.
Mountain Bike Adventure Company, *T0800-424534, www.cyclehire-tours.co.nz* Offer a good trip that goes up the Port Hills via the Gondola to then descend by bike, from $45, plus various longer tours from 3-5 days and independent hire from $30 per day, $120 per week. Other operators offering more far flung options are:
Mainland Mountainbike, *T03-3298747, www.mountainbiketours.co.nz* and
Adventure South, *T03-3321222, www.advsouth.co.nz*
Christchurch Bike Tours, *T03-3660337*. Offer a more old fashioned cycling experience touring the local parks and historical sites in typical Christchurch English fashion – on a bike with a basket and a bell. Two hrs from $28 (departs 1400 from the VIC). For other independent hire companies see Directory, page 506.

Paragliding

Paragliding is big in Christchurch, with a number of companies vying for the tourist dollar. All are safe and pretty similar in price.
Cloud Nine, *T03-3854739*. Offer tandem flights on a 2-hr trip to the Port Hills area from $125.
Eagle Paragliding, *T03-3777834*. Offer 15-20 minutes flights from a number of local sites from $120.
Nimbus, *T03-3267922, www.nimbusparagliding.cjb.net* Similarly, offer a 2-hr trip and flight daily at 1000 and 1300 for $120 and full day courses for $180.

Punting

For details see River Avon and Hagley Park, page 494.

Rafting

Adventure Canterbury, *T0800-847455*. Full-day rafting trips from $165 (see above).

Tours

TranzAlpine High Country Explorer Tour, *T0800-863975, www.high-country.co.nz* An interesting full-day trip that combines 1 hr transportation by coach across the Canterbury Plains, morning tea, a 15 km jetboat trip, a 65 km 4-wheel drive safari lunch and then a 2¼-hr trip back to Christchurch from Arthur's Pass on the famous TransAlpine from $275.
Lord of the Rings fans or indeed anyone who wants to see some classic Southern Alpine scenery could try a trip to **Mount Sunday** (Potts Station) in the Raingitata Valley with **Tussock and Beach Ecotours**, *T03-3030880, www.nature.net.nz*. Entitled 'In the Hobbits Footsteps' it includes a visit to Mt Sunday, site of Edoras in *The Two Towers*. The ecotour includes 2 nights' accommodation, all meals and a fully guided ecotour through a spectacular glaciated landscape, culminating in Mt Sunday with the opportunity to explore the site of Edoras. A beech forest walk along a mountain stream and a champagne lunch beside a sub-alpine lake is also part of the programme. Accommodation is provided in the historic Ross Cottage, a peaceful, carefully-restored building registered with the New Zealand Historic Places Trust, from $300. Covers 2 nights' accommodation, all meals, whole day guided ecotour in 4WD minivan.

The Christchurch Parachute School,
T03-3435542, www.skydiving.co.nz Operate
out of the Wingram Airfield 15 minutes south
of the city, 2-hr trip 10,000 ft, from $245.

Swimming
Atlantis Pool, *QEII Park, Travis Rd, New
Brighton, T03-9416849, www.qeiipark.co.nz*
Mon-Fri 0600-2100, Sat and Sun 0700-2000. A
new themed attraction that has the largest
wave pool in the country. It is a great place
to take the kids and has spas, sauna, steam
room and café, from $5, child $2.

Walking
In town the **River Avon** and self-guided or
guided **City Walks** (brochures from the
VIC) are recommended, while further afield
the **Port Hills Bridle Path** and **Crater
Rim Walks** provide great views and can be
tackled in part with the Gondola. Again, the
VIC has details, or see page 498. The beaches
of New Brighton and Sumner offer good and
easygoing **beach walks**. DoC has details
and leaflets covering walks throughout the
Banks Peninsula (see 'Information' above).

O Shopping

Souvenirs, arts and rafts
There is a rash of souvenir shops in and
around Cathedral Square selling everything
from furry kiwis in rugby shirts to
sheepskin slippers.
The Arts Centre, *Worcester Boulevard* is an
excellent place to pick up arts and crafts, as is
the weekend market on both Sat and Sun.
Rugby shirts are always a great buy in New
Zealand and Christchurch is home to
Canterbury of New Zealand (CCC),
*Westfield Shopping Town in Riccarton,
T03-3480144*. The best label to buy. You can
find a wide selection here and at
Champions of the World, *outlets at 767
Colombo St, T03-3774100*.
Harringtons Brewery, *199 Ferry Rd,
T03-3666323, www.canterburyfare.co.nz*
For the almost-famous Christchurch
alcoholic lemonade.

Bookshops
Whitcoulls and **Dymocks** *on the Cashel
Street Mall, just south of Cathedral Sq.*

Scorpios, *79 Hereford St, T03-3792882.* An
excellent modern independent store.
Smiths Bookshop, *133 Manchester St,
T03-3797976, www.smiths.bookshop.co.nz*
A good second-hand, multi-storeyed
bookshop.

Outdoor, camping and tramping equipment
Mainland Outdoors, *54 Lichfield St,
T03-3652178*
Mountain Designs, *654 Colombo St,
T03-3778522* and
Snowgum, *637 Colombo St, T03-3654336.*

O Directory

Airlines **Air New Zealand**, *549 Colombo St,
T03-3630600 (after hours T0800-737000).*
Qantas, *T03-3747100 (after hours
T0800-808767).* Mount Cook, *T0800-730000.*
Banks The ANZ, ASB, BNZ, National and
Westpac, all around *Cathedral Sq.* ATMs
abound. Banking hours Mon-Fri 0900-1630.
Bike hire City Cycle Hire, *T0800-343848.*
Offer a wide range of bikes, and deliver.
Trailblazers, *86 Worcester St, T03-3666033.* One
of the cheapest at about $25 per day, though
rates average about $30 half-day, $40 full.
Motorcycles hire Motorcycle Rentals and
Tours, *166 Gloucester St, T03-3770663,
www.nzbike.com* Rental Motorcycles, *28B
Byron St, T03-3723537,
www.motorcycle-hire.co.nz* From $85-$235
per day. **Currency exchange** Most of the
major bank branches offer exchange services.
Interforex, *65 Cathedral Sq, T03-3771233.*
Thomas Cook, *corner of Armagh and Colombo
sts, T03-3662087.* **Travelex**, *730A Colombo St,
T03-3654194, www.travelex.co.nz* Open til
2000.
Car hire You will find all the major national
companies at the airport and in town. Prices
average about $55 per day with unlimited
mileage; $750-$1000 credit bond. **Scotties**,
T0800-736825, also have offices in Auckland
and can offer good hire rates and buy back
sales. Others include: **Apex**, *T0800-105055*;
Hertz, *T0800-654321*; **KiwiCar**, *T0800- 5494227*;
Omega, *T0800-112121*; **Pegasus**,
T0800-803580. For cheaper deals try
Rent-A-Dent, *T0800-736823*; **Cut Price**,
T03-3663800; **Mac's** *T0800154155*; **Trusty**,
T03-3666329 and **Shoestring Rentals**,

T03-3853647. **Motorhome hire** Maui T0800-651080, Backpacker Campervan Rentals, T0800-288699, or Tomlinson Campers, T03-3745254. **Disabled services** Kiwiable, T03-3711774; Disability Information Service, 314 Worcester St, T03-3666189, dis@disinfo.co.nz. Open 0900-1630. **Internet** There are numerous places especially around Cathedral Sq. Vadal Internet Fone Shop, 51-59 Cathedral Sq (bus info corner), T03-3772381. Daily 0800-2230. E-Café, 28 Worcester St, T03-3656480, in the Arts Centre. 0800-2400. Others include: Cyber Café, 1/166 Gloucester St, T03-3655183, Mon-Fri 0900-2100, Sat/Sun 0900-2000. **Post office** (Post Restante) Cathedral Sq, T0800-501501. Mon-Thu 0800-1800, Fri 0800-2000, Sat and Sun 1000-1600. **Library**

Gloucester St .Mon-Fri 1000-2100, Sat 1000-1600, Sun 1300-1600. **Laundry**: 21 Stanmore Rd, T03-3891831. 0800-1730, Sat and Sun 0800-1400. **Luggage Storage** Vadal Internet Force 51-59 Cathedral Sq, T03-3772381. **Maps** Mapworld, corner of Manchester and Gloucester St, T03-3745399, www.mapworld.co.nz **Medical services** Christchurch Hospital, Riccarton Av, T03-3640640; 24 hr surgery corner of Bealey Av and Colombo St, T03-3657777; Dentist T03-3666644 (ext 3002); Urgent pharmacy, 931 Colombo St, T03-3664439. Open til 2300. **Taxi** Blue Star, T03-3531200, T03-3799799 (24 hrs). Gold Band, T03-3795795. First Direct, T03-3775555. **Useful addresses** Police Central Station, corner Hereford and Cambridge Terr, T03-37939999. Emergencies T111. AA 210 Hereford St, T03-3791280.

The Banks Peninsula → Colour map 5, grid C4

Jutting out into the Pacific Ocean from Christchurch, like the bulb on a jigsaw piece, is the Banks Peninsula. Distinctly out of character with the (now) connected and monotonously flat alluvial Canterbury Plains, it is a refreshing and rugged landscape of hills and flooded harbours formed by two violent volcanic eruptions. The two largest harbours, which now fill the craters and shelter their namesake settlements, are Lyttleton to the north and Akaroa to the south. The first inhabitants of the peninsula were members of the Waitaha tribe who came south from the Bay of Plenty, but their claim was not to last. Around 1577 they were violently ousted by the Ngati Mamoe from Poverty Bay, who in turn fell to the onslaught of the Ngati Tahu, another East Coast tribe, in around 1700. For over 100 years peace reigned before yet another violent battle ensued between the Tahu and the invading Toa from Kapiti Island.

The peninsula's two main settlements provide an interesting excursion from Christchurch, with Lyttelton, only 12 km away via the Lyttelton Tunnel, being by far the more accessible. Other than the obvious and refreshing hill and harbour scenery, both places offer some historic sites and activities, including cruising and dolphin watching. The bays and waters that surround the peninsula are home to the world's smallest and rarest dolphin, the Hector's dolphin. The three to four day Banks Peninsula Track from Akaroa is also a popular attraction.

Ins and outs

Getting there If you can afford it, a hire car is the best way to explore the peninsula properly (see Christchurch directory above for listings). By **road** Lyttelton is 11 km from the centre of Christchurch via the tunnel or about 20 km via the windy roads above Sumner. Both Sumner and Lyttelton are well signposted from Ferry Road at the southeastern corner of the city. The scenic Port Hills road is accessed via Colombo St via the Cashmere Hills. Akaroa is 84 km southeast of Christchurch via SH75 which skirts past Lake Ellesmere, before turning inland into the heart of the peninsula. Just past the small settlement of Little River the road climbs, offering great views from the Hilltop Hotel, before falling to the head of Akaroa Harbour and into Akaroa itself. An alternative route is via Lyttelton but it is no shorter. By **bus** Lyttelton is served by the No28 that leaves regularly from Cathedral Sq or the Casino in Christchurch. The **Akaroa Shuttle**, T0800-500929, www.akaroashuttle.co.nz, a day tour shuttle departing from the Christchurch VIC daily Nov-Apr at 0900 and 1030 (also 1600 on Fri), returning from Akaroa at 1535 and 1630 (also 0930 on Fri), from $30, child $17; in winter daily from Christchurch at 1000 (also 1600 on Fri) returning at 1600 (also 0930 on Fri). A direct shuttle departs the VIC at 0830 and 1430, $20, child $15. **Akaroa French Connection**, T03-3664556, T0800-800575, offer a scenic day-tour to Akaroa and other places of interest on the peninsula, departing daily from the the VIC at 0845, 1300 (additional 1645 on Fri) in Christchurch with the last shuttle returning from Akaroa at 1735. Full day tour (departs Christchurch VIC at 0930) from $40, ($20 transport only).

Information **Lyttelton VIC**, ① *20 Oxford St, T03-3289093. Daily 0900-1700.* The staff are full of enthusiasm and can provide all the relevant walks and activity leaflets. Of particular interest is the self-guided historical walks leaflet. They also have full accommodation listings and internet. **Akaroa VIC** (Akaroa District Promotions), ① *80 Rue Lavaud, T03-3048600, www.akaroa.com Daily 1000-1700.* The staff are very helpful and will share with you their local knowledge regarding the village and the peninsula's more out-of-the-way places.

History

Captain Cook was the first European to discover the peninsula, but actually thought it was an island and charted it as such, bestowing on it the name Banks Island after his ship's naturalist Sir Joseph Banks. This confusion remained until 1809 when further surveys by Captain Stewart of the 'Pegasus' proved otherwise. Ironically, the Banks Peninsula was in fact once an island. After the violent eruption that created it, it was eventually connected to the mainland by the advancing alluvial plains that spread east from the Southern Alps.

By 1830 the seas around the South Island were plundered for their whales and seals and the sheltered harbours and bays of the Banks were an ideal base for a number of whaling stations. Permanent settlement began with the arrival of the

Banks Peninsula

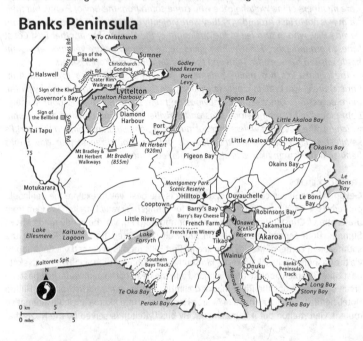

French at Akaroa in 1840 and the British in Lyttleton three years later. In effect it was this pre-emptive settlement strike by the French that spurred the British to initiate the Treaty of Waitangi and effectively place New Zealand under British sovereignty and subsequent rule. Had they not, today, the Sky Tower in Auckland would perhaps be of the Eiffel variety and it would be Bonjour, not G'day.

Lyttelton → *Phone code: 03 Colour map 5, grid C4 Population: 3,000*

Whichever way you arrive in Lyttelton, by the **Port Hills** scenic route via **Sumner,** or through the **road tunnel**, it is quite an exciting delivery and will, along with the deeply contrasting scenery, provide a pleasant sense of escape from the city buzz and the flat vistas of Christchurch. Lying on the northern shores of the volcanic crater that now forms the **Lyttelton Harbour,** this busy characterful port still has an air of history, befitting its stature as the place where the 'first four ships' arrived in 1850. It was also the port that Captain Scott and Lieutenant Shackleton used as their base to explore the Antarctic.

Sights Relics from these times and its fascinating past can be found in the **Lyttelton Museum,** ① *Gladstone Quay, T03-3288972. Tue, Thu, Sat and Sun 1400- 1600. Donation.* Also of historical interest is the **Lyttelton Timeball Station,** ① *high on the hillside off Sumner Rd, T03-3287311, www.historic.org.nz After years of disuse the Station building, which is very grand both inside and out, was fully restored and is now open daily 1000-1700 (winter Sun-Thu). $2.50, child, free.* Built in 1876, it is the only survivor of three such contraptions ever built in New Zealand, and was used as an essential visual timing device to keep mariners accurate in their calculations of longitude. From 1876 to 1934 the large ball that is clearly visible at the top of a mast on the building's turret would drop at precisely 1300 in accordance with Greenwich Mean Time.

   Raipara Island, ① *Trips depart daily at 1330, from $19, child $9.50,* was originally a Maori *pa* before it became home to Fort Jervois, once declared 'the strongest port fortress in the Empire'. It was built originally in 1886 to repel the 'Great Russian Scare'. Jervois later held the notorious First World War prisoner of war, Count Felix Von Luckner, who sunk 14 allied vessels before being captured and imprisoned. In contrast, **Quail Island,** ① *3-4 hr trips depart daily 0930 and 1330 (Sep-Apr); 0930 and 1230 (May-Aug), from $10, child $5,* was a former leper colony but now, devoid of both lepers and introduced predators, it is a safe haven abounding with native birds.
▶▶ *For Sleeping, Eating and other lisings, see pages 510-511.*

Akaroa → *Phone code: 03 Colour map 5, grid C4 Population: 642*

The name Akaroa, which is a variant on the Maori word 'hakaroa'– meaning 'Long Harbour', gives no impression of Akaroa's distinctly French roots. In 1835 French whaler Jean Langlois established a whaling station in the harbour at French Bay and, seeing its potential for settlement and as an ideal shipping port, made a down payment on the land with the local Maori. Once he had secured the deal he returned to France to organize the colonization of the newly-acquired territory. Knowing nothing of the Treaty of Waitangi, which had effectively placed New Zealand under British sovereignty only 13 days before, a group of French settlers set sail on board *L'Aube* on Feb 19th 1840. When the French arrived there was a fractious period of political 'growling, lamppost sniffing and marking' before the French eventually agreed to accept the situation, sell their claims and integrate. Perhaps through their long association and history of dealing with such situations, this integration was thankfully successful and before long Akaroa had become a pleasant and cosmopolitan European community. They brought with them both their rich character and culture which gives Akaroa its modern-day legacy of fine architecture, place names and, still, a wonderful sense of community and friendship.

Sights Akaroa is a very pretty little place with a lovely atmosphere, made even more intriguing by its French street and place names. But perhaps before getting properly acquainted with the place you should take in the superb **view** of the locality from the hill to the south, via Rue Jolie and then Onuku Road (lighthouse road). Given the village's rich history it's worth paying a visit to **Akaroa Museum,** ① *on corner Rue Lavaud and Rue Balguerie, T03-3041013. Daily Nov-Apr 1030-1630, May-Oct 1030-1600, from $3.50, child $1.* A 20-minute film provides a fine introduction backed up with collections focusing on early Maori, whaling, the French connection and the British succession. The **Custom House** at Daly's Wharf that dates from 1852, the old **Court House** and the **Langlois-Eteveneaux House** nearby, are three fine remnants that are an adjunct to the main museum.

The VIC has Heritage Trail details and also offers an excellent **Artisan's Trail** leaflet that covers the wide diversity of artists to be found around the peninsula. Of more convivial and contemporary interest is **Barry's Bay Cheese,** ① *Main Rd, Barry's Bay (at the head of Akaroa Harbour), T03-3045809.* This small family-owned operation makes a fine array of cheeses between October and May, and visitors are welcome to watch the process (alternate days between October-April) and sample the varieties, before purchasing their favourites in the shop. ➤➤ *For Sleeping, Eating and other listings, see pages 510-512.*

● Sleeping

Lyttelton *p509*
There are a few good B&Bs within walking distance of the town centre.
AL Cavendish House, *10 Ross Terr, T03-3289505, gsorell@xtra.co.nz* A well-appointed Edwardian villa with doubles, an ensuite with a spa and nice views.
A Lochranza, *14 Ross Terr, T03-3328518.* Historic (1892) B&B with 2 rooms. Both have comfortable queens, doubles and singles with good harbour views.
C-D Tunnel Vision Backpackers, *44 London Rd, T03-3287576.* Tidy and friendly, has doubles, twins and dorms, and is right in the heart of town.

Akaroa *p509*
There is some attractive and more remote accommodation throughout the peninsula. The VIC has full listings.
L-A Akaroa Village Inn, *opposite the main Wharf on Beach Rd, T03-3047421, www.akaroa.co.nz* French-influenced and the best of the hotel offerings with 40 units, several self-catering luxury apartments and courtyard cottages, most with views over the harbour. Swimming pool and spa and bike hire. They also administer the charming 1856, fully self-contained

Rebecca's Cottage which is a dream for the romantic couple.
There are a few good **motels** including:
AL-A Akaroa Criterion Motel, *75 Rue Jolie, T03-3047775, akaroacriterion@xtra.co.nz* New, spacious luxury studios and rooms close to the village centre.
LL-A Tresori Motel, *corner of Rue Jolie and Church St, T03-3047500, www.tresori.co.nz* New and impressive, also offers spotless well-appointed luxury studios and suites, naturally in a distinctly French-style. Recommended.
A L'Hotel Motel, *75 Beach Rd (wharf end), T03-3047559, hotel-akaroa@xtra.co.nz* Good units overlooking the harbour and a licensed Italian-style restaurant downstairs.

There are plenty of characterful, well-appointed **B&Bs and homestays** in and around Akaroa, with most boasting an historic and/or French flair, and you are advised to see the full listings at the VIC. Of particular historical note are:

AL Linton (Giant's House), *68 Rue Balguerie, T03-3047501, www.linton.co.nz*
AL Blythcliffe, *37 Rue Balguerie, T03-3047003, www.blythcliffe.co.nz*
AL-A Lavaud House, *83 Rue Lavaud, T03-3047121, lavaudhouse@xtra.co.nz*

● *For an explanation of the sleeping and eating price codes used in this guide, see the inside* ● *front cover. Other relevant information is provided in the Essentials chapter, see page 51.*

L Maison des Fleurs, *6 Church St,
T03-3047804, maison.des.fleurs@xtra.co.nz* A
stark contrast to all the above. Distinctly
cute, purpose-built and self-contained.
L-AL Oinako Lodge, *99 Beach Rd,
T03-3048787, www.oinako.co.nz* Modern
and purpose built but recommended.
AL Mill Cottage, *Rue Grehan, T03-3048007.*
Another good upper-range option.

C-D Bon Accord Backpackers, *57 Rue
Lavaud, T03-3047782,
bon-accord@xtra.co.nz* Under new
ownership and has tidy dorms, cosy,
good-value doubles. Peaceful and well
placed. Be sure to ask about the interesting
history of the house.
C-D Chez-la-Mer Backpackers, *Rue Lavaud,
T03-3047024, chez_la_mer@clear.net.nz*
Equally well placed and a nice historic
house with a secluded garden. It also offers
dorms, doubles, twins and singles.

Motorcamps and campsites
B-D Akaroa Top Ten Holiday Park, *off
Morgan Rd at the entrance to the village,
T03-3047471.* It is the best-equipped
motorcamp and offers flats, tourist/standard
cabins, powered/tent sites and nice views
across the harbour.

⦿ Eating

Lyttelton *p509*
There are plenty of places to eat in Lyttelton,
with most establishments on Norwich Quay
or London Road. The brightly coloured
$$ Volcano Café and Lava Bar, *corner of
London and Canterbury, T03-3287077,* good
traditional blackboard menu and good coffee.
$ Rat and Roach, *across the road,
T03-3287517. Lunch 1200-1400, dinner
1700-2030.* New establishment offering
cheap pub food.

There is no shortage of drinking
establishments, it is a port after all.
Lava Bar *(see above)* is very popular.
Irish Pub *(also on London Road)* is good with
a deck overlooking the port.
Old Post Restaurant, *on Norwich Quay,
T03-3287574.* Offers a traditional/Kiwi menu
and is recommended. Wed-Thu for dinner
and all day Fri-Sun from 1100.

Again, given the French influence, Akaroa
offers some fine restaurants and cafés, but
bear in mind that many are subject to
seasonal hours.
$$$ C'est La Vie, *33 Rue Lavaud,
T03-3047314. Daily for lunch and dinner;
dinner only in winter.* Arguably the top
restaurant in Akaroa, offering great meals
(especially seafood) by candlelight.
Other more traditional options are the
nautical surroundings and seafood.
$$ The Dolphin Café and Bar, *6 Rue
Balguerie, T03-3047658* and
$$ Harbour 71, *71 Beach Rd, T03-3047656.
Both licensed and open for lunch and dinner.*
$$ Jolly Rodger Restaurant *in the
Grand Hotel, 6 Rue Lavaud, T03-3047011. Daily
for breakfast and dinner.* A more affordable
no-nonsense dinner.
$ Turenne Coffee Shop, *corner of Rue
Balguerie and Rue Lavaud, T03-3047005. Daily
0700-1800.* Seems to be the most popular
daytime café and has good coffee, light
snacks and internet.
$ Café Eiffel, *37 Rue Lavaud, T03-3047717.*
Good breakfast.
Akaroa Bakery, *51 Beach Rd. Daily
0730-1600.* For great fresh bread.
Grand Hotel, *see above.* Has the most
happening bar in town.

▲ Activities and tours

Lyttelton *p509*
Cruises Several cruises leave from the port
from vessels both old and new.
Tug Lyttelton Preservation Society,
T03-3228911, www.nzmaritime.co.nz/tug.htm
The 1907 Steam Tug Lyttelton, lovingly
restored, has been taking passengers for
historical cruises for 28 years. Operate a
1½-hr Sunday afternoon cruise from No 2
Wharf, departing at 1430, from $12.
Sep-Jun. **Black Cat Group**, *T0800-436574,
www.blackcat.co.nz* Interesting array of
catamaran harbour trips under the banners
of 'Wildlife' and 'Island Adventure' Cruises.
The 2-hr Wildlife Cruise takes in both sides
of the harbour and out just beyond its
entrance, passes some interesting sites on
the way, including an old whaling station, a
shipwreck and the Godley Head
Lighthouse. There is usually much in the

way of wildlife to see with the highlight being the tiny and rare Hector's dolphin. Departures are from 17 Norwich Quay, Lyttelton, at 1000 (Dec-Feb); 1330 (May-Aug); 1430 (Sep-Apr), from $45, child $15. Note that there is a free shuttle that departs from the Christchurch VIC 35 minutes before departure. 'Island Adventures Cruise' takes in either Quail or Raipara Islands.

Walking As well as the historical walks around town and those up to the Christchurch (Port Hills) Gondola, the **Crater Rim Walkway** (19 km, 4 hrs) provides a longer and spectacular walk with memorable views across the Banks Peninsula and the Canterbury Plains to the Southern Alps. Again the VIC can provide directions and all the relevant leaflets.

Akaroa *p509*
Harbour/wildlife cruises All of which depart from the Main Wharf.
Akaroa Harbour Cruises, *T0800-436574 / T03-3047641, www.canterburycat.co.nz* Offer a 2-hr scenic/wildlife cruise at 1100 and 1330. Although the undoubted highlight is the probable sighting of Hector's dolphin, you can also see little blue penguin, spotted shags and fur seals. The cruise costs from $39, child $15. The same company also offer a 'Swimming with Dolphins' experience, *www.swimmingwithdolphins.co.nz* a 3-hr excursion to encounter the rare Hector's Dolphin, from $80, child $50 (watching only $45/$30). Trips depart the main wharf at 0600, 0830, 1130 and 1330.
Dolphin Experience, *61 Beach Rd, T03-3047726, dolphins.akaroa@xtra.co.nz* Offer 3-hr dolphin swimming and watching trips from $90, child $55 (viewing only $35). Trips depart Nov-Apr 0600, 0900 and 1200; May-Oct 0900 and 1200. Also on offer is a 2-hr, purely scenic/historic cruise to the harbour entrance, departing Nov-Apr 0830, 1130 and 1430; May-Oct 1100 and 1400.
Dolphins Up Close, *Main Wharf, T03-3047641*. Offer similar trips.
Bluefin Charters, *T03-3047866*. Offer independent boat charter.
Akaroa Seal Colony Safari, *T03-3047255, www.sealsafari.com* An interesting 2½ hr road trip via the rim of the crater to a fur seal

colony on the eastern bays, from $50, child $30. Trips go from the VIC at 0930 and 1300.
Shireen Helps, *T03-3048552, akaroapenguins@paradise.net.nz* Offers two tours, one a full day-tour of various historical and scenic sites with a sea kayaking and snorkelling option, from $50, child $25, or a 3-hr specialist tour of the DoC **Little Blue Penguin Reserve**, from $35, child $20.
Horse trekking Mount Vernon Stables, *T03-3047180*. 3-4 hrs, from $85.
Quad bike and 4-wheel drive Akaroa 4 Wheel Bike Safaris, *T03-3047603*. 2 hrs from $85.
Kayaking Akaroa Boat Hire, *Foreshore, Beach Rd, T03-3048758*. Kayak hire, half-day from $25.
Walking The 3-4 day, 35 km **Banks Peninsula Track**, *T03-3047612, www.bankstrack.co.nz*, is a popular tramp across private farmland, the hills and outer bays, and is recommended. It is very much an off-the-beaten-track experience, with great huts provided for accommodation. The track is open from Oct-May and costs from $180 for the 4-day trip and $120 for the 2-day. Cost includes an introductory talk, booklet, transport to the first hut and accommodation. You must take your own food. For other day-walk options on the Banks contact DoC or the VIC in Christchurch.
Bayline Services, *108 Rue Jolie, T03-3047207*. Scenic mail run departs from the VIC at 0815 Mon-Sat returning at lunchtime, from $25.

❶ Directory

Akaroa *p509*
Banks The very attractive BNZ Bank is across the road from the VIC and it has an ATM. Mon-Fri 0900-1630. **Bike hire** Akaroa Village Inn, *81 Beach Rd (opposite the Main Wharf), T03-3047421*, Chez La Mer Backpackers and Le Bons Bay Motor Camp (see above). **Internet** Akaroa Library, *141 Rue Jolie, T03-3048782. Mon-Fri 1030-1600, Sat 1030-1300*. Turenne Coffee Shop, *corner Rue Balguerie and Rue Lavaud, T03-3047005*. Café Eiffel, *37 Rue Lavaud, T03-3047717*.
Useful numbers Police, *T03-3041030*. Doctor, *T03-3047004*.

North of Christchurch

From Christchurch SH1 heads north through the unremarkable settlement of Amberley before reaching the junction with SH7 and the Waipara Valley. From here SH7 heads northeast, through the Hurunui District to Hanmer Springs and the West Coast via the Lewis Pass, while SH1 heads north to Kaikoura and eventually Blenheim. Another road, SH70, leaves SH7 just north of Culverden, offering a scenic short cut from Hanmer Springs to Kaikoura. These routes are known collectively as the (signposted) Alpine Pacific Triangle, which is designed to combine the lesser attraction of the Waipara Valley vineyards with its two star destinations, Hanmer Springs and Kaikoura. Although many people visit Kaikoura (which actually lies in Marlborough, not Canterbury) on their way to Christchurch from the north, this 'triangle' offers an attractive multi-day trip from Christchurch. There is much to see and do in both Hanmer Springs and Kaikoura, but they are very different. In landlocked Hanmer the wealth of activities includes skiing, rafting, horse trekking and, perhaps its speciality, mountain biking. All these activities of course are added to the more obvious and soporific attraction of its hot pools in the thermal resort. Kaikoura, in contrast, set on the spectacular northeast coastline and almost miniaturized in the shadow of the Kaikoura mountain ranges, is equally abuzz with activity. But here the emphasis is most definitely in the colder waters of the ocean and its inhabitants. At Kaikoura you can see and even swim with an impressive list of the oceans 'Who's Who', including albatrosses, seals, sharks (yes, sharks!), dolphins and of course Kaikoura's very own whales.

Ins and outs

Getting there and around Hanmer Springs is 136 km north of Christchurch and 214 km east of Greymouth. By **bus**, Hanmer is served by **Lazerline**, T03-3157128 (Christchurch/Nelson daily); **East West**, T0800-142622 (Christchurch/Wesport, via the Lewis Pass, and return daily), and **Hanmer Connections**, T03-3157575 (Hanmer to Kaikoura Thu, Tue, Sat and Hanmer to Greymouth daily) all serve the town.

Kaikoura is 187 km north of Christchurch, 129 km south of Blenheim (154 km Picton) on SH1, and 133 km northwest of Hanmer Springs via SH70. By **bus** Kaikoura is served from Christchurch/Blenheim/Picton by **Intercity**, 123 Worcester St, T03-3195641 (twice daily, book at the VIC); **Atomic Shuttles**, T03-3195641 (daily); **East Coast Express**, T050-8830900; and **South Island Connections**, T03-3666633. The fare to Christchurch or Blenheim costs from $15. **Hanmer Connections**, T0800-377378, go to Hanmer Springs Tue, Thu and Sat at 1400 from $30; and **South Island Connections** operate Mon-Fri. Both drop-off in the centre of the village.

Springs Junction is 95 km west of Hanmer Springs via SH7. There is a service station at Springs Junction with 24 hr EFTPOS. By **train** Kaikoura is served by the **TransCoastal**, T0800-872467, daily (Christchurch 1605, from $20; Blenheim/Picton 1025, from $19). The train station is on Clarence St. For a **taxi** call T03-3196214. The VIC caters for all transport bookings and enquiries.

Kaikoura Shuttle operate shuttles on demand to all the principal sights and also offer one or two hour tours of the region, T0800-766962. There are scheduled or on-demand shuttles to both the Hanmer and Lyford Ski fields, from $19-$29. For details contact the VIC.

Information **Hanmer Springs VIC**, ① *just in front of the Thermal Reserve off Amuri Av in the centre of the village*, T03-3157128, www.hurunui.com *Daily 1000-1700*. The VIC holds DoC walks information. **Kaikoura VIC**, ① *in the West End*, T03-3195641, www.kaikoura.co.nz *Daily 0800-1800 (Jun-Aug 0900-1700)*. Wil provide information and arrange bookings for accommodation and onward transportation. There is also a

20-min precursory audio visual about the local environment and wildlife shown every hour or on demand, $3, child $1. All **DoC** information is also held at the VIC.

Hanmer Springs → *Phone code: 03 Colour map 5, grid B4 Population: 576*

Hanmer has long been popular with Kiwi holiday-seekers, and has only recently come into its own as a top national tourist venue. Its biggest attraction is of course its **Thermal Reserve**, but it is also very popular as a base for mountain biking and walking in the **Hanmer Forest Park** nearby and, in winter, as a base for the **Hanmer and Mt Lyford Ski Fields**. After these two activities, and when winter snows lie on the ground or spring rain plays on the puddles, the hot pools are the perfect place to be. Hanmer offers a wide range of modern accommodation options, some good restaurants and numerous other activities from bungee jumping to horse trekking. The town is particularly beautiful in autumn when the forest and tree-lined streets are flush with golden hues and falling leaves. The name Hanmer derives from the name of Canterbury pioneer Thomas Hanmer, often misspelt.

Sights
The Hanmer Springs Thermal Reserve ⓘ *Amuri Av, T03-3157511. Daily 1000-2100. From $10, child $5 (day pass $13, child $6.50).* Although it may be the last thing on your agenda after activities, the Hanmer Springs Thermal Reserve is undoubtedly the top attraction. The springs were first discovered by the Europeans in 1859 and later became a commercial venture and public attraction in 1807 when the first facilities and a hotel formed the beginnings of the resort and subsequently the town as a whole. The resort is an oasis of various pools ranging from the open and landscaped to the freshwater, swimming and a children's play pool variety, all connected by steaming boulder streams. The mineral-rich waters range in temperature from a lukewarm 32°C to a balmy 42°C. Other facilities include a massage clinic, private hot pools, saunas, a steam room, a licensed café and a picnic area.▶▶ *For Sleeping, Eating and other listings, see pages 517-525.*

Hanmer Springs to the West Coast
From Hanmer Springs SH7 crosses the northern ranges of the Great Divide (Southern Alps) to the West Coast via the **Lewis Pass**, **Maruia Springs**, **Springs Junction** and **Reefton**. Although not as dramatic as Arthur's Pass further to the south, it offers some lovely scenery and a few good walking opportunities on the way. It also boasts a mountain with one of the most unusual names in the country. There are many with wonderful names, but frankly **Mons Sex Millia** has to take the prize.

At the top of the Hope River Valley from Hanmer, the road skirts the borders of the *Lake Sumner Forest Park* and begins to follow the Lewis River to its headwaters and the saddle known as Lewis Pass (864 m). In pre-European times the Ngai Tahu Maori of Canterbury used this route to access the West Coast in search of greenstone (*pounamu*). Having negotiated the pass on their return, they are said to have dispensed with their slaves – alas not with a 'thanks lads, see you next year', but a brutal death followed by a feast of their various bodily parts. A valley known as **Cannibal Gorge** remains testament to this rather grim form of the early 'transport café'.

The pass itself was named in 1860 after pioneer surveyor Henry Lewis. Ironically, Henry's daughter Eleanor married Arthur Dudley Dobson who surveyed 'Arthur's' Pass. But it doesn't end there. Arthur's sister then married the geologist and surveyor Julian Von Haast who is accredited with much of the exploration, survey work and many place names on the West Coast.

Lake Sumner Forest Park and the Lewis Pass offer some excellent **walks** from one hour to several days, and these are best outlined in various DoC leaflets, including the

Lewis Pass Region broadsheet, which is available from the Hanmer VIC. The lichen-covered beech forests are particularly superb in this region and well worth further investigation.

The five-day **St James Walkway** that begins near the Lewis Pass summit car park (and infamous Cannibal Gorge) is particularly good. There is a network of DoC huts, and the moderate track is best negotiated in summer or autumn. Just beyond the Lewis Pass, heading west, is the oasis of **Maruia Springs**, a small **thermal resort** with hot pools, comfortable accommodation, a restaurant and a bar. It is a perfect stop for tired trampers. A further 21 km west is **Springs Junction**, the only significant settlement between Hanmer and Reefton, with accommodation, a café, and also a petrol station. ► *For Sleeping see page 519.*

Kaikoura → *Phone code: 03 Colour map 5, grid B5 Population: 4,000*

So you want to see Moby Dick and friends? Well, you have certainly come to the right spot. Kaikoura is a place that is not only aesthetically stunning but one that has some of the best sea creatures in the world. They are all here: Moby, Flipper, Keiko, Jaws, the lot – you might even bump into Marine Boy having a beer in the local boozer or a mermaid on the bus. Okay, not quite. But for the wildlife enthusiast the Kaikoura coast is second only to the Otago Peninsula for richness and accessibility to some of New Zealand's biggest and most famous wildlife icons. The reason there is so much diversity matched with ease in accessibility is due to the topography and depth of the ocean floor. Just to the south of Kaikoura a trough comes unusually close to the coastline creating an upsurge of nutritious plankton soup, giving rise to the many creatures with which we are more familiar further up the food chain. At the very top of course, on the ocean throne, is the majestic and much victimized king of them all – the whale.

But even if you came to Kaikoura thinking that whales was a small and fine rugby-playing nation somewhere in Britain, or indeed that seals clap and throw beach balls to each other, you cannot fail to be impressed. From the azure waters that surround the beautiful Kaikoura Peninsula, backed by the snow-capped peaks of the Kaikoura Ranges, you can get up close and personal with them all, from whales and dolphins to seals, albatrosses and even sharks. So the place is very special and even before you arrive there is that sense of excitement.

History

Although the peninsula was known to be heavily settled by Maori before the Europeans arrived, modern day Kaikoura was, ironically, first established as a whaling station in the early part of the 1800s. Its most noted pioneer was **George Fyffe**, who succeeded his uncle as the station manager. George built Kaikoura's oldest remaining house (**Fyffe House**) in 1860, near the Old Wharf. The Fyffe name was also bestowed upon the mountain immediately behind the township. After whaling it was mainly fishing, particularly for crayfish, that took over. Today of course Kaikoura is synonymous with wildlife, thankfully now hunted only by the camera not harpoon, and it is the resident and migratory whales that remain the focus.

Sights

Of course most of what you have probably come to see lies beneath the waves and has flippers, but Kaikoura offers a number of land-based features worthy of investigation. Paramount is the **Kaikoura Peninsula** that juts out into the ocean like a well-weathered head. The cliff-top and shoreline **Peninsula Walkways** that link the northern and southern settlements of Kaikoura cross the head of the peninsula and offer superb coastal aesthetics (see below). A good spot to get an overall impression of the town, the peninsula and its mountain backdrop is from the **lookout** just off

Modern-day Whaling in Kaikoura

The whale-watching experience is a wonderful mix of expectation, unpredictability and awe. In Kaikoura the reason whales are so accessible has already been discussed (see Kaikoura introduction), but few are aware that Kaikoura is actually home to its own pod of sperm whales – the species you are most likely to see. Although it is a complex social set up and much is still not known, it is probably one or two of the young males from these resident bachelor pods that you will see. Of course this does not mean you are going to see a gang of prepubescent nippers – they are still enormous and are often joined by larger, visiting adults. A bull male can weigh as much as 50 tonnes and be up to 20 m in length. Other whale species that are seen regularly include **Humpbacks, Rights** and **Orcas**. If you are exceptionally lucky you may also see the endangered and truly industrial-size **Blue Whale**.

Your boat trip to 'hunt down' and 'encounter' the whales is a fascinating and well-orchestrated performance of hydrophonics and simple 'eye-spy'. But before all the action takes place you are invited to watch a new and very clever state of the art computer graphic that shows the incredible depths of the Kaikoura Trench and explains why the whales are so drawn to it. Once out in the bay proper, a combination of local knowledge and hydrophonics is used to locate the whales either on the surface, or on their way. It is tremendously exciting and timing is all-important. They are known to dive for certain lengths of time and once

surfaced remain there to catch their breath for around three minutes. This is your big and brief chance. With such unpredictability and in such a frenzy of expectation people watching can be as much fun as watching the whales. When the great leviathan is spotted and the word is given, almost everybody jumps from their seat and clambers to get that illusive National Geographic shot from the decks. On rough days this can be quite riotous, with copious and unintentional bouts of head-butting and hair-pulling. Only a few poor souls are left strapped to their seat, their vision of a whale long lost at the bottom of a sick-bag. Believe it or not some folk even fall asleep. It can be very amusing but for goodness sake don't let that deter you. On calm days it is much more orderly and you will also get a better view of the whale's vast bulk. Whales are a bit like icebergs; for all you can see above the surface, there is an awful lot more beneath. However, regardless of conditions, what you are guaranteed to see is the point when the whales dive, flipping their tail in the air and descending gracefully like a hot knife through butter, back into the depths. It is this vision that is so engrained in our imagination. Of course there is no guarantee you will see a whale at all and you do receive a refund if the trip is unsuccessful. But mainly you can expect to see one to three on the two hours you are out in the bay. You will also be taken to encounter dolphins, which are equally as spectacular especially in pods that can number into the hundreds at one time.

Scarborough Terrace (off SH1 between the northern and southern settlements).
There are three historical venues of note: The **Kaikoura District Museum,** ① *14 Ludstone Rd, T03-3197440, Mon-Fri 1230-1630, Sat-Sun 1400-1600, $3, child 50c,* was established in 1971 and offers an interesting insight into the early Maori and

whaling activities. If the weather closes in and you cannot get out onto the water it can provide a good activity option and help pass the time.

Fyffe House (see above) ① *62 Avoca Street, near the Old Wharf, T03-3195835. Guided tours (30 minutes) are available daily between 1000-1600, $5.* The **'Maori Leap Cave'**, ① *2 km south of Kaikoura, T03-3195023, from $8.50, child $3.50,* was only discovered this century and is a sea-formed limestone cave featuring all the usual karst scenery. It can be visited on a 40-minute guided tour. While in the area of the cave you might like to visit the **Kaikoura Winery,** ① *just south of the town,* T03-3197966, www.kaikourawines.co.nz There are hourly tours daily (from $7.50), underground cellars and tastings ($15 with transport from the VIC).

⬤ Sleeping

Hanmer Springs *p514*

There is plenty of choice in Hanmer to suit all budgets, with most of the options being modern, well-appointed and within walking distance of the town centre. You are advised to book ahead in mid-summer and at weekends in the winter ski-season.

LL-AL Heritage Hotel and Resort, *45 Conical Hill Rd, T03-3157021, www.heritagehotels.co.nz* New and ideally located overlooking the town centre. Has 64 rooms ranging from the honeymoon suite to the standard. It has all the usual facilities including a good restaurant, bar and a swimming pool. The hot pools are only 2 minutes away.

LL Braemar Lodge, *T03-3157049, www.braemarlodge.co.nz* A fine modern luxury lodge on a hillside 9 km from the town. It has beautifully appointed rooms, spa and excellent cuisine.

AL Cheltenham House B&B, *13 Cheltenham St, T03-3157545, www.cheltenham.co.nz* Well-located and offers good value rooms with ensuite bath.

A Hanmer View B&B, *8 Oregon Heights (very end of Conical Hill Rd), T03-3157947, lawsurv@xtra.co.nz* For a great view cannot be beaten and the modern facilities and rooms are good value.

A Glenalvon Lodge and B&B, *29 Amuri Av, T03-3157475, glenalvon@xtra.co.nz* A cheaper and friendly option. It has nice rooms with private bath. Self-contained modern units are also available.

The **motels** in Hanmer are generally excellent.

A Alpine Lodge, *1 Harrogate St, T03-3157311, www.alpinelodgemotel.co.nz* Modern

lodge-style and well-placed.

A Scenic Views, *10 Amuri Av, T03-3157419, scenicviews@xtra.co.nz* Just at the entrance to the town and offers peace and quiet and, as it suggests, mountain views.

A Hanmer Inn Motel, *16 Jack's Pass Rd, T03-3157516, motel@hanmer.com* Right in the heart of the town and a stone's throw from the thermal reserve.

AL-A Greenacres Chalets and Apartments, *84 Conical Hill Rd, T03-3157125, www.greenacresmotel.co.nz* Another modern option offering self-contained chalets and apartments overlooking the town, and has a spa.

A-B Willowbank Motel, *121 Argelins Rd, T03-3157211.* The cheapest motel option in town.

C-D Hanmer Backpackers, *41 Conical Hill Rd, T03-3157196.* The most well-established backpackers, just north of the town centre. Freindly place offering dorms and 2 good-value doubles.

B-D La Gite Backpackers, *3 Devon St, to the west off Jacks Pass Rd, T03-3155111, le_gite@hotmail.com* Described as a boutique backpackers (the name means 'The Resting Place' in French) it is indeed cosy with tidy doubles and dorms, polished wood floors, TV lounge with log burner, internet and off-street parking.

B-D Kakapo Lodge YHA, *14 Amuri Av, just as you come in to the village on the left, T03-3157472.* New and spacious, another fine hostel but lacks the same atmosphere. It offers the full range of rooms including motel-style ensuites and has good kitchen facilities, internet and off-street parking.

Motorcamps and campsites

B-D Mountain View Top Ten, *at the entrance to the town, T03-3157113.*
B-D AA Tourist Park, *200 Jacks Pass Rd, south*

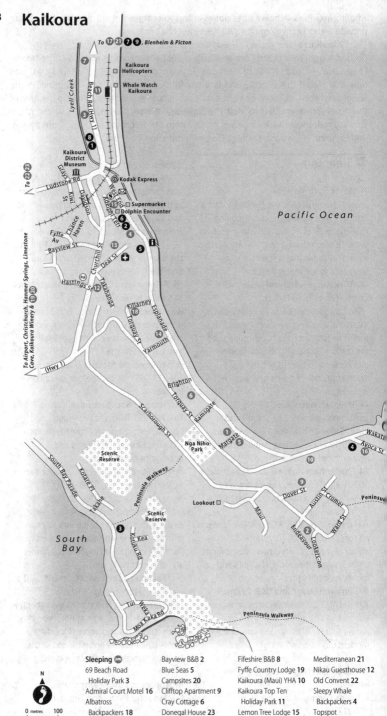

Sleeping 🛏

69 Beach Road	Bayview B&B **2**	Fifeshire B&B **8**	Mediterranean **21**
Holiday Park **3**	Blue Seas **5**	Fyffe Country Lodge **19**	Nikau Guesthouse **12**
Admiral Court Motel **16**	Campsites **20**	Kaikoura (Maui) YHA **10**	Old Convent **22**
Albatross	Clifftop Apartment **9**	Kaikoura Top Ten	Sleepy Whale
Backpackers **18**	Cray Cottage **6**	Holiday Park **11**	Backpackers **4**
Anchor Inn **1**	Donegal House **23**	Lemon Tree Lodge **15**	Topspot
	Dusky Lodge **7**	Lyell Creek Lodge **17**	Backpackers **13**

flats, cabins, powered/tent sites and clean
modern facilities.

Hanmer Springs to the West Coast
p514

A-D Maruia Springs Thermal Resort,
T03-5238840, www.maruia.co.nz Has lovely
luxury/standard studio and family units and
dorm accommodation for backpackers. The
tariff includes unlimited access to the
thermal pools. Two licensed restaurants, one
traditional/Kiwi, the other Japanese. Public
access to the hot pools daily 0900-2100,
from $10, child $5. Private pools available
1100-1700, from $30 per hr.

A Lewis Pass Motels, *SH7, around 12 km
west of the hot pools, T03-5238863,
www.lewis-pass.co.nz* Offers 3 modern
self-contained units in a pleasant
country setting.

B-C Alpine Inn, *in Springs Junction,
T03-5238813, sj.alp.inn@xtra.co.nz* Offering
studio units and separate budget chalet for
backpackers. Attached is a café and shop
selling light snacks. Internet. Daily
0800- 1930.

Kaikoura *p515*

There is plenty of choice in Kaikoura, with
motels the dominant force, but there are
also plenty of fine B&Bs. Local farmstays are
another option often overlooked. You are
still advised to book in advance in mid-
summer. The VIC has full listings.

A Fyffe Country Lodge, *SH1 (south),
T03-3196869, www.fyffecountrylodge.com* A
lovely homestead made of mud-block and
wood, with pleasant gardens and great
views. All rooms have private bathrooms
and there is a characterful restaurant
attached serving fine cuisine.

L-AL Old Convent, *Mt Fyffe Rd, T03-3196603,
www.theoldconvent.co.nz* In a quiet setting
and again full of character, friendly and has a
good range of well-appointed rooms.
A 3-course French dinner costs $50,
crayfish $60.

A Donegal House, *Fyffe Rd, T03-3195083*. It
is run very much with an Irish influence and
has good ensuite rooms, but what makes
the place are the grounds and the Irish
bar/restaurant that is attached.

A Fifeshire B&B (The Point Farm), *out*

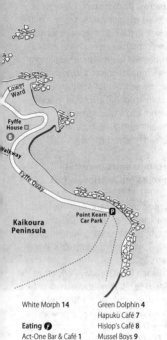

White Morph **14**

Eating 🍴
Act-One Bar & Café **1**
Craypot Café & Bar **2**
Finz Seafood &
Wine Bar **3**

Green Dolphin **4**
Hapuku Café **7**
Hislop's Café **8**
Mussel Boys **9**
Rocks Bar & Café **5**
Why Not Café **6**

towards the peninsula and its walkway, T03-3195059. It has a tidy double, twin and single and is very peaceful.

Not surprisingly there is a scattering of fine **B&Bs** and self-contained **apartments** on the peninsula itself all offering spectacular views.

AL Clifftop Apartment *5 Dover Terr, T03-3196649*. A modern, spacious timber home with a magnificent outlook that offers value twin and doubles.

L-A Lemon Tree Lodge *31 Adelphi Terr, T03-3197464, www.lemontree.co.nz* A boutique B&B that caters especially for couples or single independent travellers. Renovated 2-storey house with 4 tidy rooms, all with private deck or balcony and nice attention to detail. Outdoor hot tub. Experienced, caring and well-travelled owners.

Elsewhere, cheaper options include:
A Nikau Guesthouse, *53 Deal St, T03-3196973*. With 2 rooms with private bathroom and standard doubles. Good views across town (closed May-Sep).
B Bayview B&B, *296 Scarborough St, T03-3195480*. Both are comfortable, friendly, good value and have great views.

There are almost 20 **motels** to choose from, with most being along the Esplanade or heading north out of town on Beach St, SH1.
L-AL White Morph, *92-94 Esplanade, T03-3195014, www.whitemorph.co.nz*
AL-A Anchor Inn, *208 Esplanade, T03-3195426, www.anchor-inn.co.nz*
A Blue Seas, *222 Esplanade, T03-3195441, blue.seas@xtra.co.nz* All are recommended.
A Admiral Court Motel, *16 Avoca St, near the wharf, T03-3195525, www.kaikouramotel.co.nz* A good choice, a short walk from the start of the coastal track.
A Mediterranean, *239 Beach Rd at the northern end of town, T03-3196776, medmotel@xtra.co.nz* Another good choice.

There is no shortage of **backpacker** beds in the town.
C-D Kaikoura (Maui) YHA, *270 Esplanade, T03-3195931*. The best sea and mountain views, it has dorms, twins and doubles and a good atmosphere, and is worth the 10-min

walk from the West End.
C-D Cray Cottage, *190 Esplanade, T03-3195152*. Has good facilities, dorm and twins.
C-D Topspot Backpackers, *22 Deal St, T03-3195540, topspot@xtra.co.nz* Worth the walk is the very tidy. They have dorm and doubles and do their own value $50 seal swimming trips.
B Lyell Creek Lodge, *at the northern end of town*. A great place for couples looking for value and peace. It has 5 modern, tidy rooms, a twin and double with ensuite and 3 rooms with shared bathroom. All have TV and there is a cosy lounge.
C-D Dusky Lodge, *67 Beach Rd, T03-3195959*. Recently expanded, it is modern, spacious and friendly with dorms, twins and good value ensuite doubles with TV, internet, spa, and free bike hire. All within 3 mins to the West End and more social.
C-D Sleepy Whale Backpackers, *86 West End, T03-3197014*. Right in the heart of the West End, aesthetically unremarkable, but it is handy for all amenities and has a deck overlooking the action.
C-D Albatross Backpackers, *1 Torquay St, T03-3196090, albatrossnz@xtra.co.nz* A little further west in the old telephone exchange on a quiet suburban street. Owner Rod has shown attention to detail here providing a warm welcome for guests, a wide range of spotless, themed rooms (including a self-contained option) and good general facilities, not to mention some cool music that complements a laid-back atmosphere. Internet and off-street parking.

Motorcamps and campsites
B-D Kaikoura Top Ten Holiday Park, *34 Beach Rd, T03-3195362, www.kaikouraholidaypark.co.nz* The best motorpark and offers modern facilities, motel units, ensuite units, powered/tent sites only 3 mins from the town centre and the beach.
C-D 69 Beach Road Holiday Park, *across the road, T03-3196275*. If the above is full, or for a quieter option, try this very friendly place. There are also a number of very pleasant beachside **D** campsites on the coastal roads south of Kaikoura, T03-3195348.

🍴 Eating

Hanmer Springs p514

$$$ Heritage Hotel, *see above, T03-3157021. Breakfast 0730, lunch 1200-1430 and dinner from 1800.* The fine dining option.

$$ Old Post Office Restaurant, *near the Thermal Resort at 2 Jack's Pass Rd, T03-3157461. Daily from 1800.* Slightly cheaper and with more character, it specializes in NZ cuisine.

$$ Alpine Village Inn, *Jack's Pass Rd, T03-3157005. Daily from 1200-1400 and 1730-2030.* The local pub does hearty, good-value pub food.

$$ PT's, *in the Mall, T03-3157685. Daily 1000-2200.* Good gourmet pizzas.

There is a scattering of cafés along Amuri Ave, Conical Hill Rd and in the Mall, all of which are quite similar in fare and value.

$ Jollie Jacks Café and Bar, *12A Conical Hill Rd, T03-3157388. Daily from 1100.* Good coffee and value breakfasts, and is a good spot to watch the world go by.

Kaikoura p515

$$ Fyffe Country Lodge, *(south on SH1), T03- 3196869. Daily for lunch and dinner.* Good seafood and a fine view (especially after a late whale-watch). Cosy evening dining.

$$ Finz Seafood Restaurant and Wine Bar, *103 South Bay Par, T03-3196688. Daily from 1800 (Wed-Sun May-Sep).* Recommended.

$$ Donegal House, *Mt Fyffe Rd, T03-3195083. Daily 1100-1400 and 1800-2100.* In a lovely setting, with an Irish edge.

$$ Hapuku Café, *north on Hapuku Rd, T03-3196558.* Set on a deer and olive farm, a fine choice for organic fare, vegetarian dishes and micro-brewed beer.

In town there are plenty of affordable options for both lunch and dinner, with most specializing in seafood.

$$ Craypot Café and Bar, *70 West End, T03-3196027.* A good place to try crayfish at an affordable price.

$$ Mussel Boys, *80 Beach Rd, T03-3197160. May-Sep from 1200, closed Mon.* Serve up their standard plates of superb mussels and seafood dishes.

$$ The Green Dolphin, *12 Avoca St, at the far end of the Esplanade. Daily in summer lunch and dinner, Tue-Sun dinner only in winter.* Another firm seafood favourite serving such delights as scallops on kumara mash.

$ Act-One Bar and Café, *25 Beach Rd, T03-3196760. Daily from 1700.* For pizza look no further.

$ Why Not Café, *58 West End, T03-3196486. 0600-2100 in summer and 0600-1800 in winter.* Recommended for its coffee.

$ Hislop's Café, *33 Beach Rd, T03-3196971. Daily for lunch and dinner, closed Tue evenings in winter.* The place to find wholefoods and the best vegetarian dishes.

$ The Rocks Bar and Café, *93 West End, T03-3196414. Daily from 1000-late.* The place for the best evening entertainment, with occasional live bands, and is the main backpackers hangout. It also serves a fine value meal.

Supermarket Dreaver's 4square, *West End, T03-3195332.* **Night and Day**, *opposite the Top Ten Holiday Park on Beach Rd (SH1) open until 2300.*

🧗 Activities

Hanmer Springs p514

There are plenty to choose from, with mountain biking and skiing being the most prominent.

The Thrillseekers Adventure Centre (TAC), *9 km south of the town at the Waiau River Bridge, T03-3157046, www.thrillseeker.co.nz* is The hub of most activities. Bookings can also be made in their shop in the Mall, T03-3157346.

Hanmer Springs Adventure Centre (HSAC), *20 Conical Hill Rd, T03-3157233. Open daily.* They offer a wide range of activities and specialize in mountain biking trips, but also offer the independent hire of mountain bikes (one hr $14, full day $28), scooters, motorbikes, ATVs, fishing tackle, rollerblades and ski equipment.

Bungee jumping

Bungee jumping is available through the **TAC**. It is a fairly tame 37 m jump from the bridge over the Waiau River 9 km south of the town, perhaps most suitable for the faint-hearted or as a practice run, from $114.

There is excellent local fishing, and the VIC sells licences ($16 per day) and lists local venues and guides.

Flightseeing
Hanmer Springs Helicopters, *T0800-888308*. Offer 8-minute to 1-hr trips over the forest park and surrounding mountain ranges, from $115-$385.

Four-wheel drive
Backtrax, *T03-3157684, www.backtrax.co.nz* A 3-hr trip across farmland and the hills bordering the Waiau River will cost $120 while a longer 6-hr trip with lunch will cost from $379.
Molesworth and Rainbow Station Tours, *T03-3157181*. Offer half-day or full-day 4WD trips to the largest cattle station in New Zealand from $85.
Alpine Pacific Adventures, *T03-3157387*. Offer 45 minutes to 1½ hrs. 8WD adventures from $89, 4-hr Argo and Hike, from $125.

Horse trekking
Hanmer Forest Park and the surrounding countryside is superb horse riding country. **Hanmer Horses**, *T03-3157444*. Offer 1-hr to full-day rides from $35.
Alpine Horse Safaris, *Hawarden, T03-3144293, www.alpinehorse.co.nz* Offer standard treks and some excellent multi-day trips in the region from $356 (2-day) to $2680 (11-day).
Hurunui Horse Treks, *T03-3144204, www.horseback.co.nz* Also offer some entertaining 1-8 day options from 'Station to Station' or 'Mountain to Sea', from $160-$2425.

Jet boating
Jet boating trips (30 minutes) down the Waiau are offered by **TAC**, from $69, child $45.
Alpine Pacific Adventures, *T03-3157387*. Offer mountain lake kayaking with a full day on lake Tennyson from $165 or an overnight trip to Lake Sumner from $325 all-inclusive.

Massage
If you are exhausted even reading this list, or fancy some pampering after your activities, then a massage can be secured at the Thermal Resort 30 min from $30 (see page 519) or the **Wisteria Cottage Day Spa**, *34 Conical Hill Rd, T03-3157026*, 1 hr from $53.

Maze
Kids might like to lose themselves (or adults might like to lose their kids) in the new but fairly unremarkable **Hurunui Jones and the 'Lost Temple of Indra' Maze**, *on the roadside as you come into town. 1000-1730.* It's fun and great if you want to get lost, but you cannot help wondering if it was only ever a rock garden project gone horribly wrong. From $5.50, child $4.50.

Mountain biking
Mountain biking is a major reason why many come to Hanmer Springs, and the **Forest Park** offers some superb tracks from easy and moderate to the wonderfully muddy. The **HSAC** offer bike hire from $14 (1 hr) to $28 (full day).

Rafting
The **Waiau**, **Hurunui** and **Clarence Rivers** are good venues for rafting, and trips from half a day to multi-day are offered by **TAC** from $85 to $600.

Skiing
Skiing is another major reason why many flock to Hanmer in winter. The two fields are: **Hanmer Springs Ski Area**, *T03-3157201* (45 minutes) and **Mount Lyford**, *T03-3156178*, which is off SH70 (75 minutes). The Hanmer field has 2 rope tows, poma and lodge and accommodation facilities while the Lyford field has some challenging runs for both intermediates and the advanced as well as a good learners area, ski hire, lodge and a restaurant. Lift passes start at about $35. For more information contact the VIC or visit the website, www.nzski.com or www.snow.co.nz
HSAC hire ski equipment and **Hanmer Heli-ski and Heli-board**, *T0800-888308*, offer half-day trips from $325, full-day $650. For ski shuttles see Getting around, page 513.

Walking
There are plenty of good walking tracks around Hanmer, particularly in the Forest

Park that offers both short/long and easy/moderate options. The 1-hr **Conical Hill Lookout Walk**, with its views south across the town, is accessed from the top of Conical Hill Rd and continues through the forest to link up with Jollies Pass Rd and back into town. For more walks information contact the VIC.

Kaikoura p515

There are two things you need to bear in mind with the boat-based activities in Kaikoura. The first is simple – in mid-summer book the whale-watching and dolphin-swimming well in advance. Even the other less popular activities are worth pre-booking to avoid disappointment. The second is the notoriously fickle weather. Given its position on the Southern Ocean, Kaikoura is subject to the vagaries of wind and wave, and trips can be cancelled at a moment's notice. Again to avoid disappointment give yourself at least 2 days, just in case your trip is rescheduled. Also be sure to request your inclusion on another trip on cancellation, since this will not be done as a matter of course.

Dolphin swimming/watching

The coastal waters around Kaikoura abound with dolphins, and not just one species. They range from the common and bottlenose dolphins to the smaller dusky and rare Hector's dolphin. It is the dusky dolphin you are most likely to encounter (or swim with), and pods running into their hundreds, even thousands, are not uncommon. Even from the deck of a boat the sight of an inquisitive playful pod is superb. The duskies are also well known for breaching, and will jump out of the water or even somersault in an almost choreographed display of 'being'. Depending on their mood they may show great interest in the boat or swimmers or, on other days, show complete indifference. **Dolphin Encounter**, *58 West End, T03-3196777, www.dolphin.co.nz* The main operator. In summer the 3-hr trips leave from West End at 0530, 0830 and 1230, in winter 0830 and 1230, from $98, child $85 (viewing only $55, child $45). If you swim, and provided a pod is found (which is highly likely - refund if they are not), you will have plenty of time in the water frolicking around with the dolphins. You will be given a safety briefing and will be encouraged to make high-pitched bagpipe-like noises to attract them. This in turn will keep the 'viewing-only' passengers highly entertained. Take a towel and warm clothing, and book well in advance. Recommended.

Ecotours (general)

Blues Cruises Glass Bottom Boat Tours, *T03-3197570.* Offer the chance to dispense with the snorkel on a 1-hr trip to view the local sea life from $25, child $15.
Life on the Reef, *T0800-273334.* Offer daily (during the summer months) tours of the peninsula's shoreline at low tide with the opportunity of hunting in rock pools and encountering soporific seals that look at you as if they have seen it all before.
Kaikoura Naturally, *T0800-801040, kaikouranaturally@xtra.co.nz* Offer 3-hr guided coastal and bushwalks daily at 0900 and 1300, from $40 or $70 per couple.

Fishing

There are a number of fishing trips and charters, and the VIC has full listings.
Executive Sea Tours, *T0800-732868, www.kaikouraexecutivetours.co.nz* A new outfit earning a great reputation because not only do you go fishing (on board a very classy vessel), but you have your catch cooked on board and complimented by a glass or two of local wine or champagne. Tours depart daily in summer at 0700 for a champagne breakfast, 1300 for an afternoon lunch cruise and at 1800 for a sunset dinner, from $85 (winter one trip daily at 1300). Tours generally last about 2 hrs but the glow and the memory lasts a lot longer,
The FV Bounty, *T03-3196682, brianb@xtra.co.nz* 2 hrs from $60.

Flightseeing

Pilot A Plane, *based at the Peketa Airfield south of the town, T03-3196579.* A unique opportunity to take the controls (momentarily) on a 30-minute scenic flight, from $85.

4WD

Glenstrae Farm 4 Wheeler Adventures, *T03-3197021, T025-355628.* 4WD and Quad-bike Adventures. Offer 3-hr trips in the coastal hinterland with great views. Departs

0900, 1330 and at dusk, from $95
(Argo from $60).

Horse trekking
Fyffe Horse Treks, *T03-3195069*.
2 hrs from $45.
Lake View Horse Treks, *T03-3195997*. Inland
and coast, 1-2 hrs, from $35-$50.
Ludley Horse Treks, *T03-3195925*. From 2
hrs to 5 days, from $45.

Scenic and cultural tours
Maori Tours, *T03-3195567*,
maoritourskk@xtra.co.nz Offer plenty of local
cultural insight and protocol with visits to
local *pa* sites and a walk amidst native
bush to see how the plants were traditionally
used by the Maori. Entertaining with
plenty of participation, half-day from $65,
child $30. For a more conventional tour
option contact **Kaikoura Shuttles**,
T0800-766962.

Seabird watching
New Zealand is considered the seabird
capital of the world and a remarkable 70% of
its bird list are pelagic species. Kaikoura
offers a world-class opportunity to see many
that would otherwise involve long
excursions far offshore. Of particular interest
are the albatross, mollymawks, and
numerous petrel species. Just 2 notable
regulars include the giant petrel, which is as
big as a goose, the Westland petrel, which is
endemic to New Zealand, and the cape
pigeon that could not be more aptly named.
The birds are attracted to the boat using a
block of 'chum' (fish guts) and almost the
instant it hits the water the show begins.
Ocean Wings, *58 West End, T03-3196777*,
www.oceanwings.co.nz Run by the Dolphin
Encounter outfit, offer 2-3-hr trips on
demand, from $60, child $30.
Recommended.

Seal watching
With whales and dolphins being the main
oceanic stars, the New Zealand fur seals are
often overlooked. But encounters with these
inquisitive 'fat-bodies' can be a memorable
experience. On land they are undisputed
'beach-bum couch-potatoes', but under
water it is a completely different story,
displaying an ease and grace in motion that

would put any ballet dancer to shame. In
Kaikoura there is the choice of observing
them from land, boat, kayak, or to get up
close and personal in the water.
NZ Sea Adventures, *85 West End*,
T03-3196622, www.kaikoura.co.nz/scuba
Boat-based swimming on a 1-hr excursion,
from $65, child $40. Viewing only $30,
child $20.
Seal Swim Kaikoura, *T03-3196182*,
www.kaikoura.co.nz/sealswim 2-hr land-
based snorkelling tours daily (0900, 1130 and
1400), from $50, child $40 (Nov-Apr).
Topspot Seal Swim, *T03-3195540*. Offer the
same, again from Nov-Apr from $50,
child $40.
Sea Kayak Kaikoura, *T03-3195641*,
www.seakayakkaikoura.co.nz A kayak can
provide a great milieu from which to
encounter seals. This outfit have half-day
guided tours taking in both the scenery and
seals of the peninsula with dive and
snorkelling additional options. Trips depart
from the VIC daily at 0830, 1230 and
(summer) 1630, from $65, child $40.
Freedom hire costs from $45 for a half day,
$65 for a full day.

Sharks
Your close (caged) encounter with Jaws and
his toothy mates can be arranged through
Shark Dive Kaikoura, *T03-3196888*,
www.sharkdive.co.nz 3-hr (10 minutes in
'the cage') trips leave daily (Nov-Apr). All
equipment supplied, from $130.
Unfortunately the last few seasons have
been poor for sightings let alone encounters,
and there is some concern that this may well
be an indication of their general decline.

Star gazing
Kaikoura Night Sky, *T03-3196635*. From $35,
child $25. For a fine close up of the moon
and a little insight into nebulae.

Surfing
Although the peninsula itself offers few fine
surf breaks the coast to the north is excellent.
**Kaikoura Surf School and Board Silly
Adventures**, *T0800-787352, T025-6458211*.
Offer lessons from $30 per hr ($65 all
inclusive), advanced coaching and
independent board hire, from $35 half-day.

Tree planting
Trees for Travellers, *ask for details at the VIC, www.treesfortravellers.co.nz* A neat program that allows visitors to help with local native bush restoration. You can plant your own natural memento for $20.

Walks around Kaikoura
The 2-hr return **Peninsula Walk** that links the 2 settlements via the cliffs or shoreline is excellent and recommended. You can either walk along the cliff-top or the shoreline (depending on the tide) and start at the Point Kearn car park (at the end of Avoca Street), or alternatively at the South Bay car park. You will encounter seals, lots of interesting rock pools, and some superb coastal scenery. A much longer jaunt is the celebrated 3-day, 45 km, **Kaikoura Coast Track** that combines sights inland and along the coast.
Sally and David Handyside, *T03-3192715, www.kaikouratrack.co.nz* Offer this as a package from $120.
Mount Fyffe (1602), which is directly behind Kaikoura, offers spectacular views and can be accessed from the end of Postman's Rd (junction Athelney Rd/SH1 north of Beach Rd) or Grange Rd (SH1 north); 8-hr return, DoC huts en route ($5, book at the VIC).
There is also a good lookout and short walk, **Fyffe Palmer Track**, at the end of Mount Fyffe Rd (8 km). To get there, drive out of town on Ludstone Rd (north) then turn right onto Mount Fyffe Rd and follow it to its terminus. The VIC has DoC broadsheets on all these walks and others.

Whale watching
The first commercial whale watching operation in New Zealand was started in 1987 by the Maori-owned and operated **Whale Watch Kaikoura**, *T03-3196767, T0800-655121, www.whalewatch.co.nz* The company now has 4 purpose-built vessels and can accommodate about 60,000 visitors annually. Their base is at the 'Whaleway Station' (next to the Railway Station), accessed off Beach Road (SH1) just beyond West End. They offer between 3-4 2-3½-hr trips daily (seasonal departures) from $110, child $60. Recommended. The boats all leave from South Bay, 10 minutes from the Whaleway Station. You can expect to see at least one whale on your trip as well as dolphins, seals, albatrosses and other unusual seabirds, but if no whales are seen at all there is an 80% refund. A recent addition to the on-board entertainment is an excellent high tech computer generated animation entitled 'World of the Whales' that provides an imaginative view of the geography and remarkable depth of the Kaikoura Canyon. Trips are, of course, weather-dependent and can be cancelled at any time. Note: your inclusion on a later trip is not automatic and needs to be requested.

If you don't like the idea of a boat trip, or just fancy seeing the whales from a different (and better) perspective, then you should go whale-watching from the air. This can be particularly good in calmer sea conditions when you can see the whole whale from above rather than just the tail end and flukes. At just over 150 m you can also spot dolphins and enjoy the added bonus of spectacular aerial views across the peninsula and the coast. Photographers will need a good telephoto lens, fast film and a polarising filter.

Wings Over Whales, *based at the Peketa Airfield 6 km south of Kaikoura, T03-3196580, T0800-226629, www.whales.co.nz* Offer entertaining and personable flightseeing trips from 30-45 minutes at 0900/1100/1300 and 1500, from $135, child $75. Recommended.
Kaikoura Helicopters, *based at the 'Whaleway Station', T03-3196609, www.worldofwhales.co.nz* Offer 30-40 minute-flights from $165-$230, child rates negotiable.

❶ Directory

Hanmer Springs *p514*
Banks There is an ATM at the **Bank of New Zealand**, *beside the VIC, T03-3157220. 1000-1400.* Traveller's cheques are accepted and exchanged at the Four Square foodmarket, in the main shopping centre on Conical Hill Rd. **Internet** Hanmer Inn

Motel, *16 Jacks Pass Rd*, *T03-3157516*.
Mountain View Top Ten, *at the entrance to*
the town, T03-3157113. **Medical**
facilities Medical centre, *20 Amuri Av,*
T03-3157503. **Post office** in the Four
Square Foodmarket. **Useful addresses**
Police, *station is at 39 Amuri Av, T03-3157117*.

Kaikoura *p515*
Banks BNZ, *42 West End* with an ATM.
Internet Kodak Express, *on West End (open*
daily 0900-1730). Internet Outpost, *19 West*
End. Slower, but stays open later (until 2100).
Post office *41 West End, T03-3196808*
(open Mon-Fri 0830-1700, Sat 0900-1200).
Useful addresses Police: *T03-3195038*.

West of Christchurch → *Phone code: 03*

Until recently there were basically two main reasons tourists 'headed for the hills' west
of Christchurch. The most obvious reason is to reach the West Coast via SH73, the
Craigieburn Forest Park and Arthur's Pass, while the other is to ski the popular Mount
Hutt ski fields near Methven. However, since the release of the Lord of the Rings trilogy,
there is now another very good reason in the surprising form of a large and conspicuous
lump of rock. Mount Sunday, which sits predominantly in the Rangitata River Valley and
in stark contrast against the mountainous skyline of Southern Alps, became the perfect
filming location and set for Edoras and Meduseld, King Theoden's grand hall in the
realm of Rohan. Although you would now never guess any set ever existed except in your
own imagination, it remains one of the most scenic drives in the country and, even
without all the hype, was always a great place to visit.

Ins and outs

Getting there Methven is 90 km southwest of Christchurch via the celebrated 'Inland
Scenic Route' (SH73) and SH72. By **bus**, **Intercity**, T0800-764444, operates daily from
Christchurch. For other winter shuttles to Mount Hutt and Christchurch, contact
Methven Travel, T0800-684888, T03-3028106, www.methven.net.nz

From Christchurch it is 240 km from to the West Coast. (Arthur's Pass is 158 km.) **Coast**
to Coast, T0800-800847, www.coast2coast.co.nz, (departs Christchurch 0800, arriving
Arthur's Pass 1030 and Greymouth at 1250, from $60 return, Arthur's Pass from $25)
and **Alpine Coaches**, T0800-274888, www.alpinecoaches.co.nz, (departs Christchurch
at 1330, arriving Arthur's Pass 1630, Hokitika 1800), from $40 (Arthur's Pass from $25).

TransScenic's, T0800-872467, www.tranzscenic.co.nz, daily **rail** service **Tranz-**
Alpine is touted as one of the most scenic rail journeys in the world and is a very
popular way to get from Christchurch to Greymouth. The Alpine leaves Christchurch at
0815, arriving Arthur's Pass 1042 and the Greymouth at 1245. It makes the return
journey from Greymouth at 1345, to Arthur's Pass at 1557, arriving in Christchurch at
1805. A standard return is $119, child $62 (Arthur's Pass $78, child $46).

Getting around Methven Travel (above) offer taxi services and a ski bus to the slopes
in winter. They also provide transportation to the Mount Somers Walkway. **Mountain**
Transport, 28 Spaxton St, T03-3028443, kdanna@paradise.net.nz, and **Mount Hutt**
Taxi and Shuttle, T03-3021728, T027-4318604, also offer a door-to-door service
between Methven and the ski fields, from $25 return. **Mount Hutt Tours**, T03-3028106,
and **Leopard Coachlines**, T03-3028707, T025-339963, both offer a slightly cheaper
alternative for around $22, child $17. **Mountain bikes** can be hired from the VIC or **Big**
Al's in The Square, T03-3028003, from $28 per day.

Information Methven VIC, ① *Main St, T0800-764444, www.methven.net.nz Daily*
0900-1700 (winter 0730-1930). Has free town maps and information about the ski
fields. They also stock **DoC** information covering regional walks, have internet, and

administer transport and activity bookings. For other specific **ski** information and on-line snow reports contact the Mount Hutt Ski-field, T03-3028811 or the websites www.snow.co.nz, www.nzski.com **Arthur's Pass VIC (DoC),** ① *in the heart of the village on the southern side of SH73,* T03-3189211, *www.doc.govt.nz Daily 0900-1600.* There are various displays about the national park, a video ($1), walks information and all local accommodation and service details. Ask for the 'Village Information' broadsheet and map. Before embarking on any long walks or tramps check the weather forecast and ask the staff about up-to-date track conditions. Intentions sheets are provided.

Methven and Mount Hutt → *Colour map 5, grid C3 Population: 1000*

The biggest attraction to the small, but congenial agricultural town of Methven is its location close to the **Mount Hutt Ski-field**. At an elevation of 2075 m and covering an area of 365 ha, 'The Hutt' is highly regarded by the ski fraternity. The reason for this lies not only due to its proximity to Christchurch, but also for its reputation for having some of the best snow in the country and the longest and most consistent season in the Southern Hemisphere (min May-October). It also has a new and modern base lodge with brasserie, bar, cafés, shops and snowboarding facilities.

In summer, although the town is almost depressingly quiet, it still offers an escape from the city or the tourist hype and various activities including balloon flights, mountain biking, white-water rafting or walking. The region is also noted for its farmstays. ▸▸ *For Sleeping, Eating and all other listings, see pages 529-531.*

West Coast via Arthur's Pass

The route to the West Coast via SH73 from Christchurch across The Great Divide and the northern ranges of the Southern Alps is one of the most celebrated **scenic drives and rail journeys** in the country. It is most notable perhaps for its sheer range of dramatic South Island landscapes, from the flatlands of the Canterbury Plains to the east, through the rugged mountain peaks and river gorges in its centre, to the lush coastal valleys and lakes to the west. On the way, other than its aesthetics, are the **Craigieburn Forest** and **Arthur's Pass National Park**, which offer some excellent **walking, tramping, rock climbing** and **skiing** opportunities.

Sights
From Christchurch, with the almost constant sight of the mountains looming ever larger, you pass through the small and aptly named rural settlements of Darfield and Springfield to reach the foot of the Torlesse Range. Just beyond Springfield the road climbs steeply through **Porters Pass** before falling once again into the valleys and unusual karst landscapes that border the **Craigieburn Forest Park** (100 km). The area offers a small flurry of **ski fields**, including Porter Heights, Mount Olympus, Mount Cheeseman, Broken Rivers and Craigieburn. All these are 'club fields', offering a wide range of slopes and conditions. For information contact the VIC in Christchurch or Methven, or consult the excellent website, www.nzski.com There are also plenty of walking opportunities. The DoC leaflet the *Craigieburn Forest Park Day Walks* is very useful and available from the VICs above. The rugged karst landscape of Kura Tawhiti or **Castle Hill Reserve** (30 km west of Springfield) provide more interesting walks and also some excellent **rock climbing**.

Six kilometres further west is the **Cave Stream Scenic Reserve** which is easily accessible from SH73. Here you will find the rather unique opportunity of a self-guided black-water hike in a limestone cave system that has been created over the millennia by the Waimakariri River and its tributaries. The cave system was used for centuries by Maori on their transmigration west to the coast and still contains some examples of rock art and bones. The one-hour underground hike is of course more of a 'wade', but is well worth the soaking. Just be sure to take a good torch and dry clothing. The DoC interpretative panels in the car park will keep you right, and leaflets are available from the VICs.

At the northern border of the Forest Park, and just beyond the tiny settlement of Cass, both road and rail penetrate the vast open-braided **Waimakariri River Valley** before entering the **Arthur's Pass National Park**. From there it is only a short drive to the enveloped outpost village of **Arthur's Pass**.

Arthur's Pass → *Colour map 5, grid B3 Population: 111*

It was one Arthur Dudley Dobson, a pioneer surveyor, who first explored the route to the West Coast via the east Waimakariri and west Otira River Valleys in 1864. Although at the time Arthur was merely on a routine trip, his observations became an integral part of securing road access to the West Coast during the gold boom of the 1860s. Remarkably, or perhaps not, given the motivation, a basic road was built within a year, but the rail link that later served the coal and timber trade took a further 60 years to complete. Now, long after all the gold has gone, the railway remains a monument to patience, while the road continues to need constant maintenance and improvement. These modern feats of road engineering and construction become obvious just beyond Arthur's Pass in the form of the impressive, and only recently opened, **Otira Viaduct.**

Even before the rail link to Arthur's Pass was complete, the area was proving popular for **tramping** and **skiing**, and by 1930 Arthur's Pass was gazetted as a National Park. The tiny settlement of Arthur's Pass is 924 m above sea level and is used as the base for activities in the park, or as a welcome halfway stop en route to the West Coast.

The Arthur's Pass National Park → *Colour map 5, grid B3*

The Arthur's Pass National Park was designated in 1929 and is 114,500 ha in area. It extends from the vicinity of Harper's Pass in the northern Southern Alps to the mountains around the head of the Waimakariri and Otira Rivers. The park is essentially made up of high mountain ranges, gorges and expansive braided river valleys. One of the highest and most attractive mountains is **Mount Rolleston** (2270 m), which lies just to the southwest of the Arthur's Pass. Its impressive **'Bealey Face'** can be seen from the road just west of the village.

The mountain ranges are 'alpine' in nature, containing a broad range of vegetation which varies greatly from east to west in accordance with the varying climatic conditions and rainfall. To the east the forests are almost entirely made up of mountain beech, while to the west, on the other side of 'The Great Divide', it is more complex with a variety of podocarp species, beech, kamahi and kaiakawaka. The park is rich in alpine plant species, many of which thrive above the tree line and are endemic to New Zealand. Many native birds are also present, the most notable being the notoriously inquisitive and destructive native mountain parrot, the **kea**. Often, kea will come down to the village to see you before you go up into the mountains to see them, relieving you of your sandwiches in the process. If this is your first trip across to the West Coast you may also notice one other creature, one that will make its presence known in no uncertain terms: the satanic sandfly.

The park offers a network of **tramping** tracks that are equipped with over 30 DoC backcountry huts. Two of the best **day walks** are the 7-8 hour ascent of **Avalanche Peak**, directly behind the village on its southern side, or, further west still, the more difficult (mainly summer) climb to the summit of **Mount Rolleston**. The Avalanche Peak track begins from behind the DoC Information Centre, which can offer detailed information and advice on these tracks and others. Note that braided rivers and the small tributaries that feed them are notorious for **flash floods**, so extra care is required. History buffs might like to negotiate the 1½-hour **Arthur's Pass Village Historic Walk**. Leaflet from the VIC.

🛏 Sleeping

Methven *p527*

Given its popularity as a ski resort there is no shortage of beds in the town, with the majority being upper-to mid-range self-contained lodges with spas, open fires, drying rooms etc. There are also a good number of backpacker lodges and, again, these have that 'ski-lodge' feel with all the facilities. The VIC has full listings, and advanced bookings are advised in winter. Note that prices drop dramatically in summer and although Mount Hutt is closer to the slopes there is very little accommodation there, so if you want better choice and the best atmosphere you are advised to stay in Methven.

A **Chancellor Resort Hotel**, *Main St, T03-3028724, chancellor.methven@grand central.co.nz* Has 2 suites and numerous tidy studios, a sauna, 3 outdoor hot pools and in-house restaurants and bar.

AL-A **Lodge**, *Chertsey Rd, T03-3032000, www.lodgenz.com* Right in the heart of the town, it has some excellent luxury spa rooms, ensuites, and good modern facilities including restaurant, bar and internet café.

AL **Brinkley Village Resort**, *Barkers Rd, T03-3028885, brinkley@xtra.co.nz* Another modern option a little lacking in atmosphere that specializes in self-contained studios and apartments. It too has a restaurant, bar, hot tubs, pool and the welcoming open fire.

NB All the above offer cheap summer rates. There are numerous **lodges** and **motels**.

AL **Homestead**, *on the Mount Hutt Station, T03-3028130, www.the-homestead.co.nz* Has all the usual mod cons in a country setting, great cuisine, and is the closest top-range accommodation to the ski-field. Note, however, that it is not exactly what the word 'homestead' conjures up in one's imagination (think more plush motel in nice setting).

A **Abisko Lodge**, *74 Main St, Methven, T03-3028875, abisko@clear.net.nz* Friendly place with 12 en suites with great facilities including restaurant, bar, spa/sauna and a comfortable lounge with open fire.

B **Mount Taylor Lodge**, *32 Lampard St, T03-3029699, www.mounttaylorlodge.co.nz* Another new good mid-range option.

A-D **Bed Post**, *177 Main St, T03-3028508.* A modern motel close to the centre of town that also offers some good budget rooms.

As one might expect there are plenty of cosy **B&Bs** and self-contained options in and around town. Names to consider and in order of price are:

LL **Whitestone Cottages**, *3020 Methven Highway, T03-3029271, www.whitestonecottages.co.nz* A beautiful modern 2-storey home in a rural setting.

L **Powderhouse Country Lodge**, *3 Cameron St, T03-3029105, www.powderhouse.co.nz* Older restored villa with a great hot tub.

AL **Beluga**, *40 Allen St, T03-3028290, www.beluga.co.nz* Excellent B&B and self-contained cottage option.

AL-B **Methven Mount Hutt Holiday Homes**, *200 Main St, T03-3029200, mmhhh@xtra.co.nz* A good bet for couples and groups, with a list of about 20 houses and units from deluxe to standard or budget.

For summer **farmstays** consult the VIC.

A-B **Ryton Station**, *on the shores of Lake Coleridge, T0800-926-868, www.ryton.co.nz* The largest (14.589 ha) and best equipped, with chalets, holiday houses and camping, a restaurant and plenty of organized activities from fly fishing to jet boating all in a remote setting.

Budget/hostel options include:

C-D **Alpenhorn Chalet**, *44 Allen St, T03-3028779.* It is a cosy bungalow with new facilities, dorms and doubles and a spa.

C-D **Skiwi Lodge**, *30 Chapman St, T03-3028772, skiwihouse@xtra.co.nz* Well established, friendly and very comfortable with well-heated dorms and doubles. It is also good in summer given the enthusiasm offered in arranging other non-ski activities.

C-D **Redwood Lodges**, *5 Wayne Pl, T03-3028964, skired@xtra.co.nz* Provides two good-value purpose-built self-catering lodges, one with shared facilities and one with great value ensuites. All the ski facilities are provided, and it has a cosy log fire.

A-D Kohuia Lodge of Pudding Hill, *on the Inland Scenic Highway (12 km west of Methven) T03-3028416, www.kohuialodge.co.nz* A tidy modern establishment close to Mount Hutt and the skifield. It has 1-2 bedroom studio units, budget lodge rooms, powered/tent sites, restaurant, bar and jacuzzi.

Motorcamps
D Methven Caravan Park, *Barkers Rd, in Methven itself, T03-3028005.*

West Coast via Arthur's Pass *p527*
There are a number of good places to stay before you reach Arthur's Pass. In winter these are very popular with the ski fraternity, while in summer it is walking boots, not the skiing variety, that sit on the steps.

C-D Smylie's YHA, *Springfield, on Main Rd in the centre of the village, T03-3184740, www.smylies.co.nz* Cosy dorms and doubles, with modern facilities. Provides the ideal base for both winter and summer activities. In winter they rent skis and arrange transportation to the slopes. In summer rock climbing, horse trekking and hiking can all be arranged.

A-D Flock Hill Lodge, *a further 40 km east of Arthur's Pass, T03-3188196, www.flockhill.co.nz* Part of the expansive Flock Hill Station has tidy motel units, lodge backpackers and a restaurant. Activities arranged. Ideally located close to the ski fields and the Craigieburn Forest Park walks.

LL Grassmere Lodge, *10 km further west, T03-3188407.* Offers all mod cons, dinner and activities as part of the package. It can also be reached by the TranzAlpine which can stop at the edge of the property.

A-D Bealey Hotel, *4 km east of Arthur's Pass, T03-3189277, www.bealeyhotel.co.nz* Offers motel doubles and backpacker twins. Bealey is famous for its reputed moa sighting in recent years. Of course said sighting was an elaborate hoax, but it was successful enough to create a national hysteria deserving of a monument that stands looking decidedly giraffe-like beside the hotel. Bistro open daily.

Arthur's Pass *p528*
Arthur's Pass village offers a small range of accommodation options, with a B&B lodge, a motel, 2 backpackers and a campsite. There is only one bistro/à la carte restaurant and a café.

A Chalet B&B, *at the western end of the village, T03-3182936, www.arthurspass.co.nz* The most expensive, with comfortable doubles with 8 ensuites and 3 with shared facilities. There is an in-house à la carte and a bistro/restaurant.

A-B Alpine Motel, *just beyond the bridge on the right at the eastern end of the village, T03-3189233.* Has self-contained doubles. They also offer a 'car minding' service.

C-D Arthur's Pass Alpine YHA, *T03-3189230, yhaapass@yha.org.nz* The older of the 2 backpackers. Next to the café, has dorm and doubles.

C-D Mountain View Backpackers, *T03-3189258, mountain.house@xtra.co.nz* Newer and two-storied, has some excellent cottages on the grounds, a spacious lodge and tent sites. Recommended.

Campsites
Basic camping facilities are also available at the **public shelter** across the road from the VIC in the village ($5), or free at **Klondyke Corner**, 8 km east, and **Kelly Shelter**, 17 km west.

● Eating

Methven *p527*
$$ Chancellor Resort Hotel, *Main St, T03-3028724.* For fine dining year round, this is always a reliable option.

$$ Stronechrubie Restaurant, *in Mt Somers, 30 km from Methven, T03-3039814.* One of the best fine-dining restaurants in the region (outside Christchurch). With a change of ownership in 2002 it remains to be seen if standards can be maintained or even surpassed.

$$ Steel-Worx Restaurant and Bar, *36 Forest Dr, Methven, T03-3029900.* New and earning a good reputation. It is stylish, full of character and has a cosy atmosphere with a room separate from the main bar with a log-burning stove.

$ Café 131, *Main St, T03-3029131. 0900-1600 (winter 0700-1900).* Quite a classy breakfast.

$ **Ski Time Restaurant**, *Racecourse Av,
T03-3028398, www.skitime.co.nz* A funky
option with rock walls and an open fire.
$ **Ernie's Cantina**, *on Forest Dr Main St,
Methven, T03-3029192*. Also popular for good
value Tex-Mex.
Supermarkets Supervalue and
Topnotch foodmarkets, *both on McMillan St.
The former is open until 2100 in winter.*
The colourful **pubs**,
The Blue on *Barkers Rd*, and **The Brown** *just
opposite*, are both traditional favourites, with
the former the most popular for après-ski.
Steel-Worx Restaurant and Bar, *36 Forest
Dr, T03-3029900*. Smaller and already earning
a good reputation and also for its lively party
nights in winter. All offer good pub lunches.

Arthur's Pass *p528*
Other than the licensed **Chalet Restaurant**
(*see Sleeping above*) options are limited to
$ **Oscar's Haus Alpine Café**, *T03-3189234, in
the centre of town. Daily 0900-2100 (winter
1030-1600)*. It offers light snacks, homemade
pies and questionable coffee. There is also a
tearoom offering basic fare, across the road.
Daily 0800-1900.

▲ Activities

Skiing
Day Lift passes cost $72, child $35. A 3-day
lift pass costs from $203, child $100. Ski
equipment hire is available at the field itself
or in various outlets in Methven, including:
Big Al's, *The Square, T03-3028003,
www.bigals.co.nz* For transport to the field
see Getting around, above.
Methven Heliski, *Main Rd, T03-3028108,
www.heliskiing.co.nz* Offer heli-ski trips.

Hot air ballooning
Even outside the ski season Methven offers a
good range of activities year round.
Aoraki Hot Air Balloon Safaris, *T03-302 8172,
www.nzballooning.com* Offer relaxing flights
with a champagne breakfast, from $285.

Jetboating
Rakaia Gorge Scenic Jet, *T03-3186515*, and
Rakaia Gorge Alpine Jet, *T03-3186574,
www.rivertours.co.nz* Offer scenic trips and
Heli-jet options on the Rakaia River from $65.

Rafting
Rangitata Rafts, *T03-6963534,
www.rafts.co.nz* Offer day excursions down
the scenic Rangitata River, south of Methven
(Grade IV-V), from $145 (includes transport).
To keep up the adrenaline, you might also
consider a spot of mountain biking for which
the VIC can provide all the details.

Flightseeing
Mount Hutt Helicopters, *Blackford Rd,
T03-3028401, www.mthuttheli.com*
Offer
flightseeing trips and a heli-taxi service to
the ski slopes. For scenic trips by ATV contact
Planet Argo, *T0800-2746386, T03-3028464*.

Horse trekking
Staveley Horse Treks, *T03-3030809*. 1 hr
from $30 (best for beginners).
High Country Horse Adventures,
T0800-386-336, www.horsetrek.co.nz More
adventurous excursions.

Walks
There are numerous walks or longer hikes on
offer in the **Mount Hutt Forest** (14 km west),
Mount Somers, **'The Foothills'** and the **Peel
Forest** (south), with the climb to the summit
of **Mount Somers** (1687 m) being particularly
recommended. The VIC has details.

Golf
Terrace Downs, *Lake Coleridge Rd,
T0800-465373, info@terracedowns.co.nz*
Clubs can be hired from **Big Al's** in *The
Square, Methven*.

✪ Directory

Methven *p527*
Banks BNZ (ATM), *Main St*. **Postal
agent** *in Gifts Galore, Main St*. **Medical
facilities** Pharmacy, *Main St, T03-3028103*,
and the Medical Centre, *in The Square,
T03-3028105*. **Police** *T03-3028200*.

Arthur's Pass *p528*
Post office (The smallest on the planet),
Main St (only open limited hours). **Useful
addresses** There is a petrol station and a
police station in the village, *T03-3189212*. For
breakdown *T03-6189266*.

South Canterbury → *Phone code: 03*

From Christchurch SH1 heads south through the flat heartland of the Canterbury Plains to Timaru. With so much seemingly omnipresent and stunning scenery elsewhere in New Zealand, aesthetically it is often labelled as the least exciting drive in the country. Only the occasional glimpse of the distant Southern Alps far to the west and the odd wide pebble-strewn riverbed crossing breaks the monotony of the endless roadside windbreaks and expansive fields. Even the cows look bored to death. Roughly half way between Christchurch and Timaru is the only major settlement, Ashburton.

Ins and outs

Getting there Ashburton is 87 km south of Christchurch and 76 km north of Timaru on SH1. All the major **bus** companies heading south can stop in Ashburton and Timaru including **Intercity**, T03-3088219, and **Atomic Shuttles**, T03-3228883. Buses stop outside the VIC in Ashburton and the station in Timaru (AJ's Café in the station also act as booking agents, T03-6883594). Smaller shuttle companies doing the Dunedin/Christchurch route include **Southern Link**, T03-3588355, and **Supa Kut-Price Shuttles**, T03-3298069. The later offer the lowest fares. **GTS Country Link Tours**, 44 Omahau Cres, T03-4350052, take a return trip to Twizel every Fri. The **airport** in Timaru is about 12 km north of town (SH1) and is served by **Air New Zealand Link**, T0800-737000, daily from Christchurch and Wellington. For taxi from the airport contact **Timaru Taxis**, T03-6888899, from $12. For **car hire** and **taxi** services see 'Directory' below. The VIC holds local suburban **bus** (CRC) timetables.

Information Ashburton VIC, ① *on the main road, East St, T03-3081064, infocentre@ashburton.co.nz Mon-Fri 0830-1700, Sat 1000-1500, Sun 1000-1300.* It has a free town map and full accommodation and local activity listings. **Timaru VIC**, ① *in the former Landing Service Building, 2 George St, T03-6886163, info@timaru.com, www.southisland.org Mon-Fri 0830-1700, Sat-Sun 1000-1500.* **DoC** information is held at the VIC. **Geraldine VIC**, ① *32 Talbot St, T03-6931006, www.southisland.org.nz Mon-Fri 0830-1700, Sat-Sun 1000-1600.* It has full listings for local accommodation. The free leaflet *Geraldine* has comprehensive listings including the varied arts and crafts outlets. **DoC** information is held at the VIC. **Temuka VIC**, ① *72-74 King St, T03-6159537, temlibrary@xtra.co.nz* Has full accommodation listings. **Waimate VIC**, ① *75 Queen St, T03-6897771, www.waimate.org.nz* It has detailed accommodation and local activity listings.

Ashburton → *Population: 13,400 Colour map 5, grid C3*

Due to its surrounding topography and perhaps its very location right on SH1, as well as being so near Christchurch and so far from the principal tourist attractions to the south, Ashburton seldom lures tourists to stop for anything other than a hurried toilet break, quick snack and cup of coffee. But having said that, it is not a bad little place and if you take a little time (especially on Sundays), it will reveal a few worthy attractions and tempting activities to complement the warm welcome offered by its friendly residents.

Sights and activities The main attractions are its small museums and craft outlets. The **Ashburton Art Gallery and Museum**, ① *Baring Square East, T03-3081133, Tue-Fri 1000-1600, Sat-Sun 1300-1600, donation,* has the obvious focus on local history but is particularly noted for its displays of local and contemporary arts and crafts.

Also of note, though seldom open, is **The Plains Vintage Railway and Historical Museum**, which is just over the Manoran Road level crossing (off SH1) in the **Tinwald Domain and Recreation Park** ① *(south of the town centre), T03-3089621, www.plainsrailway.co.nz Open on every second Sun in the month (Oct-Jun) and most*

Sundays during the rest of the year. It offers short rides on some of its fine array of restored locos and traction engines, from $6, child $2.50. Sadly, the classic 'K88 Washington', built in the USA in 1877, is not one of them. After spending 47 years lying in a riverbed in Southland it was lovingly restored and returned to service in 1982. Looking *the* classic archetype of an old steam engine and almost like something that would be drawn from a child's imagination, it is well worth seeing. You may like to follow this with a visit to the **Vintage Car Museum**, ① *also in the Domain, T03-3087025*. It has a collection that dates back to 1905 and is again only open on Sundays. For crafts, the **Ashford Craft Village**, ① *415 West St, T03-3089085,* is worth a look and can double as a good place for lunch.

Timaru → *Colour map 6, grid B6 Population: 27,300*

The port city of Timaru, roughly halfway between Christchurch and Dunedin, provides a refreshing stop over on SH1, or a convenient starting point from which to head west, via SH8, to the 'MacKenzie Country', Mount Cook and Queenstown. The city is a pleasant one, boasting the popular **Caroline Bay beach** near the town centre, a few good parks, the region's main museum, a reputable art gallery and a few unique attractions, including some ancient seventh-century **Maori rock art** that adorn caves and rock overhangs near the city.

History With the existence of over 500 sites featuring **Maori Rock art**, particularly in the caves and rock overhangs of the Opihi and Opuha Rivers, west of Timaru, historians have estimated that the Maori settled in the area as early as 1400 AD. During the 17th century the warring Ngati Tahu, from the north of the South Island, drove the descendants of these people, the Ngati Mamoe south into Fiordland. European settlement began with the establishment of a whaling station at Patiti Point, close to the present town, in 1837. This was followed by the purchase and creation of a sheep station known as 'The Levels' in 1852 by the influential Rhodes brothers from England. For over two decades disputes arose between the brothers and the government surrounding land-ownership and development, but this was eventually settled and the two communities merged to form Timaru. With the reclamation of land in 1877, and the subsequent creation of the harbour at Caroline Bay, the town quickly developed as a major port. Today the port at Timaru is the second largest fishing port in New Zealand and is even visited by the odd cruise liner. The name Timaru is thought to be derived from the Maori *te maru* meaning 'place of shelter', however, some authorities dispute this and suggest the literal translation of *ti*, meaning 'cabbage tree', and *maru*, meaning 'shady' as the correct one.

Sights At the VIC you are immediately confronted by the original 'bluestone' façade of the **Landing Service Building** which was built in 1870 to facilitate the export of wool and other goods from the surrounding district. This building now forms the starting point for the town's **three main heritage trails**.

South Canterbury Museum, ① *Perth St, T03-6842212, Tue-Fri 1030-1630, Sat and Sun 1330-1630, free,* is the main regional museum and contains some interesting exhibits on local maritime history, Maori rock art and the exploits of aviator **Richard Pearse** (1877-1953). In 1903 Pearse is said to have made the first manned flight, nine months before the Wright Brothers of America (see Temuka below). A full replica of the impressive contraption that allowed him to do so is on display. Other relics of Pearse's various flying inventions are held at the Pleasant Point Railway Museum in Pleasant Point (see 'Around Timaru' below).

With the presence of **The Aigantighe** (pronounced 'egg and tie') **Art Gallery**, ① *49 Wai-iti Rd, T03-6884424, Tue-Fri 1000-1600, Mon, Sat and Sun 1200-1600 (gardens open dawn to dusk), free,* Timaru can boast one of the best art galleries in the country. Founded in 1956, and set in a 1908 historic home surrounded by a sculpture garden, its hallowed walls feature exhibitions from a substantial permanent exhibition, which dates back to the seventh century, as well as contemporary works by **Colin McCahon** and **C F Goldie**. The gallery also hosts an ongoing program of regional and national exhibitions. *Aigantighe* means 'at home' in Scots Gaelic.

The somewhat iconic **DB Mainland Brewery**, ① *Sheffield St (2 km north of town), T03-6882059*, offers free weekday tours and tastings at 1030.

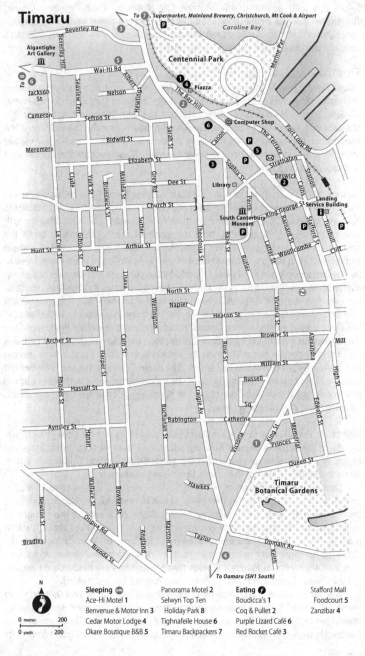

Timaru

To ⑦, Supermarket, Mainland Brewery, Christchurch, Mt Cook & Airport

South Canterbury

Canterbury

N

0 metres 200
0 yards 200

Timaru has some pleasant parks and beaches. The beach at **Caroline Bay**, to the north of the town centre, was formed as a result of land reclamation and original harbour development in 1877. Although in close proximity to the busy port, and therefore not aesthetically remarkable, the beach still remains a popular and safe haven for swimming.

The park alongside the beach has a number of attractions including a roller-skating rink, a mini-golf course, a maze and an open-air concert soundshell. Every summer, just after Christmas, this area is the focus for the **Summer Carnival**. Hugely popular amongst locals, this event attracts thousands who are entertained with organized concerts, fairground rides, sideshows and the obligatory candyfloss stalls. The addition of the new **Piazza**, leading from the Bay Hill down to Caroline Bay in 1997, added a focus for a relaxed seaside café, restaurant and wine bar scene. Of more traditional and less convivial aesthetics are the **Timaru Botanical Gardens**, ① *T03-6886163, daily 0800-dusk,* which were established in 1864. They are especially noted for their collection of rose species and are located just south of the town centre. They are best accessed on the corner of King and Queen Streets. **Centennial Park**, that follows the course of the Otipua Creek, also offers a peaceful escape and a lovely 3½ km 1-hour one-way walk that begins from the old 'bluestone' Gleniti School on Clearmont Street, west of the town centre.

Around Timaru and South to Oamaru

If you have given yourself plenty of time in the immediate area and find yourself at a loose end, the small rural communities that surround Timaru, namely, **Pleasant Point**, **Geraldine** and **Temuka** or **Waimate** off SH1 to the south, provide some singular attractions that may lure you off the beaten track.

Geraldine → *Colour map 6, grid B6 Population: 2,323*
The pleasant Anglicized country town of Geraldine, nestled amidst the Four Peaks and Peel Forest Mountain ranges, is home to a thriving arts and crafts community providing an attractive, if brief, diversion off SH1 (15 km).

Other than the obvious attraction of a scattering of **arts and craft galleries** and shops (listing from the VIC), the town has two museums. The **Vintage Car Club and Machinery Museum**, ① *178 Talbot St, T03-6938005, daily 1000-1600, $5,* has a sizeable collection of cars and tractors dating back to 1900, as well as a few notable aircraft, including its star attraction, the unique 'Spartan'. The small but lovingly maintained town **museum**, ① *Cox St, T03-6938082, Mon-Sat 1000-1200, 1330-1530, Sun 1400-1600, donations,* is housed in the former 1885 Civic Centre.

The best way to negotiate the arts and crafts outlets is with the guidance and maps available at the VIC. Of particular note is **Barkers Berry Barn**, ① *Talbot St, T03-693 9727, www.barkers.co.nz*, that offers tastings and sales from its fine range of fruity products. **The Giant Jersey**, 10 Wilson St, is also worth a look, reputedly displaying the largest jersey in the world. There are a number of good **walks** in the vicinity, part-icularly in the **Talbot Forest Scenic Reserve** next to the town, and the **Peel Forest** 19 km northwest, via SH79 (The Peel Forest Road). The VIC has details or call in at the **Peel Forest Environmental Information Centre** ① *at the OPC office base, T03-696 3832, www.peelforestopc.org.nz Mon-Fri 0900-1630.* ▶ *For Sleeping and other listings, see pages 537-539.*

Temuka → *Colour map 6, grid B6 Population: 4,000*
This small agricultural service town, 19 km north of Timaru, is the former home of farmer and eccentric inventor **Richard Pearse** (1877-1953). In April 1903, at the tender age of 26, Pearse created history by making the first-ever powered flight in a 'heavier- than-air

man-carrying aeroplane'. His flight, though neither long nor spectacular, was a world first and was completed nine months before the better-known and much-celebrated flight by the American pioneer aviator Orville Wright of the famous Wright brothers. A **memorial** to his muted achievement can be seen at Waitohi (signposted off SH1), which was the site of his brief and historic flight, and in 2003 on the 100 anniversary locals attempted to rebuild his plane and get airborne. Sadly on the day inclement weather meant nothing except umbrellas were airborne. It all seems sad really when you consider Pearse died an unrecognised recluse in a psychiatric hospital in Christchurch.

Besides the memory and memorial to its most famous son, Temuka is noted for its modern-day crafts outlets, particularly the **Temuka Pottery,** Thomas Street (tours every Wednesday at 1300). Its location is perhaps fitting given the fact that the town's name derived from the Maori Te-Umu-Kaha, meaning 'The Place of the Hot Ovens'.

Located 18 km northwest of Timaru (SH8), Pleasant Point offers a few brief diversions including the **Pleasant Point Museum and Railway,** ① *T03-6862269, www.timaru.com/railway* It is home to the world's only remaining 1925 *Model T Ford* Railcar. There are regular scheduled rides on the glistening restored loco hourly ($6, child $3), and kids will further delight at others that feature faces akin to 'Thomas the Tank Engine' and friends. Although additional rides are offered on most weekends (1030-1630) you are advised to phone for specific dates and details. After experiencing these working metal characters you may like to see another in the form of Gareth James at the **Artisan Forge,** ① *5 Maitland St, T03-6147272. Daily 1000-1700.* Gareth is one of New Zealand's few remaining working blacksmiths.

Near Pleasant Point is one of the finest examples of **Maori rock art** in the country. The weathered 14-ft drawing known as the Opihi 'Taniwha' (Maori for 'monster') is considered to be the oldest, having been created sometime in the 16th century. It is in a shallow limestone shelter on private farmland and is best viewed lying on your back. To visit the site you will need to be accompanied by a guide, which can be organized through the Timaru VIC.

Waimate → *Colour map 6, grid B6 Population: 3,000*

Although noted as being an atypical New Zealand rural township, Waimate, 47 km south of Timaru, is perhaps better known as a 'little bit of Aussie abroad', with its very furry resident population of cuddly marsupials. Known rather unfortunately perhaps as 'red necked' or bush **wallabies,** these appealing plump and bouncy little characters were originally introduced to the area in 1875 for fur and sport. But, like so many other intellectually wanting acts of 'wildlife familiarization', it has resulted in a resident population of rapacious native plant-eaters that are now considered a major pest. Given this, the activities surrounding the wallabies are in complete contrast with most folks taking delight in hunting them down. But it doesn't end there (Lord no!). In Waimate one eminent bright spark recently came up with the idea of making **wallaby meat pies**. Who knows, it might just prove to be a major tourist drawcard.

You can either take the indirect, sympathetic and close-range option, with copious amounts of petting and feeding, at the wallaby-friendly **EnkleDooVery Korna,** ① *Bathgates Rd, T03-6897197, Oct-Apr, Mon-Fri 1300-1700, Sat and Sun 1000-1700, $5, child $3,* or alternatively the more distant and direct approach, with a bullet (hunting details from the VIC). If you do take the former option you can cuddle the irresistible pouch babies. Wallabies can also be seen, petted and fed at the **Kelcey's Bush Holiday and Animal Park,** ① *Mill Rd, 7 km west of the town (signposted), T03-6898057, kelceysbush@xtra.co.nz*

Of a more steadfast and historical nature is the less cuddly but very smart **Waimate Historical Museum,** ① *in the former 1879 Waimate Courthouse, 28 Shearman St, T03-6897832. Mon-Fri 1330-1630, Sun 1400-1600, $2.* It houses a small but significant array of memorabilia and forms part of the town's **Strawberry Heritage Trail.**

Also of historical interest, but of very different structural aesthetics, is the Te **537**
Waimate historic thatched **'cuddy'** which is almost as cute as the wallabies. Built in
1854 from a single totara tree, it was the home of Michael Studholme, the first
European settler in the town. Waimate is often used as a short cut to the **Waimate
River** and **Benmore/Aviemore Lakes**, which are famous for their water-sports
activities and superb **fishing**. The huge and very uncuddly Quinnant salmon are the
prime target. The VIC has details and listings of local guides. If you are in Waimate in
February your visit may coincide with the annual **Busking Festival,** which attracts
participants from far and wide.

● Sleeping

Ashburton *p532*
A **Hotel Ashburton**, *Racecourse Rd,
T03-3083059, www.hotelash.co.nz* Modern
units with in-house restaurant, bar and spas.
There are a few **motels**, mainly on the main
drag, including:
B **Academy Lodge**, *782 East St, T03-3085503,*
B **Riverside**, *1 Main Road South, at the
southern end, T03-3088248.*
C-D **Ashburton Holiday Park**, *Tinwald
Domain, Moronan Rd, (see above),
T03-3086805.* Ideally placed with basic
cabins, powered/tent sites and backpacker
accommodation.

Timaru *p533*
The Piazza overlooking Caroline Bay is a fine
place to be based.
A-B **Panorama Motor Lodge**, *50-52 The Bay
Hill, T03-6880097, www.panorama.net* Handy
for the restaurants on the Piazza and
Caroline Bay.
AL-A **Benvenue Hotel and Motor Inn**,
16-22 Evans St, T03-6884049. Also good, has
an in-house restaurant.
B **Ace-Hi Motel**, *51-53 King St, close to the
Botanical Gardens, T03-6883054.*
A-B **Cedar Motor Lodge**, *36 King St,
T03-6844084, cedarlodge@clear.net.nz*

L **Tighnafeile House**, *62 Wai-iti Rd,
T03-6843333, tighnafeile-house@
timaru.co.nz* At the B&B top-end, a beautiful
and historic former run-holders station. A
5-min walk from Caroline Bay and 15 mins to
the town centre, it offers fine spacious
ensuites and double/twin rooms with
shared facilities.
A **Okare Boutique B&B**, *11 Wai-iti Rd,
T03-6880316, www.okare.co.nz* Another
classy and newly renovated historic house
offering a spacious double and queen with

en suite, and a king with shared facilities. Spa
and bunk room for singles or kids.
B-D **Timaru Backpackers**, *44 Evans St,
T03-6845067.* The best hostel in town and a
YHA associate that shares with a motel to
provide a wide range of rooms from
self-contained doubles to shared. Pick-ups
available from downtown.

Motorcamps
B-D **Selwyn Top Ten Holiday Park**, *8 Glen
St, T03-6847690.* In a suburban setting and,
although a good walk from the city centre,
is quiet, spacious, and has the most
modern facilities.

Geraldine *p535*
The VIC has full accommodation listings.
LL **Kavanagh House**, *SH1, Winchester,
T03-6156150, www.kavanaghhouse.co.nz*
Luxurious boutique lodge with 2 sumptuous
modern ensuites with spa or claw-bath and
open fires. It is also well known for its fine
cuisine. Recommended.
AL **Crossing**, *Woodbury Rd, in Geraldine itself,
T03-6939689.* A former old 'gentleman's
residence' (whatever that means) with
ensuites, pleasant gardens, open fire and
in-house restaurant.
B **Struan Farm Retreat**, *Thatcher Rd, Tripp,
T03-6922852, www.struanretreat.com* Also
out of town but still in range (8 km).Aptly
named and affordable. A self-contained 2
bedroom cottage in 20 acres with a lovely
atmosphere and views. The guest-friendly
animals make it especially good for kids.
B **Crown Hotel**, *31 Talbot St, T03-6938458,
Geraldine-crown@xtra.co.nz* Has character
and some good-value ensuites.
There are a handful of **motels** including:
B **Four Peaks**, *28 MacKenzie St, T03-6938339.*
Pleasant and modern.
D **Olde Presbytery**, *13 Jollie St, T03-6939644.*
Your best budget option.

Canterbury South Canterbury

B-D **Geraldine Motor Camp**, *39 Hislop St,
T03-6938147*. In a central location adjacent to
the park and cabins and powered/ tent sites.
C-D **Peel Forest Motor Camp**, *T03-6963567*.
Basic but tidy, it offers cabins, powered/tent
sites and nice walks nearby.

Waimate *p536*

AL **Te Kiteroa**, *Point Bush Rd, T03-6898291,
grakeen@xtra.co.nz* A fine old home in the
Hunter Hills, with a formal garden. It offers
well-appointed ensuites and a self-contained
former gardener's cottage. In-house
massage and aromatherapy are a speciality.
B **Locheil Motel and Guest House**, *100
Shearman St, T03-6897570*. Offers self-
contained studios and units.
C-D **Hunter's Hill Lodge**, *Hillary St,
T03-6898726, hunters.hills@xtra.co.nz*
Spacious budget accommodation.
B-D **Kelcey's Bush Farmyard**, *Mill Rd (see
above), T03-6898057*. Good for campervans
and has tidy cabins and flats.

● Eating

Ashburton *p532*

$$ **Jesters**, *9 Moana Sq, T03-3089983* and
$$ **Tuscany's (Somerset Tavern)** *across the
road from the VIC, T03-3083389* are both
good and open daily for lunch and dinner.
$$ **Cactus Jacks**, *209 Wills St, T03-3080495.
Open daily*. Good for a Tex-Mex. All
are licensed.
$$ **Kelly's Bar and Café**, *234 East St,
T03-3088811*. For a good pub lunch.
$ **Ashford Café and Wine Bar**, *in Ashford
Craft Village, 427 West St, T03-3089085.
Mon-Fri 0900-1630, Sat and Sun 1000-1600.*
Recommended for coffee and light snacks.

Timaru *p533*

The Piazza and Bay Hill Road that overlook
Caroline Bay have 2 good affordable eateries:
$$ **Boudicca's**, *T03-6888550*, offering
good Middle Eastern and traditional
Kiwi-style blackboard menu, for both
lunch and dinner; and almost next door,
$$ **Zanzibar**, *T03-6884367*, slightly more
expensive with good seafood. Both open
for lunch and dinner and licensed.
$ **Red Rocket Café**, *4A Elizabeth St,
T03-6888313. Mon-Sat from 1000-late, Sun*

from 1130. Another popular café option
with the best coffee.
$ **Coq and Pullet**, *209 Stafford St. Mon-Fri
0730-1600, Sat 1000-1300*. Has a great range
of light snacks, breads and huge cakes.
$$ **Loaded Hog**, *George St, T03-6849999.
Daily from 1100*. As ever, a good option.
$ **Stafford Mall Foodcourt**, *Stafford St*. Cheap
takeaways.
$ **The Purple Lizard Cafe**, *332 Stafford St,
T03-6888890. Mon-Fri 0730-1700, Sat
0900-1700, Sun 1000-1700*. For homesick
Scottish people there is porridge on the
breakfast menu. It might not be as good as
Granny's but it will do and the coffee is grand.

Geraldine *p535*

$$$ **Kavanagh House**, *see above*. The
obvious choice for expensive fine dining.
Bookings essential.
$$ **Totara Bar and Restaurant in the
Crown Hotel**, *see above. Daily from 1100*. A
more affordable down to earth option.
$ **Easy Way Café**, *next to the Barkers Berry
Barn Complex, T03-6938090. Daily for lunch
and dinner*. Also safe bet with frequent live
entertainment (especially jazz) and internet.
$ **Barkers Berry Barn**, *see above. Daily 0900-
1730*. Definitely the place for smoothies.

Waimate *p536*

There is not a great deal of choice when it
comes to eating, with only a handful of fairly
unremarkable take-aways and tearooms in
the town centre.
$$ **Zanders Restaurant**, *25 Queen St,
T03-6896010*. Offers à la carte.
$ **Country Kitchen**, *also on Queen St. Daily
0500-2100*. Light snacks.
$ **Savoy Tearooms**, *59 Queen St,
T03-6897147*. The place to get your gnashers
round a wallaby meat pie (with plum sauce).
You can also try goat, rabbit and thar
(another introduced species – this time a
mountain goat). They sell for a very
reasonable $3.50. Vegetarians had best catch
the bus to Timaru!

▲ Activities

Ashburton *p532*

For local activities consult the VIC. Pick-ups
are provided for other activities to the west

including **rafting and ballooning**. There are also some interesting day tours available to the **Foothills and Mount Somers.**

Timaru p533
Timaru is noted not only for its sand and surf but also for its inland rivers, which come complete with monster trout.
Aoraki Fly Fishing, *T03-6869266, www.flyfishing.co.nz* One of the best regional guides.
Timaru Marine Cruises, *T03-6886881.* Offer marine wildlife watching tours that often locate the rare and tiny Hector's dolphin. The *Caroline Cat* departs daily at 1030 from No1 Wharf in the harbour (corner of Port Loop and Ritchie St), from $30.
There are plenty of good **short-walking** opportunities in the town, with 3 Heritage Trails and the 1-hour Dashing Rocks and 45-minute Caroline Bay Walks and the Centennial Park Walk (see above). The VIC has details.

Geraldine p535
Geraldine is the base for some interesting activity operators including:
4x4 New Zealand, *T03-6938847, www.southisland. org.nz/4x4* A reputable outfit offering 4WD Alpine and scenic tours locally and throughout the region
Rangitata Rafts, *T03-6963534,* *T0800-251251, www.rafts.co.nz* Offer day excursions down the scenic Rangitata River (Grade 4-5), from $145.

O Shopping

Timaru p533
Timaru is home to the **Swanndri** - an 'iconic' New Zealand pure wool jacket or 'bushshirt' that is famously warm.
Swanndri Factory Shop, *24A Church St, T03-6849037. Mon-Fri 1000-1630, Sat 1000-1400.* Sells well-known Kiwi products including oilskins, knitwear and rugs.

O Directory

Timaru p533
Banks All the main branches have ATMs and are represented in the centre of town around Stafford St. **Car hire** Rental Vehicles Ltd, *6 Sefton St, T03-6847179.* Avis *9 Heaton St, T03-6886240.* **Internet** The Computer Shop, *331 Stafford St, T03-6849333. Mon-Fri 0900-1730, Sat 1000-1230.* **Post office** *21 Strathallan St, T03-6866040. Mon-Fri 0830-1730, Sat 0900-1300.* **Library** *King George Pl, T03-6848199.* **Taxi** Timaru Taxis, *T03-6888899.* **Useful addresses** AA *26 Church St, T03-6884189.* **Police** *North St, T03-6884199.*

The MacKenzie Country → *Phone code: 03*

The area known as the MacKenzie Country refers principally to the flat expanse of tussock grasslands that make up the watersheds of the Tekapo and Gray Rivers. It is a strange barren landscape, devoid of trees and almost analogous to the plains of heartland USA. There is really nowhere else like it in New Zealand and it bears little semblance to the lofty peaks that rise from around its edge. The name MacKenzie was bestowed upon it through the almost legendary activities of Scots pioneer and sheep drover James 'Jock' MacKenzie (see page 542).

Ins and outs
Getting there All the daily west-east buses from Christchurch and Queenstown pass through Fairlie, Lake Tekapo and Twizel including **Intercity**, T0800-767080; **Atomic Shuttles**, T03-3328883; and **Southern Link Shuttles**, T03-3588355. **Cook Connection**, T02-5583211, also offer services between Mt Cook and Timaru (via Tekapo) on Tue, Thurs and Sat. They pass through Twizel on their Mt Cook to Oamaru run on Mon, Wed and Fri (departing 0915/returning 1515, from $30 one-way). Bookings for all the above can be made with **High Country Souvenirs and Crafts**, Lake

Tekapo, To3-6806895. The **Mount Cook Landline,** To800-800-904; and **High Country Shuttles,** To800-435-050, to Twizel connect daily with Christchurch-bound Intercity and Atomic Shuttles in Mount Cook. Buses stop outside the VIC near the centre of Twizel. **GTS Country Link Tours,** 44 Omahau Cres, Twizel, To3-4350052, go to Timaru every Fri and also offer local tours.

Information The closest you find to a **VIC** in **Fairlie** are the helpful folk in the **Sunflower Centre and Café,** ① *31 Main St, To3-6858258, www.fairlie.co.nz Daily 0900-1800.* They stock leaflets and list local accommodation options. **Lake Tekapo VIC** (independent), ① *in Kiwi Treasures beside the post shopon the main street, To3-6806686, www.laketekapountouched.co.nz Daily 0800-2000.* It is very small but has free town maps, all the information about accommodation in the village, and local activity listings. **Twizel VIC,** ① *beside the Mall (northern entrance to Market Place) in the centre of the village, To3-4353124, www.twizel.com Daily 0900-1900 (winter Mon-Sat 0900-1700).* The free leaflet *Twizel – Town of Trees* has a detailed map and is very useful. Internet access. **DoC area office** (Twizel), ① *Wairepo Rd, To3-4350802, KakiVisitorHide@DoC.govt.nz Mon-Fri 0830-1730.* Can provide specialist tramping and mountain bike track information.

Fairlie → *Colour map 6, grid B5 Population: 845*

Lying relatively out on its own at the foot of the Hunter and Two Thumbs Ranges, the small rural settlement of Fairlie is often labelled as the rather dull gateway to the MacKenzie Country that lies just to the west through the portal of the **Burke's Pass**.

Sights While it is certain Fairlie will probably never set the world alight, it seems to have absolutely no intention of doing so and is, instead, perfectly happy with its pretty autumn colours and quiet existence. Quiet, that is, until winter when it is used as a base for the **Mount Dobson Ski-field,** ① *To3-6858039, www.dobson.co.nz*

If you look a little closer you will find considerable evidence that contradicts Fairlie's outward appearance and reputation for being just another dull rural town. It has in fact been home to some rather innovative folk. One such resident, **Rodolph Wigley,** for example, drove from Timaru to Mount Cook in 1906 in a De Dion Bouton single-cylinder car, taking three days and encountered atrocious conditions (and few roads) to do so. Not satisfied with this rather impressive mechanical feat, he then went on to develop a motor-coach service and later an air transport service to Mount Cook, thereby creating the **Mount Cook Company**. Still not satisfied with this thriving enterprise (and clearly still reeling with inherent tedium), he then added a threshing mill business to his list of achievements and a traction engine that could do the work of 16 bullocks at twice the speed. And it doesn't end there. Rodolph's son, Harry, went on to design a landing gear that allowed his aircraft to land on the snow and ice of the Tasman Glacier. Said gear was later to become the precursor to the landing gears in use today. So, you see it is in fact interesting after all.

Other little insights can be procured from the two small museums in town: the **1875 Mabel Binney Cottage** and the **Vintage Machinery Museum,** ① *both located on the main highway west of the town centre (open daily 1000-1700, seasonal, $2).* Further west still (5 km) is the historic 1879 limestone **Woolshed,** ① *on the privately owned Three Springs Station, To3-6858174, daily 1000-1600, seasonal.* At its peak this station accommodated nine 'blade' shearers, which to the layman is essentially a very hard working fella shearing with a very sharp pair of scissors – not the bionic electric clippers that are used today.

Lake Tekapo → *Colour map 6, grid B5 Population: 300*

Between **Lake Tekapo** and Twizel is the heart of the **MacKenzie Country**. If you have come north from the heady heights of Mount Cook there could hardly be more

The MacKenzie Muster

Every year in January the naturist friendly Aoraki Naturally Campsite, located 16 km south of Tekapo, proudly hosts an increasingly popular two-day naturist fest christened the'MacKenzie Muster'. By all accounts this is a wonderfully invigorating experience and a truly international event attracting partici-pant-less from the United States, England and Germany. Various intriguing activities are offered over the weekend all with a distinctly Scottish flavour from tossing the caber (naturally), to golf and even lawnmower races. Quite where one puts one's tees remains an enigma.

Despite inclement weather, the event in 2003 was a resounding success and the dates have once again been set for the 9th to the 12th of January 2004. Hat's (and pants) off to them! For further details contact *Aoraki Naturally, T03-6806549.*

contrast in scenery. Lake and mountain ranges quickly give way to a vast expanse of featureless tussock grasslands of the **Tekapo River** basin. Suddenly it seems you have been taken magically from the Swiss Alps to Mid-West USA, and on less than a litre of petrol. New Zealand is just like that: Switzerland one minute, the US the next, then around the corner the Highlands of Scotland – a landscape of incredible contrasts. From whichever direction you have come, SH8 delivers you to the southern shores of Lake Tekapo and the settlement of the same name. A pretty place, famous for its iconic lakeside **church** and an ever-watchful little collie dog.

Sights Just about everybody who visits Lake Tekapo pays homage to the town's stone church that sits alone, in almost picture-postcard position, overlooking the lake. If it were a stage prop for some ecclesiastical Hollywood blockbuster it could not look more perfect. Even on closer inspection it is truly blessed, with an open door revealing a cross on the altar backed by a large stained glass window – minus the stain. With a view and a backdrop like that it is heavenly enough, thank you. The church is called **The Church of the Good Shepherd** and was built in 1935, primarily as a functional place of worship, but also as a memorial to the lives of the MacKenzie Country pioneers. Sadly though, its modern-day function is almost entirely aesthetic, and the poor minister – our good shepherd – who is in attendance almost daily, must tend a very superficial and transitory flock. The vast majority of people who fall out of the tour buses in droves and are guided to the church by yelping interpreters, come only to take pictures and worship the Lord Digital and Kodak, not to pray or worship the Lord God Almighty. And watching this mass and chaotic 'sheep-dip' you can't help but wonder whether his cheery smile and kind words hide more cynical thoughts about a world gone utterly mad. Whatever you do, go early morning or late in the day to avoid the hordes.

A few pew's lengths from the church is a statue of a collie **sheepdog** which is a simple tribute to the shepherd's best friend. It's a lovely statue, with the dog facing the lake with an alert and loyal expression as if waiting for his master to appear from the mists of the lake. He has waited a long time, and may wait forever, his little nose covered in ice in winter, wet with rain in spring and bleached by the sun in summer.

Although not yet built (with a planned opening in 2005) Tekapo looks set to host an ambitious new project in the form of the **MacKenzie Heritage Centre** ⓘ *www.themackenzie.com* At an estimated cost of around $12 million it will – we are assured – be aesthetically sympathetic with the surroundings and a state of the art creation that will effectively celebrate and conserve the social and natural history of the

The Legend of James-'Jock'-McKenzie

The MacKenzie Country which lies west of the Burke's Pass from Fairlie is named after the legendary Scots sheep drover James 'Jock' McKenzie. Jock, of course, is a common label given to Scots folk, and the 'a' is optional in the 'Mac' – both Mac and Mc meaning, simply 'son of'. Anyway, the story goes that our James was caught in the Burke Pass, east of Lake Tekapo in 1855 with 1,000 sheep. Nothing unusual in that (or is there?), except for the simple fact that they were not his. Said sheep actually belonged to the Rhodes brothers from the large Levels Station near Timaru (doubtless English!). The Rhodes boys had sent out a small party to look for the flock and found James happily droving them to pastures new. Being hopelessly outnumbered, but Scottish, James managed to escape and was later recaptured in Lyttleton near Christchurch. Re-captured and suitably arraigned he was found guilty of sheep rustling and sentenced to five years in jail. But that's where it all gets a bit hazy. Apparently, James then professed his innocence, claiming the sheep

had in fact been bought and that he was taking his 'legally purchased' flock to a new claim in Otago. (Another story goes that he was in fact coerced into the theft). Initially believing this to be a load of tartan codswallop, he was jailed. But still determined, James escaped, not once, but two (some say three) times, by which time the powers that be were beginning to believe his story. Remarkably, after only nine months he was given a full pardon and released (but some say with the condition that he left New Zealand forever). Innocent or guilty, buried in the soils of New Zealand, or the glens back home in Scotland, we may never know. But still the stuff of legend he is immortalized by a monument and stone cairn on the roadside, just west of the Pass (which apparently some say was not where he was captured at all). On the monument you can read the following immortal words:

'In this spot James MacKenzie (sic) freebooter, was captured by John Sidebottom and Maoris, Taiko and Seventeen and escaped the same night, 4th March 1855'
...go Jimmy!

region. To that end no doubt its creators and more importantly, its financiers, have spent a few Sunday mornings in prayer down at the Church of the Good Shepherd.

If you have time (and a rugged vehicle) the unsealed roads on either side of Lake Tekapo are both well worth exploring. The road to the west passes **Lakes Alexandria and McGregor** which are both very peaceful (and full of trout) before winding its way north to terminate at the Godley Peak Station. On the eastern side the road travels along the lakes edge past the Mt Hay and Richmond Stations and the junction to the **Roundhill Ski Area** before continuing up in to the wilds of Macaulay and **Godley River** Basins. On a map you will see just how far the glacier formed Godley River basin goes before submitting inevitably to the peaks of the Mount Cook National Park and Mt D'Archiac (2865 m). The country up in there is the realm of the serious tramper and climber since without a helicopter it takes days to reach.

Twizel → Colour map 6, grid B4 Population: 1,179

Right in the heart of the MacKenzie Basin, near the river after which it was named, is Twizel, a former hydroelectric-scheme construction town built in the 1970s. Pioneer surveyor John Thompson bestowed the name Twizel upon the town after the Twizel

Bridge that crosses the River Tweed on the border between England and Scotland.
Twizel's most famous residents are the critically endangered and endemic Kaki, or **black stilt**, which, along with the village's proximity to the **Mount Cook National Park** and **mountain biking**, are its biggest tourist draw.

Sights Twizel presents another excellent opportunity to see cutting-edge conservation at work, so typical of DoC and the country as a whole. Twizel is home to the internationally recognized efforts to maintain the wild populations of the **black stilt** – one of the rarest wading birds in the world. They are called 'Kaki' by the Maori and are considered by them to be a *taonga* species (living treasure). Once common in the heartlands and braided-river beds throughout New Zealand, thanks primarily to man's indirect introduction of non-native predatory species, like the weasel and stoat, numbers have been decimated and currently total less than 100 wild birds. A guided visit to the **viewing hide**, located 3 km south of the village, allows the public to view the stalwart survivors and captive population of 66 that are bred in enclosed aviaries and used to replenish (or increase) the wild population. Bookings are essential and visits are by prior arrangement only. ① *Guided tours are available daily from late Oct-mid Apr (weekdays only in winter), from $12.50, child $5. Contact the VIC.*

Lake Ohau → *Colour map 6, grid B4*
Largely unbeaten by the nasty commercial stick, Lake Ohau provides a pleasant diversion off SH8 between Omarama and Twizel, and in winter a popular skiing venue. The **ski field** is best known for its scenic views, less frenzied atmosphere and the longest T-bar in New Zealand (1033 m). ① *For more skiing information T03-4389885, www.snow.co.nz* Most of the activity centres around Lake Ohau **Alpine Village** which is above the southern shores of Lake Ohau, just west of **Lake Middleton**, a small sub-lake separated from Lake Ohau by a narrow strip of land.

In summer the lake and its surroundings are popular for **walking, fishing and mountain biking.** It has six forests around its shores, with a number of tracks, access points and campsites. The best information is contained in the DoC brochure 'Ohau Conservation Area' available from the VIC in Twizel.

⬤ Sleeping

Fairlie *p540*
L-AL Dobson Lodge, *Burke's Pass, T03-6858316, dobson_lodge@xtra.co.nz* Although some distance west of Fairlie, it provides a lovely romantic self-contained stone cottage in a country setting.
B Possum Cottage, *Bedeshurst, T03-6858075, possum.cottage@xtra.co.nz* Self-contained, farm-based and very cosy alternative with an open fire.
There are a few basic but comfortable **motels** including:
B Rimuwhare, *53 Mt Cook Rd, T03-6858058, rimuwhare@xtra.co.nz*
B Fairlie Lodge, *16 School Rd, T03-6858452.*

Motorcamps
B-D Fairlie Gateway Top Ten Holiday Park *Allandale Rd, northwest of the town centre,* *T03-6858375, fairliegateway@xtra.co.nz* Also has backpacker accommodation.

Lake Tekapo *p540*
In Maori the name *Tekapo* means 'sleeping mat', but thankfully the village can offer far more than a bivvy beside the lake.
L-AL Godley Resort Hotel, *SH8, T03-6806848, www.thegodley.com* The main hotel in town. Although getting a little tired it is in prime position in the centre of the village overlooking the lake. It has comfortable suites with great views, and reputable Chinese and Japanese restaurants. It is of course very busy with tour groups in summer, which may not suit, but in winter, when rates are reduced or with the odd special deal, it can be worth considering.
AL-A Lake Tekapo Scenic Resort Motel, *T03-6806808, www.laketekapo.com*

Slightly further up the road and in the heart of the action. Modern studio units, views and spas.

AL-A Chalet Boutique Motel, *T03-6806774, www.thechalet-laketekapo. co.nz* Another fine lodge-style motel option. Lakeside (near the church) and offersplenty of activities.

Tekapo has some fine **B&Bs** including the **LL-L Tekapo Lodge**, *above the main street in Aorangi Cres, T03-6806566, www.laketekapolodge.co.nz* 4 ensuites, one with spa, and a guest lounge with open fire.

A Tekapo House, *8 O'Neill Pl, T03-6806607, rayntek@xtra.co.nz* The slightly cheaper but equally modern. 10 min from the centre of the village and has 1 ensuite, 1 double and 1 twin with shared facilities.

A Pioneer Cottage, *overlooking the lake (near the church) on Pioneer Dr, T03-6806755*. A good self-contained option and very cosy in winter with its log fire.

For other good B&B options contact the VIC.

C-D Tekapo YHA, *3 Simpson Lane, T03-6806857, yhatekapo@yha.org.nz* Popular with backpackers with a lakeside location at the western end of the village, offering great views. Doubles, twins and dorms, bike hire.

C-D Tailor-Made-Tekapo Backpackers, *9-11 Aorangi Cres, T03-6806700, tailor-made-backpackers@xtra.co.nz* Friendly and efficient, although not with the same views as the YHA, it has a good range of rooms with some good value ensuites.

Motorcamps and campsites

A-D Lake Tekapo Motels and Motor Camp, at the western end of the village, Lakeside Drive, T03-6806825. Spacious, peaceful and lakeside. A fine spot with self-contained motels, flats, cabins and sheltered powered/tent sites.

Aoraki Naturally, *17 km south of Tekapo near Irishman Creek Bridge, T03-6806549*. Should all the scenery and abounding nature lead to a sudden and dramatic desire to remove all your clothing, you would be welcome to do so here. Each year in February they proudly host a **naturist fest** christened the 'MacKenzie Muster' (see box, page 541).

Twizel *p542*

L-AL MacKenzie Country Inn, *corner of Ostler and Wairepo Rds, T03-4350869,*

bookings@mackenzie.co.nz Very plush, has 'all the right knobs and switches' and is close to the town centre.

There are a scattering of **motels**, including:

A Aspen Court Motel, *10 MacKenzie Dr, T03-4350274* and

A Mountain Chalets Motel, *Wairepo Rd, T03-4350785, mt.chalets@xtra.co.nz*

B-D High Country Holiday Lodge and Motel, *23 MacKenzie Dr, T03-4350671, www.twizel.com/highcountrylodge* A huge and cheaper motel option with backpacker facilities, which has cheap ensuites, doubles, singles and dorms. There is also a restaurant and bar on site and it is a stone's throw from Market Place.

There are not many **B&B's**, but the VIC has a full list of those that are available.

AL Heartland Lodge, *19 North West Arm, T03-4350008, european@xtra.co.nz* Has some nice rooms and a self-contained loft that is good value for up to six.

Other places worth considering are:

AL-A Lake Ruataniwha Homestay, *9 Max Smith Dr, T03-4350532, robinandlester@xtra.co.nz* A spacious modern home overlooking the lake, south west of the town centre.

A Artemis B&B *33 North West Arch, T03-4350388, atremistwizel@yahoo.co.nz* A centrally located modern home with fine views.

A Aoraki Lodge, *32 MacKenzie Dr, T03-4350300, mtdb@mtcook.org.nz* A slightly cheaper and equally reliable option.

Motorcamps

There are two motor parks in the area:

B-D Parklands Alpine Tourist Park, *122 MacKenzie Dr, T03-4350507*. In a sheltered spot and has self-contained and budget accommodation.

C-D Lake Ruataniwha Holiday Park, *4 km south of the village, T03-4350613*. In a pleasant setting near the lake.

Lake Ohau *p543*

Other than the **camping grounds**:

L-AL Lake Ohau Lodge, *T03-4389885, www.ohau.co.nz* It is set by the side of the lake and has standard self-contained studio and luxury units, a restaurant, bar and cosy open fire.

B Weatherall Motel, *T03-4389662,*

rockyhigh@xtra.co.nz Has self-contained units and shared units (30 mins from the ski-fields).
A Lake Ohau Homestay, *8 Ohau Dr, Ohau Alpine Village, T03-4389833, pesu.ohau@xtra.co.nz* The only B&B option, a mere 5 mins from the ski fields.

🍴 Eating

Fairlie *p540*
$ Old Library Café, *in the centre of town, T03-6858999. Daily from 1000-late.* Recommended, offering snacks to dinners including a great two-course 'skiers' menu for $12.50.

Lake Tekapo *p540*
$$$ Kohan Japanese Restaurant in the *Godley Resort Hotel, T03-6806688. Daily for lunch and dinner).* Your best (and only) bet if you want a bit of fine Japanese food. There are numerous café/bars and takeaways in the main street that offer light snacks and coffee, with most offering backdoor views across the lake.
$$-$ Pepes Pizza and Pasta, *T03-6806848 Mon-Fri 1800-late, Sat/Sun from 1200-late.*
$$-$ Reflections Restaurant, *T03-6806808 Daily from 1000.*
Supermarket 4Square, *at the service station is open daily until 2100.*

Twizel *p542*
The options are few with almost all centred in Market Place.
$$ The Hunter's Bar and Café, *T03-4350303.* The local's choice for lunch, dinner and entertainment. It can serve up a decent coffee.
$$ MacKenzie Country Inn, *see above. Daily from 1100.* Also offers fine dining.

▲ Activities

Lake Tekapo *p540*
Although Lake Tekapo is a small place there is plenty to do beyond grabbing a coffee, taking pictures of a church and patting an attractive bust! Being the first major stop for the east-west tour buses and independent tourist traffic, there is the instant lure to leave the car parked and reach for the skies. Various operators vie to offer the best deals on the

hire of mountain bikes, kayaks and fishing rods. For the latest deals contact the VIC.

Cruising and fishing
Lake Tekapo Adventures, *T03-6806686.* Offer an attractive range of fishing, boating, hiking and sightseeing, from 1½ hrs, $35.

Flightseeing
There are a number of flightseeing options, and the airfield in Tekapo is the starting point for 2 main operators that also pick up passengers in Mount Cook, before embarking on world-class scenic flights across the Great Divide.
Air Safaris, *on the main street, T0800-806880, www.airsafaris.co.nz* and **Tekapo Helicopters**, *T03-6806229, www.scenic-flights.co.nz* Air Safari's popular 'Grand Traverse' is a memorable 50-minute (200km) trip that takes in Mount Cook and the glaciers on both sides of the divide. It is a fairly unique combination that you would be hard-pressed to find anywhere else in the world, so if you do not have time to visit Mount Cook Village or the West Coast, where similar options abound, it is well worth considering. There will also be plenty of other options in Wanaka and Queenstown, but this trip (beyond a flight to Milford Sound) is one of the best and, at $240, child $160, is good value for money. Helicopter trips are of course are a little more expensive, provide a different kind of experience and can land on the snow. Note that the aircraft based here do not land on the snow unlike those flying from Mount Cook, but obviously, what you lose in that experience, you will gain in flight time.

Horse trekking
McKenzie Alpine Trekking *based on Godley Rd (north) below Mt John, T0800-628269, matc@xtra.co.nz* Offer horse trekking from half hr to overnight suitable for beginners or advanced riders.

Mountain climbing and trekking
Alpine Recreation, *T03-6806736, www.alpinerecreation.co.nz* Offer highly experienced guided mountain climbing and trekking trips from the 3-day Ball Pass Trek in the Tasman Glacier Valley to the Full Monty 6-day ascent of Cook, for the small mortgage of $3300.

Roundhill Ski Area information and conditions *T021-680697, www.snow.co.nz*

Star gazing

Still in the skies, there is an opportunity to go star-gazing at the **international observatory and US satellite tracking station** that sits discreetly atop Mount John at the western end of the village. Even a walk up here during the day provides some heavenly views. *T03-6806565, www.stargazing.co.nz* 1½ hrs Apr-Sep 2000, Oct-Mar 2130 and Nov-Feb 2200, from $40 (minimum 4).

Twizel *p542*

The VIC also lists over 60 *Things Twizel can offer* in the way of activities, ranging from frisbee golf to ice-skating, although 'buying a house' and 'yoga' (unless done in unison perhaps) is slightly overdoing it. It also quite rightly suggests a visit to the 'fantastic information centre' - it and its staff are great. **The Ski Shack**, Main St, T03-6858088, sells and rents out ski gear.

Mountain biking

The big and relatively new attraction based in Twizel is mountain biking. Of particular note are the Heli-biking trips to several locations including Benmore and Lake Ohau. Rides range from 1 ½ hrs to 3 ½ hrs and cost from $30-$190 (Bike hire available.) **Heli-bike Twizel**, *T03-4350626 / T0800-435-424, www.helibike.com* Independently, the numerous canals and their associated tracks that connect the waterways and hydroelectric schemes provide ideal biking opportunities. For more information

contact the VIC or consult the DoC leaflet 'OhauConservation Area'.

Mountaineering

High Country Expeditions, *T03-4350622, snorman@voyager.co.nz* A world-class mountain guide (Shaun Norman) offering half-to multi-day climbing, mountaineering and abseiling trips.

Flightseeing

A number of scenic heli-flightseeing trips leave from beside the MacKenzie Country Inn on Wairepo Road, but you are advised to look at the numerous other choices available from elsewhere before parting with the cash (see Mount Cook National Park section). There are also some excellent fishing venues in the area; the VIC has details.

Climbing

Twizel Events Centre, *Market Pl (just opposite the VIC)*, T03-4350496. *Wall open Mon, Wed, Fri 1900-2100, Sat 1700-1900 and Sun 1600-1800.* New and impressive complex with climbing wall as well as squash courts ($7), and a gym ($7), all open for casual use. A supervised 'public' session on the wall costs from $10.

❶ Directory

Lake Tekapo

Banks There is only one ATM in Tekapo, next to the petrol station. **Bikes hire** From the mini golf office behind the main shopping complex, *T03-6806961.* **Internet** *Reflections Restaurant at the top end of the village,* the **Helicopter Flights Office**, and the **Godley Resort Hotel**, *all on the Main Street.*

Mount Cook National Park

This 70,696-ha park has, by its very name, got to be one of the most spectacular in New Zealand, and a natural 'cathedral' second only to Milford Sound. With the 3754 m peak of Mount Cook as its altar, its robust ministers include Tasman (3498 m) and Mount Sefton (3158 m), surrounded by a supportive choir of 19 peaks over 3000 m. Rising up to this great chancel are the vast and impressive Hooker and Tasman Glaciers, which not only created the long nave but once blocked the very porch. All this natural architecture makes for world-class scenery and mountaineering. Indeed, it was here that Sir Edmund Hillary first started a career that was to reach its very 'peak' on the summit of Everest in 1953. The park is connected to the Westland National Park by the Great (east-west) Divide and peaks of the Liebeg Range. Yet the two parks are signif- icantly different. With such a dramatic upheaval of rock so close to the sea, the western side sees most rain and snow, creating slopes draped in dense rainforest and, higher up, huge snowfields, spawning the great Franz and Fox glaciers (to name but two). But in the Mount Cook National Park, there is almost no forest, with almost one-third of it being permanent snow and ice. In amongst the rock beds and valley floors rare alpine plants flourish, some endemic and rare, and rummaging around in this heady garden are unique bird species, like the mountain parrot and resident vandal – the kea.

The area is considered sacred by the Maori who see Aoraki (Mount Cook) as a powerful symbol of being, an ancestor from whom the Tangata Whenua – the Ngai Tahu people – are descended, and a link between the supernatural and natural world.

Ins and outs

Getting there Mount Cook **airport**, 3 km to the south of Mount Cook Village, is served by **Mount Cook Airlines**, To800-737-000, from Christchurch and Queenstown. A shuttle bus meets most flights, from $6.

Mount Cook village is 63 km from Twizel. **Intercity**, To3-3799020, **buses** offer a daily service from Christchurch (Queenstown-bound) arriving at 1200 and departing at 1230. The tour buses **Great Sights**, To800-744487, www.greatsights.com, and **Grey Line**, To800-800-904, also ply the Christchurch/Queenstown route daily, departing for Christchurch in the early afternoon. **High Country Shuttles**, To800-435-050, offer a daily service to Mount Cook from Twizel (depart Twizel 0700 and1230, Mount Cook 0930 and 1630). They connect with Atomic and Intercity services from Queenstown and Christchurch (in Twizel). **The Cook Connection**, To800-252-666, www.cookconnect.co.nz, offer a Mount Cook to Oamaru return ($80) and Mt Cook to Timaru return ($80), a minimum of 3 days a week. All the bus services stop at the YHA and the Hermitage both of which act as booking agents.

Information DoC VIC, ① *just below the Hermitage Hotel, on Bowen Dr, To3-4351818, www.mtcook.org.nz Daily 0830-1800 (winter 0830-1700)*. It has displays, an audio-visual (good in wet weather, $2.50) and information surrounding the park and its obvious attractions. There are walks leaflets, tramping information and they administer all hut bookings. An up-to-date weather forecast and intentions forms are also provided. Of immediate use is a map of the village contained in the handy leaflet *Aoraki, Mount Cook Alpine Village*, available from DoC and the Hermitage Hotel.

The road to Mount Cook

About 8 km north of Twizel the famed **SH80** skirts the western banks and azure waters of **Lake Pukaki** to pay homage to Aoraki – Mount Cook. Before entering the chancel you are first advised to look at the cathedral from afar from the southern banks of Lake Pukaki. There is a car park, unmanned information centre and **lookout point** from which, on a clear day, the mountain beckons. Unless you are really pressed for time, or the weather is foul, it really is sacrilege not to make the scenic 55 km drive to Mount Cook Village. Located so close to the base of the mountains and Hooker-Tasman Glacier Valleys, it is like a miniature toy-town that acts as the gateway to National Park. And once here, it seems a terrible waste to move on without exploring the park from even closer quarters.

Glentanner Park → *Colour map 6, grid B4*

For the first 32 km towards the mountain valleys, your excitement grows in parallel with the vista before you, as the great snow-capped edifices get larger and larger and more poignantly – you – smaller and smaller. It really is a bit like entering the gaping mouth of Moby Dick. Once again we have nature at its wonderfully dominant best! Before reaching Mount Cook Village, and just beyond the water terminus of Lake Pukaki, you will encounter the motorpark and scenic flightseeing base of **Glentanner Park,** ① *T03-4351855, www.glentanner.co.nz* You are strongly advised to stop here and muse at the **scenic flights** and other **activities** on offer, perhaps over a coffee, in its **café** overlooking the mountain. Also, if you are in a camper van and intend to stay in the valley overnight, be aware that this will be home – there is good basic DoC campsite but no fully facilitated motorpark in the National Park or Mount Cook Village.

Mount Cook Village → *Colour map 6, grid B4 Population: 300 (summer)*

From Glentanner you begin to enter the 'chancel' of the mountains and the National Park proper. In Mount Cook, about 23 km further towards the mountains and 63 km from Twizel, you will find yourself climbing out of your 'dinky-toy' car feeling like a termite. It's easy to get neck ache round here.

Sights After you have recovered from the incredible views that surround you, you will be immediately struck at how ordered and dull in colour Mount Cook, the village, is. This is not an accident, since the settlement comes within the boundary of the **Mount Cook National Park** and is therefore strictly controlled. The only real exception is the **Hermitage Hotel,** *T03-4351809,* *F4351879, www.mount-cook.com* which many claim to be the most famous in New Zealand, while others hail it merely as a blot on the landscape. Of course it is the setting that makes the hotel, with its boast of 'mountain views' taking on far more than mere honest credibility. But although the Hermitage has been well blessed by location it has also been cursed with misfortune. What you see today is not the original, in fact it is essentially the third. The original that was built in 1884 was located further down the valley and destroyed by flash floods in 1913. Relocated and rebuilt in its present position it was then gutted by fire 44 years later. Now at the beginning of the millennium it is undergoing renovation and tightly controlled (but still invasive?) expansion. No doubt you will find yourself continuously staring up at **Mount Cook** from the interior of The Hermitage or from its well-manicured lawns. Keep your eyes and ears open for **kea**, the cheeky green mountain parrots that hang about with – it seems – the sole intention of harrying anything with legs and dismantling all they possess. The DoC campsite at White Horse Hill is another good place to look for them (or the other way round).

As well as the gargantuan vista of Mount Cook and **Mount Sefton** (3158 m), the associate glacier valleys are well worthy of investigation. Directly north of the Hermitage is the **Hooker Valley**, and east, over the dwarfed **Wakefield Range**, the vast **Tasman Valley** with its own massive glacier – the longest in New Zealand. Both valleys act as the watersheds that feed Lake Pukaki and were once full of ice, hence the incredible expanse of **boulder-fields** that precede the lake's azure waters. It is incidentally the presence of fine glacial moraine ('rock flour') that gives the glacial lakes their exotic colour. There are a number of activities that focus on the glacier valleys and lakes which have already been mentioned (see Glentanner above), but they can of course also be explored by foot (see walks below).

Tramping

Mount Cook village is the gateway to the **Copeland Pass Track,** which is a 4-5 day tramp to the West Coast across the Great Divide. As attractive as this may seem, it is a tramp that requires considerable experience and proper mountaineering equipment. It is also ill advised at present due to rock falls at the higher altitudes. Conditions are expected to improve, however, especially with the planned relocation of the Hooker

∷ Sir Edmund Hillary

Sir Edmund Hillary is one of New Zealand's most famous sons, and although best known as the man that first conquered Mt Everest, he is also a noted Antarctic explorer and in more recent times is also well known for his welfare work in Nepal. Born in Auckland in 1919, he first worked as an apiarist, before serving with the air force in the Pacific during the Second World War.

It was after the war that Hilary was drawn, time and again, to the mountains of the Southern Alps in New Zealand. Being a committed mountaineer and having immense stamina and ability, it was not long before his obsession took him to the Himalayas. He almost immediately joined expeditions in 1951 and 1952, but it was on the 29th May, 1953 as a member of John Hunt's British team that Hillary and sherpa Tenzing Norgay made the first known successful ascent of the summit. It was a feat that naturally brought instant fame.

After further expeditions to Nepal in 1954 and 1955, Hillary turned his attentions to another of nature's last frontiers – the Antarctic. From 1956-58 he was a member of a team that completed the first tractor journey from Scott Base to the South Pole. After this successful expedition he returned once again to Everest where he lead several expeditions between 1961and 1965, before embarking on another journey to Antarctica to lead the first successful ascent of Mt Herschel.

It is refreshing perhaps that Hillary has gone well beyond the mere desire of climbing, or ego of summit-bagging, and has worked very hard to 'pay back' something to his much-loved Nepal. There is no doubt he has developed a great respect for its people and worked tirelessly over the years to help raise funds for the creation of schools and hospitals in the region. The first hospital was built in 1966 and he went on to form the Himalayan Trust. His sterling work lead to his appointment as New Zealand's High Commissioner to India in 1985.

Still drawn to both Nepal and Antarctica and to easing the ever-present desire to explore, Hillary served as a tour guide on commercial flights over Antarctica in the 1970s and was still active in exploration of the great continent. With a love of nature added to his love of people, Hillary was also, for a time, the proud director of the World Wildlife Fund, adding conservation to his list of interests and activities. He has published several books on his expeditions and two autobiographies. As a small nation New Zealand is proud of Hillary, perhaps because he stands for much of what New Zealand is all about: a oneness with nature and the courage to venture where others have yet to. Hillary reminds fellow New Zealanders of that today and into the future, as his face features on the nation's $5 banknote.

Hut. Although you are still currently permitted to attempt the crossing you are advised to seek advice and check with up-to-date conditions with DoC.

A far more realistic option is the overnight tramp to the new **Muller Hut,** which sits in a superb position (1768 m) on the ridge of **Mount Oliver** (1933 m) behind Mount Cook Village. Although a strenuous climb requiring a fair level of fitness, proper planning and equipment, it is a classic excursion. If you stay overnight in the new and vastly improved Muller Hut, the views at sunset and sunrise over the Hooker and Mount Cook especially are simply world class. In total it is a stiff four-hour climb each way. A further

one-hour return will see you at the top of Mount Oliver which, rumour has it, was the first peak in the region that Sir Edmund Hillary climbed - and look what it did to him! For more information and bookings contact DoC and the *Muller Hut Route* leaflet, $1.
① *Given the popularity of this hike (which has only been extenuated by the upgrading of the hut) you will need to book a few days in advance, T03-4351818.*

Walking

There are some very appealing walks in the vicinity that offer fine views and insights into the local hardy flora and fauna, with most beginning from the village. The shortest is the **Bowen Bush Walk**, which is only 10 minutes but takes you through some classic **totara forest**. It starts from behind the Alpine Guides Centre. A similar 30-minute walk, the **Glencoe Walk**, starts from behind the Hermitage Hotel and another, the 1-hr **Governor's Bush Walk**, begins from the public shelter, just to the south of the Alpine Guides Centre. The latter also offers a good viewpoint of the mountains. Two longer options are the 2-hr **Red Tarns Track** (which again begins from the public shelter) and the 2-3 hour **Sealy Tarns Track**, which is part of the Muller Hut ascent and begins from the Kea Point Track from the Hermitage. Both of these walks offer spectacular views from higher altitudes.

The **Kea Point Track** can be tackled from the Hermitage (2 hrs) or from the White Horse Hill campsite car park (1 hr), which is accessed north via the Hooker Valley Road (which in turn is accessed from beside the Kitchener Stream Bridge just at the entrance to the village complex). At the terminus of the Kea Walk is a lookout deck that offers memorable views of Mount Sefton, Footstool, the Hooker Valley, Muller Glacier and of course Mount Cook. If you want to investigate the Hooker Valley you can do this from the village or, again, from the White Horse Hill car park. Other than the spectacular views of Mount Cook towering above, the four-hour **Hooker Valley Track** takes you all the way to the ice and melt-water features of the **Hooker Glacier terminal lake.**

The **Tasman Valley** also offers some interesting walks that take in the snout of the vast, advancing glacier. From the village you will need to travel by car or mountain bike to the end of the Tasman Glacier Road (8 km) that is accessed off SH80 south of the village. There are two walks on offer: the 3-4 hr **Ball Shelter Walk** which skirts the side of the glacier, and the more remarkable 1 hr **Glacier Walk** which investigates the terminal lake and head of the glacier. Both walks start from the car park.

● Sleeping

Glentanner Park *p547*
B-D Glentanner. Excellent facilities, self-contained and standard cabins, backpacker dorm and spacious, sheltered powered/tent sites.

Mount Cook Village *p548*
LL-AL Hermitage Hotel, *T03-4351809, www.mount-cook.com* Owns most of the accommodation options on offer. Other than the rather tired and expensive traditional rooms in the hotel, there is a new luxury wing that opened in 2002 (with remarkable views and modern decor), self-contained motel doubles, studios and chalets with basic facilities. Somewhere in there you may find what you are looking for (even economically for groups of 4), but bear in mind that the price reflects the location, not necessarily the quality of accommodation. Bookings in the high season are advised. There is no faulting the hotel facilities, and the **restaurants** and bars are good, providing affordable and filling buffet meals. With all the tour buses lunch, however, can look a bit like a shark-feeding frenzy. Both the hotel and the motel complex have restaurants and bars and both offer buffet-style lunches ($36) and dinners ($47). The **café** in the hotel serves a range of light snacks and good coffee. There is also a small but expensive store and souvenir shop downstairs.

B-D Mount Cook YHA, *corner of Bowen and Kitchener Drs, T03-4351820, yhamtck@yha.org.nz* Even if it had competition would compete very favourably. It has tidy double, twin and shared rooms, modern ski-lodge style facilities including a log fire and sauna and internet. You are advised to book your bed at this hostel well in advance in summer.

Motorcamps and campsites
B-D **Glentanner Park**, *see above.*
D **White Horse Hill Campsite**, *at the end of the Hooker Valley Rd, 2 km from the village* (see walks above). Basic but sheltered (DoC) campsite.

🍴 Eating

Mount Cook Village *p548*
$$$-$$ **Hermitage Hotel**, *see above.*
$$ **Old Mountain Guide Café and Bar**, *just below the DoC Visitor Centre, T03-4351890. Open daily for lunch and dinner.* A fine alternative, offering a wholesome menu featuring lots of traditional warm-me-ups from curry to soup, with blackboard specials. It has a congenial atmosphere with open fire and a room with a pool table and internet.

🔺 Activities

Glentanner Park *p547*
Flightseeing
The biggest draw at Glentanner are the fixed-wing and helicopter flightseeing trips. The choices are vast.
Helicopter Line, *T03-4351801, www.helicopter.co.nz* Whose Mount Cook (East) operations are based at the park, offer 3 trips; a 20 minute trip with landing to the slopes of the Mt Ohau Range ($175); a 30-minute extended option over the Mount Ohau Range with a landing on the Richardson Glacier (from $265) and a 45-minute 'Mountains High' adventure (from $370). If you can possibly afford it, the 'Mountains High' trip is truly memorable. First you are flown up and over the Tasman Valley Glacier, before making a snow landing at over 2000 m to sample the atmosphere and magnificent view of Mount Cook and its associate peaks. Then, back in the air, you cross the Great Divide. From here you encounter the views of the West Coast and the fractured bed of the upper Franz and Fox

Glaciers, before skirting just below Cook's awesome summit and dropping down the Hooker Valley, over Mount Cook Village and back to base. Not even the James Bond theme music or Holst's Planets Suite playing in the background could do that justice, believe me.

Cloud 9, an adjunct operation to Helicopter Line, also offer some very appealing **Heli-hiking** trips of 3-5 hrs, from $240. You might even have a full on snowball fight or go tobogganing high above the snow line in mid summer. Bookings are advised and payment is taken shortly before any flights in case of inclement weather.
Fixed-wing trips are also offered from Glentanner by the Lake Tekapo based **Air Safaris**, *T03-6806880, T0800-806880, www.airsafaris.co.nz* (See Lake Tekapo section540.)
Mount Cook Ski Planes, *at the Mount Cook Airport just a few kilometres south of Mount Cook Village, T0800-800702, T03-4351026, www.skiplanes.co.nz* The ski-plane flightseeing option also offers the exciting prospect of a snow-landing high up amidst the peaks on the Tasman Glacier. As if the scenery in transit is not spectacular enough, you will experience a very different world at high altitude. Inevitably, when the planes are flying, it is usually a very serene atmosphere and amazingly peaceful which only extenuates your sense of awe. But obviously, as you reluctantly climb back in to the aircraft after about 10 minutes, you do so in the knowledge that the conditions up there are frequently very different. Trips on offer range from 25-minute 'Mini Tasman' with no glacier landing (from $180) to the 40-minute 'Glacier Highlights' with glacier landing, to the ultimate 55-minute 'Grand Circle', with a landing and a close up of Mount Cook (from $350). Recommended. Bookings are advised and payment is taken shortly before any flights in case of inclement weather.

Kayaking
Guided kayak trips exploring the ice walls of the glacier lakes, *T03-4350890*, from $70.

🔴 *For an explanation of the sleeping and eating price codes used in this guide, see the inside front cover. Other relevant information is provided in the Essentials chapter, see page 51.*

Other activities available from Glentanner are the excellent **Glacier Explorer Trips**, *T03-4351077, glacier007@xtra.co.nz* This involves a half-hr walk to the terminus of the Tasman Lake, followed by a fascinating two-hr boat trip to the very edges of the ice. Recommended, from $85, child $40; Glentanner has its own **horse trekking** operation, *T03-4351855,* from 30 minutes ($35) to 3 hrs ($120).

Argo Adventure Tours offer 2 hr trips on 8WD buggies, a good trip in wet weather, from $100, child $50; or 2½ hr 4WD tours are on offer with **Alan's 4WD Tours**, *T03-4351809, alan.picard@xtra.co.nz* from $80, child $35. Book at the main desk, *T03-4351855 or direct T03-4350441*. **Walking adventures**, T027-212-0727, www.discoverytours.co.nz, from $90. **Glentanner** offers mountain bike and fishing tackle hire (fishing license $13).

Mount Cook Village *p548*

Note that all the activities already mentioned above (Glentanner Park) are also available from Mount Cook Village.

Alpine Guides, *T03-4351834, www.alpineguides.co.nz* The only resident guiding company in the national park and, given the terrain, the potential challenges and hazards at hand, their presence is welcome. They offer an excellent range of multi-day **mountaineering** and **trekking** trips as well as half- to full-day (8 km) **walks** from $90, child $60 (November-March). In winter full-day **skiing** and **Heli-skiing** trips are available on the upper Tasman Glacier and other equally remote locations, from $100 for one heli lift to $550 for four. Although these trips are expensive, they provide the unique opportunity to ski on virgin snow in areas simply inaccessible to the masses.

NB Do not risk any climb without proper experience or equipment. Mount Cook National Park is serious business. If in doubt don't - and consult Alpine Guides.

❻ Directory

The **Hermitage Hotel** forms the hub of all activity and services in the village, housing two **restaurants, bars**, a small and expensive grocery **store**, and a café. The hotel also offers non-clients **internet**, **currency exchange**, a **post office, EFTPOS** and **activity** bookings. That's not a bad list to add to its comfy if overpriced beds with their world-class mountain views. The only thing it does not provide is **petrol** which can be purchased (24 hr credit card and EFTPOS) near the **Alpine Guides Centre** just to the south (unmanned). For **breakdown** assistance T03-4350844.

Waitaki Valley → *Phone code: 03*

From Oamaru you have the option of turning inland via SH83 through the picturesque Waitaki Valley to Omarama, The MacKenzie Country and Mount Cook. It is a pleasant drive, best negotiated in autumn when the poplar and lakeside weeping willows are draped in gold. Many of the orchards on the way also offer a palette of autumnal hues. The valley is best known for its lakes and the Waitaki River, which are regulated by an extensive system of hydroelectric dams that begin to dominate the waterways of the southwestern Canterbury Region. Fishing for both trout and salmon is just one of the more obvious leisure activities in the area.

Omarama → *Colour map 6, grid B4*

Located at the head of the Waitaki Valley and north of the scenic **Lindis Pass** (from Wanaka and Queenstown), Omarama provides a convenient overnight stop and starting point from which to explore the MacKenzie Country (see page 539). There are also a number of local activities that may hold you back, including **fishing** and **water sports** on Lakes Benmore and Aviemore, **gliding** from Omarama airfield and winter **skiing** at Lake Ohau.

Other than the obvious appeal of the local lakes, the **Clay Cliffs** between Omarama and Twizel are worth investigation, and echo the bizarre eroded rock and gravel formations of the Pinnacles in the Wairarapa, North Island. To reach them turn off SH8 west towards the mountains on Quailburn Road, 3 km north of the village (signposted), 15 km. There is a small charge ($5) at the gate to the cliffs. Omarama *Four Seasons Tours,* T03-4389547, offer **scenic road tours** and interpretative visits to the Clay Cliffs, Waitaki Lakes and surrounding countryside. Omarama is world-renowned for **gliding**, with the huge expanses of thermal-rich grasslands and mountain offering world-class conditions and scenic flights that are almost unparalleled. Alpine Soaring, T03-4389600, www.soaring.co.nz, offer a range of options from the airfield in the village, from $170 for 20-25 minutes. For **fishing**, two good local guides can be found in Doug Horton, T03-4389808, and Max Irons, T03-4389468. Finally, it is well worth popping your head in to the **Norman Sinclair Gallery** in the café next door to the petrol station. Norman is not only a very talented watercolourist who brilliantly captures the essence of the Otago landscape and station life, but also a great man to talk to.

Duntroon → *Colour map 6, grid C5*

From east to west the first settlement of any significance is Duntroon. With the discovery of gold in 1868 the town enjoyed a very brief boom, before the diggings proved a failure, earning them the label of the 'poor man's field'. After a return to relative obscurity, there was more excitement with the discovery of a quartz reef between the Maerewhenua and Otekaike Rivers in 1870, but, like the gold, its extraction was short-lived.

Now merely a small farming settlement, it offers a number of amenities, activities and scenic attractions. There is a petrol station and the Duntroon Tavern, Main Street, T03-4312850, or the Flying Pig Café, Campbell St, T03-4312717 (which also acts as the **information** centre), for a snack, lunch or dinner. The **Elephant Rocks**, accessed from Livingstone Rd, near the Maerewhenua River Bridge are an unusual set of limestone outcrops that are worthy of investigation and also provide good **rock climbing** possibilities, T03-4326855. There are also **Maori rock drawings** at Takiroa on the other side of the Maerewhenua River Valley dating back over 1,000 years (ask at the café for directions).

Kurow to Omarama → *Colour map 6, grid C5 From Kurow it is 52 km to Omarama and SH8*

A further 23 km west of Duntroon is **Kurow,** which nestles at the confluence of the Hakataramea and Waitaki Rivers. Most of the residents work on the hydroelectric dams of Lakes Benmore and Aviemore to the west, but for leisure they say there is one activity that stands head and shoulders above the rest - **fishing.** For insider information and guided trips contact *Waitaki Valley Fishing Guides*, 104 Gordon Street, T03-4360510. South of Kurow is another potential distraction in the form of the former 1871 homestead of the Hon Robert Campbell now open to the public by arrangement, T03-4311111. West of Kurow you soon encounter **Lake Aviemore** and the higher, more extensive and truncated **Lake Benmore**. Both have **dams**. The Aviemore Dam has a 1-km long fish spawning race that is used by up to 3000 adult trout at a time. The dam at the head of Benmore is the largest in New Zealand and can also be investigated though the lakeside picnic grounds. Safe swimming and water sports in both lakes may prove more attractive. For more information contact the **Benmore Power Station and Visitor Centre**, ① *T03-4389212. Daily 1030-1630, tours 1100, 1300, 1500.*

🍽 Sleeping

Omarama *p552*
There is a good range of accommodation in the village.

AL-A Heritage Gateway Hotel,
T03-4389805, heritagegateway@xtra.co.nz
Modern standard rooms and self-contained suites, a bar and restaurant. They can also arrange local tours and activities.

A **Ahuriri Motel**, *T03-4389451*. 14 modern and comfortable self-contained units.

B **Briar's Country Homestay**, *Ahuriri Heights, SH8, T03-4389615*. A good B&B option and the proprietors also offer garden tours.

For **backpackers** there is the popular D **Buscot Station**, *8 km north of the village, T03-4389646*. Provides dorms, en suite rooms and tent sites on a working cattle/sheep station.

D **Killermont Station**, *south (15 km), T03-4389864*. Provides a similar set up.

Motorcamps

B-D **Omarama Top Ten Holiday Park**, *T03-4389875*. It is spacious, nicely sheltered, very well equipped and has flats, cabins and powered/tent sites.

Duntroon *p553*

L **Tokarahi Homestead**, *2 km down Dip Hill Rd (47), 11 km south of Duntroon on the Dansey's Pass Rd, T03-4312500, www.homestead.co.nz* Provides luxurious, beautifully appointed accommodation in 19th-century Victorian style. A perfect peaceful, historic retreat.

D **Dansey's Pass Holiday Camp**, *at the end of Dansey's Pass Rd, T03-4312564*. Cheaper and less salubrious but no less peaceful. They also offer an interesting range of local scenic tours.

Kurow *p553*

If you are tired and cannot reach the Top Ten motorpark in Omarama then the C-D **Kurow Holiday Park** *is located at 76 Bledisloe St, T03-4360725*.

C-D **Otematata Country Inn YHA** *11 Rata Dr, T03-4387797*. A cheery motel backpacker combo with self-contained 3 bedroom cottages and private budget rooms with shared facilities. There is a restaurant and bar. The owners are keen to extol the many virtues of the immediate area and who knows, you may find yourself wanting to linger for a day or two.

🍴 Eating

Omarama *p552*

Heritage Hotel restaurant, *see above.*

$$ **Clay Cliffs Vineyardand Café**, *500 m south of the village on SH8, T03-4389654. 1100-1800 (closed in Jun)*.This café provides a bit of an escape and some fine cuisine in a peaceful setting. Additionally offers tastings and sales.

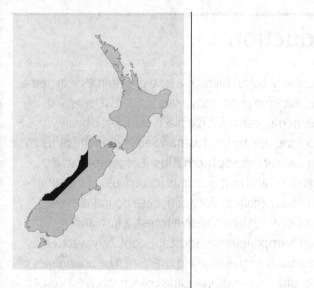

The West Coast

Introduction

The West Coast of South Island is a land of extremes – extreme climate and extreme geography, extreme ecosystems and, above all, extreme scenery. It is a place of majestic beauty. Bounded on one side by the **Tasman Sea** and on the other by the heady peaks of the **Southern Alps**, it encompasses a narrow stretch of land that accounts for only 8% of the total land mass of New Zealand. Between these boundaries lies a quarter of all New Zealand's **native forest**, a lush and predominantly impenetrable landscape copiously watered by an average annual rainfall totalling over 5 m. The boundaries of five of the country's 14 national parks breach the West Coast region. Two of these, **Paparoa National Park** and the **Westland National Park**, it can call its very own. In one – the Westland – are the huge **Fox** and **Franz Josef glaciers**.

The settlements of the region, strung along the 600 km length of SH6, from Karamea in the north to Jackson's Bay in the south, are not attractive places and stand in stark contrast to the beauty surrounding them. Nature, thankfully, has never made it easy for man to live here nor plunder its resources. The modern-day West Coast is sparsely populated, less than 1% of the country's total population lives here. Indeed, there are less people living here now than in the late 19th century.

★ Don't miss...

❶ The ancient forests and awesome limestone features of the **Oparara Basin**, page 561.

❷ Feeling the ground shake as the surf pounds **Punakaiki's Pancake Rocks**, page 565.

❸ Going 'on strike' in **Blackball**, page 571.

❹ Meeting a possum and a giant sandfly at the **Bushman's Centre** near Lake Ianthe, page 578.

❺ The colony of elegant **Kotuku (White Herons)**. Visit by jet boat, from Whataroa, page 579.

❻ Losing your watch deliberately in heavenly **Okarito**, page 579.

❼ Choosing your favourite **glacier - Franz Josef** or **Fox**, pages 583 and 584. Fly over them, land or climb upon them.

❽ The stunning coastal scenery of **Munroe, Murphy's** or **Ship Creek beaches**. Look out for **Fiordland Crested Penguins** - the rarest in the world, page 586.

❾ Jet boating from coast to mountain from **Haast**, page 592.

❿ The pristine wilderness south of Haast. Follow the **Jackson River Valley** to the Cascade, and then stop for the country's most remote fish and chip shop in **Jackson's Bay**, page 594.

⓫ Enjoying REAL **rain**.

Westport and around → *Phone code: 03*

Westport, the West Coast's oldest town, is not a pretty place. On first acquaintance its long main street, fed by a flat expanse of unimaginative orderly blocks and overly wide roads, to say the very least is uninspiring. Whether under clear blue skies, or more often a veil of rain, its drabness is all the more exposed by such beautiful surroundings. But, although the place lacks heart, its people do not. They retain the proud and stoic traditions of the old pioneers and coal miners: that down-to-earth working-class attitude, the warm welcome and the humour. Westport is most often used as an overnight base before heading north to Karamea and the Heaphy Track or south towards Greymouth. There are, however, a few attractions and activities on offer that may hold you back including rafting on the Buller River and a large seal colony at Cape Foulwind.

Ins and outs

Getting there   Wesport airport (8 km south) is served daily (except Sat) by **Air New Zealand Link**, T0800-737000. For a **taxi** to the airport (from $12), T03-7896900. The airstrip at **Karamea** is often used (from the north) for pick-up and drop-off for the Heaphy Track. The **Karamea Village Hotel**, T03-7826800 or the **Last Resort**, T03-7826617, act as agents or contact **Abel Tasman Air**, T03-5288290,which runs a quality service with small fixed wing aircraft from Nelson. The **Last Resort** also has a helicopter at its disposal. Contact Tony Ibbotson, T03-7826618.

By bus Westport is served by **Intercity** (Greymouth/Nelson), T03-3799020; **Atomic Shuttles** (Greymouth/Nelson), T03-3228883; **East-West**, (Christchurch) T03-7896251; **Southern Link Shuttles** (Queenstown/Christchurch/Nelson), T03-3588355; and **East West Shuttles**, T03-7896251 (Christchurch/Westport, departs Westport 0800 daily). Most buses stop just outside the VIC. **Intercity** stops at Craddock's Energy Centre, Caltex, 197 Palmerston St. For all services north to Karamea (and the Heaphy Track) call **Karamea Express**, T03-7826718, or **Cunningham's Coaches**, 179 Palmerston St, T03-7897177.

Information   Westport VIC, ① *1 Brougham St, T03-7896658, www.westport.org.nz Daily 0900-1900 (winter 0900-1700).* **DoC** information and enquiries are handled at the VIC. **Karamea VIC and Resource Centre**, ① *Bridge St, just as you come into the village, T03-7826652, Karamea.info@xtra.co.nz Daily 0900-1700 (seasonal hours).* The staff are very helpful and there is plenty of information on local attractions and, of course, all the latest on the Heaphy Track. Also issues DoC hut passes and has internet. Most organized activities in the area can be arranged at the VIC. Note if you have a mobile the only place you will secure a signal is in the car park of the doctor's surgery on Waverley St.

Westport → *Colour map 4, grid C1 Population: 4,500*

With such a tradition of gold and coal mining in the area it is almost rude not to visit the excellent **Coaltown Museum** ① *Queen St South, T03-7898204. Daily 0900-1630. Adult $7, child $5.* It has an extensive and nicely presented range of displays, with an emphasis on coal mining, but also gold, pioneer and maritime exhibitions. Of particular note is the interesting audio-visual presentation covering the history of coalmining in the region, the simulated walk through mine and the massive 20-ton brake drum (haulage railwagon) from the Denniston Incline. Pitched at a 47° angle (the steepest on the incline) the brake drum creates an almost fearful sight. Even if you have little interest in mining, the sheer efforts made, and feats of engineering cannot fail to impress.

In contrast and yet, in a way, related is the **Miner's Brewery**, ① *Lyndhurst St, T03-7896201. There are tours Mon-Sat at 1130 and 1330, $5*. Here various heady brews are created to quench the thirst of the modern-day miner, including – by all accounts – a fine pint of 'Good Bastards'. If you wish to explore the coal-mining heritage in more detail a *Buller Coalfields Heritage Trail* leaflet is available free from the VIC.

Cape Foulwind,① *11 km south of Westport and easily accessible and signposted from Westport,* is a buttress of land, apparently named so by James Cook in 1770, after his ship was beset by gales and rain. It was formerly called Clyppygen Hoek – or Rocky Corner – by Abel Tasman in 1642 and before that, 'Tauranga' by the Maori, which meant 'a sheltered anchorage or landing place'. The main attraction on the Cape is the thriving **fur seal colony** at the very beautiful **Tauranga Bay**. You are guaranteed to see seals here at any time of year (be it from a lookout situated quite far above the rocks) but summer, when the pups are born, is the best time to see them with over 500 in residence. The colony is best accessed from the Tauranga Bay car park. Before you set off, keep your eyes open for the rather comical and cheeky **weka** around the car park itself. Weka are a flightless, endemic, brown game-like bird about the size of a chicken. Although you are not supposed to feed them it is hard to resist.

From the seal colony the **Cape Foulwind Walkway** also takes in the lighthouse and offers great views (1½ hours, 4 km – one way). At the southern end of Tauranga Bay there is the fine **Bay House Café and Art Gallery**. It offers outdoor seating overlooking the bay and is a great place to sup a cup of coffee, or tuck into a cooked breakfast, while watching the surfers beyond.▸▸ *For Sleeping, Eating and all other listings, see page 563-565.*

The Buller Gorge → *Colour map 4, grid C1*

There are actually two gorges on the Buller River: the Upper Gorge and the Lower Gorge. They are separated by an area of relatively flat farmland around the small settlement of Inangahua, which lies roughly halfway between Murchison and Westport. Following the river is the northernmost arterial to the West Coast, SH6. This 100-km road journey from Murchison to the coast is a scenic, and at times dramatic experience, where you fall with the river through mountains and valleys draped in an ever-increasing veil of green. The drive to the coast is, in itself, pleasant enough but also holds a number of interesting attractions and stops along the way.

Sights and activities Just beyond the junction of SH6 and SH65 the road crosses O'Sullivan's Bridge and the **Upper Gorge** begins proper. Almost immediately you come across the **Buller Gorge Swingbridge**, which at 110 m is New Zealand's longest. True to the New Zealand attitude, you can not only wet yourself crossing it by foot ($5, child $2), but also fly beside it, strapped to a small chair ($25/$15). To create even more laundry for the week you can then descend to the river for a trip in a **jet boat** (from $65/$45). All this can be done while the sensible watch with great amusement from afar, the fit go for a guided **walk** and the hopeful go **gold panning** (guided $10, pan hire $5). **Swingbridge Centre**,① *right next to SH6, T03-5239809, www.bullergorge.co.nz Daily 0800-2000 (0900-1730 in winter)*. There is a café on site.

> ‡ The Buller Gorge will be your introduction to an unwelcome and almost constant companion on your West Coast journey – the ubiquitous sandfly, see page 562.

A little further on, just before Newton Livery Hotel, is the **Lookout (Earthquake White Creek Fault Slip)** where the violent (7.8 on the Richter scale) earthquake of 1929 was centred. A further 8 km on will reveal the **Brunner Memorial**, which is a small metal plaque attached to the rock, commemorating the epic journeys of one Thomas Brunner. The intrepid Mr Brunner took three months to negotiate the gorge in 1846 with little except a group of Maori guides.

⦂ A hard rain's a-gonna fall

The West Coast of the South Island, especially Fiordland, is one of the wettest places on earth. Moist, prevailing, westerly air streams fan across the Tasman Sea and on encountering the mountain ranges of the Great Divide condense and dump rain or snow in huge quantities. At lower levels the annual rainfall is a rather aquatic 1.5 m but at higher levels this can rise to staggering 5 m. Most of the rain falls on the seaward side of the mountains in what is called the 'rain shadow'. The contrast in rainfall is echoed in the types of vegetation. On the western side of the Great Divide lush rainforests of podocarp and beech predominate, while only a few kilometres west this gives way to slopes of mainly scree and tussock. With such a gradient of rainfall and topography the rivers in Westland and Fiordland are regularly subject to flash flooding. For the uninitiated this may conjure up images of rivers merely in spate, but in reality it is an incredible thing to experience. There is such a bombardment of the senses you literally freeze with fear. The mere sight of a vast, all encompassing wall of water, like boiling brown soup, full of boulders tossed like croutons on the surface is bad enough but the deafening roar and the shaking of the earth beneath your feet is almost more paralysing. Many unsuspecting trampers have been killed in such circumstances, so be advised to stay away from all riverbeds and tributaries following rain or even heavy showers.

On a more positive note – although it rains frequently on the West Coast - bear in mind it often clears quickly and the sun is never too far away. Besides, West Coast rain is real rain, industrial strength rain, so perhaps for once in your life get out there and enjoy it.

After a long bend in the river the road then passes through the old gold mining town of **Lyell** – now very much a village. Former relics of the great but brief gold rush days including an old stamper battery can be seen on the **Lyell Walkway** (two hour return). A further 17 km on will bring you to the rather unremarkable settlement of **Inangahua**. It has little more than a petrol pump and the rather dubious claim to fame of being nearly destroyed by another, more recent earthquake in 1968. If darkness is descending you can stay at the comfortable Inwoods Farm Backpackers (see page 563).

From just beyond Inangahua the **Lower Gorge** begins its dramatic descent to the sea. At **Hawk's Crag** the rock has been gouged out to form a dramatic overhang over the road. Its negotiation is really very interesting provided there is not a large petrol tanker coming the other way. ▶▶ *For Sleeping and Activities, see page 563 and 564.*

North to Karamea → *Colour map 4, grid B2*
From Westport, SH67 heads north to Karamea (100 km) and an eventual dead end at the trail head of the Heaphy Track (111 km). If you have time there are a few places of interest and several good walks on offer along the way. Of particular note is the former coal mining township of **Denniston**. Perched high (900 m) on the Rochford Plateau and accessed via Waimangaroa, (15 km north of Westport), Denniston was once the largest producer of coal in the country and the surrounding area was a hive of industrial activity. The **Denniston Walkway** (two hours, 1 km, 520 m ascent), which follows the former supply route, is the best way to explore the area and eventually takes you to the former settlement. Little remains, except a few rusting pieces of machinery, but there are great views of the impressive **Denniston Incline** (1878-1967)

on which 20-ton brake drums brought millions of tonnes of coal down over 500 m to the railhead at terrific speeds. There is a small **museum** ① *based in the old schoolhouse in Denniston (only open on Sun).*

Back on SH67 and 6 km north is the once bustling township of **Granity**. The *Drifters Café* on the main street is worth a stop and has some interesting artwork and mining remnants on display. Inland from Granity a road sweeps up the ranges to 'Porridge Hill' and two more former coal towns; **Millerton and Stockton**. Little remains of either, but again they are still worthy of some investigation. The short **Millerton Incline Walkway** (40 minutes) takes in a number of features and, as the name suggests, another incline, be it a far less impressive affair than the one at Denniston. A further 1 km north of Granity is the very pleasant **Charming Creek Walkway** (two hours, 4 km one-way), which follows the old coal line through the Ngakawau River Gorge, taking in various old tunnels and other mining features along the way.

At the mouth of the Mokihinui River SH67 turns inland and climbs precariously around the bush-clad and scenic **Karamea Bluff**, before falling again to the coast towards Karamea. ▸▸ *For Sleeping, see page 560.*

Karamea → *Colour map 4, grid B2 Population: 684*

After the rather bleak nature of the former coal mining towns, encountered on its approach, you might expect Karamea to be similarly afflicted. But this former 'frontier' settlement, perched on its namesake river mouth, and overshadowed by the rising peaks of the **Kahurangi National Park** is a far more pleasing sight and a quiet (as opposed to dead) atmosphere. Although most often used as a base for the famed **Heaphy Track** (which begins at the road terminus 15 km north) Karamea also offers some lesser known sights that are quite simply superb, in particular the limestone caves and arches of the Oparara Basin.

Sights   Oparara Basin, ① *26 km north and east of Karamea. From Karamea take the main road north for 10 km, then turn right at Break Creek Bridge (signposted) and head for the hills. Access to the basin is 16 km of narrow, winding and unsealed road. The basin is split into areas with both open and restricted public access.* This is a magical place that offers the most interesting concentration of karst (limestone) topography in the Kahurangi National Park, and some of the most spectacular in the South Island. Although the karst features will keep you spellbound, the thick veil of ancient rainforest that covers it all creates a wonderful atmosphere all of its own like some 'lost world'. There are (and certainly have been) some fantastical animals found here. Ancient moa bones have been discovered in the caves along with others belonging to the now extinct New Zealand eagle with a 3 m wingspan. Today, you may still stumble across the huge carnivorous snail (*Powelliphanta*). Also of note is the wonderfully named gradungula spider, the largest in New Zealand with a leg span of 10 cm. But, even if the prospect of such creatures leaves you cold, the Oparara Basin is still a 'must see'.

At the very end of the track is the access point to the main feature of the basin – the **Honeycomb Caves** can only be visited on a guided tour because of their delicate nature and fragile ecosystem, ① *Oparara Tours at the Last Resort, T03-7826617, two hours, $50.* They are a 15-km underground labyrinth only discovered 30-odd years ago, revealing all the usual limestone cave features plus the bones of several moa and other extinct species.

Nearby is the **Honeycomb Arch** the first of three spectacular arches that have been formed by the age-old meanderings of the Oparara River. Although this arch is indeed impressive, access is again restricted and is by kayak only ① *Oparara Tours at the Last Resort, $65.* The **Oparara Arch**, ① *free public access,* is equally if not more impressive and is reached from a path (signposted) beside the road. A pleasant 20-minute (one-way) walk alongside the intriguing tannin coloured river, and through beautiful forest, will bring you to the awesome arch entrance. Once you have

Sandflies – Satan's Spawn

There is no collective noun that adequately describes the family of flies known as Psychodidae. Psychodidae is perhaps, in itself, the wonderfully apt, Latin family name for that nasty, insect equivalent to 'Hannibal Lector' – The New Zealand Sandfly. Venture anywhere west of the main divide of the South Island and you will, without fail, not only encounter vast squadrons of them but also unconsciously enter into a state of perpetual war against them. And sadly folks, for you, I'm afraid it is a war that you cannot ever hope to win. Their staggering thirst for blood and subsequent irrepressible motivation added to their tactical superiority, fighting skills, numbers and sheer omnipresence, make them a formidable force indeed.

They say that to have the slightest chance of winning a war, or in this case to merely survive, you should 'know thine enemy' – so here goes. There are not one, but 13 species of sandfly (or blackfly) in New Zealand. Fortunately, only two of these species actually bite, but unfortunately you are still hopelessly outnumbered. You may not be surprised to learn that it is only the female that bites. Apparently they need a good feed of blood in order to lay their eggs – bless them.

So why is it that the moment you enter the great outdoors it takes about three milliseconds before what seems like the entire sandfly Luftwaffe are upon you? Well,

apparently, you are instantly detected by a combination of breath, odour, movement, shape, colour and temperature. Biting is at its peak just after dawn or before dusk on warm, overcast, low pressure days, especially when humidity is high. Your only saviour is wind – natural as opposed to your own, since you will, after all, find yourself trying anything to repel them – a strong breeze affects their strike rate. It is due to the high rainfall that sandflies are so prevalent on the West Coast and Fiordland.

So how can you bite back? Is there anything other than a spacesuit or a small thermonuclear device that is effective against the enemy? You will find a number of expensive insect repellents on the market and these are readily available throughout the region. Those that contain DEET (for short – a rather strong chemical, to say the least) are the most effective. But, given that it discolours plastic and certainly feels like it is melting your lips on application, prolonged use is perhaps not recommended. Antihistamines can also help to ease the swelling and allergic reaction from the bites. But, in conclusion, NO, there is very little you can do except grin and bear them. But, what ever you do, do not let them deter you from going to experience the West Coast. Besides, if it was not for the sandfly, just think how much more spoilt the West Coast would be by human habitation.

marvelled at the main entrance it is then well worth exploring the other end through the 140 m passage. This will involve getting your feet wet and crossing the river so special care is required.

On a far lesser scale, but in a way more beautiful, is the **Moria (Little) Arch**, accessed from the other side of the road. Again it is reached by foot through attractive forest and a 40-minutes track that is both wet and difficult in places. What it lacks in grandeur, the Moria makes up for in serenity. Perhaps before or after the arches you can visit the **Crazy Paving** and **Box Canyon Caves** that are a short, five-minutes walk from the road. Beyond their unnerving darkness (take a torch), they are the least

impressive of all the features. The **river** itself is also beautiful and well worthy of   563
investigation, particularly around the track to the small and self-explanatory **Mirror
Tarn**. A small map of the Oparara basin is available free from the VIC. ▸▸ *For Sleeping,
Eating and other listings, see pages 564-565.*

Walks → *The VIC has detailed information on these walks and others.*

Karamea is also a fine base for walking with the coastal stretch of the **Heaphy Track**
being particularly good. From the **Kohaihai River** (trailhead), cross the swing bridge
and walk through the forest to **Scotts Beach** (1½ hours return). From there you have
the option of continuing along the coastline to **Kapito Shelter** (6 hours return) or
going the whole hog with an overnight stop at the **Heaphy Hut** (5 hours one-way)
before retracing your steps. This stretch of coast is noted not only for its wild unspoilt
beaches but also for its nikau palms that gives it an almost tropical feel. Other tracks
and expeditions include the **Fenian Track** (3-5 hours) which takes in a small cave
system and a former gold mining settlement and **Mount Stormy** (1084 m, 6-8 hours
return) with its magnificent views. ▸▸ *For details on the Heaphy Track see page 480.*

● Sleeping

Westport and Buller Gorge *p558*
L-AL Otaki Lake Hideaway, *Virgin Flat Rd, 3
km off SH6 south of Westport, T03-7896841,
www.nzhideaway.com* One of the best B&Bs
in the area. It is a lone, fully self-contained
1-bedroom chalet built over a private trout-
stocked lake. Refreshingly different and
peaceful. Boat provided. Recommended.
AL River View Lodge, *Buller Gorge Rd,
T03-7896037, www.rurallodge.co.nz* Another
good out of town B&B option. It is set in
pleasant gardens overlooking the lower
reaches of the Buller River 7 km east of town
and has 4 tidy ensuites. Dinners by
arrangement.
AL Archer House, *75 Queen St, Westport,
T03-7898778, www.archerhouse.co.nz* A new
and classy B&B in the century-old former
convent. Well-appointed en-suites in a
central location.
There are plenty of **motels**:
AL-A Wesport Spa Motel, *239 Palmerston St,
T0800-375273.* The newest offering.
Spa units an extra bonus.
AL-A Chelsea Gateway Motor Lodge, *330
Palmerston St, T03-7896835.* Opposite
Wesport Spa and also with spa units.
A-B Westport Motor Hotel, *Palmerston St,
T03-7897889.* Popular, well-located and well-
established, with the added attraction of a
good in-house restaurant.
There are also plenty of **backpacker** beds:
C-D The TripInn, *72 Queen St, T03-7897367,
tripinn@clear.net.nz* A grand, spacious villa,
kept squeaky clean with a wide range of

rooms and good facilities including internet.
C-D Happy Wanderer, *56 Russell St,
T03-7898627, happywanderer@xtra.co.nz* A
vast establishment close to the town centre
with a wide range of units, self-contained
dorms, powered sites and good facilities
and internet.
C-D Basils, *next door to* Happy Wanderer,
T03-7896410. A homely, well-kept villa with
modern units, dorms, good facilities
including internet.
C-D Beaconstone Backpackers, *Out of town
and south on SH6 (17 km), T027-4310491.* An
'alternative', environmentally friendly 12-bed
lodge in a bush/coastal setting with solar
power and futon beds. Note there is no
public phone or TV. Local caving
activities arranged.
D Inwoods Farm Backpackers, *Inangahua,
Buller Gorge, T03-7890205.* Comfortable
option if you are in the area anyway.

Motorcamps
There are two main motor camps both basic
but functional.
C-D Westport Holiday Park, *37 Domett St,
T03-7897043.* Short walk from town, cabins,
powered/tent sites and dorm beds.
C-D Seal Colony Top Ten Tourist Park,
*Marine Parade, Carter's Beach (6 km on Cape
Foulwind /Carter's Beach Rd), T03-7898002.*
More popular but it is still a good 6 km from
the seal colony!

North to Karamea *p560*
C-D Old Slaughterhouse Backpackers,
35 km north of Westport at Dean Creek, Hector,

T03-7828333. A purpose-built lodge set in an elevated position overlooking the ocean and reached by a 10-min bush walk. It offers tidy doubles and shared rooms and offers a fine break on the journey north to Karamea and the Heaphy Track.

C-D Cowshed Café and Backpackers, *slightly further north, on the far side of the Mokihinui River Mouth (Gentle Annie's Beach), T03-7891826.* A great spot for both food and accommodation with quiet, dorm or self-contained lodges and camping sites. The café is imaginatively housed in a former milking shed. It has detailed information about local walks and activities including kayaking on the river from $25.

Karamea *p561*

AL-D Last Resort, *71 Waverley St, T03-7826617, www.lastresort.co.nz* The mainstay for accommodation in Karamea. It is a modern and imaginatively designed complex with lodge-style accommodation blocks all interconnected by walkway, with a large adjunct bar/café and restaurant. There are a wide variety of rooms on offer, from shared budget to self-contained ensuites. Note, however, that there are no kitchen facilities. Internet is available.

A Bridge Farm Motels, *Bridge St, T03-7826955, www.karameamotels.co.nz* With a riverside location, this is a relatively new motel and offers 6 1- and 2-bedroom self-contained suites.

C-D Karamea Village Hotel, *T03-7826800, on Waverley St.* Comfortable backpacker accommodation in a historic and lovingly restored building.

Motorcamps

C-D Karamea Holiday Park, *Maori Point, just south of the village, T03-7826758.* Offers a range of cabins and powered/tent sites.
D DoC campsite, *at the Kohaihai River mouth (15 km north) at the trailhead of the Heaphy Track, T03-7826652.*

🍴 Eating

Westport *p558*

Options are limited in the area.
$$ Bay House Café, *T03-7897133, at the southern end of Tauranga Bay, Cape Foulwind (near the seal colony).* A great restaurant,

offering breakfast, lunch and an imaginative à la carte menu for dinner and is in a superb setting over looking the bay. The best local restaurant.
$$ Serengetis Restaurant, *in the Westport Motor Hotel, Palmerston St, T03-7897889. Daily from 1800.* Recommended, see Sleeping above.
$$-$ Percy's Restaurant and Bar, *T03-7896648. Mon-Sat 1000-2100, Sun 1100-2100.* A more casual daytime option.

$ Bailies Bar, *187 Palmerston St, T03-7897289 From 1130.* Pub grub and good beer.
$ Freckles, *Palmerston St. 0900-1700.* A daytime café and good coffee.
Supermarket Supervalue, *18 Fonblanque St, T03-7898546.*

Karamea *p561*

Both the Karamea Village Hotel and the Last Resort have licensed restaurants (see above).
$$ LR Bar and café, *Last Resort. Daily.* Also offers a cheaper pub-style menu and a great atmosphere.
$ Saracens Café *across the road from the VIC. 0830-1800 (seasonal).* A good spot to watch the world go by over a coffee.

🔺 Activities

Westport and Buller Gorge *p558*

There is an increasing range of interesting and quality activity operators based in Westport.

Norwest Adventures (Underworld Rafting), *Charlestown (27 km south of Westport), T03-7896686, www.caverafting.com* Offers **adventure cave sightseeing**, caving and **underground rafting trips** to the Te Tahi and Metro limestone caves in Paparoa National Park. With such underground feature names as the 'Lambada', 'The Iron Room' and 'The Witches Cauldron' it is hard to resist. Trips leave twice daily from Westport and include a short trip by miniature rail to reach the caves. ('Metro Tour' 3 hrs from $55; 'Evening Eco-Cave Glowworm Tour', 2 hrs from $145; 'Underworld Rafting' 4-5 hrs, from $105 and 'Adventure Caving' with 120 ft abseil, 4 hrs from $220).

Buller Adventures *based east of Westport on SH6 (Buller Gorge Rd)*, T03-7897286, *www.adventuretours.co.nz* Offers **rafting** trips (half-day from $95); family rafting (3 hrs from $70); heli-rafting (from $255); **jet boating** (1½ hrs, from $65); **8-wheel** Argo ATV tours (1 hr from $30) and **horse trekking** (2½ hrs, from $55).
Burning Mine Adventures, T03-7897277. Offers **mountain biking** (4 hrs, from $45); **kayaking** (from $75); mining tours (4 hrs, from $65) and **surfing** from $35.
Out West Tours, T0800-688-937, *www.outwest.co.nz* An interesting range of 5-hr trips by **4-wheel drive** truck to the former Denniston coal mines, down the coast or inland to explore the Buller Gorge. Trips depart on demand from Brougham St.
Xtreme Adventures, T0800-526-405. **Jet ski** tours on the Buller River. 1-3 hrs from $60-$185.

Westport *p558*
Banks *Palmerston St.* **Bike hire** Becker's Sports, *204 Palmerston St, Westport*, T03-7898787. From $15 a day. Xtreme Adventures, *Westport*, T03-7896658. Hire scooters, half day from $40, full-day $70.
Internet Web Shed, *208 Palmerston St*, T03-7895131. *Mon-Fri 1000-1800, Sat 1000-1300.* Library, *across the road from the VIC. Mon-Thu 1000-1700, Fri 1000-1830 and Sat 1030-1300.* **Post office** *Palmerston St.*

Karamea *p561*
Banks There is no bank or ATM in the village. **Internet** VIC, *see page 558.* **Postal services** Karamea Hardware Store, *across the road from the VIC.* **Medical facilities** Doctor's surgery, *Waverley St*, T03-7826737. *Taxi* Karamea Motors, T03-7826757

Punakaiki and the Paparoa National Park → *Colour map 4, grid C1*

From Westport SH6 begins its relentless 600 km journey south, down the length of the West Coast. Once past the small and once-booming gold mining settlement of Charlestown, the road hits the coast proper and then skirts the northern boundary of the Paparoa National Park. Designated in 1987, Paparoa covers a relatively small area (by New Zealand standards) of 30,000 ha and features a predominantly karst (limestone) topography. From mountain top to coast, the park has everything from limestone bluffs to dramatic overhangs and caves. The most famous feature in the park are the much photographed and visited pancake rocks and blowholes of Dolomite Point at the small coastal settlement of Punakaiki. The park also offers some interesting features and notable walks inland, including the popular Inland Pack Track.

Ins and outs
Getting there Punakaiki is 60 km south of Westport and 50 km north of Greymouth. **Intercity**, T0800-767080, and **Atomic Shuttles** (Greymouth/Nelson), T03-3228883, pass through the village daily and stop briefly for passengers to grab a snack and take a quick look at the pancake rocks and blowholes. There is no **petrol** available here.

Information DoC Paparoa National Park Visitor Centre, ① *SH6 in the heart and commercial centre of Punakaiki*, T03-7311895, *www.punakaiki.co.nz Daily 0900-1800 (winter 0900-1630).* There are some interesting displays about the park and detailed information available on local attractions, activities and walking conditions.

Sights
Immediately across the road from the visitor centre is **Dolomite Point** with its oddly shaped **pancake rocks** and crowd-pleasing **blowholes**. The fluted vertical columns are a lime/mudstone feature known as 'karren', which develop their layered

appearance as a result of erosion by rain and sea spray. The track (20 minutes return) takes the form of a loop, offering various lookout points across the rocks, blowholes and down in to the surge pools. On a high tide and especially during a strong westerly, the 'show' can be amazing, with the ground physically shaking to the thunderous pounding of the waves and the sea-spray hissing from the cracks as if coming from the nostrils of some furious sea dragon. But note that when the tide is out, or there is little swell, the blowholes can be quiet and idle, leaving many visitors disappointed. Regardless of the activity the rocks are certainly intriguing and the views are stunning. Keep your eye out for **dolphins**. It is not unusual to see pods or individuals mingling with surfers with the mutual intent to catch the best wave.

If you have time there is also some stunning coastal scenery, easily accessed via the **Truman Track**, which begins beside SH6, 3 km north of Punakaiki. A 15-minute walk through coastal rainforest and nikau palms delivers you on the sands and rocky outcrops of **Perpendicular Point**. The rock formations here are fascinating with fissures, holes and mosaics, and although it is quite hard going and should only be attempted at low tide, a thorough investigation of the Point, northwards, is well worthwhile.

Turning your attention inland, the river valleys lead to some fine scenery and a number of other dramatic limestone features such as caves and overhangs. At Tiromoana, 13 km north of Punakaiki, the **Fox River** finds the sea, and a small car park north of the bridge acts as the northern trailhead for the **Inland Pack Track**. The entire track (which is usually walked from the southern trailhead in Punakaiki) is a 27 km, 2-3 day affair that takes in many limestone feature, and inland valleys. Its main highlights – the **Fox River Gorge, Caves** and **Ballroom Overhang** – can all be accessed from the Fox River mouth on an exciting 4-6 hour return walk. The track is well-formed for much of its length, but also involves crossing the river a number of times guided only by orange markers, so be prepared to get your feet wet. The Fox River Caves can be accessed with a short diversion before the first major river crossing. The main cave is over 100 m in length and decorated with the usual calcite formations. Once across the river, the track follows the base of the dramatic gorge before terminating temporarily at the confluence of the Fox and Dilemma Creek. Here you can leave the Inland Pack Track, cross the river, and then continue alongside the main Fox tributary to the **Ballroom Overhang** (1 km). Sitting like half an umbrella embedded in the riverbed, its 100 m by 30 m overhang is impressive, but spoilt somewhat by the graffiti on the walls.

Closer to Punakaiki are the **Bullock Creek** and **Pororari River** Valleys. The Pororari acts as the southern access of the Inland Pack Track which can be walked in part to join the Bullock Creek Valley and to access **Cave Creek**, a deeply incised limestone gorge and another karst feature worthy of investigation. It is also one that now serves more as a tragic memorial than a tourist attraction. In 1995 a viewing platform set high above the cavern collapsed sending 15 students to their deaths. As a result of the incident there was a complete review of all similar DoC structures countrywide and revised safety standards and protocols were subsequently put in place. Cave Creek can also be accessed via the Bullock Creek Valley, which is generally fun to explore by car, bike, or on foot. All walks in the area are subject to flooding so check with DoC at the VIC before setting off.

The area is also home to some rare wildlife. Of particular note is the **Westland black petrel (teiko)** – a gull-sized, black seabird which nests in burrows on the bush-clad slopes of Paparoa's mountains. They breed nowhere else in the world. Tours are available in season (March-December). Contact the VIC.

▸▸ For Activities, see page 567.

● For an explanation of the sleeping and eating price codes used in this guide, see the inside
● front cover. Other relevant information is provided in the Essentials chapter, see page 51.

● Sleeping

Punakaiki *p565*

Almost all the accommodation is just off SH6. The most upmarket accommodation is at the southern end of the village.

L Punakaiki Rocks Hotel, *T03-7311167, punakaikihotel@xtra.co.nz* With the appeal of an airport departure lounge, the individual units are very good. The restaurant boasts great views over the beach.

LL Punakaiki Rocks Villas, *T03-7311168*. There are two new and luxurious options from tidy studio units with private decks facing the ocean or 12 eco-designed rooms set further back from the highway in native bush.

B Hydrangea Cottages, *north of the main centre, T03-7311839, www.pancake-rocks.co.nz* One of the best self-contained cottages on the coast. Very cute and reasonably priced.

A Paparoa Park Motel, *a little further north (just off the main road), T03-7311883, www.paparoa.co.nz* Tidy and congenial place offering both studio and family units.

A Punakaiki Cottage Motels, *in the heart of the village, T03-7311008*. Older, but perfectly comfortable.

There are 2 hostels in the village:

C-D Nikau Retreat, *in Te Miko, just north of the Truman Track, T03-7311111*. Simply superb. Run by an enthusiastic manager, the establishment, with its range of stand-alone cottages set in the bush, creates a very special atmosphere. Excellent facilities, self-contained options also available. Internet.

C-D Punakaiki Beach Hostel, *Webb St (closer to the village), T03-7311852*. Two compact houses near the beach and pub. Internet.

Motorcamps

C-D Punakaiki Beach Camp, *T03-7311894*. Set next to the beach and only a short walk from the main village. It offers spacious grounds, cabins and powered/tent sites.

● Eating

Punakaiki *p565*

$$ Seascape Restaurant, *at the Punakaiki* Rocks Hotel, T03-7311167. Daily from 0700. For fine dining this the only real option in the village. The food is perfectly acceptable and the views excellent.

$ Punakaiki Tavern Bistro Café and Bar, *next to the motorcamp (SH6), T03-7311188*. The main hub of entertainment in the village offering palatable beer and the usual value pub grub. They also offer accommodation in the form of 8 basic studio units.

$ Wild Coast Café, *Main Rd (across the road from Dolomite Point and the pancake rocks), T03-7311873. Daily 0800-2100 (winter 0800-1700)*. It has good coffee and an eclectic blackboard menu. There is also a small grocery shop attached and several internet terminals.

▲ Activities

Punakaiki *p565*

There is a wide range of local activities available, above and beyond walking and tramping (see Sights above).

Dolphin watching/swimming Kiwa Sea Adventures, *T03-7687765*. From $100, child $50.

Ecotours Green Kiwi Tours, *T0800-474733, www.greenkiwitours.co.nz*

Horse trekking Punakaiki Guides, *T03-7311839*. Along the beaches or into the Punakaiki River Valley (2 hr, from $80).

Kayaking Punakaiki Canoe Hire, *T03-7311870, www.riverkayaking.co.nz* 2 hr from $30, or all day from $60, (guided trip from $60). (Also do independent hire.)

Walks and rock climbing Paparoa Guides, *T03-7311853*. Half to full-day nature walks (from $35) as well as rock climbing (from $90) and overnight wilderness trekking (from $135).

❶ Directory

Punakaiki *p565*

Banks There are no banks but EFTPOS is available in the retail and food outlets.

Internet Wild Coast Café (see above) or both the local backpackers (see above).

Greymouth and around → *Phone code: 03*

From Punakaiki the coast road continues its relentless route south, treating you to some fine coastal scenery, before turning inland through Runanga to meet the Grey River and the West Coast's largest commercial centre – Greymouth. On initial acquaintance Greymouth seems to share the drab aesthetics of most northern West Coast towns and certainly lives up to its uninspiring name. That said, the people of Greymouth are welcoming, friendly and certainly not short of heart or colour. Today, the bustling town is mostly used by tourists as a short stop over point or supply base for further investigations of the coast. It does, however, have a few local attractions and some exciting activities on offer. Inland from Greymouth the small satellite towns of Blackball and Reefton are the main highlights along the watershed of the Grey River Valley and provide further evidence of the regions gold and coal mining past. It was in Blackball in the early 1900s through the hardships of the working classes that the Labour and Trade Union movements were first formed in New Zealand. Further South the peaceful surroundings of Lake Brunner are a stark contrast to the highly commercial 'Shantytown' a working replica of an 1880s gold mining settlement.

Ins and outs

Getting there Greymouth is served from **Hokitika Airport** (40 km) with **Air New Zealand Link**, T0800-737000. The town is 258 km west of Christchurch via SH73 and Arthur's Pass; 290 km south of Nelson via SH6 and 583 km north of Queenstown, also via SH6. The major **bus** companies serving the town include: **Intercity**, T03-3799020 (Nelson/Westport); **Coast to Coast Shuttles**, T0800-800847 (Christchurch to Hokitika); **Alpine Coaches**, T0800-274888 (Christchurch to Hokitika); and **Atomic Shuttles**, T03-3228883 (Queenstown to Picton). Most buses stop at the VIC or at the **Travel Centre** in the railway station on Mackay St, T03-7687080. **Reefton** is 79 km Northeast of Greymouth and 80 km east of Wesport. Hanmer Springs is 130 km west via the Lewis Pass. Bus companies serving the town are: **Southern Link** T03-3588355 and **East-West**, T03-7896251 (Westport to Christchurch, via Lewis Pass daily). **Hanmer Connection**, T03-3157575, also runs daily between Hanmer and Greymouth via Reefton. For more information contact the VIC. By **train** Greymouth is the western terminus of the famous **TranzAlpine** from Christchurch, which is considered a world-class scenic journey, T0800-872467, www.tranzscenic.co.nz The train arrives daily at Mackay St at 1325 and departs Greymouth again at 1425. Moana (on Lake Brunner) is also on the TranzAlpine line. Westbound 1221, eastbound 1405, from $94 one way.

Information Greymouth VIC, ① *corner of Mackay and Herbert Sts, T03-7685101, www.west-coast.co.nz Mon-Fri 0830-1900, Sat 0900-1800, Sun 1000-1700.* **DoC** information is also available in the VIC. **Reefton VIC**, ① *Broadway, T03-7328391, www.reefton.co.nz Daily 0830-1800 (1630 in winter).* **DoC** have an office in the same building and there are various eco-based displays and lots of walking and tramping information available.

Greymouth → *Colour map 5, grid B2. Population: 10,000*

Greymouth enjoyed the former colonial names of Crescent City and Blaketown, before its present name (given in honour of the former New Zealand Governor, Sir George Grey) finally stuck. Not surprisingly its creation centred principally on gold prospecting and mining, but unlike so many of the other West Coast settlements that diminished with its exhaustion, Greymouth continued to thrive. This was due to the coal and timber industries, sound communication links and its status as the region's

principal port. But its watery affairs have not all been smooth sailing. The Grey River 569
Valley receives some of the heaviest rainfall in the country and on more than one
occasion the town has been badly flooded.

Greymouth

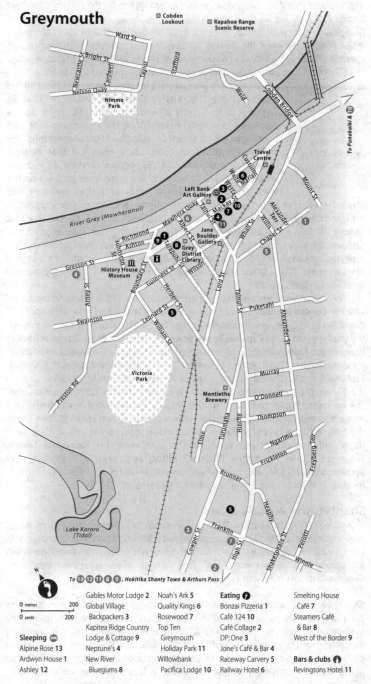

Sleeping
Alpine Rose **13**
Ardwyn House **1**
Ashley **12**
Gables Motor Lodge **2**
Global Village
  Backpackers **3**
Kapitea Ridge Country
  Lodge & Cottage **9**
Neptune's **4**
New River
  Bluegums **8**
Noah's Ark **5**
Quality Kings **6**
Rosewood **7**
Top Ten
  Greymouth
  Holiday Park **11**
Willowbank
  Pacifica Lodge **10**

Eating
Bonzai Pizzeria **1**
Café 124 **10**
Café Collage **2**
DP: One **3**
Jone's Café & Bar **4**
Raceway Carvery **5**
Railway Hotel **6**
Smelting House
  Café **7**
Steamers Café
  & Bar **8**
West of the Border **9**

Bars & clubs
Revingtons Hotel **11**

To **13 12 11 8 9**, Hokitika Shanty Town & Arthurs Pass

0 metres   200
0 yards   200

One of Greymouth's most famous sights is the **Montieth's Brewery**, ① *on the corner of Turamaha and Herbert St, T03-7684149, www.monteiths.co.nz Tours available for $10*. Considered locally as a place of sanctity, its brands of 'Original', 'Black' and 'Celtic Red', are considered by most Kiwis to be the country's greatest brews. Although not in the same league, nor enjoying the same reputation of Guinness or many other European beers, it is indeed a fine drop. In 2001 there was a major controversy when the powers that be decided suddenly to announce that operations were to be moved to Auckland (of all places). This act of insanity resulted in an outcry of such proportions that the owners wisely changed their minds.

> ⁑ *Greymouth takes the prize for the most imaginatively decorated hostels in the country. The Noah's Ark and Neptune backpackers are both excellent choices, see page 572.*

If you are more culturally inclined you should head for the small, but effective, **History House Museum**, ① *Gresson St, T03-7684028. Mon-Fri 1000-1600. Adult $3, child $1*. Its emphasis is naturally centred on the region's mining and nautical past with a copious collection of old photographs. The creatively inclined will particularly enjoy the **Jade Boulder Gallery**, ① *1 Guinness St, T03-7680700. Daily 0830-2100, winter 1700. $10*. It is one of the better jade galleries on the West Coast showcasing a range of crafted jewellery and sculptures with the added attraction of a 'Jade Discovery Walk', master sculptors at work and a huge river-polished jade boulder. Also worth a look is the **Left Bank Art Gallery**, ① *Tainui St, T03-7680088. Tue-Fri 1000-1700, Sat 1000-1500. $2*. It displays the work of mainly West Coast artisans in a wide variety of media with the expected emphasis on jade sculpture and jewellery. Both are worthy of a look and display some fine crafted examples of the West Coasts ancient *poanamu* (greenstone/jade) pieces.

For a short walk, encompassing a memorable view of the town and the coast, visit the **Cobden Lookout** (also known as the Lions Walk). The track entrance is off Bright Street, Cobden, 200 m from the road bridge. The track zigzags steadily through the southern end of the **Rapahoe Range Scenic Reserve**. The **Point Elizabeth Track** (3 hours return) follows an old gold-miners trail along the Rapahoe Range and provides another good local jaunt. Access is north of Greymouth via Bright Street, then Domett Esplanade and North Beach Road (6 km) or via Rapahoe, Seven Mile Road.

For another longer tramp the 18 km - 8-9 hour - **Croesus Track** from Barrytown (28 km north) to Blackball (25 km northeast) is recommended. It can be tackled from either end and takes in the grand views of the coast from above the tree line of the Paparoa Ranges and includes some notable gold-mining relics. Also, most importantly perhaps, it has good pubs at both ends: The **Barrytown Tavern**, T03-7311812, and the former **Blackball Hilton**, T03-7324708. Both also offer accommodation. The DoC broadsheet *Central West Coast – Croesus Track* is invaluable. ⏵⏵ *For Sleeping, Eating, and other listings, see pages 572-574.*

Shantytown → *Colour map 5, grid B2*
① *Just off SH6 (Rutherglen Rd), 11 km south of Greymouth, T03-7626634, www.shantytown.co.nz Daily 1830-1700. Adult $15, child $7.50. Gold panning is $5 extra. Kea West Coast Tours, T03-7689292, offers 3-hr guided trips from Greymouth for around $34. Greymouth Taxis, T03-7687078 offers scheduled trips from Greymouth at 1015/1215 and 1415, from $23, child $13. Book ahead.*

Shantytown is a faithful recreation of an 1880s gold-mining settlement. It comes complete with shops, a bank, saloon, goal, livery stables, fire station, working sawmill and a working steam train. Although a little commercial, it provides an interesting insight into the lives of hopeful prospectors. The steam train operates daily from 0945-1600. You can also try your hand at gold panning, or even tie the knot in the original church. More traditional facilities include a café and souvenir shop.

Lake Brunner, 37 km east of Greymouth, is the West Coast's largest lake and certainly one of the prettiest. Other than fine scenery, **Moana Kotuku** (or Heron Sea as it is also known) offers some great fishing, walking, swimming and other water-based activities. The settlement of **Moana** on its northern bank is the main base for accommodation and activities. One of the best walks – the 20-minute **Arnold River Walkway** – is accessed via a swingbridge over the Arthur River at the western end of the village (Ahau Street). Keep your eye out for the beautiful **white heron** (Kotuku), which visit outside the summer breeding season. Guided fishing trips, tackle hire and the occasional kayak can be secured through the motor camp, motel and hotel. ▶ *For Sleeping and Eating see pages 572 and 573.*

Grey Valley and Blackball → *Colour map 5, grid B2*

Between Greymouth and Reefton the Grey River heads coastward, hemmed in by the Paparoa Ranges and the northern flanks of the Southern Alps. Like much of the region, its small settlements were born during the heady days of the gold rush.

Although the small former gold-mining town of **Waiuta** (21 km south of Reefton) is of interest, it is the coal-mining town of **Blackball** (accessed from Stillwater, 11 km north of Greymouth) that holds most appeal. Founded on gold in 1866, but developed later on coal, it is most famous as the cradle of working-class protest and unionism in the early 1900s. In 1908 an almost inevitable clash occurred when a 30-minute lunch break was sought (as opposed to 15 minutes). This debacle led to the formation of the Federation of Miners and subsequently the Red Federation of Labour – essentially the nation's Labour Movement. Such was the anti-capitalist feeling that, for a few years after the First World War, you could attend Marxism classes in the town. ▶ *For Sleeping, and Eating, see pages 572 and 573.*

Reefton → *Colour map 5, grid B3. Population: 1,200*

Known as the 'Gateway to the Coast', the former gold town of Reefton is a fairly unremarkable, but pleasant little place at the end (or beginning) of the Lewis Pass arterial to the coast. Famous for very little, except its claim to be the first town in the southern hemisphere to receive a public electricity supply and street lighting in 1888, it is sustained by coal, forestry, farming and gold. The nice thing about Reefton is its unpretentious atmosphere. It seems very real. Although underrated and rarely on the tourist agenda, Reefton offers some fine fishing in the local rivers as well as a wealth of walking, tramping and mountain biking opportunities, primarily in the vast and local 180,000 ha Victoria Conservation Park – the largest forest park in the country.

Sights The two most noted walks in town are the **Reefton Heritage Walk** and the **Powerhouse Walk**. The Heritage Walk takes in a number of interesting historical buildings including the newly renovated Courthouse, beautifully decorated Masonic Lodge and the former School of Mines. On The Strand you will find the lovingly restored, former workhorse R28 Fairlie Locomotive, the sole survivor of its type. The Powerhouse Walk is an easy 40-minute walk across the river to see the former powerhouse that once proudly lit up the town. Free leaflets outlining both walks are available from the VIC.

Should you pan a large nugget, don't try to sell it to a bank without a proper mining licence.

Blacks Point Museum, ① *just beside SH7 (Lewis Pass Rd) in Blacks Point, T03-7328035. Open in summer Wed-Fri and Sun 0900-1200, 1300-1600, $4,* has extensive displays surrounding the regions goldfields history. For a fine **view** of the town and the Inangahua Valley head south on SH7, turn left after 1 km into Soldier Flat Road and left again shortly afterwards. Follow this road to the lookout point in the pine forest. ▶ *For Sleeping, Eating and other listings, see pages 573-574.*

Greymouth *p568*
See also listings for the Croesus Track, p570.
LL-AL Kapitea Ridge Country Lodge and Cottage, *Chesterfield Rd, (out of town, off SH6, 20 km south), T03-7556805, www.kapitea.co.nz* Homely comforts – worth the journey.
AL-A New River Bluegums, *985 Main South Rd (12 km south), T03-7626678, www.bluegumsnz.com* Another characterful out of town farmstay.

There are 2 main **hotels** in town:
AL-A Hotel Ashley, *74 Tasman St, T0800-807787, ashley.grey@xtra.co.nz;* and
AL-A Quality Kings Hotel, *Mawhera Quay, T03-7685085, quality.kings@cdlhms.co.nz* Both have comfortable rooms and good facilities with the Quality getting the vote not for aesthetics but for location and the Ashley the vote on the best restaurant.

For centrally located **B&B** and **homestays**:
B **Ardwyn House**, *48 Chapel St, T03-7686107;*
A **Rosewood**, *20 High St, T03-7684674, rosewoodnz@xtra.co.nz* Both are recommended.

Most of the town's **motels** are on the main drag (High St/SH6) heading south out of town.
AL-A Gables Motor Lodge, *(84), T03-7689991;* and
AL-A Alpine Rose
(139), T03-7687586; both are recommended.
A **Willowbank Pacifica Lodge**, *just off SH6 3 km north of the town, T0800-668355.* A quieter, cheaper option.
C-D Neptune's, *43 Gresson St, T03-7684425.* Run by the former owners of *Noah's Ark.* Already the former waterfront hotel/pub is showing signs of loving attention, mixed with an obvious deft touch. All things fishy is the emphasis this time, with the wide range of comfortable rooms and facilities (including baths) decorated accordingly. Neptune's is good value and particularly good for couples.
C-D Noah's Ark, *16 Chapel St, T0800-662472, noahsark@xtra.co.nz* (Formerly owned by current owners of Neptune's). A rambling old villa that has all the usual rooms and facilities but stands out a mile with its fauna-themed rooms. There is a positive zoo on site with everything from elephants and bears to the humble kiwi. Visitors often fall in love with both the place and their room and once departed continue to send themed articles to join the decor. Internet.
C-D Global Village Backpackers, *42-54 Cowper St, T03-7687272, globalvillage@minidata.co.nz* Managed by a partnership with an admiral wealth of travelling experience, its only downfall is its location from the centre of town. Kayaking is available in the river that runs alongside it. Free pick-ups.

Motorparks
B-D Top Ten Greymouth Holiday Park, *Chesterfield St, T03-7686618, www.toptengreymouth.co.nz* A spacious, well-managed place, and located alongside the beach, offering self-contained units, cabins and powered/tent sites with excellent facilities.

Lake Brunner *p571*
C-D Lake Brunner Motor Camp, *Ahau St, T03-7380600.* Has a beautiful view across the lake and has basic facilities.
A-C Moana Hotel, *Ahau St, T03-7380083.* Has modern double rooms, cabins and motel units and an expert fishing guide.
A Lake Brunner Country Motel, *on the Arnold Valley Road at the outskirts of the village towards Greymouth, T03-7380143.* It has modern self-contained chalets and can also arrange fishing and bush-walking excursions.
LL-L Lake Brunner Lodge, *Mitchell's, Kumara-Inchbonnie Rd (at the southern end of the lake), T03-7380163, www.lakebrunner.com* A historic, all mod cons, fishing retreat with 11 luxury rooms and fine cuisine.

Blackball *p571*
B-C 'Formerly the Blackball Hilton' *on Hart St, T03-7324705, www.blackballhilton.co.nz* Now a comfortable and (believe it or not) very friendly backpackers and B&B. Can also arrange a number of local activities including gold panning, horse trekking and walking (Dinner, B&B from $80)

Reefton *p571*

There are 2 principal **B&Bs** in town:
A **Quartz Lodge B&B**, *corner of Sheil and Sinnamon Sts, T03-7328383*. Perfectly comfortable.
A **Reef Cottage B&B**, *Broadway, T03-7328440*. Cute and historic.

Motels include:
B **Reefton Auto Lodge (Dawsons on Broadway)**, *74 Broadway, T03-7328406*. Modern studio units. Spa and café/bar with a lovely open fire.
B **Bellbird Motel**, *Broadway, T03-7328444*.

There are 2 **backpackers** on Sheil St:
D **Reefton Backpackers** *(64), T03-7328133*. A comfortable renovated villa with shared, single or double rooms with proper beds (not bunks).
C-D Pog Mo Thon Backpackers (Reefton Lodge), *(104), T03-7328885*. Has 2 self-contained units, double, twin and singles and assures a warm Irish welcome.

Motorcamps
C-D Motorcamp, *at the edge of town at the top of Broadway, T03-7328477*. Basic: has powered/tent sites and cabins and its coal-fired water heater is typical of the town.

🍴 Eating

Greymouth *p568*
$$$ Café Collage, *115 Mackay St (upstairs), T03-7685497. Tue-Sat from 1800*. Has a quality traditional-style menu.
$$$ Ashley's Hotel, *74 Tasman St, T0800-807787. Daily for lunch and dinner*. A la carte restaurant and brasserie with a good reputation.
$$ The Smelting House Café, *102 Mackay St, T03-7680012. Mon-Sat 0800-1700*. A local favourite located in a historic old bank building. It specializes in home-style food and serves good coffee.
$$ Jone's Café and Bar, *37 Tainui St, T03-7686468*. Another good alternative that is open late, offers a traditional-style menu with a few good vegetarian options and has occasional live jazz and blues.

Good breakfast.
$$ Café 124 on *Mackay, T03-7687503. Mon-Thu 1000-1700, Fri-Sun 0900-2100*. The newest edition to Greymouth's café scene, it is quite classy and proving popular for lunch and dinner and also for breakfast or brunch at the weekend.
$ Bonzai Pizzeria, *31 Mackay St, T03-7684170. 0700-late*. Will not let you down.
$ West of the Border, *25 Mackay St, T03-7685272. Dinner only*. Serves up hefty Tex-Mex portions.
$ Steamers Café and Bar, *corner of Mackay and Tarapuhi St, T03-7684193. Daily 1145-1430 and 1700-2100*. Does a good Sunday Roast or pub grub.
$ Railway Hotel, *Mawhera Quay, T03-7687023. Daily from 1830*. For the real 'fill your face' deal.
$ Raceway Carvery, Union Hotel, *20 Herbert St, T03-7684013. Open for lunch and dinner*. This and the Railway hotel offer all-you-can-eat BBQs from $3.
$ DP:One, *Mawhera Quay, T03-7687503 (open daily 0900-2230)*. The best (or certainly most interesting) café in town. It is a small place but full of character, ressembling something like an extrovert artist's garage. It is also the best internet venue in town.

Lake Brunner
For the more budget conscious based in Moana your only eatery options are:
$$ Moana Hotel, *see above*; or
$ Station House Café and Gallery, *overlooking the lake and train station, T03-7380158. Seasonal hours*.

Blackball *p571*
Blackball Salami Company, *T03-7324111, also on Hart St. Mon-Sat*. Award-winning sausages for your picnic basket.

Reefton *p571*
$$ Reefton Auto Lodge (Dawsons), *see above*; and
$$ Hotel Reefton, *Broadway, T03-7328447*. Both offer traditional pub-style meals.
$$ Alfresco, *across the road from the Domain Motor Camp on Broadway. Summer only*,

---

● *For an explanation of the sleeping and eating price codes used in this guide, see the inside*
● *front cover. Other relevant information is provided in the Essentials chapter, see page 51.*

Mon-Sat, lunch and dinner. Lives up to its name and serves takeaway pizza and good coffee.

$ **Reef Cottage Café**, *Broadway. Daily 1000-late*. Cosy café serving good coffee and light snacks.

🟤 Pubs and entertainment

Greymouth *p568*
Greymouth has several traditional hotels which are the focus of the town's nightlife. **Revingtons Hotel**, *Tainui St*. The most popular and has two bars the pseudo Irish **Danny Doolan's** and **Revy's Sports Bar**. **Cinema**, *in the same building as the VIC, corner of Mackay and Boundary Sts, T03-7685101*.

⛰️ Activities

Greymouth *p568*
Water Most activities are water-based with a choice of **river rafting**, **cave rafting**, and **kayaking**.
Eco-Rafting Adventures, *based at the DP:One Café, 108 Mawhera Quay, T03-7684005, www.ecorafting.co.nz* Offers half or multi-day trips on numerous West Coast rivers from $80.
Dragons Cave Rafting (Wild West Adventures), *Whall St, T0800-223456*. An exhilarating half-day black water rafting experience in the Taniwha Cave system from $120.
Jungle Boat Cruising Company, *T050-8474837, www.nzholidayheaven.co.nz* River cruises on board an imaginative range of traditional Maori craft and more conventional rafts with a distinct 'Tarzan' edge. The 3-hr trips are certainly different and offer a fine opportunity to learn more about the rich Maori culture and traditions of the West Coast, from $95.
Land On Yer Bike, *T03-7627438, www.onyerbike.co.nz* From $25-$100.
Kea West Coast Tours, *T0800-532-868, www.keatours.co.nz* Offers a range of road trips to Punakaiki, Hokitika, The Glaciers, The Grey Valley and Shantytown, from $34-$175.
Air **West Coast Scenic Flights**, *T03-7680407*. It flies locally or farther afield with a range of 1-5 hr trips, from $80 to $580.

Reefton *p571*
Spend some time in the VIC looking at the very attractive **walking**, **tramping** and **mountain biking** opportunities in the highly underrated and quiet **Victoria Forest Park**. There are numerous routes and half- to multi-day walking/tramping options that take in a wealth of former gold-mining relics. An excellent 'helicopter in/mountain bike out' trip to Big River can be arranged by the VIC. Prices on application. The DoC leaflet *Reefton-Victoria Conservation Park* is useful.
The local **fishing** is superb (information about local guides available from the VIC). **Reefton Sports Centre**, *1 km down Soldiers Rd*. Licenses and tackle hire.

🟤 Directory

Greymouth *p568*
Banks All bank branches can be found on or around Mackay St. **Bike hire** Coll's Sports/Avanti Pro Cycles, *53 Mackay St, T03-7684060*. **Car hire** Alpine Rentals, *T0800-257736*. Avis, *T0800-655111*. Both located at the train station. **Half-Price Rentals**, *170 Tainui St, T03-7680379*. Older, cheaper models. **Internet** DP:One Café, *Mawhera Quay*. Grey District Library, *Mackay St*. VIC, see page 568. **Post office** *Tainui St. Mon-Fri 0830-1700, Sat 1000-1230*.
Taxi Greymouth Taxis, *T03-76877078*. Hoki Airport Shuttles, *T03-7687078*. Offers airport pick-ups from $12, or transport further afield to Hokitika or Punakaiki, from $25.

Reefton *p571*
Internet VIC, see page 568. Library/post office, *across the road. Mon-Fri 1030-1230, 1330-1630*.

Hokitika and around → Phone code: 03

Hokitika, or 'Hoki' as it is known on 'The Coast', shares the rather drab appearance and monotonous street grid system of its former gold-mining counterparts, but at least enjoys the same warm welcome and proud, healthy heartbeat felt the length and minimal breadth of the West Coast. An important port until 1954, the town is also steeped in gold mining history. More of the precious metal passed through Hoki in the 1860s than any other town on the coast with the port being one of the busiest in the country. Between 1865-67 over 37,000 hopefuls arrived from Australia, America and Britain, requiring a staggering 84 hotels to put them all up. In 1865 pioneer surveyor Julius von Haast described Hokitika as 'a scene of almost indescribable bustle and activity'. In those heady days it seemed only the river itself could hold the town back. At one point during the gold rush there was at least one grounding every 10 weeks – and 21 in 1865 alone. Like everywhere else the gold ran out and old 'Hoki' slipped into decline. But today gold has been replaced by that other precious resource, tourism. Now it is the craft capital of the West Coast and every summer sees cosmopolitan crowds of camera-toting visitors arrive by the bus load, to watch glass-blowing and greenstone carving and to browse in its numerous galleries. South from Hokitika the influence of humanity decreases almost dramatically and the aesthetics begin to reflect the sheer dominance of nature. Mountain ranges climb steadily on the eastern horizon, gradually ascending in ever increasing beauty towards the heady peaks of The Westland National Park and to Mt Cook itself. Small villages like Ross and Hari Hari cling precariously to a history of gold mining and demonstrate in size alone how much nature rules these parts, and hopefully always will. This is where the 'real' West Coast begins.

Ins and outs

Getting there Hoki boasts the West Coast's main **airport**, 1 km east of the town centre and served at least once daily by **Air New Zealand Link (Eagle Air)**, T0800-737000. By **road** Hoki is 40 km south of Greymouth and 429 km north of Wanaka. Principal **bus** services are provided by **Intercity**, T03-7558557 (points south to Greymouth/ Christchurch); **Atomic Shuttles**, T03-3228883 (Queenstown to Greymouth/ Christchurch); **Coast to Coast**, T0800-800847 (Greymouth/ Christchurch); and **Alpine Coaches**, T0800-274888 (Greymouth/Christchurch). All stop outside the **Travel Centre**, 60 Tancred St, T03-7558557. If you are heading south this is also your last chance to join the **AA** at Addison's Furnishings, 32 Hamilton St, T03-7558589.

Information Westland VIC, ① *Carnegie Building, corner of Hamilton and Tancred Sts, T03-7556166, www.westlanddc.govt.nz Daily in summer 0830-1800 (winter Mon-Fri 0900-1700, Sat-Sun 1000-1400).* **DoC**, ① *Sewell St, T03-7558301. Mon-Fri 0800-1645.* But the VIC will stock most of what you need. **Ross VIC**, ① *4 Aylmer St, T03-7554077, www.ross.org.co.nz Daily 0830-1700.*

Hokitika → Colour map 5, grid B2. Population: 4,000

Hokitika is famous for its **arts** and **crafts**, particularly **greenstone** carving and **glass-blowing**. Tancred Street is the hub of the many artisan outlets and factory shops. Not to be missed is the **Hokitika Glass Studio**, ① *28 Tancred St, T03-7557775, daily 0900-1730 (longer in summer),* where you can see the glass being blown and crafted into rather lurid ornaments and objets d'art. Shroders, in the **Mountain Jade Complex**, ① *41 Weld St, T03-7558484,* echoes the Glass Studio and also houses a jade factory shop. There are a number of other greenstone factory shops including

Westland Greenstone, ① *34 Tancred St, T03-7558713. Daily 0800-1700.* Here, once again you can see the beautiful and spiritual stone being cut and handcrafted in to a wide array of jewellery, ornaments and traditional Maori pendants (*tiki*).

Also worthy of investigation is the **Gold Room** and **House of Wood**, both on Tancred Street. The huge natural nugget pendants in the Gold Room (at a hefty $8000) would delight the critical eye of Jimmy Saville or even Mr T.

If you fancy a go at jade carving yourself, then Gordon of the **Just Jade Experience (Backpackers),** ① *197 Revell St, T03-7557612,* will give you a full day of tuition from $80. Naturally you get to keep your masterpiece – or disaster!

Once crafted out and replete with souvenirs, you might like to absorb some local history at the **West Coast Historical Museum,** ① *in the Carnegie Building (accessed through the VIC), 7 Tancred Street, T03-7556898. Daily 0930-1700 (seasonal). Adult $5, child $1.* As you might expect there is a heavy emphasis on gold and jade, but the troubled history of the port and its numerous shipwrecks provides some added excitement.

The **Quay,** near the museum, is worth a stroll with its centrepiece the 1897 Custom House now housing a small gallery. There is a free *Hokitika Heritage Walk* leaflet available from the VIC that outlines other places of historical interest.

Far removed from both craft and history is the small, but effective, **New Zealand Eco Centre,** ① *55 Sewell St, T03-7555251. 0900-1800 (winter 0930-1600). Adult $12, child $6.* It is a small complex with a wide variety of native and non-native species, the stars of which are the New Zealand eels, the biggest eel species in the world. These unfeasibly large, ugly and lethargic octogenarians are fed daily at 1000, 1200, 1500 and 1700. Other non-aquatic creatures include native parrots and inevitably some kiwis.

The town also has its very own **Glow-worm Dell** at the northern entrance to town. Although not the best of displays, if you have not seen them yet this is your chance. ↠ *For Sleeping, Eating and other listings, see pages 580-582.*

Hokitika

0 metres 100
0 yards 100

Sleeping
Beach House &
Trappers Restaurant **1**
Blue Spur Lodge
Backpackers **11**
Fitzherbert Court **2**
Jade Court Motel **3**

Just Jade Backpackers **5**
Mountain Jade
Backpackers **4**
Shining Star Log
Chalets & Motor Camp **6**
Southland **7**
Stumpers **9**
Teichelmann's B&B **8**
Villa Polenza **10**

Eating
Café de Paris **2**
Tasman View **3**

Around Hokitika

Lake Kaniere → *Colour map 5, grid B2*

Inland from Hokitika (14 km) is the picturesque Lake Kaniere, a popular haven in summer for swimming, water sports, picnicking and walking. The lake can be explored in a number of ways, by foot, car, boat or bicycle and there are many pleasant walks and features on offer. At the entrance to the **Lake Kaniere Scenic Reserve** there is an information kiosk outlining all the possibilities. The two best short walks, both of which include lovely beaches, are the Kahikatea Walk, at **Sunny Bight** (10 minutes) and the **Canoe Cove Walk** (15 minutes). If you are feeling more energetic the **Lake Kaniere Walkway** (four hours), which also starts at Sunny Bight, follows the western shore of the lake to Slip Bay at its southern edge. The road on the eastern edge will give you access to the hardest walk (seven hours) – the ascent of **Mount Tuhua** (1125 m). Further south are the **Dorothy Falls** (64 m) near Big Bay. There is a basic campsite at Hans Bay. The DoC leaflet *Central West Coast-Hokitika* outlines all these options and a few others ($1).

Hokitika Gorge → *Colour map 5, grid B2*

Accessed directly from Hokitika (25 km) via the settlements of Kaniere and Kokatahi (end of Kowhitirangi and Whitcombe Road) or, alternatively, via Lake Kaniere (loop road to Kokatahi) is the picturesque and moody Hokitika Gorge. Other than the impressive scenery the highlight here is the **swing-bridge** across the river. Although most of the time the river slides gracefully below, it can become a raging torrent after heavy rains, making the crossing an exciting prospect. Once across the bridge you can continue through the bush for another 100 m to emerge at a rock wall that offers an even better view of the gorge.

Lake Mahinapua → *Colour map 5, grid B2*

Just 10 km south of Hokitika, and shielded from SH6 by a narrow tract of bush, is Lake Mahinapua and the **Mahinapua Recreation Reserve**, another popular spot for swimming, fishing, kayaking and walking. At the road terminus there is a pleasant picnic spot, a campsite and the trailheads to a number of short walks. Perched in concrete near the car park is a former 15-m paddle steamer that used to ply the route to 'Hoki' carrying both freight and passengers. A modern working model runs daily (seasonal) **cruises** from the outlet creek to the lake, starting 6 km south of Hokitika (see Activities, page 577).

Hokitika to Franz Josef

Stocked up with cash, petrol and photographic film, you can now follow the human artery of SH6 in to the real wild West Coast. From here, the mountains rise higher and higher and become crowned with snow and impenetrable bush creeps steadily towards the road from all directions. Also, never far away, the pounding surf crashes onto lonely, driftwood-covered beaches. It all holds the promise of great things and, provided the weather is on your side, it will not disappoint. Even if you do nothing but simply gaze in wonder from the passenger seat, the 137 km journey to Franz Josef is a stunner and will ease you gently in to West Coast time.

> **‡** *If you're hungry you could do a lot worse than a whitebait fritter and a pint of Monteiths in the Mahinapua Hotel, opposite the reserve*

Ross → *Colour map 5, grid B2*

The first settlement of any consequence is the tiny and pretty **gold-mining** town of Ross, 30 km south of Hokitika. The most interesting thing about Ross is that mining still takes place here, in a very large hole at the edge of town, where the gentle chip, chip of the early pickaxe has long given way to the hum and roar of huge diggers and trucks. Even so, Ross retains the romance of its past with evidence of fond memories and many old remnants. During the great gold rush of the 1860s it was a bustling town of over 3000 hopefuls, who chipped away relentlessly at the alluvial gravels of the Totara Riverbeds in search of the 'big one'. Ironically, in 1909, towards the end of the great gold rush, one lucky miner fulfilled that dream. His find, named the **'Honourable Roddy'**, after the erstwhile Minister of Mines, was a nugget weighing in at a healthy 3.1 kg. As you might expect, the nugget immediately took on a life of its own, at first being paraded from bar to bar then sold and sold again. Then after a short stint as a doorstop (apparently true) it was bought by the government in 1911 as a coronation gift for King George V. Sadly, this act of generosity proved its demise. After a colourful life above ground, the good and the grateful Royals melted it down for use as a gold tea service at Buckingham Palace. Or that is what we are led to believe.

Ross VIC, ① *4 Aylmer St, T03-7554077, www.ross.org.co.nz Daily 0830-1700*, has some interesting displays and photographs of the gold rush days and information on a number of short local **walks**, including the **Water Race Walk** and the **Jones Flat Walk** (1-2 hours). Both take in some former mining relics. Guided walks are available between 1000 and 1400, 30 min from $5.50 (1 hr 15 min from $12). You can also go gold panning for $6.50 (independent hire from $5). A short distance from the VIC is a renovated 1885 **Miner's Cottage** with a replica of the great 'Honourable Roddy' nugget.

Pukekura → *Colour map 5, grid B2*

About 18 km further south of Ross is the small settlement of Pukekura (population 2) and the **Bushman's Centre**, ① *T03-7554144, www.pukekura.co.nz* This place is instantly recognisable and notorious for the giant **sandfly** (*Renderus insanitus*) that hangs with menace from its walls (don't panic; despite local gossip, they could never grow that big). The Bushman's Centre is the ongoing project of local West Coaster and extrovert Peter Salter and his partner Justine Giddy. As well as a fine **café** (with its superb 'road kill soup of the day') and **shop** it has a great little interactive **museum** ($4), where you can learn about bushcraft, meet a live possum, stroke a pig, baulk at ugly eels, then wantonly throw sharp knives and axes at the wall. It's brilliant. Other activities based at the centre include **horse trekking, gold panning** and Canadian **canoe safaris** (independent hire also available).

Harihari → *Colour map 5, grid B2. 20 km south of Lake Ianthe and 80 km from Hokitika*

From Pukekura the bush continues to envelope you and you are blessed with your first occasional views of Mount Cook's snowy peak. At **Lake Ianthe** there are opportunities to stop and take in the views, enjoy a picnic on its bush-clad bank or take a leisurely 40-minute cruise on board the small kauri steamboat the 'Tamati'. Cruises cost around $15 and depart on demand from the Ianthe Jetty at the southern end of the lake, for details call T0800-119494. From the car park you can also take a short walk to visit a large **maitai tree**, the South Island's equivalent to the North Island's mighty kauri.

Harihari is a small farming settlement nestled on the open alluvial plains of the Wanganui and Poerua Rivers. It is famous due to the unexpected visitation by a 21-year-old Australian aviator called Guy Menzies in January 1931. Young Guy had set off unannounced and alone from Sydney in his Avro-Avian plane called the Southern Cross armed with little except a lot of courage and a good sense of direction. Just under 12 hours and an awful lot of sea later he crash-landed in a swamp near the town. The interesting thing is that the bold Guy had not officially told anybody of his attempt. But what was most interesting of all is that his crossing was actually completed in 2½ hours less than the much publicized success of Sir Charles Kingsford Smith, in a three-engine plane, with crew, three years earlier.

⦙ Greenstone (Pounamu)

It would take several PhDs in geology to describe the make-up, formation and various types of greenstone (nephrite), but suffice to say it is old, uncommon and as the name suggests, coloured with almost transparent olive green shades. Greenstone, or jade – as it is better known – is precious (*taonga*) to the Maori and has been revered for centuries. The Maori called it pounamu. In New Zealand greenstone is found in the South Island, predominantly in Westland. The Maori called South Island Te Wahi Pounamu (The Place of Greenstone) and they went to great lengths to find and transport the precious stone, before carving it into a range of items, both practical and ornamental. Foremost among these was the *mere* (a flat hand-held weapon), which were highly treasured and in the hands of a warrior was lethal. *Heitiki* (pendants), were also painstakingly carved, often in the form of mythical spirits and monsters. These *tiki* were passed on from generation to generation and in doing so, increased in *mana* (prestige or spiritual power). In the modern-day, greenstone is mainly used to create ornaments and tiki for the commercial tourist market. Hokitika, on the West Coast of the South Island is the best place to see it being made and to make a purchase.

If you fancy some thorough exploration of the coastline, the **Harihari Coastal Walkway** (three hours) utilizes part of the old Wanganui River pack track and is a fine walk. It traverses kahikatea and rimu forest and essentially links the two river mouths. The car park and trailhead is accessed via La Fontaine Road at the southern end of Harihari (19 km). One of the many highlights of the walk is the lookout at the top of **Mount Doughboy** (or to give it its much more attractive name – Mount Oneone) Although not especially high it does afford a great view up and down the coast. The DoC leaflet *Harihari Coastal Walk* gives detailed information.

Whataroa → *Colour map 5, grid C1*

It is little wonder that the Maori have long revered the **white heron (kotuku)**. Although a non-native and essentially an Australian import, its presence here on the West Coast seems utterly befitting of the place. Somehow, with its colour echoing the snow of the mountaintops and its graceful unhurried flight in rhythm with West Coast time, there could be no better mascot. Whataroa, 35 km south of Harihari, provides your only opportunity to see these majestic birds congregated at their sole New Zealand breeding rookery. But you will have to time it right. The birds are only in residence from mid-October to mid-March. **White Heron Sanctuary Tours,** ① *Whataroa, T0800-523-456, www.whiteherontours.co.nz All tours must be guided and the colony cannot be visited independently without a permit from DoC. Tours cost from $89, child $40 and leave daily at 0900, 1100, 1300 and 1500, in season. Offers a three hour tour by jet boat, to access the hide that looks over the colony.*

Outside the breeding season there is still an enjoyable 2½-hour **Rainforest Nature Tour** available, again by jet boat, to view the ancient Kahikatea forest and whatever birdlife that decides to show (40-minute jet boat tours on the Waitangitaona River are also available).

Okarito → *Colour map 5, grid C1. Population: 30 (formerly 3000)*

Okarito, a small coastal settlement and former goldfields port is 13 km off SH6 and 15 km south of Whataroa. This beautiful little paradise, set beachside next to the vast

3240-ha Okarito Lagoon backed by stunning views of the Southern Alps, is not surprisingly the favourite haunt of many a New Zealander. Thankfully most people shoot past the road junction from SH6 in their rush to see their first glacier – Franz Josef - 29 km to the south. But for those who take the time and the diversion, they will be rewarded not only with Okarito's simple do-nothing appeal, but also some excellent **walking**, **kayaking** and **birdwatching** opportunities. There is no public transport to Okarito and no shops in Okarito so take your own supplies.

The best walk is the steady climb (1 ½ hours) via an old, but well formed, pack track through native bush to the **Okarito Trig**. On a clear day it affords a stunning view across the bush-clad hills to the Southern Alps and the peak of Mount Cook and its associates. As if that weren't enough, you can then turn to take in the expansive views back towards the Okarito Lagoon and north up the coast. The Trig Track starts from The Strand at the southern end of the village. Once you have negotiated the Trig you can then consider carrying on along the main pack track for about an hour to reach **Three Mile Lagoon**. It is a lovely spot with a quiet beach and more coastal views. If the tide is right, you can then walk back to Okarito via the beach where huge white-veined schist rocks that have been eroded from the Kohuamarua Bluff litter the beach. Also look out for dolphins playing just offshore.

The great expanse of **Okarito Lagoon** is a **birdwatcher's** paradise with almost every mainland bird species in New Zealand visiting at some point. Over 70 species have so far been recorded. The best way to view the birds and the lagoon is either by **kayak** or boat. **Okarito Nature Tours**, ① *T03-7534014, www.okarito.co.nz* offers independent kayak rental (two hours, $35) and a range of excellent guided trips from $65 (overnight from $80) and pick-up from SH6 for a small fee. **Okarito Boat Tours**, ① *T03-7534017*, offers sedate 2-3 hour boat trips every morning at 0900 (0800 mid summer) between October-April from $65, child $25.

There are few remnants of Okarito's once bustling gold-mining past when the population remarkably ran into the thousands. Its hard to believe there were once 25 hotels, two banks, several stores, a busy school (now the *YHA*) and three theatres. Across the road from the obviously historic and incredibly cute YHA is the almost unsightly **obelisk** commemorating Abel Tasman's first sighting of New Zealand, somewhere off Okarito in 1642. ▸▸ *For Sleeping , see page 581.*

⊜ Sleeping

Hokitika *p575*

Hokitika is pretty well blessed with good accommodation but in summer, like everywhere else on the West Coast, you are advised to book well in advance.

AL-A Southland Hotel, *111 Revell St, T03-7558344, www.southlandhotel.com* The sole remaining hotel, it is comfortable enough, with its reputable restaurant/bar overlooking the beach being its best point. There are a few luxury **B&Bs** near Hokitika:

LL-L Villa Polenza, *Brickfield Rd, T03-7557801, villapolenza@xtra.co.nz* The most expensive and the best. Built in a prime location in Italian-style it offers luxuriously appointed king and queen rooms and 2 en suites. As you would expect, the cuisine is also excellent.

AL-A Teichelmann's B&B, *20 Hamilton St,*

T03-7558232, www.teichelmanns.co.nz Comfortable and friendly and right in the centre of town.

A-D Shining Star Log Chalets and Motor Camp, *11 Richards Dr, T03-7558921, shinning@xtra.co.nz* It is a superb motel with very tidy self-contained lodges designed and built by the owners. It is close the beach in a quiet location and also takes campervans and tents. The facilities are excellent and include internet.

Other **motels** include:

A Jade Court Motel, *85 Fitzherbert St, T03-7558855, www.jadecourt.co.nz;* or

A Fitzherbert Court, *191 Fitzherbert St, T03-7555342.*

B-D Stumpers, *2 Weld St, T03-7556154, www.stumpers.co.nz* Pitched somewhere between a budget motel and a backpackers, it offers tidy ensuite and standard doubles, singles and dorms (some with TV and bath).

Its central location and new in-house bar and café are an added attraction. Note in-house dining is encouraged therefore there are no kitchen facilities.

C-D Mountain Jade Backpackers, *41 Weld St, T0800-838301, T03-7557612*. Purpose built and a bit clinical, but certainly serves its purpose and has a restaurant downstairs. It takes the majority of the 'backpacker buses' so can get busy.

C-D Beach House, *137 Revell St, T03-7556859*. Beachside, offering dorms, doubles, a good restaurant and a popular 'bush-bath'.

C-D Just Jade Backpackers, *197 Revell St, T03-7557612, www.madkiwi.co.nz* Also on ther beach, smaller, more homely, and offering jade carving (from $80) a pet possum (in the garden) and private beach access as added incentives to stay.

C-D Blue Spur Lodge Backpackers, *Hampden St, 6 km east of town, T03-7558445, bluespur@xtra.co.nz* Well-appointed and well-equipped, with tidy doubles, twins and shared rooms as well as a fully self-contained cottage with 2 en suite rooms. It's a popular place noted for its peace and quiet and worth the effort to get there. Kayak hire, gold panning and bush walks on site.

Ross *p577*
B-D Empire Hotel, *Aylmer St, T03-7554005*. Basic but characterful and historic, has tent sites, backpacker cabins and en suite rooms.
B Dahlia Cottage B&B, *47 Aylmer St, T03-7554160*. A good B&B noted for its beautiful garden.

Pukekura *p578*
Across the road from the Bushman's Centre there is a fine array of accommodation options (**AL-D**) from tent sites and budget dorms, to motel units 'under canvas' with all facilities and even hot pools.

Harihari *p578*
A-D Harihari Motor Inn, *Main Rd, T0800-833026*. Tidy en suites, backpacker rooms, powered/tent sites and a licensed restaurant.
B Tomsai Motel, *T03-7533116*. Across the road is another cheaper, basic motel option that also caters for backpackers.

B-D Sanctuary Tours Motel, *T0800-523456*. Units, cabins with cooking facilities. There are tent sites but no kitchen.
C-D Whataroa Hotel, *T03-7534076*. Has rooms and powered sites.

Okarito *p579*
D Okarito YHA Hostel, *The Strand, T03-7520754*. Something of novelty with a limited number of bunks in what was the former 1870s schoolhouse. Bookings can be made via the Franz Josef VIC or payment made direct at the warden's house close to the hostel.
D Campground, *across the road, T03-7534142*. Facilities at the hostel are adequate, but showers are only available at this very pleasant, sheltered and basic campsite. Fires are permitted. Beware of sandflies and take insect repellent.
C-D Royal Hostel and Motel, *also on the Strand, T03-7534080, okarito@nzactive.com* Far better equipped, this is a homely place. It has comfortable dorms and doubles, Sky TV and a log fire very welcome after a day kayaking. The owners will also pick up from the junction with SH6 or even Franz Josef (for longer stay clients).

● Eating

Hokitika *p575*
$$$ Café de Paris, *19 Tancred St, T03-7558933. Daily from 0730*. Award-winning restaurant that sets the benchmark. It has an imaginative French-style à la carte menu for dinner, a changing blackboard menu for breakfast and lunch and good coffee. It also has an interesting history (ask about the runaway pig).
$$ Tasman View Restaurant, *attached to the Southland Hotel, Revell St, T03-7558344. Open for dinner Sat-Thu*. Popular not only for the views of the crashing waves but its seafood and good value smorgasbords on Fri.
$$ Trappers Restaurant, *131-137 Revell St, T03-7556859. Open for lunch and dinner*. Extremely wooden, very good and touts itself as the original wild food restaurant, though it is definitely not one for the avid vegan.
$ Stumpers Café/Bar, *2 Weld St, T03-7556154. Daily from 0700-2200*. A more conventional menu and aesthetics.

Supermarket New World, *116 Revell St, T03-7558390. Mon-Fri until 2000, Sat 1900, Sun 1800.*

Ross *p577*
$ **Roddy Nugget Café**, *T03-7554245, on the Main Rd..Open daily from 0700 (summer).* There is also a supermarket on Main Rd open until 2000.

Pukekura *p578*
$ **Puke Pub**, *on the main road.* Without doubt one of the finest drinking establishments on the West Coast. Full of character with pub-style grub. If you are a male-only group ask to see the mock up view into the ladies toilet – truly stunning.

Harihari *p578*
Other than the basic restaurant in the $ **Harihari Motor Inn**, *see above*, there is the $ **Glenalmond Tearooms**, *on the main road through the town.*

Whataroa *p579*
$ **White Heron Store and Tearooms**, and $ **Whataroa Hotel**, both on the main road, are the only eateries available.

● Entertainment and events

Hokitika *p575*
The main hub of entertainment is the **Stumpers Bar** (above). It attracts a diverse crowd and stages live bands most weekends. **Hokitika Wildfoods Festival** (*Mar*). Hokitika goes mad each March and enjoys such a human influx that it can jog the memories of the gold rush days. The attraction is not gold but good food and lots and lots of beer and wine. This is a celebration of the West Coast's unique lifestyle, food and hospitality (not to mention drinking capacity). On offer is a vast array of culinary delights from BBQ possum, or witchetty bug to the famed local whitebait fritter. You can even fill your face with a sphagnum moss candyfloss. A number of lesser events over the 2-3 day event (that include such diverse activities as a basketball exhibition match and a Monteiths Beer tasting) leads up the main festival and dance (monumental 'session') on the Saturday. *Tickets cost $12, T03-7558321, wildfoods@westlandddc.govt.nz*

▲ Activities

Hokitika *p575*
Cruises Paddle Boat Cruises, *T03-7557239.* Ply the creek to the picturesque Mahinapua Lake just south of the town. A 1½-hr trip will cost you from $25. Departs daily at 1400 (seasonal).

Flightseeing Wilderness Wings, *T03-7558118, www.wildernesswings.co.nz* Trips to places including Mount Cook and The Glaciers. 45 mins to 3½ hrs, from $235.

Kayaking and rafting Riverplay, *T0800-116-348, www.riverplay.co.nz* A new and professional outfit offering adventure kayaking and rafting trips ranging from half a day to 5 days. The kayak trip is an all day affair that includes 4x4 and bush walking to access the river and then the use of inflatable kayaks to negotiate class 2-3 rapids (suitable for beginners), from $170. The rafting and heli-rafting trips negotiate the Arahura, Karamea and Clarence Rivers. Trips range from a half-day family rafting at $95 to a 5-day adventure at $895.

● Directory

Hokitika *p575*
Banks Most branches and ATMs are available in the town centre. Note if you are heading south there are no further banks, or ATMs until Wanaka. **Bike hire** Hokitika Cycles and Sports, *33 Tancred St, T03-7558662.* **Car hire** Classic Car Rentals, *117 Revell St, T03-7556928, www.classiccarrentals.co.nz* From a maximum of $100 per hr including petrol and insurance, why not hire a *Porsche* or a 1938 *Alfa Romeo?* **Internet** Cybergate, *26 Weld St, T03-7556930. Daily 0900-2100.* District Library, *36 Weld St (Mon-Fri 1000-1700; Sat 0900-1200.* **Medical services** Westland Medical Centre, *54 Sewell St, T03-7558180.* **Post office** *93 Revell St, T03-7568034. Mon-Fri 0830-1700.* **Taxis** Hokitika Taxis, *T03-7555075.* **Useful addresses** Breakdown services, AA, *T0800-500222.*

The Glacier Region → *Phone code: 03*

As if New Zealand has not enough to offer in majestic scenery and ecological surprises, the two gigantic and dynamic monoliths of ice, Franz Josef and Fox Glaciers, provide a dramatic sight. They are the brightest jewels in the highly decorated crown of the Westland and Mount Cook National Parks, joined, yet separated on the map, by the jagged summits and peaks of the Southern Alps and the Great Dividing Range. Descending from a height of 3000-300 m at the remarkable speed of over 1 m a day, the glaciers create one of the best examples of glaciology in the world.

In summer there are only really two moods to the neighbouring villages of Franz and Fox. When the sun shines they are both a frenetic buzz of activity. From the moment the sun peeks from above the mountaintops, the skies fill with the sound of aircraft, the roads swarm with tour buses and the streets fill rapidly with expectant tourists. They seem excited, rushed, almost consumed with the desire to get there: to see them, walk on them, photograph them, perhaps even touch them. And yet, when the clouds gather (which is often) and the rain descends (correction; crashes down), the pace of everything slows, dramatically. Then, the streets fill with puddles and the tourists' glum faces stare at them from behind café windows. The air hangs heavy with silence. At Franz and Fox it's amazing just how much the weather and two, multi-million ton blocks of ice, dictate.

Ins and outs

Getting there There are no scheduled air services to Franz Josef. By **road** Franz Josef is 177 km south of Greymouth, 404 km north of Queenstown and 25 km north of Fox Glacier on SH6. Fox Glacier is 177 km north of Haast. **Intercity**, T03-7520242, and **Atomic Shuttles**, T03-3228883, north and southbound **bus** services all stop at Franz Josef and Fox. In Franz Josef, Scott Base Information on Main Road and Glacier Shop in the Alpine Adventure Building (also on Main Rd) both act as the local **Intercity** agents, T03-7520131.

Getting around Most of Franz Josef's services and amenities are situated on the SH6 (Main Road) with everything (except the glacier itself) being in easy walking distance. **Kamahi Tours**, T03-7520699, (book at the **Alpine Adventure Centre**) provides transportation to the head of the glacier, from $5. Hitching to the glacier and back is rarely a problem. NB Note there is no petrol available between Fox Glacier and Haast.

Information DoC Franz Josef Glacier VIC, ① *at the southern end of town (seaward side), T03-7520796. 0830-1800 (winter 0830-1700).* There are plenty of displays, walks information and most importantly up-to-date weather forecasts. On Main Rd the independent **Scott Base Information Centre** also provides local information, arranges transport and activity bookings and has internet, T03-7520288. **DoC Fox Glacier VIC,**① *on SH6, at the northern end (seaward side) of the village, T03-7510807. Daily 0830-1830 (winter 0900-1630).* It provides detailed information about regional walks, the glacier itself and the Westland National Park. Maps and an up-to-date weather forecast are also provided. **Independent VIC,** ① *in the new Mountain Helicopters base, corner of Sullivan and SH6 (opposite the BP Service Station), T03-7510046. 0800-2100 (seasonal).*

Franz Josef → *Colour map 5, grid C1. Population: 300*

Franz Josef owes its very existence and, of course its name, to the great block of ice that sits 5 km to the south of the village. Of the two principally tourist-based settlements (Franz and Fox), Franz is the larger and better serviced. As you might expect it is very much a seasonal destination, crowded in summer, quiet in winter. Although the glacier can of course be visited in the rain and the guided glacier walks are rarely cancelled, the scenic flights, and essentially, an overall impression of the glaciers from above and below, are completely dependent on favourable conditions. As a rule, you should plan to give yourself at least two days in the area. If you have scenic flights booked, these can be forwarded and while you wait for the clouds to clear, there are still a few things to keep you occupied, even in the rain. The average annual rainfall in the area is about 5 m over 180 rain days. In summer always book your accommodation well in advance.

Franz Josef Glacier Franz Josef was first sighted and officially documented by both Abel Tasman in 1642 and Cook in 1770, but first properly explored and named by geologist and explorer Julius von Haast in 1865. When he first explored its lower reaches it was almost 3 km nearer the coast than it is today. His official title of 'Francis Joseph Glacier' was given in honour of the Emperor Franz Josef of Austria. The spelling was later changed to Franz Josef in accordance with the internationally accepted version – as in Franz Josef Land in the Arctic and Franz Josef Fjord in Greenland. Until 1985, and apart from a few sporadic advances last century, the glacier had actually been receding steadily since 1865. As it stands, it is unclear what it will do next. After advancing almost 1 km, at almost 1 m a day over the last 17 years, it is now slowing down. Many are worried that global warming will see the glaciers recede at an unnatural rate due to a lack of snow at the summits.

The glacier is about 5 km south of town and accessed by the Glacier Access Road which runs alongside the cold, grey **Waiho River** that dramatically appears from beneath its face. From the car park it is a one hour 40 minute return walk along the wide rocky river bed to within 500 m of the glacier. Unless properly equipped you cannot walk on the glacier itself and to do that you are strongly advised to join one of the many and regular guided trips on offer. Perhaps the best view of the glacier is from the 280 m-high viewpoint on **Sentinel Rock** (a stubborn remnant of previous glacial erosion), which is easily accessed from near the main car park (20 minutes). ▸▸ *For Sleeping, Eating and other listings, see pages 586-591.*

Fox Glacier → *Colour map 5, grid C1. Population: 300*

Many people visiting the Glacier Region only visit one of the great monoliths, with Franz Josef being the most favoured. However, if you have time, Fox Glacier (25 km south of Franz and a further 8 km southeast) is no less dramatic. The **Fox Glacier Valley** and the chilly **Fox River**, which surges from the glacier terminus provide a significantly different atmosphere, with the more precipitous, ice-carved cliffs near the car park being particularly remarkable. The Fox Glacier was originally called the Victoria Glacier and was renamed in honour of former New Zealand Prime Minister, Sir William Fox, on a visit in 1872. The small village of Fox Glacier is the main service centre and sits on a site that was, as recently as 5,000 years ago, covered by the present glacier.

> ❈ By far the best way to view the glacier is from the air, you have numerous different options, see Activities, page 588.

Although less commercial, Fox, like its neighbour Franz, can also be explored at its terminus independently, or with along with a guide, can be walked upon or climbed over. Once again however the recommendation is to admire it from the air. There are also a number of interesting walks within the valley, at the coast and around the reflective **Lake Matheson**, which lies 4 km west of the village. ▸▸ *For Sleeping, Eating, and other listings, see pages 587-592.*

South to Haast

From Fox Glacier you leave the great glaciers and towering peaks of the National Parks behind and SH6 winds its scenic way ever southwards to Haast and to the most remote region of the West Coast – South Westland. For many years Fox was as far south as any tourist ventured, the road from there becoming rough and eventually non-existent at Paringa. With the opening of the great Haast Pass Highway in 1965 the two roads were eventually linked making the continuous journey possible. Given much of the terrain in South Westland, it is not difficult to understand why such a 'frontier' link was so late in coming. Luckily, despite the intrusion, much of South Westland remains remote, unspoilt and remarkably beautiful.

Copeland Pass → *Intercity and Atomic Shuttle buses pass the Copeland Valley entrance and can drop-off or pick-up.*

The heavily forested **Copeland Valley**, 26 km south of Fox, heralds the trailhead of the **Copeland Track**. ① *For detailed information get hold of the Copeland Track broadsheet from DoC. Hut fees are $8 per night and there is a resident warden at Welcome Flat between Nov-Apr.* Although the complete 3-4 day tramp makes a spectacular high alpine crossing into the Hooker Valley and, eventually, the haven of Mount Cook Village, recent rock falls have made the route very difficult and one only suited to the experienced mountaineer. Nevertheless, the 17 km overnight tramp up the Copeland Valley to the **Welcome Flat Hut** is recommended. This tramp acquaints you with some superb forest, river and mountain scenery and perhaps best of all, includes the **natural hot pools** at Welcome Flat. The one-way tramp to the hut takes about six hours. From Welcome Flat you then have the option of an overnight stay and a return, or the extra (three hours one-way) excursion higher up the valley to the **Douglas Rock Hut**.

Bruce Bay → *Colour map 6, grid B3*

A further 20 km on will see you rejoining the coast at Bruce Bay, a quiet, scenic spot, once famous for a false **gold claim** made during the rush of 1865. Apparently in Hokitika, three miners initiated the story that they had secured a hundredweight of gold in Bruce Bay and, as a result, over 2000 hopeful souls made the long and difficult journey south. Frustrated and angry after finding nothing and realizing it was a hoax, they then went on the rampage looting and destroying the makeshift stores and shanties. Although it is very pretty in itself, one of the most beautiful and scenic bays and beaches of the West Coast lies just over the headland, to the south. The much-photographed (from the air) **Heretaniwha Bay**'s golden curve of sand and rim of windshorn rimu epitomize the West Coast wilderness. With the **Bruce River** and trackless headland preventing easy access it is very difficult to reach, which is perhaps what makes it so special.

Paringa → *Colour map 6, grid B3*

Turning inland again the SH6 continues south to cross the **Paringa River** before arriving at **Lake Paringa**. The river is noted as the furthest point south that the intrepid early explorer **Thomas Brunner** reached in his epic 18-month journey from Nelson and the Buller Gorge in 1848. Considering it would be another 100 years before the road even reached this point, his 'feat' can only be admired. A plaque by the river honours it. At Lake Paringa you will find accommodation and a café. The lake is noted for its good trout **fishing** and the **Jamie Creek Walkway** (15 minutes) which negotiates a fine tract of beech and rimu, 1 km south of the café near the DoC campsite. ►► *For Sleeping and Eating, see page 588.*

For Sleeping and Eating, see page 588.

The West Coast The Glacier Region

The reflective waters of Lake Moeraki are a further 18 km south of Lake Paringa and 30 km north of Haast. Although popular for swimming, kayaking and bird watching most people are in an understandable rush to share the intent of its outlet river and head straight for the beach. The car park and trailhead to Munroe Beach is 200 m north of **Moeraki River** bridge. An easy, well-formed path through some beautiful coastal forest will deliver you to the pounding surf. It is a typical West Coast stunner and a place where wildlife abounds. In the breeding season (July-December), or during their moult in late summer, it is a great place to see the rare and beautiful **Fiordland Crested Penguin**. If you are lucky, and provided you are quiet and stay out of sight, you can watch them fighting their way through the crashing waves to waddle uneasily up the beach before disappearing quietly into the bush. It really is a wonderful spectator sport and there's not an iceberg in sight.

If the tide is well out try to investigate the beach and the Moeraki River mouth to the south of Munroe. It's even better. Note that there is one other species that is present in its thousands and are far less interesting or welcome – sandflies. Apply lots of repellent or you will re-emerge at the car park looking like a serious road accident.▶ *For Sleeping, see page 588.*

Knight Point

South of Moeraki SH6 rejoins the coast and climbs to Knight Point with its spectacular views of sea stacks and near inaccessible beaches. Just south of the viewpoint you should be able to see **fur seals** dozing on the beach. It was just south of Knight Point that the Haast Highway was officially opened in 1965, thereby connecting Otago with South Westland and the West Coast proper. At the base of the hill, about 3 km south, is a small car park allowing unadvertised access to **Murphy's Beach**. This is a superb spot for a beach walk. If the tide is out you can explore this beautiful sweep of sand and the rugged coast north or south. Like Wharariki Beach near Farewell Spit, in the Nelson Region, you will do so feeling guilty at leaving a single set of footprints in the sand. The rock outcrops and pinnacles to the south of the beach provide some superb photo opportunities, especially at sunset.

Ship Creek

A little further south is the more popular access to the beach at Ship Creek. Here you can choose from a number of excellent **short walks** that explore the beach, the coastal forest and a small lake held captive by the dunes. If the tide is out you can make the easy river crossing, negotiate the headland and explore the beaches heading north. In summer it is not unusual to see **Fiordland Crested Penguins** coming ashore to their breeding areas hidden in the coastal fringe. When it comes to an archetypal wild and remote coast it does not get much better than this. Ship Creek was named after a wreck that ironically occurred on the Australian Coast at Cape Otway in Victoria in 1854. On her maiden voyage, the 2600 tonne 'Schomberg' ran aground and several years later, pieces of the ill-fated vessel were washed up here over 1500 km away. From Ship Creek SH6 hugs the coast and passes some spectacular examples of coastal rimu, rata and kahikatea forest on its approach to Haast and the Haast River crossing.

⬤ Sleeping

Franz Josef *p583*

Given the amount of tourist traffic in summer and the fickle weather, you are advised to book your accommodation well in advance and add an additional night, just in case.

LL Waiho Stables Country Stay, *Docherty Creek, T03-7520747, www.waiho.co.nz* A boutique B&B 5 km south of the village. It has 2 luxury en suite rooms. The food and the company are excellent.

LL-L Franz Josef Glacier Hotels, *Main Rd,*

T03-7520729. The largest (and only) hotel in the village with over 177 rooms, a restaurant, a café and 4 bars, plus a spa. It is mainly designed to cater for tour groups.

LL Westwood Lodge, *SH6, 1 km north of the village, T03-7520111, www.westwood-lodge.co.nz* A well-appointed, modern, single-storey B&B, with 6 spacious, luxury ensuite rooms.

There are about 10 rather similar **motels**:
AL-A Bella Vista, *T03-7520008*; and
L-A Punga Grove, *T03-7520001; www.pungagrove.co.nz* Both at the northern end of Cron St, just to the east of Main Rd.
AL-A Alpine Glacier Motor Lodge, *T03-7520224, corner of Cron and Condon sts.* In the village centre.
AL-A The Glacier Gateway Motor Lodge, *T03-7520776.* Quieter and on the southern edge of town (nearest the glacier).
AL-A Glenfern, *T03-7520054.* This modern place is another good option near the Tatare River 3 km north of the village.
AL-D Rainforest Retreat, *Cron St, T03-7520220, www.rainforestretreat.co.nz* Offers a fine selection of affordable eco-based log cabins and also has good campervan facilities and tent sites. Recommended.

There are many **backpacker hostels** available in the village, most being on Cron St. The 2 favourites are:
C-D Chateau Franz, *(8) T03-7520738, chateaufranz@xtra.co.nz;* and
B-D Glow Worm Cottages, *(27), T0800-151027, T03-7520172, glowwormcottages@hotmail.com* Both offer the best in facilities, character and atmosphere.
Other options include:
C-D YHA, *4 Cron St, T03-7520754, yhafzjo@yha.org.nz;* and
C-D Black Sheep, *to the south of the village, T03-7520007, www.Franzjosef.co.nz* It is a big place that is used by most of the backpacker buses so has a party atmosphere (centred around the *Baah Bar*!).

Motorcamps and campsites
D Forest Park (Rainforest Retreat) , *T0800-873346, www.forestpark.co.nz* See above.

B-D Franz Josef Holiday Park, *SH6, 1 km south of the town, T03-7520766.*
A-D Mountain View Top Ten, *SH6, T0800-467897.* Provided you are not a travel writer, they will provide a warm welcome and a smile.

Fox *p584*
AL Glacier Country Hotel, *Main Rd, T03-7510847.* An old hotel but has recently undergone refurbishment. It has a wide range of fairly unremarkable rooms from studio to single. Restaurant and bar with large open fire. Internet.
AL-C Fox Glacier Resort Hotel, *Cook Flat Rd, T03-7510839, fox.resort@xtra.co.nz* Slightly tired but cheaper. It's still popular and spacious with standard en suites, economy twins and backpacker rooms with en suites.
AL-D Fox Glacier Lodge, *Main Rd, T03-7510888.* Has a tidy lodge with 5 en suites (2 with spa) and powered sites with shared facilities.
A Homestead Farm B&B, *Cook Flat Rd, T03-7510835.* One of the few B&Bs in the village offering all the comforts of home in a century old farmhouse.

Many **motels** in Fox are on Cooks Flat Rd.
LL-L Te Weheka Inn *opposite the DoC VIC on Main Rd, T03-7510730, www.teweheka.co.nz* Has a striking attractive, modern design and tidy luxury suites. Tariff includes breakfast.
L The Westhaven Motel, *Main Rd, T03-7510084, www.westhaven.co.nz* Slightly cheaper and offers a wider range of room options, some with spa.
On Cooks Flat Rd are a few more established and cheaper options including (listed in order of proximity to the village):
A-B Rainforest Motel, *T03-7510140;*
B Lake Matheson Motel, *T03-7510830* and
A Mount Cook View Motel, *T03-7510814.*
There are 2 main **hostels** in the village:
C-D Fox Glacier Inn, *Sullivan's Rd, T03-7510022, foxinn@xtra.co.nz* The newest with tidy family, double or shared rooms, a café, restaurant and bar. Tents also welcome.
C-D Ivory Towers, *also on Sullivan's Rd, T03-7510838, ivorytowers@xtra.co.nz* An old favourite with a cosy atmosphere and great facilities, including a spa. Bike hire and internet. Their double rooms are especially good value.

B-D **Fox Glacier Holiday Park**, *Cooks Flat Rd, T03-7510821*. The main motor park in the village. Very spacious, it has cabins, lodge rooms, flats, powered/tent sites and a backpacker dorm. Good facilities.

Paringa *p585*
B-D **Lake Paringa Motels**, *T03-7510894*. Basic studios and units and an on-site café. It also rents out dinghies, canoes and issues fishing licenses.
D **DoC campsite**, *1 km south of the motel*. On the shores of the lake.

Lake Moeraki *p586*
LL-L **Moeraki Wilderness Lodge**, *beside SH6 at the Moeraki River outlet, T03-7500881, www.wildernesslodge.co.nz* An exclusive eco-based B&B establishment. The lodge has 22 rooms all with private facilities and an in-house restaurant. Guided nature/history walks and canoe trips are also available, with some being part of the package. The restaurant is open to non-guests.

❼ Eating and drinking

Franz Josef *p583*
$$ **The Landing**, *Main Rd, T03-7520229*. Daily from 1000-late.
$$ **Beeches Café, Restaurant and Bar**, *Main Rd, T03-7520721*. Daily from 0700. Both offer standard fare for breakfast, lunch and dinner.
$$ **Alice May Bar and Restaurant** *on Cron St, T03-7520740*. Daily from 1100. English pub-style, with arguably more atmosphere and better value food. It's also the main drinking and after-hours entertainment establishment in the village. Has some fine ales.
$$ **Franz Josef Glacier Hotel restaurants**, *T03-7520729*. Provide another à la carte option, but often busy with bus tours. Bookings are recommended.
$ **The Cheeky Kea Café**, *Main Rd, T03-7520139*. *0700-2100*. A slightly cheaper option than most and is good for a no nonsense snack or breakfast.
$ **Café Franz**, *Alpine Adventures Centre*. *0700-1800 (seasonal)*. Good coffee and internet.
$ **The Blue Ice Café/Pub**, *T03-7520707*.

Serves up a good pizza and evening meals. All-out war on the free pool table its other speciality.
Grocery supplies **Fern Grove Food Centre**, *on the Main Rd*. *0800-2200 (seasonal)*. Well-stocked but expensive.

Fox Glacier *p584*
$$ **The Plateau**, *T03-7510058*. *Daily 0900-late (seasonal)*. The village's newest eatery and is earning a good reputation. The menu is imaginative enough but more attractive still is the open fire and the wine list.
$$ **Café Neve**, *Main Rd opposite the Alpine Guides Centre, T03-7510110*. *0800-late (seasonal)*. It is pretty expensive, but still a pleasant place for breakfast, light snacks, home baking and coffee with outdoor seating that offers a good spot to watch the world go by.
$$ **Cook Saddle Café and Saloon**, *Main Rd, T03-7510700*. *Open from 1000*. It offers a good meat-lover's menu and has a bar.
$$ **Hobnail Café** *in the Alpine Guides Centre, T03-7510005*. *Daily 0700-1600 (seasonal)*. Offers a hearty, value breakfast and some fine home baking.
$ **Café at Lake Matheson**, *see above*. *0700-2100*. Another option if you plan to go walking there and it is especially welcome after the popular sunrise photo opportunities. $10 breakfast.
Fox Glacier Inn, *see above*. Good for a beer and a chat.
Grocery supplies **General Store**, *Main Rd, T03-7510829*. *Daily from 0800-1900*. Supply essential groceries (at sadly elevated prices).

Paringa *p585*
$$ **Salmon Farm Café**, *just north of the Paringa River, T03-7510837*. *Daily 0730-1700 (winter 0830-1600)*. A popular 'quick-stop' eatery. Either feed the salmon in the tanks below or eat one in the café.

⛰ Activities

Franz Josef *p583*
There are many operators based in Franz offering a wide range of methods and modes of transport with which to acquaint yourself with the great glacier. Competition is pretty fierce so shop around. Most people

do one, or preferably, all of three things: they **walk** to the glacier's terminal face independently, they take a **guided walk** on to the glacier (**glacier walking**) or they take to the **air**. What you do will of course depend on your budget and the weather. Although a glacier walk is both exciting and very informative, if you can possibly afford it, take an extended scenic flight around Mount Cook and down the face of the glacier, landing briefly on the snow at its crown. The atmosphere up there, and the silence on a calm, clear day, is simply unforgettable.

Flightseeing

Fixed wing or helicopter? Twin engine or single? Snow landing or no landing? Weather permitting, these are the questions to ask yourself. Generally speaking fixed wing aircraft will allow longer in the air for the price and cover more 'air', but you miss out on that unique feel of a helicopter. Apparently, helicopters have twin or single engines (a twin being safer). Most helicopters offer 10-min snow landings whereas most fixed-wing planes do not. All modes are intrinsically safe and all companies are accommodating regarding weather cancellations (payment takes place pre-flight and post-booking) even arranging another flight at sister locations.

Helicopter The cost of a helicopter flight ranges from around $145-$165 for 10-20 mins to $220-$310 for 30-40 mins.
Helicopter Line, *Main Rd*, *T0800-807767*, *www.helicopter.co.nz* Offers flights from 20-40 mins all with snow landings and a 3-hr Heli-hike option. They are a nationwide company and their helicopters are twin-engine.
Glacier Southern Lakes Helicopters, *Main Rd*, *T03-7520755*, *T0800-800732*, *www.heli-flights. co.nz* Offer 10-40-min flights with snow landings on flights over 10 mins. They are a local South Island based company (founded in 1970).
Fox and Franz Josef Heli-services, *Alpine Adventure Centre, T03-7520793, T0800-800-793, www.scenic-flights.co.nz* Offers flights from 20-40 mins, again with

These helicopters are smaller but still relatively comfortable. The company pride themselves in their flexibility and the fact they are locally owned and operated. Being perhaps the most competitive in price they better suit the budget traveller. Charters are also available.
Mountain Helicopters, *T0800-369423*, *www.mountainhelicopters.co.nz* Another good local company offering flights from both Franz and Fox and from 10-40 mins. It offers competitive charter prices for independent climbers.

Fixed-wing **Air Safaris**, *Main Rd*, *T03-7520716, www.airsafaris.co.nz* Offer a 30-min 'Twin Flight' taking in both glaciers and the immediate high peaks from $160, child $110 and a 50-min 'Grand Traverse' flight over 10 glaciers and the upper peaks of both National Parks from $240, child $160. Neither flight has a snow landing. They have been operating for 30 years.
Ski Plane Adventures (Aoraki Aero Company), *T03-7520714*, *aoraki@aorakiaero.co.nz* Offers flights with a snow landing (50 or 60 mins from $240/$300). Both companies are based in Fox Glacier but can provide pick-ups from Franz.)

Glacier walking, hiking and ice climbing

Glacier walking is an extraordinary experience and a magical way to explore a glacier properly. By climbing across the surface and descending into small crevasses you get a better feel of how they work and can witness the beautiful blue colour of the ice. The tours are also very informative. Fox is generally accepted as the better glacier for ice climbing, while Franz is steeper and more heavily crevassed which makes for better glacier walking.
Franz Josef Glacier Guides, *Main Rd*, *T03-7520763, www.franzjosefglacier.com* Has been operating since 1990 and are a highly experienced and professional outfit offering 4-8 hr excursions as well as Heli-hike and high level alpine-hut trips. The 8-hr trip takes

you to the impressive icefalls further up the glacier face, while the basic low altitude 2-3 hr tour takes in the glacier face. For tours on the glacier their famous strap-on 'Ice-Talonz' crampons make for comfortable walking. Trips leave throughout the day from 0900 and you are requested to check in 30 mins before departure. Prices are from $35 (Glacier Face Walk); Half-day Glacier Trip $60 (4 hrs) / Full-day $100 (8 hrs).

The Guiding Company, *Main Rd (Alpine Adventures Centre), T03-7520047, www.nzguides.com* A more recent outfit offering similar trips for about the same price. It also offers an ice climbing option. **Alpine Guides**, *Fox Glacier, see below.* Ice climbing and Heli-hiking.

Heli-hiking

For the keen tramper (hiker) being at the base of all these stunning mountains and the 2 glaciers is almost too much to bear and with time a premium you might like to consider heli-hiking. Although inevitably expensive the combination of the views and exploring the upper reaches of the glaciers makes it well worth it.

The Guiding Company, *T0800-800102,* and **Glacier Guides**, *T0800-484337.* Both offer heli-hiking options from 2-3 hrs with about 10 mins in the air from $240.

The Helicopter Line, *see above.* Offers a similar experience for around the same price. **Alpine Guides**, *in Fox, see below.* Other self-guided walking options are outlined in various DoC leaflets from the VIC.

Walking

Other than the glacier terminal walk there are a number of other walking options in the glacier valley. The wonderfully christened **Lake Wombat** (after a gold miner's nickname) and another (don't ask) **Alex Knob** (1000 m), can be accessed about 350 m down the Glacier Access Road. The route, which traverses the valley wall, takes you through classic rata and kamahi forest, rich in birdlife. The 'kettle' lake, Lake Wombat can be reached in about 45 mins, while the stunning view of the glacier from Alex Knob will take another fairly strenuous 3 hrs.

A little further along the Glacier Access Road is the access point to the **Douglas Walk** and **Peter's Pool**. Named after a young camper

who set up his tent there in 1894, it is an easy walk and the lake can be reached in about 10 mins. The track continues to reunite with the road further up the valley (1 hr). Located 1 km from the junction of the Glacier Access Road and SH6 is **Canavan's Knob Walk** (40 mins return), which, like Sentinel Rock in the glacier valley, withstood the actions of the ice that completely covered it until about 10,000 years ago. Now covered only in rimu trees it offers views of the glacier and the mountains.

Other activities

Climbing wall *Opposite the YHA on Cron St, T03-7520047.* From $30 with tuition and all equipment.

Fishing Alpine Adventure Centre *on Main Rd.* Arrange fishing on pretty **Lake Mapourika**, 8 km north of Franz.

Horse trekking South Westland Horse Treks, *just south of Franz on Wahio Flat Rd, T03-7520223, www.horsetreknz.com* Offers 1, 2 or 3 hr horse treks from $40.

Kayaking Ferg's Kayaks, *Cron St, T03-7520230, T0800-423262.* Offers 2½ hr kayaking trips in the area from $45.

Tandem skydives Skydive New Zealand, *T0800-751-0080.* Offers 9,000 ft and 12,000 ft tandem skydives amidst what must be the most stunning scenery in the country, from $225-$265.

Tours Kamahi Tours, *Heli-services Office, Main Rd, T03-7520793.* Offers conventional road and walking tours of 1-3 hrs, from $35.

Fox *p584*

Helicopter In Fox there are 4 helicopter companies (3 of which also operate from Franz Josef).

The Helicopter Line, *Main Rd, T03-7510767, www.helicopter.co.nz* Offers flights from 20-40 mins all with snow landings and a 3 hr Heli-hike option.

Glacier Southern Lakes Helicopters, *Main Rd, T03-7510803 (T0800-800-732), www.heli-flights.co.nz* Offer flights from 10-40 mins with snow landings on flights over 30 mins;

Fox and Franz Josef Heli-services, *Alpine Guides building, T03-7510866, www.newzealandnz.co.nz/helicopters/* Offers flights from 20-40 mins, again with snow landings on flights of 30 mins or more.

Mountain Helicopters, *Fox Glacier Store,*

T03-7510045, www.mountainhelicopters.co.nz
Are another small, local company. Again as such it is perhaps the most competitive in price because it is better suited to the budget traveller. Charters also available. The cost of a helicopter flight ranges from around $145-$165 for 10-20 mins to $220-$310 for 30-40 mins.

Fixed-wing **Air Safaris**, *Main Rd, T03-7520716, www.airsafaris.co.nz* Offers a 30-mins 'Twin Flight' taking in both glaciers and the immediate high peaks from $160, child $110 and a 50-mins 'Grand Traverse' flight over 10 glaciers and the upper peaks of both National Parks from $240, child $160. Neither flight has a snow landing. Air Safaris have been operating for 30 years.
Ski Plane Adventures (Aoraki Aero Company), *T03-7520714, aoraki@aorakiaero.co.nz* Offers flights with a snow landing (50 or 60 mins from $240/$300).

Glacier walking, hiking and ice climbing
Fox is generally accepted as the better glacier for ice climbing.
Alpine Guides, *Alpine Guides Building, Main Rd, T03-7510825, T0800-111600), www.foxguides.co.nz* Has been operating since 1975 and is a highly experienced and professional outfit offering 2-8 hr excursions as well as Heli-hike, ice climbing, multi-day mountaineering and high level (overnight) alpine-hut trips. Trips leave throughout the day from 0900 and include a basic guided excursion to the glacier terminus ($25). Prices are from $45 (4 hrs) to $415 (8 hrs Heli-hike). Its ice climbing instruction days are a speciality ($180).

Walking
The closest short walk is the (25 min return) **Minnehaha Walk**, which starts beside the road just south of the village. It is a pretty rainforest walk that takes in a small **glow worm dell** ($2); best viewed with a torch at night. The glacier valley walks and the glacier itself is accessed via Glacier Road, which leaves SH6 about 1 km south of the village. The **Glacier terminus** can be accessed from the car park (1 hr return) which is about 8 km from Fox village. About

3 km down Glacier Road is a small car park on the left which is the trailhead for the River (1 km, 30 mins return) and **Chalet Lookout Walk** (4 km, 2 hrs return). The very pleasant **River Walk** begins with a swing bridge crossing over the cold, grey, Fox River. Once across the river the track then climbs through the rainforest, offering the occasional view of the glacier, before reaching the car park and terminus of the Glacier View Road (which runs along the southern bank of the river). From here it is a steady climb through forest and across crystal clear streams to reach the lookout point. The walk itself is as good as the view. However, do not expect to get good photographs of the glacier from here since there is too much bush in the way. The walk around **Lake Matheson** (4 km west from Cook Flat, then Lake Matheson Road, 1 ½ hrs return) and to the **seal colony** at **Gillespies Beach** (20 km west via Cook Flat Road) are another 2 excellent options. The marked route (6 hrs return) up **Mount Fox** (1021 m), 3 km south of the village provides great views across the higher peaks and surrounding forest.

⊙ Directory

Franz Josef *p583*
Banks There are no banks in the village but there is an ATM outside the Blue Ice Pub at the southern end of main St. The **Mobil Service Station** (Glacier Motors Ltd), *T03-7520725, open from 0800,* nearby has EFTPOS and will cash travellers' cheques and give advance cash on credit cards. Foreign exchange at **Fern Grove Souvenirs**, *Main Rd, (across the road from Alpine Adventures), T03-7520731.* **Bike hire** Chateau Franz or Glow Worm Cottages (see Sleeping, above).
Postal agent Mobil Service station, *see above.* **Internet** Café Franz, *Alpine Adventure Centre.* Franz Josef Glacier Guides/ Helicopter Line, and the Scott Base Information Centre, *both on Main Rd.* Also in most backpackers. **Useful numbers** Police, *Whataroa, T03-7561070.* Doctor, Whataroa, *T03-7561080.* Weatherline *T0900-99903,* or check out the satellite map on www.nzcity.co.nz

Banks There are no banks or ATMs but EFTPOS is accepted in most places. Foreign currency exchange available at **Alpine Guides**, *Main Rd, T03-7510825. Daily 0800-2100 (winter 0830-1730).* **Bike hire** Fox Glacier Holiday Park. Fox Glacier Lodge.

Ivory Towers Backpackers. *See Sleeping, above.* Full day from $20. **Internet** Glacier Country Hotel. Ivory Towers Backpackers. *See Sleeping above.* **Postal agents** Alpine Guides, *Main Rd, T03-7510825. Daily 0800-2100 (winter 0830-1730).*

The Haast Region → *Phone code: 03 Colour map 6, grid B3*

The Haast Region of South Westland contains some of the most unspoiled ecosystems in New Zealand. The stunning scenery, from mountaintop to coastal plain, includes pristine streams that terminate in vast river mouths fringed with dense tracts of ancient coastal (Kahikatea) forests. Within the forest lie swamps and hidden lakes and all along their fringe endless swathes of beach covered in sculpted driftwood. Wildlife, too, abounds, from the playful keas of the summits to the sleepy fur seals on the coast. Few tourists stop long enough in the Haast region to truly appreciate or explore properly. But if you do Haast is an ideal base and gateway to a timeless environment.

Ins and outs

Getting there North and southbound **Intercity** and **Atomic Shuttle** services stop in Haast Township and/or the DoC VIC. **Haast Shuttles,** T03-7500827 provides local transportation and specialist cyclist shuttle services.

Information DoC Haast VIC, ① *next to SH6 a few hundred metres past the Haast River Bridge, T03-7500809, haastfc@doc.govt.nz Daily 0900-1800 (1630 in winter).* As if the sculpted water features outside were not impressive enough the interior displays are memorable and all the usual information on local walks and natural attractions are provided. Ask to see the 20-min 'Edge of Wilderness' Video which is a fine introduction to the local landscape ($3).

Haast → *Colour map 6, grid B3. Population: 300*

From the north, a lush corridor of coastal forest and the 750 m Haast River Bridge brings you to the rather splintered settlement of Haast. The Haast River is a fitting introduction to the village and the stunning wilderness that surrounds. On the coastal plain of Haast the annual rainfall, at 5 m, is similar to that of much of the West Coast. But above 1500 m, the average can be over three times that and, after a deluge, the great river can turn into a menacing torrent. Haast is the epitome of a West Coast village – remote, unobtrusive and the home of characters full of pride and moulded by the wild, rugged and harsh environment that surrounds them.

Haast is named after the geologist/explorer/surveyor Julius von Haast who first explored the then almost inaccessible coast in 1863. He did so via the pass to the east, which also bears his name and now provides the modern day road access. Locals, however, will pull your leg and tell you the name actually derived from a misquotation by Captain James Cook on his voyage of 1770. On sailing past he was, by all accounts, so appalled at the sight and inhospitable nature of the place, he ordered all the ships flags to be flown at half-mast. Perhaps tired and, for once, short of a name, he entered 'Half-mast' in his log. A century later, when the log was reopened, the fold in the page disguised the full name and it became known as Haast.

On initial acquaintance Haast (the 'settlement') is a bit confusing. Immediately on the southern side of the bridge is a huddle of buildings that form **Haast Junction**. This is home to the DoC visitors' centre, a petrol station and the World Heritage Hotel. A further

❝ ❞ Within the forest lie swamps and hidden lakes and all along their fringe endless swathes of beach covered in sculpted driftwood. Wildlife, too, abounds, from the playful keas of the summits to the sleepy fur seals on the coast...

4 km south of Haast Junction, on the Jackson's Bay Road, is **Haast Beach** another small conglomerate, including another petrol station, a motel, foodstore and some private homes. From there the road continues for 50 km before reaching a dead end and the remote village of **Jackson's Bay**. East of there an unsealed road accesses the **Arawata River** and the **Cascade Saddle**, a memorable day trip. The main settlement of Haast – or **Haast Township** – is 4 km inland and east of Haast Junction on SH6. Here you will find the major residential area, shops and most of the accommodation. ▸▸ *For Sleeping, Eating and other listings, see pages 595-596.*

Jackson's Bay Road → *Colour map 6, grid B3*
Other than the obvious attractions of the coast to the north, the true wilderness of the **Arawata** and **Cascade River** Valleys south of Haast via the Jackson's Bay Road, is considered legendary. Though this stunning landscape is well worthy of some thorough investigation, the tiny pioneering settlement of **Jackson's Bay** is the main attraction.

From Haast Junction and Haast Beach, Jackson's Bay Road hosts the tiny, principally whitebaiting settlement of **Okuru** on the Okuru River before carving a straight 20 km path through native forest to the Arawata River. On the way the covert streams crossing the road have some intriguing names including *Dizzy*, *Dancing* and *Dismal*. In the heart of this forest is the stubborn plug of bedrock known as **Mount McLean**, which, like **Mosquito Hill** near Haast, withstood the assaults of old glaciers. At the **Arawata Bridge** you are afforded a grand view up the valley before the road forks inland to the Cascade River Valley, or west along the coast to Jackson's Bay.

The unsealed **Cascade Road** follows the beautiful Jackson River Valley (a tributary of the Awawata). The river provides a wonderful place to go fishing or simply kick back and admire the scenery. But perhaps your first stop should be the **walk** to the hidden **Lake Ellery**. Beginning just beside the Ellery River Bridge a well-disguised track follows the river to the lake edge. It is neither well signposted nor well maintained; so expect to get both muddy and lost. But the beautiful reflections of the forest on the river and tranquil atmosphere of the lake itself, makes the one-hour return walk well worthwhile. Once at the lake head you can go no further and must return the way you came.

From Lake Ellery River the Cascade Road rises steadily crossing the Martyr River and the evocatively named **Monkey Puzzle Gorge**, before reaching a high point in the valley and the road terminus. From here you are afforded an expansive view down to the **Cascade Valley** and the dramatic glacial sculpted sweep of the hills to the coast. Inland the Olivine Range and Red Hills herald the boundary of the **Mount Aspiring National Park**. The **Red Hills** are a particularly interesting and noted geological feature. The colouration is caused by high concentrations of magnesium and iron in the rock that has been forced up by the actions of the Austral and Pacific tectonic plates. What makes this mountain range of special interest is that their other half (Dun Mountain) now lies in the Nelson Region! ▸▸ *For Sleeping, see page 595.*

Fighting hard to survive its wild remoteness is the historic little village of Jackson's Bay at the end of Jackson's Bay Road. Jackson's Bay has an interesting and troubled history. Now a small fishing settlement of about 20 registered vessels moored in what is the nearest thing to a natural harbour the length of the West Coast, it was first settled by a hardy group of 400 in 1875. A cosmopolitan bunch of Scandinavians, Germans, Poles, Italians, Irish, Scots and English, they set about trying to establish agriculture and the small port. However, due to the weather, poor soils and a general lack of interest from beyond, the project was a catastrophic failure. Within weeks whole families fell ill, or simply gave up and moved out. Only three years after landing the community shrank from 400 to a mere handful. Only a few of the most prosperous survivors managed to stay by founding large cattle runs.

The iron-framed grave of pioneer settler Claude Morton Ollivier, who died of pneumonia only weeks after his arrival, is a fitting testament to the Europeans' failed attempts. It is the oldest known European grave on the West Coast and is next to the main road above the beach.

Other than a wander around Jackson's Bay itself you might like to try the 1½ hour return **Smoothwater Track**. Beginning about 500 m north of the village it climbs the forested hill to take in the fine views north, before crossing a saddle and dropping down again to the Smoothwater River Valley and neighbouring Smoothwater Bay. One attraction not to miss in Jackson's Bay is the **Cray Pot Café**, on the waterfront (see next page). Also full of character (and often characters) is the other café where you can secure a proper coffee or hire **kayaks** for $40 per day, T03-7500880 (summer only). The area is well known for its resident **dolphins.**➤➤ *For Eating, see page 595.*

The Haast Pass → *Colour map 6, grid B3*

From Haast Township SH6 turns inland and follows the bank of the **Haast River** before being enveloped by mountains and surmounting what was, until 1960, the insurmountable. The Haast Pass at 563 m is an ancient Maori greenstone trail known as Tiori-patea which means 'the way ahead is clear'. Ironically, being the principal water catchment of the Haast River and plagued by frequent floods and landslips, the name is one of misplaced optimism as the modern-day road can testify. However, although sometimes treacherous and difficult to negotiate, the crossing captures the mood of the place, with names such as the **Valley of Darkness** and **Mount Awful**. Even beside the road there is suggestion of this, with other evocative titles like **Solitary Creek No 2** and the first of three waterfalls, **Roaring Billy**, 28 km inland from Haast. Best viewed on a short (signposted) loop walk Roaring Billy plunges down mountain slopes on the opposite side of the river, and although it's only a steady flow most of the time, after heavy rains it most certainly lives up to its name.

A further 25 km, just before the 'Gates of Haast' another waterfall – the competitively named **Thunder Creek Falls** – drop a vertical 28 m into the Haast River. They too can be accessed and photographed from a short loop track beside the road.

The gorge, known as the **Gates of Haast,** is just a little further on and you can see the huge boulders and precipitous rock walls that proved such a barrier to road construction for so many years. Above the Gates the road and the river level off and the mountains take on a less menacing appearance, as do the waterfalls, with **Fantail Falls** (again signposted and accessed next to the road) proving far less threatening, with moderate plumes of white water tumbling over a series of rocky steps. From Fantail Falls it is only a short distance before the **Haast Pass** itself and the boundary of Westland and **Otago**. From here the scenery dramatically changes and you leave the West Coast behind.

● Sleeping

Haast and Jackson's Bay Road p592
AL-D Haast World Heritage Hotel, *Haast Junction, T0800-502444, www.world-heritage-hotel.com* Long established but fairly unremarkable, it has 54 en-suite units, and budget accommodation but is best known for its restaurant and bar.
A-B Acacia and Erewhon Motel, *Jackson's Bay Rd, Haast Beach, T03-7500803*. Modern and friendly, it has 3 elite (upper floor with coastal view), 4 studio and 5 standard units all self-contained.
L-AL Collyer House B&B, *Jackson's Bay Rd, further south on the banks of the Okuru River, T03-7500022, www.collyerhouse.co.nz* The best in the region. It is wonderfully peaceful and offers 4 luxury en suite rooms with terrific views. Activities can be arranged.
L-A McGuires Lodge, *between Haast Junction and Haast Township, T03-7500020, www.mcguireslodge.co.nz* A fine range of en suite units suitable for single travellers to families, an outdoor spa and the best restaurant in the area. Recommended.
A-B Heritage Park Lodge, *Marks Rd, Haast Township, T03-7500868, heritageparklodge@xtra.co.nz* Has a range of modern units and suites and a licensed restaurant on-site.
A-D Haast Highway Accommodation, *T03-7500703*. Has a range of units, cabins, powered/tent sites and also acts as the local YHA associate.
C-D Wilderness Backpackers, *Pauareka Rd, T03-7500029*. The favoured backpackers. Spacious, single-storey building with good value doubles, a pleasant atmosphere and Internet access.

Motorcamps and campsites
A-D Haast Beach Holiday Park, *in Okuru (15 km), Jackson's Bay Rd, T03-7500860*. Excellent. It offers a number of motel units, self-contained and standard cabins, but is mainly noted for its location, friendliness and fine modern facilities.
A-D Haast Highway Accommodation, *see above*.

● Eating

Haast p592
$$ Haast World Heritage Hotel Café and Bar, *Haast Junction, T0800-502444. Daily 0700-1000*. The best (and only) option. Hearty pub-grub.
$$ McGuire's Lodge, *between Haast Junction and Haast Township, T03-7500020*. New licensed restaurant, it is by far the best in the region offering fine venison, lobster and whitebait in intimate surroundings with a log fire. During the day lighter meals and quality coffee are also available. Recommended.
$$ Smithy's Tavern, *Marks Rd, Haast Township, T03-7500034*. Another venue for pub-grub.
$$ Fantail Café and Restaurant, *Haast Township, T03-7500055. 0730-2200*. Also offers basic meals all day.
Supermarket *in Haast Township. 0730-1930 (seasonal)*.
Also a **general store** next to the motel in *Haast Beach, T03-7500825*.

Jackson's Bay p594
$$ Cray Pot Café, *Jackson's Bay. 0830-1930 (winter 0900-1830)*. A quirky cross between a rail carriage and a barge. It serves up the best fish and chips on the West Coast. You can eat in (recommended) or take away. Stand outside and the sandflies will eat you before you eat your chips.

▲ Activities

Haast p592
River Safaris, *in the 'Red Barn' between Haast Junction and Haast Township, T0800-865382, www.jetboat.com* Reputedly offers 'the world's only sea to mountain river safari' on the Waiatoto and Haast River. The 1-hr trips on their purpose built (covered) jet boat depart daily at 0845, 1045 and 1445 and cost from $75, child $50. Recommended.
Waiatoto River Safaris, *also at the Red Barn, T0800-538723, www.riversafaris.co.nz* As the name suggests, provides an opportunity to explore the Waiatoto River south of Haast. The 2-hr trips depart at 0845, 1200 and 1515,

The West Coast The Haast Region

● For an explanation of the sleeping and eating price codes used in this guide, see the inside
● front cover. Other relevant information is provided in the Essentials chapter, see page 51.

from $109, child $69.

Heli Ventures, *Haast Township, T03-7500866, www.heliventures.co.nz* Ideally located for some stunning scenic helicopter flights but may suffer due to the fact many have already parted with their scenic flight savings in Franz or Fox. But hopefully, if you have not, it is well worth looking at the trips on offer. There is some superb local fishing on offer especially south of Haast on the Arawata River.

Wanna Go Fishing, *T03-7500134, www.wannagonz.com* Offers guided trips from half day $400 to full at $650.

Round About Haast Tours, *Jackson's Bay Road, T03-7500890, www.roundabouthaast.co.nz* Operated by locals Mauryne and Bob Cannell, the tours

are an ideal way to acquaint yourself with the area, its history and folklore. The tours last from 3-4 hrs and cost from $55.

ⓘ Directory

Haast *p592*

Banks and useful addresses Johnston Motors (Caltex), *in Haast Junction, beside the VIC, T03-7500846,* has EFTPOS and provides AA recovery and an independent breakdown recovery service (a godsend!). Petrol is available 24 hrs with EFTPOS and credit cards. **Mobil Service Centre**, *Haast Beach, T03-7500802,* also provides the same services and acts as car hire and postal agents. **Police**, *T03-7500850.* **Internet** Wilderness Backpackers, *Pauareka Rd, Haast Township.*

Otago

Introduction

If the Otago Region were a girl she would be a very engaging sort from a good Scots background and good-looking. Her topography and scenery varies from the towering peaks of **Fiordland** and **Mount Aspiring National Parks** in the west, to the gently rolling hills, harbours and golden beaches of the **Otago Peninsula** to the east. Her two large blue eyes would be **Lakes Wakatipu** and **Wanaka**. And down her entire length carves the vein of New Zealand's second longest river, the **Clutha**. In personality and mood too, there is also huge variety: from the student city buzz of **Dunedin** to the quiet whispers of **Glenorchy** or **Clyde**. Otago is also down-to-earth and wears her heart on her sleeve. She has distinct seasons: cold and snowy in winter; miserable with rain in spring; and boasting beautiful golden hues in autumn. Otago owes her considerable pedigree to her predominantly Scots heritage and the discovery of gold, a resource that was once her lifeblood. Now, though, the region pumps fast and furious with sheer adrenaline. Although Otago's head is in Dunedin, her heart is in **Queenstown** – the adventure sports capital of the world. Otago is not only pretty, she also knows how to have a good time.

★ Don't miss...

1 The Scots heritage and architecture of **Dunedin**, page 600. Try 'rolling your R's' with the locals.

2 The grace of the **albatross** or the charms of the **yellow-eyed penguins** on the Otago Peninsula, page 610.

3 Gold panning in the historic **Central Otago goldfields**, page 618.

4 Canyoning, tandem skydiving or skiing in **Wanaka**, page 645. Take a scenic flight to Milford.

5 Walking to the base of the **Rob Roy Glacier** – the best day walk in the region, page 651.

6 The remarkable view from the **Remarkables**, page 628.

7 Making the jump in **Queenstown**, page 633.

8 Visiting the real Paradise north of **Glenorchy**, page 641.

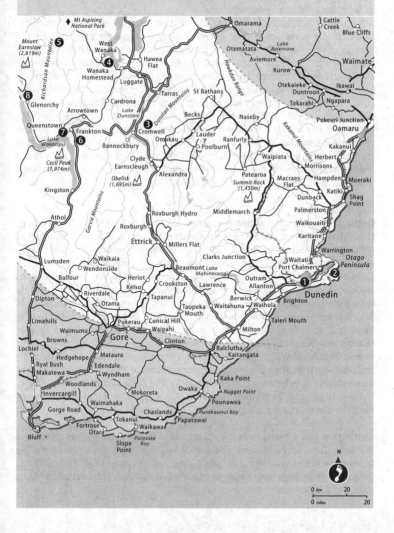

Dunedin → *Phone code: 03. Colour map 7, grid B6. Population: 95,000*

There is perhaps nowhere else in the world – and certainly nowhere so far from its roots – that boasts a Scottish heritage like Dunedin, the South Island's second largest city. For those who have walked the centuries-old streets of Edinburgh in Scotland, let alone lived there, a trip to Dunedin (which actually means 'Edin on the hill') is somewhat disconcerting. Immediately, you will notice the echo of Scottish architecture – grand buildings of stone, built to last, that go far beyond the merely functional and, in true Scots tradition, defy inclement weather. The streets are blatant in their similarity, even sharing the names of Edinburgh's most famous – Princes Street, George Street and Moray Place – and presiding over the scene, in its very heart, a statue of one of Scotland's greatest sons, the poet Robert Burns. Now, as you ponder his gentle expression of intellect, with the seemingly omnipresent seagull perched on his head, you cannot help but wonder what he would say about this pseudo-Scots city, so very far from home.

Although a lively and attractive city, Dunedin has seen better days. In the 1860s, thanks to the great Otago gold boom, it enjoyed prosperity and considerable standing. But as ever the gold ran out, decline set in and very quickly Dunedin, like so many other places in the South Island, had to learn how to survive where once it thrived. Having said that, modern day Dunedin has many assets, of which its university and rare wildlife are perhaps the best known. In term-time the city boasts a population of 18,000 students who study at Otago University, New Zealand's oldest seat of learning, while the Otago Peninsula, Dunedin's beautiful backyard, is home to another form of wildlife – the only mainland-breeding colony of albatross, the rare yellow-eyed penguins and Hooker's sea lions. There is also one other undeniable asset to Dunedin, and one that can perhaps be attributed to its Scots heritage: without doubt it has the friendliest people and offers the warmest welcome in New Zealand.

▶▶ *For Sleeping, Eating and other listings, see pages 605-609.*

Ins and outs

Getting there Dunedin **airport** is about 27 km south of the city; **Air New Zealand Link**, To800-737000, www.airnewzealand.co.nz; fly daily to Christchurch, Wellington, Auckland and Rotorua. **Origin Pacific**, To800-302302, www.originpacific.co.nz, fly several times daily to Christchurch with onward connections to most major towns and cities. **Freedom Air**, To800-600500, www.freedomair.co.nz, provide Trans-Tasmam flights daily to Eastern Australia. By **road**, Dunedin is 362 km south of Christchurch and 217 km north of Invercargill via SH1. Queenstown is 283 km south then west via SH8. By **bus** Dunedin is served by **Intercity**, 205 St Andrew St, To3-4778860 (Christchurch/ Invercargill/ Queenstown/Wanaka); **South Island Connections**, To3-3666633 (Christ- church); **Atomic Shuttles**, To3-4774449 (Christchurch/Invercargill/Queenstown/ Wanaka); and **Southern Link**, To3-3588355 (Queenstown/Wanaka). Both Atomic Shuttles and Southern Link Shuttles stop at the train station. The **Catlins Coaster**, To2-1682461, To800-304333, and The **Bottom Bus**, To3-4347376, www.bottombus.co.nz, serves the Catlins to Invercargill and provides pick-up/drop-off.

Getting around Citibus, To3-4775577, are one of several suburban **bus** companies that serve Dunedin and its surrounds. The VIC has timetables. City buses stop in the **Octagon**, the distinctive heart of the city. For bus services to the Otago Peninsula see Otago Peninsula page 610, **Super Shuttle**, To800-748885, or the major taxi firms (from $15-$20 one-way).

their real namesakes in Edinburgh, **Princes St** and **George St** combine to form the main thoroughfare through the city centre, with the **Octagon** forming its heart. Generally the Central Business District (CBD) is easily negotiated by foot, and even by car makes a pleasant change to the charmless, flat streets of Auckland or Christchurch. You will find most restaurants and cafés at the northern end of George St or around the Octagon. **Dunedin VIC**, ① *on the Octagon at Number 48, below the magnificent Municipal Chambers Building, T03-4743300, www.dunedinnz.com, www.cityofdunedin.com Mon-Fri 0800-1800, Sat and Sun 08450-1800.* It is an efficient centre that can provide free city **maps** and advice on local tours and activities, particularly to the Otago Peninsula. Also acts as transport booking agents and has internet. **DoC**, ① *77 Lower Stuart St, T03-4770677. Mon-Fri 0800-1700.*

History

The largest Maori *pa* in the area was on the Otago Peninsula at Otakau which saw its fair share of inter-tribal disputes before being ravaged by diseases brought by the early European whalers and sealers. Otakau is also the source of the name Otago that came about through a mispronunciation by the early pioneers. The first seeds of Dunedin's settlement and creation were sown in 1842 by Scots parliamentarian George Rennie who, concerned at the levels of poverty and unemployment in Scotland, presented a plan for Presbyterian colonization in a 'New Edinburgh' of the south. Although this idea was initially declined, it was adapted and later accepted by a 300-strong Free Church colony that arrived in 1848, under the leadership of Captain Cargill (of Invercargill fame) and the Reverend Dr Thomas Burns. With the discovery of gold just over a decade later the population exploded (between 1861 and 1865 its population grew by 500% to 10,000) and the town developed into a cosmopolitan, commercial centre becoming the largest and most prosperous city in New Zealand by the late 1860s (it was even the first place outside the USA to have a tram system). Despite the loss of gold as a resource, Dunedin has been more successful than most in retaining a strong economic base and is now a pleasant mix of old and new.

Sights

Architecture

A good way to get an immediate feel for Dunedin is with a quick tour of its finest architecture. Perhaps already acquainted with the statue of **Robert Burns** presiding over the Octagon and the grand **Municipal Buildings** that house the VIC, you could start your tour with a visit to the original **Otago University Administration Building and clock tower** on Leith Street. This grand edifice is perhaps the most famous and most photographed icon in the city. The University, which was New Zealand's first, was founded in 1869.

The **train station** at the end of Lower Stuart Street is another fine historic example, echoing that typical Scots desire to take train station architecture way beyond the purely functional. Built in 1906, its grand towered exterior cannot fail to impress, but the interior too is rather splendid complete with stained glass windows, Royal Doulton tiles, mosaics and brass fittings. The almost omnipresent New Zealand Rail (NZR) logos are proudly displayed with more repetition than a large herd of branded, prize cattle. **The New Zealand Sports Hall of Fame**, ① *on the first floor, T03-4777775, www.nzhalloffame.co.nz, daily 1000-1600, from $5, child $2,* celebrates the legacy of more than a century of New Zealand champions and is a worthy attraction for any avid sports fan.

The city's churches are also worth more than just a passing glance, particularly the **First Church of Otago**, ① *Moray Pl, T03-4777150. Daily from 0800-1800,* which is a distinctly pointed affair, and **St Paul's** in the Octagon which houses the only stone-vaulted ceiling in the country. **St Joseph's Cathedral**, on the corner of Rattray and Smith Street, and the **Knox Church**, on George and Pitt Streets, are also noted for their robust architectural aesthetics.

Museums and galleries

Just a few hundred metres from the train station, and boasting a couple of monstrous historic steam trains, is the **Otago Settlers Museum**, ① *Cumberland St, T03-4775052. Daily 1000-1700. $4, child free.* The emphasis is placed firmly on people and transport, with many fine exhibits both temporary and permanent. One recent temporary exhibition was a fascinating display all about Scotland's second national drink – tea – which is a reflection of the museum's interesting and imaginative approach. There is also a fine collection of archives and over 20,000 photographic portraits of the early pioneers. If only to muse at their hardy, hopeful expressions and eyes full of memories would be reason enough to visit. The museum also offers **heritage walks** around the city that can be tailored to your own interests from $11-$15, children free.

Otago Museum, ① *419 Great King St, T03-4747474, www.otagomuseum.govt.nz Daily 1000-1700, donation ($5 encouraged). 'Discovery World' and some temporary exhibitions are extra. Café on site. Guided tours of the museum are available daily at 1530 from $10.* Established in 1868, this museum is one of the oldest in the country, with a staggering 1.7 million items. The museum's primary themes are culture, nature and science, all housed in newly renovated surroundings and displayed in the now almost obligatory state-of-the-art fashion. The new *Southern Land-Southern People* exhibit is particularly good and has been designed to become the museum centrepiece. In essence, it is intended to reflect the uniqueness, beauty and diversity of Southern New Zealand. The traditional Maori and Pacific heritage, maritime, natural history and archaeology displays are also impressive and there is (of course) a hands-on 'Discovery World' to keep the kids engrossed for hours.

Aside from the safe, but unintentionally wobbly, grand staircase in its foyer, the **Dunedin Public Art Gallery**, ① *T03-4743240, www.dunedin.art.museum daily 1000-1700, free,* provides a grand and stable platform to display a fine collection of traditional and contemporary art. It is the oldest art gallery in the country and of special note is its collection of New Zealand works that date from 1860 to the present day. There are also some works by the more familiar iconic names like Turner, Gainsborough and Monet.

The **Milford Galleries**, ① *18 Dowling St, T03-4778275, Mon-Fri 0830-1700, Sat 1100-1500,* are considered to be one of the country's leading dealer galleries and represent more than 130 of New Zealand's foremost artists.

At 42 Royal Terrace is the 1906 'Edwardian time capsule' of **Olveston House**, ① *T03-4773320. Guided tours are recommended and available daily at 0930, 1045, 1200, 1330 and 1600, $13, child $4.* Bequeathed to the city in 1966 by the last surviving member of the wealthy and much-travelled Theomin family, the 35-room mansion comes complete with an impressive 'collection of collections', containing many items from the Edwardian era. It gives an interesting insight into Dunedin of old and the lives of the more prosperous pioneer!

Breweries and wineries

Although Dunedin hosts many fine Scottish churches it also, not surprisingly, pays homage to that other great Scottish religion, the alcoholic beverage. South Island's iconic **Speights Ale** is the worship of many a 'Good Southern Man' and its communion is to be found in the hallowed walls of the surprisingly small Speights Brewery, ① *200 Rattray St, T03-4777697, www.speights.co.nz Heritage tours and tastings are available daily but, unlike the churches these days, bookings are essential. From $12, child $4.*

If beer is not your tipple perhaps you might like to visit the **Weston Vintage Winery**, ① *25 Forresbank, Wakari, T03-4675544*. Although not quite in the same league as its many New Zealand counterparts it can boast of being the world's most southerly winery. Also for chocoholics there is **Cadbury World**, ① *280 Cumberland St, T03-4677800, T0800-223287, www.cadburyworld.co.nz Tours every half hour from 0900-1530, from $14, child $8*, that recently opened its doors to the drooling public. Though they could never quite live up to the fantasy of Charlie and the Chocolate Factory the interactive tours offer an interesting and mouth-watering insight into the production of the irresistible stuff and can even impress with mere statistics. There are, for example, 120 million chocolate bars sold in New Zealand every year which equates to almost 40 bars per head of population or an estimated 4 kg each per year. Naturally, there is a well-stocked shop that does very well thank you.

The Taieri Gorge Railway and the Otago Central Rail Trail

① *Trips depart daily Oct-Mar at 1430 (additional trip on Sun at 0930) and Apr-Sep at 1230, from $57 return (extended trip to Middlemarch $65. One-way $36.50/$41.50*. The Taieri Gorge Railway is considered a world-class train trip encompassing the scenic splendour and history of Otago's hinterland. The former goldfields supply line was completed in 1891, and as one negotiates the **Taieri Gorge** with the aid of 12 viaducts and numerous tunnels, it very quickly becomes apparent why it took over 12 years to build. The four-hour trip gets off to a fine start amidst the splendour of Dunedin's grand train station before heading inland to the gorge and Pukerangi. An informative commentary is provided along the way and you are allowed to disembark at certain points of interest. Also, if you ask really nicely, you may also be able to ride alongside the locomotive engineer. Licensed snack bar on board. If you wish, you can extend the rail journey by coach across the rugged **Maniototo Plateau** to **Queenstown** (6½ hours), from $110. Another popular alternative is to take a **mountain bike** (no extra charge) and disembark at **Middlemarch** (only selected trains, but one-way fares available). From there you can negotiate the 150-km **Otago Central Rail Trail** (the former goldfields railway from Middlemarch to Clyde). It is a wonderful bike ride that includes over 60 bridges, viaducts and tunnels and much of Central Otago's classic scenery. **Horse trekking** is also an option. For more details call in at the train station or T03-4774449, www.taieri.co.nz DoC in conjunction with the Otago Central Rail Trail Trust also provides an excellent leaflet *Otago Central Rail Trail Middlemarch-Clyde* that is available from DoC or the VIC.

Other attractions

There are many New Zealand 'firsts' in Dunedin, including the **Botanical Gardens**, ① *North Rd. Open from dawn to dusk*. Nurtured since 1914, the 28-ha site is split into upper and lower gardens that straddle Signal Hill. Combined they form an interesting topography and all the usual suspects, with a particular bent on rhododendrons, plants from the Americas, Asia and Australia, native species, winter and wetland gardens. If you tire of the flora there is also a modern aviary complex, housing many exotic and native birds including the 'cheeky' kea and kaka parrots. Also on site are information points, a café and a small shop, all in the Lower Garden. Access to the Lower Garden is from Cumberland Street while the Upper Garden is reached via Lovelock Lane. The **Centennial Lookout** (6-km 1½ hours' walk) and **Lookout Point** offer grand views of the harbour and the city, and are accessed via Signal Hill Road (beyond Lovelock Avenue).

You might also like to visit the famed **Baldwin Street**, ① *head north via Great King Street then veer right at the Botanical Gardens on to North Rd. Baldwin is about 1 km (10th street) on the right*, which at a gradient of nearly 1 in 3 (19° angle), is reputed to be the steepest street in the world. It's worth a look, if only to work out the building methodology and what happens when the residents are eating at a table, in the bath or shooting some pool.

Otago Dunedin

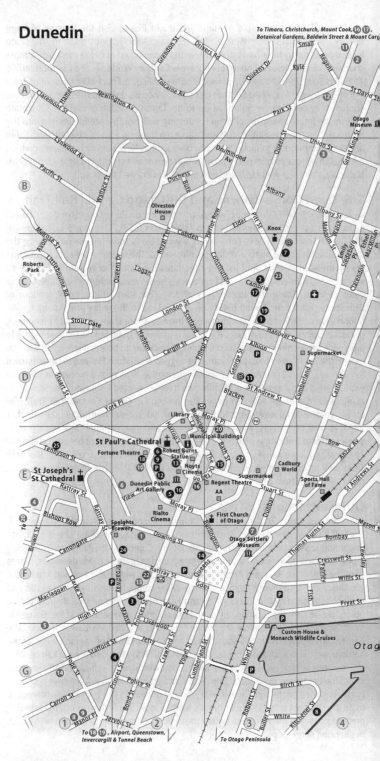

⑤

The aptly named **'Gut-Busters'** race is held annually in February during the Dunedin Festival to see who can reach the top and back again in around two minutes. Doubtless the street has been the scene of much fun over the years, but in 2001 the irresistible desire to defy or master gravity turned to tragedy when a young student took a 'wheelie-bin' (used for rubbish) to the top of the street, climbed in and launched herself down the hill toboggan-style. Sadly, the result was fatal and Baldwin Street claimed its first life.

Tunnel Beach ① *1 km, 1 hour return, south of the city centre near Blackhead (car park seaward end of Green Island Bush Rd off Blackhead Rd),* is a popular spot and a precursor to the splendid coastal scenery of the Otago Peninsula. A steep path through some bush delivers you to some impressive weathered sandstone cliffs and arches. For details see DoC's *Tunnel Beach Walk* broadsheet. If you do not have your own wheels take the Corstorphine bus from the city centre to Stenhope Crescent (start of Blackhead Road) and walk from there.

🛌 Sleeping

Dunedin *p600*

Dunedin City has a good range of options, and you might also like to consider those available on the Otago Peninsula (see page 610). For both, pre-booking in summer is advised.

L-A Southern Cross, *corner of Princes and High sts,* T03-4770752, *reservations@southerncross.co.nz* Dunedin's premier hotel, well located in the heart of the city centre, with 131 rooms and 8 suites. Its history dates back to 1883 when it was the original Grand Hotel, but it now boasts all the mod cons of the Scenic Circle Chain with an in-house bar/restaurant.

LL Corstorphine House, *23A Milburn St, Corstorphine,* T03-4876676, T03-4876672, *www.corstorphine.co.nz* A popular 1863 Edwardian luxury lodge offering 6 en suites with great views across the city. The house is beautifully appointed throughout, is surrounded by 12 acres of private gardens and has a reputable in-house restaurant.

Otago Dunedin

L Fletcher Lodge, *276 High St, T03-4775552, www.fletcherlodge.co.nz* This is another recently upgraded luxury establishment set in an elegant historic mansion. There are 5 en suites all richly furnished with antiques.

AL-B Leviathan Hotel, *27 Queens Gardens, T03-4773160, T0800-773773, leviathan@xtra.co.nz* Another historic, renovated place that is friendly, great value and well located (near the train station). It has a range of rooms from self-contained suites (with spas) to budget rooms. Restaurant and internet. Recommended.

AL-A Hulmes Court, *52 Tennyson St, T03-4775319, www.hulmes.co.nz* A well established slightly cheaper option set in an 1860s Victorian mansion close to the city centre, and comes complete with a friendly ex-stray cat called Solstice. Having recently expanded to include an adjoining property it now offers 8 en suites, as well as doubles, twins and single. The caring owners have plenty of local knowledge and can offer valuable advice on activities and tours.

AL Mandeno House *667 George St, T03-4719595, www.mandenohouse.com* For something more modern this place will not disappoint. Within walking distance of the city centre its interior design has a strong hint of Glasgow's most famous architect Charles Rennie Mackintosh and as such has a distinct air of class and sophistication. Two queen suites and a twin, Sky TV, breakfast and off-street parking.

AL Nisbet Cottage, *6A Eliffe Pl, Sheil Hill (east of the city centre), T03-4545169, www.wingsokotuku.co.nz* Conveniently located at the base of the Otago Peninsula and offers 3 very private rooms, one with a superb view across the city. The German couple also operate Otago Nature Tours (see Otago Peninsula activities) and can organize multi-day nature tours to the Catlins and Stewart Island.

B Albatross Inn, *770 George St, T03-4772727, albatross.inn@xtra.co.nz* A pleasant and spacious budget B&B with 13 rooms, well located close to the city centre.

There are plenty of **motels** to choose from, with most being along the main drags in and out of town, particularly George St.

AL-A 97 Motel, *hidden away at 97 Moray Pl, T03-4772050, info@97motel.co.nz* One of the best, it offers a wide variety of standard and executive units that are quiet, well-appointed, and all within a stone's throw of the Otagon.

A 858 George St, *no prizes for guessing the number, T03-4740047, www.858georgestreetmotel.co.nz* An aesthetic award-winner and is recommended.

A Allan Court Motel, *590 George St, T03-4777526, allan.court@earthlight.co.nz,* and the

A Regal Court, *at 755, T03-4777729.* Elsewhere, other recommended options are:

A Commodore Luxury, *932 Cumberland St, T03-4777766, commodore.motels@xtra.co.nz;*

B Manor Motel, *22 Manor Pl, T03-4776729, manormotel@cartwright.co.nz;*

There is no shortage of choice when it comes to **backpacker hostels** and as you might expect the vast majority are housed in traditional suburban villas.

C-D Elm Lodge, *up the hill from the Octagon at 74 Elm Row, T03-4741872.* Noted not so much for its accommodation (though there is no problem there) but for its superb adjunct operation the **Elm Nature Tours**, run by the friendly and nature-loving owners. (See Otago Peninsula Activities, page 615.) The accommodation is comfortable with dorms and doubles and fine views and all comes amidst a very congenial atmosphere. Elm also runs another overflow establishment the **Elm Lodge Too** further up the hill. Pick-ups and internet.

C-D Stafford Gables YHA, *71 Stafford St, T03-4741919.* A rambling old villa with lots of character, offering a good range of rooms. Parking, rooftop garden, internet.

C-D Manor House, *28 Manor Pl (near the YHA), T03-4770484, www.manorhousebackpackers.co.nz* Another historic colonial villa that has modern kitchen and dining areas with dorms, twins and doubles. Quiet location, bike hire, off-street parking and in-house wildlife tours.

C-D Adventurer Backpackers, *37 Dowling St, T03-4777367, T0800-422257.* Yet another spacious, historic villa and a popular choice with the highly active. Dorms, singles, twins and doubles. Open fire, No TV! Internet. Located close to the Octagon.

C-D Billy Brown's Backpackers, *423 Aramoana Rd, Hamilton Bay, T03-4728323, billybrowns@actrix.co.nz* If you fancy a day or two away from the city centre, you would do well to consider this new, small, relaxing, rural hostel with friendly owners and fine views across the harbour, just outside Port Chalmers (15 mins north of Dunedin). Also offers free bike hire.

Motorcamps and campsites

B-D Leith Valley Touring Park, *103 Malvern St (towards the northern end of town), T03-4679936.* In a sheltered setting next to the Leith Stream. It has modern self-contained cabins, powered tent sites.

B-D Dunedin Holiday Park, *41 Victoria Rd, T03-4554690.* Another option lying alongside St Kilda Beach at the other end of town. It has modern facilities, en suite units, standard cabins, flats and powered and tent sites.

❼ Eating

There is plenty of choice in Dunedin, with over 140 restaurants and cafés, with most being along George St or around The Octagon. You will also find 2 **Star 24 hr** shops in George St.

$$$ Bell Pepper Blues, *474 Princes St, T03-4740973. Lunch Wed-Fri, dinner Mon-Sat from 1830.* A few minutes' walk from the Octagon but worth it. The menu is highly imaginative and the service and presentation is excellent.

$$ Etrusco at the Savoy, *8A Moray Pl (first floor), T03-4773737. Daily from 1730.* Very grand and a fine Italian choice that is good value despite the plush surroundings.

$$ High Tide, *29 Kitchener St, T03-4779784. Tue-Sun from 1800.* Provides a convenient escape from the city centre and overlooks the harbour. It has a mainly seafood but can cater for those looking for other traditional NZ/Euro dishes.

$$ Abalone, *1st Floor corner of George and Hanover Sts, T03-4776877. Mon-Fri 1200-late, Sat 1700-late.* A chic and well-established traditional choice.

$$ The Two Chefs, *428 George St, T03-4779117. Mon-Sat from 1800.* Locally popular and well established. Traditional

European/NZ fare.

$$ French Café and Italian Café, *a joint venture at the top of Moray Pl (118), T03-4771100, www.frenchcafe.co.nz* Great if you are feeling a little indecisive. Here Chef and manager Kieran Walsh has struck a fine balance between choice, atmosphere and affordability. The more expensive of the two is the French Café with its tempting range of traditional French Provencal dishes. It also offers vegetarian options and has the added appeal in summer of a pleasant deck outside in the garden. The Italian is the cheaper option and naturally can serve a good pizza.

$$ Little India, *82 St Andrew St, T03-4776559;*

$$ Indian Summer, *corner Upper Stuart and Moray Pl, T03-4778880.* Both are affordable and enjoy a good reputation.

$ London Lounge, *above the Albert Arms, corner of George and Hanover sts, T03-4778035. Mon-Thu 1100-2230, Fri and Sat 1100-2300, Sun 1130-2130.*

$ Ale House at the Speights Brewery, *200 Rattray St, T03-4719050. Daily from 1130.* Both recommended for traditional pub grub. The latter is especially generous in both choice and servings.

$ Reef Seafood Restaurant and Bar, *329 George St, T03-4717185.* For fish and chips.

On George St you will also find plenty of cheap Asian eateries and takeaways designed to keep poverty-stricken students mildly plump and chirpy, with numerous Thai and Chinese options particularly between St Andrew and Fredrick Sts.

$ Ananda Indian Café and Takeaway, *365 George St, T03-4771120. Mon-Sat 1130-1430 and 1700-2100.* Noted for vegetarian dishes.

$ Joseph Mellor Restaurant, *Tennyson St, T03-4796172. Daily from 1200-1400 and again from 1800-2130.* From Mar-Nov it serves very affordable and imaginative dishes created by trainee chefs. Well worth considering. Lunch $9.50 and dinner $19.50. Where else would you get seared Cervena Medallions Baden-Baden for that price? Recommended.

❼ Cafés

Mazagran Expresso, *36 Moray Pl, T03-4779959.* Recommended specialist coffeehouse.

Tangente, *111 Moray Pl, T03-4770232.*

Mon-Tue and Sun 0800-1530, Wed-Sat 0800-late. Designer café/restaurant that is pretty faultless. Specializes in organic fare and offers a wide ranging blackboard menu with some great vegetarian dishes and brunch options. It also has a great atmosphere, wine list and service, all making a return trip likely.

There are plenty of other cafés around the Octagon.

The Nova (29), *next to the Dunedin Art Gallery, T03-4790808. Mon-Wed 0800-late, Thu and Fri 0700-late, Sat 0900-late, Sun 1000-2300.* A good place for brunch, breakfast and even sells porridge.

The Percolator, *142 Lower Stuart St, T03-4775462. Sun-Thu 0900-2300, Fri and Sat 0900-late.* Also recommended.

Governor Café, *438 George St, T03-4776871. Daily 0800-late.* No great shakes aesthetically but is very popular, with a cosmopolitan clientele, good-value meals (especially breakfasts) and an internet suite next door.

Arc Café, *135 High St, T03-4741135. Mon-Sat from 1200.* A very popular place with local artists, 'musos' and laid-back students. It's great for a coffee and offers regular live gigs. Free email but you will have to wait.

Palms Café, *18 Queens Gardens, T03-4776534.* In a nice spot overlooking the war memorial and popular with locals. It offers a value 4-course à la carte menu and does specials on weekdays between 1700 and 1830. A la carte open daily from 1800. Lunches Wed-Sun.

Jizo, *56 Princes St, T03-4792692. Mon-Sat 1130-2100.* A pleasant Japanese café offering standard and affordable sushi.

☻ Pubs, bars and clubs

Robert Burns, *George St.* Popular and lively Scots pub.

Albert Arms, *across the road (corner of Hanover St).* Another popular drinking establishment, especially with the younger set, and they often stage live gigs.

The café/bars that surround the Octagon are also popular, especially at the weekends and with the mobile phone brigade:

The Ra Café and Bar, *21, T03-4776080;*
Bennu Café and Bar, *12 Moray Pl, T03-4745055.* Both are particularly well

frequented and also offer good food.

Woolshed Bar and Grill, *318 Moray Pl, T03-4773246,* A good all-round drinking, eating and music venue.

Bath St, *1 Bath St, T03-4776750.* For the full 'shake of the pants'.

☻ Entertainment

There is a healthy music, arts and cultural scene in Dunedin, and the best place to view current event and gig listings is in the *Otago Daily Times* or the free weekly *Fink* magazine available free from the VIC.

If you have never had the guts to try the traditional Scottish dish 'haggis' then **The Bard Celtic Bar**, *T03-4749674,* can oblige (quite literally) on Tue-Thu (Oct-Mar) with all the usual tartan attire and ceremony from 1830, from $25.

Theatres

Fortune Theatre Company, *corner of Moray Pl and Stuart St, T03-4771292, www.fortunetheatre.co.nz* Two venues: the Mainstage and Studio Theatres. They play from Feb to Dec, Tue-Sun.

Regent Theatre, *on the Octagon, T03-4778597.* Hosts the annual film festival and touring national and international shows.

Casino

Dunedin Casino, *in the Southern Cross Hotel, T03-4774545. Sun-Thu 1100-1500, Fri/Sat 1100-1600.*

Cinema

Multiplex, *on the Octagon.*

Rialto, *Moray Pl, T03-4742200 (Mon/Tue cheap night, $8).*

Metro, *in the Town Hall, T03-4743350, www.artfilms.co.nz* A venue that boasts 'No raincoats, no popcorn, no dinosaurs – just the finest films'. Hosts the best in Euro-Arthouse Film.

☻ Festivals and events

The most noted annual events are the **Dunedin Summer Festival** (*Feb*), followed close on its heels by the **Dunedin Food and Wine Festival** and **Scottish Week** (*Mar*). The **Dunedin Film Festival** (*Jul/Aug*) is focused on the Regent

Theatre while **Rhododendron Week** blossoms in *Oct*. For more information on these or other annual events contact the VIC or www.CityofDunedin.com

▲ Activities and tours

For the highly popular attractions and tours beyond Dunedin to the Otago Peninsula see the Otago Peninsula, page 615.

Flightseeing
Mainland Air, *Dunedin airport, T03-4862200, www.mainlandair.com* 30 mins from $95.
Dunedin Helicopters, *T03-4897322*. Offers flights locally and to Queenstown or Wanaka.

Golf
Dunedin claims yet another first, having created the first Golf Club in the Southern Hemisphere in 1871.
Otago Golf Club, *125 Balmacewen Rd, T03-4672099*. From humble beginnings the club was officially formed in 1892 and is regarded as one of the best 18-hole courses in the country. The clubhouse also houses an interesting collection of early memorabilia, cups and medals. Green fees from $50.

Horse trekking
Bums 'n' Saddles, *in Blackhead, south of the city, T03-4880097*. Negotiate a network of coastal beach tracks, 2 hrs from $30.

Mountain biking
Other than the obvious attraction of the *Otago Central Rail Trail* (see *Sights* above), there are a number of other shorter tracks available in the area. These are outlined in *Mountain Bike Rides in Dunedin*, available free from the VIC.

Surfing
Southern Coast Surf Clinic, *T03-4556007, www.surfcoachnz.com* Lessons locally are available from $30 per hr.

Sightseeing tours
Citysights Newton Tours, *T03-4775577*, provides a fun 1½-hr double-decker bus tour of the major city sights and depart from the VIC daily at 1000, 1245 and again at 1530. From $20, child $10. Newtons also offers a range of trips to the Otago Peninsula (see relevant section below).
Dunedin City Heritage Tours, *T0800-346370*. Offers a variety of scenic and informative 4-hr road trips in classic jaguar limousines and depart from the VIC daily at 1245, From $88, child $57.
Country Tours, *T03-4675041*. A knowledgeable and friendly operator that offers individually designed trips from half- to multi-day, and specialize in garden and nature tours in Dunedin and beyond. Accommodation can also be arranged.
Arthur's Tours, *T0800-840-729, www.arthurstours.co.nz* A similar operator. Given its colourful history it is not surprising to find ghosts lurking somewhere on the heritage walks agenda and should you be interested in the alleged facts you can join **'The Hair Raiser'** ghost walks, *departing from the VIC at 1800 on Wed and Fri, from $10. T03-4772258*.

Walking
Other than the **Centennial Lookout** (Signal Hill) and **Tunnel Beach** (see Sights above), another recommended local walk is to the summit of **Mount Cargill** with its wonderful views across the city and the Otago Peninsula. It can be accessed by foot (4 km, 3 ½ hrs return) from Bethunes Gully (Norwood Street off North Road past the Botanical Gardens), or via Cowan Road (off Pine Hill Road, off SH1 heading north). For details see the DoC broadsheet *Mt Cargill and Organ Pipes Walk*, available from DoC or the VIC.

⊙ Directory

Banks Represented along Princes and George Sts, with many accommodating currency exchange services. **Thomas Cook**, *346 George St, T03-4777204. Mon-Fri 0830-1700, Sat 1000-1230.* **Bike hire** Cycle Surgery, *67 Stuart St, T03-4777473.* Avanti Pro, *Lower Stuart St, T03-4777259*. From $30 per day. **Car hire** Pegasus, *867 Cumberland St, T03-4776296*. Jackie's Rent-a-Car, *23 Cumberland St, T03-4777848*. Reliable Rentals, *(delivers), T03-4883975*.
Internet Dunedin Library, *Moray Pl. Mon-Fri 0930-2100, Sat 1000-1600, Sun 1400-1800.* The Arc Café, *135 High St.* Free email but in doing so gets very chaotic. **The Governors Café**, *438 George St. Daily from*

1100. Another good bet, with cheap email next door. **Modak's**, *339 George St*. **Post office** *243 Princes St, T03-4773518.* Mon-Fri *0830-1730.* Offers post restante services. **Medical services** Dunedin Hospital, *201 Great King St, T03-4740999*; Urgent doctor

95 Hanover St, T03-4792900 (pharmacy next door). **Useful addresses** Police, *25 Great King St, T03-4776011.* AA, *450 Moray Pl, T03-4775945.* **Taxis** City Taxis, T0800-771771. Dunedin Taxis, T03-4777777. Southern Taxis, T03-4766300.

Otago Peninsula → *Phone code: 03*

The beautiful Otago Peninsula, that stretches 33 km northeast from Dunedin out into the Pacific Ocean, is as synonymous with wildlife as Dunedin is with Scotland. If there were any place that could honour the title of being the wildlife capital of the country, this would be it. It is home to an array of particularly rare species including the enchanting yellow-eyed penguin and the soporific Hooker's sea lion, as well as the more common New Zealand fur seals. But without doubt the peninsula's star attraction is the breeding colony of royal albatross on Taiaroa Head, at the very tip of the peninsula. This colony is the only mainland breeding albatross colony in the world and offers an extraordinary opportunity to observe these supremely beautiful masters of flight and long-haul travel. A day trip to see all these wildlife delights is highly recommended and will leave a precious and lasting memory. Besides the wildlife the principal attractions on the Otago Peninsula are historic Larnach Castle and the stunning vista of Sandfly Bay, as well as activities such as sea kayaking, cruising and walking. → *For Sleeping, Eating, and other listings, see pages 615-617.*

Ins and outs

Getting there The best way to see the peninsula is by car, but if you have no wheels of your own or are not familiar with the wildlife, an organized **tour** is recommended (see page 615). Some of the tours on offer can take you to several wildlife sites (and sights) that are out of bounds to the general public. **By road** there are two main routes that penetrate the peninsula. On the western side, hugging the numerous small bays and inlets of the Otago Harbour, is the Portobello Road which serves the peninsula's main village, Portobello. From Portobello this road then continues past the small settlement of Harington Point to terminate at Taiaroa Head and the albatross colony. An alternative route to Portobello via Highcliff Road accesses two of the peninsula's major physical attractions, Larnach Castle and Sandfly Bay, and straddles the hilltops of the peninsula offering some memorable views. Note that both roads are sealed but very windy and dangerous. It is important to slow down and not maintain the pace and buzz of Dunedin city streets. Both Highcliff Rd and Portobello Rd are easily accessed via Cumberland St (city) across the railway line and then by skirting the Otago Harbour on Wharf St and Portsmouth Dr. For a free map of the Otago Peninsula ask at the VIC.

Information One of the principal *raisons d'être* of the **Dunedin VIC** (see page 601) is arranging half- to full-day trips out to the peninsula. There are a number of options regarding the length of time of visit, the route and the sight itinerary, so it pays to study the options carefully before parting with your cash. The DoC office in Dunedin can provide further information on walks and wildlife.

Albatrosses

Although **Taiaroa Head** is an interesting historic site in its own right, it is the colony of royal albatross that has really put the small, rocky headland on the map. Ever since the first egg was laid in 1920, the site, which is the only mainland breeding colony in the world, has become an almost sacred preserve of these magnificent seabirds. The colony, now numbering almost 100, is fully protected and managed by the DoC and the Otago Peninsula Trust. With the opening of **The Royal Albatross Centre**, ① *T03-4780499, www.albatrosses.com, daily 0830-2100 (seasonal)*, in 1972, thousands of people have been given the opportunity to view the birds from an observatory and to learn about their fascinating lifestyle and the threats we place upon them. Even before you enter the centre, if the conditions are right, you can see the great birds wheeling in from the ocean on wings that span over 3 m (the largest of any bird) and with a grace that defies the effort. If there is such a thing as airborne ballet this is it.

The Albatross Centre has some superb exhibits that include static and audio-visual displays and even a **live close-circuit TV feed** from the occupied nests in the breeding season. It takes about eight months for the parent birds to rear one of these avian B52s so your chances of seeing the industrial size carpet-slipper chicks are high. The activity of the adults does vary depending on courting, mating, incubating and feeding, with the best viewing times generally being between late-November and April. But having said that you would be fairly unlucky not to see at least one on any given visit at any time of year. The centre also has a café and a shop.

There is plenty of **other wildlife** to see on and around Taiaroa Head. Of particular note are the **rare Stewart Island shags** that also breed on the headland. They are beautiful birds, but when it comes to flight are the complete antithesis of the albatross. Also known as 'the flying brick', on a very windy day, it is not completely out of the ordinary for one to 'take out' you, your child and your ice cream from the viewing area near the centre. Around the base of the headland, **fur seals** and **little blue penguins** can regularly be seen and, if you have binoculars, the ocean will reveal a plethora of petrels and other seabirds.

The coast and headlands immediately south of Taiaroa Head are private land and out of bounds to the public, however, Nature's Wonders do offer wildlife watching tours of the area (see Activities and tours page 615).

Yellow-eyed penguins

The Otago Peninsula is a haven and breeding site for the yellow-eyed penguin, one of the rarest penguin species in the world. For many, the conditioning we have of the penguin/ice relationship and their near symbiosis is shattered amidst the golden sands and grasses of the peninsula's bays and inlets. The 'yellow eyes' or *hoiho* (to give them their Maori name), have been using the peninsula and the southeast coast of the South Island for centuries as a spillover from the subantarctic islands that are their traditional home. But rarity, range and biology aside, it is the mere sight of these enchanting, congenial characters' daily comings and goings that is the irresistible attraction. At a number of sites on the peninsula (almost all on private land and protected) you can watch them returning home at dusk from their daily fishing trips or leaving again at dawn – all highly entertaining. Like fat amphibious little surfboards they emerge from the surf and take a few minutes to cool off. Then, usually in small groups, they scuttle up the beach into the undergrowth.

There are a number of locations and tours on which you can experience this delight. Most people visit the award-winning Yellow-eyed Penguin Conservation Reserve or **Penguin Place**, ① *just before the Albatross Colony at Harington Point. For bookings contact Penguin Place direct, T03-4780286, www.penguin-place.co.nz or the Dunedin VIC. Daily from 0800 (May-Sep from 1500). From $27, child $12.* This is the most commercial operation, set on a private reserve with an expanding colony of about 200 birds that has been carefully created and managed as a workable (and reputedly successful) mix of tourism, commercialism and conservation. Once provided with an introductory talk you are then delivered by four-wheel drive truck to the beach where an amazing network of covered tunnels and hides allows you to view the birds discreetly. Although the breeding season and adult moult periods (from mid-October to late February and early May) are the best times to see large numbers, you are almost guaranteed to see at least half a dozen birds all year round especially around dusk. Although Penguin Place provides a fun and informative experience, and is certainly the best location for photographs, its commercialism can, at times, let it down. Somehow, in the company of so many camera-toting individuals, and in such confined spaces, it can all be a bit too busy and staged. The same outfit runs the Twilight Wildlife Conservation Tour (see tours page 615) and can provide backpacker-style accommodation.

For a less commercial experience see Elm Wildlife Tours and Otago Nature Guides below. To see penguins independently you can visit the **DoC** hide at Sandfly Bay at dawn or dusk (see below).

Otago Peninsula

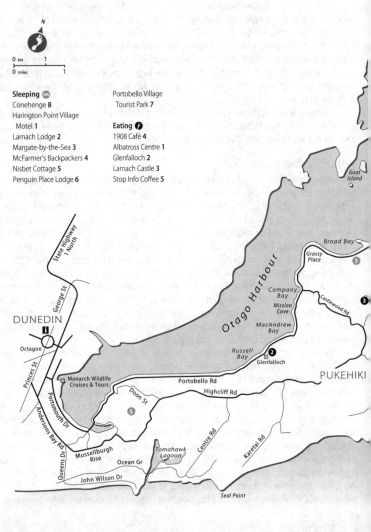

0 km 1
0 miles 1

Sleeping
Conehenge **8**
Harington Point Village
  Motel **1**
Larnach Lodge **2**
Margate-by-the-Sea **3**
McFarmer's Backpackers **4**
Nisbet Cottage **5**
Penguin Place Lodge **6**

Portobello Village
  Tourist Park **7**

Eating
1908 Café **4**
Albatross Centre **1**
Glenfalloch **2**
Larnach Castle **3**
Stop Info Coffee **5**

Hooker's sea lions and New Zealand fur seals

The Otago Peninsula is also home to the endemic Hooker's sea lion, which is the rarest of the world's five species of sea lions. Fortunately these huge creatures, that can be over 3 m in length and weigh up to 400 kg, are making a comeback to mainland New Zealand after being eliminated by Maori hunters centuries before the arrival of Europeans. In 1995 they bred again on the peninsula for the first time in 700 years. To encounter these ocean-going couch potatoes almost anywhere along the coast is an unforgettable experience. Seemingly devoid of any fear (and who wouldn't be, given those proportions and an impressive set of dentures housed in a mouth the size of a large bucket), they haul up on beaches and even the roads to rest. Having done so, they then display an overwhelming desire to do very little, except sleep, break wind (gas), scratch, or eye you up occasionally with an expression of complete

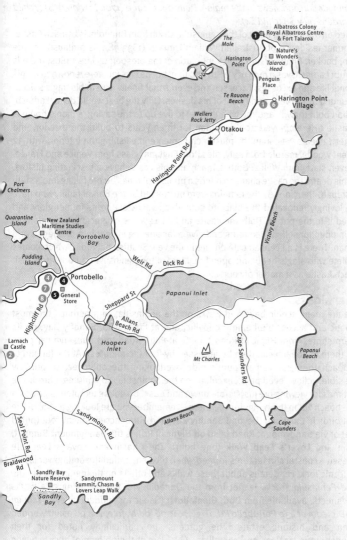

indifference. If you are lucky enough to see one do not go any nearer than 10 m and never get between the said 'Jabba the Hut' and the water, since they are hardly going to say 'excuse me' as they head for home and the results would be like a rolling pin over a Gingerbread Man. Despite their looks they can move like a slug from a slingshot and you would certainly lose the argument. Otago also has a number of **fur seal colonies**, the most accessible of which is around Taiaroa Head. Below the main car park you can usually find one or two hauled up in an almost enviable soporific state. Again, you can take a closer look but do not approach within 10 m.

Larnach Castle

① *Larnach is signposted off Castlewood Rd (from Portobello Rd). T03-4761616, www.larnachcastle.co.nz Daily 0900-1700. The castle also provides some of the best accommodation and views in the region. Daily 0900-1900 (1700 in winter), $14, child $6 (gardens only $8, child $4).*

Perched on the highest point of the peninsula, 16 km from Dunedin, is Larnach Castle, the former residence of Australian William Larnach (1833-98). As a minister of the Crown, banker, financier and merchant baron of the prosperous late 1880s, there is no doubt Larnach was a man of wealth and title, but he was far more renowned for his personal life and excesses. Excesses and events that finally lead to his tragic suicide surrounded by the very monument of his desires. Only the best would do for Larnach, who had both the will and the wherewithal to live up to the saying 'a man's home is his castle'. He employed 200 workmen for three years to build the exterior, and another 12 years was spent by master craftsmen embellishing the interior, with 32 different woods, marble from Italy, tiles from England, glass from Venice and France, and even slate from Wales. Both Larnach and his castle have a fascinating history. After his death, the castle changed hands a number of times before falling into a state of disrepair. Then in 1967 the remains were purchased by the Barker family who have since lovingly renovated the place to something very close to its former glory and opened it to the public. Both the castle and its 14 acres of gracious grounds now remain open for self-guided tours and give a fascinating insight into the period and the man. There is a licensed café on site in the very Scottish ballroom, which comes complete with stag's head and open fire. Most of the peninsula tour operators visit Larnach Castle as a matter of course.

Other sights

There are many scenic bays and walks on the peninsula, with perhaps the most dramatic and accessible being the idyllic, and at times wild, **Sandfly Bay**, on its eastern shore. From Highcliff Road take Seal Point Road to the reserve car park. From there the beach can then be accessed by foot (20 minutes). At the far end of the beach there is a small public hide overlooking the only free, or publicly accessible, yellow- eyed penguin colony on the peninsula (40 minutes return). The best times for viewing are just before dawn and dusk. Do not be tempted to go down to the beach when the penguins are there – remember you are looking at one of the rarest birds in the world. Beyond Sandfly Bay, and either accessible by foot (poled route) or via Sandymount Road (also off Highcliff Rd), is the **Sandymount Summit, Chasm and Lover's Leap Walk** (one hour). The Chasm and Lover's Leap are impressive coastal cliff features formed when the sea eroded the soft, lower layers of volcanic rock. For details about these walks and others on the peninsula get the *Otago Peninsula Tracks* leaflet from the Dunedin VIC and the peninsula walks broadsheets, available from DoC. **Glenfalloch** (Gaelic for 'hidden valley'), ① *9 km from Dunedin at 430 Portobello Rd, T03-4761006, daily, free,* is a pleasant wooded garden and historic estate. The gardens are particularly noted for their rhododendrons, azaleas and camellias, which are at their bloomin' best between mid-September and mid-October. There is also a restaurant on site.

Near Portobello, on the shores of Otago Harbour, is the **New Zealand Marine**
Studies Centre, ⓘ *Hatchery Rd, T03-4795826, www.otago.ac.nz/marinestudies Daily*
1200-1630, $7, child $3. On display there are a number of aquariums and 'touch
tanks', with a range of native New Zealand sea creatures from sea horses to the
octopus. There is even the opportunity to taste nutritious seaweed, and
knowledgeable and friendly staff are on hand to answer any questions.

● Sleeping

Otago *p610*

L-B **Larnach Lodge**, *T03-4761616,*
www.larnachcastle.co.nz The
accommodation available at Larnach Castle
is some of the best in the region with views
that are unsurpassed. The lodge offers a
range of beautifully appointed 'themed'
rooms from 'The Scottish Room' with its
tartan attire, to the 'Goldrush Room' which
comes complete with a king-size 'cart bed'
made out of an original old cart found on the
property. The views across the harbour and
peninsula from every room are simply
superb. Breakfast is served in the old stables,
while dinner is optional in the salubrious
interior of the castle. Cheaper 'Stable Stay'
rooms with shared bathrooms in the former
coach house are also available. Book well in
advance. Recommended.
A **Nisbet Cottage**, *6A Eliffe Pl, T03-4545169,*
www.nznatureguides.com A comfortable
and private B&B run by a friendly German
couple who also operate Otago Nature
Tours. Ideal for that personalized
peninsula experience.
AL **Conehenge**, *High Cliff Rd, T03-4780911,*
kolig@ihug.co.nz A modern purpose-built
property set above Portobello village
amongst an intriguing rock sculpture
garden. The well-travelled friendly hosts
ensure a warm welcome and lost of good
local advice regarding sights and activities.
Cosy private en suite.
A **Margate-by-the-Sea**, *5 Margate Av,*
Broad Bay, T03-4780866. Cosy and
self-contained with spa.
A **Homestead**, *238 Harington Point Rd (2 km*
north of Portobello), T03-4780384,
thehomestead@clear.net.nz Set in a lovely
position near the water's edge overlooking
Portobello Bay, 3 modern self- contained
units with Sky TV. Includes breakfast.
A **Harington Point Village Motel**,
Harrington Point, T03-4780287. Further out
on the peninsula and conveniently placed

for both the albatross and Penguin Place
yellow-eyed penguin colonies. Small,
modern and comfortable.

There are 2 **backpacker** options:
C-D **McFarmer's Backpackers**, *774*
Portobello Rd, T03-4780389. Has dorms and
doubles and is close to all village amenities.
C-D **Penguin Place Lodge** (Yellow-eyed
penguin reserve), *Harington Point,*
T03-4780286. Basic, but modern, with single,
twin and doubles with shared facilities.

Motorcamps and campsites
C-D **Portobello Village Tourist Park**, *27*
Hereweka St, Portobello, T03-4780359,
portobellotp@xtra.co.nz It has self-contained
tourist flats, powered/tent sites and a
bunkroom. Bike hire is available.

● Eating

Otago *p610*
There are only 2 restaurants and a scattering
of cafés on the peninsula. Both Larnach
Castle and The Royal Albatross Centre have
cafés (see above).
$$ **Glenfalloch Restaurant**, *430 Portobello*
Rd, T03-4761006. Daily from 1100. A licensed
café-style establishment set in the pleasant
Glenfalloch Gardens.
$$ **1908 Café/Restaurant**, *7 Harington Point*
Rd, Portobello, T03-4780801. Mon-Sun for
lunch and dinner. Pleasant enough with a
good Euro/NZ menu and a seafood edge.
$ **Stop Info Coffee**, *699 Highcliff Rd,*
T03-4781055. 0900-1700. Has snacks,
breakfast, acceptable coffee and internet.
Groceries There is a well-stocked **general**
store, *on the main street in Portobello,*
T03-4780555.

▲ Activities and tours

Cruising
There are a number of opportunities to
cruise the Otago Harbour.

Monarch Wildlife Cruises and Tours, *corner of Wharf and Fryatt sts, T03-4774276, www.wildlife.co.nz* Award-winning outfit offers a variety of trips from 1-7 hrs throughout the day and evening taking in all the harbour sights, with the main highlights being the Marine Studies Centre Aquarium at Portobello and the wildlife of Taiaroa Head. For a short trip you can join the boat at the Wellers Rock Jetty near Taiaroa Head. Road trips taking in the latter are also available. Regular daily departures, 1 hr cruise (Wellers Rock) $30, child $10, up to 7 hrs from $185, child $90.

Sea kayaking

Otago Harbour and Taiaroa Head provide some of the best sea kayaking in the country with the added attraction of viewing and accessing wildlife in a manner simply not possible by land. Where else in the world can you kayak while viewing albatross at the same time?

Wild Earth Adventures, *T03-4736535, www.wildearth.com* Provides an excellent range of tours, the most popular of which is their 4-5-hr 'Taiaroa Ocean Tour' around the heads. From $139 (Connections available with Elm Wildlife Tours). Recommended.

Wildlife

Etours, *T03-4761960, www.inmark.co.nz/e-tours* Interesting day ($95) tours of the peninsula by bike which really allows you the opportunity to get a feel for the place. Departs 0900. Self guided tours and hire available.

Elm Wildlife Tours, *Elm Backpackers Lodge, see above, T03-4741872, www.elmwildlifetours.co.nz* Provides an excellent award-winning eco-tour of the peninsula. Their 5-6-hr trip takes in the Albatross Centre, a New Zealand fur seal colony and their own Yellow-eyed penguin-breeding beach at the remote Cape Saunders. The tour is fun, informative, yet nicely uncommercial, and gives you access to some of the most scenic private land on the peninsula. From $49 (albatross observatory tour extra). Pick-ups available. Recommended.

Nature's Wonders, *near Taiaroa Head, T0800-246446, www.natureswonders naturally.com* Has expanded its operation in

recent months to include a cross-country 8x8 Argo tour and walk to the penguin colonies on private land. Albatross sightings, fur seals and occasionally sea lions are also encountered. The tour lasts about 40 min and costs from $30, child $25. Coach transport from Dunedin from $25.

Newton Tours (Citibus), *T03-4775577, www.transportplace.co.nz* A basic sightseeing bus trip to the peninsula, allowing the opportunity to get off at Larnach Castle, the albatross centre and the Penguin Place Yellow-eyed penguin colony. It can also drop off at the Monarch Wildlife Cruise jetty. Regular daily departures from the city are from $56-$89.

Otago Explorer, *T03-4743300*. Tours to Larnach Castle depart from the city daily at 0900 and 1500, from $30.

Otago Nature Guides, *T03-4545169, www.nznatureguides.com* Specializes in personalized, small group tours at dawn to see the Yellow-eyed penguin colony at the beautiful Sandfly Bay. Tours in conjunction with its fine B&B accommodation in Nisbet Cottage (see above) are recommended. Extended trips to the Catlins and Stewart Island are also available. German spoken.

Otago Peninsula Experience, *T03-4767261, www.classicjaguar.co.nz* Offers a wildlife tour in a classic 1960s Jaguar and includes Larnach Castle as an optional extra on the itinerary, 3hr 30 min-7hr 30 min from $59-$175, child $40/$108. Departs 1015.

Royal Albatross Centre, *see p611.*
There are a number of tours available. The 90-min 'Unique Taiaroa' tour includes an introductory video, a viewing of the colony from the hilltop observatory, and a look at the remains of Fort Taiaroa. This is a series of underground tunnels, fortifications and a 'disappearing gun' that were originally built in 1885 in response to a perceived threat of invasion from Tsarist Russia. Dec-Mar; $30, child $15. Apr-Sep, $25, child $12. The second tour on offer is the 60-min 'Royal Albatross' which includes all the above except the fort. Dec-Mar $24, child $12. Apr-Sep, $20, child $10. For those with no interest in seabirds and merely the forts, paranoia and guns you may like to join the 30-min 'Fort Taiaroa Tour' ($12, child $6). The 30-min 'Albatross Insight Tour' involves a guided tour of the centre and an

introductory talk about the birds while viewing them on close-circuit TV, as opposed to first hand from the observatory ($8, child $4). Note that the observatory is closed between 17 Sep and 23 Nov each year, to allow the new season's birds to return and renew their pair bonds. **Sam's 4x4 Adventures**, *T03-4780878, www.samsoffroadtours.com* A personalized 4-wheel drive road tour of the peninsula. 4-hr morning ($75) or 2½-hr evening tour

($40). Peninsula accommodation package also available.
Twilight Wildlife Conservation Tours, *T03-4543116, wildsouth@clear. net.nz* Offers a relaxed and friendly tour of the albatross colony (entry optional), various wildlife sites, peninsula beaches and the Penguin Place reserve (see above). The Monarch Wildlife Cruise (see below) is also an optional extra. Tours depart from Dunedin Mar-Oct 1330 (Nov-Feb 1430). From $50, child $39.

Central Otago → *Phone code: 03*

The barren, rugged and almost treeless landscapes of Central Otago have a dramatic sense of space and loneliness. Looking at these vistas now and passing through the quiet, unassuming towns of its back roads and river valleys, it is hard to imagine the immensity of the chaotic gold boom years that once made Otago the most populous region in the land. After gold was first discovered in 1861 by Gabriel Read, an Australian prospector, near Lawrence in the Clutha River Valley, Central Otago erupted into a gold fever that spread like wildfire across its barren landscape. It was a boom and a resource that would last until the turn of the 20th century, seeing the establishment of many towns including Alexandra, Clyde, Cromwell, Roxburgh, Ranfurly and St Bathans, and the construction of the impressive Taieri Gorge Railway and what is now the Otago Central Rail Trail which both formed vital communication links with Dunedin.

With the lure of Wanaka and Queenstown to the west, Central Otago sees little except transitory tourist traffic. But, if you have a couple of days to kill, a more thorough exploration of this historic gold-mining region can be rewarding and provide some respite from the crowds heading elsewhere. Attractions of particular note include the Taieri Gorge Railway trips, a walk around historic St Bathans or Clyde, and the Otago Central Rail Trail. The latter is becoming increasingly popular, with its 68 bridges, numerous tunnels and viaducts to add to the pleasant scenery. The trail also offers some of the best mountain biking in the region. Other equally less gold-orientated activities include fishing, walking and horse trekking.

Ins and outs

Getting there There are 3 main **roads** into Central Otago which essentially converge to form a loop. From Palmerston, 55 km north of Dunedin (via SH1 and the coast), SH85 turns inland to follow the 'Pig Root' to Ranfurly and Alexandra, with a small diversion to St Bathans. At Alexandra SH85 joins SH8 that follows the Clutha River Valley, south through Roxburgh, Raes Junction and Lawrence, before rejoining SH1 near Milton, 60 km south of Dunedin. At Mosgiel, 15 km south of Dunedin, SH87 follows close to the Taieri George Railway and Otago Central Rail Trail to merge with SH85 just east of Ranfurly. One of the best ways to get a taste of Central Otago is by **train** via the Taieri Gorge Railway and then by **mountain bike** from Middlemarch to Clyde on the now disused line that forms the Otago Central Rail Trail. Alternatively you can combine rail and bus to Queenstown (see Dunedin activities). Roxburgh, Alexandra, Clyde and Cromwell are all on the main highway to Queenstown (SH8) and are served by **Intercity**, T03-4428238, and **Atomic Shuttles,**T03-4429708, on the Queenstown and Wanaka to Dunedin route. **Catch-a-Bus,** T03-4428178, and **Wanaka**

Connexions, To800-879-926, both provide additional shuttle services to Queenstown and Wanaka. For information and bookings contact the VIC.

Information **Alexandra VIC,** ① *in the new museum complex on Kelman St (from early 2004) and until then on the main drag, 22 Centennial Av,* To3-4489515, *info@tco.org.nz Mon-Fri 0900-1700, Sat and Sun 1000-1500.* It is an excellent centre almost as full of information as the staff are with enthusiasm for the region. There are free maps, leaflets and displays outlining the many historical aspects of the region and its most popular activities, including mountain biking, fishing and horse trekking. **DoC Central Otago Regional Office,** ① *43 Dunstan Rd,* To3-4488874. **Cromwell and Districts VIC** (and Museum), ① *47 The Mall (along with just about everything else),* To3-4450212, *www.cromwell.org.nz Daily 1000-1600.* The staff here are very enthusiastic and helpful and will do their best to make sure you see the financial and health benefits of staying in Cromwell as opposed to Queenstown. The website www.cromwell.org.nz is excellent. For **ski field information** contact Cardrona, To3-4437341, Coronet Peak, To3-4424620, The Remarkables, To3-4424615, Treble Cone, To3-4437443, and Waiorau, To3-4437542 (www.nzski.com). The *Time for Real Adventure – Cromwell and Lake Dunstan,* is an excellent leaflet that is available from the VIC listing everything from climate statistics to local walks. The **Otago Goldfields Heritage Trust,** To3-4451516, has a useful website, www.nzsouth.co.nz/goldfields Many of the region's towns and goldfields heritage sites come within the boundaries of the Otago Goldfields Park administered by DoC.For the serious historian the Otago *Goldfields Heritage Trail* booklet, available free from all of the region's VICs, provides a solid route guide from which to explore the diverse historical sites scattered throughout the region. The websites www.centralotagonz.com and www.tco.org.nz, may also prove useful. The **Otago Central Rail Trail** has its own website, www.otagocentralrailtrail.co.nz

Alexandra → *Colour map 7, grid A5. Population: 4,500*

At the junction of the Clutha and Manuherikia Rivers, Alexandra was one of the first gold-mining towns to be established in Central Otago. Its creation was due to the first strikes made in 1862 by Horatio Hartley and Christopher Reilly in the once rich Dunstan fields, in what is now the neighbouring town of Clyde. The river junction became known as Lower Dunstan and later, as the hopefuls descended, became the settlement of Alexandra. Once the gold ran out at the end of the 1800s the orchardists moved in, making fruit growing Alexandra's modern-day industry. The town is at its best in autumn when the riverside willows and poplars, ironically, bathe the valley in another golden hue. Alexandra serves as the principal gateway to the **Otago Central Rail** and **Dunstan gold mining heritage trails**, which are a major attraction for mountain bikers and four-wheel drive enthusiasts.

Sights Almost instantly noticeable and visible from almost everywhere is the 11-m diameter **clock** on part of the **Knobbies Range** to the east of Alexandra. Completed in November 1968, its creation came about through no particular reason other than the pure and simple desire of one Alexander Jaycee. Somehow, after managing to get his idea endorsed by the town's residents, he then found the support and finances to build it – which was no mean feat in itself, requiring 1,264 man hours of work. Although hardly ugly, it does seem a little out of place, and certainly does not reflect the general atmosphere or the pace of life in the town. One gets the feeling that if it ever stopped no one would be particularly bothered about going up there to give it a tap.

Besides the clock and its simple riverside aesthetics, the main attraction in town is the new **Alexandra Museum,** ① *Kelman St,* To3-4486230. *Opening times and prices under review at time of going to press.* It concentrates naturally on gold mining, but also includes some interesting displays on the role of the early Chinese settlers and sheep farmers as well as the work of local artisans.

A short walk from the centre of town will take you to the **Shaky Bridge** that crosses the Manuherikia River on Fox Street (just below the clock). Originally built in 1879, it was once used by wagons and horses. Now purely a footbridge, although aesthetically pleasing, it does not provide the impending adrenaline rush that its name suggests, however, the smart Shaky Bridge Vineyard Café and Restaurant on the far side provides added incentive.

As well as orchards the area has its fair share of **vineyards** including the Blackridge, ① *76 Conroys Rd, T03-4492059, daily 1000-1700,* that claims to be the most southerly winery in the world. Ask at the VIC for the free *Central Otago Wine Map.*

If you are a **Lord of the Rings** fanatic Alexandra will no doubt provide the launching pad to visit the remote **Poolburn Reservoir** which sits on the Rough Ridge Range 40 min east of the town. There, an expansive area of rocky outcrops (tors) and tussock surrounding the reservoir, provided the perfect backdrop for the realm of **'Rohan'**. Note that the area is by no means easy to reach and you are advised to seek detailed directions from the VIC before venturing out independently. If you do not have a reliable vehicle of your own then you can always join one of the local tour operators that will no doubt have started to offer trips out there perhaps taking in the former gold mining village of **Ophir** on the way. ▸ *For Sleeping, Eating and other listings, see pages 621-623.*

Clyde → *Colour map 7, grid A5. Population 1,000*

Just 10 km west of Alexandra is the pretty and historic village of Clyde. Backed by the concrete edifice of the Clyde Dam that incarcerates **Lake Dunstan**, it offers a pleasant stop on the way to Queenstown or Wanaka. Originally called Dunstan and the hub of the rich Dunstan Goldfields, it assumed its present name in the late 1860s. Clyde in Scots Gaelic is *Clutha* – which is the river that once flowed freely through the Cromwell Gorge and is the longest in the South Island. Amidst Clyde's very pleasant aesthetics are a number of historic old buildings including the **Town Hall** (1868), various pioneer cottages and a handful of its once 70 hotels. The **Old Courthouse** on Blyth Street is another fine example that was built in 1864. Sadly now not open to the public many interesting artefacts were displayed inside, including the original courtroom dock, leg irons, handcuffs, and a set of scales. These scales, which no doubt were the focus of many an argument, are thought to have weighed over 70,000 ounces of gold. It is not surprising that during the **gold boom**, with so many hopefuls harbouring such a sense of greed, there were many disputes and disturbances in the town. Perhaps the worst of these was the $26,000 gold and banknotes robbery that caused uproar in 1879.

Nearby, on Fraser Street, is the **Clyde Historical Museum and Briar Herb Factory**, ① *T03-4492092. Tue-Sun 1400-1600, or at other times by arrangement. $2, children free.* The herb factory originally began operations in the 1930s processing local thyme, but has since grown into a museum housing not only the original herb-processing machinery, but also a variety of exhibits illustrating the life of the early settlers. These include the workshops of blacksmith, farrier and wheelwrights, and stables with various horse-drawn vehicles.

The trilogy of historical sites is completed by the **Clyde Station Museum,** ① *at the former railway station on Fraser St, T03-4492400. Sun 1400-1600, or by appointment, $2.* It houses some lovingly restored locos. Although perhaps a bit morbid, the **cemetery** in Clyde (Springvale Road) can be an interesting place for reflection. Having been in use since the 1850s, the headstones provide some fascinating reading, particularly the ages, surnames and origins of the former settlers. Once you have enjoyed the atmosphere and historical aspects of the village, you might like to take the 30-minute walk to the **Clyde Lookout hill** (signposted) above the town and enjoy the views. ▸ *For Sleeping and Eating, see page 621.*

Otago Central Otago

From Clyde, SH8 negotiates the Cromwell Gorge and plays tag with a section of Lake Dunstan, which on the map looks like the antenna of a large blue sea creature. At its head, 23 km to the north, is the tidy little town of Cromwell. Cromwell is faced with five very large dilemmas – a pear, an apple, a peach, a lemon and its proximity to Queenstown. It is the latter of course with which it struggles the most. Just how do you stop any tourist so intent on reaching perhaps the busiest tourist town in the country? Well, it seems some bright spark (there is always one) thought a sculpture of four man-eating pieces of fruit might be a good idea. But you have to wonder if this has only added to the dilemma. Sure, people stop, they stare, make the suitable ohh and ahh noises, then take the inevitable photographs, but that is often the problem – they go no further. That's Cromwell. Forever and around the globe, Cromwell has become that place with the whooping fruit, ingrained forever in a million memories with a silly photo. But Cromwell is ideally situated between Wanaka, Queenstown, the Lindis Pass to Mount Cook and SH8 to Dunedin. The accommodation here is much cheaper than Queenstown and the place is far less stressful. It is also in a great position to access five ski fields (see Information above). So it makes a lot of sense, despite the fruit, to base yourself here. Another thing – it is also one of the sunniest, warmest places in the South and has to be given considerable credit for being the only place in the world that has a reserve set aside especially for **beetles**.

Another former **gold town**, Cromwell was originally called 'The Junction' due to its position at the confluence of the Clutha and Kawarau Rivers. These important bodies of water, which are now masked with the creation of Lake Dunstan, form an integral part of the South Island's hydropower scheme. (The **museum**, attached to the VIC, focuses on the early history and building of the dam and is worth a look. Entry by donation.) The decision to build the **Clyde Dam** in the 1980s, using Cromwell as the accommodation base, brought many changes to the town and gave rise to a mix of old-world charm and modern, tidy aesthetics. A wander through its very congenial Mall (almost in the shadow of the giant fruit), followed by another in its historic precinct, provides a stark and interesting contrast. With the dam now established they say Cromwell's future lies in tourism, and of course its horticultural status as the **'Fruit Bowl of the South'**. ▸▸ *For Sleeping, Eating and other listings, see pages 621-623.*

Sights The main attraction in the town itself is the **Old Cromwell Town Precinct**, at the end of Melmore Place, at the point where the two rivers merge. Since the 1980s and encouraged by the disruption of the dam work, many of the former buildings have been restored or reconstructed and now house local **cafés** and **craft shops**. The precinct also serves as a base for **Lake Cruises**, and some of the restored buildings are open for viewing between 1000-1630, entry is free and the VIC has various free leaflets. *In Search of the Main Street* is particularly useful.

As you might expect, there are also numerous former gold-mining sites and relics surrounding Cromwell. **Bannockburn**, **Bendigo** and the **Carrick Goldfields** are of particular interest. The VIC has details and maps. The **Goldfields Mining Centre**, ① *in the Kawarau Gorge (SH6 west), 6 km towards Queenstown, T03-4451037, www.goldfieldsmining.co.nz, daily 0900-1700. $14, child $6*, provides the opportunity to explore historic gold workings, a Chinese settlers' village, gold stamper batteries and a sluice gun. You can also pan for gold, go horse trekking or jet boating ($78, child $42).

As well as its many orchards, the immediate area is also home to a number of **vineyards**. In Bannockburn, just to the south of Cromwell, you will find the **Felton Road Winery**, ① *Felton Rd, T03-4450885, 1000-1700, closed weekends May-Oct*; **Bannockburn Heights**, ① *Cairnmuir Rd, T03-4450887 (café/bar daily 1000-1800)*; **Carrick**, *Cairnmuir Road, T03-4453480, www.carrick.co.nz, daily 1100-1700*; and the **Olssen's Garden Vineyard**, *306 Felton Rd, T03-4451716 (tastings daily 1000-1700, closed weekends May-Sep)*. The intriguingly-named **Mount Difficulty Vineyard**,

1000-1700, is a small boutique winery that is fast contributing to the region's reputation for fine Pinot Noir, if not its expansive views.

● Sleeping

Alexandra *p618*

The VIC has full accommodation listings and can book on your behalf. There are a number of **motels**, most on the main drag north, towards Clyde. These include:

A **Centennial Court**, *96 Centennial Av, T03-4486482;*

A-B **Alexandra Heights**, *125 Centennial Av, T03-4486366.*

B **Alexandra Garden Court**, *Manuherikia Rd, T03-4488295*, is recommended.

For **B&Bs** try:

L **Rocky Range**, *Half Mile, T03-4486150, www.rockyrange.co.nz* Very pleasant.

A **Iversen**, *47 Blackman Rd, T03-4492520*. For a lovely orchard stay.

C-D **Central Tranquaillity Backpackers**, *16 Theyers St, T03-4487098*. The main budget hostel in town, offering 2 comfortable units with shared facilities. Book ahead.

C-D **Ophir Lodge Backpackers**, *1 McDonald St, in the historic village of Ophir (28 km north), T03-4473339, blgaler@xtra.co.nz* A fine alternative with cabin dorms, 1 twin, a double and tent sites. The added attractions here other than the peaceful and friendly atmosphere of the village, are the local walks, bike trails and fishing and (of course) the local pub.

Motorcamps and campsites

B-D **Alexandra Holiday Camp**, *on the Manuherikia Rd, T03-4488297*. Has cabins, backpackers, powered/tent sites and also hires kayaks and mountain bikes.

B-D **Pine Lodge Holiday Camp**, *Ngapara St, T03-4488861*. Smaller, but has flats, units and powered/tent sites. Both parks are about a 10-15-min walk from the town centre.

Clyde *p619*

LL-AL **Olivers Lodge**, *34 Sunderland St, T03-4492860, www.olivers.co.nz* Offers some charming individually styled rooms right in the heart of the village all of which ooze character. The old shower and sunken bath

in the Smokehouse room are simply superb. Classy restaurant also on site.Recommended.

A **Dunstan House**, *Sunderland St, T03-4492295, www.dunstanhouse.co.nz* This historic former hotel has been nicely refurbished and offers elegant en suites decorated in turn-of-the-century style.

A **Antique Lodge Motel**, *56 Sunderland St, T03-4492709*. A good motel option.

C-D **Hartley Arms Backpackers**, *Sunderland St, T03-4492700, hartleyarms@xtra.co.nz* Friendly place set in a historic cottage right in the thick of things.

Motorcamps

C-D **Clyde Holiday Complex**, *Whitby St, T03-4492713*, has 1 cabin and powered/tent sites. For other accommodation options contact the VIC in Alexandra.

Cromwell *p620*

There is a surprisingly good range of accommodation in Cromwell and, given its popularity as a base close to (but cheaper) than Queenstown, the number of beds is increasing. The VIC has a full list of options and can book on your behalf. In summer it would still be wise to book ahead.

AL-A **Golden Gate Lodge**, *Barry Av, T03-4451777, www.goldengate.co.nz* The closest thing to a hotel in town. Smart and spacious, it is designed to reflect the region's gold-mining heritage and offers well-appointed studios, suites (some with spa) and units and restaurant.

AL **Lake Dunstan Lodge**, *Cromwell Rd (SH8), T03-4451291, www.lakedunstanlodge.co.nz* A smart, modern home in a peaceful location on the shores of Lake Dunstan, offering tidy twin and queen rooms, with balconies, a spa pool and some great home cooking.

AL **Villa Amo**, *Shine La, Pisa Moorings on Lake Dunstan, T03-4450788, VillaAmo@xtra.co.nz* A modern spacious place and a good option in the upper B&B range. It is owned by the Eco-experience operators (see below).

A **Cottage Gardens B&B**, *corner of Main Highway and Alpha St, T03-4450628, eco@xtra.co.nz* Also a good choice.

There is a scattering of standard **motels**:
A **Lake Dunstan Motel** *3 Mead Av,
T03-4451696, www.lakedunstanmotel.co.nz;*
B **Colonial Manor** *corner of Barry and Mead
Aves, T03-4450184.* Both new.
B **Anderson Park Lodge**, *Gair Av,
T0800-220550.* Cheaper and fairly
unremarkable.

Motorcamps and campsites
B-D **Cromwell Top Ten Holiday Park**, *1
Alpha St, T03-4450164,
cromwell.holiday.park@xtra.co.nz* Has a wide
range of modern motel, en suite/standard
cabins and powered/tent sites in a quiet
setting beside the golf course.
C-D **Chalets and Holiday Park**, *102 Barry Av,
T03-4451260, thechalets@xtra.co.nz* Former
revamped dam workers' residences. It has
bunkrooms and cheap but comfortable
singles and doubles with shared facilities.

🍴 Eating

Alexandra *p618*
Clyde, see below, provides far better dining
options than Alexandra.
$$ **Briar and Tyme Café and Bar**, *next door
to the VIC at 26 Centennial Av, T03-4489189.
Daily (Tue-Sat in winter).* An historic single-
storey villa offering imaginative and
affordable Euro/NZ lunches and dinners.
$$ **Red Brick Café**, *just off Ennis St,
T03-4489174, Mon-Sat for a good lunch or
dinner.* The exception to the plethora of
unremarkable cafés and takeaways in the
centre of town.
$$ **The Vineyard Café**, *near the Shaky Bridge,
Graveyard Gully Rd, T03-4485111.* Proving to
be a fine venue for an al fresco lunch or a
coffee all year and for dinner in summer.

Clyde *p619*
$$ **Oliver's Restaurant**, *in the former 1863
general store, 34 Sunderland St, T03-4492860,
www.olivers.co.nz Daily for lunch and dinner
(bookings advised).* Award-winning, the food
is just as pleasant as the surroundings.
$$ **Dunstan House**, *Sunderland St,
T03-4492295.* Offers café-style cuisine that
focuses mainly on local produce in an
equally historic setting.
$ **Blues Bank Café and Bar**, *also on
Sunderland St in the former bank,*

T03-4492147. Tue-Sun from 1100-late. A funky
little place, with a light, imaginative menu
and good coffee.
$ **The Post Office Café and Bar**, *2 Blyth St,
T03-4492488. Daily from 1000.* Nice aesthetics
and light meals.

Cromwell *p620*
$$ **Bannockburn Heights Café and Wine
Bar**, *on Cairnmuir Rd, 8 km from the town
centre in Bannockburn, T03-4453211. Daily for
lunch and dinner.* It is in a nice setting, boasts
its own wines and beers. Recommended.
$$ **Gentle Annie's Restaurant**, *in the Golden
Gate Lodge, on Barry Av, T03-4451777. Daily
from 0700-2100.* The best bet for à la carte.
$ **Junction Pizza Company**, *The Mall (61A),
T03-4450777.* Won't disappoint.
$ **Cromwell Town and Country Club**,
Melmore Terr, T03-4451169. Fri and Sat.
Provides a good cheap feed.

⛰️ Activities

Alexandra *p618*
Alexandra is the principal starting point for
the **Otago Central Rail Trail and
Dunstan Trails**. The VIC can provide
information and free leaflets on the methods
and negotiation of both, mainly by mountain
bike or 4-wheel drive. Accommodation
listings are also available from the VIC. The
Otago Central Rail Trail has its own website,
www.otagocentralrailtrail.co.nz, that may
prove useful. Various transport operators
provide luggage and bike pick-up or
drop-offs and bike hire (and/or guided tours)
for both trails.
Kayak and Outdoors, *21 Shannon St,
T03-4488048, www.kayakandoutdoor.co.nz*
Offers both kayaking and mountain biking
tour options as well as an attractive local
accommodation package for groups at the
self-contained Glencarron Lodge.
Fat Tyre, *025-802-378, www.fat-tyre.co.nz*
Offers guided half-day or multi-day rides to
suit all abilities.
Altitude Adventures, *88 Centennial Av,
T03-4488917, www.altitudeadventures.co.nz*
Offers a 2-3-hr, fast single track ride from
$55, a full day trip for a very reasonable $79
and a bike and boat combo with an early
morning cruise down the Roxburgh Gorge to
the dam, followed by an afternoon of

backcountry biking from $145.

Dunstan Trail Rides, *118 Waikerikeri Valley Road, Clyde, T03-4492445.* Offer horse trekking on the Dunstan Trail from $25 per hr, 2 hrs $40.

Fishing permits and a list of local guides are available from the VIC.

Cromwell *p620*

Lake Dunstan Eco-experience, *T03-4450788, EcoExperience@xtra.co.nz* Offesr an interesting 3-4-hr trip up Lake Dunstan to the Bendigo wetlands which are home to numerous water birds and waders.

Southern Lakes Pack Horse Trekking, *T03-4451444.* Local horse trekking operators. There are plenty of good **walks** in the area and the *Walk Cromwell* brochure available free from the VIC will literally keep you on track. The area also provides some excellent **fishing**, **mountain biking** and **4-wheel drive** opportunities, again, contact the VIC.

There are also several **orchard and vineyard tour** operators including: **Freeway Orchards**, *T03-4451500;* **Jackson Orchards Tours**, *T03-4450596;* **Grape Escape**, *based in Clyde, T03-4487669.* Great half day from $60, full day from $85.

❶ Directory

Alexandra *p618*

Internet Library. *Mon-Fri 0900-1700, Sat 1000-1200.* **Cobblestone Cafe.** *Daily in season from 0830-1800. Both on Tarbert St in the centre of town.*

Cromwell *p620*

Banks BNZ and National Bank, *in the Mall. and the Westpac.* **Internet** Library. The Resource Centre. Composite Computers. *All in the Mall.* **Postal agent** Paper Plus, The Mall. **Useful addresses** Breakdown services: CR Motors, *Murray Terr, T03-4451844.* **Police:** *T03-4451999.*

Queenstown → *Phone code: 03 Colour map 7, grid A4 Population: 15,000*

Oh dear, where do you start. Here goes. Ladies and Gentlemen, fasten your seat belts and welcome to Queenstown – Adrenaline Central, Thrillsville, New Zealand; the adventure capital of the world. You are perhaps studying this guide in your hotel room, or perched in your hostel bunk, with a pained expression trying to decide which of the 150-odd activities to try and, more especially, how your wallet can possibly cope? But first things first. Look out of the window. Now where else in the world do you have such accessible scenery as that? And all that is free!

Queenstown has come a long way since gold secured its destiny in the 1860s. It is now the biggest tourist draw in New Zealand and considered one of the top (and almost certainly the most scenic) adventure venues in the world. It simply has so much to offer. Amidst the stunning setting of mountain and lake, over 1,000,000 visitors a year partake in a staggering range of activities from a sedate steamboat cruise to the heart-stopping bungee jump. You can do almost anything here, from a gentle round of golf to paddling down a river in what looks like a blow-up carrot. Add to that a superb range of accommodation, services, restaurants and cafés, and you simply don't know where to turn. And it's all-year-round, day and night. In winter the hiking boots are simply replaced by skis, the T-shirt with a jumper and, after sunset, the activity guide with the wine glass, knife and fork. It just goes on and on.

Ins and outs

Getting there Queenstown **airport** is 8 km east of the town in Frankton, T03-4422670. **Air New Zealand**, T03-4411900, have direct daily flights to Auckland, Christchurch, Wellington and Dunedin and also offer regular international flights to Sydney in summer and both Sydney and Brisbane in winter. **Qantas**, T09-3578836, also offer winter services out of Sydney and Brisbane. Several small domestic operators offer flights to Milford, including **Air Fiordland**, T03-4423404, and **Milford**

66 99 Here goes. Ladies and Gentlemen, fasten your seat belts and welcome to Queenstown – Adrenaline Central, Thrillsville, New Zealand; the adventure capital of the world...

Sound Scenic Flights, T03-4423065 (see Activities section).

By **road,** Queenstown is 486 km from Christchurch, 283 km from Dunedin, 68 km from Wanaka and 170 km from Te Anau (Ilford Sound 291 km). The town is served daily by **Intercity,** T03-4422800, www.intercitycoach.co.nz (Dunedin/Christchurch via Mount Cook/Te Anau/Franz Josef); **Atomic Shuttles,** T03-4429708, www.atomictravel.co.nz (Dunedin/Christchurch/Invercargill/Greymouth); **Southern Link,** T03-3588355 (Dunedin/Christchurch); **Mount Cook Landline,** T0800-800904, (Christchurch via Mount Cook). Fares to Dunedin start from $30, Christchurch $45. **Topline Tours,** T03-2498059, and **Tracknet,** T03-2497777, go to Te Anau from $35. **Catch-a-Bus,** T03-4799960, goes daily to Dunedin from $30. The backpacker orientated **Bottom Bus,** T03-4429708, www.bottombus.co.nz, serves Dunedin and the Southern Scenic Route to Invercargill and Te Anau on Tue/Thur/Fri and Sun. **High Country Shuttles,** T0800-435050, connects daily with Christchurch-bound Intercity and Atomic Shuttles in Mount Cook, from $40. Intercity, Atomic Shuttles, and the recommended **Wanaka Connections,** T03-4439122, go 6 times daily to Wanaka, from $25. ▸▸ *For bus trips to Milford Sound see page 666.*

Getting around The **Shopper Bus,** T03-4426647 (stops outside *McDonald's*), and the **Airport Bus,** T03-4426647 (door-to-door), serve the airport from $3.50. A taxi will cost about $20. The Shopper Bus stops at most major hotels and accommodation establishments and with a $10 day-pass can be a good way to negotiate the **town** (timetable free from the VIC). **Ski Shuttle** T03-4428106, and **AA Alpine Taxis,** T03-4426666, are the principal ski field shuttle operators serving Cardrona, Coronet Peak, The Remarkables and Treble Cone, from $25-$30. **The Arrow Express,** T03-4421900 (stops outside *McDonald's*) and **Double-Decker Bus Tours** (top of the Mall) go several times a day to Arrowtown, from $10 each way, child $6. **Backpacker Express,** T03-4429939, runs daily to Glenorchy. For taxi, car rental and bike hire see Directory, page 640. You are advised to book car rental well in advance in summer.

Tramping track transport For detailed information and trailhead bookings contact the **Information and Track Centre** (see Information below). **Tracknet,** T03-2497777, are the specialist tramping track operators to **Te Anau (Kepler/Milford/Dusky).** For **Glenorchy** and beyond **(Routeburn/Greenstone-Caples/Rees-Dart)** contact **Backpacker Express,** T03-4429939, info@glenorchyinfocentre.co.nz For **water-taxi transport** via Lake Wakatipu and up the Rees/Dart, contact **Glenorchy Cruising,** T03-4429951, WAKATIPU@xtra.co.nz, or **Backpacker Express** (see above).

Information and orientation Queenstown is compact and easily negotiable by foot. The main street for information and activity bookings is Shotover St while **The Mall,** bordered by Camp St to the east and Marine Par on the waterfront, is the principal shopping and restaurant centre. The **Esplanade** (lakeside) and **Steamer Wharf** also have retail, information and activity outlets. **Queenstown Gardens,** on the southern edge of Queenstown Bay, offers sanctuary from the chaotic town centre.

There is total information overload in Queenstown. For non-biased advice head straight away to the very efficient and busy **Queenstown Travel and Visitor Centre**, ⓘ *below the Clock Tower, corner of Shotover and Camp Sts, T0800-668888, T03-4424100, qvc@xtra.co.nz Daily 0700-1900 (winter 1800). The website www.queenstown-nz.co.nz is excellent.* **DoC**, ⓘ *37 Shotover St, T03-4427935, queenstownvc@doc.govt.nz* Next to the **Information and Track Centre**, ⓘ *www.infotrack.co.nz Daily 0830-1900, winter Mon-Fri 0900-1700, Sat and Sun 0930-1630.* It can provides all local walk and up-to-date major tramping information and deal with transportation and hut information and bookings. It also provide up-to-date weather forecasts. **Real Journeys Visitors Centre**, ⓘ *Steamer Wharf, T0800-656503, T03-4427500, www.realjourneys.co.nz* Deals with a multitude of pleasures and trips to Milford and the Fiordland National Park. Also owns and operates the *TSS Earnslaw Steamship.* ▸▸ *See also Activities , pages 627 and 633.*

History

The first European known to have visited the vicinity was Scots sheep farmer Donald Hay, who explored Lake Wakatipu in 1859, and also gave his name to Lake Hayes near Arrowtown. From this point on several sheep drovers set up camp along the eastern shore of Lake Wakatipu at Queenstown Bay. With the discovery of gold in the Shotover River Valley by prospectors/shearers Thomas Arthur and Harry Redfern in 1862, the race was on. Within a year over 2000 hopefuls were camped in the area and searching the Shotover and Kawarau for gold. The Shotover is known to be the richest gold-bearing river of its size in the world. Despite that, it only took about a decade before the gold was exhausted and the population declined, reaching a meagre 190 by 1900, most of whom were farmers. By the mid-1900s the town was well on its way to being a popular tourist resort. The name Queenstown is believed to have been bestowed in 1863, when at a public gathering it was agreed that the town and its location were 'fit for a Queen'. Various heads of state have since marvelled at the place.

Sights

Perhaps the best place to start is the **Skyline Gondola**, ⓘ *Brecon St, T03-4410101, www.skyline.co.nz 0900-dusk. There are a number of 'fare' options. A gondola only costs $15, child $5. Gondola and Luge (5 rides) costs $29, child $23.* Perched on **Bob's Peak**, over 450 m above the town, it boasts a world-class view and has a host of activities on offer including The Ledge Bungy, The Luge, The Sky-Swing, paragliding and helicopter flightseeing. There are also shops, a café (open 0930-2100), a restaurant (see Eating below) and a 27-minute film of New Zealand's many attractions ($8 child $4). A good time to go up is just before sunset when the golden rays slowly creep up the **Remarkables Range** and the town's lights come on. Then you could perhaps enjoy a meal before watching the bungee jumpers and the novel 'Sky-Swing' below the main building. At night it is quite hard to believe such a place and such activities exist. You can also **walk** (one hour one-way) up to the Skyline Complex via the **Ben Lomond Track** which starts on Lomond Crescent (via Brunswick St off the Lake Esplanade).

While at the base of the gondola you might like to see the obligatory **kiwi** and friends in the **Birdlife Park**, ⓘ *Brecon St, T03-4428059. Daily 0900-2100 (winter 0900-1700), $13, child $5.* Set in 8 hectares of quiet(ish) pine forest it displays all the usual suspects, including kiwi, morepork (owl), parakeets, tui and of course the 'cheeky kea'. Of the 16 endangered species, the rarest is the delicate black stilt, sadly, one of only about 150 remaining.

Also in Brecon Street is **Caddy Shack City Mini-Golf**, ⓘ *T03-4426642. 1000-dusk. $15, child $10.* Here, a plethora of weird and wonderful holes will keep small kids (and big kids) amused for hours on rainy days or evenings. **Queenstown Gardens** offer some respite from the crowds and has oaks, sequoias and 1500 roses planted in 26 named rose beds. On the way you might like to pop into the historic

1865 **Williams Cottage**, on Marine Parade, which has been restored and now serves as a small museum.

There are also a number of **wineries** around Queenstown that boast surprisingly fine wines (especially Pinot Noir) and claim to be the most southerly vineyards in the world. **The Peregrine**, ⓘ *T03-4424000, www.peregrine.co.nz* **Chard Farm**, ⓘ *T03- 4426110, www.chardfarm.co.nz* and **Gibbston Valley**, ⓘ *T03-4426910, www.gv wines.co.nz*; all on SH6 on the way in to Queenstown are the three most noted. The VIC has details and tours are available (for further information, see tours, page 638).

Finally, if you have run out of money, or simply want a good laugh, head for the **Kawarau Bridge Bungee** (23 km east on SH6) and watch the jumpers. It is a

Queenstown

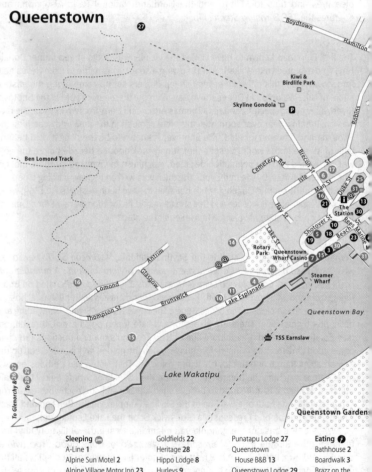

Sleeping	Goldfields 22	Punatapu Lodge 27	Eating
A-Line 1	Heritage 28	Queenstown	Bathhouse 2
Alpine Sun Motel 2	Hippo Lodge 8	House B&B 13	Boardwalk 3
Alpine Village Motor Inn 23	Hurleys 9	Queenstown Lodge 29	Brazz on the
Blue Peaks Lodge 3	Kawarau Falls Holiday	Queenstown	Green 1
Bumbles Backpackers 4	Park 24	Motor Park 14	Cow 8
Creeksyde Campervan	Lakeside Motel 10	Queenstown YHA 15	Ferg's Burgers 24
Park 5	Lodges 11	Scallywags 17	Gantley's 31
Dairy Guesthouse 6	Matakauri Lodge 26	Southern Laughter 17	Habebes 10
Eichardt's Private 31	Millennium 12	Stone House Inn 18	HMS Brittannia 11
Esplanade 25	Novotel Gardens 7	Thomas's & Backpackers	Joe's Garage 12
Glebe Luxury	Point Luxury	30	Leonardo's 13
Apartments 20	Apartments 21	Waterfront 19	Little India 14

fascinating mix of fear and fun and watching the spectators is just as entertaining. **627**

▶ *For Sleeping, Eating and other listings, see pages 629-640.*

Activities

The choice is of course vast. There are over 150 activities to choose from, with everything from the tipples of a wine tour to the ripples of jet boating. And Queenstown is not just geared up for the young and the mad. There are activities to suit all ages, from infant to octogenarian and from the able to the disabled. If a 91-year-old can do a bungee jump, surely the possibilities are endless? Of course it is the bungee that made Queenstown famous, and no doubt if you are prepared to make 'the jump' and have been saving your pennies to do so, then it is here, in Queenstown, you must finally pluck up the courage. Heights vary from about 40 m to 134 m, and if there is any advice here (other than psychological and financial counselling), it is – if you are going to do it, make sure you do it in style and go high!

The **'big four'** activities in Queenstown are considered to be the **bungee**, **jet boating**, **rafting** and **flightseeing**. But you can use your imagination and manage your finances way beyond just those – and make sure you shop around. Do not be swayed by reputations or the Las Vegas-style advertising and marketing that confronts you the moment you arrive. The 'in thing' at the moment of course are tours by four-wheel drive or by air to see the numerous **Lord of the Rings** locations which for some adds to its appeal.

In summary, try to consider a variety of pursuits according to the budget at hand and the sheer variety available. For example consider something that costs nothing and is rather sedate, like a good walk taking in a stunning view (see box, page 628), since this as just as much 'Queenstown' as anything else. Then by all means get the pulse racing with something high on the **'adrenalinometer'**, like a bungee, then perhaps something easy-going or an activity you can do nowhere else like a cruise on the *TSS Earnslaw*. Above all, don't only consider what you are 'supposed' to do, but also what most others do not. Queenstown is special and deserves far more of your attention and imagination.

Of course there are numerous **'combos'** on offer (see below), and this is

To Supermarket & **31**
Queenstown Hill Walkway
To **21**
To **23** & Airport

McNeill's Cottage
 Brewery **17**
Minami Jujisei **18**
Naff Caff **19**
O'Connells
 Food Hall **20**
Pasta Pasta
 Cucina **21**
Pog Mahone's **23**
Sky Alpine Casino **26**
Skyline **27**
Tatler **29**
Vudu Café **30**

Bars & clubs 🌸
Bunker **4**
Chico's **6**
Cigar Bar **7**
Edge **9**
Loaded Hog **15**
Lone Star &
 Rattlesnake **16**
Pig & Whistle **22**
Red Rock **25**
Tardis **28**
Triple M **5**
World **31**

WG Rees Memorial
Amusement Park
Ice Skating

Otago Queenstown

❧ The Best View in Queenstown

Although it takes a rugged drive and a fair scramble (in summer) to get there, the view of Lake Wakatipu and Queenstown from the **Remarkables Lookout** is worth every rut and step of the journey. Before considering this trip make sure the weather is clear and settled, since you will be over 2000 m above sea level. Assure that you are well prepared, with warm clothing and proper walking boots and that your car will survive the 1500 m climb up the unsealed road to the ski fields (in winter you may need chains). The ski field road is accessed off SH6 about 2 km south of Frankton. If the ski field is open you might consider taking a shuttle from Queenstown, *T03-4426534*. From the Remarkables ski field buildings you are basically trying to reach the top of the Shadow Basin Chair Lift, the base of which is in the main car park. If the lift is open you have the option of using it, but in summer (or if you fancy the climb) then follow the path that zigzags up the slopes behind the main building to the 'Mid-Station'. From the Mid-Station continue on the path in a rough line with the chairlift until you reach its terminus. The lookout is about 200 m directly behind and further up from this point. On a clear day surrounded by snow, you won't forget it!

From the lookout (two hours 30 minutes return) it is then possible to climb and scramble with care, further south along the ridge to the weather station. From here you will have even greater views including Lake Alta, the entire ski field below and north, to Mount Aspiring. On an exceptional day you may even see Mount Cook almost 200km away.

often a good way to go, saving you significant dollars. Some will take up about four hours, others are an exacting 12, it's all up to your stamina, your budget and of course your sheer 'guts'. One word of warning however. If you are unsure of an activity and whether you can, or indeed will, actually do it, do not part with your cash. You cannot expect a refund.

In Queenstown you will be confronted with numerous sales and promotional outlets that can sniff your dollars in a dead calm, so be careful. The big players are **A J Hackett** (Lord of the bungee) and **Shotover Jet,** with numerous others biting at their heels. ① *A J Hackett and Shotover share an office in 'The Station', suitably situated right where the buses stop, at the corner of Shotover and Camp Street, T03-4427122, www.AJHackett.com 0700-2100, winter 0800-2000.* Bookings can be made direct, but most accommodation establishments, especially backpackers, will book on your behalf. The Station is also the main pick-up and drop-off point for the relevant activities. The best advice is first to take a wander into the unbiased VIC below the Clock Tower, have a chat and avail yourself of the leaflets and all the information.
▸▸ *See also listings section page 633.*

Activity combos There are a huge number of combo packages available, from the main players like A J Hackett and Shotover to independents like Adventure Marathon. Most gravitate (no pun intended) between the big four – bungee, rafting, jet boating and flightseeing, with the odd 'luge' or movie thrown in. Bear in mind there are also others on offer like fish/trek, plus heli-skiing or hiking. If you are short of time a combo is probably the best way to go, and with prices ranging from about $170 to $420 the savings can be quite attractive. One of the best, but most demanding combos, is the **Awesome Foursome** , a full day (and at 12 hours it is exactly that) which includes the

$415. ① *For details contact Queenstown Combos, T03-4427318, www.combos.co.nz*
A slightly less demanding value package is the **High Five:** 3½-hour jetboat, helicopter, skyline, movie and luge. ① *Shotover, T03-4427318, for $179.* The half-day (5 hr) helicopter-raft and jet boat **Triple Challenge** is also good value at $269, ① *Queenstown Rafting, T03-4429792, www.rafting.co.nz* If you are still intent on a bungee this could perhaps be combined with one of the Hackett multiple jumps. Again, the best advice is to shop about and take your time. ⏵ *For all Activities and tours listings, see page 633.*

● Sleeping

Despite a healthy range of accommodation and a total of 8,000 beds, it is essential to book 2 or 3 days in advance in mid- summer or during the height of the ski season (especially during the Winter Festival in mid-Jul). This particularly applies to backpacker accommodation. For a good browse of options visit the web at www.queenstownaccommodation.co.nz

Hotels
There is plenty of choice, with over a dozen major ones in town and as ever an alarming number on the way. **LL Eichardt's Private Hotel**, *T03-4410450, www.eichardtshotel.co.nz* One of the newest (refurbished) hotels in town sitting right on Marine Parade and catering to the luxury boutique market. Already reeling in some lauded international awards it offers all the decor, fine lavish furnishings and amenities one might expect for the exorbitant price and has quite genuinely perhaps the edge when it comes to a caring, personable service.
LL-AL Heritage Hotel, *91 Fernhill Rd, T03-4424988, www.heritagehotels.co.nz* Offers a wide range of modern suites, has all the usual facilities and is particularly recommended for it's quiet position and fine views. It even has a health club.
LL-AL Millennium Hotel, *corner Frankton Rd and Stanley St, T03-4418888, millennium.queenstown@cdlhms.co.nz* Relatively new and very well positioned close to town. Again it has a wide range of suites and all the usual modern well-appointed facilities.
LL-AL Novotel Gardens, *corner of Earl St and Marine Par, T03-4427750, reservations@novotelgardens.co.nz* Would not win any beauty contests from the

outside but is modern and in an ideal position at the edge of the town centre, right on the waterfront and a stone's throw from the peace and quiet of Queenstown Gardens.
AL-A A-Line Hotel, *27 Stanley St, T03-4427700, aline@scenic-circle.co.nz* Offers well-appointed A-frame-style units with great views within 2 mins of the town centre.
B-D Hotel Esplanade, *78 Park St, T03-4428611.* A very good budget hotel that overlooks the lake in a quiet area of town. It is a no-nonsense place but perfectly comfortable, good value for money and has a magnificent outlook for the price.
LL-AL Millbrook Resort, *T03-4417000, www.millbrook.co.nz* Sumptuous out-of-town choice with its world-class golf course and luxury facilities. It has suites, villas and cottages, 2 restaurants, a bar, and a health and fitness complex.

Self-contained apartments
Like the main cities, Queenstown has realized the preference for luxury, fully self-contained and serviced apartments. Just 3 of the recommended examples are:
LL-AL Glebe Luxury Apartments, *corner Stanley and Beetham Sts, T03-4410310, stay@theglebe.co.nz* New and central.
LL-AL Point Luxury Apartments, *239 Frankton Rd, T03-4411899, www.thepoint.net.nz*
L-AL Lakefront Apartments, *26 The Esplanade, T03-4418800, lakefront@xtra.co.nz* Long-established and waterside.

B&Bs
With about 80 B&Bs the choice is huge with most being in the upper to luxury range. The VIC has full listings.
LL Matakauri Lodge, *Farrycroft Row (off the Glenorchy Rd), T03-4411008,*

www.matakauri.co.nz Stunning and deservedly popular, it is a magnificent place set in private bush 5 km west of Queenstown, with uninterrupted views across Lake Wakatipu. Accommodation is in modern villa-style, fully self-contained suites. The spacious lodge offers a library and four fireplaces, perfect for that après-ski.

LL **Punatapu**, *1113 Rapid Gate (7 km out on the Glenorchy Rd), T03-4426624, www.punatapu.co.nz* An equally sumptuous place with an individually styled 'hamlet' of suites around a central courtyard. Again the views are stunning and there is a swimming pool, spa, sauna and the works!

LL **Pear Tree Cottage**, *51 Mountain View Rd (at the other end of town), T03-4429340, www.peartree.co.nz* Enchanting place at the base of the Coronet Peak ski field. A quiet, lovingly restored 1870s cottage, tastefully appointed with 2 bedrooms. In summer flowers abound.

LL **The Loose Box**, *a little further out, overlooking Lake Hayes near Arrowtown, T03-4421802, www.theloosebox.com* New and elegant luxury retreat, very well-appointed, has all mod cons and is full of beautiful antiques.

LL **Remarkables Lodge**, *south along SH6, T03-4422720, www.remarkables@xtra.co.nz* A well-established luxury lodge with a fine reputation. It offers modern facilities and great cuisine and is expensive but worth it.

LL-L **Dairy Guesthouse**, *10 Isle St, T03-4425164, www.thedairy@xtra.co.nz* Central choice with 10 cosy ensuites in period-style house restored and modelled on a 1920s dairy. Nicely appointed with antiques, Asian textiles and Persian rugs.

L **Stone House Inn**, *47 Hallenstein St, T03-4429812, www.stonehouse.co.nz* Built in 1874 from local stone it is full of character and offers nicely appointed en suites, an open fire, jacuzzi and a nice view righrt across the town.

A **Queenstown House B&B**, *69 Hallenstein St, T03-4429043, queenstown.house@xtra.co.nz* Offers comfortable en suites, good views and a memorable breakfast.

A **Chalet Queenstown** *nearby on Dublin St, T03-4427117.* A small Swiss chalet-style B&B-come-hotel which is well-positioned and good value.

C-D **Scallywags**, *27A Lomond St, T03-4427083.* Budget B&B half way between a B&B and backpackers and is good-value, friendly, slow-paced and quiet. Dorms, twins and doubles.

Motels

There are over 70 to choose from, so shop around. The VIC has full listings. Prices are generally more expensive than elsewhere, especially in mid-summer, so do not necessarily expect the value for money that you are used to.

AL-A **Alpine Village Motor Inn**, *633 Frankton Rd (on the way into town), T03-4427795, alpinevillage@xtra.co.nz* A large place best noted for the views of The Remarkables from the rooms or chalets. In-house restaurant.

A-B **Goldfields**, *57 Frankton Rd, T03-4427211, goldfieldsmotel@xtra.co.nz* A pleasant, good value option.

AL **Hurleys**, *T03-4425999, F4425998, www.hurleys.co.nz* Has tasteful fully self-contained studios supported with great facilities, centrally located.

AL **Blue Peaks Lodge**, *corner Stanley and Sydney St, T03-4429224, www.bluepeaks.co.nz* Offers apartments as well as standard units and is also recommended.

A **Alpine Sun Motel**, *18 Hallenstein St, T03-4428482, alpine.sun@xtra.co.nz* Basic but comfortable and well positioned. Elsewhere, on the waterfront, offering superb views (which you pay for), are:

AL **Waterfront**, *109 Beach Rd, T03-4425123, www.thewaterfront.co.nz;*

AL **Lodges**, *8 Lake Esplanade, T03-4427552, www.thelodges.co.nz;*

AL **Lakeside Motel**, *T03-4428976, medward@es.co.nz*

B-D **Queenstown Lodge**, *Sainsbury Rd (a little further out at the west end of town), Fernhill, T03-4427107, www.qlodge.co.nz* Friendly ski-lodge style place. It is quiet, has off-street parking, a pizza restaurant, spa, sauna and excellent views.

Backpacker hostels

As you can imagine Queenstown is not short of backpacker hostels and with 20 establishments both old and new, staid or funky, there is plenty to choose from. This is not the complete listing, just those that we recommend or that stand out. In summer you should book at least 3 days in advance.

C-D **Queenstown YHA**, *80 Lake Esplanade (at the western end of town), T03-4428413, yhaqutn@yha.org.nz* Deservedly popular and with a wide range new of comfortable shared, twin and double rooms and modern facilities. Internet.

C-D **Bumbles Backpackers**, *2 Brunswick St, T03-4426298*. Well-established, spotlessly clean and efficient. Has a nice range of well-heated dorms, singles, twins and doubles, all with modern facilities and good views. Storage, drying rooms and internet.

B-D **Thomas's Hotel and Backpackers** *Corner of Beach and Rees St, T03-4427180*. In an ideal position, with comfortable dorms and a wide range of doubles, some very good value with TV and phones and a grand view. The shared backpacker facilities are good, there is an in-house café and then of course there is Thomas the cat.

C-D **Southern Laughter**, *4 Isle St (towards the Gondola, but still well positioned for town), T03-4418828*. Small, but well established, has a nice atmosphere and facilities. The Larsson cartoon theme will keep you chuckling on rainy days.

C-D **Hippo Lodge**, *4 Anderson Heights, T03-4425785, hippolodge@xtra.co.nz* A superb place with the best backpackers' view in town. It is modern, friendly, clean and well equipped, with dorms, twins and doubles, making it worth every step of the climb to get there. Parking can be a problem.

Motorcamps and campsites

A-D **Creeksyde Campervan Park**, *54 Robins Rd, T03-4429447, creeksyde@camp.co.nz* The most centrally located and has modern motel units, flats, cabins, lodge rooms and good facilities including spa. It gets busy in summer, so pre-book.

C-D **Queenstown Motor Park**, *Man St, T03-4427252, info@motorpark.co.nz* Huge and efficient with cabins both old and new, powered/tent sites and a shop nearby. Also good for information and activity bookings.

C-D **Kawarau Falls Holiday Park**, *about 6 km east and south on SH6, T03-4423510, kaw.falls@xtra.co.nz* Quieter and beautifully positioned, set right next to the crystal clear river mouth from Lake Wakatipu. It is an ideal place to escape the stresses of town. It also has a Backpacker Lodge, with 3 grades of cabins, some self-contained. The shared facilities are fine.

🍴 Eating

There are over 100 eateries in Queenstown with a choice and quality to compete with any of the larger cities in New Zealand. There are Chinese, Mexican, Indian, Korean, Lebanese and Italian restaurants alongside the traditional New Zealand fare with many doubling as bars and nightspots. Again, although prices can be slightly elevated, there are restaurants to suit all budgets as well as 2 unique eating options in the form of the Gondola restaurant and the TSS Earnslaw (see Sights above).

$$$ **Skyline Restaurant,** *at the Skyline Gondola Complex, Brecon St, T03-4410101. Daily, lunch buffet 1200-1400, dinner from 1800.* Offers a 6-course 'Taste of New Zealand' buffet which includes roast meats, seafood, local produce and salads followed by dessert and cheeseboard. The views, obviously, are exceptional, even at night.

$$$ **The Boardwalk,** *1st Floor, Steamer Wharf, T03-4425630. Daily from 1200.* Well known for its superb seafood and great views. They are still dining out on the fact that it was Bill Clinton's choice when he visited in 1999.

$$$ **Gantley's**, *Arthur's Point Rd, T03-4428999, www.gantleys.co.nz Daily from 1830.* A very romantic affair set in an historic stone building 7 km out of town towards Arrowtown. Award-winning, the equal of the others above and its wine list, like its cuisine, is superb.

$$$-$$ **Tatler**, *at the west end of the Mall, T03-4428372.* Modern, stylish and popular not only for traditional NZ fare including salmon, venison and South island oysters. There is also some fine and regular live jazz orchestrated by the owner who is herself a jazz vocalist.

$$ **Brazz On the Green**, *1 Athol St, T03-4424444. Daily from 1100.* One of the newest in town, modern and classy, and given its open fires, especially popular with the après-ski crowd in winter. Traditional

NZ/Euro menu and a fine place to watch the world go by.

$$ **McNeill's Cottage Brewery**, *14 Church St, T03-4429688. Daily from 1130.* A nice mix of heritage and atmosphere, it's another atmospheric award-winner with a good selection of gourmet pizzas, open fire outside, live bands at the weekend and of course some fine home brewed ales.

$$ **Bathhouse**, *T03-4425625. Daily from 1000.* Perched on the edge of the beach, next to Queenstown Gardens, is this very romantic place. With an imaginative menu, it is a lovely spot for both lunch and dinner.

$$ **HMS Britannia** *in The Mall, T03-4429600.* Good if you have kids or simply enjoy good seafood. It is a wee bit on the expensive side but the portions are huge and the walls are something of a museum exhibit.

$$ **The Cow**, *Cow Lane, T03-4428588.* Also popular, though more for its exterior aesthetics and atmosphere. Set in a former stone milking shed it is a little cramped but full of character. Pizza and pasta is the speciality.

$$ **Pasta Pasta Cucina**, *6 Brecon St, T03-4426762. Daily from 1200.* Another popular pizza place.

$$ **Little India**, *11 Shotover St, T03-4425335,* Good Indian food: either sit-in or takeaway.

$$ **Minami Jujisei**, *45 Beach St, T03-4429854.* Decent Japanese choice.

$$ **Pog Mahone's**, *14 Rees St, T03-4425382;*
$$ **Loaded Hog**, *Steamer Wharf, T03-4412969;*
$$ **Pig and Whistle**, *19 Camp St. All open daily from about 1100.* All are great for pub food, atmosphere and beer. The latter is a very pleasant al fresco spot.

$ **Habebes**, *Wakatipu Arcade, Rees St, T03-4429861. Daily 1100-1800.* Very popular day café for cheap vegetarian and Middle Eastern takeaways.

$ **Giuseppes**, *Fernhill Rd (west of town).* Considered the best place in town for a good value pizza, but you need car to get there.

$ **O'Connell's Food Hall**, *Camp St. Daily from 0800.* The usual cheap buffet lunch outlets.

$ **Ferg's Burgers**, *Cow Lane.* The late night munchy option.

Supermarkets **The Alpine Food Centre**, *Upper Shotover St. Mon-Sat 0800-2000, Sun 0900-2000.* Handy for groceries and tramping food supplies. **First Choice**, *1 km out along Gorge Rd (Skippers and Coronet Peak Rd), T03-4411252. Mon-Sun 0800-2100.* The largest and most convenient. **New World**, *Franktown (6 km), T03-4423045.* This is the cheapest.

Cafés

Naff Caff, *1/66 Shotover St, T03-4428211. Daily from 0730.* One of Queenstown's best and offers great light snacks, coffee and a value breakfast.

Leonardo's, *further up towards town next to the VIC, T03-4428542.* It's small but in a perfect position for that essential caffeine hit after arriving back from all the activities based at the 'The Station'.

Joe's Garage, *Camp St.* Also noted for its great coffee.

Vudu Café, *Beach St, T03-4425357.* Also has a loyal local following and is good for breakfast too.

Entertainment

For something different try the **Maori Feast and Concert**, see Activities below.

Pubs and bars
Queenstown is very much a party town, and at **New Year** particularly goes off like a firecracker. It can all be a lot of fun, but at its busiest don't go out looking for refined culture and conversation. With so much adrenaline and testosterone flying around it doesn't go far beyond the standard yelps about the 'awesome' bungee jumping, or the double-flip-half-hernia on the snowboard, maaaan. The well-established favourites like the **Loaded Hog**, Irish **Pog Mahone's**, British-style **Pig and Whistle** and quaint **McNeill's Brewery** (all above), are all well known for a good beer and atmosphere. Slightly more upmarket and more popular with the upwardly mobile (with mobiles) is the **Cigar Bar** *in the Steamer Wharf*,
The Tatler, *The Mall*, and the hard to find **Bunker**, *Cow Lane*.
Red Rock, *48 Camp St, T03-4426850*, is a well-known place to 'acquaint oneself with the opposite sex' as is **The Lone Star**, *Brecon St*, and **Rattlesnake** (upstairs). They all

provide regular live music and DJs beats and are the favoured haunts of the younger set.

Clubs
As far as late-night drinking and dancing goes, try **Chico's**, *at the bottom of The Mall (open until 0230)*, or **The Tardis** and **The Bunker**, *Cow Lane*. **The Edge**, *on the corner of Camp and Memorial Sts, open from 2200 every night*, is a new nightclub. **Triple M**, *54 Shotover St*, and **The World**, *Shotover St*, are the most commercial, chat-up (or throw-up) venues with regular happy hours. *Both stay open until about 0230.*

Casinos
Queenstown Wharf Casino, *Steamer Wharf, T03-4411495. 1100-0300.*
Sky Alpine Casino, *Beach St, T03-4410400.*

Cinema
Embassy Cinema, *The Mall, T03-4429990.*

⊛ Festivals and events

Lindauer Queenstown Winter Festival www.winterfestival.co.nz (*Jun/Jul*) Queenstown's most famous and popular event (9 days), which of course has its focus on skiing, but also involves many other forms of entertainment, from live concerts, arts and fashion events, to madcap races. Later in the month is the internationally recognized **K2 Snowboard Challenge** (*Jul*). **Spring Carnival** (*mid-Sep*) More extreme and zany ski competitions at the Remarkables Ski Area. **Queenstown Jazz Festival** (*Labour weekend in Oct*) Now in its 15th successful year. **Christmas** and particularly **New Year** see the town a-buzz with Kiwis and foreigners alike. **Glenorchy Races** (*1st Sat in Jan*) A local affair generally regarded as reflecting Glenorchy's true colours as a wild west frontier town. **Central Otago Wine Festival** (*Feb*) Gourmands gather in the town's gardens to sample the delicacies produced by 15 local vineyards. **Millbrook Outdoor Concert** (*Feb*) Last year featured the Little River Band. Tickets must be booked well in advance and cost about $60. **Arrowtown Autumn Festival** (*late Mar*) and the **Ben Lomond Assault** (*late Mar*) Colourful and increasingly popular and exhausting race to the town's famous 1747 m lookout.

More strain on 2 legs. **Silverstone Race to the Sky** (*mid-Apr*) Four-wheel races in the Cardrona Valley, the highlight of which is a car race to the summit to see who is 'king of the mountain'.

Throughout the year there are many multisports events from triathlons to mountain traverses, peak to peaks, jet boat races, marathons and even horse cavalcades. For more details visit www.queenstown-nz.co.nz

▲ Activities *See also p627*

Ballooning
Sunrise Balloons, *T03-4420781, www.ballooningnz.com* Offers a 3-hr flight with Champagne breakfast for $295, child $195. It is expensive, but given the scenery it is a great venue (0530 summer/0830 winter).

Bungee jumping
The first commercial bungee jump in the world was created at **Kawarau Bridge**, about 12 km east of Queenstown, by A J Hackett and associates in 1988. Although perhaps the most famous spot and certainly the most accessible, at 43 m it is now dwarfed by most of the others. Since 1988 Hackett has created 3 other sites, the 71-m **Skippers Canyon Bridge**, the 47-m urban '**Ledge**' bungee beside the Skyline complex above Queenstown; the 102-m **Pipeline Bungee** over the Shotover River, again in Skippers Canyon; and, perhaps the mightiest and certainly the best, the awesome and the highest (ground based) 134-m **Nevis Highwire**. Jump prices range from $125 for the Ledge to $175 for the Nevis. This includes a 'T' shirt, but videos are usually extra. There are a number of **combos** on offer like Hackett's 'Bungee Thrillogy' from $289, which includes the Nevis, Kawarau and Ledge bungee sites. A second (within 24 hrs) jump at most sites is half price.
A J Hackett, *at 'The Station', corner of Shotover and Camp sts, T03-4424007, www.AJHackett.com*
Not surprisingly there is also a **Bungy Rocket**, *2 km up the Coronet Peak Rd, T03-4429894*. If you are not already acquainted the bungee rocket is like a cross

between a bungy and a yo-yo with you being strapped to a chair and catapulted into the air at an alarming speed. It is entertaining of course but in Queenstown perhaps your money would be better spent doing the 'real' thing. It costs $65 with the kind option of a second ride and chance to see your breakfast again for about half price.

Canyoning

Twelve-Mile Delta *T0800-222696, www.xiimile.co.nz* Although Wanaka is famed for its canyoning activities, this outfit offers both daytime and 'full moon' trips that involve abseiling as well as canyoning, from $115, child $95.

Routeburn Canyoning *T0800-222696, www.gycanyoning.co.nz* Offers a similarly attractive package that involves a part walk and canyoning session on the Routeburn Track near Glenorchy. As well as the great 30-min walk and scenery along the initial stage of the track the trip involves abseiling, scrambling, rappelling and plunging your way down a mountain river. Full day from $225. Note, this canyoning lark is not one for the agrophobic or the 'damn it darling, my shoes are wet'.

Children's activities

If you have kids and want to do the family thing, or conversely leave them in somebody else's capable hands, then the 2 companies to contact are:

Family Adventures, *T03-4425112*, and **Activekids**, *T03-4421003, activekids@xtra.co.nz* Family Adventures offer full- or half-day 'sedate' rafting trips for families from $150, child $100, while Activekids offers qualified care and day trips to Arrowtown and around Queenstown for those 7 years and up.

Climbing, abseiling and mountaineering

The possibilities are endless, and the Mount Aspiring National Park provides world-class venues. Although most of the operators are based in Wanaka.

Queenstown Mountain Guiding, *corner of Shotover and Rees sts, T03-4413400, www.mountainguiding.co.nz* Offers a wide variety of trips from glacier walks and Heli-hikes to expeditions and instruction

courses. They also guide on Mount Aspiring, Mount Cook and Mount Tasman. Prices range from about $100 for a full-day trip to about $650 for a 3-day mountain climb.

Queenstown Events Centre, *Joe O'Connell Drive, Frankton, T03-4423664*. Has a 12-m high **climbing wall**. $10, child $5. Mon-Fri 0900-2100, Sat and Sun 0900-1700. There are also instructor supervised nights on Tue and Thu.

Cruising

It won't take you long to spot the delightful *TSS Earnslaw* (TSS incidentally stands for Two Screw Steamer), plying the waters of Lake Wakatipu from the Steamer Wharf in Queenstown Bay. The TSS Earnslaw, named after the highest peak in the region Mount Earnslaw (2819 m), was launched at the most southerly end of **Lake Wakatipu**, Kingston, in 1912 and burns one-ton of coal an hour. Despite her propensity to belch half of New Zealand's 'Kyoto nasty smoke quota' into the air she is a lovely sight indeed and there are a number of cruising options available. A standard 1-hr 35-min cruise heads west across the lake to its southern edge to the **Walter Peak Station**. They depart from the Steamer Wharf Oct-Apr every 2 hrs from 1000-2000 (reduced winter schedule), from $35, child $15. A 3 ½ hr cruise, plus a farm tour of the Walter Peak Station which is designed to give an insight into typical Kiwi farming life (and to access lots of affectionate animals), costs $53, child $15. With a BBQ it is $15 extra. A 4-hr evening dinner cruise costs $92, child $46. There are also 40-min horse trekking and wagon rides available at Walter Peak.

Real Journeys, *beside the Steamer Wharf, are the owner-operators and take bookings, T0800-656503, www.fiordlandtravel.co.nz* There are also numerous cruise/bus and cruise/fly options on Milford and Doubtful Sounds that operate out of Queenstown (see Milford and Doubtful Sound, pages 673 and 677).

Lion Cruises, *78 Lower Shotover Rd, T03-4423499*. Offer 1½-hr lake cruises aboard the lovingly restored 1908 Lion motor launch, for around $50.

Fishing

The region provides some excellent trout and salmon fishing, and there are numerous guides offering simple half-day to full-day Heli-fishing trips.

Stu Dever, *T03-4426371.*

Queenstown Fishing Guides, *T03-4425363, www.wakatipu.co.nz*

Over the Top Helicopters, *T03-4422233, www.flynz.co.nz*

Glenorchy Cruising, see Glenorchy, page 641. Prices vary from around $120 per hr to between $350 and $650 for the full day. Heli trips range from half-day $660 to full-day $2730, both for two. A fishing licence costs $16 per day.

Flightseeing

There are numerous options available and you are advised to shop around. If you do not have time to reach **Milford Sound** by road then a scenic flight is highly recommended. Note that there are numerous fly, fly/cruise/fly and bus/cruise/fly options on offer to Milford.

Fixed-wing Operators offering flights to Milford and Fiordland include:

Air Fiordland, *T03-4423404, www.airfiordland.com*

Queenstown Air, *T03-4422244, www.queenstownair.co. Nz*

Air Milford, *T03-4422351, www.airmilford.co.nz*

Milford Sound Scenic Flights, *T03-4423065, www.milfordflights.co.nz*

Air Milford, *T03-4422351, www.airmilford.co.nz*

Air Wakatipu, *T03-4423148, www.flying.co.nz*

Prices range from a 20-min local flight costing from $129 to the full 4-hr Milford Sound and Mount Cook experience, costing from $329.

A recent addition to the many local flightseeing options is the **Lord of the Rings 'Trilogy Trail'** offered by the personable owners and staff of **Glenorchy Air**, *Queenstown Airport, T03-4422207, www.glenorchy.net.nz / www.trilogytrail.com* This down-to-earth company have been around for many years and were regularly utilized by the Rings cast and crew during extensive filming in the region. The 2-hr Trilogy trip takes in the

mountains and valleys of Skippers Canyon and the Rees-Dart, with a landing near Paradise (quite literally), and then a journey south to Mavora Lakes with plenty of informative commentary and behind-the-scenes stories as you go. The aircraft are perhaps a little cramped, but regardless, one cannot fail to be awestruck, even if such fictional location names as Isengard, Lothlorien, Amon Hen and Fanghorn Forest mean very little! Even without the complex world of Tolkien to fuel your imagination this has to be one of the most spectacular and affordable scenic flight experiences in the world. From $260, child $130. There is also an extended 5-hr Trilogy Trail offered, taking in other locations including the spectacular Rangitata Valley-Mt Sunday ('Edoras') from $615 and a 3hr 30min road trip only to local filming sites from $115.

Helicopter flights **Glacier Southern Lakes**, *T03-4423016, www.heli-flights.co.nz*
The Helicopter Line, *T03-4423034, www.helicopter.co.nz*
Over The Top Helicopters, *T03-44232233 / T0800-123-359, www.flynz.co.nz*
Heliworks, *T03-4414011, www.heliworks.co.nz*

Prices range from a 25-min local flight across **The Remarkables** from $132, to the full 'Milford Extravaganza' from around $900. Over the Top provide a great range of Milford, Queenstown, Heli-fishing and Heli-skiing options. For more information on flightseeing trips to Milford Sound and Fiordland see Milford p669.

Actionflite, *T0800-360264, www.actionflite.co.nz* If you fancy a flight with a difference try the 3-hr aerobatics 'Pitts Special'. Labelled as the **'Ferrari of the skies'**, it reaches speeds of up to 300 kph with 3G turns. Fantastic. Trips cost from $235 for 15 min.

Fly-by-Wire

The Fly-by-Wire, *corner of Shotover and Rees St, T03-4422116, T0800-359299, www.flybywire.co.nz* The sister operation to the original experience, created in Paekakariki, Wellington Region, from $145 (see Wellington, 421).

Millbrook Resort, *Malaghan's Road, Arrowtown, T03-4417010, proshop@millbrook.co.nz* One of the best courses in New Zealand. It was designed by former Kiwi ace Bob Charles and opened in 1993. It is renowned for its long fairways, water hazards and, of course, its views. Green fees from $110.

Arrowtown itself also has a nice course at *Centennial Avenue, T03-4421719.* From $40.

Frisbee Golf Course, Queenstown Gardens. Of course Queenstown would have one of these, but don't be surprised if a dog disappears with your frisbee. Contact **Outside Sports**, *Camp St, T03-4428883, $2.* They also sell frisbees, but no dog treats.

Horse trekking

Moonlight Stables, *15 mins from Queenstown near Lake Hayes, T03-4421229.* A 1½-hr ride costs from $60, child $35. Full day and fishing trips also available.

Shotover Stables, *T03-4429708.* Offer 1 hr 45-min or full day treks from $60/$35. Horse and carriage rides are available in town from $20. Departs Steamer Wharf at 1200-1600 and from 1800 to late (seasonal).

For other operators see Glenorchy, p 644.

Jetboating

Such is the marketing, somehow you seem familiar with the Shotover Jet before you even arrive in Queenstown. That indelible blurred image of a red boat full of smiley faces and Captain cool in shades at the wheel. Jet boating is one of the big four activities in Queenstown and, other than the thrills of the precipitous **Shotover Gorge**, there are also other independent operations on the **Kawarau** and the superb aesthetics of the **Dart River**.

Shotover Jet, *The Station, Shotover St, T03-4428570, T0800-SHOTOVER (7468-6837), www.shotoverjet.com* The originals, having been in existence for over 30 years, offer the almost 'must-do' operation on the Shotover River – the only folks permitted to do so on the lower reaches. An efficient, safe and thrilling 30-min, 70-kmph 'blat' down the river will see you too with a smiley face, interrupted only intermittently with one of shock as you are given the impression of coming perilously close to rock walls and

jagged logs. The highlights of all the trips are the superb 360 degree turns that always soak some poor soul in the boat. Shotover Jet picks up from town several times a day for the 15-min ride to the riverside. From $85, child $45.

Kawarau Jet, *Marine Pde (lakeside), T03-4426142, www.kjet.co.nz*

Twin River Jet, *T03-4423257, www.twinriversjet.co.nz* Both zoom out across Queenstown Bay and down the Kawarau and up the lower reaches of the Shotover. 1 hr from $75, child $40.

Dart River Safaris (recommended) or **Dart Wilderness Adventures** in Glenorchy (see Glenorchy, p 641). One of the best scenic jet boating trips in the world. 3-6 hrs from $145, child $72.50.

Kayaking

Some superb day to multi-day sea kayaking is offered on Milford and Doubtful Sounds (see p 671 and 676). Locally kayaks can usually be hired on the waterfront. For the very enjoyable ('blow-up carrot') **Funyak trips** on the Dart River see p 644; full-day costs from $215.

Mountain biking

There are many options, from the manic Heli-bike to the low level mundane.

Adventure Biking, *T03-4429708, boxer@paradise.co.nz* Offer a 3-hr easy to moderate trip from Queenstown that takes you from Moke Lake to Seffer Town – an area steeped in gold mining history, costing from $69.

Gravity Action, *T03-4411021, www.gravityaction.com* Offer half-day rides on the famous **Skippers Pack Track,** departing Queenstown at 0830 and 1230, from $79, child $59. Heli and raft combos are also available.

Vertigo Heli Adventures, *14 Shotover St, T03-4428378.* Offer 3 downhill heli/bike combo adventures on the Gondola Track, Deer Park Heights and the Remarkables, from 2-3 hrs, $89-$229. For bike rentals see Directory below.

Off-Road, rallying, trial-bike and snowmobile adventures

New Zealand Nomad Safaris, *T03-4426699, T0800-688222 www.nomadsafaris.co.nz* Offer

2 excellent 4-hr 4x4 tours entitled 'Safari of the Rings' that take in the main regional film locations for the **Lord of the Rings trilogy**. The Wakatipu Tour concentrates on local sites with plenty of diversity from the stunning vistas over Deer Park Heights ('used as the dramatic backdrop to the scene depicting the escaping refugees of Rohan'); Kawarau River ('River Anduin and the Pillar of the Kings'), Arrow River (Ford of Bruinen) and the dramatic road to Skippers Canyon (Ford of Bruinen). Departs 0830 and 1300, prices from $120.

The longer road trip to Glenorchy takes in the stunning scenery around Glenorchy and the Dart River Valley, which was used as the backdrop to Isengard and Lothlorien. Departs 0815 and 1330, from $120 Both tours in combination cost $240. Both tours are very relaxed with entertaining knowledgeable guides some of whom were extras during filming.

Other **non-LOTR orientated trips** are of course also available touring the Skippers Canyon and remote Macetown goldfields. They also stop for a bit of gold panning. From $85, child $50.

Goldseekers, *T03-4425949*. Offer traditional 4-hr tours locally with gold panning from $88, child $50.

Off Road Adventures, *61A Shotover St, T03-4427858, www.offroad.co.nz* Offer 4WD tours where you drive and they guide. 1-hr from $100, half day from $250 Kids are welcome. They also hire out trail bikes and can organize local tours from $229.

Monster Mountain Rally, *Cardrona (Hwy 89) near Wanaka, T0800-872559, www.mmrally.co.nz* Can satisfy many a budding Colin MacRae with an adrenaline pumping trip strapped in the passenger seat of a performance rally car. There is plenty of fast-paced but safe action on gravel roads and through water and even a little bit of the airborne. Two hrs from $135 ($150 includes transport from Queenstown, heli transport also available).

Nevis Snowmobile Adventures, *T03-4424250, www.snowmobilenz.co.nz* Self-drive or guided Heli/snowmobile adventures available in winter. Expensive but great fun (mid-Jun-Oct) 3 hrs costing from $420.

When you arrive in Queenstown it won't be long before you see the colourful chutes of the tandem paragliders descending gracefully down into the town from Bob's Peak and the Skyline Complex. It's a wonderful way to see the views, but all a bit 'Queenstown' when your instructor answers his mobile phone mid-flight!

Tandem Paragliders, *T03-4418581, T0800-759688, www.queenstown-tandem-paragliding.co.nz* From $170. If the flight has you hooked you might then like to have lessons or try at another venue with the **Elevation Paragliding School**, *T0800-359-444*, or **Flight Park**, *Franktown, T0800-467-325, www.tandemparagliding.com* 2 hrs from around $165.

Queenstown Paraflights *NZ Main Pier, T03-4428507*. If you would rather be alone and feel safer over water, then you might like to try paraflying across the lake. 15 mins from $75, child $70.

Antigravity, *T03-4418898, T0800-4264450, www.antigravity.co.nz* For 10-20-min tandem-hang-gliding trips with stunning views from the Coronet Peak skifields across to the Remarkables. From $175.

Sky Trek, *T03-4426311, skytrek@queenstown.co.nz* Similar trips cost from $165.

Rafting

There are a glut of rafting operators in Queenstown all trying to lure you with their ineluctable inflatables.

Queenstown Rafting, *T03-4429792, www.rafting.co.nz* Ply the rapids of the Shotover, Kawarau and Landsborough with such enchanting highlights as 'The Toilet' and 'The Sharks Fin'. Depart Queenstown 0830 and 1315, 1-5 hrs, $129. Activity Combos also available.

Extreme Green Rafting, *T03-4428517, www.nzraft.com* The oldest company also rafts the Shotover or Kawarau. Departures 0815 and 1245. 1-5 hrs, from $129 (heli-raft $190).

Challenge Rafting, *T03-4427318, www.raft.co.nz* Offer half-day or raft combo trips, again on the Shotover and Kawarau from $129. Minimum age for rafting is 13 .

Pioneer Rafting, *Wanaka (see p 645)*. A more eco-orientated trip.

Family Adventures, *see Children's activities, above*.

River sledging and surfing

River surfing is basically the cunningly simple concept of replacing a raft with your own personal bodyboard. It is great fun and provides a far more intimate experience with the water. There are two companies: **Mad Dog**, *T03-4427797*, and **Serious Fun**, *T03-4425262, www.riversurfing.com* River sledging basically involves more drifting as opposed to surfing and provides more buoyancy.

Frogz Have More Fun, *Wanaka, see p 645, T03-4439130, www.frogz.co.nz* Pick up from Queenstown. All trips are about 4 hrs (2 hrs on the water) and cost from $129 ($119 for 1 hr 30 min on the water).

Skiing

Queenstown is as much a winter ski resort as it is a summer madhouse. From June to September the 2 local ski fields of **Coronet Peak** and **The Remarkables** spring into action. Coronet Peak (1649 m) is the larger of the 2 and the more accessible (25 mins via SH6 west and Lower Shotover Rd). It also has a longer season, night skiing (Fri and Sat 1600-2200), and a brasserie, bar, café and crèche. Slopes are suitable for beginners and advanced skiers, with intermediate skiers being the best catered for. *Day lift pass costs $75, child $37, T03-4424620, www.nzski.com* The Remarkables ski field is higher (1935 m) and accessed from SH6, south of Frankton (45 mins). The road is steep and often requires chains. Shuttle buses from Queenstown are recommended. Being the highest in the region, the snow conditions are often superior, and then, of course, there are the stunning **views**. Slopes cater for all levels of skier and snowboarder as well as cross-country. *A day lift pass costs $72, child $35, T03-4424615, www.nzski.com* **NZSuperpass**, 2-day ($138, child $69) to 10-day ($610, child $305) gives full access to both ski fields and also Mount Hutt in Canterbury. 1-day ski/boots/poles rental $37, child $26. 1-day snowboard and boots $50, child $39. Group Lessons 1 hr 50 min from $45, child $32; personal from $70 per hr. Also

within range of Queenstown are the **Cardrona** (45 km), *T03-4437341*, and **Treble Cone**, *T03-4437443* (95 km). The standard group fares (4) to Coronet are around $35, Remarkables $80 and Cardrona $150 1-way. For detailed information on both ski fields get your hands on the *Queenstown Winter Resort Guide* from the VIC, or visit the website www.nzski.com or www.snow.co.nz Finally, for **snow reports**, T0900-99766 or websites above ($0.99/min). For ski equipment hire see Directory below. For transportation see Getting around above.

Tandem skydiving

Queenstown offers one of the most scenic skydiving venues on earth, for the 'bungee without the bounce' – or the elastic rope for that matter.

Nzone *35 Shotover St, T03-4425867, www.nzone.biz* The new rather flash set up in town these days offers jumps from 9-15,000 ft from $245. Allow 3 hrs.

Tours

Vineyard, garden and general sightseeing tours offer a more sedate diversion from the mainstream adrenaline activities.

Wine Time, *T0508-946384*. Full- or half-day lunch and dinner tours.

Central Otago Wine Tours, *T03-4426622, www.winetoursnz.com* Take you to local vineyards and further afield to the Cromwell vineyards. Half- to full day from $119.

Queenstown Wine Trail, *T03-4423799, www.queenstownwinetrail.co.nz* Visits all the main **Kawarau Valley** vineyards, 4 hrs from $75, child $35.

Kawarau Jet, *T03-4426142*. Visit the vineyards via jet boat. 4 hrs from $150.

Queenstown Garden Tours, *T03-4423799*. A good 4 hrs local garden tour from $75.

Tramping

Queenstown is a principal departure point for the **Routeburn**, **Greenstone-Caples** and **Rees-Dart Tracks**. For detailed information, hut and transportation bookings visit the Information and Track Centre (see Information above).

Ultimate Hikes (*Encounter Guided Day Walks*). Guided walks on the Routeburn, Greenstone and Milford tracks from 1-6 days. They offer a wide range of 10 hr day 'encounter' or multi-day options both locally on the Routeburn or further afield on the Milford or Mt Cook from $125, child $75. Another attractive local option is the **Ben Lomond trek** (see below).

Cecil Peak Adventure Experience (Queenstown Heli Hikes), *T0800-443-544, www.helihikes.co.nz* Combines a hike with a scenic helicopter flight and boat trip across lake Wakatipu that offers some fantastic views back across to Queenstown, not to mention a lovely picnic beside the rather dubiously named 'Fanny Falls'. 5 hrs, from $279.

Guided Nature Walks, *T03-4427126, www.nzwalks.com;* and

Arrowtown Lodge, *T03-4421101*, also offer a wide range of professionally guided trips from half- and full- to multi-day from $85.

Walking

For guided walks see above. In the town itself you can learn something of its interesting past on the 1-hr historical perambulation followed by a welcome libation in McNeill's Cottage Brewery with **Quirky Queenstown Historical Walking Tours**, *T021-152-0674*. Trips depart from the west end of the Mall at 1130, 1330 and 1530. The immediate Queenstown area offers many excellent walks from 1 hr to half a day. The DoC Visitor Centre on Shotover Street displays and can advise on the many local alternatives. If you have half a day, reliable wheels and walking boots, the walk to the lookout above the **Remarkables ski field** is highly recommended.

Other recommended walks

Queenstown Hill Accessed from York Street (look for DoC sign), this is a 2-3-hr moderate walk up to a scenic lookout above the town. The millennium gate on the way up is a nice and unusual piece of craftsmanship.

Ben Lomond (1747 m) dominates the scene above Bob's Peak and the Gondola and provides stunning views of the town and Lake Wakatipu. The full walk can be negotiated through forest from Lomond Street (from the Esplanade), but the best bet is to take the Gondola and join the track from there, 6-8 hrs return. Details available from DoC.

Ben Lomond Guided Walks, *T03-4429434, www.benlomond.co.nz* A new and reputable outfit that offers a 2-day fully guided walk to Ben Lomond with the added attraction of an exhilarating 4WD trip through Skippers Canyon, accommodation in a high country station lodge and all meals from $495, child $395. Recommended.

Twelve-Mile Delta to Bob's Cove, an easy 2-hr jaunt on the shores of Lake Wakatipu, accessed from the main Glenorchy Road (12 km).

Mount Crichton Scenic Reserve inland and just a bit further along the road also offers good options. Again DoC can provide details and leaflets.

More activities

Amongst the multitude of activities available at the Skyline (Gondola) Complex above the town is the **Luge**, the rather tame cousin of the famous course in Rotorua. The gondola trip and 5 rides will cost $29, child $23 (0930-dusk). The new invention with our activity junkie Hackett, *T03-4424007*, is the **Ledge Sky-Swing**, which is the delightful concept of being strapped into a harness and dropped from a great height and at mighty speeds, making the average park swing look like utter tedium. From $85.

One of the few opportunities to enjoy a **Maori Concert and Feast** is available in Queenstown, *1 Memorial St, T03-4428878*. If you missed out in Rotorua this is your chance. The *hangi*-style feast (1 hr 30 min) begins after a traditional 'powhiri' (Maori welcome) at 1900 with a concert at 2030-2130 (1 hr). From $45.

Kingston Flyer, *T03-2488848, www.kingstonflyer.co.nz* Puffs along for 1 hr 15 mins on a 14-km track from Kingston, 47 km south of Queenstown from September to mid-May. Daily 1015 and 1345, morning pick-ups available from Queenstown. Ride only $25, child $10. **Clay-bird Shooting**, *T0800-273251*. 2 hrs from $125.

Also available: **water-skiing**, **skating**, **gold panning** (details from the VIC).

And if you can simply take no more action, try a soothing massage or beauty treatment with **Body Sanctum**, *12 Man St, T03-4429085*. From $45.

Small Planet Recycling Co, *17 Shotover St, T03-4426393.* For second-hand outdoor and ski equipment.

Outside Sports, *top of the Mall (open 0700-2200), T03-4428883, www.outdoorsports.co.nz* For new sports/outdoor/ski equipment.

Whitcoulls, *Beach St, T03-4429739.* The principal bookshop and stationer in town.

O Directory

Airlines Air NZ, *Queenstown Travel Centre, 41 Shotover St, T03-4411900.* **Banks** All the major banks are represented and ATMs are available in The Mall, Shotover St, Beach St, Rees St, Steamer Wharf and the O'Connell's Shopping Centre.

Bike hire Queenstown Bike Hire, *Lakefront Esplanade, T03-4426039;* Outside Sports, *corner of The Mall and Camp St, T03-4428883, from $50 a day (open 0800-2100);* Small Planet, *17 Shotover St, T03-4426393,* from $35 per day. **Car hire** Avis, *9 Duke St, T03-4427280;* Budget, *Chester Blding, corner of Shotover and Camp Sts, T03-4429274;* Hertz, *2 Church St, T03-4424106;* NZ Rent-A-Car, *corner of Shotover and Camp Sts, T03-4427465;* Pegasus, *The Mall, T03-4427167;* Queenstown Car Rentals, *26 Shotover St, T03-4429220;* Thrifty, *Queenstown Airport, T03-4428100.* **Currency exchange** There is a Travelex in the VIC and additional outlets at the BNZ, *Rees St (daily 1000-2000);* Thomas Cook, *corner of Camp St and The Mall;* ANZ Postbank, *Beach St.* Travelex, *at the airport, daily until 1900.*

Internet The cheapest is usually Budget Communications, *2nd Floor, O'Connell St Shopping Centre.* Others include: The E Café, *50 Shotover St,* which plays good music, and the biggest is Internet Outpost, *27 Shotover St. Most outlets are open in summer from 0900-2300.* **Laundry** Internet laundry, *1 Shotover St, T03-4418309. Daily 0800-2200.* Library *Corner of Shotover St and George Rd.* **Medical Services** Hospital, *Douglas St, Frankton, T03-4423053. No Accident and Emergency Department.* Doctor, *Athol Street Surgery, T03-4427566; Queenstown Medical Centre, Isle St, T03-4410500.* **Police** Non-emergency, *11 Camp St, T03-4427900.* Emergency, T111. **Post office** *Corner Camp and Ballarat Sts, T03-4427670. Mon-Fri 0830-2000, Sat 0930-2000, Sun 1000-1800. Post Restante.* **Ski and Snowboard hire** Outside Sports, *corner of The Mall and Camp St, T03-4428883. 0800-2100;* Brown's Ski Shop, *39 Shotover St, T03-4424003;* Extreme Green Ski and Snowboard Rental, *39 Camp St, T03-4428517, www.nzraft.co.nz* **Taxis** AA Taxis, *T03-4418222;* Alpine Taxi, *T0800-4426666;* Queenstown Taxis, *T03-4427788;* Prestige Tourist Services, *T03-4429803.* A Mercedes complete with interpreter. Ranks can be found at the top of The Mall and lower Shotover St.

Around Queenstown → *Phone code: 03*

Ins and outs

Getting there and around The Arrowtown **Double Decker Bus Tour** departs from the top of The Mall in Queenstown daily at 1000 and 1400, allowing 1 hr in Arrowtown and returning from outside the Museum. It visits Lake Hayes and the Kawarau Bungy Bridge on the way, T03-4426067, $34, child $15. The **Arrow Express** runs regularly between Queenstown and Arrowtown from outside McDonald's in Queenstown and the museum in Arrowtown, T03-4421900, $18, child $10 return (from 0945-1700). It is happy to take bikes and even the occasional gold pan. **Backpacker Express**, 2 Oban St, T03-4429939, info@glenorchyinfocentre.co.nz, offers a comprehensive transport system between Queenstown, Glenorchy and the major tramping track trailheads by road ($15 one-way) and a water-taxi. **Glenorchy Cruising**, T03-4429951, also provides water-taxi services to various points along the Dart-Rees Track.

building, To3-4421824, www.arrowtown.org.nz Daily 0900-1700. The free brochures
Welcome to Historic Arrowtown and *Historic Arrowtown* are both comprehensive guides
to the history and historic sites of the village and the surrounding area. **DoC VIC
(Glenorchy)**, ⓘ *at the end of the Main Rd, To3-4429937. Daily 0830-1630 (closed
weekends in winter).* Although providing all the relevant local walks and tramping
information/bookings, if your intentions are merely to pass through Glenorchy on your
way to one of the major tracks, you are advised to avail yourself of the information, and
secure hut bookings at the Queenstown offices. Likewise for accommodation and
activities, although the **Glenorchy Store** in the Holiday Park, 2 Oban St, can provide
some information, the Queenstown VIC is your best bet. For more general pre-visit
information on Glenorchy the website, www.Glenorchy.com, is also useful. For
information on the Routeburn and Greenstone and Caples Tracks see page 642.

Arrowtown → *Colour map 7, grid A4. Population: 1,700*

Arrowtown provides some respite from the stress and adrenaline highs of Queenstown.
Yet another former **gold mining** settlement, its pleasant tree-lined streets with their old
historic buildings lie nestled below the foothills of the Crown Range – an apt name
given their once rich reserves of gold. The origins of Arrowtown go back to 1862 when
prospector William Fox made the first rich strike in the Arrow River Valley – a find that
soon brought over 7,000 other hopefuls to the area. The first few weeks of mining
produced 90 kg alone. Although first called Fox's, once the settlement was firmly
established it was renamed Arrowtown after the river that revealed its riches. Once the
gold was exhausted, the town's economy was centred first on agriculture and, in more
recent years, the more lucrative resource of tourism. Looking down its quaint but
almost Hollywood-style main street, one hopes this modern form of gold will not
destroy its true aesthetic wealth and soul. Autumn (end of March) sees the village at its
most colourful both in scenery and spirit when the hugely popular **Arrowtown Autumn
Festival** takes place, ⓘ *To3-4421570, www.autumnfestival.co.nz*

Sights The **Lakes District Museum and Gallery**, ⓘ *49 Buckingham St, To3-4421824,
museum@queenstown.co.nz, 0830-1700, $5, child $0.50,* offers plenty of insight into
the 'calm before the storm', and then depicts the area's rather chaotic and feverish
gold mining boom. If you're feeling lucky you can also hire out gold pans ($3 includes
instruction sheet).

Outside the museum the tree-lined avenue of **Buckingham Street** reveals several
old historic cottages that add to the much-photographed aesthetics. At the far end of
Buckingham Street the **Chinese Settlement** offers further insight with several
mud-walled huts, and a reconstruction of a general store. The Chinese were subjected
to much prejudice and derision by the European miners and, much of the time,
instead of seeking claims of their own, would sift through the tailings looking for fine
gold undetected or simply left by the other rapacious miners.

In the hills up-river from Arrowtown, and accessed via a difficult 13-km track, is
the former mining settlement of **Macetown**. Its remnants are the focus for a number of
interesting tours by foot, four-wheel drive or on horseback. *» For Sleeping, Eating and
other listing, see pages 642-645.*

Glenorchy → *Colour map 7, grid A3. Population: 200*

North of Queenstown (48 km) via the superb **Wakatipu Lake** scenic drive is the tiny
former frontier village of Glenorchy. Backed and surrounded on both sides by the
rugged peaks of the **Fiordland** and **Aspiring National Park,** the glacier-fed **Rees** and
Dart Rivers and ancient beech forests, it is little wonder it has been labelled the

Otago Around Queenstown

66 99 Glenorchy is named after Glen Orchy, through which the Orchy River runs on its way to Loch Awe in the highlands of Scotland. With such similar scenery to their native land it is obvious why Scots pioneers were especially drawn to the place...

'Gateway to Paradise'. Indeed, part of the attraction here, other than the pure scenic delights or activities is a visit to **Paradise** itself – an aptly named little farming settlement 20 km further north. So stunning are the mountain backdrops around here and so lacking in any signs of human habitation that the Dart River valley became a principal filming venue for the **Lord of the Rings** trilogy as Isengard, home of the evil wizard Saruman, and the forests of Lothlorien.

Activities available in Glenorchy include **jet boating** and **horse trekking**. The village also serves as the main access point to the **Routeburn, Greenstone/Caples** and **Rees-Dart** tramping tracks. Both four-wheel drive and scenic flight tours from Queenstown explore the Lord of the Rings film locations (see Queenstown Activities, page 633).▶▶ *For Sleeping, Eating and other listings, see pages 643-645.*

● Sleeping

Arrowtown *p641*
The VIC has full listings of the many charming B&Bs in the village and its surrounds.
LL-L Arrowtown House, *10 Caernarvon St, T03-4420025, www.arrowtownhouse.co.nz* Right in the heart of town, in the original church grounds. A very smart boutique luxury lodge with 5 well-appointed en suites.
AL-A The Old Nick B&B, *70 Buckingham St, T03-4420066, www.oldnick.co.nz* As the name suggests, this place is set in the village's old police station built in 1902 although it is now a place to escape to rather than from. It has 2 fine rooms with shared spa bathroom and several others in the former stables with en suite bathroom. It is within a short walk of the village centre and all in all is good value.
AL-A Arrowtown Lodge and Hiking Company, *7 Anglesea St, T03-4421101, www.arrowtownlodge.co.nz* If you enjoy walkingyou might consider these walking or walking/accommodation packages. There are 4 cottage-style en suites all designed in keeping with the village's historic past.
B New Orleans Hotel, *27 Buckingham St,*

T03-4421745. Basic but friendly, has a few cheap and comfortable doubles and twins.
C Royal Oak Hotel, *46 Buckingham St, T03-4421700.* Has the cheapest beds in town.

C-D Riverdown Boutique Backpackers, *7 Bedford St, T03-4098499.* Look no further than this new 6-bed place for backpacker accommodation. It is simply immaculate and has the feel of a cosy B&B rather than a hostel and is a little known gem. One can only hope the word doesn't get out too much! Shared, double and twin. Off street parking. Book well ahead. (Closed in winter.)

Arrowtown has a scattering of **motels** including: A **Settlers Cottage Motel,** *22 Hertford St, T03-4421734, settlersmotel@clear.net.nz* Reasonably characterful units.
A-B Viking Lodge Motel, *21 Inverness Cres, T03-4421765, viking@inq.co.nz* It has self-contained A-frame units and a swimming pool.

Motorcamps and campsites
D Arrowtown Holiday Park, *Suffolk St, T03-4421876.* Centrally located with powered/tent sites.

Given its size, there is not a huge amount of choice in Glenorchy, but that lends to its atmosphere.

A-D Kinloch Lodge, *on the opposite side of the Dart River, accessed via the Dart Valley Rd (Routeburn Track Rd), 862 Kinloch Rd, T03-4424900, www.kinlochlodge.co.nz* One of the most idyllic and peaceful places in the region, this historic 1868 cottage has proved immensely popular with trampers for many years. It has both characterful self-contained and dorm accommodation and can also be reached by water-taxi. Evening meals are offered and it has a shop on site.

A Glen-Roydon Lodge Hotel, *corner of Argyle and Mull Sts, T03-4429968, www.glenroydon.com* Offers ski-lodge-style en suites with a shared lounge and open fire. There is also an in-house restaurant/café and bar.

A-D Glenorchy Hotel, *across the road from Glen-Roydon Lodge, T03-4429902, relax@glenorchy.org.nz* Offers traditional NZ-style hotel doubles, en suites or a self-contained cottage. It also has backpacker dorms. The cheap in-house restaurant and bar is popular, with the outdoor upper-deck views proving a top spot.

A-B Mount Earnslaw Motels, *87 Oban St, T03-4426993, www.earnslaw.bizland.com* Glenorchy's most modern motel offers tidy en suite units.

Motorcamps and campsites
C-D Glenorchy Holiday Park and Backpackers, *2 Oban St, T03-4427171*. Has a self-contained villa, standard cabins, bunkrooms and powered/tent sites. There is also a small store and information centre.

❷ Eating

Arrowtown *p215*
$$ **Saffron**, *18 Buckingham St, T03-4420131. Daily 1130-2130*. Has a good modern Pacific-rim menu and a fine wine list.
$$ **Stables Café and Restaurant**, *28 Buckingham St, T03-4421818. Daily from 1100-late*. Older and more historic but especially popular for al fresco dining.
$$ **Café Mondo**, *Ballarat Arcade, Buckingham St, T03-4420227. Mon 1000-1730, Tue-Wed 0800-1730, Thu-Sun 0800-late*. Locally popular especially for traditional café-style breakfast, brunch or lunch and seems to attract a diverse crowd. The coffee is some of the best in the village and there is internet and occasional live music.
$ **New Orleans Hotel**, *Buckingham St*. Cheaper pub-style food.
$ **Royal Oak Hotel**, *Buckingham St*. Especially welcoming to kids and BBQ meals.
$ **Arrowtown Bakery**, *11 Ballarat Avenue, Buckingham St*, Light snacks and especially great pies.
$ **Wind in the Willows Bookshop Café**, *Ramshaw Lane (turn right at the top of Buckingham St), near the river, T03-4420055. Daily*. For something more peaceful.

Glenorchy *p641*
$ **Glenorchy Café** *on Mull St, T03-4429958*. A funky little place that offers light snacks and a good breakfast – all of which can be enjoyed to the dulcet tones of 80s hits, played on an ageing record-player. Internet is also available.

▲ Activities and tours

Arrowtown *p641*
4WD tours
New Zealand Nomad Safaris, *T03-4426699, www.nomadsafaris.co.nz* Provide an exhilarating 2-hr (4½ hrs from Queenstown) 4WD trip to Macetown. There are over 25 river crossings and a stop for a spot of gold panning in the Arrow River (summer only), from $85. Also popular 'Safari of the Rings Tours' from $120 (see Queenstown activities, page 627).
Walking and tramping
See **Arrowtown Lodge**, in Sleeping, above.
Pottery
Gone Potty, *18 Buckingham St, T03-4420890*. If it is raining you might like to consider

● Since the Lord of the Rings trilogy hit cinema screens the Arrow River has also taken its place on the must-see list of film location venues. Although you would never guess it, it was here, only a few hundred yards up river from the town centre, where the sinister Nazgul were filmed charging at Arwen and Frodo.

madly colouring your own ceramic (the finished product is fired for you and can picked up within a few days).

Glenorchy *p641*
Jet boating
Other than the stunning scenery and the services on offer to the tramping fraternity, the big attraction in Glenorchy is the jet boating operations that ply the **Dart River**. Unlike the highly commercial rides of the Shotover and Kawarau in Queenstown, the remote Dart penetrates parts of the **Aspiring National Park** simply not accessible by road, and provides one of the most scenic jet boat trips in the world.
Dart River Safaris, *Mull St, T03-4429992, www.dartriver.co.nz* (Transportation provided from Queenstown.) There are 2 safaris on offer: the '*Dart River*' and the '*Heritage Trail*'. Since the hysteria surrounding the *Lord of the Rings*, the tours have wisely now included some detail and explanation about film locations en route but thankfully they have not gone over the top. After all, the scenery speaks for itself without the added fictional world of JRR Tolkien. Both trips involve a wonderfully scenic ride to Glenorchy by bus, then a transfer to 4WD to negotiate the back roads beyond the settlement of Paradise taking in the 2 main LOTR film locations on the way. Then there is a short (or extended) walk through the beech forest at the start of the terminus of the Rees/Dart track followed by the fun-filled jet boat trip up river then downstream all the way back to Glenorchy. The *Dart River* trip takes roughly 3-hrs (6 hr from Queenstown) and costs from $170, child $90 (ex Glenorchy $159/$80). Departs Queenstown daily 0800 and1230 ; Glenorchy 0900 and 1330. *The Heritage Trail* takes about an hr or so longer with a longer walk much more pampering and picnic lunch to add to the usual 4WD/jet boat trip. from $325, child $243. Departs Queenstown daily at 0930; Glenorchy at 1015.

Dart River Safaris also offer a wilderness '**Funyak**' (www.funyaks.co.nz) option which is a part jetboat (32-km 1¼-hr), part paddle (2 hr) on a blow-up carrot (well, okay – a kayak), from $255, child $191. It's a great day out and the scenery is memorable to say the least. Lunch included and transport from Queenstown available (departs Queenstown 0930; Glenorchy 1015).

Several **combos** are also worth considering including reductions on a Milford Sound fly/cruise/fly; horse trekking; 3-hr guided walk and a 4WD gold mining heritage trip to the ghost town of Sefferton. Note there is a bad weather refund policy on all trips.
Dart Wilderness Adventures, *T03-4429939, www.glenorchyinfocentre.co.nz* Somewhat overshadowed by Dart River Safaris but a fine operator in its own right, it also offers a 70-km 3-hr trip on the Dart River again with some detail afforded to LOTR film locations for $145, child $73. Again pick-ups are available from Queenstown ($10/$5).

Horse trekking
Dart Stables, *Glenorchy, T03-4425688.* Offer 2-hr ($95), 5-hr ($145), and 2-day/ 1-night ($360) horse trekking trips through scenic forest trails near the Rees and Dart Rivers. Again there is some emphasis on LOTR film locations and this is perhaps one of the best ways to really experience them.
High Country Horses, *T03-4429915, www.high-country-horses.co.nz* Another company based in the Rees Valley.

Flightseeing
Glenorchy Air, *T03-4422207.* Offers flightseeing trips around both national parks and to Milford Sound to add to the hugely popular *LOTR Trilogy Trail Trip* (see Queenstown activities).

Fishing and nature cruises
Glenorchy Cruising, *T03-4429951*, or **Backpacker Express**, *see p 640*. Both offer fishing and nature cruises to the lake islands.

Tandem skydiving
Vertical Descents. From 9-12,000ft from $245. Pick-ups from Queenstown several times daily.

Walking
If you wish to explore the area under your own steam there are several short walks on offer immediately around Glenorchy, with the 2-km wetlands boardwalk (**Glenorchy Walkway**) just at the northern outskirts of the town (accessed from Islay St) being particularly recommended. The reflections

and views of **Mount Earnslaw** are superb and there is an abundance of birdlife. By road you can head north of Glenorchy and explore the **Rees** or **Dart River** (Routeburn) **Valleys**, or better still visit **Paradise** and head to the western trailhead of the **Rees-Dart Tramping Track**. Both film locations for *Isengard* and *Lothlorien* were centred around the open fields just beyond the settlement of Paradise. From the trailhead, you can also take a short walk through the beech forest on the tramping track's first section. Again the views of Mount Earnslaw from the Paradise Rd are excellent and you can also have some fun with silly photos at the Paradise road sign. For more information on walking in the area contact the DoC visitor centre in Glenorchy.

○ Shopping

Glenorchy *p641*
Made in Glenorchy Fur Products, *Main St,*

www.glenorchy-fur.co.nz Oh, have you been wanting to get your dear mother or girlfriend that special homecoming present? Well, if so you have found 'ideal presents utopia'. Of particular appeal is the fine range of possum fur nipple warmers. They are the genuine article, come in a fine array of colours and are most appealing. And should your mother or dearest not feel the urge to accept or indeed model them on a regular basis, then they make a wonderful pair of eyeshades for the next flight back to New Zealand after the fall-out. Just don't expect to make friends withthe person sitting next to you..

● Directory

Arrowtown and Glenorchy *p641 & 641*
Internet Café Monody, see above. **Library**, *Buckingham St, Arrowtown. Mon-Fri 1000-1700, Sat 1030-1230.* Glenorchy Café, *Mull St, Glenorchy.* **Postal agent** Mobil Station, *Mull St, Glenorchy.*

Wanaka and around → *Phone code: 03*

Wanaka is almost unfeasibly pleasant, and has to rank as one of the most desirable places in New Zealand. With the lake of the same name lapping rhythmically at its heels and its picture-postcard mountain backdrops bordering the Aspiring National Park, it is easy to understand why Wanaka is such a superb place to visit, or indeed live. In recent years Wanaka has seen a boom in both real estate sales and tourism, but it is reassuring that its manic neighbour, Queenstown, will always keep growth in check. As it is, Wanaka is just perfect: not too busy, not too quiet; developed, but not spoilt and a place for all to enjoy. It is also not just a place frequented by the rich and famous. Although now you would never guess it, Wanaka's history goes back to the 1860s when it played an important role as a service centre for the region's itinerant gold miners. Today, its principal resources are activities and its miners are tourists. Year-round, there is a multitude of things to do, from water sports and tramping in summer to skiing in winter. But it can also be the perfect place to relax and recharge your batteries beside the lake. Wanaka is that kind of town.

Ins and outs

Getting there Wanaka is accessed via Queenstown **airport** which is served by **Air New Zealand Link**, T0800-737000. The airfield for the Wanaka Region is 11 km east of the town via SH6. **Aspiring Air**, T03-4437943, fly between Queenstown and Wanaka.

Wanaka is served daily by **Intercity**, T03-4437885 (Christchurch/Dunedin); **Atomic Shuttles**, T03-3228883 (Christchurch/Dunedin Queenstown), and **Southern Link**, T03-3588355 (Christchurch/Dunedin/Queenstown). **Wanaka Connexions**, T0800-879926, www.wanakaconnexions.co.nz, also run daily between Queenstown, Wanaka and Dunedin. Typical one-way fares are Christchurch from $45, Dunedin from

$35 Fox Glacier from $37 and Queenstown from $25. **Intercity** services can be booked at the **Paper Place**, 84 Ardmore St, T03-4437885. **United Travel**, 99 Ardmore St, T03-4437414, can also be of assistance. All the major bus companies heading up or down the West Coast must pass through Makarora and Oamaru. Wanaka is 424 km southwest of Christchurch via SH1 and SH8; 276 km northwest of Dunedin via SH8; and 117 km north of Queenstown via SH8 and SH6. Or, alternatively, 70 km from Queenstown via the Cardrona Valley Road.

Getting around Local shuttle services are available to Wanaka airfield ($12-15), the ski fields (from $22 return), local sights (Puzzling World from $3) and the Mount Aspiring trailheads (from $45) with **Alpine Shuttles** (Good Sports), T03-4437966; **Edgewater Adventures**, T03-4438422, and **The Bus Company**, T03-4431855, also offer a range of local services. **Mount Aspiring Express**, T03-4438422, specialize in national park, walks and trailhead connections (Raspberry Creek, twice daily from $45 return, Mount Roy $5, Diamond Lake $10). With Mount Aspiring Express you can also drive up/bike back ($5 extra – not hire). During the summer months **Cook Connection**, T0800-252666, www.cookconnect.co.nz, go from Oamaru to Mt Cook and return a minimum of 3 days a week (Mon/Wed/Fri), from $45 one-way (Omarama $25). Note that in winter there is currently no public transport to Mt Cook from Oamaru. **Coastline Tours**, T03-4395265, www.coastline-tours.co.nz **Oamaru 3 W Tours**, T03-4349957 and the **Penguin Express**, T03-4395265, offer shuttles to the penguin colony and other local attractions from $15.

Information Wanaka VIC, ① *in the Log Cabin on the lakefront, 100 Ardmore St, T03-4431233, www.lakewanaka.co.nz daily 0830-1830 (winter 0930-1630).* This office also administers most of the local activity and adventure bookings through Lakeland Adventures, T03-4437495, www.lakelandadventures.co.nz There is also a café on site that looks over the lake. The **DoC VIC (Wanaka)**, ① *Upper Ardmore St at the junction with McPherson St, T03-4437660, www.doc.govt.nz daily 0800-1645.* It deals with all national park/tramping hut bookings and local walks information. Up-to-date **weather forecast** also available. **DoC VIC (Makarora)**, ① *T03-4438365. daily 0800-1700 (closed weekends in winter).* It has information on the northern sector of Aspiring National Park and the Haast Pass, and local short walks, also issues hut passes ($5-$10). Given the isolation and the potential for very wet weather conditions in the area you are advised to consult DoC before embarking on any of the major walks or tramps. Intentions sheets are provided. **Oamaru VIC (I-Site)**, ① *corner of Itchen and Thames Sts, T03-4341656, www.tourismwaitaki.co.nz Mon-Fri 0900-1800 (1700 Easter-Nov), Sat and Sun 1000-1700 (1600 Easter-Nov).* The centre has town maps and a wealth of information surrounding the historical buildings, local tours and things to see and do. The leaflet *Historic Oamaru* is very useful, and all local DoC walks leaflets are also available. Note the **Penguin Colony** has its own Information Centre, ① *at the base of MacAndrew Wharf (Waterfront Rd), T03-4331195, www.penguins.co.nz* It can supply general information after hours.

Wanaka → *Colour map 6, grid C3. Population: 3,700*

One of the most immediate ways to get acquainted with the area is to make the short 45-minute climb up **Mount Iron** (240 m), just 2 km before the township on the main road. A stubborn lump of rock left by the glaciers, its 360-degree views are very impressive and provide an ideal way to get your bearings. The track is well marked and there is a car park by the roadside. Wanaka town centre borders the very pretty **Roy's Bay** that opens out beyond Ruby Island into the southern and indented bays of **Lake Wanaka**. The lake, which is 274 m above sea level and over 45 km long, occupies an ancient glacier bed. The aesthetics speak for themselves, but the glistening waters are also a prime attraction to boaties, water-skiers, kayakers and windsurfers. Even before you consider these activities you will find yourself simply admiring its beauty from Wanaka's attractive **lakefront**.

On the way into town you cannot fail to miss New Zealand's 'Leaning Tower of Wanaka', the centrepiece of **Stuart Landsborough's Puzzling World**, ① *T03-4437489, www.puzzlingworld.com daily 0830-1730, from $6, child $4.50 (with maze $9/$6)*. This is a madcap and indeed puzzling conglomerate of mazes, illusions and holograms that is worth a muse. The toilets and 'Hall of Following Faces' are particularly engaging. Shop and café on site.

A further 8 km east on SH6, surrounding Wanaka airfield, is the NZ Fighter Pilots Museum and the Wanaka Transport and Toy Museum, which also houses the **Wanaka Beerworks**, ① *T03-4431865, www.wanakabeerworks.co.nz daily 0930-1800, from $5, child, free*. In these days when beer and transport make uncomfortable relations, it seems unusual to find a brewery at a transport museum, but so be it. It is a craft brewery producing very palatable award-winning beers for many Central Otago outlets. There are daily tours at 1400, tastings and, of course, sales.

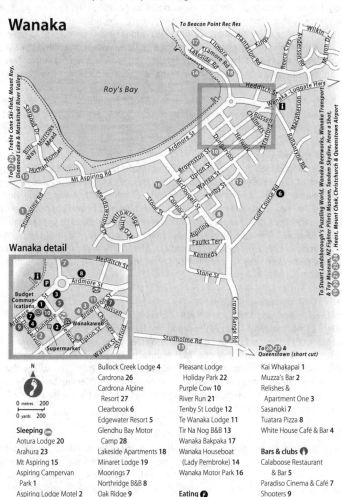

Wanaka

Otago Wanaka and around

N

0 metres 200
0 yards 200

Sleeping 🛏
Aotura Lodge 20
Arahura 23
Mt Aspiring 15
Aspiring Campervan
  Park 1
Aspiring Lodge Motel 2
Brookvale Manor 3

Bullock Creek Lodge 4
Cardrona 26
Cardrona Alpine
  Resort 27
Clearbrook 6
Edgewater Resort 5
Glendhu Bay Motor
  Camp 28
Lakeside Apartments 18
Minaret Lodge 19
Moorings 7
Northridge B&B 8
Oak Ridge 9
Parklands Lodge 24

Pleasant Lodge
  Holiday Park 22
Purple Cow 10
River Run 21
Tenby St Lodge 12
Te Wanaka Lodge 11
Tir Na Nog B&B 13
Wanaka Bakpaka 17
Wanaka Houseboat
  (Lady Pembroke) 14
Wanaka Motor Park 16

Eating 🍴
Ambrosia 6

Kai Whakapai 1
Muzza's Bar 2
Relishes &
  Apartment One 3
Sasanoki 7
Tuatara Pizza 8
White House Café & Bar 4

Bars & clubs 🍸
Calaboose Restaurant
  & Bar 5
Paradiso Cinema & Café 7
Shooters 9
Slainte Irish 10

Wanaka Transport and Toy Museum, ⓘ *To3-4438765, www.wttmuseum.com, daily 0830-1800, from $6, child $3,* provides a good wet-weather option and is the largest privately owed vehicle and toy collection in New Zealand. There are over 15,000 items on display, including a staggering 9,000 toys and 200 vehicles, comprising a tank, fire engines, trucks and the obligatory tractors. There is even a collection of spark plugs!

Of more interest is the **NZ Fighter Pilots Museum**. Although its main purpose is to honour the lives (and death) of New Zealand fighter pilots, this museum provides a fascinating insight into general aviation history. The museum's enviable and much-loved collection of flyable, classic Second World War fighters and trainers includes a Spitfire, Hurricane and a Mustang, all of which are the star attraction of Wanaka's main biannual event, the 'Warbirds over Wanaka' which attracts thousands of spectators. Real enthusiasts will also delight in other unusual aircraft on display; the 'Polikarpovs', housed in a separate hanger, are particularly unique. Attached to the museum is the fun-filled **Compaq Computer Flightzone**, ⓘ *To3-4437010, www.nzfpm.co.nz Daily 0900-1600, from $8, child $4* Here, you can have endless virtual dogfights with the bad guys. For the technophobe this becomes a rather frustrating exercise and does make you wonder if you are even fit to drive a car! The sound effects are great, as is the chance to fly upside down and spot the enemies lurking.. Around the museum you might like to sit and watch terrified faces turn to ecstatic ones at the base of **Wanaka Tandem Skydive,** *To3-4437207, www.skydivenz.com*

Near the airfield is the **Have a Shot** complex, ⓘ *To3-4436656, www.haveashot.co.nz,* with its range of 'smack it or shoot it' activities from clay-birds to archery and a full golf range. ▸▸ *For Sleeping , Eating and other listings, see pages 652-660.*

Hawea → *Colour map 6, grid B4*

North of Wanaka on SH6 towards the West Coast is **Lake Hawea** and the small holiday settlement of Hawea. Lake Hawea, like its neighbour Lake Wanaka, occupies an ancient glacier valley, and only a narrow strip of moraine known as The Neck separates the two. Lake Hawea is noted for its fishing and beautiful scenery, with mountain reflections that disappear towards its remote upper reaches, 35 km north of Hawea settlement. The lake level was raised by 18 m in 1958 as part of the Clutha River hydropower system. Hawea itself nestles on its southern shore and, although a fairly new settlement, was formerly the site of an important and strategic Maori *pa*. ▸▸ *For Sleeping, see page 653.*

Makarora → *Colour map 6, grid B3*

From Lake Hawea and the narrow Neck you revisit Lake Wanaka and head north through some beautiful 'Scottish' scenery to its northern edge and the small settlement of Makarora. At about 67 km from Wanaka, and almost on the border of the Otago and West Coast Regions, Makarora acts as the portal to the northern tramps and activities within the **Mount Aspiring National Park**. The village itself offers little except a small conglomerate of tourist services reflecting the desires of most visitors who either pass through quickly or head for the hills. ▸▸ *For Sleeping and other listings, see pages 653-660.*

Oamaru → *Colour map 7, grid A6. Population: 12,000*

Oamaru is an unusual and appealing coastal town on the South Island's east coast, somehow befitting its position gracing the shores of 'Friendly' Bay. Primarily functioning as a port and an agricultural service town, its modern-day tourist attractions lie in the strange combination of stone, architecture and penguins. Thanks to the prosperity of the 1860s to 1890s, and the discovery of a wealth of local limestone that could be easily carved and moulded, the early architects and

Mount Aspiring National Park

Like most of New Zealand's majestic national parks Mount Aspiring has an impressive list of vital statistics. First designated in 1964 the park has been extended to now cover 355,000 ha or 3,500 sq km, making it New Zealand's third largest. It stretchess for about 140 km from the Haast Pass to the Humbolt Range at the head of Lake Wakatipu and it is 40 km at its widest. It contains five peaks over 2600 m, including Aspiring itself – at 3027 m, the highest outside the Mount Cook range. It contains over 100 glaciers, including the Bonar, Therma and Volta. It enjoys an annual rainfall of between 1,000 mm-6,000 mm a year. It is home to some unique wildlife like the New Zealand falcon, the kea and the giant weta. It is part of a World Heritage Area of international significance… the list just goes on. But, it is not figures that best describe this park. It is without doubt the names, words and phrases associated with it. How about Mount Awful, Mount Dreadful or Mount Dispute. Or Mount Chaos perhaps? Then there is The Valley of Darkness; Solitude Creek; Siberia River. How about Rob Roy, the Pope's Nose or the mind boggling Power Knob. Are you getting the picture? This is a wilderness worthy of investigation and well beyond mere imagination; a park of stunning and remote beauty. The locals call the place 'Tiger Country'. Enough said… get in there and enjoy… but go prepared. For more information contact the DoC Information Centre in Wanaka or Makarora (see Wanaka and Around Wanaka sections) or visit the website www.doc.govt.nz

stonemasons of Oamaru created a settlement rich in imposing, classic buildings, earning it the reputation of New Zealand's best-built town. Many old buildings remain, complete with Corinthian columns and gargantuan doorways, giving it a distinctly grand air. Add to that a small and congenial colony of yellow-eyed and blue penguins that waddle up to their burrows on the coast like dignified gents in 'tux and tails', and the town's appeal becomes truly unique.

Sights Most of the historic buildings and associated attractions are located in the **Tyne-Harbour Street Historic Precinct** (begins at the southern end of Thames St), which boasts the largest and best-preserved collection of historic commercial buildings in the country. Although the *Historic Oamaru* leaflet will provide enough information for a self-guided tour, there are one-hour **guided walks** available on demand through the VIC, from around $8, child $4. You will find that most of the buildings demonstrate a range of architectural styles from Venetian to Victorian and are now occupied with a variety of tourist lures, from antique and craft outlets to second-hand book stores, auto collections and cafés. The **Harbour and Tyne Market**, ① *2 Tyne St, every Sat and Sun from 1000-1600 (Sun only in winter)*, specializes in local crafts, food and produce. Another interesting attraction is the **Oamaru Steam Train**, ① *T03-4345634*, that is lovingly owned and operated by the local and very enthusiastic Steam and Rail Society. The shiny engine comes complete with a proud conductor in period uniform and hisses into action from beside the VIC to the Harbour on Sundays, from $5, child $2. As if there were not enough history on the streets, the town is also home to the **North Otago Museum**, ① *58-60 Thames St, T03-4348060, Mon-Fri 1300-1630, Sat 1000-1300, donations*, which has a modest collection, focusing on Maori history and the inevitable early settler collections. Of special interest are the information and displays about *Oamaru Stone*, the white limestone for which the town is so famous.

In one of Oamaru's original banks is the **Forrester Art Gallery**, ① *9 Thames St, T03-4341653, Mon-Fri 1030-1630, Sat 1030-1300, Sun 1300-1630, donations.* It features local contemporary works as well as national and international touring exhibitions. The VIC has listings of other notable galleries in the area.

There are a number of historic **homesteads** that are open to the public, including the Victorian country mansion, **Burnside**, T03-4324194; the 1885 **Kuriheka**, T03-4395358; the **Tokarahi**, T03-4312500, and the Oamaru stone buildings of the **Totara Estate**, T03-4347169. Most of these offer regular self guided or guided tours from $4-$15. Ring for details and opening times. **Oamaru 3W**, T03-4349957 offers excellent two-hour to three-hour guided tours to **Totara** and the **Parkside Whitestone Quarry** from $25. Recommended.

If you get fed up with stone then head for the very pleasant **Oamaru Public Gardens**, ① *off Severn St, dawn to dusk, free.* Rated as one of the top 10 public gardens in the country, and first set aside in 1876, its 30 acres boast rose and Chinese gardens, fountains, statues and, of course, the ubiquitous duck pond. The area also has a number of private gardens open to the public and again the VIC can provide the details.

No visit to Oamaru would be complete without visiting its **penguin colonies**. The town has two species in residence – the enchanting **little blue penguin** (the smallest in the world) and the rare, larger, **yellow-eyed penguin**. There are two colonies and observation points, one at **Bushy Beach**, where you can watch the yellow-eyed penguins from a hide for free, or the official harbour-side, **Oamaru Blue Penguin Colony**, ① *T03-4431195, from $10, child $8,* that you must pay to access. Obviously the free option is an attractive one, but if you know nothing about penguins and were always under the impression they lived on icebergs and wore bow ties, then you are advised to join a tour, or visit the official colony or VIC before venturing out alone. The only time to view the penguins is from dusk (specific times are posted at the colony reception). There is a large covered stand from which you are given a brief talk before the penguins come ashore and waddle intently towards their burrows. The colony is accessed via Waterfront Road past the Historic Precinct (signposted).

The **Bushy Beach** yellow-eyed penguin colony and viewing hide is accessed on foot via the walkway at the end of Waterfront Road (30 minutes), or alternatively by car via Bushy Beach Road (end of Tyne Street from the Historic Precinct). The best time to view the birds is an hour or so before dawn and dusk when they come and go from their fishing expeditions. If you think one penguin species is just like another then think again, the two are very different in character and you are advised to see both. If you want a closer more informative experience you are advised to join Jim Caldwell's **walking tours** during the summer. Tours last 40 min and depart at 1800 and 1900, from $8. Book at the VIC. The **Penguin Express**, T03-4395265, combines transport with tours and entry fees to both colonies from $18. **Oamaru 3W**, T03-4349957, also offer tours to both from $16.

As well as its historical aspects and penguin-watching, Oamaru has a number of other **activities** on offer including fresh and salt-water fishing, kayaking, heritage and fossil trails, gold-mining and farm tours, jet boating, horse trekking and glider flights. The VIC has all the details. ►► *For Sleeping, Eating and other listings, see page 660.*

Oamaru to Dunedin → *Colour map 7, grid A/B6*

If you are heading south and have time, take the quiet and **scenic coast road** from Oamaru, through **Kakanui** to rejoin SH1 at Waianakarua. The area hosts a number of market gardens so keep your eyes open for fresh, good value produce at roadside stalls. **Kayak hire** is also available for the lower reaches of the **Kakanui River**, T03-4395404, from $8 per hour. About 10 km south of Waianakarua are the **Moeraki Boulders**, a strange and much-photographed collection of spherical boulders that litter the beach. Although Maori legend has it that these boulders are *te kai hinaki*, or food baskets and sweet potatoes, science has determined that they are in fact

The Rob Roy Glacier Walk

If you haven't time or the energy for any of the major tramps, there is one day-walk in the Mount Aspiring National Park that is accessible from Wanaka and quite simply a 'must do'. From Wanaka drive (or arrange transportation) to the **Raspberry Creek** Car Park in the West Matukituki Valley (one hour). From there follow the river, west to the footbridge over the river and up in to the **Rob Roy Valley**. From here the track gradually climbs, following the chaotic Rob Roy River, through beautiful rainforest, revealing the odd view of the glacier above. After about one hour 30 minute you will reach the tree line and enter a superb hidden valley rimmed with solid rock walls of **waterfall** and **ice**. It is simply stunning and well deserving of the label '**The Jewel of the Park**'. Keep your eyes (and ears) open for kea and in the forest for the tiny rifleman. After some thorough investigation of the area, you can then retrace your steps back down the valley to the Matukituki River and the car park (5hrs return). Mt Aspiring Express can shuttle you to Raspberry Creek for $45 return, T03-4438422.

'septarian concretions', a rather classy name for 'darn big rock gob-stoppers' left behind from the eroded coastal cliffs. To understand exactly how they are formed requires several PhDs in geology and physics, but you will find something near a layman's explanation at the **Moeraki Boulderpark Visitor Centre and Café**, T03-4394827, that is signposted just off SH1. Rather predictably shaped like the boulders themselves, it is open daily for lunch and dinner offering light meals and refreshments. The path to the boulders starts at the car park, where an interpretative panel explains the formation of the boulders to the geologically wanting. You are requested to provide a donation of $2. **Coastline Tours,** T03-4347744 operate from Oamaru and include the boulders on their range of itineraries from $15-$45.

There are other, smaller boulders to be seen at **Katiki Beach** and Shag Point a few kilometres south, beyond the village of Moeraki. Sadly, there used to be many more, with most having been pilfered as souvenirs, prompting the protection of the larger boulders at Moeraki. The small fishing village of **Moeraki**, 3 km from the boulders, can be reached along the beach by foot (three hours return) or by car via SH1. Once a whaling settlement first settled as long ago as 1836, it now offers far more acceptable forms of fishing, as well as swimming, **wildlife cruises** (to try to see the rare Hector's dolphin) and some very pleasant **coastal walks**. The historic **lighthouse** is also worth a visit and for seafood don't miss **Fluer's Place**, 169 Haven St, T03-4395980. The coastline at **Shag Point** south of Moeraki is also a good spot to observe **NZ fur seals** but do not go too close.

With the boulders still fresh in your mind your imagination can really run wild a further 20 km south on SH1 in **Palmerston**. There, dominating the scene above the town, is the rather spectacular phallus adorning **Puketapu Hill** (343 m). A monument to the late John McKenzie, a Scots runholder who rose to high office and pushed through the Land Settlement Act in the 1890s, the monument and its accompanying views can be reached from the northern end of town (signposted). If you resist closer inspection perhaps you can gaze from afar while sampling the almost legendary mutton pies from the **McGregors Tearooms**, T03-4651124. Children and budding Lepidopterists may also like to alight upon the **Palmerston Butterfly House** in Stronsa St. From Palmerston it is a further 55 km through gently rolling hills to Dunedin. ➤ *For Sleeping and Eating, see page 654.*

Wanaka p645

Although Wanaka has about 2,800 beds you are advised to book at least 3 days in advance in summer (especially at New Year) and during the winter ski season.

LL-AL Edgewater Resort, *Sargood Dr, T03-4438311, www.edgewater.co.nz* Set overlooking Roy's Bay, is this modern and classy place. Its aesthetics cannot be faulted and it offers a wide range of en suites from the standard to luxurious. Lots of activities can be arranged in-house.

AL Mt Aspiring Hotel, *Mt Aspiring Rd, T03-4438216, www.wanakanz.com* Newly refurbished and within walking distance of the town centre. A popular choice, with comfortable, good-value studios and suites, some with spa. Restaurant, bar and internet.

A Cardrona Hotel, *Crown Range (Cardrona) Rd (26 km from Wanaka), T03-4438153, info@cardrona-hotel.co.nz* A little way out but simply superb. The hotel is over 140 years old and still retains much of its former character. As it is, the 16 comfortable double rooms in the old stables are charming and front a beautiful enclosed garden and courtyard. There is a great rustic restaurant and bar attached. Bookings are essential.

There are plenty of **motels** including:

LL-AL Clearbrook, *corner Helwick and Upton St, T03-4434413, www.clearbrook.co.nz* The units are nicely appointed and the complex is right in the heart of the town centre.

A Aspiring Lodge Motel, *corner of Dunmore and Dungarvon Sts, T03-4437816, www.pacificahotels.co.nz* Offers good standard and executive suites and a spa.

A Brookvale Manor, *35 Brownston St, T03-4438333, www.brookvale.co.nz* 1-bedroom and studio suites, pool, spa.

A Tenby St Lodge, *24 Tenby St, T03-4439294, tenbystlodge@amcom.co.nz* Backs on to the golf course and offers 10 quiet, well appointed en suites.

A Cardrona Alpine Resort, *T03-4437411, www.cardrona.com* Units that are actually within the ski field complex, and sleep 1-8 from $320.

Apartment complexes are very much an increasing feature in Wanaka.

LL Lakeside Apartments, *5 Lakeside Rd, T03-4430088, www.lakesidewanaka.co.nz* 4-5 star fully serviced apartments in a central position with lake views, pool and spa.

LL-AL Moorings, *17 Lakeside Rd, T03-4438479*. Modern and classy boutique apartments overlooking the lake.

There are many **B&Bs** and **homestays** available, from the luxury lodge or self-contained cottage to the basic B&B. The VIC has full listings.

LL Aotura Lodge, *17 km from Wanaka on the banks of the Clutha River, T03-4435000, www.aotura.co.nz* Also worth looking at in the same luxury price range. There are 4 excellent, very private suites on offer amidst spacious grounds.

LL Arahura, *Faulks Rd, Mt Barker, T03-4437439, F4436503, www.arahura.com* A top-quality country house lodge (out of Wanaka township) with 4 well-appointed double en-suites, singles and twins, tennis court, pleasant gardens and heated pool.

LL Minaret Lodge, *34 Eely Point Rd, T03-4431856, www.minaretlodge.co.nz* New on the scene and set in a peaceful 2-acre park-like setting a short walk from the town centre. The modern mud-brick lodge has 4 en suite guest rooms in chalets behind the property and one two-room suite. Sauna and spa.

LL River Run, *Halliday Rd, T03-4439049, www.riverrun.co.nz* Set on an escarpment with sweeping views across the mountains, this huge 420-acre property provides a perfect retreat with imaginatively appointed rooms and furnishings, often using recycled materials in traditional NZ style. There are 5 en suites and the cuisine is superb.

LL-AL Oak Ridge, *corner of Cardrona Valley and Studholme Rds, T03-4437707, www.oakridge.co. nz* Purpose-built like a luxurious motel, it has well-appointed units that look out across spacious lawns and a swimming pool to the mountains. The Asian/Scots owners add an interesting flavour beyond the very reputable restaurant attached. Living areas are very spacious and comfortable with a large log fire.

L Parklands Lodge, *Ballantyne Rd, T03-4437305, www.parklandswanaka. co.nz* A modern, spacious, single-storey place with

6 luxury en suites, pool, spa and 5-hole golf course, set in 10 acres of farmland.

AL **Northridge B&B**, *11 Botting Pl, T03-4438835, s.atkinson@xtra.co.nz* Commanding views and very pleasant surroundings.

AL **Te Wanaka Lodge**, *23 Brownston St, T03-4439224, www.tewanaka.co.nz* Excellent alpine-style lodge complex with well-appointed en suites, self-contained cottage, spa, open fire, wine cellar and library.

B **Tir Na Nog B&B**, *Studholme Rd, T03-4437111, tirnanog@xtra.co.nz* A pleasant self-contained cottage with spa.

B Wanaka Houseboat (Lady Pembroke), *T03-4437181, www.houseboat.co.nz* In Wanaka accommodation options even extend on to the water. This is fully functional and sleeps up to 10 in 2 king-size bedrooms and 2 bunk rooms.

The **hostels** in Wanaka are all generally of a high standard. Three of the best are:

C-D **Bullock Creek Lodge**, *50 Brownston St, T03-4431265, bullockcreeklodge@clear.net.nz* Has dorms, doubles and singles all with en suites, TV, decks, a great outlook and is close to the town centre.

C-D **Purple Cow**, *94 Brownston St, T03-4431880, www.purplecow.co.nz* A large place with stunning views across the lake. A wide range of comfortable dorms, twins and doubles all with en suites. Great facilities, internet, walks information and nice friendly atmosphere.

C-D **Wanaka Bakpaka**, *117 Lakeside Rd, T03-4437837, wanakabakpaka@xtra.co.nz* Five mins walk from the centre of town but worth it. It has great views, a good range of dorm, twins and doubles (some new) and clean, modern facilities. It is very much a tramper's retreat with great walking advice and information. Kayaks for hire ($18 per hr) and internet.

Motorcamps and campsites

There are several choices here from the convenient, to the luxury and the stylish.

AL-C **Aspiring Campervan Park**, *Studholme Rd, T03-4436603, www.campervanpark.co.nz*

An entirely different and new concept in motorcamps. Charges a hefty $30 for a powered site, but has all mod cons with new and modern facilities including a spa that looks out towards Mount Aspiring. Modern lodge, motel and tourist flats are also available. Internet.

AL-D **Pleasant Lodge Holiday Park**, *at the western end of the town 3 km towards Glendhu (217 Mount Aspiring Rd), T03-4437360.* In an elevated position overlooking the lake and has all the usual facilities including spa, bike and fishing rod hire.

C-D **Glendhu Bay Motor Camp**, *Mount Aspiring Rd 11 km from town, T03-4437243, glendhucamp@xtra.co.nz* For the best aesthetics, offers lakeside sites with views up to Mount Aspiring. Facilities are really too basic given its obvious popularity and there seems far too much reliance on its position. There is no denying the attraction on that front. Gets very busy in mid summer and in the ski season (book ahead).

C-D **Wanaka Motor Park**, *212 Brownston St, T03-4437883.* Closest to town, sprawling and rather unremarkable, it has adequate facilities, cabins and powered/tent sites.

Hawea *p648*

Two comfortable self-contained options:

A **Lake Hawea Lodge Motel**, *60 Capell Av, T03-4431714.* Slightly cheaper.

A **Lake Hawea Motor Inn**, *1 Capell Av, T03-4431224.*

Makaroa *p648*

B-D **Makarora Tourist Centre**, *T03-4438372, www.makarora.co.nz* Offers motel, cabin, backpacker and camping facilities.

A **Larrivee Homestay**, *near the VIC, T03-4439177, andrea_larrivee@hotmail.com* Comfortable and also offers a self-contained cottage and can do dinner.

Oamaru *p648*

A **Quality Hotel Brydone**, *115 Thames St, T03-4349892, qhbrydone@xtra.co.nz* Fairly unremarkable but comfortable, has standard doubles or suites. The popular 'T' Bar and restaurant housed in the hotel is the biggest attraction.

● *For an explanation of the sleeping and eating price codes used in this guide, see the inside*
● *front cover. Other relevant information is provided in the Essentials chapter, see page 51.*

Most of Oamaru's **motels** are on Thames Highway, heading out of town.

A **Bella Vista Motel**, *206 Thames St, T03-4342400*. New and centrally located. AL-A **Heritage Court Motor Lodge**, *346 Thames Highway, T03-4372200*. Tidy and modern accommodation.

B **Alpine Motel**, *285 Thames St, T03-4345038, alpine.motel.oamaru@xtra.co.nz*; and

B **469 Café and Motels**, *469 Thames Highway, T03-4371443, tskitto@ihug.co.nz*

There are an ever increasing number of fine **B&Bs** and **homestays** on offer with many being in historic surroundings.

LL **Pen-Y-Bryn Lodge**, *41 Towey St, T03-4347939, www.penybryn.co.nz* A vast, lovely and historic Victorian villa, which is actually the largest single-storeyed timber dwelling in the South Island. It offers luxury en suites and a sumptuous 5-course dinner included in the price.

A **Clyde House**, *32 Clyde St, T03-4372774, www.clydehouse.co.nz* Built of original Oamaru Stone and offers a peaceful setting and comfortable doubles. Dinner by arrangement.

B **Glenhaven B&B**, *5 Forth St, T03-4370211*. Very friendly and has a separate en suite and a triple room in the house. Anybody interested in cars or toys will be fascinated with the Matchbox car collection.

B **Blue Penguin Lodge**, *2 Chelmer St, T03-4347027, bplodge@xtra.co.nz* A spacious former 1910 gentleman's residence. The rooms and the facilities are great value.

There are several **hostels** in and around town, all pretty comfortable, clean and friendly. Again the VIC has full listings.

C-D **Red Kettle YHA**, *corner of Reed and Cross Sts, T03-4345008, yhaoamaru@yha.org.nz* Offers dorm and twins and a welcoming open fire.

C-D **Swaggers**, *25 Wansbeck St, T03-4349999, swaggers@es.co.nz* A large suburban house a twin and 8 dorm beds.

C-D **Empire Hotel** *13 Thames St, T03-4343446, empirehotel@hotmail.com* and Ccentrally located, Victorian-style house which has the added attraction of free internet and even penny farthings.

B-D **Oamaru Gardens Top Ten Holiday Park**, *Chelmer St (signposted off Severn St, SH1), T03-4347666*. Backs onto the Oamaru Public Gardens and has flats, cabins, units, powered/tent sites and standard facilities.

Oamaru to Dunedin *p650*

D **Coastal Backpackers**, *south of Oamaru, T03-4395411, seaside@coastalbackpackers.co.nz* A popular and peaceful place within walking distance of the beach (All Day Bay). It has good-value doubles, twins and dorms, and canoes, body-boards and bikes can be hired. The nearest shop is 4 km away, so stock up.

D **Happy Valley Backpackers**, *15 km south of Oamaru just off SH1 (200 m down Happy Valley Rd), T03-4395041, rissmang@xtra.co.nz* Another good option with accommodation centred in a renovated old barn. A dorm, 1 double, tent sites and full kitchen facilities.

C-D **Olive Grove Holiday Park and Backpackers**, *SH1, just beyond the settlement of Herbert, before Moeraki and beside the Waianakarua River, T03-4395411*. Another fine spot to stay for a night.

B **Moeraki Motels**, *in Moeraki itself, T03-4394862*. Has basic but comfortable self-contained units and cottages.

C-D **Moeraki Motor Camp**, *T03-4394759*. Motel units, flats, cabins and powered/tent sites. Shop on site.

B-D **Joy's Guest House, B&B, Chalet and Backpackers**, *Moeraki, T03-4394762*. Also offers free English lessons!

⊙ Eating

Wanaka *p645*

$$$ **Ambrosia**, *76 Golf Course Rd, T03-4431255, www.ambrosiawanaka.co.nz* Chef Carlos was the head chef in one of Auckland's top restaurants Cin Cin and no doubt his lauded culinary talents will be welcome and prove popular.

$$$ **White House Café and Bar**, *corner of Dunmore and Dungarvon Sts, T03-4439595*. Daily from 1100. Deservedly popular with an imaginative Mediterranean/Middle Eastern menu with vegetarian options. Fine wine list, outdoor eating and a big fat cat that jumps on your lap.

$$ **Kai Whakapai**, *Lakefront, T03-4437795*. Daily from 0700. The best place for daytime eating. Has freshly baked breads, pies,

pastas, pizzas and a good vegetarian selection. Breakfasts are also good value, the coffee is great and there is outside seating from which to watch the world go by on the waterfront.

$$ Relishes *1/99 Ardmore St, T03-4439018. 0900-1500 and 1800 til late.* Another good option offering a good value blackboard menu, outdoor dining in summer and fireside dining in winter. Good coffee and breakfasts.

Sasanoki *145 Ardmore St, T03-4431188. Daily.* Modern kiwi fare with a Japanese influence.

$$ Bombay Palace *Upstairs on the Pembroke Mall, T03-4436086.* A good Indian choice.

$$ Tuatara Pizza Co *72 Ardmore St, T03-4438186.* For gourmet pizzas.

$ Muzza's Bar, *corner Brownston and Helwick Sts, T03-4437296.* Good value pub food.

$$ Cardrona Hotel , *see Sleeping above, T03-4438153. Daily from 1100.* Historic and cosy and well worth the 26-km journey for lunch or dinner.

Supermarkets New World, *Dunmore St. Daily 0800-2030.*

Hawea *p648*
Country Café, *T03-4438207.* Serves light meals and refreshments and sells petrol.

Oamaru *p648*
Oamaru has a surprisingly good range of eateries offering everything from seafood to Thai. Most of are on or around Thames St.

$$$ T'Bar Restaurant, *in the Quality Hotel, 115 Thames St, T03-4349892.* Offering a nice ambience and good traditional NZ/ European menu.

$$ Last Post Bar and Restaurant, *12 Thames St, in the former Oamaru Stone-built Post Office*; and

$$ Star and Garter, *opposite the VIC on Itchen St, T03-4345246.* Both offer casual dining at reasonable prices.

Oamaru has quite a high Chinese population which has a very noticeable influence on the standard of the local Chinese restaurants.

$$ Golden Dragon, *500 Thames Hwy;* and **$$ Golden Island**, *243 Thames Hwy.* The two most noted.

$ Northside Dairy, *447 Thames Hwy, T03-4370641.* Recommended takeaway food.

$ Emma's Café, *30 Thames St, T03-4341165 Tue-Sun 0900-1800.* For light snacks, a hearty

breakfast and good coffee. The locals' choice.   **655**

$ Whitestone Cheese Factory, *corner Torridge and Humber Sts, T03-4348098. Daily 0900-1700.* As well as the innovative blackboard menu in the café, you can of course sample and purchase their impressive range of 18 cheeses.

$ Criterion Hotel, *in the Tyne St precinct.* Pub grub and good beer in historic hotel.

$ Annie Flannigan's, *84 Thames St, T03-4348828.* Popular seudo-Irish pub. Live folk and rock mainly at weekends.

🎭 Entertainment

Wanaka *p645*
Slainte Irish Bar, *21 Helwick St, T03-4437663.* Proving popular and offers live music.

Shooters Bar. Also new and highly commercial. Seems very much to be aimed at the young and rapacious. Its saving grace is its fine position over looking the lake.

Calaboose Restaurant and Bar, *2 Dunmore St, T03-4436262.* A more sedate atmosphere.

Apartment One, *above Relishes Restaurant, 99 Ardmore St, T03-4434911.* Especially popular for its laid back atmosphere, balcony overlooking the lake and its cocktails, après ski and open fire in winter.

Paradiso Cinema and Café, *3 Ardmore St.* Famous for its one-of-a-kind movie offerings and comes complete with easy chairs and homemade ice cream. Front man (and Scot) Calum McLeod often provides an entertaining introduction. The café is just as laid back.

Oamaru *p648*
Penguin Entertainers Club, *Sea Side, Harbour St* is another little-known spot for occasional visiting live acts. For dates and directions contact T025-373-922, F4345637. Also popular with the locals is the modern **ten pin bowling complex** at the **Armada Motor Inn**, *500 Thames Hwy, T03-4370017.* It also has takeaway pizzas.

✹ Festivals and events

Wanaka *p645*
The big annual event in the region is the increasingly popular **Warbirds Over Wanaka**, which is New Zealand's premier **air show**, held at the end of Mar biannually

(due 2004). The venue is of course the airfield, which hosts a wide variety of visiting 'birds', but also blows the dust off the NZ Fighter Pilots Museum's very own Spitfire. Entry is from $20, child $5 (3-day $70). For more information, T03-4438619, www.nzfpm.com

Oamaru *p648*

The annual **Oamaru Victorian Heritage Celebrations** take place in the Historic Precinct on the third weekend in Nov. It's all fun, top hats and penny-farthings.

▲▲ Activities

Wanaka *p645*

Most of the above can be booked at the **VIC/ Lakeland Adventures** office (see 'Information' above).

Good Sports, *Dunmore St, T03-4437966, www.good-sports.co.nz* Hire out bikes, kayaks, 'funyaks', 'sit-on kayaks', fishing rods and tackle, plus the full range of ski and snow-sports equipment. The 2 main activity operators are:
Lakeland Adventures, *T03-4437495, www.lakelandadventures.co.nz* (Fishing, jet boating, cruising) that host the VIC; and
Edgewater Adventures, *59A Brownston St, T03-4438422, www.adventure.net.nz* (Trekking, cruising, fishing, 4-wheel drive tours, jet boating).

Canyoning

Most of the activities available in Wanaka you can also do elsewhere, but canyoning is a local speciality and recommended. It basically involves negotiating a mountain river with the assistance of gravity and in suitable attire. Methods of descent include scrambling, abseiling or just plain jumping – all great fun.
Deep Canyon, *T03-4437922, www.deepcanyon.co.nz* 'Do' the Emerald creek, Niger Stream and others (6-7 hrs) from $175 (16 years of age minimum). Transport and lunch included.

Cruising

Lakeland Adventures, *see above.* Offer scenic cruises of varying duration to explore the waters and islands of lake Wanaka from 1-3 hrs $50-$90 child $25-$45.

Fishing

The local fishing is excellent and there are many operators and guides including:
Kiwi Pete, *T025-2892044* (half day from $180);
Alpine Fishing Guides, *T03-4437655, www.cobwebs.co.nz/fishing* ($385 per boat);
Southern Lakes Fishing Safaris, *T03-4439121, www.southernlakesfishing.co.nz* (full day $395);
Wanaka Fishing Safaris, *T03-4437748, www.trout.net.nz* (full day $395);
Edgewater Adventures, *T03-4438422, www.adventure.net.nz* The most commercial operators offering the most competitive prices.
Lakeland Adventures, *see above.* Most of the above can also organize more adventurous **Heli-fishing trips** throughout the region. Prices start at about $85 per person per hr and about $300 for a privately guided half-day trip.
Good Sports, *Dunmore St.* Independent **licences** ($16) can be bought here.
Lakeland Adventures, *see above.* Offer independent rod hire from $20 per day.

Flightseeing

Wanaka is a superb base from which to reach **Milford Sound** by air, with the bonus of the stunning aesthetics of the **Aspiring National Park** on the way. Most flights from Queenstown and other centres (that cost about the same) do not follow quite the same spectacular flight path.
Aspiring Air, *at the airfield, T03-4437943, www.nz-flights.com* Offer a range of flights from a 20-min local flight for $100 to their highly recommended 4-hr *Majestic Milford Sound* flight. Leaving at 0845 or 1345 and arriving back at 1300 or 1800 this epic involves a superb flight over Wanaka, up the Matukituki River Valley, past Mount Aspiring and then out across the national park and out to sea, before flying up the chancel of Milford Sound and Milford Sound village. Included in the trip is a 45-min cruise on the Sound. It is a truly memorable experience and well worth the $330, child $200. Other alluring options include a scenic flight over Mount Cook (from $315) or several activity combos from jet boating in the Haast Region (from $400) to West Coast glacier landings (from $520).
Wanaka Flightseeing, *at the airfield, T03-4438787, www.flightseeing.co.nz* Offer

similar trips from $165-$335 including an interesting flight/jetboat experience with Dart River Jetboats in Glenorchy (see page 644), from $335, child $200. Recommended.

Golf
Wanaka's very scenic course is on *Ballantyne Rd, just behind the town, and welcomes visitors, T03-4437888*. Green fees are a very reasonable $20, club hire $15.
Rippon Vineyard, *T03-4438084, www.golfcross.co.nz* Hosts Wanaka's **Golf Cross** course which uses an oval ball and goals as opposed to holes.

Horse trekking
The Wanaka region offers some superb horse trekking possibilities.
Lake Wanaka Horse Trekking, *T03-4437777*, offer two daily 2-hr guided treks suitable for the beginner, from $55, child $45; while **NZ Backcountry Saddle Expeditions**, *near Cardrona, T03-4438151, backcountry.saddle. expeditions@xtra.co.nz* Offer 2-hr to 2-4 day treks, from $55, child $35 (full day $150).

Jet boating
Lake Wanaka and its surrounding scenic rivers would almost have to incorporate a jetboat trip somewhere, and there are a number of operators.
Wanaka Jet, *T03-4438408*. Offer 1-hr scenic trips on the Clutha and elsewhere, with an interesting commentary, from $65, child $35. A 3-hr combined fishing trip is also available at $125 per hr.
Clutha River Jet (Lakeland Adventures), *on the Lakefront, T03-4437495*. Also offer 1-hr trips down the Clutha for $70, child $35.
Wilkin River Jets, *Makarora*. Ply the Makarora and Wilkin Rivers (see page 648).

Kayaking
Alpine Kayak Guides, *T03-4439023, www.alpinekayaks.co.nz* Daily, guided white water day-trips on the Clutha, Matukituki and Hawea Rivers that are especially suitable for beginners. Transport and free pick-ups included, from $140 full day, $99 half day.
Self Exposure, *T03-4434085, www.selfexposure.co.nz* A new and enthusiastic local company offering overnight and heli trips. Prices on application.

Lakeland Adventures *see above*. Independent kayak hire from $10 per hr.

Mountaineering and rock climbing
With Mount Aspiring and so many other attractive mountain climbs so close to Wanaka it is not surprising to find a number of quality mountaineering guiding companies offering a range of packages.
Alpinism and Ski Ltd, *11 Rimu Lane, T03-4436593, www.alpinismski.co.nz* Offer guided trekking excursions throughout the region, and year-round to a number of peaks including Mount Aspiring and further afield to Mount Cook and the Westland National Park. Once you have flown over Aspiring you will appreciate that having a guide makes a lot of sense! The price of a guided climb of Aspiring on a 2:1 client: Guide ratio is $1625 (5 days without flights). Mountaineering courses, snow tours and trekking are also offered.
Mount Aspiring Guides, *T03-4439422, www.mtaspiringguides.co.nz* Offer a range of trips and packages all year round (Aspiring $2,195 2:1 Client: Guide with flights).
Adventure Consultants, *T03-4438711, www.adventure.co.nz* (Aspiring $2,450 2:1 Client: Guide with flights) Very good for mountaineering and ice-climbing courses.
Wanaka Rockclimbing, *T03-4431996, www.rockclimb.net.nz* Specialize in rock-climbing instruction, courses and ascents, from $99.
Wanaka Rock, *T03-4436411, www.wanakarock.co.nz* Another outfit earning a good reputation for introductory (1 day from $165), intermediate (1 day from $185) and multi-day technical courses, costing from $450.

Mountain biking
Alpine and Heli Mountain Biking, *T03-4438943, www.mountainbiking.co.nz* Take the nasty, uphill part out of a trip and take you by helicopter to some of the country's highest and most scenic track trailheads including Mount Pisa, Mount Alpha and the Treble Cone ski field. 4WD from $165 (heli from $295). Half-day road trips are also available from $130.
Self Exposure, *T03-4434085, www.selfexposure.co.nz* Offer some attractive overnight and heli trips. Prices are

available on application.

Cardrona Alpine Resort, *T03-4437341,
www.cardrona.com* Stays open in summer
to allow climbers, trampers and bikers to
access the mountains. The chairlift operates
daily from 1000-1600 and there are 2
purpose-built downhill bike tracks. Cardrona
is 34 km southeast of Wanaka on the Crown
Range Road.
Independent mountain bike hire:
Lakeland Adventures, *see above.*
Mountain Bikes Unlimited, *99 Ardmore St,
T03-4437882.*
Outdoor Sports *17-23 Dunmore St,
T03-4437966.* Prices start at about $25 for a
half day.

Off-road, 4WD and rallying
Criffel Peak Safaris, *Mount Barker Road,
T03-4431711, criffelpeak.safaris@xtra.co.nz*
The local ATV 4-wheel drive quad bike
adventure specialists, offering guided 2-5-hr
trips on farm and hill trails with great views,
from $75-$200.
EWA Land Adventures, *T03-4438422,
www.adventure.net.nz* Offer 2 hr 30 min
4-wheel drive tours taking in some stunning
views from $95.
Monster Mountain Rally, *Cardrona, Hwy 89,
T0800-872-559, www.mmrally.co.nz* Offer
the chance to experience rally driving
strapped in the passenger seat of a
performance rally car. There is plenty of fast
paced but safe action on gravel roads and
through water and even airborne. 2 hrs from
$150 (includes transport from Wanaka).

Paragliding and paraflying
Paragliding is huge around Wanaka with the
slopes of Mt Roy in particular providing ideal
terrain and conditions. On a fine day it is not
unusual to see over twenty colourful shutes
drifting across the skyline. Just makes you
want to give it a try!
Wanaka Paragliding, *T03-4439193,
www.wanakaparagliding.co.nz* Paragliding
on nearby Mount Iron, tandem from $80
(mountain tandem from $178). A full day
introductory course will cost from $188
(Sep-Apr).
Paragliding trips over lake Wanaka
(speedboat) are also available from the
waterfront (15-20 min) from about $180,
T03-4431680.

Rafting and river sledging
Pioneer Rafting, *T03-4431246.* Offers fairly
sedate eco-trips on the Clutha, full- or
half-day from $95, child $55. Multi-day trips
further afield are also available.
White-water sledging is growing in
popularity and provides a far more intimate
experience with the water on a modified
boogie board.
Frogz Have More Fun, *T0800-338737,
www.frogz.co.nz* A French-owned outfit
offering 1-2-hr trips on the Clutha, Hawea
and Kawarau Rivers, from $119 (minimum
age 10-14 years depending on the river).

Skiing
Wanaka has 2 great ski fields within 50 km of
the town, Cardrona to the south and Treble
Cone to the northwest.
Cardrona, *34 km from Wanaka on the Crown
Range (Cardrona) Rd, T03-4437341,
www.cardrona.com* It has a base area at
1670 m, and ski and board runs suitable for
all levels, with the intermediates being
especially well catered for. Facilities include
bars and restaurants and, unusually,
apartment accommodation. The ski season
runs from 23 Jun-7 Oct but the resort (and
some lifts) remain open in summer for
trampers and mountain bikers. Lift passes
from $62, child $31. **Waiorau Snow Farm**,
on the other side of the valley, T03-4437542,
www.snowfarm.co.nz A base for cross-
country skiing with international standard
tracks. It is open from mid Jun to the end of
Sep and a pass costs from $25, child $10.
Treble Cone Ski field, *20 km north west of
Wanaka via Glendhu, T03-4437443,
www.treblecone.co.nz* Well known for its
good snow and interesting terrain, not to
mention its stunning views of Lake Wanaka
and Mount Aspiring. It also offers more
ski-able terrain than any other ski or board
area in South Island and has the longest
vertical rise in the Southern Lakes Region.
Little wonder it is considered one of the best
fields in the country. It is open from
0900-1600 late Jun-early Oct (no access in
summer). Lift passes are from $63, child $32.
Full clothing, ski and board hire are available
on the mountain and there is a café, bar,
childcare centre and ski/board schools.
For general information and snow reports:
www.snow.co.nz / www.nzski.com or

www.skilakewanaka.com
Daily transport from Wanaka is available with
Ski Shuttle (transport and lift day-packages
available), *T03-4424630*. Other shuttle
operators are listed in Getting around above.
Harris Mountain Heli-skiing, *T03-4438589*,
www.heliski.co.nz 3-7 run days from $645.
Base, *corner of Helwick and Dunmore sts*,
T03-4436699, www.base.net.nz. Ski
equipment hire.
Good Sports, *Dunmore St, T03-4437966*. Also
arrange transport.
Racer's Edge Planet Snow, *99 Ardmore St*,
T03-4437882, www.racersedge.co.nz Average
prices – skis/boots from $32, child $12/
Snowboard and boots from $39, child $20.

Skydiving
The Wanaka Region is one of the most scenic
in the country, which gives that added edge
to any jump.
Tandem Skydive Wanaka, *T0800-786877*,
T03-4437207, www.skydivenz.com Operate
out of the airfield from heights of 9,000
($245) and 12,000 ($295), allowing 30-50
seconds of free-fall at around 200 kph,
followed by a gentle and peaceful 6-7-min
parachute ride to earth. Weight limit 100
kg/age limit 7 years. Many people in the
business recommend Wanaka, as we do!
Pick-ups from Wanaka are free.

Wakeboarding
Lake Wanaka is the perfect place for
wakeboarding and big enough for you to be
able to find a quiet spot.
Wake Wanaka, *T03-4434350*. More details
and lessons.
Sun and Snow Business, *103 Ardmore St*,
T03-4438855. Independent hire

Walking
Other than the **Mount Iron Walk** (see
above) and the walk to **Rob Roy Glacier**
(highly recommended, see page 651), there
are many other possibilities. Two popular
alternatives are the ascent of Mount Roy or
the easier, but still quite demanding, climb
to the top of **Rocky Mountain past
Diamond Lake**. From lakeside, the vision
of Mount Roy (1585m), which dominates the
western edge of Roy's Bay, can hardly be
missed, but its ascent can reward you with
some tremendous views. A well-formed path

zigzags its way to the summit from a car park
6 km north of Wanaka towards **Glendhu
Bay**. The walk takes about 5 hrs return, and
Mount Aspiring Express, *T03-4438422*, offer
a shuttle service to the car park: $10 return.
Further up this road, past Glendhu and
before the entrance to the Treble Cone Ski
field, is the **Rocky Mountain and
Diamond Lake Walk**. The appeal here is
the view of Mount Aspiring and the
Matukituki River Valley, as well as Lake
Wanaka itself. The geology is also
fascinating, with rocks that form unusual
mounds and folds across the landscape. It is
a stiff climb, but the path is marked and it is
definitely worth the effort. At the end of
Hospital Flat you will see the signposted car
park. From there it is 20 mins to the fairly
unremarkable lake before the track skirts
around the slopes to the top. On the descent
be careful not to stray off the path far from
the lower lookout. You need to double back
here to rejoin the track. The walk takes about
3 hrs return and again **Mount Aspiring
Express**offer a shuttle from $25 return. For
detailed walks information grab a copy of
the *Wanaka Walks* broadsheet from
Edgewater Adventures or the local walks
leaflets from DoC.
Mount Aspiring National Park
offers endless opportunities for walking
and tramping.
Mount Aspiring Guides, *99 Ardmore St*,
T03-4439422,
www.MountAspiringGuides.com and
Edgewater Adventures, *59A Brownston St*,
T03-4438422, www.adventure.net.nz Both
offer an extensive range of guided day and
multi-day walk options.

Other activities
Wanaka Sightseeing *T03-4431855*. Offer
very pleasant 2-5 hr sightseeing tours of the
region from $25.
Alpine Shuttles, *T03-4437966*. Offer half- or
full-day wine or garden tours.
Clean Green Images, *T03-4437951*,
www.cleangreen.co.nz Photo nature tours
from $60.
Aspiring Images, *T03-4438358*,
grussell@xtra.co.nz General eco- and
4-wheel drive nature/photography tours
from $30 per hr.

Of special note in this area is the superb 3-day **Gillespie Pass Tramp** and 'The Siberia Experience' run by **Southern Alps Air** (in conjunction with **Wilkin River Jet Boats**, *housed in the café and shop, T0800-345666, T03-4434385, www.siberiaexperience.co.nz, www.southernalpsair.co.nz* This evocatively named jaunt is a combination of scenic flight, tramp and jetboat, which gets consistently good reviews. You are first flown (25 mins) into the beautiful and remote **Siberia Valley**, from where you tramp for about 3 hrs to the Wilkin River to be picked up by Jetboat with a 30-min scenic ride back to Makarora. At $225, child $150, it is good value. They also offer scenic flights to Milford, Mount Cook or over Aspiring National Park from 20 mins ($160) to 2¼ hrs ($550).

Wilkin River Jet Boats, *T03-4438351, wilkinriverjets@xtra.co.nz* Offer 1 hr trips on the scenic Wilkin from $60, child $30, as well as water-taxi services for trampers from $45.

◐ Directory

Wanaka *p645*
Banks National, *T03-4437521*. Westpac, *T03-4437857*. They also have ATMs. **Bike hire** Good Sports, *Dunmore St,*

T03-4437966, www.good-sports.co.nz from $25-$50 per day. Lakeland Adventures, *on the Lakefront, T03-4437495*. **Car hire** Aspiring, *T03-4437883*. Adventure Rentals, *31 Dunmore St, T03-4436051*. Good Sports, *T03-4437966*. Lakeland Adventures, *T03-4437495*. Wanaka Car Rentals, *T03-4438422*. **Post office** *39 Ardmore St, T03-4438211. Mon-Fri 0830-1730, Sat 0900-1200*. **Medical facilities** Aspiring Medical Centre, *28 Dungarvon St, T03-4431226*. Wanaka Medical Centre, *21 Russell St, T03-4437811*. **Useful** addresses Police: *28 Helwick St, T03-4437272*.**Taxi** Wanaka Taxi, *T03-4437999*. **Internet** Budget Communications, *38 Helwick St, T03-4434440 Daily 1000-2200*. WanakaWeb, *3 Helwick St, T03-4437429. Daily 0900-2100*.

Oamaru *p648*
Banks Most of the major bank branches and ATMs on Thames St, with some housed in grand historic buildings. The National Bank, in the former 1871 Bank of Otago building, is the best example. **Internet** VIC, *see above*. Quality Hotel Brydone, *see above*. Small Bytes Computing, *187 Thames St*. Lagonda Coach Travel tearooms, *see above*. **Post office** *Severn St, near the intersection with Thames*.

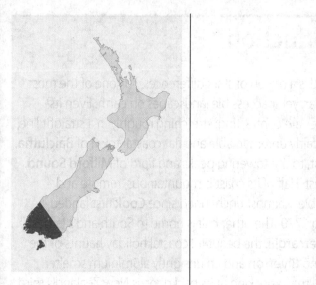

Southland and the Fiords

Introduction

Southland is a region of stark differences. It is one of the most spectacular, yet inaccessible landscapes on earth. Even its boundaries are contrasting; stretching roughly in a straight line, from the fairly unremarkable and flat coastal town of **Balclutha**, in the east, to the towering peaks and fiord of **Milford Sound**, to the west. Half of its coast is mountainous, remote and inhospitable – almost unchanged since **Cook** first landed (briefly) in 1770. The other half is home to Southland's largest town **Invercargill**, the beautiful coastal holiday haunts of the **Catlins** and **Riverton** and an unsightly aluminium smelter. Amidst all that, knocking at its backdoor, is New Zealand's third island and newest national park, **Stewart Island**.

Most visitors head for the hills, and who can blame them? The **Fiordland National Park**, which is part of the internationally acclaimed **Te Wahipounamu World Heritage Area**, is a staggering 2.6 million hectares of some of the world's most magnificent scenery and covers 10 percent of the country as a whole. And, although the vast majority of it is wonderfully inaccessible, it still contains over 5000 km of walking tracks. But don't be fooled into thinking the less spectacular parts are not worth a look. There, too, you will find a warm welcome and some pleasant surprises. Where else on earth, for example, can you meet a 150 year-old **tuatara**, a reptile that has outlived the fiords themselves? Or see, unusually in daylight hours, the weird and wonderful **kiwi**, that flightless national icon.

★ Don't miss...

❶ A major tramp in the **Fiordland National Park** – perhaps the 'moderate' Kepler, the 'challenging' Dusky or the new Hump Ridge Track, page 667.

❷ Driving to magnificent **Milford Sound** via the unforgettable Milford Road from Te Anau, page 666.

❸ **Kayaking** under the waterfalls of Milford Sound, page 671, or amidst the dolphins of Doubtful Sound, page 675.

❹ Overnighting on **Doubtful Sound** where the silence is deafening, page 675.

❺ Cruising beautiful **Lake Manapouri**, and then going underground to the power station, page 676.

❻ 'Henry' the tuatara in the Southland Museum, **Invercargill**, page 680.

❼ Wild kiwi on **Stewart Island** – New Zealand's newest national park, page 691.

❽ The quiet back roads and stunning scenery of the **Catlins Coast**, page 696.

❾ The sunrise over **Nugget Point**, page 700.

Southland and the Fiords Introduction

Te Anau → *Phone Code: 03 Colour map 7, grid A3 Population: 3000*

On the shores of New Zealand's second largest lake, Lake Te Anau, and at the edge of the magnificent wilderness of the Fiordland National Park is the 'walking capital of the world', Te Anau. In summer it is like a busy gatehouse with crowds of eager trampers, intent on and excited at the prospect of visiting its enormous garden. In winter it is like an unused holiday house, with only its resident caretaker, quietly waiting and wanting to turn the heating on again. As you drive into Te Anau, often wedged between a convoy of tour buses, it can initially seem a rather dull little town, but once you acquaint yourself with its bustling centre, spacious open areas and beautiful lake views, your desire to move on quickly will fade. And although what lies beyond the town is what you have really come to see, it is worth giving Te Anau a little time. And, given the fickle weather in these parts, you my have little choice.

Ins and outs

Getting there **By air** Te Anau is served from Queenstown by **Air New Zealand Link** (agents are the Te Anau Travel and Information Centre, Lakefront Dr, T03-2497516), **Air Milford,** T03-4422351, and **Air Fiordland,** T03-2497505. The airfield is between Te Anau and Manapouri. For airfield transport contact **Te Anau Taxis,** T03-2497777. By car, Te Anau is 177 km southwest of Queenstown via SH6, 152 km from Invercargill via SH99 (Southern Scenic Route) and 290 km west of Dunedin via Gore and SH94. The town is served by **Intercity** (Christchurch/Invercargill/Dunedin daily) T03-2497505; **Topline Tours,** Caswell St (Queenstown daily, from $35), T0508-832628, www.toplinetours.co.nz; **Catch-a-Bus** (Dunedin daily), T03-4714141; **Scenic Shuttle** (Invercargill, daily Nov-Apr, Mon-Fri May-Oct), T03-2497654, T0800-277483; and the backpacker orientated **Bottom Bus** (Queenstown/Dunedin/Invercargill), T03-4347370. All buses stop in the town centre. **Back Track Transport,** T03-2497457, offer a rather unique way to get to Te Anau via Lake Wakatipu (Queenstown) and the Steamer TSS Earnslaw. Once ashore at the remote Walter Peak Station you can then travel by coach via the pretty Von Valley and Mavora Lakes to Te Anau.

Getting around (Trampers' track transport) Both local fixed-wing and helicopter companies offer chartered transportation (or packages) to Milford and beyond (see Activities, page 669). **Air Fiordland,** Town Centre, T03-2497505 (Hollyford/Milford); **Waterwings Airways,** Lake Front (Milford/Dusky), T03-2497405; **South-West Helicopters,** T03-2497402, offer helicopter charters throughout the region.

Tracknet, office at the Te Anau Lake View Holiday Park, Te Anau-Manapouri Hwy, T03-2497777, offer shuttle **bus** services and packages to Queenstown ($35 one way); Milford-Te Anau Downs ($35); Routeburn/Greenstone/Hollyford turn-off ($20); Kepler control gates ($5). All shuttle services run from Oct-May except the Milford Track service which is year-round, T03-2497777, www.greatwalksnz.com **Topline Tours** (see above) also offer shuttle services to tramping trailheads. By **boat**, **Sinbad Cruises,** based on the lakefront, T03-2497106, sinbad@teanau.co.nz, offer an appealing way to reach the start of the Milford Track (from $65) or Kepler Track (from $20) on the 36 ft Gaff ketch 'Manuska'. **Lakeland Boat Hire,** Te Anau, T03-2498364, stevesaunders@xtra.co.nz, run a regular water-taxi service to Brod Bay and the Kepler Track from $15 one-way.

Information Te Anau has a worryingly large number of information centres and booking offices. The most unbiased information is available from: **Fiordland VIC (I-Site),** ① *Lakefront Dr, T03-2498900, vin@realjourneys.co.nz Daily 0830-1800 (winter 0830-1700).* It deals with all local information and serves as the agents for domestic air and bus bookings. **Real Journeys**, ⓘ *downstairs from VIC. Daily summer 0830-2100.* Deals with local sightseeing trips on Lake Te Anau (including the Te Anau Caves) and to Milford and Doubtful Sounds. **DoC Fiordland National Park Visitor Centre**, ⓘ *at the southern end of Lakefront, T03-2497924, greatwalksbooking @doc.govt.nz Daily 0830-1800 (seasonal).* The principal source for track information, track bookings office and up-to-date weather forecasts. There is also a small museum and audio-visual theatre ($3).

Other information and booking offices: **Te Anau Travel and Information Centre**, ⓘ *Lakefront Dr, T03-2497516, teanau.travel@xtra.co.nz* The handling agents for Air New Zealand, including check-in for Te Anau flights. Take bookings for most local trips. **Tick-it Te Anau (Air Fiordland)**, ⓘ *town centre, T03-2497505, www.airfiordland.com 0730-2000 (seasonal).* Have a local sightseeing booking office in their main office.

Lake Te Anau → Colour map 7, grid A3

At 61 km long, 10 km at its widest point and a total of 344 sq.km in area, **Lake Te Anau** is the largest lake in the South Island and second largest in the land. Looking from the lakeside up its length to the Earl Mountains it certainly seems worthy of those dimensions and perhaps the label of the prettiest in the country. Directly opposite Te Anau, unseen in the bush, is the meanderings of the **Kepler Track** which begins at the southern end of the lake and skirts its southwestern edge, before climbing steadily towards the Kepler Mountains and the spectacular views from the **Luxmore Hut**. Also along the western edge between the Middle and South Fiords are the 200 m **Te Ana-au Caves**. Long revered by Maori, but only rediscovered by the Europeans in 1948, they provide the usual spectacular rock formations, fossils, whirlpools, waterfalls and glow-worms. The caves can only be accessed by boat and guided trips (2 ½ hours) leave from the wharf at Te Anau up to six times a day. After arriving by launch you are given a short video presentation before joining your guide on a short bush walk to the caves. The caves themselves are then explored by foot and on the water by punt. The 2015 (summer) or 1845 (winter) evening trips are recommended. Book with **Real Journeys**, Lakefront Drive, T03-2497416. From $45, child $15 ($52 for 2015).

On the southern shores of the lake on the road to Manapouri, is the **DoC Te Anau Wildlife Centre**, which is an important breeding centre for **takahe** and other rare native species. The story of the takahe is a fascinating one. Thought to be extinct for over 50 years, a small group were rediscovered in the Murchison Mountains above Lake Te Anau in 1948, by ornithologist and medical practitioner Dr Geoffrey Orbell.

Te Anau

Sleeping
Anchorage 1
Arran 2
Cats Whiskers B&B 3
Croft 4
Fiordland Lodge 14
Holiday Inn & Restaurant 5
Lake Front Lodge 6
Lakefront Backpackers 7
Lakeside Motel 8
Lake Te Anau
 Backpackers 9
Mountain View Top
 Ten Holiday Park 10
Red Tussock Motel 11
Te Anau Lakeview
 Holiday Park &
 Steamers Backpackers 12
Te Anau YHA 13

Eating
La Toscana Pizzeria 1
Moose Restaurant & Bar 2
Olive Tree Café 3
Quality 4
Ranch 7
Redcliff Café & Bar 5
Snack Attack 6

Although much of what goes on behind the scenes at the centre (in their efforts to maintain the new breeding colony in the Murchison Ranges) is off-limits, the open-air aviaries and grounds are very appealing and well worth the visit. Once again it is very refreshing to see such efforts being made in wildlife conservation in New Zealand and to witness unique species in such a relaxed atmosphere. There are takahe, kea, morepork, and kaka to name but a few. Entry is very reasonably by donation, T03-2497921. Across the road from the Wildlife Centre is the 35-ha **Ivor Wilson Park** (open dawn to dusk) which offers a number of pleasant tracks and picnic spots amongst native bush and surrounding Lake Henry. Open dawn to dusk. For children or urbanites **Glen Monarch Farm Tours**, located off SH94 (17 km) offer an entertaining introductory kiwi farm tour with the obligatory sheep shearing and working dog demonstrations as well as plenty of animal petting, (3 hr) from $45 (plus $20 per vehicle transport from Te Anau), T03-2497041.

The Milford Road → *Colour map 7, grid A3*

The 119 km trip into the heart of the **Fiordland National Park** and **Milford Sound** is all part of the world-class Milford Sound experience. In essence it is a bit like walking down the aisle, past the interior walls of a great cathedral, to stand aghast at the chancel and the stunning stained-glass windows above. This may sound like an exaggeration but if nature is your religion, then the trip to Milford is really nothing short of divine. Of course much depends on the weather. Ideally it should be of either extreme – cloudless, or absolutely thumping it down. Under clear blue skies it is of course magnificent, but many say that the trip through the mountains is better during very heavy rain. It is an incredibly moody place so don't necessarily be put off by foul weather.

From Te Anau you skirt the shores and enjoy the congenial scenery of Lake Te Anau before heading inland at **Te Anau Downs** (30 minutes). This is principally a boat access point to the Milford Track (there is a **motel**, T0800-500805, and a **hostel**, T0800-478679, www.teanau- milfordsound.co.nz). Another 30 minutes will see you through some low-lying alluvial flats and meadows as the Earl Mountains begin to loom large. After penetrating some beech forest you suddenly emerge into the expanse of the **Eglinton River Valley** with its stunning views towards the mountains. This is known as the 'Avenue of the Disappearing Mountain' and it speaks for itself.

At the northern end of the valley you then re-enter the shade of the beech forests and encounter **Mirror Lake**, a small body of water overlooking the Earl Mountain Range. The lookout point is a short walk from the road. On a clear day you can, as the name suggests, capture the mood and the scene twice in the same shot.

● *If you are an independent traveller without your own transport, you'll need to rely on tour buses. Almost 30 make the daily pilgrimage to Milford Sound in summer, especially from about 1100 onwards, so go early or late in the day.*

Several kilometres further on is **Knobs Flat** where there is a DoC shelter and information/display centre and toilet facilities. For much of the next 25 minutes you negotiate the dappled shadows on a near constant tunnel of beautiful beech forest before reaching **Lake Gunn**, which offers some fine fishing and a very pleasant 45 minutes' nature walk through the forest. The copious growth of mosses and lichens here provide the rather unsubtle hint that the place can get very wet, very often!

From Lake Gunn you are really beginning to enter 'tiger country' as the road climbs to **The Divide** one of the lowest passes along the length of the Southern Alps. Here a shelter and an assortment of discarded boots marks the start of the **Routeburn** and **Greenstone/Caples Tracks**. The car park also serves as the starting point to a classic, recommended (three hours return) walk to **Key Summit** which looks over the Humboldt and Darran Ranges. Round the corner there is the **Falls Creek (Pop's View) Lookout**, which looks down the **Hollyford Valley**. Depending on the weather this will be a scene of fairly quiet serenity or one of near epic proportions as the swollen Hollyford River rips its way down to the valley fed by a million fingers of white water.

Fiordland National Park

Fiordland National Park is 1.25 million ha and the largest of New Zealand's 14 national parks. In 1986 it was declared a World Heritage Area on account of its outstanding natural features, exceptional beauty and its important demonstration of the world's evolutionary history. Four years later, in 1990, Fiordland National Park was further linked with three others – **Mount Aspiring**, **Westland** and **Mount Cook** **(Aoraki)** to form the (United Nations) World Heritage Area of South West New Zealand. It was given the Maori name **Te Waipounamu** (*Te* 'the'/ *Wai* 'waters'/ *Pounamu* 'greenstone' or 'jade'). (Twice the size of Singapore with 0.06% of the population.) Hopefully we can rest assured, that with such official labels and protection it will remain the stunning wilderness it is.

Following the river is the **Lower Hollyford Road** and access to **Lake Marian** (1 km), a superb (three hours return) walk up through forest and past waterfalls into a glacial hanging valley that holds the lake captive. Photographers will find the best light in the early morning. A further 7 km on is the **Hollyford (Gun's) Camp**, and the Hollyford Airfield, important access and accommodation points for the **Hollyford Track** (See page 705), the trailhead for which is at the road terminus 6 km further on. The short 30 minutes' return walk to the **Humboldt Falls**, which again are spectacular after heavy rain, starts just before the car park.

Back on the main Milford Road the mountains begin to close in on both sides as you make the ascent up to the **Homer Tunnel**, an incredible feat of engineering, and a bizarre and exciting experience, like being swallowed by a giant drain. It seems to have changed little since the last bit of rubble was cleared and is only lit by road markers. This simply adds to the appeal as long as you are not claustrophobic, or indeed on a bike! (If you are you had better pedal like mad or shut your eyes for its entire 1200 m length and think of the ocean).

However, keep your eyes open for **kea** (native mountain parrots) that frequent the main stopping areas at either end of the tunnel. If they are not there, it is worth stopping a while to see if they turn up. Watching these incredibly intelligent birds go about their business of creating general mayhem in the name of food and sheer vandalism is highly entertaining. There will be plenty of photo opportunities and despite the obvious temptation DO NOT feed them. A parrot fed on white bread, crisps and chocolate is, obviously, a very sick parrot.

Once out of the tunnel you are now in the spectacular **Cleddau Canyon** and nearing Milford Sound. Instantly you will see the incredibly precipitous aspect of the mountains and bare valley walls. The rainfall is so high and rock and mudslides so frequent that the vegetation has little chance to establish itself. As a result the rainwater just cascades rapidly into the valleys. Note the creeks that cross under the road. There are so many they don't have names, but numbers! These all count up steadily to form the **Cleddau River** which, at **The Chasm** (20 minutes return), is really more waterfall than river, and has, over the millennia, sculpted round shapes and basins in the rock. From the Chasm it is five minutes before you see the tip of the altar of **Mitre Peak** (1692 m) and spire of **Mount Tutoko** (2746 m), Fiordland's highest peak. It's now only five minutes before your appointment with the Minister of Awe at the Chancel of **Milford Sound**.

Southland and the Fiords Te Anau

🛏 Sleeping

Bear in mind that there are some excellent overnight cruise options on both Milford and Doubtful Sounds see pages 673 and 677.

LL-L Holiday Inn (formerly the Centra), *Lakefront Dr, T03-2499700, holidayinn.teanau@xtra.co.nz* Lakeside, and the most high profile hotel in town. It has had a number of renovations and offers standard rooms, self-contained villas and 4 deluxe suites. A la carte restaurant, spa, pool and sauna.

There are a generous number of **B&Bs and homestays**, most out in the country.

LL-L Fiordland Lodge, *472 Te Anau-Milford Highway, (5 km north of Te Anau), T03-2497832, www.fiordlandlodge.co.nz* A fine new option that offers 10 very tidy en suite guest rooms, 2 self-contained log cabins, restaurant and a large open fire. All you feel inclined to do is sit and watch the ever-changing scene from the huge windows overlooking the lake and mountains. The owners also offer a wide range of guided excursions. The VIC has full listings of others. Recommended.

AL Croft B&B, *Milford Rd (on the edge of town, 3 km north), T03-2497393, www.thecroft.co.nz* With 2 new self contained cottages set in private gardens on a farm with memorable views across the lake. Very peaceful and plenty of pets dying to make your acquaintance.

AL Cat's Whiskers B&B, *2 Lakefront Dr, T03-2498112.* Conveniently placed town B&B.

There are plenty of **motels** around town, the best and most expensive being on Lakefront Dr and the older and cheaper tending to be elsewhere, particularly one street back on Quintin Dr. On Lakefront Dr, from the town centre heading south:

AL-A Radfords Motel *56, T03-2499186, www.radfordslakeviewmotel.co.nz;*

L-A Lake Front Lodge *58, T03-2497728, www.LakefrontLodge.co.nz*

A Lakeside Motels *36, T03-2497435, www.lakesideteanau.com* (set amongst beautiful gardens);

A Red Tussock Motel, *10 Lakefront Dr (at the southern end), T03-2499110;* (a recent addition and recommended).

In Quintin Dr you have the options of the cheaper but comfortable:

A Arran, *T03-2498826, www.arranmotel.co.nz;* and

A-B Anchorage, *T03-2497256, www.teanaumotel.co.nz*

There are plenty of **backpacker hostels** most of which are geared up to cater for trampers and muddy boots.

C-D Te Anau YHA, *29 Mokonui St, T03-2497847, yhatanau@yha.org.nz* After years out of town has been relocated and purpose-built right in the centre. It is the most popular backpacker option (deservedly so) with a wide range of rooms and a very comfortable lounge.

C-D Lake Te Anau –Te Anau Lakefront Backpackers, *48-50 Lakefront Dr, T03-2497713, www.teanaubackpackersco.nz* A large bustling place with all the usual facilities plus some excellent double or quad ex-motel units and new fully self contained units at reasonable prices. Spa and internet. Bike hire.

C-D Steamers Beach Backpackers, *across the road from the DoC Visitor Centre, T03-2497737, www.teanau.info.co.nz* The strangest looking backpackers in town, owned and operated by the Te Anau Lake View Holiday Park. Perhaps looks a little over the top but you'll find both fore and aft perfectly comfortable and fine facilities on deck.

There are also a number of perfectly acceptable backpackers on the roads north to Milford or south to Manapouri.

A-D Eglington Experiences, *Knobs Flat (north, 62 km, and within the boundary of the Fiordland National Park, T03-2499122.* Eco-orientated and has studio motel units, shared backpacker dorms, powered sites and campsites. Bar the sandflies it is a great place to be based.

C-D Barnyard Backpackers, *80 Mt York Rd (south off SH95, 9 km), T03-2498006.* Tidy log cabins, van or campsites on a deer farm, open fire, horse trekking, internet and transport.

Motorcamps and campsites

See also backpackers above.

A-D Mountain View Top Ten Holiday Park, *128 Te Anau Terr, T03-2497462, www.teanaumountainview.co.nz* A proud multi-award winner and one of the best holiday parks in the country. The facilities are excellent and kept exceptionally clean and well maintained. You are even personally escorted to your site. It lives up to its name as having a 'bed for every budget'.

A-D **Te Anau Lake View Holiday Park**, *1 Te Anau-Manapouri Hwy (at the other end of the town over looking the lake, SH95, T03-2497457, www.Teanau.info* More spacious and offering a wide range of options from new motel units, to cabins, powered sites and tent sites. Internet café, sauna and spa, Sky TV. The added attraction here, other than the modern facilities is the organization of activities and ease of tramping track transportation in conjunction with the in-house 'Tracknet' company.

🍴 Eating

For fine dining the à la carte restaurants in $$$ **Holiday Inn** (McKinnon Room), *T03-2499700*, and
$$$ **Quality Hotel** (Bluestone), *T03-2497421*, are an option and both open daily.
$$$ **Redcliff Café and Bar**, *12 Mokonui St, T03-2497431. Daily 1600-late.* Far more intimate and congenial, and offers some particularly good lamb and venison dishes.
$$ **Moose Restaurant and Bar**, *Lakeside Dr, T03-2497100. Daily from 1100 for lunch and dinner.* It has lost a little of its former atmosphere but can still serve up a good meal and has the town's most popular bar attached.
$$ **La Toscana Pizzeria**, *108 Town Centre, T03-2497756. 1730-2200.* Good value and recommended.
$ **Olive Tree Café**, *52 Town Centre, T03-2498496. Daily 0800-2100.* Good coffee.
Supermarkets Super Value, *1 The Lane. Daily 0800-20000.* **Four Square**, *Town Centre. 0830-2130, seasonal.*

⛰ Activities

The vast majority of visitors to Te Anau use it as a portal to Milford and Doubtful Sounds and the major tramping tracks. Note that there are other activity operators in Milford Sound, Manapouri and Queenstown offering a wide range of other trips in the region (see pages 677 and 627).

Cruising

Sinbad Cruises, *lakefront, T03-2497106, sinbad@teanau.co.nz* Offer an appealing way to cruise the lake in the 36 ft Gaff ketch 'Manuska'. Trip options include 5-hr day cruise, cruise/walk, Heli/cruise and overnight cruises from $55.

Diving

Tawaki Dive (Dive Milford), *T03-2499006, www.tawakidive.co.nz* Unique full-day fiord diving trips for the experienced, from $235.

Fishing

As you might imagine the fishing in the region is superb, provided you can take your eyes off the stunning backdrops.
Kiwi Reel-Rifle, *T03-2499071, www.kiwireelrifle.com* The most commercial operators in Te Anau (and the cheapest). Offer a half day trip for $115, full day $380 and a *Dawn and Dusk* option from $300. Tuition and tackle available.
Fiordland Guides, *T03-2497832, www.fiordlandguides.co.nz* More specialist services. Charge about $90 per hr or $580 for 2 people on a full day trip. Overnight camping trips are also an option.
Fish Fiordland, *T03-2498070, www.fishfiordland.co.nz;* and
Fish and Trips, *T03-2497656, www.fiordland-flyfishing.com* Both offer a full day trip for $500 all-in.

Flightseeing

Without doubt the best way to see the **Fiordland National Park** is from the air.
Air Fiordland, *Town Centre, T03-2497505, www.airfiordland.com* From $150-$480.
Waterwings Airways, a **floatplane** *that operates from the lakeshore, Lakefront Dr, T03-2497405, waterwings@teanau.co.nz* Both are fixed-wing operators offering a range of options principally to **Milford and Doubtful Sound** including flight only to flight/cruise and coach in/fly out, from 1-4½ hrs and $225. Waterwings also offer flights with kayaking and hiking options while both Air Fiordland and Waterwings can also be chartered to see some of the remote locations used for filming in the *Lord of the Rings Trilogy*.
Southern Lakes Helicopters, *Lakefront Dr, T03-2497167, slheli@teanau.co.nz* The

principal **helicopter** operator in Te Anau. **Fiordland Helicopters**, *T03-2497575, www.fiordlandhelicopters.co.nz;* and **South West Helicopters**, *T03-2497409, www.southwesthelicopters.co.nz*

All the above offer a dynamic range of flights and packages from 10 mins (from around $100) to 1½ hrs ($600). Again the principal locations are Milford and Doubtful Sounds though a trip to see the remote wilderness of the **Dusky Sound**, a heli-hike-cruise trip to the Mount Luxmore Hut on the **Kepler Track** or a scenic flight and jet boat combo are all available (at a price!).

Waterwings, *in conjunction with Kiwi Reel-Rifle Ltd (see above),* also now offer a new and attractive 'Masters of the Monument' **fly/kayak** option that takes in filming locations from the *Lord of the Rings* from $180.

4WD

High Ride 4 Wheeler Adventures, *T03-2498591, www.highride.co.nz* Offer scenic (3-4-hr) backcountry safaris on 4-wheel drive ATVs from $120. Also offer horse trekking (with transportation from Te Anau). 2½ hrs, from $70.

Golf

Golf Fiordland, *T03-2497247.* Can take care of all the arrangements, for a reasonable fee. **Te Anau Golf Club**, *T03-2497474.* Green fee $25.

Horse trekking

Westray, *55 Ramparts Rd, T03-2499079.* 2 hrs from $60, child $45.
High Ride, *see above.* Also offer trekking with transportation.

Jet boating

Luxmore Jet, *T03-2496951, www.luxmorejet.co.nz* Offer memorable 1-hr scenic trips down the **Upper Waiau River** that connects Lake Te Anau and Lake Manapouri, from $75, child $40.

Kayaking

Fiordland Wilderness Experiences, *T03-2497700, www.fiordlandseakayak.co.nz* Offer a day excursion on **Milford and Doubtful Sounds** from $110. The Milford trip is especially good taking in the scenery of the Milford Road.

Rosco's Milford Sound Sea Kayaks, *see page 674.* An excellent company based in Milford Sound.
Kiwi Reel-Rifle Ltd, *T03-2499071, www.kiwireelrifle.com* Offer an attractive 2-3 hr moonlight paddling experience on Lake Te Anau or Manapouri from $85. **Lakeland Boat Hire Te Anau**, *T03-2498364.* Offer independent hire from $25 per hr. Other spectacular kayaking options are available in Milford and Doubtful Sound from Manapouri (see pages 673and 677).

Mountain biking

Fiordland Bike and Hike, *T03-2497098, www.bikefiordland.co.nz* Offer a great tour that takes in the downhill sections of the Milford Road and includes a cruise on Milford Sound, from $119 (departs Te Anau at 0800). Recommended. Their local mountain biking tours start from $69 for 3-4 hrs.

Sightseeing tours

All the highly commercial Queenstown-based scenic day coach tours (see page 627) pass through Te Anau and you can join these to reach **Milford or Doubtful Sounds**. The VIC has details and you are advised to book in advance.
Trips and Tramps, *T03-2497081.* More locally and far more personable. Offer day-trip to Milford Sound (including cruise ticket). It departs Te Anau at 0830 and returns at 1800 and costs $142, child $90. They also do a Milford Track day walk option from $126.
Milford Wilderness Explorer, *T03-2497505, www.airfiordland.com* Also offer personalized trips with cruise options from Te Anau from about $115, child $70.
Fiordland Bike and Hike, *see above.* For a far more intimate mountain biking tour of the Milford Road.

Walking

The biggest local attraction here is of course the 67 km (2-3 day), **Kepler Track** which can be walked in whole or part. One of the most popular day or overnight walks is to capture the view from the **Luxmore Hut**, which is the first DoC hut on the track (in the traditional anticlockwise direction). To access the hut by foot, walk along the southern edge of the lake to the control gates. From there it is a fairly strenuous 11 km (6 hrs) one-way walk along the lake edge and up above the tree line to the hut. One very appealing way to cut out much of the strain is to get a water-taxi (T03-2498364, $30 return) or to join a walk/cruise trip (see Cruising above) from Te Anau to **Brod Bay**. It is then a 16 km (8 hrs) return trip.

Trips and Tramps *T03-2497081, www.milfordtourwalks.co.nz* Offer **Milford Track** day-walks (5 hrs and 11 km walking) on the Milford Track from $120, child $77. **Fiordland Bike and Hike**, *T03-2497098, www.bikefiordland.co.nz;* and **Fiordland Guides**, *T03-2497832, www.fiordlandguides.co.nz* Both also offer a range of guided walking options. A walk to Lake **Marian** on the Milford Road is also recommended.

Bev's Tramping Gear, *16 Homer St, T03-2497389, bevs.hire@max.net.co.nz* and **SportsWorld**, *38-40 Town Centre.* Both hire a vast range of walking, tramping and camping equipment at competitive prices.

Banks There are 2 banks (Westpac/BNZ) in the town centre both have ATMs and offer currency exchange services. **Bike hire** Fiordland Bike Hire, *7 Mokonui St, T03-2497211.* From $10 per hr ($25 per day). **Breakdown services** Mobil, *80 Town Centre, T03-2497247 (24 hr).* **Car hire** Hertz, *T03-2497516.* Te Anau Taxi and Tours, *T03-2497777.* Mini-van hire from $65 per day. **Internet** E-stop, *Jailhouse Mall, Town Centre. 0900-2100, seasonal.* Air Fiordland (tic-it Te Anau), *Town Centre. 0900-1900, seasonal.* Mountain View Holiday Park, *Te Anau Terr.* Lake Te Anau Backpackers, *48 Lakefront Dr.* Fiordland Electrical, *Luxmore Dr (24 hr).* **Laundry** Fiordland Electrical, *see above, (24 hr).* **Medical services** Doctor *Luxmore Dr, T03-2497007. Mon-Fri 0800-1800/Sat 0900-1200.* **Post office** *'Paper Plus', Town Centre.* **Taxi** Te Anau Taxi and Tours, *T03-2497777.* **Useful addresses** Police: *Milford Rd, and T03-2497600.*

Milford Sound → *Colour map 7, grid A2 Population: 200*

There are simply not the words in a thesaurus to describe the sight of Milford Sound; let alone its moods. Come rain or shine, calm or storm, dawn or dusk, it is ever-changing, always dramatic, and never dull. In every sense Milford Sound is quite simply New Zealand at its glorious and unparalleled best. Given the enormity (quite literally) of the attraction you will probably be immediately struck with how underdeveloped Milford Sound is. With its conservative scatter of low-key buildings it seems only the boat terminal stands out like a sore thumb. This is quite deliberate. The fact that Milford is the jewel in the crown of the Fiordland National Park and administered by DoC means that further development is strictly controlled, hence the lack of accommodation. How utterly refreshing it is to see a place of such outstanding natural beauty so unspoilt and not completely over-run with rapacious developers out to make a buck. Or the well-heeled building their dream homes, eating up the acres and then calling in the 'Animal Control' man. In Milford only nature (and sandflies) rule and you had better respect it.

However, that said, this is still one of New Zealand's biggest tourist attractions. In mid-summer the place is a hum of propeller and diesel engines, as the masses are brought in to 'take the cruise'. On any given day in the high season there can be well over 100 coaches doing the trip from Queenstown and Te Anau which, against a backdrop of such enormity can be a surreal sight in itself. This is one place where 'Ant Travel' or 'Humblin Coaches' would seem entirely appropriate. Without proper investigation Milford can almost be too much for the senses, so it's best to arrive independently. By all means take a cruise, and more especially a scenic flight, but if you can linger a while, and wait until the buses have left, you can appreciate this incredible place even more.

Getting there You can reach Milford Sound by air, by bus, independently by road, or in real style by foot, via the Milford Track. But the best way to arrive, if you can afford it, is to take a scenic flight/cruise combination from Wanaka or Queenstown. Then, if you do not have your own wheels, hire a car from Queenstown or Te Anau and give yourself at least two days to explore the area properly. Your arrival by **air** will almost certainly be in combination with a scenic flight or tour option from Wanaka, Queenstown or Te Anau (see Flightseeing, page 674). The landing and take-off from the airfield in Milford, 1 km from the Visitor Centre, is a memorable experience.

There are a vast array of **bus** and **coach** operators serving Milford Sound, with an equal number of tour options, from simple bus-in/bus-out, to bus/cruise/bus or bus-in/cruise/fly-out and even bus/overnight cruise options. Most operators are based in Queenstown, from where they make the 12 hr, 291 km day-trip by road picking up passengers from Te Anau on the way. This is one of the most spectacular bus trips in the world, provided the weather is favourable. However, if dark clouds are gathering, or the forecast is for heavy rain (which it frequently is) do not despair. Even if it is pouring down this can actually add to the drama and spectacle of the Milford Road as channels of water fall from the precipitous outcrops and in all directions like a some sort of surreal giant's car wash. In fact, the heavier the better. Many people actually prefer Milford in awful weather and quite right too – with an average of about 7 m annually it really knows how to rain here. ‣‣ *See also Tour operator listings, page 674.*

> ⁑ *Whatever you do, don't forget to bring insect repellent. The sandflies in Milford are legendary.*

Information If you have arrived independently and not yet pre-booked any activities you can choose from the array of options at the **Milford Sound Visitors' Centre** ① *(Boat Terminal). 0900-1700.* You are, however, advised to research the huge number of options prior to your visit. The VICs in Queenstown and Te Anau will assist.

Sights

Milford Sound is, in itself of course, just one huge sight but there are individual aspects worth noting. The centrepiece of the Sound is **Mitre Peak**. At 1,692 m it is not that high by New Zealand standards but, as with the entire corridor of Milford Sound, it is the sheer rate of ascent created by the actions of the glaciers that creates such an impact. Opposite Mitre Peak is **The Lion** (1,302 m) and further up the ridge behind it **Mount Pembroke** (2,045 m). **Milford Sound** itself is 15 km in length and about 290 m at its deepest. The mouth of the fiord is only about 120 m wide, due to melt action and the terminal moraines of the former glaciers. In heavy rains the fiord can seem like one great waterfall but by far the most impressive at any time are the 160 m **Bowen Falls** which can reached by a short 10-minute boardwalk from beside the boat terminal. In a storm you would be unable to stand beyond the fringe of the trees such is the power of the water and spray these falls can generate. Similarly, about midway along the eastern well of the fiord are the **Stirling Falls** (154 m) whose mist and rainbows can only be visited by boat or kayak.

The fiords are home to some fairly unusual and hardy wildlife. **Fur seals** are commonly seen lazing about on the rocks on almost every cruise, but it is below the water's surface that the most noted species are found. Milford Sound is home to an unusual **Milford Deep Underwater Observatory**, ① *T0800-326969, www.milforddeep.co.nz*, opened in 1995 and no mean engineering feat. In the sheltered waters of **Harrison Cove**, about a third of the way out of The Sound on its eastern edge, the observatory can be visited independently ($45), or in combination with a cruise from $65. From the observatory's interesting interpretative centre you can descend 8 m into a circular viewing chamber where a wide array of sea creatures can be seen at close quarters. There are many rare species in Milford including the

66 99 Here you can mix it with all types including the inevitable towny sitting all alone, looking like Stan Laurel... because he was "never told about the sandflies and tried using my girlfriend's 'Ponse Mystique' perfume to ward them off".

very rare **black coral** (which is actually white), a species that can live for over 300 years. Another white resident you may encounter is **'Charlie'** the Kotuku (**white heron**). Charlie has been using Milford Sound as his winter residence for over 12 years. In summer Charlie reunites with his mate in Okarito on the West Coast, which is New Zealand's only breeding colony. The best place to spot Charlie is around the boat harbour or on the beach where he will probably be busy fishing or just watching the tourists go by. ▸▸ *For further Activities see below.*

🛏 Sleeping

C-D **Milford Sound Lodge**, *just off the Milford Road about 1km east of the airfield, T03-2498071, www.milfordlodge.com* For the independent traveller this really is the only place to stay in Milford Sound. Being the only option it can be a very cosmopolitan place and in mid-summer outside the Milford Pubs opening hours forms the hub of Milford's leisure activity. Here you can mix it with all types, from the rich to locals and trampers, to the almost inevitable towny sitting all alone looking like Stan Laurel after dropping a piano on his foot because he "was never told about the sandflies and tried using my girlfriend's 'Ponse Mystique' perfume to ward them off". Despite those inevitable 'damned biting things' (poised for attack by the squadron every time you venture outside) it has a comfortable range of double/twins, dorms and powered/tent sites. This really is the place to see a tent put up in world record time. Bathroom facilities are shared. All in all it's a great place to be. There is an in-house restaurant offering breakfast and pub-style evening meals, a great kitchen, large comfortable lounge, small grocery store and internet.

Mitre Peak Lodge *near the boat terminal.* More salubrious, but caters only for clients of Milford Track guided walks, T03-4411138.

🍴 Eating

Other than the Milford Sound Lodge your eating options are the day-time **Milford Pub and Café**, *next to the Mitre Peak Lodge and main car park, T03-2497657. Summer 0830-1700 (bar 1100 til 'close' (local jargon for when most of the punters have all left and the local operators have had their fill); winter 0900-1630, bar 1630 til close.* It sells a full range of pub-style food from generous breakfasts to toasted sandwiches. Pass the salt and sandflies. Note there are also lunch options on some cruises.

⛰ Activities

Cruising
Day cruises Real Journeys, *T03-2497416, T0800-656501, www.fiordlandtravel.co.nz* and **Milford Sound Red Boat Cruises**, *T0800-264536, www.redboats.co.nz* The 2 principal cruise operators on the sound. The majority of cruises explore the entire 15 km length of The Sound to the Tasman Sea, taking in all the sights on the way, including the waterfalls (from very close range), precipitous rock overhangs, seal colonies and the underwater observatory (optional). There is an interesting commentary, with free tea or coffee, and you are encouraged to ask the crew questions. Free access is allowed all around the boat with the most hardy souls

and budding National Geographic photographers braving the wind on the upper decks. Additional luncheon options are also available. Real Journeys offer a 'Small Boat Daytime Cruise', a standard (larger boat) 'Scenic Cruise' and a longer 'Nature Daytime Cruise'. Prices range from $58 (child $15) to $65. A cruise which includes a 30-min stop at the underwater observatory is an additional $20. Red Boat Cruises offer very similar cruises and rates.

Mitre Peak Cruises T0800-744633, www.mitrepeak.com Another smaller independent operator offering a low-passenger number (smaller boat), nature-orientated day cruise, from $56. There are also numerous options that include air or bus transportation from Wanaka, Queenstown or Te Anau.

Overnight cruises On the overnight cruises you take in all the usual sights, but can enjoy an extended trip, meals, comfortable accommodation and other activities including boat-based kayaking. Given the fact you are not joined on the water by the fleets of day cruise ships you are also more likely to see the local wildlife, including dolphins.

Real Journeys, see above, offer a small boat 'MV Friendship Overnight Cruise' (1630-0900; $175); a larger boat the 'MV Milford Wanderer' (1645-0915; from $175) that has 4 bunk cabins; and the top of the range 'MV Milford Mariner Overnight Cruise' (16 hrs; $275) which has double cabins and includes dinner and breakfast. All prices are for twin share but sole occupancy at an elevated rate are available.

Diving

Tawaki Dive (Milford Dive), Te Anau, T03-2499006, www.tawakidive.co.nz Offer full-day fiord diving trips for the experienced, from $195 (includes equipment hire).

Flightseeing

Flightseeing trips to Milford are readily and principally available from Wanaka, Queenstown and Te Anau. The most popular option is the combination **fly/cruise** trip that combines an extended scenic flight with one of the regular daytime cruises. Expect to pay about $300-350 (Queenstown/ Wanaka). Note, however, that although exciting and well worth the money, this does not allow much time (2 hrs) in Milford itself. Another

popular trip, missing out the long bus journey back, is the **bus-in/ cruise/ fly-back** option, which costs from $430 (Queenstown). Note also that the flight into and around Milford Sound rates right up there with the glacier and Mount Cook flights of the West Coast.

Air Fiordland, T0800-103404, www.airfiordland.com;
Air Milford, T0800-462252, www.airmilford.co.nz;
Fiordland Helicopters, T03-2497575, www.fiordlandhelicopters.co.nz; and
Milford Helicopters, T03-24983, are the principal operators based in Milford, Queenstown and Te Anau, offering a wide array of options with some flights taking in the Sutherland Falls on the Milford Track and Doubtful Sound.

Kayaking

A far more serene and atmospheric way to see The Sound is by kayak, giving you an incredible sense of scale.

Milford Sound Sea Kayaks, based at Deep Water Basin (just east of the airfield), T03-2498500, www.kayakmilford.co.nz Operated by the intrepid Rosco Gaudin and offers a range of day-safaris, fly/kayak, paddle/walk (part of the Milford Track) twilight and even full moon trips from 4-7 hrs (flight options are also available ex Queenstown). The standard paddle costs from $119 (from Te Anau and $98 from Milford.

Fiordland Wilderness Experiences, Te Anau, T03-2497700, www.fiordlandseakayak.co.nz Offer a day excursion on The Sound from $110 which takes in the scenery of the Milford Road.

Kiwi Reel-Rifle, Te Anau, T03-2499071, www.kiwireelrifle.com Also offer day trips ex Te Anau and independent kayak hire, from $50 per day.

⌕ Tour operators

From Queenstown the principal upmarket operators serving Milford Sound can be booked through
Real Journeys, 74 Shotover St, Queenstown, T03-4427509, www.realjourneys.co.nz Expect to pay around $165 for a coach/cruise day-trip, from $395 for a coach/overnight cruise combo (twin share) and $423 for the

bus/cruise/fly option.
There are a few companies operating out of Queenstown (via Te Anau) that cater for smaller groups, thereby offering a more personable experience.

BBQ Bus, T03-4421045, www.milford.net.nz Enjoy a good reputation and are recommended. Their day trip from Queenstown (departs 0645, pick-ups in Te Anau, return to Queenstown at 1900), includes lunch in the Hollyford Valley, a cruise on the Sound and a visit to the native wildlife centre in Te Anau if time allows, all from $170. There is also a return flight option.

Kiwi Discovery, Camp St, Queenstown, T03-4427340; and

Kiwi Experience, 37 Shotover St, Queenstown, T03-4429708. Also from Queenstown these backpacker orientated outfits offer similar coach/cruise options from $150. A fly/cruise/coach option with

Kiwi Experience costs from $305. Will also pick you up in Te Anau (knocking around $30 off the Queenstown rate).

There are also many options available by bus from Te Anau, many linking up with the Queenstown tours. Again Real Journeys (see the Te Anau section) are the principal operators. The VIC lists others. From Te Anau for the coach/cruise option expect to pay around $110, and for a coach/overnight cruise around $335.

Trips and Tramps, T03-2497081. Offer day trips to Milford Sound (including cruise ticket). It departs Te Anau at 0830 and returns at 1800 and costs $142, child $90. They also do a Milford Track day walk option from $126.

Milford Wilderness Explorer, T03-2497505, www.airfiordland.com Offer a personalized trips with cruise options from Te Anau from about $115, child $70.

Manapouri and Doubtful Sound → Colour map 7, grid A2 Population: 400

As you drive into Manapouri with its stunning vistas across the eponymous lake, you are immediately struck by how unobtrusive it is. If it were anywhere else in the developed world, it would probably be an unsightly mass of exclusive real estate and tourist developments. Thankfully it is not, though perhaps the recent history of this pretty little village, the main gateway and access point to activities on Lake Manapouri, Doubtful Sound and the incredible and challenging Dusky Track, has something to do with that. Though you would never guess it, Manapouri has been the sight of some major altercations between the advocates of economics and conservation. Hidden away at the West Arm of the lake, and smack-bang in the heart of Fiordland National Park, is the country's largest hydroelectric power station, which has, over the years, created much controversy. Yet it is the very development of the power station that allows the tourist and conservationist access to some of the most remote parts of the park. Now it is home to an uneasy mix of power station workers and eco-friendly tourist operators and service providers.

Ins and outs

Getting there Manapouri is 20 km south of Te Anau via SH95. Several **bus** companies pass through Manapouri on their way south via SH99 to Invercargill, including **Scenic Shuttles**, (Invercargill, daily Nov-Apr, Mon-Fri May-Oct), T03-2497654, T0800-277483; **Bottom Bus**, T03-4429708; and **Topline Tours**, T0508-832628, www.toplinetours.co.nz   **Real Journeys**, T03-2496602, is also regularly shuttling back and forth to Te Anau.

Getting around Fiordland Explorer Charters, T03-2496616, offer **water-taxi** services on Lake Manapouri for trampers or mountain bikers who wish to explore the

Wilmot Pass, or access the Dusky Track trailhead. **Real Journeys**, Pearl Harbour, Manapouri, T03-2496602, info@realjourneys.co.nz, offer excellent day (8 hr) and overnight (24 hr) excursions to Doubtful Sound via Lake Manapouri and the Wilmot Pass (see below).

Information There is no Information Centre in Manapouri per se, but **Real Journeys** ① *on the wharf (Pearl harbour), T03-2496602, www.realjourneys.co.nz,* is the base for all water activity on the lake and Doubtful Sound tour operations. For additional information contact the **VIC**, T03-2498900 or **DoC**, T03-2497924, in Te Anau.

Lake Manapouri

Lake Manapouri is stunning not only because of its backdrop of bush and mountain but also its moods. From the beach beside the village the whole scene echoes the constant change of Milford Sound. It is of course not so dramatic in its topography, but no less dynamic. There are 35 islands which disguise its boundaries and, at a forbidding 420 m deep, is the second deepest lake in the country (the deepest is Lake Hauroko in southwestern Fiordland). To really appreciate the size and complex nature of Lake Manapouri it is necessary to get out on the water, which, thankfully, is a matter of course on the route to Doubtful Sound.

Manapouri Underground Power Station At the terminus of West Arm, and forming the main access point via Wilmot Pass to Doubtful Sound, is the Manapouri Underground Power Station. Although an unwelcome development to the conservationist, one cannot fail to admire the environmentally sympathetic way in which this incredible feat of engineering has been achieved and is maintained. Started in 1963 and completed eight years later, now only a few unsightly pylons, connected to a switchyard, control building and water intakes, belie the mammoth constructions underground – all supplied by a fairly unobtrusive barge that goes back and forth across the lake to Supply Bay near Manapouri. A 2040 m, 1:10 tunnel set in the hillside allows access to the main centre of operations – a large machine hall housing seven turbines and generators, fed by the water penstocks from 170 m above. What is most impressive is the 9.2 m diameter, tailrace tunnel that outputs the used water at the head of Doubtful Sound – an amazing 10 km from Lake Manapouri and 178 m below its surface. Started in 1964 the tailrace took four years to build. **Real Journeys** (see Activities below) make three-hour trips to the power station (it is also a port of call on the Doubtful Sound day-excursion, see below) – the bus drives down the dank and forbidding access tunnel and makes a very tight turn at the bottom where passengers are decanted out to look at the interior of the machine hall. Even the worst luddite will be impressed.

Wilmot Pass → *The road can be explored independently by mountain bike (provided you are fit enough) and acts as the northern trailhead to the Dusky Track*

The 22 km road from West Arm to Doubtful Sound across the Wilmot Pass is a spectacular drive, encompassing remote mountain and beech and podocarp forest scenery, lookout points and waterfalls. The unsealed road, which took two years to complete, was built as part of the hydropower project. At a cost of nearly $5 for every 2.5 cm, it is easily the most expensive road in the country. With its numerous twists and turns and heady topography, together with a local annual rainfall of over 7 m, it is also a very hard road to maintain. Like the power station the road forms part of Real Journeys' Doubtful Sound day trip (see below).

Doubtful Sound

Doubt nothing, this fiord, like Milford Sound, is all it is cracked up to be – and more. Many who have made the trip to Milford feel it may be very similar and therefore not worthy of the time or expense to get there. But Doubtful Sound has a very different atmosphere to Milford. With the mountain topography in Fiordland getting generally lower the further south you go, and the fiords becoming longer and more indented with coves, arms and islands, Doubtful Sound offers the sense of space and wilderness that Milford does not.

Doubtful is, after Dusky, the second largest fiord and has 10 times the surface area of Milford and at 40 km is also over twice as long. It is also the deepest of the fiords at 421 m. There are three distinct arms and several outstanding waterfalls including the heady 619 m **Browne Falls** near Hall Arm. This is only marginally less than the near-vertical Sutherland Falls on the famed Milford Track. At the entrance to Hall Arm is the impressive 900 m cliff of **Commander Peak** (1274 m), the only true echo of Milford's dramatic corridor.

Doubtful Sound hosts its own pod of about 60 **bottlenose dolphins** which are regularly seen by visitors as well as **fur seals** and **fiordland crested penguins**. But is also noted for its very lack of activity. On a calm night the silence is deafening.

Captain Cook originally named it Doubtful Harbour during his voyage of 1770. He decided not to explore past the entrance, fearful that the prevailing winds would not allow him to get back out; hence the name. It was not until 23 years later that Italian explorer Don Alessandro Malaspina, leading a Spanish expedition, dropped anchor and sent a small crew on a whaleboat into the fiord to make observations. Although a brief excursion it was both brave and meticulous and left a number of present-day names in its wake – Malaspina Reach being the most obvious.

⊜ Sleeping

Doubtful Sound p676
LL **Murrell's Grand View House**, 7 Murrell Av, T03-2496642, www.murrells.co.nz A rambling house near the mouth of the outlet and surrounded by spacious gardens. It offers double en-suites and fine cuisine.
AL **Beechwood Lodge**, 40 Cathedral Dr, T03-2496993, www.beechwoodlodge.com A new B&B that sits over looking the lake. It offers 2 well appointed guest en suite bedrooms and has a glorious lounge from where you can watch the ever-changing moods of the lake.
B-D **Lakeview Motor Inn**, Manapouri-Te Anau Highway, T03-2496652, www.manapouri.com This older place overlooks the lake and has serviced units, plus 2 self-contained and 11 budget rooms, a café and internet.
A-D **Manapouri Lakeview Motel and Motor Park**, Manapouri-Te Anau Highway, T03-2496624. Wonderfully quirky place whose elderly (and clearly) European owners tend a range of 'disney-esque' cottages, old Morris Minors and even a period costume collection. It has the cottages of course, which are a delight plus more conventional cabins, powered sites and good facilities. The lake shore is just across the road.
B-D **Manapouri Glade Motel and Motor Park**, at the end of Murrell Av and right on the headland at the Waiau River mouth, T03-2496623. 3 self-contained cottages, cabins and powered/tent sites. Lovely short walks.
D **Deep Cove Hostel** very remote, at the head of Doubtful Sound, T03-2496602. A possibility outside school term-time but phone first for details.
Real Journeys offer a 2-night package in season that includes a 3-hr cruise on Doubtful Sound, T03-2496602.

⊘ Eating

There are few options in Manapouri and you would be better to head back to Te Anau for evening dining.
$ **Beehive**, in the Lakeview Motor Inn T03-2496652. Mon-Sat 1100-2130 (seasonal). Has a licensed café and bar, serving acceptable pub-style grub into the evening.
$ **Cathedral Café**, Cathedral Dr (next to the general store and petrol station). Tries hard to serve good coffee and snacks during the day.

▲ Activities

Tours of the Sound
This trip is recommended not only because of the stunning natural scenery and the wildlife but because you are afforded such a stark contrast in the very bowels of the earth.

Real Journeys Pearl Harbour, *T03-2496602, www.realjourneys.co.nz* The main commercial tour operator to the Manapouri Power Station and Doubtful Sound. They offer 3 trips; the Manapouri Power Station trip (see above, 3 hr 15 min, adult $53, child $15), the Wilderness Day Cruise, see below, (10 hr) and the popular overnight Overnight Cruise.

Fiordland Explorer Charters, *also based in Pearl Harbour, T03-2496616, explorercharters@xtra.co.nz* Offer a smaller scale more personalized operation and day-excursion (7 ½ hrs) daily at 1000, from $160, child $80.

Wilderness Day Cruise After boarding a modern launch at Manapouri you cross the lake to West Arm (interesting commentary and free tea/coffee). From West Arm you then board a bus and negotiate the Wilmot Pass, stopping at a viewpoint over Doubtful Sound before descending past rivers, waterfalls and the hydropower tailrace outlet to the Doubtful Sound wharf. From there you board another launch for a superbly scenic and informative cruise through The Sound to the Tasman Sea. If time allows, you negotiate one or two of the fiords 'arms' and throughout the cruise can often see the resident dolphins. Once returned to the wharf, reunited with the bus and Lake Manapouri's West Arm, you then leave the dramatic scenery and daylight behind and negotiate the underground access tunnel to the machine hall of the hydropower station. There you stop for 30 min to learn how it all works before re-emerging into daylight and catching the launch back to Manapouri. Trips depart daily at 0930 (Te Anau at 0815) and cost from $190 child $45 (Te Anau $204, child $52).

Overnight Cruise This trip involves all of the above, plus an overnight stay on The Sound, aboard the new and comfortable *Fiordland Navigator*. Designed along the lines of a traditional New Zealand trading scow, it comes complete with sails and offers private en suite cabins or quad-share bunks. There are friendly nature guides on board and also kayaks with which you can do your own scheduled exploring. Trips depart daily Nov-Apr at 1230 from $285, child $142 . Both these trips link in with Queenstown and Te Anau departures.

Ecotours

Fiordland Ecology Holidays, *based on the main road in Manapouri, T03-2496600, www.fiordland.gen.nz* Have developed an excellent range of holiday options from 3 days to 2 weeks on board their 12 passenger, 65 ft yacht *Breaksea Girl*. The yacht is very comfortable and well equipped and the tours offer a very sensitive insight into Fiordland's unique wildlife. Trips cost from $800 -$5600.

Adventure Kayak and Cruise, *Waiau St, T03-2496626, www.fiordlandadventure.co.nz* Offer day or overnight rental or fully equipped kayaks on Lake Manapouri (from $40 per day) as well as full day trips to Doubtful Sound, from $169.

Fiordland Wilderness Experiences, *based in Te Anau* (see page 670). Offer 2-5 day trips to Doubtful, Breaksea and Dusky Sounds from $275. They also offer independent rental for the experienced, from $50 a day.

Kiwi Reel-Rifle Ltd, *T03-2499071, www.kiwireelrifle.com* In conjunction with Waterwings offer a new and attractive 'Masters of the Monument' fly or kayak option that takes in the prominent geological feature near Lake Manapouri used as a filming location in the *Lord of the Rings*, from $180.

Mountain biking

The Wilmot Pass is a superb (but challenging 500 m ascent) road to explore by mountain bike. For bike hire see Te Anau page 670.

Walking and tramping

The Wilmot Pass is the principal access point to the northern trailhead of the **Dusky Track** (see page 704). There are also a number of walks available around Manapouri most of which negotiate the **Garnock Burn** catchment and start on the southern bank of the Lake Manapouri outlet at Pearl Harbour. The most popular walk is the (3 hrs) **Pearl Harbour Circle Track** that follows the riverbank, up stream, before negotiating the forest ascent to a lookout point, then descending back to Pearl Harbour. The Circle Track also allows access to the longer **Back Valley** and **Hope Arm Hut tracks** that explore Hope Arm (Lake Manapouri) and the inland **Lake Rakatu**. For details pick up the *Manapouri*

Walks leaflet ($1) from the DoC VIC in Te Anau. For dinghy hire across the river (call at the post centre next to the petrol station and café) or contact **Adventure Charters**, *T03-2496626.*

The Southern Scenic Route

From Manapouri SH99 leaves the vast majority of tourist traffic behind, as most retrace their steps to Queenstown or cross-country east, to Dunedin. The Southern Scenic Route, which first heads south to the coast via Tuatapere and Invercargill, then north, via the beautiful and underrated Catlins coast to Dunedin, provides an attractive alternative. The highlights of this trip, other than the sheer peace and quiet, are the potential stops in Tuatapere to walk the new and celebrated Hump Ridge Track, an overnight stay in the pleasant seaside resort of Riverton, a day or two in Invercargill, before a trip to Stewart Island (page 688) and then, perhaps most recommended, the thorough exploration of the Catlins coast (page 696).

Ins and outs

The Southern Scenic Route which is sometimes advertised as encompassing the entire journey from Dunedin to Milford Sound is a total of 440 km. By bus the route is served by **Scenic Shuttle** (Invercargill, daily Nov-Apr, Mon-Fri May-Oct), T03-2497654, T0800-277483, and the backpacker orientated **Bottom Bus** (Queenstown/ Dunedin/Invercargill), T03-4347370. Local shuttle services and transport to and from Invercargill are listed in the places below.

Information Tuatapere VIC, ① *corner Half Mile and Clifden Rd, 31 Orawia Rd, T03-2266739, info@humpridgetrack.co.nz Daily 0900-1700 (winter Mon-Fri 0900-1700).* The staff are very enthusiastic and helpful and there is infinite detail about the new Hump Ridge Track, www.humpridgetrack.co.nz The also administer all track bookings. Internet. **DoC** has an office in Tuatapere but you will find all the relevant administration at the VIC. **Riverton VIC,** ① *across the river (from the west) on Palmerston St (172), T03-2349991, therock@riverton.co.nz Daily 0900-1700.* **Invercargill VIC,** ① *next to Queen's Park and housed in the Southland Museum and Gallery Building, Victoria Av, T03-2146243, www.southland.org.nz Mon-Fri 0800-1800, Sat and Sun 0900-1800.* Has listings of local activities including flightseeing, sightseeing tours, golf, horse trekking and windsurfing. **DoC,** ① *regional office, 7th Floor, State Insurance Building, 33 Don St, T03-2144589. Mon-Fri 0800-1700.* (Information is also held at the VIC.) Can also organize hut bookings for Stewart Island tramps.

Manapouri to Tuatapere

Still reeling from the highs of Fiordland's stunning scenery, your journey south could include the main drag of Vegas and still seem boring, so just accept that fact and sit back and enjoy the peace and quiet of the road. SH99 has to be one of the quietest main roads in the country and between Manapouri and Milford it's unusual to pass more than half a dozen cars even in summer. Generally speaking you will encounter very little with two legs. Instead what you will see is paddock upon paddock of sheep.

Although birdwatchers can find considerable pleasure at the **Redcliffe Wetland Reserve** just north of Blackmount (38 km) there is little to justify a stop until **Clifden** (66 km). As well as its limestone caves (see below), Clifden boasts one of the oldest and longest **suspension bridges** in the country (built in 1899). Though a little

The Tuatara

To describe the noble and endemic tuatara as the most ancient reptile on earth is impressive enough, but when you consider that these 'living fossils' are even older than the landscape itself, it seems truly remarkable that they exist at all. They belong to a very singular order of reptiles known as beakheads that once roamed the earth (be it very slowly) over 225 million years ago. Once common throughout the country, but subject to predation and a widespread loss of habitat, the tuatara, has sadly joined the long list of New Zealand creatures in decline and now exists on only 30 offshore islands. They grow to a maximum of 610 mm, live in burrows and feed mainly on ground-dwelling insects. Given their status and natural habitat, your best chance of seeing a tuatara is in one of the country's zoos or museums. The Southland Museum in Invercargill is without doubt the most famous venue, having the most successful breeding and research programme in the world. They also boast perhaps the most famous tuatara in the land – 'Henry'. In appearance and mannerism tuatara generally (but Henry in particular), seem the very epitome of the word ancient and a true mascot of an old, far less manic world. No click-of-a-switch, press-button reactions here; no loud noises; no 'Reality TV' – 'When reptiles carry away your children' or films by Steven Spielberg; no bloodthirsty chases, hideous maulings, or perverse 'Crocodile Hunter'-induced poison bites. No, not necessary. Somehow, Henry, who is at least 120 years old, without expression or movement and in a time zone all of his own, makes a mockery of all this human nonsense. Yet he and his ilk are not like the human centenarian awaiting death in some old folks' home, most probably devoid of dignity or normal function. He looks more like a proud bronze bust, head held high and starring, waiting, waiting and waiting, his existence set to a schedule well beyond anything we adhere to. He clearly looks like he has all the time in the world to watch in utter complacency as you you come and go and, one could swear, a look that even says, 'and not only you punk, but the human race, period'.

disappointing in global terms, it is still worth a look and makes a nice picnic spot by the river. Near Clifden (signposted off Clifden Gorge Road to Winton) are its very uncommercial and undeveloped **limestone caves**, which can be explored carefully with a good torch and a little courage.

Just south of Clifden is the 30 km unsealed road to **Lake Hauroko**, the deepest body of water in New Zealand. Its remoteness is undoubtedly appealing and there is an interesting **walk** up a precipitous bluff to a lookout point. The area is also known for its many Maori (Ngai Tahu) burial sites. Lake Hauroko also provides jetboat access to the **Dusky Track**, one of the country's most challenging and remote treks. **Lake Hauroko Tours**, based in Tuatapere, T03-2266681, reinfo@es.co.nz, can provide access. On your way back from Lake Hauroko you may consider the short diversion north (off the Hauroko Road just before SH99) to sample the delights of **Dean Forest**. There, a pleasant short walk takes in its most famous native, a 1000-year-old totara tree. Once back on SH99 it is a further 13 km to Tuatapere, considered the gateway to the southeast corner of the Fiordland National Park (not that there are any roads!).

Tuatapere is a quiet little town that wants to start making a big noise. The reason for this and the town's new intended raison d'être, is the 53 km **Hump Ridge Track**, New Zealand's newest 'Great Walk' and one that is advertised as being on a par with any of the others in Fiordland, or indeed the country (see page 705). The track starts at the western end of **Bluecliffs Beach**, which, in itself, is a nice spot to spend a couple of hours. Nearby, on the first section of the Hump Ridge Track is the 36 m high, 125 m long   **Percy Burn Viaduct**, the largest wooden viaduct in the world. But even as it stood, this former saw-milling and farming town and (mysteriously) self-proclaimed **'sausage capital'** of the country, had a few other notable local attractions, including some fine jet boating operations down the **Wairaurahiri River**. ►► *For Sleeping, Eating and other listings, see pages 685-687.*

> ⦂ *Southland is noted for its paua (abalone) industry, used both for food and decorative jewellery. The Southern Paua and Pacific Shell Factory and Shop, 35 Bath Rd, T03-2348825 and the Riverton Paua Shoppe, 134 Palmerston St, T03-2349043 are the principal outlets.*

Tuatapere to Invercargill

A further 10 km south and SH99 reaches the coast at the evocatively named **Te Waewae Bay**. Here you can stop at **McCraken's Rest** to admire the beach and the views west over southern Fiordland, or east, to **Monkey Island**. Monkey Island was the anchor site of the great Maori *waka* (canoe) Takitimu which, as legend tells, was wrecked on the bar of the Waiau River. Te Waewae Bay itself is quite a serene sight in fine weather and often the playground for Hector's dolphin and the odd whale, but in winter the wind can come sweeping in from the Antarctic with a vengeance. This phenomenon is starkly highlighted in the next port of call – the intriguing village of **Orepuki** – where the macrocarpa trees have been sculpted into amazing, tangled shapes by the wind. Apparently, it is not in fact the wind that is directly responsible for this but the tree's aversion to sea salt swept in the air.

The tiny former gold rush village of Orepuki is worth a little investigation, not only for its trees, but because it looks like the village that time forgot. The buildings seem to have changed little in decades. Also, 500 m north of the village is the Orepuki Gemstone Beach, which, for the geologist may reveal garnets, jasper, quartz, nephrite as well as the odd worm fossil or even sapphires. From Orepuki the road garrottes the Wakaputa Point before rejoining the coast again at the beachside settlement of **Colac Bay**. A place rich in Maori history, it is now mainly frequented by surfers. Unless you have a board, you are best moving on to the far more ample amenities and sights of Riverton, a further 11 km east.

Riverton → *Colour map 7, grid B3 Population: 1900*

Riverton – or Aparima, to use its former Maori name – is the oldest permanent European settlement in Southland and one of the oldest in the country. Located on the banks of the common estuary formed by the Aparima and Purakino Rivers, it was formerly a safe haven for whalers and sealers and was first established as early as the 1830s. Now having gradually developed into a popular coastal holiday resort Riverton is a fine place to stop for lunch, a short walk on the beach, or even to consider as a quieter alternative base to Invercargill, now only 42 km to the east.

Sights Given the rich history of the area the, **Wallace Early Settlers Museum**, ① *172 Palmerston St, T03-2348520, daily 1030-1600, donation,* is worth a look. It houses

⬤ *On a brief visit to Invercargill, Mick Jagger allegedly described it as the 'asshole of the*
⬤ *world'.*

displays and photographs focusing on the early Maori, whaling and gold mining days, with over 500 portraits of the early pioneers. It also provides genealogical research assistance. Nearby the **South Coast Environment Centre**, ① *T03-2348717, daily 1330-1630*, promotes the local environment and wildlife with displays and information.

The **Riverton Rocks** and **Howell's Point**, at the southern edge of Taramea Bay provide safe swimming, fishing, short walks and fine views across to Stewart Island. If you are looking for a good place for lunch then try the excellent Beachhouse Café and Bar (see below). Other local **walks** are outlined in the free *Riverton Scenic Walks* leaflet; available free from the VIC.▸▸ *For Sleeping and Eating, see pages 685 and 686.*

Invercargill → *Colour map 7, B4 Population: 53,209.*

Invercargill suffers the same affliction of many towns in New Zealand and particularly those of South Island – it looks pretty awful. Stuck at the very rear end of New Zealand and sandblasted by the worst extremes of the southern weather, even its climate and geography are against it. However, despite all that, Invercargill has many good points, and although you will hear different, it is not quite the underdog it is reputed to be. For a start, it is the capital of the richest agricultural region in South Island and in 2000 had the strongest economic growth in the country.

Ins and outs

Getting there Invercargill **airport** is 2 ½ km south of the city and served by **Air New Zealand Link**, T0800-737000, www.airnewzealand.co.nz, and **Origin Pacific**, T0800-302302, www.originpacific.co.nz There are direct flights daily to Christchurch and Dunedin. **Stewart Island Flights** (Southern Air), T03-2189192, www.stewartisland flights.com, and **Southeast Air**, T03-2145522, southeast.air@xtra.co.nz, also serve Oban and Mason's Bay on Stewart Island. By **bus** Invercargill (579 km from Christchurch and 217 km from Dunedin via SH1; 187 km from Queenstown via SH6 and 168 km from Te Anau via SH99 Southern Scenic Route) is served by **Intercity** (Christchurch/Dunedin), T03-2146243; **Atomic Shuttles** (Christchurch/Dunedin), T03-2146243; **Knightrider**, (Christchurch/Dunedin) T03-3428055; **Scenic Shuttle** (Invercargill, daily Nov-Apr, Mon-Fri May-Oct), T03-2497654, T0800-277483; and the backpacker orientated **Bottom Bus** (Queenstown/Dunedin/Invercargill), T03-4347370, www.bottombus.co.nz Also plying the Southern Scenic Route is the **Catlins Coaster**, (Catlins/Dunedin) T0800-304333, www.southern-nz.co.nz Most buses leave from the **train** station on Leven St, T03-2140599, and bookings can be made at the VIC. Note there is now no train service south of Dunedin. For **ferry** services from Bluff to Stewart Island see page 688.

Getting around Scenic Shuttle, T03-2187381, T0800-277483, connect with Invercargill airport flights and will pick-up from your accommodation ($6). **Invercargill Passenger Transport**, 100 Leven St, T03-2182320, provide local suburban bus services, from $1.50-$3.50. Campbelltown Passenger Services, T03-2127404, provide shuttle services to Bluff and the Stewart Island ferry ($12). For taxis, car and bike rental see page 687. **Lynette Jack Tours**, T03-2157741, is a noted local and regional sightseeing tour operator.

History

Although the south coast was settled by European sealers and whalers as early as 1835, it was not until 1857, that the Chief Surveyor for Otago, one John Turnbull Thompson, was ordered by Governor Sir Thomas Gore Browne, to choose a site and

Invercargill

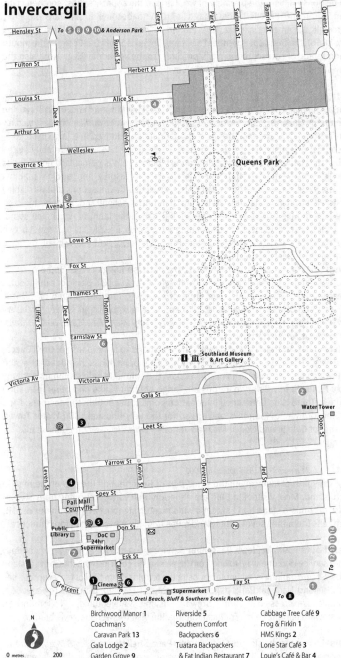

Queens Park

Southland Museum & Art Gallery

Water Tower

Pall Mall Courtville

Public Library

DoC

24hr Supermarket

Cinema

Supermarket

To ⑨, Airport, Oreti Beach, Bluff & Southern Scenic Route, Catlins

To ⑧

To ⑤⑧⑨⑩ & Anderson Park

Streets: Hensley St, Fulton St, Louisa St, Arthur St, Beatrice St, Avenal St, Lowe St, Fox St, Thames St, Earnslaw St, Victoria Av, Lewis St, Herbert St, Alice St, Wellesley, Gala St, Leet St, Yarrow St, Spey St, Don St, Esk St, Tay St, Crescent, Grey St, Park St, Swinton St, Raming St, Lees St, Queens Dr, Russel St, Kelvin St, Dee St, Liffey St, Thomson St, Thomson St, Leven St, Cambridge, Doon St, Jed St, Deveron St

N

0 metres 200
0 yards 200

Sleeping 🛏
Ascot Park **14**
Balmoral Lodge **12**
Birchwood Manor **1**
Coachman's
  Caravan Park **13**
Gala Lodge **2**
Garden Grove **9**
Gum Tree Farm
  Motor Park **10**
Homestead Villa **3**
Moana Court **11**
Queens Park Motel **4**
Riverside **5**
Southern Comfort
  Backpackers **6**
Tuatara Backpackers
  & Fat Indian Restaurant **7**
Tudor Park Country
  Stay **8**

Eating 🍴
148 on Elles **8**
Cabbage Tree Café **9**
Frog & Firkin **1**
HMS Kings **2**
Lone Star Café **3**
Louie's Café & Bar **4**
Tillermans **5**
Waxy O'Shea's **7**
Zookeepers Café **6**

take responsibility for the planning of what is now the country's most southerly city. When Southland seceded from Otago in 1861 to become a separate province, Invercargill became its capital. It is named in honour of Captain William Cargill (1784-1860), the first superintendent of Otago. 'Inver' is Scots Gaelic for 'at the mouth of' and refers, of course, to the city's proximity to the Waihopai River. Note also the many street names dedicated to Scottish rivers.

Sights

The main highlight in the town is the excellent **Southland Museum and Art Gallery** ① *on the edge of Queen's Park, Victoria Av, T03-2189753, www.southlandmuseum.co.nz Mon-Fri 0900-1700 Sat and Sun 1000-1700. Donation.* Housed in a large pyramid in the southern hemisphere (27 m) it boasts all the usual fine Maori and early settler exhibits and national and international art exhibitions, but is particularly noted for its 'Roaring Forties Antarctic and Sub-Antarctic Island' display and audio-visual (25 minutes, $2) shown several times daily. Also excellent is the museum's **tuatara** display and breeding programme. The 'Tuatarium' is an utter delight and an opportunity to come face to face with a reptilian species older than the land on which you stand. Henry, the oldest resident at an estimated 120 years plus, usually sits only a foot or two away from the glass. You can try to stare the old fella out, but you will fail, because Henry has had plenty of practice.

Beyond the museum is **Queen's Park**, the city's saving grace. Its 80 ha of trees, flowerbeds and duck ponds provide a lovely setting for a walk, a picnic or a quiet doze. **Anderson Park**, McIvor Road, 7 km north of the city centre (signposted off SH6) is another 24 ha of beautiful parkland, with an interesting public art gallery. ① *Gallery open daily 1330-1700, T03-2157432. The VIC has a very useful free 'Parks and Gardens' and 'Heritage Trail' leaflets.*

If beaches and sand are your thing, then the huge 30 km expanse of **Oreti Beach**, 10 km west of the city (past the airport) will not disappoint. It has the added attraction of allowing vehicles (with sensible drivers) on the sand and safe swimming. Nearby **Sandy Point**, Sandy Point Road, offers a range of short walks and other recreation activities. There is an unmanned information point at the entrance to the park. For a fine view of the city (Sundays only) head for the very unusual 1889 **Water Tower**, ① *corner of Gala St and Queen Dr. 1330-1630.* ⤮ *For Sleeping, Eating and other listings, see pages 685-687.*

Bluff → *Colour map 7, grid B3 Population: 2000*

At 27 km south of Invercargill, the small port of Bluff heralds the end of the road in South Island. Most visitors to Bluff are either on their way or returning from Stewart Island, or come to stand and gawk at a wind blasted signpost at the terminus of SH1, which tells them they several thousand miles from anywhere. Next stop Antarctica!

Ins and outs Campbelltown Passenger Services, T03-2127404, offer a regular daily shuttle service ($12 one-way) to and from Invercargill to coincide with the Stewart Island Ferries. Secure parking is available opposite the terminal from $5. For **ferry** services see Stewart Island National Park, page 688, or contact **Foveaux Express**, T03-2127660, www.foveauxexpress.co.nz or **Stewart Island Adventures**, T0800-000511, www.stewartislandnz.co.nz For local information visit the website www.bluff.co.nz

Sights En route to the signpost is the quirky **Paua Shell House**, ① *258 Marine Parade, daily 0900-1700,* which has over years become a bit of a New Zealand legend. For reasons best known to themselves, the elderly residents of this concrete crustacean took shell collecting to its extreme. Externally the house is nothing, compared to the interior. Enough said – you just have to see it! Sadly, Myrtle died in 2000 and Fred in 2002. The family are deciding whether to maintain the icon as a visitor attraction.

Those with more time on their hands and a disturbing interest in aluminium smelting can take a free guided tour of the monstrous **Tiwai Smelter**, ① *opposite Bluff harbour, T03-2185494, 1000 Mon-Fri.* A far more aesthetically pleasing alternative is **Bluff Hill** (270 m), which provides nice panoramic views past its chimney across Southland and back towards Stewart Island. If it is raining the **Maritime Museum**, ① *Foreshore Rd, T03-2127534, Mon-Fri 1000-1630, Sat and Sun 1300-1700, $2,* is worth a look to soak up the town's long history.

Bluff's biggest event of the year is the famous **Bluff Oyster Festival**, ① *bluffoysterfest@icc.govt.nz,* usually held in May. It is a celebration of the world-class Bluff oysters and other local seafood delights. Of course there is lots of fine wine to wash it all down and plenty of entertainment, including live bands (noise annoys an oyster?) and oyster opening and eating competitions. The festival's raucous finale is the Southern Seas Ball. ▸▸ *For Sleeping and Eating, see page 686.*

◉ Sleeping

Tuatapere *p681*

B-D Rarakau Farmstay and Lodge, *Papatara Coast Rd, Bluecliffs Beach (right at the entrance to the Humpridge Track), T03-2258192, www.rarakaulodge.com* This excellent place offers lodge bunkrooms, double B&B or private rooms. Cooking facilities or meals available and campervans are negotiable.

C-D Five Mountains Holiday Park Backpackers and Camping, *6 Clifden Rds, T03-2266418.* The principal backpackers in Tuatapere.

C-D Tuatapere Motor Park, *beside the river on Half Mile Rd, T03-2266502.* Campervans well catered for.

Riverton *p681*

A-D Riverton Rock, *136 Palmerston St, T03-2348886, www.riverton.co.nz* An excellent mid-budget establishment in a restored historic villa. It offers a range of very well appointed, themed rooms including one with a superb original Victorian Bath. There is also an open fire in the 'paua' bunkroom. Modern facilities and good value. Campervan facilities available.

AL River Lodge B&B *93 Towack St, T03-2348732, rbjmdore@actrix.co.nz* Offers 3 doubles and a studio with spa in a peaceful setting over looking the bay.

C-D The Globe Backpackers, *144 Palmerston St, T03-2348527, globebackers@xtra.co.nz* Centrally located in the town's oldest hotel.

Invercargill *p682*

For farmstay options contact the very helpful **Western Southland Farm Hosting Group**, *T03-2258608, www.nzcountry.co.nz/farmhost*

LL-A Ascot Park Hotel, *corner of Tay St and Racecourse Rd, T03-2176195, ascot@ilt.co.nz* The city's top hotel and a large modern establishment offering a wide range of rooms and fine facilities in a quiet setting. Spa, pool and in-house restaurant and bar.

A Tudor Park Country Stay, *21 Lawrence Rd, Ryal Bush, T03-2217150, tudorparksouth@hotmail.com* A B&B option 15 mins north of the city. Set in 4 ha of beautiful garden it is a neo-Tudor home with comfortable ensuite rooms. Meals available.

A Gala Lodge, *177 Gala St, T03-2188884.* Another 3-bedroom option with friendly, caring hosts across the road from Queen's Park.

There are plenty of **motels** in Invercargill, some up-market and modern, others older and budget-oriented.

A Homestead Villa, *corner Avenal and Dee Sts, T03-2140408, villa@southnet.co.nz* A *Balmoral Lodge, 265 Tay St, T03-2176109, (recommended); and*

AL-A Birchwood Manor, *189 Tay St, T03-2188881, www.birchwoodmanor.co.nz* **B Garden Grove**, *161 North Rd, T03-2159555, ggrove@ihug.co.nz* and **B Moana Court**, *554 Tay St, T03-2178443.* **A Queen's Park Motel**, *85 Alice St, T03-2144504.* Another good motel option within a short walk of Queen's Park.

B-D Tuatara Backpackers, *30-32 Dee St, T0800-8828272, tuataralodge@xtra.co.nz* A modern hostel ideally located in the centre of town. It has just undergone further expansion and now offers a full range of rooms with some very tidy shared standard double/twins and a few luxurious and value double en suites. Good kitchen facilities, popular street-side café with fast internet and value meals and breakfasts, Sky TV and off-street parking. Recommended.

C-D Southern Comfort Backpackers, *30 Thomson St, T03-2183838.* An old, spacious villa near the museum and Queen's Park. It is a traditional Southland favourite and offers dorms, doubles and free bike hire.

Motorcamps

D Gum Tree Farm Motor Park, *77 McIvor Rd (northern edge of town off SH6), T03-2159032, gumtreefarmmp@xtra.co.nz* Small, cosy and very friendly.

C-D Coachman's Caravan Park, *705 Tay St, T03-2176046.* The central option.

Bluff *p684*

A Land's End Hotel, *at the very end of SH1, T03-2127575, www.nzcountry.co.nz/landsend* A boutique hotel with comfortable, well-appointed ensuite rooms and a wine bar/café with open fire.

B-D Flynn's Club Hotel, *104 Gore St, T03-2128124.* A wide range of basic but comfortable rooms, plus a bar selling meals.
Campsites

D Argyle Park Camping Ground *is on Gregory St, T03-2128704.*

For **eating** there is the **Land's End** (above), which serves breakfast, lunch and dinner and will happily serve up the famous oysters when in season (Mar-Aug).

⦿ Eating

Tuatapere *p681*

$ Highway 99 Café/Bar and Takeaway. Fine for a quick daytime snack. But, its biggest attraction is neither its coffee nor its sausages, but 'Brandy' the cockatoo, with a level of conceit so great it would make the great Mohammed Ali seem modest. As you enter the shop you will be told in no uncertain terms that 'Brandy is a very (very) pretty boy'.

Riverton *p681*

$$ Country Nostalgia Café, *108 Palmerston*

St, T03-2349154. Wed-Mon for lunch and dinner. Award-winning and yet affordable.

$ Beachhouse Café and Bar, *126 Rocks Highway, T03-2348274. Daily 1000-late.* Overlooks the bay and is understandably popular. It also has internet.

Invercargill *p682*

There isn't a huge amount of choice in Invercargill.

$$$ Birchwoods Restaurant, *Ascot Hotel, T03-2176195. Lunch Mon-Sat 1200-1400, dinner Mon-Sun from 1800.*

$$$ 148 On Elles, *148 Elles St, T03-2161000. Closed Sun.* Both come recommended.

$$ Louie's Café and Bar, *142 Dee St, T03-2142913. Tue-Sun from 1800.* Affordable evening dining.

$$ Tillermans, *16 Don St, T03-2189240. Mon-Fri 1200-1400 and 1800, Sat from 1800.* Pleasant arty ambience.

$$ HMS Kings, *80 Tay St, T03-2183443. Daily lunch and dinner.* Serves up a great seafood chowder amidst the nets and anchors.

$$ Lone Star Café, *corner of Leet and Dee St, T03-2146225. Mon-Sun from 1730.* Recommended Tex-Mex.

$$ Fat Indian, *just next-door down Picadilly Lane (38 Dee St), T03-2144001.* Backpackers from the Tuatara regularly recommend this place.

$ Zookeeper's Café, *50 Tay St, T03-2183373. Daily from 1000-late.* The best café in town with has a nice atmosphere, good coffee and good value evening meals.

$ Frog and Firkin, *Dee St, next to the cinema, T03-2144001. Lunch 1200-1400, dinner Mon-Sat from 1700.* Pub-grub.

$ Waxy O'Sheas, *90 Dee St, T03-2140313.* More of the same at Invercargill's Irish pub.

$ Cabbage Tree Café, *379 Duns Rd (west, out towards Otatara and Oreti Beach), T03-2131443. 1100 to late.* Lunch or dinner in a relaxed rural setting.

Supermarkets On the eastern fringe of the city centre on Tay St. Most open until 2100 or 2200.

Bluff *p684*

$ Drunken Sailor, *Mon-Thu 1130-1600, Fri and Sat 1130-2100, T03-2128855.* A recent addition offering traditional fare and good views.

⦿ Bars and entertainment

Invercargill *p682*
The *Southland Times* is the best source of local events and entertainment information.
Zookeeper's Café, **Tillerman's**, *16 Don St* and **Waxy O'Sheas**, *see above*, are all popular spots with the locals and usually have live gigs at the weekend.
The Globe, *Tay St, opposite the Zookeeper's Café*, is currently the most popular (and the nation's most southerly) nightclub.
Cinema, *29 Dee St, T03-2141110.*
Ten Pin Bowling Centre, *corner of Kelvin and Leet Sts (licensed bar), T03-2144944.*

▲ Activities

Tuatapere *p681*
Waiau Jet Tours, *Hwy 99 Café Bar, 73 Main St, Tuatapere, T03-2266996;*
W Jet, *Clifden, T03-2266845, www.wjet.co.nz*
Hump Ridge Jet, *Otautau, T03-2258174, www.humpridgejet.co.nz* All offer exciting 6 ½-hr **jetboat** trips down a 10 km section of Lake Hauroko, before negotiating its 27 km 'outlet' river to the coast. It is a Grade III river, which to the layperson means very little, but what it does boast is the steepest lake-to-coast river fall in the country. From $189, child $89. Heli-jet, 2-day trips and water taxi services to both Dusky and Hump Ridge Tracks are also available.
Lake Hauroko Tours, *T03-2266681.* Also offer transport and launch trips to and from the tracks.

Riverton *p681*
Kiwi Wilderness Walks, *T03-2348886, kiwiwalks@riverton.co.nz* A popular operator

that provide guided eco-walks of Stewart Island (5-day, 4-night, from $1495) Hump Ridge (4-day, 3-night, from $995) and Dusky Tracks. The all-expenses -paid guided trips are best suited the older or less independent traveller but are no less exciting. The highlight of the Stewart Island trip is the good chance of observing kiwi in daylight, an unforgettable experience. Recommended.
Southern Scenic Horse Treks *T03-2348407.* Located between Tuatapere and Riverton and have several stranger-friendly horses including Willow who featured somewhere in the background of *Lord of the Rings*. Treks cost from $30 per hr.

⦿ Directory

Invercargill *p682*
Banks The main banks (most of whom offer **currency exchange**) *are on or around Don St in the city centre.* **Bike hire** Wensley's Cycles, *corner of Tay and Nith Sts, T03-2186206.* **Car hire** The airport has branches of most major players. Others include Riverside Rentals, *corner of Bay and North Rds, T03-2159030.* Rent-a-Dent, *T03-2144820.* **Internet** VIC, *see page 679.* Library. *Mon-Fri 0900-2000, Sat 1000-1300.* Tuatara Backpackers, *30-32 Dee St.* Com zone, *just opposite Tuatara, T03-2140007. Daily 0930-late.* Global Byte Café, *150 Dee St, T03-2144724 Mon-Fri 0800-1700, Sat and Sun 0900-1600.* **Post office** *51 Don St in the city centre, T03-2147700. Mon-Fri 0830-1700, Sat 1000-1230.* **Medical services** Doctor, *103 Don St, T03-2188821. Mon-Fri from 1700, 24-hr Sat and Sun.* **Taxi** Blue Star, *T03-2186079.* Taxi Co, *T03-2144478.* **Useful addresses** Police: *Don St, T03-2144039.*

Stewart Island (Rakiura National Park) → *Colour map 7, grid C3 Population: 390*

Lying 20 km southwest off Bluff, across the antsy waters of Foveaux Strait, is the 'land of the glowing skies' (Rakiura) or Stewart Island. Often called New Zealand's third island (making up 10% of its total area) and about the same size as Fiji, Stewart Island was described over a century ago by pioneer botanist Leo Cockayne, as 'having a superabundance of superlatives'. There is much truth in that. It can be considered one of the country's most unspoilt and ecologically important areas. Such are its treasures that only the country's national parks can compare, which is why it was only a matter of time before it entered the fold in May 2001, with 85% of the island now enjoying the limelight as the newest of New Zealand's 14 national parks.

Ins and outs

Getting there Stewart Island can be reached by **air** (20 min) from Invercargill to Half-moon Bay or the western bays of Masons, Doughboy, West Ruggedy or Little Hellfire (trampers) with **Stewart Island Flights**, T03-2189129, www.stewartislandflights.com, from $145 return ($80 one way). Scheduled flights Oct-Apr 0800/1300/1700 (May-Sep 0900/1300/1600). Only 15 kg of personal baggage can be flown over on a full flight (additional gear can be flown over on subsequent flights).

The principal operator ferry operator, **Foveaux Express**, T03-2127660, www.foveauxexpress.co.nz, sail Sep-Apr; 0930/1700 and May-Aug; 0930/1630 from the port of Bluff. The crossing by fast catamaran takes about 1 hour and costs $84 return, child $42 ($45/$22.50 one way). The smaller launch service operated by **Stewart Island Adventures**, T0800-000511, www.stewartislandnz.co.nz, departs Bluff at 1000 daily, from $80, child $40 return ($45/$22.50 one way). Secure parking is available in Bluff for $5 per day. **Campbelltown Passenger Services**, T03-2127404, offer a regular daily shuttle service to and from Invercargill to coincide with the Stewart Island ferries ($12 one-way). Bookings advised.

‡ Before booking anything independently, check with the Invercargill VIC, T03-2146243, for special rates and packages.

Getting around Once on the island you will find that most things are within walking distance, but many accommodation establishments will provide pick-ups. **Oban Taxis and Tours**, T03-2191456, (0700-1930; later by special arrangement); and **Sam and Billy the Bus**, T03-2191269, provide independent transportation. Oban Taxis and Tours also offer car hire (from $70 per-day) and scooters from $20 per-hr. **The Stewart Island Adventure Centre**, on the Wharf, T03-2191134, can also arrange tours, boat trips, water-taxis and car rentals. Stewart Island Flights have a depot on the waterfront, T03-2189129. A **shuttle** to/from the airfield is included in the fare.

There are numerous water-taxi operators including **Stewart Island Water Taxi**, T03-2191394, www.portofcall.co.nz; **Seaview Water Taxis**, T03-2191014; **Seabuzzz**, T03-2191282, www.seabuzzz.co.nz; and **Rakiura Waterways/Blue Water Taxis**, T03-2191414. Fares range between $20 and $50 one-way. **The Adventure Centre** on the wharf (Foveaux Express), T03-2191134, bookings@foveauxexpress.co.nz are the principal centres for land/water transportation and activity and non-independent walking/tramping information and bookings.

Information and orientation **Oban** on Half-moon Bay is the principal settlement on the island. It is further connected to several smaller settlements including Golden

Dong Won 529

Although you will almost certainly be blissfully unaware of it, Stewart Island actually holds the rather dubious honour of suffering New Zealand's worst and most recent major maritime oil spill. In October 1998 the Korean fishing vessel Dong Won 529 ran aground on the Breaksea Islands on their most southeasterly point. Sadly for the captain, had he not been negligent, and in possession of all his required faculties, he could so easily have missed them, even had he given himself another 20 m! The result was not thankfully the loss of any lives, but the loss of the ship and, most importantly, its 380 tonnes off diesel fuel.

Although generally well prepared for most aspects of oil spill response and clean up, for years the New Zealand government had made limited progress in bringing itself up to speed in the vital area of oiled wildlife response and preparedness. Ironically it was also Stewart Island that was felt to be the least likely location for a major spill.

Of course, its very remote location, the potential weather and most of all, the sheer variety and sheer scale of seabirds that might be affected, presented an instant and potentially disastrous situation. In simple terms, in Stewart Island an oil spill in the wrong place at the wrong time could result not in a few hundred birds, or indeed a few thousand, but potentially tens of thousands. The only thing in everybody's favour (and most especially the wildlife), was the fact it was diesel oil and not crude. Had it been the thicker, more tenacious and potentially more damaging crude oil, the consequences would have been catastrophic. Within hours after the ship's crew were rescued a full national oil spill response was initiated and experienced oiled wildlife responders brought in. The island became a frantic buzz of activity as helicopters hit the spill with dispersants and DoC crews and local residents were sent out to determine the impact on wildlife. Meanwhile in Invercargill, the oil spill response HQ was set up and a temporary oiled wildlife treatment centre created in the city's old swimming pool complex. Thankfully, the first few vital days and hours passed with no affected wildlife sighted. Favourable weather and the dispersant seemed to quickly disperse the diesel. After a week the threat to wildlife was significantly decreased and miraculously not one oiled bird was received for rehabilitation. Although almost unheard of even with diesel, this was put down to the remote and inaccessible nature of the coastline and the wildlife itself. The fact that the birds in the area were predominantly 'tube-nosed' petrels may have also have been a factor, since they may have been able to smell the diesel and avoid it. However, even if any birds had been affected they would most likely come ashore and disappear down their breeding burrows never to be seen again. After the incident was over an impact assessment was initiated and thankfully the results seemed to be encouraging. It seemed on this occasion Stewart Island's precious wildlife and New Zealand as a whole, had been very lucky. Next time (and there will be a next time) things will almost certainly be different.

Bay, Horseshoe Bay, Leask Bay and Butterfield Bay, by about 20 km of mainly sealed road. Almost all of Oban's amenities and (non-B&B) accommodation establishments can be reached easily by foot from the wharf. The principal streets are Elgin Terrace (the waterfront) and Main Road. **DoC Visitor Information and Field Centre,** ① *Main Rd,*

T03-2190009, www.stewartisland.co.nz www.doc.govt.nz Mon-Fri 0800- 1700, Sat and Sun 0900-1600. It is the principal source of accommodation and walk/tramping information and bookings on the island. There is a small interpretative display, which is no doubt going to expand with the new national park status. They also provide toilets, a pay phone, storage lockers, sell maps and hire personal locator beacons. An excellent free location map of the village and its surrounds is available at the VIC and is an essential on your arrival.

History

According to Maori legend, Stewart Island is the anchor stone of the canoe of the mythological hero and explorer Maui and is therefore known as 'Te Puka-o-te-waka-a-Maui'. As early as the 13th century there is evidence that the island's rich natural resources were being utilized by the Maori, with the particular attraction being attributed to the vast numbers of muttonbirds (sooty shearwater) or 'Titi'. The first European visitor (no prizes for guessing), in 1770 sailed past and mistook the island to be the mainland, calling it Cape South. Thirty-nine years after Captain Cook, it took one William Stewart, the first officer aboard the whaling ship Pegasus, to get it right and bless the island with its modern name. In the first half of the 18th century, whalers and sealers were beginning to establish themselves in the region and they were soon followed by fishermen and saw-millers who soon settled the island permanently.

In 1864 the island was officially bought from the Maori by the British, for the standard price of £6000. Besides a brief and sudden increase in population, thanks to a very unproductive gold rush in the late 1800s, the island has remained fairly uninhabited, with the current 390 residents mainly involved in fishing or tourism.

Stewart Island

Stewart Island has an indented coastline of river inlets, bays and offshore islands not dissimilar to parts of southern Fiordland. In many ways it is equally unspoiled and its heavily bush-clad landmass is host to a wealth of ecological habitats and a rich bio-diversity. The most common species on the island are sadly, as ever, the non-natives and the introduced. The most unwelcome and destructive of these are the possums, the rats and feral cats. Also, for over a century, white-tailed deer have roamed the bush, put there to occupy the hunting interests of us humans.

The island is home to 21 threatened plants, some of which are endemic or occur only on the island. With the absence of dominant and introduced trout, there are 15 native fish species and when it comes to birds the island is surrounded by a vast array of pelagic species, including **mollymawks** (a kind of albatross), **petrels** and **shearwaters** (muttonbirds), many of which breed on the offshore islets in vast numbers. Even on the main island (and fighting to survive the ravages of introduced vermin), its impressive bird breeding list includes two of the rarest and most unique in the world: a distinctly odd and enchanting, flightless parrot, called a **kakapo** (of which only about 60 remain) and perhaps most famous of all – *Apteryx australis lawryi* – better known as the **Stewart Island Brown Kiwi**, the largest and only diurnal kiwi in New Zealand. It is to see these whimsical birds on the beach by daylight that many visit the island. The thing is, though, you may have to watch them sidestep a **yellowed-eyed penguin**, which is one of the rarest penguins in the world. And, in turn, they may get their flippers in a twist to avoid the attentions of a dosing **Hookers sea lion**, which is one of the rarest sea lions in the world. You've probably got the picture; Rakiura is a very special place indeed.

Sights and activities

Other than to see **kiwi**, the **boat trips** and **kayaking**, people visit Stewart Island for two main reasons: either to bask in its **tranquillity** and do very little around the pleasant little village of Oban; or attempt one of its challenging, very long and very wet **tramping tracks**. Yes, it rains a lot here.

Around Oban

Perhaps the best place to start is by foot with a short, steady climb to **Observation Rock** (southern end of Oban village, up Ayr Street). From here you get a grand view of **Paterson Inlet** and the impenetrable forests that deck its southern shores and disappear beyond the horizon. This vista gives an idea of the rest of the island's wild and unspoilt make-up. In Oban itself the **Rakiura Museum**, ① *Mon-Sat 1000-1200, Sun 1200-1400, $2,* can entertain between rain showers, showcasing many aspects of the island's interesting history, including the very early Maori and their continued harvesting of muttonbirds (Titi), to whaling, saw-milling, gold mining and fishing.

The beach on the **waterfront** (Elgin Terrace) is a fine place to simply sit and watch the world go by, play industrial size chess, or decide on one of the many **water-based trips** that are available.

You could head north of Oban towards Horseshoe Bay, which is a very pleasant walk in itself. On the way you can spend some time exploring or **swimming** at **Bathing Bay**, a lovely sheltered beach accessed via Kamahi Road off Horseshoe Bay Road. This walk can be extended to **Horseshoe Point** (three-four hours), accessed from the southern end of **Horseshoe Bay**. On the southern entrance to Half-moon Bay the (three hours) **Harrold Bay to Ackers Point Lighthouse Walk**, accessed at the end of the southern bay road (Elgin Terrace), is another fine alternative. Harrold Bay is the site of **Ackers cottage** (1835), one of the oldest stone cottages in New Zealand. DoC has a very useful *Day Walks* leaflet available from the VIC ($1) which outlines other alternatives.

Guarding the entrance of Paterson Inlet is Ulva Island, a nature reserve criss-crossed with trails and home to abundant and extremely tame and exuberant birdlife. The island provides the most popular **day or half-day trip** from Oban, with a number of water-taxi operators offering organized trips taking in the mussel and salmon farms in **Big Glory Bay**, as well as seal and shag colonies (four hours guided trips, $45, T03-2191066). Most companies also offer independent transportation from $20 return. A trip to Ulva is recommended. Ulva and Paterson Inlet also provide one of the many excellent **sea-kayaking** venues. You could also consider a **paddle/tramp** option with the trip up to the DoC Freshwater Hut and access from there to Mason's Bay.

▲ Tramping

With 245 km of walking tracks, Stewart Island is a popular venue for trampers. These tracks range from the many short 'warm-up' walks around Oban, to the Northwest Circuit, a mammoth 125 km, 10-12 day tramp around the island's northern coast. Some other, far more remote, routes are sometimes negotiated, including the fascinating **'Tin Range'** route on the island's southwestern corner, but these require expert planning, logistics and a high level of fitness. Overall, tramping on Stewart Island presents its own challenges, not only because the island is so underdeveloped, remote and rugged, but also because it is particularly wet underfoot. There are numerous DoC huts that vary in size and standard, with the more remote obviously being the most basic. Hut details and bookings, maps and detailed track **information** is available with DoC and it is highly recommended that you obtain all the details and if necessary fill in an intentions form for the longer or more remote

Oban

To Horseshoe Bay, Maori Beach & Port William

Hicks Rd

Mill Creek

Halfmoon Bay

Mapau Rd

Horseshoe Bay Rd

Kamahi Rd

Miro Cres

Ship to Shore

Rata St

Oban Taxis & Tours

The Adventure Centre

Main Rd

Sam & Billy the Bus

Dundee St

Argyle St

Waterfront

Wnre St

To Airstrip & Rakiura Track

Elgin Terr

Ayr St

View St

Rakiura Museum

Stewart Island Flights Depot

To Golden Bay Rd

Leonard St

Excelsior Rd

Rankin St

Observation Rock

Nichol Rd

Wohlers Rd

Patterson Inlet

Ackers Cottage

Ackers Point Lighthouse Walk

To Ackers Point Lighthouse

N

0 metres   200
0 yards   200

Sleeping	Pilgrim Cottage 6	Eating
Ann's Place 1	Port of Call 7	Church Hill Café & Bar 1
Bay Motel 4	South Sea Hotel 8	Lettuce Inn 2
Butterfield Beach House 2	Stewart Island	Lighthouse Wine Bar 3
Ferndale Campsite 3	Backpackers 9	Justcafe 4
Miro Cottage 5	Stewart Island Lodge 10	Kai Cart 5

Mason's Bay to Freshwater Landing

This is a 14 km four-hour walk with no road access that can be approached in various ways. You can walk to Mason's Bay from Oban (37 km, three days one-way), taking in part of the Rakiura Track, then reach Mason's Bay via Freshwater Landing. Once at Mason's Bay you can then walk or fly back to Oban. Or take a water-taxi or kayak to Freshwater Landing then make the return walk to Mason's Bay (28 km, two days return). The recommended alternative is to fly into Mason's Bay, then make the leisurely return walk to Freshwater Landing (14 km, four hours) giving yourself an extra day to explore Mason's Bay (and give yourself the best chance of seeing **kiwi**). You can then get a water-taxi from Freshwater landing to Golden Bay and Oban. The track is low-level all the way, with a nice mix of open flax and tussock country and intriguing corridors of enclosed manuka tree. You will not manage to negotiate this trip without getting your feet wet and it is notoriously muddy, but there are boardwalks in the worst sections. The DoC Mason's Bay hut has 20 bunks but is popular and runs on a first come first served basis, so take a tent if you can.

Rakiura Track → *You can purchase a Great Walks or campsite pass ($10/$6) from the VIC before departure or book over the net, greatwalksbooking@doc.govt.nz*

The Rakiura is one of New Zealand's 'Great Walks' immediately accessible by foot from Oban and is a 29-36 km track requiring two to three days. The appeal of the Rakiura, other than ease of access, is the mainly rimu and kamahi forest scenery, and views and secluded beaches of **Paterson Inlet**. There is also an abundance of **birdlife**. In the forest this includes kaka, tomtit, bellbirds, tui, and shining cuckoo, while wading birds including New Zealand dotterel and seabirds, including shags and little blue penguins, that can be seen on the coast. The track can be negotiated clockwise or anticlockwise from Oban. In a clockwise direction the walking distances and times are as follows: Halfmoon Bay to Port William Hut, 12 km, four-five hours; Port William Hut to North Arm Hut, 12 km, six hours; North Arm to Halfmoon Bay 12 km, four-five hours. Port William and North arm huts are well equipped and have 30 bunks each. There are designated campsites with water and toilets at Maori Beach, Port William and Sawdust Bay.

The Northwest Circuit → *A Northwest Circuit Pass allowing 10 nights in any hut on the route is available from the VIC for $40.*

At 125 km and requiring at least 10 days, this is one of the longest tramps in the country and done in total, is not for the faint-hearted. The appeal, other than the sense of achievement and feeling of complete solitude, is the remote and rugged coastal scenery with its stunning bays and features, some with such evocative names as Hellfire Pass and Ruggedy Beach. The side trip to climb **Mount Anglem** (980 m), the island's highest peak, is also a recommended highlight. The track is also noted for its wildlife. That the track is notoriously muddy and wet at times but don't let that put you off. There are 10 DoC huts on the route with 6-10 bunks.

The track distances and minimum times are as follows: Halfmoon Bay to Port William, 12 km, four hours; Port William to Bungaree Hut, 6 km, three hours; Bungaree Hut to Christmas Village Hut, 11 km, five hours; Mount Anglem side trip, 11 km, six hours; Christmas Village Hut to Yankee River Hut 12 km, six hours; Yankee River Hut to Long Harry Hut, 11 km, five hours; Long Harry Hut to East Ruggedy Hut, 7 km, three hours; East Ruggedy Hut to Hellfire Pass, 14 km, seven hours; Hellfire Pass Hut to Mason's Bay Hut, 15 km, seven hours; Mason's Bay Hut to Freshwater Landing Hut 14 km, three hours; Freshwater Landing Hut to North Arm Hut 11 km, five hours; North Arm Hut to Halfmoon Bay, 12 km, five hours.

The Southern Circuit is a 74 km 6-7 day tramp that takes in many similar (but more remote) aspects of the Rakiura Track and the delights of the rugged coastline from Doughboy Bay to Mason's Bay and Mason's Bay itself. Access to the recommended start and finish point of Freshwater Landing is by water-taxi. Four DoC huts and an interesting bivvy at Doughboy Bay provide accommodation. DoC can provide detailed information about the tramp.

● Sleeping

Stewart Island *p688*

Most of the accommodation on the island takes the form of comfortable upper to mid-range B&Bs and homestays and budget options but there is one hotel and a handful of motels. Note that none of the budget hostels take advance bookings in summer and beds must be secured on the day of departure from Bluff or Invercargill airport. Note also that there is much gossip surrounding certain bachelor-owned/operated hostels and the 'comfort' of single women travellers. The best advice is to check out a few hostels on your arrival (particularly those recommended below) and decide for yourself.

L **Port of Call**, *Jensen Bay, T03-2191394, www.portofcall.co.nz* Set in an idyllic spot overlooking the entrance to Halfmoon Bay, very cosy and friendly. It offers a charming en suite double, great breakfasts and views from the deck that are almost unsurpassed elsewhere.

L **Stewart Island Lodge**, *14 Nichol Rd, Halfmoon Bay, T03-2191085, www.stewartislandlodge.co.nz* Well established as one of the best upper-range B&Bs on the island. It provides 5 luxury en suites and famously good cuisine, amidst the perfect peaceful setting.

A **South Sea Hotel**, *corner of Elgin Terr and Main St, Oban, T03-2191059, www.stewart-island.co.nz* The main hotel on the waterfront. Although its in-house rooms are comfortable enough, its modern motel studio units out back are even better. In-house restaurant and bar, which is the local hub of evening entertainment.

AL **Bay Motel**, *9 Dundee St, Halfmoon Bay, T03-2191119, bay.motel@xtra.co.nz* The newest motel on the island with tidy units,

good facilities, views across the bay and within a short walk of all amenities.

A **Pilgrim Cottage** and

A **Butterfield Beach House**, *T03-219114*. Two modern, tidy and affordable self-contained options, owned by the same couple. Kiwi trips a speciality.

A **Miro Cottage**, *113 Miro Cres, Oban, T03-2191180, janlance@xtra.co.nz* Another fine self-contained option with 2 bedrooms and close to town.

C-D **Anne's Place**, *Mill Creek, T03-2191065*. A no-nonsense, no TV, budget option run by a former VIC representative, so her knowledge knows no bounds. If Anne is full she can refer you on to another reputable hostel.

C-D **Stewart Island Backpackers**, *Ayr St, T03-2191114, www.stewart-island.co.nz* In town this is a sprawling but highly functional place, with a wide range of dorms and units.

D **Ferndale Campsites**, *Halfmoon Bay, T03-2191176*. Basic but close to all amenities.

● Eating

Stewart Island *p688*

Stewart Island has only a few eateries, with the famed muttonbird (*Titi*) being the speciality dish round these parts. By all accounts it is very tasty, being a bit like venison and certainly more oily than chicken. But if you see these beautiful seabirds up close, never mind the chicks (which resemble fluffy brown slippers), you'll be picketing these establishments with a placard round your neck!

$$ **Church Hill Café Bar and Restaurant** *next to(not in) the church on the headland above the wharf, T03-2191323. Daily from 1030 (seasonal)*. The best bet for fine dining.

$$ **South Sea Hotel**, *see above. 0800-0930/ 1200-1400/ 1800-2100, seasonal.* Provides a fine menu of no-nonsense lunch and dinner

● *For an explanation of the sleeping and eating price codes used in this guide, see the inside* ● *front cover. Other relevant information is provided in the Essentials chapter, see page 51.*

options including the unique muttonbird for around $20.

$$ Lighthouse Wine Bar, *Main St, Oban, T03-2191208. From 1800, seasonal.* Good for a sit-in pizza.

$ Justcafe, *Main St, T03-2191208.* The place for good coffee and a light meal, while absorbed with the internet.

$ Kai Cart *on Ayr St, T03-2191442.* Class fish and chips for lunch or dinner.

Groceries Ship to Shore, *on the waterfront.* The only general store.

The Lettuce Inn, *31 Main St, T03-2191243.* Good for fresh meat, fruit and vegetables.

⊕ Entertainment

South Sea Hotel, *Elgin Terr.* Without doubt the place to be for a beer and unpredictable entertainment. But what kind of night you will have depends on whom you bump into and whether they are in good spirits or bad. They are great and welcoming bunch most of the time, so just place your cards on the table and give as good as you get! Should it all get too much you will find comfort and solitude in the new boutique **cinema**. It is entirely in tune with the feel of the place. For details about what is on and when, just ask the locals.

▲ Activities

As you can imagine there are a wide range of possibilities from **fishing** and **diving**, to simple daytime **sightseeing**, overnight or luxury multi-day **adventures**. The **DoC VIC** or the **Adventure Centre** on the wharf list all the operators and charter possibilities.

Oban Tours and Taxis, *T03-2191456,* hire out diving gear.

Seabuzz, *T03-2191282, 1100 daily.* Offer a 1-hr glass-bottom boat trip. From $25.

Bravo Adventure Cruises, *T03-2191144.* A 4-hr twilight bush-walking trip to attempt to see **kiwi**. From $60. Short of Mason's Bay this may be your best chance of seeing the kiwi in half-light (see page 693).

Sam and Billy the Bus, *T03-2191269.* 1½ hrs scenic bus trip. Sam, the naturalist/ historian and Billy the wheels-cum-petrol junkie have been providing entertaining and informative trips around Oban and its neighbouring settlements for 15 years. Tours depart from the centre of the village 1100-1430 (seasonal), from $20.

Oban Tours and Taxis, *Main Road, Oban T03-2191456.* Similar sightseeking tours available or you may decide to do a self-guided trip by scooter.

Completely Southern Kayaks, *T03-2191275, jo.paine@clear.net.nz* Provide a range of guided single to multi-day **sea kayaking** trips around Ulva and Paterson Inlet and independent hire.

Walking There are 2 good companies offering guided walks, including the 'kiwi experience':

Ruggedy Range Wilderness Experience, *Oban, T03-2191066, www.ruggedyrange.com*;

Kiwi Wilderness Walks, *based in Riverton, T0800-248886, www.riverton.co.nz*

Ulva's Guided Walks, *T03-2191216, www.ulva.co.nz* Also offer an informative trips to Ulva Island.

● Directory

Stewart Island *p688*

Banks Ship to Shore, *on the waterfront.* Have EFTPOS and accept NZ travellers' cheques. There are no banks or ATMs on the island. **Postal agents** Stewart Island Flights depot, *on the waterfront (Elgin Terr), T03-2191090.* **Internet** Justcafe, *Main St. 0800-2200 seasonal.* Stewart Island Backpackers, *Ayr St.* **Medical centre** *Argyle St, T03-2191098.* **Police** *T03-2190020.*

The Catlins → Phone code: 03, Colour map 7, grid B3/4

If you love remote and scenic coastlines you are going to love the Catlins. The added bonus here is their location. Like the Wairarapa in the southwest of the North Island, the area is generally off the beaten track and certainly under-rated. You can negotiate the Catlins from the north or the south via the publicized Southern Scenic Route, encompassing a 187 km network of minor roads, about 30 km of which are unsealed (see warning below). The journey between Invercargill and Dunedin (or in reverse) is often attempted in one day, which is definitely a mistake. A more thorough, comfortable and less frustrating investigation will take at least two days, preferably three. But, if you can really only afford one day, the highlights not to be missed are – from the north – Nugget Point (for sunrise); the opportunity to see the seductively named Hookers sea lions at Cannibals Bay (morning); the Purakaunui Falls and Purakaunui Bay (for lunch); then Curio Bay and Slope Point in the afternoon.

❖ *Given the combination of 'difficult' road conditions, stunning scenery and often a time constraint, the Catlins have become a notorious black spot for accidents. 'Prangs' are so commonplace that most car rental companies do not provide insurance coverage in the region. Read the small print and check before setting off.*

The Catlins is also noted for its rich flora and fauna. Of particular note are the pinnipeds, or seals. The Catlins is the only mainland region of New Zealand where you can observe the New Zealand fur seals, Hookers sea lions and Southern elephant seals in the same location. The region is also within the very limited breeding range of the rarest penguin on the planet – the yellow-eyed Penguin (hoiho) – and the rare and tiny Hector's dolphin. Incredibly, with a little luck all these species can be observed quite easily, independently and at relatively close (safe!) range. The tracts of dense coastal forest that still remain are made up predominately of poDoCarp and silver beech (but Curio Bay is home to a scattering of petrified fossil trees that are over 160 million years old) and are home to native birds like native pigeon (kereru), yellowhead (mohua) and fernbird. The forests also hide a number of attractive waterfalls.

The Catlins - Invercargill to Papatowai

Sleeping
Bayfarm B&B **1**
Catlins Farmstay **2**
Curio Bay Camp Ground **3**

Fernlea B&B **10**
Governors Cottage **4**
Hilltop Backpackers
  & Internet **5**

Papatowai Motor Park **6**
Southern Scenic Motel **7**
Tautuku Lodge **8**
Waikawa Holiday Lodge **9**

Getting there Bottom Bus, T03-4429708, www.bottombus.co.nz, and the **Catlins Coaster,** T021-682461, www.catlinscoaster.co.nz, provide transport and tour options via Queenstown and Te Anau. Being on SH1 Balclutha and Gore are serviced by all the major north/south or east/west bus companies. Refer also to activity operators page 703. **Petrol** is available at Owaka and Papatowai.

Information Both the VICs in **Invercargill** and **Balclutha** can supply detailed information about the Catlins including accommodation. *The Catlins* is a useful free booklet as are the websites www.catlins.co.nz and www.catlins-nz.com **Owaka VIC,** ① *at the Catlins Diner, Main St, T03-4158371, www.catlins-nz.com Mon-Fri 0830-2030 Sat 0800-2030, Sun 0900-2130.* **Waikawa VIC,** ① *Dolphin Magic Information Centre, T03-2468444. Daily Oct-Apr.* **DoC** also has leaflets ($1) on Catlin's walks and ecological highlights. **Balclutha VIC,** ① *4 Clyde St, T03-4180388, balvin@nzhost.co.nz Mon-Fri 0830-1700, Sat and Sun 0930-1500.* The centre can provide all the northbound information surrounding the Catlins and Southern Scenic Route. Internet. **Gore VIC,** ① *corner of Hokonui Dr and Norfolk St, T03-2039288, goreinfo@goredc.govt.nz Mon-Fri 0900-1700 Sat and Sun 1000-1600.* Has a list of local walks including the popular 1½ hour Whisky Falls Track.

History

The first human settlers in the region were the South Island Maori who utilized the abundant coastal resources and hunted the flightless moa as long ago as 1350 AD. Within 200 years most of the moa had been plundered and the settlers turned their attentions to the fur seals, fish and other seafood. The thick almost impenetrable coastal forests of the region prevented easy access inland so the population waxed and waned but was never substantial. The forbidding forests were also thought by the Maori to be the home of a race of hairy giants known as Maeroero (a group of early Scots settlers looking for a pub?). The Maori were joined, first by small groups of European whalers, then timber millers who began their relentless rape of the forest from the 1860s. Once depleted, as with most other parts of New Zealand, it was the farmers who then moved in. Thankfully a few tracts of the original coastal forest escaped the axe and can still be seen.

Invercargill to Papatowai → *Colour map 7, grid B4/5*

From Invercargill the Southern Scenic Route (SH92) crosses the Southland Plains to join the coast and the **Mataura River** mouth at the former coastal whaling station of **Fortrose** (42 km). At Fortrose you leave SH92 and begin to negotiate the coastal road networks of the Catlins towards **Otara** and Waikawa. The first potential diversion is to **Waipapa Point**. From just beyond Otara take the signposted road cross-country to a car park beside the lighthouse. The gently sloping beach is backed by dunes and decked with rock pools and offshore reefs. These reefs were the cause of New Zealand's second worst shipping disaster in 1881, when the *SS Tararua* ran aground with the loss of 131 lives. It was this tragedy that prompted the erection of the **lighthouse**. Completed in 1884, it was the last wooden lighthouse built in New Zealand. Keep your eyes open for Hookers sea lions, which sometimes haul up on the beaches here for a doze. If there are none in evidence, don't worry, you will very probably see them further north.

Once back on the main route near Otara continue to Haldane and follow signs for **Slope Point**, which is actually the southernmost point in New Zealand, contrary to what most visitors believe. The real geographical point and obligatory signpost can be reached here via a short 10-minute walk from a roadside car park. From the car park you are also treated to the impressive views of the dramatic headlands that herald a distinct change from Waipapa's lowly dunescapes. Also note the macrocarpa trees which seem to get much photographic attention.

From Haldane the road skirts the Haldane Estuary before delivering you at the beautiful **Porpoise Bay**, a popular spot for swimming and surfing. From the junction it is a short drive (right) to the headland and **Curio Bay**.

The headland overlooking both bays is a superb spot to simply admire the coastal scenery, crashing waves and try to spot the tiny **Hector's dolphins**. Some patience may be required for this but eventually you may see a pod (especially near the rocks that protect Porpoise Bay). They are a delight to observe as they breach the surface in exuberant playfulness.

At Curio Bay, about 500 m west, is the **fossil forest**. At first glance it is difficult to make out the petrified stumps and logs that scatter the rock platform, but a more thorough investigation by foot reveals the distinct features of these Jurassic ancestors.

Although it is hard to drag yourself away from Curio Bay, the road now turns briefly inland to rejoin the Waikawa River Estuary at **Waikawa**. Here you will find a small **information centre** in the old church that also hosts Dolphin Magic (see Activities, page 703) and a small café, ① *T03-2468444. Daily Oct-Apr*. Across the road is the Waikawa Holiday Lodge Backpackers (see page 701) and the small **District Museum**, ① *1300-1600 daily (seasonal)*, which contains some relics from the whaling and saw-milling years.

From Waikawa the road then heads north past the former saw-milling village of **Niagara**. A few hundred metres past the village you then join the main SH92 Catlins road (from Tokanui and Fortrose) and turn right through more dramatic topography and coastal forest towards **Chaslands** and Papatowai. The **Chasland Scenic Reserve** boasts some of the best forest in the area with large rimu and kamahi. Look out for the left turn to **McLean Falls** (1 km south of the Cathedral Caves turn-off). The falls car park is reached via the unsealed Rewcastle Road (3 km). The picturesque three-stepped falls (often said to be the most beautiful in the Catlins) are reached easily by foot (40 minutes return).

The 30-m high **Cathedral Caves** at the north end of Waipati Beach are accessible only at low tide (posted at the road junction or available from the local VICs). The 2 km access road will deliver you to a car park where the caves are accessed via a short (30 minutes) forest and beach walk. Although the forest is part of **Waipati Scenic Reserve**, note that part of the area is Maori owned. After several land claim disputes a small fee is now requested to access the caves.

Just before the beautiful Tautuku Bay is the **Lenz Reserve** and the **Traill's Tractor Historic Walk** (10 minutes). Tautuku was a prolific logging area and the walk takes you to a former milling site and an original 'Traill's Tractor' logging machine, that took over from horse-drawn trams in the steeper country. The walk starts from the Flemming River Bridge. Nearby is the hidden little scenic delight of **Lake Wilkie**. Formed in a dune hollow and surrounded by lush bush, it can be viewed from a lookout a mere five

● *The village of Niagara, just north of Waikawa, is said to have been named somewhat*
● *facetiously after the famous falls in North America – see the tiny falls at the bridge.*

minutes' walk from the car park. You then have the option to complete a 30-minute circuit of the lake's coastal edge. The boardwalk provides another view across the lake and comes complete with interpretative signs that outline the botanical features of the unique habitat. Note there is no access to the beach from this point.

About 1 ½ km south of Lake Wilkie is the new **Tautuku Estuary Walk** (30 minutes return) which offers access to the estuary and coastal forest. The beach (which is a cracker) is best accessed via the **Tautuku Dune/Forest Walk** (15 minutes) which is just opposite the Tautuku Outdoor Education Centre on SH92. A stunning view of the whole bay and its thick fringe of coastal forest can be seen from the road as you climb **Florence Hill** at its eastern edge. Just offshore are the **Rainbow Isles**, which owe their name to the effects of the sun on sea-spray, squirted skywards by a small blowhole on the main island. The Maori call it *rerekohu,* meaning 'flying mist'. From Florence Hill it is a short 2 km drive to **Papatowai**, – the Catlins 'mid-point' and base for services and accommodation. ⠢ *For Sleeping, Eating and Activities, see pages 701-703.*

Papatowai to Owaka → *Colour map 7, grid B5*

There are a number of notable walks around Papatowai, the most popular of which is the **Picnic Point Track** (40 minutes), which takes in both coast and forest and with a short diversion to the unusual **Kings Rock** formation.

From McLennan and the river of the same name you can access both the **Maitai** (north) and **Purakaunui Falls** (east). They are both easily reached from the road (Maitai first via SH92), and significantly different and worthy of investigation. About 4 km east of the Purakaunui Falls is the access road to **Purakaunui Bay**. This is one of the most beautiful and supremely quiet spots on the Catlins Coast and is excellent for a short walk, surfing, a picnic or an overnight stay at the basic campsite. **Be careful on this road, it is very narrow and winding.**

If you want a change from all the coastal scenery the **Catlins River Track** (five hours one-way) provides an excellent opportunity. Access is about 3 km south of Catlins Lake via Tawanui where there is a **DoC campsite**. Follow the road to **The Wisp** (farm lease) and the picnic site trailhead. The section between Wallis Stream and Franks Creek (1½ hours) is recommended.

Back on the coast many visitors are drawn along the western bank of the Catlins Lake and the Owaka Heads to see **Jack's Bay** and **blowhole**. At 55 m deep, with an opening of 140 m by 70 m, it is quite an impressive sight, even without a storm to spur it into action.

Owaka and around → *Population: 400, Colour map 7, grid B5*

Returning back to Catlins Lake and SH92 it is then a short drive to the Catlins' largest settlement and supply centre, Owaka, which offers a host of basic facilities including a good restaurant, petrol, a grocery store, accommodation, visitors' centre and even internet. But if the weather is fine, and you still have time on your hands before sunset, don't hang around. Instead, head back to the coast. **Pounawea**, 4 km south of Owaka offers a very pleasant (45 minutes) **nature walk** through poDoCarp forest and saltmarsh.

Just east of Pounawea is **Surat Bay**, which is reached across other side of the Owaka River (bridge 2 km south of Owaka). Although beach access is awkward (ask at the signposted Surat Bay Lodge), its golden swathes of sand and those of its neighbour, **Cannibals Bay** (access road from SH92, a few kilometres north of Owaka), provide the reasonable likelihood of encountering some dozing Hookers sea lions.

Cannibals Bay was mistakenly named in the late 1800s by geologist James Hector, who took the human remains from a Maori burial site to be something far more sinister. A very pleasant **walk** from here negotiates the length of Cannibals Bay (from the car park) to the **False Islet** headlands. Then, once you have taken in the views, from the west to Jack's Bay and then east, to the rocky outcrops of the Nugget

Point, continue on to Surat Bay, before returning across the neck of the headland to Cannibals Bay (two hours). ▸▸ *For Sleeping, Eating and other listings, see pages 702-703.*

Nugget Point, Roaring Bay and Kaka Point → *Colour map 7, grid B5*

Back on SH92 the road turns inland again towards Balclutha. About 3 km east of Owaka is **Tunnel Hill**, which is a historic reserve featuring the 246-m long tunnel, once the most southerly railway tunnel in New Zealand. Completed in 1915 it was the most prominent feature on the Catlins branch railway line that ran between Balclutha and Tahakopa near McLennan. The line closed in 1971.

Just beyond the hill is the turn-off to Nugget Point, without doubt the highlight of the Catlins Coast. To get a proper feel for 'The Nuggets' they are best visited at sunrise, when the spectacular rock pillars and outcrops take on the orange glow of the sun. The track to the 1870 **lighthouse** starts at the terminus of a delightful road that skirts the beach and rock platforms of Molyneux Bay. It takes about 10 minutes to reach the lighthouse and its associated lookout point, but by far the best view is to be had from the hill, about 100 m short of it. Care must be taken here, but the views from the top are outstanding. The islets and rocky, inaccessible coastline, offers an important haven for **wildlife**, and is home to seals (all three species: fur, Hookers and elephant), yellow-eyed and blue penguins, sooty shearwaters, gannets and occasionally royal spoonbills. Even below the waves life abounds, and the area boasts a wide diversity of underwater habitats. Keep your ears open for the plaintive wails of fur seal pups playing in and around the rock pools below the track and in the distance, look out for squadrons of shearwaters, skimming the waves in search of food. It really is a magical place.

Just inland from The Point is **Roaring Bay** that has a small public hide where **yellow-eyed penguins** can be seen coming ashore at dusk, or leaving again for their routine fishing trips at dawn. If you are lucky enough to see one, bear in mind you are looking at the rarest penguin in the world so be discreet and do not approach them. Back along the edge of Molyneux Bay is **Kaka Point** (8 km), a charming little coastal settlement that, along with Owaka, provides the necessary visitor amenities and accommodation. From Kaka Point it is about 40 km to Balclutha and SH1 to Dunedin. ▸▸ *For Sleeping, Eating and Activities, see pages 702-703.*

Balclutha → *Colour map 7, grid B5 Population: 4000*

Balclutha (which is actually in South Otago) is 80 km southwest of Dunedin on the banks of the **Clutha River**, which, with its origins at Lake Wanaka, is the South Island's longest (322 km). Known as 'Big River Town' its name actually refers to the Scots Gaelic for 'town on the Clyde' after Glasgow's great river. The town's first known white resident was Scot Jim McNeill who used to run a ferry service across the river between 1853 and 1857. The modern-day concrete bridge that provides the vital road link with Southland is not the original bridge. The first effort, which was constructed in 1866, was washed away in floods. **Fishing** is of course a popular local pursuit and the VIC has details of this and other local activities. The **South Otago Museum**, ① *1 Renfrew St, T03-4182382, Mon-Fri 1000-1600 Sun 1300-1600, free*, is particularly noted for its collection of bottles and displays surrounding the history of the local **Kaitangata** Coal Mine. ▸▸ *For Sleeping, Eating and Activities, see pages 702-703.*

Gore → *Colour map 7, grid B4 Population: 9000 The VIC, see page 697, has a list of local walks including the popular 1½ hr Whisky Falls Track.*

Gore, on the banks of the Mataura River, is Southland's second largest town and most famous for its unusual mix of **trout fishing**, **country music** and formerly (we can only presume), **illegal whiskey distilling**. So although on first acquaintance you might think the place to be a just another quiet backwater, beware. At times, particularly during the 10-day annual **New Zealand Gold Guitar Awards**, ① *T03-2081978,*

lingerie shop. During the festival both amateur and professional artists compete and provide live entertainment, while the true fanatics get the chance to dust off their cowboy boots and line dance the night away.

Other than the rod and reel, other local attractions include the **Hokonui Moonshine Museum** and the **Gore Historical Museum** ① *both housed in the Hokonui Heritage Centre next to the VIC, T03-2087032. $5.* There, the heady days of Gore district's insobriety and chaos, alongside its times of prohibition and prudence, are all revealed, along with all the usual more mundane aspects of the region's history. Just opposite the VIC is the recently renovated **Eastern Southland Gallery**, ① *T03-2083851, Mon-Fri 1000-1700, Sun 1400-1600,* showcasing the quite impressive private collection of expatriate kiwi John Money and donated works by one of New Zealand's most well known contemporaries Ralf Hotere. Also still in the planning is a **Fishing Museum** where the monster brown trout and the fishermen that come from around the globe to catch them will be celebrated. However, it seems the great funding fish has yet to be landed. Should you fancy a spot of **fishing** yourself, you'll get a license at the VIC ($16 for a day). The VIC also has an extensive list of **local guides** and **tackle hire** outlets.

Also of note in the region is **Moth Restaurant and Bar,** ① *operated by the Croydon Aircraft Company, SH94, Mandeville, west of Gore on SH94, T03-2089662, www.themoth.co.nz* Not only does it provide good food but also the unique opportunity to combine your visit with a flight in a Tiger Moth (from $60). Although you may get a taste of what to expect from the website (and certainly all the latest information), the sound of the aircraft fails to have the desired affect – much more like a bovine with severe flatulence. If you have animal-loving children, **The Reservation,** ① *at the top of Coutts Rd, T03-2081200, daily 1000-1730, $4, child $1,* has a small menagerie of warm and fuzzies, from windless bovines, to chinchillas and Clydesdale horses, all of whom are available for copious stroking and generous feeding. Café on site. ▸▸ *For Sleeping, Eating, and other listings, see pages 702-703.*

● Sleeping

Invercargill to Papatowai *p697*
South Catlins Farmstay Group, *T03-2469876, christine@xtra.co.nz* A co-operative group of 9 farmhouses and 5 self-contained cottages throughout the South Catlins region and an excellent source of information. They can also arrange farm tours and garden visits.
A Fernlea B&B, *Motokua (20 mins from Invercargill).* A lovely self-contained cottage (sleeps 4) with its own private garden on a large dairy farm.
A-B Catlins Farmstay, *midway between Cathedral Caves and Curio Bay, T03-2468843, www.catlinsfarmstay.co.nz* In a 1000-acre working farm, offers 2 doubles and a twin. The owners also have several fine (**A-B**) self-contained cottages in the area that are well worth enquiring about.
A Govenors Cottage (Waikawa Cottages), *Curio Bay, T03-2468843, www.cottagestays. co.nz/governors/cottage.htm* Another fine

2-bedroom self-contained option.
A Southern Scenic Motel, *Papatowai, T03-4158600, catlinsbb@xtra.co.nz* A stylish modern place with 4 studio units, all with their own balcony. Close to amenities and coastal walks.
B Papatowai Motels and Store, *T03-4158147.* A cheaper option nearby.
D Curio Bay Camp Ground, *on the headland overlooking Porpoise Bay, T03-2468897.* Has powered/tent sites, showers and a small store.
D Tautuku Lodge, *set in the Lenz Reserve at Tautuku, T03-4158024, dianan@clear.net.nz* Owned by the Forest and Bird Society. The lodge sleeps 10 but there is also a smaller cabin sleeping 4. Supply your own bedding.
C-D Waikawa Holiday Lodge, *Waikawa, T03-2468552.* Backpackers providing comfortable budget doubles and dorms in a spacious house. In-house shop and café across the road at Dolphin Magic.
C-D Hilltop Backpackers, *Papatowai, T03-4158028, hilltop@ihug.co.nz* An

excellent place offering doubles (with a great view) and dorm beds. Log fire, modern facilities, hot tub, bikes, canoes, internet and much more.

B **Papatowai Motels and Store**, T03-4158147. Has three self-contained units

C-D **Papatowai Motor Park**, *behind the motel, T03-4158500.*

Papatowai to Owaka *p699*

AL **Greenstone Farmstay**, *Purakaunui Falls Rd, T03-4158259, greenwoodfarm@xtra.co.nz* An en suite Queen, twin and singles in a modern villa homestead on a 1900-acre farm. Dinners on request. Ideally located near the falls and Purakaunui Bay.

C-D **Falls Backpackers**, *Purakaunui Falls, T03-4158724, sparx@es.co.nz* Offers a double, and shared twin rooms. Walking distance from the falls.

D **DoC campsite**, *Purakaunui Bay.* Basic but in a superb setting – worth buying a tent for!

Owaka and around *p699*

B **Catlins Retreat B&B**, *27 Main Rd, T03-4158830.* A century-old villa located right in the heart of Owaka. It has a spa, open fire and its BBQs are a speciality.

C-D **Blowhole Backpackers**, *24 Main St, T03-4158998.* Popular and homely, has both doubles and dorms.

There are a small number of **motels**:

A **Catlins Area Motels**, *34 Ryley St, T03-4158821;* and

B **Catlins Gateway Motel**, *corner of Main Rd and Royal Terr, T03-4158592.* Both recommended. The later has some nice new 1-bedroom units.

A **Kepplestone B&B**, *9 Surat Bay Rd, T03-4158134, www.kepplestone@hostlinknz.com* Tucked away near the coast and Surat Bay. A delightful B&B with a range of en suite rooms and fine cuisine.

C-D **Surat Bay Lodge**, *Surat Bay Rd, T03-4158099, www.suratbay.co.nz* A small, peaceful backpackers which is a stone's throw from the beach. It also runs its own nature, farm, walking and canoe tours (2-3 hrs) from $25-$65. Recommended.

C-D **Pounawea Camp Ground**, *Park Lane, Pounawea near Owaka, T03-4191110.* Basic motorpark.

Nugget Point, Roaring Bay and Kaka Point *p700*

A **Nugget View and Kaka Point Motels**, *11 Rata St, Kaka Point, T03-4128602, nugview@catlins.co.nz* Just what the name suggests with 10 comfortable studio units. They also run a small backpackers at 17 Rata St and offer boat based eco-tours to The Nuggets.

A **Nugget Lodge Motels**, *2 km from Nugget Point right on the beach, T03-4128783.* Run by a former DoC field officer with plenty of local knowledge. On offer are 2 new, modern units, one overlooking the bay.

C-D **Fernlea Backpackers**, *Moana St, Kaka Point, T03-4128834.* Small, homely and well-established. The view from the balcony is wonderful.

C-D **Kaka Point Motor Park**, *on the edge of the town on Tarata St, T03-4128818.* Quiet place offering 2 modern cabins.

Balclutha *p700*

A **Rosebank Lodge Motor Hotel**, *265 Clyde St, T03-4181490.* Has comfortable units, spa, sauna and an in-house restaurant.

A **Highway Lodge Motel**, *165 Clyde St, T03-4182363.* Another modern option that sits at the start of the Southern Scenic Route and the Catlins coast.

A **Lesmahagow**, *Main Rd, Benhar, T03-4182507, www.lesmahagow.co.nz* You will find a warm Irish welcome and all the comforts at this B&B. It is located just north of the town in a peaceful setting and has cosy doubles and singles.

C-D **Naish Park Motor Camp**, *56 Charlotte St, T03-4180088.* The only option for campervans in town which should adequately serve your needs. It also has a few cabins.

Gore *p700*

A **Croydon Lodge**, *corner of SH94 and Waimea St, T03-2089029.* A large motel set in extensive grounds with a 9-hole golf course, à la carte restaurant and bar.

A **Oakleigh Motel**, *70 Hokonui Dr, T03-2084863, www.oakleighmotel.co.nz* Another more upmarket motel in town.

C-D **Old Fire Station Backpackers**, *19 Hokonui Dr (across the road from the VIC), T03-2081925.* Small backpackers with double/twin, singles and dorms.

C-D **Gore Motor Camp**, *35 Broughton St, T03-2084919*. Basic cabins, powered/tent sites.

🍴 Eating

Invercargill to Papatowai *p697*
If you are not in a B&B or self-contained place then eating out in the South Catlins really takes the form of a stove or a BBQ with the sandflies.
General store, *Papatowai sells. Daily 0830-2200, winter Sun-Thu 0900-1800, Fri and Sat 0900-1830*. Basic takeaways.

Owaka *p699*
$$ **Lumber Jack Bar and Café**, *on Owaka's main street, T03-4158747. Daily from 1200 (1600 in winter)*. A new and fairly classy place, with a traditional NZ menu and good coffee.

Kaka Point *p700*
Point Café and Bar, *on the Esplanade, T03-4128800. Daily 0800-2000*. The newest eatery/bar in the area. Both the food and the bar are very good and the place has been an instant hit. It also has a grocery store attached.

Balclutha *p700*
$$ **Rosebank Lodge**, *see above. Daily for breakfast, lunch and dinner*. The restaurant here is recommended.

Gore *p700*
$ **Moth Restaurant and Bar**, see page 701. *Tue-Sun from 1100-2100*.
$ **Table Talk Café**, *76 Main St, Gore, T03-2087110*. Has a modern NZ menu and serves a good all-day breakfast.
$ **Howl at the Moon**, *2 Main St, T03-2083851. Daily from 1200*. A café/bar with a reasonable blackboard menu.
$ **The Green Room Cafe**, *59 Irk St, T03-2081005*. Locally recommended for good coffee. Also has internet.

⛰️ Activities and tours

The Catlins *p696*
Catlins Wildlife Trackers Eco-tours, Papatowai, *T03-4158613,*
www.catlins-ecotours.co.nz Have been operating for over 11 years and offer award winning 2- (from $290) and 4- (from $580) day ecotours that explore the region's forest, coast, natural features and wildlife. Very informative; accommodation also provided.
Catlins Encounters is a new adjunct to the already very successful **Elm Wildlife Tours** *operating out of the Elm Backpackers in Dunedin, T0800-356563,* www.elmwildlifetours.co.nz The entertaining 2-day/1-night camping (or alternative) trip takes in all the best sights and encompasses a lot of local knowledge and there will be a very good chance to see both yellow-eyed penguins and Hookers sea lions. Departs Dunedin Sun/Tue/Fri from Nov-Apr and reaches Curio Bay (camp) before turning back, from $169 (includes BBQ dinner).
Catlins Natural Wonders, *Balclutha, T0800-353941, www.catlinsnatural.co.nz* Another eco-based tour operator offering day trips (from $110) 4 times a week (depart from Dunedin 0830/Balclutha 1000) and 2-day trips (from $200) from Invercargill to Dunedin on Thu which include a choice of accommodation at extra cost.
Nugget Point Eco-Tours, *based in Kaka Point, T03-4128602, www.catlins.co.nz* Offer water-based wildlife spotting and fishing trips around the Molyneux Bay and Nugget Point area, from $50.
Catlins Tours, *based in Invercargill, T03-2304576, catlins@southnet.co.nz* Provide a more generalized tour Mon-Sat.
Dolphin Magic, *based in Waikawa, T03-2468444, dolphinmagic@xtra.co.nz* Trips (1½ hrs) to see general marine life with the chance of spotting the rare Hector's dolphin. Depart Waiwaka Dolphin Information Centre Oct-Apr 1000/1400 (from $50) and a (2½ hrs) twilight trip at 1700 (from $75).

☎️ Directory

Banks There are no banks in the Catlins but EFTPOS is available at the general stores and petrol stations the main centres. **Internet** Hilltop Backpackers, *Papatowai*. VIC, *Owaka*. Lumberjack Café and Bar, *Owaka*. Green Room Café, *Gore*. Table Talk Café, *Gore*.

Tramping in Southland and the Fiords

Information

For information (including DoC self-guided leaflet), the latest conditions on all the tracks listed below and hut bookings contact the **DoC VIC** in Te Anau and the VIC in Tuatapere (see pages 664 and 679). The following websites are also useful: www.DoC.govt.nz, www.hollyfordtrack.co.nz, www.humpridgetrack.co.nz (on-line bookings). Most mainstream bookshops stock specialist guides on the Milford or Fiordland Tracks. DoC also stock maps.

The Dusky Track → *Grade of Difficulty 9/10 Colour map 7, grid B1*

Now this is a track for 'real trampers': the sort with tree trunk legs, well-worn boots and copious facial hair. The Dusky offers the widest range of 'experiences' of any track in Fiordland, from stunning glacial valley and mountain scenery, to the possibility of complete immersion in icy water. It really is magnificent and thoroughly recommended. Perhaps the true attraction, other than the relative peace, is the sense of awe at the remote **Dusky Sound**, at the very heart of the Fiordland National Park. It is a true wilderness that has changed little since Captain Cook first set foot there over two centuries ago.

The Dusky attracts less than 1000 trampers a year, which is a reflection of its remote and difficult nature. Both its location and grade of difficulty make it a true challenge and one that should only be attempted in summer. Note the track is subject to bad flooding year round. Always consult with DoC before any attempt and fill in an intention sheet (Te Anau). Locator beacons are also recommended.

Walking times and distances: Allow 8-10 days from Lake Hauroko to Supper Cove to West Arm (Lake Manapouri), or 4 days one way to Supper Cove: Hauroko (Hauroko Burn Hut) to Halfway Hut: 12 km, 4-6 hours. Halfway Hut to Lake Roe Hut: 7 km, 3-5 hours. Lake Roe Hut to Loch Maree Hut: 10 km, 4-6 hours. Loch Maree Hut to Supper Cove: 12 km, 6-8 hours. North Access (Wilmot Pass Road Access Point to Loch Maree): Wilmot Pass Road Access Point to Upper Spey Hut, 8 km, 4-5 hours (add 45 minutes to West Arm Wharf and Hut). Upper Spey Hut to Kintail Hut: 7 km, 6 hours. Kintail Hut to Loch Maree Hut: 11 km, 4-7 hours.

Trailhead transport and access The Dusky Track can be accessed from the south via **Lake Hauroko** (64 km west of Tuatapere) or from the **Wilmot Pass** Road (40 mins from West Arm Wharf), accessed via boat and **Lake Manapouri**. By **road** Lake Manapouri is reached from Manapouri (SH95), 21 km south of Te Anau. **Scenic Shuttles**, T03-2497654, can provide transport to Manapouri and Tuatapere (departs Te Anau 0830). **Lake Hauroko Tours**, Tuatapere, T03-2266681, reinfo@es.co.nz, offer road and **jetboat** access to the southern trailhead via Lake Hauroko. Departs Mon and Thu from Tuatapere at 0900, from $50. **Real Journeys**, T03-2496602, and **Fiordland Explorer Charters**, T03-2496616, explorercharters@xtra.co.nz, both based in Pearl Harbour, Manapouri, provide daily boat transportation to and from West Arm and Wilmot Pass Road. It is also possible to fly in or out of Supper Cove or Lake Hauroko by **floatplane** (Waterwings Airways, Te Anau, T03-2497405, or **helicopter** (**Southern Lakes Helicopters**, T03-2497167, or **South West Helicopters**, Te Anau/Tuatapere, T03-2497402). Prices on application. For more trailhead transport and trailhead access details see 'Tramping Track Transport' in the Te Anau section, page 664.

The Hollyford Track → *Grade of Difficulty 6/10 Colour map 6, grid C2*

The Hollyford Track is essentially a low-level (**bush**) 56 km four-day (one-way) tramp that negotiates the **Hollyford River Valley** and bank of **Lake McKerrow** to the remote **Martins Bay**. It is not a tramp for those expecting spectacular high-level views, but does offer fine scenery and a superb sense of wilderness. The undeniable highlight is the **Martins Bay Hut** at the mouth of the Hollyford River. Two days at Martins Bay taking in the coast and **seal colony** is a fine remote West Coast experience. The tramp is most often tackled in conjunction with **jetboat** returns/shortcuts via Lake McKerrow and a **flight** out from Martins Bay Lodge to Milford or Hollyford Valley airfield is highly recommended. Note that guided walks are available. Also note that the Hollyford can be extended or combined to include the long (9-10 day) and arduous **Pyke-Big Bay Track**. Martins Bay to Big Bay Hut offers a good day trip but the route is vague.

This is not a tramp to be tackled during or after heavy rain. The sections between The Trailhead car park and the Hidden Falls Hut (first hut) are especially tricky in wet weather. Some river crossings have **3-wire bridges** and the sandflies at the Martins Bay Hut are legendary!

Walking times and distances: Allow 4-5 days to Martins Bay Hut one-way. Road End to Hidden Falls Hut: 9 km; 2-3 hours. Hidden Falls Hut to Alabaster Hut: 10 ½ km; 3-4 hours. Alabaster Hut to Demon Trail Hut: 14 ½ km; 4-5 hours. Demon Trail Hut to Hokuri Hut: 9 ½ km; 5-6 hours. Hokuri Hut to Martins Bay Hut: 13 ½ km; 4-5 hours.

Trailhead transport and access For air transportation contact **Air Fiordland**, To3-2497505 (up to $415); for jetboat **Hollyford Track**, To800-832226 (To3-4423760); road to trailhead **Tracknet**, To3-2497777 ($38); **Trips 'n' Tramps**, To3-2497081. For more trailhead transport and trailhead access details see 'Tramping Track Transport' in the Te Anau section, page 664.

The Hump Ridge Track → *Grade of Difficulty 5/10 Colour map 7, grid B2 The Hump Ridge Track is administered by the Tuatapere Hump Ridge Track Trust*

The Hump Ridge Track opened in late 2000 and is New Zealand's newest tramping track. It is a 53 km three-day 'moderate' circuit track at the southeastern end of the Fiordland National Park. Whether it can live up to all the promotional hype remains to be seen, but there is no doubt it offers an great tramping experience. Its mix of both coastal and poDoCarp/beech forest landscapes added to the historic appeal of its four viaducts are the main attractions. The 125 m **Percy Burn Viaduct** is reputed to be the largest wooden viaduct in the world. **Wildlife** to look out for include kea and bellbirds. Fur seals and the endangered Hector's dolphins can be seen on the coast. The track is **boardwalk** through the areas most subject to any flooding, but you are still advised to check on track conditions before departure.

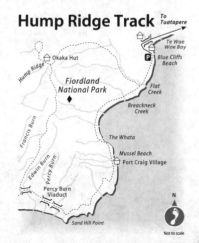

Hump Ridge Track To Tuatapere

Te Wae Wae Bay
Okaka Hut
Blue Cliffs Beach
Hump Ridge
Fiordland National Park
Flat Creek
Breackneck Creek
Francis Burn
The Whata
Mussel Beach
Port Craig Village
Edwin Burn
Percy Burn
Percy Burn Viaduct
Sand Hill Point

N

Not to scale

Walking times and distances: Allow three days: Bluecliffs Beach car park to Okaka Hut: 18 km; 8-9 hours. Okaka Hut to Port Craig Village Hut: 18 km; 7 hours. Port Craig Village Hut to Bluecliffs Beach: 17 km; 6-7 hours.

Trailhead transport and access The Hump Ridge Track starts and finishes at the western end of Blue Cliffs Beach on Te Wae Wae Bay (signposted from Tuatapere). An anticlockwise approach is generally recommended. Road transportation to the trailhead can be arranged through **Lake Hauroko Tours**, Tuatapere, T03-2266681, reinfo@es.co.nz, or the VIC in Tuatapere (see page 679). Independent vehicles can be left at the Tuatapere Hump Ridge Track office in Tuatapere, T03-2266739, or the **Rarakau Farmstay and Lodge**, Papatotara Coast Rd, Bluecliffs Beach, T03-2258192, www.rarakaulodge.com

The Kepler Track → *Grade of Difficulty 6/10 Colour map 7, grid A3*

The Kepler Track is a 60 km, 3-4 day **'Great Walk'**, that is easily accessible from Te Anau, providing a convenient and viable alternative to the Milford Track. It traverses the edge of the beautiful **Lake Te Anau** before ascending to the **Luxmore Hut** – reputed to offer one of the best 'hut views' in Fiordland. From the Luxmore Hut the track negotiates the scenic, open tops of the **Luxmore Range**, before falling through forest in to the **Iris Burn Valley** and back to civilisation via Shallow Bay on **Lake Manapouri**. The highlights are of course the views from the Luxmore Hut and the scenic combination of lake, mountain and river valley scenery. The forest is classic silver beech and poDoCarp, which at night often echoes to the cry of kiwi. New Zealand robin and blue duck are also seen occasionally. This track attracts over 10,000 trampers a year so book well in advance and expect company! The Kepler offers an excellent two-day (return) part-track walk to the Luxmore Hut and back.

Walking times and distances: Allow 4 days: Control Gates to Luxmore Hut: 14 km; 6 hours (Brod Bay campsite 1½ hours). Luxmore Hut to Iris Burn Hut: 18 ½ km; 5-6 hours. Irish Burn Hut to Moturau Hut: 17 km; 5-6 hours. Moturau Hut to Rainbow Reach: 6 km; 1 ½ hours.

Trailhead transport and access The Kepler Track starts at the Lake Te Anau outlet **control gates**, 5 km south of Te Anau and finishes at **Rainbow Reach** 11 km south of Te Anau near SH95. By **road** from Te Anau town to control gates ($5) or Rainbow Reach

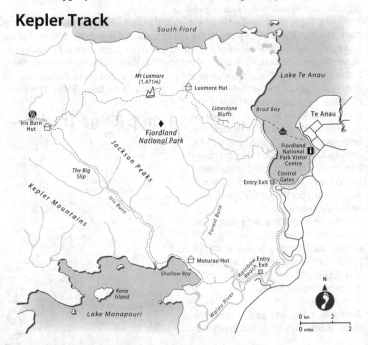

Kepler Track

($9) contact **Tracknet**, T03-2497777 ($5). Tracknet also provide transportation from Queenstown. By **boat** the Kepler can be accessed opposite Te Anau at Brod Bay (missing out first 5 ½ km lakeside section of track), contact **Sinbad Cruises**, T03-2497106, or **Lakeland Boat Hire**, T03-2498364, from $20 (one-way). The Luxmore Hut can be reached by helicopter with **Southern Lakes Helicopters**, T03-2497167, $125 per person (minimum 2 people). For more trailhead transport and trailhead access details see 'Tramping Track Transport'in the Te Anau section, page 664.

The Milford Track → Grade of Difficulty 6/10 Colour map 7, grid A2 and A3

Ever since the *National Geographic* magazine hailed the mighty, 53 km, four-day, Milford Track as the **'World's Greatest Walk'** in the early 1980s, it has become a victim of its own reputation. It is now the hiking equivalent of the Old Course, St Andrews in Scotland – the home of golf. Of its utter scenic splendour there is no doubt, but there is also human traffic and commercialism.

That of course does not mean that it cannot be treated as a challenge. It is essentially a difficult tramp and should be tackled with enthusiasm, but more importantly, also, a sense of realism.

Highlights on the Milford are many, including the stunning vista of the **McKinnon Pass** (1073 m) and the 580 m **Sutherland Falls**. Then, of course, at track's end is the stunning and unforgettable **Milford Sound**. The Milford Track attracts up to 20,000 trampers a year so book well in advance (at least two months) and expect company! Bookings are on a first-come-first-served basis and start on 1 July for the following summer. Trampers should be of a suitable fitness level, allowing for four (six-hour, 20 km) days of walking with a heavy pack. The track is very well maintained but is still steep and rough in places. In winter the McKinnon Pass can be impassable due to snow and ice and there can be a severe avalanche danger. In winter always consult DoC before setting off, check weather forecasts, fill in an intentions sheet and consider taking locator beacons (can be hired from the DoC Visitor Centre).

Walking times and distances (independent trampers): Allow 4 days: Glade House Wharf to Clinton Hut: 5 km; 1 ½ hours Clinton Hut to Mintaro Hut: 16 ½ km; 5 ½ hours. Mintaro Hut to Dumpling Hut: 14 km; 6 hours. Dumpling Hut to Sandfly Point: 18 km; 6 hours.

Trailhead transport and access The Milford Track starts (by boat from Te Anau Downs) at **Glade House** (south) and finishes (by boat) at **Sandfly Point** near Milford Sound (north). The track can be tackled in either direction in winter (Apr-Oct) but if you are an independent tramper must be negotiated from south to north in summer (Oct-Apr). By **road** Te Anau Downs (and Milford Sound) is served by a number of Te Anau operators (see Te Anau 'Tramping Track transport' section, page 664. **Tracknet**, T03-2497777 (Te Anau Downs $15; Milford Sound, departing Te Anau 0930/1500/1700, from $38) are recommended. Tracknet also provide transportation from Queenstown. By **boat** **Glade House** can be accessed from Te Anau with Sinbad Cruises, T03-2497016 (1030; $68) or from Te Anau Downs with

Milford Track

Sidebar (right margin): Southland and the Fiords Tramping in Southland and the Fiords

Real Journeys, T03-2497416 (1030/1400; from $38). **Waterwings Airways,** T03-2497405, can deliver you to Glade House by **floatplane**. Prices on application. From Milford Sound **Red Boats,** T03-2497926 (1400/1500/1600; $25.50) and **Rosco's Sea Kayaks** provide pick-ups and drop-offs to **Sandfly Point** to Te Anau, at 1430; $65). Sinbad Cruises and Tracknet (see above) do complete transportation package deal for $120.

😴 Sleeping

Dusky Track p704
All 7 huts (Halfway, Lake Roe, Loch Maree, Supper Cove, Kintail, Upper Spey and West Arm Hut) are **Category 3** ranging from 12-20 bunks with mattresses and toilet facilities. There are no gas cookers but there are potbelly stoves in each hut. Huts must be booked through **DoC** and cost $5, child, $2.50 per night. For **post-walk accommodation** see Manapouri/Te Anau and Tuatapere sections. For more booking information see the DoC website www.DoC.govt.nz

Hollyford track p705
All the DoC huts are Category 3 ($5) from 12-20 bunks with wood fires but no gas cookers.
B **Charlie's Place**, *northwestern bank of Lake McKerrow between the Hokuri and Martin's Bay Hut*, T025-893-570, *www.purewilderness.co.nz* A comfortable, friendly and unique oasis mid-tramp. Kayaks for hire. Sadly, Charlie may be selling his little piece of wilderness soon so it remains to be seen if the new owners choose to keep it private. The Hollyford Guided Walk accommodation which includes The **Martins Bay Lodge** (between the Hokuri and Martins Bay Huts, accessible by jetboat and open to the public) are of a much higher standard than the DoC Huts. Guided trips Fully catered and guided fly in/walk out or walk in /walk out tramps are available with **Hollyford Track**, *T03-4423760, www.hollyfordtrack.co.nz* From Te Anau a 3-day (fly out) adventure costs from $1,395.

Hump Ridge Track p705
Both huts (Okaka and Port Craig Village) are maintained and managed by the Hump Ridge Track Trust. Wardens are seconded to each hut from Oct-Apr. The huts are very modern with 40 bunks, mattresses, lighting, cooking, heating and toilet facilities (limited hot water). Huts must be booked through

the Track Trust direct, or through the VIC in Tuatapere. They cost $40, child, $20 per night. For post walk accommodation see Tuatapere sections.
B-D **Rarakau Farmstay and Lodge**, *Papatotara Coast Rd, Bluecliffs Beach*, T03-2258192, *www.rarakaulodge.com* Well placed and recommended (see Tuatapere Sleeping, page 685).

Kepler Track p706
DoC Great Walk Tracks apply. All 3 huts (Luxmore, Iris Burn and Moturau) are of a good standard ranging from 40-60 bunks with mattresses and cooking facilities. Note huts do not have heating or cooking facilities in winter (May-mid Oct). They cost $10 per night or $25 for 3 nights, all year round. **Campsite at Brod Bay**, costs $12, child $6. All bookings should be made with DoC well in advance, especially in mid summer. For trailhead accommodation see Te Anau, page 664. For more booking information see the DoC website www.DoC.govt.nz

Guided walks
Fiordland Guides, *Te Anau, T03-2497832, www.fiordlandguides.co.nz*
Trips 'n' Tramps, *Te Anau, T03-2497081, www.milfordtourswalks.co.nz* Offer guided walks on the Kepler. Prices on application.

Milford Track p707
The 3 DoC huts (Clinton, Mintaro and Dumpling) are of a good standard with 40 bunks with mattresses, cooking, heating and toilet facilities. Wardens are seconded to all huts in summer. The cost of the 3 nights' accommodation is $105, (Child, $52.50). In winter Apr-Oct the huts revert to backcountry hut standard/category (no heating or cooking facilities) and cost $10, child $5. The Guided Walks companies have separate huts (Glade House, Quintin Hut and Milford Lodge). Given the popularity of the Milford, as an independent tramper you cannot stay consecutive nights in one hut and must

move on.

There is no camping allowed.

All bookings should be made with DoCs Great Walks booking office (Te Anau), well in advance (preferably the year before), especially for a mid summer excursion.

Guided Walks

Milford Track Guided Walk, *T03-4411138, www.milfordtrack.co.nz*

Ultimate Hikes, *T03-4351809, www.ultimatehikes.co.nz*
Offer full guided walk packages, from $1490.
Trips 'n' Tramps, *Te Anau, T03-2497081, www.milfordtourswalks.co.nz* and
Koromiko Trek, *Te Anau, T03-2498167 (winter T03-4810571).*
Offer guided day-walks and packages from $125 (from Te Anau).

Background

History

The Maori legends

According to Maori legend New Zealand was created by the great Polynesian demigod **'Maui-Tikitiki-a Taranga'** who hailed from the original Polynesian homeland of **Hawaiki**. Maui was well known for his trickery and guile and through the magical powers of a magic jawbone given to him by his 'sorcerer' grandmother, he was blessed with many god-like powers, with which to confront the world around him. Once, while out fishing with his five brothers, Maui used a piece of his magic jawbone as a fishhook and his own blood as bait. Soon he caught an almighty fish and struggling to pull it to the surface placed a spell upon it to subdue it forever. This great fish became **Te-Ika-a- Maui** (The Fish of Maui) and in essence the North Island of New Zealand. The shape of the North Island is said to resemble the body of the fish with the mouth being Palliser Bay at its southernmost tip, the fins Taranaki and the East Cape and its tail Northland. The mountains and valleys were created when Maui's jealous brothers hacked hungrily at the fish with their greenstone *mere* (clubs). The South Island is **'Te-Waka-a-Maui'** (The Waka of Maui) and Stewart Island **'Te-Punga-o-te-Waka-a-Maui'** (The anchor)

Maori trace their ancestry to the homelands of 'Hawaiki' and the great Polynesian navigator **Kupe**. On a brave scouting mission, across the uncharted oceans to the southeast, Kupe made landfall on a new and as yet undiscovered land (Maui's fish) at a spot now called the Hokianga in Northland, around 800 AD. Finding the new land viable for settlement, Kupe named it **Aotearoa – The Land of the Long White Cloud**. Leaving his crew to colonise, Kupe then returned to Hawaiki to encourage further emigration. A century later the first fleet of *waka* left Hawaiki on the great migration to settle Aotearoa permanently. It was the crew of these great canoes that formed the first *iwi* (tribes) of a new race of people called the **Maori**.

Early beginnings

Due to its geographic isolation New Zealand was one of the last 'viable' lands to be settled by humans. Although it is a matter of debate, most modern historians speculate that the first peoples to discover and settle permanently in New Zealand were the ancestors of early Polynesians, who gradually spread southeast to the Pacific Islands from Indonesia around 1000 AD. The ancestral land called Hawaiki is thought to be Tahiti and the Society Islands. This late ocean-going migration is quite incredible if you consider that just across the Tasman, in Australia, the aborigines had already been happily ensconced for over 50,000 years. Again, exactly when and how these early Polynesians arrived and how they actually lived is in doubt. What is known is that they arrived sporadically in **double-hulled canoes** and initially struggled with the colder climate of New Zealand. Finding their traditional root crops like yam and **kumara** (sweet potato) hard to establish, they had to change their principal diet and methods of hunting. Fishing and seafood gathering took precedence over cultivation, and seals and abundant flightless land birds (mainly moa) became principal food items. With such plentiful food, for many decades the early Maori thrived, but like the first aboriginal settlers of Australia they made the fatal mistake of plundering the environment without thought for the future or sustainability. They also brought with them **dogs** and **kiore** (rats) which, in the absence of predators, and along with hunting, reaped havoc on the flightless native birds.

Before long, especially in the South Island, much of the native bush had been burnt down and the hapless moa, along with a number of other species, were hunted to extinction. This period of colonisation was to become known as the **Archaic Period**. Facing starvation, many of the tribes that had ventured south returned to the warmer environment of the North Island where traditional crops could still be grown and seafood could easily be gathered. By the time the first European explorers arrived the Maori had developed their own culture, based on the tight-knit family unit and a tribal system not dissimilar to the Celts and Scots. In a desire to protect family, food resources and land the Maori, like the Scots, saw their fair share of brutal inter-tribal conflict. The Maori developed a highly effective community and defence system built within fortified villages or *pa* and cannibalism was also common. By the 16th century they had developed into a successful, fairly healthy, robust race, free from European diseases or intercontinental greed and were, by this time, like the aborigines millennia before them, beginning to develop a sustainable future in tune with the environment around them. This period is known as the **Classic Period.**

However despite the Maori successes in colonisation, in many ways, when the first human footprint was made on New Zealand shores, the subsequent environmental damage was inevitable and irreversible. A 'classic' dynamic of cause and effect was set in place that would compromise the land forever. The Maori had proved the nemesis of the unspoiled and isolated biodiversity of the land. Now, with the sails of European ships appearing above the horizon and the first European shoe-print – it was, effectively, to become the turn of the Maori themselves to be facing threat.

European Exploration

Although there is a vicious rumour that the French or Spanish were actually the first Europeans to sight New Zealand, the first documented discovery was made by in 1642 by Dutch explorer **Abel Tasman**. Commissioned by the Dutch East India Company, Tasman was sent to confirm or otherwise the existence of the hotly rumoured Great Southern Continent (**Terra Australis Incognita**) and if discovered, to investigate its viability for trade. Doubtless with great satisfaction, he first set eyes on the new continent (Aotearoa) off what is now Okarito in Westland, on 13 December 1642, before heading north and anchoring in **Golden Bay** at the northern tip of the South Island. However, the excitement quickly turned to despair when the first encounter with the Maori proved hostile, with a loss of life on both sides. Without setting foot on land Tasman turned tail and fled up the west coast of the North Island en route to Tonga and Fiji. He christened the new land 'Staten Landt' which was later renamed **'Nieuw Zeeland'**. It was Tasman's first and last encounter with the new land, but his visit led to New Zealand being put on the world map.

The next recorded European visit occurred with the arrival of the ubiquitous British explorer **Captain Cook** on board the **'Endeavour'** in **1769**. It would be the first of three voyages to New Zealand. Cook's first landing, on 7 October in **Poverty Bay** was 'eventful' to say the least, with what proved to be a classic culture clash with the resident Maori (see page 343). Ignorance and fear on both sides led to a mutual loss of life, but unlike Tasman, Cook persevered with his public relations efforts and after further encounters managed to establish a 'friendly' relationship with the new people he called *tangata* Maori (The 'ordinary people').

Cook spent a further six months in New Zealand coastal waters mapping and naming the geographical features as he went. From Poverty Bay he first sailed south via The Bay of Plenty and Cape Kidnappers to Cape Turnagain (on the border of modern day Southern Hawke's Bay and the Wairarapa), before heading back north, around the North Island, then south again to the Cook Strait and **Ship Cove** in the Queen Charlotte Sound. Ship Cove was clearly a favourite of Cook's and would be revisited on every subsequent voyage. After refitting the Endeavour in Ship Cove, Cook returned to Cape Turnagain (via Cape Palliser), before sailing down the eastern coast of the South Island, passing Stewart Island (which he mapped as a headland), sighting the entrance to Dusky Sound in Fiordland, before returning via the West Coast back to Cook Strait. Perhaps reluctantly he then left for Australia, but not before naming Cape Farewell, just south of Farewell Spit.

Cook's second voyage in **1773** on board the **'Resolution'** saw him land briefly in Dusky Sound (virtually unchanged to this day) before returning to Ship Cove via the west coast of the South Island and from there on to South America. On his third and last voyage, three years later, he returned to Ship Cove and his beloved 'Sounds', before heading for Hawaii (**Sandwich Islands**), where he was killed by the natives. Modern-day New Zealand owes a great deal to Captain Cook; not least the long list of place names that he bestowed upon what was perhaps his favourite destination. There are at least six statues around the country that now immortalize the great man.

European Settlement and the Clash of Cultures
After news spread of the Cook voyages, and perhaps more so due to the observations of his colleague and ship's naturalist Joseph Banks, it did not take long for European **sealers** and **whalers** to reach New Zealand and rape the rich marine resources. Many set up stations around the south coast and Sub-Antarctic Islands and by the 1820s the New Zealand fur seal and numerous species of whale had been brought to the verge of extinction. As the industries subsequently declined they were quickly joined or replaced with a limited but still repetition of timber and flax **traders**. Others including adventurers, ex-convicts from Australia and some very determined (and some would say, much needed) missionaries joined the steady influx in. **Samuel Marsden** gave the first Anglican sermon in the Bay of Islands on Christmas Day, 1814.

Inevitably, perhaps, an uneasy and fractious integration occurred between the Maori and the new settlers and, in the familiar stories of colonised peoples the world over, the consequences for the native people were disastrous. Western diseases quickly ravaged over 25% of the Maori population and the trade of food, land or even preserved heads for the vastly more powerful and deadly European weapons resulted in the **Maori Musket Wars** of 1820-35, a swift and almost genocidal era of inter-tribal warfare. With such a melting pot of divergent cultures, greed and religion simmering on a fire of lawlessness and stateless disorganisation, contrary to the glowing reports being given back in Europe, New Zealand was initially an awful place to be. Crime and corruption was rife. The Maori were conned into ridiculously unfavourable land for weapons deals and, along with the spread of Christianity and disease, their culture and tribal way of life was gradually being undermined. Such were the realities of early settlement that Kororareka (now known as Russell) in the Bay of Islands, which was the largest European settlement in the 1830s, earned itself the name and reputation as the 'Hellhole of the Pacific'. Amidst all the chaos the settlers began to appeal to their governments for protection.

Treaty of Waitangi
By 1838 there were about 2000 British subjects in New Zealand and by this time the country was under the nominal jurisdiction of New South Wales in Australia. In 1833 **James Busby** was sent to Waitangi in the Bay of Islands as the official 'British Resident'. He was given the responsibility of law and order, but without the means to enforce it. Matters were made worse with the arrival of boatloads of new British immigrants sent under the banner of the privately owned and non-government supported **New Zealand Company**. Four years after Busby's arrival British settlers petitioned William IV for protection, citing the fact that Frenchman Baron de Thierry was threatening to pre-empt any British attempt to claim sovereignty of New Zealand. Fearful of losing any possibility of control, Britain appointed **Captain William Hobson** as Lieutenant Governor to replace Busby in New Zealand. His remit was to effect the transfer of sovereignty over the land from the Maori Chiefs to the British Crown. In many ways the circumstances bore an uncanny resemblance to the situation in Britain before it became a United Kingdom. In essence the fact that the Maori were, like the Scots, a culture based on family (clan or tribe) and fought ferociously to protect *that* rather than a whole nation, would undoubtedly be in their favour. The lure

for the Maori would of course be material gain in return for land and 'full protection' as British citizens. For many Maori *iwi* (tribes) whose power was inferior to that of others, this would of course be an attractive proposition. With the help of Busby who was now familiar with the ways and desires of the Maori, Hobson created what was to become the most important and controversial document in New Zealand history, **The Treaty of Waitangi**.

In the hastily-compiled document there were three main provisions. The first was the complete cession of sovereignty by the Maori to the Queen of England. The second was the promise of full rights and possession of Maori lands and resources (but with the right to sell, of course). The third, and perhaps the greatest, attraction, given the chaotic environment, was the full rights and protection of Maori as British citizens. After two days of discussions, a few amendments and amidst much pomp and ceremony, over 40 Maori Chiefs eventually signed the Treaty on 5 February 1840. With these first few signatures from the predominantly Northland tribes, Hobson went on a tour of the country to secure others.

To this day the Treaty of Waitangi remains a very contentious document. From its very inception it was inevitably going to be a fragile bridge between two very different cultures. Given the many differences in communication, translation and meaning, at best it was spurious or vague, but worse still could, as a result, be easily manipulated in both actual meaning and subsequent enactment. Indeed, a modern day lawyer would look at the Treaty and rub his little hands with glee. In essence the best politician, public relations consultant or rabid optimist could only have sold it as a 'beginning' or a 'start' on the 'difficult road to stable biculturalism', while many a realist would have (and still would) declare it an unworkable 'scam'.

By September of 1840 Hobson had gathered over 500 signatures, all in the North Island. Feeling this was enough to claim sovereignty over New Zealand he did so, and declaring the right of discovery over the South Island, made New Zealand a Crown Colony, independent of New South Wales and Australia. But the refusal and subsequent omission of several key (and powerful) Maori chiefs paved the way for regional disharmony and eventually war.

The Maori (Land) Wars

In 1840 Hobson established Kororareka (the Hell-hole of the Pacific') as the first capital of New Zealand, but given its reputation and history, he moved the seat of government to Auckland within a year. With the increased influx of settlers, all greedy for land and resources, human nature very quickly superseded the legal niceties and undermined the fragile bridge of the new bicultural colony. In a frenzy of very dubious land deals between Maori and *Pakeha* (white settlers), as well as misunderstandings in methods of land use and ownership, resentment between the two was rife. This, plus the heavy taxes that were being demanded by the new and financially strapped government, strained the bridge to breaking point. The Maori were essentially beginning to feel disenfranchised and began to rebel against British authority.

One of the first disputes was initiated by a particularly fractious and persistent chief called **Hone Heke** who was one of the original chiefs to sign the Treaty in the Bay of Islands. In 1844 he protested in a way that he knew would hit hard at the British psyche by cutting down the flagpole that so proudly flew the Union Jack in Kororareka (later renamed Russell). He did this not once, but (almost admirably) four times. Hone Heke's actions led to a bloody war with the British that was to last two years. Sadly, this clash was just the beginning. In 1852 the **Constitution Act** was created and in 1853 the country was divided into six provinces, each with a Provincial Council exercising the functions of local government which included land purchases and sales.

At the same time immigration was increasing and with the spread of disease, the Maori were becoming well outnumbered. Once again it seems, as with many native peoples around the world, they were becoming a resented minority and a displaced people. Exacerbated by the provincial administration, the continued greed of the settlers and inter-tribal conflicts, the Maori continued to lose land at an alarming rate and often in return for only meagre material gains.

Some of the more savvy Maori chiefs became reluctant to sell land and, in 1858, several Waikato tribes went a step further by electing their own Maori king. This became known as the **King Movement**. Although initially designed to preserve cultural identity and serve as a land policy maker, supporters were encouraged to resist all land sales and *Pakeha* settlement. The British reacted with complete derision, seeing the movement only as a barrier to further colonisation. The Land Wars (or Maori Wars) inevitably ensued. Troops from both Britain and Australia were sent to aid the NZ militia in an attempt to quash the uprising, which spread outside the Waikato to Northland and Taranaki. The East Coast later joined the fold with the formation of a Maori 'Hauhau' religious movement. One of the most noted Maori rebels was **Te Kooti** who for a time became the most wanted man in the land (see page 228).

It proved to be a bloody time in New Zealand's early history with the fierce and fearless Maori warriors putting up a determined and courageous fight. Their traditional methods of fighting from a fortified *pa*, with trenches, proved so effective (and later, so admired by the British) it became the chosen method of defence and attack in ground warfare until after the Second World War.

With far superior weaponry and organisation the British quickly subdued the rebels. In return for their disobedience, and despite the Treaty, they confiscated huge tracts of land. This land was then sold to new or already established settlers. By 1900 over 90% of the land was outside Maori ownership or control. They were a defeated people and, with little or no power and continued integration, their culture was rapidly crumbling.

Natural Resources, Consolidation and Social Reform

Although development in the North Island suffered as a result of the conflicts, both timber, agriculture and gold came to the rescue. On an already solid base of productive agriculture, and with the lucrative rape of the upper North Island's **kauri forest** already in full swing, the discovery of **gold** in the Coromandel in 1852 sealed the economic boom. South Island too, which had been a relatively peaceful haven compared to the North, joined the party, with the discovery of gold from 1857 in the Nelson, Otago and West Coast Regions.

With much of the economic focus being on the South Island, the seat of a new central (as opposed to provincial) government was moved to Wellington which became the capital in 1876. With gold fever the prime attraction, the *Pakeha* population grew dramatically. With so much good fortune in the south, Dunedin's headcount alone grew from 2000 in 1861 to 10,000 four years later, making it the largest town in the land. Although the gold boom lasted only a decade, the infrastructures that the boom set in place paved the way for agricultural, timber and coal industries to take over.

In the agriculture sector alone, especially through sheep and dairy cattle, New Zealand was becoming an internationally significant export nation and prosperity continued. Towards the end of the 19th century led by the enigmatic Liberal Party leader **Richard 'King Dick' Seddon**, New Zealand's colonial settlers went through a dramatic and sweeping phase of **social reforms**. Well ahead of Britain, the USA and most other Western nations, women secured the vote and pioneering legislation was enacted, introducing old-age pensions, minimum wage structures and arbitration courts.

But while the *Pakeha* prospered the Maori continued to suffer. The **Native Lands Act** of 1865 was established to investigate Maori land ownership and distribute land titles, but again, thanks mainly to Maori tribal structure and the split of land to individual as opposed to communal blocks, this only exacerbated the disintegration of the Maori culture and undermined its cohesion. Maori were given the vote in 1867 but only held four out of 95 seats in the parliamentary House of Representatives. By 1900 the Maori population had decreased to less than 50,000 and with the integration of Maori and *Pakeha* and many Maori/*Pakeha* marriages, the pure Maori were becoming even more of a minority.

Prosperity and The World Wars

By 1907 New Zealand progressed to the title of **'Dominion'** of Britain rather than merely a 'colony' and by the 1920s was in control of most of its own affairs. By virtue of its close links with Britain, New Zealand and the newly formed (trans-Tasman) **Australia and New Zealand Army Corps (ANZAC)** became heavily embroiled in the Boer War of 1899-1902 and again in the First World War, at Gallipoli and the Western Front. Although noted for their steadfast loyalty, courage and bravery, the ANZACs suffered huge losses. Over 17,000 never returned with one in every three men aged between 20 and 40 being killed or wounded. Almost a century on there remains a palpable sense of pride in both Australia and New Zealand for those lives lost and quite rightly so; their First World War casualties remain the greatest of any combat nation.

New Zealand joined the Western world in the **Great Depression** of the 1920s but it recovered steadily and independently progressed in an increasing atmosphere of optimism. Again from a solid base of agricultural production it prospered and immigration, particularly from Britain, grew steadily. The population had now passed one million. In 1935 New Zealand became the fist nation to enact a social welfare system, which included free health care and low-rental council properties. These pioneering acts of social reform, along with the economy, resources and common attitude, secured one of the highest standards of living in the world and New Zealand was an envied, prime 'new-life' destination.

However, along with the rest of the world, water was temporarily thrown on the fires of progress and prosperity with the outbreak of the Second World War. Once again, New Zealand and the loyal ANZACs answered the call. This time, in both Europe and Asia, it was the turn of the **28th Maori Battalion** to earn a widespread admiration and respect for their tenacity and courage. It seemed their warrior spirit, if not their culture was still alive and well. Like most warring nations the war effort extended to the home shores where women replaced men in the vast majority of industrial and social practices. With the spread of the conflict across the Pacific, it proved a nervous time for the nation and although many would be correct in saying it was not for the first time, the people of New Zealand were under a renewed threat of invasion. However, with the dropping of the atomic bomb in Japan the threat ceased and the war was over.

Post 1945

Shortly after the war, in 1947, New Zealand was declared an independent nation but thanks to the war and its important agricultural exports, it maintained close defence and trade links with the Great Britain, the USA and Australia. In 1945 it became one of the original member states of the **United Nations** (UN) and later joined the **ANZUS Defence Pact** with the USA and Australia. Domestically, the country again prospered but the nagging problems of race relations, land and resource disputes between Maori and *Pakeha* still had to be addressed.

By the early 1970s the vast majority of Maori had moved to urban areas in search of work but with many being unsuccessful, social problems proved inevitable. In an attempt to spawn a new sense of spirit, the government passed the **Waitangi Day Act** in 1960 making 6 February a day of thanksgiving in celebration of the Treaty and the cohesive bicultural society it was supposed to have created. This was further emphasised with an official public holiday in 1973. But some Maori (and *Pakeha*) merely saw the day as an opportunity for protest and although the public holiday remains, the traditional pomp and ceremony annually enacted at Waitangi in the Bay of Islands, was scrapped for much more low key governmental diplomatic posturing. In

1975 more significant progress was made with the formation of the **Waitangi Tribunal** which was established to legally and officially hear Maori claims against the Crown. This method of addressing the problems continues to this day, but as ever, the misinterpretations of the Treaty and its translation remain a major stumbling block.

New Zealand joined most of the developed world in the economic slump of the '70s and '80s. The traditionally strong agricultural exports to Europe declined, the price of oil and manufacturing imports rose and it was hit hard by the stock market crash of 1987. In response to the economic decline the government of the day, under **Robert Muldoon's** National Party deregulated the country's economy, paving the way for free trade. The most important and lasting trade agreement was the **Closer Economic Relations Trade Agreement** made with Australia in 1983, but New Zealand was beginning to see itself playing a far more significant role in the Asian markets as opposed to the traditional European ones.

In 1984 the Labour government, under its charismatic leader **David Lange**, took control and made further sweeping and radical changes to the economy. These were dubbed **'Rogernomics'** after the then finance minister Roger Douglas. Although the policies of privatization, free enterprise and the deregulation of the labour market improved the situation, unemployment rose and the policies began to prove unpopular with the voting public. Fearful of losing re-election votes Lange sacked Douglas, but the party reinstated him, and this resulted in his own shock resignation in 1989, leaving the party in disarray. Subsequently, the National Party led by the far less charismatic **Jim Bolger** swept to power in 1990.

One of the most important landmark decisions made on foreign policy in the 1980s was New Zealand's staunch **anti-nuclear** stand. In 1984 Lange refused entry to any foreign nuclear-powered ships in its coastal waters. This soured its relationship with the US who reacted by suspending defence obligations to NZ made under the ANZUS pact in the 1950s. This anti-nuclear stance is still maintained with considerable pride and is one that was only strengthened when the French Secret Service bombed the Greenpeace vessel **Rainbow Warrior** in 1985, causing national and international outrage. Relations with France were further soured in 1995 with the rather arrogant and insensitive testing of nuclear weapons in French Polynesia.

Throughout the 1990s the National Party continued successfully to nurture the free market economic policies first initiated by Labour. In 1993 a national referendum voted unanimously in favour of a mixed-member proportional representation (**MMP**) system of government. This system, which has proved successful in Germany, gives electors two votes: one for a candidate in their own electorate and the second for their favoured political party. Maori can choose to vote in either a general or Maori electorate. There is a 120-seat parliament with 60 general electorate seats, five Maori and 55 allocated to parties according to the percentage of party votes received.

Whether this system of government has been good for the country as a whole is debatable, but what did result, through some ugly internal politics and fragile power-sharing agreements, were two women prime ministers. The first in New Zealand's History was **Jenny Shipley** of the National Party who engineered a 'coup' to seize party leadership from Jim Bolger in 1997 and currently in power is **Helen Clark** of the 1999-elected Labour Party. The new system can also not exactly be accused of restricting a diverse representation. One Green Party MP, Nandor Tanczos, is a Rastafarian and a Labour Party MP, Georgina Beyer, is transgender.

A highly significant event outside politics in 1995 was New Zealand's win in the coveted **America's Cup** yachting race. It was first time the Cup had been won by any nation other than the US and, given the country's love of yachting, it was the cause of unprecedented national celebration and pride. Over 300,000 people lined Queen Street in Auckland to congratulate the heroic yachties' return. With the successful defence of the Cup again in 2000 it seemed yachting would join – or some would say replace – rugby as the nation's world-dominating sport. Amidst much hype and after considerable amounts of money were spent to transform Auckland's waterfront into a state-of-the-art sailing arena, the Kiwi populace prepared themselves for what would surely be another convincing win in 2002/3. But it was a dream that turned, quite dramatically, into a nightmare as amidst tactical errors, design faults and even the mast snapping, former Kiwi team member Russell Coutts led a far superior outfit in the form of the Swiss *Alinghi* team to a highly embarrassing 5-0 whitewash. With that, sadly, and for now anyway, it seems the words 'America's Cup' suddenly went out with the tide.

Into the new millennium

Given its size and isolation New Zealand enjoyed its 15 minutes of international fame on 1 January 2000 when it was the first country to see the dawn of the new millennium.

Since the infamous terrorist attacks of 11th September 2001 and more recently the US-led military interventions in Afghanistan and Iraq that were, we are told, such a fundamental part of its ongoing, self-styled global **'War Against Terrorism'**, it seems New Zealand, through its steadfast determination (unlike the Howard government of Australia) not to align itself with that US policy, will almost certainly pay a heavy price, both in recognition and the nuts and bolts of trade agreements and economics. Ask the average Kiwi what they think of all this global politicking however and they will say that for them and their country little has changed. New Zealand is a great country, easily forgotten on the world stage and too easily mocked. Most are very proud of Helen Clark's intelligent and (some say) truly democratic leadership, courageously demonstrated in her stoic stance against war in Iraq and reaction to US and UK policy and its ramifications in current world affairs. The majority of Kiwis did not want to join the campaign in Iraq and its government rightfully and steadfastly exercised that opinion. Kiwis are proud of their country and by their very nature and number are traditionally more concerned about community and the environment than misguided patriotism, rhetoric ad populum, power and politics. Surely, if you look at the bigger picture, through history and to the long term, it is just as wise to be as concerned about non-native species getting through customs as explosives and drugs?

So returning to the shadows (bar the considerable and on-going hype surrounding the filming of *Lord of the Rings*) New Zealand remains largely a 'low-key' nation largely left to its own devices, blessed by an outstanding natural environment, healthy independence and the huge asset of a low and cosmopolitan population. Its current economic struggles lie in a poor exchange rate and its biggest social challenge is the continued and difficult journey down the road of biculturalism as well perhaps as some sensible long-term decisions pertaining to future levels of immigration.

But perhaps New Zealand's greatest challenge lies in the conservation and protection of its environment, for which it is most famous and much loved. Dubbed the 'Clean Green Land' it remains to be seen whether its government and people can truly embrace the reality that its relatively healthy ecological condition is mainly due to its lack of population, as opposed to the common and traditional human attitudes that have proved to be so ruinous elsewhere. One can only hope that this wise and determined attitude can blossom, even though it is very much against the international grain. Without doubt, New Zealand is a premier tourist destination with a great deal to offer. Like its much larger neighbour Australia, tourism is fast becoming the biggest and most important growth industry. Encompassed within that industry is the sensible, desirable and sustainable realm of ecotourism, which it is hoped can assist in the country's efforts to conserve its many unique and vulnerable species. At the forefront of these conservation efforts is the ongoing program to conserve the iconic kiwi as well as the country's impressive position on international whaling and the creation of a South Pacific Whale Sanctuary. So, from the creation of the great fish by the Maori demigod Maui, to its current efforts to protect them, the land and the people remain on an inextricable and co-dependent voyage into the new millennium.

Culture

People and population

The population of New Zealand currently stands at about 3.8 million. The population densities are unevenly spread between the two islands, with North Island home to about 2.8 million and the South Island about 920,000. Greater Auckland alone is home to just over 1 million, almost a third of the total population. New Zealand is essentially a bicultural society made up of Maori and Europeans, and many Caucasian (*Pakeha*) nationalities are present. Maori make up about 15% of the total population, with the vast majority living in the North Island. Pacific Islanders make up the second largest non-Caucasian group at around 6% with almost all living in Greater Auckland. Asians make up 3% of the total population and are the fastest-growing minority group. Again, the vast majority of Asians choose to live in Greater Auckland. New Zealanders are famous for being 'the world's greatest travellers' and at any one time a large proportion of citizens are absent or living abroad. Over 400,000 live and work in Australia alone. Through their close trans-Tasman ties Australian and New Zealand citizens are free to live and work in both countries.

Religion

The dominant religion is **Christianity**, with Anglican, Presbyterian and Roman Catholic denominations the most prominent. Other minority religions include Hinduism, Islam, Judaism and Buddhism. The Maori developed two of their own minority Christian-based faiths; Ratana and Ringatu, both of which were formed in the late 19th to early 20th centuries. Reflecting the increasing trend in most developed nations, at least a quarter of the total population are atheists or have no religion and this number is growing.

Music

For such a small country New Zealand has a thriving **rock** scene with **Dunedin** considered the hotbed of talent. In the '70s and '80s **Split Enz** was New Zealand's best-known group, reaching international recognition. Other notable bands include **Crowded House** and the **Exponents**. In the late 90s **OMC** (Otara Millionaires Club) shot to fame with their catchy hit 'How Bizarre', but despite their success have since broken up. Many alternative bands and singers like **Bic Runga** and **DJ Amanda**, who are fast developing a unique Kiwi or rap sound, mixed with mainly Polynesian influences, thrive within the mainstream. **Neil Finn**, formerly of Crowded House, and **Dave Dobbyn** spearhead the most successful ageing-rocker solo careers. In the classical arena **Dame Kiri Te Kanawa** has for many years been New Zealand's most noted international opera star. Traditional domestic or world music outside of Maori performances and Irish pubs is quite hard to find, however the **Pacific Festival** held in Auckland in March is one notable exception.

Film

Even before Kiwi Peter Jackson, director of *Lord of the Rings* changed the face of New Zealand film making, the nation had produced a number of notable feature films and is (or was) home to a few other internationally recognized actors and directors. Perhaps the most famous film (though many would describe it more as an alarming and uncomfortable experience) is *Once Were Warriors* (1994) – an adaptation of Kiwi writer Alan Duff's portrayal of a highly dysfunctional urban Maori family, directed by Lee Tamahori. For those looking for a reality check of the worst social aspects of the advertised, pleasant 'clean green land' it is a must-see, superbly demonstrating that

New Zealand is not immune to the death of traditional cultures, poverty, alcoholism
and domestic abuse.

On a lighter note, yet still depicting harsh times, is the romantic classic *The Piano* (1993) directed by New Zealand's most noted director **Jane Campion.** Starring Holly Hunter, Sam Neill and Hollywood tough guy, Harvey Keitel, it tells the haunting story of a Scottish immigrant (Hunter) and her daughter (Anna Paquin) who are brought to New Zealand in the early 19th century in an arranged marriage to troubled colonial landowner (Neill). Finding Neill to be as romantic and warm-hearted as the mud they seem to spend all their time trudging through, she turns to the brooding, yet caring employee (Keitel) for love and affection. Part of the attraction is also his willingness to transport her prized possession – a grand piano – inland from the beach where she and her daughter were so unceremoniously off-loaded. It is a deserving multi-award winner that is well acted and has a superb musical score. However, it may leave you thinking New Zealand is a very harsh, wet place of little more than tangled bush and mud – which essentially it once was. Although actor **Sam Neill** was not born in New Zealand, he grew up in the South Island and now lives in Queenstown, so is considered by many to be an adopted son. Another actor who was born in New Zealand, but grew up in Australia, is **Russell Crowe**, who recently shot to fame for his macho role in *Gladiator*. He now seems set to become one of Hollywood's golden boys and of course must always be envied for dating Meg Ryan.

But it was the creative talent and determination of North Islander **Peter Jackson** that put the country firmly on the movie-making map in 1999-2000 with the filming and release of the much lauded **Lord of the Rings** trilogy. At a cost of over $300 million it was a far cry from Jackson's other lesser-known projects, which including the New Zealand classic *Heavenly Creatures*, an intriguing tale of two troubled teenage girls. Perhaps it was his talent, his passion and his unflappability that made what was for him a childhood dream-a film version of JRR Tolkien's *Lord of the Rings* (LOTR) into such a success, but ask any Kiwi and they will add two other essential ingredients with pride and alacrity to what was a mammoth technical and logistical filming project. The first is the very nature and variety of the Kiwi landscape, from its foreboding volcanoes to classic snow-capped mountain ranges that were so suited to Tolkien's realm of 'Middle Earth' and the collective global imagination of what it would really look like. Indeed, as the saying now goes, it was the Kiwi landscape that should have won an Oscar for 'best supporting role'. The other essential ingredient for the film's technical success is the famed Kiwi ingenuity and down to earth enthusiasm – traits so obvious and refreshing in Jackson's own rather plump persona. In tune perhaps with the fictional characters he so brilliantly portrayed on film, you would not catch the boffin-like Jackson posing in tux and tails at an award ceremony or emerging from some stretch limo with a vacuous, leggy model by his side. Whether on set or in Tinsel Town he is far more likely to be discussing scenes with an equally down-to-earth actor or technician, a mate, in a pair of training shoes and munching on a ham sandwich, than 'Lording' it amidst the usual superficiality and hyperbole.

There is no doubt Jackson will now be seen as the true founding father of film in New Zealand and that many more films and directors will follow suit to utilise the landscape and boundless, innate Kiwi skills. In 2002/3 filming for *The Last Samurai* starring Tom Cruise was already under way in the shadow of Mount Taranaki and Jackson himself had already secured funding for his next big project - another childhood passion-*King Kong*.

But whether you are an avid fan of LOTR desperately keen to pay homage to the many film locations, or don't know a *Hobbit* from an *Uruk-Hai*, or *Isengard* from *Amon Hen*, one thing is for sure. Despite all the hype and the massively increased profile of the New Zealand landscape, in reality and aesthetically nothing has changed and the country exists as it always has - undeniably in your face and breathtakingly beautiful. Neither a Lord, nor any Lord of the Rings can ever change that - only nature itself.

Lord of the Rings film trilogy facts and figures

1 *Lord of the Rings* film trilogy director Peter Jackson was born in 1961 near Wellington, North Island. His first film *Bad Taste* was made in 1988 and started out as a joke amongst friends. It was about alien invaders that ate humans. His first major production and successful endeavour on the international scene was a film titled *Heavenly Creatures* (1994).

2 When Jackson secured US$270 million funding for his film version of Tolkien's three-part novel with New Line Productions in the US, it was considered to be the riskiest endeavour in motion-picture history.

3 Filming began in 1999 and surprisingly took only 15 months of intense on-location work. There were over 2400 employed in the production team and around 26,000 extras. The final cost was US$310 million.

4 The weapons used by the central characters of the film were forged from steel employing the same methods that were used 500 years ago. In total 2000 weapons, 10,000 arrows and 1000 suits of armour were made.

5 The chain mail used in the film was labouriously put together using lightweight polybutylene piping cut into individual rings. Two people linked over 12.5 million rings for the cast. These two were unofficially labeled as the real Lords of the Rings.

6 The character Gollum was played by actor Andy Serkis and was the most complex digital character ever created on film. Joe Letteri the visual effects supervisor said after filming 'We were portraying him as a 60-year-old heroin addict.'

7 The first film *Fellowship of the Ring* released in 2001 ended up being the highest grossing film of the year grossing US$860 million. Jackson receives about 10% of that revenue.

8 The varied and often extreme scenery of New Zealand provided over 150 filming sites in New Zealand (see box, page 59). Most are around Queenstown, Otago and all had to have every trace of filming removed.

9 It has been suggested that the long established Literary Estate of Tolkien and the Tolkien Society, both based in England, are somewhat uneasy about establishment of New Zealand as 'Middle Earth' in the minds of 'Rings' fans. In order to appease, perhaps, Mark Burton, New Zealand's minister of Tourism stated; "New Zealand has to promote itself as the land where the Hobbits were filmed – not the land of the Hobbits".

10 The Lord of the Rings *Location Guidebook* written by Kiwi and LOTR fanatic Ian Brodie, is only available in New Zealand (due to rights issues) and became the nation's greatest domestic bestseller in 2002.

11 The battle scene in the Two Towers was digitally enhanced using state of the art computer technology and a remarkable software program called *Massive*. Essentially it gave each individual screen warrior its own artificial intelligence. The idea was that each warrior would react in a predictable, yet varied manner when confronted by the enemy. However, during the first experiment of the program on screen, much to the creator's horror, most of the individuals fled the battlefield – doing the intelligent and logical thing to preserve their own lives. Proof perfect perhaps that machines and computers lack that innate human trait – utter stupidity.

Maori culture and traditions

The Maori are essentially a tribal race consisting of the *whanau* (family unit), extending to the **hapu** (sub-tribe) and then the **iwi** (full tribe). Together they are referred to as the **tangata whenua**, which directly translated means 'people of the land'. The Maori relationship with their ancestors (or **tipuna**) is considered to exist through their genetic inheritance, and an individual's own genealogy (or **whakapapa**) can be traced right back to the gods via one of the original migratory canoes (or **waka**). There are over 40 **iwi** in New Zealand with the largest being the **Ngapuhi** (descendants of Puhi) in Northland who have over 100,000 members, to one of the smallest, the **Ngai Tahu** (descendants of Tahu) in South Island, who have only about 30,000 members. The Maori's very family-based social structure is in many ways remarkably similar to the early Scottish clan system that developed almost in parallel at the other end of the earth. Indeed, the Maori culture has some uncanny similarities to the Scots in their love of music, song (**waiata**), dance (**haka**), oration (particularly storytelling), socialising and unfortunately, to their equal detriment, fighting amongst themselves and against outside invaders with fearless courage and determination. The word **Maori** does in itself not denote a common background but derives from a term of differentiation used between the ordinary people (natives) and the European explorers.

Traditional Maori life is bounded by the customs, concepts or conducts of **tapu** (meaning taboo, or sacred) and **noa** (meaning mundane, or the opposite of *tapu*). If something is *tapu*, whether an object, place, action or person, it must be given the accordant respect. To do otherwise can result in ostracism, bad luck or sickness. A good example would be a burial place that is forever *tapu*, or a food resource that is given seasonal *tapu* to encourage sustainability. One good example for the visiting tourist is the summit of **Moehau**, the Coromandel Peninsula's highest peak. It is currently *tapu* which means, that despite the views, or absence of any guard (beyond the spiritual that is) it would be very culturally insensitive to go clambering all over it. Another is **Green Lake** (Rotokakahi) near Rotorua. The island on the lake is an ancient Maori burial ground and the lake is therefore *tapu*. As such you cannot use it for any recreational activity and you must not set foot on the island.

Noa is a term heard less often, but plays an important role in the balance or cancellation of *tapu*. For example, at some point the summit of Moehau may, through ceremony, have its *tapu* rendered *noa*. Once *noa* you can clamber away to your little heart's content! Of course in the modern day your average 'Maori Joe' cannot just place a *tapu* on anything he chooses – his beer for example, or the Visa bill! If this were the case there would be social mayhem! Placing a *tapu* is a matter that requires deliberation by the *iwi* and enactment by the **elders**, very often after a meeting or **hui**. All things whether living or otherwise possess **mauri** (see next page), **wairau** (spirit) and **mana**. The meaning of *mana* goes well beyond words, but in essence means prestige, standing, integrity or respectability. It is a term that is often used by both Maori and *Pakeha*, and is even sometimes heard outside New Zealand. If a Maori warrior won a fight or a battle this would increase his *mana*, if he lost, it would undermine it, and so on. Objects too have *mana*. The pendants (or **tiki**) that you buy (for others, never yourself) can hold spiritual *mana* or can increase in *mana* as they are passed on to others. It is a lovely term and perhaps the one most tourists take away or remember once they leave.

Maoritanga (The Way of the Maori)

The Maori language, lifestyle, social structure, customs, spirituality, legends, arts and crafts are all enjoying something of a revival in modern-day New Zealand. The unique Maori culture and history are all very well represented in museums throughout the country, with both **Auckland Museum** and the state-of-the-art **Museum of New**

Zealand (Te Papa) in Wellington, in particular, offering a fascinating insight. Although there are thought to be no 'true' full-blooded Maori left in New Zealand, the majority of those of undisputed Maori descent remain staunchly and rightly proud of their ancestry and cultural identity. It is a sad fact that their cultural journey in the face of what many would call a 'European invasion' has been, and continues to be, a difficult and troubled one. To that end it is important for the visitor to be aware of the basics and to realise that New Zealand culture, in total, goes a lot deeper than the practice or development of a cosmopolitan mix of cultures imported from elsewhere. In a country that essentially has a very short human history and one that some critics declare as 'historically wanting', Maoritanga is, in essence, as old as it gets.

The Marae

The *marae* is essentially the sacred 'place of meeting' or of simply 'being', that exist around a **wharae tupuna** (or ancestral meetinghouse). It is traditionally used as a communal centre, meeting place or sometimes a retreat. Strict customs and protocols (or **kawa**) surrounds the *marae* and for any tourist who wishes to visit or stay it is important to be aware of these customs and the protocols. It is akin to taking your shoes off in a Japanese house, offering the correct welcome, introduction and so on. Visitors are welcomed on to the *marae* with a **powhiri** (a welcome), which is multi-faceted. First, a warrior will greet you (or all visitors – **manuhiri**) with a **haka**, which is a traditional dance that can look decidedly threatening. In essence this is a challenge (or **wero**). Do not return the gestures, unless you want to be considered uncouth, culturally ignorant, or have the desire to get your head removed. At the end of the *wero* there is a peace offering (or **teka**), which is placed on the ground between you and the warrior. Once accepted, a female elder will then initiate the **karanga** (a chant), that both welcomes and addresses the visitor and their ancestors.

On moving forward you must bow to acknowledge the ancestors. At the entrance to the *whare* the chief will then offer a **whaikorero** or *mihi* (a welcoming speech). If you can, you, or traditionally the leader (chief) elect of your group, are supposed to respond accordingly. You, or your chief, then perform the **hongi** – the touching (not rubbing) of noses unique to Maori. The *hongi* is an action, which is equivalent to a hug, or a kiss and is often accompanied with a handshake. The equivalent of English 'hello' is the Maori **'kiaora'**.

Once this protocol is enacted you are then a welcome guest in the *marae* and free to talk, stay, or feast. The feast (or **hangi**) is a superb experience of earth-oven, steamed meat and vegetables with a very distinctive, succulent taste. A **karakia** (or prayer) is traditionally said beforehand.

The Pa

The *pa*, or the traditional **fortified settlements** built by the Maori are worth special mention. Built predominantly on a headland or hill and from wood and often networked by trenches, they were used to protect against invasion by hostile tribes and also the *Pakeha* during the **Maori Land Wars**. Within the *pa* boundary are the *marae*, *whare* and food storage facilities. So effective was this system defence and so impressed were the colonial British forces, that the design was echoed in the First World War in the trenches of the Western Front. There are many subtle remains around the country with one of the best being the distinct earthworks and *kumara* (sweet potato storage) pits on **One Tree Hill** in Auckland. The volcanic plugs of the Auckland area made ideal *pa* sites.

Song and dance

Like the aborigine of Australia the Maori did not keep a written history, but rather passed down the essence of their culture and historical journey by song – **waiata** – and chants – **karakai**. The two most common song types are **waiata tangi** (songs of mourning) and **waiata aroha** (songs of love).

:black_small_square: Maori Values

To the Maori everything has a *mauri*, an essence that gives everything its special character and everything is viewed as a living entity. *Mauri* pervades and infuses everything: things living and non-living, earth and sky. Sometimes a sacred stone, which is placed at a secret location in a forest or river, represents it and sometimes it has no tangible presence at all, but always the *mauri* must be nurtured, cared for and respected. When *kia moana* (seafood) is taken from the sea, a tree is felled or any other thing is harvested a **karakia** should be said beforehand and thanks given afterwards.

The concept of *mauri* leads to a sense of unity between man and nature. The unity extends to the opposing principles that make up the cosmos, as is expressed in the creation tradition the tradition expounds how **Rangi** the sky father and **Papa** the earth mother were once united and how **Tane Mahuta** the god of the forest tore them apart to let in the daylight. The separation brought great sorrow to Rangi the sky father and Papa the earth mother. This sorrow continues in the clinging mists and falling rain, and rising of the dew.

Water is therefore fundamental to the Maori world view. It is considered a basic essence, a part of every living thing, the linking medium between individuals and their environment. The water of a *hapu* or *iwi* is a fundamental source of their mana and plays a central role in many rituals.

Maori dance is known as **haka**. The most famous form of this has been given somewhat false iconic status in the modern day by the sporting rugby legends the **All Blacks** before the start of each game. This particular form of *haka* is a war chant made as a challenge to all opposition and is quite a sight to behold. Whether you were Captain Cook or a 120-kg lock forward in the English rugby team, to be confronted with a Maori doing a *haka* is to know you're in for quite a battle!

There are other far less threatening forms of dance called **taparahi**. These include the **poi** dance, commonly seen in traditional Maori performances; the *poi* being balls of strings that are swung or twirled in harmony and synchronicity to the music. Traditional musical instruments are the flute or **putorino**. The beat is kept by the stamping of feet.

Arts and crafts

The artistic styles and media used by the Maori were already fairly well developed on their arrival in New Zealand and influenced heavily by Polynesian tradition. However, in the absence of clay for pottery and metals with which to fashion rock or wood, they developed their own unique style.

Wood or greenstone (pounamu) **carving** was the commonest form of craft both for functional purposes (like **waka**) or for decoration, on panels, **pou** (equivalent to Native American totem poles), or adorning **whare whakairo** (meeting houses). **Kauri** or **totara** were the commonest native wood types and it was fashioned into highly distinctive patterns using **greenstone (pounamu)**, shells, or sharp stones. Sadly the early Christian missionaries often discouraged the Maori from producing their carvings, which they saw as containing obscene or inappropriate imagery. This is especially the case in Northland where elaborate carving is far less commonly seem on the *marae*. Other forms of carving were the creation of pendants or **tiki**, which were made predominantly from whalebone or pounamu. These pendants often depict spiritual ancestors – or **hei tiki** – as well as legendary or sacred animals. Weapons like **taiaha pouwhenua** (long clubs) and **patu** (short clubs) were fashioned from wood, while **mere** (short, close-combat clubs) were traditionally fashioned from greenstone.

One of the best places to see traditional and contemporary Maori arts and crafts in creation is at the **Maori Arts and Crafts Institute**, at the Whakarewarewa Thermal Reserve in Rotorua. Aside from carving and other three-dimensional works, Maori rock art is in evidence, particularly around Timaru in the South Island. There are also some very interesting contemporary Maori artworks showpieced in the Rotorua Museum.

Moko
The unique Maori facial tattoo (or **moko**) was traditionally applied, doubtless with considerable pain, using bone chisels, a mallet and blue pigment. The moko was predominantly the decoration of the higher classes with men covering their entire face (and sometimes their buttocks) while the women were decorated on the chin. Today Maori (especially those in the Maori gangs like the Mongrel Mob and Black Power) still apply *moko*, but this is done of course using modern tattooing techniques. To get the best idea of its design and permanence (let alone to imagine the pain), take a look at the superb realist paintings of the Maori elders done in the late 1800s by renowned New Zealand painters **Gottfried Lindauer** and **Charles F Goldie**. Examples are on display in major art galleries throughout the country, with the Auckland Art Gallery being especially good.

Language
The Maori language is still spoken throughout New Zealand and generally encouraged and spoken with pride within the *whanau* and *iwi* (Maori family and tribes), but has never been given the respect it deserves in mixed (*Pakeha*/Maori) schools over the years, hence its general decline.

To the layperson who cannot understand a word, it is an intriguing language to listen too, unusually repetitive in sound and hardly melodic. There is much accentuation and repetition of vowels and the 'w' and it is wise to be aware of a few basic rules before arriving in the country. Perhaps the most important feature is the pronunciation of 'wh' as the English 'f'. For example Whanau above is not pronounced 'Wha-now' , but 'Fha-now' and Whangarei is not pronounced 'Wangarei', but 'Fhongarei'. Likewise Whakapapa, or Whakarewarewa gets similar treatment and the 'a' is pronounced more like a 'u'.

Other than that it's a bit like pronouncing your vowels like the Scots twins and folk-rockers *The Proclaimers* with songs like *Letter From America* – with lots of power and opening your mouth as wide as the Homer Tunnel. A limited Maori word glossary is on page 742. Good luck (and no, thankfully, there is not a town in New Zealand called Whuck, or indeed Whuckit).

Land and environment

Geography
New Zealand consists of three main islands – **North Island, South Island** and **Stewart Island** – with a handful of other small far-flung subtropical and **sub-Antarctic islands** (the largest being a group called the **Chathams**, which lie 853 km east of the South Island) completing the family. The total land area is 268,704 sq km (slightly larger than the UK).

New Zealand's geographical boundaries extend from 33° to 53° south latitude and from 162° east longitude, to 173° west longitude, which results in a broad climatic range from north to south. It is bounded north and east by the **South Pacific Ocean**, on the west by the **Tasman Sea** and on the south by the great **Southern Ocean**. The

Geographical features   Although compact in size, New Zealand's landscape is rich and varied: glaciers, braided rivers, lakes, fiords (flooded glacial valleys), sounds (flooded riverbeds) – found predominantly in the South Island – lowlands, alluvial plains, wetlands, large natural coastal harbours and a rash of offshore islands. Given the fact New Zealand is located at the meeting point of the Pacific and Indo-Australian Plates, it is also a distinctly 'shaky' land of frequent earthquakes and constant **volcanic activity**. The **Taupo Volcanic Zone** in central North Island is one of the most active in the world. A string of volcanoes stretches from the currently active White Island in the Bay of Plenty, to the moody Mount Ruapehu in the heart of North Island. The area also has numerous **thermal features,** including geysers, mineral springs, blowholes and mud pools, most of which can be found around Rotorua and Taupo. One of the largest **volcanic eruptions** in human history occurred in New Zealand in 186 AD, the remnants of which is the country's largest lake – Lake Taupo. The most recent eruption occurred in 1995 (and again in 1996), when Mount Ruapehu – North Island's highest peak – had a moderate stomach upset. The country's most dramatic **earthquake** in recent history occurred in Napier on North Island's East Coast in 1931.

Due to the 'uplift' created by the clash of the two tectonic plates, South Island has many more mountain ranges than the North and boasts the country's highest peak, **Mount Cook**. *Aoraki*, as the Maori call it, stands less than 40 km from the West Coast at a height of 3,753m. The country's longest river is the **Waikato**, which stretches 425 km from Lake Taupo to the Tasman Sea.

Geology

New Zealand is an ancient land that has been so isolated from any other land mass for so long that its biodiversity is described by some scientists as the closest one can get to studying life on another planet. The oldest rocks, which make up part of the New Zealand we know today, were first rafted away from the great Gondwana landmass over 100 million years ago by a process called continental drift. The modern landscape is the dramatic result of geological uplift and volcanic activity created by New Zealand's location on the boundary of the Pacific and Indo-Australian Plates. Further 'sculpturing' occurred as a result of natural erosion, particularly the glacial erosion of numerous ice ages in the last two million years. Thanks to its long isolation, much of New Zealand's biodiversity is not only ancient, but also highly unique, with such incredible oddities as the kiwi, tuatara and weta still in evidence today. A useful comparison is with the endemic biodiversity of Great Britain: having been separated from continental Europe for a mere 10,000 years it has only one endemic plant and one endemic animal species. In contrast, as a result of over 80 million years of isolation, the vast majority of New Zealand species are endemic. Around 90% of its insects and marine molluscs, 80% of its trees, ferns and flowering plants and 25% of it bird species, all 60 reptiles, four remaining frogs, two species of bat and eel are found nowhere else on earth. So there is little doubt New Zealand could aptly be described as a 'paradise created'. But on the tragic day that man arrived, a mere 1000 years ago, it was not only 'paradise found', but was to become 'paradise lost'. Our arrival has caused more devastation to this 'clean green land' than anything else in 80 million years of evolution.

Wildlife

Urban

Birds   It is a tribute to the little bird itself to start with the humble, clever and ubiquitous **house sparrow**. As you emerge bleary-eyed from the airport terminal, the chances are you will see one before you do a taxi. Whether on high or at your feet, they are waiting and watching and have your every move and bag contents under close observation. After human beings and, in essence, thanks to them, these master scavengers are one of the most successful and omnipresent species on earth. In New Zealand, the humble sparrow was introduced in 1867 and like anywhere else the land provides a happy hunting ground.

New Zealand's urban landscape is home to many introduced plants and animals and Europeans especially will notice many familiar species. In the average garden these include birds like the **song thrush**, the **blackbird**, the **starling** and the **chaffinch**. Almost all of these were, of course, introduced. One notable exception that is absent is the European **robin**. However, old habits die hard and they are still seen in two dimensions, annually, on the front of New Zealand Christmas cards.

Elsewhere, in the parks and open spaces, you will see (or more likely hear) the **Australasian magpie**, as well as the comical **pukeko** and on the urban waterways, the obligatory **mallard duck** and **black swan**. The Australasian magpie is the size of a crow. He's dressed in black and white – like a butler – and is melodious and very intelligent. They are, as the name suggests, an Australian import and very unpopular in New Zealand. While nesting they are fiercely territorial and every year newspapers are full of Hitchcockian tales of people being attacked. The **pukeko** is a much more amicable import from Australia, where it is known as the swamphen. They look like a cross between a chicken and a spider, with outrageously long feet, with which they walk on water. They are a gorgeous blue/purple colour and sport a robust red beak. Get used to the 'pookie', as you will see them everywhere.

Often mistaken for the similar-looking pukeko, the **takahe** is much larger (and certainly much rarer). The black swan takes the place of the mute swan in Europe and is common throughout. They are smaller than the mute variety, but just as daft and just as delighted to share your sandwiches. The most common urban 'seagull' is the antsy and stern-looking **red-billed gull**. They are also encountered on the coast and will show up at your feet before your stomach even grumbles. The same applies of course to the **feral pigeon**. They too are commonplace, especially in sight of flat-whites and menus. Out and about almost anywhere in the North Island you will also see the street-wise **Indian myna**, a chestnut coloured, medium-sized passerine that, like the sparrow, is an introduced, almost human-reliant 'opportunist'. Their speciality is dodging traffic, which they can do with precision while catching dead insects on the road.

Mammals When it comes to mammals in suburbia you will find that Mrs Tiggywinkle (alias the **hedgehog**) moved in long ago. By all accounts 'she' paid a visit, liked both the climate and the menu and decided to stay. While the hedgehog at least adds slugs and other such unwelcome garden pests to its menu of native bird's eggs, the notorious **cat** is just the wanton, careless and prolific killer of old. Domestic and feral cats maul literally millions of native and non-native birds every year and next to **humans**, the **stoat**, the **possum** and the **rat**, they are native wildlife's worst enemy.

Coastal

Seabirds Of course the coast is never far away in New Zealand and it is home to some of New Zealand's 'wildlife royalty', specifically the world's only mainland colony of **royal albatross**, found only on the Otago Peninsula near Dunedin. If you are from the northern hemisphere this is simply a must-see, since without an expensive trip to Antarctica, this is perhaps your only chance. To watch them in flight or see their fat, infant chicks awaiting their next inter-continental meal (looking like large, bemused, fluffy white slippers) is simply unforgettable. It is amazing to think that said 'slippers' must grow wings that will span over 3 m and that those wings will then subsequently take them around the world more times than Michael Palin or Richard Branson.

New Zealand is actually known as the seabird capital of the world and a

remarkable 70% of its total avian 'who's who' is pelagic (the world average is 3%).
The list is long. Numerous types of **mollymawk**, which are similar to albatrosses, are common, especially off the southern tip of the South Island, where another family of seabirds, the **shearwaters**, also abound. If you go to **Stewart Island** you may get the opportunity to see many of them, but you are more likely to find one boiled, next to your ketchup and chips. The prolific **sooty shearwater (or Titi)** has been hunted by the Maori for centuries and is still harvested today for food. Other seabirds include numerous species of **petrel**, including the Westland, Pycroft's and Cook's, all of which are found nowhere else in the world. One, the **taiko**, which was collected during Captain Cook's voyages, was not encountered again for nearly two centuries, when it was finally tracked down to its sole breeding site on the Chatham Islands. Most petrels and shearwaters nest in burrows and in huge numbers on the many offshore islands. They come ashore mainly at night, so your best chance to see them is offshore from boats or promontories, especially in Otago and Southland. Sometimes you will see huge rafts of petrels or shearwaters surface feeding, looking from a distance like a huge brown oil spill. One member of the petrel family you may bump in to while out sea fishing is the **giant petrel**. He's big (about the size of a goose), uniform brown, and looks like an industrial-strength mole-grip on wings. So don't mess! Throw out your fish scraps and smile politely.

Penguins Another huge treat for any visitor from the northern hemisphere are New Zealand's penguin species. Believe it or not, there are in fact three species perfectly at home in New Zealand and without an iceberg in sight! The **little blue** is the commonest, being found all round the coast. It is also the smallest of the penguin species and almost certainly has to be the cutest. They come ashore to their burrows at dusk, and there are many places where you can observe them doing this. Oamaru in Otago is one of the most noted sites.

Some reserves, like **Tiri tiri Matangi** Island near Auckland have nest boxes in which you can take a quick peek at little blues during the day. This can be highly entertaining as the enchanting little souls will merely look up at you with a pained expression as if to say 'Oh god, go away, you mustn't see me this fat'. Sometimes, if you encounter them on a path at night, by torchlight, they will look utterly bemused, stick their heads in the grass and point their bums in the air. Dead cute. Almost as enchanting are the endangered **yellow-eyed penguins** of the Otago and Southland coasts. Enough is said about them in the subsequent chapters, but like the Albatross they are a must-see. Less easily encountered is the rarest penguin in the world, the **Fiordland crested penguin**. You best chance to see one of these is on the West Coast between Fox Glacier and Haast, again mainly as they come ashore at dusk or leave again at dawn.

Other notable seabird attractions include the colonies of greedy **gannets** at Murawai (near Auckland), Cape Kidnappers (near Napier, in Hawke's Bay) and on Farewell Spit, off the northern tip of South Island. Several species of **shag** (cormorant) are also present in New Zealand. The most common are the large **black shag**, the black and white **pied shag** and again, as the name suggests, the petite (and again black and white) **little shag**. Some very rare, endemic and more colourful cousins include the **spotted shag**, the **Stewart Island shag** and **king shag**. Many other rare birds also inhabit the coastline including the **New Zealand dotterel** and one of the world's rarest birds, the **fairy tern**, of which tragically only around thirty remain.

Marine mammals When it comes to **whales** the word common can only be used with extreme caution, with many species being more prevalent around the New Zealand coast than most countries worldwide. **Kaikoura** is, of course, synonymous with the whale and presents one of the best whale watching opportunities in the world. As well as its resident pods of **sperm whale**, it plays host to **humpback whales, southern right whales, orca** and occasionally, even the endangered and massive, **blue whale**.

New Zealand is proud to host the great whales and is a world leader in promoting their conservation and the respect they so richly deserve. It certainly does not share the view that these awesome creatures that have been around for millions of years are – as one Japanese minister at the International Whaling Commission conference recently put it – 'cockroaches of the sea'. Now there's a man who needs a shark encounter without the cage! New Zealand is also a world leader in dealing with mass **whale strandings**, which are all too common, particularly in the natural trap of **Golden Bay**, at the northern tip of the South Island.

Still in the XXL department are the three sub-Antarctic pinniped species (or seal). The **hooker's sea lion** (or New Zealand sea lion), the **leopard seal** and the **southern elephant seal**. Although actual breeding is rare on the mainland, all three regularly visit the southern coast. The best place to see these soporific barrels of bad breath and wind (gas), are the Otago and Southland Coasts. Indeed, the Catlins coast in Southland often presents the opportunity to see all three species in one day – which is unheard of out of the sub-Antarctic Islands.

Given plenty of mention throughout the text is the **New Zealand fur seal**, which is a character of infinite charm and one that you will almost certainly encounter at close range. Out of the water, their ability to look fat and lazy, break wind and scratch their privates (all at the same time), while looking at you through one eye as if you are a complete waste of space, is frankly legendary. Quite right too – having had their brains battered to near extinction around New Zealand's waters throughout the 19th century perhaps we deserve such derision. A little word of warning: do not go within 10 m of any seal that you encounter on the beach. In the water they are even more agile and can swim faster and with more grace than anything in Speedos. Underwater or on it is also the best place to encounter **seals**. Whether diving independently or on an organised seal swim, they will often check you out like a dog in the park.

Dolphins are also a major feature of New Zealand's coastal wildlife, with dolphin watching and swimming being one of the country's many world-class activities. Apart from New Zealand's 'speciality' species, the tiny and endemic **Hector's dolphin** (one of the rarest in the world), and at least four others are regularly seen, including the **dusky dolphin**, **common dolphin**, **striped dolphin** and **bottlenose dolphin**.

Offshore Islands

The New Zealand coast features literally thousands of offshore islands that are proving crucial to the conservation of the country's native wildlife. Many combine to form an invaluable flotilla of **'arks'**; ultimately the only true hope for many species. Once the Department of Conservation has eradicated formerly -ntroduced predators, for example cats, rats and possums, which involves an expensive and time-consuming poisoning and/or capture programme – the remaining small pockets of resident birds, plants and animals are encouraged to re-colonise, and captive endemic breeds can also be re-released. Some of the many species that are now reliant on the management of these 'arks' include birds like the kakapo, the kokako and takahe. Other non-avian species include the precious tuatara.

The most crucial of the island's reintroduction programmes concerns the ancient flightless parrot, the **kakapo**; the flagship of New Zealand's conservation efforts. Only about 62 named individuals remain and each is closely monitored. The vast majority are kept on three island reserves, **Codfish Island** (off Stewart Island), **Maud Island** in the Marlborough Sounds and **Little Barrier Island**, near Auckland in the Hauraki Gulf. But the intense efforts being made to save the kakapo is, at best, merely plugging up the holes. Many species are in essence their own worst enemies, taking years and very specific habitat and environmental requirements to breed successfully. Tragically, many say it is only a matter of time.

However, to visit one of these vital reserves is to at least get a taste of the New Zealand of old and to experience the 'paradise lost'. On one of these islands you enter a world of unique and ancient wildlife that shows little fear of humans, creating a near bombardment of the senses. To encounter a kiwi at night or listen to the sublime dawn chorus of the near flightless **kokako** is one of the greatest wildlife experiences in the world. While most of the offshore islands are, understandably off limits to visitors, New Zealand is very refreshing in its attitudes towards the education and access to its endangered wildlife for the average person. The islands of **Tiri Tiri**

National parks & Forest parks

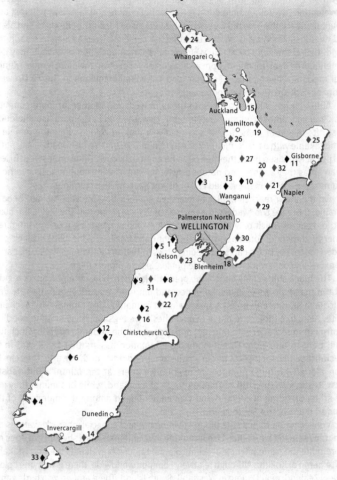

Fiordland **4**	
Kahurangi **5**	
Mt Aspiring **6**	
Mt Cook **7**	
Nelson Lakes **8**	
Paparoa **9**	
Stewart Island **33**	
Tongariro **10**	
National park ◆	Urewera **11**
Abel Tasman **1**	Westland **12**
Arthur's Pass **2**	Whanganui **13**
Egmont **3**	

Forest park ◆	
Catlins **14**	
Coromandel **15**	
Craigieburn **16**	
Hanmer **17**	
Haurangi **18**	
Kaimai Mamaku **19**	
Kaimanawa **20**	
Kaweka **21**	
Lake Sumner **22**	
Mt Richmond **23**	

Northland **24**	
Raukumara **25**	
Pirongia **26**	
Pureora **27**	
Rimutaka **28**	
Ruahine **29**	
Tararua **30**	
Victoria **31**	
Whirinaki **32**	

Matangi (see page 134) and **Kapiti Island** off the Wellington coast (see page 422) are just two examples.

Rivers, lakes and wetlands

New Zealand is riddled with rivers, lakes and low-ying wetlands all of which are home to both common, rare and unique species of animals and plants. From the rafts of mallard and black swan on **Lake Taupo**, to the endangered **brown teal** on the quiet backwaters of **Great Barrier Island**, there is much to hold your interest. Other than the brown teal, other waterfowl of particular note include the beautiful **New Zealand shoveler** and the unique **blue duck**. A resident of remote and fast flowing forest and mountain rivers, the blue duck uses highly specialised feeding methods to find algae and river insects and it is so unique it has no close relatives anywhere else in the world. Called the *whio* by Maori, which is an apt pronunciation of its call, they can sometimes be seen (or heard) from a kayak or raft, or even on the more remote tramps near mountain rivers. The rivers that feed **Lake Waikaremoana** in the **Te Urewera National Park** are just some good places to search.

Although not strictly confined to areas of wetland, another far more common duck you will almost certainly encounter in New Zealand is the **paradise shelduck**. Most often seen in pairs the male is relatively dark in colour, while the female is unmistakable with a predominantly chestnut plumage and a white head. In city parks and publicly-utilised lakes they can often be approached with little protest, but in less urban areas they are shy and notoriously loud, often circling continuously overhead issuing a repetitive, high-pitched call until you have left their territory.

On the lower reaches of glacial rivers, where they become vast braided beds of moraine, there are two **'waders'** that are very unique and special. The first is the **black stilt**, or kaki, of which only about 80 individuals remain, making it one of the rarest waders in the world. You can see these beautiful and fragile-looking 'birds in black' on a guided tour of the DoC's captive breeding hides in **Twizel**, Canterbury. These are part of the excellent conservation programme put in place to protect them.

The black stilt's close cousin the **pied stilt** is much more common and a regular sight in the shallows of lakes, estuaries and natural harbours. Again they are very delicate in stature and boast a smart, almost formal-looking plumage of black and white. Also, like their pure black relative they have legs like busy knitting needles. Another unique wader with unusual appendages is the endemic **wrybill**, which has a bill bent to one side. This remarkable adaptation assists this small bird in its specialist search for insects under small stones and driftwood. In winter they can be seen along with huge numbers of migratory waders at the **Miranda Naturalist's Trust Reserve** on the **Firth of Thames** south of Auckland, while in summer they join the stilts, breeding 'incognito' and well camouflaged among the moraines of the braided rivers of the South Island.

Very common in both the urban environment and especially around water is the non-native **sacred kingfisher**. Like its European counterpart it is a shy bird but does not share quite the same bright iridescent colours. Far less prevalent is the unmistakable **white heron** or Kokutu. Although relatively common worldwide, there is only one colony in New Zealand, near Okarito in Westland, South Island. There around 200 birds gather between September and November to breed, before scattering throughout the country during the winter months. You can see these magnificent birds on one of the daily tours that visit the Okarito breeding colony from Whataroa, north of Franz Josef. In winter, if you find yourself in Milford Sound, look out for 'Charlie', a famous heron that has spent the last 12 winters in and around the boat terminal. Somehow, the sight of white heron in Westland seems like some eminently suitable signature to such a majestic scenic backdrop. Little wonder the Maori have always held the white heron in such high esteem. The other far more common and smaller heron you will certainly see throughout New Zealand is the non-native **white-faced heron**.

Of course New Zealand's waterways are also home to many endemic fish and insects. Two native **eels**, the short-finned eel and the long-finned eel have been sacred to the Maori for generations and once provided an important food source. They are huge, reaching up to 2 m in length and are thought to live up to 100 years old. You can see them in many nature reserves and animal parks where they are often fed by hand. The DoC **Mount Bruce Wildlife Centre** in the Wairarapa and **Rainbow Springs** in Rotorua are just two good examples.

Lowlands and forest

Less than 25% of New Zealand is under 200 m so, despite appearances there is not as much room as you think. When man arrived and set to with his short-sighted slash and burn policy, New Zealand's landscape was irrevocably altered and has now lost over 85% of its natural forest cover. The impact on the whole ecosystem has been immense; most of the native forest that remains is confined to inaccessible areas and mountain slopes, with almost a quarter of that being in South Islands' West Coast region alone.

One of the most evident yet hardly common species of the forests and low lying bush is the native **New Zealand pigeon** or **kereru**; a large, handsome, colourful character, with a signature plumage of almost iridescent greens, browns, purples and white, with bright red eyes. Often heard crashing about in the leaf canopies before being spotted, they exhibit the congenial air of one who is over-fed and bring new meaning to the word plump. Little wonder the Maori prized the kereru as an important source of food. Today, despite being protected, their numbers are declining, mainly due to habitat loss and illegal hunting. The kereru can be also seen in gardens and parks, but if it remains illusive you can still see them at most animal parks and zoos. 'Pig', a rather daft Kereru residing in **Wellington Zoo**, is amenable to visitors and nearly died once after swallowing a pencil!

The stitchbird, bellbird and tui are also found in the lowland and forest habitats and are New Zealand's three representatives of the **honeyeaters**. A New Zealand endemic, the **tui** is quite common throughout the country and you are bound to see, and certainly hear them. From a distance they look a dull-black colour with a distinctive white bib (that also earned it the name of the 'parson's bird'), but on closer inspection their plumage is a superb mix of iridescent blues and greens. Their song is almost legendary, a delight to listen to, but almost impossible to describe. In essence they boast a remarkable range of audible whistles, grunts and knocks – a bit like Björk on a good night. Much of the tui's repertoire is beyond our audible range which is why they often look as if someone kept the camera rolling but momentarily pressed the 'mute' button. One of the best places to see tui in large numbers is during spring in the blooming cherry trees behind the **Wairakei Golf Club**, near Taupo. There up to 30-odd birds can be seen in action, which is quite a sight and sound. The **stitchbird** and **bellbird** are not as common as the tui but are equally colourful and just marginally less melodic. They are best seen on the offshore island reserves.

Of all the smaller birds encountered most folks' favourite is the enchanting little **fantail**. These charming little birds are a bit like butterflies on speed and your visit to New Zealand will more than once be enhanced by their inquisitive nature. While walking down any bush or forest park they will often appear from nowhere and with manic audible 'peeps' fly about your person as if interested in making your acquaintance. They do this not once but for some time, flitting about and fanning their tails manically. In actuality, fantails are only interested in the insects you are disturbing within their individual territories, which is why, after a while, they suddenly seem to lose interest. Another little charmer, that is less common and shares this behaviour, is the **tom tit**: a small, native black-and-white character that in many ways resembles the European robin. Trampers will become familiar with the tomtit, especially in South Island. New Zealand does also have its own robin, the dull-coloured **New Zealand robin** which can often be seen in the forests of both North, South and Stewart Islands.

The **morepork** is New Zealand's only native owl species. It is a small owl that feeds mainly on insects but is not impartial to the odd lesser-sized avian. Being very illusive and nocturnal, they are most often heard rather than seem and it is their distinctive butcher's shop request – 'more pork, more pork' – that earned them the name. The only other raptors (birds of prey) present in New Zealand are the native New Zealand falcon and the 'imported' **Australasian harrier**. Commonly seen soaring above hillsides and fields throughout the countryside, the harrier is often mistaken by the novice to be some sort of eagle. But eagles are much larger; the **Haast eagle**, which is now extinct but once ruled the skies in New Zealand, was over 26 times the harrier's weight and had a wing span of over 3 m, so large it would probably have been able to tackle a child.

Also with a curvaceous beak, the adorable **kaka** is one of New Zealand's three native parrot species. Once common throughout the country they are now confined mainly to old-growth beech and podocarp forests. Although unmistakable in both call and plumage the average visitor would be lucky to see one in the wild, making your best bet the zoos or DoC wildlife centres at **Mount Bruce** in the Wairarapa or Te Anau in Fiordland. At Mount Bruce, a small group has been successfully captive-bred and were released locally. Now, although essentially wild, they remain in the vicinity, returning to the same spot at the same time each day to be fed. This daily spectacle provides the kind of quality entertainment for which parrots can always be relied upon and also offers a superb photo opportunity.

Even tamer than the kaka but sharing its love for a free lunch is the **weka**, a sort of flightless brown rail. Again, without any predators, the weka evolved to dispense with the need for flight and focused its hunting activity entirely on the forest floor. In modern times it is not just the forest, but the human car park and campground that offers rich pickings. If you are joined at any point by this appealing albeit uninvited guest, bear in mind they can be very persistent and notoriously quick with the steal.

Of course the lowlands and forests are also home to many non-avian species, but most of the true endemics are either reptiles or insects. Two notable exceptions are the much celebrated and impressively sounding **peripatus** and **powelliphanta**, both of which are as old as the land itself. Peripatus is like a cross between a worm and a centipede, while powelliphanta is a carnivorous land snail with a shell the size of a saucer. Both of course are remarkable creatures and were on the scene millions of years before man.

Mammals It is remarkable to think that New Zealand played host to only one mammal before we arrived, a small bat, of which two species evolved. The **long-tailed bat** and the **short-tailed bat** are rarely seen by the casual observer, living in small local populations, and even then mainly on only a few remote offshore islands. Of course in New Zealand today, besides the bat, there is now a thoroughly cosmopolitan and unsavoury list of mammalian guests. This extraordinary list of reprobates includes possums (an estimated 70 million – 20 to every person), stoats, weasels, rabbits, hares, wallabies, ferrets, rats, mice, pigs, cats, horses, deer, goats and the infamous Paul Holmes (watch NZ TV every weeknight at 1900).

Highlands

With over 75% of the country being above 200 m, this is a vast habitat that due to its very inhospitable landscape could never exactly be overrun with species. However, New Zealand's mountains and glacial valleys, like the rest of its ecosystem, boast a fair number of endemic animals and many unique plants that can often be spotted by the casual observer.

Most noted of the birds is of course, the notorious **kea** – the only alpine parrot in the world. This highly intelligent, entertaining, 'avian thug' lives high above the tree line, where it nests amongst rocks and feeds on just about anything edible. Although you may only ever hear them from a distance, if lucky you may encounter them at close range. If you do you are almost certainly in for a treat. Nicknamed the 'cheeky

The Mystical Kiwi

Of course the iconic kiwi is deserving of a special piece and no doubt you are dying to see one. Along with the platypus of Australia, or perhaps the peacock, it has to be one of the most curious and endearing creatures on earth – one, perhaps, that even Charles Darwin, given a party pack of recreational drugs, a bottle of vodka and a considerable bet, could still not devise. Almost half-bird half-mammal it evolved over millions of years of isolation to fill a specific niche free of any predators. Although related to the ostrich of Africa, the emu of Australia and the extinct, native New Zealand moa, it is in many ways unusual and in some absolutely unique. Flightless of course; they have no wings and their feathers are more like hairs. They are nocturnal and like rabbits, live in burrows. They have long whiskers almost like those of a cat, which, along with an acute sense of hearing and smell, are its ammunition in the hunt for food. It is the only bird with nostrils at the end of its beak and of course its egg-to-body weight ratio is legendary. The egg of a kiwi averages 15% of the female's body weight, compared to two percent for the ostrich. Females tend to be larger than males and when it comes to the brown kiwi, the male tends to do most of the incubating. They mate for life, sleep for almost 20 hours a day and live as long as thirty years. There are four identified species of kiwi. The brown kiwi, is the most common species and the one you are most likely to see in captivity. Although relatively widespread in central and northern North Island there is only an isolated population of 160 birds occurring in the South Island at Okarito. The **little spotted kiwi** is extinct on the mainland and survives only as 1,000 birds on Kapiti Island and 200 on four smaller islands. The **great spotted kiwi** is only found on the South Island and an estimated 20,000 remain. Lastly the **tokoeka** is found on Stewart Island, Fiordland and around Haast. The tokoekas of **Stewart Island** are the only kiwi that can be seen during the day, which creates something of a touristical pilgrimage to try to see them (see box, page 688). Of course the best and only chance the vast majority of visitors get to observe these quirky characters in one of the many darkened 'kiwi houses' scattered around the country. Some of the best are to be found at the Whangarei Museum, the DoC Wildlife Centre at Mount Bruce in the Wairarapa, Wellington Zoo, Orana Park in Christchurch and in Queenstown. Like so many New Zealand species, even the iconic kiwi is not immune from the tragic threat of extinction and it is feared that they too will no longer be found anywhere in the wild on mainland New Zealand within two decades. For more information on kiwi and the efforts being made to conserve them, consult the web site www.kiwirecovery.org.nz

kea' – thanks to their inherently inquisitive nature and extrovert behaviour – they are particularly fascinated by cars, rucksacks and shoelaces, in fact anything that can be dismantled, demolished or preferably eaten. To have a flock descend in the middle of your picnic is a bit like an encounter with a special class of infants, all unsupervised, out of control and with severe behavioural disorders. I say children because that is truly how they behave and it certainly relates best to your subsequent reaction. They are so appalling, carefree and fun-loving that it is almost impossible not to just let them get on with it.

Another creature of the slopes and mountain valleys is the equally clever, but far less frivolous, **New Zealand falcon**. Quite elusive and capable of demolishing its prey like a surface-to-air-missile you would be lucky to see one, but once spotted they are unmistakable. Nothing else in New Zealand flies with such stealth or purpose, nor when it arrests momentarily (most probably still grasping its latest victim) is so stern in looks. Even keas don't mess with a falcon's lunch!

Another bird of the mountains and remote glacial valleys is the remarkable and flightless **takahe**. They are the most appealing of birds and look like some congenial, almost 'clueless', prehistoric, purple chicken. Another ancient species once thought to be extinct, they were dramatically rediscovered deep in the Murchison Mountains of Fiordland in 1948. There is now an intensive breeding programme to attempt to secure their conservation, with only about 100 birds remaining in the wild and about the same again kept in captivity or on predator-free islands. Without doubt the best place to see them is **Tiri Tiri Matangi** Island near Auckland, where several families (totalling about 20 birds) are allowed to roam free. Being incredibly tame and inquisitive it is both memorable and remarkable to sit amongst them and reflect on just how privileged you are in being able to do so. But, as with so many of the species on the brink, you do so perhaps with a deep sense of guilt and the overriding and worrying question – but for how much longer?

Insects

New Zealand has an impressive range of creepy-crawlies, ranging from the noisy and the colourful to one that is the size of mouse. Although lacking in butterflies and far more replete with moths, one large and perhaps familiar butterfly that you will see, especially in Auckland and the upper North Island, is the **monarch butterfly**. Famous the world over as a migratory species, these tawny-red and black-striped beauties, with a wingspan of 10 cm first arrived in New Zealand around 1840 (some say much earlier). It is very common in the urban and suburban habitats, but rarely seen in the bush or south of Christchurch. Although well known in the Americas for their swarming and long inter-state migrations, the butterflies found in New Zealand infrequently demonstrate either of these behaviours. However, like their American cousins and unlike most butterfly species, they often over-winter and live for several months.

One moth species that has a remarkable tendency to commit suicide by flying into any artificial light source at night is the large, native **puriri moth**. A beautiful lime-green colour with a wingspan of up to 15 cm, it is the country's largest moth species but is only found in the native forests of the North Island. Although the adults only live for a few days the caterpillars spend several years in tunnels bored in to trees.

By far the noisiest insect in the country is the **cicada**, which in summer and en masse can create an ear-splitting din in almost any area of bush or forest throughout the country. There are many species in New Zealand with one of the most common being the clapping cicada which was one of the first insects noted by Joseph Banks, the naturalist accompanying Captain Cook on his first new Zealand voyage in 1769-70. They are fascinating creatures, about 30 mm in length with a wingspan up to 80 mm. The larvae of the very vocal adults can live in the ground for many years before aspiring to split eardrums. It is only the males that sing and the noise is created by the vibration of a unique ribbed structure called a 'tymbal' which resonates the sound in the almost hollow abdomen. Despite there being so many in any given area of bush or even one tree, take some time to focus on one song and try to locate the insect on the tree trunk branch or underside of leaves.

There are a number of spider species in New Zealand with the two most notable being the **katipo** and the **avondale**. The **katipo spider** is about 10 mm in length and, along with the average politician, is the only poisonous creature in the land. Looking the part, with a shiny black body, long legs and a red spot on its abdomen, it is a relative of the famous black widow and can deliver a nasty bite that can be incapacitating, but rarely fatal. You will doubtless be relieved to learn that they are a coastal species that frequent the undersides of logs rather than toilet seats!

The **Avondale spider** is a sub-species of the well known Australian huntsman. It is relatively harmless, but very large at over 10 cm in length. A unique, localised sub-species, found only in the suburb of Avondale in Auckland, it is an amenable easily-handled species that was bred en masse in captivity and used in the film *Arachnophobia*.

Perhaps the most remarkable native insect in New Zealand is the **glow-worm**. Although essentially a gnat, it is the worm-like larvae that frequent the damp limestone caves and sheltered cavities on both the North and South islands that are most famous. The sight of an ethereal 'galaxy' of glow-worms (often called 'grottoes') on the roof of a cave in the darkness, particularly at Waitomo in the Waikato is a truly memorable sight. What you are actually seeing, to put it bluntly, are the shiny bottoms of the larvae, which emit a bright blue/green light. It is a clever and remarkable mechanism and a chemical reaction known as bioluminescence used to attract insect prey; the prey flies towards the light and is caught in sticky threads that the worm hangs from like a row of fishing lines from the roof of the cave. To enter a grotto at night then emerge into a clear starlit sky is a very firm reminder of the incredible world in which we live.

Not to be outdone by a mere glowing bottom, the New Zealand **weta** is perhaps the king of all the New Zealand insects. They are an ancient creature that has been around for millions of years. A number of species are found in gardens, forests caves and rock crevices throughout the country ranging from the common tree wetas, to the cave weta and ground weta. But without doubt the most impressive is the **giant weta**. At up to 9 cm in length and weighing in at up to 80 gm they are about the size of a mouse and the largest insect in the world. With their huge abdomens, beady black eyes, long antenna and 'alien' like legs you will either love or hate the weta. Your best bet to see one either live or dead is in the country's zoos or museums. Once you see one it will incite one of two reactions: an instant and impressive 100-m dash or a deep desire to make their acquaintance. Weta are not dangerous despite a fine set of mandibles used to crunch up leaves, shoots and small insects.

Of course, if you go anywhere near the West Coast of the South Island you will become very intimate with the infamous New Zealand **sandfly**.

Vegetation

Like the country's animal life, much of New Zealand's plant life is very beautiful, very ancient and very unique, making it a veritable paradise for any 'budding' botanist. Over 80% of the country's flowering plants are not endemic to any other land. But like the fauna, much of the country's plant life is in a worrying state of decline, not as a result of predation, but by the clear felling and burning that has taken place since the arrival of man. Tragically, only about 15% of the New Zealand's original forest cover remains. Even a brief description of New Zealand's plant species is beyond the scope of this guide, but the following are some of the most notable species that you are likely to see or hear about.

Fern species

Alongside the iconic kiwi, the **ponga** or **silver fern** is New Zealand's other great national emblem and just one of a vast array of over 80 fern species. Depicted on everything from the national rugby jersey to the side of America's Cup yachts, the silver fern is a common sight in both the natural and commercial world. It is found throughout the mainly subtropical bush landscape, forming stands of almost prehistoric -ooking umbrellas. A lush green colour on top, it is the silver underside that has created their notoriety, and not just in pure aesthetics. One well-known aspect of 'bush survival and rescue' is to lay out the fronds upside down in a clearing so as to capture the attention of a helicopter from above. Ferns generally have always been a very significant and sacred symbol of the Maori culture, especially in their tendency to 'unfurl' into 'being'. Often alongside the ubiquitous ponga, you will find the taller and more classic desert island-type **nikau palm**, the **cabbage tree**, and numerous creepers, palm lilies, tree ferns and mosses.

Forest trees

The ancient New Zealand forest is traditionally one of **podocarp** and **beech trees**. Without doubt the most celebrated, yet overly utilised of the one hundred-odd forest tree species is the **kauri**. Occurring predominantly in the north of the North Island and a member of the podocarp family, it was once the dominant tree of the Auckland province and the Coromandel Peninsula. With vast trunks often over 15 m in diameter, and 30 m tall, free from knots and blemishes, the kauri was prized by both the Maori for canoe building and by the early Europeans for masts and other ship-building materials. The tree's resin ('kauri gum') was also used as a derivative of varnishes and paint products and also made a medium suitable for carving into elaborate ornaments. Sadly, over 90% of the trees were harvested and only a few ancient individuals remain. Most noted of these is the impressive 1,200-year old **'Tane Mahuta'** ('Lord of the Forest') which still stands proudly in the **Waipoua Forest** in Northland. Other notable podocarp species, utilised (and over-utilised) for canoes, boat building and timber generally, are the native **matai** (black pine), **rimu** (red pine), **totara, miro** and New Zealand's tallest tree – the **kahikatea** (white pine). The kahikatea can grow to over 60 m.

Another plant heavily utilised by the Maori is the tough-stemmed **flax** plant, found predominantly in wetlands the length and breath of the country. It was used for everything from footwear to building.

Flowering trees

Two very colourful flowering trees, well known throughout the country, are the yellow flowering **kowhai** (New Zealand's national flower) and the red flowering **rata**, a climber that literally strangles its host tree to death. New Zealand's best known flowering tree is the beautiful **pohutukawa**; a gnarled-looking coastal evergreen that bursts into bright crimson flower for three weeks in December, earning it the affectionate label as New Zealand's Christmas tree.

Endemic flowers

Of the many endemic flowers in New Zealand a large number are found in the high alpine areas, including the **Mount Cook lily**, the largest of all the buttercups. With flowers as big as its leaves it is an impressive sight provided, that is, you can find it amongst the 60-odd species of mountain daisy!

Conservation

Describing New Zealand's rich and unusual animal and plant species is an act of celebration, but it is also a sorry tale. Although the country is often dubbed **'clean and green'**, many agree that it is a boast that is far more a result of low population rather than attitude. Since the arrival of man we have had a dramatic and tragic effect on the entire landscape and biodiversity of New Zealand. As a result of our presence 32% of indigenous land and freshwater birds and 18% of seabirds are now extinct. The most recent extinction occurred in 1907 with the last sighting of the beautiful huia, a relative of the kakako, which is now also endangered. Tragically, the loss of the huia occurred not only as a result of a decline in habitat, but man's ridiculous desire to adorn himself with its feathers. Many other unique and well known species have also disappeared, like the legendary **moa**, which was essentially hunted to extinction by the Maori. In the present day many others currently sit quietly on the brink and alas, the clean green land is gathering grey clouds and storms are brewing. As it stands, with endemic bird species alone, there are only 36 fairy terns remaining, 62 kakapo, about 70 Campbell Island teal, 70 taiko, 80 black stilt and 200 takahe, to name but a few. Even the kiwi, the very emblem of the nation and its people is severely under threat and without more financing, it too is expected to be completely absent on mainland New Zealand within the next two decades. To lose the kiwi itself – the very bird after which its native humans are named – seems unimaginable. One can only hope, that given its prestige, it may stir the people into action.

Government initiatives

Sterling efforts are being made in the war of conservation by governmental departments, for example the Department of Conservation, as well as independent organizations and individuals. Numerous captive breeding and predator eradication programmes have been initiated to stop, or at the very least slow down, the decline of so many species. Indeed, New Zealand is on the 'front line' of the global conservation war and thankfully there have been some fine and victorious battles. The **black robin**, an endemic little bird found only on the Chatham Islands, is one such example and one of the most famous conservation successes in human history. From a population of only nine individuals in the mid 1970s, it has essentially been saved and now numbers around 250. But these battles all defy the short-sighted, financial and technologically driven society of the modern day. Since the very act of conservation is a drain on funds rather than a source, DoC is always under-funded and under-researched and it seems, tragically, a war that can perhaps never be won. Ecotourism does offers a viable path in some areas but it is just part of a long and difficult climb towards salvation.

Paradise Lost

In the New Zealand of today, the great clean, green land – the paradise, but really the paradise lost – it almost makes the heart cry to experience the deathly hush of forests once alive to the sound of birds. At times it really is like standing in an ancient church that has been sacked of all its contents and robbed of both congregation and choir. Instead of a heads held high in celebration, the whispers of prayer and beautiful arias of worship, the pose is one of despair, the atmosphere one of remorseful reflection and the sound, one of eternal silence. To lose the kakapo, the kokako or the kiwi itself, all species that have been around for millions of years is too tragic to contemplate.

Books

For detailed and excellent information on the full range of New Zealand titles, subjects and authors contact the Book Publishers' Association of New Zealand, T09-4802711, www.bpanz.org.nz For general titles and worldwide availability try www.amazon.com

Non-fiction, pictorial, natural history and environment

As you might expect, there is a vast array of pictorial books celebrating New Zealand's stunning scenery. The best known photographers are **Craig Potton, Andris** Apse and **Robin Morrison**, to name but a few. Their numerous books are of a very high production quality and contain some exquisite photographs. There are a few good wildlife guidebooks and field guides. **Geoff Moon's** New Zealand Birds is an old favourite while the new Field Guide to New Zealand

Wildlife by **Rod Morris** and **Terence Linsey** (Collins) is recommended. From afar the pictorial websites of www.photonewzealand.com www.andrisapse.co.nz www.craigpotton.co.nz are all excellent.

History, politics and culture

The History of New Zealand by **Keith Sinclair** is a dated but celebrated historical work that is a complete history starting from before the arrival of Europeans. Maori: A Photographic and Social Study and Being Pakeha, both by **Michael King**; The Old-Time Maori by **Makereti**; The Treaty of Waitangi by **Claudia Orange**; and The New Zealand Land Wars by **James Belich** are all equally celebrated works covering the often contentious historical issues of the Maori and Pakeha. For an overall insight The New Zealand Historical Atlas: Ko Papatuanuku e Takoto Nei is highly visual, easy to read and generally recommended.

Biographies and travelogues

For tramping, the Moirs Guides (NZ Alpine Club) and New Zealand's Great Walks by **Pearl Hewson** (Hodders) are recommended. Also check out titles by **Craig Potton**, www.craigpotton.co.nz For cycling, the word is that **Bruce Ringer**'s New Zealand by Bike (Mountaineers) is excellent. For skiing try the annual Ski and Snowboard Guide available free from Brown Bear Publications based in Christchurch, PO Box 31-207, Ilam, T03-3885331 from www.brownbear.co.nz

Guide books and reference

The Mobil New Zealand Travel Guide by **Diana and Jeremy Pope** offers a general place-orientated guide, with interesting background reading and historical insights into each place listed. If you can get your hands on an old copy of Wise's New Zealand Guide, available in most second-hand bookshops, it is brilliant. For B&B guides the New Zealand Bed and Breakfast Guide by J

Thomas (Moonshine) and the Friar's B&B Guide are recommended. **Lord of the Rings** fans will be delighted to find the compact New Zealand best seller the Lord of the Rings Location Guide by **Ian Brodie** readily available in most bookshops and VICs ($20). Providing a comprehensive look at the numerous film locations around the country and how to get there (with GPS references) it also contains movie images and cast contributions. The book is only available in New Zealand, www.harpercollins.co.nz.

Fiction

The **New Zealand Book Council**, PO Box 11-377, Wellington, T04-4991596, www.bookcouncil.org.nz, is an excellent source of information on New Zealand literature and fiction. They provide listings of books, places of literary interest to visit and literary events.

There are many celebrated fiction writers in New Zealand and when **Keri Hulme** won the Booker Prize in 1985 for The Bone People and children's writer **Margaret Mahy** the Carnegie Medal twice that same decade for The Haunting and The Changeover, New Zealand writing was put on the international map. Previous to that it was really only the celebrated short stories by the Wellingtonian writer **Katherine Mansfield** (1888-1923) that had received international recognition. The Collected Stories of Katherine Mansfield is her best-known literary export. Other notable names and titles include **Maurice Shadbolt's** Season of the Jew, a story about dispossessed Maori identifying with the Jews of ancient Israel. **Maurice Gee** is another well-known writer. His Going West is the story of unravelling relationships amidst the backdrop of Auckland and Wellington. The Plumb trilogy is recommended, as are his entertaining children's works. **Witi Ihimaera's** Bulibasha is an affectionate look at Maori sheep shearing gangs in Eastland and **Alan Duff's** much acclaimed Once Were Warriors is a disturbing and powerful insight into Maori domestic life in Auckland's suburbs. The film of it provides a reality check and is the complete antithesis of New Zealand's clean green, peaceful image.

Footnotes

Maori words and phrases

Aotearoa New Zealand
Ariki tribal leader
Atua spiritual Being
Harakeke flax plant, leaves
Hawaiki ancestral Polynesian homeland
Hapu sub-tribe/ to be pregnant
He Ao a land or a world
He tangata the people
Iwi tribe
Kaikaiawaro a dolphin (Pelorus Jack) who cruised the Sounds and became a guardian for iwi
Kaitiaki protector, caretaker
Kapa haka group of Maori performers
Kiaora welcome
Kaumatua elders
Kawa protocols
Kete basket
Kowhaiwhai rafter patterns
Mana integrity, prestige, control
Manawhenua people with tribal affiliations with the area
Maoritanga Maori 'ness'
Marae sacred courtyard or plaza
Mauri life essence
Moana large body of water, sea

Moko tattoo
Muka flax fibre
Ngati people of
Pa a fortified residential area
Poi ball attached to flax string
Pounamu sacred greenstone
Rangatira Tribal leader
Taiaha A fighting staff
Tangata people/person
Tangihanga death ritual
Taonga treasure, prized object (often passed down by ancestors)
Tapu sacred, out of bounds
Te Ika-a-Maui North Island
Tipuna ancestor
Tukutuku wall panels
Utu cost
Wahakatauki proverb or saying
Waiata song, flute music
Wairua soul
Waka canoe
Whakairo carvings
Whakapapa origins of genealogy
Whanau extended family/to give birth
Whare house
Whenua land

Index

Footnotes Index

Acknowledgements

Thanks once again to all the staff and representatives of the many regional visitor information centres and regional tourism offices who provided invaluable advice and assistanc.

Also thanks to Chris and Don Stuart in Auckland, John, Sharon and Jim in Christchurch and Tony and Brigitte Robinson and Sally Van Natta in Santa Barbara, for their valued friendship and for providing sanctuary from the rigours of the road.

Thanks too to all the team at Footprint and Sarah Thorowgood in particular for her much appreciated patience and hard work.

Finally a special thanks, as ever, to my mother Grace for her steadfast encouragement and support, my brother Ghill for the many 'tonic' email attachments and to my partner Rebecca, who knows that although she is not always able to join me on the road is always with me in my thoughts and in my heart.

This edition is dedicated to Jeanne Aird and Kaija Robinson, just two people with big hearts, whom, through the tragic circumstances forced upon them, were unable, or will never be able to see or experience life as I have.

Map index

Map symbols

Administration

- Capital city
- Other city/town

Roads and travel

- Highway
- Major road
- Minor road
- 4WD/track
- Footpath
- Railway with station

Water features

- River
- Lake, ocean
- Beach, sand bank
- Waterfall
- Ferry

Cities and towns

- Sight
- Sleeping
- Eating
- Bars & clubs
- Building
- Main through route
- Main street
- Minor street
- Pedestrianized street
- Tunnel
- One way street
- Bridge
- Steps
- Park, garden, stadium
- Airport
- Bus station
- Metro station
- Bank
- Hospital
- Museum
- Police
- Post office
- Tourist office
- Cathedral, church
- Mosque
- Internet
- Telephone
- Golf
- Parking
- Detail map
- Related map

Topographical features

- Contours (approx), rock outcrop
- Mountain
- Volcano
- Mountain pass
- Escarpment
- Gorge

Other symbols

- Archaeological site
- National park/wildlife reserve
- Viewing point
- Vineyard
- Campsite
- Refuge
- Deciduous/coniferous trees

Complete listing

Footprint publishes
travel guides to over 150
destinations worldwide. Each guide
is packed with practical, concise
and colourful information for
everybody from first-time travellers
to travel aficionados. The list is
growing fast and current titles are
noted below.
Available from all good bookshops
and online

www.footprintbooks.com

(P) denotes pocket guide

Latin America and Caribbean
Argentina
Barbados (P)
Bolivia
Brazil
Caribbean Islands
Central America & Mexico
Chile
Colombia
Costa Rica
Cuba
Cusco & the Inca Trail
Dominican Republic
Ecuador & Galápagos
Guatemala
Havana (P)
Mexico
Nicaragua
Peru
Rio de Janeiro
South American Handbook
Venezuela

North America
Vancouver (P)
New York (P)
Western Canada

Africa
Cape Town (P)
East Africa
Libya
Marrakech & the High Atlas
Marrakech (P)
Morocco
Namibia
South Africa
Tunisia
Uganda

Middle East
Egypt
Israel
Jordan
Syria & Lebanon
Australasia

Footnotes Complete listing

Credits

Footprint credits

Editor: Sarah Thorowgood
Assistant editor: Laura Dixon
Map editor: Sarah Sorensen

Publisher: Patrick Dawson
Editorial: Alan Murphy, Sophie Blacksell, Claire Boobbyer, Caroline Lascom, Felicity Laughton, Davina Rungasamy
Cartography: Robert Lunn, Claire Benison, Kevin Feeney
Series development: Rachel Fielding
Design: Mytton Williams and Rosemary Dawson (brand)
Advertising: Debbie Wylde
Finance and administration: Sharon Hughes, Elizabeth Taylor

Photography credits

Front cover: Image State, Whirinald Forest
Back cover: Darroch Donald
Inside colour section: Darroch Donald

Print

Manufactured in Italy by LegoPrint
Pulp from sustainable forests

Footprint feedback

We try as hard as we can to make each Footprint guide as up to date as possible but, of course, things always change. If you want to let us know about your experiences – good, bad or ugly – then don't delay, go to **www.footprintbooks.com** and send in your comments.

Publishing information

Footprint New Zealand
2nd edition
© Footprint Handbooks Ltd
November 2003

ISBN 1 903471 74 5
CIP DATA: A catalogue record for this book is available from the British Library

® Footprint Handbooks and the Footprint mark are a registered trademark of Footprint Handbooks Ltd

Published by Footprint

6 Riverside Court
Lower Bristol Road
Bath BA2 3DZ, UK
T +44 (0)1225 469141
F +44 (0)1225 469461
discover@footprintbooks.com
www.footprintbooks.com

Distributed in the USA by

Publishers Group West

New Zealand

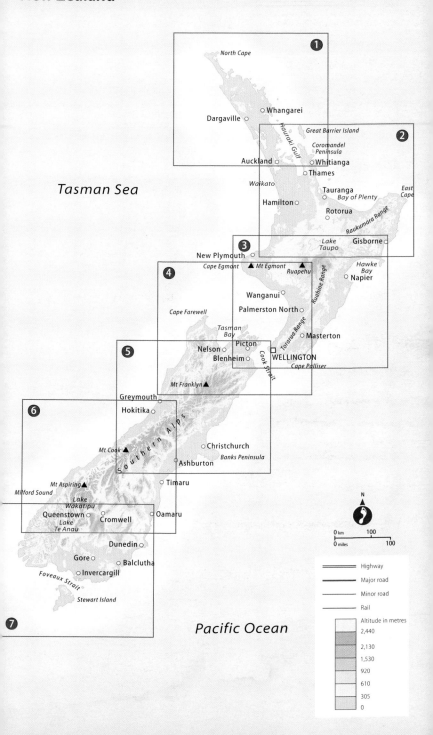

Tasman Sea

North Cape

❶

Whangarei

Dargaville

Great Barrier Island

❷

Hauraki Gulf

Coromandel
Peninsula

Auckland

Whitianga

Thames

Waikato

Tauranga

Bay of Plenty

East
Cape

Hamilton

Rotorua

Raukumara Range

Lake
Taupo

Gisborne

❸

New Plymouth

Cape Egmont ▲ Mt Egmont ▲

Ruapehu

Hawke
Bay

Napier

❹

Wanganui

Palmerston North

Ruahine Range

Cape Farewell

Tasman
Bay

Nelson

Picton

Torora Range

Masterton

❺

Blenheim

Cook Strait

WELLINGTON

Cape Palliser

Mt Franklyn ▲

Greymouth

❻

Hokitika

Southern Alps

Christchurch

Mt Cook ▲

Banks Peninsula

Ashburton

Mt Aspiring ▲

Milford Sound

Timaru

Lake
Wakatipu

Queenstown

Cromwell

Oamaru

Lake
Te Anau

Dunedin

Gore

Balclutha

Invercargill

Foveaux Strait

Stewart Island

❼

Pacific Ocean

N

0 km   100

0 miles   100

Highway

Major road

Minor road

Rail

Altitude in metres

2,440

2,130

1,530

920

610

305

0

Map 1 North Island

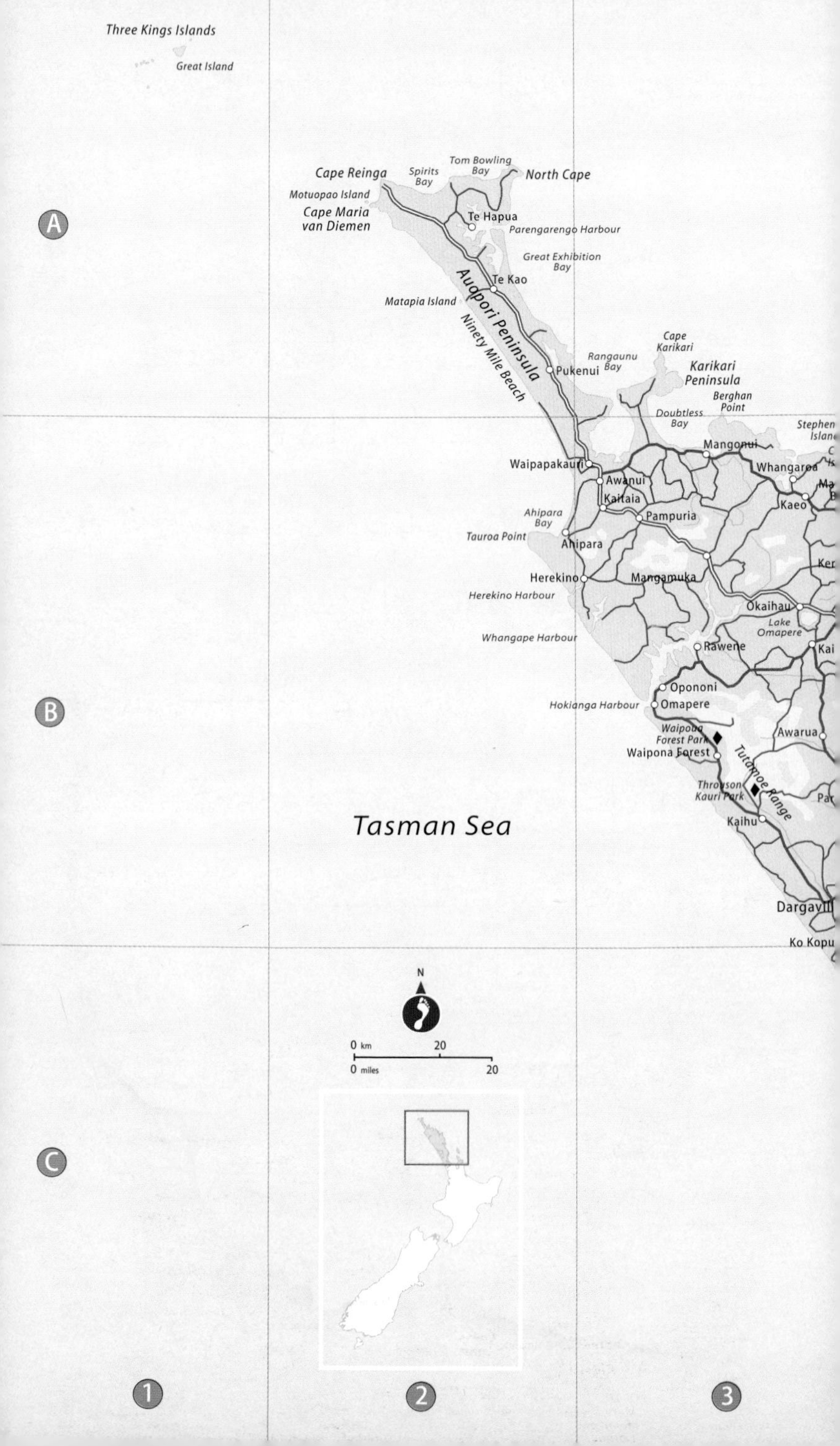

Three Kings Islands

Great Island

Cape Reinga
Spirits Bay
Tom Bowling Bay
North Cape
Motuopao Island
Cape Maria van Diemen
Te Hapua
Parengarengo Harbour

Great Exhibition Bay

Te Kao

Matapia Island

Aupori Peninsula

Ninety Mile Beach

Rangaunu Bay

Cape Karikari

Karikari Peninsula

Berghan Point

Pukenui

Doubtless Bay

Stephen Island

Mangonui

Waipapakauri

Whangaroa

Awanui
Kaitaia
Kaeo

Ahipara Bay

Pampuria

Tauroa Point

Ahipara

Ker

Herekino

Mangamuka

Herekino Harbour

Okaihau
Lake Omapere

Kai

Whangape Harbour

Rawene

Opononi
Omapere

Awarua

Hokianga Harbour

Waipoua Forest Park
Waipona Forest

Tutamoe Range

Pa

Throvson Kauri Park

Kaihu

Tasman Sea

Dargavill

Ko Kopu

N

0 km   20
0 miles   20

Map 2 North Island

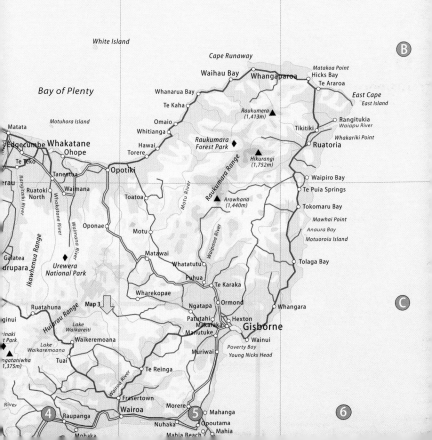

N

0 km   20
0 miles   20

A

South Pacific Ocean

B

White Island

Bay of Plenty

Cape Runaway

Matakaoa Point
Hicks Bay
Waihau Bay   Whangaparaoa   Te Araroa

Whanarua Bay   East Cape
East Island

Te Kaha

Omaio   Raukumera
(1,413m)   Rangitukia
Waiapu River

Whitianga   Tikitiki   Whakariki Point

Hawai   Raukumara
Forest Park   Ruatoria
Matata   Torere
Motuhora Island
Edgecumbe   Whakatane   Hikurangi
Ohope   (1,752m)
Te Teko   Opotiki
Taneatua   Waipiro Bay
Te Puia Springs
Ruatoki   Waimana
North   Toatoa   Tokomaru Bay
rau
Galatea   Oponae   Arowhana   Mawhai Point
rupara   (1,440m)   Anaura Bay
Motu   Motuoroiu Island
Urewera
National Park   Matawai   Tolaga Bay

Ruatahuna   Whatatutu
ginui   Map 3   Puhua
Lake   Wharekopae   Te Karaka
Waikareiti
inaki   Ngatapa   Whangara
t Park   Lake   Waikaremoana   Patutahi   Hexton
Waikaremoana   Makaraka
ngataniwha   Tuai   Manutuke   Gisborne
(1,375m)
Wainui
Muriwai   Poverty Bay
Te Reinga   Young Nicks Head

River   Frasertown
Wairoa   Morere   Mahanga
Raupanga   Oputama
Nuhaka   Mahia
Mohaka   Mahia Beach

C

4   5   6

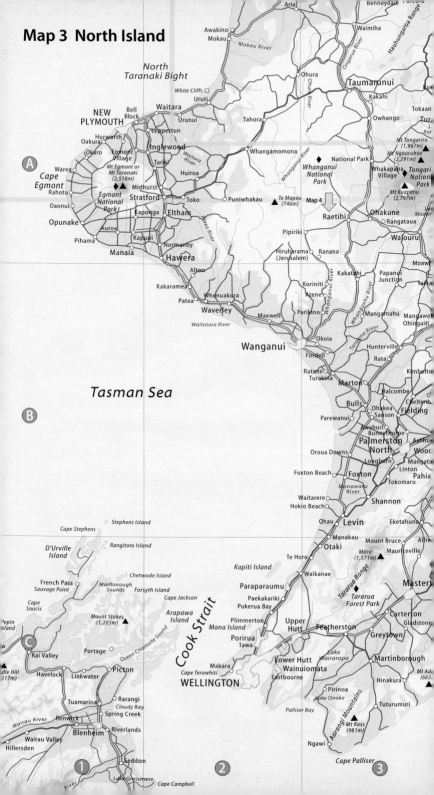

Map 3 North Island

Arial
Benneydale
Waimiha
Haubungaroa Range

Awakino
Mokau
Mokau River
Ongarue River
Ohura
Taumarunui
Kakahi
Tokaan
Tur
Ongarue River
Owhango
L Rot

White Cliffs
Uruti
Tahora
Whangamomona
Whanganui River
National Park
Mt Tongariro
(1,967m)
Mt Ngauruhoe
(2,291m)

NEW PLYMOUTH
Bell Block
Waitara
Urunui
Teppertun
Whangamomona
Whanganui
National Park
Whakapapa
Village
Tongari
Nation
Park

Oakura
Hurworth
Inglewood
Egmont
Village
Waitara
River
Mt Egmont or
Mt Taranaki
(2,518m)
Tariki
Huiroa
Whangamomona
Te Mapou
(746m)
Map 4
Mt Ruapehu
(2,797m)

Okaro
Warea
Cape Egmont
Rahotu
Egmont
National
Park
Midhurst
Stratford
Toko
Puniwhakau
Raetihi
Ohakune
Rangataua

Oaonui
Eltham
Kaponga
Pipiriki
Wajouru

Opunake
Auroa
Kapuni
Normanby
Hiruharama
(Jerusalem)
Ranana
Papanui
Junction
Moawl

Pihama
Manaia
Hawera
Alton
Korinti
Kakatahi
Taih

Kakaramea
Patea
Whenuakura
Atene
Parikino
Mangamahu
Mangawe
Ohingaiti

Waverley
Maxwell
Whanganui River
Okoia

Waitotara River
Wanganui
Fordell
Hunterville
Rata

Ratane
Turakina
Marton
Kimbolto
Halcombe
Cheltenh

Tasman Sea

Bulls
Ohakea
Sanson
Fielding
Parewanui
Awahuri
Bunnythorpe
PALMERSTON NORTH
Asthus
Wooc

Oroua Downs
Longburn
Mangata
Foxton Beach
Foxton
Linton
Pahia
Tokomaru

Waitarere
Hokio Beach
Manawatu River
Shannon

Ohau
Levin
Eketahuna

Stephens Island
Cape Stephens
Rangitoto Island
Manakau
Otaki
Mount Bruce
Alfre
Mauriceville

D'Urville Island
Te Horo
Mitre
(1,571m)
Maste

French Pass
Sauvage Point
Marlborough
Sounds
Chetwode Island
Forsyth Island
Kapiti Island
Waikanae
Paraparaumu
Tararua Forest Park

Cape Soucis
Mount Stokes
(1,205m)
Cape Jackson
Paekakariki
Pukerua Bay
Carterton
Gladstone

Rai Valley
Portage
Arapawa Island
Plimmerton
Mana Island
Upper Hutt
Featherston
Greytown

dle Hill
217m)
Havelock
Linkwater
Picton
Queen Charlotte Sound
Porirua
Tawa
Martinborough
Mt Ad
663

Tuamarina
Rarangi
Cloudy Bay
Spring Creek
Makara
Cape Terawhiti
WELLINGTON
Lower Hutt
Wainuiomata
Eastbourne
Hinakura

Renwick
Riverlands
Pirinoa
Lake Onoke
Tuturumuri

Wairau Valley
Blenheim
Palliser Bay
Aorangi Mountains
Mt Ross
(981m)

Hillersden
Seddon
Ngawi

Wairau River
Lake Grassmere
Cape Campbell
Cape Palliser

North Taranaki Bight

Cook Strait

Whanganui National Park

Tararua Range

Lake Wairarapa

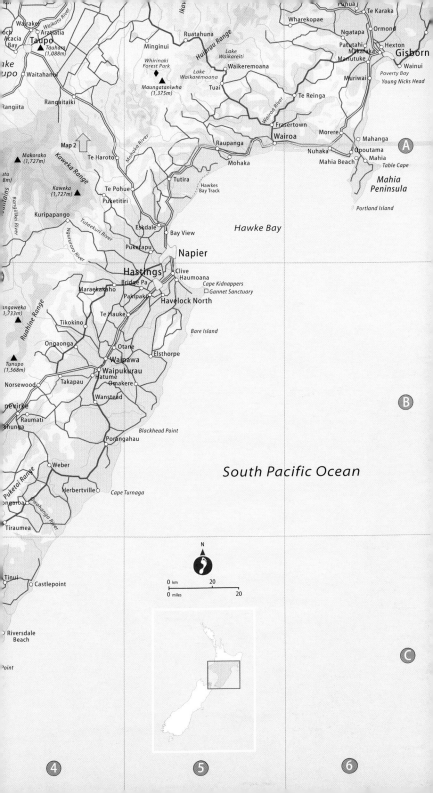

Map 4 South Island

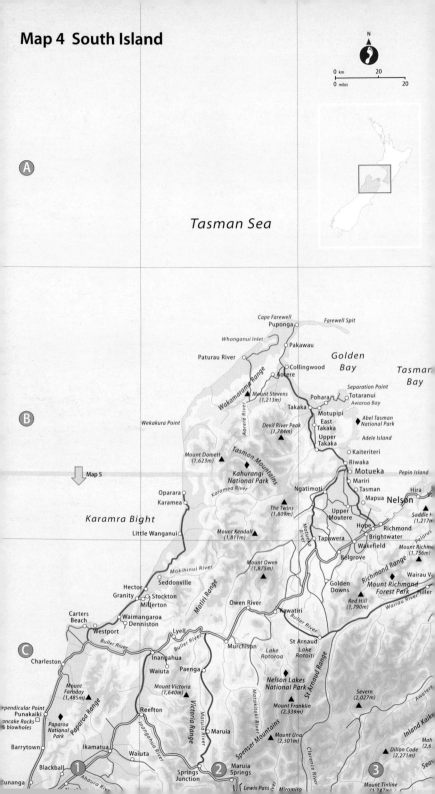

A

Tasman Sea

N

0 km   20
0 miles   20

B

Cape Farewell
Puponga   *Farewell Spit*
Whanganui Inlet
Pakawau   *Golden*
Paturau River   Collingwood   *Bay*   *Tasman*
Onekaka   *Bay*
Wakamarama Range   ▲ Mount Stevens   Pohara   *Separation Point*
                       (1,213m)   Totaranui
Aorere River   Takaka   *Awaroa Bay*
Wekakura Point   Devil River Peak ▲ Motupipi
                       (1,784m)   East   ◆ Abel Tasman
                                         Takaka   National Park
Mount Domett ▲   *Tasman Mountains* Upper   *Adele Island*
(1,623m)   Takaka
                       Kahurangi   Kaiteriteri
Map 5   *National Park*   Riwaka
                       Karamea River   ○ Motueka   *Pepin Island*
Oparara   Mariri
Karamea   Tasman
                       The Twins   Mapua   **Nelson**   Hira
Karamea Bight   (1,809m)   Upper   Saddle H
                                          Moutere   (1,217
Little Wanganui   Mount Kendall ▲   Hope   ◆ Richmond
                       (1,811m)   Tapawera   Brightwater
                                                       Wakefield Mount Richm
                       Mokihinui River Mount Owen   (1,756m)
                                          (1,875m)   Belgrove
Hector   ▲   *Richmond Range*
Granity Seddonville   Mount Richmond Wairau V
Millerton Stockton   Golden   *Forest Park*   Miller
Carters Waimangaroa   Downs Red Hill *Wairau River*
Beach   Denniston   (1,790m)
C   Westport *Buller River* Lyell Owen River Kawatiri
Charleston   *Matiri Range*   *Buller River*
                                          Murchison St Arnaud *St Arnaud Range*
         Inangahua   *Lake   *Lake
         Waiuta   Paenga   Rotoroa*   Rotoiti*
Mount Faraday ▲   Mount Victoria   *Severn*
(1,485m) *Paparoa Range* (1,640m)   ◆ *Nelson Lakes* (2,027m)
Perpendicular Point   *National Park*
Punakaiki   Mount Franklin
Pancake Rocks   *Victoria Range*   (2,339m)
& blowholes   Reefton *Maruia River*
         ◆ *Paparoa*   *Spenser Mountains* *Inland Kaik*
Barrytown *National Park* Maruia   Mount Una
         Ikamatua   (2,301m)   *Mah*
Blackball   Waiuta   Dillon Code ▲ (2,6
                                           Maruia   (2,271m)
○unanga *Ahaura River* ① Springs ②   Springs ③   Mount Tinline
                          Junction   *Clarence River* (1,747m)
                          Lewis Pass Miromiro *Seav*

Matakitaki River

Map 5 South Island

Map 4
Map 6

A

B

C

Karamra Bight

Oparara
Karamea
Karamea River

Little Wanganui

Mokihinui R

Hector
Granity
Seddonville
Stockton
Millerton
Carters Beach
Waimangaroa
Denniston
Westport
Lyell
Buller River
Buller River
Inangahua
Paenga
Charleston

Mount Faraday (1,485m)
Mount Victoria (1,640m)
Paparoa Range
Victoria Range
Reefton

Perpendicular Point
Punakaiki
Pancake Rocks & blowholes
Paparoa National Park
Ikamatua
Waiuta
Waru

Barrytown
Inangahua River
Springs Junction

Blackball
Ahaura River
Runanga
Ngahere
Mount Tec (1,867m)
Greymouth
Shantytown
Dobson
Paroa
Moana
Kopara
Mount Ajax (1,834m)
Lake Se Forest
Kumara
Lake Brunner
Hokitika
Lake Kaniere
Inchbonnie
Lake Sumn
Mount Long (1,901r)
Lake Mahinapua
Turiwhate
Ruatapu
Lake Kaniere
Otira
Arthur's Pass National Park
Ross
Kowhitirangi
Arthur's Pass
Arthur's Pass
Pukekura
Browning Pass
Cass
Chest Peak (1,935m)
Lees Valle

Abut Head
Rotokino
Wanganui River
Harihari
Craigieburn Forest Park
Esk River
Puketeraki

Okarito Lagoon
Okarito
Whitcombe Pass
Mount Whitcombe (2,644m)
Rakaia River
Porters Pass
Ox
Wilberforce River
Lake Coleridge
Springfield

Whataroa
Mount Arrowsmith (2,795m)
Lake Coleridge
Sheffield
Waim

Beach
Franz Josef Glacier
Fox Glacier
Franz Josef Glacier
Mount D'Archiac (2,865m)
Mount Hutt (2,188m)
Coalgate
Darfield

Fox Glacier
Fox Glacier
Mount Potts (2,194m)
Lake Heron
Mount Hutt
Hororata
Greendale
Dunsand

Westland National Park
Jacobs River
Mount Cook National Park
The Thumbs (2,545m)
South Branch
Methven
Lauriston
Rakaia
Southb

Bay
Mount Cook (3,754m)
Godley River
Two Thumbs Range
Mount Somers
Chertsey

Copland Track
Mount Cook
Mount Musgrave (2,246m)
Rangitata River
Mayfield
Winchmore
Ashburton
Rakaia River

Pasman River
Lake Tekapo
Woodbury
Carew
Tinwald
Willowby
Hakatere

Mount Ward (2,644m)
Gondsborough River
Glentanner
Mackenzie Country
Lake Tekapo
Burke
Geraldine
Rinds
Lowcliffe
Canterbury B

Dun Fiunary (2,499m)
Lake Pukaki
Fairlie
Orari
Winchester
Pleasant

nt Huxley (,499m)
Lake Pukaki

1
2
3

Canterbury B

Matiri

Maruia River

North Branch

Mount Doe (1,623m)

Map 6 South Island

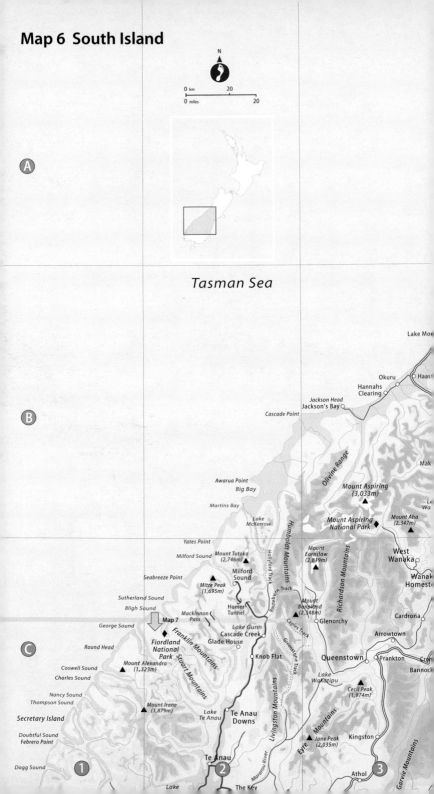

N

0 km 20
0 miles 20

Tasman Sea

A

B

Lake Mo⌐

Okuru ○ Haas⌐
Hannahs
Clearing ○
Jackson Head
Jackson's Bay ○
Cascade Point

Olivine Range

Mak⌐

Awarua Point
Big Bay

Mount Aspiring
(3,033m) ▲

Martins Bay
Lake
McKerrow

Mount Aspiring ◆
National Park

Mount Aha
(2,347m) ▲

Le⌐
Wa⌐

West
Wanaka ○

Yates Point

Milford Sound Mount Tutoko
(2,746m) ▲

Mount
Earnslaw
(2,819m) ▲

Milford
Sound

Wanak⌐

Seabreeze Point

Mitre Peak
(1,695m) ▲

Wanak⌐
Homest⌐

Sutherland Sound

Bligh Sound

Mackinnon
Pass

Homer
Tunnel

Mount
Bonpland
(2,348m) ▲

Cardrona ○

B

George Sound

Map 7

Lake Gunn

Glenorchy ○

Arrowtown ○

Cascade Creek

Round Head

Fiordland
National
Park

Glade House

Knob Flat

Queenstown ○ Frankton ○ Cro⌐

Bannoc⌐

Coswell Sound

Mount Alexandra
(1,323m) ▲

Lake
Wakatipu

Cecil Peak
(1,974m) ▲

Charles Sound

Nancy Sound
Thompson Sound

Mount Irane
(1,879m) ▲

Lake
Te Anau

Te Anau
Downs

Kingston ○

Secretary Island

Jane Peak
(2,035m) ▲

Doubtful Sound
Febreto Point

Te Anau ◆

Athol ○

Dagg Sound

① **②** **③**

The Key

C

Richardson Mountains

Humboldt Mountains

Hollyford Track

Routeburn Track

Caples Track

Greenstone Track

Franklin Mountains

Stuart Mountains

Livingston Mountains

*Eyre
Mountains*

Garvie Mountains

Maraou River

Lake

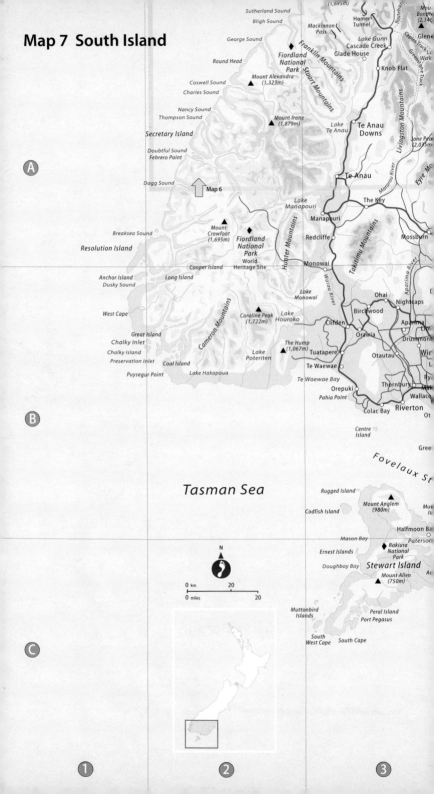

Map 7 South Island

Sutherland Sound
Bligh Sound
George Sound
Round Head
Coswell Sound
Charles Sound
Nancy Sound
Thompson Sound
Secretary Island
Doubtful Sound
Febrero Point
Dagg Sound
Breaksea Sound
Resolution Island
Anchor Island
Dusky Sound
West Cape
Great Island
Chalky Inlet
Chalky Island
Preservation Inlet
Puysegur Point

Cooper Island
Long Island
Coal Island
Lake Hakapoua

(1,695m)
Homer
Tunnel
Mackinnon
Pass
Lake Gunn
Cascade Creek
Glade House
Knob Flat

Franklin Mountains
Stuart Mountains
Livingston Mountains

Mount
Bonfa
(2,31

Glen

Routeburn Track
Caples Track
Lo
Wak

Greenstone Track

Fiordland
National
Park

Mount Alexandra
(1,323m)

Mount Irane
(1,879m)

Lake
Te Anau

Te Anau
Downs

Te Anau

The Key

Lake
Manapouri

Manapouri

Jane Peak
(2,035m

Eyre Mo

Mararoa River

Map 6

Mount
Crowfoot
(1,695m)

Fiordland
National
Park
World
Heritage Site

Caroline Peak
(1,722m)

Lake
Houroko

Lake
Monowai

Cameron Mountains

Hunter Mountains

Takitimu Mountains

Redcliffe

Monowai

Waiau River

Ohai

Birchwood

Clifden

Oravia

Mossburn

Nightcaps

Aparima

Lim

Drummond

Wir

L

Apārima River

The Hump
(1,067m)
Lake
Poteriten

Tuatapere

Te Waewae

Otautau

Thornbury

Mat

Ry

Wallace

Te Waewae Bay

Orepuki
Pahia Point

Colac Bay

Riverton

Ot

Centre
Island

Gree

Fovelaux St

Tasman Sea

Rugged Island

Codfish Island

Mason Bay

Ernest Islands

Doughboy Bay

Mount Anglem
(980m)

Mu
Is

Halfmoon Ba

Paterson

Rakiura
National
Park

Stewart Island

Mount Allen
(750m)

Ac

N

0 km   20
0 miles   20

Muttonbird
Islands

South
West Cape

South Cape

Peral Island
Port Pegasus

A

B

C

1   2   3

For a different view of Europe, take a Footprint

Footprint

Bologna

Ben Donald